St. James Guide to

BLACK ARTISTS

St. James Guide to

BLACK ARTISTS

With a Preface by
Howard Dodson

Editor
Thomas Riggs

Published in Association with
the Schomburg Center for Research in Black Culture

ST. JAMES PRESS

AN IMPRINT OF GALE

DETROIT • NEW YORK • TORONTO • LONDON

Thomas Riggs, *Editor*

Barbara Bigelow, Elizabeth Oakes, Robert Rauch, John Wolff, Janet Zupan,
Contributing Editors

Laura Standley Berger, Joann Cerrito, Dave Collins, Nicolet V. Elert, Miranda Ferrara,
Kristin Hart, Janice Jorgensen, Margaret Mazurkiewicz, Michael J. Tyrkus,
St. James Press Staff

Peter M. Gareffa, *Managing Editor, St. James Press*

Mary Beth Trimper, *Production Director*
Shanna Heilveil, *Production Assistant*

Cynthia Baldwin, *Art Director*
C. J. Jonik, *Desktop Publisher*
Pamela A. Reed, *Photography Coordinator*
Randy Bassett, *Image Database Supervisor*
Mikal Ansari, Robert Duncan, *Imaging Specialists*

∞ The paper used in this publication meets the minimum
requirements of American National Standard for Information Sciences—
Permanence Paper for Printed Library Materials, ANSI Z39.48-1984.

Cover photo: *Maryland Crab Feast* by Tom Miller. Courtesy of Steven Scott Gallery, Baltimore, and the artist.

St. James Guide to Black Artists / editor, Thomas Riggs.
     p. cm.
  Includes bibliographical references and index.
  ISBN 1-55862-220-9 (alk. paper)
  1. Artists, Black--Biography. I. Riggs, Thomas, 1963-.
N40.S78 1997
709'.2'396--dc21
[B]
97-3068
CIP

Printed in the United States of America
Published simultaneously in the United Kingdom

St. James Press is an imprint of Gale
10 9 8 7 6 5 4 3 2 1

CONTENTS

PREFACE

Art represents the human struggle, its renewed excitement, its unmet demands as well as ever fresh wonder. It is like science, exercising its own disciplines and will toward discovery. It strives for the representation of unseen forms, the revelation of new relationships, the transformation of our sensory powers and the content of our imagination.

—Pierre Mabille

Over the last three decades the names and works of African American artists Romare Bearden, Jacob Lawrence, Augusta Savage, and Elizabeth Catlett, among others, have become familiar to many Americans. Less familiar are the names of Brazilian artists Terciliano, Jr., and Mestre Didi; Jamaicans John Dunkley and Edna Manley; Haitians Wilson Bigaud and Hector Hyppolite; and Nigerian Sokari Douglas Camp. Like their African American counterparts, these twentieth-century African and African-diasporan artists—painters, sculptors, collagists, printmakers, and other practitioners of the visual arts—have assumed increasingly prominent roles as creative artists in their respective national cultures. Many have also won the grudging respect and admiration of art critics, as well as art collectors and consumers, around the world.

A century ago the majority of Americans would have scoffed at the notion that there were or ever had been "black artists" or "black art." Most Americans at that time (both black and white) knew little if anything about African peoples' centuries-long (indeed millennial-long) tradition of creativity in the visual arts. The reigning racist ideology of the time maintained that African peoples had neither history nor culture. Seen as inherently inferior to whites, culturally as well as intellectually, black people were thus perceived as incapable of higher intellectual and aesthetic pursuits. Their detractors did not believe they were capable of practicing the "fine arts"—opera, painting, sculpture, ballet, and other forms of artistic expression created and practiced by Europeans and imitated and revered by white Americans.

A cursory reading of human history should have revealed the fact that these propositions were untenable. But in this politically charged era, when the major European powers were consolidating their recently won control over the African continent and strengthening their hold on colonized African peoples in the Caribbean, they needed ideological justifications for their actions. Similarly, Euro-Americans simultaneously invented systems of internal colonialism to control and exploit disenfranchised African Americans. Both Europeans and American colonialists looked upon African peoples as beings outside the human family. They rationalized and justified their "right" to exercise dominion over black folk by contending that blacks had no history and culture. Obviously, nothing they produced would be considered art and certainly not fine art.

Humankind had its origins on the African continent, however. As a consequence, it is likely that art (like history and culture), as a human enterprise, had its origins there as well. Scientific evidence confirms that some 25,500 to 27,700 years ago, African artists living in present-day Namibia produced an extensive body of rock paintings that still exist today. Subsequently, painters, sculptors, jewelers, and other visual artists throughout ancient Africa created and bequeathed to humankind startling evidence of their creative genius. Nowhere is the evidence of such creativity more abundant than in the remains of predynastic and dynastic Egyptian civilizations, where exquisite paintings, sculptures, jewelry, and other artworks abound.

Over the last century the world has been introduced to the extraordinarily rich and complex visual arts traditions of African societies. Researchers in the fields of anthropology, archaeology, African history, and art history have contributed significantly to a growing appreciation of and respect for the visual arts traditions of Africa and the African diaspora. A century or more of stunning exhibitions of traditional and contemporary works by black artists from continental Africa and the African diaspora has heightened public interest in these art forms and challenged some of the most pervasive myths about the intelligence, histories, and cultures of people of African descent worldwide.

Unfortunately the vast majority of black artists who produced these works, both from continental Africa and the African diaspora, have languished in obscurity and anonymity—the visual arts equivalents of James Weldon Johnson's *Black and Unknown Bards*.

Traditional works of art by continental African artists continue to this day to be identified by ethnic or religious group or collector rather than by artist. New World African artists of the seventeenth, eighteenth, and nineteenth centuries have suffered a similar fate. Over the last century, however, artists of Africa and African descent have become the subjects and objects of serious study. So has the art these artists produced. Cultural renaissances have occurred in African and African diasporan societies around the globe during this century. In virtually every instance, visual arts movements and schools have been created to celebrate and promote the work of black artists. As a consequence, the twentieth century has produced and identified more artists of African descent than all the previous centuries combined.

The *St. James Guide to Black Artists* is a unique compendium of information on artists of African descent. Though focused on the twentieth century, selected nineteenth-century artists are also included. About three-fourths of the entrants are African Americans, and the remainder are from Africa, the Caribbean, and other parts of the diaspora. In addition to basic biographical and career information and brief essays on each entrant's art, *Black Artists* includes hundreds of photographs of artists and their works.

In collaborating with St. James Press to produce this compendium, the Schomburg Center is continuing a tradition established by its founder, Arturo Alfonso Schomburg, almost a century ago. Best known as a bibliophile and historian, Schomburg was also a committed and steadfast exhibitor, promoter, patron, and student of black artists and their works. His pioneering activities in defense and support of black artists date back to the first decade of the twentieth century. He acquired artworks by African and African diasporan artists for inclusion in his now legendary collection of Africana research resources. The first recorded exhibition that he curated (1914) included works by African and African American artists. A 1918 "Exhibition of Books, Manuscripts, Paintings, Engravings, Sculptures, etc." included works by African American artists such as William E. Braxton, Albert A. Smith, and Laura Wheeler Waring, among others. This exhibition, the first of an annual series on black history and culture, was held at Brooklyn's Carlton Avenue YMCA under the sponsorship of the Negro Library Association, which Schomburg had cofounded with his mentor John E. Bruce. By 1921 the annual series of exhibitions had moved to the 135th Street branch of the New York Public Library in Harlem, the future repository of Schomburg's distinguished collection. Three exhibitions held there in 1921, 1922, and 1923 exhibited 261 paintings, sculptures, and works on paper by sixty-five black artists from New York, Washington, D.C., Philadelphia, Chicago, and Boston. Exhibiting artists ranged from Meta Vaux Warrick Fuller and Edwin A. Harleston to Palmer Hayden and James Lesesne Wells.

A central part of the cultural euphoria in Harlem during the 1920s, often referred to as the Harlem Renaissance or the New Negro Movement, these initiatives, under Schomburg's leadership, brought hundreds of black American artists to the attention of the American public. The annual Harmon Foundation exhibits, which used the New York Public Library's 135th Street branch as their originating and New York City venue, built on these foundations and between 1926 and 1933 did more to identify black American artists and celebrate and promote their works than any other single private entity in the first half of the twentieth century. In the 1930s the federally financed Works Progress Administration (W.P.A.) picked up where the Harmon Foundation left off.

Schomburg continued his efforts on behalf of black artists and black art until his death in 1938. He was instrumental in organizing the exhibition (and eventually the acquisition) of the Blondeau Collection of African art at the 135th Street branch. It became the foundation of the center's extensive African art collection.

Most diasporan artists of the sixteenth, seventeenth, eighteenth, and nineteenth centuries who ventured into the pristine world of the fine arts imitated the styles and conventions of European classical art. Most were seemingly committed to demonstrating their technical proficiency, reflecting the sensibilities and styles of their mentors or patrons.

The standards by which their works were judged were those of the European classicists in painting, sculpture, and other arts. Nothing distinguished their subject matter, their media, their technique, and their aesthetic principles from these European norms. Few if any black artists in the United States, Haiti, Brazil, Cuba, Jamaica, and France explored African or African diasporan themes. Like their European and Euro-American counterparts, they neither questioned nor challenged European conventions. Some, like those in Brazil prior to the twentieth century, worked for the various religious orders and created works that were ordered or commissioned by the church. Most of the religious art in colonial Brazil was painted or sculpted by black artists. It did not differ markedly from that found in European cathedrals. Others, such as Juan de Pareja and Sebastian Gomez in seventeenth-century Spain, were apprentices of European artists and were trained in their styles, tastes, and techniques.

Evidence of pre-twentieth-century deviations from European classical standards and norms is most prevalent in those New World colonial societies where neo-African religions were created. In places like Brazil, Cuba, and Haiti, artists who were practitioners of Candomblé, Santeria, and voodoo reinvented the role carried out by artists in traditional African societies. They used their artistic talents to create the kinds of objects that were deemed essential for carrying on these New World African religious practices.

World War I ushered in the first major break in the dominance of classical European art in the definition of fine arts. African diasporan artists, headed by those who were active participants in the Harlem Renaissance, began to explore indigenous and continental African subject matter and themes and adapted traditional African stylistic devices to modern needs. European artists such as Picasso, Matisse, and Modigliani discovered the beauty and aesthetic quality of traditional African art and used it to invent new national standards and a modernist art movement. Seemingly liberated from the tyranny of European classicism, Euro-American artists in Mexico, Brazil, and the United States began to search for more authentic indigenous idioms and vocabularies. The post-World War I era can be seen as a period of artistic self-determination in which black artists, like their European and Euro-American counterparts, rebelled against the hegemony of European classicism and sought to express themselves in authentic, indigenous voices that mirrored their present and future visions rather than simply paying homage to the achievements of the classical European past.

Black artists of the post-World War I era have been among the most innovative and adventurous explorers of the neo-African and modernist approaches to the fine arts. Most movements and trends in the post-World War I art world have had their African or African diasporan practitioner. The works of black surrealists such as Wifredo Lam, as well as black abstract artists like collagist Romare Bearden, sculptor Richard Hunt, and painters Herve Telemaque and Emilio Cruz, are comparable to those of any other artists working in their genre. But what has distinguished nontraditional black artists of the twentieth century, regardless of their national or geographical origin, has been their attempt to invent and develop idioms that express their individual, national, or pan-African cultural identity. Throughout the African and African diasporan world, individual artists as well as schools and movements have sprung up to take on this challenge. The result has been an extraordinarily vast and diverse body of art by black artists around the world.

In Jamaica, for instance, a handful of artists of the 1930s, who were eventually joined by a revitalized, nationalistic Institute of Jamaica, pioneered in the development of a dynamic and vital Jamaican art movement. In the forefront of this initiative was the English-born sculptor and painter Edna Manley, who was the daughter of a Jamaican mother and an English father. She was also the cousin and wife of Norman Manley, leader of Jamaica's People's National Party, an early exponent of Jamaican independence. What Norman and the People's National Party did for Jamaican politics, Edna did for Jamaica's artistic development. She, along with fellow pioneers Carl Abrahams, Albert Hine, Cecil Baugh, and Alvin Mariott, led the search for a Jamaican nationalist aesthetic, exploring the Jamaican identity and African and Jamaican folk themes through their work. During the 1940s Edna Manley also taught other artists who explored similar themes.

By the late 1930s the Institute of Jamaica, an organ of the British colonial government formed in 1879 to promote art, science, and literature, had come under attack by young nationalists. The appointment in 1938 of Jamaican nationalist Phillip Sherlock as secretary of the institute transformed it into a catalytic force in the development of Jamaican art and artists. Edna Manley and Audrey Clarke presided over the institute's Arts and Crafts Committee, and free art classes, which nurtured local, indigenous visions, were offered at the institute. Hundreds of contemporary Jamaican artists benefited from these classes. The Jamaican School of Arts and Crafts (1950), the National Gallery of Jamaica, and the Edna Manley School of Art have provided the institutional infrastructure for the continuing evolution of Jamaican art and artists. In a little more than two generations, black artists of Jamaica have developed a truly national school of artistic expression that is at the forefront of Caribbean arts movements. Comparable though less developed movements have emerged in most formerly colonized areas in Africa and the Caribbean.

Haiti's visual arts tradition dates back at least to the regime of Henri Christophe (1807-1818), and throughout the nineteenth century Haitian political leaders and cultural institutions supported and promoted the work of academically trained Haitian artists, many of whom were educated in France and worked in French classical traditions. On the other hand, "peasant painters"—"naive," "primitive," or "self-taught" artists—trace their heritage back to the era of slavery. They have continued to be a vibrant, foundational part of the Haitian visual arts scene up to the present day.

In the mid-1940s these two traditions came together to forge a Haitian national art movement that brought the work of Haitian artists to the attention of the world. The catalyst was the founding of the Centre d'Art in 1944 by Dewitt C. Peters with the support of the Haitian-American Institute in Port-au-Prince. Peters, an American, was an English teacher living in Port-au-Prince. The center provided material supplies, training, exhibitions, and marketing support for the work of Haiti's artists—folk and "modern." Within a mere decade or two, thousands of works by Haitian artists had found their way into the marketplace, and a distinguished group including Hector Hyppolite, Wilson Bigaud, Rigaud Benoit, and Philomé Obin had achieved a degree of international recognition. Schools proliferated throughout the island in the 1950s and 1960s and served as training grounds and promoters of distinctive regional or aesthetic styles. Many of the peasant painters became part of these movements, but many more continued to work in their village or mountain habitats, creating works for their personal enjoyment or for various voodoo rituals. Every dimension of Haiti's unique and tumultuous historical, economic, political, social, and cultural life has been captured visually by its black artists.

New forms of art that are distinctly African also began to emerge on the continent during the 1950s. One of the first experimental centers devoted to fostering this kind of enterprise was founded by Frank McEwen, director of the National Art Gallery of Rhodesia (now Zimbabwe) in 1957. Located in Salisbury (now Harare), the National Art Gallery Workshop provided a context in which essentially untrained artists from throughout Zimbabwe could come and explore, primarily through carved stone sculptures, their respective artistic and spiritual visions. No tradition of stone sculpture-making existed in Zimbabwe prior to this time. The result has been the development of the internationally renowned "Shona Sculptures of Zimbabwe." The works of artists of the "Zimbabwe school," such as Albert Mamvura, Henry Munyaradzi, Moses Masaya, and Brighton Sango, are frequently exhibited in Europe and the United States, represented by major art galleries, and acclaimed by art critics throughout the Atlantic world.

Summer workshops for artists established in Ibadan, Nigeria, in 1961 and 1962, and the Mbari Mbayo artists' club in Oshogbo, Nigeria, from 1962 to 1964, led to the emergence of the Oshogbo school of artists. Painters and sculptors associated with this workshop have been commissioned to produce contemporary works of art using traditional idioms and techniques, which have also been incorporated into the architectural design and decorative strategies of modern commercial and religious institutions in Nigeria. Wax-resistant dyed cloths and wall hangings have been widely acclaimed as vibrant new art forms emanating from the Oshogbo school.

A significant number of Western-trained continental Africans have been practicing on the continent over the last four or five decades. Most have been going through various stages of experimentation, frequently producing works that are more geared to the international art market than to an indigenous African public. These works, while often African in subject matter, rely more heavily on the stylistic traditions of art from other continents. These African "modernists" and "postmodernists" are also making unique contributions to the continental African and universal art vocabulary.

African American artists have been extremely creative and productive over the last forty years as well. Indeed, this has likely been the most dynamic and expansive period in African American art history. An impressive coterie of artists who were nurtured during the Harlem Renaissance, Harmon Foundation, and W.P.A. eras burst onto the national scene during the 1950s and 1960s. Individual and group shows featuring artists such as Jacob Lawrence, Aaron Douglas, Elizabeth Catlett, Charles White, Romare Bearden, and Hale Woodruff announced to the national and international world that African American art and its artists had indeed come of age. In so doing they paved the way for the next major flowering of African American art and cultural creativity, which would occur during the late 1960s and early 1970s.

The "black power" phase of the African American struggle for political and economic freedom had a profoundly liberating effect on African American visual and performing arts. The black arts, or black aesthetic, movement became the artistic counterpart of the black power political and economic agenda. Thousands of African American artists embraced black nationalist ideologies and tried to reflect them in their works. Poets, novelists, dramatists, and lyricists, as well as painters, sculptors, collagists, and other visual artists, created works that grappled with nationalist and pan-Africanist issues, ideals, values, and imagery. For many African American artists the events taking place on the African continent during the 1950s and 1960s became a major source of personal identity and artistic inspiration. Unlike their peers of the previous six decades, who had more frequently than not made the pilgrimage to Paris in search of new aesthetic ideas and identities, many artists went to newly independent Ghana and other West African countries. John Biggers, Herman "Kofi" Bailey, and Tom Feelings are among those artists of the 1960s who moved to Africa in search of aesthetic and cultural authenticity and identity.

The vast majority of African American visual artists of the 1960s and 1970s found abundant cultural and aesthetic inspiration in the political and social revolution that was taking place under their noses, first in the American South and then nationally. The public nature of the civil rights and black power movements made them ripe candidates for visual representation and interpretation. The cultural symbols and iconography invoked or invented to express the transformation in aesthetic sensibilities that occurred among African Americans during the 1960s and 1970s (such as dashikis, Afros, and Kente Cloth) also attracted the attention of black American visual artists. Many, like those associated with the Chicago-based Africobra and the New York-based Weusi groups, believed their art should be committed to fostering black political and cultural liberation. While many of their predecessors eschewed the labels "Negro" or "black" artists and art, these artists of the 1960s and 1970s unashamedly referred to themselves as "black artists" and consciously sought to develop a "black aesthetic" in their art.

Unlike the 1920s, when black American artists were concentrated in Harlem, Chicago, and a few cities on the East Coast, the black arts movement of the 1960s and 1970s was genuinely national in scope. During the period from the late 1960s to the early 1980s, more than a hundred African American museums were established throughout the country to exhibit the works of local, national, and internationally acclaimed black artists. Mainstream museums, such as the Corcoran, the Whitney, the Brooklyn, the High Museum (Atlanta, Georgia), and the Smithsonian, have been obliged both to acquire the works of African American artists (historical and contemporary) and to organize and present major individual and group shows of their works. They have also opened their doors to major exhibitions of works by African and African Caribbean artists. In addition, African American vernacular artists have been discovered over the last decade. Their works have both heightened public awareness of an enduring folk idiom in African American art and inspired new African American and American modernist expressions.

The artists selected for inclusion in the *St. James Guide to Black Artists* are representative of the diverse forms of artistic expression and trends in African, African diasporan, modern, and postmodern art. Part of a long and enduring tradition of art-making in the African world, they and their works eloquently attest to the fact that African peoples, like all members of the human family, have been actively and creatively involved in producing art of extraordinary beauty, meaning, and power regardless of where and under what circumstances they have lived. *Black Artists* celebrates them and their achievements.

—Howard Dodson
Director, Schomburg Center for Research in Black Culture

EDITOR'S NOTE

The *St. James Guide to Black Artists* contains biographical and career information, as well as brief critical essays, on nearly four hundred of the most prominent black artists. About three-fourths, or three hundred, were alive at the time of publication. Also included are a small number of important artists from the nineteenth century. Illustrating the book are nearly three hundred photographs of artists and their works.

All the entrants in the book are visual artists. The book focuses mostly on painters, sculptors, and printmakers—those working in what were traditionally considered the "fine arts"—but important artists in other media, such as photography, have also been included. Though the great majority of entrants are from the United States, about one hundred are from Africa, the Caribbean, Brazil, and elsewhere.

The selection of entrants was based on the recommendations of our distinguished advisers. We could not, however, include all the artists recommended to us. We hope that many new artists will be added to future editions of the book.

The editor would like to thank the many people involved in the project, including the nine advisers and seventy-one writers, many of whom spent a great amount of time researching artists for the book. Because of the primary research done for the entries, the *St. James Guide to Black Artists* contains information not available in any other source.

Thanks must also be given to the artists and galleries who kindly responded to our requests for biographical and career information. Many artists supplied personal statements about their art, and, unless otherwise indicated in the caption, all photographs were also provided by the artists themselves.

I would like to thank personally John Wolff and Janet Zupan, who compiled the book's biographical and career sections and who performed various other editorial jobs; Robert Rauch, Elizabeth Oakes, and Barbara Bigelow, who edited much of the text; and Dave Collins, Joann Cerrito, and Janice Jorgensen, who coordinated the various in-house responsibilities, including the proofreading.

Finally, special thanks must go to the New York Public Library's Schomburg Center for Research in Black Culture. The *St. James Guide to Black Artists* is being published in association with the Schomburg Center, and the center generously assisted in various stages of the book's production. Howard Dodson, director of the center, served as the chair of the advisory board and wrote the book's preface. Mr. Dodson was involved from the early planning stages of the book, and his advice and help were invaluable. Other members of the Schomburg Center deserve mention. Theresa Martin, Mr. Dodson's secretary, was essential in so many transactions between the center and St. James. Tammi Lawson, head of the center's Art and Artifacts Division, helped select photographs for the book and also spent untold hours assisting writers on research for their essays; we greatly appreciate her time and the support she gave to the project. St. James is proud to publish this book with the Schomburg Center, indisputably one of the world's finest resources on black art and culture.

—Thomas Riggs
Editor

ADVISERS

Howard Dodson, chair
Director
Schomburg Center for Research in Black Culture

David C. Driskell
Distinguished University Professor of Art
University of Maryland

Edmund Barry Gaither
Director
Museum of the National Center of Afro-American Artists

Leslie King-Hammond
Dean of Graduate Studies
Maryland Institute, College of Art

Samella Lewis
Professor Emerita
Scripps College

Richard A. Long
Atticus Haygood Professor of Interdisciplinary Studies
Emory University

Richard J. Powell
Chairman, Department of Art and Art History
Duke University

Roslyn A. Walker
Senior Curator
National Museum of African Art
Smithsonian Institution

Jeanne Zeidler
Director, University Museum
Hampton University

CONTRIBUTORS

Petrine Archer-Straw
Terry Bain
Dedria A. Humphries Barker
Deirdre Bibby
David Boxer
Patricia Brady
Crystal Britton
Eddie Chambers
Deirdre Cross
Alissandra Cummins
Monique G. Curnen
Patricia J. Darish
Howard Dodson
Henry John Drewal
Carolyn Richardson Durham
Claude L. Elliott
Laurie Fitzpatrick
Jacqueline Francis
Edmund Barry Gaither
Nicole Gilpin
Betty Kaplan Gubert
Eric Hanks
Elizabeth Harney
Joanne Harris
Michael D. Harris
Stephanie Harvie
Salah Hassan
Harry Henderson
Kyra E. Hicks
Freida High
Coria A. Holland
Ihor Holubizky
Regina Holden Jennings
Leslie King-Hammond
Amy Kirschke
Udo Kultermann

Babatunde Lawal
Lizzetta LeFalle-Collins
Theresa Leininger-Miller
Nashormeh N.R. Lindo
Worth W. Long
Audrey Mandelbaum
Frank Martin
Christine Miner Minderovic
Madeline W. Murphy
Barthosa Nkurumeh
Nkiru Nzegwu
Sylvester Okwunodu Ogbechie
Regenia A. Perry
Aaronetta H. Pierce
Veerle Poupeye
Delores Jackson Radney
Marilyn Richardson
Brady M. Roberts
Jontyle Theresa Robinson
Helen M. Shannon
Thomas M. Shaw
Neale A. Shultz
M. Franklin Sirmans
Robert Steele
Sonya Stinson
Louise Davis Stone
William E. Taylor
Gabriel Tenabe
Glenn Townes
Leo Twiggs
Dorothy Valakos
Paul Von Blum
Roslyn Adele Walker
A.M. Weaver
Regina L. Woods
Jeanne Zeidler

St. James Guide to

BLACK ARTISTS

LIST OF ENTRANTS

Carl Abrahams
Tayo Adenaike
Terry Adkins
Aleijadinho
Tina Allen
Charles Alston
Amalia Amaki
Emma Amos
Benny Andrews
Emanoel Araújo
Octávio Araújo
Pastor Argudin y Pedroso
William Ellisworth Artis
Ellsworth Ausby

Herman "Kofi" Bailey
Malcolm Bailey
James Ball
Antônio Bandeira
Ellen Banks
Henry Bannarn
Edward Bannister
José Barbosa
Ernie Barnes
Richmond Barthé
Jean-Michel Basquiat
Gloretta Baynes
Romare Bearden
Phoebe Beasley
Gwendolyn Bennett
Rigaud Benoit
Wilson Bigaud
John Biggers
Camille Billops
Willie Birch
Robert Blackburn
Betty Blayton-Taylor
Skunder Boghossian
Leslie Bolling
Shirley Bolton
Frank Bowling
David Bustill Bowser
David Boxer
Sonia Boyce
William Ernest Braxton
Edgar Brierre
Murat Brierre
Karl Broodhagen
Everald Brown
Grafton Tyler Brown
Samuel Joseph Brown, Jr.
Vivian Browne

Beverly Buchanan
Jimoh Buraimoh
Selma Burke
Calvin Burnett
Millie Burns
Margaret Burroughs
David Butler
Carole Byard

Sokari Douglas Camp
Elmer Simms Campbell
Arthur Carraway
Carol Ann Carter
Nanette Carter
Yvonne Pickering Carter
George Washington Carver
Yvonne Parks Catchings
Elizabeth Catlett
Eddie Chambers
Dana Chandler
Barbara Chase-Riboud
Albert V. Chong
Claude Clark
Ed Clark
Irene Clark
LeRoy Clark
Robert Colescott
Houston Conwill
Eldzier Cortor
Raimundo da Costa e Silva
Ernest Crichlow
Allan Rohan Crite
Emilio Cruz
Manuel da Cunha

Alonzo Davis
Bing Davis
Charles Dawson
Roy DeCarava
Avel DeKnight
Beauford Delaney
Joseph Delaney
Nadine DeLawrence
Henry DeLeon
James Denmark
Murry DePillars
Milton Derr
Rashid Diab
Thorton Dial
Mestre Didi
Jeff Donaldson
Aaron Douglas

Robert M. Douglass, Jr.
John Dowell
David Driskell
Robert S. Duncanson
John Dunkley
Édouard Duval-Carrié

Felix Eboigbe
William Edmondson
Melvin Edwards
Uzo Egonu
El Anatsui
Ibrahim El Salahi
Erhabor Ogieva Emokpae
Ben Enwonwu
Tomás Esson
Minnie Evans
Frederick Eversley

Lamidi Fakeye
Malaika Favorite
Mhlaba Zwelidumile Mgxaji Feni
Amos Ferguson
Thomas Fleet, slave of
Sherman Fleming
Frederick Flemister
Agboola Folarin
L'Merchie Frazier
Allan Freelon
Robert Freeman
Roland Freeman
Meta Vaux Warrick Fuller

Reginald Gammon
Herbert Gentry
Milton George
Sam Gilliam
Ablade Glover
Christopher Gonzalez
Paul T. Goodnight
Russell Gordon
Rex Gorleigh
Gladys Barker Grauer
Renée Green
Jefferson Eugene Grigsby, Jr.

David Hammons
James Hampton
Marvin Harden
Inge Hardison
John Wesley Hardrick
Edwin Harleston
William A. Harper
Michael D. Harris
Bessie Harvey
Maren Hassinger
Cynthia Hawkins
Palmer Hayden
Vertis Hayes
Benjamin Hazard
Barkley Hendricks

Janet Oliva Henry
Leon Hicks
Freida High
Lubaina Himid
Adrienne Hoard
Geoffrey Holder
Alvin Hollingsworth
Charnelle D. Holloway
Varnette Honeywood
Earl J. Hooks
Humbert Howard
Mildred Howard
Julien Hudson
Manuel Hughes
Margo Humphrey
Richard Hunt
Clementine Hunter
Hector Hyppolite

Ovia Idah

Harlan Jackson
May Howard Jackson
Oliver L. Jackson
Suzanne Jackson
Martha Jackson-Jarvis
Wadsworth A. Jarrell
Wilmer Jennings
Leandro Joaquim
Malvin Gray Johnson
Marie E. Johnson
Sargent Claude Johnson
Stephanie A. Johnson
William H. Johnson
Joshua Johnston
Serge Jolimeau
Ben Jones
Loïs Mailou Jones
Napoleon Jones-Henderson
Barbara Jones-Hogu
Tam Joseph

Kapo
Kofi Kayiga
Paul Keene
Souleymane Keita
Mohammad Omer Khalil
Bodys Isek Kingelez
Gwen Knight
Khalid Kodi
Vincent Kofi

Laura Jean Lacy
Wifredo Lam
Artis Lane
Doyle Lane
Akinola Lasekan
Christian Lattier
Jacob Lawrence
Hughie Lee-Smith
James Lewis

Joseph Lewis
(Mary) Edmonia Lewis
Norman Lewis
Samella Lewis
Georges Liautaud
Glenn Ligon
Arturo Lindsay
Jules Lion
Thomas Lloyd
Jon Lockard
Juan Logan
Ed Love
Al Loving

Maria Magliani
Gregory Maloba
Edna Manley
Kerry James Marshall
Richard Mayhew
Valerie Maynard
Manuel Mendive
Yvonne Cole Meo
Tom Miller
Lev Mills
Priscilla Mills
Moke
Evangeline Montgomery
Ronald Moody
Philip Moore
Scipio Moorhead
Clarence Morgan
Norma Morgan
Keith Morrison
Petrona Morrison
Archibald Motely
Thomas Mukorobgwa

Abdias do Nascimento
Teixeira Nash
Iba N'Diaye
Nefertiti
Senga Nengudi
Valente Malangatana Ngwenya
Joseph Norman
Amir Nour

Philomé Obin
C. Uche Okeke
Asiru Olatunde
Ademola Olugebefola
Omari Ra
Aina Onabolu
Mary Lovelace O'Neal
Bruce Onobrakpeya
Ouattara
Hayward Oubre
John Outterbridge
Joe Overstreet

William Pajaud
Gordon Parks

Marion Perkins
James Phillips
Delilah Pierce
Elijah Pierce
Anderson J. Pigatt
Howardena Pindell
Adrian Piper
Keith Piper
Rose Piper
Horace Pippin
Michael B. Platt
Stephanie Pogue
Prentice Herman Polk
Charles Ethan Porter
James Porter
Georgette Powell
Harriet Powers
Debra Priestly
Nelson Primus
Nancy Elizabeth Prophet
Noah Purifoy
Martin Puryear
Rachelle Puryear

Teodoro Ramos-Blanco
Helen Ramsaran
Patricia Ravarra
Patrick Henry Reason
Robert Reid
John Rhoden
Gary Rickson
John Riddle
Faith Ringgold
Haywood "Bill" Rivers
Malkia Roberts
John H. D. Robinson
Mahler Ryder

Alison Saar
Betye Saar
Robert St. Brice
Chéri Samba
Raymond Saunders
Augusta Savage
Elizabeth Scott
John T. Scott
Joyce Scott
William Edouard Scott
Charles Searles
Charles Sebree
Gerard Sekoto
Ahmad Mohammed Shibrain
Durant Sihlali
Thomas Albert Sills
Gary Simmons
Carroll Simms
Jewel Woodward Simon
Lorna Simpson
Merton Simpson
William H. Simpson
Clarissa Sligh

Albert Alexander Smith
Al(fred) Smith
Alvin Smith
Frank Smith
Vincent Smith
William E. Smith
Gilda Snowden
Sylvia Snowden
Genilson Soares
Amadou Sow
Therman Statom
Raymond Steth
Nelson Stevens
Renee Stout
Thelma Johnson Streat
Richard Stroud
Robert Stull
Kaylynn Sullivan Twotrees

Papa Ibra Tall
Ann Graves Tanksley
Henry Ossawa Tanner
Terciliano, Jr.
Alma Thomas
Matthew Thomas
Mildred Thompson
Robert Thompson
Dox Thrash
Mose Tolliver
Bill Traylor
Curtis Tucker
Yvonne Edwards Tucker
Leo Twiggs
Twins Seven-Seven

Obiora Udechukwu

Rubem Valentim
James Van Der Zee

Ruth Waddy
S. Irein Wangboje
Eugène Warburg
Barbara Ward
Denise Ward-Brown
Laura Wheeler Waring
Gregory Warmack
Barrington Watson
Osmond Watson
Carrie Mae Weems
Joyce Wellman
James Lesesne Wells
Pheoris West
Rene Westbrook
Charles White
Jack Whitten
Aubrey Williams
Frank Williams
Michael Kelly Williams
Pat Ward Williams
William T. Williams
Philemona Williamson
Ed Wilson
Ellis Wilson
Fred Wilson
John Wilson
Vernon Winslow
Beulah Woodard
Hale Woodruff
Shirley Woodson

Richard Yarde

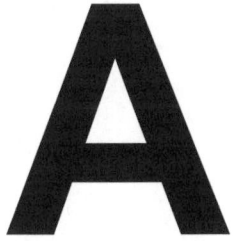

ABRAHAMS, Carl
Jamaican painter

Born: Saint Andrew, Jamaica, 1913. **Education:** Calabar High School, Kingston, Jamaica; studied painting with English painter Augustus John. **Military Service:** Royal Air Force, 1940-44. **Awards:** Silver Musgrave Medal, Institute of Jamaica, 1973; First Prize, Alcoa Fine Arts Exhibition, 1975; Purchase Award, National Gallery of Jamaica, Kingston, 1977; First Prize, best mural, Banana Board, 1985; Institute of Jamaica Gold Medal, Kingston, 1987. **Agent:** Douglas Reid, Grosvenor Galleries, 1 Grosvenor Terrace, Kingston, Jamaica.

Individual Exhibitions:

1964	Sheraton Art Gallery, Kingston, Jamaica
1969	70, The Gallery, Kingston, Jamaica
1973	Bolivar Gallery, Kingston, Jamaica
1982	Mutual Life Gallery, Kingston, Jamaica
1992	Grosvenor Galleries, Kingston, Jamaica

Selected Group Exhibitions:

1962	*The Art of Jamaica,* Kaiser Center Gallery, Oakland, California
1976	*Five Centuries of Art in Jamaica,* National Gallery of Jamaica, Kingston
1977	National Gallery of Jamaica, Kingston
1978	University of Caracas, Venezuela
1982	Jamaican High Commission, Ottawa, Canada
1983	Art Gallery, Commonwealth Institute, London
	Jamaican Art 1922-1982, Smithsonian Institution Traveling Exhibition Service and National Gallery of Jamaica (traveling through 1985)
	National Gallery of Jamaica, Kingston
1988	National Gallery of Jamaica, Kingston
1992	National Gallery of Jamaica, Kingston

Collections:

National Gallery of Jamaica.

Publications:

On ABRAHAMS: Book— *Carl Abrahams, Artist and Visionary: An Introduction to His Life and Work* by Nora Louise Strudwick, Pomegranate Press Limited Publications, 1983. **Articles**—"The Ironic Vision of Carl Abraham" by Ignacy Eker, in *The Sunday Gleaner,* 10 August 1975; "Carl Abraham in Retrospect" by Archie Lindo, in *The Star,* 12 August 1975; "Retrospective Art of Carl Abrahams On Show," in *The Daily Gleaner,* 12 August 1975.

*   *   *

Carl Abrahams began his career as a cartoonist, learning by correspondence course from England and patterning his style after that of Cliff Tyrell, the foremost cartoonist practicing in Jamaica at the time. This "apprenticeship" as a cartoonist no doubt accounts for many of the traits of his mature paintings, in particular, his quick, economical drawing style, love of narrative, caricatural approach to expression, and dry wit and humor.

In 1937 Abrahams met and befriended the English painter Augustus John, who was then in Jamaica painting. His exposure to John's informed conversations about art and to his paintings, ravishing images of Jamaican womanhood, gave Abrahams the impetus to become a professional painter. Although he had attempted to paint before, his efforts were limited to schoolboy copies of the old masters from art books. (A copy of Frans Hals's *Laughing Cavalier* still exists.) After meeting John, however, Abrahams set about developing a personal style by immersing himself in art books and by adapting a variety of painting techniques to his cartoonish drawing style.

Abrahams's progress was slow, and it was interrupted by World War II and his service, between 1940 and 1944, in the Royal Air Force. It was not until the mid-1950s that his true talents began to emerge. From the 1950s there are some witty self-portraits, anecdotal narratives such as his *Grand Finale of the Tea Party* (1959), a humorously observed barroom brawl between two peg-legged men, and his first acknowledged masterpiece, *The Last Supper* (1955), in which he reworked the clichéd Christian theme but also imparted a new vitality with cleverly individualized caricatural expressions given to each of the participants. *The Last Supper* was a precursor of a wave of religious works, from the 1960s on, that present the elements of the Christian story in fresh interpretations that always manage to be convincing. It is perhaps the artist's own devout and utterly sincere religious feelings that are able to lift many of these works from potential bathos to a truly religious, at times even ecstatic, art.

Although Abrahams's style has remained essentially naturalistic, with the added dynamism of caricatural distortions, he has absorbed many modernist influences. Cubism (and its variants) is a case in point. Many of Abrahams's larger works, including his early murals, show a cubistic division of space. Others, such as *Lady with a Fan* and *Persian Cat*, both from the late 1950s, reveal a marked rectilinear structuring of the human form. His well-known *Grief of Mary* (1965) accommodates a complex cubistic partitioning of the face in an extraordinary diagramming of inward pain. There is even a small group of completely abstract paintings done in a cubist-inspired style, while in still others his subjects seem composed of tubing and mechanical parts, perhaps suggesting acquaintance with the works of Fernand Léger.

In other paintings Abrahams uses seemingly endless meandering lines to unfold landscape elements in an apparently undetermined manner akin to the automatism of the surrealists, while motifs in certain of his abstract paintings recall the work of Paul Klee and Joan Miró. The surrealism of the fantastic landscapes of the Jamaican painter John Dunkley, one of the few modern artists Abrahams has admired, seems to have been an early influence and has probably contributed to the surreal developments in his own art.

Abrahams's iconographic interests are vast. Religious narratives and iconlike paintings; surreal fantasies that touch on a wide variety of subjects, including political satire; portraits, in both painting and sculpture; landscapes and still lifes; genre works, including backyard scenes in which the activities of Jamaica's rural and poor are wittily characterized; classical mythology, often disguising erotic fantasies; history, both factual and imagined; and contemporary events—Abrahams's brush has touched them all. Yet he is inimitable among Jamaican artists, his paintings marked as they are by the workings of a unique if quirky imagination. He is considered by many to be Jamaica's greatest living painter.

—David Boxer

ADENAIKE, Tayo
Nigerian painter and graphic artist

Born: Augustine Omotayo Adenaike, Idanre, Ijebu-Imushin, Ogun State, 27 April 1954. **Education:** Federal Government College, Warri, 1966-72; National Art Workshop, Ahmadu Bello University, Zaria; University of Nigeria, Nsukka, B.A. 1979, M.F.A. 1982. Studied art at Schwabisch-Hall, Germany, 1986. **Career:** Teacher, Institute of Management and Technology, Enugu, 1979-80; art director, MAAN Limited, Enugu, 1982-84; art editor, *Okiki*, 1983. Since 1985 creative director, Dawn Functions Nigeria Limited, Enugu, Nigeria. Designed more than thirty book covers for Fourth Dimension Publishers, Enugu. **Awards:** Second National Painting Prize, Federal Government College, Warri, 1972; University of Nigeria departmental painting prizes, 1974 and 1979; Federal Government of Nigeria scholarships, 1974 and 1980. **Address:** Dawn Functions Nigeria, Limited, 84 Nza Street, Independence Layout, P.O. Box 2890, Enugu, Enugu State, Nigeria. **Online Address:** http://www.afrika.com.adenaike.

Individual Exhibitions:

1980	*Childhood Fears,* Goethe Institute, Lagos
1981	Africa Centre, London
1982	*Distorted Souls,* Goethe Institute, Lagos
1983	National Council for Arts and Culture, Lagos
1984	Italian Cultural Institute, Lagos
1986	*We Live in the Deep,* Goethe Institute, Lagos (traveling)
	Italian Cultural Institute, Lagos
1990	Italian Cultural Institute, Lagos
	Mbari Art, Washington, D.C.
1991	Greensboro Cultural Center, North Carolina
1992	*Solemn Notes,* New Orleans
1993	African American Gallery, Charleston, South Carolina

Tayo Adenaike, 1992.

1994	*Recent Watercolors,* Contemporary African Art Gallery, Denver
1996	Contemporary African Art Gallery, Denver

Selected Group Exhibitions:

1978	International Trade Fair Exhibition, Lagos
1980	Exhibition Hall, National Theatre, Lagos
	East Zone Exhibition, Enugu
	Afrikanische Kunst Haute, Frankfurt, Germany
1982	Goethe Institute, Lagos
1984	Thirty-Fourth Birmingham Festival of Arts, Alabama
1988	Sinsemillia Gallery, Lagos
	Italian Cultural Institute, University of Nigeria, Lagos
1991	Nsukka and Italian Cultural Institute, University of Nigeria, Lagos
1992	Bona Gallery, Enugu, Lagos

Collections:

African Heritage Museum, Mattye Reed African Heritage Center, Greensboro, North Carolina; Agrip International, Lagos, Nigeria; Museum für Volkerkunde, Frankfurt, Federal Republic of Germany;

National Council for Arts and Culture, Lagos, Nigeria; National Gallery of Modern Art, Lagos, Nigeria; New Orleans Museum of Art; National Museum of African Art, Smithsonian Institution, Washington, D.C.; University of Lagos, Centre for Cultural Studies, Lagos, Nigeria.

Publications:

By ADENAIKE: Books—*Homage to Uli,* exhibition catalog, Lagos, National Council for Arts and Culture, 1983 (illustrated); *We Live in the Deep,* exhibition catalog, Lagos, Goethe-Institute, 1986 (illustrated). **Articles**—"The Influence of Uli Art on Contemporary Nsukka School Painting (Part 1)," in *Nigeria Magazine* (Lagos), 1982, pp. 38-52 (illustrated); "The Oshogbo Experiment," in *Seven Stories About Modern Art in Africa* (London) Whitechapel, 1995, pp. 202-07.

On ADENAIKE: Book—*Fragments: Watercolours and Drawings by Tayo Adenaike,* exhibition catalog, Washington, D.C., 1990 (illustrated). **Article**—"AKA's Second Harvest" by Ifeanyi Afuba, in *West Africa* (London), 17 August 1987, pp. 1584-86.

*

Tayo Adenaike comments:

   To continue to be a painter after formal art school education is problematic. One is faced with the question of what to paint, what medium or media to use, how the audience will react, and more importantly, what impressions would be left behind for future generations.

   Over the years I have found some answers in exploring the limitless possibilities of traditional Uli art, in the use of mostly watercolor, and in exhibiting in galleries, where I am faced with diverse and critical but highly appreciative audiences.

   Essentially my art is human, and I paint what I think of what I see or hear.

*   *   *

   Nigerian painter Tayo Adenaike's soft and luminous watercolor works are rich in multilayered symbolic meaning, paying homage to the Nigerian traditional cultures of the Igbo and Yoruba peoples. The enigmatic quality of the artist's work is derived in part from his synthesizing of geometric, animal, and vegetable motifs traditionally used by Igbo women to decorate both body and building in an art form known as Uli.

   Adenaike was trained in Nsukka, Nigeria, where the Uli conventions—including variations in form—have been revitalized by male artists since the 1970s. One of a number of contemporary Nigerian painters drawing inspiration from Uli imagery, Adenaike fashions his own stylistic idioms by infusing traditional, organic forms with his own Yoruba background.

   Compositional simplicity and economic use of form are trademarks of Adenaike's paintings and may well contribute to the visual dynamism of his works. His palette includes a variety of color combinations, the use of which results in muted overlays of color fields often invoking a sense of fluid motion. In his painting *In the Deepest Waters, a Fish Never Loses Its Way,* Adenaike presents images that depart somewhat from his typical reflection of Igbo and Yoruba motifs. This organic composition recalls an expression from

Tayo Adenaike (art piece).

his youth referring to the importance of remaining connected to one's home. His detailed rendering of scales on the fish in the lower middle ground of the work reveals his mastery of watercolor. Curvilinear forms suggesting movement and current in the waters guide the fish into a circular green and yellow open space.

   Although Adenaike is well known for his artistic blending of Uli symbols with aspects of his Yoruba heritage, he simultaneously depicts the essence and beauty of the broader human experience. The artist synthesizes myth and folklore from his traditional past and offers visual commentary on the political and economic turmoil in his country. *Keeping Mute* examines both the verbal and visual traditions of the Yoruba people while invoking the geometric and lyrical forms associated with the Igbo. The influence of Yoruba shrine painting is evidenced in his work through the treatment of figures, the disembodiment of human parts, and the use of earth tones. On the left side of the picture plane Adenaike projects a disembodied eye that bears witness to the tumultuous nature of contemporary Nigerian society and serves as a symbol for a Yoruba proverb. Balancing the composition is the image of a human head with closed eyes in the middle right ground. On each side and behind the head are haunting dark and light silhouetted figures appearing to torment the head. This representation, which honors

3

proverbs and shrine painting, implies resolution between visionaries and the unenlightened.

Integrating elements of the traditional past has become a powerful element for contemporary African artists seeking innovative and alternative means for artistic expression. By exploiting the design elements of Uli, Tayo Adenaike has positioned himself as an emerging leader in the art world, drawing on a rich tradition of the past for images addressing the present and future.

—Regina Holden Jennings

ADKINS, Terry (R.)

American sculptor and performance artist

Born: Washington, D.C., 1953. **Education:** Fisk University, Nashville, B.S. 1975; Illinois State University, Normal, M.S. 1977; University of Kentucky, Lexington, M.F.A. 1979. **Career:** Instructor, Kentucky State University, Frankfort, 1977; visiting professor, California State University, Chico, 1991; assistant professor, SUNY New Paltz, New York; associate professor, SUNY New Paltz, New York, 1996. Guest lecturer, University of California, Davis, 1991, Montclair State College, New Jersey, 1992, The Chrysler Museum, Norfolk, Virginia 1993, University of Pennsylvania, Philadelphia, 1993, High Museum of Art, Atlanta, Georgia, 1993, Brown University, Providence, Rhode Island, 1994, Skidmore College, Saratoga Springs, New York, 1995, University of Connecticut, Storrs, 1997. Visiting artist, Koprod International, Zurich, 1989, Guggenheim Museum, New York, 1993, California State University, Humboldt, 1995, Anderson Ranch, Aspen, Colorado, 1996. Falk Visiting Artist, University of North Carolina, Greensboro. Artist-in-residence, Studio Museum in Harlem, New York, 1982, Special Arts Services, NYSCA, New York, 1988. **Awards:** Virginia Museum Fellowship, 1980; National Program Studio Artist, P.S. 1, Queens, New York, 1984; National Endowment for the Arts Fellowship, 1986; Artist Exchange Fellowship, Projekt Blinz 39, Zurich, 1986; SECCA 7 Fellowship, Winston-Salem, North Carolina, 1989; Joan Mitchell Foundation Fellowship, Brooklyn, New York, 1994; New York Foundation for the Arts grant, 1995; commission award, Perspectives in African-American Art, Seagram Americas, New York, 1996; printmaking fellowship, Anderson Ranch, Aspen, Colorado, 1996. **Address:** 429 Clinton Avenue, Brooklyn, New York 11238, U.S.A.

Individual Exhibitions:

1980	James Wise Gallery, Norfolk State University, Virginia
1981	Arts and Humanities Center, Richmond, Virginia
1986	Projekt Binz 39, Zurich
1987	Galerie Emmerich-Baumann, Zurich
1988	Liz Harris Gallery, Boston
1989	Galerie Andy Jllien, Zurich
1990	LedisFlam, New York
	Miami-Dade Community College, Florida
	Valencia Community College, Orlando, Florida
1991	Anderson Gallery, Virginia Commonwealth University, Richmond
1992	LedisFlam, New York

1993	Weatherspoon Gallery, University of North Carolina, Greensboro
	Chrysler Museum, Norfolk, Virginia
	LedisFlam, New York
1995	Hammonds House Resource Center for African-American Art, Atlanta, Georgia
	Whitney Museum of American Art at Philip Morris, New York
1997	William Benton Museum of Art, University of Connecticut, Storrs

Selected Performances:

1981	Washington Project for the Arts, Washington, D.C.
1982	University of Cincinnati, Ohio
1983	New Music America Festival, Washington, D.C.
1985	P.S. 1, Institute for Art and Urban Resources, New York
1987	Kulturzentrum Rote Fabrik, Zurich
1988	Institute for Contemporary Art, London
1989	Koprod International, Zurich
1990	Valencia Community College, Black Box Theater, Orlando, Florida
	Rigiblick Theatre, Zurich
1991	Hall of Science, New York
	California State University, Chico
1992	Weatherspoon Gallery, University of North Carolina, Greensboro
1996	Whitney Museum of American Art at Philip Morris, New York

Selected Group Exhibitions:

1980	Mississippi Museum of Art, Jackson
1984	The Clocktower, New York
1987	Salama-Caro Gallery, London
1989	Kenkeleba Gallery, New York
1990	Studio Museum in Harlem, New York
1992	Hillwood Art Museum, Brookville, New York
1993	David Klein Gallery, Birmingham, Mississippi
1995	Phoenix Museum of Art, Arizona
1996	Real Art Ways, Hartford, Connecticut
1997	International Gallery, Smithsonian Institution, Washington, D.C.

Collections:

Arts and Humanities Center, Richmond, Virginia; Chrysler Museum, Norfolk, Virginia; Fisk University, Nashville; Hammonds House Resource Center for African-American Art, Atlanta, Georgia; High Museum of Art, Atlanta, Georgia; Hirshhorn Museum and Sculpture Garden, Washington, D.C.; Illinois State University, Normal; Jersey State Museum, Trenton, New Jersey; Metropolitan Museum of Art, New York; The New School, New York; Tougaloo College, Mississippi.

Publications:

By ADKINS: Book—*Visionary Recital,* exhibition catalog, Atlanta, Georgia, Hammonds House, 1995.

On ADKINS: Articles—"Terry Adkins" by Keith Morrison, in *New Art Examiner,* 9(5), 1982; "Terry Adkins at Valencia Community College" by Gregory R. Miller, in *Art Papers,* July/August 1990; "Terry Adkins at LedisFlam" by Michael Brenson, in *New York Times,* 15 February 1991; "Review of Terry Adkins at LedisFlam" by Robert Mahoney, in *Arts,* May 1991; "Sculptures Bring Out the Scavenger in Terry Adkins" by Catherine Fox, in *The Atlanta Constitution* (Georgia), 28 April 1995.

*   *   *

Terry Adkins makes enigmatic sculptures from found materials and detritus. He has worked in other media, but his sculptures are the basis of his artistic output. Although he migrated to the North, the spirit of the African American South, from which he came and where he was educated, pervades his work. In this respect he is like his friend and contemporary Anthony Murrell.

Adkins seeks to imbue the finished product with a fusion of the spirit in the object and the spirit invested in the reconfiguration. In this sense his works share a characteristic with traditional African sculpture, in which wood (only that deemed worthy of carving) is often drenched in a libation or incised or carved to add elements of spirituality. For Adkins paint is a libation, and the object, often found wood, carries a history, a spirit that exists with or without the hand of the artist. Thus, like David Hammons, Nari Ward, and others, Adkins works with the spirit of preexisting objects in creating his unique brand of contemporary art.

As an idiom this genre took its cue from Marcel Duchamp, who placed a bicycle wheel on a stool and thus created the readymade. Within the past two decades the style has been mined by artists of color in such a vigorous way that it has become almost a contemporary African American aesthetic within the historical canon. It is eclectic and is in line with African American music, especially jazz and blues. In fact, music is an integral force in many of these artists' works. One of Hammons's strongest works is called *Blue Train,* and Ward's grand installation of discarded baby carriages is titled *Amazing Grace.* Adkins's work *Last Trumpet* (1995) consists of four eighteen-foot conical brass horns that can be played, thus referring to the utilitarian quality of African art. *Ezekiel* is a nine-foot-tall disk (spoked like Duchamp's wheel) with bells that can be used as an instrument. Although he works in his own vernacular, Adkins also represents a spiritual and conceptual link to the Abstract Expressionists of the 1950s, particularly to artists like Ed Clark, Norman Lewis, and Franz Kline, who often sought to give visual expression to the popular music of the moment. Yet for Adkins his own moment is crucial and open to inquiry, and nothing reveals the answer. He has said, "Most of my influences lie outside the umbrella of history."

Adkins is also a saxophonist who often performs within his exhibitions. In 1990 he performed *Recent Anthem: Dedicated to John Carlos, Lee Evans, and Jimi Hendrix,* which included his own rendition of "The Star-Spangled Banner" in a funked-up Hendrix fashion. Although he is concerned with the wide-reaching spiritual effect of music and creates objects on a large scale, Adkins's work can be distinctively intimate. He has made numerous wall sculptures like *Were Bell, Shaken Green,* and *Frenesi,* the last the title of an Artie Shaw recording, in which he has compressed his ideas into minimal works that use collage and improvisation. On any scale the spirit of something resides in Adkins's sculpture, and it is there for the viewer to see.

—M. Franklin Sirmans

ALEIJADINHO

Brazilian sculptor, architect, and wood-carver

Born: António Francisco Lisboa, near Ouro Prêto, Brazil, 1738. **Education:** Apprenticed in architecture to father, a Portuguese stonemason. Studied stone carving under Francisco Xavier de Brito. **Career:** Commissioned architect and sculptor. Victim of unknown degenerative disease, perhaps leprosy or syphilis, beginning at age 39. **Died:** 1812.

Publications:

On ALEIJADINHO: Books—*Antonio Francisco Lisboa-O Aleijadinho,* by Rodrigo José Ferreira Brétas, Rio de Janeiro, 1951; *Aleijadinho et la sculpture baroque au Brésil,* by Germain Bazin, Paris, 1963. Articles—"The Colonial Architecture of Minas Gerais in Brazil" by Robert C. Smith, in *Art Bulletin,* 21, June 1939, pp. 110-59; "Da participaçao de Antonio Francisco Lisboa na arquitetura sacra Mineira" by José Marianno Filho, in *Estudos de Arte Brasileira,* 1942, pp. 45-53; "Estilo Aleijadinho and the Churches of Eighteenth-Century Brazil" by John B. Bury, in *Architectural Review* 111, February 1952, pp. 92-100.

*   *   *

Aleijadinho, an accomplished architect, sculptor, and wood-carver of the Baroque period, was born António Francisco Lisboa. The illegitimate son of a black mother and of Manoel Francisco Lisboa, an influential Portuguese master carpenter in Brazil in the early eighteenth century, Aleijadinho has come to be regarded as the outstanding Brazilian artist of his time. He learned to build from his father, but his artistic genius far exceeded that of his mentor. His massive body of work encompassed the design and construction of numerous churches, wood carvings in their interiors, ornamental carvings in stone, and wood and stone statues.

The name Aleijadinho, which means "Little Cripple," was conferred on him as the result of a disease that caused him to lose his fingers and toes. Despite this loss, at about the age of forty, historical documents report that the artist continued to carve and chisel, using the stumps of his hands. In fact, his greatest masterpieces were produced after the loss of his fingers.

Among Aleijadinho's masterpieces are *The Way of the Cross* and *Atrium of the Prophets,* both in the sanctuary of the Church of Bom Jesus at Congonhas do Campo. *The Way of the Cross* consists of six chapels built on the hillsides of Congonhas do Campo between 1795 and 1798. Each chapel contains a scene from the life of Jesus: the Last Supper, the Mount of Olives, his arrest, his flagellation and the crown of thorns, his carrying the cross, and the Crucifixion. The works are composed of scenes that have a total of sixty-six statues carved from wood, painted with delicate colors and with enamel eyes. Upon finishing the walk of *The Way of the Cross,* a person arrives at the terrace of the Church of Bom Jesus. The statues of the prophets, executed between 1800 and 1805, are of stone. These twelve statues are placed on the staircases of the terrace ascending to the sanctuary of the church. Among the outstanding statues of this group is *Daniel with the Lion,* which has been compared to Donatello's *David.* The best of the figures, however, is that of the prophet Jonah, showing him at the moment he is expelled from the belly of the whale. Each of the prophets is cloaked in vestments of Eastern cultures as represented in Florentine engravings of the Renaissance.

There is a tremendous body of Aleijadinho's architectural work in his birthplace of Ouro Prêto in Minas Gerais state. His influence on the design of the Church of São Francisco in Ouro Prêto was profound. The facade of the church, the main portal and its monumental facade, the medallion over the entrance, the high altar, and the cornices are the work of Aleijadinho. The facade of the Church of Our Lady of Carmo, also in Ouro Prêto, has been attributed to Aleijadinho as well. Other examples of his architectural work are the parochial church in Tiradentes and the Church of São Francisco at São João del Rei, whose facade is considered one of his highest achievements.

Aleijadinho's carvings inside churches included altars, pulpits, fountains, and archways, done in both wood and stone. He added to the rococo style, changing the design, proportions, and colors of the high altars. Examples of his new designs for altars are found at São Francisco in Ouro Prêto. Cherubim and angels by Aleijadinho adorn the interiors of these churches as well. His bas-reliefs reproduce Biblical scenes and stories, as with *Parable of the Avaricious Man and His Treasure* and *Christ and the Samaritan Woman* at the Church of Our Lady of Carmo at Sabará. *Holy Women of the Sepulchre,* on the main altar of the Church of Saint Francis of Assisi at Ouro Prêto, is an especially detailed scene in wood.

—Carolyn Richardson Durham

ALLEN, Tina

American sculptor and painter

Born: 1955. **Education:** The School of Visual Arts, New York, B.F.A.; University of Southern Alabama. Advanced studies, Pratt Institute, New York, and University of Venice, Italy. **Career:** Commissioned sculptor. Member, board of directors, International Center for African American Asian Relations, Los Angeles, Support Committee for the African National Congress, American Lung Association of Los Angeles County. **Awards:** Fannie Lou Hamer Award, New York; Urban League Award, New York, 1988; Genesis-Generation Spirit Award, 1989; Artists' Salute to Black History Month Award, 1995. **Address:** c/o M. Hanks Gallery, P.O. 5386, Santa Monica, California 90409, U.S.A.

Selected Individual Exhibitions:

Akhinyah Studio Gallery, Illinois; American Roots Gallery, New York; New Orleans Civic Center; Ophelia's Gallery, Alabama; Options the Gallery, Florida; Richardson Gallery, New York; Riverside Art Museum, California; Savacou Gallery, New York; Texas Southern University, Houston; Third World Art Gallery, New York; Third World Arts Festival, California; United Nations Showing, New York; Wanda Wallace Gallery, California.

Selected Group Exhibitions:

Cristie's, New York; East End Art Show, Stamford, Connecticut; Gallery Tanner, Los Angeles; Third World Art Gallery, New York.

Tina Allen at work. Photo courtesy of Phillip Ghee.

Collections:

Afro-American Museum, Hempstead, New York; Essence Communications, New York; Fine Arts Museum of the South, Mobile, Alabama; Huntsville Museum of Art, Mobile, Alabama; Museum of African American Art, Los Angeles; Pratt Institute, New York; Schomburg Center, New York.

Publications:

On ALLEN: Articles—"Tina Allen: Abstract Figurative Artist Taking Leaps and Bounds Around the Globe," in *Legends* (Los Angeles) I (1), December-January 1994; "Tina Allen" by Curtia James, in *Essence*, January 1995; "Japan Gives ICAAAR-U.S. Visitors a Hearty Welcome," in *Los Angeles Sentinel,* 1 August 1996, p. B-9.

*

Tina Allen comments:
So dislodged, insecure, and confused have many people become that the simple bedrock of personal judgment and firsthand clear

observation gives way to the opium of slick artificial mass conditioning and manipulation. We abdicate our responsibility of creating our own original meaning to the visual stimulus we encounter, slipping unconsciously into wholesale acceptance of this ever changing junk food visual diet. We buy from the snake oil salesman, who promises all innovation is good, better, best. The experience is guaranteed to leave the healthy prostrated with exhaustion and reeling with contempt. Some weary souls, unwilling to ignore the obvious, murmur inaudibly that this or that visual is vulgar. "Yes" it is vulgar, through and through! Some fully conscious individuals become brave and challenge the prodigious books, articles, and support data, which grow daily like a Babylonian tower. All this is necessary to keep the illusion in place that some authorities in fact know what's best and can subscribe and anoint value to any object, simply by manipulating public opinion. It's risky business attracting the ire of the sophisticated and pseudosophisticated, hell-bent on avaricely consuming every new fad and whim of an aggressive art market. Still some have the strength of character to state publicly that there is a jaded, useless, and unhealthy quality that pervades too much of our visual landscape, and it needs to stop on a mass scale. Some simply say, "The Emperor is Nude!"

Consider the arsenal of visual expressions hammering at our souls, fighting for our attention at a bewildering rate. It is not always true that what doesn't kill you makes you stronger. Should the Mayday signals of a tattooed and graffitied world with its careless appearance and irreverent narcissism have charm? I think not. Only for those who subscribe to celebrated decadence. Perhaps for "black holes" who want visual proof to support their pessimism and comfort them in their inertia.

The time has come when all hands on board have to throw their ores in the water and row with earnest, if we hope to keep our ship from sinking. After many years of cavalierly offering our children water in a dirty glass, it's not surprising that the fruit of our trees has become inedible. It comes as no news that we no longer uniformly turn out personalities willing to carry the future on their shoulders. For too many youth, the axiom of the day has become, "do less, become less, and get paid at any cost." These are not bad children, they're just sad children.

Subtle internal change, visual modification, and spiritual illumination as opposed to inertia, easy condemnation, and time-worn deception should be the tonic that returns us to Plato's pharmacy. The lighthouse warns us that it's time to return to a universe of service and love. Let's close the lid on Pandora's box, leaving the depressing lackluster "shoot yourself in the foot" philosophies of Schopenhauer and Nietzsche to those who think it's chic to be cynical, and return with haste to the notion that there is a higher power capable of controlling our id. Yes, it feels good to develop conscience, values, and a love and respect for life and beauty in our young.

I look forward to the day when beauty is like a fragrance—you sense it, you don't see it, but you're positive it's there. We need to see with our souls; from that crow's nest, we have a clearer vision. Art should address this longing from within and create Rosetta stones of a sort to unlock the meaning of true beauty that nurtures and heals.

I believe in the conduit theory to get the ego out of the way. The time has come to draw a line in the sand and to consciously develop an appetite for a new aesthetic of beauty. This new aesthetic would evolve to a level of emotional symbolism surrounding the survival of mankind. We can now take the corset off the stylistic adventures of artists and allow them to grow naturally, rather than forcing them to determine the commercially advantageous route. We can encourage "meaning in art" without becoming mundane or stagnant. We are producing strange fruit, full of hate, and the long-term effects of our denial will be a generation filled with appetites for the macabre.

Artists have the right to express anything, in any way—and I have the right to reject it. Given the overriding concern for the future of humanity and the spiritual health of our souls, we cannot ignore the devastating effects of celebrated "nothingness." The rights of a few should be appropriately protected—but not at the cost of our children's visual landscape. Everything new is not always better and certainly not a clear advancement in thought.

When a generation refuses or forgets to nurture its young and develop people willing to carry the future on their backs, the game of life is over.

*   *   *

Tina Allen is a sculptor who has strong feelings about why she creates art. Her primary mission is to destroy negative stereotypes of African Americans. Her medium is bronze. Most of Allen's work can be classified as historical-figurative. It should be noted, however, that she has created a large and growing body of work that might fall into the category of abstract-figurative.

The two principal features of Allen's historical-figurative work are the use of famous persons of African descent as subjects and a larger-than-life scale. Among her subjects are former slave and abolitionist Harriet Tubman, author Alex Haley, legendary civil rights activist Martin Luther King, Jr., labor leader A. Philip Randolph, and South African political prisoner-turned-president Nelson Mandela. The scale of Allen's works is quite large. For example, her rendering of Alex Haley is twelve feet tall, while A. Philip Randolph stands more than nine feet in height.

The large size of the artist's works emphasizes the importance of these figures, but the essence of each subject's African heritage is

Tina Allen: *Delta Spirit.* **Photo courtesy of Phillip Ghee.**

also stressed. Their hair, lips, and noses are not exaggerated but accentuated to demonstrate pride in the physical beauty of African ancestry.

In contrast to Allen's historical-figurative work, her abstract-figurative style stresses form over detail. Here she's mostly interested in capturing the essence of the subject to convey her ideas on the nature of black beauty. Allen idealizes African American women in many of these pieces. In *Door of Life,* a bronze piece with a marble patina, the body is twisted, as if dancing. The subject is an African woman's hips. The message is twofold. First, Africa is the mother of humanity. The oldest human remains were found there. Second, all human beings pass through the door of life, our mother's birth canal. Consequently, we ought to respect womanhood. The piece's marble patina and two-step pedestal reinforce the importance and idealization of the subject.

Another example is *Body of Woman.* In this piece a woman's body is stretched and curved to form an encasement around a pyramid with a high-polished golden bronze patina. The pyramid is a symbol of stability and the greatness of African culture. For Allen it represents the highest expression of African American organizational abilities—that black America's foundation is on something solid and stable. The gold patina further exalts the pyramid. The look on the woman's face is one of peaceful contentment and devotion to her role as protector.

Steal Away is a piece named after a gospel song. (According to the artist, the title is a reminder of how African slaves would steal away to freedom via the underground railroad.) It is a female body with a polished bronze patina, big thighs, and broad hips. She leans backward and up; instead of arms she has nubs that look like two flames when viewed from the front. Her pose is one of celebration, freedom, and the glorification of the black female figure. Again the golden patina and two-step pedestal are used to reinforce the ennobling effect of the figure.

—Eric Hanks

ALSTON, Charles (Henry)

American painter, muralist, sculptor, and printmaker

Also known as Spinky. **Born:** Charlotte, North Carolina, 28 November 1907. **Education:** Columbia College, New York, c.1925-29, A.B. 1929; Teacher's College, Columbia University, New York, c.1929-31, A.M. 1931; National Academy of Art, New York; Pratt Institute, Brooklyn, New York, 1944-45. **Family:** Married Myra Logan. **Career:** Illustrator, *Mademoiselle,* New York, 1940-c.1944, *New Yorker,* 1937; instructor/professor, Art Students League, New York, 1950-71, Museum of Modern Art, New York, 1956-57, City College of New York, 1970-77. **Awards:** Arthur Wesley Dow Fellowship, Columbia University, 1929; Rosenwald fellowships, 1939-40, 1940-41; National Institute of Art and Letters grant, 1958; named to American Academy of Arts and Letters, 1958; Distinguished Alumnus Award, Teachers College, Columbia University, 1975. **Died:** 27 April 1977.

Individual Exhibitions:

1953   John Heller Gallery, New York
1955   John Heller Gallery, New York

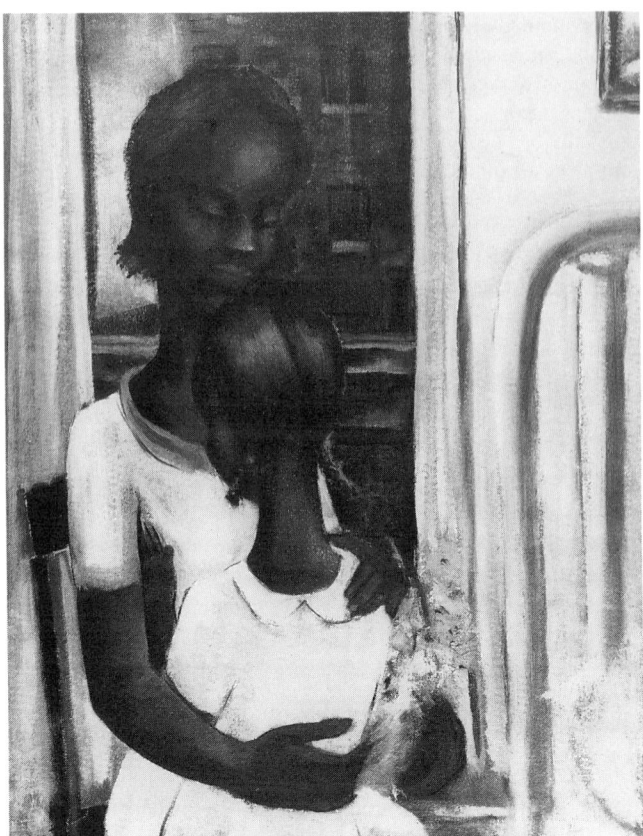

Charles Alston: *Big Sister,* 1935. Photo by Manu Sassoonian; courtesy of the Schomburg Center for Research in Black Culture.

1956   John Heller Gallery, New York
1958   John Heller Gallery, New York
1960   Feingarten Gallery, New York
1968   Fairleigh Dickinson University, Madison, New Jersey
        Gallery of Modern Art, New York
1990   Kenkeleba Gallery, New York (retrospective)

Selected Group Exhibitions:

1934   Harmon Foundation, New York (traveling)
1936   Harmon Foundation, New York (traveling)
1939   Baltimore Museum of Art, Maryland
1940   Tanner Galleries, Chicago
1950   Metropolitan Museum of Art, New York
1975   Art Students League, New York
1976   Los Angeles County Museum (traveling)
1985   Center Gallery, Bucknell University, Lewisburg, Pennsylvania
        Bellevue Art Museum, Bellevue, Washington
1989   Smithsonian Institute, Washington, D.C. (traveling)

Collections:

Atlanta University, Georgia; Barnett Aden Gallery, Washington, D.C.; Butler Institute of American Art, Youngstown, Ohio; Detroit Institute of Art; Golden State Mutual Life Insurance, Los Angeles; Harlem Hospital, New York; Howard University, Washington, D.C.;

Metropolitan Museum of Art, New York; National Association for the Advancement of Colored People, New York; National Portrait Gallery, Washington, D.C.; Schomburg Center, New York; Whitney Museum of American Art, New York.

Publications:

On ALSTON: Books—*Charles Alston,* exhibition catalog, Madison, New Jersey, Farleigh Dickenson University, 1968; *Charles Alston: Artist and Teacher,* exhibition catalog, New York, Kenkeleba Gallery, 1990. **Articles**—"Fifty Seventh Street in Review: Charles H. Alston" by Dore Ashton, in *Art Digest* (New York), 1 May 1955; "Alston: American Artist" by Warren Marr II, in *Crisis* (New York), February 1969.

*   *   *

Charles Alston restlessly experimented in figurative and abstract modes over his long career. A painter, sculptor, muralist, illustra-tor, and teacher, Alston was a leader in Harlem's art community. Among his students in the 1930s was the young Jacob Lawrence, who mingled with black literati and artists at Alston's studio, called 306 after its street address.

Alston's early art challenged the conventions of representational realism, evidence of his exposure to African sculpture and European modernist styles influenced by non-Western aesthetics. Alston responded to the call of the philosopher and cultural critic Alain Locke for black American artists to make "racial art." In the 1920s and 1930s, Locke advocated an art whose form would be based on the geometry and symmetry of traditional African sculpture, while its content would take up historical and social themes pertinent to black American life. Locke planned for racial art to serve two cultural objectives: it would place black American artists at the forefront of modernism, and its visual power would generate racial pride.

Alston's entire career was dedicated to this idea. *Head,* a 1937 wooden bust, and *Two Sisters,* an oil painting executed around 1935, were inspired by the bold design of West African masks and

Charles Alston: *Stud Poker*. Photo courtesy of the Schomburg Center for Research in Black Culture.

Mexican statuary. In 1936 Alston created two murals for New York's Harlem Hospital, the symbolic allegories *Magic and Medicine* and *Modern Medicine.* Magic is represented by Fang statuary and black African dancers following drumbeats and by a conjure woman in a rural American setting. In the modern section black surgeons and nurses in hospital scrubs employ microscopes and petri dishes to fight sickness and disease. Alston said that his inspiration came from the fifteenth-century art of Piero della Francesca and from that of the Renaissance master Michelangelo. His flatly painted forms, compressed in shallow pictorial space, are also modernist inventions; they are equally indebted to the murals of the influential Mexican artists José Clemente Orozco, Diego Rivera, and David Alfaro Siqueiros. Just as these artists painted the popular history and myths of Mexico, so Alston made Africa and the American South the sources of a black past and culture.

Working from photographs he took while traveling in the South, Alston made genre portraits of the region's people. With angular and planar facial depictions and reduced and simplified volumes, these genre paintings are effective translations of African mask and statuary styles.

Alston continued to test the limits of abstraction and nonobjective painting in the 1950s. His canvases of the time barely suggest forms but instead investigate the relationship of closely related tones, unmodulated color, and indeterminate pictorial space and depth.

The figure was never permanently absent from Alston's work, however. It reappeared in the "Blues Singer" and the "Family" series, which engaged the artist in the 1950s and 1960s. The subjects of these series are related to the genre portraits of the previous decades; they, too, are figural abstractions with strong sculptural qualities. Even as Alston symbolized strength by exaggerating and distorting the physiognomy of figures, he often generalized and greatly minimized facial characteristics to make a political statement about the anonymity of blacks in a white majority nation. During this period he also made recognizable portraits of historical figures, as in the 1967 paintings *Frederick Douglass* and *Martin Luther King, Jr.* Alston painted textured close-ups of the leaders' faces, a strategy that draws the viewer close to the monumentalized subjects.

Alston broke racial barriers throughout his career. In the 1930s he was among the first African American supervisors on the Federal Art Project of the Works Progress Administration, and his Harlem Hospital murals, prior to their site installation, were the first by an African American to be exhibited at the Museum of Modern Art. He was also the first African American instructor at the Art Students League and at the Museum of Modern Art. During the civil rights era Alston was a founding member of Spiral, a black artists group formed to make a visual contribution to the struggle for racial equality.

—Jacqueline Francis

AMAKI, Amalia (K.)

American mixed-media artist

Born: Atlanta, Georgia. **Education:** Georgia State University, Atlanta, B.A. 1971; University of New Mexico, B.A. 1980; Emory University, Atlanta, M.A. 1992, Ph.D. 1994. **Career:** Museum assistant, University Art Museum, Albuquerque, New Mexico,

1978-80; contributing writer, *Art Papers,* Atlanta, 1985-87, *Southern Homes,* Norcross, Georgia, 1985-91; art critic, *Creative Loafing,* Atlanta, 1986-87; instructor, Spelman College, Atlanta, 1987-88; instructor, Morehouse College, Atlanta, 1988-90; adjunct instructor, Atlanta College of Art, 1990; instructor, Spelman College, Atlanta, 1992-93; adjunct instructor, Kennesaw State College, Georgia, 1993; appraiser, Atlanta Life Insurance Company Collection, 1993; adjunct instructor, Atlanta College of Art, 1994; curator, Robert W. Woodruff Library, Atlanta University Center, Atlanta, 1994-95. **Address:** 1790 Willis Mill Road, S.W., Atlanta, Georgia 30311-3818, U.S.A.

Individual Exhibitions:

1983	Morris Brown College, Atlanta
1986	Nexus Contemporary Arts Center, Atlanta
1991	Hughley Gallery, Atlanta
1992	Spelman College, Atlanta
	Albany Museum of Art, Georgia
1993	Brenau University, Gainesville, Georgia
	Seven Stages Gallery, Atlanta
	The Light Factory, Charlotte, North Carolina
	Beach Institute, Savannah, Georgia
	BAGIT Gallery, Chicago
1994	Atlanta Financial Center
1995	Houston Center for Photography
1995	*Seventy-Five Mixed-Media Works,* Emory University, Atlanta

Selected Group Exhibitions:

1984	Schatten Gallery, Emory University, Atlanta
1991	Artspace Gallery, Atlanta
1992	New Visions Gallery, Atlanta
	Atlanta Photography Gallery
1993	*Photographs APG,* Robert Woodruff Arts Center, Atlanta
1994	*Points of Observations: Six Atlanta Artists,* University of West Florida, Pensacola
	Ann Nathan Gallery, Chicago
	Museum of Fine Arts, Houston
1995	American Cultural Center, Charlotte, North Carolina
	Georgia Museum of Art, Athens

Collections:

Albany Museum of Art; Apex Museum; Atlanta-Fulton County Library, Georgia; High Museum of Art, Atlanta; Museum of Fine Arts, Boston; Spelman College Collection, Atlanta.

Publications:

By AMAKI: Articles—"The Invisible Artist," in *Creative Loafing* (Georgia), 2 February 1985; "Ambivalent Spaces, Planar Depth," in *Creative Loafing* (Georgia), 16 March 1985; "Ways of Seeing: The Crisis of Contemporary Black Artists," in *Selected Essays: Art and Artists from the Harlem Renaissance to the 1980s,* Atlanta, National Black Arts Festival, 1988; "Harlem Renaissance: Art of Black America Relies Too Much on Era's Outgrowth," in *The Atlanta Journal and Constitution,* 23 August 1988.

On AMAKI: Articles—"Amalia Amaki: American Reminiscences, Buttons and Blues" by Clarence White, in *Art Papers,* May/June 1994; "Strange Fruit" by Amy Jinkner-Lloyd, in *Creative Loafing,* 12 March 1994; "Collages Are Not Button Down Art: Amalia Amaki Savors the Familial Intimacy of Common Treasures" by Catherine Fox, in *The Atlanta Journal/Atlanta Constitution,* 20 March 1994; "Amalia Amaki/Liz Hampton" by Mildred Thompson, in *Art Papers,* November/December 1994.

*   *   *

Some aspect of revisiting the past dominates most of Amalia Amaki's works. This revisiting is observed in *Three Hummers* (1994-95, photographs, buttons, simulated pearls, beads, and jewelry fragments, 21" x 7") and *Fan Series: A Small Token of Great Regard* (1994, buttons, simulated pearls, fabric, jewelry fragments, 20" x 15"). Amaki's mother is responsible for her choice of materials. Buttons and other sewing notions refer to her preschool years, when she routinely played with sewing notions as her marbles. The artist's mother was too busy to entertain her, and her three older sisters were either in school or with their friends. Her father was at work. So Amaki was left alone to while away the hours with her marbles. Her mother, however, felt that the marbles were not "correct" items of play for a gentile, Atlanta-born child. In exchange for the marbles, Amaki's mother gave her child her special tins of buttons. Because the tins of sewing notions were so special to her mother, they were also special to Amaki and thus began a love affair that lasts until this day.

Amaki's works are full of familial ties. Her perception of the objects and subjects of these ties is discernible in *Three Hummers* and *Fan Series: A Small Token of Great Regard.* Presented as a totem, *Three Hummers* appears to be a tribute to Amaki's three foremothers— mother, grandmother, and great-grandmother. Like Amaki, I remember my mother and grandmother humming their favorite songs. Early in the morning and late at night, I recall how comforting it was to hear them hum. Although Amaki may have heard her great-grandmother humming, most likely the legacy and the memory were passed down as in the placement of these individuals in the piece, one superimposed atop the other. The women and the items that surround them are carriers of her stories that are not completely known and will never be known. What the artist attempts, however, is a glimpse into their lives. Who touched the lives of these women? Who touched the buttons? Where had these women been? Where had these buttons been? On a daily basis these women were probably often taken for granted. Buttons, too, are taken for granted until you lose one. Amaki weaves an intriguing counterpoint with subjects and objects, and she reminds us to revere the commonplace and mundane.

From her "Fan" series is *A Small Token of Great Regard.* In her inimitable way Amaki takes a device that is used for producing a current of air and incorporates multiple messages in its design. We are reminded that Amaki grew up in Atlanta and attended the Wheat Street Baptist Church. Fans were often part of a complete Sunday outfit. Additionally, enterprises such as funeral homes and neighborhood grocery stores advertised on paper fans that were placed in the storage racks on each of the pews. Amaki played with these fans when she was a youth. She takes us back to those days, and she also includes a photograph, buttons, and a note card on which the words "A token of high regard" are printed. The artist uses artistic license and places these unrelated items in a homogeneous setting. Even though the buttons, when applied to a surface, alter

the original field, the photographic image and the printed word dictate the size of the button area, the colors utilized, and the type of button cluster. Nevertheless, the buttons maintain a certain independence because they are, obviously, a nontraditional material. They assume a jewel-like, light-reflective quality despite their utilitarian association. Amaki endeavors to combine the sacred, the secular, and the familial in a setting that is powerful and provocative.

—Jontyle Theresa Robinson

AMOS, Emma

American painter and printmaker

Born: Atlanta, Georgia, 1938. **Education:** Antioch College, Yellow Springs, Ohio, B.A. 1958; London Central School of Art, diploma 1960; New York University, M.A. 1965. **Career:** Since 1980 professor of art and since 1994 undergraduate director, Mason Gross School of the Arts, Rutgers University, New Brunswick, New Jersey. Member, Printmaking Workshop, New York, 1964-82, Spiral (club and art discussion group with Romare Bearden, Norman Lewis, Hale Woodruff, and Charles Alston), 1964-66; creator, writer, and co-host, *Show of Hands,* WGBH (television), Boston, Massachusetts, 1977-78; collective member and contributor, *Heresies,* New York, 1984-96; advisory board member and contributor, *M/E/A/N/I/ N/G,* 1990-96; chair, board of governors, 1994-96, and co-chair (with David Reed) since 1996, Skowhegan School of Painting and Sculpture, Maine; trustee, Richard Florsheim Art Fund, since 1995. **Awards:** National Endowment for the Arts Fellowship (drawing), 1983; New York Foundation for the Arts Fellowship (painting), 1989; Rockefeller Foundation Fellowship (painting, Bellagio, Italy), 1993; Catalog Publication Award, Richard Florsheim Art Fund, 1993; Art Matters Fellowship (painting), 1994. **Address:** 21 Bond Street, New York, New York 10012, U.S.A.

Individual Exhibitions:

1960	Alexander Gallery, Atlanta, Georgia
1974	Davis Fine Arts Gallery, West Virginia State College, Institute, West Virginia
1979	Art Salon, New York
1980	Gallery 62, National Urban League, New York
1983	Jazzonia Galleries, Cleveland, Ohio, and Detroit
1986	Galleri Oscar, Stockholm
1987	Parker/Bratton Gallery, New York
1988	Isobel Neal Gallery, Chicago
	Jersey City Museum, New Jersey
	Shifflett Gallery, Los Angeles
1989	Zimmerman/Saturn Gallery, Nashville, Tennessee
	Ingrid Cusson Gallery, New York
	Clemson University Gallery, Genoa, Italy
	Douglass College Women Artists Series, New Jersey
1990	Newark Museum, Newark, New Jersey
	Zimmerman/Saturn Gallery, Nashville, Tennessee
1991	Bronx Museum, New York
	McIntosh Gallery, Atlanta, Georgia
1992	Pump House Gallery, Bushnell Park Foundation, Hartford, Connecticut
1993	College of Wooster Art Museum, Wooster, Ohio (traveling through 1995)

Emma Amos, 1995. Photo courtesy of Becket Logan.

1994   Art in General, New York (traveling through 1995)
1996   Sherry Washington Gallery, Detroit

Selected Group Exhibitions:

1992   *Dream Singers, Story Tellers: An African American Presence,* New Jersey State Museum, Trenton
        Reading Prints, Museum of Modern Art, New York
1994   *Engaged Vision,* Terry Dintenfass Gallery, New York
        Romare Bearden and Friends: Emma Amos, Charles Alston, Herbert Gentry, Norman Lewis, Alitash Kebede Gallery, Los Angeles
        Interamericano De Artistas Plastico, Museo De Las Artes, Universidad de Guadalajara, Guadalajara, Mexico
1995   *Division of Labor: Women's Work in Contemporary Art, 1970-95,* Bronx Museum of the Arts, New York
1996   *A Women's Place,* Monmouth Museum, Lincroft, New Jersey
        Six Artists: The 1990s, New Jersey State Museum, Trenton
        Bearing Witness: Contemporary Works by African American Women Artists, Atlanta, Georgia
        Thinking Print: Books to Billboards, 1980-95, Museum of Modern Art, New York

Collections:

Bellevue Hospital Fine Arts Collection, New York; Colgate-Palmolive Collection, New York; College Board Collection of Prints by American Artists, New York; Columbia Museum, Columbia, South Carolina; Dade County Museum of Art, Florida; Franklin Furnace, New York; Jane Voorhees Zimmerli Art Museum, New Brunswick, New Jersey; Johnson & Johnson Inc., New Brunswick, New Jersey; Lang Communications, New York; Library of Congress, Washington, D.C.; Minnesota Museum of Art, Minneapolis; Museum of Modern Art, New York; New Jersey State Museum, Trenton; Newark Museum, New Jersey; New York Health and Hospitals Corporation, New York; Rutgers University Hospital, New Brunswick, New Jersey; Skandinaviska Enskilda Bankn, Stockholm; Schomburg Collection, New York Public Library; Spelman College, Atlanta, Georgia; Studio Museum in Harlem, New York; Tulsa Civic Center, Tulsa, Oklahoma; Wadsworth Atheneum, Hartford, Connecticut; Williams College Museum, Williamstown, Massachusetts.

Publications:

By AMOS: Articles—"Some Dos and Don'ts for Black Women Artists," in *HERESIES,* (15), 1982; "Juicy Overflowing Studios: Questions Too Rude to Ask Older Artists" (interviews with Joseph Delaney and Claire Moore), in *Art and Artists,* November 1982; "Letters: Invisible Women," in *New York Times,* 23 April 1989; "Forum 1989," in *M/E/AN/I/N/G,* May 1989; "Contemporary View on Racism in the Arts," in *M/E/AN/I/N/G,* May 1990; "Dos and Don'ts for Art Students," in *HERESIES* (25), 1990; book cover and essay in *Bad Girls, Good Girls: Women, Sex & Power in the Nineties,* Maglin and Perry, editors, New Brunswick, New Jersey, Rutgers University Press, 1996.

On AMOS: Books—*Emma Amos: Paintings and Prints 1982-92,* exhibition catalog, by Thalia Gouma-Peterson, Bell Hooks, and Valerie Mercer, New York, Studio Museum in Harlem, 1993. **Articles**—"Laws of Falling Bodies: Emma Amos, 'The Falling Series,' Jerry Clifford Community Gallery, The Bronx Museum of the Arts" by Arlene Raven, in *The Village Voice,* 7 May 1991; "When Deep Memories Are Unshakable" by William Zimmer, in *New York Times,* 12 April 1992; "A Catalyst for Sophistication" by William Zimmer, in *New York Times,* 9 February 1992; "Emma Amos: 'Painting White,'" in *Essence,* September 1994; "Light, Canvas, Action! When Artists Go to the Movies!" in *ARTnews,* December 1994; "Black (and White) Snapshots" by Bell Hooks, in *Ms.,* September/October 1994; "Everything from Emma Amos, Art in Review" by Pepe Karmel, in *New York Times,* 3 March 1995; "Emma Amos, Studio Museum" by Ruth Bass, in *ARTnews,* May 1995; "Emma Amos at the Studio Museum in Harlem," in *Art in America,* January 1996. **Video**—*Emma Amos, Action Lines,* hosted by Anna Deavere Smith, L & S Enterprises, Inc.

*   *   *

Emma Amos was born and spent her early years in Atlanta, Georgia. Surrounded by the supportive environment of her family and the intellectual community at the colleges of Atlanta University Center (where her father had a drugstore), the artist developed a sense of personhood from which emanates the woman-centered art she has developed since completing her education.

Emma Amos: *X Flag,* **1993. Photo courtesy of Becket Logan.**

In 1963 she was asked to join Spiral, a group whose main thrust was art-making and the politics of being an African American artist. Amos was the only woman member. In existence for three years, the group had one exhibition at their 147 Christopher Street space in Greenwich Village. Negritude and abstract expressionism were important topics for discussion. Amos's first foray into abstract expression occurred during her sojourn in London. She saw and was influenced by the work of the American abstract expressionists, including Norman Lewis, a founding member of Spiral.

A decisive period in Amos's career was the civil rights movement. She shifted to more politically oriented works with strong womanist proclivities. In 1991 she completed a body of work entitled the "Women Artists" series. These paintings acknowledge women artists and the significance of the history of women. *Elizabeth Catlett, India, and Emma* (intaglio printed silk collagraph, watercolor); *Camille, Remember Me* (silk collagraph); *Have Faith* (silk collagraph, copper); *Howardena* (intaglio printed silk collagraph); and *Giza and Faith* (acrylic on linen canvas, African fabric borders) are five works from the series. *Elizabeth Catlett, India, and Emma* pays homage to the sculptor Elizabeth Catlett and features an image of her onyx sculpture *Recognition.* Amos's daughter, India, is portrayed holding a photograph of her artist/mother above her head. The mother/daughter relationship is revealed in both Catlett's sculpture and the images of India and Emma. In *Camille, Remember Me* the artist includes three images—a self-portrait of Amos wearing a t-shirt with the word "artist" inscribed on it; a laser-transfer photograph of a group of Amos's mother's friends; and Camille Billops, visual artist, filmmaker, and archivist. Artist Faith Ringgold is recognized in *Have Faith* and *Giza and Faith.* Giza Daniels Endesha, Amos's former student at Rutgers who died of AIDS, is also memorialized in this work.

The 1994 work *Tightrope* (acrylic on linen, African fabric, laser-transfer photographs of Mrs. Gauguin's breasts from *Two Tahitian Women with Mangoes* [reproduced in the four corners] 82" x 58") reveals the import of the various influences on her art. These influences include her personal search for and focus on gender-oriented issues; the Atlanta years; travels abroad; and her association with the art and political concerns of Spiral. Amos portrays herself in *Tightrope* above the ground. Perched precariously on this rope, the possibility of falling is real and immediate. We wonder about the artist and where this journey will take her as she moves across to the other side. Will the trip across the tightrope yield safety, or will she plummet into change and discord? The artist creates and is a part of the tension. The association with Spiral is evident in the use of African textiles, symbols, and motifs. It is a "pieced work" that recalls African cloth appliqués or African American quilts.

Amos, who is an art professor at Rutgers University in New Jersey, has been a champion for bringing issues related to women to prominence in the twentieth century. Her role in focusing on gender issues in art will be critical as she moves toward the next century.

—Jontyle Theresa Robinson

ANDREWS, Benny
American painter

Born: Madison, Georgia, 13 November 1930. **Education:** Fort Valley State College, Ft. Valley, Georgia, 1948-50; School of the

Benny Andrews.

Chicago Art Institute, 1954-58, B.F.A. 1958; University of Chicago, 1955-56. **Military Service:** United States Air Force: staff sergeant. **Family:** Married 1) Mary Ellen Smith in 1959 (divorced 1976), two sons and one daughter; 2) Nene Humphrey in 1986. **Career:** Since 1969 art instructor, professor, Queens College, New York. Director, Visual Arts Program, National Endowment for the Arts, Washington, D.C., 1982-84. Since 1987 member, board of directors, The MacDowell Colony, Artists Talk on Art, Provincetown Work Center, Creativedrama Society, Atlanta Bureau of Cultural Affairs Gallery. **Awards:** John Hay Whitney Fellowship, 1956-66; New York Council on the Arts fellowships, 1971-81; MacDowell Colony fellowships, 1972-73, 1975-78; National Endowment for the Arts Fellowship, 1974-81; O'Hara Museum Prize, Tokyo, 1976; Bellagio Study and Conference Center Fellowship, Rockefeller Foundation, Bellagio, Italy; President's Research Award, Queen's College, 1990. **Address:** 130 West 26th Street, New York, New York 10001, U.S.A.

Individual Exhibitions:

1962	Forum Gallery, New York
1964	Forum Gallery, New York
1966	Forum Gallery, New York

Benny Andrews: *Confinement II,* 1996.

1971	Studio Museum, New York
1972	ACA Galleries
1973	ACA Galleries
1975	ACA Galleries
	Herbert F. Johnson Museum
1976	Lerner-Heller Gallery, New York
1977	Ulrich Museum, Wichita, Kansas
1978	Wadsworth Atheneum, Hartford, Connecticut
	Lerner-Heller Gallery, New York
	High Museum, Atlanta, Georgia
1982	Albany Museum of Art, Albany, Georgia
1983	Sid Deutch Gallery, New York
1985	Brooks Museum, Memphis, Tennessee
	Stanback Museum, Orangeburg, South Carolina
1985	Armstrong Gallery, New York
	Gallery 291, Atlanta, Georgia
1987	Shifflett Gallery, Los Angeles
1988	Studio Museum, New York
1989	Studio Museum, New York
	Danville Museum of Fine Arts and History, Virginia
1989	Sherry Washington Fine Arts, Detroit
1989	McIntosh Gallery, Atlanta, Georgia
	Gross McCleaf Gallery, Philadelphia
1992	Butler Institute of Art, Youngstown, Ohio
	Mississippi Museum of Art, Jackson
	Triton Museum of Art, Santa Clara, California
	Susan Conway Carroll Gallery, Washington, D.C.
1993	New Jersey State Museum, Trenton
	Fine Art Museum of the South, Mobile, Alabama
	Arkansas Art Center, Little Rock
1995	Dayton Art Institute, Ohio
	Harriet Tubman Museum, Macon, Georgia
	Brandywine Print Image Gallery, Philadelphia
	Bill Hodges Gallery, New York

Selected Group Exhibitions:

1984	National Academy, New York
1987	Georgia Museum, Athens
	Hecksher Museum, New York
1990	Columbus Museum, Columbus, Georgia
1992	R.F. Brush Art Gallery, Canton, New York
1993	Fine Arts Museum of the South, Mobile, Alabama
	New Jersey State Museum, Trenton
1994	Morris Museum of Art, Augusta, Georgia
1995	High Museum of Art, Atlanta, Georgia
	Glass Museum, New York

Collections:

Memphis Brooks Museum of Art, Tennessee; Brooklyn Museum of Art, New York; Chrysler Museum of Art, Norfolk, Virginia; Columbus Art Museum, Columbus, Ohio; Detroit Institute of Art; Fine Art Museum, Mobile, Alabama; High Museum of Art, Atlanta, Georgia; Hirshhorn Museum, Washington, D.C.; Little Rock Art Center, Little Rock, Arkansas; Metropolitan Museum of Art, New York; Morris Museum of Art, Augusta, Georgia; Museum of Modern Art, New York; New Jersey State Museum, Trenton; Newark Museum of Art, New Jersey; Philadelphia Academy of Art; Studio Museum, New York; Ulrich Museum of Art, Wichita, Kansas; Wichita Museum of Art, Wichita, Kansas; Wadsworth Atheneum, Hartford, Connecticut.

Publications:

By ANDREWS: Articles—"One Understanding Black Art," in *New York Times,* 27 June 1970; "The B.E.C.C.," in *Arts Magazine,* Summer 1970; "Prison Art after a Decade," in *American Artists,* March 1977; "A Wonderful Potpourri of Styles," in *Art Journal,* Summer 1980; "Soyers' Work at the Form," in *Artworld,* November 1985; "Benton's America at the Equitable," in *Artworld,* November 1985; "Is There a Black Esthetic?" in *Art Papers,* November/December 1985; "Decentralization: the Greening of America," in *Art Papers,* March/April 1986; "The Mule Is about Keeping On," *American Visions,* April 1988.

*   *   *

Benny Andrews could be called a minimalist. His drawings, oils, and collages, created over the past forty years, were all done in a similar manner, and Andrews has been quoted as saying that he was not interested in how much he could do on canvas but how little. At the beginning of his career, Andrews always wanted to express black experience through his art, but he found during his studies at the Chicago Art Institute that it was a difficult thing to do. Boris Mango and Jack Levine were the people at the Institute who inspired him to continue to make art in his own way. Andrews began his own style of painting in the 1960s, when the collage movement started to flourish. He was using geometrical forms in his art, and abstract expressionism became a personal movement for him. Even though he has very little going on in his pieces, the message is as effective as if the composition were on a much larger scale. His drawing *Mourners* (Study for *Appalachee Red*) from 1977 shows only the outline of man and a woman with their backs to the viewers. Their stooped postures in front of a small casket make one feel the sadness and the agony of losing a loved one. *The Preacher*, also from 1977, is a simple drawing that reminds viewers of early-morning Sunday sermons. Andrews is a humanist and crusader, whose portraits depict his personal feelings about human life, suffering, desperation, and about hardworking African Americans and blacks all over the world.

During the 1960s and 1970s Andrews was also busy organizing a crusade on behalf of the black artist. The Black Emergency Cultural Coalition became the mouthpiece for the black artist. His 1971 painting *No More Games,* located in the New York Museum of Modern Art collection, is about the plight of black artists. It is a collage of oil and cloth on canvas, a composition of a dejected male sitting on a box, waiting for something to happen. On the second panel is a body covered with an American flag—perhaps this person was lynched. Edmund B. Gaither characterized another Andrews painting entitled *Trash* as "false religion plus sexism plus militarism plus false democracy equals deception equals trash or waste."

Andrews wanted to express himself differently from other artists in order to create his own unique individuality. His works are delicate, subtle, and intimate. Whatever the medium, they are always linear, narrative, and abstract. He draws from his past private life in Georgia and his social life in New York. The inclusion of rugged surfaces, found scraps of papers, cloth, and built-up sections gives the paintings a "surreal reality" in relation to the past and present of a person.

His collages are at times illusionary and representational. Christian imagery is prevalent in his work, and many of his collages and paintings have referred to the southern black life, where there was

Emanoel Araújo.

no interference with religion. A social realist, Andrews believes that art elevates people, glorifies people's pasts, and builds self-pride.

—Gabriel Tenabe

ARAÚJO, Emanoel

Brazilian sculptor

Born: Santo Amaro da Purificacao, Bahia, 15 November 1949. **Education:** Fine Arts School of Bahia Federal University, Salvador-Bahia, 1960-64, degree 1964. **Military Service:** Santo Amaro da Purificacao, Bahia, 1958-59, artillery. **Career:** Director, Art Museum of Bahia, Salvador, 1981-83. Since 1992 director, Pinacoteca São Paulo. Since 1996 Ministre of Culture, Brasilla. Distinguished Visiting Professor, City University of New York, 1988-89. **Awards:** Prize of National Young Print, Museum of Contemporary Art of São Paulo, Brazil, 1966; Prize of Exemption of Jury, Rio de Janeiro, Brazil, 1967; Great Silver Medal, Campinas, Brazil, 1967; Third Salon of Ouro Preto First Prize, Ouro Preto, MG-Brazil, 1969; II Salon of Contemporary Art of São Paulo First

Prize, Brazil, 1970; Jornal do Brasil Prize, Rio de Janeiro, 1970; Greeting Card Prize, National Museum of Fine Arts, Rio de Janeiro, 1970; Odorico Tavares Prize, Salvador, Brazil, 1970; Third Graphic Art Biennale of Firenze Gold Medal, Firenze, Italy, 1972; Best Printmaker of the Year Prize, São Paulo Art Critic Association, 1973; Panorama of Prints and Drawings Grand Prize, 1977, and Panorama of Sculpture Prize, 1981, Museum of Modern Art of São Paulo, 1977; Best Sculptor of the Year, São Paulo Art Critic Association APCA, 1983. **Agent:** Hack Hoffemberg, 40 East 62nd Street, New York, New York 10021, U.S.A. **Address:** Rua dos Ingleses, 143, Bela Vista, São Paulo, SP 01329-000, Brazil.

Individual Exhibitions:

1959	Santo Amaro da Purificacao, Brazil
1960	Public School of Bahia-Salvador
1961	Public Library of Salvador
1962	Macunaima Gallery, Rio de Janeiro
1963	Aremar Gallery, Campinas, Brazil
1965	Bonino Gallery, Rio de Janeiro
	Astréia Gallery, São Paulo
	Querino Gallery, Salvador
1966	Bonino Gallery, Rio de Janeiro

Emanoel Araújo: carbon steel structure.

	Astréia Gallery, São Paulo
1967	Hakusuisha Gallery, Osaka, Japan
	Guignard Gallery, Belo Horizonte, Brazil
1968	Bahia Art Museum, Salvador
1969	Guignard Gallery, Belo Horizonte, Brazil
	Bonino Gallery, Rio de Janeiro
1970	Documenta Gallery, São Paulo
1972	Bonino Gallery, Rio de Janeiro
1973	Oscar Seraphico Gallery, Brasilia
1975	Brazilian American Cultural Institute, Washington D.C.
	Bonino Gallery, Rio de Janeiro
1976	Arte Aplicada Gallery, São Paulo
	Arte Memoria Gallery, Belo Horizonte, Brazil
1977	IAB Gallery, Porto Alegre, Brazil
	Oscar Seraphico Gallery, Brasilia
1978	Federal Savings Bank, São Luis, Brazil
1979	Bonino Gallery, Rio de Janeiro
	Cristina Faria de Paula Gallery, São Paulo
	Bahia Art Museum, Salvador
1980	Guignard Gallery, Porto Alegre, Brazil
1981	*O Construtivismo Afetivo de Emanoel Araújo,* Art Museum of São Paulo
1983	Skultura Gallery, São Paulo
1984	Cesar Aché Gallery, Rio de Janeiro
1985	Art Office of Bahia, Salvador
1986	Cesar Aché Gallery, Rio de Janeiro
1987	*Large Scale Sculptures,* Art Museum of São Paulo
	Skultura Gallery, São Paulo
1988	G.R. N'Namdi Galleries, Inc., Birmingham, Michigan
1989	Manhattan East Gallery of Fine Arts, New York
1990	*Thirty Years of Art,* Galeria Skultura, São Paulo
1991	Calouste Gulbenkian Foundation, Lisbon, Portugal
1992	Bärengassen Museum, Zurich
1993	Museu Banespa, São Paulo
	Club Transatlântico, São Paulo

Selected Group Exhibitions:

1965	*Contemporary Printmakers of Brazil,* "Casa de la Paz," Mexico City
1968	*Salon of Modern Art of "Distrito Federal,"* Brasilia
1975	*"Paulista" Salon of Contemporary Art,* São Paulo
1976	Art Museum of São Paulo
1978	Museum of Modern Art of São Paulo
1981	*Contemporary Printmakers of Brazil,* Estoril, Portugal
1984	Biennale Foundation of São Paulo
1985	Museum of Modern Art of São Paulo
1988	*Uptown/Downtown,* Gallery Art 54, New York
1990	Bronx Museum of the Arts, New York

Collections:

Art Museum of São Paulo; Art Museum of Brasilia; Itamaraty Palace, Brasilia; Los Angeles County Museum; Museum of Austin, Texas; Museum of Modern Art of Firenze, Italy; Museum of Modern Art of Rio de Janeiro; Museum of Modern Art of São Paulo; Museum of Sidney, Australia; Rockfeller Foundation, New York; University of Kansai, Japan; Weisman Foundation, Los Angeles.

Publications:

On ARAÚJO: Book—*Bahia Prints Album* by Odorico Tavares, São Paulo, Cultrix Edition, 1965; *Emanoel Araújo: Um Vulcão Rumo ao Classicismo,* São Paulo, Brazil, Galeria Nara Roesler, 1996.

*   *   *

Emanoel Araújo builds opaque colored crystals in the sky. His angular forms thrust upward and outward as they merge with and emerge out of one another, enclosing interior negative spaces and transforming exterior ones. Obliquely aligned shapes, their colors dense and rich, cut through space.

Araújo's work may appear to be solely nonrepresentational—plays of form and color—but appearances can deceive. His works are not only about significant form; they also are forms with significance. Specific sacred entities—African gods who thrive in contemporary Brazil—are present. Araújo captures their essence in works he calls "Afro-minimalist" or "Neo-Ancestral."

One of Araújo's works is entitled *Totem Ogun,* dedicated to the god of iron and war, who embodies strength, force, quickness, and directness. Like his metal, Ogun is hard and sharp. He builds civilizations, or he destroys them. All of these attributes reverberate in Araújo's sculpture that celebrates Ogun's powers and presence. Araújo builds bladelike forms on top of a pyramid, a symbol of Egypt, Africa's most famous civilization. These shapes thrust upward, first one way, then sharply angled to another, like a pivoting cannon or an active phallus—both images supremely evocative of Ogun. Ogun's colors (dark blue and black) make the work appear heavy and dense like his metal.

Eshu is another god present in Araújo's work. He is the divine mediator and trickster who serves as a messenger between gods and humans. Eshu stands at crossroads and thresholds. He embodies action as well as contradiction. As one of his praises claims, "he can throw a stone tomorrow and kill a bird yesterday." Araújo's *Ritoexu* captures many of these aspects. Eshu's colors (red and black) sym-

Octávio Araújo.

bolize his unpredictability and the heat of his sudden transformations. The sprouting, rising forms recall Eshu's primary icon, a projection at the top that refers to many things, among them the link between this world and the next. Volumes intersect at various angles, like the roads guarded by Eshu.

Araújo captures the essence of these African gods in colors, forms, movements, and rhythms—not in realistic representations. A Yoruba proverb says that "only half a speech is necessary for the wise, in their minds it becomes whole." Araújo materializes such wisdom in his Afro-minimalist forms.

Araújo manifests many of the attributes of the gods he evokes in his works. He is clearly a man of action, probably one of the most successful and productive artists in Brazil today. His public sculptures can be seen all over the country—many of them, appropriately enough, at crossroads and city squares. His outer calm and relaxed manner mask an inexhaustible energy. He is driven to achieve and make his mark in the art world beyond Brazil's shores. His style may, therefore, appear international and universal, yet its content, like the work of other Brazilian artists of African descent, is deeply rooted in ancestral traditions. Such seeming contradictions recall aspects of both Ogun and Eshu, his invisible patrons and visible themes.

—Henry John Drewal

ARAÚJO, Octávio (Ferreira de)

Brazilian painter and printmaker

Born: Terra Roxa, State of São Paulo, 22 March 1926. **Education:** Vocational Institute for Boys, São Paulo, 1939-43. **Military Service:** 1946-47: artillery, corporal. **Family:** Married Klara Gourianova in 1960, one son and one daughter. **Career:** Assistant, studio of C. Portianari, Rio de Janeiro, 1952-56; announcer, Radio Moscow, Moscow, 1962-68. **Awards:** First Prize, divided with Roberto Dellamonica, *Saloon Para Todos* Magazine, Rio de Janeiro, 1958; First Prize, Rio de Janeiro, 1959. **Agent:** Klara Gourianova, R. Carlos Affonseca, 53, São Paulo 05353-120, Brazil. **Online Address:** allans@mandic.com.br.

Individual Exhibitions:

1972   *Octávio Araújo Twenty Years Later,* Assis Chateaubriand
             Art Museum, São Paulo
1974   Brazilian Institute of Architects, Porto Alegre
1975   Art Gallery of the Brazilian-American Cultural Institute,
             Washington, D.C.
1979   *Ten Years of Painting,* Andre Art Gallery de São Paulo

Octávio Araújo: *Apotheosis of Afrodite.*

1981   Andre Art Gallery de São Paulo
1996   Benedicto Calixto Museum Foundation, Santos

Selected Group Exhibitions:

1971   Modern Art Museum, São Paulo
1974   Modern Art Museum, São Paulo
        Brazilian Graphic Art of Today, General Direction Fine
           Arts, Madrid (traveling)
1975   Modern Art Museum, São Paulo
1976   New York Botanical Garden Museum, New York
        Stozzi Palace, Florence, Italy
        World Festival of the Negro and African Art and Culture,
           Lagos, Nigeria
1980   *Salon Comparaison,* Grand Palais, Paris
1981   Grand Palais, Paris
1989   California Afro-American Museum, Los Angeles

Collections:

Modern Art Museum, São Paulo; Municipal Library, São Paulo;

Museum of São Paulo State; Pushkin Museum of Western Art,
Moscow; Lasar Segall Museum, São Paulo.

Publications:

On ARAÚJO: Books—*Octávio Araújo: Ten Years of Painting,*
exhibition catalog, São Paulo, Andre Art Gallery de São Paulo and J.
R. Teixeira Leite, 1979; *The Drawing and the Feminine,* exhibition
catalog, São Paulo, Andre Art Gallery and J. Klintowitz, 1981;
Masters of Brazilian Drawing by J. Klintowitz, São Paulo,
Folkswagen of Brazil, 1983; *Brazilian Engravers* by J. Klintowitz,
São Paulo, Folkswagen of Brazil, 1984. **Articles**—"The Roots of
Octávio's Art" by P. Maranca, in *Ultima Hora* (São Paulo), May
1972; "The Surreal, Designed, Engraved, Photographed" by A. P.
D'Horta, in *O Estado de São Paulo,* October 1972; "Art and Sci-
ence in Octávio Araújo," in *Planeta Magazine,* March 1973; "The
Formal Case of Octávio Araújo" by A. Zago, in *O Estado de São
Paulo,* 10 July 1979; "Octávio Araújo: The Solitude Far from All
the 'ism'" by O. Kruse, in *Jornal da Tarde* (São Paulo), September
1979; "The Magic Art of Octávio Araújo" by L. Sanches, in *Folha
de São Paulo,* September 1979; "The Fantastical Art of Octávio

Araújo" by E. Sacramento, in *Diario Do Grande ABC* (São Paulo), 5 May 1982.

*

Octávio Araújo comments:

During 1950 I studied engraving at the Academy of Fine Arts of Paris and the Print Cabinet of the Louvre. My award by *Para Todos* magazine was a trip to China for one year, taking a course in traditional Chinese engraving, as announced by the magazine, but it wasn't true. Roberto Dellamonica and I had the right to remain there only for fifteen days. As a compensation Jorge Amado, then the editor of the magazine and the initiator of the Saloon, arranged for us an invitation to the USSR, where I knew Klara, our interpreter, an employee of the Association of Plastic Artists of the USSR and my future wife. At that time the only way to return and stay there in order to marry her was try to get a scholarship. This is what I did and in 1960 received it from the Ministry of Culture of the USSR. As soon as I got the job at the Brazilian broadcast of Radio Moscow and invitations to illustrate the Latin American literature, I refused my postgraduate scholarship. In 1968 my family and I went to Brazil.

I don't see any important reason to talk about myself or my work as painter and designer. The life and the work of someone speak by themselves with more objectivity and eloquence than any comments made with the claim of clarifying what is evident by itself. Concerning the influences received along my fifty years of work as an artist, I was first interested in the Italian, German, and French Renaissance and in Flemish primitives. At the same time I felt a great enthusiasm for Bosh, Rembrandt, Velasquez, Goya, and also for the ancient Greek and Benin sculpture. Later I became interested in French romanticism and impressionism. Afterwards my attention was drawn to van Gogh's painting, German expressionism, and European symbolism and surrealism. I don't belong to any specific artistic tendency. Each artist reflects in his achievement, with more or less intensity, certain characteristics of the time in which he lives, and, sometimes, the artist transcends his present time and announces the future.

*   *   *

Octávio Araújo facetiously describes himself as an "imperfect Brazilian"—his heritage includes African, Indian, and Portuguese, but not Asian, elements. He adds mischievously that he compensates for this by adding yellow colors to his works. But such issues do not often occupy his thoughts. He is more interested in creating other, surreal, worlds.

Araújo's early work was in the style of German expressionism. He then went to Italy, where he "touched" a drawing by Leonardo da Vinci and in turn the work touched him ("it became a virus—I had to draw and paint"). He traveled to China and then Russia, where he met his first surrealist artists, and he has worked in that style ever since.

Araújo is a surrealist on many levels. Not only are his images culled from disparate, totally unrelated sources, but the meticulousness of his painting and printing techniques also suggests eras long past. Even before the pigment is dry, his paintings look as if they have been around for centuries. He evokes several epochs—the medieval world of Hieronymus Bosch, the Renaissance world of Leonardo and Sandro Botticelli, the mystical world of the nineteenth-century symbolists, and the twentieth-century surrealism of Salvador Dali. Yet his work is different from all of these. It is a very personal, independent vision. Like his floating images, Araújo's work is not connected to a particular nation, culture, or era in any so-called logical way. Rather, he transcends such boundaries, forcing viewers to react instinctively, to let their minds and imaginations wander freely.

Araújo's choice of images reflects his thinking at various times in his life. In the 1960s and 1970s he began to read much about Africa, African art, and African influences in Brazil to learn more about this part of his ancestry. These themes appear prominently in works like his 1975 lithograph *Aphrodite: Syncretic Representation,* which juxtaposes Greek and African (Kota) images of beauty and purity. The images symbolize the essence of life itself and the themes of nature and fertility. The dice refer to games of chance, but they also are meant to evoke Afro-Brazilian divination systems that involve the throwing and reading of cowrie shells.

The artist later turned to other ideas. Araújo explains that "it is cyclical." Depending upon whether his thoughts are close or far from these themes, he may go back to them or leave them. One gets the sense of this reverie as his mind washes over a lifetime of dreams. When talking of his landscapes, Araújo explains that they are "inventions of the mind." His incredible sense of observation and technical skill pull the observer deeper and deeper into the work. They mesmerize the viewer and create a dreamlike state that matches the works themselves.

Araújo escapes into his work and enters other worlds. His striking realism and disquieting images carry viewers far from issues of race, color, and class to battle with the apparitions of their dreams and nightmares. In that sense, his work touches on universal truths that are independent of social or historical conditions. As he says, he tries to create an ambiance of ambiguity in his work, since "there is mystery and magic in life."

—Henry John Drewal

ARGUDIN Y PEDROSO, Pastor

Cuban painter and muralist

Born: Havana, Cuba, c.1889. **Career:** Housepainter and muralist, Havana, Cuba. **Awards:** Fine Arts of Decorative Painting Award, Madrid Academy, Spain, 1915. **Died.**

Individual Exhibitions:

1935	Harmon Foundation, New York (retrospective)
	Bereen Manual Training and Industrial School, Philadelphia (retrospective)
	New York Public Library (retrospective)

Selected Group Exhibitions:

1926	*Philadelphia Sesquicentennial*
1931	*International Colonial Exposition,* Paris
1935	Harmon Foundation, New York
	New Jersey State Museum, Trenton

Collections:

Club Atenas, Havana, Cuba; Museum of Andalusia, Seville, Spain; Schomburg Center, New York.

Publications:

On ARGUDIN Y PEDROSO: Articles—"The Face Everybody Knows" by W. B. Courtney, in *Collier's Magazine,* 12 February 1949, p. 36; "Candid Negro Art," in *Art Digest,* 1 September 1935, p. 19.

*   *   *

Pastor Argudin y Pedroso was a Cuban portrait and genre painter who remains little known in the United States. Of the few of his works that have been published, most are poor black-and-white reproductions; several additional pieces are known only by name.

Born in 1889 in Havana to parents who had been slaves, Argudin initiated his artistic career as a house painter who drew on newly painted walls. It may have been around this time that he executed a mural in the Church of Our Lady, Havana (a parish church of the poor). After Spanish painter Francisco Piera discovered Argudin, a government scholarship allowed the budding artist to study abroad. He remained in Europe for about twenty years, with stops in Italy, Spain (where he won awards in fine arts and decorative painting from the Madrid Academy in 1915, had a solo exhibition at the Pavilion de Cuba, Seville, and had a piece placed in the Museum of Andalusia, Seville), and France (where he was the only Cuban represented at the International Colonial Exposition in 1931).

Two of Argudin's earliest known works date from this time. *The Gardens of Versailles* (1919) depicts a broad, curving avenue flanked by trees with a row of statues on the left and conical hedges on the right. The shadowed pathway begins in the lower left and opens to sunlight in the center of the composition. Painted in short brushstrokes, its dappled surface demonstrates impressionist influences. *Breton Women: Concarneau* (also known as *Bretons Coming from the Marketplace,* 1924) is more realist in subject matter and technique. The composition is divided bilaterally. On the left on shadowed stone steps rest two women who are chatting after having set down their ceramic vessels near their feet. The younger woman, dressed in a dark gown and boots, and white collar, apron, and bonnet with lappets, gestures in animated conversation. Seated below her and leaning against a stone or brick wall, an older woman, hands folded in lap, listens attentively. In the center right a young woman walks away from the pair down a narrow, sunlit corridor. Carrying her vessel in her right hand, she cocks her left hand on hip. This work evokes the mid-nineteenth-century genre peasant pieces of Jean-François Millet and Josef Israels. Argudin exhibited such work in cities throughout Europe and at the Philadelphia Sesquicentennial (1926).

Around the early 1930s Argudin began correspondence with a Puerto Rican immigrant librarian named Arthur Schomburg. It was probably Schomburg who introduced Argudin to influential figures in the art world. In February 1935 the Harmon Foundation—aided by the Honorable Cayetano de Quesada, Consul for Cuba—hosted a solo exhibition of forty works by Argudin painted in Europe, Cuba, and the United States. Among those works believed to have been on display were *Abraham Lincoln* (c.1925), a grave, bust-length, three-quarters portrait of the Civil War era president set against a plain background. Dressed in a dark suit, Lincoln's middle-aged, lined face appears contemplative. (Club Atenas in Havana, a

cultural, political, and civic organization, acquired the work.) The show then traveled to the Berean Manual Training and Industrial School in Philadelphia in April. By the spring of 1935 the artist's pastels (*Senegalese Warrior, Children from the Congo Playing the Tambourine, Dance of Celom,* and *Girl Warrior*) were being shown at the New Jersey State Museum in Trenton, where they received considerable attention from the public, according to *Art Digest.* Next Schomburg coordinated a solo exhibition of the painter's work at the 135th Street branch of the New York Public Library that July and acquired Argudin's copy of Diego Velázquez's *Juan de Pareja* (c.1930-35), as well as *Portrait of the Curator, Arthur A. Schomburg* (1935), for the institution. After this auspicious beginning Argudin seems to have returned to Cuba and disappeared from public view in the States.

—Theresa Leininger-Miller

ARTIS, William Ellisworth
American sculptor, ceramist, and illustrator

Born: Washington, North Carolina, 2 February 1914. **Education:** Art Students League, New York, 1933-35; Alfred University, Alfred New York; Syracuse University, New York, B.F.A., M.F.A.; New York State University, College of Ceramics; Long Beach State College, California; Pennsylvania State University, University Park; Chadron State College, Chadron, Nebraska, B.S.; New York State College of Ceramics; Greenwich House Ceramic Center. **Military Service:** U.S. Army, 1941-45: technical sergeant. **Career:** Teacher, Harlem YMCA, Nebraska State Teachers College. Member, American Ceramic Society, National Sculpture Society, College Art Association of America, National Art Education Association, New York Society of Arts and Crafts. **Awards:** John Hope Prize, 1933, 1935; Atlanta University Purchase awards, 1944, 1947, 1952, 1959, 1962, 1965; Rosenwald Fellowship, 1947; Sculpture Purchase Prize, Atlanta University, 1951; Outstanding Afro-American Artist, 1970; Outstanding Educator of America, 1970; Smith-Mason Gallery Award, 1971. **Died:** April 1977.

Individual Exhibitions:

1921	Carl von Vechter Gallery of Fine Arts, Nashville
1940	Museum of Modern Art, New York

Selected Group Exhibitions:

1933	Harmon Foundation, Talladega College, Alabama
1934	College Art Association, New York
1935	New Jersey State Museum, Newark
1940	Whitney Museum, New York
	Museum of Modern Art, New York
1942	Grace Horn Galleries, Boston
1944	Atlanta University, Georgia
1947	Syracuse Museum of Fine Arts, New York

Collections:

Atlanta University, Georgia; Howard University, Washington D.C.;

Joslyn Art Museum, Omaha, Nebraska; National Portrait Gallery, Smithsonian Institution, Washington, D.C.; Slater Memorial Museum, Norwich, Connecticut; Walker Art Center, New York.

Publications:

On ARTIS: Articles—"Negro Artists in the Fifth Harmon Exhibition," in *Southern Workman,* 62, April 1933, pp. 175-181; "New Yorkers Win Honors at Atlanta Show," in *Art Digest,* 15 April 1951, p. 13; "Leading Negro Artist," in *Ebony,* 18, September 1963, pp. 131ff; "William Ellisworth Artis: Afro-American Sculptor, Ceramist and Teacher" by Robert P. Johnson, in *Minority Voices: An Interdisciplinary Journal of Literature and the Arts,* Spring 1977, pp. 42-52 (illustrated).

*   *   *

William Ellisworth Artis, a sculptor, ceramist, and educator, is best known for a series of terra cotta and stoneware heads of black youth he created in the 1930s and 1940s. Artis's earliest known pieces are *Head of a Girl* (c. 1933), exhibited by the Harmon Foundation and the Art Student's League in 1933, and *Weariness* (1934), shown at the Salon of America Exhibit at Radio City in New York in 1934 (and awarded an honorable mention). Artis's models' faces typically have an introverted impassivity and a spiritual appeal. *Head of a Negro Boy* (1937, terra cotta) and *Head of a Boy* (1940, terra cotta) both depict a sensitive visage with almond eyes looking slightly to the side, thin eyebrows, a broad forehead, and full, sensual lips. With their smooth skin and stoic expressions, they are reminiscent of ancient Nok terra cotta heads and Benin bronzes of obas. The former piece, of a younger child in a golden hue with an almost bald head, has the suggestion of a hairline with a small, ribbed curve above the brow. The latter head wears a knit cap. Though the two pieces are very much alike, subtle details hint at individual characteristics, somewhat in the manner of sculpture by Augusta Savage, with whom Artis studied in the early 1930s.

Head of a Woman (1946, stoneware) is a streamlined, Art Deco-influenced head with pupilless eyes, a veil of smooth hair, and a long neck cocked at an angle atop a modular, Brancusi-like base. Such stylizations may also reflect the influence of fellow sculptor Sargent Claude Johnson. While most of Artis's figurative pieces are of anonymous subjects (such as his terra cotta *Two Heads of Children, Portrait Busts of a Brother and Sister,* and *Woman with Kerchief,* 1949), he also produced portraits of such notables as *Dr. Louis Tompkins Wright* (1891-1952) (1946, terra cotta), now in the National Portrait Gallery collection.

Artis was a technical sergeant in the U.S. Army during World War II. After the war he had the opportunity to study on the G.I. bill with Ivan Mestrovic, an expatriate Yugoslav sculptor, at Syracuse University. Mestrovic's influence is apparent in several of Artis's compact, monumental works from this time, including *The Quiet One* (1951). Inspired by a documentary film of the same name about childhood maladjustment in Harlem, the marble statue depicts a boy in a T-shirt sitting with his head buried in his knees, arms wrapped tightly around his legs, and hands clasped about his ankles. *Time* magazine (April 9, 1951) asserted that this piece dominated the sculpture section in the Atlanta University annual, "withdrawn, miserable and taut with life."

In the late 1940s Artis's style changed significantly when he began to produce functional objects (such as ceramic tile room dividers) and experiment with abstract forms and special glazes.

Through the 1960s his ceramic jars, jugs, and vases seemed to reach upward, some from stemlike bases to bulbous bodies with conical lids. This movement toward stretching organic shapes may have been affirmed when Artis worked as an assistant to Claire Falkenstein and Piotr Kowalski at the International Sculpture Symposium at Long Beach State College in the summer and fall of 1965.

Elongation also became evident in Artis's figurative work of the late 1960s and early 1970s, even while the sculptor continued to produce somber, terra cotta heads such as *Michael* (1962) in the manner of his early work. *Supplication* (1971, terra cotta), for instance, depicts a young boy in a loose-fitting, long-sleeved top looking upward with his head tilted back, arms raised with elbows bent and hands gently cupped open. With its expression of hope and entreaty, the work is a profound statement of human aspirations.

Recognized as a gifted ceramist and sculptor in terra cotta, stone, marble, and plaster, Artis was also an exemplary instructor who taught at several institutions. He served as associate professor at Charon State College in Nebraska (1954-65) and Mankato State College in Minnesota (1966-75). For his pedagogical contributions, he was named Outstanding Educator of America in 1970.

—Theresa Leininger-Miller

AUSBY, Ellsworth (Augustus)

American painter

Born: Portsmouth, Virginia, 5 April 1942. **Education:** Pratt Institute, 1960-61; School of Visual Arts, New York, 1961-64, B.F.A., 1977. **Family:** Married 1) Lorraine Eskeles, 1966 (died), three daughters; 2) Jamillah Jennings, one son. **Career:** Since 1978, professor, School of Visual Arts, New York. **Awards:** C.A.P.S. Fellowship, New York, 1980; C.E.P.A. Fellowship, 1980-81; National Endowment for the Arts Fellowship, 1984-85. **Address:** PO Box 15, Brooklyn, New York 11211, U.S.A.

Individual Exhibitions:

1970	Cinque Gallery, New York
1972	Peale Gallery, Pennsylvania Academy of Fine Arts
1973	Artist House, New York
1975	Soho Center for the Arts, New York
1976	Cinque Gallery, New York
1983	Skylight Gallery, Center for Art and Culture of Bedford Stuyvesant
1987	National Museum of Art, Lagos, Nigeria
1993	Norfolk State University
1997	Wagner College, Staten Island, New York

Selected Group Exhibitions:

1969	Brooklyn Museum, New York
1970	Boston Museum of Fine Arts
1971	Whitney Museum of American Arts, New York
1984	High Museum of Art, Atlanta, Georgia
	Brooks Memorial Art Museum, Tennessee
	Los Angeles Municipal Art Gallery

Ellsworth Ausby: untitled.

1993   Aljiria Arts, New Jersey
1995   Reichhold Art Gallery, St. Thomas, Virgin Islands
         Gettysburg Art Gallery, Pennsylvania
1996   Rotunda Gallery, Brooklyn, New York

Collections:

Aldrich Museum of Contemporary Art, Ridgefield, Connecticut; Center for Arts and Culture, Brooklyn, New York; Cinque Gallery, New York; New York City Technical College, Brooklyn; Rice University, Houston, Texas.

Publications:

On AUSBY: Articles—"Ausby Paints that Special Feeling" (interview) by Orde Coombs, in *Encore,* 1, September 1972, pp. 56-57; "Ellsworth Ausby" by April Kingsley, in *The Soho Weekly News* (New York), December 1975; "Ellsworth Ausby" by John Parrault, in *The Soho Weekly News* (New York), 27 February 1980.

*   *   *

The process of making art is not as simple as it seems; various forces have an impact on the artist's conscience. Ellsworth Ausby frees his art from those technical and formal conventions that indubitably obscure purity of visual expression. He is aware of the need for the artist to maintain an autonomy from existing movements and local social events. He has said on this subject, "I know all the major painters in New York. They are my contemporaries. Sometimes we run into one another. It is subliminal, not intentional. In my kind of synthesis, I have always striven for authenticity; no single artist has executed a considerable influence on my art. Teaching in college has exposed me to a variety of art from different periods. You cannot be controlled by the art culture. If you are, you are not an original thinker."

Indeed the contemporary American art circle still contains a menu for propaganda, which is discernible even from its denominations, namely American art (not European American art), African American, Native American, and Latin American art. Ausby believes that his art reflects that he is an American artist—an African who has gone through an acculturation in America. He has to assimilate what he needs in a process of growth. This is probably why, despite more than three decades of artistic odyssey, Ellsworth Ausby has yet to receive attention as one of the foremost artists in contemporary America.

Ausby's excursion into abstract art can be traced to the late 1960s. By 1969 his painting had begun to appear less figurative. An objective transformation from frontality of figures to nonfigurative art was soon to become resonant. Analysis of his art from the 1970s to the present reveals certain recurrent tendencies, such as the use of frontality of structure, approximate symmetry, simplicity of form, and decorative dexterity. He emphasizes the primacy of the diagonal, the horizontal, the vertical, and the curve in an effort to remove extraneous details from his work. These are arguably the basic compositional blocks, but they approximate his intellectual freedom.

Although painting is his principal concern, Ausby has produced some sculptures, portraits, and monoprints, as well. There are two public metal sculptures to his credit. In the 1970s he produced elemental hangings of forceful strips reminiscent of woven structures. Instead of stretching the canvases, he mounted them on the wall to activate the wall into the visual plane. Use of primary colors was not common to his work in this period. Many of these scrolls, such as *Five Fingers and Purple Thumb,* rely heavily on balance of tension, color variegation, and color weight. Another scroll, *Sha-bazz,* conveys his black nationalist sentiments. As part of this effort to find a visual language, Ausby also made some totemic paintings—ten wooden columns painted in acrylic.

Ausby describes his travel to Nigeria for Festac '77 as one of the most meaningful events in his life in that it was a chance to meet black people from all over the world and to evaluate all areas of the arts. Consequently he traveled to Egypt in 1989. The study visit resulted in a series of monoprints and numerous acrylic paintings on canvas. These works are seemingly abstract. The viewer will notice in them this principal format: a pyramidal form at the bottom of the composition, a horizontal thrust at the upper middle, and presumably a baseline structure of a landscape suspending a few other geometric structures.

Features of his compositions are customarily carried on to subsequent works. The diagonal thrust that suspends the semicircular component in the sculpture *Space Odyssey,* installed at the New York Technical College, is fully developed in the 1995-96 "Untitled" series. In this series the internalized central idea, used here as metaphor for fertility, changes from one piece to another in both dynamism and value. The paintings in this series do not seek to satisfy our referential needs but to extend our scope of symmetry and sequential art. In fact most of the paintings could be appreciated from any side with equal interest. The fluctuation between primary and secondary hues lends this collection undeniable simplicity and clarity.

In some of his nonrepresentational work, the use of "Untitled" as a title for each unit and the absence of easily identifiable images seem to limit the work's vocal range. There is this suggested reliance on the viewer as an active participant, who must possess knowledge of the artist and the world he explores through his art.

—Barthosa Nkurumeh

BAILEY, Herman "Kofi"

American painter and printmaker

Born: Chicago, 1931. **Education:** Howard University, Washington, D.C.; Alabama State College; University of Southern California, M.F.A. **Died:** 1981.

Exhibitions:

National Center of Afro-American Artists, Boston; Spelman College, Atlanta.

Publications:

On BAILEY: Articles—"Editors Notes" by Hoyt W. Fuller, in *Negro Digest,* 16, July 1967, p. 4; "Atlanta," in *Journal of Black Poetry,* 1, Winter/Spring 1970, pp. 115; "News Atlanta," in *Rhythm Magazine,* 1(1); "Herman Kofi Bailey" by Lorenz Graham, in *Black Art Quarterly,* 4, April 1981, pp. 25-28.

*　　*　　*

Herman "Kofi" Bailey was concerned that there were not enough positive images of African Americans, and he made it his task to create images of leaders in the global fight for the self-determination of black people. He also created images that captured poignant moments in the everyday lives of blacks. Feeling that art should aid in the uplift and education of the black race, he selected his subject matter carefully. Thus, his individual aesthetic was second to the humanistic purpose in his work. He adopted a technique that used quick strokes of the conté crayon to illustrate the subject. His attention was focused on creating realistic renderings that could be easily recognized by his public, as in *Nkrumah.* Kwame Nkrumah, the first leader of an independent Nigeria, became a revered world figure and symbol of freedom from colonial rule. Although Bailey's portrait shows him only from the chest to the head, the chosen vantage point places Nkrumah above eye level so that the viewer must gaze up to him, thereby elevating his status.

In the color lithograph *Homework* (1973) Bailey captured the intense concentration of a little girl as she completes the task of homework. As she leans closer to the table to immerse herself even further in her work, she seems completely absorbed. She is a young child, as shown by the two braids gathered high on the sides of her head. Her hair is disheveled, the disorder that comes from a day's work and play at school and perhaps another period of play after school before settling in to the serious business of homework. In the lithograph Bailey stresses the importance of study and education for young black children. But he also believed that children must play, and children engaged in play, alone or in a group, was

another favorite subject. Other subjects included lovers, and he drew many portraits of his family and friends, as in *Sarah* (1978).

Bailey's art is of and for the people. He targeted his audience and was not concerned with technically challenging the figurative form or pushing the limitations of the medium in new directions. Bailey believed in the pan-African concept that black people around the globe should work toward the uplift of the race in everything they do. He felt that as an artist his gift for creating likenesses should be used in the service of his people and should be instructional as well as inspirational in giving people the determination to seek self-empowerment. Toward that end he taught and participated in community art activities, first in southern California and later in Atlanta, Georgia. Bailey did not care about his association with galleries or museums but was more concerned that his work engender pride and the acceptance of self by blacks. After his move to Atlanta, he reproduced some of his lithographs for wider distribution.

Bailey thus created images that promoted a pan-African worldview, and in doing so he celebrated and embraced positive aspects of the lives of black people. These included the tenderness and love between black males and females and among family members as well as life's everyday occurrences, such as the concentration of a child on homework or the joy of childhood play.

—Lizzetta LeFalle-Collins

BAILEY, Malcolm

American painter

Born: New York, 1947. **Education:** High School of Art and Design, 1965; Pratt Institute, B.F.A. 1969. **Career:** Teacher, Cooper Union, New York. **Awards:** Yaddo Scholarship, 1969-70; Pratt Institute Scholarship.

Individual Exhibitions:

1966	Cinque Gallery, New York
1971	Whitney Museum of American Art, New York

Selected Group Exhibitions:

1969	Brooklyn College, New York
	Whitney Museum Annual, New York
1970	Boston Museum of Fine Arts

Publications:

On BAILEY: Book—*Malcolm Bailey: Paintings and Drawings*

Untitled, exhibition catalog, New York, Cinque Gallery, 1966. **Articles**—"Black Art: What Is It?," in *The Art Gallery,* April 1970, pp. 32-35; "Object: Diversity," in *Time,* 6 April 1970, pp. 80-87.

*   *   *

Malcolm Bailey's work is characterized by graphic immediacy. Cool and elegant, it belongs to the genealogy of the color-field and minimalist movements. Yet the unmodulated color spaces of Bailey's linear drawings and paintings also include legible figures that are central elements in his political critiques.

A New York native, Bailey gained the attention of the city's art communities in the late 1960s, while he was still a student at the Pratt Institute. The founders of the Cinque Gallery—Romare Bearden, Ernest Crichlow, and Norman Lewis—recognized Bailey's talent, and in 1969 he became the gallery's first exhibitor. He subsequently participated in black art shows and in shows such as the 1969 and 1972 annual exhibitions of the Whitney Museum of American Art. He also had a one-man exhibition at the Whitney Museum in 1971, at a time when few major museums showed interest in mounting solo exhibitions for black artists.

Bailey's "Separate but Equal" series (1969) captured the attention of audiences. The series referred to the 1896 U.S. Supreme Court decision in *Plessy v. Ferguson:* the landmark ruling allowed that racial segregation was permissible when "separate but equal" accommodations were available for nonwhite citizens. Separate but equal was the law of the land until overturned by *Brown v. Board of Education of Topeka* in 1954. In both title and imagery Bailey sought to criticize nineteenth-century judgment and to highlight the consequences of legalized inequality. Among the paintings of the "Separate but Equal" series is *Hold: Separate but Equal.* In the painting Bailey drew cross-sectional views of a slave ship and its cargo—seated and bent human forms silhouetted in provocative black and white. The ship, which is powerfully presented, symbolizes the immoral commerce of slavery and the ills of contemporary racism. As many observers have stated, the "Separate but Equal" series makes it clear that blacks and whites in an unequal society are in the same doomed boat.

The objectification of women became a subject for Bailey in the 1970s. *Untitled* (1970), for example, is a delicately colored drawing of a cow, a dog, and a Mickey Mouse caricature, all viewed from the rear, and of a white female nude seen in profile. In each figure centers of thought, reproduction, and excretion are labeled, with the woman treated in the same manner as the animals. Art historian Elsa Honig Fine has discussed *Untitled,* also part of a series, in this way: "A comment upon male chauvinism and male sexual fantasies, the series was Bailey's attempt to work through his own sexism."

Like many artists of the twentieth century, Bailey has reflected on the alienation of the individual in modern society. In both *Untitled, Number 4* (1971) and *Untitled, Number 7* (1972), a tiny silhouetted figure free-falls from a precipice into a solid-colored void. In each instance the light-value cliffs are revealed to be portions of larger human figures viewed in silhouette and bisected by the edges of the pictorial support. In *Untitled, Number 4* the two large-scale forms are further disguised by their upside-down orientation and complicated by a swath of pattern within their borders. Dwarfed by everything else in the pictorial environments and overwhelmed by the stark color contrasts, the tiny figures in each picture seem to personify vulnerability and isolation.

By placing the schematic diagram into the context of fine arts, Bailey has joined a select company of modernists—among them Francis Picabia, René Magritte, and Larry Rivers—who used the look of distanced objectivity to challenge formalist norms.

—Jacqueline Francis

BALL, James (Presley)

American photographer

Born: Virginia, 1825. **Education:** John B. Bailey, private tutor, White Sulphur Springs, c. 1845. **Family:** Married 1) c. 1849 (divorced c. 1864), one son and one daughter; 2) Fannie Cage in 1864; 3) Annie E. Ewing, July 1887. **Career:** Itinerant daguerreotypist, Ohio, Pennsylvania, Virginia, 1845-47. Daguerreotypist, Ball's Daguerrean Gallery of the West, Cincinnati, Ohio, 1847, Ball and Brothers, Cincinnati, Ohio, 1851-57, Ball and Harlan, Cincinnati, Ohio, 1857, Ball and Thomas, Cincinnati, Ohio, 1858-71, J.P. Ball & Son, Minnesota, 1887, J.P. Ball & Son, Helena, Montana, 1888-1901, Globe Photo Studio, Seattle, 1892-1902. Worked in London, Liverpool, Paris, 1856. **Awards:** Diploma in Bronze Medal, Ohio Mechanics Institute Exhibition, 1857. **Died:** c.1904.

Individual Exhibitions:

1855   *Ball's Splendid Mammoth Pictorial Tour,* Ohio Mechanics Institute, Cincinnati and Boston

Selected Group Exhibitions:

1852   Ohio Mechanics Annual Exhibition, Ohio Mechanics Institute, Cincinnati (and 1854, 1855, 1857)

Collections:

Cincinnati Art Museum; Cincinnati Historical Society; International Museum of Photography and Film at George Eastman House, Rochester, New York; Montana Historical Society, Helena; Ohio State University, Columbus; Schomburg Center, New York; Swann Galleries, New York; University of Washington, Seattle.

Publications:

On BALL: Books—*Ball's Splendid, Mammoth Pictorial Tour of the United States,* exhibition brochure, Cincinnati, Achilles Pugh (printer), 1855; *The Negro in Montana 1800-1945: A Selected Bibliography* by Lucille Smith Thompson and Alma Smith Jacobs, Helena, Montana State Library, 1970; *Black Photographers Bear Witness: 100 Years of Social Protest* by Deborah Willis and Howard Dodson, Massachusetts, Williams College Museum of Art, 1989; *J. P. Ball, Daguerrean and Studio Photographer* by Deborah Willis, New York, Garland Publishing, Inc., 1993.

*   *   *

In 1856 the *London Times* reported that Queen Victoria was so charmed by the portrait James Presley Ball took of her "that she removed one taken by the most eminent artist in London from her boudoir and hung the American artist's in its place." Such was the renown of Ball, "from that fertile province of pork, Cincinnati," that his sitters included Charles Dickens, Frederick Douglass, Jenny Lind, Ulysses S. Grant's family, and many black and white citizens throughout the United States.

Born in Virginia in 1825, Ball learned daguerreotypy around 1840 from Boston-based African American photographer John B. Bailey. One of Ball's earliest known works (c. 1840) is a half-plate daguerreotype of Myers & Co. Confectioners. It is a remarkably clear image featuring a horse and cart standing in the dirt street and a group of top-hatted men standing before the confectionary. This piece, like many of Ball's daguerreotypes, is enclosed in a brass mat and embossed "J. P. Ball/Cincinnati." Such works were frequently housed in navy or red velvet-lined leather or Union cases.

Between perfunctory attempts at business in Cincinnati in 1845, 1847, and 1849, Ball was an itinerant artist in Pennsylvania and Virginia, then opened his first successful studio in "Porkopolis" on New Year's Day in 1851. The business employed Ball's brothers, Tom and R.G., and his brother-in-law, Alexander Thomas, as well as landscapist Robert S. Duncanson, who hand-tinted photographs from the early to mid-1850s. By 1854 Ball employed nine men (including a white man) and averaged $100 a day in sales in his "Great Daguerrean Gallery of the West." That year an engraving of his studio was featured with a full-length article in *Gleason's Pictorial.* Ball's portrait daguerreotypes often feature frontal, three-quarters-length poses of husbands and wives, sisters, or a single subject against a plain background.

In 1855 Ball, an ardent abolitionist, commissioned a team of unknown African American artists to paint an enormous, 2,400-square-yard panorama, *Ball's Splendid, Mammoth Pictorial Tour of the United States Comprising Views of the African Slave Trade; of Northern and Southern Cities; of Cotton and Sugar Plantations; of the Mississippi, Ohio, and Susquehanna Rivers, Niagara Falls, &C.* No longer extant, the work depicted the slave trade from its inception in Nigeria to its height in the American South to freedom in Canada. Quaker Achilles Pugh published a pamphlet describing each of the fifty-three scenes in detail. Thousands paid to see the work at the Ohio Mechanics Institute and Boston's Armory Hall, and Ball reportedly gave part of the proceeds to benefit children's schools.

After touring Europe and opening establishments in London, Liverpool, and Paris in 1856, Ball exhibited his European pictures in a new gallery he co-owned with another African American photographer, Robert Harlan. Together the two won a bronze medal for a photograph and a diploma for a daguerreotype from the Ohio Mechanics Institute exhibition of 1857. The partnership dissolved after eighteen months, yet Ball continued to flourish as a portraitist. While few of his images of African Americans remain, a surviving family album contains sensitive *cartes-des-visit* of his grandmother, brothers, brother- and sister-in law and their children, as well as portraits of unidentified women and children.

In 1860 a tornado destroyed Ball's studio, but numerous white families contributed funds to set him back up in business, which reached its height during the Civil War. Ball photographed many Union soldiers and their families using such features from conventional British painted portraits as the three-quarters pose and props like a Doric column, an elaborately carved Victorian chair, and theatrical drapery. Notable patrons included General William Lytle, Congressman Timothy C. Day, entrepreneur Samuel Pike, artist Thomas D. Jones, civil engineer R. C. Phillips, and the Revs. Max Lilienthal and Moncure D. Conway. After the death of his brother Tom (the senior member of the firm) and the end of the war, Ball may have lost much of his abolitionist patronage in the face of increased competition. Around 1872 he and his family moved west in search of greater opportunities, following the wake of silver and gold rushes.

As one of the few black photographers in Minneapolis, Ball prospered and was commissioned as the official photographer for a celebration of the twenty-fifth anniversary of the Emancipation Proclamation in September 1887. A month later he served as delegate for a civil rights convention, then moved to Helena, Montana. There he and his son produced numerous cabinet cards of white civic and infantry groups, families, business partners, infants in their baptismal gowns, and children, women, and men with props such as cloth-covered tables, wooden gates, books, broken columns, hay bails, and bicycles. Some of these portraits feature painted backdrops of parlors or pastoral scenes, or frames with scroll or shell motifs. Notable sitters included the Hon. Lee Mantle (Montana senator), Joe (a Chinese cook for the Ming family), African American porter William C. Irvin in his Masonic uniform, and William Biggerstaff (a former slave), before and after hanging for murder and in his coffin.

While most of Ball's images were studio work, he also photographed outdoor scenes, such as the Old Helena Library, a group portrait in front of St. Paul's Church, and the cornerstone laying ceremony of the state capitol. A popular citizen, Ball served as a black delegate to the Republican party convention and as president of the Afro-American Club in Montana. He declined a nomination for the position of coroner.

Around 1900 Ball, with his daughter-in-law Laura and son (who also worked as a lawyer), opened the Globe Photo Studio in Seattle and continued to practice commercial photography. Ball also sold advertisements for the *Seattle Republican* and organized Shriner's lodges in Seattle and Portland before seeking relief from crippling rheumatism in Hawaii, where he likely passed away around 1904.

—Theresa Leininger-Miller

BANDEIRA, Antônio

Brazilian painter

Born: Ceara, Brazil, 1922. **Died:** Paris, 1967.

Selected Exhibitions:

1953   Museu de Arte de São Paulo, Brazil
1967   Secretary of Culture of the State of Ceara, Fortaleza, Brazil
1968   *Bienal de Artes Plasticas,* Salvador

*   *   *

Antônio Bandeira is highly regarded for his paintings. A Brazilian by birth, he went to Paris to live during the 1940s and subsequently exhibited his work in both collective and individual shows. Except for a stay in Brazil between 1950 and 1954, he lived continuously in Paris after 1946.

Like other Afro-Brazilian artists of his generation, Bandeira found it necessary to leave Brazil in order to succeed. The need for self-imposed exile can be explained by the discriminatory nature of the

Brazilian cultural milieu, to which Afro-Brazilians had limited access, as well as the repressive political ambiance of the time. Afro-Brazilian artists enjoyed greater acceptance elsewhere, and for that reason they emigrated to a number of other countries.

Bandeira's paintings are characterized by the beauty of their poetic abstraction. His canvases are often said to resemble sparkling representations of cities seen from a distance, and they are noteworthy for their elaborate textures. *The Afro-Brazilian Touch* (1988), the largest exhibition ever to be assembled on the African influence in Brazilian art, included works by Bandeira. *Black Trees,* an oil on canvas, and the mixed-media work *Composition,* both from private collections, were part of the exhibition.

—Carolyn Richardson Durham

BANKS, Ellen

American painter

Work also appeared under the name E. Banks-Feld. **Born:** Boston, Massachusetts, 7 June 1941. **Family:** Married Bernard T. Feld in 1985 (died 1993). **Career:** Professor of painting, Museum School of Fine Arts, Boston, Massachusetts, 1972-96. **Awards:** Blanche E. Coleman Award, 1972; Ford Foundation grant, 1979; George Gund Foundation grant, 1982; Bunting Fellowship, Radcliff College, 1983-84; National Endowment for the Arts grant, 1987; book grant, Nexus Press, 1988; Massachusetts Artists Fellowship, 1991. **Agent:** McIntosh Gallery, Atlanta, Georgia; Spandow Gallery, Fischerstrasse 28, Brose-Passage/Handwekrhof, 13597 Berlin, Germany; Caroline Corre Gallery, Paris. **Address:** 328 Flatbush Avenue, #208, Brooklyn, New York 11238, U.S.A.

Individual Exhibitions:

1973	Rose Art Museum, Brandeis University, Waltham, Massachusetts
1975	Howard University, Washington, D.C.
1979	DuBois Institute, Harvard University, Cambridge, Massachusetts
1981	Wetering Gallery, Amsterdam, Holland
1982	Museum of the National Center of Afro-American Artists, Boston
1983	Addison Gallery of American Art, Andover, Massachusetts
1984	Bunting Institute, Radcliff College, Cambridge, Massachusetts
1985	University of Campinas, Campinas, Brazil
1986	Sofia and Varna, Bulgaria
1987	Campinas Gallery, Campinas, Brazil
1988	Nexus Contemporary Art Center, Atlanta, Georgia
1989	McIntosh Gallery, Atlanta, Georgia
1990	Akin Gallery, Boston, Massachusetts
1992	Amerika Haus, Berlin
1993	Frielander Tor, Neubrandenburg, Germany
1994	Kuntspeicher, Fredersdorf, Germany
1995	Markishe Museum, Berlin
1996	Spandow Gallery, Berlin

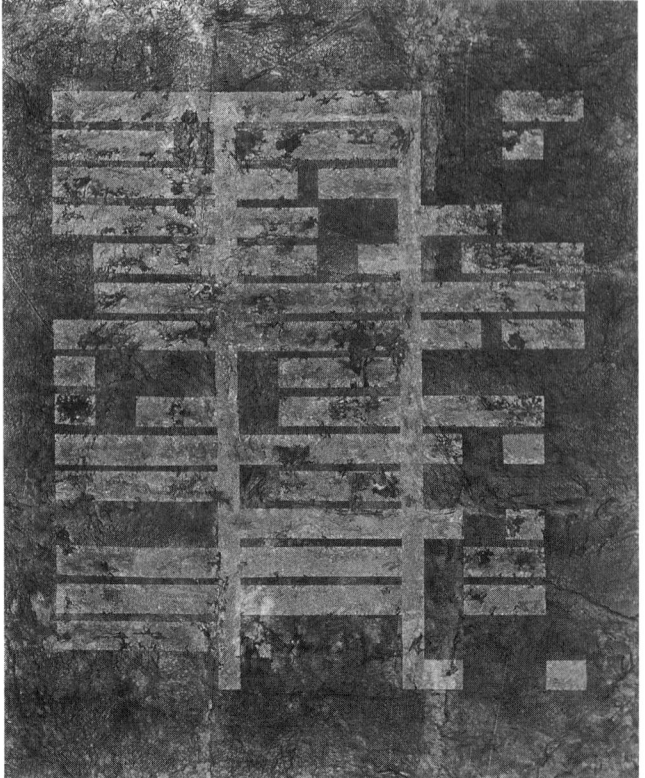

Ellen Banks: *Improvisation,* **1993.**

Selected Group Exhibitions:

1980	Boston Atheneum, Boston
1985	Nexus Gallery, Philadelphia
1987	Massachusetts College of Art, Boston
1988	A.I.R. Gallery, New York
1989	Drawing Center, New York
1990	Centre d'Action Culturelle, Musée de Beziers, France
1991	Galerie Caroline Corre, Paris
1993	Fine Arts Center, Neubrandenburg, Germany
1994	Stephen Rosenberg Gallery, New York
1995	Art Initiatives, New York

Collections:

Addison Gallery of American Art, Andover, Massachusetts; Boston Public Library; Bunting Institute, Radcliff College, Cambridge, Massachusetts; Chicago Art Institute; Institute for Contemporary Social Studies, Bulgaria; List Visual Arts Center, Massachusetts Institute of Technology, Boston; Museum of Fine Arts, Boston; Museum of Modern Art, New York; Museum of the National Center for Afro-American Artists, Boston; New York Public Library; Rose Art Museum, Brandeis University, Waltham, Massachusetts; University of Campinas, Brazil; Yale School of Art and Architecture, New Haven, Connecticut.

*   *   *

Ask Ellen Banks to describe Bach's music, and she might tell you that the toccatas are about three feet tall and nine feet long, and the fugues are about three feet square. She might go on to describe colors and backgrounds and textures, maybe even brush strokes and paint viscosity, and eventually you'd be imagining something very much like a painting by Ellen Banks.

Banks grew up listening to her father play Bach and other music (he was a pianist and organist who played in a local church) and developed not just a love for it but a passion. Banks herself began to play, and there was a time when Banks had to decide whether to become an artist or a musician. "I loved playing music for people," Banks has said. "It's so immediately gratifying."

Eventually, though, Banks's love of painting won out over her love of music. She received her B.F.A. from Massachusetts College of Art in Boston. She studied with Hans Jaffe, who wrote a biography of Mondrian, and César Domela of the De Stijl group, of which Mondrian was a leader. Banks admits to a great admiration for Mondrian's work and has become a gifted abstract artist, whose paintings show evidence of Mondrian's influence. But describing her work in this way is too simplistic, largely because the music she played and loved growing up never left her. In the early 1980s she began to investigate the possibilities offered by music in painting. She began work on reinterpreting the scores of her favorite composers using paint and brush and canvas rather than piano.

Since then she has worked on many nonobjective paintings of musical compositions, including Bach compositions, Scott Joplin's "Maple Leaf Rag," Chopin's nocturnes, Brahms's "Improvisations," and a series of spirituals. The paintings are not meant to represent the experience of listening to the music but the experience of play-

ing it—the visual impact rather than the musical impact of reading and interpreting the scores. Banks says of her musical paintings, "I feel I have made a contribution of something new to the field." Indeed, she has.

—Terry Bain

BANNARN, Henry (Wilmer)

American painter and sculptor

Born: Wetunka, Oklahoma, 17 July 1910. **Education:** Minneapolis School of Art, Minnesota; Art Students League, New York. **Career:** Instructor, Alston-Bannarn Workshop, New York, 1934-36; Harlem Community Art Center, New York, 1937-39; Phyllis Wheatley House, Minneapolis, Minnesota. **Awards:** Second Prize, Minnesota State Fair, 1928; First Prize, Minneapolis Institute of Arts, 1932; First Place Award, Minnesota State Artists Annual Exhibition, 1940; First Place Award, Atlanta University, 1943; John Hope Landscape Award, 1945, 1948; Second Place Award, Atlanta University, 1954. **Died:** 1965.

Individual Exhibition:

1940   Hanley Gallery, St. Paul, Minnesota

Selected Group Exhibitions:

1935   *An Art Commentary on Lynching,* Arthur Newton Galleries, New York
1936   Pennsylvania Academy of Fine Arts
1939   Baltimore Museum of Art, Maryland
1940   Newton Gallery, Arthur University
        American Negro Exhibition, Chicago
1943   Atlanta University Annual Exhibition
1945   Atlanta University Annual Exhibition
        The Negro Artist Comes of Age, Albany Institute of History and Art, New York
1948   Atlanta University Annual Exhibition
1955   Atlanta University Annual Exhibition

Collections:

Clark College-Atlanta University, Atlanta, Georgia; Howard University, Washington, D.C.

*   *   *

The painter, sculptor, and art educator Henry W. Bannarn was among a small number of academically trained African American artists—a group that included Charles Alston, Gwendolyn Bennett, Augusta Savage, and James Lesesne Wells—who were pivotal in the training of artists during the 1930s and 1940s. Bannarn taught drawing at the Phillis Wheatley House in Minneapolis, Minnesota, and sculpture at the Harlem Community Art Center in New York City.

Bannarn attended the Minneapolis School of Art on a scholarship. He could not survive financially on his artwork, however, and

Ellen Banks: *Improvisation,* 1995.

he performed menial jobs such as working as a dining car attendant and for a valet service. He was employed by the Works Progress Administration as an art instructor at the Harlem Community Art Center, where Robert Blackburn and Ronald Joseph studied in their formative years. In this capacity Bannarn served as a role model and nurtured the next generation of artists. His ability to demonstrate traditional techniques provided a core education for many aspiring artists.

From 1938 through 1941, *Who's Who in American Art* listed Bannarn's address as 306 West 141st Street. This was also the address of Alston's studio, which functioned as a meeting place for literary, performing, and visual artists. In this capacity Bannarn and Alston provided an intellectual forum, which had not previously existed, where artists forged a collective community and exchanged technical information, as well as discussing aesthetics and critiquing one another's work.

Bannarn exhibited consistently from 1933 through 1955 and won many cash prizes. He exhibited with the Harmon Foundation in 1933 and participated in the historic 1935 NAACP exhibition *An Art Commentary on Lynching,* held at the Arthur U. Newton Galleries in New York. In 1940 he had a one-man exhibition of sculpture, paintings, and drawings in Minneapolis at the Harriet Hanley Gallery. In 1945 he participated in the *Negro Artist Comes of Age* exhibition, sponsored by the Albany (New York) Institute of History and Art. He received cash awards in 1943, 1945, 1948, and 1955 in the annual competitive exhibitions at Atlanta University.

The artistic achievements of Bannarn are not well documented. It seems that his reputation rests on his versatility and mastery of a variety of media. He painted oil and watercolor portraits and landscapes in the traditional academic style, as well as genre scenes of African Americans engaged in a variety of activities. He sensitively carved and molded sculptural figures in wood and stone. The simplicity of form, frontal perspective, and compactness of these works recall the style of William Edmondson and are reminiscent of Egyptian art.

Bannarn's subjects were inspired by his observations of the commonplace as well as his interest in social history. His career was eclipsed during the transitional period when representational art and social realism were no longer popular in American art. Nonetheless, Bannarn was a significant figure in the development of art education at a time when tuition-free classes were provided at community art centers. These programs opened up opportunities for several African Americans who later became professional artists and contributed to the aesthetics of American art.

—Claude L. Elliott

BANNISTER, Edward (Mitchell)

American painter

Born: Nova Scotia, November 1826. **Education:** Lowell Institute, Boston, 1860s. **Family:** Married Christiana Cartreaux. **Career:** Self-employed artist. Cofounder, Providence Art Club (later known as Rhode Island School of Design), 1880. **Awards:** Bronze Medal for *Under the Oaks,* Centennial Exhibition, Philadelphia, 1876. **Died:** 9 January 1901.

Selected Exhibitions:

Atlanta University, Georgia; Barbizon School, Providence; Boston Art Club; Centennial Exhibition, Philadelphia (1876); Howard University, Washington, D.C.; Museum of Fine Arts, Boston; National Center of Afro-American Artists, Boston (1972); Providence Art Club (1901, retrospective), Rhode Island.

Collections:

Bannister House (apartment complex), Providence, Rhode Island; Frederick Douglass Institute of Negro Arts and History, Washington, D.C.; National Museum of American Art, Washington, D.C.; New York Public Library; Rhode Island School of Design; Schomburg Center, New York.

On BANNISTER: Books—*Edward Mitchell Bannister, 1828-1901,* exhibition catalog, Rhode Island School of Design, Museum of Art, 1966; *Ten Afro-American Artists of the Nineteenth Century* by James A. Porter, Washington, D.C., Howard University, 1967; *Edward Mitchell Bannister, 1828-1901,* exhibition catalog, New York, Kenkeleba Gallery, 1992. **Articles**—"Negro Has Given Much Art, Survey Shows," in *Boston Traveler,* February 1933; "Edward Mitchell Bannister" by John S. Brown, in *Crisis,* November 1933; "Edward M. Bannister" by Muriel B. Wellington, in *The Negro History Bulletin,* October 1941; "Blacks Duncanson and Bannister Honored in Fine Arts Exhibit" by Edgar Drisco, in *Boston Globe,* 16 January 1972; "Edward M. Bannister, Afro-American Painter (1828-1901)" by Joseph T. Skerett, Jr., in *Negro History Bulletin,* 41, May/June 1978, p. 829; "Edward M. Bannister," in *A History of African-American Artists, From 1792 to the Present* by Romare Bearden and Harry Henderson, New York, Pantheon Books, 1993; "To Be Free, Gifted and Black: African American Artist, Edward Mitchell Bannister" by Juanita Marie Holland, in *The International Review of African American Art,* 12(1), 1995, pp. 5-25 (illustrated).

*   *   *

Edward Bannister's determination to become a successful artist was largely fueled by an article he read in the *New York Herald* in 1867. The article stated that "the Negro seems to have an appreciation for art while being manifestly unable to produce it." Ironically, less than a decade later, in 1876, Bannister became the first African American artist to receive a national award. He also held the distinction of being the only African American artist of the late nineteenth century who developed his talents without traveling to or studying in Europe.

Information concerning Bannister's early life is sketchy. In 1848 he moved to Boston, where he held a variety of menial jobs before he became a barber and learned to paint. It is recorded that he painted in the Boston Studio building and also attended evening classes with the noted sculptor-anatomist William Rimmer at the Lowell Institute. Only a few paintings by Bannister from the 1850s and 1860s have survived, preventing a stylistic assessment of his early period in Boston. While Bannister lived there, however, he saw and was apparently influenced by the Barbizon-inspired paintings of William Morris Hunt, who had studied in Europe and who exhibited frequently in Boston during the 1860s. In fact, American landscape painters generally were becoming aware of the simple rustic motifs and pictorial poetry of French Barbizon paintings by Camille Corot, Jean-François Millet, and Charles-François Daubigny in the mid-nineteenth century.

In 1870 Bannister moved from Boston to Providence, Rhode Island. In spite of his limited artistic studies, it is remarkable that within five years after his arrival in Providence one of Bannister's

Edward Bannister: *Last Glow,* 1881. Photo courtesy of the Schomburg Center for Research in Black Culture.

paintings was accepted in the Philadelphia Centennial Exposition of 1876. The painting, *Under the Oaks,* was awarded the first-prize bronze medal. The location of the painting has not been known since the turn of the century.

Following the Centennial Exposition, Bannister's reputation grew, and numerous commissions enabled him to devote himself full-time to painting. He executed a large number of landscapes, most of which depict quiet, bucolic scenes rendered in somber tones and thick impasto. While Bannister's initial influence probably stemmed from the works of Hunt, his paintings are reflective of an artist who loved the quiet beauties of nature and represented them in a realistic manner. Bannister's middle period landscapes of the 1870s were generally executed in broad masses of heavy impasto with few details. They also evoke a tranquil mood that became one of the hallmarks of Bannister's style. Later landscapes of the 1880s employed a more gentle impasto and loosely applied broken color similar to impressionistic techniques.

Many of Bannister's landscapes are small and have darkened considerably with age. His paintings contain no social or racial overtones, and the small figures seen frequently in his landscapes appear to be Caucasian. Although the majority of Bannister's paintings are landscapes, he also painted portraits, figure studies, religious scenes, seascapes, still lifes, and genre subjects. Bannister was attracted primarily to picturesque motifs, including cottages, castles, cattle, dawns, sunsets, and small bodies of water, and in his works he portrayed nature as a calm and submissive force.

In spite of his limited training and experience, Bannister was among Providence's leading painters and citizens during the 1870s and 1880s. He was one of the founding members of the Providence Art Club, which still displays the certificate that he was awarded at the Philadelphia exposition. Bannister's only known surviving portrait is that of his wife, Christiana. It hangs in the boardroom of the Bannister House apartment complex in Providence. One of Bannister's most intriguing paintings is *Newspaper Boy,* of 1869, which is also one of his few genre subjects. The name and racial identity of the subject are not identified in the work, which was painted in Boston the year before Bannister moved to Providence. Newspaper boys and children of the streets were a popular subject of painting in Europe and America at the time.

On 9 January 1901 Bannister died while attending a prayer meeting at his church. His grave in North Burial Ground in Providence is marked by a rough granite boulder ten feet high. It bears a carving of a palette with the artist's name and a pipe. A bronze plaque also adorns the monument and is inscribed with a poem that reads in part, "This pure and lofty soul . . . who, while he portrayed nature, walked with God."

—Regenia Perry

BARBOSA, José
Brazilian painter and wood-carver

Born: Olinda, Brazil, 1948.

Selected Exhibitions:

1981	Escritorio de Arte, Sao Paulo, Brazil
1984	Galeria Bonino, Rio de Janeiro, Brazil
1987	Artespaço, Recife, Brazil
	Montesanti Galeria, Sao Paulo, Brazil

Publications:

On BARBOSA: Book—*A Mao Afro-Brasileira: Significado da Contribucao Artistica e Historica,* Sao Paulo, Tenege, 1988.

*   *   *

José Barbosa, who lives and works in São Paulo, Brazil, specializes in wood carving and painting. His intricate wood carvings, which are usually done in cedar, combine a vast number of symbolic elements. The intricate carving and the symbolic elements come from a long tradition of Afro-Brazilian works in wood with religious significance.

Barbosa's work *Porta da paisagem,* for example, is an elaborately carved door consisting of oil painting on wood with bronze, copper, and mirrors. He combines straight and curvilinear lines to produce an intricate design. In the center of the lower portion of the door is a female figure on which is superimposed a smaller winged figure partially covered with a design similar to a peacock's quill. A radiant sun with a face emerges at the stem of the body of the larger figure. This larger figure, enclosed within curvilinear lines, is surrounded by vegetation and birds of various descriptions in the trees. In a rectangular section immediately above the female figure are birds, resembling peacocks, who gaze back toward their luminescent feathers, which have various distinct textures. An open hand extends downward toward a bird in flight, and the beak of this bird is joined to the crown of the female figure in the lower part. In the upper portion of the door is a window (a mirror). On either side of the window are figures, a warrior with a lance in his hand on the left and an angel on the right. Each of these figures has a fish engraved immediately above. On the uppermost portion of the door is the figure of a reclining woman, with her back toward the viewer. The symbols on the door seem to have both religious and erotic meanings.

Another wood carving by Barbosa is *Deusa* ("Goddess"), which incorporates copper, tin, shells, glass, and mirrors. The mask or face of the goddess is surrounded by vertical lines that resemble hair or a headdress. The figure is in the form of a cross, with the transverse part resembling outstretched arms with carved winged figures and mirrors. The mirrors are isosceles triangles. The mirror on the right stands on its base, while the mirror on the left stands on its apex. Each mirror reflects light but also appears to reflect smaller triangles. In the center of the carving is a section in which hang shells and various trinkets. Immediately below, in the section corresponding to the abdominal region of the goddess, are the carved petals of a flower. The stem of the flower simultaneously appears to be the separation between the goddess's legs. The entire figure is supported on a pedestal resembling the feet and legs of the goddess. The materials used to decorate the goddess—mirrors, shells, and copper—are those associated with the goddess of fertility, love, and money in Afro-Brazilian religious cults.

—Carolyn Richardson Durham

BARNES, Ernie
American painter

Born: Ernest Eugene Barnes, Jr., Durham, North Carolina, 15 July 1938. **Education:** North Carolina College (now North Carolina Central University), Durham, North Carolina, 1956-59. **Family:** Married 1) Andrea Burnett in 1957 (divorced), one daughter and one son; 2) Thaleen Norton in 1965 (divorced 1981), one son and two daughters; 3) Bernadine C. Gradney in 1984. **Career:** Football player, San Diego Chargers, 1960-63, Denver Broncos, 1964-65; writer/illustrator, *San Diego,* 1962-63; official artist, American Football League, 1966. Since 1970 founder, president, artist, Company of Art, West Hollywood, California. Official artist of the XXIII Olympiad, Los Angeles, 1984. **Awards:** Sports Artist of the Year, United States Sports Academy, 1985; Treasure of Los Angeles Award, 1996. Honorary doctorate: North Carolina Central University, 1990. **Address:** Company of Art, 8613 Sherwood Drive, West Hollywood, California 90069, U.S.A.

Individual Exhibitions:

1966	McKenzie Gallery, Los Angeles
1971	Agra Gallery, Washington, D.C.
1972	Heritage Gallery, Los Angeles
	California Science and Industry Museum, Los Angeles
1974	Orr's Gallery, San Diego, California
1975	Bedford-Stuyvesant Restoration Center, Brooklyn, New York
1977	Heritage Gallery, Los Angeles
1978	North Carolina Museum of Art, Raleigh
	Spectrum Fine Art Gallery, New York
1983	Spectrum Fine Art Gallery, New York
1984	Heritage Gallery, Los Angeles
1990	Grand Central Art Galleries, New York

Collections:

Seton Hall University, South Orange, New Jersey; St. Benedict's Preparatory School, New Jersey.

Ernie Barnes. Photo courtesy of the Company of Art, West Hollywood, California.

Publications:

By BARNES: Book—*From Pads to Palette,* Waco, Texas, WRS Publishing, 1995.

On BARNES: Articles—"Barnes, A Former Player, Paints a Penetrating Portrait of Pro Football" by Neil Amdur, in *New York Times,* 9 May 1971; "One Artist's Life After Sports" by Dave Anderson, in *New York Times,* 6 May 1979; "An AFL Journeyman, Olympic Artist Barnes is an All-Pro at the Easel" by Franz Lidz, in *Sports Illustrated,* 1984; "The Athlete as Artist" by Eileen Keerdoja and Paul Vercammen, in *Newsweek,* 26 March 1984; "Ernie Barnes: An Athletic Artist" by Diane K. Shah, in *New York Times,* 7 May 1984; "An Ex-Pro Football Lineman, Ernie Barnes Comes Out of the Trenches to Score as an Olympic Artist" by Lois Armstrong, in *People,* 9 July 1984; "Take One" by Rebecca Bricker, in *People,* 30 June 1986; "Neo-Mannerist Paintings by Ernie Barnes at Grand Central," *Antiques and the Arts Weekly,* 9 November 1990; "All of the Same Sidewalks: Ernie Barnes' Vision of the Beauty of the Ghetto," in *Crisis,* January 1991; "Portrait of the Artist" by Tracie Fellers, in *Herald Sun,* 6 November 1994; "Ebony Bookshelf," in *Ebony,* December 1994; "From Pigskin to Palette" by Clea Hantman, in *San Diego,* March 1995; "Q & A: Ernie Barnes Arrives" by Tomika DePriest, in *Atlanta Tribune,* 7 August 1995; "Barnes A Two-Sport Artist" by Larry Weisman, in *USA Today,* 17 May 1996.

*

Ernie Barnes comments:

I am bound by the strongest ties with the organic life of all people. And being an artist has created in me the desire to continually affirm beauty. I am well aware that art has no concrete connection to beauty, but beauty is profoundly interwoven into the fabric of the individual and his environment. I can think of no other word that better equips one's perception of the human being. ! am referring to the intrinsic beauty that is achieved through mental toughness and the spiritual energy which allows us to turn out peak performances despite the burden of racist behavior.

As the mother of our emotions, art integrates itself into our behavior, when we learn through the senses—how to see, touch, and listen. Only then can art be applied to life when judging one another. The closed eyes of my subjects represent a mirror in which to judge oneself. It facilitates the identification with another's life and makes the heart all that it is capable of feeling.

(From *The Beauty of the Ghetto,* exhibition catalog, West Hollywood, California, Company of Art, 1990.)

*   *   *

Ernie Barnes's 1995 autobiographical account of his dual careers in football and art chronicled his unique path in endeavors usually seen as entirely unrelated. He moved from being a successful lineman in professional football in the early 1960s to being a highly accomplished figurative painter. His depictions of athletics and of scenes from daily life add luster to the long tradition of American genre painting, and his portrayals of African American themes specifically have made him one of the best-known contemporary black artists.

Barnes grew up shy and reserved. Few who knew him would have imagined his future as either a professional athlete or an artist. In high school he discovered his natural athletic prowess, which supplemented his early artistic inclinations. His sports accomplishments led to a scholarship to historically black North Carolina College, where his undergraduate years were valuable for both of his subsequent careers. Majoring in art, he learned the fundamentals of drawing and painting, including techniques for rendering perspective and light and shade, as well as design, art history, and human anatomy. His teachers encouraged him to develop an individual style by drawing on his personal experience, and he has incorporated this perspective in all his subsequent artwork.

In college Barnes also excelled in football, culminating in his being drafted in 1959 by the Baltimore Colts. Barnes played five years with three professional teams. His gridiron experiences, especially the intense camaraderie with other players, have profoundly affected his life and his art. The remarkable teamwork of people of different races and backgrounds has informed many of his paintings. Moreover, in football he experienced and observed human movement, which provided the foundation for the dynamic energy characterizing his artwork.

In 1964 Barnes discovered the work of Charles White, which encouraged him to emulate White's dignified portrayals of African Americans and helped him augment the broader tradition of black figurative art. Following his retirement from football, he used his athletic contacts to advance his artistic career, becoming the official artist of the American Football League and thus gaining major exposure in exhibitions. His early professional paintings focused on football, but he later produced works with more diverse themes. His paintings for the television series *Good Times* and his work as the official artist for the 1984 Olympic Games increased his public visibility.

Barnes is a traditional painter whose work can be characterized as neomannerist, that is, derived from the style popular in Italian art between the Renaissance and the Baroque period. His works use

Ernie Barnes: *Homage to Charles.*

carefully conceived distortions of color and perspective and include elongated figures. The dramatic sense of movement emerges from his involvement in athletics, an element that he characterizes as "tension generated by paradox and conflict." Barnes also acknowledges the formal and thematic influences of George Bellows, Thomas Hart Benton, and Andrew Wyeth, as well as the entire tradition of black genre painting.

Like many other black artists, Barnes uses his art to express themes relevant to African American life and culture. Paintings like *Homage to Charles, The Story Teller, Commencement,* and *Study Break* highlight the value of learning. Sports-themed paintings like *Half Time, Inner City Football, The Neighborhood Games,* and *Night Game* are conspicuously multiracial, reinforcing his message of tolerance, cooperation, and community solidarity. His genre paintings, similar to the earlier works of Archibald Motley, showcase the positive elements of black life. Paintings like *Sugar Shack, Club 55, Quintet, Palace Barber Shop, A Joyful Noise, Eight Ball,* and *The Gospel Truth* portray the joys of African American pool halls, barbershops, musical and dance clubs, and churches—in short, the beauty of the ghetto. Like many other black artists, Barnes is especially affected by music, a theme pervading his artwork.

Throughout his artistic career Barnes has created favorable images of whites and other people beyond the black community. Having lived and worked outside this community, he is uniquely equipped for the task. Works like *Sam and Sidney, Skateboard, Coffeebreak,* and *Arms of Comfort* reinforce his status as a humanistic artist of the late twentieth century. Above all he has successfully used his art to counter destructive racial stereotypes and to foster durable human understanding. Few artistic objectives are as worthy in the increasingly multicultural society of America.

—Paul Von Blum

BARTHÉ, Richmond

American sculptor and painter

Born: St. Louis, Missouri, 29 January 1901. **Education:** School of the Art Institute of Chicago, 1924-28; Art Students League, New York, 1931; Xavier University, New Orleans, M.A. 1934; St. Francis College, Brooklyn, New York, A.F.D. 1947. Private study with Charles Schroeder and Albin Polasek. **Career:** Traveled frequently to Italy and Iolaus, Jamaica. Member, Chicago Art League and Sculpture Guild. **Awards:** Eames McVeagh Prize, 1928; Rosenwald Foundation Fellowship, 1928-29; Guggenheim Memorial Foundation Fellowship, 1940-41; Edward B. Alford Award. Honorary master's degree, Xavier University, New Orleans, 1934. **Died:** 6 March 1989.

Individual Exhibitions:

1925	Delphic Studios, New York
1933	Caz-Delbos Gallery, New York
1934	Salons of America, New York
1935	New Jersey State Museum
1938	Arden Gallery, New York

Richmond Barthé: *West Indian Girl,* 1931. Photo by Manu Sassoonian; courtesy of the Schomburg Center for Research in Black Culture.

Selected Group Exhibitions:

1933	Whitney Museum of American Art, New York
1935	Whitney Museum of American Art, New York
1939	Whitney Museum of American Art, New York
	Baltimore Museum, Maryland
1947	World's Fair, New York
	Margaret Brown Gallery, Boston
	Grand Central Gallery, New York
1971	Newark Museum, New Jersey
1976	Los Angeles County Museum (traveling)
1985	Bellevue Art Museum, Washington (traveling)

Collections:

Armstrong High School Richmond, Virginia; Atlanta University, Georgia; Harlem River Houses, New York; Lake Country Children's Home, Gary, Indiana; Metropolitan Museum of Art, New York; New York Public Library; New Theatre, London; Oberlin College, Ohio; Pennsylvania Academy of Fine Arts; Schomburg Center, New York; Anson Phelps Stokes Foundation, New York; United States Treasury Project; University of Wisconsin; Virginia Museum; Whitney Museum of American Art, New York.

Publications:

On BARTHÉ: Articles—"Richmond Barthé: Sculpture" by H.A.

William, in *Opportunity VI,* November 1928, p. 334; "Richmond Barthé," in *Tarrytown News,* March 1940; "Story of Barthé," in *Art Digest,* 1 March 1939; interview with Elizabeth Catlett, *International Review of African-American Art,* 23 October 1982; "Richmond Barthé," in *A History of African-American Artists, From 1792 to the Present* by Romare Bearden and Harry Henderson, New York, Pantheon Books, 1993, pp. 136-146.

*   *   *

Richmond Barthé is enshrined among the artists of the Harlem Renaissance. Most of the black artists of the time were painters, and Barthé was one of the few sculptors. He participated in the Harmon Foundation exhibition in 1929. Barthé is always considered an African American, but his full heritage was somewhat more complex. In addition to being part African, he was also part French and Native American.

As a young man Barthé was extraordinarily good-looking. The rather full photographic record of him until the 1940s shows his photogenic face, often with a broad smile. He seems also to have been a smart dresser, for the photographs often depict him wearing a jacket, usually with a handkerchief carefully folded and placed in his breast pocket. His smile did not fade even in later years. In addition to sculpture Barthé had a deep interest in dance. He was a friend of the choreographer Katherine Dunham and at one stage in his life aspired to be a professional dancer. The figure in his work *Benga* moves with the gracefulness of a dancer.

As an artist Barthé used his gifts to explore and depict the culture of people of African descent. He became known for his sensual castings of the human figure, both male and female, although he had a specific interest in the male nude. He worked primarily in clay, from which bronze figures were cast.

Barthé's interests and subjects, however, were wide-ranging. Although some of his works were religious, most were secular. One of his pieces, *The Blackberry Woman,* shows a figure in motion with a load perfectly balanced on her head. He also did the bust of Booker T. Washington in the Hall of Fame of New York University. His sculpture in high relief called *The Negro Looks Ahead* is frequently reproduced, and it serves as the cover illustration of the brochure describing the Schomburg Center for Research in Black Culture in New York City.

Like many creative African Americans, Barthé lived for a period outside the United States. Sometime during the 1940s he went to Jamaica, where he had a home. Upon his return to the United States, he was surprised that younger people still knew who he was and knew of his accomplishments as a sculptor.

Barthé's legacy as a sculptor is difficult to assess. He was one of the first men of African descent to have a career as a formally trained sculptor. Because of his success other younger men may have seen him as a role model and realized the possibilities and opportunities that sculpture presented. One of his students, John Rhoden, went on to make an impact in sculpture.

Critical judgment of Barthé's work seems to be summed up by the word "conventional." His subject matter was that of the classical sculptor—the human figure—and he never seems to have ventured into nonhuman subjects or into abstraction. But the assessment of being conventional may be the key to understanding Barthé's success. He so mastered the conventional rules of content, style, and technique in Western sculpture that he made a mark for himself and led the way for others.

—Thomas M. Shaw

Richmond Barthé: *Paul Robeson as Othello,* **1974. Photo by Manu Sassoonian; courtesy of the Schomburg Center for Research in Black Culture.**

BASQUIAT, Jean-Michel
American painter

Born: Brooklyn, New York, 22 December 1960. **Education:** City as School, Brooklyn, New York. **Died:** 12 August 1988.

Selected Exhibitions:

1979	Mudd Club, New York
1980	Times Square Show, New York
	Club 57, New York
1981	Mazzoli Gallery, Modena, Italy
	New York/New Wave, P.S.1 Gallery, New York
1982	Annina Nosei Gallery, New York
	Fun Gallery, New York
	Gagosian Gallery, Los Angeles
	Gun Gallery, New York
1984	Museum of Modern Art, New York
	Mary Boone Gallery, New York
1985	*Basquiat/Warhol/Clemente,* Tony Shafrazi Gallery, New York
1992	Whitney Museum of American Art, New York (retrospective)

Publications:

On BASQUIAT: Books—*Basquiat Drawings,* edited by John Cheim, Bulfinch, Little, Brown, 1990; *Jean-Michel Basquiat* by Richard Marshall, New York, Abrams, 1992. **Articles**—Article by Cathleen McGuigan, in *New York Times Magazine,* 10 February 1985; "Banking on Basquiat" by Allan Schwartzman, in *Arts Magazine,* 63, November 1988, pp. 25-26; "Saint Jean Michel" by Frederick Ted Castle, in *Arts Magazine,* 63, February 1989, pp. 60-61; "The Umbilicus of Limbo" by Catherine Liu, in *Flash Art,* 146, May/June 1989, pp. 102-105; "The Drawings of Jean-Michel Basquiat" by Peter Winter, in *Art International,* 10, Spring 1990, pp. 94-95; "The Basquiat Battle" by Richard W. Walker, in *Art News,* 90, May 1991, p. 38; "Royal Slumming: Jean-Michel Basquiat Here Below" by Thomas McEvilley, in *Artforum,* 31, November 1992, pp. 92-97 (illustrated); "A Boost for Basquiat" by Judd Tully, in *Art News,* 92, March 1993, p. 27; "A Day at the Races" by Lorraine O'Grady, in *Artforum,* 31, April 1993, pp. 10-12; "The Wild Child" by Deidre Stein, in *Art News,* 93, March 1994, p. 21 (illustrated); "Mount Holyoke College Art Museum/South Hadley: Jean-Michel Basquiat, the Blue Ribbon Paintings" by John Arthur, in *Art New England,* 16, February/March 1995, pp. 46-48 (illustrated); "Basquiat's Wave" by David Bowie, in *Modern Painters,* 9, Spring 1996, pp. 46-47 (illustrated); "Double Feature (Collaborative Paintings of Andy Warhol and Jean-Michel Basquiat)" by Trevor Fairbrother, in *Art in America,* 84, September 1996, pp. 76-83 (illustrated); "A Cautionary Tale: Memorializing Basquiat" by Bill Stamets, in *New Art Examiner,* 23, November 1996, p. 19 (illustrated); "What's Wrong with this Picture: Reviewing Basquiat (How White and Black Directors Portray Blacks)" by Bill Gaskins, in *New Art Examiner,* 23, November 1996, pp. 18-19.

*   *   *

The decade of the 1980s saw the creation of a bullish art market encouraged by the Reagan economy of easy money, in which art stars promoted by a new generation of savvy New York dealers sold works for up to six figures. Jean-Michel Basquiat was the fastest rising and most controversial artist of the decade. He attained blue-chip status as the youngest of the new-expressionist painters, had several solo shows in New York City and Europe, and dined nightly with Andy Warhol, all before the age of twenty-five. Critics dismissed him as an art world mascot and a fraud. Supporters proclaimed him a genius and named him the Wild Child. Either way, Basquiat's life often overshadowed his art. His death at age twenty-seven of a cocaine-heroin overdose transformed Basquiat's life into legend.

A prominent fixture of the East Village bohemia of the late 1970s, Basquiat adopted the persona of the artist ingenue from the mean city streets. In reality, he came from an upper-middle-class neighborhood in Brooklyn and attended an alternative high school, City As School, for gifted but difficult students. He first attracted attention with his SAMO (short for "same old shit") graffiti tag and for cryptic poetic sayings that he and friend Al Diaz sprayed throughout Manhattan. Basquiat's first paintings were described by Rene Ricard in his 1981 *Artforum* article "The Radiant Child" as "a logical extension of what you could do with a wall."

Basquiat quickly adopted the neoexpressionist style, a European import that had revived and energized the New York art world, and he immediately attracted the attention of important art critics.

Ricard said, "I asked someone once why he liked Jean-Michel's work and why it was being singled out for acclaim, and he said, 'because it looks like art.'" The works were large and colorful, splashed with crowns, stick figures, and African mask faces, and sprinkled with enigmatic words and brief phrases. Bell Hooks, a black painter, writer, and art critic, maintained in "Altars of Sacrifice," a 1993 article in *Art in America,* that Basquiat's expressionist borrowings from Pablo Picasso, Jackson Pollock, and Willem de Kooning were actually a reclamation of the African primitivism that these artists had copied in the first place. Basquiat, Hooks said, worked from ancestral memory and was thus "grappling with both the pull of a genealogy that is fundamentally Black."

Basquiat's content centered on the relationship between black cultural concerns within a white, Eurocentric frame of reference. Hooks stated that Basquiat's visibility depended on assuming "the blackness defined by the white imagination . . . he had to sacrifice those parts of himself [that whites] would not be interested in or fascinated by." Paintings from 1981 and 1982, such as *Irony of Negro Policemen* and *Native Carrying Some Guns, Bibles, Amorites on Safari,* superficially bear out this idea. Upon reflection, however, the meaning of Basquiat's symbols and words, which he chose quickly and unconsciously, as in jazz improvisation, double back on themselves endlessly as he deconstructs white myths about black people and vice versa. Basquiat's subtle dialogue erodes the racist and classist frame of reference of any viewer. His investigations reached their greatest depth in *Crowns,* where his vision focused on the white male world and a black man's place within it. *Crowns* can be read biographically as Basquiat freshly kinged and then thrown into an art world full of malevolent, warring kings (other male artists).

After Basquiat's initial burst of creativity and fame, two distinct periods, middle and late, followed. A few later works stand out, but overall the intensity and sustained power of his early painting diminished. Although some later images revisited the earlier cavalier time of splashed paint and stick figures, most were characterized by a harnessing of Basquiat's lines into cartooning. Large canvasses such as *Pegasus* swarm with amusing words, symbols, and little drawings, like an unfiltered, nervous mental buzz that paint only occasionally intrudes upon. In Basquiat's last images from 1988, expressly done for dealer Vrej Baghoomian and intended for a European tour, he was heavily assisted by artist Rick Prol. Largely linear with shapes colored in, these canvases boldly go nowhere. One image stands out, however—*Riding with Death* is both ominous and portentous because of Basquiat's early death.

—Laurie Fitzpatrick

BAYNES, Gloretta

American painter, fiber artist, and mixed-media artist

Born: Cambridge, Massachusetts, 21 October 1954. **Education:** Massachusetts College of Art, Cambridge, 1972-76, B.F.A. 1976. **Career:** Since 1993 assistant to the director, Museum of the National Center of Afro-American Artists; since 1993 associate curator, *Sequential Art, The Next Step 2: An Exhibition of Contemporary African American Comic Book Artists,* Museum of the National Center for Afro-American Artists. Chairwoman, since 1997, and artist-in-residence, since 1989, African American Artist in Resi-

Gloretta Baynes (with *Yam Mask*), 1994. Photo courtesy of Peggy Tuitt.

dence Program (AAMARP), Northeastern University, Boston. **Award:** Outstanding Young Woman of America, 1980. **Address:** 76 Atherton Street, Jamaica Plain, Massachusetts 02130, U.S.A.

Selected Exhibitions:

1972	Cambridge Public Library, Massachusetts
	Cambridge Trust Bank, Massachusetts
1976	Massachusetts College of Art, Boston
1981	*Young Black Artists under 36,* Northeastern University, Boston
1982	Regis College, Wellesley, Massachusetts
1989	Charrette Corporation, Boston
1990	*Tribute to Martin Luther King,* Boston City Hall
1991	*Tribute to Martin Luther King,* Boston City Hall
	Boston State House
1992	Mazmanian Gallery, Framingham State College, Massachusetts
1993	New World Bank, Boston
	Trustman Gallery, Simmons College, Boston
	Women's Institute for Housing and Economic Development, Boston
1994	*The Time Is New,* Winfrisky Gallery, Salem State College, Massachusetts
	Grossman Gallery, Museum of Fine Arts, Boston
	World Trade Center, Boston
	Northeastern University, Boston
1995	Cinque Gallery, New York
	Montclair University, New Jersey
1996	Pine Manor College, Chestnut Hill, Massachusetts
	Harriet Tubman Gallery, Boston
	Museum of Fine Arts, Boston
	Copley Society, Boston
	Imajica, Northeastern University, Boston (solo)

Publications:

On BAYNES: Articles—"Pick of the Week: Imajica" by Cheryl Sinapis, in *Boston Globe,* 12 September 1996, p. 24; "Hot Tickets" by Joan T. Collins, in *Boston Herald,* 15 September 1996, p. 38; "Baynes World Has Radiance" by Joanne Silver, in *Boston Herald,* 8 November 1996, p. S11; "Artist Chairs NU Program" by Gillian Hodgen, in *Northeastern News,* 19 February 1997, p. 18. **Television**—"Imajica/Artist Gloretta Baynes," on *About the Arts* produced by James Brown, BNN, 8 December 1996.

*

Gloretta Baynes comments:

The first recollection I have about drawing is when my mother was combing my hair when I was five or six. My father, Henry, made a quick sketch of me with my hair standing all over my head. I didn't think it was very flattering at the time. In retrospect it actually was a very good study. We lived in Cambridgeport, a quiet residential area of Cambridge. There was always an allowance available for drawing paper and pencils, even in a household of five children. I would happily walk to Central Square to the local drug store for my supplies.

My first mural was on the cafeteria walls of Cambridge High Latin. I don't think they were expecting the young angry black couple with their fist raised in a black power salute or the posters made of Angela Davis to sell to raise money for the Black Student Union. I was fortunate to be mentored by the black students of Harvard and Tufts universities. In fact, my first commissioned piece was a Kwanza card for the African Studies department at Harvard.

The first artist I met was Vuzi Madonna, who lived down the street from me. His significant other was also an artist, and they never turned me away when I knocked on their door. Gary Rickson mentored me and taught me the significance of jazz and art articulation.

In 1972 I received a scholarship to attend Massachusetts College of Art. I majored in fashion design and illustration, and I received honors for two years. I look back in wonder at the exceptional artists I met during my formation years at Massachusetts Ar— Paul Goodnight, George Cook, Calvin Burnett, Napoleon Jones Henderson, and a host of others. The nurturing I received from the Black Artist Union has carried me throughout the years.

In 1988 I was invited to become a member of the African American Artist in Residence Program by Dana Chandler. I was given a wonderful opportunity to collaborate with others, work in different media, and develop large scale projects.

The work currently displayed is a personal exploration of color

Gloretta Baynes: *Afro Blues #1,* 1994. Photo courtesy of Hakim Raquib.

in texture and content. The dominant colors are cool blues and purples—soothing, streaming, tranquil . . . flowing like waves through peaks and valleys into infinity. The images are simple but reflect a deep emotional content based on my personal experiences and convictions.

Sisters and *African Madonna* are based on family. My father died when I was eleven. The strength, determination, and beauty of my mother to successfully raise five children is an amazing feat. That strength of character and resiliency is instilled in my work.

The "Afro Blue" series was created after hearing an exotic and sensual rendition of John Coltrane's "Afro Blue" by Stan Strickland. The works represent harmonious relationships, equal partnership, and profound and ecstatic spiritual experiences.

Yam mask and *Timburrawa* are images from Papua, New Guinea. The Yam mask is used to celebrate a bountiful harvest. The Timburrawa is a guardian figure for a spirit house.

My fabric abstracts are studies of color, form, and spontaneity. In contrast, *Matsuda* and *Toshiba Cranes* are intricately developed images, with each stroke deliberately placed.

When I was younger I enjoyed lavishly illustrated fairy tales. As I got older I would search through comic-book racks for a super-heroine who looked like me. The black fairy tale series and goddess characters are a result of that frustration.

The "Ascension" series represents personal growth and self-love. "The spiritual manifests itself not only in invisible forms but also in physical forms . . . one passes through a world of forms

ascending from reality to abstraction. In this manner one approaches spirit, or purity itself" (Piet Mondrian).

My personal journeys are just beginning.

* * *

Gloretta Baynes studied at the Massachusetts College of Art and at Boston University. She is active as both a visual artist and an arts administrator. In the latter capacity Baynes is assistant to the director of the museum of the National Center of Afro-American Artists, and she is the chair of the African American Master Artists in Residence Program at Northeastern University (AAMARP). Baynes also is a resident artist in AAMARP. Her media are the airbrush applied to both paper and fabric and pen-and-ink drawings.

In their preoccupation with heroics Baynes's artworks on paper are strongly allied with the work of comic book and sequential artists. Like them she uses a simplified form to emphasize clarity of action and dramatic purposefulness. Her heroines, their hair often squared in a Grace Jones style, are often masculine women who demonstrate their physicality. In some works, such as *Alice in Wonderland,* however, she presents a fantastic world with the brilliance and directness of Walt Disney cartoons or of fine children's book illustrations.

Women are the predominant image in Baynes's art, and they often carry an erotic suggestiveness in their attitudes and in the muted but warm colors with which she portrays them. This erotic implication is even more apparent in works such as *Afro Blues,* in which a pair of figures embrace.

Baynes is more experimental in her airbrush works on fabric. Here she uses templates to re-create the patterns of African stamped cloths, and she gives wide latitude to her interest in creating subtle patterns and shapes over the expanse of the fabric's surface. In one recent series she has gone much further than before in drawing on African, and perhaps Native American, icons to give visual focus to her hangings. Her most totally resolved and technically brilliant works, however, may be a series of decorative themes featuring cranes against patterned backgrounds. These works, using a closely harmonized palette, achieve a wonderful feeling of sensuous, elegance, and visual peace.

—Edmund Barry Gaither

BEARDEN, Romare (Howard)
American painter and mixed-media artist

Born: Charlotte, North Carolina, 2 September 1914. **Education:** New York University, 1932-35, B.S. 1935; studied under George Grosz, Art Students League, New York, 1936-37; studied advanced mathematics at Columbia University, New York, 1943; studied philosophy and art history at Sorbonne, Paris, 1951. **Military Service:** United States Army, 1942-45. **Family:** Married Nanette Rohan in 1954. **Career:** Caseworker, New York City Department of Social Services, 1938-42, 1946-49, 1952-66. Concentrated on songwriting, 1951-54; established studio on Canal Street, New York, 1956. Beginning 1964 art director, Harlem Cultural Council, New York; cofounder, with Norman Lewis and Ernest Crichlow, Cinque Gallery, New York Public Theater, 1969; set and costume designer,

Romare Bearden: *Christ's Entry into Jerusalem,* **1945. Photo by Manu Sassoonian; courtesy of the Schomburg Center for Research in Black Culture.**

Alvin Ailey Ballet Company, New York, 1977. Artist-in-residence, Spelman College, Atlanta, Georgia, 1968, University of Delaware, Newark, 1970; visiting lecturer, Williams College, Williamstown, Massachusetts, 1969; instructor, Yale College, New Haven, Connecticut, 1980. Traveled in Italy, Switzerland, Algiers, and Morocco, 1950. Member, American Academy of Arts and Letters. **Awards:** American Academy of Arts and Letters Painting Award, 1966; National Institute of Arts and Letters grant, 1966; Guggenheim Memorial Foundation Fellowship, 1970; Ford Foundation Fellowship, 1973; Medal of the State of North Carolina, 1976; Frederick Douglas Medal, New York Urban League, 1978; James Weldon Johnson Award, Atlanta Chapter of NAACP, 1978. Honorary doctorates: Pratt Institute, New York, 1973; Carnegie Mellon University, Pittsburgh, 1975; Maryland Institute of Art, Baltimore, 1976; North Carolina Central University, Durham, 1977; Davidson College, North Carolina, 1978. **Agent:** Cordier and Ekstrom Inc., 980 Madison Avenue, New York, New York 10021, U.S.A. **Died:** 1988.

Individual Exhibitions:

1935	"G" Place Gallery, Washington, D.C.
1940	A.D. Bates Studio, New York
1944	*10 Hieroglyphic Paintings,* "G" Place Gallery, Washington, D.C.
1945	Galerie John Duvuloy, Paris (with Pietro Lazzari) "G" Place Gallery, Washington, D.C.
	Samuel Kootz Gallery, New York
1946	Samuel Kootz Gallery, New York
1947	Samuel Kootz Gallery, New York
1948	Niveau Gallery, New York
1955	Barone Gallery, New York
1960	Michel Warren Gallery, New York
1961	Cordier and Ekstrom Gallery, New York
1964	*Projections,* Cordier and Ekstrom Gallery, New York
1966	Carnegie Institute, Pittsburgh, Pennsylvania
	Bundy Art Gallery, Waitsfield, Vermont

	Corcoran Gallery of Art, Washington, D.C.
1967	Fine Arts Building, Spelman College, Atlanta
	Collages, J. L. Hudson Gallery, Detroit
	Cordier and Ekstrom Gallery, New York
1968	*Paintings and Projections,* State University of New York at Albany
1969	Williams College, Williamstown, Massachusetts
	Iowa State University, Iowa City
1970	Cordier and Ekstrom Gallery, New York
	Tricia Karliss Gallery, Provincetown, Massachusetts
1971	*The Prevalence of Ritual,* Museum of Modern Art, New York (traveling retrospective through 1972)
	Cordier and Ekstrom Gallery, New York
1973	Cordier and Ekstrom Gallery, New York
1974	Galerie Albert Loeb, Paris
	Madison Art Museum, Wisconsin
	Everson Museum, Syracuse, New York
	Of the Blues, Cordier and Ekstrom Gallery, New York
1976	Firehouse Gallery, Nassau College, New York
	Graphics Gallery, Toronto
	Cordier and Ekstrom Gallery, New York
1977	Union College, Cranford, New Jersey
	Odysseus: Collages, Cordier and Ekstrom Gallery, New York
1978	Cordier and Ekstrom Gallery, New York
	Davidson College, North Carolina
1980	*Retrospective: 1970-1980,* Mint Museum, Charlotte, North Carolina (traveling)
1981	*Collages: Profile: The 30s,* Cordier and Esktrom Gallery, New York

Selected Group Exhibitions:

1945	Whitney Museum of American Art, New York
1948	*6 American Painters,* Galerie Maeght, Paris
	Abstract and Surrealist American Art, Art Institute of Chicago
1951	*Survey of American Art,* Metropolitan Museum of Art, New York
1955	Whitney Museum of American Art, New York
1968	*30 Contemporary Black Artists,* Minneapolis Institute of Art, Minnesota
1969	*New American Painting and Sculpture,* Museum of Modern Art, New York
1970	*5 Famous Black Artists,* Museum of the National Center of Afro-American Arts, Boston
1981	*6 Black Americans,* New Jersey State Museum, Trenton
	The Human Form, Maryland Institute College of Art, Baltimore, Maryland
	24 Black American Artists, Goucher College, Baltimore, Maryland

Collections:

High Museum of Art, Atlanta; Madison Art Center, Wisconsin; Metropolitan Museum of Art, New York; Museum of Fine Arts, Boston; Museum of Modern Art, New York; Newark Museum, New Jersey; Philadelphia Museum of Art; Princeton University, New Jersey; Rochester Memorial Art Gallery, New York; Schomburg Center, New York; Whitney Museum of American Art, New York.

Publications:

By BEARDEN: Books—*The Painter's Mind,* with Carl Holty, New York 1969; *6 Black Masters of American Art,* with Harry Henderson, New York 1972; *Prevalence of Ritual,* portfolio of 5 silkscreens, New York, 1977. *A History of African-American Artists, from 1792 to the Present,* with Harry Henderson, Pantheon, New York, 1993. **Articles**—"The Negro Artist and Modern Art," in *Opportunity,* December 1934; "Problems of the Negro Artists," in *Critique,* October 1948; "Rectangular Structure in My Montage Paintings," in *Leonardo* (Paris), January 1969; "The Artist and His Education," in *Harvard Art Review* (Cambridge, Massachusetts), Spring 1969.

On BEARDEN: Books—*Romare Bearden: Paintings and Projections,* exhibition catalog, by Ralph Ellison, Albany, New York 1968; *Romare Bearden: The Prevalence of Ritual,* exhibition catalog, introduction by Carroll Greene, New York, 1971; *The Art of Romare Bearden: The Prevalence of Ritual* by John Williams and M. Bunch Washington, New York, Abrams, 1973; *Of the Blues,* exhibition catalog, by Albert Murray, New York 1975; *Romare Bearden: Odysseus: Collages,* exhibition catalog, introduction by Calvin Tomkins, New York, 1977; *Romare Bearden: Collages: Profile: The 30s,* exhibition catalog, edited by Albert Murray, New York, 1981; *Romare Bearden: His Life and Art* by Myron Schwartzman, New York, Abrams, 1990; *Memory and Metaphor: The Art of Romare Bearden,* New York, Oxford University Press and the Studio Museum in Harlem, 1991; *A Graphic Odyssey: Romare Bearden as Printmaker* by Gail Gelburd, New York, Council for Creative Projects, and University of Pennsylvania Press, 1992; *Romare Bearden in Black-and-White: Photomontage Projections* by Gail Gelburd and Thelma Golden, New York, Whitney Museum of American Art, 1997. **Articles**—"Romare Bearden—Projections" by Dore Ashton, in *Quadrum* (Brussels), (17), 1965; "Black Persephone" by Ralph Pomeroy, in *Artnews* (New York), October 1967; "Romare Bearden—Paintings and Projections" by Ralph Ellison, in *New Yorker,* 28 November 1977; "Romare Bearden: 'I Paint Out of the Tradition of the Blues'" by Avis Berman, in *Artnews* (New York), December 1980; "Romare Bearden" in *Vogue* (New York), February 1981; "Romare Bearden" in *Smithsonian* (Washington, D.C.), March 1981; "Romare Bearden" in *Newsweek* (New York), 30 March 1981; "Romare Bearden: Rites and Riffs" by M. S. Campbell, in *Art in America* (New York), December 1981; "Romare Bearden Sees in a Memory" by Myron Schwartzman, in *Artforum,* 22, May 1984, pp. 74-70; "The Unknown Romare Bearden" by Lowery Stokes Sims, in *Art News,* 85, October 1986, pp. 116-20 (illustrated); "Obituary," in *Art in America,* 76, May 1988, p. 202; "Rhythm-a-ning" by Bruce Nixon, in *Artweek,* 22, 17 January 1991, pp. 15-16; "Remaking Bearden" by Eric Gibson, in *The New Criterion,* 10, November 1991, pp. 61-65; "Precious Memory" by Mario Cutajar, in *Artweek,* 23, 30 January 1992, p. 1; "Romare's Renaissance" by Richard W. Walker, in *Art News,* 91, February 1992, p. 21; "Cut and Paste: Romare Bearden's Collages Reflect His Life in Many Worlds" by Hugh Kenner, in *Art and Antiques,* 9, May 1992, p. 96 (illustrated); "A Look at Romare Bearden and the Textile Metaphor" by W. Logan Fry, in *Fiberarts,* 19, September/October 1992, pp. 22-23 (illustrated); "Signifying Identity: Art and Race in Romare Bearden's Projections" by Lee Stephens Glazer, in *Art Bulletin,* 76, September 1994, pp. 411-26 (illustrated);"Romare Bearden: In Tune with Jazz" by Eric Gibson, in *Art News,* 94, September 1995, p. 102.

Romare Bearden: Untitled, 1975 (executed to commemorate the Schomburg Center for Research in Black Culture's 50th anniversary). Photo by Manu Sassoonian; courtesy of the Schomburg Center for Research in Black Culture.

Romare Bearden's famous 1974 collage *Carolina Shout,* named for a Harlem stride-piano composition by James P. Johnson, takes as its subject a baptism ceremony in a Southern black church. Dark, masklike silhouettes of heads and gesturing hands punctuate a pulsating hot-pink ground, while below their bodies appear submerged in the sustaining cool blue-green of ritual evocation. Present in this one image are the wellsprings of Bearden's art: the ceremonial dimension of the everyday lives of people of color, at work, at church, and at play; and the blues aesthetic, the affirmation of the black experience through the dissonant, elegant, soaring, and plaintive textures, voices, and rhythms of jazz. In *Romare Bearden 1970-80,* novelist Albert Murray noted, "The figures suggest an ecstatic high point in a downhome church service. At the same time, the title . . . implies that the movements and gestures are not unrelated to the dance hall, the juke joint, the honky tonk, and the barrel house. So even as the figures evoke Sunday Morning Service, there are overtones of . . . Saturday Night." *Carolina Shout* is indeed a song of praise, a shout of triumph, an exultation. "Art celebrates a victory," Bearden once said.

The vibrant choreography of daily life in black communities was for Bearden "perhaps the richest because it is the one lifestyle that is talking about life and about the continuation of life . . . and through all the anguish—the joy of life." Bearden drew for his art upon the fullness of his own experience of black America, from boyhood summers spent in rural Mecklenberg County, North Carolina, to memories of his grandmother's boardinghouse near the steel mills of Pittsburgh, to the spirited Harlem of his adolescence and early adulthood, then in its heyday as a black cultural and intellectual mecca. Bearden's artistic development grew from an early cubist-inspired figuration through the abstract works of the 1950s and 1960s, with their lyrical use of line and color, to the signature collages of his later years. He first began collage work in the mid-1960s and soon made the medium uniquely his own, with his soulful mix of paint, cloth scraps, colored papers, and magazine photographs.

A man of broad outlook and wide-ranging talents, Bearden nurtured his creative vision on everything from Chinese landscapes to the carved wood sculpture of West Africa, from patchwork quilts to the whole of European painting from Duccio di Buoninsegna through Jan Vermeer to Piet Mondrian and Pablo Picasso. George Grosz, with whom Bearden studied as a young man, was an important influence: Grosz's corrosive, satirical drawings of Weimar Germany helped Bearden see that his art could address the social conditions of American blacks. But Bearden's outlook was essentially joyous, as evinced by his attraction to the exuberant canvases of American cubist Stuart Davis, whose synthesis of the avant-garde and the vernacular was another significant influence. It was Davis who encouraged Bearden to apply the rhythms and structures of jazz to his visual compositions. "At Davis' suggestion, I listened for hours to recordings of Earl Hines at the piano," explained Bearden. "Finally, I was able to block out the melody and concentrate on the silences between notes. I found that this was very helpful to me in the transmutation of sound into colors and in the placement of objects in my paintings and collages. . . . I could have studied this integration and spacing in Greek vase painting but . . . Jazz has shown me ways of achieving artistic structures that are personal to me."

The spaces in Bearden's work seem to reverberate not only with silence but with ancestral voices. His men and women, with their often composite faces, evoke the presence of generations. Place, too, provides Bearden with a patchwork of meaning. *The Street* (1975) pulses with a cacophonous jumble of urban color and sound.

Street musicians jam, a watchful child stares, a stooped elderly woman picks her way down the sidewalk. Inside a tenement, a mother caresses a child, a couple make love. Photographed 'real' eyes stare out from collaged faces; hands, oversized and powerful, emerge from painted clothes to strum chords, embrace, or touch. In *Southern Limited* (1976) the wail of a passing train fills the flat pink expanse of rural sky, a bird dips, a man hoes a field, the brooding faces of gingham-clad women loom, serious and dark, above the landscape. Trains constantly pass through Bearden's landscapes: trains going to glory, freedom trains, soul trains, trains as emblems of the artist himself, revisiting the space and time of his earliest memories. "Time is a pattern," Bearden was quoted as saying. "You can come back to where you started from with added experience and you hope more understanding. You leave and then return to the homeland of your imagination."

Freedom and bondage, death and renewal, the exalted spirit present in the humble rites of daily living—these are Bearden's blues, his persistent themes, given to us in scraps of shape and color alive with the presence and memory of his people's stories and sounds, an epic of the actual, told with improvisatory freedom and unbridled hope.

—Dorothy Valakos

BEASLEY, Phoebe
American painter and collage artist

Name also appears as Arlene A. Beasley. **Born:** Cleveland, Ohio, 3 June 1943. **Education:** Ohio University, Athens, B.A. 1965; Kent State University, Ohio, 1967-69, graduated 1969. **Career:** Teacher, Cleveland Board of Education, 1965-69; artist, Sage Publications, 1969-70. Since 1970 senior account executive, KFI/KOST Radio, Los Angeles. First African American female president, American Women in Radio and Television, 1977-78. Designed International Tennis Trophy and Medal, 1984 Summer Olympic Games. Official artist, 1987 Los Angeles Marathon. Designer, sickle cell disease campaign poster. **Awards:** Merit Award, Achievement Award, and Genii Award, American Women in Radio and Television, 1975; Woman of the Year, Los Angeles Sentinel, 1989; Black Women of Achievement Award, NAACP Legal Defense and Educational Fund, 1991; presidential seal for Clinton inaugural. **Address:** 610 South Ardmore, Los Angeles, California 90005, U.S.A.

Selected Exhibitions:

Alex Gallery, Washington, D.C.; Arizona State University, Tempe; Cinque Gallery, New York; Museum of African American Art, Howard University, Washington, D.C.; Museum of Science and Industry, Chicago; North Carolina Central University.

Publications:

On BEASLEY: Articles—"Phoebe Beasley," in *Black Art Quarterly,* 5, February 1982, pp. 4-11; "Art Card Raises Funds" by Leigh Ann Clifton, in *Artweek,* 24, 18 November 1993, p. 2.

*   *   *

Phoebe Beasley works in the realm of collage, utilizing paint, tissue paper, cloth, and found objects to recreate worlds she knows and worlds she admires. She sometimes works in straight collage and other times uses a clear acrylic foundation, then applies various materials on both the front and back of the piece. Backlight provides a stained-glass quality to the composition, as in *105 Count Down #1.*

Beasley has written of her themes, or subjects, that they are "what I know, based on my point of reference, just like any other artist. And certainly they are from my culture. But, there is a universality in my work of what it's like living alone, being poor, and getting old." The people in her collages may be ordinary, working-class folks or they may be extraordinary, well-known, and well-loved celebrities, such as in her piece *Zora and Langston,* which portrays authors Zora Neale Hurston and Langston Hughs.

The overall effect of Beasley's work has been described in terms of jazz. She applies blocks of color and pattern to her work that quickly draw the eye from one part of the painting to another—and back again—establishing a beat, a rhythm, something to dance to. "The block print patterns set up rhythms on the surface," says Beasley. The subjects of her collages inhabit the music of the piece. They bring you onto the surface of the work like a dance partner pulling you onto the floor. Once the rhythm is established, and you begin to dance, and your body begins to sing along, then Beasley has made the work a part of you, ensuring that her "idea will reverberate clearly."

One of the greatest influences on Phoebe Beasley's work is the collage artist Romare Bearden. Beasley says of artists who have come before her, "It's important to keep alive art heroes like Romare Bearden and Charles White and Elizabeth Catlett. They didn't receive a lot of recognition. But . . . we need to know how valuable a contribution they made—not just to African art, but to art." Beasley says that early in her career when gallery owners were rejecting her work, they sometimes asked, "Why do you always paint black subjects?" Questions such as these, as well as the everyday concerns of a person living in the world, continue to make her portrayal of real life necessary.

—Terry Bain

BENNETT, Gwendolyn (Bernette)

American painter and illustrator

Work also appeared under the names Gwendolyn Bennett Jackson and Gwendolyn Bennett Crosscup. **Born:** Giddings, Texas, 8 July 1902. **Education:** Columbia University, New York, 1921; Pratt Institute, New York, 1922-24, B.A. 1924; Barnes Foundation, Merton, Pennsylvania, 1928. **Family:** Married 1) Dr. Alfred Jackson, 1928-36; 2) Richard Crosscup, 1941-79. **Career:** Editorial boardmember, *Fire!!,* New York, 1926; assistant professor, Howard University, Washington, D.C., 1924-25; editor, *Opportunity,* New York, 1926-28; journalist, Department of Information, New York, 1932-38. Director, Education Welfare Council, Harlem Community Art Center, New York, 1939-44, George Carver Community School, New York, 1943-47. Correspondent, Consumers Union, New York, c.1948-1960. Antiques dealer, Pennsylvania, late 1960s through early 1970s. **Awards:** Delta Sigma Theta Sorority Fellowship, 1925; Barnes Foundation Fellowship, 1928. **Died:** 30 May 1981.

Publications:

On BENNETT: Book—*Gwendolyn Bennett: Portrait of an Artist Lost* (dissertation) by Sandra Goran, Atlanta, Georgia, Emory University, 1980. **Articles**—"Artists League Lectures," in *Art Digest* 13, 15 April 1939; "The Negro As Artist," in *Art Digest* 29, 15 December 1945; "Gwendolyn Bennett in the WPA Years" by Sandra Goran, in *Midatlantic Writers Association,* December 1988.

*   *   *

Gwendolyn Bennett, while little known for her visual art, contributed significantly to the African American arts community as a poet, fiction writer, journalist, arts teacher, and administrator during the 1920s and 1930s.

Talented in both literature and art, Bennett participated in Brooklyn's Girls' High School's drama and literary societies (becoming the first African American to do so), and she won first place in an art contest with a poster design. In the early 1920s Bennett took fine arts classes at Columbia University and at Pratt Institute, where she graduated in art education and fine arts in 1924. While she was an undergraduate, her poem "Nocturne" was published in the November 1923 issue of *Crisis* magazine; "Heritage" was published the next month in *Opportunity* magazine.

Bennett taught design, watercolor, and crafts at Howard University from 1924 to 1925, then spent the following year studying art in Paris at the Académies de la Grande Chaumière, Julian, and Colarossi, and the École du Panthéon, on a $1,000 Delta Sigma Theta sorority fellowship. Her short stories—"Wedding Day" published in *Fire!!* and "Tokens" in Charles S. Johnson's *Ebony and Topaz: A Collectanea*—both express the loneliness she experienced in Paris and feature African American expatriates who remained in France after serving in World War I.

After Bennett returned to Washington, D.C., in 1926, a fire in her stepmother's home destroyed most of the paintings and batiks she had produced abroad. She spent the next two years editing "The Ebony Flute," a "literary and social chit-chat" column for *Opportunity.* During the summer of 1927 Bennett taught art classes at Nashville's Tennessee and Industrial State College and served as editor of the magazine *Black Opals.*

Bennett's poetry typically dealt with racial uplift and pride in her African heritage. "To Usward," a tribute to the New Negro generation and a call to those who have "a song to sing," was published in both *Opportunity* and *Crisis* in May of 1926. She also produced symbolist-inspired and romantic lyrics, such as "Quatrains" (1927). This verse expresses the strain Bennett felt, torn between art and literature: "Brushes and paints are all I have / To speak the music in my soul / While silently there laughs at me / A copper jar beside a pale green bowl." From 1927 through 1936, twenty-two of Bennett's poems appeared in various periodicals, as well as in *Anthology for Magazine Verse for 1927 and Yearbook of American Poetry, Caroling Dusk,* and *The Book of American Negro Poetry.*

It is more difficult to assess Bennett's artistic skill since so few of her works have been published. Five of her black-and-white illustrations graced monthly periodical covers between 1923 and 1930. Three untitled pen and ink drawings are of Christmas scenes: three white Christmas carolers in a holly wreath vignette, published in *Crisis,* December 1923; the three kings paying homage to the Madonna and child, published in *Opportunity,* January 1926; and the three kings kneeling and offering gifts, published in *Opportu-*

nity, December 1930. *Pipes of Pan* (1924) is a line drawing of a young black man sitting cross-legged and leaning against a tree, listening with eyes closed to music produced by three nymphs and three satyrs. By contrast, another work—this one published two years later—seems to depict an erotic, Harlem nightclub scene. A black woman in a low-cut dress sways seductively against a plain, dark background. In the lower half of the composition (on what may be a railing or screen) are silhouetted figures of a man and two bare-breasted women gyrating among palm trees, a grass hut, and the sun's rays. All of these illustrations reflect the influence of Art Nouveau, with their whiplash and swelling reverse curves, expressive lines, interlaced patterns, and detailed natural forms.

Bennett was likely inspired by art movements she witnessed in Paris, and later, at the Barnes Foundation in Merion, Pennsylvania, where she studied art on scholarship in 1928. One of her few extant oil paintings, *Winter Landscape* (also known as *Winterset,* c. 1936), is a cubist-influenced work with its geometric, snow-covered hills and bushes and stark bare trees. Elton Fax said that Bennett's work in the landscape genre "while not abstract was somewhat avant garde in color and design. Her color was daring and warm and she obviously was intellectually influenced by Braque and Picasso though she was not an imitation of either."

Bennett rarely exhibited or promoted her visual work and focused the rest of her life more on writing and administration than on art. In the early 1930s she worked as a journalist for the Department of Information and Education of the Welfare Council of New York. Her feature articles appeared in the *Amsterdam News,* the *New York Age,* the *Baltimore Afro-American,* and *Better Times.* Bennett subsequently served as a teacher, then project supervisor, in the Federal Art Teaching Project and in 1939 was director of the Harlem Community Art Center. She was also active in the Harlem Artists Guild, the National Negro Congress, the Artists Union, the Negro People's Theater, and the Negro Playwright's Company.

In 1941 Bennett gave a lecture series on African American art, music, journalism, and poetry at the School for Democracy. Three years later she was suspended from the Art Center by the U.S. House Un-American Activities Committee (HUAC) for her leftist sympathies. She then cofounded and directed the George Carver Community School, an adult education center for Harlem African Americans. Following a HUAC investigation for communist leanings, the school closed in 1947. From the end of the 1940s until the late 1960s, Bennett worked for the Consumers Union as a correspondent.

—Theresa Leininger-Miller

BENOIT, Rigaud

Haitian painter

Born: Port-au-Prince, Haiti, 1911. **Career:** Worked as taxi-driver, musician, and pottery decorator early in life. Member, Centre d'Art, Haiti. **Died:** 1987.

Individual Exhibition:

1969   Centre d'Art, Port-au-Prince, Haiti

Selected Group Exhibitions:

1964   Centre d'Art, Port-au-Prince, Haiti
1969   Davenport Art Gallery, Iowa
        Centre d'Art, Port-au-Prince, Haiti
        Hayward Gallery, London (traveling)
1973   New York Cultural Center
1974   Davenport Art Gallery, Iowa
1978   Brooklyn Museum of Art, New York (traveling)
        Smithsonian Institution Traveling Exhibition Service, Washington, D.C.
1980   Davenport Art Gallery, Iowa
1983   Chicago Public Library Cultural Center
        Davenport Art Gallery, Iowa
1984   Centre d'Art, Port-au-Prince, Haiti
1985   Davenport Art Gallery, Iowa
        Yale University Art Gallery, New Haven, Connecticut
1989   Museum of Art, Fort Lauderdale, Florida

Collections:

Davenport Museum of Art, Iowa; Flagg Collection, Milwaukee, Wisconsin; Holy Trinity Cathedral (mural), Port-au-Prince, Haiti; Musée d'Art Haitien du Collège St. Pierre, Port-au-Prince, Haiti; Museum of Modern Art of Latin America, Washington, D.C.

Publications:

On BENOIT: Book—*Tracing the Spirit: Ethnographic Essays on Haitian Art* by Karen McCarthy Brown, University of Washington Press, Seattle, and Davenport Museum of Art, Iowa, 1995.

*   *   *

One of the most significant of the untrained Haitian painters to emerge in the mid-twentieth century, Rigaud Benoit is known for his surprisingly refined and elaborate figurative scenes. By virtue of his lengthy painting career, which began in the late 1940s, Benoit was also one of the more prolific artists of his generation. Before he began his career as an artist, one of his many odd jobs included painting ceramics, which would play a role in the refinement of his mature style.

After he became associated with the Centre d'Art, a gathering place for artists in Port-au-Prince, Benoit's paintings of the late 1940s demonstrated the pervasive influence of the Haitian master Hector Hyppolite. Benoit's *Nude* (c.1948) recalls Hyppolite's paintings of the goddess Ezili from the mid-1940s. Flat decorative areas of high-keyed colors form the backdrop for the goddess, who is surrounded by vevelike flowers, signifying her spirituality. In another Benoit painting of this early period, *La femme qui pense* (1947), the broadly painted areas of solid color recall Hyppolite's bold patterns and scumbled surfaces, as do the omnipresent floral still lifes.

By 1950 Benoit was beginning to develop more complex and precisely painted narrative scenes. The work *Cockfight* employs what would become his signature—the barren trees and low, stylized mountains of Haiti—to create a stagelike setting for the dozens of figures in the genre scene. Thus, as Benoit's predilection for precision and order, derived from his experience as a painter of ceramics, became increasingly important, his style changed dramatically from the painterly works of the late 1940s. Nonetheless,

Rigaud Benoit, 1979. Photo courtesy of Davenport Museum of Art.

the influence of Hyppolite, especially on Benoit's voodoo-inspired subjects, was lasting. Indeed, as late as the early 1970s, Benoit paid homage to the older artist in his work *The Recall of Hector Hyppolite.*

During the 1960s Benoit's style evolved fully into precise and calculated compositions, with clearly defined space and volumetric, individualized figures rendered from finished preparatory drawings. The influence of surrealism also became recognizable in his work at this time. In *Chalice* (1968) a hollow, plantlike body lying on the ground sprouts a fantastical chalice of flowers from its midsection that fills the upper half of the composition. Rendered with alternating areas of brightly colored impasto flowers and cool, thin layers of translucent glazes, the work shows a dreamlike transformation that is simultaneously horrific and sensually appealing. Although surreal in its startling, dreamlike imagery, *Chalice,* like virtually all of Benoit's paintings, is imbued with Haitian spirituality. In her book *Tracing the Spirit,* Karen McCarthy Brown has deciphered the significance of the central vertical flower and stem in *Chalice* as a potomitan, the center pole in a voodoo temple that connects with Ginen (Africa), home of the ancestors. The plantlike shell of the horizontal body is that of an ancestor blossoming forth with new life. The intersection of these horizontal and vertical elements creates a cross, or a crossroads, between the world of the living and of the dead in voodoo cosmology.

Haitian voodoo festivals are also an important theme in Benoit's paintings. In *Bal du Carnival* (1979) flat, geometric planes define the architectural stage on which a visually and socially complex drama unfolds. Carnival is celebrated just before Lent, and it provides an occasion for uninhibited celebration. Benoit delights in describing the brilliantly colored costumes of the celebrants, who come from different racial backgrounds. As Brown notes, carnival presents an opportunity in the highly stratified Haitian society for the small proportion of mulatto elite of mixed French and African origin to mingle with dark-skinned Haitians.

Benoit's meticulously ordered compositions, skillful draftsmanship, and delicate and varied paint application in culturally expressive scenes have made him one of the most highly regarded Haitian artists of the second half of the twentieth century. His prominence is assured by decades of consistently strong and original paintings that reach an increasingly growing international audience.

—Brady Roberts

BIGAUD, Wilson
Haitian painter

Born: 1929. **Died.**

Rigaud Benoit, *Bal du Carnival*, 1979. Photo courtesy of Davenport Museum of Art.

Wilson Bigaud was a poster boy for the prodigious success of the Centre d'Art, which was itself an important catalyst in the flowering of Haitian art in the middle of the twentieth century. A genuinely talented first-generation painter of the Haitian indigenous, or naive, movement, Bigaud was introduced to the Centre d'Art at the age of fifteen by Hector Hyppolite and was nurtured by a group of artists there whose works came to define the sensibility of Creole culture. This culture, a synthesis of African religious and cultural ideals, Roman Catholic religious practices and visual imagery, and possibly autochthonous Indian practices, had been created as a response by African slaves to the harsh conditions of their life in the diaspora.

The Centre d'Art was founded in 1944 by DeWitt Peters. He attempted to harness Haiti's Creole culture as a basis for stimulating and nurturing an artistic tradition among the indigenous population, whose creativity had been sidelined by an official art that sought inspiration from established French traditions. The Centre d'Art became a locus for the development of a uniquely indigenous Haitian style, and it also produced some of the most famous Haitian artists of the twentieth century. Bigaud, whose precocious talent and early accomplishments invited comparisons to genius, loomed large in this movement.

Bigaud's grasp of pictorial form revealed itself at an early age. Although he may have received informal training by observing the more famous members of the Centre d'Art, such as Hyppolite and Philomé Obin, Bigaud brought a unique response to composition. He not only showed an ability to assimilate formal styles and techniques, but he also quickly developed a personal style based on pictorial verisimilitude. His technique and pace of development placed his early work beyond the tendencies then prevalent among his contemporaries at the Centre d'Art. For example, his mural *Marriage at Cana* (1951) in the Cathedral Sainte-Trinité, which is regarded as the high point of his career, was completed when the artist was just twenty-two years of age. In the painting Bigaud presented the biblical narrative of the miracle at Cana in a Haitian setting.

Bigaud painted his most accomplished pictures between 1951 and 1957 before succumbing to mental illness, for which he was institutionalized in 1957-58. His early works were praised for their striking, dramatic lighting and their Christian themes. The works included the mural on the marriage at Cana and several interpretations of Haitian voodoo lore and ritual practices. They combined naturalism with a predilection for fantasy and the supernatural and were painted in dark, evocative tones whose effects were heightened by broad flashes of bright, luminous color.

After 1958 Bigaud returned to painting. His late period, however, was uneven, and his style and themes changed dramatically. His later works were notable for the use of airy pastel colors, in marked contrast to his earlier somber tones. Bigaud aimed for social commentary, and many of the paintings concentrated on everyday Haitian life, replete with images of women, cockfights, carnival dances, and conflicts revolving around institutions such as marriage. In some, estranged lovers forcibly interrupt wedding ceremonies, much to the consternation of those in attendance. As in his earlier works, even though the themes and colors were markedly different, his style was characterized by pictorial verisimilitude and a judicious use of volumes and space. Although the figures in the later pictures were meticulously rendered, there is no sign of the monumental composition or evocative imagery of his early paintings. In addition, the reverential attitude that characterizes his murals with Christian themes and his images of voodoo rituals was replaced with a sardonic humor evident in the deleterious circumstances of his subjects. The later works, however, were not as well received as the earlier ones, owing in part to their repetitiveness but also perhaps because of a misunderstanding of the artist's attempts to use the paintings as therapeutic devices in the wake of his psychological problems.

Bigaud's conscious adoption of a naive style may have affected his natural development as a painter, since the products of his late period did not achieve the impact of his early pictures. In spite of this, however, his narrative style has remained popular in Haitian art, and his paintings have been widely copied.

—Sylvester Okwunodu Ogbechie

BIGGERS, John (Thomas)
American painter, sculptor, and printmaker

Born: Gastonia, North Carolina, 13 April 1924. **Education:** Lincoln Academy, Kings Mountain, North Carolina, 1937; Hampton Institute, Hampton, Virginia, 1941-46; Pennsylvania State University, B.S. 1948, M.S. in art education 1948, Ph.D. in education 1954. **Military Service:** United States Navy, 1943-45; honorable discharge 1945. **Family:** Married Hazel Hales in 1948. **Career:** Instructor, Alabama State Teachers College, Montgomery, 1949; professor, Alabama State Teachers College, Montgomery, 1954-67; professor, art department head, distinguished professor, Texas Southern University, Houston, 1949-83. Visiting professor, University of Wisconsin, Madison, 1965. Illustrator, *Good Earth,* Reader's Digest Series, 1966. Member, Houston Fine Arts Commission, Texas, 1968-72, Texas Fine Arts Commission, 1970-73. **Awards:** Purchase prize, Museum of Fine Arts, Houston, 1950; purchase prize, Atlanta University Annual Exhibition, 1950, 1953; Schlumberger Prize, Museum of Fine Arts, Houston, 1951; Nieman Marcus Prize for Drawing, Dallas Museum of Art, 1952; Ella Lyman Cabot Trust stipend for special study of graphic arts at the University of Southern California and Pennsylvania State University, 1952-53; purchase prizes for prints and sculpture, Atlanta University, Georgia, 1953; Rental Service Award for *Grace,* Contemporary Arts Museum, 1955; UNESCO fellowship for study of traditional cultural patterns in West Africa, 1957; Best Texas Book Design for *Ananse: The Web of Life in Africa,* Dallas Museum of Art 1963; Chicago Book Clinic Award for excellence of design, 1963; Excel-

lence of Design Award for *Ananse: The Web of Life in Africa,,* Southern Book Competition, 1963; Best Texas Book Design Award, Dallas Museum of Art, 1963; Piper Professor Award for outstanding scholarly and academic achievement, Minnie Stevens-Piper Foundation, 1964; E. Harris Harbison Award for Distinguished Teaching, Danforth Foundation, 1968; Distinguished Alumni Award, Pennsylvania State University, 1972; Mayor's Award for Outstanding Contributions as Visual Artist, Houston, Texas, 1981; Texas Artist of the Year, Art League of Houston, 1988; honorary doctor of humane letters, Hampton University, Virginia, 1989; Van Der Zee Award, Brandywine Graphic Workshop of Philadelphia, 1992; Margaret Hawkins Art Award, 1994. **Address:** 3338 Prospect Street, Houston, Texas 77004, U.S.A.

Individual Exhibitions:

1951   Pennsylvania State University, University Park
1955   Pennsylvania State University, University Park
1962   *Drawings of West Africa: Dr. John Biggers,* Museum of Fine Arts, Houston
        Paintings by Dr. John Biggers, Jewish Community Center, Houston
        Illustrations, Fort Worth Art Center, Texas
1963   *Drawings by John Biggers,* Dallas Public Library
        Shreveport Public Schools, Louisiana
        Jewish Community Center, Houston
        Laguna Gloria Art Museum, Austin, Texas
        Lubbock Museum of Fine Arts, Lubbock, Texas
        United States Information Agency (traveling)
1969   Graceland College, Lamoni, Iowa
1975   Texas A & M University, College Station
1978   *The Web of Life in Africa, An Exhibition of Drawings and Paintings by John T. Biggers,* African-American Cultural Center, Dallas
1983   California Museum of Afro-American History and Culture, Los Angeles
1984   Texas Southern University
1987   *John Biggers: Patchwork Quilts and Shotguns,* Transco Energy, Houston
        Balene, Incorporated, Houston, Texas
1989   Delta Fine Arts Center, Winston-Salem, North Carolina
1990   Hampton University, Virginia
        Pyramid Gallery, Little Rock, Arkansas
1991   *John Biggers: Mural Sketches,* Diggs Gallery, Winston-Salem University, North Carolina
1993   Northeast Texas Community College, Mount Pleasant
        Fayetteville Museum of Art, North Carolina
1995   *The Art of John Biggers: View from the Upper Room,* Museum of Fine Arts, Houston (traveling)

Selected Group Exhibitions:

1943   *Young Negro Art,* Museum of Modern Art, New York
        Virginia Museum of Fine Arts, Richmond
1945   Baltimore Museum of Art, Maryland
1953   Contemporary Arts Museum, Houston
1956   Howard University, Washington, D.C.
1972   Winston-Salem Delta Fine Arts, Winston-Salem, North Carolina
1975   California Museum of Science and Industry, Los Angeles

John Biggers: *Family Ark.* Photo courtesy of the Schomburg Center for Research in Black Culture.

1976   Los Angeles County Museum of Art (traveling)
1985   Museum of Fine Arts, Houston
1989   Dallas Museum of Art
1992   American Federation of Arts, New York
1994   San Antonio Museum of Art, Texas

Collections:

Atlanta University, Georgia; Barnett-Aden Collection, Washington, D.C.; Dallas Museum of Art; Hampton University Museum, Virginia; Howard University, Washington, D.C.; Museum of Fine Arts, Houston; National Museum of American Art, Smithsonian Institution, Washington, D.C.; Lubbock Museum, Texas; Texas Southern University, Houston.

Publications:

By BIGGERS: Book—*Ananse: The Web of Life in Africa,* Austin, Texas, University of Texas Press, 1962. **Article**—"Searching for Roots," in *Impressions,* Fall 1958.

On BIGGERS: Books—*Seventeen Black Artists* by Elton Fax, Dodd, Mead, New York, 1971; *Five Decades: John Biggers and the Hampton Art Tradition,* exhibition catalog, Hampton, Virginia, Hampton University Museum and Rebecca Ritter, 1990; *The Storyteller: The Work of Dr. John T. Biggers,* exhibition catalog, Houston, Texas, Museum and Arts Houston and Leann Davis Alspaugh, 1992; *The Art of John Biggers: View from the Upper Room,* exhibition catalog, Houston, Texas, Museum of Fine Arts and Alvia J. Wardlaw, 1995.

Articles—"Lone Star Artist," in *Time,* 30 June 1952; "American Artist Wins UNESCO Fellowship," in *United States Commission for UNESCO News,* 28 December 1956; "Strength, Tears, and Will: John Biggers's *Contribution of the Negro Woman to American Life and Education*" by Alvia J. Wardlaw Short, in *Callaloo,* 5, 1979; "Dr. Biggers' Art is Exhibited in L.A.," in *TSU Today,* 2, April 1983, p. 5; "John Biggers: Bridges, A Retrospective," in *In the Arts,* 3, 1983; "Artist Series: An Interview with John Biggers" by Patricia Johnson, in *Trends: Journal of Texas Art Association,* Fall 1983; John T. Biggers: Artist Who Influenced a Generation" by Thad Martin, in *Ebony,* 39, March 1984, pp. 87-90; "John Biggers: Filling the Sacred Vessel" by Alvia J. Wardlaw, in *The Texas Humanist,* July-August 1984, pp. 34-36; "The John Biggers Profile: Patchwork Quilts and Shotguns" by Alvia J. Wardlaw, in *Wave,* February 1987; "John T. Biggers," in *A History of African-American Artists, From 1792 to the Present* by Romare Bearden and Harry Henderson, New York, Pantheon Books, 1993, pp. 427-36.

*   *   *

John Biggers's art has been described as "American Kongo," and he has been called the "black Grant Wood." Since the beginning of his career, Biggers's paintings, drawings, sculpture, and prints have been inspired by southern African American culture and its roots in Africa. Early paintings completed as a student at Hampton Institute established themes that remained central to the artist's work throughout his career. His first painting, *Crossing the Bridge* (1942), is about people moving in search of a better life; the second painting, *Crucifixion* (1942), is a strong political and social statement on the oppression of blacks in the South; the third painting, *Mother and Child* (1943), is a tender portrayal of the centrality of women in the universe; and *Gleaners* (1943) celebrates the dignity of ordinary people.

Much of Biggers's work until 1947 was biting social commentary (*Victim of the City Streets,* 1946) or documentation of the everyday hard work and perseverance of African American people (*Laundry Woman,* 1940s; *Coming Home from Work,* 1944; *Going to Church,* 1944). While studying at Pennsylvania State University, Biggers completed several murals, one of which he has said was a breakthrough in his evolution as an artist. *Baptism* (1947-48) depicts humble rural people being transformed by the process of baptism. For the artist this work coincided with the transformation of his own anger into a more positive, universal outlook.

John Biggers chose to spend his career in the South, close to the earth and the culture that inspired his work. *First Shotgun* (1949) was completed the same year he moved to Houston, Texas. With this painting he began his fascination with the shotgun house of the rural South and of African cultures. In numerous paintings, drawings, and lithographs that followed, he transformed the shotgun house into a temple and a symbol of strength, stability, and security.

As his work progressed, Biggers developed a visual vocabulary of symbols drawn from everyday life, and later from African art, which convey ideas and concepts about the human condition. A wash pot such as his mother used to wash clothing became a symbol of women and also of the cleansing of the human spirit. Biggers's interest in the transformation from mundane to spiritual, from specific to universal, is captured repeatedly by such images as the wash pot and railroad tracks and also by the metaphor of baptism. Fascinated with the concept of "sacred geometry," his paintings after the 1980s often contained carefully constructed groups of three, four, or seven. Turtles, birds, quilt patterns, African combs, and xylophones are some of the repeated symbolic images in Biggers's work. Throughout this later work, reference is also found to the four basic elements—fire, water, earth, and air.

Biggers's work incorporated more African symbols and imagery after his pioneering trip in 1957 to West Africa to study art and culture. He also began to use a brighter and more vibrant color palette and to convey more motion in this work, which became less narrative and more abstract. Pieces created after he experienced an exhibition of Dogan art in 1974 reflect his growing understanding of African art and culture. They are complex compositions that use painstaking geometric patterns and many layers of paint to achieve depth and transparency.

Mural painting has been a hallmark of Biggers's career, and he completed more than twenty-three. He is a master drawer who also considers himself a storyteller. For him murals provided a useful storytelling format, for they enabled him to present multiple concepts in a fashion that is very accessible to a large number of people. Through this body of work, the progression of this artist's style and philosophy is readily apparent. He began with figurative, narrative statements about the experience of ordinary people in the South. As he traveled, studied, and reflected, he connected this experience more and more to other cultures and to the earth, to the predicable yet mysterious cycle of life. His painting grew more complicated both in composition and in technique, and the imagery grew more abstract. In his work in the early 1990s, Biggers has begun to incorporate Native American and Asian symbols in his continuing quest to better convey the unity of all people and the interdependence of humans, plants, and animals in this universe.

—Jeanne Zeidler

BILLOPS, Camille (J.)
American sculptor and filmmaker

Born: Los Angeles, 12 August 1933. **Education:** California State College, B.A. 1960; City College of New York, M.F.A. 1973. **Family:** One daughter; married James Hatch. **Career:** Lecturer, Rutgers University, New Jersey, 1973-87, City College of New York, 1970-75, Koahsiung Teachers College, Taiwan, 1982-83; instructor, Governor's School for the Humanities, University of Tennessee, 1986-90. Since 1975 founder and co-director, Hatch Billops Collection. Publisher of *Artist and Influence.* Juror on panels, New Jersey State Council on the Arts, 1981, New York Foundation for the Arts (film), 1987, Boston Film and Video Foundation, 1988, Atlanta Arts Festival, 1989, North Carolina Film Festival, Mint Museum, 1994. Served as executive director, Hatch-Billops Collection, 1974-87. Guest editor, Black American Literature Forum, 1991, 1985, 1986. **Awards:** First Prize for documentary/drama, Second Prize for direction, National Black Programming Consortium, 1991; Sojourner Truth Lecture Award, Claremont College, California, 1992; Black Maria Film and Video Festival Award, 1992; Atlanta Film Festival Juror Award, 1992; Sundance Film Festival, Grand Jury Prize for best documentary, 1992; James Van Der Zee Award, Brandywine Graphic Workshop, 1994. **Address:** 491 Broadway, New York 10012, U.S.A.

Individual Exhibitions:

1965	Gallerie Akhenaton, Cairo, Egypt
1973	Ornette Coleman's Artist House, Soho, New York
1974	North Carolina State University, Winston-Salem
1976	Amerika Haus, Hamburg, Germany
	Foto-Falle Gallery, Hamburg, Germany
1977	Rutgers University, Newark, New Jersey
1980	*Harlem Book of the Dead Performance Piece,* Buchandlung Welt, Hamburg, Germany
1981	Bronx Museum of Art, New York
1983	Otto Rene Castillo Center, New York
	American Center, Karachi, Pakistan
	American Cultural Center, Taipei, Taiwan
	Chau Yea Gallery, Kaohsiung, Taiwan
	Pescadores Hsien Library, Makung, China
1984	Southeast Arkansas Arts and Science Center, Pine Bluff
1986	Gallery at Quaker Corner, Plainfield, New Jersey
	Calkins Gallery, Hofstra University, Hempsted, New York
1990	Clark College, Atlanta University
1993	University of North Carolina, Charlotte
1997	Aljira Gallery, Newark, New Jersey

Selected Screenings:

1983	*Suzanne Suzanne,* Atlanta Film Festival
1987	*Suzanne Suzanne,* Whitney Museum of American Art
1989	*Suzanne Suzanne,* Society for Cinema Studies, University of Iowa
1991	*Finding Christina,* Festival of Festivals, Toronto
1992	*Finding Christina,* Sundance Film Festival, Park City, Utah
	Finding Christina, Cinema du Reel, Centre George Pompidou, Paris
	Finding Christina, Philadelphia Festival of World Cinema

Camille Billops, 1994.

Camille Billops is a versatile visual artist. She is a ceramist and a filmmaker, a designer of costumes and sets, and an actress in the theater. All of her films and some of her drawings and sculptures are about people she knows. Her film *Suzanne Suzanne* is about a niece who was a heroin addict. *Finding Christina* is a film about finding Billops's daughter who was given up for adoption. Billops has traveled to Egypt, India, Japan, China, and Southeast Asia, and many of her works show the influence of other cultures. Her ceramic piece *Three-Headed Fountain* (1969), for example, consists of three heads located at the top of the vessel, with, toward the bottom of the piece, three protruding cups in alignment with the mouths of the heads. The heads are a combination of human and animal and resemble Egyptian Coptic vessels.

Billops is best known for her work in ceramics. Her most intriguing ceramic structures are sculptures of people formed by hand from clay slabs. *Remember Vienna III* (1988) consists of two figures, one male and one female, facing each other. The figures are boxlike, having four flat sides, but when the viewer looks at them straight on, they appear as two-dimensional, almost cartoonish characters. The figures are dressed up, and the viewer can sense an attraction between the two. The woman's head is turned away, her eyes focused on the male but with eyelids lowered. There are also two figures in *Remember Vienna,* but this couple is more casually dressed and the male looks a bit sinister. Another interesting thing about this couple is that they appear to be able to fit perfectly together, like two puzzle pieces. Thus, the spacing between the figures in these sculptures dictates the viewer's response.

Older Women And Love, Wellesley College
1993 *Suzanne Suzanne,* Los Angeles Film Festival
1994 *Suzanne Suzanne,* Cornell University

Selected Group Exhibitions:

1972 Studio Museum in Harlem, New York
1976 Boston Museum of Art
1978 Schnectady Museum, New York
1981 Kenkeleba House, New York
1985 Museum of Science and Industry, Chicago
1986 Museum of Art and Science, New Jersey
1987 Robeson Gallery, Rutgers University, Newark, New Jersey
1989 Bernice Steinbaum Gallery, New York
1990 Zimmerman/Saturn Gallery, Nashville
1996 Modern Art Museum, Fort Lauderdale, Florida

Collections:

The Museum of Drawers, Bern, Switzerland; Photographers Gallery, London; The Studio Museum in Harlem.

Publications:

On BILLOPS: Articles—"A Visitor to Ceylon, Camille Billops, Universal Citizen," in *The Times of Ceylon,* Columbo, Sri Lanka, 1968; "Power Exchange: Camille Billops," in *Heresies Magazine,* 1979; "American Artist to Hold Exhibit in Kaohsiung, Taipei," in *China Post* (Taiwan), 24 May 1983; "Billops Sees Hidden Faces of Black Faces" by Beth Monin, in *Nashville Banner,* 30 October 1990; "Encounters: The Film Odyssey of Camille Billops" by Barbara Lekatsas, in *Black American Literature Forum* 25(2), Summer 1991; "Reel to Teel" by Leslie Camhi, in *Village Voice* (New York), 7 March 1995.

*   *   *

Camille Billops: *Mammy's Little Coal Black Rose* ("Minstrel" series), 1992.

Billops has used a similar male-female theme in some of her colored pencil drawings. *#2 Kaosiung Series* (1982), for example, is a drawing of a couple facing one another; the woman's head is turned away, with her eyes focused on the male, but the male appears forceful and aggressive. (Or is the man teasing his woman friend? Most of Billops's works leave a lot of room for interpretation.) *Franco & Tessa I* (1990) shows a male and female holding onto each other and dancing. Again, she is looking at him with her head turned away, and the drawing portrays a coy, flirtatious behavior.

Billops also likes to use stripes, as is shown by her figures in the "Remember Vienna" series. *Prisoners* (1987), another four-sided sculpture, consists of four different compositions in which the subjects are wearing striped shirts. The four-sided sculpture *The Story of Mom* (1981) uses Billops's godmother as the subject. The sculpture is a nude, although striped, female standing on one leg. A small child who appears distraught and overwhelmed clasps the supporting leg, an image provoking a myriad of responses. The colored pencil drawing *From the Story of Mom* (1986) shows a striped woman at the wheel of a car, with a cross breaking the pattern created by the horizontal stripes on her upper arm. The viewer can sense the tension in the image. Since showing a striped human figure does not identify the person as black or white, stripes become a useful design tool for creating an attitude. Perhaps Billops is addressing issues larger than race.

Billops uses her art to express strong feelings about racism, however. *Old Black Joe* (1991) looks like the cover of late 1800s sheet music. The main image is a white man in blackface—a minstrel. In the background are a pair of black shoes, with the toe area drawn into smiling mouths showing teeth. The images represent a revival of racial stereotypes and serve as a reminder of a common racist symbol. Billops's film *KKK Boutique Ain't Just Rednecks*, which explores racism, is loosely based on Dante's *Inferno*.

—Christine Miner Minderovic

BIRCH, Willie

American painter and sculptor

Born: New Orleans, 1942. **Education:** Southern University, Baton Rouge, Louisiana, 1960-61; Southern University, New Orleans, B.A. 1969; Maryland Institute, Baltimore, Maryland, M.F.A. 1973. **Awards:** New York Foundation for the Arts Fellowship, 1986; National Endowment for the Arts, 1989-90; Lila Wallace International Artist Fellowship, 1992; Guggenheim Fellowship, 1993. **Agent:** Arthur Roger Gallery, 432 Julia Street, New Orleans, Louisiana 70130, U.S.A. **Address:** 2022 North Villere Street, New Orleans, Louisiana 70116, U.S.A.

Individual Exhibitions:

1968   Southern University, New Orleans
1971   Equitable Trust Bank, Baltimore, Maryland
        Institute of Black Ministry, Philadelphia
1975   Art Works Gallery, Baltimore, Maryland
1977   New Muse Community Museum of Brooklyn, New York

1978   New York State Office Building in Harlem Gallery, New York
1979   Tim Blackburn Gallery, New York
1984   Miami-Dade Library, Florida
1988   Amelie A. Wallace Gallery, Old Westbury, New York
1989   Tompkins Square Gallery, New York Public Library, New York
1990   Gallery 1199, New York
1991   Sculpture Center, New York
        College of Saint Rose, Albany, New York
        NYNEX, White Plains, New York
1992   Exit Art, New York
        Arthur Roger Gallery, New York
1993   Sculpture Center, New York
        Afro-American Historical Museum, Philadelphia
        Arthur Roger Gallery, New York
        Paa Ya Paa Gallery, Kenya
        York College Art Gallery, New York
1994   Luise Ross Gallery, New York
1995   Arthur Roger Gallery, New York
1996   Southeastern Center for Contemporary Art, Winston-Salem, North Carolina

Selected Group Exhibitions:

1989   *Artist in Residence Then and Now,* Studio Museum in Harlem, New York
        A Tribute to the Brooklyn Community, Boricua College, Brooklyn, New York
1991   *Origins,* Tyler School of Art, Temple University, Philadelphia
1992   *The Lower Manhattan Sign Project,* Repohistory Group, New York
        Remeria/America 1492-1992, Hunter College Art Gallery, New York
        Voices from Mantua, Painted Bride Art Center, Philadelphia
1993   *Figurines,* Luise Ross Gallery, New York

Collections:

Atlanta Life Insurance Company, Atlanta, Georgia; Children's Museum, Chicago; Harlem Hospital, New York; Henry Street Settlement, New York; Metropolitan Museum of Art, New York; Miami-Dade Public Library, Miami, Florida; New Orleans Museum of Art, Louisiana; Pennsylvania Academy, Philadelphia; Southern University, New Orleans; Universal Pictures, Los Angeles.

Publications:

On BIRCH: Articles—Review (Sculpture Center) by Robert Taplin, in *Art in America,* 79, July 1991, pp. 122-23; review (Afro-American Historical and Cultural Museum) by Robin L. Rice, in *New Art Examiner,* 21, November 1993, p. 39; review (Sculpture Center) by Jenifer P. Borum, in *Artforum,* 32, January 1994, p. 93; "Willie Birch" by Gylbert Coker, in *New Art Examiner,* 22, September 1994, pp. 44-45; "Willie Birch" by Tom Csaszar, in *Sculpture* (Washington, D.C.), 15, April 1996, pp. 59-60; "Artist and the Community: Willie Birch" by Linda Johnson Dougherty, in *Art Papers,* 20, May/June 1996, p. 46 (illustrated).

*   *   *

Willie Birch: *Knowing Our History, Teaching Our Culture.*

From the diminutive to the monumental, Willie Birch's two-dimensional paper collages and three-dimensional papier-mâché constructions come from within the African diaspora and are intended as iconographic discourses imbued with sociopolitical content and a reverence for the metaphysical. His works capture significant aspects of the African American experience, from lifestyles in Northern urban centers to legacies of oppression in the South. There are messages of urgency directed toward urban youth and the depiction of the economic history of slavery and its debilitating effects. His work raises questions of identity and social and economic equity.

As a modern-day storyteller Birch combines image and text to create commentary on various aspects of life. His tales range in subject matter from the political to the quotidian. His relocation from Brooklyn to his hometown of New Orleans in the mid-1990s has prompted a body of work that gives a panoramic glimpse of the underbelly of racial tension along with the wealth of African elements retained in Southern culture. Diverse African cultural symbols are reflected within the Louisianan black community in anecdotes, behavior, and decorative practices. Birch attempts to capture and translate the multifaceted aspects of life within his extended community, the works serving as historical records of particular periods of time. His commemorative suite of churches, for example, is a testimony to hate crimes committed against blacks and serves to promote healing.

Birch executes his sculptures in papier-mâché, but their surface treatments resemble lightweight sheet metal in brass or bronze rendered with subtle angularity. He emblazons his sculptures with an effervescent and vibrant palette, and form and color converge into unified wholes. Aspects of his palette and use of form also appear in his two-dimensional works. Birch shifts between the use of text, commenting on the images and emblems portrayed, and its absence. He embraces the directness of folk art and contemporary populist African art. Akin to outsider art, Birch's elaborate tableaux and sculptures replicate aspects of personhood, the vibrancy of life, and the impact of circumstance.

Birch's travels, particularly to Kenya, have resulted in a distinctive body of work, for he has chronicled his experiences there with garmentlike constructions. He has captured the way contemporary communities in Kenyan urban centers choose to express themselves through varied modes of dress. Birch uses these papier-mâché garments to commemorate selected political and cultural figures in addition to people he has had a close affiliation with. The works become portraits, and in many of them Birch has replaced text with materials that allude to qualities of the particular individuals.

Birch's figural styles are reminiscent of clay figures found in an *mbari*, the spirit house of the Igbo. The *mbari* structures were traditionally constructed to placate the most powerful deities. Signs—changes in the community, weather conditions, or the appearance of certain animals—preceded their construction, the signs indicating that the deities were demanding a commemorative dwelling. Traditional *mbari* figures range from the formal to the informal, each category possessing specific qualities and styles. Some of Birch's forms bear a resemblance to traditional figures. His forms possess naturalistic proportions and appear frozen in motion, conveying a reality that incorporates contemporary themes. The surfaces are inlaid with text, numbers, symbols, and found objects, and some are representational simplifications of the human form.

Many of Birch's sculptures are replicas of *ibeji*, or twins. The traditional Yoruba sculptures are constructed as spiritual embodi-

ments of twins who have died. Birch's *ibeji* works are commemorative in nature, denoting the spirit of jazz and literary greats, friends and relatives, and political figures. Birch carries out the tradition of adorning his *ibeji* to make them decorative and rich in texture. Vitrines in the form of geodesic disks are inlaid in the area of the navel to serve as points of entry into the other world. They contain found objects such as shells, bones, and vegetative matter. Such disks are considered by many cultures to be a chakra, a major source of the life force.

Like a modern-day shaman Birch combines multiple African traditions within an individual piece in an attempt to make contact with the spiritual realm. His statues and portraits are both poignant and didactic, for belief systems and concepts prevalent within the African American community are symbolically disclosed through them.

—A. M. Weaver

BLACKBURN, Robert (H.)

American printmaker

Born: Summit, New Jersey, 10 December 1920. **Education:** Harlem Community Arts Center, New York, 1935-39; Art Students League, New York, 1940-43; Wallace Harrison School of Art, New York, 1950-53; Jaques Desjobert Workshop, Paris, 1953-54. **Career:** Professor, Columbia University, New York, 1970-90. Instructor, College of the City of New York, 1949, New School for Social Research, New York, 1950; faculty member, Cooper Union Art School, New York, 1949-67, New York University, 1965-71, Wooster Community Art School, New York, 1966, Pratt Institute, New York, 1974, National Academy of Design, 1986-87; adjunct professor, School of Visual Arts, New York, Maryland Institute of Art, 1982-92, Brooklyn College, New York, 1991-92; lecturer, Trinity College, Hartford, Connecticut, 1976, Mason Gross School of the Arts, Rutgers University, New Brunswick, New Jersey, 1977-79, Montclair State College, Upper Montclair, New Jersey, 1978, Albany State College, New York, 1983, University of California, Santa Cruz, 1984, Tamarind Institute, University of New Mexico, 1990, Oswego College, New York, 1991, Manhattanville College, New York, 1991, Albright College, Reading, Pennsylvania, 1992; visiting professor, Little Rock University, Arkansas, 1991; Detwiller Visiting Artist, Lafayette College, Easton, Pennsylvania, 1994; Eric Kenagy Fellow, Goshen College, Goshen, Indiana, 1994. Council member, Society of American Graphic Artists, New York, 1968-70, Society of American Graphic Artists, New York, 1975-78; board of directors, New York Foundation for the Arts, 1971-86, Artist's Space, New York, 1975-78, Friends of Cinque, New York, 1975-78, Tiffany Foundation, New York, 1974-93. **Awards:** Purchase Award, Library of Congress, Washington, D.C., 1950; Sarasota Art Association Award, Florida, 1950; Purchase Award, Brooklyn Museum, New York, 1951; John Hay Whitney Traveling Fellowship, 1953-54; Purchase Award, Oakland Museum of Art, California, 1959; Purchase Award, Washington Printmakers Association, 1960; Bay State Printmakers Award, 1961; Purchase Award, Audubon Artists Annual Exhibition, 1964; Purchase Award, Howard University, Washington, D.C., 1968; Creative Artist Program (CAPS) Award, 1974; 1st Augusta Savage Memorial Award, 1980; Skowhegan Governor's Art Award for Lifetime Service to the

Robert H. Blackburn (with Printmaking Workshop artists). Photo courtesy of Robin Thomas.

Arts, Maine, 1987; New York State Governor's Art Award, 1988; College Arts Association Award, 1989; Distinguished Teaching Award, College Art Association, 1990; Eugene Grigsby Award, National Art Education Association, 1990; Mayor's Award for Art and Culture, New York, 1992; John T. and Catherine D. MacArthur Foundation Award, 1992; certificate of merit, Municipal Arts Society, New York, 1996. Honorary doctorates: Parsons School of Design, New York, 1990; University of Maryland, College Park, 1990; New School for Social Research, New York, 1990; CW Post-Long Island University, New York, 1992; City College of New York, 1994. **Address:** The Printmaking Workshop, 55 West 17th Street, New York, New York 10025, U.S.A.

Individual Exhibitions:

1951   Brooklyn Museum, New York
          Library of Congress, Washington, D.C.

1956   Philadelphia Print Club, Paris
1959   Oakland Museum of Art, California
1960   IBM Gallery, New York
        Sarasota Art Association Gallery, Florida
1961   Pennsylvania Academy of Fine Art
1962   Terrain Gallery, New York
        Meltzer Gallery, New York
1963   Associated American Artists Gallery, New York
        Meltzer Gallery, New York
1964   *Audubon Artists Annual Exhibition,* CW Post Gallery,
        Long Island University, New York
        Meltzer Gallery, New York
1965   Meltzer Gallery, New York
1966   Bridge Gallery, New York
        Wooster Community Art Center, Connecticut
        Hampton Institute Gallery, Virginia
1967   Hampton Institute Gallery, Virginia
1968   Howard University Gallery, Washington, D.C.
1969   Society of American Graphic Artists, Associated Ameri-
        can Artists Gallery, New York
        University of Nevada Gallery
1970   Brooklyn Museum of Art, New York
        Joe Grippi Gallery, New York
        Center for African Arts, Boston Museum of Fine Arts
        Upsula College Art Gallery, New Jersey
        Stout State University Gallery, Wisconsin
        University of Alberta Gallery, Canada
1971   Wichita Art Associate, Kansas
1973   University of Maryland Gallery
1975   Associated American Artists, New York
        Kennedy Galleries, New York
1976   Noho Gallery, New York
        Brooklyn Museum of Art, New York
        Pratt Institute Gallery, New York
1977   Society of American Graphic Artists, Associated Ameri-
        can Artists Gallery, New York
1978   Black Enterprises Gallery, New York
        Langston Hughes Community Center, New York
        Brotherhood Synagogue, New York
        Montclair State College, New Jersey
        Howard University Gallery, Washington, D.C.
1979   Appalachian Gallery, Maryland
1980   Terrain Gallery, New York
        Society of American Graphic Artists, New York
        National Conference of Artists, Harlem State Office, New
        York
        Hamilton College Gallery, New Jersey
1981   Richard Gallery, New York
1982   Jazzonia Gallery, New York
1983   Bedford Stuyvesant Restoration Center, New York
        Asilah Festival, Morocco
1984   University of California, Santa Cruz
        In a Stream of Ink (traveling through 1988)
1985   *Tribute: Robert Blackburn,* Association of Community-
        Based Artists of Westchester, New York
        Tweed Court House, New York
        *Through a Master Printer: Robert Blackburn and the
        Printmaking Workshop,* Columbia Museum of Art,
        South Carolina (traveling through 1988)
1988   *Robert Blackburn: Master Printer/Artist,* Miami-Dade
        Public Library, Florida

1990   *Robert Blackburn: A Life's Work,* Alternative Museum,
        New York
1991   Upstairs Gallery, New York
        A.J. Lederman Fine Art, New Jersey
1993   Watermark/Cargo Gallery, New York
        Hartwick College, New York
        National Gallery of Art, Washington, D.C.
1994   *Robert Blackburn—Master Printer, Master Artist,*
        Lafayette College, Easton, Pennsylvania
        *Robert Blackburn: Inspiration & Innovation in American
        Printmaking,* Wilmer Jennings Gallery at Kenkeleba,
        New York

Selected Group Exhibitions:

1986   *Choosing: An Exhibit of Changing Perspectives in Mod-
        ern Art and Art Criticism by Black Americans,* Hamp-
        ton University, Virginia
        *Unbroken Circle: African American Artists of the 1930s
        and 1940s,* Kenkeleba House, New York
1987   *Masters and Pupils: The Education of the Black Artist in
        New York, 1900-1980,* Jamaica Arts Center, New York
        Expressions: Afrikan-Art against Apartheid, Fashion
        Moda, New York
        Eight Black Artists, Hudson Guild Art Gallery, New York
1992   *Bob Blackburn's Printmaking Workshop—Artists of Color,*
        Albright-Knox Art Gallery, Buffalo, New York (through
        1995)
1993   *Seven over Seventy,* Krasdale Food Gallery, New York
        Forty Years of African American Printmaking, G.R.
        N'Namdi Gallery, Birmingham, Michigan
1994   *African American Printmakers,* Goshen College, Goshen,
        Indiana

Collections:

Asilah Museum, Morocco; Bronx Museum, New York; Brooklyn
Museum, New York; Hampton Institute, Virginia; Howard Univer-
sity, Washington, D.C.; Kenkeleba House, New York, Library of
Congress, Washington, D.C.; Munson-Williams-Proctor Institute,
New York; Oakland Museum of Art, California; The Printmaking
Workshop Print Collection, New York; Tel Aviv Museum, Israel;
United Negro College Fund, New York.

Publications:

On BLACKBURN: Books—*Robert Blackburn: A Life's Work,*
exhibition catalog, by Nina Parrish and Harriet Green, New York,
Alternative Press, 1990; *Bob Blackburn's Printmaking Workshop—
Artists of Color,* exhibition catalog, by Noah Jemison, New York,
Long Island University, Hillwood Art Museum, 1992. **Articles**—
"Bob Blackburn and the Printmaking Workshop" by Hildreth York,
in *Black American Literature Forum,* Spring/Summer 1986;
"Printmaking for the Love of It" by Grace Glueck, in *New York
Times,* 12 July 1988; "Ink, Paper, and Purpose," in *Modern Matu-
rity,* August-September 1990; "A Guiding Spirit for Printmakers"
by Phyllis Braff, in *New York Times,* 2 February 1992; "Bob
Blackburn: Interview" by Robert Berlind, in *Art Journal,* Spring
1994.

*   *   *

Born in 1920 in Summit, New Jersey, Robert Blackburn studied art in New York City at the Art Students League after graduating from DeWitt Clinton High School. Throughout much of his career, he has been at the center of the black art world and has worked with many of the major two-dimensional artists.

His unique position in the art world resulted in part from his Blackburn Printmaking Workshop. Located in the Chelsea neighborhood of Manhattan, it has served as a center for many artists. Blackburn first went to "the street" (17th Street) in 1948 after having migrated downtown from Harlem. He started the workshop primarily as a place in which to create and disseminate his own work at a time when there were very few opportunities for black artists. Though now located at a different site, he has been on 17th Street ever since.

Blackburn studied with the best. He studied under Rex Goreleigh at the Harlem Community Art Center at the same time as Jacob Lawrence. In the New York public schools, Countee Cullen was one of Blackburn's English teachers. Other teachers important in his life were Riva Helfond (his first teacher in lithography), Henry "Mike" Bannarn (his first inspiration), and Charles "Spinky" Alston. While still a student in junior high school, he worked at the Harmon Foundation.

Blackburn's extensive facilities still cater to those artists who want to use and master traditional methods of lithography, etching, and woodcut. Hundreds of examples of the work done by artists who have passed through the workshop decorate the walls of the building, and Blackburn recorded the artists who have worked there in many thick albums filled with photographs. They are an impressive visual display of the importance of the workshop's place in the art world.

At a time when computer-generated images occupy a greater prominence in the visual world, the workshop holds to its traditions. The workshop has become the home for a community of artists, including many loyal supporters. One of the younger generation of artists who has found a home in the workshop is a Nigerian who prefers to be known simply as Augustino. Jayne Cortez and Mel Edwards have worked there, too.

The importance of the very act of making prints cannot be underestimated. Prints are less expensive on the open market than one-of-a-kind drawings or paintings in part because of the multiple images. This means that more people can afford to own them, and thus an image created in this way potentially has a wide impact. The act of making prints makes art more accessible and aids in the dissemination of the art.

As a visual artist and principal administrator of the workshop, Blackburn wears two hats. He has also taught at every major art school in New York, including New York University, Columbia University, the School of Visual Arts, and Pratt Institute.

—Thomas M. Shaw

BLAYTON-TAYLOR, Betty

American painter and mixed-media artist

Born: Betty Blayton, Newport News, Virginia, 10 July 1937. **Education:** Syracuse University, New York, 1954-59, B.F.A. 1959; City College of New York, 1961; Art Students League, New York, 1960-62; Brooklyn Museum School, 1964-67. **Family:** Married

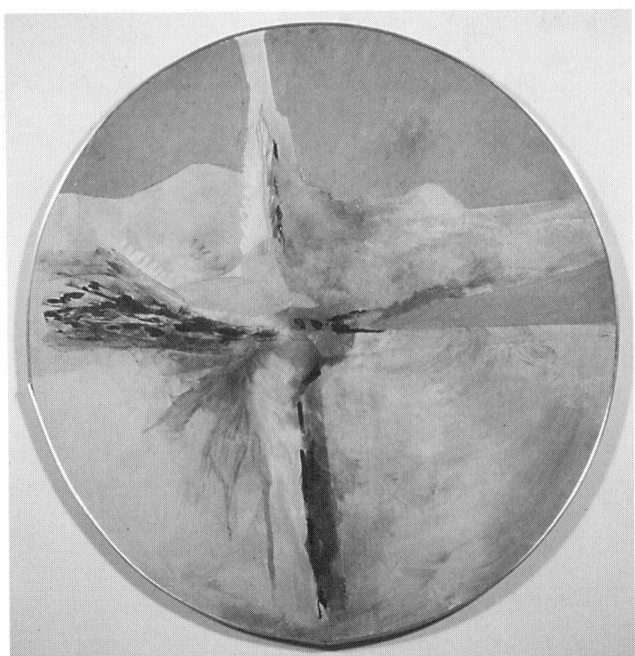

Betty Blayton-Taylor: *To Soar.*

Ivanhoe A. (Rheet) Taylor in 1967. **Career:** Illustrator, General Services Administration, Washington, D.C., 1958-59; art teacher, Charlotte Amalie High School, St. Thomas, Virgin Islands, 1959-60; recreation leader, Department of Recreation, New York, 1960-63; art instructor, Haryon-Act, New York, 1964-67; since 1968 president/CEO, Children's Art Carnival, New York. Artist-in-residence, Fisk University, Nashville, 1978, Norfolk State College, Virginia, 1980, Tougaloo College, Mississippi, 1982. Founding member, Studio Museum in Harlem, New York, 1965-77. **Awards:** Empire State Woman of the Year in the Arts Award, 1984; Blackwoman in the Arts Award, 1988; National Council of Negro Women of New York Award, 1980; City of New Orleans, Amorary Citizen Award for teacher of education, 1980; certificate of appreciation for Youth Career Development Project for Employment Support, National Council of Negro Women of New York, 1980; Apple Polisher Award, Association for a Better New York, 1982; Empire State Woman of the Year in the Arts Award, 1984; Harlem Commonwealth Council Community Service Award, New York, 1986; Eugene Grigsby Award, National Arts Education Association, 1990; New York City Award, Harlem School of the Arts, 1990; Family Award, New York Urban Coalition, 1991; West Side Award, 1991; New York State commission, 1994-95; Fulfilling the Dream Award, 1995. **Address:** 2001 Creston Avenue, Bronx, New York 10453, U.S.A.

Individual Exhibitions:

1968	Capricorn Gallery, New York
1975	Caravan House Gallery, New York
1980	Fisk University Gallery, Nashville
1983	Community Gallery, Syracuse University, New York
1984	Tougaloo College Gallery, Mississippi
1990	Bedford Stuyvesant, Brooklyn, New York
1993	Luben House Gallery, New York

Selected Group Exhibitions:

1967   *Manhattan Counterpoints,* Lever House Gallery, New York
1968   American Greeting Card Gallery, New York
        Thirty Contemporary Black Artists, Minneapolis Museum, Minnesota
1969   *Six Partners*, Marc Gallery, New York
1971   *8 x 8,* Riverside Gallery, New York
        Acts of Art Gallery, New York
1976   Howard University Gallery, Washington, D.C.
1978   Studio Museum in Harlem, New York
1993   Isabel Neal Gallery, Chicago

Collections:

Fisk University, Nashville; Metropolitan Museum, New York; Philip Morris Corporation Gallery, Richmond, Virginia; Studio Museum in Harlem, New York; Tougaloo College, Mississippi; Virginia State College, Norfolk; Whitney Museum, New York.

Publications:

By BLAYTON-TAYLOR: Books—*Make Thoughts Become,* New York, Not-for-Profit Press, 1978; *SWAP/Studies of Nations Art of People,* New York, CAC Production, 1989. **Article**—"People Who Make Things Happen," in *Art Gallery Guide* (New York), 1969.

*   *   *

Longevity is the word that best describes contemporary artist Betty Blayton-Taylor. Her family members have a history of living well past the age of ninety. In addition Blayton-Taylor's contributions to the world as an artist will live on for decades through her students.

Blayton-Taylor is the chairman and president of the Children's Art Carnival in New York City. The prestigious and respected art school has graduated such luminaries as the late and controversial artist Jean-Michel Basquiat and John Steptoe to name a few. Blayton-Taylor has held the post for nearly thirty years and expects to remain at the helm for at least another thirty.

But running an internationally recognized art school and drawing pictures for a living was something Blayton-Taylor never dreamt she would be doing when she started out as a commercial illustrator nearly forty years ago. It was then that she realized her interest in contemporary art was more than just a passing fancy and a way to pay the bills. Recognizing her appreciation for the dramatic and her exceptional visualization, Blayton-Taylor attended and graduated from Syracuse University in 1959. It wasn't until 1968, however, that her abstract paintings landed in an exhibit called *Thirty Contemporary Black Artists* at the Minneapolis Museum in Minnesota. Most of the her canvas paintings revealed the issues of the time—civil rights, discrimination, and racial unrest. As it turned out the Minneapolis exhibit would be the first of more than nearly two dozen exhibits that would span thirty years and be featured in galleries across the country. Many of the shows were simply titled *Betty Blayton, One Woman Show.*

The year of her first exhibit also saw the emergence of her art school for children. In addition to the few celebrated public artists that have passed through the hallways of her small Manhattan school, a number of Blayton-Taylor's students have gone on to successful careers in the private sector. Among her former students are senior executives at Fox Television and Motown Records. Many of her former students are also active supporters, both financially and culturally, of the not-for-profit school, which employs a staff of about thirty-two and teaches more than 12,000 art students annually. Blayton-Taylor said it is through her students' successes that she realizes how essential it is to encourage young people to set goals for themselves and achieve their dreams. She also tells her students that art is a medium they can use to truly express themselves by fearlessly visualizing what is on their minds. It is this philosophy and sense of self that has gained Betty Blayton-Taylor enormous respect and adulation as one of America's most revered artists.

—Glenn Townes

BOGHOSSIAN, (Alexander) Skunder
Ethiopian painter

Born: Addis Ababa, Ethiopia, 1937. **Education:** Addis Ababa, Ethiopia, 1943-55; Saint Martins School, Central School and Slade School of Fine Arts, London; École des Beaux Arts, Académie de la Grande Chaumière, Paris, 1957-66. **Career:** Assistant to Professor, Goetz, Académie de la Grande Chaumière, Paris, 1959-60; instructor, painting and design, Fine Arts School, Addis Ababa, 1966-69, painting and African design, Atlanta Center for Black Art, Atlanta University, Georgia, 1970; assistant professor, School of Fine Arts, Howard University, Washington, D.C. 1974-77. Since 1978 associate professor, School of Fine Arts, Howard University, Washington D.C. Participated in Second Congress of Negro Writers and Artists, Rome, 1959. **Awards:** National Art Exhibition Prize, Addis Ababa, Ethiopia; Haile Selassie First Prize for the Fine Arts, Addis Ababa, Ethiopia, 1967; Contemporary African Painters in Munich First Prize, Germany, 1967; Twenty-Ninth Annual Show of Black Artists First Prize, Spelman College, Atlanta, Georgia, 1970; District of Columbia Certificate of Appreciation, 1984; United Nations Special Committee Against Apartheid Certificate of Appreciation, 1984; City of Miami Beach, Florida, Certificate of Appreciation, 1985.

Individual Exhibitions:

1963   Mbari Gallery, Munich
        Gallery Lambert, Paris
1964   Deberkow Gallery, Frankfort
1965   Merton D. Simpson Gallery, New York
1968   Municipality Hall, Addis Ababa
1969   Creative Art Center, University of Addis Ababa
1971   Creighton University, Omaha
1972   Studio Museum in Harlem, New York
        Gallery of Art, College of Fine Arts, Howard University, Washington, D.C.
1973   Belvedere Art Gallery, Addis Ababa, Ethiopia
        Union Carbide Hall, New York
1974   German Cultural Institute
1975   American Museum, Philadelphia
1978   Gallery of Art, College of Fine Arts, Howard University, Washington, D.C.

Skunder Boghossian: *Dumb Deaf & Blind,* 1972. Photo courtesy of Porter Troupe Gallery.

Alternative Center for International Arts, Incorporated, New York
1980   Trisolini Gallery, Ohio University, Athens, Ohio
1983   Nyangara Gallery, Washington, D.C.
1984   Fondo del Sol, Washington, D.C.
1989   Gallery of Art, College of Fine Arts, Howard University, Washington, D.C.

Selected Group Exhibitions:

1959   *Second International Congress of Negro Artists and Writers,* Rome
1960   Cimaise Gallery, Paris
1961   Merton Simpson Gallery, New York
1973   Paa Ya Paa Art Gallery, Nairobi, Kenya
1974   African-American Institute, New York
        Field Museum, Chicago (traveling)
1984   Museum of the National Center for Afro American Artists, Massachusetts

Fondo del Sol, Washington, D.C.
1985   Corcoran Gallery of Art, Washington, D.C.
1989   D.C. Art Center, Washington, D.C.

Collections:

Harmon Foundation, National Archives and Records Services, Washington, D.C.; Musée d'Art Moderne, Paris; New Ministry of Foreign Affairs Building, Addis Ababa, Ethiopia; Studio Museum in Harlem, New York.

Publications:

On BOGHOSSIAN: Books—*Creative Impulses/Modern Expressions: Four African Artists* by Salah Hassan, Ithaca, Africana Studies and Herbert F. Johnson Museum, Cornell University, 1993; *New Currents, Ancient Rivers: Contemporary African Artists in a Generation of Change* by Jean Kennedy, Washington, D.C., Smithsonian Institutional Press, 1992, pp. 123-41 (illustrated); *Af-*

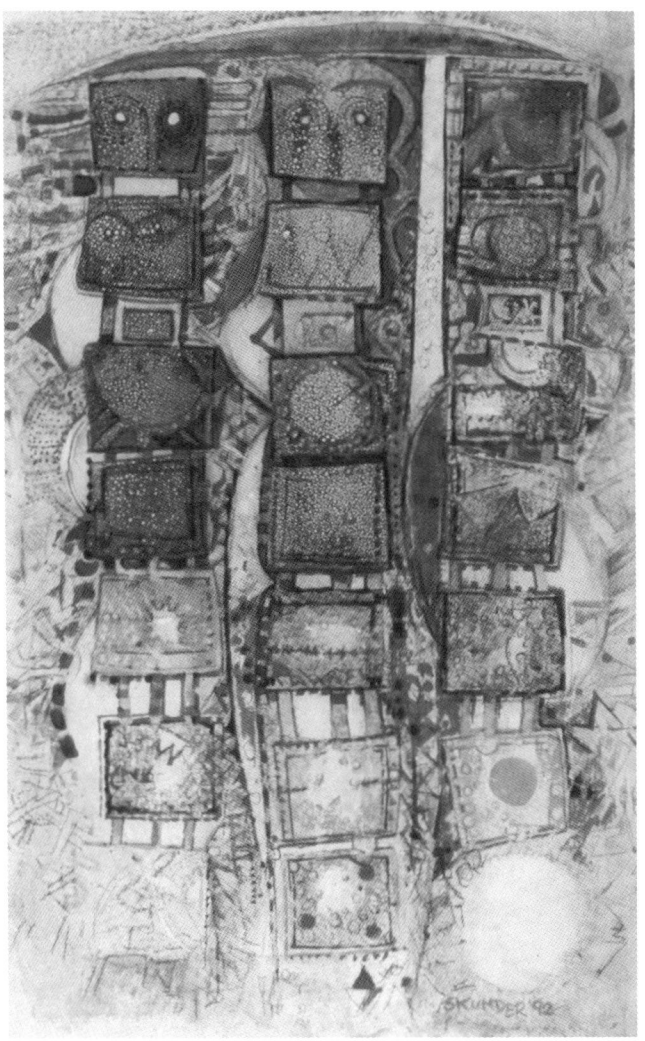

Skunder Boghossian: *Original Spring*, 1992. Photo courtesy of Porter Troupe Gallery.

rican Art: The Years Since 1920 by Marshall Ward Mount, Bloomington, Indiana Press, 1973, 1989; *Spaces,* exhibition catalog, Athens, Lawhead Press and Tom Porter, 1980.

*   *   *

Skunder Boghossian is one of Africa's best-known contemporary artists and is exhibited internationally. For the past twenty years his art and style have defined modern Ethiopian painting. He was the first Ethiopian artist to be honored by both the Musée National d'Art Moderne in Paris (1963) and the Museum of Modern Art in New York City (1965) with the purchase of his works. In 1992 the Smithsonian Institution's National Museum of African Art acquired several of his paintings.

Born in Ethiopia, Boghossian lives and works in Washington, D.C., where he has taught painting at Howard University since 1974. In 1955 he received an Ethiopian government scholarship to study at Saint Martins School, Central School, and the Slade School of Fine Arts in London. In 1957 he moved to Paris, where he attended and taught at the École des Beaux Arts and the Académie de la Grande Chaumiere. Boghossian returned to Ethiopia in 1966, and for the next three years he taught at the Fine Arts School of

Addis Ababa, where, despite his short stay, he had a lasting impact on a younger generation of artists. After moving to the United States, he continued to influence modern Ethiopian painting through artists such as Wosene and Germai Hewitt, who followed to study with him at Howard University.

Boghossian's period in Paris, which during the late 1950s and the early 1960s was a meeting place of diverse intellectual trends, provided him with vigorous experiences and shaped his personal philosophy and artistic style. He formed an association with the Senegalese scholar and philosopher Sheikh Anta Diop and with other major figures in the pan-African and Negritude movements. In Paris, Boghossian worked closely with artists from Africa, Latin America, and the United States, specifically African American artists. He was particularly influenced by Paul Klee, André Breton, Georges Braque, Wilfredo Lam, and Max Ernst, in addition to a number of West African artists.

As is evident from his works, Boghossian uses highly diverse techniques and media to enhance the power of expression in his paintings. His works combine relief with bark cloth and goatskin. He works in oil, acrylic, gouache, crayon, and pen and ink. Boghossian's *Time Cycle II* (1982) offers the finest example of his innovative techniques and experimentation with media. Like Ernst he begins a painting by creating accidental effects. He has developed a method of splashing water on the canvas and then spraying it with paint so as to create a surface alive with energy. His works are vibrant in color and are enriched with symbols, motifs, forms, and shapes drawn from his own Ethiopian heritage and the larger African continent, as well as from his contemporary surroundings. Boghossian's work synthesizes his country's rich and powerful traditions, including wall and scroll paintings and illuminated manuscripts dating to the eighth century, with European techniques. The best example of such synthesis is his *The Spirit Is Landing* (1987-89), in which he included painted scrolls on the vibrant background that has become his distinguishing mark.

—Salah Hassan

BOLLING, Leslie (Garland)

American sculptor

Born: Dendron, Virginia, 1889. **Education:** Hampton Institute, Virginia; Virginia Union University. **Career:** Worked as a porter in Richmond, Virginia. **Died:** 1955.

Individual Exhibitions:

c.1928   Carl Van Vechten Gallery
1932   Richmond Academy of Arts, Virginia
1933   Harmon Foundation, New York
         Second Annual Exhibition of Virginia Artists, Richmond
         National Gallery of Art, Washington, D.C.

Collections:

Virginia Museum of Art, Richmond; Yale University, New Haven, Connecticut.

*   *   *

The earliest African American woodcarver to receive national recognition during his lifetime, Leslie Bolling became noted for his distinctive and keen portrayals of various aspects of Southern life. He was the most talented woodcarver among the self-taught artists of his generation. The genre nature of his subjects places his works in the category of American realism that includes such artists as Eastman Johnson and John Rogers.

Bolling achieved the status of a major artist during the 1930s and 1940s, although he considered himself simply a porter who whittled in his spare time as a hobby. Bolling's fame is based on a group of small wood carvings, from twelve to eighteen inches in height, that depict various aspects of African American life as observed by the artist. His works were executed using a few simple tools, and he worked without models or formal artistic instruction. Bolling first received public attention when he entered seven of his works in the National Exhibition of 1933 at the Smithsonian Institution.

Wood from the female poplar tree was Bolling's favorite material, and his only tools were a half dozen pocket knives, of which some were in a poor state of preservation. His working technique involved squaring up a block of wood, cutting the front and side view of the figure out with a scroll saw, and completing the modeling with his jackknife. Bolling's sculptures are generally characterized by a rough, unfinished appearance, with numerous chisel marks evident on the surfaces. The completed carvings were waxed to enhance the light-colored wood, and paint was used sparingly and infrequently to accentuate details.

The subjects that Bolling depicted were the people of his immediate environment in Richmond, Virginia, and included the mailman, workman, redcap, preacher, shopper, housewife, and an occasional religious figure such as Salome. His studio was a corner of a bedroom in his home and contained only a desk with his vise, scroll saw, and an assortment of knives.

The "Days of the Week" series by Bolling is his masterpiece. Six of the figures represent females engaged in an activity appropriate to the day of the week—washing clothes, mending, ironing, scrubbing, cooking, and so forth—while the seventh figure depicts a preacher on Sunday. The variety of expressions, moods, and poses of the figures were expertly conceived, and Bolling's sense of scale and anatomical proportioning were unusually competent for a person with no formal artistic training. The series was completed around 1937, and the locations for most of the figures from the group are unknown.

Bolling exhibited regularly in the Harmon Foundation Show in New York City, and he was the first African American artist to have a one-man show at the Academy of Arts in Richmond. Examples of his work then appeared in a book by E. J. Tangerman entitled *Design and Figure Carving,* published in 1939, and Bolling was also praised and patronized by the novelist and critic Carl Van Vechten.

The wood carvings of Bolling are almost too sophisticated to be labeled folk art. Because he never studied art, however, they must be placed in that category. Although many of Bolling's figures show traces of humor, they are never undignified, overly sentimental, or caricatures. He was a keen observer who was apparently attracted to stout, buxom females with large, round buttocks, which may have symbolized for Bolling the strength of African American womanhood. Bolling carved slowly, and he completed only about six pieces a year. Most of his carvings were purchased for private collections in the United States, Canada, and England.

There is nothing in the history of American art that compares with Bolling's works. They bear no relationship to the West African tradition of wood carving, and they are as fresh and original as the Negro spirituals that grew out of slave work songs. It is unfortunate that the locations of most of Bolling's sculptures are not known and that little information is available about the activities of his later years. Most of the museums and galleries that are recorded as having exhibited or purchased his works during the 1930s have no record of their existence or list them as lost. Thus, attempts to locate Bolling's wood carvings have, except for a few cases, been unsuccessful.

—Regina A. Perry

BOLTON, Shirley (Lee)

American painter and illustrator

Born: Lexington, Georgia, 9 January 1945. **Education:** University of Georgia, B.F.A. 1966, M.F.A. in graphic art design 1970, Ed.D. in art education 1970. **Career:** Professor of art, University of West Florida, Pensacola. Member, National Conference of Artists, College Arts Association of America. **Awards:** Popular Ballot Award in painting, Atlanta University Annual Exhibition, Georgia, 1969, 1970; James V. Herring Award in painting, National Exhibition of Black Artists, Washington, D.C., 1971. **Died:** 10 August 1984.

Selected Exhibitions:

1964	Atlanta University, Georgia (through 1970)
1970	University of Georgia (solo)
1971	*National Exhibition of Black Artists,* Washington, D.C.
	High Museum of Art, Atlanta
	National Bank of Washington
	Citizens and Trust Bank Building, Atlanta
	Carnegie Museum of Art, Pittsburgh
1972	Newark Museum, New Jersey
	Warbeke Gallery, Mount Holyoke College, South Hadley, Massachusetts
	Southern Illinois University, Carbondale
	Museum of Arts and Sciences, Macon, Georgia
	Black Exposé, San Francisco
1973	High Museum of Art, Atlanta
	Florida Faculties Traveling Show
	Banks-Haley Gallery, Albany, Georgia
	University of West Florida Gallery, Pensacola

Collections:

Atlanta University, Georgia; High Museum, Atlanta, Georgia; University of Georgia.

Publications:

By BOLTON: Article—"Art as Creative Learning for the Rural Disadvantaged," in *Studies in Art Education,* Winter 1969.

On BOLTON: Article—"Black Artist," in *Savannah Magazine,* April 1972, p. 16.

*   *   *

Shirley Lee Bolton's career is marked by three distinct periods—detailed drawing, figural studies, and abstraction. *Tenement* (oil and collage, 1969) and *Black Man* (oil on canvas, 1970) are prize-winning works from the second period of her career. The second period was inspired by her association with the National Conference of Artists (NCA) and her tenure at the University of Georgia. NCA was organized in 1959 at Atlanta University and has among its membership African American artists, art historians, and art educators. Dr. Bolton was active in NCA in the 1970s and attended a number of its national conferences. Influential members of NCA at this time were E. J. Montgomery, Samella Lewis, Margaret Burroughs, Malkia Roberts, Jewel Simon, and Jenelsie Holloway.

Bolton studied at the University of Georgia and received her B.F.A. in 1966, M.F.A. in 1970, and Ed.D. in August 1970. These were critical years for the artist. A number of important artists/activists/scholars, such as Leo Twiggs, Benjamin Colbert, Charles Dallas, Roosevelt Lenard, and Floyd Coleman, who was completing his doctorate in art education at the University of Georgia, were in school in Athens, Georgia, at the same time. These individuals had a profound impact on Bolton's art and ideas, especially Coleman, who is now chair of the art department at Howard University. Although there were no planned, regular meetings, these individuals would often meet over dinner or lunch at the home of one of the group, and discussions about politics, art, and education would ensue. Bolton, who was an excellent gourmet cook, would prepare the meal.

Though Bolton's doctorate is in art education, her undergraduate and master's degrees were in graphic design and painting. It is these interests that shaped the third and final period of her art career. Her graphic design work already included lyrical abstractions, which alternated counterchanging patterns and shifting optical illusions. The abstraction commenced in the early 1970s and continued unabated until her untimely death in 1984. Bolton's art became increasingly free of figural forms towards the end of her life. Before she died of multiple sclerosis on 10 August 1984, she was completely immersed in abstraction. She would use an airbrush to place color on her canvases. The canvases were in different layers, protruding and receding, creating their own sense of movement and rhythm. Then superimposed on the canvases of airbrushed colors as a kind of visual support were vertical lines of contrasting or complementary colors. The dimensions of some of these canvases could be as large as four feet wide and six feet long. She would listen to popular, jazz, and classical music (and had a special affinity for Credence Clearwater Revival), while she created these layered compositions. The influence of this music on her canvases is clear. In the triptych *Themes from Capricorn*, Bolton explores her astrological sign, as she did in many of her works. The concept of tripartite or quadripartite movements or themes as in suites, sonatas, or symphonies is prominent. Bolton manipulated the senses of sight, touch, and hearing. She endeavored to assist individuals in hearing colors.

When she was stricken with multiple sclerosis, Bolton had an impressive following. Her achievements as an artist/educator are legion. She taught at the University of South Carolina at Columbia. At the time of her death, she was a professor at the University of West Florida in Pensacola, where she taught design and African American art history.

—Jontyle Theresa Robinson

BOWLING, Frank

Guyanese painter

Born: Bartica, Essequibo, Guyana, 29 February 1936. **Education:** Slade School of Arts, London University, Royal College of Art, London, 1959-62, M.F.A., 1962. **Career:** Tutor, Camberwell School of Arts and Crafts, London, 1963-83. Lecturer, Reading University, 1964-66; instructor, Columbia University, New York , 1968-69; assistant professor, Douglass College, Rutgers University, New Jersey, Massachusetts College of Art, Boston; lecturer, School of Visual Arts, New York, 1975-76. Tutor, Byam Shaw School of Painting and Sculpture, London, 1975-86. Artist-in-residence, Skowhegan School of Painting and Sculpture, Maine. Co-founder, Young Commonwealth Artists Group; contributing editor and critic for *Arts Magazine,* 1969-72. **Awards:** Royal College of Art Silver Medal, 1962; Calouste-Gulbenkian Foundation Painting Purchase Award, 1963; First World Festival of Negro Art Grand Prize, 1966; Edinburgh Open 100 Painting Prize; Guggenheim Memorial Fellowship, 1967, 1973; New York State CAPS Award, 1975; Arts Council of Great Britain Award, 1977; Pollock Krasner Award, 1992. **Address:** 8A John Islip Street, London SWIP 4PY, England.

Individual Exhibitions:

1962	Grabowski Gallery, London
1963	Grabowski Gallery, London
1966	Terry Dintenfass, New York
1971	Whitney Museum of American Art, New York
1973	Gallery Center for Inter American Relations, New York
	Noah Goldowsky Gallery, New York
1974	Noah Goldowsky Gallery, New York
1975	Tibor de Nagy Gallery, New York
	William Darby, London
1976	Tibor de Nagy Gallery, New York
	Watson/de Nagy and Company, Houston, Texas
1977	William Darby, London
	Acme Gallery, London
1978	Polytechnic Art Gallery, Newcastle upon Tyne, England
1979	Tibor de Nagy Gallery, New York
1980	Tibor de Nagy Gallery, New York
1981	Vecu, Antwerp, Belgium
1982	Tibor de Nagy Gallery, New York
1983	Tibor de Nagy Gallery, New York
1986	Serpentine Gallery, London
	Tibor de Nagy Gallery, New York
	Arcade Gallery, Harrogate
1988	Castlefield Gallery, Manchester, England
	Municipal Art Gallery, Limerick, Ireland
	Crawford Art Gallery, Cork Ireland
	Senate House, University of Liverpool, England
1989	University Art Gallery, Reading
	Royal West of England Academy, Bristol
	Tibor de Nagy Gallery, New York
1991	Wilmer Jennings at Kenkeleba, New York
1993	National Academy of Sciences, Washington, D.C.
	Heimatmuseum, Eckernforde, Schleswig Holstein, Germany
1995	AFTU/Bill Hodges Gallery, New York
	Cut Gallery, Waterloo, London

Selected Group Exhibitions:

1964   *The London Group,* Tate Gallery, London
1971   Whitney Museum of American Art, New York
1976   Hirshhorn Museum and Sculpture Garden, Washington, D.C.
1979   Mappin Art Gallery, Sheffield, England (traveling)
1982   Currier Gallery, Manchester, New Hampshire (traveling)
1989   Tibor de Nagy Gallery, Chicago
        Umana Yana, Georgetown, Guyana
1992   Whitechapel Gallery, London
1994   Camille Love Gallery, Atlanta, Georgia
1995   Skoto Gallery, New York

Collections:

Arts Council of Great Britain; Calouste-Gulbenkian Foundation, Lisbon, Portugal; Crawford Municipal Art Gallery, Cork, Ireland; Herbert F. Johnson Museum, Cornell University, Ithaca, New York; Lloyds of London; Metropolitan Museum of Art, New York; Museum of Fine Arts, Boston; Museum of Modern Art, New York; Tate Gallery, London; Whitney Museum of American Art.

Publications:

On BOWLING: Books—*Frank Bowling,* exhibition catalog, by Robert M. Doty, New York, Whitney Museum of American Art, 1971*; Frank Bowling, Selected Paintings 1967-77,* exhibition catalog, London, Acme Gallery, 1977; *Caribbean Expressions,* exhibition catalog, by Julia Nicholson, England, Leicester Museum, 1986; *Frank Bowling,* exhibition catalog, by Ronald Alley, London, Serpentine Gallery, 1986; *Frank Bowling,* exhibition catalog, by Christine Eccles, Manchester, England, Castlefield Gallery, 1988; *Soundings Towards the Definition of an Individual Talent,* exhibition catalog, by Mel Gooding, London, Hayward Gallery, 1989; *Some Remarks about Bowling's Art,* exhibition catalog, by Valentin Tatransky, London, Greenwich Citizens Gallery, 1991; *The Search for Freedom,* exhibition catalog, by Corrine Jennings, New York, Kenkeleba House, 1991; *A/Cross Currents, Synthesis in African American Abstract Painting,* exhibition catalog, Senegal, Dakar Biennale, 1992. **Articles**—"Color, Material, Form" by Robert M. Doty, in *New York Times,* June 1983; "Abstract Art in Britain Today" by Peter Davies, in *Art and Artists,* May 1986; "Formalism Versus New Art: A Conversation Between Frank Bowling, Paul Harrison and Jeremy Thomas," in *Artscribe,* 44, December 1983.

*   *   *

Frank Bowling is an artist who has been painting for the better part of four decades. Born in British Guiana (Guyana), he went to London at the age of fourteen to complete his schooling. He was first a poet, but he turned to painting in his late teens. After periods of study at art schools in London, he began his career as a painter in earnest with solo exhibitions in London in the early 1960s.

Bowling has come to be universally known and respected for his abstract paintings, often large, expansive works rich with color and texture. He came to abstract art at the beginning of the 1970s via figurative painting, however. His art of the late 1950s and the 1960s resonated with distinctly political narratives. Bowling himself has cited the death of the African nationalist leader Patrice Lumumba in 1961 as being one of his themes during this period.

By the mid-1960s Bowling had taken the first of the innumerable transatlantic flights that have enabled him to maintain studios in both New York City and London. It was in New York around 1966 that Bowling met, engaged with, and was influenced by abstract artists, both African American and European American. Thus began Bowling's enduring love affair with modernism, something to which he has remained steadfastly loyal decade after decade. He has been quoted as citing critic Clement Greenberg as a major influence on this seismic development in his painting: "Clem was able to make me see that modernism belonged to me also, that I had no good reason to pretend I wasn't part of the whole thing." The central and pivotal esteem in which Bowling places modernism is evident in his statement that "I believe that the black soul, if there can be such a thing, belongs to modernism."

It is perhaps this attachment to modernism that makes Bowling, particularly within a British context, a unique artist. He has consistently refused to rule himself out of the main currents of contemporary international art practice. Herein also lies one of his most interesting aspects. As a black artist he confounds and frustrates stereotypes of what work he should be producing or might be expected to produce. Through his painting he relentlessly expresses the view that, for him, art should not be burdened by considerations of race, racism, or racial and national identity.

Bowling's earliest abstract paintings have been described as consisting of "thin, luminous washes infused with metallic pigment, often dripped or poured." He also experimented with acrylic gels, applying liberal quantities of paint to create undulating, tactile surfaces in which he embedded an assortment of objects. It was perhaps these paintings, reminiscent of large wall maps detailing the altitude of terrain, that prompted one observer to suggest that "Bowling's paintings are not landscape, but land."

Critics struggle to locate Bowling's work satisfactorily. Some speak of "obvious" or "strong" Caribbean influences. Others mention tropical colors. But such labels do little or nothing to aid in a fuller understanding of Bowling's paintings. Such influences, of course, occasionally have a place, but they are by no means the whole story. Bowling can cite an endless, almost bewildering range of influences. Some are obvious; others less so. And the titles of his paintings offer additional, occasionally cryptic, pointers. Regarding the titles of his paintings, Bowling has described them as "private jokes, evocative. You'd have to know the connection between the activity of the painting and the literary connections that stretch across the cultural divide. They are meant to be ironic and evocative. An awful lot is personal and in riddles."

Certainly within Britain, Bowling has in recent years become known more by reputation than anything else, although his curriculum vitae testifies to a career of extensive international exhibition activity. As one admirer has written, Bowling has already "produced a body of painting like nothing else in contemporary art. An achievement that deserves to be more widely known and appreciated." One thing is certain, however. It is that Bowling has earned an important place in the postwar history of black artists in Britain.

—Eddie Chambers

BOWSER, David Bustill
American painter

Born: Philadelphia, 16 January 1820. **Education:** Attended private school, Philadelphia, 1830-33; apprenticed to cousin Robert Douglass, Jr., beginning 1833. **Family:** Married Elizabeth H. Bowser, one daughter and one son. **Career:** Sign-painter, Philadelphia. **Awards:** First Prize Medal, Colored American Institute, Philadelphia, 1851 and 1852. **Died:** 2 July 1900.

Selected Exhibitions:

c.1844	Philadelphia Museum
1848	Franklin Institute, Philadelphia
1851	Colored American Institute, Philadelphia
1852	Colored American Institute, Philadelphia

Collections:

Albino Kuhn Library and Gallery, University of Maryland, Baltimore; Atwater Kent Museum, Philadelphia; Cigna Museum, Philadelphia; Harper's Ferry National Historical Park; Mercer Museum, Doylestown, Pennsylvania; Philadelphia Historical Society.

Publications:

On BOWSER: Articles—"David Bowser, A Colored Artist" by G.E.S., in *Anglo-African,* 28 June 1862; "David Bustell [sic] Bowser Expired Saturday Last," in *Philadelphia Tribune,* 7 July 1900; "Obituary," in *The Times* (Philadelphia), 2 July 1900; "Obituary: David B. Bowser," in *Public Ledger* (Philadelphia), 2 July 1900; "A Negro Artist's Oil Painting of Lincoln," in *Lincoln Lore* (Indiana), 15 February 1954.

*   *   *

David Bustill Bowser was one of the most commercially successful African American artists in Philadelphia in the nineteenth century. As a child Bowser showed remarkable artistic talent in the private school of his cousin, Sarah Mapps Douglass, and later as an apprentice to another cousin, painter Robert Douglass, Jr. Forced to learn a trade to make a living, Bowser reluctantly practiced hairdressing for eighteen months before spending several years as a barber on steamboats along the Mississippi and Red Rivers. Although he longed to travel to Europe, the frustrated artist returned to Philadelphia to care for his parents. There he resumed hairdressing until he was able to devote himself exclusively to art.

Little is known about Bowser's early work, except that his first commission was from Jacob C. White, Sr., a leading African American citizen of the time. Bowser is known to have received two first prize medals for marine and landscape painting at the Colored American Institute exhibitions of 1851 and 1852. One surviving, untitled landscape (1856) is a serene, ovoid composition of a tiny single figure. The figure is walking across a bridge above a calm body of water toward a modest dwelling in the woods. With a predominant blue-green palette, it is evocative of the Barbizon school.

Widely noted as a skilled ornamental artist, Bowser fulfilled commissions for painted banners from the Native American Party parade in 1844, the Odd Fellows chapter (Smithsonian Institution, 1855), and a local fire department. Shown at the Philadelphia Museum, the latter works were heralded as the best on exhibition. From the 1840s through the 1860s Bowser painted countless signs and other paraphernalia (hose reels, engine panels, and procession apparel) for volunteer fire companies, fire insurance businesses, and military companies in Philadelphia, Baltimore, and Richmond. Typical images based on sample designs included state seals, bald eagles, phoenixes, seascapes, and the U.S. shield, evident in at least four extant pressed felt top hats for the United States Fire Company that were worn with matching oilcloth capes in parades. Bowser produced similar procession attire for the wealthy Phoenix Fire Company and the Phoenix Hose Company. A boldly colored hat for the latter enterprise features a patriotic eagle with wings outspread against a burning blue sky, the striped white clouds and red flames of which suggest the American flag. This type of work ended in 1871 when professional squads replaced volunteer units.

Bowser also specialized in portraits of eminent persons, including John Brown (1858), whom the artist hosted in his home. He portrayed the head of the abolitionist with his long white beard, unruly hair, and distant eyes against a plain, dark background. In addition, Bowser produced twenty-one oil paintings and retouched photographs of Abraham Lincoln (often signed in bright red), commissioned by African Americans such as Philadelphia's Vigiliant Committee president Robert Purvis and whites like Civil War financier and U.S. Treasury secretary Jay Cooke. One work depicts the tall emancipator in an overcoat and top hat freeing a kneeling female slave. Another represents the president on a banner for the 15th Avenue Presbyterian School beneath the motto, "With malice towards none, with charity for all."

During the Civil War Bowser executed at least ten United States Colored Troops pictorial flags in the manner of Robert Douglass. Nine of these are in extant photographs. With captions like "Liberty or Death," "We Shall Prove Ourselves Men," and "Rather Die Freemen Than Live to Be Slaves," these banners each featured a heroic black man in allegorical scenes or with nationalistic emblems. "Freedom for All," for instance, depicts a soldier conversing with Liberty personified as a white woman in Greco-Roman garb while the obverse of the flag displays a patriotic eagle. Perhaps Bowser's most compelling image is a painted silk banner (c. early-mid 1860s) of the 22nd U.S.C.T. with the Virginia state motto, *Sic Temper Tyrannis* ("Thus Always to Tyrants"). A fierce African American Union officer prepares to bayonet the chest of a sitting white Confederate soldier who has dropped his sword and flag in terror. This dramatic scene boldly heralds a monumental black man as the new American hero. Bowser himself worked as an emancipator, aiding fugitive slaves in their escape to Canada, eradicating Philadelphia's segregated streetcars, and serving in the city's delegation to the Pennsylvania Equal Rights League.

In the 1870s and 1880s Bowser designed regalia for the African American Grand United Order of Odd Fellows, an organization he once headed. He and Robert Douglass, Jr. were at least two artists who inspired a new generation of painters, Henry O. Tanner among them.

—Theresa Leininger-Miller

BOXER, David (Wayne)

Jamaican painter, assemblage artist, and installation artist

Born: Saint Andrew, Jamaica, 17 March 1946. **Education:** Cornell University, Ithaca, New York, 1965-69, A.B. 1979; The Johns Hopkins University, Baltimore, Maryland, 1970-75, M.A. 1972, Ph.D. 1975. **Career:** Medical technician, Ministry of Health, Kingston, Jamaica, 1964-69; film editor, Harvey Film Productions, Kingston, Jamaica, 1969-70; film director/producer, Jamaica Broadcasting Corporation, Kingston, 1970; director/curator, National Gallery of Jamaica, Kingston, 1975-90. Since 1990 director emeritus/chief curator, National Gallery of Jamaica, Kingston. **Awards:** Centenary Medal of the Institute of Jamaica, 1980; Commander of the Order of Distinction Award, Jamaican National Honors, 1991; Santo Domingo Biennial Gold Medal, Dominican Republic, 1992; Musgrave Medal, 1995. **Address:** 7 Devon Road, Kingston 10, Jamaica, West Indies.

Individual Exhibitions:

1970	Bolivar Gallery, Kingston, Jamaica
1972	Bolivar Gallery, Kingston, Jamaica
1973	Institute of Jamaica, Kingston
1975	Just-Above-Midtown Gallery, New York
1976	John Peartree Gallery, Kingston, Jamaica
1978	Gallery on the Hill, Kingston, Jamaica
	Giammaca Gallery, Kingston, Jamaica
1979	Museum of Modern Art of Latin America, Washington, D.C.
1981	John Peartree Gallery, Kingston, Jamaica
1984	Frame Centre Gallery, Kingston, Jamaica
1985	Artist's Studio and Gallery, Kingston, Jamaica
1988	Artist's Studio and Gallery, Kingston, Jamaica
1990	Artist's Studio and Gallery, Kingston, Jamaica
1996	Artist's Studio and Gallery, Kingston, Jamaica
	Bienal Internacional de São Paulo, Brazil (retrospective of installations)

David Boxer: *Violon d'Ingres,* 1987. Photo courtesy of Jacqueline Gannie.

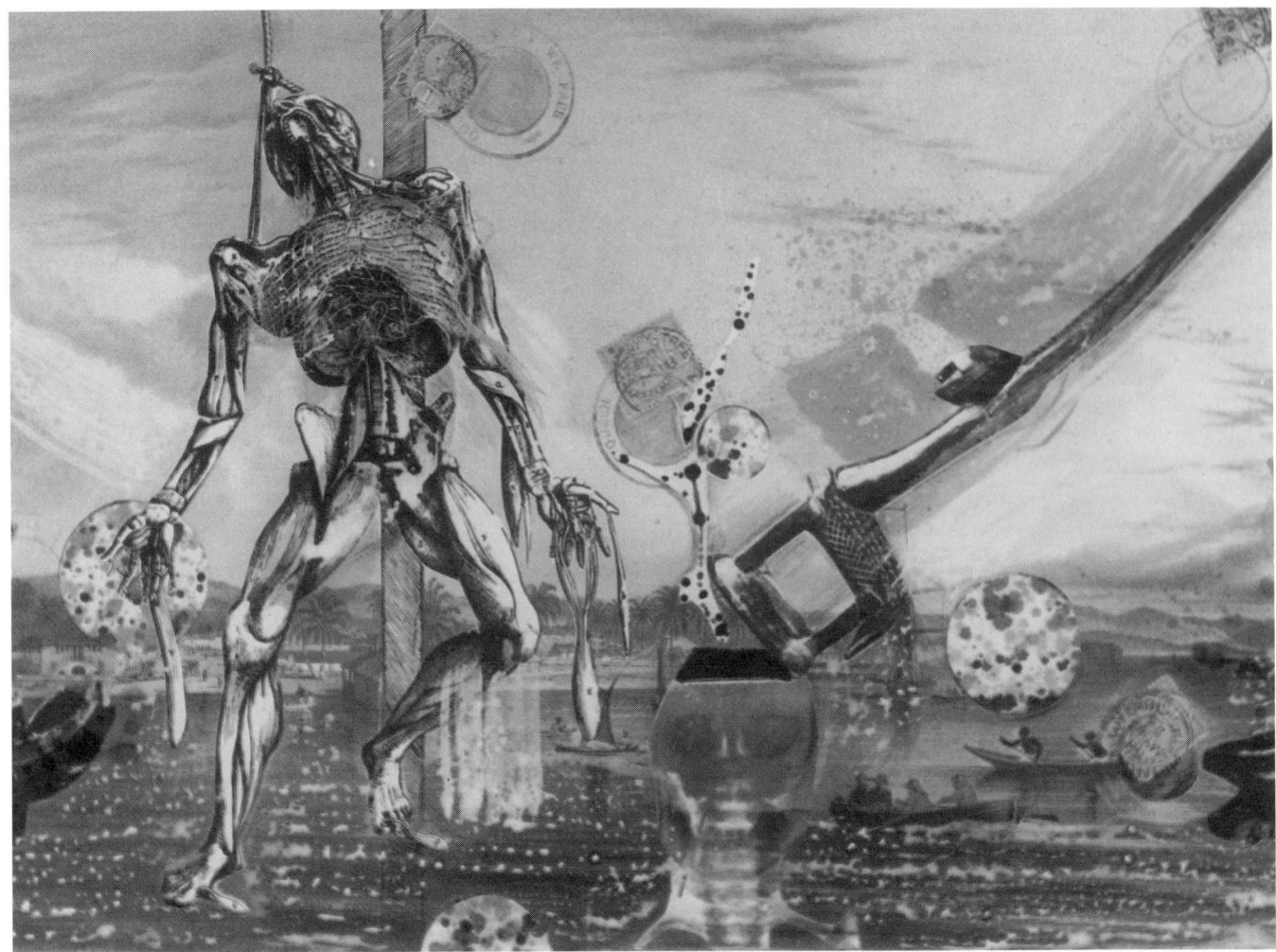

David Boxer: *Memories of Colonization: Kidd Triptych* (detail), 1995. Photo courtesy of Maria La Yacona.

Selected Group Exhibitions:

1981   Bass Museum, Miami
1982   *Jamaican Art 1922-1982,* Smithsonian Institution Tour-
            ing Exhibition Service and National Gallery of Jamaica
            (traveling)
1986   Commonwealth Institute, London (traveling)
1987   Mutual Life Gallery, Kingston, Jamaica
1991   *Aspects III, Eight Jamaican Avant Garde Artists,* National
            Gallery of Jamaica, Kingston
1992   Galeria de Arte Moderno, Santo Domingo
1995   *New World Imagery: Contemporary Jamaican Art,* Na-
            tional Gallery of Jamaica, Kingston (traveling)
            Hayward Gallery, London
            National Gallery of Jamaica, Kingston

Collections:

Museum of the Americas, Washington, D.C.; National Gallery of
Jamaica, Kingston; Stedelijk Museum, Amsterdam.

Publications:

By BOXER: Books—*Ten Jamaican Sculptors,* exhibition catalog,
Kingston, National Gallery of Jamaica, 1975; *Five Centuries: Art in
Jamaica Since the Discovery,* exhibition catalog, Kingston, National
Gallery of Jamaica, 1976; *The Self and Each Other,* exhibition cata-
log, Kingston, National Gallery of Jamaica, 1977; *The Formative
Years: Art in Jamaica, 1922-1940,* exhibition catalog, Kingston,
National Gallery of Jamaica, 1978; *Fifteen Intuitives,* exhibition
catalog, Kingston, National Gallery of Jamaica, 1987; *Arawak Vi-
brations, Homage to the Jamaican Taino,* exhibition catalog,
Kingston, National Gallery of Jamaica, 1994.

On BOXER: Articles—"Tribute to An Artist" by Edna Manley,
in *The Daily Gleaner,* 7 July 1973; "David Boxer—Macabre or
Magnificent?" by Betty Russell, in *The Jamaica Daily News,* 13
July 1973 (illustrated); "The Boxer Exhibition" by Basil McFarlane,
in *Jamaica Journal,* 7(4), December 1973; "David Boxer, Artist of
the New Image" by Verena Reckford, in *Xaymaca,* December 1975,
pp. 3-5 (illustrated); "David Boxer's Requiem: Painting of the
Month" by Andrew Hope, in *Sunday Gleaner,* 27 February 1977;

"Man of the Year" by Andrew Hope, in *Sunday Gleaner Magazine,* 14 January 1979; "The Intuitive Eye: The Editor Interviews David Boxer," in *Jamaica Journal,* 44, June 1980.

*   *   *

David Boxer has contributed to the development of Jamaican art as an influential artist and through his work as an art historian and curator. As an artist he is self-taught, although he studied briefly with the abstract expressionist Fred Mitchell at Cornell University.

Boxer's first significant painting, *Viet Madonna* (1967), a haunting mother-and-child image inspired by news photographs of napalm victims, is an early exploration of the themes of conflict and war that reappear throughout his work. Boxer's work temporarily moved in another direction in the late 1960s, however, when he painted soft-edged, delicately colored informal abstractions. Most of these paintings were inspired by classical music, another lasting influence on his work.

In the early 1970s Boxer shocked the conservative Jamaican art world with macabre assemblages such as *Rack with Seven Heads* (1971) and *Shopping Cart with Eight Heads* (1971). These were followed by equally disturbing neofigurative paintings, most notably the "assaulted self-portraits" that introduced the autobiographical into his oeuvre. While these works can be placed in the larger context of neofiguration in Latin American and Caribbean art, they were also influenced by Boxer's doctoral studies on the early work of Francis Bacon. Like many other Jamaican artists, he was deeply affected by the sociopolitical problems that engulfed the country in the mid-1970s. This resulted in allegorical works such as the triptych painting *Passage* (1977), which, in an abstract form, reminds one of the scenes of hell by Hieronymus Bosch.

Although Boxer had used assemblage and collage before, these techniques became more important in the 1980s. To create his collages, assemblages, and installations, Boxer appropriates and manipulates images and objects from various sources. These include art reproductions, medical illustrations, surgical instruments, music sheets, news photographs, stamps, x-ray photographs, maps, antique furniture, archaeological artifacts, video footage, decaying organic substances, and even live fish. With this eclectic arsenal of visual material, he has developed a complex, surreal iconography that he uses to explore existential issues facing the individual in a multicultural society.

In the collage suite *Memories of Colonization* (1982), for instance, Boxer superimposed a ghostlike assortment of African masks and medical illustrations upon engravings of English palace interiors. The anti-imperialist overtones of the collage represented a new, more overtly political direction in his work. In his first installation, *Headpiece* (1985), Boxer further explored the themes of genocide and cultural confrontation in a sequence of dramatic tableaux that juxtaposed images of chaos and order. This installation also included his first video montage. Boxer's interest in moving images is also reflected in his *Fourth of July over Baghdad* (1991), a filmic series of thirty collage paintings inspired by CNN's coverage of the Persian Gulf conflict and its dehumanized, abstract representation of the horrors of war.

Although Boxer incorporates painted elements in most collages and assemblages, painting as such has remained an important aspect of his work. The imagery of his paintings is disguised by the tangled chance surface patterns he calls "nervfelds," which replaced the medical gauze he often used in his earlier work. These so-called nervfelds also reinforce the near monochromatic quality and spatial ambiguity of his paintings. Although his painting process is highly improvisatory, his compositions are typically controlled by geometric structuring devices reminiscent of Bacon's "cages."

Boxer's paintings tend to address personal rather than political issues and often have erotic overtones. Their meaning is rarely explicit, however, but relies on syncretic, allegorical references to the same sources he uses in his multimedia works. His *Pieta* (1984), for instance, which was painted as a memorial to a close friend, appropriates traditional Christian iconography.

As the chief curator of the National Gallery of Jamaica since 1975, Boxer has been responsible for the institution's collection, exhibition, and publication programs. In 1979 he introduced the term "intuitive" as an alternative to "primitive" or "naive," and he has advanced the recognition of Jamaica's intuitive artists. He is the leading Edna Manley scholar and published a definitive monograph on her work in 1990. He has also aided in bringing young Jamaican artists to national and international attention. Several of these artists, such as Omari Ra ("African") and Anna Henriques, have been noticeably influenced by his work.

—Veerle Poupeye

BOYCE, Sonia

British painter and mixed-media artist

Born: 1962. **Education:** East Ham College of Art and Technology, 1979-80; Stourbridge College of Art and Technology, Birmingham, 1980-83, B.A. (honors) in fine art.

Individual Exhibitions:

1986	Black Art Gallery, London
1987	AIR, London (traveling)
1988	Whitechapel Art Gallery, London
1991	Vanessa Devereux Gallery London

Selected Group Exhibitions:

1987	Cornerhouse Gallery, Manchester, England
1988	University of Essex Gallery, Colchester, England
	Angela Flowers Gallery, London
	Cooper Gallery, Barsley and Rochdale Art Gallery
	Winnipeg Art Gallery, Canada
	Chisenhale Gallery, London
1989	Hayward Gallery, London
1990	Photographers Gallery, London
	McLellan Galleries, Glasgow (traveling)
1995	Photography Gallery and Workshop, Glasgow

Publications:

On BOYCE: Articles—Review (Black-Art Gallery, London) by David Lee, in *Arts Review* (London), 38, 26 September 1986, p. 509; review (AIR Gallery, London) by Mary Rose Beaumont, in *Arts Review* (London), 39, 16 January 1987, pp. 11-12; review (Vanessa Devereux Gallery, London) by Charles Hall, in *Arts Review* (London), 43, 29 November 1991, p. 603; "Portable

Fabric Shelters" by Godfrey Worsdale, in *Art Monthly,* 187, June 1995, pp. 41-42.

*   *   *

Sonia Boyce, born of Caribbean parents in the 1960s in Britain, grew up speaking a seemingly foreign language of art until she was in college. There Boyce was moved by visiting feminist artist Margaret Harrison's claims that female experiences are legitimate artistic subject matter. Boyce was later introduced to a textbook featuring African American artists since the 1700s, the first book she had seen with evidence that the language of art was not foreign but her own to claim.

To survive as the only black student in her art college, Boyce sought refuge in drawings of home, family, and domestic life. Her large-format chalk and pastel works in the early 1980s examined both racial and gender issues related to black women. She specifically used the home and family as central settings for examining the base of black women's power within a hostile, white patriarchal British society. For instance, *Aunt Enid, the Pose* (1985) shows a black woman in her best Friday night dress posing next to a simple table with a potted flowering plant. The pastel highlights both the class and cultural aspirations of some immigrant women. *Big Woman's Talk* (1984) focuses on a child's wish to be included in the adult world. This closely cropped painting shows a young girl leaning on her mother's lap while the mother is presumably engaged in conversation with a close girlfriend. One can almost anticipate the gentle nudge the mother will give her nosy daughter to return to her child's play world.

Boyce credits Mexican artist Frida Kahlo's use of self-portraits to express cultural and political themes as a major influence on her own autobiographical work. *She Ain't Holding Them Up, She's Holding On (Some English Rose),* from 1986, depicts a life-size black woman lifting two generations of family. The women's red rose print dress symbolically claims her right to British privilege while she simultaneously clings to West Indian roots.

Boyce deliberately, and almost exclusively, shows black people in her paintings. She dismisses the notion that focusing on black subjects diminishes her contributions to the fine arts. She believes that black women can represent a universal. Black men, however, are not absent from her portfolio. *Cricket Days—Domino Nights* (1986) is a large (four feet by nine and a half feet) mixed-media portrait featuring twenty-three formally dressed men and boys seemingly waiting to step down from the picture frame to loosen their stiff ties and enjoy a serious game of dominoes. The men seem to be posing physically outdoors and figuratively outside of home— a woman's domain.

In the late 1980s Boyce's work moved toward collage as a means of examining a more complex black life. *Talking Presence* (1988) shows a nude couple sitting at night on their private windowsill as they contemplate their place in the outside industrial community, which features such landmarks as London Bridge, the Houses of Parliament, and the City. The picture suggests that these elements of the British establishment are within the dreams of black British citizens.

Boyce is not alone in her quest to bring a black perspective to the arts in Britain. Other black British artists of Boyce's generation include the painter and mixed-media installation artist Keith Piper, Tanzanian-born mixed-media artist Lubaina Himid, sculptor Veronica Ryan, mixed-media political artist Eddie Chambers, and Nigerian sculptor Sokari Douglas Camp. Boyce credits Himid with intro-

ducing her to the black arts community in 1982 and encouraging her to exhibit her works.

Boyce continued to evolve and re-create her style in the 1990s. Her works from this period include drawings, digital photography, and photocopying. Boyce also has experimented with combining pastels and computerized images. Her works continue to explore narrative and nonnarrative aspects of everyday urban black British life.

—Kyra E. Hicks

BRAXTON, William Ernest
American painter

Born: Washington, D.C., 10 December 1978. **Education:** Adelphi College, New York. **Career:** Office assistant, valet, and Pullman porter. **Died:** 1932.

Selected Exhibitions:

1925   New York Public Library
1928   Harmon Foundation, New York
1929   Smithsonian Institution, Washington, D.C.
        National Gallery of Art, Washington, D.C.
1948   *Graphic Arts by Negro Artists,* Howard University, Washington, D.C.

Collections:

Schomburg Center, New York.

Publications:

On BRAXTON: Articles—*Crisis,* 3, January 1912, p. 98; *Crisis,* 5, February 1913, p. 169; "African American Artists, 1800-1950," in *Ebony,* 23, February 1968, p. 121; article by C. D. Johnson, in *Ebony,* 1927, p. 78; *Southern Workman,* 53, April 1924, p. 149.

*   *   *

William Ernest Braxton is considered to have been the first African American expressionist painter. He studied painting at Adelphi University under John Bernard Whittaker, and his favorite medium was oils. Following the tradition of other late nineteenth- and early twentieth-century American painters—including Edward Mitchell Bannister, William Eduoard Scott, and Samuel Collins—he did portraits and subject studies as well as landscapes and seascapes. He rendered his themes in muted tones and thick impasto.

Most of Braxton's extant paintings are in a relatively small format. Painted in oil on artist board, they range in size from about twelve by sixteen inches to thirty by thirty-four inches. Braxton used a muted palette of ocher, brown, black, and gray tones, employing bold brush strokes and liberally using the knife to create shaded, textured surfaces. Although his palette was frequently dark, he inserted a jewel of color, often a tone of red or white, as a focal point to create a point of contrast and hence bring the composition alive. Examples of this technique are evident in *Snow Scene,* with a red barn standing out against a backdrop of whites, and *Woman with a Red Umbrella.*

Braxton's landscapes are reminiscent of Bannister in that they seem to have an attraction to quiet, bucolic scenes. Intensely personal, his landscapes reflect a contemplative, almost melancholy nature. The titles of his landscapes are often purely subjective and based on either the subject matter or what curators and researchers have called them. Hence, several of the works are known by more than one title. Braxton's portraits were often so ambivalently rendered that they verge on the abstract. The figures in *Old Lady in Gloves* (1923; also known as *Woman in Black*) and *Red Ribbon in Her Hair,* for example, are barely recognizable as women. His untitled painting of a black woman in profile with a white head scarf holds an uneasy air of dark mystery, the figure almost unapproachable.

Braxton was one of the favorite painters of Arthur Alphonso Schomburg, a collector and bibliophile who was also a supporter of the visual arts. Schomburg commissioned Braxton to paint a portrait of his second wife, Elizabeth, in 1911. He also was instrumental in organizing several exhibitions in which Braxton participated, and in the spring of 1925 Braxton had an exhibition of fifty-six oils, pastels, and drawings at the 135th Street branch of the New York Public Library. Like Schomburg, Braxton was interested in the history of African Americans, and many of his drawings reflected the nationalist philosophy of the new Negro era and the calls by W. E. B. Du Bois and Alain Locke to paint and celebrate the black experience and black ancestral arts. Along with Schomburg, J. Bruce Grit, and other African American scholars, Braxton helped form the Negro Society for Historical Research, and he became the group's art director.

Braxton was among the first black artists to use an etching press. He created etchings of prominent blacks, often done from photographs, that were reproduced in *Crisis* and *Opportunity* magazines, both of which featured the works of black artists on their covers. Schomburg also commissioned Braxton to produce many etchings and drawings of blacks for his private collection. Braxton depicted black leaders such as Toussaint-Louverture, Booker T. Washington, Frederick Douglass, and Nat Turner, as well as writers of African descent such as Aleksandr Pushkin, Phillis Wheatley, Alexandre Dumas *père,* and Paul Laurence Dunbar. The last appeared as the frontispiece for the 2 June 1924 issue of *Opportunity.*

Braxton is also known for his pencil drawing of Juan de Pareja, done after the Spanish painter Diego Velázquez. Pareja, who was originally a slave of Velázquez, was an artist in his own right and later won his freedom. Braxton's portrait was probably done as an illustration for one of Schomburg's papers on forgotten artists of African descent. It was included, along with his *Photo of a Man,* in an exhibition organized by James V. Herring at Howard University in 1948 and entitled *Graphic Arts by Negro Artists from Colonial Times to the Present.* Braxton also exhibited with the Harmon Foundation and is mentioned in the catalogs for *Exhibit of Fine Arts* (1929) and *Exhibition of Productions* (1933), as well as posthumously in *Negro Artists* (1935).

—Nashormeh N. R. Lindo

BRIERRE, Edgar
Haitian painter and sculptor

Born: Port-au-Prince, Haiti, 1933. **Family:** Brother of Murat Brierre. **Career:** Worked as a tailor in Port-au-Prince. Joined the Centre d'Art, 1967.

Selected Group Exhibitions:

| 1974 | Milwaukee Art Center, Wisconsin |
| 1982 | Studio Museum in Harlem, New York |

Collections:

Le Centre d'Art, Port-au-Prince, Haiti; Flagg Collection, Milwaukee, Wisconsin; Musée d'Art, Hatien du Collège St. Pierre, Port-au-Prince, Haiti; Studio Museum in Harlem, New York.

*   *   *

In the world of art, it sometimes happens that two or more people of the same family, especially siblings, are endowed with extraordinary talent and drive. Both achieve success in the terms they set out for themselves. Though perhaps more common in the theater and in music—think of such families from the stage as the Redgraves and the Sheens and from music, the Jackson siblings and the Dorsey brothers—the situation also occurs in visual art. In Europe Jan and Hugo van Eyck, the Flemish artists of the northern Renaissance, come to mind. In the United States of the nineteenth century, the founder of the painting dynasty Charles Wilson Peale and his sons stand out. In the twentieth century, the extended Wyeth family is an example of an artistic dynasty. Among African American families, Joseph and Beauford Delaney are prime examples.

Haiti has had families of gifted painters, like the Obins of Cape Haitian. But among Haitian metal sculptors, it is the Brierre brothers, Murat and Edgar. Edgar Brierre was the older sibling, who made his first artistic contributions in painting. These paintings of landscapes and rural scenes were carefully executed.

It was not until he followed his younger brother, Murat, into the metier of sculpting metal in 1972 that Edgar found his own unique niche. Murat had already begun to produce sculptures in the mode invented by Georges Liautaud and was the more prolific of the two, in part because his career as a sculptor began earlier. But Edgar may have been the one who set an example, perhaps encouraging and making possible the ultimate achievements of his younger brother. Edgar's works in metal have a power that may evolve from his religious beliefs. He was deeply involved in voodoo, and the demons and deities of his sculpture arise from his own religious convictions.

The precise relationship between the sculptures of these two brothers remains to be determined. Rather than a true "signature," both brothers signed their work with their last name only. Unfortunately this confusion over the authorship of the brothers' metal sculptures encouraged Edgar to stop creating art. His sculpture, however, remains among the most accomplished of any Haitian artist working in metal.

—Thomas M. Shaw

BRIERRE, Murat
Haitian sculptor

Born: Mirebalais, Haiti, 1938. **Career:** Brickmason, cabinetmaker, tile setter, and blacksmith. **Family:** Brother of Edgar Brierre. **Died:** 1988.

Individual Exhibitions:

1967	Haitian Art Gallery, New York
1968	Centre d'Art, Port-au-Prince, Haiti
	Bradley Galleries, Milwaukee, Wisconsin
	Georgetown Graphics Gallery, Washington, D.C.
	Menschoff Gallery, Chicago
	John Michael Kohler Arts Center, Sheboygan, Wisconsin
	Roko Gallery, New York
1969	Centre d'Art, Port-au-Prince, Haiti
	Showcase Gallery, Washington, D.C.
	Botolph Group, Boston
1970	Centre d'Art, Port-au-Prince, Haiti
1971	Centre d'Art, Port-au-Prince, Haiti
1972	Centre d'Art, Port-au-Prince, Haiti
	Roko Gallery, New York
1973	Centre d'Art, Port-au-Prince, Haiti
1979	Areta Contemporary Design, Boston

Selected Group Exhibitions:

1969	Davenport Art Gallery, Iowa
1974	Davenport Art Gallery, Iowa
1978	Brooklyn Museum, New York (traveling)
1980	Davenport Art Gallery, Iowa
1982	Studio Museum in Harlem, New York
1983	Chicago Public Library Cultural Center
1985	Davenport Art Gallery, Iowa
1987	Musée du Panthéon National, Port-au-Prince, Haiti
1988	Galeries Nationales d'Exposition du Grand Palais, Paris
1989	Museum of Art, Ft. Lauderdale, Florida

Collections:

Centre d'Art, Port-au-Prince, Haiti; Davenport Museum of Art, Iowa; Flagg Collection, Milwaukee, Wisconsin; Musée d'Art Haitien du Collège St. Pierre, Port-au-Prince, Haiti; New Orleans Museum of Art, Perry E. Smith Collection; Studio Museum in Harlem, New York.

Publications:

On BRIERRE: Book—*Tracing the Spirit: Ethnographic Essays on Haitian Art* by Karen McCarthy Brown, University of Washington Press, Seattle, and Davenport Museum of Art, Iowa, 1995.

*   *   *

As an important innovator of modern Haitian metal sculpture, Murat Brierre expanded the scale, formal complexity, and emotional range of this highly original form of indigenous expression. Brierre borrowed from and advanced techniques developed by Georges Liautaud, progenitor of the metal tradition in Haiti. Surplus oil drums, hammered flat, provide the raw material for the sculptures. Once the drum is flattened, a design is drawn on the sheet with chalk and then incised with a razor or similar tool. Next,

Murat Brierre: *Four Sirens,* c.1966. Photo courtesy of Davenport Museum of Art.

in a laborious process, the metal sheet is cut with a hammer and chisel. Finally, detail work and finishing with a file complete the process.

Brierre's sculptures typically range from three to six feet in length and portray themes from Christianity, voodoo, and folklore. A recurrent motif in Brierre's oeuvre is voodoo *lwas,* or spirits, which personify the mysteries of nature and human activity. An important deity for the seafaring Haitians is La Sirene, wife of Agwe, the sea spirit whose corollary in classical mythology would be Poseidon (Neptune). In one of Brierre's depictions of the sea spirit, *Four Sirens* (c.1966), the large central figure and the figure on the left have the whimsical appearance and simple design of Liautaud's benevolent figures. More malevolent forms rising from within and on the right of the sculpture, however, indicate the broad range of expression that can be found even within single works by Brierre. The transformation of La Siren in the work suggests the changing aspects of the sea, which can be either a provider or a destructive force. The iconic central figure, emphasized by the negative space of the cutout metal, may be an ancestor risen up from Ginen (Africa) through the sea.

Brierre returned to this theme in 1977 in the work *Four Sirens,* but by the mid-1970s his sculpture had evolved to include greater areas of cutout space that surrounded long, elegantly curving lines of metal in organically unified compositions. As Selden Rodman has pointed out in *Where Art Is Joy,* in Brierre's cutout metal sculpture *Lwa* (c.1975) the fluidity of the spirit metamorphosing seems to defy the prosaic industrial medium.

Crucifixions have also been a recurring motif for Brierre. A symbol with various meanings in the voodoo mélange of African religions and Roman Catholicism, the crucifix can signify the crossroads between earthly and spiritual realms, between life and death. In one of his crucifixes from around 1970 Brierre's prominent signature on Christ's chest alludes to the artist's romantic identification with the Savior.

Brierre's expressiveness and formal innovations in large-scale sculpture contributed to his reputation as one of the leading Haitian sculptors of the period from the mid-1960s through the 1980s. Sometimes elegant in design, at other times created with the powerful simplicity of Liautaud, Brierre's works exhibit an exceptional sensitivity to the graphic potential of metal sculpture by emphasizing the outlines and shapes of the metal forms and, most importantly, the design of the cutout areas. His conception of metal sculpture as a whole, or gestalt, of the positive and negative spaces influenced the works of the most important contemporary metal artists, as, for example, the baroque explorations of Serge Jolimeau.

—Brady Roberts

BROODHAGEN, Karl (Rupert)

Barbadian painter, sculptor, and drawer

Work also appeared under the name Broodie. **Born:** British Guiana (now Guyana), 4 July 1909. **Education:** Goldsmiths College, London, 1952-54. **Family:** Married Morestina Smith in 1940, one daughter, three sons (two deceased). **Career:** Professional tailor, c.1925-47; founder, art department, 1947, head of art department, 1947-74, Combermere School, Barbados, West Indies. Continued teaching at Combermere School, 1974-96, with no formal title. Visiting instructor, Trinidad Arts Society, Port of Spain, 1957, Grenada Arts Society, St. Georges, 1959, San Fernando Arts Society, Trinidad, 1961, Visual Arts Society of the Cayman Islands/Cayman National Cultural Foundation, 1996. Since 1944 member, Barbados Arts and Crafts Society (now Barbados Arts Council). Since 1957 member, Barbados Museum and Historical Society. **Awards:** British Council Scholarship, Goldsmiths College, 1952; Queen's Jubilee Medal, Barbados, 1977; Gold Crown of Merit, Barbados, 1982; International Award of Excellence, Drexel International Forum, 1991; Outstanding Contribution to the Development of Fine Arts in Barbados Award, National Cultural Foundation, 1991; Outstanding Lifetime Contribution to Developing the Arts Award, Shell Antilles and Guianas, Ltd., St. Lucia, 1992. **Address:** Glenrosa, Strathclyde, St. Michael, Barbados.

Individual Exhibitions:

1952	Barbados Museum and Historical Society
1953	Hans Crescent Hostel, London
1956	British Council Gallery, Bridgetown, Barbados
1960	Barbados Museum and Historical Society
1970	Pelican Gallery, Bridgetown, Barbados (since 1970 annual exhibition with his son Virgil Broodhagen)
1985	Queen's Park Gallery, Barbados (retrospective, sculpture)
1991	Queen's Park Gallery, Barbados (retrospective, painting)

Selected Group Exhibitions:

1944	Ice House Building, Bridgetown, Barbados
1947	Young Men's Christian Association, Barbados
1972	*CARIFESTA I,* Georgetown, Guyana
1976	*CARIFESTA II,* Georgetown, Guyana
1979	*CARIFESTA III,* Havana
1981	Barbados Community College
1993	Caribart, Curacao

Collections:

Adams-Burrow-Cummins (ABC) Highway, Barbados; Barbados Gallery of Art, Bridgetown, Barbados; Drexel University, Philadelphia; Government headquarters, Bridgetown, Barbados; Government of Antigua, St. John's; Government of St. Kitts, Basserterre, St. Kitts; Hilton Hotel, Bridgetown, Barbados; Independence Arch, Bridgetown, Barbados; Louis Lynch Secondary School, Bridgetown, Barbados; Samuel Jackman Prescod Polytechnic, Barbados; UNESCO, Paris; University Chapel, U.C.W.I. Mona, Jamaica; University of the West Indies, Cave Hill, Barbados.

Publications:

On BROODHAGEN: Articles—"The Art of Karl Broodhagen," in *Sepia Art* (London), November 1953, pp. 5-6; "Karl Broodhagen: Man and Work" by John Wickham, in *Bajan* (Barbados), pp. 24-28; "Karl Broodhagen" by David Gall, in *International Review of African American Art,* 7(1), pp. 57-64.

*

Karl Broodhagen comments:

My carvings are more creative in the sense that, with an idea, I work with a couple of sketches directly, and change as the work develops. For example, the *Benin Head*. At a certain stage it looked like a Benin head. I finished it that way.

[As for] *Serenity*: I set out to make a girl with plaits, to keep the feeling of the block of wood. It looked serene, so I called it *Serenity*. I look more for charcter in men, and beauty in women, not cosmetic beauty, the aforementioned qualities.

(From *Tribute: An Exhibition of the Sculpture of Karl Broodhagen,* Barbados, National Cultural Foundation, 1985.)

*   *   *

Karl Broodhagen's response to and harmonious existence within his immediate environment inspired his work. His irrepressible curiosity, modesty, and unreserved enthusiasm made him the consummate artist and teacher, and he well deserved the title "father of Barbadian art," despite his Guyanese origins. The confluence of Caribbean cultures he embodied, combined with a true generosity of spirit, enabled him to share his talent, knowledge, and vision with many people. His work served as a signpost for a profound revolution in the Caribbean artistic consciousness, and in Barbados he reintroduced a lost sculptural heritage, using indigenous resources.

In the 1930s, inspired by memories of his artistic family, Broodhagen began to experiment with oils. Like others conditioned within a colonial society, he initially accepted the assumption of European superiority and authority in the creation of a visual language.

Instinctually responding to the multicultural face of the West Indian community, however, he soon discovered his raison d'être as an artist by exploring the rich racial mélange that defines the Caribbean.

Although he was largely self-taught, a few photographs and a book by Albert Toft fueled Broodhagen's curiosity and guided his first attempts at clay modeling. Apart from neoclassical memorial works imported from Europe, the clay heads of the Austrian expatriate Fela de Kuh were the first actual sculptures Broodhagen saw. His early portraits, which directly transcribed Caribbean features without attempting to pierce the tensions pervading the Caribbean psyche, have been somewhat arbitrarily dismissed as "photographic" and lacking depth. In turning to sculpture, however, Broodhagen quickly came to recognize that photographic exactitude was not required. Heads of the young novelist George Lamming (1945) and the prominent politician Grantley Adams (1947) were more assertive explorations of character than form.

The year 1952 was a watershed for Broodhagen. He modeled a bust of John Beckles in terra-cotta, a seminal work in his career. The huge dome of the forehead, the prominent nose and full-lidded eyes, and the heavy jowls convey the weightiness and mobility of a lived-in face not present in his earlier work. The artist rigorously excluded the superficiality of his subject's moods and emotions, which he regarded as transitory distractions. Rather, his work exhibits an intuitive grasp of the subject's elemental being, with a sure, sensitive rendering of the physiognomy.

Later that year Broodhagen became the first black artist from Barbados to receive art training in London. It was Broodhagen's encounter with non-European cultures, particularly African art, in museums, however, that inspired him. His exposure to Benin bronzes and to Ife and Egyptian forms among others led to the revelation of ancestral memory, and Broodhagen was inspired to articulate a new ethos in his work.

While Broodhagen's work was not radically transformed by this experience, it triggered a process of rediscovery and redefinition of his African Caribbean identity. The artist synthesized these concepts in a series of works that included *Neferdine* (1961) and *Benin Head* (1971), representing his so-called naturalistic style. The monumentality and simplicity of the frontal, symmetrical heads is compelling, expressive of power and intimacy, with the stylized texturing of the hair forming an integral part of the whole.

Denied an opportunity to further his studies in Africa, Broodhagen returned home to produce some of his most successful paintings—portraits of women influenced by the sensuous patterning of Paul Gauguin's Tahitian work. The portrait of Ann-Marie Asing (1957), for example, is a sharply delineated study exuding controlled power and tension. Within an arabesque of bold color and line, Asing is effectively defined by her restless ivory hands.

Broodhagen's work reached its zenith with his celebrated *Emancipation Statue* (1985). Commissioned to commemorate the 150th anniversary of Emancipation, the ungainly bulk of the nude male freeing himself from the bondage of slavery aroused more ire than acclaim. Surrounded by controversy, the figure swiftly acquired trousers, but it soon came to symbolize the storm of uncertainty encompassing a people proud of their independence but still shadowed by the menace of disenfranchisement.

Broodhagen's contemplation of African cultures was in the vanguard of social change, but it was the artist's striving for balance that enabled him to imbue his work with an irreducible integrity that still resonates today.

—Alissandra Cummins

BROWN, Everald

Jamaican sculptor and painter

Born: St. Ann, Jamaica, 1917. **Education:** Staceyville Primary School, Clarendon, Jamaica. **Career:** Carpenter and priest. **Awards:** Bronze Festival Medal, 1970; Silver Musgrave Medal, Institute of Jamaica, 1974; National Gallery of Jamaica Artist Fellowship, 1978. **Address:** Murray Mountain, St. Ann, Jamaica.

Selected Group Exhibitions:

1969	Creative Arts Centre, Kingston
1972	Kingston and St. Andrew Parish Library, Kingston
	Art Gallery, Organization of American States, Washington, D.C.
1976	*Eight Jamaican Primitives,* Havana, Cuba
1977	Institute of Jamaica, Kingston
1978	Museum of Modern Art of Latin America, Washington, D.C.
1982	Harmony Hall, Ocho Rios, Jamaica
1983	National Gallery of Jamaica, Kingston, and Smithsonian Institution, Washington, D.C. (traveling)
	National Gallery of Jamaica, Kingston
1986	National Gallery of Jamaica, Kingston
	Art Gallery, Commonwealth Institute, London
1987	National Gallery of Jamaica, Kingston

Collections:

Museum of Modern Art of Latin America, Washington, D.C.; National Gallery of Jamaica, Kingston; Olympia International Art Centre, Kingston; Wadsworth Atheneum, Hartford, Connecticut.

*   *   *

The painter and sculptor Everald Brown ranks with John Dunkley and Mallica "Kapo" Reynolds as one of Jamaica's foremost intuitive artists. He began exhibiting in the late 1960s and was soon included in major local and international exhibitions.

Brown was born in rural Jamaica and moved to West Kingston in 1947. There he became involved in Rastafarianism, which was then in its formative stage. Like many Rastafarians, he was attracted to the rites of the Ethiopian Orthodox Church as an ecclesiastical framework for his beliefs. Around 1960 he established a small church community as an unofficial mission of the Ethiopian Orthodox Church.

Brown's earliest documented works were the crude wall paintings and ritual objects he made for his church. These included a series of four allegorical paintings entitled *The Rainbow Valley* (c. 1961) and a wooden prayer staff he still uses today. These early works combined Rastafarian, Ethiopian Orthodox, revivalist and Judaic imagery with Brown's own visionary designs and augured the individualistic eclecticism of his mature work. His church, which he called The Assembly of the Living, attracted many local and overseas visitors, which aided his entry into the mainstream art world.

The images Brown presents in his paintings and sculptures are given to him in dreams and visions, which he shares with his family, especially his wife, Jenny. In the 1970s he collaborated closely with his son Clinton, who is also a painter. The painting *Ethiopian Apple* (1970), a prime example of his use of polymorphic images and a central piece of the National Gallery of Jamaica's collection, is typical of the early 1970s. The title is a pun on the name Otaheite apple, a popular fruit in Jamaica. The emblematic central figure in the composition is at once an Otaheite tree and a hieratic figure that symbolizes humanity's oneness with nature, a principal tenet of Brown's personal beliefs and Rastafarianism in general. Verbal and visual punning is common in Jamaican popular culture, especially in Rastafarian circles, where it is usually based on mystical association. In Brown's work punning becomes a powerful imaginative device that has led him far beyond the established Rastafarian iconography.

Although Brown is better known as a painter, he is also an accomplished sculptor. His carvings of the early 1970s, such as *Lion Rider* (c. 1972), are of particular interest for their elegant, dynamic forms. His famous musical instruments also date from the early 1970s. While he initially made them for performances with his family, they can be regarded as painted sculptures. Their general form is symbolic, usually a dove or a star, and they are covered with intricate symbolic patterns. The instruments culminated in the spectacular dove-shaped *Instrument for Four People* (1986), which combines a drum, a guitar, a harp, and a rumba box.

Frustrated with the increasingly politicized and violent climate in West Kingston, Brown moved in 1973 to the remote district of Murray Mountain in Saint Ann, not far from where he was born. When his plans to reestablish his church did not materialize, he embarked on an increasingly personal spiritual search based on mystical communion with the environment. His work changed accordingly, and he began to use associative processes inspired by the suggestive karst landscape and limestone formations that surround him, which he calls "the imprints of time." His *Bush Have Ears* (1976), for instance, depicts a near monochromatic hilly green landscape that is, on closer inspection, filled with a myriad of figures hidden in the calligraphic patterns that cover the surface.

Although he has yielded to a certain amount of mass production, especially of his musical instruments, which are in demand in the Jamaican tourist sector, Brown continues producing major works. In recent years these have included the *Instrument for Four People* (1986) and *Duppy Tree* (1994).

—Veerle Poupeye

BROWN, Grafton Tyler

American printmaker and painter

Born: Harrisburg, Pennsylvania, 22 February 1841. **Career:** Worked for Kuchel and Dresel (lithographers), San Francisco, c.1861-67. Founder, G.T. Brown and Company (lithography business), San Francisco, 1867. Draftsman, Saint Paul Engineer Office, Minnesota, 1882-96. Member, Amos Boman Geological Party, 1882, Portland Art Club, 1889. **Died:** 2 March 1918.

Exhibitions:

1871   Grant Lodge of the State of Nevada
       Mechanics Institute Fair

1972   *Grafton Tyler Brown: Black Artist of the West,* Oakland
       Museum, California

1986   Museum of History and Industry, Seattle

Collections:

British Archives, Victoria, British Columbia; California Afro-American Museum Foundation; Hampton University Museum, Virginia; National Museum of American Art, Washington, D.C.; Oakland Museum, California; State Museum of Washington, Olympia; Wells Fargo Museum, Los Angeles and San Francisco.

Publications:

By BROWN: Book—*Illustrated History of San Mateo County,* G.T. Brown and Company, n.d., (illustrated by author).

On BROWN: Book—*Grafton Tyler Brown, Nineteenth Century American Artist* by Thurlow Tibbs, 1988. **Articles**—"Review of Brown Exhibition," in *The Victoria Colonist* (British Columbia), 5 July 1883; "Grafton T. Brown," in *A History of African-American Artists, From 1792 to the Present* by Romare Bearden and Harry Henderson, New York, Pantheon Books, 1993, p. 52-53; "Grafton Tyler Brown: Selling the Promise of the West" by Lizzetta LeFalle-Collins, in *The International Review of African American Art: Nineteenth Century African American Artists of the North and West,* 12(1), 1995.

*   *   *

The San Francisco lithographer, cartographer, and painter Grafton Tyler Brown was a prolific producer of commercial lithographs and maps during the 1860s, when many African Americans remained enslaved, and during the 1870s, when, after being freed, they had few skills that would effectively aid them in realizing their freedom. Brown's early work, maps of claims and city boundaries in the Nevada Territory, and his later views of towns and ranches in the Bay Area documented settlements, developments, and the selling of the American West. His finely done *Virginia City* (1865) stands as one of the most important drawings of that town. The view was drawn by Brown when he was sent to the Nevada Territory to document the area by his initial lithographic employer, C. C. Kuchel of San Francisco. This and other views were finely rendered scenes that stood as official documents because of their exactness and recognizability. They emphasized both the ordering of the landscape through architecture and enclosures and the taming of the wilderness through the clearing of the land for future development.

Buying his employer's business after his death in 1865, Brown held accounts for bill heads, stock certificates, and other commercial lithography that included accounts from Levi Strauss, Wells Fargo Mining, and Ghirardelli Chocolate. His business was brisk among mining companies. While the boom that was initiated by the discovery of gold at Sutter's Mill in 1848 had dried up for the individual miner, large companies mining gold, silver, and other metals remained big producers in northern California and in Nevada and the adjoining territories, and Brown flourished from their business.

To help sustain themselves, draftsmen and lithographers like Brown often obtained subscribers for their bird's-eye views of cities by soliciting individual businessmen to use vignettes of their firms as borders. Businessmen found that including their firms along the borders of a city view helped market their establishments within the context of the stability of the city. Such views encouraged commerce within the city and drew families and individuals who were looking to relocate to the Western frontier. The drawings helped to win the confidence of potential settlers who wanted assurance that basic services would be satisfied by commercial enterprises and that they would have access to many of the goods they had grown accustomed to in the East. It was Brown's city views and the techniques he developed as a lithographer, along with his experience in plein air drawing, that helped prepare him for the move from the world of commercial lithography to that of the professional fine art painter.

Brown left San Francisco for Canada in 1882, joining the Amos Boman geological survey party to work in the Fraser River area. After completing his tasks with the surveyors, he opened a painting studio in Victoria in British Columbia and advertised himself as a landscape artist. He painted more than twenty-two views of Victoria locales and also painted views of places in Washington, Oregon, and California and in Yosemite and Yellowstone National Parks. *View of Lake Okanagan, British Columbia* (1883) is an excellent example of his painted landscapes that show the vastness and unspoiled nature of the Western environment. Such landscapes seem to revere the land for its natural beauty rather than for its potential for exploitation and development. Brown later settled in the Saint Paul area of Minnesota, where he worked as a civil engineer. His career as an artist seemed to have ceased then, for there are no major landscapes known from this period of his life.

—Lizzetta LeFalle-Collins

BROWN, Samuel Joseph, Jr.

American painter, printmaker, and sculptor

Work also appeared under the name Sam Brown. **Born:** Wilmington, North Carolina, 16 April 1907. **Education:** Pennsylvania Museum and School of Industrial Art (now Philadelphia University of the Arts), Philadelphia, 1926-30, B.A. in art education 1930; University of Pennsylvania, Philadelphia, M.F.A. **Career:** Teacher, Bok Vocational School, Philadelphia, and in other schools in Camden, New Jersey, and Philadelphia, 1938-1971. Appointed to Public Works Arts Project, a component of Works Progress Administration's Federal Arts Project, 1933. Member, Philadelphia Water Color Club, National Forum of Professional Artists, International Graphic Arts Educational Association, Delaware Valley Artists Guild. **Awards:** First Prize, National Competition Serigraphy in Colors; First Prize, Latham Foundation National Competition; First Prize in sculpture, Willingborg Art Show, New Jersey; One of the Best 100 Designs, *House Beautiful* cover competition, 1928, 1930, 1933. **Died:** 23 October 1994.

Selected Exhibitions:

1928	Philadelphia Museum of Art
1930	Philadelphia Museum of Art
1933	Pennsylvania College of Art, Philadelphia (solo)
	Harmon Foundation, New York
1934	Pennsylvania Museum of Art, Philadelphia

	Corcoran Gallery of Art, Washington, D.C.
1935	Howard University, Washington, D.C.
	Museum of Modern Art, New York
	New Jersey State Museum, Trenton
1936	University of Pennsylvania, Philadelphia
	Temple University, Philadelphia
1937	Philadelphia Museum of Art
	Baltimore Museum of Art, Maryland
	Museum of Modern Art, New York
1939	*New Horizons in American Art,* Museum of Modern Art, New York (traveling)
1941	South Side Community Center, Chicago
1946	Barnet Aden Galleries, Washington, D.C.
1966	Bryn Mawr Baptist Church, Pennsylvania
1968	River Park Community Gallery, Philadelphia
1969	John Wanamaker Store Gallery, New York
	National Forum of Professional Artists, Philadelphia
1970	National Forum of Professional Artists, Philadelphia
	James A. Porter Gallery of African American Art, New York
1971	Newark Museum, New Jersey
	National Convention of Negro Physicians

Collections:

Hamilton Elementary School, Philadelphia; Howard University; Huey Elementary School, Philadelphia; Hyde Park Elementary School; International Ladies Garment Workers, Philadelphia; Metropolitan Museum of Art, New York; National Archives, Washington, D.C.; Philadelphia Museum of Art; Temple University, Philadelphia.

Publications:

On BROWN: Articles—"Advance on the Art Front" by Alain Locke, in *Opportunity,* March 1939; "Howard University Gallery: Paintings by Three Artists are Displayed," in *Washington Star,* 18 February 1940; "Chicago's New Southside Art Center" by Alain Locke, in *American Magazine of Art,* August 1941; "Negro Art Given Full Length Review in Show," in *Art Digest,* 15 December 1941; "Samuel Brown Exhibits Mexican Watercolors," in *Philadelphia Art Alliance Bulletin,* 10, December 1946.

* * *

Samuel Joseph Brown's pursuit of art began when he was a small child. He won his first art award while in the fourth grade at the James Logan Elementary School in Philadelphia. His earliest training in art was at the Public Industrial Art School of Philadelphia to which he was recommended by his seventh grade teacher. Brown worked as an artist for a commercial printing company while attending the South Philadelphia High School, and his early training included silkscreen printing and sign painting.

After graduating from high school, Brown attended the Pennsylvania Museum School of Industrial Art (now the Philadelphia University of the Arts), where he majored in art education. He graduated from the museum school in 1930 and had his first solo show there that same year. In 1933 he was appointed to the Public Works Arts Project, a component of the Works Progress Administration's Federal Arts Project. This proved to be a major stepping-stone for Brown to an exciting and prolific career as an artist and educator.

Many of his early works for the project included murals in churches and restaurants. Commissioned by the Philadelphia Regional Office of the Federal Arts Project to paint portraits, Brown was one of the few African American artists to participate in the program on a national level.

During this time he also participated in numerous group shows at such venues as the Harmon Foundation in New York, the Baltimore Museum of Art, the University of Pennsylvania, Howard University, the Corcoran Gallery of Art, and the Museum of Modern Art. In 1939 the Museum of Modern Art organized an exhibition entitled *New Horizons in American Art,* which traveled to Paris. His painting of a Philadelphia woman, *Mrs. Simmons,* was the only work by an African American artist to be exhibited at the Paris showing. His work attracted favorable attention from Fiske Kimball, the director of the Philadelphia Museum of Art, who recommended Brown for a number of commissions. The museum also selected several of his paintings for its collection, including his self-portrait, *Smoking My Pipe,* and *The Lynching.*

Although he worked in a variety of media including linoprints, lithographs, dryprints, vitrograph prints, and serigraphs, Brown found his oeuvre in watercolors. His proficiency is demonstrated especially in portraiture but also in landscapes and abstract painting. The work he created displays a facility, knowledge, and control of the medium that qualifies his as masterworks.

Brown's work with the WPA led to many private commissions, particularly portraits. He produced numerous images of social and civic leaders of the Philadelphia area, as well as those whom he referred to as "living on the Main Line" (an affluent community on the outskirts of Philadelphia proper). He also painted pictures depicting the lives of children and the ordinary, hardworking people he knew from his family, community, and church. Examples include *Little Boy Blue, The Twins,* and *Child with a Toy Horn.*

His painting *So Tired* depicts a black woman on her knees, cleaning the floor. The figure is slightly out of perspective, her posture iconic. The woman's hands are as important as her face, balancing her and the composition and conveying a hardworking blues history. Gazing out of the piece from the kneeling position, she seems resigned to her fate of hard work and monotony. Brown has forced the viewer to meet her on her terms, to feel her pain and angst. Yet there is a quiet power and fortitude reflected in the glazed, faraway look in the woman's eyes, which are set in a face veiled in sorrow. This painting touched Eleanor Roosevelt when she saw it at an exhibit held at the Corcoran Gallery in Washington, D.C., in 1934. Twelve years later, in 1946, she visited Brown at his Philadelphia studio and wrote of the visit and her recollection of the painting, *The Scrub Woman,* which she called "exceptionally striking."

In addition to making works for exhibitions, artists who participated in the WPA were also responsible for graphic designs and illustrations for various publications. Brown's illustrations appeared in such magazines as the *Crisis* and *Opportunity.* His work was also reproduced in *Art Digest, Art News,* Alain Locke's *Negro Art,* James Porter's *Modern Negro Art,* and *Fortune,* among others.

The social consciousness reflected in his subject matter serves to confirm his commitment to making art that functioned both as a record of the people he encountered and as a barometer of his perceptions of the political climate in which he lived during the Great Depression, World War II, and the postwar era. The images Brown painted, drew, and printed are poignant and serenely beautiful. His use of dramatic highlights and shadow make these simple compositions come alive. His technique was unusual in that the figures in his paintings are often somewhat distorted, their per-

spectives and postures slightly off or exaggerated as if they are physical reflections of the uneasy social climate in which they existed. This evoked strong criticism of his style. James Porter noted that "many judged the work shockingly amateurish and grotesque."

Brown worked concurrently in abstraction and realism, frequently drawing on sociohistorical themes. He often addressed the historical injustices suffered by the victims of racism and war. *The Lynching* is a searing commentary on the tragic legacy of mob violence against black Americans and the continuing failure of the law to prevent it. The viewer is placed in the uneasy position of looking up into the tree and is forced to participate in the raw emotionalism of the moment through the position of the victim, the distorted perspective of the composition, and the raw horror of the act. Dr. J. Clay Smith said of Brown, "Samuel J. Brown is not trained as a lawyer, but several of his canvases are legal briefs, calling for social and economic justice for Afro-Americans."

—Nashormeh N.R. Lindo

BROWNE, Vivian (E.)
American painter and graphic artist

Born: Laurel, Florida, 26 April 1929. **Education:** Hunter College of New York, B.S. 1950, M.A. 1958; Art Students League, New York; Pratt Institute; New School for Social Research. **Career:** Teacher of fine arts, Booker T. Washington High School, Columbia, South Carolina, 1950-53, Queens Junior High School, Brooklyn, New York, 1953-56, Newton High School, Queens, New York, 1956-65; superintendent of art, New York Board of Education, 1966-68, assistant to the director, 1968-71; chair, art department, Rutgers University, Newark, New Jersey, 1975-78. Beginning 1985 professor of art, Rutgers University, Newark, New Jersey. Visiting assistant professor, University of California, Santa Cruz, 1983-84. Organizer, *Women Artists Series,* Rutgers University, Newark, New Jersey. Representative, Artists Delegation to the People's Republic of China, 1976. **Awards:** Painting Fellowship, Huntington Hartford University, 1964; achievement award, National Association of Business and Professional Women, 1965; MacDowell Colony Painting Fellowship, 1980; Artist Honoree of the Year, NYFAI, 1988; Distinguished Teacher of Art Award, College Art Association, 1989. **Died:** 1993.

Selected Exhibitions:

Bronx Museum of the Arts (1985); Douglass College Art Gallery, Rutgers University, New Jersey (1983 and 1993); Franklin and Marshall College, Lancaster, Pennsylvania (1983); June Kelly Galleries (1993, posthumous); Museum of Modern Art, New York; P.S.1, New York; Robeson Gallery, State University of New Jersey (1993, posthumous); Soho 20, New York (1982, 1989, 1993, posthumous); Studio Museum in Harlem, New York.

Publications:

On BROWNE: Articles—"And So It Is" by Henri Ghent, in *School Arts,* 68, April 1969, pp. 21-26; "Talking to Vivian Browne" by

Leo Hamalian, in *BALF,* 19, Spring 1985, pp. 48-49; "Review" by Michael Brenson, in *New York Times,* 23 June 1989; "Review" by Arlene Raven, in *Village Voice,* 20 June 1989.

*   *   *

Like many artists Vivian Browne displayed changes in techniques and subject matter, but her basic, underlying theme remained constant. Browne's paintings show the vulnerable relationship between living things and their environments. Her choice of living subjects was either humankind or the world of plants, the difference being that humans can ultimately choose their environment whereas a tree, for example, cannot. In either case Browne's work explores the constant struggle between the subjects and their imposed surroundings.

In her painting *Seven Deadly Sins* (1967) there are, curiously, eight faces, but only one figure is engaged in an identifiable activity—drinking from a bottle. The figures are out of proportion, and it seems unclear which body corresponds to each of the sins (lust, envy, pride, greed, sloth, anger, and gluttony) depicted. One face appears to have the body of a dog, while another is putting his bare foot up to his mouth. The painting is a group portrait that represents all of humanity and implies the outcome of sinful activity—a nightmarish place, maybe hell. The overall effect is eerie and grotesque. *Two Men* (1966) and *Dancer* (1968) also feature human subjects. The heads and upper bodies of the figures are much larger than the legs and feet. In *Two Men* one man seems to be communicating with the viewer while the other has his head thrown back in despair. *Dancer* shows another disproportionate figure—a man dancing alone. The viewer gets the impression that the dancer would like to join in with others but, for whatever reason, cannot. *Getting Out* (1969) shows a face looming out of a dark background. All of these paintings impart a feeling of alienation.

Browne created many paintings in which trees are juxtaposed with images of large steel communications towers. Both the trees and towers are seen from angles that make the viewer aware of the similarity in their essential structures—man-made constructions are often engineered using patterns or designs borrowed from nature. The similarity between the structures adds a sense of irony—that a borrowed object could pose a threat. It is interesting that the earth, in which both of these subjects are presumed to be anchored, cannot be seen. To the viewer the trees and towers exist only in the sky. *Versatile Source* (1987) shows a tree painted against a light background—a beautiful outdoor scene—while the tower is seen against a dark, threatening background. The title of the painting and the use of a light versus dark background allows the viewer to make a quick interpretation. *Gigantea I & II* (1989) is a diptych in which the communications towers are superimposed over giant trees, an incongruity that creates tension and confusion. In her series of paintings *Bald Ring, Burning of the Bush,* and *Global Warning* (all 1987), Browne carried the theme of nature versus technology a little further, for pieces of the tower fall onto the tree.

Browne also used an abstract approach to nature. *Tuolumne* (1985) shows a large tree viewed by looking upward from the lower trunk. The very top of the tree is not apparent, and the earth cannot be seen. Here, like many artists, Browne takes something quite usual and, by showing it from an atypical angle, makes it unrecognizable or abstract. In *Tuolumne* the eye is drawn to the lightest area on the trunk and the darkest area in the branches. This light and dark contrast enhances the abstraction. Even more abstract are *Trees, Not Flowers, Not Words* (1984) and *...collisions, rumblings and*

waters (1984). These paintings are filled with movement, and the brush strokes appear haphazard, even though they are not. Order within chaos comes to mind, the order being nature and the chaos, of course, man's intrusion upon nature. *Untitled* (1987) could be a tree represented in cubist style, pine needles and pieces of bark, or a forest after a damaging storm. In contrast to her pieces that speak to the struggle to exist, works such as *Pinacea* (1987) and *Metasequoia* (1987) set the viewer at ease. We are reminded that nature is perfect and beautiful.

—Christine Miner Minderovic

BUCHANAN, Beverly
American sculptor, painter, mixed-media artist, and photographer

Born: Fuquay, North Carolina, 8 October 1940. **Education:** Bennet College, Greensboro, North Carolina, 1958-62, B.S. 1962; Columbia University, New York, M.S. in parasitology; Columbia University, New York, M.P.H. 1969; Art Students League, New York, 1972. **Awards:** National Endowment for the Arts grant, 1980; Guggenheim Memorial Foundation Fellowship, 1980; Pollock-Krasner Foundation Award, 1994; National Endowment for the Arts Fellowship, 1994. **Agent:** Steinbaum Krauss Gallery, 132 Greene Street, New York, New York 10012, U.S.A.

Individual Exhibitions:

1972   Cinque Gallery, New York
1977   Mercer University, Macon, Georgia
1978   Truman Gallery, New York
1981   Kornblee Gallery, New York
1982   University of Alabama, Birmingham
1987   Heath Gallery, Inc., Atlanta, Georgia
1990   Bernice Steinbaum Gallery, New York
1991   Hoffman Gallery, Portland, Oregon
1994   *Beverly Buchanan: ShackWorks: A Sixteen Year Survey,* traveling retrospective
1996   Steinbaum Krauss Gallery, New York

Selected Group Exhibitions:

1988   High Museum of Art, Atlanta, Georgia
1989   University Galleries, Illinois State University, Normal
1990   Stein Gallery, Tampa, Florida
1991   Diggs Gallery, Winston-Salem State University, North Carolina
1992   Columbia Museum of Fine Art, Columbia, South Carolina
1993   Steinbaum Krauss Gallery, New York
1994   New Jersey Center for Visual Arts, Summit
         House and Home: Spirits of the South, Addison Gallery of American Art, Phillips Academy, Andover, Massachusetts (traveling)
1995   Brattleboro Museum of Art, Brattleboro, Vermont
1996   Sweet Briar College, Sweet Briar, Virginia

Beverly Buchanan, 1993. Photo by Nancy Revnes, courtesy of Steinbaum Krauss Gallery, New York.

Collections:

Amerada Hess, New York; ARCO, Pennsylvania; Carnegie Museum of Art, Pittsburgh; Chrysler Museum of Art, Norfolk, Virginia; Columbia Museum of Art, South Carolina; High Museum of Art, Atlanta; Metropolitan Museum of Art, New York; Montclair Museum of Art, Montclair, New Jersey; Museum of Art and Sciences, Macon, Georgia; Newark Museum, New Jersey; Tampa Museum of Art, Florida; Winston-Salem State University Sculpture Garden, Winston-Salem, North Carolina.

Publications:

On BUCHANAN: Books—*Beverly Buchanan (Parameters Seven),* exhibition catalog, Norfolk, Virginia, Chrysler Museum, 1992; *Beverly Buchanan,* exhibition catalog, Pittsburgh, Pennsylvania, Three Rivers Arts Festival at Bell of Pennsylvania Building, 1992; *Beverly Buchanan: In Celebration of Improvisational Architecture,* exhibition catalog, Madison, New Jersey, Shering-Plough, 1992; *Beverly Buchanan: ShackWorks: A 16 Year Study,* exhibition catalog, Montclair, New Jersey, Montclair Art Museum, 1994. **Articles**—"Beverly Buchanan," in *Art Papers,* November-December 1992, and "Story Shacks," in *Port Folio,* 19, September 1992, both by Linda McGreevy; "Celebrating Shack Dwellers," in *Athens,* 5(4),

October 1993, and "Artist Lifts Southern Shacks out of the Mud, to Level of Art," in *Georgia Journal,* 14(1), Spring 1994, both by Tom Hudson; "Portfolio: Beverly Buchanan" by Anthony C. Murphy, in *American Visions,* 9(4), August/September 1994.

*   *   *

Beverly Buchanan was born in and still resides in the South. She grew up on the campus of South Carolina State University in Orangeburg, where her father, Walter Buchanan, was dean of the School of Agriculture. Vistas of the rural south were close by and had a profound impact on the subject matter in her art. Strongly influenced by Betye Saar, she works in a variety of media, including sculpture, drawing, painting, and mixed media. She has achieved much success during the last two decades of the twentieth century and has exhibited nationally and internationally. Her works are in major museums and collections throughout the United States and abroad. She is well known for creating works in a series. Two series of note are "ShackWorks" and "Black Walls," which have brought her critical acclaim.

"Black Walls" is a series of paintings on paper from the 1970s and represents her fascination with walls and portions of walls. The "ShackWorks" series, especially from the 1980s and 1990s, locates Buchanan experientially and artistically. Born in Fuquay,

North Carolina, Buchanan witnessed ramshackle, dilapidated structures dotting the provincial, southern landscape. Her experience provided a different view regarding these buildings and the people that inhabited them. In addition to the obvious commentary these structures made on the socioeconomic plight of the poor in the South, she saw them as beautiful and enduring. The "ShackWorks" series consists of photographs, paintings, and sculptures. When Buchanan shows us these shacks, they are observed as architecture, but they also are presented as individualized "portraits," almost like people, as seen in *4 Shacks with Black-Eyed Susans* (1995, oil pastel on paper, 25 1/2" x 38").

This painting is a "family" of shacks nestled together and surrounded by flower heads that have orange rays and dark conical disks. Buchanan's selection of oil pastel as her medium makes the shacks, which are drawn in burgundy, appear rich, almost regal, in the overgrown grass and flowers. Her subtext of houses used by sharecroppers, migratory workers, and the poor does not militate against or deny the dignity and grandeur that she sees in the commonplace and mundane. She skillfully manipulates color and medium to convey her message.

Commencing in the mid-1980s, Buchanan began to work on actual sculptures of shack houses and barns. These sculptures are more than just miniatures of shacks and barns. They are evocations of the rural South and the people who call the land their own. Some of the "ShackWorks" sculptures become room-size installations. They have lyrical, sonorous names—*Robert Mathis's Yellow Root House & Table, Shack South Inside Out, Orangeburg County Family House, Hastings House,* and *Shotgun Shack.* A commissioned "ShackWorks" sculpture was erected in a park in southwest Atlanta, on Ralph David Abernathy Boulevard, in walking distance of the Atlanta University Center, where it created an interesting dialogue among denizens of the area. This particular piece from the "ShackWorks" series had the appearance of a small house and was often vandalized because intruders felt that they were breaking into an actual structure. After it was restored several times, the decision was made to dismantle the sculptural "ShackWork."

—Jontyle Theresa Robinson

BURAIMOH, Jimoh (Olatunji)

Nigerian mosaicist, graphic artist, and painter

Born: Oshogbo State, 1943. **Education:** Oshogbo art workshops, Oshogbo, 1964; Ahmadu Bello University, certificate in sculpture 1974; University of Berlin, University of Munich, 1976. **Career:** Institute of African Studies, University of Ife, Ile-Ife, Nigeria, 1968-72. Artist-in-residence, Ahmadu Bello University, Zaria, 1974; lecturer, Haystack Mountain Crafts School, Deer Isle, Maine, 1974; opened African Heritage Gallery, Oshogbo, Nigeria, 1975. Member, Associazione Internazionale Mosaicisti Contemporanei, Italy. **Address:** African Heritage Gallery, P.O. Box 113, Oshogbo, Oshun State, Nigeria.

Individual Exhibitions:

1967	Goethe Institute, Lagos
1968	Sheraton Hotel, Lagos
1970	Goethe Institute, Lagos
1973	Goethe Institute, Lagos
1975	Goethe Institute, Lagos
1977	Goethe Institute, Lagos
1979	Commonwealth Institute Art Gallery, London
1982	Goethe Institute, Lagos
1984	National Museum, Lagos
	USIS, Ibadan, Nigeria
1985	Howard University, Washington, D.C.
1988	Italian Cultural Institute, Lagos
1990	African Centre, London
	Nigerian High Commission, London

Selected Group Exhibitions:

1988	Heritage International Hotel, Oshogbo, Nigeria
	Aljira, Newark, New Jersey
	Jiraj Art Gallery, Lagos
1989	Museum Alexander Konnis, Bonn, Germany
	Centro Wifredo Lam, Havana
	Kunst aus Nigeria, Bonn, Germany
	Zeitgenössische Nigerianishe Kunst, Bonn, Bocholt, and Mönchengladbach, Germany
	Home Design Centre, Lagos
1990	National Museum, Lagos
	National Theater, Lagos

Collections:

Cleveland State University, Ohio; Iwalewa-House, Bayreuth, Germany; Mbari Art, Washington, D.C.; Museum für Völkerkunde, Frankfurt, Germany; National Gallery of Modern Art, Lagos; Studio Museum in Harlem, New York; University of Lagos.

Publications:

By BURAIMOH: Articles—"Painting with Beads," *African Arts* (Los Angeles), 5(1), Autumn 1971, pp. 16-19 (illustrated; some color); "Att mala med pärlor," in *Moderne Konst i Africa,* Lund, Sweden, Kalejdoskp, 1978, pp. 100-02 (illustrated); "Unique Creativity" (interview), in *West Africa* (London), no. 3745, 29 May-4 June 1989, p. 875.

On BURAIMOH: Books—*Jimoh Buraimoh: Creator of Bead Painting in Africa,* exhibition catalog, Victoria Island, Lagos, Goethe Institute, 1982 (illustrated); *Beadworks, Drawings, and Deep Etchings: Jimoh Buraimoh, the Creator of Bead Paintings in Africa,* exhibition catalog, Lagos, Italian Cultural Institute, 1988 (illustrated). **Article**—"Jimoh Buraimoh's Bead Paintings" by Lade Adeyanju, in *Curio Africana; Journal of Art and Criticism* (Ile-Ife, Nigeria), 1(2), 1989, pp. 89-99.

*   *   *

Jimoh Buraimoh comes from a family of artists. His mother, a well-known mat weaver and dyer, first taught him about the qualities and powers of color, which would later inform his beadwork. He assisted her in dying raffia fibers and in planning the intricate designs of wedding mats, and he also wove raffia broom handles, often with elaborate, colorful patterns.

Buraimoh began his career as an electrician in the Duro Ladipo theater group—that is, as an artist of light and color. While on tour, he saw a large wall mural being painted by the Urhobo artist Bruce Onobrakpeya and became "fascinated. . . . I loved what he was doing." He participated in an artists' workshop at Oshogbo in 1964 doing prints and paintings, but he decided that he wanted to define himself through a different medium. During a visit to Amsterdam he was inspired by a mosaic. He returned to Oshogbo, bought various pieces of colored broken pottery in the market, made a shallow wooden box that he filled with cement, and laid in colored shards, shells, and stones to create his first mosaic tablet. He began to create mosaic tables and later large wall mosaics commissioned for hotels, businesses, and universities. With advice from Jean Kennedy, an American who encouraged many Nigerian artists in the 1960s and 1970s, Buraimoh began to affix beads to cloth. He first made a series of lamp shades, sewing and gluing beads onto the fabric so that the light shined through them. His earliest bead "paintings," done in 1966, were sewn onto vinyl automobile seat covers. Later, in order to work in larger forms, he strung and glued beads onto canvas and then Masonite and plywood board.

Buraimoh uses strung beads to form the outlines in his compositions and then uses loose beads to fill in areas and suggest the tints and shades of three-dimensional form and space. He also uses loose beads to suggest continuities or, in sharply contrasting colors, to define ruptures. Among his early works in this form are *Bishop Ajayi Crowther* and *Imam*. His choice of two religious figures seems to have resulted from his family upbringing and early schooling (he attended both Koranic and Christian schools simultaneously).

During 1968-69 Buraimoh did several bead paintings on the theme of insects. As he explains, he was fascinated by the iridescent colors of these creatures. But by far the vast majority of his paintings are concerned with people, not flora and fauna. Heads and faces dominate his compositions, something he has explained by saying, "It is your head that you have to worship . . . it is destiny." The physical head (*ori*) and its spiritual counterpart (*ori inu*) are central in Yoruba philosophy and in the beaded images of Buraimoh's paintings.

By the early 1970s Buraimoh was experimenting with different styles and approaches, often combining beads and painted backgrounds. He used colors that "jumped" and paint to "blend . . . to pull the painting together." In his earlier bead- and paintworks the painting had been somewhat haphazard, although it gave a quality of low relief to the images. By 1975, after formal studio work at Ahmadu Bello University, he began to "put more energy into [the] carefulness, tidiness, and presentation" of his work. He continued with this combination of beads and pigment until 1990, when he decided to create works with beads alone, making the works "flatter."

Buraimoh's later works have continued and elaborated upon his interest in humanity. A large beaded mural entitled *People of the Universe* was commissioned by the Winston-Salem State University in North Carolina and installed over the entrance to a new dormitory there in the fall of 1994.

Since then Buraimoh has worked on a series of bead paintings about masks, inspired primarily by various Yoruba traditions. One painting honors an ancestral Egungun masker. His largest painting to date, it is about life-size. But he also has used the concept of masking to express his views on contemporary political situations. For example, one of his favorite pieces, entitled *Hidden Agenda*, refers to "two-faced" politicians and soldiers who say one thing

and do another. In a sense he has continued to return to the themes of visible faces and heads (*ori*) and of hidden inner intentions (*ori inu*) as sites of character and destiny. Thus, Buraimoh exemplifies how, building upon a vibrant visual tradition, Yoruba artists can create works that are transcultural, transnational, pan-African, and universalist in intention.

—Henry John Drewal

BURKE, Selma (Hortense)
American sculptor

Born: Mooresville, North Carolina, 31 December 1900. **Education:** Winston-Salem University, B.A.; St. Agnes Training School for Nurses, Raleigh, North Carolina, R.N. diploma 1924; Women's Medical College, Philadelphia, 1928; Columbia University, New York, M.F.A. 1941; Livingston College, Ph.D. 1970. **Career:** Art instructor, Friends Council on Education, Philadelphia, 1930-49, Saint George's School, New York, 1936-49; teacher-demonstrator, Board of Education, Pittsburgh, Pennsylvania, 1968-76. Art instructor, Sidwell School, Forest House, New York, 1946, Oakwood School, Schenectady, New York, 1950, Sidwell School, Washington, D.C., 1950, Plymouth Meeting Friends School, 1963, Haverford College, Livingston College, Solebury School, Swarthmore College, 1963-76. Founder, Selma Burke School of Sculpture, New York, 1940, Selma Burke Art Center, Pittsburgh, 1968. **Awards:** Rosenwald Foundation Fellowship, 1938; Columbia University Scholarship, New York, 1939-41; two sculpture awards, Howard University, Washington, D.C. 1940; Fine Arts Commission Award for profile of President Franklin Delano Roosevelt, District of Columbia Competition, 1943; Urban League Award, 1943; Alford Purchase Prize for sculpture, Atlanta University, Georgia, 1944; citation, Pennsylvania Governor Schaffer, 1967; citation, Pennsylvania House of Representatives, 1970; Dr. Martin Luther King Citizens Award, Pittsburgh, 1971; National Conference of Artists Award, Chicago, 1972; National Association of Negro Business and Professional Women's Clubs, Inc., Award, 1972; Pittsburgh Pupil's Program Student Affairs Nomination Award, 1971-72; V.I.P. Award, Pittsburgh, Pennsylvania, 1972; International Poetry Award, Pittsburgh, Pennsylvania, 1972; *Sculptress of World Renown,* Citizens of Mooresville, 1972; Kent State University Award for Excellence in Art, 1973; Fifty-State Bicentennial Medal Collection Hallmarked First Edition Proof Set, 1973; citation, Alpha Kappa Alpha Sorority, 1974; proclamation Selma Burke Day, City of Pittsburgh, Pennsylvania, 20 July 1975; award, Black Women's Association, Pittsburgh, Pennsylvania, 1975; fine arts award, Alabama State University, Montgomery, 1976; citation, Milwaukee County Commission, 1976; Top Hat Award, New Pittsburgh Courier, Pennsylvania, 1976; Cinque Gallery Award, New York, 1976; Weidner Prize for Sculpture, Philadelphia Academy of Fine Arts, 1976; Women's Caucus Award, Washington, D.C., 1978; Citation for Contribution to Negro Arts in America, President Carter, Washington, D.C.; citation, Moore College, Philadelphia, 1979; Ambassador of Fine Arts Award, Bucks County Chamber of Commerce, 1979; Honorary doctorates: Livingston College; University of North Carolina; Moore College of Art. **Died:** 29 August 1995.

Individual Exhibitions:

1945   Carlen Galleries, Philadelphia
1945   Modernage Gallery, New York
1952   Artists Gallery, New York
1973   William Penn Museum, Harrisburg
1974   Princeton University
        Carnegie Museum, New York
        Johnson C. Smith University
        Vassar Club, New York
        Virginia Union University

Selected Group Exhibitions:

Art Institute of Chicago; Brooklyn Museum, New York; Delaware Museum; Detroit Institute of Fine Arts; High Museum, Atlanta; Metropolitan Museum of Art, New York; Syracuse University, New York; Virginia Union University, Richmond; West Virginia Museum of Fine Arts; Whitney Museum, New York.

Publications:

On BURKE: Article—"Without Color" by Harry Schwalb, in *Art News,* 93, September 1994, p. 27.

*   *   *

In the company of a small number of distinguished African American women sculptors is Selma Hortense Burke, who achieved a high level of national recognition during her lifetime. Her accomplishments as a significant sculptor and art educator of the twentieth century and her long list of notable commissions are perhaps more noteworthy than any singular achievement. She is admired for her consummate mastery of several sculptural media, her indefatigable dedication to arts education, and her philosophical approach to creating art.

Although her life spanned almost an entire century, it was in the early stages of midlife when Burke actively pursued art as a career. Her employment as the private nurse of a wealthy heiress who later became a supportive patron left Burke financially stable during the lean years of the Great Depression. She arrived in New York City during the burgeoning of African American artistic expression and eventually became involved with the Harlem WPA project. Burke was also a member of the Harlem Artists Guild. In 1940 she opened the Selma Burke School of Sculpture and at age 41 earned her M.F.A. from Columbia University.

Her experiences as an African American woman and her intensive studies in France, Germany, and Austria in the late 1930s can be seen as critical determinants in Burke's aesthetic development. In Paris she studied the human figure with Aristide Maillol, who had a major impact on the development of modernist art of the twentieth century. Although completed in 1968, Burke's *Mother and Child* reveals her sensitivity to the human body and can be readily associated with her European influences. Her use of pink alabaster renders a smooth texture to the skin and drapery of the figures. The child's left arm reaching out to mother's face and the mother's supportive hold under the left leg and right arm of the child suggest the dynamic connection and enduring tenderness of the mother/child relationship.

The refinement of her craft as a sculptor led to the natural progression towards portraiture. Once she returned to the United States,

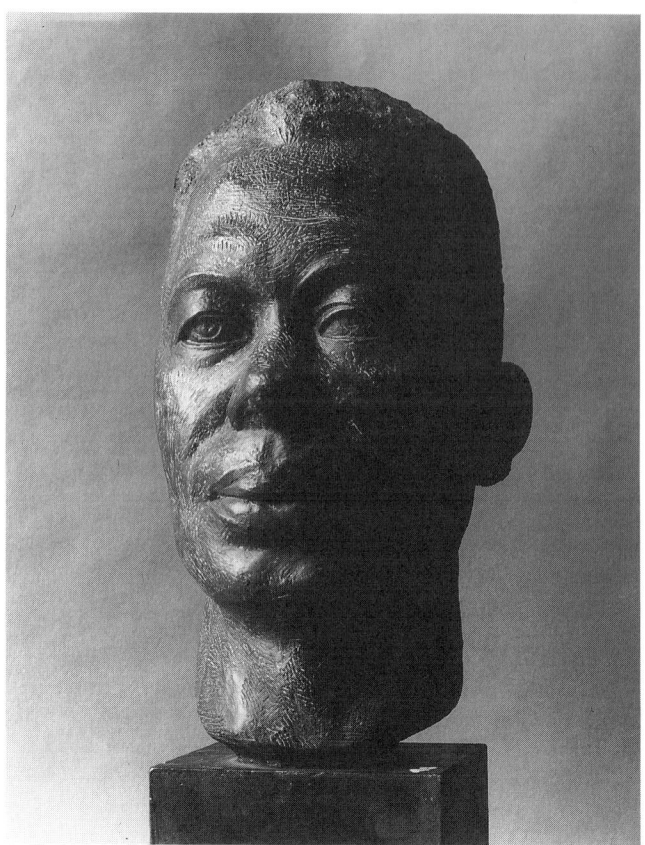

Selma Burke: *Jim.* Photo courtesy of the Schomburg Center for Research in Black Culture.

Burke received commissions for portraits of Franklin Delano Roosevelt, Mary McLeod Bethune, Martin Luther King, Jr., Duke Ellington, and a number of other luminaries. *Jim* is one of her most exemplary busts as it demonstrates her high level of skill in portraiture. The subject's disciplined and tenacious character is reflected in strong facial lines, solid features, and his intense depth of expression.

Burke's work has been described as neoclassical, and though her oeuvre encompasses mostly busts and torsos, her tendency was to interpret rather than replicate models. Her approach to sculpting the human form was to seek a kind of perfection and to imbue her figures with idealistic features, only simplifying them to give them strength. One of the artist's most notable works is *Falling Angel,* where she depicts an angel expelled from heaven. The angelic figure, which is rendered in bronze, is jettisoned in space and gliding to earth with a serpent in her grip. The long, thick elements that represent the angel's feathered wings add a density to the free falling body. Upon the face of the angel Burke crafts an expression of supplication.

In later years Burke continued to receive commissions and remained dedicated to sharing her artistic gift through education. Numerous awards, citations, and honorary degrees embellish her career achievements as a premiere artist of the twentieth century. More than these accolades, Selma Burke's sculptures remain as evidence of her considerable contributions to American figurative sculpture and African American art history.

—Regina Holden Jennings

BURNETT, Calvin (Waller)

American painter and printmaker

Born: Cambridge, Massachusetts, 18 July 1921. **Education:** Massachusetts School of Art, Boston, Massachusetts, 1938-42, B.F.A. 1950; Massachusetts College of Art, Boston, 1949-51, B.S. in education 1951; Boston University, 1957-60, M.F.A. 1960; Boston University, 1961-70, doctoral candidacy. **Family:** Married Torrey Milligan in 1960, one daughter. **Career:** Freelance commercial artist, Boston, 1945-56; instructor/professor, Massachusetts College of Art, Boston, 1956-86. Laborer, Charleston Navy Shipyard, Boston, 1942-45. **Agent:** Sragow Gallery, 73 Spring Street, New York, New York 10012, U.S.A.; Liddell Associates, 423 West Broadway, South Boston, Massachusetts 02127, U.S.A. **Address:** 87 Fisher Street, Medway, Massachusetts 02053-2232, U.S.A.

Individual Exhibitions:

1946	Boris Minski Gallery, Boston
1957	Massachusetts Institute of Technology, Cambridge
1959	Marlboro College, Marlboro, Vermont
1965	Lowell State College, Lowell, Massachusetts
1966	West Virginia State College, Institute, West Virginia
1970	Framingham State College, Framingham, Massachusetts
1982	Massachusetts College of Art, Boston (retrospective)
1993	Boston Public Library
1995	National Center of Afro-American Artists, Roxbury, Massachusetts (retrospective)

Selected Group Exhibitions:

1971	Pennsylvania State University, University Park
1979	Studio Museum in Harlem, New York
1980	Smithsonian Institute, Washington, D.C.
	Howard University, Washington, D.C.
1981	Atlanta University, Georgia
1983	Massachusetts School and College of Art, Boston
1988	Boston University
1991	Hanson-Larsen-Campell, Martha's Vineyard, Massachusetts
1993	Simmons College, Boston
	Fuller Museum, Brockton, Massachusetts

Collections:

African-American Museum and Cultural Center, Wilberforce, Ohio; Atlanta University, Georgia; Bazalel National Museum, Israel; Boston Public Library; DuSable Museum, Chicago; Ebony Publishing, Chicago; Franklin Pierce College, Chicago; Fogg Art Museum, Cambridge, Massachusetts; Howard University, Washington, D.C.; Museum of Afro-American History, Boston; Museum of Fine Arts, Boston; National Center of Afro-American Artists, Boston; National Urban League, Baltimore, Maryland; Oakland Museum, California; Simmons College, Boston; United States Army Archives, Washington, D.C.; Wellesley College, Wellesley, Massachusetts.

Publications:

By BURNETT: Book—*Objective Drawing Techniques,* New York, Reinhold, 1965.

Calvin Burnett: *Self-Portrait with Hanged Dolls.*

On BURNETT: Articles—"And No Birds Sing" by Dorothy Adlow, in *Christian Science Monitor* (Boston), 1954; "Skill Adds to Communication" by Della Taylor, in *Charleston Gazette* (Charleston, West Virginia), 1966; "Some Boston Printmakers" by Mildred Housen, in *Connoisseur* (London), 1967; "Black Artists . . . at Brandeis" by Daldwell Titcomb, in *Harvard Summer News* (Waltham, Massachusetts), 1969; "Burnett, Powers, and Morgan" by Robert Taylor, in *Boston Globe,* 1980; "The Post-Modern Manifesto" by Sarah Wright, in *Real Paper* (Boston), 1981.

*   *   *

The Boston-based Calvin Burnett is a painter, drawer, printmaker, collage artist, and educator. He has also illustrated several books and has written an instructional drawing book. Like many artists in his generation, Burnett was influenced by abstract art. His own work reflects the emerging social consciousness of the post-World War II African American art community.

Abstract expressionist in style, Burnett's oil painting *Insect* depicts what the title suggests. The subject's wings and long tail are readily identifiable. There is a suggestion of legs, although the angu-

Calvin Burnett: *KKKKK.*

lar lines that could represent legs also blend into the orange-yellow background. The insect is not in flight; the viewer does not get a sense of movement from the insect. The background, however, is very lively. The image suggests an insect imbedded in amber, conveying the idea of being trapped in time.

Three Crippled Drunks is a visually demanding print. Three men are walking, apparently drunk, entwined. The largest man, on the left, is using a crutch, and the man on the right is using a cane; both of these men are supporting the third man in the middle. The print consists of four layers of color, and along with the gestures of the figures so expertly drafted by the artist, the picture appears full of fumbling, intoxicated movement.

A disturbing and powerful work by Burnett is *KKKKK*. There is nothing subtle in this collage/drawing. The peaked, triangular shape of a Ku Klux Klan headdress is repeated several times in the picture plane. A triangular shaped flap is torn out of some draped, white fabric (a sheet?). The remaining hole is a triangle, as well as the flap of fabric hanging down. A separate, similarly shaped triangle is overlapping the flap, and another triangle is lightly drawn on top. Peering through the hole with one knowing eye is a black person. Spray painted across the fabric are the letters "KKK." An equally upsetting work is *Self Portrait with Hanged Dolls,* a graphite self-portrait of the artist. The upper right corner of the picture plane contains an upside down head of a baby doll and the hanged body of a rag doll. Burnett's art presents the haunting themes of cruelty, danger, and vulnerability. He has the ability to express human anguish in a powerful and suggestive manner.

—Christine Miner Minderovic

BURNS, Millie
American photographer and printmaker

Born: Brooklyn, New York, 25 December 1950. **Education:** Rochester Institute of Technology, New York; Parsons School of Design; School of Visual Arts, New York. **Career:** Artist/instructor/photographer, Children's Art Carnival, New York, 1989-90; gallery curator, Dance Theater Workshop, New York, 1990-93. Artist-in-residence, Children's Museum, Manhattan, New York, 1988-89; guest artist, Rotunda Gallery, Brooklyn, New York, 1992. **Awards:** Artist grant, Artist in the Marketplace, 1986-87; fellowship, Dorland Mountain Art Colony, Temecula, California. **Address:** 1024 Greene Avenue, Brooklyn, New York 11221-2911, U.S.A.

Selected Exhibitions:

1981   *Third Biennial Exhibition,* Newark Museum, New Jersey
1989   *Photosensitive,* Library of Arts, Washington, D.C.
1990   *A Decade of the Marketplace,* Bronx Museum of Arts
         Photographs of Millie Burns, En Foco, Inc., New York
1991   YWCA Gallery, Brooklyn, New York
1992   *Vision of Solitude,* One Square Mile Gallery, Seacliff, New
         York

Collections:

Art Information Center, New York; Brooklyn Museum, New York;

Canadian Imperial Bank of Commerce, New York; Museum of Hudson Highlands, New York; Museum of Modern Art, New York; New York Public Library; Percent for Art Program, Pennsylvania; Rotunda Gallery, Bronx, New York; Studio Museum in Harlem, New York.

Publications:

On BURNS: Articles—"Refreshing Talent in Two Snug Harbor Exhibits" by Marlene Schiller, in *Staten Island Advance,* 14 August 1984; "Photographs by Women Artists at Rotunda Gallery" by Stephanie Rauschenbush, in *The Prospect Press,* April 1987.

*   *   *

Millie Burns is part photographer and part painter. "I use my camera like a paintbrush," says Burns, "capturing that magical quality of light that exists in every place at one time or another." Burns does not "capture" an image but "sets [it] apart from the continuum of change." She removes nothing from the landscape but describes it for us by selection and revelation. For Burns a photograph is a method of communication that describes people, places, and events by visual rather than verbal report.

"I don't always choose what I shoot," says Burns, "it often chooses me. I celebrate the world around me through everyday objects and sights and transform these into things deserving closer scrutiny." After the image is shot and has been "set apart," Burns takes further time to transform the photograph into a final composition. She hand-colors and tones her silver gelatin prints or sometimes prints color transparencies as black-and-white photos.

A native of Brooklyn, New York, Millie Burns studied photography at the Rochester Institute of Technology, Parsons School of Design, and the School of Visual Arts. But Burns doesn't stay long in any one location. Her subjects are scattered across the globe, from California to Morocco (where her work is in the permanent collection of King Hass II of Morocco) and back to Brooklyn. What she chooses to shoot, or what chooses her, usually consists of some kind of landscape, made extraordinary by allowing the ordinary subjects to speak for themselves in the final image. "With strong, personal feelings I approach my subjects with both wonder and respect, allowing them to speak with directness and clarity." Though Burns gives much of the credit for the photograph to the subject, she is not a passive spectator. "Photography allows me to be a passionate observer and express my vision of solitude, seasons, and time, of the serene beauty in scenes left to themselves when man has departed or not been there at all."

—Terry Bain

BURROUGHS, Margaret (Taylor)
American painter

Work also appeared under the names Margaret Taylor and Margaret Taylor Goss. **Born:** Margaret Taylor, St. Rose, Louisiana, 1 November 1917. **Education:** Chicago Teachers College (now Chicago State University), 1935-37; Art Institute of Chicago, 1938-48, B.A. in education, 1946, M.A. in art education, 1948; Esmerelda Art School, Mexico City, 1952-53; Teachers College, Columbia

Margaret Burroughs, 1987.

University, summers 1958-60. **Family:** Married 1) Bernard Goss in 1939 (divorced 1947), one child; 2) Charles Gordon Burroughs in 1949, one adopted son. **Career:** Art teacher, DuSable High School, 1946-69; professor of humanities, Kennedy-King Community College, 1969-79. Since 1939 co-founder, officer, board of directors, South Side Art Community Center. Executive director, DuSable Museum of African-American History, Chicago, 1961-85; instructor, African and African-American art history, Chicago Institute of Art, 1968. **Awards:** NCA Award, 1963; American Forum for International Study Fellowship, 1968; New City Award, Better Boys Federation, 1968. Honorary doctorates: Columbia College; North Central College, Lewis University, 1972; Chicago State University, 1983; School of the Art Institute of Chicago, 1987; North Central College, 1988; Rhode Island College, 1990; De Paul University, 1995. **Address:** 3806 South Michigan Avenue, Chicago, Illinois 60653, U.S.A.

Individual Exhibitions:

1986   Nicole Gallery, Chicago
1987   Southside Community Art Center, Chicago

Selected Group Exhibitions:

1949   California Civic Museum, San Francisco
1950   Market Place Gallery, New York
1953   Kenosha Museum, Wisconsin
1961   Pulavy Place, Kazimierz-Dolney, Poland

1967   House of Friendship, Moscow
1970   Wright Art Center, Beloit, Wisconsin
1975   High Museum, Atlanta, Georgia (traveling)
1976   Los Angeles County Art Museum (traveling)
1980   Corcoran Gallery, Washington, D.C.
1992   Nicole Gallery, Chicago

Publications:

By BURROUGHS: Book—*Jasper the Drummin' Boy,* Viking, 1947 (written and illustrated under the name Margaret Taylor), Follett, 1970 (reprint under the name Margaret Burroughs, illustrated by T. Lewin); *Did You Feed My Cow?,* Crowell, 1955 (written and illustrated under the name Margaret Taylor), Follett, 1969 (reprint under the name Margaret Burroughs).

On BURROUGHS: Article—*Chicago Defender,* 9 September 1991, pp. 5, 22, 14 May 1992, p.26; "Dr. Margaret Burroughs Celebrates Her Fifty Years as Artist," in *Chicago Defender,* May 14, 1992; "DuSable Founder Blazes New Trails of Art, Culture" by Melita Marie Garza, in *Chicago Tribune,* February 10, 1993.

*   *   *

Margaret Burroughs is known for her roles as an educator, museum founder and director, writer, political activist, and role model for African Americans and women of all colors. Born in St. Rose, Louisiana, in 1917, she and her family moved to Chicago, where she has lived since. She attended the Chicago Teachers College, where she earned her degrees, and she also did postgraduate work at Columbia University.

Margaret Burroughs has been a cultural leader in the community. Since she was in her early twenties, she has founded the

Margaret Burroughs: *Two Pharoahs,* 1990. Photo courtesy of Art Richardson.

National Conference of Artists, the South Side Community Art Center, and numerous other arts organizations. In 1961 she and her husband founded the Du Sable Museum of Art, a museum of African American art in Chicago. She views her museum, which presents the United States with the positive side of the nation's African American legacy, as a prime tool for combating racism. She and her husband have been collecting for the museum since 1959, and Burroughs has stated that "the collection for the museum grew adequately because every time anyone went over to Africa, we asked people to bring us something back." Her travels throughout the world have been extensive and have included many visits to Africa, which have allowed her the opportunity to broaden her knowledge of African culture and enhance the Du Sable Museum's collection.

Burroughs has her own unique style. Her paintings are colorful, imaginative, and sincere. An avid storyteller, she has incorporated the use of storytelling into her portrayals. Most of her pieces deal with social commentary, oppression, and race-related themes. In *Faces* the artist has used an abundance of warm colors, such as reds, yellows, and oranges, to create clear expressions of skin color. The painting is of three faces, all of which contain sharp piercing eyes that beckon the viewer to look further into the piece. *Me and Picasso* (1989) uses semirealism and cubism, as well as vibrant colors, which suggest a strong likeness to the work of Picasso. Comprised of blues and purples, the painting is a still life of fruits and vegetables. Her energy is best felt in the vitality of her recent paintings, but Burroughs has also completed many prints, including woodcuts and linocuts. To further her goal of making art accessible to every home, she has turned to prints in black-and-white, which allow people who cannot afford to buy originals to buy art at modest prices.

—Gabriel Tenabe

BUTLER, David

American painter and sculptor

Born: Good Hope, Louisiana, 1898. **Career:** Sawmill laborer.

Publications:

On BUTLER: Articles—Article by M.T. Thomas, in *Contributions,* 1973, pp. 36-37; *New York Times,* 26 June 1977; *National Sculpture Review,* 25, Fall 1976, p. 3; *Ms. Magazine,* 5, January 1977, p. 27; *Art in America,* 66, January/February 1978, p. 116;"Remember Your Dream," in *American Craft,* 51, December/January 1991-92, pp. 44-45 (illustrated).

*   *   *

David Butler is the quintessential folk artist-environmentalist. Following his retirement as a sawmill laborer, Butler began to create art. He lived a reclusive life in the tiny town of Patterson, Louisiana, where he surrounded his house with an incredible assortment of snipped, folded, and painted tin sculptures and whirligigs. He was dubbed the Tin Man by his friends and neighbors.

Butler stated that his impulse to create stemmed from his desire to look at beautiful things. His yard was a phantasmagoria of gaily painted but recognizable rams, pregnant pigs, rabbits, peacocks, skunks, camels, birds, dogs, turkeys, snakes, and cocks. Santa with reindeer and nativity scenes, along with seven-headed monsters, mermaids, flying elephants, and other hybrid creatures, completed the menagerie. To the viewer Butler's animals and people often seemed to be in friendly confrontation with one another, as if they were communicating through a special language known only to themselves. The scale of his creations ranged from six inches in height for animals and birds to between six and eight feet for constructions and whirligigs. Butler used an axle and crankshaft to create the animation that played such a vital role in the visual aesthetics of his works. The pieces could be wind driven or turned manually to achieve greater velocity. Butler also embellished the screen doors of his house and made a remarkable group of tin window shutters with pierced and cutout designs of both secular and religious subjects.

Butler's technique for making the figures involved sketching a rough outline of the design with chalk on tin. He then cut the design out with a tin snip, and he made openwork patterns by tapping an old meat cleaver against the tin with a hammer. He used a nail and a hammer to make tiny holes for attaching supplementary pieces of folded tin and a variety of found objects.

Butler painted his works with enamel house paint, limiting his palette to pure red, blue, green, orange, and yellow, with dramatic black and white accents. The same creature often displayed two entirely different color schemes on its opposite sides. He frequently used polka dots and stripes to decorate the figures.

Light-hearted humor was an important aspect of Butler's oeuvre, and through his attachment of auxiliary tails, wings, and legs to a number of his pieces the figures attained an aspect of three-dimensionality. Many of the most ferocious members of Butler's menagerie were delightful and charming, and even a skunk became an affable creature.

As in the case of Simon Rodia, with his Watts Towers in Los Angeles, and Samuel Perry Dinsmoor, with his *Garden of Eden* in Lucas, Kansas, Butler remained essentially a folk artist-environmentalist. He displayed few of his figures on the interior of his house, preferring instead to locate them in his yard, placed in orderly rows and attached to substantial posts that were placed firmly in the ground. Although Butler's menagerie was apparently the center of his universe, he delighted in sharing his figures with others and continued to replace them with successors that were equally delightful. It was this aspect of impermanence and a frequently changing scenario in Butler's realm that distinguished him from most folk artists-environmentalists.

Essentially a sculptor, Butler was also a talented folk painter and constructivist. His deft hands and rudimentary tools guided the creation of hundreds of objects that have become some of the most avidly collected works by museums and private collectors of folk art. Unfortunately, his art-filled yard was stripped bare by collectors after he was forced by frail health to leave, and his tiny house was later consumed by fire.

—Regina A. Perry

BYARD, Carole (Marie)

American sculptor and painter

Born: Atlantic City, New Jersey, 22 July 1941. **Education:**

Fleischer Art Memorial, Philadelphia, 1961-63; New York Phoenix School of Design, 1964-68, diploma in fine arts and illustration; Westbeth Graphic Artist Workshop, New York, 1972. **Career:** Simulator pilot, National Aviation Facilities Experimental Center, New Jersey, 1960-64. Instructor, New York Phoenix School of Design, 1968-71, Metropolitan Museum, New York, 1972-73, New York Foundation for the Arts, 1978, Maryland Institute College of Art, 1983. Department head and instructor, Baltimore School for the Arts, 1980-84; adjunct faculty, Parsons School of Design, New York, 1987-92. **Awards:** Ford Motors Travel Fellowship, Institute of International Education, 1972; National Endowment for the Arts fellowships, 1986, 1994; New York State Council on the Arts grant, 1989; Caldecott Medal for *Working Cotton,* American Library Association, 1993. **Address:** 55 Bethune Street, 309c, New York 10014, U.S.A.

Individual Exhibitions:

1976	Janet Carter Gallery, New York
1977	University of Massachusetts, Amherst
1980	Institute of International Education, New York
1985	Reese Palley Gallery, Atlantic City, New Jersey
1992	Artscape, New Haven, Connecticut
	Art in General Gallery, New York
	Woodland Pattern Gallery, Milwaukee, Wisconsin
1993	Franklin and Marshall College, Lancaster, Pennsylvania

Selected Group Exhibitions:

1980	Museum of Afro-American Artists, Boston
1989	Memorial Arch, Grand Army Plaza, Brooklyn, New York
	Downtown Art Gallery, Nashville
1990	Art in General Gallery, New York
	Soho 20, New York
	Alternative Museum, New York
1991	National Museum of Women in the Arts, Washington, D.C.
1992	Walker Art Center, Minneapolis
1995	Newhouse Center for Contemporary Art, Staten Island, New York
1996	Spirit Square Center for Arts and Education, Charlotte, North Carolina

Publications:

On BYARD: Articles—"Byard in Baltimore," in *In the Arts,* 1(2), 1983; "Manhattan Profile/Carole Byard" by Sheila McKenna, in *Newsday,* 1 November 1989; "Carole Byard: Artist Profile" by Sylvia Marantz, in *Library Talk,* 3(4), October 1990; "Carole Byard, A Woman Artist of Color, The 60's, The 70's, Today," in IKON, 11, September 1990. **Video**—*Strong Medicine, Carole Byard and C. Sligh* by A. Sundberg, Minneapolis, Minnesota, 1993.

*

Carole Byard comments:

There is something about earth that moves me.
The clean tan sands of the Atlantic shore;
the majestic, magical mounds of the Sahara;
bright, red rusty Senegalese earth;

Carole Byard: *The Gathering.* Photo courtesy of Ellen Eisenman.

turquoise, ochre, magenta mystical New Mexico, with her Plaza Blanca
white sands, red roads earth.

I take the earth in my hands,
sift the tiny creek stones of The Scoharle,
The river Mississippi, Ashokan, The Rio Grande.
I touch the ground,
taste the earth my father's, father's, father's, father's feet touched at Goree and Elmina
dungeons . . . last Africa footprint.
Pressing my face against the dusty stones of tombs,
a crypt, Pyramids at Giza, and rubble, sacred places,
searching for smells and
visions of ancestor artists' call and response.
Answers.
I shall find myself if I can in this earth.
I squeeze the earth when she is soft and sticky
unruly wet clay of the Catskills.
Running between my fingers, down my arms in Abiqui,
the muddy arroyo rouge is playful unchecked,
staining my clothes, caking my fingernails, I wear the earth.

I shall lose my self if I must,
In this earth of memories and power.
She has marked me and I can't seem to get enough.
Here is where things grow, my garden, my temple is here.
And I am nourished.
Suck the berry, swallow the sap,
burn the sage, bury my mother here.

In this earth of living things,
sustenance and movement,
roll over, change your ways, be redeemed.
Search for secrets.
There are things inside of things.
Secrets, sweetness hidden, tucked down below and
I make a bed of my own, a space for my head,
a resting place.
At dawn, my work begins.

*   *   *

A spirited, unconventional painter, illustrator, teacher, and sculptor, Carole Byard is one of the most innovative African American artists to emerge in recent years. Her work is driven by her desire to move people and to make them aware of the struggles of African Americans and women for a place at the table. Her work "is not meant to match the sofa," she once told *Essence* magazine.

As an illustrator of twelve children's books, one of which, *Working Cotton,* won the prestigious Caldecott Medal in 1993, Byard is highly regarded. She has taught at many institutions, including the Metropolitan Museum of Art and the Parsons School of Design in New York City. Her work is mentioned in extensive publications. Byard is fully committed to the struggle to change the way African Americans and women are regarded, and her concepts creatively defy the emptiness of most American sculpture.

Although Byard was born in Atlantic City, New Jersey, her mother came from Panama and her grandparents from Barbados. In high school an art teacher, Priscilla Gerard, who demanded the very best, helped Byard realize that she had talent and, by showing her the works of Vincent van Gogh and Paul Cézanne, taught her that art had great expressive dimensions. Byard's high school experience turned her toward becoming an artist. She won a four-year scholarship to the Columbus (Ohio) College of Art and Design, but family illness prevented her from attending. Instead, she had to get a job, and she worked as a simulator pilot at the National Aviation Facilities Experimental Center near Atlantic City. Continuing to paint, she won prizes in many exhibitions, even though she was the only black competing. Gerard kept encouraging her to become an artist,

Carole Byard: *Praise Song for Charles.* **Photo courtesy of Ellen Eisenman.**

and in 1971 Byard won a Ford Motors/Institute of International Education fellowship that enabled her to travel to nations in Africa. What she remembers is how friendly the people were, and in one village she painted a mural for the temple. On her return she won a residency at the Studio Museum in Harlem.

Byard's most striking work has been as sculptor. In 1992 she and photographer Clarissa Sligh collaborated in creating an unusual portrait of Malcolm X at the Walker Art Center in Minneapolis, Minnesota. The mural consists of a circular room within a square one. The outer room contains visual texts, a specialty of Sligh's, and an audio loop that broadcasts the sounds of civil rights marches and riots and the voices of President John F. Kennedy, the Reverend Martin Luther King, Jr., and police chief Eugene "Bull" Connor. The inner room contains a life-size portrait of Malcolm X sculpted by Byard from laminated two-by-fours. The figure has the stance of a warrior, and its stomach contains a video monitor on which Byard, reared in the North, and Sligh, reared in the South, recall their reactions to the televised civil rights marches. In their collaboration they saw Malcolm X as a healing figure "because his ideas and his words were designed to make us grow and change."

Another unusual work is *Praisesong for Charles,* constructed on a triangular plot of land bordered by stones, on which long barkless tree limbs are mounted, each topped by a lamenting mask. The haunting image, African in its character, expressed Byard's grief over the loss of her friend Charles Abramson, an installation artist and Yoruba priest.

Painting an adolescent black youth led to the creation of Byard's most unusual work, *The Perception of Presence*. Ignoring sculpture's contemporary focus on abstract linear shapes, Byard developed a striking concept. She created twenty-four life-size busts of young black men, each different and each mounted on a shoulder-high stand. A room filled with these figures produces a stunning sense of their humanity, their power, their brooding silence, and their wasted lives in today's society. No single figure could match the impact of the large group. Contributing to the impact is the fact that the heads are molded in canvas and mud on armatures of two-by-fours, reflecting Byard's readiness to invent. If she had tried to make the heads out of granite or black marble, she could not have done it. By building two-by-four structures and then applying canvas and mud, she was able to create a powerful work.

—Harry Henderson

CAMP, Sokari Douglas

Nigerian sculptor

Born: Ngogo George Douglas Sokari, Buguma, Nigeria, 18 December 1958. **Education:** Central School of Art and Design, London, B.A. (honors) 1983; Royal College of Art, London, M.A. 1986. **Awards:** Amy Sadur Priedlander Prize, 1981; Saatchi and Saatchi Award, 1982; Princess of Wales Scholarship, 1983; Henry Moore Bursary, 1983. **Address:** Morecombe Street Studios, Morecombe Street, London SE17 1DX, England. **Online Address:** http://www.arc.co.uk/sokari/home.html; e-mail: mark@arc.co.uk.

Individual Exhibitions:

1982	Africa Centre, London
1984	Angela Flowers Gallery, London
1985	October Gallery, London
1986	Milton Keynes Exhibition Gallery, England
1987	Africa Centre, London
	Dorman Museum, Middlesbrough, England
1988	Alall Bluecoat Gallery, Liverpool, England
	National Museum of African Art, Washington, D.C.
1990	Sue Williams Gallery, London
1991	Chelsea Arts Club, London
1992	Sue Williams Gallery, London
1993	Redfern Gallery, London
1994	Museum of London
	Barbican Centre, London
1995	Contemporary African Art Gallery, New York
	Museum of Mankind, London
1996	Angel Road Gallery, Nottingham, England

Selected Group Exhibitions:

1983	ICA, London
1985	Royal Festival Hall, London
1986	Royal Academy of Arts, London
	Dowse Art Museum, Lower Hutt, New Zealand
	Whitechapel Art Gallery, London
1989	West African Music Village, Kew Gardens, London
1990	Sue Williams Gallery, London
1996	Kunst Hallie Krems, Austria
	Royal West of England Academy

Collections:

Centro Atlantico de Art Moderno, Las Palmas, Spain; Glenbow Museum, Canada; Unilever, London.

Publications:

By CAMP: Books—*Echoes of the Kalabari: Sculpture by Sokari Douglas Camp,* (exhibition catalog), Washington, D.C., National Museum of African Art, 1989 (illustrated); *Sekiapu: Masquerades and Sculptures,* (exhibition catalog), London, Africa Centre, 1987 (illustrated).

On CAMP: Books—*Sokari Douglas Camp: Kinetic Sculpture and Drawings,* exhibition catalog, London, October Gallery and Christiane Bergob, 1985 (illustrated); *Alali-Festival Time/Sokari Douglas Camp,* exhibition catalog, England, Dorman Museum, 1987 (illustrated); *Time and Motion,* exhibition catalog, England and Stephanie Brown, 1989 (illustrated). **Articles**—"Sculpting Sounds and Rhythms," in *New African* (London), February 1984, pp. 43-44 (illustrated); "Echoes of the Kalabari: Sculpture by Sokari Douglas Camp," in *African Arts* (Los Angeles), 23(1), November 1989, pp. 86-87; "Sokari Douglas Camp" by Dennis Duerden, in *Art Monthly* (London), May 1990; "Sokari Moves Ahead" by Toyin Akinosho, in *Sunday Times* (Lagos), 1 July 1990. **Audiocassettes**—*Interview with Sokari, Voice of America interview with Sokari Douglas Camp, Nigerian sculptor*, Washington, D.C., National Museum of African Art and Maimonna Mills, 1988; *Interview with Sokari Douglas Camp, Nigerian sculptor,* Washington, D.C., National Public Radio, 1988.

*   *   *

Sokari Douglas Camp was born in Buguma, near the Niger Delta, a principle trading center for the Kalabari region in southern Nigeria. The Kalabari live by fishing and trading, and Camp's father, who was a chief, traded fish, while her mother traded palm oil. At an early age she went to live with her older sister in England, and when her sister died in childbirth, her brother-in-law became her guardian. Camp spent her youth being educated in England and traveling to Nigeria to visit her family. These experiences have allowed her to bring a cultural dualism to her sculpture. She is an artist in the Western sense, but her work draws heavily upon her Kalabari cultural foundations for imagery and narratives.

Camp remembers seeing a carving by the Nigerian artist Ben Enwonwu in a Baptist church when she was six or seven years old, a moving and inspiring experience. Camp herself is more inspired by the movement of dance and the activities of people, particularly in her native Kalabari region, than by physical objects. She remembers her mother and other women making things with their hands—for example, thatching or using raffia to tie things together—and she sees her work as being a similar activity, putting various materials together.

Camp began creating metal sculpture on the death of her father. Among the Kalabari one of the greatest things a person can provide the deceased is a brass bed to be sent off on. Although she could not

Sokari Douglas Camp: *Big Masquerade with Boat and Household on His Head,* **1995. Photo courtesy of Peter White.**

work in brass, Camp had done welding, and she decided that steel was the grandest material she could work in and control. It was thus that she came to make *Church Ede* (1984). The work is a welded-steel four-post canopied structure, with a depression in the mattress area to suggest the body. Three mourning female figures, who are waving handkerchiefs, are suggested by twisted metal. The work was shown in Camp's one-woman exhibition at the Smithsonian Institution's National Museum of African Art in Washington, D.C., in 1988, the first exhibition of contemporary African art at the museum.

Camp's sculptures use open spaces cut from metal sheets to represent the colored, patterned clothing worn by the women in her culture, and life-size works like *Masquerader with Feather Headdress* (1987) show characters from masquerades. Many of the works have painted surfaces, and the movement and sound of a number of the works bring to life mythical and historical characters and water spirits of the important Kalabari festival.

Artists in the Kalabari culture deal with power objects and spiritual purposes. When she began doing works suggesting masquerades, Camp was concerned that she was tampering with something religious. She resolved her concerns, however, and has combined her knowledge and imagination to create objects that give glimpses of spiritual performances and performers. Because she is a woman, she has always been relegated to being an observer of masquerade performances, and there are certain things she has not been allowed to see or know. Many of the Kalabari women in her tableaux are also represented as observers, as in *Small Iriabo (Clapping Girl)* and *Woman,* both part of *Audience Ensemble* (1986). It was in London, in conjunction with her exhibition in 1987 at the Africa Centre, that Camp saw forbidden aspects of a masquerade performance by a Sekiapu men's association, and her Smithsonian exhibition was shown concurrently with Kalabari ancestral screens, something she had been absolutely forbidden to see in Nigeria.

Camp feels that being forced to be an observer has prevented her from having a complete view of the spiritual aspects of the art of her culture and has denied her the fulfillment that might have come from participation. That fulfillment now comes from creating art. Of course, as a woman Camp also would have been denied the opportunity to create sculpture in her Kalahari homeland, but living in the West has opened up this possibility for her.

Camp's way of looking at the world and her most lasting influences and experiences come from her African existence and inform her sculpture. In many ways she represents the complexity and fluidity of contemporary artists born in Africa but working in the international art world.

—Michael D. Harris

CAMPBELL, Elmer Simms
American illustrator

Born: St. Louis, Missouri, 2 January 1906. **Education:** University of Chicago; Chicago Institute of Fine Art; Art Students League, New York. **Family:** Married Vivian Campbell (died 1970). **Career:** Beginning 1933 cartoonist, *Esquire, New Yorker, Judge.* Creator of Esky, cartoon character in *Esquire.* Lived in Neerach, Switzerland, 1957-70. **Awards:** Hearst Prize, 1936; honorable mention, American Negro Exposition, 1940. **Died:** 27 January 1971.

Selected Exhibitions:

1924	Minneapolis Artists Exhibit
1929	Harmon Foundation
	National Gallery of Art
1935	Arthur H. Newton Galleries
1940	American Negro Exposition, Chicago
1941	South Side Community Art Center

Collections:

Schomburg Center, New York.

Publications:

On CAMPBELL: Articles—"The Onlooker: Talent Rewarded" by A.L. Jackson, in *The Chicago Defender,* 18 October 1924; "E. Simms Campbell—Caricaturist" by Elmer Carter, in *Opportunity,* March 1932; "Elmer Simms Campbell, One of the Few Who Have Crashed the Color Line to Success," in *Washington Tribune,* 12 June 1937; "Colored Cartoonist 'Doodles' to Get Clever Gag Ideas," in *Evening Star* (Washington, D.C.), 22 March 1941; "Cuties Artist Makes Address at Howard University," in *Times Herald* (Washington, D.C.), 22 March 1944; "Cuties by Campbell" by Arna Bontemps, in *Negro Digest,* 1944; "Country Gentleman," in *Ebony,* 2, August 1947, pp. 9-12; "Cartoonist for Playboy," in *Jet,* 39, 18 February 1971, pp. 12-13.

*   *   *

The cartoons of Elmer Simms Campbell, an internationally known illustrator, served as a familiar commentary on the American scene for almost half a century. Campbell was born in St. Louis, Missouri, in 1906 into an educated family. His father, an assistant principal of a high school, was not the source of his artistic talent. His fascination with drawing came from his mother, who was a watercolorist. From a very young age, Campbell used to sit at his mother's side and sketch. Campbell was fourteen when his family moved to Chicago, and he recalled taking his most prized possession with him, his sketchboard.

E. Simms Campbell attended the University of Chicago and graduated from the Chicago Art Institute. He also held honorary degrees from Lincoln and Wilberforce Universities. He began illustrating for magazines while he was studying in college, working nights on a professional humor magazine, *College Comics.* Campbell's talent was recognized by the cartoonists Ed Graham and C.D. Russell. Both men encouraged him to develop his craft. In 1932-33 he studied at the famed Art Students League under George Grosz.

After completing his studies Campbell worked briefly in St. Louis for an advertising agency. He developed his own signature style of illustrations and cartoons and began selling regularly to *Esquire* and other magazines, including the NAACP's *Crisis* magazine, and the Urban League's *Opportunity* magazine. Campbell recognized that creating cartoons was hard work and likened it to ditch-digging, without the benefit of fresh air. Campbell was able to travel the world with other cartoonists, when he took part in U.S.O. shows in Japan, Germany, and France. He eventually moved to Switzerland, where he remained for fourteen years.

Campbell's cartoons were published regularly in *Esquire* starting in 1933. He was known for his harem sequence, which featured lush odalisques and rich colors. His work also appeared in the *New*

Elmer Simms Campbell: *War Knows No Color Line.* Photo by Manu Sassoonian; courtesy of the Schomburg Center for Research in Black Culture.

Yorker, Life, Judge, Collier's and the *Saturday Evening Post*. He created the character "Esky," the white-mustached, pop-eyed, bulbous-nosed connoisseur of female beauty, who appeared on several *Esquire* covers.

Campbell also illustrated children's books and wrote numerous articles on American jazz. He won many awards for his work, including a Hearst prize. His work was first exhibited in Minneapolis, when he was only eighteen years old, and five years later the Harmon Foundation featured some of his images in a group show.

Campbell infrequently dealt with black subject matter, although he did include a series of paintings and essays in *Esquire* that described life in the Harlem Renaissance, including "Home of Happy Feet" and "Blues Are the Negro's Lament." His drawing of a lovely young African American woman was featured on the July 1929 cover of *Opportunity,* as was his sultry portrait of a *Blues Singer Backstage* in the October issue that same year. His blues singer is reminiscent of the painters of the American scene; it is realistic, moody, and slightly angular. Campbell's drawings also accompanied various essays and pieces of fiction in *Opportunity.* Included in this category are a drawing to accompany the short story "Escape" and highly stylized drawings of musicians to accompany "Jim Europe—A Reminiscence." These drawings were published in the March 1930 issue and capture the excitement and exhilaration of the Jazz Age, a subject Campbell was familiar with as an artist, an essayist, and a jazz aficionado.

—Amy Kirschke

CARRAWAY, Arthur

American painter

Born: Fort Worth, Texas, 1927. **Education:** California School of Fine Arts, 1950-53; Institute of African Studies, University of Ghana, Ligon, 1971-72; Academy of Advertising Art, San Francisco. **Awards:** Nomination, Future Leader in the Arts, Committee for San Francisco Future, 1953; Purchase Prize and First Prize, Los Angeles County Fair, 1953; Purchase Prize, Oakland Art Museum, 1968; San Francisco Art Festival Prize, 1955; special scholarship for painting, California Society of Classical Arts, 1957.

Selected Exhibitions:

1953	Los Angeles County Fair
	San Francisco Art Association Annual Exhibits (through 1956)
1954	San Francisco Museum of Art
1955	San Francisco Museum of Art
	The Six Gallery, San Francisco
1958	Crocker Art Gallery, Sacramento, California
1965	Gump's Gallery
1968	Oakland Museum of Art, California
	Wallace Creek Civic Arts Gallery

Publications:

On CARRAWAY: Articles—"Arthur Carraway, Charles Searles, and Houston Conwill: Work of Three North American Black Painters" (dissertation) by Rosalind Jeffries, Yale University, 1979.

*   *   *

Arthur Carraway was a longtime San Francisco painter. As a result of his travels to various regions in Africa while a merchant seaman, he early on incorporated imagery based on Makonde sculpture in his work. But he was more directly affected by the African sculpture he saw later when he traveled to East Africa under the auspices of the United Nations. His decision to continue to use African motifs also was renewed through his knowledge of the vocabulary of myth and magic learned at the Institute of African Studies at the University of Ghana at Legon in 1971-72.

Carraway moved to San Francisco from Fort Worth, Texas, in 1945, during the second major wave of black migration from the South. He arrived at a time when abstract expressionists such as Hans Hofmann and Clyfford Still were beginning to exert influence on San Francisco painting, which had previously had a strong tradition in social realism, led by artists such as Diego Rivera. Studying art at the California School of Fine Arts from 1950 to 1953 placed him at the center of the debate between figuration and abstraction.

Like many other African American artists who experimented with pure abstraction, Carraway rejected the idea that he must disavow the figure in his work. Instead, he found ways of engaging his materials by using scumbled pigment, which resulted in a dry but heavy consistency in the paint. As his shapes seem to emerge from their dark blanket of color, they suggest an attitude of spontaneous gaiety that can often overpower the more subdued flat foreground of the compositions. In his "Fetish Form II" series (1968) a figure emerges from the background as if coming from a dreamlike realm.

Although Carraway's figures have the bulk and self-contained symmetry of Makonde forms, he disturbs their clean and finite shapes. The figures often stand on spindly legs fixed onto an unknown ground, or they seem to sprint through space like ancient wall paintings. In the early works Carraway favored light grounds that he had painted over darker ones. The white or light paint intruded upon the central shapes, causing their edges to become blurred and irregular. He experimented with texture and movement as it revealed itself from layers of painted surfaces. In his effort to capture the movement of forms in nature, his paintings share characteristics with those of Norman Lewis.

Carraway's later technique involved making brisk strokes of colored paint onto areas of the canvas and then working into them or completely covering them. In this way only a slight hint of the underpainting comes through the usually cool, modulated hue of the top coat, as can be seen, for example, in *African Symbol of Wisdom* (1968). The warm underpainting seems to resist being obliterated by the grayish mass and fights to retain its visibility. The resulting effect is a push-and-pull tension, something that also is evident in the work of Lewis.

—Lizzetta LeFalle-Collins

CARTER, Carol Ann

American mixed-media artist, painter, and installation artist

Born: Carol Ann Williams, Indianapolis, Indiana, 14 January 1947. **Education:** Ball State University, Muncie, Indiana, 1965-66; Herron School of Art, Indiana University, Indianapolis, 1966-70, B.F.A. 1970; Yale Summer School of Music and Art, Norfolk, Connecticut, 1969; University of Notre Dame, South Bend, Indiana, 1972-

74, M.F.A. 1974. **Family:** Married 1) Dennis L. Carter in 1970 (divorced 1982), one son; 2) Matti Mattsson in 1995. **Career:** Associate professor, Saint Mary's College, Notre Dame, Indiana, 1975-86, Pennsylvania State University, University Park, 1987-88, University of Michigan, Ann Arbor, 1988-95. Since 1996, professor, University of Kansas, Lawrence. **Awards:** Lilly Endowment Open Faculty Research Fellowship, 1984; Ford Foundation Postdoctoral for Minorities, 1986; National Endowment for the Arts grant, 1988; international travel grant, University of Michigan, 1993; Fulbright Fellowship, 1994; Langston Hughes Visiting Professorship, University of Kansas, 1995. **Agent:** G.R. N'Namdi Galleries, 230 W. Huron Street, Chicago, Illinois 60610, and 161 Townsend, Birmingham, Michigan 48011, U.S.A. **Address:** 700 Maine Street, Lawrence, Kansas 66044-2342, U.S.A.

Individual Exhibitions:

1981   Loyola University, Chicago
1985   Central State University, Wilberforce, Ohio
1986   Southern Ohio Museum, Portsmouth, Ohio
        Ohio Wesleyan University, Delaware, Ohio
        Jackson State University, Jackson, Mississippi
1989   Isobel Neal Gallery, Chicago
        Detroit Institute of Arts
1991   College of Wooster Museum, Ohio
1992   Cinque Gallery, New York
1993   University of Rhode Island, Kingston
1995   University of Kansas Art and Design Gallery, Lawrence
1996   Kansas City Artists Coalition, Missouri

Selected Group Exhibitions:

1982   Snite Museum, Notre Dame, Indiana
1983   Kentucky State University, Frankfort
        Gallery Route 1, Point Reyes Station, California
1986   Webster College, Saint Louis, Missouri
1987   Amber Gallery, Richmond, Virginia
        Pennsylvania State University
1988   College of the Holy Cross, Worcester, Massachusetts
        University of Wisconsin, Green Bay
1991   G.R. N'Namdi Gallery, Birmingham, Michigan
        Bowling Green State University, Ohio

Collections:

Atlanta Life Insurance Company, Atlanta, Georgia; Chevron Oil Company, Louisville, Kentucky; First National Bank of Louisville, Kentucky; First Source Bank, South Bend, Indiana; Indianapolis Museum of Art, Indiana; Las Vegas Museum, Nevada; Michiana Regional Museum, South Bend, Indiana; Santa Reparata Print Studio, Florence, Italy; Snite Museum, University of Notre Dame, Indiana; University of Michigan, Ann Arbor; Wabash College, Crawfordsville, Indiana.

Publications:

On CARTER: Articles—"Living Fearlessly with and within Difference: Emma Amos, Carol Ann Carter and Martha Jackson-Jarvis" by Sharon Patton, in *The African-American Aesthetic in the Visual*

Arts and Post Modernism, Washington D.C., Smithsonian Institution Press, 1996.

                                    *

Carol Ann Carter comments:

Since 1984 one of the most apparent characteristics of my work has been that of transition. In technique, process, overall character, and purpose, it has moved from intaglio printmaking (1975-84) to mixed-media painting (1985-94) to collaborative installation (1994-present). These changes or transitions closely follow and reflect actual travel away from "home," most notably to Nigeria in 1984 and Scandinavia several times between 1992 and 1996. The work's purpose seems to be to guide me in exploring the points of contact between worlds—male/female, black/white, high/low, form/context, and privilege/poverty. The journeys to and from these positions create a bridge for understanding my own space or territory in this culture. My work becomes a vehicle for the passage.

I am curious about how our cultural patterns and sensibilities are constructed and the degree to which we are able to exercise choice and control in the selection of our realities. I ask my audience (and that includes my students) to look again at its perceptions of what is fixed and what is flexible, the grays between black and white and the shifting distances between the "truth," the "lie," and the "other."

                            *   *   *

Carol Ann Carter is a mixed-media artist whose work has been greatly influenced by her experience as a traveler, particularly in Nigeria and in Scandinavia. A continuing theme in Carter's art is that of journeying: both the open-ended process of exploring new territories of media and techniques, and the movement between cultures and concepts that on the surface appear to be worlds apart.

Carter's journey as an artist began in her childhood home in Indianapolis, Indiana, where she was encouraged to paint wall murals and furniture and to make her own textiles. When her professional career began in the 1970s, she focused on intaglio prints that often incorporated the imagery of overlapping pieces of fabric in their designs. In 1984 Carter traveled to Nigeria on a Lilly Endowment fellowship to study the traditional men's weaving and the intricate embroidery techniques of the Hausa people. This experience marked a turning point in her artistic career, and she began to focus on expressing in her work the kind of energy and passion that she had observed in Nigerian art. Her later work in mixed-media painting shows the influence of these traditions, as well as of African American interpretations of Western women's decorative arts, such as sewing and quilting. All of these influences reflect her growing interest in the connections among cultural ideas and identities—Western and African and male and female.

Carter produces assemblage works of art, in which found objects are used to construct sculpturelike creations rather than being mounted on a flat surface, as in a collage. Her work has continued the development of this form among black artists such as Faith Ringgold and others, whose interest in the medium and in African folk traditions arose during the 1960s and 1970s. To create her assemblage sculptures, Carter begins by hand dying pieces of cloth and edge sewing them to create a larger textile. By incorporating ordinary objects, such as buttons, sequins, and plastic flowers, into rich textiles created in the tradition of formal African artistry, Carter's work blurs the distinction between "high" and "low" arts. The addition of found objects to dyed fabrics is also akin to the artistry of Yoruba women, who combine beans, small

Carol Ann Carter (with Matti Mattsson): *Platform with Steps and Ramp,* 1996.

stones, and seeds with their hand-dyed textiles to create richly textured fabrics known as *adire eleso.*

Carter's aesthetic vision has been referred to as the "iconography of the mundane," an approach to art that echoes the African concept of *mana,* or the sense of the spiritual in all things, even the most ordinary materials. For example, her mixed-media painting *Woman's Apron* (c. 1990-91), which incorporates several types of fabric and found objects, speaks to the issue of gender roles and elevates an ordinary work garment to high art.

Carter's travels to Scandinavia between 1992 and 1996 coincided with her movement into collaborative installations, works that involve the placement of a variety of objects, some of which are created by other artists. In this form, creation and the interpretation of place become the art. One example is *Living Room,* which combines wall panels of varying colors and patterns, a patched kilim rug, fabric draped over chairs, and other objects. The work reflects Carter's sense of being in transition as an artist. Writer Lucy R. Lippold said of *Living Room,* "As the objects and surfaces interact, their meanings change." The statement might also be applied to the artist herself and to her journey of reexamining her sense of identity and place through the intimate exploration of the ideas and materials she finds along the way.

—Sonya Stinson

CARTER, Nanette
American painter and mixed-media artist

Born: Columbus, Ohio, 30 January 1954. **Education:** L'Accademia di Belle Arti, Perugia, Italy, 1974-75; Oberlin College, Ohio, B.A. 1976; Pratt Institute of Art, Brooklyn, New York, M.F.A. 1978. **Career:** Teacher, Dwight-Englewood School, New Jersey, 1978-87. Since 1987 freelance artist. Since 1992 instructor, City College of New York. **Awards:** National Endowment for the Arts Fellowship, 1981; Jerome Foundation Award, 1981; New York State Council on the Arts Award, 1984; New Jersey State Council on the Arts Award, 1985; fellowship, Bob Blackburn's Printmaking Workshop, New York, 1989; New York Foundation for the Arts grant, New York, 1990; Pollock-Krasner Foundation grant, New York, 1994. **Address:** 788 Riverside Drive, New York, New York 10032, U.S.A.

Individual Exhibitions:

1983	Ericson Gallery, New York
1984	G.R. N'Namdi Gallery, Detroit
1985	Cinque Gallery, New York
1986	G.R. N'Namdi Gallery, Detroit

1988	Montclair Art Museum, New Jersey
1989	G.R. N'Namdi Gallery, Detroit
1990	Jersey City Museum, New Jersey
	June Kelly Gallery, New York
1991	Westminster Gallery, Bloomfield College, New Jersey
	Southampton College, New York
1992	Kebede Fine Arts, Los Angeles
	Franklin Marshall College, Lancaster, Pennsylvania
	G.R. N'Namdi Gallery, Columbus, Ohio
	G.R. N'Namdi Gallery, Birmingham, Michigan
1993	Sande Webster Gallery, Philadelphia, Pennsylvania
1994	June Kelly Gallery, New York

Selected Group Exhibitions:

1983	Albright-Knox Museum, Buffalo, New York
1984	Abrons Center for the Arts
1986	Clocktower Gallery, New York
1987	Kenkeleba Gallery, New York
1988	June Kelly Gallery, New York
1992	National Museum of Women in the Arts, Washington, D.C.
1993	Delaware Art Museum, Wilmington
	Paine Webber Art Gallery, New York
	Painted Bride Gallery, Philadelphia
1994	Museum of Art, Rhode Island School of Design, Providence

Collections:

Jersey City Museum, New Jersey; H.F. Johnson Museum of Art, Cornell University, Ithaca, New York; Library of Congress, Washington, D.C.; Museum of Art, Rhode Island School of Design, Providence; Newark Museum, New Jersey; Oberlin College, Ohio; Schomburg Center, New York; Studio Museum in Harlem, New York; Zimmerli Arts Museum, Rutgers University, New Brunswick, New Jersey.

Publications:

On CARTER: Articles—"Artist at Work: Nanette Carter" by Theodore Wolff, in *Christian Science Monitor,* 11 September 1986; "Art for Our Sake" by Evette Porter, in *Essence,* May 1990.

*   *   *

Nanette Carter likes to focus on nature and to observe its similarities to human life. This focus can be observed in works created since 1992. Carter primed all of her canvases black in order to create the sense of infinity and great space. Black suggests that painted objects project, which allows the artist to capture the rhythms of life and nature in all their fluidity and tactility. Carter's canvases become windows through which we perceive this endless panorama.

In January 1992 she created *Crisscross* (oil, metal on canvas). Nature predominates in this mixed-media work, which appears as small topographical views of sections of the earth. The artist skillfully shifts us from one section of the earth to another, thus encapsulating several panoramic views of the earth's land mass into one small creation. Hallmarks such as rhythm, fluidity, and tactility are powerful and present. *Segments #49* is reminiscent of cosmic timekeepers. It recalls segments of brilliant sunsets and sunrises and breathtaking, spectacular moon phases. Large areas of black could

represent eclipses. Carter's provocative series is exquisitely rendered. *Segments #51* (oil on collaged canvas) serves as segue between *Crisscross* and *Segments #52*. Aspects of both perspectives appear in the work. In *Segments #52* (1993, oil on collaged canvas, 62" x 67") the perspective switches. It seems that we are in outer space in a vista that pulsates with energy. Flares of flaming combustion light up a tundra of intergalactic miasmas.

As early as 1994 she began her "Window View-Scapeology" series, in which her canvas becomes windows with compartments. Various ideas and symbols are presented in these compartments. If turned one way, the symbols can represent land. If turned another, they may represent an outerspacescape, waterscape, landscape, or cloudscape.

Carter, who was in graduate school in the 1970s, was unfamiliar with any African American women artists. She only saw the work of Elizabeth Catlett, who has been a strong influence on this young artist, after she completed her education. Nanette Carter had no knowledge that she was a critical part of a continuum. She was unaware of Catlett's decades-long tradition of creating works about the African American female in a positive, uplifting spirit. Despite this she has created a strong body of work and has received national recognition for her adept and skillful abstractions.

—Jontyle Theresa Robinson

CARTER, Yvonne Pickering

American painter, assemblage artist, printmaker, and performance artist

Born: Washington, D.C., 6 February 1939. **Education:** Traphagen School, graduated 1959; Howard University, Washington, D.C., A.B. 1962, M.F.A. 1968. **Career:** Professor of design and painting (beginning 1971) and chair of the art department (beginning 1986), University of the District of Columbia, Washington, D.C. **Award:** Visual Arts Award, D.C. Commission of the Arts and Humanities, 1981-82. **Address:** 1337 Tenth Street N.W., Washington, D.C. 20001.

Selected Exhibitions:

Anacostia Museum, Smithsonian Institution, Washington, D.C. (1990); Bronx Museum of the Arts, New York (1989-90); California Afro-American Art Museum, Los Angeles (1989-90); Corcoran Gallery of Art, Washington, D.C.; Gibellina Museo Civico D'Arte Contemporanea, Palermo, Italy (1990); Greensboro Cultural Center, North Carolina (1994); George Mason University, Fairfax, Virginia; Howard University, Washington, D.C.; Maryland Institute College of Art, Baltimore; National Museum of Women in the Arts, Washington, D.C. (1994); *National Women Artists of Color,* Art in General, New York (1994); New Visions Art Gallery, Atlanta, Georgia (1990); Washington State Convention and Trade Center Galleria, Seattle, Washington.

Selected Performances:

Dance Place, Washington, D.C.; Dock Street Theater, Charleston, South Carolina; Harris Theater, George Mason University, Fairfax, Virginia; National Museum of Women in the Arts.

Publication:

On CARTER: Article—"Three Artists, Three Ways" by M. Sunderland, in *Ocular,* Fall 1981; review by Curtia James, *Art Papers,* 1991.

* * *

Yvonne Pickering Carter moves rapidly from medium to medium. She works on abstract paintings, assemblages, prints, and performance pieces, and she may "recycle" what is useful from one into the next. Sometimes even a "finished" piece is subject to movement and change. Especially in her "Notes and Tracings" series, she has torn many of her early watercolors and reassembled them into stitched compositions.

Carter's interest in the visual arts didn't really unfold until she attended Howard University, where she met painter James A. Porter, black art historian and artist David Driskell, and printmaker James L. Wells. It was her friend William Carter who encouraged her to work more with paper, and his influence is evident throughout her work.

Much of Carter's work is on paper. She folds, creases, tears, sews, and paints paper. But each new series of her work represents some change in approach. Her "Linear" series offers long, calligraphic strokes in paneled groups that she says imply "a certain degree of privacy and sacredness." Later, in her "Folded" series, she used less vivid colors and the paper itself—its shadows and folds and movements—dominated the work. For her "Shrine" series she created minimalist compositions made up of silver teachest paper. It would seem that very little is typical about the work of Yvonne Pickering Carter, yet in the early 1980s she began her "N.T." (Not Typical) series, wherein she "went back to the heavy application of paint that I was doing in school that I abandoned in the '70s when I went to paper."

For her performance pieces Carter creates complex costumes, which she refers to as "paintings," that use moiré, netting, painted canvas remnants, ribbons, and tulle instead of paint and paper. The costumes are an extension of her painting, but the performance itself allows Carter to dance. "When I first went to Howard," she says, "I was taking as many dance courses as I could. I never lost the connection with the desire to dance. . . . There was something about movement that was important to me." And it is the word "movement," perhaps more than any other, that best describes Yvonne Pickering Carter's work.

—Terry Bain

CARVER, George Washington
American painter

Born: Near Diamond Grove, Missouri, c.1864. **Education:** Simpson College, Indianola, Iowa, 1890; Iowa State College of Agriculture and Mechanic Arts (now Iowa State University), Ames, B.A. in agricultural science, 1894, M.A. 1896. **Career:** Director, Department of Agricultural Research at Tuskegee Normal and Industrial Institute (now Tuskegee University), 1896-1935; collaborator, Division of Plant Mycology and Disease Survey of the Bureau of Plant Industry, U.S. Department of Agriculture. Developed *Carver's Hybrid* cotton. Established the George Washington Carver Foundation (for research in natural science), Tuskegee, Alabama, 1940. **Awards:** Spingarn Medal, National Association for the Advancement of Colored People, 1923; George Washington Carver National Monument established 1951 (posthumously). **Died:** 5 January 1943.

Publications:

On CARVER: Books—*George Washington Carver: An American Biography* by Rackham Holt, rev. ed., Doubleday, 1962; *George Washington Carver: The Man Who Overcame* by Lawrence Elliot, Prentice-Hall, 1966; *Wizard of Tuskegee* by David Manber, Crowell, 1967; *George Washington Carver: Scientist and Symbol* by Linda O. McMurry, Oxford University Press, 1981. **Articles**—"Black Leonardo," *Time,* 24 November 1941, pp. 81-82, 18 January 1943, p. 89; "No Greener Pastures," *Reader's Digest,* December 1942, pp. 71-74; "Death Comes to Dr. Carver," *Christian Century,* 20 January 1943, p, 68; "One of Our Greatest Americans," *Commonweal,* 16 April 1943.

* * *

Most schoolchildren know George Washington Carver for his accomplishments as a chemist. As Carver said, "I set out to find ways and means to utilize the peanut. I discovered two hundred and seventy uses for it." When he finished with the peanut, he turned to sweet potatoes, another staple crop in the diet of African Americans in the rural Southeast. As a chemist he experimented with natural substances that he found on his daily walks through the fields. From them he produced "veneers, paints and stains from yucca and palmetto; paper, paints, foods and beverages from common herbs and shrubs; stains, dyes, pigments, and cosmetics from plain clays; rare colors from barnyard wastes; and roofing materials, rubber, inks, beverages, pharmaceuticals, and explosives from peanuts and sweet potatoes; starch, gums, dextrins, and food products from cotton stalks; dyes from many plants, and many other products."

What many people do not realize is that Carver was also an artist. As a child he was adept at needlework, and as an adult he crocheted delicate doilies in his spare time. He also wove pine needle baskets from the long-needle trees that dotted Macon County, the home of Tuskegee Institute. Since he created so many veneers, paints, and pigments, it followed that, with his artistic tendencies, he would become a painter. Carver painted the source of many of his discoveries and what he loved—plants and flowers. He was known to pick a fresh flower from the fields and woods on his daily early morning walk and place it in the buttonhole of his jacket. He actively cultivated red amaryllises and experimented with their cross-pollination in an attempt to develop other colors. As a result the red amaryllis continues to be seen in many gardens in the town of Tuskegee.

Of his painting, as with his ability as a chemist, Carver gave the credit to God, saying that he would speak to God and receive his will and that his hands would express God's message. The paintings have an airy feeling of filtered light. Most use a light background, with a single type of flower or plant highlighted. Carver was after the exactness of a botanical painter, and his paintings, therefore, are highly accurate in their representations. It seems that Carver did not make a distinction between the importance of his experiments with organic materials and their creative uses in art, thereby effectively combining science and art.

Carver chose to remain near his beloved fields and woods at Tuskegee even though he was offered many research appointments nationally and internationally. Examples of his crocheted work and pine needle baskets are in the collection of the George Washington Carver Museum on the campus of Tuskegee University The whereabouts of most of his paintings are unknown, however. It was said that one painting, *A Rose,* was sought by the Luxembourg Galleries during his life and promised to them at his death.

—Lizzetta LaFalle-Collins

CATCHINGS, Yvonne Parks
American painter

Born: Atlanta, Georgia, 1935. **Education:** Spelman College, Atlanta, A.B. 1955; Columbia University, New York, M.A. in art education, 1958; University of Michigan, Ann Arbor, M.A. in museum practices, 1970; University of Michigan, Ph.D. in art education, 1981. **Family:** Married James Albert A. Catchings, two daughters and one son. **Career:** Instructor, Spelman College, Atlanta, 1956-57, Marygrove College, Detroit, 1970-72; assistant professor of art, Valdosta State College, 1987-88. Since 1988 specialist, Detroit Board of Education. Since 1956 presenter, National Art Education Association. National treasurer, the Smart Set, 1976-78. Since 1981 art chair, the Links. **Awards:** Jerome Award, Spelman College, Atlanta, 1955; Delta Sigma Theta Fellowship, 1968-69; fellowship, University of Michigan, 1968-70; honorable mention, Atlanta University Art Exhibition, 1954, 1955, 1958, 1959; Jewelry Award, Scarab Club, Detroit Art Teachers Club, 1964; First Award for Print, Delta Sigma Theta Sorority, 1975; First Award in Art and Letters, Delta Sigma Theta Sorority, 1978; Mayor's Award of Merit, Detroit, 1978; James D. Parks Award, National Conference of Artists, 1979; Fulbright Hayes Award for study in Zimbabwe, 1982; Service Award, Afro-American Museum, 1983; Outstanding Black Woman in Michigan, Detroit Historical Museum, 1985.

Selected Individual Exhibitions:

Hilton Hotel, Detroit; Plymouth United Church of Christ, Detroit.

Selected Group Exhibitions:

Art Teachers Club, Scarab Club Galleries, Detroit; Beaux Art Guild, Tuskegee, Alabama; Columbia University, New York; Contemporary Studio, Detroit; Festival of Fine Arts, Ebenezer, A.M.E. Church, Detroit; Marygrove College, Detroit; Northwestern High School, Detroit; Piedmont Park Art Festival, Atlanta; Wayne State University, Detroit.

Publications:

By CATCHINGS: Books—*You Ain't Free Yet! Notes from a Black Woman,* DuSable Museum of Art, Chicago, 1976.

On CATCHINGS: Articles—*Arts and Activities,* January 1960; *The Instructor,* May 1960; *The Michigan Chronicle,* March 1971; *The Instructor,* April 1961; *The Michigan Reading Journal,* Fall 1984; *The Instructor,* December 1962; *Detroit Society for Genealogical Research Journal,* Spring 1975; *Black Art: An International Quarterly,* Spring 1978.

*   *   *

Though Yvonne Catchings does not limit herself to any one medium, she is primarily a painter and is accomplished in oil, acrylic, watercolor, and mixed media. Her techniques are varied enough that her work is difficult to classify. She has been called an abstract expressionist not because of a deliberate attempt by Catchings to abstract but because her approach to her subjects is often abstract.

For example, in her watercolor painting *Dogwood,* she portrays brilliantly colored flowers and leaves close up against a dark background. The flowers and leaves take up the entire space of the painting, and the negative-space background is almost nonexistent between the crowded positive space. For the viewer the idea of "dogwood tree" is nearly replaced by the abstract notion "pattern of flowers and leaves." There is no evidence that Catchings intended to abstract a dogwood tree, yet that is what she has accomplished by choosing what portion of the tree to paint.

Catchings's most extreme and most rare form of abstraction can be seen in the painting *The Detroit Riot* (1968), which is a mixed-media piece made up of completely abstract objects—a red background and charred wood foreground reminiscent of both fire and conditions after a fire. The painting seems to be a single distilled emotion, perhaps recalling an incident but representing that incident only in the abstract. The painting is probably most notable in that it sets Catchings squarely in the realm of abstract expression.

Catchings also creates abstraction in many paintings by the use of fluidity and contrasting transparency and opacity. Brushstrokes sometimes move and flow from one object to the next with broken and fluid boundary lines. And boundary lines might be the only opaque objects in the painting. Concrete objects, such as people and buildings, might be rendered as transparent, as in her painting *Search for Peace* (1974), where the solid lines surrounding the objects seem to dance. These lines only suggest the crowd of people and the cathedral-like structure to the left or the hills in the background to the right. Even the central crucifix seems to float above the scene—as if it stands only because it was painted to stand or because it is being held by the invisible hand of God.

—Terry Bain

CATLETT, Elizabeth
American painter and sculptor

Born: Washington, D.C., 1919. **Education:** Howard University, B.S. (cum laude) 1937; State University of Iowa, M.F.A. 1940; Institute of Chicago, 1941; Art Student's League, New York, 1942-43; Escuela de Pintura y Escultura, Esmeralda, Mexico, 1947-48. **Family:** Married Charles White (divorced). **Career:** Promotion director, George Washington Carver School, Harlem, New York. Instructor, National University of Mexico. **Awards:** First Prize, American Negro Exposition, Chicago, 1941; Julius Rosenwald Foundation grants, 1945-47; Second Prize in sculpture, National Exhibition, Atlanta University, Georgia, 1946; Second Prize in sculpture,

Elizabeth Catlett: *Homage to the Panthers,* 1970. Photo courtesy of the Schomburg Center for Research in Black Culture.

Atlanta University Annual, Atlanta, Georgia, 1956; Tlatilco Prize, *First Sculpture Biennial,* Mexico, 1962; honorable mention, *Second Latin American Print Exhibition,* Havana, Cuba, 1963; Xipe Totec Prize, *Second Sculpture Biennial,* Mexico, 1964; First Prize in sculpture, Atlanta University Annual, Georgia, 1965; First Purchase Prize, *National Print Salon,* Mexico, 1969; Howard University Alumni Award, Washington, D.C., 1979; Outstanding Achievement in the Visual Arts Honor Award, National Women's Caucus for Art Conference, San Francisco, 1981; James Van Der Zee Award, Philadelphia Museum of Art, 1983; Purchase Prize, *Salon de la Plastica Mexicana,* Mexico, 1985; Works by Women Award, *National Sculpture Conference,* Cincinnati, Ohio, 1987; Amistad Research Center Award, New Orleans, 1990; Artist of the Year Award, New York City Art Teachers Association, 1991; Candace Award for Art, National Coalition of One Hundred Black Women, New York, 1991. Honorary doctorate: Morgan State University, Baltimore, Maryland, 1993. **Online Address:** http://www.artnoir.com.

Individual Exhibitions:

1947   Barnett-Aden Gallery, Washington, D.C.
1962   Gallery, National School of Fine Arts, Mexico City
1970   Modern Art Museum, Mexico City

1971   Brockman Gallery, Los Angeles
         Studio Museum in Harlem, New York
1972   Howard University Galleries, Washington, D.C.
         National Center of Afro-American Artists, Dorchester, Massachusetts
         Atlanta Center for Black Art, Georgia
         Rainbow Sign Gallery, Berkeley, California
1973   Carl Van Vechten Gallery, Fisk University, Nashville
         Jackson State College, Mississippi
1974   Southern University, Baton Rouge, Louisiana
1975   Scripps College, Claremont, California
1978   Alabama A & M University, Normal (traveling)
         Nexus Gallery, New Orleans
1979   Your Heritage House, Detroit
         Pyramid Gallery, Detroit
1980   Chi-Wara Gallery, Atlanta, Georgia
1981   Malcolm Brown Gallery, Shaker Heights, Ohio
1982   Gallery Tanner, Los Angeles
1983   New Orleans Museum of Art
1984   Southeast Arkansas Art and Science Center, Pine Bluff
         Kilcauley Center, Youngstown State University, Ohio
         Arkansas Arts Center, Little Rock
         Howard University, Washington, D.C.
         African American Museum, Dallas
         Nassur Museum, Monroe, Louisiana
1985   Spelman College, Atlanta, Georgia
         Norfolk State University, Virginia
1986   Mississippi Museum of Art, Jackson
1987   Arizona State University Museum, Tempe
         Museum Diego Rivera, Guanajuato, Mexico
1989   Jamaica Arts Center, Queens, New York
1990   Junior Black Academy Gallery, Dallas
1991   Pelloon Gallery, Washington, D.C.
         Columbus Museum of Art, Ohio
         Malcolm Brown Gallery, Shaker Heights, Ohio
         Montgomery Museum of Art, Alabama
1993   James E. Lewis Museum of Art, Morgan State University, Baltimore
         June Kelly Gallery, New York

Selected Group Exhibitions:

1974   Anacostia Neighborhood Museum, Washington, D.C.
1975   Studio Museum in Harlem, New York (traveling)
1976   Los Angeles County Museum of Art
1984   *Since the Harlem Renaissance: Fifty Years of Afro-American Art,* Center Gallery of Bucknell University, Lewisburg, Pennsylvania (traveling)
1988   Museum of Modern Art, New York
1989   Bronx Museum of the Arts, New York
         Smithsonian Institution Traveling Exhibition Service, Washington, D.C.
1990   *A Courtyard Apart: The Art of Elizabeth Catlett and Francisco Mora,* Museum of African-American Art, Detroit
1992   Newark Museum, New Jersey (traveling)
1993   National Museum of American Art, Washington, D.C.

Collections:

Atlanta University, Georgia; Barnett-Aden Collection, Tampa, Florida; Cleveland Museum of Art, Ohio; Fisk University, Nashville; Hampton University, Virginia; High Museum of Art, Atlanta, Georgia; Howard University, Washington, D.C.; Institute of Fine Arts, Mexico; Library of Congress, Washington, D.C.; Metropolitan Museum of Art, New York; Mississippi Museum of Art, Jackson; Museum of African American Art, Tampa, Florida; Museum of Modern Art, New York; Museum of Modern Art, Mexico; National Institute of Fine Arts, Mexico; National Museum of American Art, Washington, D.C.; National Museum of Prague, Czech Republic; New Orleans Museum of Art; Schomburg Center, New York.

Publications:

By CATLETT: Article—"The Role of the Black Artist," in *The Black Scholar,* 6(9), June 1975.

On CATLETT: Books—*Elizabeth Catlett: Museo de Arte Moderno,* exhibition catalog, Mexico City, National Institute of Fine Arts and

Raquel Tibol, 1970; *Elizabeth Catlett,* exhibition catalog by Elton Fax and Jeff Donaldson, New York, Studio Museum in Harlem, 1971; *An Exhibition of Sculptures and Prints by Elizabeth Catlett,* exhibition catalog by David C. Driskell and Fred F. Bonds, Nashville, Carl Van Vechten Gallery of Fine Art, 1973; *Elizabeth Catlett* by Samella Lewis, Handcraft Studios, 1984; *Elizabeth Catlett: Works on Paper, 1944-1992,* exhibition catalog by Richard J. Powell, Virginia, Hampton University Museum, 1993. **Articles**—"Art and Identity: Elizabeth Catlett" by Melanie Herzog, in *School Arts,* December 1962; "Lady Encore, Elizabeth Catlett," in *Encore,* February 1973; "Elizabeth Catlett" by Samella Lewis, in *Black Art: An International Quarterly,* 1(1), 1976; Interview with Glory Van Scott, in *Artist and Influence,* 10, December 1981; "Elizabeth Catlett: The Power of Human Feeling of Art" by Thalia Gouma-Peterson, in *Women's Art Journal,* Spring/Summer 1983; "Elizabeth Catlett," in *A History of African-American Artists, From 1792 to the Present* by Romare Bearden and Harry Henderson, New York, Pantheon Books, 1993, pp. 418-426. **Films**—*The Work of Elizabeth Catlett* by Juan E.C. Mora, Elizabeth Catlett Productions, Inc., Third World Newsreel, New York, 1978.

*   *   *

Born in Washington, D.C., in the opening years of the twentieth century, Elizabeth Catlett holds a B.A. from Howard University, where she was a student of Lois Mailou Jones, Professor Emerita. In 1930 Jones began her teaching career at Howard. That same year she received an award for her 1929 drawing *Negro Youth* from the Harmon Foundation, a crucial institution that organized art competitions for black American artists. Witnessing someone of Jones's talent and resolve was important for the impressionable student. The imprimatur of Jones's national reputation and focus on Catlett's choice of black subjects is clear. With an artist of Jones's energy, talent, temperament, and consciousness in her métier, Catlett, in the early years of her career, began to forge what Freida High Tesfagiorgis, an artist, critic, and historian, refers to as an "Afrofemcentrist" analytic.

In various media, including sculpture and prints, Catlett has sought to reveal this Afrofemcentrist analytic through the dignity and impressive history of black women in the diaspora. In 1940 she won first prize in sculpture for a mother and child figure at the American Negro Exposition in Chicago. A print that epitomizes her determination to eradicate prevalent and spurious misconceptions and to unmask the grossly minimized role of the black woman in history is *Harriet* (1975, linoleum block print, 12½" x 10 "). Catlett created prints about Harriet Tubman and other black women in the 1940s, 1950s, and 1970s. In Harriet she draws a dynamic, forceful woman pointing the way to freedom. Concomitantly Catlett militates against the weapon of ideological warfare in the guise of the clichéd "castrating female." Catlett has made these warrior women the subject of her art, reminding us that black women have made outstanding contributions throughout the diaspora.

Catlett has received innumerable sculptural commissions in America and abroad. Her work is in major public and private collections. The lithograph *Negro es Bello* (*Black is Beautiful,* 1968, 8" x 11") is perhaps one of her most well-known prints. It is a powerful yet poignant portrayal of a young black child. In *Negro es Bello* a determined Catlett underscores the beauty of the black head. She suggests, through emphasis on the shape of the head and the prominence of the features, that this youth is beautiful. She reminds us that the beauty of black people should be affirmed.

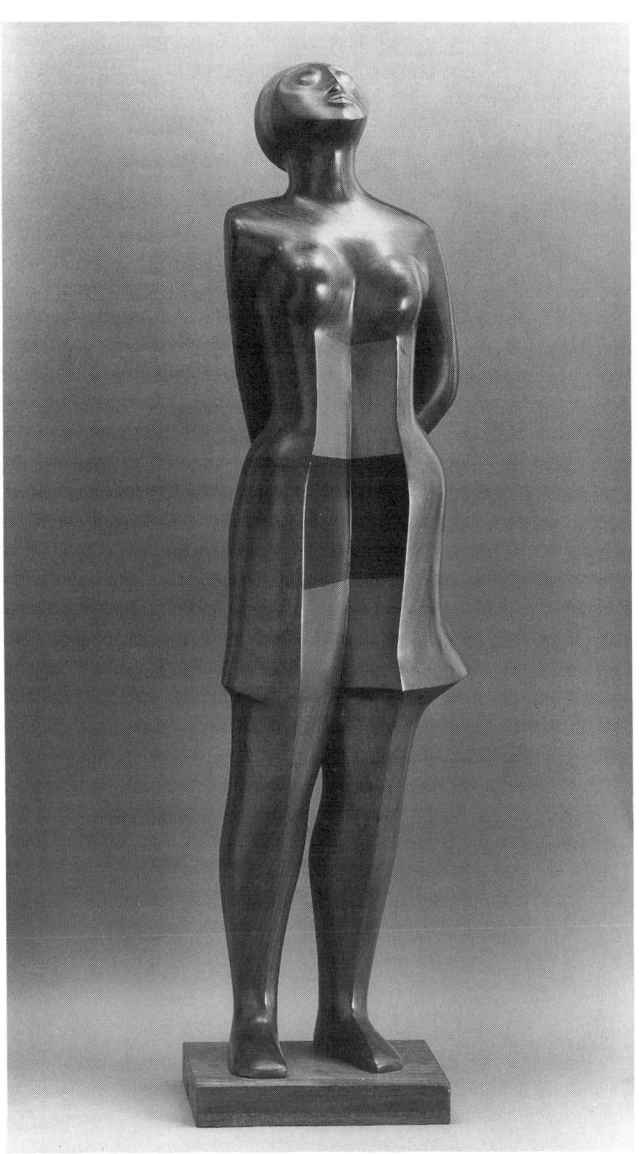

Elizabeth Catlett: *Political Prisoner,* **1971. Photo by Manu Sassoonian; courtesy of the Schomburg Center for Research in Black Culture.**

In 1993 the Metropolitan Museum of Art in New York City purchased for its permanent collection *Woman Fixing Her Hair* (1993, mahogany wood, opal, 28" x 19" x 15½"). Made of exquisitely grained mahogany wood, this is a woman seated with her legs apart, feet firmly planted on the ground in front of her. She has magnificent, full, ample hips and thighs, upright breasts, and a slightly turned head and face, with opal eyes that are the pinnacle of a triangle formed by her arms and hands, raised to fix her hair.

Catlett, married to the artist Francisco Mora, is also a mother and resides in Cuernavaca, Morelos, Mexico. Although she has lived in Mexico since the 1940s, Catlett has been consistent in her portrayal of the black woman and her experiences throughout her career as an artist. Remaining steadfast in her ideas, subjects, and consciousness decade after decade, she has influenced generations of black women artists, an influence that will undoubtedly continue through the next century.

—Jontyle Theresa Robinson

CHAMBERS, Eddie

British mixed-media artist

Born: Wolverhampton, England, 9 September 1960. **Education:** Coventry Lanchester Polytechnic, 1979-80; Sunderland Polytechnic, 1980-83, B.A. 1983. **Career:** Founder and coordinator, African and Asian Visual Artists' Archives, 1988-92; curator, Institute of International Visual Arts, 1992-1994; freelance curator, 1994-95. Since 1995 curator-in-residence, University of Sussex. **Address:** 62 Islington Road, Southville, Bristol BS3 1PZ, England.

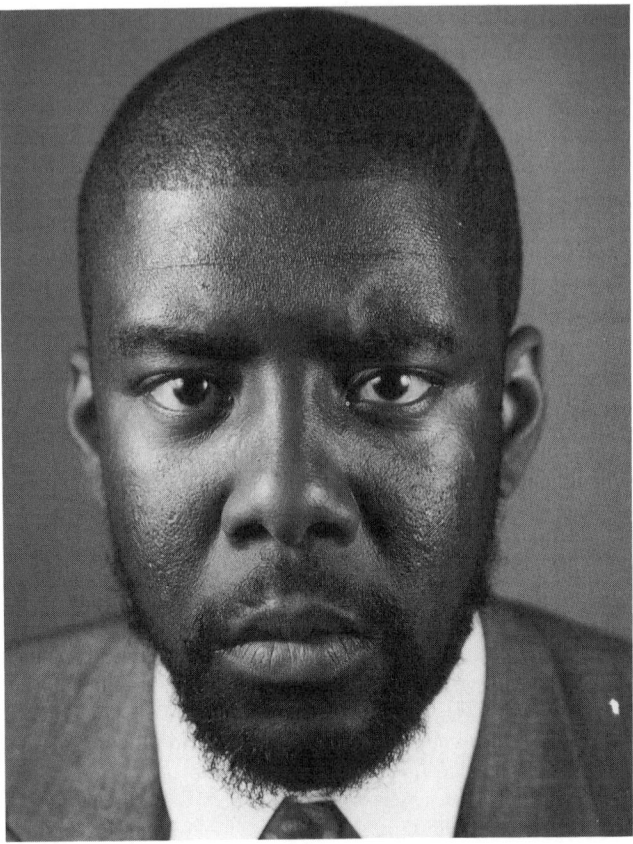

Eddie Chambers. Courtesy of Jamie Woodley and Sarah Quick.

Individual Exhibitions:

1984	*Breaking that Bondage, Plotting that Course,* Black-Art Gallery, London
1985	Grapevine Arts Centre, Dublin
	Watershed Concourse Gallery, Bristol
1988	Africa Centre, London

Selected Group Exhibitions:

1982	Africa Centre, London
	Ikon Gallery, Birmingham
	35 King Street Gallery, Bristol
1983	Midlands Arts Centre, Birmingham
	Midland Group, Nottingham
	Spectro Arts Centre, Newcastle-upon-Tyne
1984	Black-Art Gallery, London
	Mappin Gallery, Sheffield (traveling)
1985	Black-Art Gallery, London
	Bluecoat Gallery, Liverpool
1987	Brixton Village, London
	Chisenhale Gallery, London (traveling)
1989	Hayward Gallery, London (traveling)

Collections:

Arts Council of Great Britain; Mappin Art Gallery, Sheffield.

*   *   *

The contrast between Eddie Chambers and his artwork is notable. Like many black British artists, his life is full of cultural contradictions. His artwork is not, however, for it is direct, uncompromising, and confrontational. Chambers is concerned with communication, promoting a message about black pride and race consciousness through his work. To do this well, beyond the cliché statement, has required intellectual rigor, an awareness of the subtleties and ironies of life, and a sophisticated command of printmaking and design techniques. Yet the immediacy of slogans such as "Black Art an Done," "No Art but Black Art," and "No War but Class War" belie the nuanced maturation of his ideas as each new project is executed.

Chambers's commitment to black activism has been consistent throughout his professional life as both artist and curator. Clarity of expression was evident even while he was still an art school undergraduate in the 1970s. He eschewed classes in painting and life drawing and what he regarded as the other conventional planks of art school training in favor of printmaking, woodworking, and "low-status" art forms such as the political poster. He was thus more closely aligned with the agitprop concepts of postrevolutionary Russia than with traditional art. Because taking art to the people has always been part of Chambers's ethic, he has leaned toward the didactic message and mass production, whether in the form of text-based exhibitions, posters, or catalogs.

Although he has always been committed to the international struggles of black people and was a founding member of the Blk. Art Group and the Pan-Afrikan Connection, which advocated collective creativity, his source of inspiration has been more Marcus Garvey than Marxism. His poster making, assemblage, and installation art of the 1980s, with their promotion of black iconography, bold references to Garvey's quotations, and predominance of the "freedom colors"—red, gold, black, and green—were evidence of this. In the wake of the Brixton riots in 1981 and the government report that followed, Chambers's work, along with that of his peers Keith Piper, Tam Joseph, and Donald Rodney, seemed to mirror and vent the mood of second-generation blacks in Britain.

In the past decade Chambers's vision for black art has been realized through a collaborative curatorial approach that inverts the hierarchies normally inherent in exhibition practice. At once curator and artist, he has engaged the works of a number of black artists in order to create exhibitions that explore and engineer a larger picture of black history and identity. Whether in the form of the one-person shows of Eugene Palmer (1993), Michael Platt (1994), and Lesley Sanderson (1995) or in the larger group shows such as *Black Art: Plotting the Course* (1988), *The Dub Factor* (1992), and *Black People and the British Flag* (1993), these exhibitions have all contributed to Chambers's exploration and demonstration of a black aesthetic both nationally and internationally.

But Chambers is by no means an advocate of black separatism. His aim is to challenge Western art's cultural exclusivity and, more specifically, to ensure the visibility of black art in Britain. Further, his curatorial work addresses social issues in an attempt to critique British social and political life. Whereas earlier exhibitions such as *The Slaughter of Another Golden Calf* (1985) and *The Black Bastard as a Cultural Icon* (1985) interrogated history, his later curatorial work, as with *Us and Dem* (1994), has examined contemporary social and political issues and agitated for a reevaluation of black-white relations within British culture.

Chambers has brought the same confrontational style to each of these exhibitions, but his methods of communication have become more considered. By paying careful attention to the conceptual and documentary evidence of his exhibitions, he has come to channel his artistic creativity into the selection, design, and presentation of the work. It is a curatorial role that he considers necessarily interventionist to the end of promoting a politicized art, at once narrowing the gap between black art curating and art making and between black issues and British audiences.

—Petrine Archer-Straw

CHANDLER, Dana (C.)

American painter and muralist

Work also appeared under the name Akin Duro. **Born:** Lynn, Massachusetts, 7 April 1941. **Education:** Massachusetts College of Arts, Boston, 1962-67, B.S. 1967; graduate student, University of Massachusetts. **Career:** Since 1971 professor, Simmons College, Boston. Since 1974 artist-in-residence, Northeastern University, Boston. Cultural critic, *Bay State Banner;* cultural commentator, WILD, Boston. Since 1968 panelist, lecturer, moderator, critic. **Awards:** NAACP Man of the Year Award, Boston, 1970; citation for mural work, Kevin White, Mayor of Boston, 1973; National Endowment for the Arts Fellowship, 1974; Roxbury Action Program Community Service Award, 1974; Citation for the Arts, Governor Edward King, 1979; METCO Parents Award, Boston, 1981; Parks Award, National Conference of Artists, 1982; Citation for the Arts, Boston City Council, 1983; Citation for the Arts, Mayor Flynn, 1985; Citation for the Arts, State Legislature, 1985. **Ad-**

dress: Simmons College, 300 The Fenway, Boston, Massachusetts 02115, U.S.A.

Selected Individual Exhibitions:

1968	Piper Gallery, Boston
	Emerson Gallery, Boston
1970	Edna Stebbins Gallery, Boston
	Copley Gallery, Boston
1971	Gallery Amadeus, Boston
	Skiffin Gallery, Boston
1974	Salem State College Gallery, Massachusetts
1976	Northeastern University Gallery, Boston
	University of South Alabama Gallery, Mobile
1987	Gordon College, Wenham, Massachusetts
	Massachusetts College of Art, Boston

Selected Murals:

1968	Massachusetts and Columbus Avenues, Boston (destroyed)
	Intervale Street and Blue Hill Avenue, Boston
1970	Camden Street, Boston (destroyed)
1972	Zeigler and Warren Streets, Boston
1973	Grove Hall Library (inside), Boston
	43 Warren Street, Boston
1974	Dearborn School, Roxbury, Massachusetts
1982	Martin Luther King Middle School, Boston
1986	Martin Luther King Mural, Boston

Selected Group Exhibitions:

1968	Studio Museum in Harlem, New York
1970	Newark Museum, New Jersey
1971	Museum of the National Center of Afro-American Artists, Boston
1972	Carnegie Institute, Pittsburgh, Pennsylvania
	Museum of the National Center of Afro-American Artists, Boston
1973	New York Cultural Center, New York
1976	Museum of Fine Arts, Boston
	Institute of Contemporary Art and State House Bicentennial Collection
1987	New York State Museum, Albany, New York
	David and Alfred Smart Gallery, University of Chicago
	Arkansas Art Center, Little Rock

Collections:

African American History Museum; Boston Museum of Fine Arts; Museum of the NCAAA, Boston.

Publications:

On CHANDLER: Books—*T.C.B. (Taking Care of Business),* exhibition catalog, Boston, NCAAA Museum, 1971; *If the Shoe Fits, Hear It!,* exhibition catalog, Boston, Northeastern University, 1976; *Upon My Fortieth Year, 1976-1981,* exhibition catalog, Boston, Northeastern University, 1981.

* * *

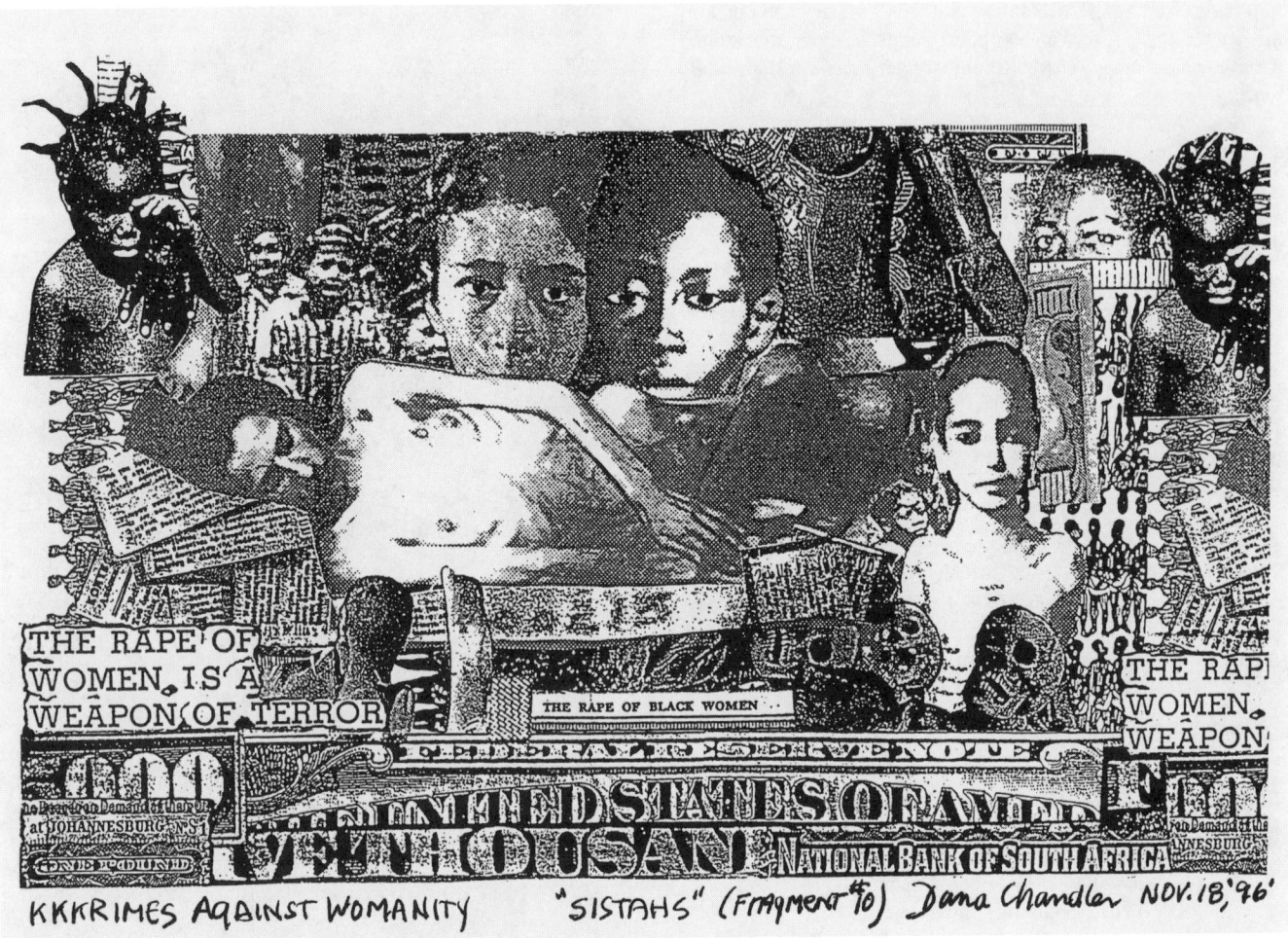

THE RAPE OF WOMEN IS A WEAPON OF TERROR

THE RAPE OF BLACK WOMEN...

THE RAPE WOMEN WEAPON

KKKRIMES AGAINST WOMANITY   "SISTAHS" (FRAGMENT #0)   Dana Chandler   NOV. 18, '96'

Dana Chandler: *Sistahs* **from the series "KKKrimes against Womanity," 1996.**

The colorful, expressive, and sometimes complex images of artist Dana Chandler first came to life during a 1960s protest that got wildly out of control. Chandler watched white police officers set upon a group of protesting mothers at a welfare office in the Grove Hall section of Boston. The officers then began to unleash their anger on "every African American in sight," Chandler recalled. He felt the collective anger and fear of the victims of the attack. These emotions spilled from his mind and soul onto the canvas. Depicting social upheaval and the inequities in the American social system are now his trademark. "After that day on June 5, 1967, my mission became very clear," he said. "Whether you were part of the protest or coming home from work, the police attacked everyone with black skin. It was a blatant reminder. This scene depicted visually that the police were an occupying force."

Although some may consider his work a form of protest art, he prefers to describe it as "activist" or "aesthetic journalism." For Chandler the paint is like film, and his canvas is a frame that contains the final snapshot or painting. The images he creates represent a broad message that takes on multiple themes, he said.

The Boston-based artist is known for illustrating these concerns in a direct and often controversial manner. For example, his pieces often show male genitals in chains or shaped into guns to demonstrate the castration and emasculation of African American men in today's society.

Some of his work is abstract coupled with a collage effect, such as a piece that shows different colorful pieces of fruit that appear separate but at the same time melded together. He also employs a figurative realism in his artwork.

A 1970 trip to West Africa also had a profound effect on his work that remains apparent today. One theme is the beauty of African women both on the continent and throughout the world. Chandler's current focus on women as a subject is what he describes as "man's inhumanity to women." In a show at Simmons College in Boston where he is a professor, he focused on this issue in *Crimes against Womanity.* "At some point an artist has to take that banner up," he said.

Two major themes in Chandler's work are the middle passage and religion. Chandler also pays homage to important figures in African American history. In a lithograph piece, he created the images of Medgar Evers, Nelson Mandela, Elijah Muhammed, Muhammed Ali, and Martin Luther King.

Chandler, whose work has also appeared under the name Akin Duro, is known in Boston for his work with the African American Master Artists in Residency Program (AAMARP), an artist collaborative that he founded and directed. When a fire destroyed his studio space and his work, Northeastern University in Boston offered him space to create art and exhibit. He opened the studio space to local artists and community groups. Although he is no longer director, AAMARP still operates as a gallery and community gathering place for neighborhood groups. Visitors from around the globe have made AAMARP one of their must-see stops while touring Boston.

—Coria Holland

CHASE-RIBOUD, Barbara

American sculptor

Born: Barbara De Wayne Chase, Philadelphia, Pennsylvania, 26 June 1939. **Education:** Temple University, Philadelphia, B.F.A. 1957; American Academy in Rome (John Hay Whitney Foundation fellow), 1958; Yale University, New Haven, Connecticut, M.F.A. 1960. **Family:** Married 1) Marc Riboud in 1961 (divorced 1981), two sons; 2) Sergio Tosi in 1981. **Awards:** National Endowment for the Arts grant, 1973; Outstanding Alumni Award, Temple University, 1975; Academy of Italy Award with Gold Medal, 1978. Honorary doctorates: Temple University, Philadelphia, Muhlenberg University, Pennsylvania, University of Connecticut, 1996. Knight of the Order of Arts and Letters of the French Republic, 1996. **Agent:** Alexandra Boutin, 3, rue Auguste Compte, 75006 Paris, France.

Individual Exhibitions:

1970	Massachusetts Institute of Technology, Boston
1973	Berkeley Museum, California
	Detroit Institute of Arts
	Indianapolis Art Institute, Indiana
	Kunsthalle, Freiburg, Germany
1974	Musée de l'Art Moderne de la Ville, Paris
	Kunsthalle, Baden Baden, Germany
	Kunstmuseum, Dusseldorf, Germany
1976	Musée Reattu
1977	Kunstmuseum, Freiburg, Germany
1980	Bronx Museum, New York
	Museum of Modern Art, Sydney
1994	Kiron Arts and Communications, Paris

Selected Group Exhibitions:

1977	Museum of Arts and Crafts, New York
1979	Sydney (traveling)
1980	Public School 80, New York
1981	Indianapolis Museum of Art, Indiana
1983	Rothschild Foundation, Paris
1992	Bomani Gallery, San Francisco
1995	Utsukushi-ga-hara Open-Air Museum, Japan
1996	African-American Historical and Cultural Museum, Philadelphia (traveling)
	Spelman College, Atlanta, Georgia (traveling)
	Studio Museum in Harlem, New York

Collections:

Berkeley Museum, Los Angeles; Centre Georges Pompidou, Paris; Kiron Arts and Communications, Paris; Lannon Foundation, Los Angeles; Metropolitan Museum of Art, New York; Museum of

Barbara Chase-Riboud.

Modern Art, New York; National Collections, France; New York Public Library; St. John's University, New York.

Publications:

On CHASE-RIBOUD: Articles—"People, B.C.R." by I. Lewis, in *Essence,* June 1970; "The Riboud Family: Collective Individualists" by Gwen Mazer, in *Harper's Bazaar,* December 1972; "American Primitive" by Sheila Walters, in *Tuesday,* May 1974; "New Black Novelist Explores Thomas Jefferson," in *People Magazine,* 8 October 1979; "Barbara Chase-Riboud" by Susan McHenry, in *Ms.,* October 1980; "Triumphant Return for Author-Artist" by Elmer Smith, in *Philadelphia Daily News,* 22 September 1995.

*   *   *

Barbara Chase-Riboud is a woman of many talents. She is a poet, writer, and sculptor, whose beautiful and powerful sculptures reside in many collections, including the Metropolitan Museum of Art in New York; the National Collections, France; the Centre Georges Pompidou, Paris; and the Museum of Modern Art, New York. Born in Pennsylvania, she lives in France and Italy but has remained steadfast in her focus on African American culture through all phases of her creative expressions, including her writing, lecturing, and sculptural works.

Chase-Riboud is renowned for her large sculptural works and for mixing materials not commonly used together, such as silk and bronze, in very dynamic combinations. One such work is *Tantra,* fabricated in gold, silk, and bronze and completed in 1995. It measures 190 x 100 x 60 cm. "Tantra," a Hindu word, connotes a circular assembly of signs and symbols. The silk in *Tantra* is dyed to match the bronze. All the silk is tied by the artist. The bronze is made directly from a full-size wax sculpture model. Shell Oil or Mobil Oil of France manufacture the artificial petroleum-based wax. With a blow torch and hot knife, the artist melts the wax so that it becomes large sheets, measuring 1/8" x 4 or 5'. She cuts welds, folds, and molds together these huge wet sheets. The detailed undercuts and baroque character in her sculpture are the result of this direct process. She moves directly from wax to sculpture with nothing in between. She works out the lost wax process with Pietra Santa, her foundry in Tuscany, Italy. The artist does almost everything herself, only occasionally employing an assistant for making the sculpture armature or for welding. She is competent in creating these large sculptural pieces alone and has debunked the myth that women, especially black women, are not proficient in making large-scale, monumental sculptural works. It is no accident that Chase-Riboud is fond of Mary Edmonia "Wildfire" Lewis (c.1843-after 1911), the first documented American woman sculptor of African-Native American descent. Lewis lived and worked in Italy in the 1800s. Chase-Riboud, who also lives and works in Italy, follows in the path of her sister artist.

Chase-Riboud is presently engaged in seeking support for the monumental work *Harrar,* which is dedicated to the eleven million victims of the Middle Passage. This work, if funded and supported by the United States government, would be placed on Theodore Roosevelt Island in Washington, D.C. in 1998, the 380th anniversary of the landing of the first African deportees in America in 1619. The conceptualization of *Harrar* has taken more than ten years of reflection. It is two bronze-cast obelisk-shaped forms, between which is suspended a wheel of bronze chain consisting of eleven million links, each link representing one Middle Passage victim. The pillars and the suspended chain form an "H" shape, representing the ancient African city of Harrar. On the sculpted surface of the obelisks, Chase-Riboud proposes engraving the name of every nation, kingdom, clan, village, city, and river source from which the martyrs were deported. The artist desires that, eventually, each link, which represents a nameless victim, will be claimed by a living American—an individual, a wife, a husband, a group, a church, a city so that the unknown victim from the past becomes linked with the present.

—Jontyle Theresa Robinson

Barbara Chase-Riboud (chair-art piece).

CHONG, Albert V(alentine)
Jamaican photographer, installation artist, and sculptor

Born: Kingston, Jamaica, 20 November 1958. **Education:** School of Visual Arts, New York, 1978-81, B.F.A. 1981; University of California, San Diego, 1988-91, M.F.A. 1991. **Family:** Married Frances Charteris in 1982, one son and one daughter. **Career:** Instructor, School of Visual Arts, New York, 1986-88; visiting scholar, Mira Costa College, Oceanside, California, 1989-91; professor University of Colorado, Boulder, 1991-96. Since 1996 professor, Rhode Island School of Design, Providence. **Awards:** Silver and Bronze Medals for photography, Jamaica Festival of the Arts, 1977; Creative Artist Program Fellowship, 1982; California Arts Council Fellowship, 1990; Western States Arts Federation Regional Fellowship, National Endowment for the Arts, 1991; National Endowment for the Arts Fellowship, 1992; Junior Faculty Development Award, University of Colorado, 1993; Office of Vice Chancellor for Faculty Affairs grant, University of Colorado, 1993; Pilot Fund grant, Arts International, National Endowment for the Arts, 1993; CO Visions Recognition Award in the Visual Arts, Colorado Council on the Arts, 1994. **Agent:** Margaret Porter Troupe, 301 Spruce Street, San Diego, California 92103, U.S.A. **Address:** 135 Carpenter Street, Providence, Rhode Island 02903, U.S.A. **Online Address:** Albert.Chong@risd.edu.

Individual Exhibitions:

1993	Bronx Museum of Art, New York
1994	Ansel Adams Center of Photography, San Francisco, California
	Sangre de Cristo Arts Center, Pueblo, Colorado
	La Torre de Tejuana (Insite), Tejuana, Mexico
	University of Colorado Art Galleries, Boulder
	Chelsea Galleries, Kingston, Jamaica

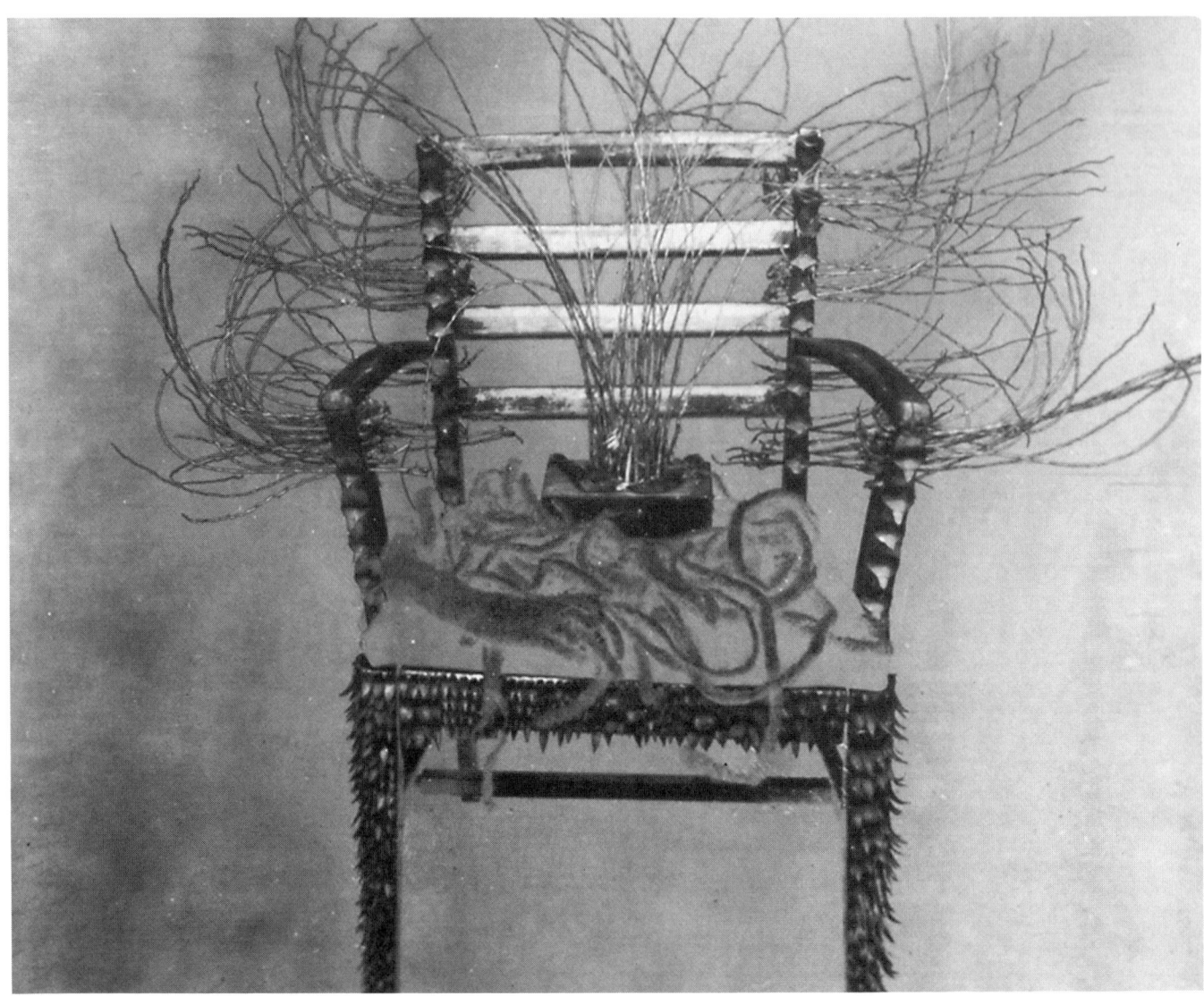

Albert Chong: *Throne for Ogun with Spirit Box & Dreadlocks,* 1990.

1995	Cleveland Museum of Art, Ohio
	InterAmerican Art Gallery, Miami, Florida
1996	Project Row Houses, Houston
	Throckmorton Fine Arts, New York

Selected Group Exhibitions:

1989	Studio Museum in Harlem, New York
	Walker Art Center, Minneapolis, Minnesota
1994	Wifredo Lam Center, Havana, Cuba
1995	Bronx Museum of Art, New York
	Ansel Adams Center of Photography, San Francisco (traveling)
	Center for Fine Arts, Miami (traveling)
	Royal Festival Hall, London (traveling)
1996	CEPA Gallery, Buffalo, New York

Collections:

Allen Memorial Art Museum, Oberlin College, Oberlin, Ohio; Artists of Color Collection, University of Colorado, Boulder; Baltimore Museum of Art, Maryland; Bibliotèque Nationale, Paris; Catskill Center for Photography, Woodstock, New York; Erie Art Museum, Erie, Pennsylvania; Lehigh University Art Galleries, Bethlemhem, Pennsylvania; Museum of the National Center of Afro-American Artists, Boston; Schomburg Center, New York; Tampa Museum of Art, Florida.

Publications:

By CHONG: Book—*Ancestral Dialogues: The Photographs of Albert Chong* edited by Michael Read, Friends of Photography, 1993.

On CHONG: Articles—"'Thrones for Ancestors': The Albert Chong Photo Exhibit" by Mary Motian-Meadows, in *Colorado Arts,* (90) June 1994; "Albert Chong—Blending Art and Spirituality" by Mary Jean Porter, in *Lifestyles* (Pueblo, Colorado), *Sunday Pueblo Chieftain,* 10 April 1994.

*

Albert Chong comments:

Photographs of spiritually infused objects, still lifes evocative of magic rites and rituals that resemble shrines and altars to obscure deities; images of a shamanic figure weaving through a personalized interior landscape reminiscent of the European colonial portraits of native peoples, except instead of the fake opulent European-style backdrops, there is crushed burlap, and the subject is the artist; installations revolving around political, personal, spiritual, and cultural issues. One involves the cross and its negative uses with Christianity in the conquest and colonization of nonwhite peoples.

Another installation work was a dinner prepared for Ancestral Spirits with the food, drinks, and even the cigars that they cherish. The audience was invited to sit at the table with the Ancestors, sip of the rum, gin, and water, and smoke the cigars.

The "Throne Series" is of found chairs that are embellished and dedicated to Ancestral and other spirit forces. Offerings of food, drink, and objects that are culturally or spiritually infused are made on or around the thrones that are meant to attract, appease, and seat the deities.

Other works are one-of-a-kind artist books and photographic images on metals that explore the possibilities of three-dimensional-looking images on reflective metals such as copper; slide projections on bodies; and an ongoing project, portraits of friends who are artists.

Another body of work deals with the exploration of the Jamaican culture via the genre of photographic portraiture. Many individuals from the district of Bamboo in the Parish of Saint Ann were photographed and some of their statements recorded with the images.

Albert Chong: *Cousin Shirley*, 1995.

The social life of the district, the odd assortment of individuals that revolve around the small country store, and the stories they tell about their lives in Jamaica. This photographic project is accompanied by video footage. The work was as much about my interactions with the locals as it was about documentary portraiture. I hope to continue this project in other parts of the island and hope to publish the work in book form, tentatively titled *Yard: A Jamaican Portrait.*

In November of 1996 at Brooklyn Academy of Music's Majestic Theatre as part of the Next Wave Festival, I presented, in collaboration with Johnny Coleman, Quincy Troupe, and The Hittite Empire, a work titled *Black Fathers and Sons,* a multi-media installation/performance work.

*   *   *

A photographer, as well as an assemblage and installation artist, Albert Chong arranges common objects that have been empowered by ritual and spiritual meanings associated with his African and West Indian cultures. He explores a postmodernist approach to photography, making the photographs rather than just taking them. In this way, like the assemblage artist, he uses common and familiar objects and recontextualizes them, thus broadening their possibilities and the viewer's identification with them.

Born in Kingston, Jamaica, Chong first became interested in photographs, particularly historical ones of his family and community members, when he realized their importance to the self-definition of the subjects they portrayed. The photographs documented the people's presence in a world that constantly denied the importance of their existence, showing that "they were there," as Chong has stated. In *Sisters* (1986) Chong used an old torn photograph of his mother and her two female cousins as small children that shows their African and Chinese heritages. The photo rests on a burlap bag, in which the obeahman, a spiritual leader in Jamaican culture, carries his roosters, and on other ritual objects used in the obeah ceremony, such as cowrie shells, chicken feathers, and flowers, with an animal skull framing them. Although his mother had asked him to repair the picture, Chong copied and recontextualized it—affirming the existence of the three small girls and illuminating their young lives.

By rereading family photographs Chong evaluates the subjects' particular situation and time and their context in the world around them. Whether or not viewers know who the subjects are, they relate to them and attempt to decipher a sense of their stories in the instance of the photograph. Viewers also bond with the familial subjects on a human level, especially if they are children, as is the case in many of the photographs.

Chong also has done self-defining photographs, in which he runs and leaps in the nude through the frame, as if fleeting memories from the past had become blurred, sweeping ritualistic figures, making them even more mysterious and incomprehensible. This can be seen, for example, in *The Fire Keeper Dancing with the Flames* (1982-84).

In some of Chong's works objects stand alone and become important in and of themselves. The contrasts of egg shells and skulls, birth and death, and regeneration and degeneration occupy most of the compositions from the 1990s, as in *Dancing Around the Throne for Antelope Spirit* (1992). In this work Chong is the dancer—a phantasmagoric form moving through the composition and seeking to make contact with his ancestral past. The work is part of a larger series in which the throne is the central icon. The throne itself is a chair that Chong views literally and spiritually to "seat the spirits of my ancestors and [the thrones] were also used as shrines and altars on which to make offerings to elemental forces and to the Gods and Deities of Africa as they manifested themselves in the new world."

In 1994 Chong installed a work at the Torre de Tijuana in Mexico entitled *Yin/Yang, Us/Them* that was, as he stated, the "mandala of the Taoist Chinese symbol for the equilibrium and harmony of the world." Apples, oranges, and feathers formed the core of the work in the symbol of yin and yang, with coconut shell vessels forming a ring around the perimeter. In this installation apples and oranges were a metaphor for difference, but what also resulted was an inviting work that fused the embodiment of harmony in the traditional Chinese symbol with the suggestion of plenty that is a direct result of living a harmonious life. Chong saw the work as a tribute to the cultural differences and similarities specifically between Mexico and the United States, with a hope that both would respect each other's cultures and coexist harmoniously.

In all of his photographs, those with family images and those without, Chong encourages a reclamation and reevaluation of the past. He believes that it is in the past that one finds a clearer sense of self in a mainstream world that can overpower and confuse.

—Lizzetta LeFalle-Collins

CLARK, Claude

American painter

Born: Rockingham, Georgia, 11 November 1915. **Education:** Pennsylvania Music School, Philadelphia, 1935-39, certificate 1939; Barnes Foundation, Merion, Pennsylvania, 1939-44; Sacramento University, California, 1955-58, B.A. 1958; University of California at Berkeley, 1958-62, M.A. 1962. **Family:** Married Daima May Lockhart in 1943, one son and one daughter. **Career:** Artist, Works Progress Administration, Philadelphia, 1939-42; substitute teacher, Philadelphia Public Schools, 1945-48; assistant professor of art, Talladega, Alabama, 1948-55; special education instructor, Alameda College, Oakland, California, 1959-68; art instructor, Merritt College, Oakland, California, 1968-81. **Awards:** Silver Medal, St. Nicholas League, 1933; Barnes Foundation Fellowship, 1942. **Address:** 788 Santa Ray Avenue, Oakland, California 94610, U.S.A.

Individual Exhibitions:

1944	Phillip Ragan Gallery, Philadelphia
1945	Bonestell Gallery, New York
1946	Roko Gallery, New York
1949	Talladega, Alabama
1956	Crocker Art Gallery, Sacramento, California
1971	Fisk University, Nashville, Tennessee (retrospective)
1990	Hammonds House, Atlanta, Georgia (retrospective)
1993	Pro Arts Gallery, Oakland, California
1995	Bomani Gallery, San Francisco
1996	Apex Gallery, Atlanta, Georgia (retrospective)

Selected Group Exhibitions:

1939	Worlds Fair, Flushing Meadows, New York
1941	Downtown Gallery, New York
1945	Brooklyn Museum, New York
1953	Sorbonne, Paris, France
1975	Philadelphia (circuit)
1976	Los Angeles (circuit)
1985	Los Angeles County Museum
1986	Portsmouth, Virginia
1989	Lehman College Art Gallery, Bronx, New York

Collections:

Afro-American Museum, Wilberforce, Dayton, Ohio; Apex House, Atlanta, Georgia; Atlanta University, Georgia; Barnes Foundation, Merion, Pennsylvania; Du Sable Museum, Chicago; Fisk University, Nashville, Tennessee; Hammond House, Atlanta, Georgia; Hampton University, Hampton Roads, Virginia; Talladega College, Talladega, Alabama; Van Vechten, Tennessee.

Publications:

By CLARK: Books—*Black Art Perspectives,* Oakland, California, Merritt College Press, 1970.

On CLARK: Article—"Barnes Foundation" by Vincent Jubilee, in *Journal of Negro Education* (Washington, D.C.), 15(1), Winter 1982.

*

Claude Clark comments:

I attempt to use fauna and flora in an environment to create the essence of some visual spiritual values of the universe. My visions led me to a single purpose: to research the heritage of African peoples. As we seek to know ourselves, our culture, we are ready to help others.

Early on I was convinced that a creative spirit must soar far beyond compartments of religion and politics. Such freedom has enabled me, in celebration of creativity, to learn and to know that, through the roots of African art, I learned of the source of most western and eastern art. So it is that I *celebrate* all art of the soul and spirit.

*   *   *

Claude Clark became interested in art because he wanted to document the contributions of black people. He is known for the careful thought and planning of his compositions rather than for spontaneous action, no doubt because of his training at the Philadelphia Museum School of Art in 1935-39 and at the Albert Barnes Foundation in 1939-44. Clark's early works are marked by heavy dark lines that outline fluid shapes, recalling the work of the French painter Georges Rouault and traditional Japanese narrative works. While Clark's early style was influenced primarily by French expressionism, his study at the Barnes Foundation and his friendship with Albert Barnes in subsequent years shaped his appreciation and promotion of traditional African art. His study at the Barnes Foundation also helped inform his knowledge of the role that African art had played in the development of the modern European art that so affected his work. In addition, it encouraged him to concentrate on images of Africans in the Americas (primarily the United

Claude Clark (with *Creative Source*), 1995. Photo courtesy of Jonathan Eubanks.

States and the Caribbean). Moreover, he came to understand and practice Alain Locke's decree that the work of African American artists should reflect the native culture found in their folk roots in the South. Thus, rural life in the South and in the Caribbean have been favorite themes throughout Clark's career.

Clark came to know the paint medium well, initially having to mix his paints from dry pigment and oil because premixed colors were too expensive. For this reason he experimented with different consistencies to arrive at a variety of surfaces, from thick impasto to watercolors. Known primarily for his "juicy colors," as a *New York Times* reviewer once called them, he created powerful landscapes and figurative studies that revealed his concern with the condition of the African American community. In his early works he painted in undulating shapes that seemed to fuse with one another but were prevented from doing so only by the dark lines that contained them. Lines were used to ensure that there was separation between the colors, but the edges were sharpened or relaxed at will. Clark's subjects ranged from floral studies, which were exercises in color experimentation, to landscapes and urban scenes. Some of his most interesting works were his watercolors of jitterbug dancers, in which the compositions seemed to swing as the dancers slid across the paper.

Clarke participated in the Federal Art Project of the Works Progress Administration from 1939 to 1942 before leaving Phila-

delphia to teach at Talladega College in Alabama from 1948 to 1955. Clark agrees that his most successful works were created in the 1940s because of the time he had then to devote to his art career. After he moved to Talladega, his emphasis shifted to teaching, which continued when he moved to Oakland, California, in 1958 and enrolled in a master's degree program in painting at the University of California, Berkeley, in the same year. Clark's experiences there changed his style. At the university the emphasis was on abstraction, and Clark was encouraged to drop the lines around his images. What he lost in linear definition, however, he made up with texture. His smooth surfaces became rugged, and the undulating shapes became angular and hard. Clark's minor at the university was social studies, with an emphasis on anthropology, and he came to realize that his explorations in abstraction were too far removed from what he wanted his art to do—to document the lives and culture of black people. Toward that end, after graduating from the university in 1962, Clark focused on educating African American students about their art heritage by teaching in innovative programs that encouraged art-making and appreciation among the underserved and in nontraditional settings, as among prison inmates.

Clark's greatest achievement was almost single-handedly founding, in 1967, one of the first art curriculums with emphasis totally on the black experience. With the establishment of the new Peralta Community College system in the East Bay area in 1966, the Black

Claude Clark: *Saturday Night (Woman Giving Child a Bath), 1939.* Photo courtesy of Jonathan Eubanks.

Panthers demanded that black educators like Clark be considered for positions. The black studies curriculum at Merritt College in Oakland became the standard on which other programs in the state of California were patterned. In 1969 Clark wrote *A Black Art Perspective: A Black Teacher's Guide to a Black Visual Art Curriculum,* offering educators a detailed annotated outline for preparing and presenting courses in African and African American visual culture from a black point of view. In the 1990s an updated version was prepared by Clark and his wife. Clark believes that blackness is a culture and not just a color, and his main purpose in pursuing art has been to teach about black life from his people's point of view, to record the eras in which he and his people have lived, and to give his people a sense of the broader diaspora.

—Lizzetta LeFalle-Collins

CLARK, Ed(ward)
American painter

Born: New Orleans, Louisiana, 1926. **Education:** Art Institute of Chicago, 1947-51; L'Academie de la Grande Chaumiere, Paris, 1952-54. **Career:** Artist-in-residence/art teacher, University of Delaware, 1969, Art Institute of Chicago, University of Oregon, 1973, Skowegan School of Painting and Sculpture, 1974, Ohio State University, 1976, Louisiana State University, 1978, Syracuse University, 1980. **Awards:** Prix d'Othon Friesz, Musée des Arts Decoratifs, 1955; National Endowment for the Arts grant, 1972; C.A.P.S. grant, New York State Council on the Arts, 1975; Adolph Gottlieb Award, 1981; Master Award, National Endowment for the Arts, 1985.

Individual Exhibitions:

1980	Studio Museum in Harlem, New York
1981	Jazzonia, Detroit
1982	Randall Gallery, New York
1983	Randall Gallery, New York
1987	Alitash Kebede Fine Arts, Los Angeles
1988	Manhattan East Gallery of Fine Arts, New York
1989	Gallery Kesser-Bohbot, Hamburg
1990	Spiral Gallery, Brooklyn, New York
1991	Galerie Resche, Paris
1992	Wilmer Jennings Gallery, New York
1993	Alitash Kebede Fine Arts, Los Angeles
1994	A.F.T.U. Bill Hodges Gallery, New York
	Syracuse University, New York
1995	G.R. N'Namdi Gallery, Birmingham, Michigan

Selected Group Exhibitions:

1984	Studio Museum in Harlem, New York
1985	Gallery of the Avant-Garde, New York
1987	*The Art of Black America,* Tokyo
1988	Buckam Fine Arts, Flint, Michigan
1989	California Afro-American Museum, Los Angeles
1990	Carl Murphy Fine Arts Center, Mortan State University, Baltimore
1991	Studio Museum in Harlem, New York
1992	Art Institute of Chicago
1993	*Diversity and Style, African American Artists,* University of Michigan, Dearborn
1994	Museum of Science and Industry, Chicago

Collections:

Aldrich Museum of Contemporary Art, Ridgefield, Connecticut; California Afro-American Museum, Los Angeles; Evans-Ribbs Collection; Louisiana State University, New Orleans; Museum of Modern Art, Salvador, Bahia, Brazil; Museum Solidarity, Titograd, Yugoslavia; Schomburg Center, New York; Studio Museum in Harlem, New York; Syracuse University, New York; University of Kentucky, Lexington.

Publications:

On CLARK: Book—*Edward Clark: A Complex Identity,* exhibition catalog, by Anita Feldman, New York, Studio Museum in Harlem, 1980. **Articles**—"Ed Clark's Luminous Expanses" by April Kingsley, in *American Rag* (New York), 1(2/3), 1980; "Edward Clark, Directions" by Judith Wilson, in *Art in America,* 69(1), 1981, pp. 119-21; "In Search of Vision: Edward Clark and Candida Alvarez" by Dawoud Bey, in *Uptown,* 2(2), p. 6; "Ed Clark" by Judith Wilson, in *Issue 4,* Fall 1985; "Ed Clark: Recent Paintings-Gallery Art 54," in *Art News,* March 1987, p. 138.

*   *   *

Ed Clark (with "Paris Series"), 1995.

Ed Clark, as he is called by friends and admirers, could be credited as the architect of the shaped canvas. In the mid-1940s, during his early studies at the Art Institute of Chicago, Clark was very much an impressionist painter. Like other American artists, travel to Paris in 1952 was the beginning of a new direction for Clark, who developed interests in abstraction, a departure from the representational art that he was used to in the United States.

He was impressed by a Russian-born artist, Nicolas de Stael, a leading postwar abstractionist. In 1953 Clark painted his first abstract, entitled *The City,* which was almost called a hard-edge composition. Even though it was a city scene, Clark was able to break into different shapes and sizes with color in the work, which was distorted to the extent that it became less representational.

In 1957 he created a series of paintings, intermingling canvases with painted fragments of paper that overlapped and went beyond the frame of the canvas. At the time Clark had started to paint imaginative sceneries, with large strokes of the brush, perhaps from his recollection of his earlier days at the beach of New Orleans. The "Untitled" series (1957, oil on canvas with paper collage on wood) could be the beginning of Clark's freedom of expression.

Mary Schmidt has said about Clark that "his strength as a painter has been his ability to do the work of imagination, an ability that has permitted him to maneuver past the pitfalls of painterly and postpainterly abstraction. His art has never succumbed to rhetorical posturing or fashionable irony. Instead he has persisted, with devotion and skill, in opening the way to triumphant ordering that is both convincing and free."

Clark's *Broken Rainbow* (1986) shows a new dimension and direction in his career. In this painting he used large strokes of a broom to create the illusion of waves. As Lawrence Campbell puts it, "an example of how a process of painting can result in an appearance of nature closer and more faithful to it than if the painter had sat down in front of the sea and endeavored to fit its image on canvas."

Ed Clark's quest to explore his newly found field led him to develop and create some elliptical, diamond-shaped, round, and square canvases, with bold broad strokes in either heavy or light harmonious colors. Large broom-like brushes are used to spread the pigment across the canvas, as it lays on the floor. The paintings are in some occasions hung to float from the ceiling, a practice that Sam Gilliam also adopted during the late 1960s. It was a provocative and fascinating departure from the academic style of stretched canvas.

Ted Joans thought that Clark's painting was an attempted erotic reaction in space, tone, texture, and color—a painted feeling, a means to reunite the self with the world of desire. The free uninhibited use of color and brush strokes has made Clark one of the major American abstractionists and provided another avenue for the modernist movement to explore.

—Gabriel Tenabe

CLARK, Irene

American painter

Born: Washington, D.C., 1927. **Education:** 414 Workshop, Chicago; San Francisco Art Institute. **Career:** Gallery director, Exhibit Gallery and Studio, Chicago. Member, African-American Historical and Cultural Society. **Awards:** John Hope Purchase Award, Atlanta Annual, Georgia; First Purchase Award, Atlanta University, Georgia; Lake Meadows Art Fair Award, 1960; Beaux Art Ball Award, Chicago, Georgia. **Died.**

Selected Exhibitions:

African Historical Society (1972); Atlanta University, Georgia; Chabot College; Grant Street Art Fair; Howard University, Washington, D.C.; Kaiser Cement Gallery, New York; Left Bank Gallery, San Francisco; Lioga Duncan Gallery, New York; Institute of Technology, Crown Hall, Illinois; North Shore Art League, Chicago; Oakland Museum, California (1968); Old Triangle Fair; San Francisco Art Festival; Southside Art Center; Tamapais High School, Mill Valley, California; Walnut Creek Art Festival.

Collections:

Atlanta University, Georgia; Oakland Museum, California.

*   *   *

While Irene Clark's paintings cannot be categorized by any particular style, her work is undeniably contemporary African American. Although she was trained in the academy, her paintings reflect the influence of primitive, or folk, style, and her work is sometimes described as neoprimitive. She grew up at a time when genre paintings and portraits by many notable black artists, while not considered mainstream, were becoming well known and influential in the African American art community. Inasmuch as she uses African themes and the African American community as her subjects, her work also reflects modern African American consciousness.

Old Negro Rhyme (1958) is a painting whose subjects are derived from a rhyme dating to the 1920s and 1930s. (In the 1960s a version of the rhyme was incorporated into a contemporary pop song.) The rhyme, officially titled "Once Upon a Time" by Langston Hughes, and the painting refer to a monkey and a rooster. African American folklore has a rich storytelling tradition that often adds images and anecdotes from various African cultures. As with other traditions, animals are commonly used either as symbols or as trickster types. *Rolling Calf* is based on a Jamaican folktale telling of a restless spirit that eventually reveals itself as an animal. The painting depicts five different animals that resemble a pig, a cat, a dog or jackal, a horse, and a large sheep whose front legs end in human feet and back legs in cloven hooves.

Other paintings by Clark offer the viewer less fantastic images. *Mansion on Prairie Avenue* is a painting that shows not an event but rather a scene from an African American community's everyday life (no specific location is indicated). The work depicts a large three-story Victorian-style house, with people standing at the windows on each floor. All of the adult subjects are female, a few with scarves on their heads, and there are several small children. It is obvious that conversations are taking place. Outside the house young children are playing with hoops. The paint for the house appears to have been applied thickly and then scored to create the illusion of stone blocks and roofing shingles. A bottle sticking up out of the front yard is a jarring detail in an otherwise friendly scene. The viewer gets the impression of perseverance. *Playmates* demands a more complicated reaction from the viewer. A solemn young girl, whose face is reminiscent of a Picasso-like African mask, is gently holding a doll, which appears to be happier than the girl.

Other than a stark background, there are no visual clues in the painting to help the viewer determine the emotional state of the girl.

Clark's paintings provoke the viewer's intellect and sensibilities. At first glance her paintings may appear to be whimsical, but a closer look reveals details that provide room for interpretation.

—Christine Miner Minderovic

CLARK, LeRoy
Trinidadian painter

Born: 1938. **Address:** 28 West Hill, Port of Spain, Trinidad.

Individual Exhibitions:

1966	Port of Spain
1972	Studio Museum in Harlem, New York
1976	Howard University, Washington, D.C.
1977	World Bank, Washington, D.C.
1979	Teachers Training College, Port of Spain
1988	Aquarela Galleries
1989	Aquarela Galleries
1991	Aquarela Galleries
1992	Aquarela Galleries
	A Retrospective, National Museum Art Gallery

Selected Group Exhibitions:

1966	*Biennale,* São Paulo, Brazil
1967	Expo '67, Canada
1969	Loeb Student Center, New York University
	Hudson River Museum, New York
1971	Bell Traveling Exhibition, Illinois
1974	Cornell University, New York
1975	*Young Artists International,* New York
1990	*Four Artists in Venezuela,* Caracas
1991	Drexel University, Philadelphia
1992	Espace Carpeaux, Courbevoie, France

Collections:

National Collection, Jamaica; National Museum and Art Gallery, Royal Victoria Institute, Trinidad; Studio Museum in Harlem, New York.

*   *   *

A painter, poet, philosopher, and teacher, LeRoy Clarke has created an expansive body of surrealist paintings, drawings, and poetry that explores his personal philosophy on the complexities of African Caribbean identity. Clarke considers his entire body of work to be an epic consisting of several movements that document the journeys and struggles of the poet. In these movements the poet seeks "the apotheosis of the self," the realization of his greatest abilities, and central to this quest is the comprehension and embracing of African memories and culture. Initiated in 1970, the epic is made up of eight movements: *Fragments of A Spiritual, Douens, In*

the Maze I Make a Single Line to My Soul, Eye Am, El Tucuche, Utterance, Pantheon, and *Revelations.* The epic is a work in progress, to which future movements are to be added as they occur to the artist.

Clarke's canvases are a dense interweaving of color, abstracted human figures, and anthropomorphic shapes drawn from the landscapes and folklore of his native Trinidad, as well as the African Caribbean religions of Santeria and voodoo. According to J. D. Elder, Clarke also "employs the cosmic symbols of the ecology—water, mountains, vistas, air, fire, and ether," and his work is most often compared to the Latin American surrealists Roberto Matta and Wifredo Lam. His complex layering of shape, color, and pattern creates varying depths within the canvas. In works such as *Lakoja, Our Waters Meet,* and *Oya, Breath of the Invisible,* from the 1996 movement *Pantheon,* Clarke combines layers of color, figures, and symbols to give the paintings an organic quality and a pulsating, living energy. In "Pelt Yuh Stones Nuh . . . ," the artist himself describes how this vibrancy is achieved:

> through syllables of violet, the science of turquoise,
> through populous ochres and energetic reds
> through fathomless greens, through supplicant blue,
> through the arterial vegetation of the rainbow.

One of the core images that bears special significance in Clarke's work and that serves as the theme for a large body of his ink drawings is the Douens. In Trinidadian folklore the Douens are the spirits of children who died before they were baptized. The Douens have big heads, swollen stomachs, and feet turned backward, and because they cannot stand the light of the sun, they can inhabit only the twilight. Clarke uses the Douens as a metaphor for "the dilapidation of the African spirit," and his work stands as both a warning and a challenge to his people against the evils of douenophilia, what Elder describes as "a growth disease in which the personality's evolution towards maturity is arrested." Besides their feet, which impede their progress and, as Tracy Wilson explains, keep them "trapped in a state of unbeing," Clarke's Douens are afflicted by distended heads and stomachs, for during slavery and colonization they were filled with foreign knowledge and food that displaced self-knowledge and that did nothing to nourish the African spirit. According to Wilson, it is through his artwork that Clarke seeks to redeem his people and build "an African consciousness forged with remembrance."

The drawings that accompany the poetry of the *Douens* movement are powerful graphic works, executed with tremendous detail and extensive patterning. They are peopled by distorted figures that seem to be a cross between human, beast, plant, and machine, and they bear an interesting comparison to the work of Lam from the mid-1960s. In this movement, as in all of Clarke's work, it is important to be aware of the intimate relationship between word and image. The two are intertwined and are at the center of the artist's philosophy that "art is the language of life, the languaging of one's life." As the Trinidadian musicologist and painter Patricia Bishop has observed, Clarke's paintings "have as much to do with words as they do with image . . . you can't deal with the canvas without dealing with the word."

Clarke is undoubtedly one of the most important artists working in the Caribbean. His work has been widely exhibited, published, and collected throughout the United States and Latin America, including the West Indies. With many publications to his name, including numerous articles, and a rich body of paintings and drawings, Clarke continues to make significant contributions to the development of an African Caribbean aesthetic and to send a compelling and challenging message of cultural empowerment through his art.

—Monique G. Curnen

COLESCOTT, Robert

American painter

Born: Oakland, California, 1925. **Education:** Student of Fernand Léger, Paris, 1940-50; University of California, Berkeley, B.A. 1949; University of California, Berkeley, M.A. 1952. **Career:** Associate professor of art, Portland State University, Oregon, 1957-66; visiting professor, American University of Cairo, 1966-67; professor of art history, American College, Paris, 1967-68; professor of art, College Art Study Abroad, Paris, 1967-69, California State College, Stanislaus, California, 1970-74; visiting lecturer of painting and drawing, University of California, Berkeley, 1974-79; visiting professor of art, University of Arizona, Tucson, 1983-84; instructor of painting and drawing, San Francisco Art Institute, 1976-85; professor of art, University of Arizona, Tucson, 1985-90. Since 1990 regents' professor of art, University of Arizona, Tucson. Since 1984 public lecturer throughout the United States. **Awards:** Visual Arts Award, SECCA Winston-Salem; American Research Center grant, 1964-65; National Endowment for the Arts grant, 1976, 1980 and 1983; Guggenheim Foundation grant, 1985; Roswell Foundation Artist's Residency grant, 1987; "Robert Colescott Day" declaration, City of Houston, December 2, 1988; Tamarind Institute Resident Artist grant, 1989; Marie Walsh Sharpe Foundation award, 1991.

Robert Colescott. Photo courtesy of G.R. N'Namdi Gallery.

Individual Exhibitions:

1953	Miller Pollard, Seattle
1957	Zoe Dusanne, Seattle
1958	Portland Art Museum, Oregon
1960	Portland Art Museum, Oregon
	Museum of Art, Eugene, Oregon
	Fountain Gallery, Portland, Oregon
1961	Salem Art Museum, Oregon
	Reed College Art Gallery, Portland, Oregon
1965	Victoria Municipal Art Gallery, British Columbia
1966	Fountain Gallery, Portland, Oregon
	Portland Art Museum, Oregon
1972	Friedlander Gallery, Seattle
1973	Spectrum Gallery, New York
1975	Razor Gallery, New York
1977	Razor Gallery, New York
1978	John Berggruen Gallery, San Francisco
1979	Hamilton Gallery, New York
1981	Semaphore Gallery, New York
1982	Semaphore Gallery, New York
1983	Freedman Gallery, Albright College, Reading, Pennsylvania
1985	Institute of Contemporary Art, University of Pennsylvania, Philadelphia
	Hadler/Rodriguez Gallery, Houston, Texas
	Greenville County Museum of Art, Greenville, South Carolina
	Semaphore Gallery, New York
	Dart Gallery, Chicago
	Knight Gallery, Charlotte, North Carolina
1986	Koplin Gallery, Los Angeles
	Semaphore East Gallery, New York
1987	Roswell Museum and Art Center, San Francisco
	Semaphore Gallery, New York
	Phyllis Kind Gallery, Chicago
1988	*The Eye of the Beholder: Recent Work by Robert Colescott,* Marsh Gallery, Modlin Fine Arts Center, University of Richmond, Virginia (traveling)
1987	*Robert Colescott: A Retrospective, 1975-1986,* San Jose Museum of Art, (traveling)
1989	Phyllis Kind Gallery, New York
	Robert Colescott, A Retrospective, Seattle Art Museum
	Greg Kuccra Gallery, Seattle
	University of Texas, El Paso
1990	Overholland Museum, Amsterdam, Holland
	Arthur Roger Gallery, New Orleans
	Phyllis Kind Gallery, Chicago
	Linda Cathcart Gallery, Los Angeles
	Howard Yezerski Gallery, Boston
1991	Phyllis Kind Gallery, New York
	University of Colorado Museum, Boulder
1992	G.R. N'Namdi Gallery, Birmingham, Mississippi
	Phyllis Kind Gallery, New York
1993	Laura Russo Gallery, Portland, Oregon
	Linda Cathcart Gallery, Santa Monica, California
	Phyllis Kind Gallery, New York

1994	Phyllis Kind Gallery, New York
1995	Scottsdale Center for the Arts, Arizona
	Horwitch LewAllen Gallery, Santa Fe, New Mexico
	Katonah Museum of Art, Westchester County, New York
1996	G.R. N'Namdi Gallery, Birmingham, Mississippi

Selected Group Exhibitions:

1991	Aldrich Museum of Art, Ridgefield, Connecticut
1992	*Spirit Made Visible,* John Natsoulas Gallery, Davis, California
	Museum of Modern Art, New York
1993	Brooklyn Museum, New York
	The Purloined Image, Flint Institute of Arts, Flint, Michigan
	Arthur Roger Gallery, New Orleans
1994	Corcoran Gallery of Art, Washington, D.C.
	Whitney Museum of Contemporary Art, New York
1995	Aspen Art Museum, Colorado
	Horwitch LewAllen Gallery, Santa Fe

Collections:

Akron Art Museum, Ohio; Boston Museum of Fine Art; Brooklyn Museum of Art, New York; Columbia College, Portland, Oregon; Contemporary Museum of Art, Honolulu; Corcoran Gallery of Art, Washington, D.C.; Delaware Museum of Art, Wilmington; Denver Museum of Art; Greenville County Museum of Art, South Carolina; High Museum of Art, Atlanta, Georgia; Hirshorn Museum, Washington, D.C.; Indianapolis Art Museum, Indiana; Kresge Art Museum, Michigan State University, East Lansing; Metropolitan Museum of Art, New York; Museum of Modern Art, New York; Newark Museum of Art, New Jersey; Oakland Art Museum, California; Portland Art Museum, Oregon; Reed College, Portland, Oregon; Rose Art Museum, Brandeis University, Waltham, Massachusetts; Roswell Museum, New Mexico; San Francisco Museum of Modern Art; Seattle Art Museum; Tucson Museum of Art, Arizona; University of Massachusetts, Amherst; University of Oregon, Eugene; Victoria Art Gallery, British Columbia; Whitney Museum of American Art, New York.

Publications:

By COLESCOTT: Article—"Cultivating a Subversive Palette," in *Reimaging America: The Arts of Social Change,* edited by Mark O'Brien and Craig Little, Philadelphia, New Society Publishers, 1990.

On COLESCOTT: Books—*Those Africans Look Like White Elephants: An Interview with Robert Colescott,* exhibition catalog, New York, Semaphore Gallery and Joe Lewis, 1982; *Robert Colescott: A Retrospective 1975-1986,* exhibition catalog, California, San Jose Museum of Art, Lowery S. Sims and Mitchell D. Kahan, 1987; *The Eye of the Beholder: Recent Work by Robert Colescott,* exhibition catalog, Virginia, University of Richmond, Katherine Weiss and Susan Arnold (interview), 1988; *Robert Colescott: Another Judgment,* exhibition catalog, Charlotte, North Carolina, Night Gallery, Kenneth Baker and Anne Shengold, 1985; *Here and Now, Robert Colescott,* exhibition catalog, South Carolina, Greenville County Museum of Art and Thomas W. Styron, 1984; *In Celebration of Black History Month: Twelve Artists and Their Work* by Dennis Evans, Sowder and Associates, Incorporated, Minneapolis, Minnesota, 1984; *Paris Connections: African American Artists In Paris,* exhibition catalog, San Francisco, Bomani Gallery and Q.E.D. Press, 1992. **Articles**—"Robert Colescott: Pride

Robert Colescott: *You're Driving Me Crazy,* **1984. Photo courtesy of G.R. N'Namdi Gallery.**

and Prejudice" by Mitchell Kahan, in *Art Papers,* May/June 1985, pp. 22-23; "Colescott Sees Humor in Human Behavior" by Suzanne Muchnic, in *Los Angeles Times,* 24 April 1986, part VI; "Robert Colescott: Saints and Other Stereotypes" by Merle Schipper, in *Artweek,* 10 May 1986; "Invented Stereotypes: The Painting of Robert Colescott" by M. VanProyon, in *Artweek,* 18(15), 18 April 1987; "Ironic, Irreverent, Confrontational Robert Colescott: A Retrospective" by E. Wright, in *The Baltimore Afro-American,* 16 January 1988; "Robert Colescott's Perspectives on Black and White" by Paul Richard, in *Washington Post,* 20 January 1988; "Turbulent Restatements from Robert Colescott" by John Russell, in *New York Times,* 3 March 1989, weekend section; "Colescott on Black and White" by Ken Johnson, in *Art In America,* June 1989, pp. 148-153, 197; "Robert Colescott: Urban Artist in the Desert" by Jay M. Rochlin, in *Arizona Alumnus,* Fall 1989, pp. 9-13; "Robert Colescott at Phyllis Kind" by Brooks Adams, in *Art in America,* July 1991; "L'Ecole de Paris Is Burning: Robert Colescott's Ironic Variations" by Faye Hirsh, in *Arts Magazine,* September 1991, pp. 52-57. **Videos**—"David D'Arcy Interview with Robert Colescott," on *Morning Edition, National Public Radio,* 14 March 1989; "Video Interview," Linda Freeman Productions, March 1991.

*   *   *

The work of Robert Colescott stands as an original and independent manifestation of present-day American art that reconstitutes the black narrative. Creative in its unique and extravagant expressiveness, it reaches previously unknown levels in revealing an African American identity. Colescott's contribution over three decades has been a challenge to both the various versions of contemporary art and the multilevel traditions of black art. His work thus transcends borderlines in contemporary American society.

Colescott studied at the University of California, Berkeley, and in Paris with Fernand Léger. He spent four years in Paris after the completion of his studies and then two years in Cairo. It was in Cairo that he came in contact with an important nonwhite tradition, which gave him a strong sense of self-affirmation and identity. His early paintings represented the "clash of African and European cultural standards of beauty," as he himself has defined his work in those years.

Colescott's development after his return to the United States soon culminated in works in which masterpieces of the European past were reinterpreted in terms of a dialogue between tradition and the contemporary life of the black community. He combined elements from such artists as Édouard Manet, Vincent van Gogh, and Pablo Picasso with the narrative of black themes, events, and symbols to create an often humorous new configuration. The reuse of familiar themes was filled with new life and at the same time with a reevaluation of black historic and contemporary reality.

The relevance of Robert Colescott's work in the 1970s and 1980s to American art is evident. In contrast to the hierarchical standards of American modernism, he reintroduced the missing black presence, and at the same time he revealed the prevalent imbalance between race and gender representation. Going beyond the formalistic reinterpretations of past images by other American artists, Colescott transcended surface satire and provoked complex reactions, making people aware of the often absurd and racist patterns of American life. An important but still often misunderstood theme in several of Colescott's works is his focus on the relationship between black men and black women, including interracial sexual politics and the manifestation of machismo in black men.

Since the mid-1980s Colescott's development has taken on still another direction. Completely self-assured in his attitude and painterly exuberance, he has achieved a new complexity by relating historical points of departure to more subtle and sophisticated topics. While still referring to and deconstructing images from the European and American past, Colescott has come to focus with increasing intensity on contemporary class, race, and gender issues so as to reveal the political and social hypocrisy that continues to dominate wide areas of American life. His work is an open door into a harmonious symbiosis of art and society that is still in the making. In this regard Ken Johnson has written, "What Colescott is after, then, is anti-discrimination in the broadest sense, not only racially but aesthetically and psychologically. . . ." Colescott's work has a unique significance and is a strong manifestation of an American art in which existing borderlines are transcended. It offers an open-ended vision that in itself has the power to create a new tradition.

—Udo Kultermann

CONWILL, Houston

American sculptor, painter, installation artist, and performance artist

Born: Lexington, Kentucky, 1947. **Education:** Howard University, Washington, D.C., B.F.A. 1973; University of Southern California, Los Angeles, M.F.A. 1976. **Awards:** Guggenheim Memorial Foundation Fellowship, 1982; National Endowment for the Arts fellowships, 1982, 1988; Prix de Rome Fellowship, 1984; New York Foundation for the Arts Fellowship, 1985; Louis Comfort Tiffany Award, 1987; Award for Excellence in Design for *Rivers,* Art Commission of the City of New York, 1992; Certificate for Special Congressional Recognition, for *Revelations,* San Francisco, 1993.

Individual Exhibitions:

1975   Lindhurst Gallery, University of Southern California
1976   *JuJu,* The Gallery, Los Angeles
        JuJu Funk, Lindhurst Gallery, University of Southern California
1978   Just above Midtown, New York
1979   Space Gallery, Los Angeles
1981   Public School #1, Long Island City, New York
1982   Public School #1, Long Island City, New York
        Institute for Art and Urban Resources, Long Island City, New York
1983   Islip Museum, East Islip, New York
        Just above Midtown Downtown, New York
1984   Roanoke College, Salem, Virginia
        Studio Museum in Harlem, New York
1986   *The Passion of Saint Matthew,* Alternative Museum, New York
1988   High Museum of Art, Atlanta, Georgia (traveling)
1989   Smithsonian Institution, Washington, D.C.
        Hirshhorn Museum and Sculpture Garden, Washington, D.C.
        Museum of Modern Art, New York
1992   Brooklyn Museum, New York

Selected Group Exhibitions:

1979   Bronx Museum, New York
1982   Sculpture Center, New York
        Studio Museum in Harlem, New York
1985   Pennsylvania State University, University Park (traveling)
        American Academy in Rome
1986   Nassau County Museum of Fine Art, New York
1989   Bronx Museum of the Arts, New York
1991   *Places with a Past: New Site-Specific Art in Charlestown,*
        Spoleto Festival
1994   *Public Intervention,* Institute of Contemporary Art, Boston
1996   Museum of Modern Art, New York

Selected Performances:

1978   *Thanatopsis: Contemplations on Death,* Space Gallery,
        Los Angeles
1979   *Warrior Chants, Love Songs and New Spirituals,* Watts
        Tower Art Center, Los Angeles
1983   *Cakewalk,* Just above Midtown, Downtown, New York
1984   *The Joyful Mysteries 1984-2034 A.D.,* Studio Museum in
        Harlem, New York
1992   *The New Merengue,* Brooklyn Museum, New York
1993   *Underground Railroad Praise Song,* Underground Rail-
        way, Atlanta, Georgia (traveling)
1994   *Vision at Leni Lenape,* Libation for the Freedom Ring,
        Philadelphia

Collections:

Bellevue Hospital, New York; Centro Wifredo Lam, Havana, Cuba; City College of New York; High Museum of Art, Atlanta, Georgia; Home Life Insurance Company, New York; Howard University, Washington, D.C.; Museum of Contemporary Art, Los Angeles; Museum of Modern Art, New York; Prudential Life Insurance Company, New York; Schomburg Center, New York; Studio Museum in Harlem, New York.

Publications:

On CONWILL: Books—*The Passion of Saint Matthew,* exhibition catalog, New York, Alternative Museum, Madeleine Burnside and Mary Schmidt Campbell, 1986; *Cakewalk,* exhibition catalog, New York, Just above Midtown Downtown, Lucy R. Lippart, and Rosalind Jeffries, 1983; *Art at the Edge: Houston Conwill,* Atlanta, Georgia, High Museum of Art and Susan Krane, 1989. **Articles—**"JuJu Ritual—Cycles of Life" by Suzanne Muchnic, in *Artweek,* 9, 25 February 1978, p. 4; "Notes of a Griot" by Richard Powell, in *Newworld Magazine,* February/March 1979; "Ritual as Art: The Work of Houston Conwill" by Yvonne Cole Meo, in *Black Art Quarterly,* 3, Fall 1979; "Site Sculptors: Burton, Conwill, Fleichner, and Mills" by Ed Spriggs, in *Artpapers,* 1981; "Houston Conwill at P.S. 1" by Judith Wilson, in *Art in America,* October 1981; "Houston Conwill at Just above Midtown" by Donald B. Kuspit, in *Art in America,* February 1984; "Creating a Necessary Space: The Art of Houston Conwill 1975-83" by Judith Wilson, in *The International Review of African American Art,* June 1984; "Houston Conwill, Joseph DePace, and Estella Conwill Majozo in the Brooklyn Museum Lobby" by George Melrod, in *Art in America,* June 1992.

*

Houston Conwill comments:

I am a sculptor, Joseph DePace is an architect, and Estella Conwill Majozo is a poet, and together we form an interdisciplinary team of collaborating artists concerned with the function of art in bringing meaning to our lives and serving as a catalyst for social change. We create site specific installations that rechoreograph the history of the African diaspora within a place with an impulse toward freedom. This is done in the West African tradition of the griot. Our works are multilayered and are intended to open the exclusivity of the historical canon to multiple perspectives. We promote the preservation and communication of wisdom across generations and cultures and intend for our works to serve as vehicles for education, reversing stereotypes and presenting positive role models.

We seek to form a synthesis of multicultural sources, including world art, music, dance, architecture, poetry, theater, film, popular culture, and folk and festival arts. We use language, light, water, natural elements, and glass, as well as video, photography, and performance.

We create maps of language that present symbolic journeys of transformation, fostering greater cultural awareness, racial harmony, and understanding. They are composed from ideographs and symbols as well as collaged and edited lyrics from world music—including spirituals, blues, gospel, soul, jazz, funk, samba, merengue, reggae, calypso, rock and roll, rap, and freedom songs—and quotations from speeches of heroic models.

Their humanistic words address issues of world peace, social justice, human rights, and ecology. They also address the universal enemies: oppression, racism, violence, and poverty. They challenge us to break down barriers between people of diverse backgrounds and to build bridges of compassion, clarifying a common meeting ground for all humanity.

*   *   *

African rituals, blues music, and a desire to explore his African American heritage have always been important to Houston Conwill's art. During his undergraduate studies at Howard University, this painter, sculptor, and site-specific installation artist studied with three artist-professors who were instrumental in the development of his early artistic career. Under the influence of Ethiopian painter Skunder Boghossian, who paints on leather, Conwill executed his first paintings in acrylics on the rough sides of leather strips. From Africobra painter Jeff Donaldson, he became aware of a black aesthetic and folk expression through the use of bright colors, and while serving as a studio assistant to color-school painter Sam Gilliam, Conwill learned to liberate his paintings from the two-dimensional frame and stretcher. It was in Los Angeles, however, where Conwill lived while completing graduate school, that he developed a distinctive, independent style employing abstract imagery and black power aesthetics.

During the late 1970s in California, Conwill and his wife staged performances in which conga drums and flutes were played with tapes of blues, jazz, and spirituals during narrative rituals that incorporated ju-ju bags (West African symbols for good luck). It was during this same period that Conwill invented "petrigraphs," scroll-shaped forms that were initially flat and subsequently rolled up, cast from plastic rhoplex, and studded with two- and three-dimensional objects related to the African American experience. The highly textured petrigraphs were placed in nichelike spaces in small artworks.

Houston Conwill: *The New Ring Shout* (central rotunda, Federal Office Building, New York City). Photo courtesy of Bernstein Associates.

Following his relocation to New York in 1980, Conwill completed his first major East Coast work, located outside the Nexus Contemporary Art Center in Atlanta. *Passages Earth/Space H-3* was an extension of the petrigraph in that it combined that form with the interest in Earth art that was prevalent at the time in California. *Passages* (9' x 9' x 9') was an underground chamber containing forty-nine catacomblike niches, each containing a scroll or ju-ju bag. After it was on view for six months, the excavated "time capsule" was reburied, perhaps to be discovered by "children of the future." During the early 1980s, Conwill also performed narrative, ritual-like actions in environments he created, refined the honeycomb grids on which he had been working, experimented with architectonic elements including arches, circles, and hollow triangles showing pictographic images in relief, and employed sizzling colors.

The years 1983 and 1989 were pivotal in Conwill's career: in 1983 the cosmogram was introduced, and in 1989 he formed a collaboration with an architect and a poet. Since that time most of Conwill's projects have been designed and executed in collaboration with his sister, Estella Conwill Majozo, a poet, and Italian American architect Joseph DePace. The cosmogram motif was inspired

by ceremonial ground-drawings of the Kongo people of Zaire. These were based on the four corners of the universe, and each one suggested an avenue to spiritual fulfillment.

The first cosmogram, created in 1983 at the Just above Midtown Gallery in New York, was based on the cakewalk dance, which was first performed by slaves in the antebellum South to entertain, while simultaneously mocking, their masters. After the Civil War, the cakewalk emerged as a stage act, and during the late 1890s it became a ballroom dance craze popularized by whites. Following the appearance of the cakewalk theme at the Just above Midtown Gallery, where the audience walked through the circular diagram while viewing it, the theme reappeared in *The New Cakewalk* of 1988 in a glass circle at the High Museum of Art in Atlanta and in the *Cakewalk Humanifesto: A Cultural Libation* of 1989 at the Museum of Modern Art in New York. That installation featured a dance floor diagram identifying cities in the South that were associated with the civil rights struggle and was accompanied by a honeycomb wall of blues lyrics.

Markings on the Sand, completed in 1989 at the Hirshhorn Museum and Sculpture Garden in Washington, D.C., was the earliest cosmogram not inspired by a dance. Following this, Conwill,

DePace, and Conwill Majozo completed the following three cosmograms at public libraries in New York, Chicago, and Charleston, South Carolina, respectively: *Rivers,* in honor of poet Langston Hughes; *DuSable's Journey,* a tribute to the Haitian man who became Chicago's first permanent resident; and *The New Charleston,* a piece celebrating both the city and the popular 1920s dance of the same name.

A 1995 project by Conwill and his collaborators also took them back to their original dance theme. *The New Ring Shout* commemorates the eighteenth-century African burial ground in New York City that was partially excavated in 1992. The piece is dedicated to the approximately 20,000 blacks buried there, and it takes its name from a dance performed throughout North America and the Caribbean. In the center of the building's rotunda, a terrazzo and polished brass cosmogram are transposed over a map of New York City. Quotations by seven men and seven women, who alternate as dance partners, are seen in conjunction with fourteen signposts in the city's geography.

The multicultural and multilayered cosmograms created by the partnership of Conwill, DePace, and Conwill Majozo are unique, important, and though-provoking monuments that celebrate a blend of African American history, music, dance, oratory, folklore, and political manifestos, as well as the pluralism of world cultures. Performances and/or dances are usually enacted during the installation ceremonies for the cosmograms. As audiences walk or dance while viewing the works, they become participants in the total experience.

—Regenia Perry

CORTOR, Eldzier

American painter and printmaker

Born: Richmond, Virginia, 10 January 1916. **Education:** Art Institute of Chicago, 1936 and 1941; Institute of Design, Columbia University, New York, 1942-43; Columbia University, New York, 1947. **Career:** Teacher, Centre d'Art, Port-au-Prince, Haiti, 1949-51, Pratt Institute, Brooklyn, New York, 1972-74. **Awards:** Rosenwald Foundation Fellowship, 1944-45; Bertha Aberle Florsheim Award, 1945; William H. Bartels Award, Chicago, 1946; honorable mention, Carnegie Institute, Pittsburgh, 1947; Guggenheim Memorial Foundation Fellowship, 1950. **Address:** 35 Montgomery Street, New York, New York 10002, U.S.A.

Selected Exhibitions:

Art Institute of Chicago; Carnegie Institute, Pittsburgh; Howard University, Washington, D.C.; Metropolitan Museum of Art, New York; National Center of Afro-American Artists, Boston; Studio Museum of Harlem, New York.

Publications:

On CORTOR: Books—*Seventeen Black Artists* by Elton C. Fax, New York, Dodd, Mead and Company, 1971; *Three Masters—Eldzier Cortor, Hughie Lee-Smith, Archibald Motley,* exhibition catalog, New York, Kenkeleba Gallery and Corinne Jennings, 1988.

Articles—"Negro Art in Chicago" by Willard F. Motley, in *Opportunity,* 18, January 1940, pp. 19-22; "Eldzier Cortor," in *History of African-American Artists, From 1792 to the Present* by Romare Bearden and Harry Henderson, New York, Pantheon Books, 1993, 272-279.

*   *   *

As with his contemporaries, the social realists, Eldzier Cortor's earliest and most remarkable work was concerned with the poverty created by the Great Depression. Like many other blacks from the South, Cortor migrated to Chicago. He attended Englewood High School, along with the artist Charles White, before beginning formal art education at the Art Institute of Chicago in the early 1930s. The European exhibitions at the Art Institute often stressed the tenets of formal classicism, and Cortor's early work showed this influence, especially in the many drawings titled "Classical Study." On the strength of his work at the Art Institute he was employed by the Works Progress Administration, which provided him access to materials and other artists. He also taught at the South Side Community Arts Center, where he developed an interest in political and historical events that prompted him to draw cartoons. The Field Museum in Chicago provided a large collection of African sculpture that was particularly influential on the young painter, and their effect is recognizable in his handling of the female nude in paint. But it was the Art Institute, where Cortor received a Julius Rosenwald Fellowship, that enabled him to work and study in the Sea Islands off the coast of Georgia and thus develop what would become his signature style. He later spent extensive time in Cuba, Jamaica, and Haiti on a Guggenheim Fellowship.

After his time in the Sea Islands statuesque black nudes became the focus of Cortor's artistic output. Like Amedeo Modigliani, Cortor clearly admired the female nude, which is revealed in the sinuous, elongated renderings of the women who populate most of his works. As graceful and beatified as Cortor makes his female bodies, however, he is clearly being voyeuristic. In the 1940s he created many such works, simply titled "Room," in which a woman, always dignified, appears amid the cramped quarters of a single-room tenement apartment. It is as if Cortor is testifying to the strength of spirit needed in the urban ghetto, just as he showed the strength necessary in the fields of the South in *Southern Gate* (1942). In this work the juxtaposition of the beautiful woman among chaos creates a surreal characterization of Ernest Hemingway's "grace under pressure." A seminude (a cloth hangs around her waist) female stands in front of a gate not unlike those of large plantation houses, with the eerie dark sky creating a tone of tragedy.

As with the work of Richmond Barthé, Cortor's nudes present the beauty of the black body in repose, a skill highly prized by the critic Alain Locke. Yet Cortor is merely making the black female nude his subject, without taking into account the loaded history and myth behind the surface. Nonetheless, the overall psychological and sociological tension found in the "Room" series is unequaled in his later work, where Cortor seems to have become more occupied with graphic depiction than any corresponding underlying mood.

Cortor's art represents the changing landscape of New Deal life and Locke's call for artists to look for inspiration from Africa and their own folk tradition in the South. What is most intriguing is the way in which Cortor evinces so many complex concerns so simply.

—M. Franklin Sirmans

COSTA E SILVA, Raimundo da

Brazilian painter

Contemporary of Leandro Joaquim. **Born:** Rio de Janeiro, 18th century. **Died.**

Publications:

On COSTA E SILVA: Book—*A Mao Afro-Brasileira: Significado da Contribucao Artistica e Historica,* São Paulo, Tenege, 1988. **Article**—"Negros Pardos e Mulatos na Pintura e na Escultura" by Leite Teixera and José Roberto, in *Brasileira do Séc* (São Paulo), 18, 1988.

* * *

Raimundo da Costa e Silva lived in Rio de Janeiro during the eighteenth century and was a contemporary of Leandro Joaquim. Little is known of his life other than that he was an artilleryman in the army and lived to be an octogenarian. He learned the arts of sculpture and wood carving at an early age from his father, and he later came to be a painter, specializing in painting on glass. He also painted portraits. Above all it was Costa e Silva's religious paintings that brought him distinction.

Costa e Silva's oil painting on canvas *Nossa senhora do Carmo* (1787; "Our Lady of Carmo") depicts the crowned Virgin lavishly dressed in gold brocade and holding a fair-haired toddler. Both the mother and child have their heads tilted, as if looking from the painting but avoiding a direct gaze at the viewer. The painting is displayed at the National Museum of Fine Arts in Rio de Janeiro. Another painting of the same subject hangs in the Church of the Third Order of Carmo in Rio de Janeiro. Although the painting is similar, in this work the gazes of the Virgin and the child directly meet the eyes of the viewer. Another religious work attributed to Costa e Silva is the oil on canvas *Nossa senhora da conceição* ("Our Lady of the Conception") at the Church of the Third Order of Nossa Senhora da Conceição da Boa Morte in Rio de Janeiro. The figure in the work stands with her hands clasped prayerfully and her head surrounded by an aura of light. Her features are delicate and youthful, and her face has a beatific expression. Her robes of brocade are richly embroidered with flowers. Another oil on canvas of the same subject attributed to Costa e Silva hangs in the Church of Nossa Senhora Mae dos Homens in Rio de Janiero. This painting depicts the barefoot Virgin standing on a crescent moon held aloft by a group of cherubs. Angels in the background surround the figure, which is ascending to heaven. The eyes of the Virgin are cast downward, and her hands are clasped in a prayerful pose. In this painting the Virgin's robes do not exhibit the baroque ornamentation of other paintings by Costa e Silva. A further painting attributed to Costa e Silva is in the Museum of the Church of Nossa Senhora do Carmo da Lapa do Desterro, also in Rio de Janeiro. This oil on canvas, *Virgin of Carmelo,* is another rendering of the Virgin and child. Both figures wear crowns and gaze from the painting directly at the viewer.

Other paintings by Costa e Silva are *Bautismo do Cristo* ("Baptism of Christ") in the Church do Santissimo Sacramento and *Sagrada familia* ("Holy Family") in the Church of São José. *A Ceia do Senhor* ("The Lord's Supper") at the Metropolitan Cathedral is considered Costa e Silva's best work.

—Carolyn Richardson Durham

CRICHLOW, Ernest

American painter and illustrator

Born: Brooklyn, New York, 19 June 1914. **Education:** School of Commercial Illustrating and Advertising Art, New York; New York University; Art Students League. **Career:** Artist, New York Federal Art Project, North Carolina Art Project, Greensboro. Former director, Society for American Culture. Cofounder, Cinque Gallery, New York, 1969. Teacher, Art Students' League, New York, 1979-1994. **Awards:** School of Commercial Illustrating and Advertising Art Scholarship, New York.

Individual Exhibitions:

1938 Harlem Community Center, New York
1939 New York World's Fair
   Augusta Savage Studios, New York
1940 *American Negro Exposition,* Chicago
   Library of Congress, Washington, D.C.

Ernest Crichlow: *White Fence,* **1967. Photo by Manu Sassoonian; courtesy of the Schomburg Center for Research in Black Culture.**

Collections:

Boys and Girls High School, Brooklyn, New York; Medgar Evers College, Brooklyn, New York.

Publications:

On CRICHLOW: Articles—"Afro-American Issue," in *Art Gallery,* April 1968; "Negro Artists Prove Skill in DC Display," in *Washington Post,* 5 January 1941; "Two Artists in Exhibits Downtown," in *New York Amsterdam News,* 21 May 1938; "Advance on the Art Front," in *Opportunity,* May 1939; "Art by Negroes," in *Art Digest,* 15 December 1941; "Leading Negro Artists," in *Ebony,* September 1963; "The Cinque Gallery," in *Art Gallery,* April 1970; "Art Lessons" by Jonathan Mandell, in *Newsday,* 16 January 1991.

*   *   *

Ernest Crichlow can be called a social realist and expressionist painter, although he is also known for his illustrations and many children's books. Among the titles of his children's books are *Two in a Team, Maria, Lift Every Voice,* and *Magic Mirrors.* Crichlow also completed a twenty-five panel mural in 1976 at the Boys and Girls High School in Brooklyn. In the 1930s Crichlow gained inspiration from Jacob Lawrence, Romare Bearden, Norman Lewis, and Augusta Savage, who opened her studio to many black artists including Lewis and Lawrence. Savage was an important mentor to Crichlow during this period, when he started to paint and rub elbows with other black artists.

Crichlow's paintings are not rigid, and he always manages to capture the mood, time, and the social and economic conditions of African Americans. His print *Lovers III* (1938) shows a time of racial tension in America, when African Americans were sometimes held against their will by members of the Ku Klux Klan. One of Crichlow's few remaining prints, this composition reveals the tale of a black woman accosted in a bedroom by a hooded member of the Ku Klux Klan. It is an ominous lithograph, small but powerful, that stands as a revealing expose against the traditional themes of the American scene. It is social commentary in the highest degree.

Crichlow created many paintings and prints for the Work Progress Administration's program. His focus in all these works was on the "indomitable inner strength, intrinsic beauty, dignity, and essential humanity that exists in the African American community," as Mel Edwards puts it. In a painting of his mother, Crichlow gives a highly expressionistic portrayal of her sitting gracefully on a chair, rubbing her hands to ease the pain of her arthritis. His subject matter often revolves around home life—the family, children, and even gardening.

Unlike Jacob Lawrence, who recorded history through pictorial forms both in painting and in prints, Crichlow used cool colors in his painting to express the mood and time. The Caribbean island of Jamaica was as an important place for him. It was said to be a "continuous source of both subject and spirit." He has also traveled to many parts of Africa.

Though Crichlow often painted children, he turned increasingly to adults later in his career. He always tried to captivate a wholeness within his paintings, where it takes more than a glance to interpret the painting's true meaning. His works of adults were described by Lynn Kenny as "violent and despairing; he doesn't feel the world getting any better." Whatever he may feel, Crichlow has continued to paint and make remarkable contributions to the art world.

—Gabriel Tenabe

CRITE, Allan Rohan
American painter, printmaker, and illustrator

Born: Plainfield, New Jersey, 28 March 1918. **Education:** School of Fine Arts, Boston Museum, 1929-36; Painter's Workshop, Fogg Art Museum, c.1940; Harvard University, Cambridge, Massachusetts, A.B. 1968. **Career:** Lecturer, Oberlin College, Ohio, 1958, Regis College, Denver, Colorado, 1958, Eye of the Beholder, Isabell Stewart Gardner Museum, 1994; instructor, Roxbury Community

Allan Crite: *Our Lady of Africa,* 1951. Photo by Lee White; courtesy of the Schomburg Center for Research in Black Culture.

College, New York, 1977-78. Art historian, Semitic Museum, Harvard University, Cambridge, Massachusetts; engineering draftsman and illustrator, Technical Equipment, Naval Shipyard, Boston, 1940-70; muralist, Rambusch Decorating Company, 1949-50, librarian, Grossman Library, Harvard University, Cambridge, Massachusetts, 1974-89. **Awards:** Boston Museum School Scholarship, 1935; Boit Prize, 1935; Harvard University Medal, Cambridge, Massachusetts, 1986; Men of Vision Award, Museum of African-American History, Massachusetts, 1992; Certificate of Appreciation, Life Contributions to Visual Art, Saint Bartholomew's Episcopal Church, 1994. Honorary doctorates: Suffolk University, 1978; Emmanuel College, Boston, 1983; Massachusetts College of Art, 1988. **Address:** 410 Columbus Avenue, Boston, Massachusetts 02116, U.S.A.

Selected Exhibitions:

1929	Boston Society of Independent Artists
1930	Harvard University, Cambridge, Massachusetts
	Harmon Foundation, New York
1935	Harmon Foundation, New York
1936	Texas Centennial
	Museum of Modern Art, New York
1939	Howard University, Washington, D.C.
	Corcoran Gallery of Art, Washington, D.C.
	Institute of Contemporary Art, Boston
1939	Dillard University, New Orleans
1940	American Negro Exposition, Chicago
1942	Atlanta University, Georgia
1943	Grace Horne Galleries, Boston
1945	Symphony Hall, Boston
1948	Boston Printmakers
1968	St. John and St. James Church, Boston
1970	James A. Porter Gallery
1971	Newark Museum, New Jersey
	National Center of Afro-American Artists
1978	Boston Museum of Fine Arts
1979	Afro-American History and Culture Museum, Philadelphia
1994	Afro-American History and Culture Museum, Philadelphia
1995	Harvard University, Cambridge, Massachusetts

Publications:

By CRITE: Books—*Were You There When They Crucified My Lord?* Harvard University Press, Cambridge, Massachusetts, 1944; *All Glory: Brush Meditations on the Prayer of Consecration,* Society of Saint John the Evangelist, Cambridge, Massachusetts, 1947; *Three Spirituals from Earth to Heaven,* Harvard University Press, Cambridge, Massachusetts, 1948.

On CRITE: Articles—"Allan Crite Exhibit in Gallery of Art," in *The Hilltop* (Cambridge, Massachusetts), 22 February 1919; "Advance on the Art Front" by Alain Locke, in *Opportunity,* May 1939; "American Negro Given Full-Length Review in New York," in *Art Digest,* 15 December 1941.

*   *   *

Allan Rohan Crite's depictions of the everyday lives of Boston's African American community in the 1920s and 1930s transformed

Allan Crite: *Christ with Cross,* 1946. Photo by Lee White; courtesy of the Schomburg Center for Research in Black Culture.

the American art scene and society's view of people of color in a way that no other artist has ever replicated. Crite's classic painting, *Parade on Hammond Street,* shows black men, women, and children dressed in their Sunday best, their faces beaming with pride as they watch a parade led by a young man, resplendent in white regalia and in full stride. *Parade on Hammond Street* is an example of how Crite depicted African Americans in Boston in a natural yet beautifully elegant manner. His close attention to detail in creating the features of his subjects are apparent in each of his paintings.

School's Out is another example of the graceful charm and distinct clarity of his work. The painting portrays the excitement of young children, escorted by their mothers, leaving school at the end of the year. He captures the youngsters in a flurry of activity—running, jumping, clapping, and waving—in such a natural way that it seems more than an imitation of real play in a child's life. This universal image of children is a cornerstone of his life's work.

A visionary, Crite was one of the first artists to focus on average black Americans. His depictions of their lives earned him the title of "reporter-artist" in his neighborhood because his paintings are like color photographs. Similar to photographs, his paintings reveal the fine detail of a building that serves as a backdrop in pieces such as *School's Out.* The fine lines and cuts of the clothing his subjects wear, which reflect the style of the dress at the time, are shown in full detail, including color, texture, and fit.

Crite still lives in the neighborhood he captured in his paintings and maintains a museum that has features his work, a retrospective that spans more than six decades. His Depression-era canvas snapshots of life in black Boston are in the collections of the Museum of Fine Arts, the Museum of Modern Art, and the Smithsonian.

During the mid to late 1940s, Crite entered a new phase in his career as an artist by turning to religious themes in his paintings and lithographs. Drawing on his strong Episcopalian roots, Crite created spirituals for his church drawings. The pieces he created were and continue to be revolutionary. The drawings showcase Afro-Asian- and Asia Minor-inspired themes, and the features of his subjects are not the Rubenesque-inspired characteristics that seem to dominate religious paintings and church drawings.

His drawings were the subject of his book of religious illustrations, *Three Spirituals from Earth to Heaven,* published in 1948 by Harvard University Press. Crite also created the majestic-theme spirituals, using oil on wood and crafting them into three-panel altar pieces. His piece, *Adoration,* is a tabletop, triple panel, high-altar depiction of the Virgin Mary and the baby Jesus. The panels close, revealing a presentation on the outside of the three kings. He continues to paint in this style today.

His lithographs of nudes done on off-set press constitute another phase in his career. In one untitled piece he drew a group of young men and women dressed in regular street clothing, and on the other side of the canvas, he created the same group with the same expressions but nude. He refers to this piece as an example of "using fantasy to cover reality." A master artist, Crite's work as a painter, printmaker, and illustrator of religious subjects has had a profound and lasting effect on how the black experience is depicted in the world of art.

—Coria Holland

CRUZ, Emilio
American painter and performance artist

Born: Bronx, New York, 15 March 1938. **Education:** Art Students League, New York; Seong Moy, Provincetown, Massachusetts; University of Louisville, Kentucky; New School for Social Research, New York. **Family:** Married 1) Modesta Villega in 1956 (divorced 1957), one son; 2) Patricia Marshall, 1971. **Career:** Ramblerny School for Performing Arts, 1967; teacher, South Bronx Multi-Purpose Service, 1967-68; artist, Metropolitan Educational Council of Arts, 1969; professor, School of the Art Institute of Chicago, 1970-82, Parsons School of Design, 1988, Cooper Union, 1988. Since 1994 professor, Pratt Institute. Since 1995 professor, New York University. Visiting artist, Ox-Bow, 1973, State University of New York, Purchase, 1987. **Awards:** Walter Gutman Foundation Award, 1962; John Whitney Fellowship, 1964; Cintas Foundation Fellowship, 1965; Fulbright Scholarship, 1964; National Endowment for the Arts Fellowship, 1970; Illinois Arts Council Fellowship, 1981; Artemercato Internanzionale Accademia Italia Award, 1984; World Culture Prize—Statue of Victory, Centro Studi Richerche Delle Nazioni, Artemercato Internationale Accademia Italia, 1984; National Endowment for the Arts grant, 1987; Joan Mitchell Foundation grant, 1994. **Agent:** Steinbaum Krauss Gallery, 132 Greene Street, New York, New York 10012, U.S.A.

Individual Exhibitions:

1959	Sun Gallery, Provincetown, Massachusetts
1964	Zabriskie Gallery, New York
1965	Zabriskie Gallery, New York
1969	Loretto Hilton Gallery, Webster College, Missouri
1973	Walter Kelly Gallery, Chicago
1974	One Illinois Center, Metropolitan Structures, Chicago
1975	Walter Kelly Gallery, Chicago
1976	Walter Kelly Gallery, Chicago
1977	Krannert Center, University of Illinois
1978	Walter Kelly Gallery, Chicago
1985	Hand in Hand Gallery, New York
	Alternative Museum, New York
1986	Anita Shapolsky Gallery, New York
1987	Studio Museum in Harlem, New York
1988	Kingsborough College, Brooklyn, New York
1990	Anita Shapolsky Gallery, New York
1991	Galerie Françoise et Ses Fréres, Baltimore, Maryland
1997	Steinbaum Krauss Gallery, New York
	Pennsylvania Academy of Fine Arts, Philadelphia

Selected Performances:

1976	*Musical Homage to Ants and Other Symbiotic Creatures,* Illinois Institute of Technology, Chicago
1980	*Homeostatis Once More the Scorpion,* MoMing Dance Center, Chicago
1981	*The Absence Held Fast to Its Presence,* Randolph Street Gallery, Chicago
1982	*The Absence Held Fast to Its Presence,* Washington Project for the Arts, Washington, D.C.
1987	*Cage,* Rhode Island School of Design

Selected Group Exhibitions:

1991	Museum National de Bellas Artes, Santiago, Chile
1992	Jukui Fine Arts Museum, Japan
	Porter Randall Gallery, La Jolla, California
	Socrates Sculpture Park, Long Island City, New York
	Porter Randall Gallery, La Jolla, California
1993	Fine Arts Gallery, University of Maryland, Baltimore (traveling)
	Galerie Françoise et Ses Fréres, Baltimore, Maryland (two-person exhibition with Kathy Acker)
	Biennial of Painting, Cuenca, Eduador (traveling)
	Studio Museum in Harlem, New York
	Wadsworth Atheneum, Hartford, Connecticut

Collections:

Albright Knox Museum; Brooklyn Museum, New York; William Benton Museum of Art, Storrs, Connecticut; Greenwich Public Library, Connecticut; Hirshhorn Museum of Art, Washington, D.C.; Herbert F. Johnson Museum of Art, Ithaca, New York; Kingsborough College, New York; Rhode Island School of Design Museum of Art, Providence; Cintas Collection, Museum of Florida International University, Miami; Museum of Art Association of Provincetown, Massachusetts; Museum of Modern Art, New York; Museum of the University of Texas at Austin; Museum of the University of Tucson, Arizona; National Gallery of American Art, Smithsonian Institution, Washington, D.C.; New England Center for Contemporary Art, Connecticut; New Jersey State Museum, Trenton, New Jersey; Newark Museum, Newark, New Jersey; Portland Museum of Maine; Studio Museum in Harlem, New York; Wadsworth Atheneum, Hartford, Connecticut; World Trade Center, New York.

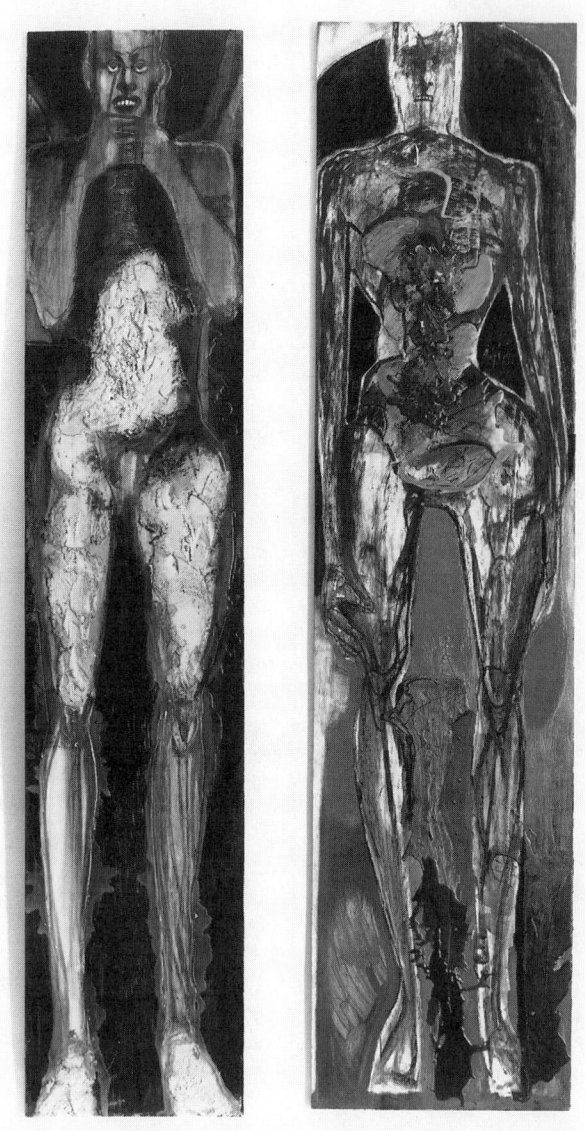

Emilio Cruz: "Homo Sapien" series, 1994. Photo courtesy of Steinbaum Krauss Gallery, New York.

Publications:

On CRUZ: Books—*Emilio Cruz, Recent Paintings and Drawings,* exhibition catalog, New York, Alternative Museum, 1985; *Tradition and Conflict: Images of a Turbulent Decade, 1963-1973,* exhibition catalog, New York, Studio Museum in Harlem, 1985. **Articles**—"In the Galleries: Fay Lansner, Emilio Cruz, Anne Arnold" by Vivien Raynor, in *Arts 37,* April 1963, p. 54; "Reviews and Previews: Emilio Cruz, Solo at Zabriskie" by G. R. Swenson, in *Art News 64,* November 1965, p. 13; "Inside the Galleries: Emilio Cruz" by William Berkson, in *Arts 40,* December 1965, p. 59.

*   *   *

Emilio Cruz has been described as an Expressionist painter. Expressionism is a style of painting that stresses the artist's emotions

over strict adherence to the rules of realism and proportion. Cruz draws on ideas and beliefs from many different cultures to create his art. Western philosophy, Eastern philosophy, art history, paleontology, myths, and his own dreams inform his work. But the strongest single artistic influence—the thread that runs through most of Cruz's work—is his own set of beliefs. He believes that art, to be relevant, must feed the spirit: "Integrity is formulated by acknowledging those things that we find inform us about the nature of the human spirit. The word inspired means 'in the spirit.' [Being] in the spirit is always avante garde."

Cruz also believes that humans have arrogantly placed all living things in danger of total destruction. Pollution, war, violence, and nuclear devastation cast a dark shadow over his world of art.

In 1990 Cruz executed his "Homo Sapiens" series. The paintings comprise several panels, each eight feet tall and two feet wide, depicting human figures, male and female, with their skeletons exposed. Each figure is standing upright, but they all strike different poses and bear different facial expressions. Some critics feel that Cruz is portraying mortality as the common bond among all human beings. The figures may look different on the outside, but they all have skeletons; all of us will die regardless of our ethnicity, race, gender, or religious background. Cruz also highlights the importance of the spine by making it the prominent feature of each figure, suggesting perhaps that the inner spiritual essence of a person ought to be the main thing on which we focus. The artist was quoted as saying that the spine is the seat of human consciousness and the location of the oldest part of the brain. The "Homo Sapiens" series reinforces the concept of the timelessness of the human spirit.

A piece that seems to show Cruz's concern for the destructiveness of the human race is *Green Leaf Turned Grey Laments Its Roots.* A large solitary leaf with a thin pale green and light brown stem grows out of a hard slab of brown dirt. Sunlight is noticeably absent. The leaf appears to be enclosed in a dark gray box. Death and gloom permeate the piece; it evokes the harshness of a nuclear winter, an environment—created by humans—that is not able to sustain life.

In two paintings titled *The Beast of My Story I* and *The Beast of My Story II,* Cruz appears to be mining his own dreams for subject matter. In both pieces the surrealistic figures are strange and menacing looking animals. Their heads are turned backwards, their mouths are opened like snarling dogs, and sharp projections rise along the lengths of their backs, making them look like ancient reptiles. Cruz blends the conscious with the unconscious and fantasy with reality to confront the most frightening beasts of all—our imaginations.

—Eric Hanks

CUNHA, Manuel da
Brazilian painter

Born: Rio de Janeiro, Brazil, 1737. **Died:** 27 April 1809.

Publications:

On CUNHA: Book—*A Mao Afro-Brasileira: Significado da Contribucao Artistica e Historica* (São Paulo), Tenege, 1988. **Articles**—"Biografia de Manuel da Cunha" by Moreira de Azevedo and Manoel

Duarte, in *Revista do IGHB,* 33(2), 1870, pp. 206-11; "Aspectos da Arte Colonial Brasileira" by Antonio Barbosa, in *Revista do IGHB,* 56, 1898; "Negros Pardos e Mulatos na Pintura e na Escultura" by Teixera Leite and José Roberto, in *Brasileira do Séc,* 18.

* * *

The son of an African woman, Manuel da Cunha was born a slave. According to art historians, the majority of practitioners of the arts in Brazil during colonial times were slaves. Cunha studied art with João de Souza in Rio de Janeiro and later went to Lisbon, Portugal, for further study with the financial support of his patron, the businessman José Dias da Cruz. When he came back to Rio de Janeiro, Cunha dedicated himself to religious painting and to portraiture. In addition he taught art in his home.

José Roberto and Teixiera Leite describe the artistic style of Cunha as "heavy" and note that other art historians have stated that his work came about as the result of the sheer force of his will. Cunha painted the *Descent from the Cross* on the ceiling of the Chapel of Nosso Senhor dos Passos. *Our Lady of the* Victories, which hangs in the Church of the Third Order of São Francisco in Rio de Janeiro, depicts the Virgin with the Christ child surrounded by choirs of angels who sing and play violins, lutes, and flutes. An oil painting on wood, it is divided into the realms of heaven and earth with earth depicted as the scene of strife and conflict. The earthly realm occupies a small part of the painting, while the heavenly realm with blond cherubim and angels is an ethereal area. A dove, symbolic of the Holy Spirit, spreads its wings in flight at the apex. Another oil painting on wood, also at the Church of the Third Order of São Francisco, is *The King of Naples, Fernando I, Commands the Captain to Palermo.* It depicts the captain, in the foreground, receiving a blessing with members of his troops assembled behind him. Some, apparently dead, lie huddled on the floor, their lances and swords in disarray. Others in the background march in military formation across an esplanade. In the far background, outside the arches of the palace, is a tent on the battlefield. *In the Land of the Prince of France* hangs in the same church. This dark and somber work shows a group of men gathered around a fountain.

Cunha's best works are his portraits. Notable among these are *The Portrait of the Count of Bobadela* in the Convent of Saint Teresa, *Saint Andre Avelino,* and the *Portrait of Inácio da Silva Metela* at the Santa Casa da Misericórdia in Rio de Janeiro.

—Carolyn Richardson Durham

DAVIS, Alonzo (Joseph)

American painter

Born: Tuskegee, Alabama, 2 February 1942. **Education:** Pepperdine College, B.F.A. 1964; University of California, Los Angeles, 1966; Otis Art Institute, Tuskegee, Alabama, B.F.A. 1971, M.F.A. 1973. **Career:** Dean, Memphis College of Art, Tennessee. Teacher, Los Angeles Unified School District, 1965-70; instructor, Pasadena City College, California, 1971, Mount San Antonio College, Walnut, California, 1971-73, University of California, Los Angeles, 1973. Artist-in-residence, Dorland Mountain Arts Colony, Temecula, California, 1981 and 1986, Arkansas Arts Center, Little Rock, 1984, East-West Center, Institute of Communication and Culture, Honolulu, Hawaii, 1988-89, Portland State University, Oregon, 1994. Owner and co-director, Brockman Gallery, Los Angeles, 1967-73. **Awards:** Arts Management Fellowship, Coro Foundation, Los Angeles, 1980; New Works in Performance Award, Sacramento Metropolitan Arts Commission, 1990; Majestic Foundation Artist Retreat Award, Boerne, Texas, 1991; DiverseWorks Award, Houston, Texas, 1992; artist fellowship, Department of Arts and Cultural Affairs, San Antonio, Texas, 1992; Virginia Center for the Creative Arts Fellowship, Mount San Angelo, Sweet Briar, Virginia, 1995. **Address:** P.O. Box 12248, Memphis, Tennessee 38182-0248, U.S.A. **Online Address:** ArtAlonzo@aol.com.

Individual Exhibitions:

1975	Just above Midtown Gallery, New York
	Bowers Museum, Santa Ana, California
1976	Transition Gallery, Idaho State University, Pocatello
1978	William Grant Still Community Arts Center, Los Angeles
1979	Modern Nordisk Konst, Gothenberg, Sweden
1980	American Center, Helsinki, Finland
1981	Watts Towers Arts Center, Los Angeles
1984	Brockman Gallery, Los Angeles
1987	Isobel Neal Gallery, Chicago
	Triton Museum, Santa Clara, California
1988	Cuba College, Woodland, California
	East-West Center, Honolulu, Hawaii
1989	German Museum, Davis, California
	San Antonio Art Institute, Texas
1990	Brockman Gallery, Los Angeles
	Institute for Design and Experimental Art, Sacramento, California
1992	Lawrence University, Appleton, Wisconsin
1993	Carnegie Arts Center, Leavenworth, Kansas
1994	Carver Cultural Center, San Antonio, Texas

Selected Group Exhibitions:

1971	Studio Museum in Harlem, New York
1979	Howard University Gallery, Washington, D.C.
1989	Sacramento City College, California
	California Afro-American Museum, Los Angeles
1991	Blue Door Gallery, San Antonio, Texas
1992	Natsoulas Gallery, Davis, California
	National Afro American Museum and Cultural Center, Wilberforce, Ohio
1995	Horwitch LewAllen Gallery, Santa Fe, New Mexico
1996	Austin Museum of Art, Laguna Gloria, Texas
	Anchorage Museum of Art and History, Alaska

Publications:

On DAVIS: Book—*Alonzo Davis,* exhibition catalog, Los Angeles, Brockman Gallery, 1982. **Articles**—"Alonzo Davis" by Cheryl McKay Dixon, in *The International Review of African American Art,* 6(3), 1986, pp. 16-32; "Davis in a Good Place in Sacramento" by Holly Johnson, in *Sacramento Union Newspaper,* 14 January 1988, p. D4; "Brockman Gallery" by Kay Lindsey, in *Art Papers* (Georgia), July/August 1990, pp. 23-24; "Alonzo Davis" by Michael Kelley, in *Commercial Appeal* (Tennessee), 1993, pp. A1, C1-2; "Alonzo Davis," in *Number: An Independent Quarterly of the Arts* (Tennessee), October 1993.

*   *   *

Alonzo Davis, dean of the Memphis College of Art in Tennessee, was for thirty years a resident of California, where in 1967 he and his brother, ceramist Dale, founded the Brockman Art Gallery in Los Angeles. One of few venues to expose the art of African Americans at that time, especially on the West Coast, the gallery proved to be a launching area for the many artists who exhibited and sold their work there. It was always difficult for Davis to juggle his career as an artist and the needs of the gallery, and in the early 1990s he decided to close it.

Davis was encouraged by the artist Charles White, who became a mentor for many artists in southern California, to work in the series form in order to fully explore concepts before moving on to another theme. Davis's early works centered on the civil rights movement, and he developed the "Yellow Bus" series by using the icon of a school bus to highlight a boycott in the state of his birth, Alabama, and the desegregation of schools across the country. Davis produced nine series that explored several compositional symbols, including "Vote," which used the arrow as an icon for focusing on upwardly mobility. In Los Angeles in the 1970s and 1980s he also was a part of a mural movement, painting works such as the "Crenshaw Wall" series (1979), the "Olympic Mural" series (1984), on the ramp of the heavily traveled Harbor Freeway, and the *Peace*

Mural (1986) on Martin Luther King, Jr., Boulevard. The murals were especially directed at instilling pride and encouraging a sense of purpose in the lives of the youth of Los Angeles.

Before moving to Sacramento in the mid-1980s to direct the public art program for the Sacramento Arts Commission, Davis began the "Blanket" series, his longest running work, in which he used matte and iridescent acrylic paints. Painting on paper, he let the surfaces dry, tore the paper into strips, and wove them together like cloth, replicating African American quilting patterns or Ghanaian kente cloth but with the energy of Hawaiian textiles. On these large "blankets" he sparsely attached elements such as beads and feathers. Even after he left California to take the position as dean at the San Antonio (Texas) Art Institute, he continued to develop this idea, and he has stated that his most recent works are a continuation of the series, although they now incorporate patchwork elements suggested by vast farmlands as seen from the air on his trips crisscrossing the country.

In 1992 Davis responded to the civil unrest in Los Angeles with a site-specific temporary work that used fireworks with some of his earlier props. Entitled *L.A. Burns 1,000 Points of Light,* the work was meant to signify how the program of a thousand points of light initiated under the administration of President George Bush had no relevance to life in South-Central Los Angeles. The later "Tar Paper" series is characterized by site-specific installations of acrylic paintings of layered tar paper shapes. One such work is *Scatterseed* (1995), a wall installation. Davis also burns designs into the paper, giving them a scorched-wood effect. Returning to the idea of empowering his artwork with fetishlike attributes, Davis attaches power poles, bundles, leather, stones, and twine, among other materials. Resembling wings or cocoonlike shapes, the paintings are attached to the wall, thus creating an illusion of flight or transformation. Such "spirit catcher" works, which have been influenced by Davis's residencies in Hawaii, Texas, New Mexico, and New Zealand, are meant to enfold and protect the spirit.

Davis has received commissions for public artworks in several transportation hubs. These have included Atlanta's Hartsfield airport in Georgia (1996), the Revere Station on the Blue Line Subway in Boston (1995), and the Lak'Esh, Southern Pacific Railroad/Union Station in Sacramento (1991).

—Lizzetta LeFalle-Collins

DAVIS, (Willis) Bing

American ceramist, mixed-media artist, painter, and photographer

Born: Willis Hoke Davis, Greer, South Carolina, 30 June 1937. **Education:** DePauw University, Greencastle, Indiana, 1955-59, B.A. 1959; Miami University, Oxford, Ohio, 1965-67, M.E., 1967; Indiana State University, Terre Haute, 1975-76; Dayton Art Institute, Ohio, 1963-65. **Family:** Married 1) Pat Davis in 1966 (divorced 1973), one son; 2) Audrey Masden in 1977, one daughter. **Career:** Teacher, Dayton Public Schools, Ohio, 1959-67; art director, Living Arts Center, Dayton, Ohio, 1967-70; assistant professor of art, DePauw University, Greencastle, Indiana, 1970-76; assistant dean of graduate school, associate professor of art, Miami University, Oxford, Ohio, 1976-78. Since 1978 chair, Art Department, Central State University,

Wilberforce, Ohio. Artist-in-residence, Columbus Cultural Arts Center, Ohio, 1989; visiting artist, Center for Fine Arts, Miami, Florida, 1988, National Conference Association of American Cultures, Washington, D.C., 1988, Phillips Academy, Dakar, Senegal Project, Andover, Massachusetts, Middle Tennessee State University, Murfreesboro, 1989, Slippery Rock University, Pennsylvania, 1989. Has served on numerous boards and panels, including Minority Arts Task Force, Columbus, Ohio, Ohio Arts Council, Columbus, 1983-88, DePauw University, 1985-88, Dayton Arts Institute, Ohio, 1883-88, National Endowment for the Arts, Washington, D.C., 1980-84, Association of American Cultures, Washington, D.C., National Conference of Artists, Washington, D.C., National Black Arts Festival, Atlanta, Georgia, National Endowment for the Arts, 1989-91. National President, National consortium on Arts and Letters for Historically Black Colleges and Universities, Washington, D.C., 1985-88. **Awards:** U.S. Office of Education grant, 1973; National Endowment for the Humanities Summer Fellowship, 1974; Individual Artists Fellowship, Ohio Arts Council, 1979; Ohio Individual Artists of the Year, co-winner, 1980; Architectural Commission Award, Kansas City, Missouri, 1983; Creativefest Award, Chamber of Commerce, Dayton, Ohio, 1984; Alumni Citation Award, DePauw University, Greencastle, Indiana, 1984; International Art Award, National Conference of Artists, Dakar, Senegal, 1985; Black Leadership Award, Southern Christian Leadership Conference, Dayton, Ohio, 1985; National Black Artists Exhibit purchase Award, Louisville, Kentucky, 1986; Black Creativity Exhibit First Place Award, 1986; Dr. Martin Luther King Jr. Living-the-Dream Artist-in-Residence, Columbus Cultural Arts Center, Ohio, 1989; Black Cultural Artist of the Year, Ohio Black Expo, Columbus, Ohio, 1988; Outstanding Achievement in Crafts, co-winner, Ohio Designer Craftsmen, Columbus, Ohio, 1989; WROU-FM Black Achievement Award, 1996. **Address:** 201 Lexington Avenue, Dayton, Ohio 45407, U.S.A.

Individual Exhibitions:

1961	Trotwood Theater, Ohio
1963	Antioch College Area Theater, Yellow Springs, Ohio
1965	Art House Gallery, Cincinnati, Ohio
1970	J.F.K. Gallery, University of Dayton, Ohio
1971	Bolinga Black Cultural Center, Wright State University, Dayton, Ohio
1972	DePauw University, Greencastle, Indiana
	Purdue University, West Lafayette, Indiana
1973	Wabash College, Crawfordsville, Indiana
1975	Vincennes University, Vincennes, Indiana
	Turman Gallery, Indiana State University, Terre Haute
1976	Sinclair Community College, Dayton, Ohio
	Studio Museum of Harlem, New York
	Purdue University, West Lafayette, Indiana
1977	Gallatin Gallery, Ann Arbor, Michigan
	Antioch College, Yellow Springs, Ohio
	Kilcawley Gallery, Youngstown State University, Ohio
1978	Gallatin Gallery, Ann Arbor, Michigan
	University of Arkansas, Pine Bluff
1980	Earlham College, Richmond, Indiana
	Indianapolis Art League, Indiana
	Pan-African Institute, Kent State University, Ohio
	Spiva Art Center, Joplin, Missouri

1995   Fitten Center for the Arts, Hamilton, Ohio
        Ohio Wesleyan University, Delaward
1996   20 North Gallery, Toledo, Ohio
        YMI Cultural Center, Asheville, North Carolina

Selected Group Exhibitions:

1985   Art Center Gallery, DePauw University, Greencastle,
            Indiana
        National Museum of Art of Senegal, Dakar
1986   Mosley Gallery, University of Maryland, Eastern
            Short
        Museum of Science and Industry, Chicago
1988   Dillard University, New Orleans
1989   Middle Tennessee State University, Murfreesboro
1990   Center for Afro-American and African Studies, Univer-
            sity of Michigan, Ann Arbor
        National Center for African-American Artists, Boston
        National Afro-American Museum and Cultural Center,
            Wilberforce, Ohio
1991   West Virginia State University, Institute
1994   National Gallery, Accra, Ghana
1996   Herndon Gallery, Yellow Springs, Ohio
        Gallery Antiqua, Miami

Bing Davis.

Collections:

African Cultural Institute, Lome, Togo; Columbus Gallery of Fine Arts, Ohio; Dayton Art Institute, Ohio; Evansville Museum, Indiana; National Afro-American Museum, Wilberforce, Ohio; National School of Art and Manufacturing, Libreville, Gabon, Central Africa; Purdue University, West Lafayette, Indiana; Schomburg Center, New York; Syracuse University, New York.

Publications:

By DAVIS: Articles—"Symbols, Visions, Images," in *Dialogue* (Ohio), April 1981; "American Ceramist Discovers Clay Is Alive and Well in Africa," in *The Crafts Report,* September 1987, p. 18; "A Personal Statement," in *African Affairs Bulletin,* Winter 1995.

On DAVIS: Book—*"Symbols, Visions, Images,* exhibition catalog, Ohio, Tangement Gallery, 1981; *Willis Bing Davis: A Retrospective,* exhibition catalog, Ohio, Dayton Art Institute, 25 July 1981. **Articles**— "The Thin Line Between Arts and Crafts," in *Art Space Magazine* (Ohio), 1986; "ODC Presents Awards to Miller and Davis," in *Ohio Designer Craftsmen* (Ohio), Summer 1989, p. 2; "Arts Center Plans A Celebration of African Influences," in *Artalk* (Ohio), December 1994; "Art for Education's Sake," in *Ohio Art Line* 20(1), 1995; "Tying into Black Heritage" by Franki V. Ranson, in *Dayton Daily News* (Ohio), 13 January 1995; "Masks That Reveal Us" by Catherine Agrella, in *Asheville Citizen-Times* (North Carolina), 20 October 1996; "For Bing Davis, Art Satisfies the Soul" by Debra K. Gaskill, in *Xenia Daily Gazette* (Ohio), 18 November 1996. **Video**—*The Art of Bing Davis* (Ohio), Central State University, Wilberforce, 1978.

*

Bing Davis comments:

In my works I am concerned with taking a given medium and making a personal statement based on my perception, observations, and response to my environment. I feel that my art should be a natural extension of my existence, bringing to fruition personal images, symbols, and forms that most accurately express my perception of life.

I approach my works with a deliberate abandonment based on a comfortable degree of technical skill, placing the greater emphasis on the impact of the completed visual image rather than the technical aspects of the process used.

In terms of subject matter, I address myself to the unlimited resource of possibilities of my existence. The conscious inclusion of social commentary in my works is the first step toward speaking to a universal condition. The rich artistic heritage of African art with its religious, social, and magical substance is what I select as an aesthetic and historical link.

*   *   *

Willis Davis, or "Bing" as he is affectionately called, has been noted for being an abstract expressionist. In the last three decades, Davis has developed a new aesthetic, in which he combines craft and art together. According to the artist this movement intends to return craft and art to their ancestral roots and dissolve the bridge between art and life.

Bing Davis: *Ancestral Spirit Vessel #20,* 1987. Photo courtesy of Jerry Anthony.

Davis uses a broad spectrum of materials, including clay, cloth, beads, pastels, photographs, and found objects. In many of his stoneware pieces, such as *Puberty Ritual Image* and *Ancestral Spirit Vessel,* spiritual themes are strongly expressed. Davis has molded a combination of his personal feelings with the images and thoughts embedded in him through ancestral connections. These pieces are sometimes cylindrical or rectangular. Some patterns mix and match different shapes and textures to form a mystical idea from his imagination.

Most of his pieces have a similarity to the works of traditional African artists, such as Skunder Boghossian, Bruce Onabrapkeya, Joyce Scott, Jimoh Buraimoh, and Twin Seven-Seven. Even though these are painters and printmakers, their works share with Davis's a sense of ritual and tradition. The works of Skunder Boghossian and Bruce Onobrakepeya also incorporate themes of a spiritual nature. Boghossian's works exhibit his interest in the art and culture of Ethiopia, Europe, and West Africa, and both Boghossian and Davis use masks and effective line work to unfold stories. Davis also absorbed the art of the Mayas and Eskimos into his works. In the pieces from his "Ceremonies and Rituals" series, it is clear that he believed that art is more than decoration and that the base of art is spiritual. Many of Davis's pieces could be hung at a shrine or an altar.

Like Romare Bearden and Benny Andrews, who are known for working with collages, Davis transgressed from the traditional way of making collages and has used different materials to transform his pieces. One can see a correlation to the art of Sorells Adewale, who incorporates scrap, paper, iron, wood, and cloth to make assemblages in the form of a collage.

Davis relates his work to his life experiences and his knowledge of the traditional artworks and spiritual meaning found in the African culture. He has in fact traveled to Africa, and the connection between his art and his life can be seen in *Ancestral Spirit Dance.* In this painting Davis uses his lines and colors, such as blues and purples with earth tones such as brown added, to produce a strong sense of abstract expressionism. Davis has linked this piece to an ancestral ritual dance that he attended in 1973. Davis's art has now fully transformed fully into the realm of the untraditional abstract expressionists, whose work carries a story, spirituality, and motion.

—Gabriel Tenabe

DAWSON, Charles (Clarence)
American painter, illustrator, and sculptor

Born: Brunswick, Georgia, 1889. **Education:** Tuskegee Institute, Alabama; Art Students League, New York; Art Institute of Chicago, graduated. **Career:** Newspaper staff artist, freelance painter and illustrator. Designed exhibit and painted murals, Urban League Social Work Exhibit, A Century of Progress, Chicago, 1933-34; designer, National de Saible Memorial Society exhibit booklet, 1933-34; curator, Carver Museum, Tuskegee, Alabama. **Award:** Harmon Award for Distinguished Achievement, Harmon Foundation. **Died:** 1940.

Exhibitions:

1929	Harmon Foundation, Tuskegee, Alabama
	National Gallery of Art
	Smithsonian Institution, Washington, D.C.
1932	Howard University, Washington, D.C.
1933	Harmon Foundation, New York
	Findlay Art Gallery, Chicago
	Illinois Host House, Chicago
	National DeSaible Memorial Exhibit
	Urban Social Work Exhibit, Century of Progress, Chicago
1934	National DeSable Memorial Exhibit
1940	Art Institute of Chicago
	American Negro Exposition, Chicago
1941	South Side Community Art Center, Chicago

Collections:

Carver Museum, Tuskegee, Alabama.

Publications:

By DAWSON: Book—*ABC of Great Negroes* (26 linoleum blocks). **Article**—"The Negro in Art," in *The Southern Workman,* 58, January 1929, pp. 12-13.

On DAWSON: Article—"Painter Charles C. Dawson Has Been Finding Beauty in Black Subjects for Eighty-One Years" by Barbara Parry, in *Philadelphia Inquirer Magazine,* 19 July 1971.

*   *   *

Originally from Georgia, Charles C. Dawson was educated at the Tuskegee Institute in Alabama. He later took art courses at the Art Students' League in New York City and at the Art Institute of Chicago. At Tuskegee, Dawson was often called upon to use his skills in graphics to create images and calligraphy for brochures and other printed materials. During his time there the institute was involved in developing students' skills in science, animal husbandry, agriculture, and the trades. A program in typography was the benefactor of many of Dawson's skills in graphic design. He drew the illustrations, and students in the print shop typeset and printed them for campuswide distribution. The program was in keeping with the idea of self-sufficiency that Booker T. Washington promoted in all areas of life. Thus, it was at Tuskegee that Dawson learned the skills of illustration and, more significantly, the production and distribution of printed materials, which proved beneficial to his later development when he relocated to Chicago. In Chicago he worked as a staff artist for a newspaper, but he also continued to work as a freelance painter and illustrator, offering his services to a wide range of African American clients, from businesses to social organizations. He entered his paintings into art competitions, including the Harmon Foundation exhibition of 1929.

In 1933 Dawson participated in Chicago's Century of Progress Exposition. He entered large mural-size portraits of black historical figures such as Washington, W. E. B. Du Bois, and George Washington Carver in the Urban League Social Work Exhibit. The portraits were eventually exhibited on the Tuskegee campus, where they remained into the 1970s. There also was a major Harmon Foundation exhibition in New York City in 1933. Alain Locke wrote in the exhibition catalog, "Welcome as is the very real and vital racialism that is now stirring in the world of the Negro artist, it is artistically important as a sign of aesthetic objectivity and independence, and thus a double emancipation from apologetic timidity and academic imitation." By the time of the Chicago and Harmon Foundation expositions racialism in African American art had taken a firm hold. Because of a growing sense of pride in their race, African American artists were choosing to insert their self-image into their work.

As a portraitist Dawson capitalized upon racialism in art and on opportunities to document prominent African American personalities on canvas. The main concern for any portraitist is to achieve the likeness of his sitter. Dawson was strong in this area, although he sometimes romanticized the sitter's appearance to satisfy his clients, which may account for his use of an abundance of white paint to achieve a muted pastel quality. He did not seem to separate his work in portraitures from his commercial illustrations, viewing both as businesses.

In producing paintings of African Americans, Dawson became one of the resident artists and illustrators in Chicago who were called upon to create images for a variety of projects. For example, he designed a booklet for the National Du Sable Memorial Society exhibition in 1933 and 1934, and he painted the *Evolution of Negro Music,* used as the official poster of the Pageant of Negro Music in 1934. At a time when there were few books that visually heralded the deeds of African Americans, he privately published a volume of twenty-six linoleum block engravings entitled the *A.B.C. of Great Negroes.* Each letter of the alphabet contained a portrait of an African American leader. Because Dawson could visually connect the person with the name, the book was sought after by collectors and by libraries, especially those that had a significant number of African American patrons. Ever the businessman, Dawson also sold the engravings individually, and, as a self-promoter, he also sold paintings such as *Quadroon Madonna* to schools and other educational venues.

With the federally funded Works Progress Administration, Dawson painted watercolors and drew graphite compositions that focused on the lives of children. In later years he continued to paint members of the black middle class from whom he received the commissions that supported him. Although he was no innovator, he is recognized as an accomplished illustrator.

—Lizzetta LeFalle-Collins

DeCARAVA, Roy (Rudolph)
American photographer

Born: New York, 9 December 1919. **Education:** Textile High School, 1934-38; Cooper Union Art School, 1938-40; Harlem Art Center, New York, 1940-42; George Washington Carver Art School, New York, 1944-45. **Military Service:** United States Army: topographical draftsman, 1943. **Family:** Married Sherry Turner in 1970, three daughters. **Career:** Sign painter and display artist, New York, 1936-37; technical draftsman, New York, 1939-42; commercial artist and illustrator, 1944-58. Freelance photographer, New York, for various advertising agencies, recording and television companies, and magazines such as *Scientific American, Fortune, McCall's, Look, Newsweek, Time, Life,* 1959-68 and since 1975; contract photographer, *Sports Illustrated,* New York, 1968-75. Founder and director, *A Photographers Gallery,* New York, 1954-56, Kamoinge Workshop for black photographers, New York, 1963-66. Adjunct professor of photography, Cooper Union Institute, New York, 1969-72; associate professor, Cooper Union Institute, New York, 1975-78; professor of art, Cooper Union Institute, New York, 1978-88. Since 1988 distinguished professor of art, Hunter College, New York. Member, Curatorial Council, Studio Museum in Harlem, New York, 1976. **Awards:** Guggenheim Fellowship in photography, 1952-53; Art Service Award, Mount Morris United Presbyterian Church, New York, 1969; Benin Creative Photography Award, 1972; Artistic and Cultural Achievement Award, Community Museum of Brooklyn, New York, 1979; citation, American Society for Magazine Photographers, 1983 Distinguished Career Photography Award, Friends of Photography, 1991; Special Citation for Photographic Journalism, American Society of Magazine Photographers, 1991. Honorary doctorates: Rhode Island Institute of Fine Arts, 1985; Maryland Institute, 1986; Wesleyan University, Middletown, Connecticut, 1992. **Address:** 81 Halsey Street, Brooklyn, New York 11216, U.S.A.

Individual Exhibitions:

1950   Forty-Fourth Street Gallery, New York
1951   Countee Cullen Branch, New York Public Library
1954   *Guggenheim Photographs,* Little Gallery, New York Public Library

1955   Photographers Gallery, New York
1956   Camera Club of New York
1967   *US,* Countee Cullen Branch, New York Public Library
1969   *Thru Black Eyes,* Studio Museum in Harlem, New York
1970   Sheldon Memorial Art Center, University of Nebraska, Lincoln
1974   University of Massachusetts, Amherst
1975   Museum of Fine Arts, Houston
1976   *Nation's Capitol in Photographs,* Corcoran Gallery of Art, Washington, D.C.
        Benin Gallery, New York
1977   Witkin Gallery, New York
        Light Work Gallery, Syracuse, New York
1978   *Mirrors and Windows,* Museum of Modern Art, New York
        Port Washington Public Library, New York
1980   *Silver Sensibilities,* New House Gallery, Staten Island, New York
        Friends of Photography, Carmel, California
        Akron Art Institute, Ohio
1982   Clarence Kennedy Gallery, Boston
        Ziikha Gallery, Wesleyan University, Middletown, Connecticut
1983   Studio Museum in Harlem, New York
1988   Museum of Modern Art, Stockholm (traveling)
1990   *Recent Photographs,* Witkin Gallery, New York

Group Exhibitions:

1953   *Always the Young Strangers,* Museum of Modern Art, New York
1955   *The Family of Man,* Museum of Modern Art, New York (traveling)
1964   Museum of Modern Art, New York
        Photography in the Fine Arts, Metropolitan Museum of Art, New York
1967   National Gallery of Canada, Ottawa (traveling)
1969   Studio Museum in Harlem, New York
1974   Whitney Museum of American Art, New York
1978   Museum of Modern Art, New York (traveling)
1980   Center for Creative Photography, University of Arizona, Texas
1983   *Photography in America, 1910-83,* Tampa Museum, Florida
1985   *American Images 1945-80,* Barbican Art Gallery, London
1986   *Jazz pa Fotografiska,* Fotografiska Museet, Stockholm

Collections:

Andover Art Gallery, Phillips Academy, Massachusetts; Atlanta University, Georgia; Center for Creative Photography, University of Arizona, Tucson; Corcoran Gallery of Art, Washington, D.C.; Harlem Art Collection, New York; Metropolitan Museum of Art, New York; Museum of Fine Arts, Houston; Museum of Modern Art, New York; Sheldon Memorial Art Gallery, University of Nebraska, Lincoln.

Publications:

By DeCARAVA: Books—*The Sweet Flypaper of Life,* with text by Langston Hughes, New York, Washington, D.C., 1955; *Roy DeCarava: Photographs,* 1981; *The Sound I Saw,* (jazz photos), 1983.

ON DeCARAVA: Books—*Roy DeCarava, Photographer,* exhibition catalog by James Alinder, Lincoln, Nebraska, 1970; *Seventeen Black Artists* by Elton Fax, Dodd, Mead, 1973; *Roy DeCarava: Photographs,* exhibition catalog by Alvia Wardlaw Short, Houston, 1975. **Articles**—"Negro Winners," in *Art Digest,* 1 May 1946; "Recognition for the Invisible Man" by Michael McManus, in *Artweek,* 18, 17 January 1987; "Roy DeCarava," in *Artweek,* 19, 30 January 1988, p. 12; review (The Photographers' Gallery, London), in *Arts Review* (London), 40, 12 February 1988, p. 73; "Roy DeCarava" by Steven Jenkins, in *Artweek,* 22, 21 March 1991, p. 3; "Shadow and Substance" by Maren Stange, in *Art in America,* 84, March 1996, p. 35 (illustrated); "Time Stands Still: The Photographs of Roy DeCarava" by Max Kozloff, in *Artforum,* 34, May 1996, pp. 78-83 (illustrated); "Roy DeCarava" by Margaret Loke, in *Art News,* 95, May 1996, p. 133 (illustrated).

*   *   *

As Langston Hughes had done with words, Roy DeCarava documented Harlem through photography. From his earliest photographs he captured the reality of people's everyday lives—ceremonies and celebrations in the midst of depravation and debris in *Graduation* (1949), the cradling of a child by his father sitting on a stoop in *Man* (1952), and the acrobatics of the workplace in *Three Men with Hand Trucks* (1963).

DeCarava was a product of the Harlem Community Art Center. The many artists who frequented the center and who participated in its programs helped foster the cultural identity of Harlem. They included Charles Alston, Augusta Savage, Charles White, and Jacob Lawrence, as well as the writers Hughes, Countee Cullen, Claude McKay, and Robert Blackburn. DeCarava began as a graphic artist, and his starkly perceptive *Strikers* (c.1951) and *Close Up* (1949-50) recall the intrinsically intimate views of Lawrence but with the graphic and social bite of Ben Shahn. These serigraphs signal the economy of form and vacuum of space as well as the social commentary that would mark his later photographs.

DeCarava lived and worked at a time in which the black residents of Harlem struggled to overcome the effects of the Great Depression of the 1930s and the continued overt racism and Jim Crow attitudes of the 1940s and 1950s. *Strikers* and *Close Up* are, therefore, visual manifestations of DeCarava's identification with the disenfranchised and dispossessed masses who were attempting to carve out a living. Conscious of the limited means of his Harlem neighbors and potential patrons, DeCarava chose serigraphy and then photography as his mediums so as to create affordable prints. By day he worked as a salaried employee, but after hours he was an independent photographer, taking pictures of the world around him and capturing the highlights and low moments of life in Harlem.

DeCarava's artwork took a turning point because of the suggestion of a fellow photographer, Homer Page. He suggested that DeCarava alter his printing technique from one that yielded stark contrasts between black and white to a softer one that produced dark grays and a narrower range of tonal areas. What resulted was a more muted photograph, one in which the viewer had to search to lift recognizable objects from the composition. Objects no longer jumped out at the viewer on first glance. Because they required more time and introspection, these photographs created a more intimate relationship with the viewer.

By the 1950s photography was taking on a new meaning in the world of art, largely because of Henri Cartier-Bresson's view of the "man in the street as the vital embodiment of human values and cultures." The photographer was not just one who documented life around him, but he was also an artist. DeCarava's photographs of Harlemites and their everyday lives as works of art were an instant success with critics. He provided a straight-forward, unromanticized insider's view of the people's lives. As a keen observer of the daily spectacle, he knew how to maintain economy of shape while engaging his viewers to complete the narrative he put forth.

Many of DeCarava's works from the 1960s and 1970s concentrated on the extension of the body—hands, legs, ankles, bellies, and backs. These focused views asked the spectator to analyze the meaning or importance of a small gesture. The viewer had to ask what could be learned from a detailed shot—what iconographic images like a cigarette, a ringed finger, or a gloved hand could mean. Compositions with a partial shot of legs, feet, or hatted heads required a viewer who was willing to fill in the information that had been left out. In DeCarava's compositions the spectator must become a participant.

—Lizzetta LeFalle-Collins

DeKNIGHT, Avel (Cynolair)

American painter

Born: New York, 9 April 1933. **Education:** École des Beaux-Arts, Paris; Académie de la Grande Chaumiere; Académie Julian. **Military Service:** United States Army: World War II. **Career:** Instructor, National Academy School of Fine Arts, New York, 1981-95. Resident exhibition coordinator and designer, Brooklyn Museum, New York. Guest curator, Corner Gallery, Brooklyn Museum, 1978-80, New York Urban League, 1980, Western Electric, 1981, Bankers Trust, New York, 1981. **Awards:** New York Village Art Center Prize, 1953; Paton Prize, National Academy of Design, 1958, 1967; Childe Hassam Fund Purchase Prize, American Academy of Arts and Letters, 1960; exchange grant, United States State Department, 1961; Grumbacher Award, National Audubon Artist Society Award, 1964; Watercolor Society Prize, 1967; Grand Prize and Gold Medal, 1967 Centennial Exhibition; Audubon Artists Annual Prize, 1968; Purchase Prize, American Federation of Arts; Medal of Honor, Audubon Artists; Purchase Prize, Ranger Fund; Samuel F.B. Morse Medal; Palmer Memorial Prize. **Died:** 16 May 1995.

Individual Exhibitions:

1968	Larcada Gallery, New York
1971	Larcada Gallery, New York
1973	Babcock Galleries, New York
1977	Babcock Galleries, New York
	University of Pittsburgh, Johnstown (retrospective through 1987)
1980	New York Urban League

Group Exhibitions:

1953	Village Art Center, New York
1960	Gallery 10, New Hope, Pennsylvania
1970	Museum of Fine Arts, Boston

1971	Whitney Museum of American Art, New York
	Finch College Museum of Art, New York
	Black American Artists, Illinois Art Council
	Remnants of Things Past, Cummer Gallery of Art, Jacksonville, Florida
1972	*Landscapes,* Museum of Modern Art, New York
1973	Babcock Gallery, New York
1988	*Faces and Figures,* Metropolitan Museum, New York

Collections:

Lehigh University, Bethlehem, Alabama; Massillon Museum, Ohio; Metropolitan Museum of Art, New York; Miles College, Birmingham, Alabama; National Academy of Design, New York; Norfolk Museum of Arts and Sciences, Virginia; Rutgers University, New Brunswick, New Jersey; Springfield Museum of Art, Missouri; University of Vermont; Walker Art Center, Minneapolis.

Publications:

On DEKNIGHT: Articles—"Two GI's Go Back to Paris," in *Ebony,* 2, March 1947, pp. 16-18; "Who's News," in *Art Digest,* 15 November 1953; "Reviews and Previews: Avel DeKnight," in *Art News,* 55, February 1957, p. 52; "Galleries Cross Country," in *Art News,* 59, March 1960, pp. 52-53; "Art: Russia-Bound Artist," in *Jet,* 20, 1 June 1961, p. 48; "Review and Previews: Avel DeKnight" by Rosalind Brown, in *Art News,* 67, November 1968, p. 13; "Artists in the Art News," in *Art News,* 68, March 1969, p. 6; "Eye on New York," in *Art Gallery,* 17, November 1973, pp. 63-65 (illustrated); "Watercolor Page: Avel DeKnight," in *American Artist,* September, 1976, pp. 44-47 (illustrated); "Reviews and Previews" by Laurie Anderson, in *Art News,* 70, November 1977, p. 12; "Avel DeKnight" by Karl Lunde, in *Arts,* 52, November 1977, p. 11 (illustrated).

*   *   *

The surreal lyrical paintings of Avel de Knight evoke an imaginary atmospheric world populated by figurative images that allude to a romantic and deeply poetic sensibility. He was a product of the École des Beaux-Arts and the Académie de la Grande Chaumiere in Paris, and his works were clearly influenced by the nineteenth-century French symbolist school. While this approach might be considered backward looking, given the period of his primary activity (the 1960s through the 1980s), De Knight's conviction and fidelity to the romantic ideal gave his works a communicative power that overrides their sometimes derivative and amorphous effects.

De Knight's images were produced in a range of media, including oils, watercolors, gouache, and casein. In his employment of all of these media he used a subtlety of expression to explore the complex visual relationships he created. His search for a means of depicting the dream-like ideals associated with memory, fantasy, and interior reality resulted in images populated by mythical, mysterious, or winged figures and by strongly horizontal compositions that intentionally or subliminally alluded to the idea of sleep and of the subconscious.

The "Mirage Paintings" series of the late 1970s and the early 1980s is one of the most captivating of De Knight's groups of works. In these works symbolist visions, evidently influenced by the haunting imagery of Odilon Redon and by the ideas of French symbolist poetry, were syncretized with Afro-centrist representations to create a lyricism of great poetic possibility. The works captured De Knight's responses to his travels in Muslim Russia and, later, North Africa. His interest in Africa and in images associated with the African diaspora was the product of the engagement of his social conscience after the civil rights activities of the late 1960s and the 1970s. Sociopolitical statements, however, were not De Knight's essential concern. His works show a continued faith in the power of beauty, and although in the atmosphere of the art world of the 1970s and 1980s such a faith might have been construed as naive, his works retain a communicative power, authority, and sophistication that merit careful analysis.

In works such as *Halo of Memory* (1980), De Knight showed the tranquil profile of a beautiful African youth, evidently an allegorical figure, centrally placed in an arched compositional format. The youth gazes dreamily out of the composition to face the viewer's right, as if looking into the past. The figure is surrounded by a series of small, turbulent, iridescent, luminous bodies that coalesce into soothing horizontal bands of color and fade into a frozen, stratified sunsetlike visual motif. Glowing azure wings of memory emerge from the figure's brow, suggesting the flight of the mind (flights of fancy) and thus evoking the ideas of imagination and reverie. These subtle allusions and dream images underscore De Knight's poetic sensibility and imaginative power.

Another work, *Ancestor Tree, II*, again uses the motif of an African youth in profile. Although he also faces the viewer's right, in this case the youth gazes upon a tree composed of ethereal lights and flowers, which are in fact the glowing spirits of the past, ancestral links to our common humanity. Such a work may be interpreted as an homage to the animist traditions of De Knight's own African ancestors. The youth, who serves to anchor a circular compositional format—which itself alludes to the cycles of life, generation, decay, and regeneration—is the embodiment of a people's future, for he is shown in African tribal dress, his face shrouded in mysterious shadow. The image is bisected by pale blue horizontal bands of color that abstract and intercept the figural representations of the youth and tree and that darken in intensity as they move progressively toward the apex of the composition into a transitional, tertiary palette of mauve, rose, and violet, only to fade to a cool pallor at the culmination of the arrangement. These graduated abstractions of colored bands are as much a part of De Knight's message as the figural representations concerning journey, change, subtle shifts, and movement, and they allude to both physical and exterior change and to metaphorical and interior vicissitudes.

In works such as *Mediterranean,* fantasy figures are shown in illusory moonlit landscapes. De Knight's three-tiered compositions often elicit abstract values and indicate an intricate design-oriented awareness in his mystery-filled vague worlds where fantasy and reality merge and intertwine in a harmonious exchange to delineate a new reality. De Knight's richly evocative images help the viewer form an idea of how the communicative and poetic powers of the mind are linked with humanistic values to produce the subtle and sensitive civilizing influences of an evolved culture.

—Frank Martin

DELANEY, Beauford

American painter

Born: Knoxville, Tennessee, 1901 (sources also list 1904, 1905, 1907, 1910). **Education:** Massachusetts Normal School, beginning

1924; Copley Society, Boston. Studied under Thomas Hart Benton, John Sloan, Don Freeman. **Career:** South Boston School of Art, beginning 1924. Moved to Paris in 1950s. Suffered mental breakdown in 1961 and was hospitalized, 1971-79. **Awards:** Exhibition Prize, Village Art Center, New York, 1948; Fairfield Foundation grant, 1964. **Died:** 26 March 1979.

Exhibitions:

1930	Whitney Galleries, New York
1932	135th Street Branch, New York Public Library
	42nd Street Branch, New York Public Library
1933	Cooperative Art Market and Roxy Theatre
	Harmon Foundation
1938	Eighth Street Playhouse, New York (solo)
1940	American Negro Exhibition, Chicago
1941	Vendome Galleries, New York (solo)
1941	McMillen Galleries, New York
1948	Artists Gallery, New York
1950	Roko Gallery, New York
1954	Salon des Réalitiés Nouvelles, Paris
1955	Galerie Clan, Madrid
1956	Galerie Prisme, Paris
	Galerie Arnaud, Paris
	Iserlohn, Germany
1957	Bordighera, Italy

Beauford Delaney: *Portrait of Albert Amons,* **1943. Photo courtesy of the Schomburg Center for Research in Black Culture.**

1958	Leverkusen, Germany
	University of Wisconsin, Madison
1959	Galerie Breteau, Paris
1960	Salon des Réalitiés Nouvelles, Paris
	Galerie Paul Facchetti, Paris
	Musée des Arts Decoratifs, Paris
1961	Centre Culturel Americain, Paris
	Lincoln Gallery, London
1962	Galerie Breteau, Paris
1963	Musée d'Art Moderne, Paris
	Salon des Réalitiés Nouvelles, Paris
1964	Galerie Internationale d'Art Contemporain, Paris
1967	Morgan State College, Baltimore, Maryland
1969	Galerie Culturel Americain, Paris
1970	University of Texas
1971	Newark Museum, New Jersey
1973	Gallery Darthea Speyer, Paris
1978	Studio Museum in Harlem, New York (retrospective)

Collections:

Mr. James Baldwin; Mr. Henry Miller; Morgan State College, Baltimore, Maryland; Newark Museum, New Jersey; Schomburg Center, New York; Whitney Museum of American Art, New York.

Publications:

On DELANEY: Books—*Beauford Delaney Exhibition*, exhibition catalog, Paris, Galerie Darthea Speyer (includes statements by James Baldwin, James Jones, Georgia O'Keeffe, and Henry Miller), 1973; *Beauford Delaney: A Retrospective*, exhibition catalog, New York, Studio Museum in Harlem and Richard A. Long, 1978; *Amazing Grace: A Biography of Beauford Delaney*, Leeming, Oxford University Press, New York, 1997. **Articles**—"Paintings by Beauford Delaney," in *Life*, 1938, p. 216; "The Fortnight in New York: The Panorama" by Paul Bird, in *Art Digest*, 13, 15 November, 1938, p. 34; "New Exhibitions of the Week," in *Art News*, 39, 1 February 1941, p. 21; "The Amazing and Invariable Beauford Delaney" by Arthur Miller, in *Remember to Remember* (New York), 1945; "Paris Letter" by Michael Peppiatt, in *Art International*, 17, April 1973, pp. 68-71; "Beauford Delaney," in *A History of African-American Artists, from 1792 to the Present* by Romare Bearden and Harry Henderson, New York, Pantheon Books, 1993, pp. 280-87.

*   *   *

Beauford Delaney was one of the early black American abstract expressionists. During the 1930s, however, he produced some pastel portraits that showed his true feelings for his subjects. They were formal, posed, and elegantly painted in bright and light colors. An example of these is *Portrait of a Woman*—a painting that may be of one of his friends or relatives.

In the early 1940s in New York, Delaney was inspired by van Gogh and the fauve style. His portraits at that time were mostly of his friends in Greenwich Village, though there were also some of homeless people on the streets of New York. In these portraits the paint was applied in thick layers, using a combination of oranges, pink, red, brown, and a touch of green, which Robert Smith called the radiant intensity of genius.

Some writers and critics have aligned Delaney's work with European expressionists such as Jules Pascin or Chaim Soutine, but Delaney's works went beyond these artists. He defined his own expressionistic landscape and figurative forms by breaking them into segments with brilliant and powerful colors in a rhythmic passion. *The Figure in a Landscape* and *Face* are good examples of his works during the late 1940s or early 1950s. He used heavy impasto red and yellow and separated them with either black or white lines to show details of the trees, the sidewalk, and the figure. Delaney's paintings became nonrepresentational, reminiscent of the abstract expressionist movement in New York during those days. Delaney, unlike other African American painters, never remained on the same style for long. He was quoted as saying, "the abstraction, ostensibly, is simply for me the penetration of something that is more profound in many ways than rigidity of a form."

In the 1960s Delaney completely changed his style to abstraction. It was not known why he became an abstract painter. Some have attributed the change to his financial problems and his attachment to art dealers who may have encouraged him to paint in certain styles that they promoted. Delaney was also very close to some younger American abstractionists, such as Edward Clark and Herbert Gentry. It was said that Delaney spent a lot of time in the warmth of vibrating yellows, oranges, red, blue, and green. *Autumn* and *Fall* in the Morgan State University collection are examples. Despite all the stylistic changes in Delaney's art, one thing that never changed was his passion for brilliant colors.

—Gabriel Tenabe

DELANEY, Joseph
American painter

Born: Knoxville, Tennessee, 1904. **Education:** London School of Art, Washington, D.C.; Art Students League, New York (under Thomas Hart Benton). **Career:** Artist, New York Federal Art Project, 1936-39. **Died:** 24 November 1991.

Selected Exhibitions:

1936	New York Federal Art Project (through 1939)
1937	Washington Square Show, New York City (through 1940)
1940	*American Negro Exposition*, Chicago
1941	McMillen, Inc., Galleries, New York
1942	Atlanta University, Georgia
1944	Greenwich House, New York
1948	Hotel Diplomat
1967	City College of New York
1986	*Homecoming '86*, Knoxville, Tennessee

Collections:

Arizona Collection; British American Galleries; Knoxville Museum of Art; Metropolitan Museum of Art, New York; National Academy of Design; Riverside Art Museum, California; University of Tennessee, Knoxville.

Publications:

On DELANEY: Articles—"American Negro Art Given Full Length Review in New York Show," in *Art Digest,* 14 December 1941; "Negro Art Scores without Double Standard," in *Art Digest,* 1 May 1946; "Obituary," in *Art in America,* 80, March 1992, p. 150.

*   *   *

Documenting the places, faces, and events of the city that captured his heart for most of his eighty-plus years, the art of Joseph Delaney reflects his love of the human figure, beautiful women, and New York City. Growing up in Knoxville, Tennessee, the ninth of ten children born to Reverend and Mrs. Samuel Delaney, Joseph Delaney's values were shaped by the Christian doctrine of his family, especially his father, a Methodist minister. By age eighteen, however, he was ready to leave the restrictions of the Knoxville community and try his luck in the larger world. Delaney lived the life of a homeless traveler, roaming through Kentucky and Illinois, where he eventually signed on for a three-year stint with the Illinois National Guard. While stationed in Chicago he made friends with numerous jazz musicians and began an ongoing series of drawings depicting musicians and singers. His love of storytelling often showed through as visual storytelling in his portraits, such as those of Eubie Blake and Mahalia Jackson, and in his somewhat biographical works, such as *Hobo Jungle Feast.*

After a brief return to Knoxville, where he once again found sorely needed family support and odd jobs, Delaney decided to pursue his long-time dream of an art career. In 1930 he moved to New York City, lured by the example of his older brother Beauford's pursuit of an art career.

Enrolled in classes at the Art Student's League of New York, Joseph Delaney was enthusiastic about the association with other artists and felt that this environment connected him to the pulse of the contemporary art world. He became part of an academic setting in which artists such as Jackson Pollock taught, worked, and interacted. Delaney befriended Pollock, and a sketch of Pollock by Delaney appears in Steven Niafeh and Gregory White Smith's biography of Jackson Pollock.

While Delaney's formal study at the Art Student's League lasted only a few years, he retained a lifetime membership and a philosophical association with the League. He treasured the instruction he received there from two teachers in particular—Thomas Hart Benton and George Bridgeman. Delaney greatly admired Benton both as a successful artist and as a teacher. From Benton he gained respect for the importance of mastering the basic fundamentals of art. Effective application of the tools of the trade allowed Delaney to open his vision to composition, design, and an expressionistic style that distinguished his work.

Part of that style came from his appreciation of the human figure. George Bridgeman, an anatomical art instructor, taught Delaney about the muscle and skeletal systems that shaped the human form. Understanding anatomy seemed to strengthen the power of the lines in Delaney's drawings of the human figure. Delaney wrote in "Know What You See, Flesh and Bones, Simple Anatomy" that "The bones and muscles are only guides to help you say what you want to with the figure, like words for a poem." Delaney's portfolio includes a multitude of drawings and sketches of men and women of all shapes and sizes, since for forty-five years he drew the human figure almost daily.

Beginning in 1931 Delaney began participating in the Washington Square Outdoor Art Show. In a published documentary, "Thirty Six Years Exhibiting in Washington Square Outdoor Art Show," Delaney describes the importance of this experience in his life. Loving New York as he did, he was energized by working outside in this powerful and competitive exposure. He loved watching the comings and goings of the people and their environment and recording the changes. He enjoyed the critical evaluation from his fellow artists as they responded to the works exhibited by each other. The exchange with the public was also affirming to him when it was good and troublesome to him when it was not, particularly when someone offered a paltry sum to purchase one of his paintings. Much of Delaney's time at the Washington Square exhibit was spent drawing portraits of passersby, including celebrities such as Eartha Kitt and Tallulah Bankhead.

The outdoor exhibition substituted for the lack of gallery support and allowed the artists the opportunity to be "discovered." Delaney survived in New York partly because of the government-supported arts project of the Works Progress Administration and, years later, the Comprehensive Employment and Training Act (CETA). Numerous memorable drawings such as *Around Henry Street* and *Senior Citizens Center* were actually assignments from the CETA program.

Delaney's narrative paintings of the places, events, and festive parades in New York captured the people's energetic, patriotic, and celebratory feelings about their city. Notable examples are *V. J. Day, Times Square, Easter Parade, Yankee Parade, Hostage Parade*, and *The Macy's Parade.* Whether easel-size or mural-size, these paintings use simple lines to form the faces and figures of the people. As the forms overlap, the lines express the repetition and the rhythm of the marchers, automobiles, and onlookers. In *V. J. Day, Times Square* Delaney's characters capture the legacy of New York City, while the rainbow caption, "Peace on Earth," brings to mind the elusive American dream. *Marble Collegiate Church, Central Park Skating,* and *Madison Square Park* continue his documentation of his beloved city.

The fluid lines that form the simplistic, sometimes ghostlike figures in Delaney's large works become more defined, even voluminous, in his scores of portraits of women of all colors, races, and walks of life. Again his visual storytelling reveals insight into the women; at other times the images are void of all but the striking portrait of the face.

Delaney returned to Knoxville in 1986 for his last major exhibition, which was part of Tennessee's statewide celebration, Homecoming '86. He remained as guest artist-in-residence at the University of Tennessee until his death on 24 November 1991. The University of Tennessee and the Knoxville Museum of Art have outstanding collections of the work of their native son, Joseph Delaney.

—Aaronetta H. Pierce

DeLAWRENCE, Nadine
American painter, sculptor, and installation artist

Born: Hartford, Connecticut, 1952. **Education:** Rhode Island School of Design, Providence, B.F.A. 1975. **Died:** 1993.

Individual Exhibitions:

Carol Getz Gallery, Coconut Grove, Florida; Matrix Gallery, Alternative Museum, New York; Sisson Gallery, Henry Ford Community College, Dearborn, Michigan; Spiral Gallery, New York; Studio Museum in Harlem, New York; Sherry Washington Gallery, Detroit; Frances Wolfson Gallery, Miami.

Collections:

Printmaking Workshop, New York; Studio Museum in Harlem, New York.

*   *   *

As an artist Nadine DeLawrence drew upon ancient themes and images from various traditions, but she joined them with modern sculptural and painting techniques to form a connection with past cultures and myths. A modern technique DeLawrence used for her sculptures was welding together sheet aluminum that had been cut into shapes. For her paintings she covered the surface of her work with words, symbols, and disorderly colors.

Classical influences in DeLawrence's work, such as mythical subject matter and compositional symmetry, began in 1974 during her undergraduate studies while in a European honors program in Italy. Those influences remained, as remarked upon by Michael Chisolm, commenting on DeLawrence's 1989 solo exhibition at the Frances Wolfson Art Gallery at Miami-Dade Community College: "This emphasis on a collective unconscious and its atavistic implications recall the traditional role of the artist in pre-Christian, non-Western culture as the interpreter, guardian, and, sometime creator of myth." Also relevant to DeLawrence's work, as noted by Chisolm, are Egyptian cultures, abstract expressionism, and the formalist minimalism of 1960s American art.

DeLawrence's art seems to ask the viewer to stop, to take time and think about what is being looked at, and to examine the story or history beneath the surface of the piece. In the wall relief *Daedalus,* for example, her choice of rich historical or mythical subject matter asks that we examine not only the work before us but also what we know of the myth of Daedalus. Is the golden surface of the wall relief a warrior's shield, a reflecting device to be used to send messages from peak to peak, or a symbol of the sun, which Daedalus warned his son, Icarus, against flying too near with waxen wings? Certainly it is all three. This confluence of images is typical of her work and is one of the principal components that makes her art extraordinary.

—Terry Bain

DeLEON, Henry

Puerto Rican sculptor and filmmaker

Born: Puerto Rico, 1945. **Education:** Brandeis University, Waltham, Massachusetts; Boston Trade School, 1973-75. **Awards:** Deborah Joseph Cohen Memorial Award in sculpture, 1968; Abram L. Sachar International Fellowship for travel and study abroad. **Address:** c/o Museum of the National Center of Afro-American Artists, 300 Walnut Avenue, Roxbury, Massachusetts 02119, U.S.A.

Selected Exhibitions:

Boston City Hall; Institute of Contemporary Art, Boston; El Museo del Bario, New York; Museum of Fine Arts, Boston (1970); Museum of the National Center of Afro-American Artists, Boston; Newark Museum, New Jersey; Rose Art Museum, Brandeis University, Waltham, Massachusetts (1969); Studio Museum in Harlem, New York (1969).

*   *   *

Henry DeLeon's art is a mirror image of his introspective nature, reflecting what he has experienced and witnessed during his lifetime. His sculptures explore the everyday realities of love, religion, spirituality, friendship, and man's inhumanity to man. The cultural influences of his native Puerto Rico and of his poverty-stricken childhood in East Harlem in New York City are also ever present in his work.

DeLeon's career began in the late 1960s while he was a student at Brandeis University in Waltham, Massachusetts. Until he attended Brandeis, he had no interest in art, but there a teacher and mentor introduced him to this new world. Art then became his world, and, just as he shapes the sculptures he creates, his life is shaped by his work.

During the 1960s, a time of turbulence that forever changed the landscape of society in the United States, DeLeon found stability in art. He found his niche in working with his hands, particularly with stone. DeLeon found that for him stone had an unmatched quality. It also required him to work outside, which he found calming and exciting at the same time. On his material DeLeon molded, shaped, and chiseled the thoughts and feelings he believed were channeled through him by nature and by God. He has described the creative process as being as liberating as prayer and as natural as the earth.

DeLeon later traded stone for wood. He made the switch after a fire in 1976 destroyed his home and his life's work. DeLeon has now had a twenty-year affiliation with wood—primarily walnut, oak, and cedar. He has said that he often yearns to lay his hands on stone again and that he plans to return to the material one day. For now, however, wood is his primary material in the creative process.

Fueled by the cross fires of emotion, rage, and spiritualism, DeLeon's sculptures clearly reflect the issues of today. In his piece *9 millimeter youth* he speaks to the plague of gang violence and warfare that dominates and eventually destroys the lives of so many African American and Latino young men in urban America. The sculpture, an abstract image of a gun and raised fist that are equal in height and space but appear as one, sends a chilling but all too familiar message of death and destruction. Another work, *The Crucifixion,* is an expressionist piece that borrows from the strong Roman Catholic tradition in DeLeon's predominantly Latino community in East Harlem. In this depiction of the crucifixion of Christ, DeLeon crafted a linear figure surrounded by spiked pieces of wood that point heavenward to represent a crown of thorns.

In a sculpture titled *Birth,* DeLeon focused on the wonders of reproduction and the life cycle. The sculpture, crafted from pine, represents the mother's breasts, the father's scrotum, and the egg interwoven with a wood-shaped coil that symbolizes the spiral of life. *Forbidden Fruit* takes its name from a Billie Holiday song about lynching. The sculpture is as stark as it is beautiful and fluid, with a chain symbolizing the rope used to kill hundreds of African Americans in the segregated South.

Many of DeLeon's pieces are mobile, which speaks to the metamorphosis and the continuous physical and mental journeys that humans experience as they travel through life. His pieces are simple, yet as complex as life itself.

—Coria Holland

DENMARK, James

American painter, woodcutter, and collage artist

Born: Winter Haven, Florida, 23 March 1936. **Education:** Florida A & M University, Tallahassee, Florida, B.A.; Pratt Institute of Fine Arts, New York, 1973-76, M.F.A. 1976. **Awards:** Living Legends Award, National Urban League, 1980; Thirty-Ninth Annual Printing Industry Award, Schomburg Center, New York.

Individual Exhibitions:

Acts of Art Gallery, New York; Bratton Gallery, New York; Center for Art and Culture of Bedford Stuyvesant, Brooklyn, New York; Design Masters, Harlem, New York; Gallery 62, New York; Gallery W, Washington, D. C.; Norsam Gallery, New York; Roots in Art Gallery, Scarsdale, New York; Savacou Gallery, New York; Sewickley Academy's Campbell Gallery, Sewickley, Pennsylvania; Spectrum Gallery, New Rochelle, New York; Spiral Gallery, Brooklyn, New York.

Selected Group Exhibitions:

Boston Museum of Fine Arts, Boston; Contemporary Arts Museum, Houston; Everson Museum of Art, Syracuse, New York; Flint Institute of Art, Flint, Michigan; High Museum of Art, Atlanta, Georgia; Minneapolis Institute of Art, Minneapolis, Minnesota; Museum of Art at Rhode Island School of Design, Providence; Orozco Chapel, Guadalajara, Mexico; San Francisco Museum of Art; Bomani Gallery, San Francisco.

*　　*　　*

James Denmark, like many artists, has worked with various media and in many styles but is perhaps best known for his collages. He also sculpts and creates pictures from woodcuts and watercolors. He grew up among family members who were very artistic and, after graduating from college, became an art teacher. Early in his career as an artist, Denmark worked primarily in watercolors and charcoal. Like the art of other African American artists who came into adulthood after World War II and during the civil rights era, some of Denmark's works of art reflect the African American consciousness of that time.

James Denmark.

James Denmark: *Spiritual Eclipse.*

Denmark was already an established artist when he received his M.F.A. degree from Pratt Institute. During his time at Pratt, Denmark was surrounded by a well-endowed art community and influenced by several ideologies, specific artists, and movements. In particular he studied and looked to the ideas and styles of African American masters such as Romare Bearden, Ernest Crichlow, Jacob Lawrence, and Norman Lewis. Denmark was also greatly influenced by mainstream abstract expressionists such as Willem de Kooning, Jackson Pollock, and Clyfford Still. With his newly expanded artistic involvement, Denmark's style underwent a prominent change. He began to experiment with the essentially improvisational medium of collage. Using paper, found objects, and fabric, Denmark developed a personal, identifiable style.

Henri Matisse served as the obvious muse for Denmark's collage entitled *Chickie.* Reminiscent of a Matisse paper cutout of a black, reclining nude woman, Denmark's figure has on an African-style head wrap and is reclining on pieces of fabric with traditional African prints. *Seated Woman* is also reminiscent of a Matisse painting, especially in terms of the color choices.

A less figurative work, although it contains two figures, is Denmark's *Paradise.* Somewhat abstract, the work has an unusual balance. The eye is drawn to the most conspicuous shapes, which are located at the central horizontal plane. Due to the context in which the shapes exist, their particular shape, and the fact that the shapes rest upon stems/trunks, the viewer knows they are trees or giant plants. Above the "tree" plane are purple-hued mountains and a blue sky with white clouds. There are two birds in flight, and

upon noticing the birds, a viewer might recognize that some of the clouds are bird-shaped. The effect is vaguely Escher-like. At the bottom left of the picture plane, a man is presenting an object to a woman, who is sitting. The use of basic geometrical planes, the color, and the balance of the composition enhance the dimension of what is paradise.

In some of Denmark's collages, for example *Orchids* and *Mother and Son,* black, faceless human figures stand out as silhouettes against angular, boldly patterned backgrounds. The garments on the figures can be either part of the background or part of the figure—an effect that demands the attention of the viewer. In his collage, *Brothers and Sisters,* the background is subtle while the six figures in the foreground are visually demanding. The garments on the figures simultaneously stand out and blend together. Denmark has a natural affinity for the medium of collage and is a master colorist.

—Christine Miner Minderovic

DePILLARS, Murry (Norman)
American painter, printmaker, and illustrator

Born: Chicago, 21 December 1938. **Education:** Kennedy-King Community College, Chicago, A.A. in fine arts, 1966; Roosevelt University, Chicago, B.A. in art education, 1968, M.A. in urban studies 1970; Pennsylvania State University, University Park, Ph.D. in art education, 1976. **Military Service:** United States Army, 1961-63. **Career:** Master instructor, Chicago Committee on Urban Opportunity, 1968; assistant director, Educational Assistance Program, University of Illinois at Chicago Circle, 1968-71; assistant dean of student affairs, Virginia Commonwealth University School of the Arts, 1971-76, dean/professor of art education, 1976-95. Since 1995 executive vice president, Chicago State University. Advisory board, *New Art Examiner,* 1983-84; board of directors, College Art Association, 1990-94. Since 1985 member, AfriCobra. **Awards:** Elizabeth Catlett Mora Excellence Award, National Conference of Artists 1978; Man of Excellence plaque, Ministry of Education, Republic of China, 1980; Award for Excellence in the Education, Preservation and Promotion of Jazz, Richmond Jazz Society, 1981; Alumni Fellow, College of Art and Architecture, Pennsylvania State University, 1989; Plaque of Appreciation, Kappa Alpha Psi Fraternity, Eta Xi Chapter, 1990; Outstanding Service Award, Near Westside Community Center, 1995; Presidential Medallion, Virginia Commonwealth University, 1996. **Agent:** Darice Wright, Satori Fine Art, 230 West Superior, Chicago, Illinois 60610, U.S.A. **Address:** Executive Vice President, Chicago State University, ADM/315, 9501 South King Drive, Chicago, Illinois 60628, U.S.A.

Individual Exhibitions:

1969	Afam Studio and Gallery, Chicago
1973	Art Gallery, Virginia State University, Petersburg
1974	Museum, South Carolina State College, Orangeburg
1975	Paul Roberson Cultural Center, Pennsylvania State University, University Park
1976	Union Gallery, Purdue University, Lafayette, Indiana
	Studio Museum in Harlem, New York
	Art Gallery, Stillman College, Tuscaloosa, Alabama

Murry DePillars: *For "BU"—Art Blakey,* c.1991. Photo courtesy of Elizabeth Lecor.

1992	Center for Afroamerican and African Studies Gallery, University of Michigan, Ann Arbor
1995	Newcomb Hill Artspace, University of Virginia, Charlottesville
1996	Satori Fine Art, Chicago

Selected Group Exhibitions:

1990	Lee Hall Gallery, Clemson University, Clemson, South Carolina (traveling)
1992	Museum of Science and Industry, Chicago
	Center for Afroamerican and African Studies Gallery, University of Michigan, Ann Arbor
1993	Southside Community Art Center, Chicago
	Norman Parrish Gallery, Washington, D.C.

1994	Art Department Gallery, San Francisco State University
1995	Lyons Matrix Gallery, Austin, Texas
1996	Betty Rymer Gallery School of the Art Institute, Chicago
	Mary and Leigh Block Gallery, Northwestern University, Evanston, Illinois

Collections:

Art Institute of Chicago; Institute of Positive Education, Chicago; Kuumba Theatre Workshop, Chicago; National Gallery of Art, Dakar, Senegal; Penn Center, St. Helena, South Carolina; Southside Community Art Center, Chicago; Studio Museum in Harlem, New York.

Publications:

By DePILLARS: Articles—"The Emerging Voice of the Black Artists," in *Black Art: An International Quarterly,* 1, Fall 1976, pp. 50-52; "Art History and Black Culture," in *Minority Voices,* 1(1), Spring 1977, pp. 19-28; "Renaissance to Renaissance," in *Minority Voices,* 4(1), Spring 1980, pp. 39-48; "Wanted: A New Role for the Black Visual Artists," in *Western Journal of Black Studies,* 6(1), Spring 1983, pp. 26-34; "Multiculturalism in Visual Arts Education: Are America's Educational Institutions Ready for Multiculturalism?" in *Art, Culture, and Ethnicity* (Reston, Virginia), National Art Education Association, 1990, pp. 115-133; "Bodyphobia: Censorship by Litigation and Suggestion," in *Anonymity and Identity,* Virginia Commonwealth University's Anderson Gallery, 1993, pp. 6-8; "A Celebration of the African American Legacy in the Visual Arts," in *International Review of African American Art,* II(2), 1994, pp. 7-14.

On DePILLARS: Articles—"DePillars Traces Transition from Artist to Black Artist" by Jacqueline A. Long, in *Virginia Statesman,* 5 April 1973, pp. 6-7; "DePillars' Works Depict Afro-American Heritage" by Paula Ruth, in *Daily Collegian,* 12 August 1974, p. 3; "DePillars Is Artist with Message" by F. D. Cositt, in *Richmond Times-Dispatch,* 15 June 1975, p. H4; "Murry DePillars, High Energy: The Dean of VCU's School of the Arts Brings a Taste of Chicago and Greenwich Village to Richmond" by Robert Goldblum, in *Style Weekly,* III(9), 2 April 1982, pp. 25-27.

*   *   *

Despite his busy administrative schedule as an executive vice president of Chicago State University, Murry DePillars has continued to write and paint. He matured as an artist in Chicago in the 1960s, when the city was a center of radical political and cultural activities. Apart from being the cradle of the Black Panther Party, whose militant approach to the civil rights struggle attracted national and international attention, Chicago was the venue of the 1968 Democratic Party Convention, which was disrupted by anti-Vietnam War protesters. The city also nurtured the black arts movement, the Organization of Black American Culture, and the African Commune of Bad Relevant Artists (Africobra), among others, which

Murry DePillars: *The Dancers,* 1993. Photo courtesy of Elizabeth Lecor.

not only used art to combat social and racial injustices but also initiated the search for an aesthetic that would truly reflect the history, heritage, ethos, and realities of the black experience in the Americas.

DePillars's drawings and paintings are empowered by a rich intellect, a consciousness of his African heritage, and a recognition of the potentials of art as an instrument of cultural education and social change. As he once stated, "The decisive factor in my work is the social and political plight of blacks throughout the world." He became known in the 1960s and 1970s for reversing, through a series of naturalistic, cartoonlike drawings, stereotypical images of African Americans in the public imagination. For instance, in *Aunt Jemima* (1968) he transformed the image of a docile mammy into a black Amazon conscious of her rights and ever ready to fight for social justice by using her trademark pancake spatula as a weapon. In *The People of the Sun* (1972) Uncle Remus storms out of a book of African American folktales as if fed up with his life as a passive ethnographic specimen and henceforth determined to assert his rights to self-determination.

In the 1980s DePillars joined Africobra, a group committed not only to distilling from the African legacy the fundamentals of a black aesthetic but also to using the resulting expression to celebrate blacks' spirituality, love of colors, and sense of rhythm. Since then he has deemphasized the social realism that characterized his early works in favor of schematized compositions and stylized figures. Apart from being a keen observer of everyday life, he seeks inspiration from ancient African civilizations, traditional African art, and black history and music. His "Queen Candance" series (1980s) is dominated by an elegant and colorfully dressed black female who is pregnant and who strolls proudly across the picture plane, recalling the power and glory of the queen mothers of the ancient Nubian kingdom of Cush who challenged the imperial ambitions of the Roman legions in Africa toward the end of the first century B.C.

DePillars's later works are more decorative and stylized, reflecting a creative exploration of traditional African sculpture and textile designs. Intricate forms dissolve in a pattern of colors to create a kaleidoscope in which the visual suggests the aural by evoking the improvisations, syncopations, modulations, and multiple rhythms associated with jazz. His acrylic painting *For BU . . . Art Blakey* (1992) exemplifies this new direction. Dedicated to the jazz legend Art Blakey, the painting vibrates with synergetic colors and patterns, conjuring up the beats of the trap drums—an instrument on which Blakey displayed phenomenal skills as the leader of the Jazz Messengers. Rendered in silhouette, the figure of the drummer recedes from the viewer, hinting at his passage to the great beyond and at the same time his enduring contributions to jazz.

If some of DePillars's works tend to recall elements of cubism, futurism and orphism—and the similarities are coincidental—it is evidently because he is drawing inspiration directly from African art, from which these Eurocentric movements also benefited. The significant difference is that, like other members of Africobra, DePillars is exploring his African artistic legacy at a much deeper level.

—Babatunde Lawal

DERR, Milton
American painter

Born: Milwaukee, Wisconsin, 1932. **Education:** Layton School of Art, Milwaukee, Wisconsin, 1949-51; studied with an independent group of painters and sculptors, Tokyo, Japan, 1954-56; studied with George Demetrios, 1957-60; School of the Museum of Fine Arts, Boston, 1956-60, diploma 1960; School of the Museum of Fine Arts, Boston, 1961. **Career:** Since 1964 faculty member, School of the Museum of Fine Arts, Boston. Visual art consultant, Elma Lewis Center of Afro-American Artists, 1969-73; director, Community Service Art Program, Massachusetts College of Art, 1970-73; art director, Model Cities Higher Education Program, Inc., 1969-74. Artist-in-residence, Concord-Carlisle High School, 1979-84. **Awards:** Printmaking and drawing awards, School of the Museum of Fine Arts, Boston, 1956-61; Clarissa Bartlett Traveling Scholarship for travel and study in Japan, School of the Museum of Fine Arts, Boston, 1961-64; winner, Boston 200 Bicentennial Painting Competition, 1976; Hassam and Speicher Purchase Award for drawing, American Academy and Institute of Arts and Letters, 1980; Gund Foundation grant, 1984; Mellon grant, Boston Museum School, 1988. **Address:** 791 Tremont Street, E314, Boston, Massachusetts 02118, U.S.A.

Individual Exhibitions:

1976   *Landscapes,* The Gallery, Boston
1977   *Drawings and Watercolors,* The Gallery, Boston
1978   *Drawings,* DuBoise Institute, Harvard University, Cambridge, Massachusetts
1980   AAMARP Gallery, Northeastern University, Boston
1987   Gallery at the Piano Factory, Boston
1988   CRT Craftery Gallery, Hartford, Connecticut

Selected Group Exhibitions:

1970   *Fourteen Black Artists,* Studio Museum in Harlem, New York
1975   Boston Museum of Fine Arts
1977   *Northeastern University First Annual Exhibition,* Boston City Hall
1980   Museum of the National Center of Afro-American Artists
1981   Northeastern University Gallery
1983   *Northeastern University Group Exhibition,* Federal Reserve Bank of Boston
1984   Copley Society, Boston
1985   Federal Reserve Bank of Boston
1988   Museum of Fine Arts, Boston
      National Center of Afro-American Artists

Collections:

Bentley College, Waltham, Massachusetts; National Museum of Afro-American Art, Roxbury, Massachusetts; University of Vermont, Putney.

Publications:

On DERR: Book—*Milton Derr Exhibition: The Journey,* exhibition catalog, Connecticut, CRT's Craftery Gallery, 1988.

*   *   *

The art of Milton Derr (a.k.a. Milton Johnson) communicates intense emotion and often provides compelling social commentary. A superb draftsman, Derr describes himself primarily as a figura-

Milton Derr, 1993.

tive painter whose style falls somewhere between expressionism and impressionism. While the human figure is usually the focal point in his paintings, it often appears against the backdrop of a landscape or other design element. This classically trained artist's works also include prints, illustrations, and decorative and interior design. The color field is a strong factor in his work.

Derr's themes are often derived from his readings in subjects such as economics and world history. While some of his works portray black subjects, his approach has been to universalize the black experience by focusing on themes that transcend race and by employing generally accepted modern art techniques in the European tradition. Thus, he has been included among the so-called blackstream artists of the 1960s and 1970s. This group of artists is distinguished both from those African Americans who rejected conventional European-based art styles and aesthetics and from the mainstream black artists who not only embraced conventional techniques but also avoided black subject matter. Other blackstream artists include the collagist Benny Andrews, painter Joe Overstreet, and sculptor Barbara Chase-Riboud. Derr has said that his art depicting black subjects and social commentary represents at once the most "forceful" aspect of his work and the most "restrictive" in terms of commercial appeal.

One of Derr's best-known works is *Another Birthday* (1969), an oil painting of an elderly black figure in which the heavy application of vivid color paradoxically becomes a gloomy or burdensome element. The painting effectively conveys the loneliness that often accompanies old age. *Limited,* a woodcut depicting a crippled man on crutches, expresses the despair felt by the wounded and physically impaired.

Among Derr's many book illustrations is his work in *The Little Fishes,* a young adult novel by Erik Christian Haugaard about a twelve-year-old beggar in Naples during World War II. The haunting pen-and-ink wash illustration on the cover and the lyrical continuous-line sketches throughout the book portray the writer's themes of loneliness, hunger, and death, the legacies of war that children suffer. The similarity in style and emotional intensity between the drawings in *The Little Fishes* and *Another Birthday* seems to confirm Derr's preference for a universal, nonracial aesthetic.

Derr's travels in Europe and Japan, where he spent five years in the early 1960s, have figured greatly in the development of his multicultural perspective. While in Japan on a fellowship, he studied with a group of elderly artists who gave him lessons in aesthetics and discipline that remain a powerful influence on his work and life. His studies of Eastern art and cultures—Japanese, Chinese, and Korean—also have had a major influence on his sense of design, especially his fascination with patterns. His collection of works includes not only paintings of black leaders such as Martin Luther King, Jr., and W. E. B. Du Bois but also Japanese-inspired decorative folding panels.

—Sonya Stinson

DIAB, Rashid

Sudanese and Spanish painter and printmaker

Born: A. Rashid M. Diab, Wadmedani, Sudan, 1 January 1957. **Education:** Faculty of Fine Art, Khartoum, Sudan, 1974-1978, B.F.A. 1978; Faculty of Fine Art, Madrid, 1980-1991, M.F.A. 1984, M.F.A. 1986, Ph.D. 1991. **Family:** Married Mercedes Carmona Andreu in 1994, one daughter, one son. **Career:** Teacher assistant, Institute of Music and Drama, Khartoum, Sudan, 1978-84. Since 1990 teacher, Faculty of Fine Art, Madrid. **Awards:** Honorary Scholarship, Ministry of Exterior Affairs, Spain, 1979; Spanish Government Scholarship, 1980; Honorary Scholarship, Spanish-Arab Institute of Culture, Madrid, 1985; Cultural Foundation of Abu Dabi Medal, 1986; Third Biennial of R.O.C. Prize, Taipei, Taiwan, 1987; Third Biennial of Cairo Medal, 1988; Salon de Otoño de Madrid Prize, 1989; Cuban Fund of Cultural Goods Medal, Havana, 1989; Institute of Collaboration with the Arab World scholarship, 1991; Maximo Ramos Prize, El Ferrol, Spain, 1991; Tenth Biennial of Drawing Prize, Zamora, Spain, 1991. **Address:** C/ Magallanes 10 Bajo A Madrid 28015, Spain.

Rashid Diab: *Red Space II,* 1993. Photo courtesy of Alejandro Lamas.

Individual Exhibitions:

1976	African Centre, London
1986	Cultural Foundarion, Abu Dabi
	Al-Khalig Hotel Gallery, Oatar
1987	Orfaly Gallery, Bagdad
	Abila Gallery, Syria
1988	Gallery Sharga
	Faculty of Fine Arts, Complutense University, Madrid
	Dushahri Gallery, Kuwait City, Kuwait
1989	Xeito Gallery, Madrid
	Gallery Watatu, Nairobi, Kenya
1990	Gris y Negro Gallery, Madrid
1991	La Caixa, Barcelona, Spain
	L'Espace Miro, Paris, France
1992	Annual Exhibition, Khartoum, Sudan
	Alif Gallery, Washington, D.C.
	Savannah Gallery, London
	Expo' 92, Sevilla, Spain
	Tecni Arte, Madrid
	Tolmo Gallery, Toledo, Spain
1993	Gallery Watatu, Nairobi, Kenya
	Herbert Johnson Museum
	Savannah Art Gallery, London
	Islamic Cultural Center at Madrid, Spain (retrospective)
1994	Museum of the National Center of Afro American Artists, Boston
	Alif Gallery, Washington, D.C.
	Zaragoza Grafica, Spain
1995	A & T State University, Greensboro, North Carolina
	Mattye Reed African Heritage Center, North Carolina
	Camarena Palace, Caceres, Spain
	Hector Mora Gallery, Elche, Spain
1996	Arca Gallery, Torrelodones, Madrid
	Ra del Rey Gallery, Madrid
	Darat Al Fanon, Amman, Jordan

Selected Group Exhibitions:

1980	*Third Cultural Art Festival,* Khartoum, Sudan
1987	Raggab Gallery, Cairo, Egypt
1988	Sudan Art Aid, Oxfam Foundation, London
1989	*Contemporary Art from the Islamic World,* London
1991	National Museum of Art, Asilah, Morocco
1993	London Contemporary Art Fair 1993, London
	International Exhibition of Etching, Abila Gallery, Syria
1995	*Fifth Biennial International,* Cuba
	White Chapel, London
	Right to Hope, United Nations Gathering, Johannesburg, South Africa

Collections:

African Centre of Madrid, Spain; Arab League, Madrid; Diputacion de Zamora, Spain; Institute of Arab World, Paris; Jordan Royal

Fine Arts Museum; Life Museum of Fine Art, Tunis; Ministry of Foreign Affairs, Madrid; Modern Museum of Etching, Cairo; Musée d'Art Contemporain of Chamalienes, Paris; Museo de Arte Castellano-Leones, Spain; Museo of Bello Piñeiro, El Ferrol, Coruña, Spain; Museum of Royal Academy of Fine Arts, San Fernanco, Madrid; Museum of Contemporary Art, Nairobi, Kenya; Museum of Fine Arts, Alexandria, Egypt; Museum of Modern Art, Iraq; Museum of Modern Art, Tunis; Nacional Council of Arts and Letters, Khartoum, Sudan; National Library, Madrid; Royal Museum of Fine Arts, Amman, Jordan; Spanish-Arab Institute of Culture, Madrid; Wilfredo Lam Centre of Havana, Cuba.

Publications:

By DIAB: Articles—"Sudanese Contemporary Painting," in *Art from the Islamic World,* London, Escorpion Publishing, pp. 245-252; "Contemporary African Art from the Sudanese Perspective," in *Atlantica Magazine, Augumn 1994;* "Arab Contemporary Art," in *Correo del Arte,* November 1988.

*

Rashid Diab comments:

I was born and raised in a small town, Wad Medani, on the banks of the Blue Nile in Sudan. Since I was a small child, I loved to travel; I always wanted to be somewhere discovering new places, different types of life, and other people. I had the constant thought of how I could create a real intimate relationship with the distances, the space. The reason why things have specific dimensions and a certain time and shape . . . these questions became like an obsession for me, and the only way to solve these problems was to paint and to continue to do so. Painting has been a necessity for me. I know that the desire to paint is something inside me . . . part of my inner self . . . part of my unconsciousness. As time passed, this need to paint and draw transformed into something like a biological instinct, which strengthened my relationship with the world around me.

At the age of four years, I began to spend a long time molding clay into animal forms—lions, elephants . . . and some human figures. In the beginning I encountered significant difficulty in developing this instinct or desire; I didn't receive any direct support from my family or any outside help, since no one in my immediate family had any interest in art, and with the lack of an artistic atmosphere, there was no gathering, no related art activities, nothing at all. It was an environment that I remember as discouraging, but it didn't affect me negatively. Quite on the contrary, I think it made me look into my inner self and search for my own language.

Since the initial stage I was really keen about achieving a good level of expertise in techniques and general knowledge about art. My first idea was to enter directly into the School of Fine Art in Khartoum since it was a terrible period having to study subjects like chemistry, mathematics, etc. All I wanted to do was to dedicate my entire time to artwork. Unfortunately I was disappointed with the atmosphere at the school, as well as with the syllabus that I had to learn. In spite of the full dedication I had, I missed the freshness because I felt obligated to adopt new influences both in learning, having to study foreign art such as Western art in general, and in practicing. I had to keep offering a new type of painting, such as still lifes and landscapes, in a very academic way.

I talk as though I were painting because I always have a very general idea. I start to weed out the unnecessary clutter. Studying art for me had a positive side, that of being with other art students.

But it was disappointing as well because it was an unfulfilled dream, even when I came to Spain. Since I came to Spain in December 1979 with a scholarship to further my studies in art, I was certain that I had a diverse artistic heritage, which I have continued to maintain, and that I had an extensive vocabulary of images and patterns in my mind. As I stated before, my foremost philosophy of art is my relationship to space and time. I have kept my unique theme, but over the years I have acquired a more adequate technique to express myself better.

Art for me is knowledge in the sense that I think an artist must first be a vivid reader and conscious of his contribution. Every stroke, every line, whatever may be in the artist's mind, whether or not it is apparent in his work, transferred or not from his mind to his art, is part of his life. That is why within the same work, an artist could be a father of all schools or tendencies during the partial time between when the work begins and when he thinks it has finished. The lapse in time will take me through fractions of seconds and centuries. It really doesn't matter if it is in past, present, or future. Rather, what matters is how I can achieve the color, shape, and form to express this fraction of time.

It is not a mere coincidence of other times or incarnations of some moment, it is more than that. It is actually a reflection of the human being as a conclusion, a material result of the species, which I try to express in my work. Through colors and form I try to illustrate these moments of sorrow, happiness, hope, despair, etc., but the most important element is that of nostalgia for this universal world and its true reflection and the culmination of the past twenty years living far from home.

*   *   *

Rashid Diab is an accomplished Sudanese painter, master printmaker, and art critic who has lived in Madrid, Spain, since 1982. He graduated with honors from the College of Fine and Ap-

Rashid Diab: *Homage to My Poet Friend,* **1994. Photo courtesy of Alejandro Lamas.**

plied Arts in Khartoum in 1978. He then traveled to Madrid on a scholarship from the government of Spain, where he completed several graduate degrees, including M.F.A.'s in painting and in etching and a Ph.D. from the Complutensian University of Madrid for his thesis on contemporary Sudanese art. One of the most successful of the younger Sudanese living abroad, he is a prolific artist who has participated in more than twenty solo and group exhibitions. His works are included in the permanent collections of several museums in Africa, the Middle East, Europe, and Asia. He owns and directs the Medani Galeri, a studio that has become a well-known print shop and a meeting place for talented artists in Madrid.

Diab's work reflects a synthesis of his Sudanese heritage and an awareness of contemporary artistic developments in Europe. His imagery and symbols range from Arabic illuminations and calligraphic designs, animals, human figures, and traditional folk and historical motifs to mythical and masklike African motifs. This is illustrated not only in his etchings and paintings but also in his rarely exhibited but successful experiments in other artistic media, such as furniture and interior design. Diab's distinct use of calligraphy and calligraphic designs can be seen in several of his works, in which the written word, sometimes verses from the Koran, becomes part of the overall design and the Arabic letter forms acquire an independent aesthetic value.

Diab's experience in Spain has enriched his artwork. He has moved to new mediums and studied and mastered techniques such as silk screening, etching, and engraving. During his early days in Spain, Diab was busy painting the faces of people he had left in the Sudan and the aspects of Sudanese social customs, occasions, and rituals he missed in his new and strange environment. *Fragments of My Palace* (1984) and *La Trayectoria* (1987) are typical works that represent the essence of Diab's early subject matter and style. In *La Trayectoria,* for example, a repeated part of a short Koranic verse runs through the upper frame of the work. The calligraphy here is rendered in a distinct style popular among Muslim clerics and students in traditional Koranic schools in the Sudan and differs from the style known in other parts of the Islamic world. Diab's use of Arabic calligraphic designs is reminiscent of the Khartoum school style found in the works of Ibrahim al-Salahi, Ahmad Shibrain, and Osman Waqiallah. The color scheme in Diab's work of this period also echoes the earthy style popularized by al-Salahi's earliest work and emulated by other Khartoum artists in the 1960s and early 1970s.

In his later works Diab has been inspired by the painting techniques of the Renaissance he has seen in Spanish and other European museums. He has been particularly drawn to the Renaissance artists' ability to control color, light, and contrast and their distribution over the space of the canvas. Diab's works remain autobiographical, however, and represent a continuity of subject matter. The constantly unfolding thread of the artist's memory of his past, his people, and his native country's landscape, observed in earlier works, persists. In composition and the use of space, and even in perspective, his series "Memories of an Immigrant Bird" (1989) is a poetic expression of the artist's daydreams and memories of bygone times. Diab's bold experimentation with color can be seen in the group of works entitled "The Series of the Red Space" (1991), executed in oil on canvas, or in "People" (1992-94), a series of monoprints. The forms and lines within the composition of the work, though conceived as abstract representations of people or of genre scenes, dissolve into overlapping and sometimes bold layers of color.

Diab's painterly talent, improvisational spirit, and great sense of color have enabled him to achieve powerful and emotionally charged images in his works. Moving from one medium to another, he has remained faithful to his vision as a colorist and a painter. The forms in Diab's work acquire prominence as color formations rather than referential meanings or symbolic gestures. The overall composition and color relationships within his work take precedence over small composite details, motifs, or other elements of design. Diab's art, whether it is an etching or a painting, exhibits a mastery of medium combined with a precision of statement and a magical vision that give the overall work a distinctive style.

—Salah Hassan

DIAL, Thorton (Sr.)
American painter and sculptor

Born: Livingston, Alabama, 10 September 1928. **Family:** Married Clara Mae Murrow in 1951, three sons and one daughter. **Career:** Worked for thirty years at Pullman Standard. Has held a variety of jobs, including work in construction, carpentry, cafe ownership, farming, ranching, factory work, bricklaying, and commercial fishing. **Agents:** Dolly Fiterman Fine Arts, 100 University Avenue Southeast, Minneapolis, Minnesota 55414, U.S.A.; Ricco-Maresca Gallery, 152 Wooster Street, New York, New York 10012, U.S.A.; **Address:** c/o Ricco-Maresca Gallery, 152 Wooster Street, New York, New York 10012, U.S.A. **Online address:** http://artnetweb.com/artnet web/gallery/galhome.html; rmgal@aol.com.

Individual Exhibitions:

1990	Kennesaw State College, Marietta, Georgia
	Fay Gold Gallery, Atlanta, Georgia
	Southern Queens Park Association/African-American Hall of Fame, Jamaica, New York
1991	Ricco-Maresca Gallery, New York
1992	Luise Ross Gallery, New York
1993	Museum of American Folk Art, New York (traveling)
1994	New Museum of Contemporary Art, New York
	Milwaukee Art Museum, Wisconsin
1995	Kennesaw State College, Marietta, Georgia
1996	Michael C. Carlos Museum, Emory University, Atlanta, Georgia
1997	Tennessee State Museum, Nashville

Selected Group Exhibitions:

1988	High Museum of Art, Atlanta, Georgia
1989	Intar Latin American Gallery, New York
1990	*The Dial Family: Paintings by Thorton Dial, Sr., Thorton Dial, Jr., Arthur Dial, Ronald Lockett,* Ricco-Maresca Gallery, New York
1991	Museum of York County, Rock Hill, South Carolina
1991	Malmo Konsthall, Sweden (traveling)
1992	*Power of the Dials,* Sloss Furnace Historical Monument, Birmingham, Alabama
	Metropolitan State College Center for the Visual Arts, Denver, Colorado
	Center for the Arts, Vero Beach, Florida
1993	High Museum of Art, Atlanta, Georgia
	Phyllis Kind Gallery, New York
	Florida State University Gallery and Museum, Tallahassee

Thornton Dial (with Clara Mae Dial, left, and Dolly J. Fiterman), 1993. Photo courtesy of Collection Dolly J. Fiterman.

Collections:

Dolly Fiterman Fine Arts, Minneapolis; High Museum of Art, Atlanta, Georgia; Hirschhorn Museum and Sculpture Garden, Washington, D.C.; Phyllis Kind Gallery, New York; Milwaukee Art Museum, Wisconsin; Museum of American Folk Art, New York; National Museum of American Art, Smithsonian Institution, New York; New Orleans Museum of Art; Philadelphia Museum of Art; Ricco-Maresca Gallery, New York; Luise Ross Gallery, New York; Studio Museum, New York; United Nations, New York.

Publications:

By DIAL: Book—*Thorton Dial: Image of the Tiger,* exhibition catalog, New York, Museum of American Folk Art and Abrams, Inc., 1993.

On DIAL: Articles—"The Ascension of Thornton Dial" by Eileen M. Drennan, in *The Atlanta Journal/The Atlanta Constitution,* 29 July 1990, pp. N1-2; "Self-Taught Artist Makes Compelling Case for Human Rights" by Catherine Fox, in *The Atlanta Journal/The Atlanta Constitution,* 13 March 1990: p. F9; "Outsider Art USA" by Paolo Bianchi, in *Kunstforum International,* March/April 1991, pp. 204, 206; "Don't Touch That Dial," in *Manhattan Spirit 8,* 46, 2 December 1992, p. 31; "Thorton Dial" by Sue Scott, in *ARTnews*

92, April 1993, p. 137; "Thornton Dial at Luise Ross" by Ann Wilson Lloyd, in *Art in America,* 81(5), May 1993, pp. 123-24; "Bits, Pieces and a Drive to Turn Them into Art" by Dinitia Smith, in *New York Times,* 5 February 1997, p. C-9, C-13.

*

Thorton Dial comments:

The Dial art show is about the strategy of the world. If this touch anybody, it got to touch them all. If my art don't rub off on somebody, it ain't art. It got to be a feeling, it got to be a mind. It ain't just my feeling, it come from just about everybody. I speak about life, I think about the world, life always going on for everybody. God made a man to understand life, if you got college degrees or if you got just common sense, mother's wit. Mother's wit is where ideas come from. Since I got the opportunity to speak like I can, I give the best I know. I can't read and spell but I got a mind and I can speak with any man. I might say something in my art that somebody ain't never heard before. Life is so hard for people when they don't understand.

I make art that ain't speaking against nobody or for nobody neither. Sometimes it be about what is wrong in life. I do that because I want the world to be right. If people can see it and understand. It don't make the world right just because I want it right. I hope that I can just make them study over it. If a person can't understand something, somebody got to understand for them. That's what I be all about, building a black road. That's what the black star is all about. Everything travel by the black star if the lights is out.

Every color I put on a board is put on there according to the way of life. There's color on there somebody going to like and color somebody ain't going to like. I be putting it all down on there, what people done did, what they think about, what they know about. We ain't doing nothing man ain't already thought about. God gave different people different power. He gave me a good mind to think. Some people can't think. I have had that mind, I was down a long time and couldn't do no better, but I climbed up. When you been down like I been, you appreciate up and you use it when you get it.

My way of life is to do what's on my mind to do. I ain't been nowhere but I believe I can strategize about the whole world. Everything works the same everywhere.

Life go on for man any time. Since the beginning of the world man been struggling to learn about things. Anything you pick up, somebody know about. You picking up the spirit of somebody. My art got my spirit. I picked up a whole lot in my day. Leaves fall off a tree got a spirit in them. Cows, dirt, rocks, the whole world, all that stuff carry on life. An old house got old tin fall off. Everything help somebody carry on life. Old tin fall off, but it done did a many people some good before it fall. It can still do somebody some good.

Old life is just make new life. That's what recycle is all about. When God died he rose again.

There got to be light in the darkness of the world. God gave light to the dark world, and then he gave signs. He gave me the power to see the signs—from the water in the sea, from the ground in the earth. That's what knowledge is. He put people on earth to lead and people on earth to preach.

God gave man so much knowledge so he can't fall. The world ain't fell yet, is it? When God get tired of us, he'll cut us all off.

I done give you the strategy of the world. I don't know nothing else to say.

(From *Strategy of the World,* Jamaica, New York, Southern Queens Park Association, Inc., 1990.)

*   *   *

Perhaps best known for his images of tigers contending with the world around them, self-taught artist Thornton Dial burst into the public's imagination in 1987. As is customary with folk artists, however, he did not seek its attention; the art world went to him. For thirty years he was a steelworker, and for years he released his creative energy by producing painted objects, which he displayed or buried in his backyard in Bessemer, Alabama. Not until 1987 did

Thornton Dial: *Remembering the Road,* **1992. Photo courtesy of Collection Dolly J. Fiterman.**

he turn his attention to easel painting at the urging of the white art collector who that year had "discovered" him. Still most of his paintings, like his sculptures, are "constructed"; they are built, layer upon layer, using impasto and found materials, such as carpeting, rope, metal, plywood, bottles, plastic—all drawn from the immediate world around him. In his words, "Old life makes new life."

As a laborer in the deep South who had performed odd jobs over the years in construction, farming, and fishing, Dial had seen the entanglements of race relations and the ongoing struggle for freedom up close. He has lived through segregation, migration North, and the civil rights movement of the 1960s. His themes were spawned by those eras, but he also turned his attention to love, women, and sexuality. He wrestles with topics that are popular in every black household, but to those discussions he adds an element of pragmatism and sophistication. He is confident that he has something to say in his art that has not yet been heard and certainly hasn't been seen.

Though a knowledge of the artist is helpful in understanding his visual language, as with any nonrepresentational artist, some references come more easily than others. Dial expresses himself mainly through human and animal forms, including such traditional folk art symbols as the snake, the monkey, birds, fish, and the tiger, which is often used as a metaphor for self. The images in *The Tiger Cat* (a steel, tin, and enamel structure, 1987) are clear—chickens and a rabbit gracefully perched on the tiger cat's back and human skeletons hanging below in the tiger's belly. Whether the message is that the tiger, once a wild and free predator (as indicated by the humans he has consumed), has been tamed or that it has rebelled, consumed its oppressors, and freed the animals on its back, the dual nature of the tiger suggests a struggle, possibly that of Dial's ancestors, who were enslaved and fought for their freedom.

Dial differs from other folk artists, such as Clementine Hunter who preserved the South in memory paintings, in his interpretation of life's trials and in his depictions of events that reach well beyond his personal experiences. In his paintings, drawings, and assemblages, he has tackled the middle passage, *African Ladies Dancing,* the Iraqi invasion of Kuwait, and the Los Angeles riots of 1992. He doesn't merely document; he infuses art with abstract qualities, making intellectually appealing statements about human struggle, and often his works are not easily distinguished from those of mainstream master artists.

Images of men are noticeably rare in his work. Instead he pairs women with animals, as in *Life Go On* (acrylic on canvas, 1990), in which the naked woman holds a fish and a bird in her arms, while another bird nests on her head. Perhaps the woman is fishing for love, with the bird on her head suggesting that she's already found it. The warm background and the long brush strokes lend a flowing, rhythmic calm to Dial's exploration of female sexuality. Temptations of the flesh fight against a commitment to monogamy and stability, and . . . life goes on.

Dial's style has evolved more substantively and more quickly than the styles of many other folk artists, whose creations are marked by a repetition of approach, themes, and materials. Some critics say that Dial's art has entered the realm of the contemporary. Surely the art world's rave reception of his creations has given him the confidence to pursue wider-ranging subjects. As he continues to explore Southern themes, he and his tiger delve into popular art, world events, travel, and politics.

Dial's use of the tiger as a symbol can be deceptively simple. *Struggling Tiger Proud Stepping* (enamel, oil, rope, tin, and wood on canvas and wood, 1991) is, on first glance, a loud painting with a forceful mix of earth tones protruding from the surface. The tiger strutting in the upper right corner may not be visible at first, but once seen he's a dominating presence, stepping out of the jungle of chaos below him. A closer look reveals a knotted rope binding together the discordant images of frightened woman, proud tiger, and thick jungle. Does the rope represent yet another of life's many struggles?

Dial's ability to draw the viewer into his compelling artistic tales by merging striking but familiar images with bold color schemes and a keen sense of perception underlines why the art world landed on his doorstep in the 1980s and why they haven't left.

—Joanne Harris

DIDI, Mestre

Brazilian sculptor

Family: Married Juana Elbien in 1964. **Career:** Religious priest of the Nago tradition. Traveled to Africa in 1967. **Awards:** Homage and special accommodation, *XXIII Biennale,* São Paulo, Brazil, 1996.

Individual Exhibition:

1996   *XXIII Bienale,* São Paulo, Brazil (retrospective)

Publications:

On DIDI: Articles—"Sala de Mestre Didi Reunira Obras Realizadas em 33 Anos," in *Folha de Sao Paulo,* 1996; "Mestre Didi Vai ser Homenageado na Bienal de SP" by Angelica de Moraes, in *O Estado de Sao Paulo,* 1996.

*   *   *

Deoscoredes Maximiliano dos Santos, better known as Mestre Didi, is a multitalented artist—a writer, historian, and sculptor—as well as a devoted follower of the *orisa* (Yoruba divinities) and of his ancestors from Yorubaland in West Africa. As a titled son of Shango, the thunder god, he has been a major presence at the Candomble Axe Opo Afonja in Salvador, Brazil, where he was the priest of Obaluaye. He also has held an important position in the Egungun ancestral masking society on the island of Itaparica. Since adolescence he has been creating sacred objects in wood, concrete, and stone for various *candomble* altars. This cultural and religious background has been the inspiration for all of his art.

His multimedia sculptures celebrate a variety of divinities. They are re-creations of sacred ritual forms as well as materializations of ancient legends. Inspired by his own deep faith and the traditions of his forebears, he takes the icons, colors, and materials of the gods and creates new spatial and aesthetic imagery. He thus blurs sacred and secular distinctions as he evokes powerful forces. His primary media are tightly bound bundles of palm ribs, raffia fibers, leather, gourds, beads, and cowrie shells worked into forms inspired by straight (*sasara*) and looped (*ebiri*) Yoruba ritual brooms—sacred implements used for purifying spaces, places, and persons and for assuring well-being and good fortune. The works symbolize deities

151

associated with the curing of diseases (Omolu, Obaluaye, and Soponna) and the elderly matron Nana Buku, as well as the rainbow serpent deity Osumare, which is associated with riches. In the complex work entitled *Osanyin and Osumare,* his imagery fuses references to several *orisa,* including serpents symbolic of Osumare that swirl around the central shaft while a majestic bird floats above. The bird suggests many things. It is a primary symbol of the spiritual powers of women, the healing power of herbs controlled by Osanyin, the flight of mind and soul, and the sign of prayers offered and answered.

The scale of his works varies greatly. Some are small, reminiscent of personal icons on domestic altars. Others are life-size. They claim and embrace space like spiritual companions, hovering beside their viewers like protecting, guiding presences. Whether small or large, they embody a meticulous mind and open spirit.

There is an elegance and delicacy in his forms—the flow of lines in space, the shimmering beads that punctuate the slender shapes, and the floating birds with outstretched wings. The fluid lines, created from flexible palm ribs, suggest the Afro-Brazilian tradition of *pontos riscados,* linear signatures drawn with sacred chalk or gunpowder to attract, call, and welcome spiritual forces to ceremonies in their honor. Here his evocations rise and swirl in the air, making the imagination soar.

—Henry John Drewal

DONALDSON, Jeff (Richardson)
American painter and printmaker

Born: Pine Bluff, Arkansas, 15 December 1932. **Education:** University of Arkansas, Pine Bluff, B.A. in studio art 1954; Institute of Design, Illinois Institute of Technology, M.S. in art education and administration, 1963; Northwestern University, Evanston, Illinois, Ph.D. in art history, 1974. **Military Service:** United States Army, 1955-57. **Family:** Two children. **Career:** Art instructor, Lamer High School, Jackson, Mississippi, 1954-55, Chicago Public Schools, 1957-59; chairman, art department, Marshall High School, Chicago, 1959-65; assistant professor, Northeastern Illinois University, Chicago, 1965-68; visiting professor, Northwestern University, Evanston Illinois, 1968-70; director, Gallery of Art, and chairman, Department of Art, Howard University, Washington, D.C., 1970-76; director, World Black and African Festival of Art and Culture, Lagos, Nigeria, 1975-80; art director, Jazz America Marketing Corporation, Washington, D.C., 1978-82; professor, Department of Art, Howard University, Washington, D.C., 1980-85; associate dean, Howard University, Washington, D.C., 1985-90. Since 1990 Dean, College of Fine Arts, Howard University, Washington, D.C. Grants reviewer, National Endowment for the Arts, National Endowment for the Humanities, Arts International Travel. Consultant, Time-Life Books. **Awards:** Outstanding Faculty Award, Northeastern Illinois University, 1967; First Place Painting Award, Art and Soul Competition, 1968; First Place Painting Award, Black Expressions Competition, 1968; Distinguished Service Award, University without Walls, 1971; Catlett Award of Excellence, National Conference of Artists, 1977; Bryant Recognition Award, Midwest Theatre Alliance, 1984; Outstanding Arkansans Award, University of Arkansas, 1985; African American Leadership Award, African Heritage Studies Association, 1985; Spirit

of Sinai Award, Mount Sinai Hospital Medical Center, 1994. **Address:** Howard University, College of Fine Arts, Washington, D.C. 20059, U.S.A.

Individual Exhibitions:

Cynthia Tilson Gallery, Milwaukee; ETA Gallery, Chicago; Hammonds Gallery, Atlanta.

Selected Group Exhibitions:

Afro-American Museum, Wilberforce, Ohio; Ascension Gallery, Washington, D.C.; Cheekwood Center, Nashville; Corcoran Museum, Washington, D.C.; Florida A & M University, Tallahassee; Howard University, Washington, D.C.; Museo d'Arte Contemporanea, Palermo, Italy; Museum of Contemporary Art, Chicago; Museum of Science and Industry, Chicago; Parish Gallery, Washington, D.C.; Southside Art Center, Chicago; Steinbaum Gallery, New York.

Collections:

Afro-American Art and Culture Museum, Philadelphia; Arizona State University, Tempe; Atlanta University, Georgia; Cornell University, Ithaca, New York; ETACA Foundation, Chicago; Fisk University, Nashville; Howard University, Washington, D.C.; Musée Dynamique, Dakar, Senegal; National African American Museum, Wilberforce, Ohio; National Center of Afro-American Artists, Boston; Schomburg Center, New York; Southside Art Center, Illinois; Studio Museum in Harlem, New York; University of Arkansas, Pine Bluff.

Publications:

By DONALDSON: Articles—"Henry O. Tanner, American Artist," in *Negro Digest,* February 1970; "Ten in Search of Nation," in *Black World,* October 1970; "TransAfrican Art," in *The Black Collegian,* October/November 1980; "AfriCobra, 1981," in *The Black Collegian,* October/November 1981; "Upside the Wall, in *The Peoples Art: Murals 1967-78,* African American Museum, 1986; "Nine African American Printmakers," in *Art Exhibeo,* Wayne State University Press, 1988; "AfriCobra: Then and Now," in *New Art Examiner,* March 1990; "AfriCobra and TransAtlantic Connections," in *Seven Stories about Modern Art in Africa,* WhiteChapel, London, 1995; "Ten in Search of a Nation," in *Theories and Documents of Contemporary Art* edited by K. Stiles and P. Selz, University of California Press, Berkeley, 1996.

On DONALDSON: Articles—"Jeff Donaldson" by Keith Morrison, in *New Art Examiner,* February 1982, p. 19; "Jeff Donaldson" by Paul Richard, in *The Washington Post,* 12 December 1982, p. C3; "Jeff Donaldson—Image-maker with an Afrocentric Lens" by Harriet Jackson Scarupa, in *New Directions,* Fall 1990, p. 20; "An Interview with Jeff Donaldson" by Alice Thorson, in *New Art Examiner,* March 1990, p. 26; "Blackness Is the Soul of Donaldson's Art" by Catherine Fox, in *Atlanta Journal/Constitution,* 12 November 1993, p. 17; "Jeff Donaldson, On the Growth of a TransAfrican Esthetic" by Ken Oda, in *KOAN,* December 1993, 2(4), pp. 10-14.

*   *   *

Jeff Donaldson: *Jam Packed, Jelly Tight*, **1988.**

Jeff Donaldson is an African American painter, printmaker, educator, and scholar, who helped articulate the philosophy and aesthetics of the black art movement of the 1960s and 1970s. Donaldson, who serves as the dean of the College of Fine Arts at Howard University, was a cofounder in 1968 in Chicago of AfriCobra (an acronym for African Commune of Bad Relevant Artists, a name derived from combining "Afri," as it relates to Africa, with "Cobra," the acronym for Coalition of Black Revolutionary Artists), an active and influential group of African American artists. As emphasized in AfriCobra's 1970 manifesto, which Donaldson authored, the group's objectives were to develop a new African American aesthetics as well as a commitment to the principles of social responsibility, involvement of artists in their local communities, and promotion of pride in black self-identity.

Through his writings, artwork, and curatorial interventions, Donaldson has devoted his career to the recovery and display of a distinctly black aesthetics, synthesizing and linking the diverse visual traditions of Africa and its diaspora, from ancient Egyptian to contemporary African and African American arts. In theory and practice Donaldson has been a major driving force in the growth of TransAfrican art, an international contemporary aesthetic and style uniting people of African descent all over the world. Donaldson uses "TransAfrican," a term he helped coin, to define a whole range of new forms of expression born in the aftermath of the independence movements in Africa and the Caribbean and the black power

movement in the United States. This was a time when "artists of African descent throughout the world began to look at Africa as a source of their aesthetics and to imbue and invigorate the traditional iconography, symbolism and philosophical basis of African art with contemporaneous ideas, ideals and symbols from their own time and place." This is exemplified by art movements and groups such as Group Fwomaje in Martinique, Bogolan Kasobane in Mali, and Vohou-Vohou in the Ivory Coast. As vice president of the international committee and chair of the USA-Canada zone of the Festac festival from 1972-77, Donaldson pursued his vision of TransAfrican art.

Born and raised in Pine Bluff, Arkansas, Donaldson's life-long interest in an Afrocentric art was nurtured by his early tutelage under John Howard, his mentor at Arkansas A. M. & N. College, who was a student of the great Harlem Renaissance artist Hale Woodruff. This interest was later strengthened through study and travel in Africa and through his commitment to researching and teaching African and African American art history. After graduating with a master's degree in fine arts from the Institute of Design of the Illinois Institute of Technology in Chicago, Donaldson received a doctoral degree in African and African American art history from Northwestern University. Through his involvement in the Organization of Black American Culture (OBAC), a group he helped form in Chicago, Donaldson organized the visual art workshop, which painted the *Wall of Respect* in 1967, a significant mural that celebrated important black historical and contemporary figures. The mural became a rallying symbol for Chicago's black activists and initiated a movement of outdoor murals in the 1970s in major cities throughout the United States, such as *The Wall of Dignity* mural in Detroit.

Donaldson's works reflect his commitment to the principles of technical excellence and social responsibility outlined in AfriCobra's manifesto. To this he added the TransAfrican aesthetic identified as "color that shines. Color that is free of rules and regulations." Donaldson's *Victory in the Valley of Esu,* painted in 1971, was inspired by an article he read in the *Washington Post* about an old African American couple who refused to sell their home, which was destined to be demolished as it stood in the path of a highway planned to connect the city to the suburbs. In portraying the determination of this couple, Donaldson drew on African spiritual symbols and designs. "Esu" in the title is a reference to the god of crossroads in Yoruba mythology. The victory of the couple is symbolized by their swift journey through the valley of Esu in recognition of their moral strength. Donaldson juxtaposes a photograph of the photograph of the couple from the *Washington Post's* article against a larger, colorfully painted version of the same couple to symbolize the bigger-than-life status attained by the couple through their act of defiance. Several layers of meaning are ascribed to the painting through the use of symbols and designs borrowed from African visual resources, such as the six-pointed stars framing the photograph, which symbolize the sign of Ifa in the Yoruba divination system. The woman's ankh, an ancient Egyptian symbol of life, is combined with the aura around her head, which resembles a pharaoh's crown. The man is depicted in a dignified posture, wearing suspenders painted in red, green, and black, the well-known colors of the African liberation.

Donaldson's trademark use of color is best seen in works such as *Jam Packed and Jelly Tight.* Originally painted in 1988 as a visual homage to the Chicago-born progressive jazz group AACM (Association for the Advancement of Creative Musicians), this painting transcends the direct adaptation of specific African symbolism seen in the earlier work by creating colorfully rich visual patterns that convey a jazzlike rhythm, a visual "syncopation." Like jazz's multiple rhythms, the painting's title conveys multiple meanings. The "Jam" of the title refers not only to a jam session of jazz musicians but also to the artist's daughter Jamila, whose nickname is Jam and for whom the painting was intended as a gift. The title also makes reference to one of AfriCobra's goals, which was the creation of "images that are filled with forms."

—Salah Hassan

DOUGLAS, Aaron

American painter, muralist, and illustrator

Born: Topeka, Kansas, 1899. **Education:** University of Nebraska, Lincoln, B.F.A. 1922; studied under Winold Reiss in New York, 1924-27; L'Academie Scandinave, Paris, 1931; Columbia University Teachers College, New York, M.A. 1944. **Family:** Married Alta Mai Sawyer c.1926. **Career:** Art teacher, Fisk University, Nashville, beginning 1937. Founder/chair, Department of Education, Fisk University, Nashville, 1937-66. Traveled in Haiti, Dominican Republic, Mexico, Canada, Portugal, Senegal, Liberia, Ghana, Nigeria, Italy, Spain, England. **Awards:** Barnes Foundation Fellowship, 1928-29; Julius Rosenwald Founda-

tion travel grant, 1938; Carnegie Grant-in-Aid for the Improvement of Teaching Project, 1951. Honorary doctorate: Fisk University, 1973. **Died:** 2 February 1979.

Individual Exhibitions:

1934	D'Caz-Delbo Gallery, New York
1937	Howard University, Washington, D.C.
1938	American Contemporary Art Gallery, New York
1939	American Contemporary Art Gallery, New York
1942	University of Kansas, Lawrence (traveling)
1947	People's Art Center, St. Louis, Missouri
1948	Chabot House, Los Angeles
	Fisk University, Nashville
1952	Fisk University, Nashville
1953	Fisk University, Nashville (retrospective)
1955	Riley Art Galleries, New York
1964	University of California, Berkeley
1970	Mulvane Art Center, Washburn University, Topeka, Kansas
1971	Fisk University, Nashville (retrospective)

Selected Group Exhibitions:

1944	Atlanta University, Georgia
1945	Albany Institute of History and Art, New York
1967	City College of New York
1971	Newark Museum, New Jersey
1976	Los Angeles County Museum of Art (traveling)
1978	Studio Museum in Harlem, New York
1982	Studio Museum in Harlem, New York
1983	Virginia Museum, Richmond (traveling)
1984	Fisk University, Nashville
	Center Gallery, Bucknell University, Lewisburg, Pennsylvania (traveling)
1985	Bellevue Art Museum, Washington (traveling)
1987	Studio Museum in Harlem, New York (traveling)

Collections:

Amistad Research Center, New Orleans; Bennett College, Greensboro, North Carolina; Evans-Tibbs Collection, Washington, D.C.; Fisk University Museum of Art, Nashville; Governor's Residence, Madison, Wisconsin; Hampton University Museum, Virginia; Gallery of Art, Howard University, Washington, D.C.; Schomburg Center, New York; Texas Southern University, Houston.

Publications:

On DOUGLAS: Books—*Modern Negro Art* by James A. Porter, New York, Dryden Press, 1943, pp. 104-05; *Paintings by Aaron Douglas,* exhibition catalog, Nashville, Fisk University, 1971; *Aaron Douglas: Art, Race, and the Harlem Renaissance* by Amy Helene Kirschke, Jackson, University Press of Mississippi, 1995. **Articles**—"A Final Farewell to Aaron Douglas" by Romare Bearden, in *New York Amsterdam News,* 24 February 1979; "Aaron Douglas," in *A History of African-American Artists, from 1792 to the Present* by Romare Bearden and Harry Henderson, New York, Pantheon Books, 1993, 127-35.

*   *   *

Within weeks of his arrival in Harlem in 1925, artist Aaron Douglas was recruited by W.E.B. DuBois, who edited the *Crisis* for the NAACP, and Charles S. Johnson, editor of the Urban League's *Opportunity,* to create illustrations to accompany editorials on lynching, segregation, theater, jazz, poems, stories, and political issues in their respective magazines. Douglas, a Kansas City high school teacher, had chosen to join the young artists of the Harlem Renaissance after viewing a copy of *Survey Graphic,* which had devoted a special issue to Harlem.

Creating a new and positive African-influenced black image, Douglas tried to reach this new black middle class public with the language of African art as one of his most important tools. Douglas felt his work could touch his black audience in a unique way. In magazine illustrations he created some of his most forceful and interesting works and evolved his artistic language, a language immersed in African art, in a way no other American artist had to date. These illustrations anticipate the style in his murals, which came later, but are simpler and bolder because of the format in which they were published. For both covers and interior drawings, the magazine illustrations are usually just a few simple figures that illustrate a basic idea or show images of African Americans, but they are heavily influenced by Egyptian art as a way to make the connection with Africa. Stark figures in black and white silhouette, so often featured in the *Crisis* and *Opportunity,* were particularly

Aaron Douglas: *Aspects of Negro Life: The Negro in an African Setting,* 1934. Photo by Manu Sassoonian; courtesy of the Schomburg Center for Research in Black Culture.

forceful. Douglas hoped to remind his audience of their African ancestry and to inspire in them an interest in their common heritage.

Douglas also attempted, with the help of several of his friends, to start a more radical magazine, *Fire!!* Only one issue of *Fire!!* ever appeared, yet it was important because it showed an effort on the part of its organizers to break from the confines of Harlem leadership, both black and white, and express themselves freely and without censorship to a younger, separatist, more militant black audience. Douglas penned their artistic statement, which called for black artists to create racial art and stressed the need for black patronage.

Some of Douglas's most interesting art was executed in the form of book covers and book illustrations. He contributed illustrations to the *New Negro* in 1925 and was particularly pleased with his work in Paul Morand's *Black Magic* of 1929. Douglas provided eight of his most sophisticated African-inspired drawings for the volume. The influences of Egyptian art and the art of the Ivory Coast are obvious.

Douglas's career culminated in his 1934 Marxist-inspired Work Progress Administration murals, which are now at the Schomburg Center in Harlem. These large murals chronicle the struggle of black men and women from Africa through slavery, emancipation, and their role as workers in the machine age. Douglas's murals appealed directly to a public suffering from the harsh conditions of unemployment and poverty.

Douglas was unique in his efforts as the first black artist in the United States to consistently create racial art, including his attempts to reach a vast readership through black magazines. Created during a time of limited artistic freedom for African Americans, Douglas's works are based on studies of the African heritage. The artist confronted the problem of trying to reach a public that was still difficult to define and locate. A limited patronage and a geographically isolated audience were challenges Douglas met with success in his efforts to address important issues to a growing black middle class.

—Amy Kirschke

DOUGLASS, Robert M., Jr.

American painter

Born: Philadelphia, Pennsylvania, 8 February 1809. **Education:** Studied with Thomas Sully, at the British Museum, and at the National Gallery, London. **Family:** Married Sarah. **Died:** 26 October 1887.

*   *   *

Like many artists of his era, Robert M. Douglass began his art career as a sign painter, but he is best known for his portraits. He studied with Thomas Sully, a well-known portraitist, who encouraged him to study abroad. Even though Douglass was born a free man, he was unable to obtain a passport because he was an African American. Eventually, however, he did travel abroad and study at the British Museum and the National Gallery in London. Later Douglass traveled to France and the West Indies.

Douglass's works of art, other than an 1827 seal of the state of Pennsylvania and a portrait of a relative, have never been recov-

ered. His known works, whose existence has been documented by newspaper articles and personal letters, include a banner made for the Grand Order of Odd Fellows in Philadelphia, a portrait of Nicholas Fabre Geffrard (president of the Republic of Haiti, 1859-1867), and some drawings of missionary stations in Jamaica. The following reference to Douglass as an artist appeared in the 20 July 1833 issue of the *Emancipator*:

> This Gentleman is a very respectable colored gentleman, in Philadelphia, and has for several years carried on the business of sign and ornamental paintings. . . . He has lately turned his attention to portrait painting, in addition to his other employment. In this too he has been eminently successful. We have seen several of his paintings that would scarcely suffer in comparison with those of many who are considered among the finest artists of our country.

Another known work, which identifies Douglass as an abolitionist, is his lithograph of William Lloyd Garrison (1833). Douglass made the lithograph from his own painting of Garrison. He then printed many copies and sold them in New York and Philadelphia for fifty cents each. It is thought that the money he made from this endeavor was in turn given to the abolitionist movement. Douglass also created "likenesses" of several other philanthropists of the day. His art studies were often sponsored by the abolitionist groups in which he was active. Douglass is considered a pioneer among African American artists because he was one of the first to have a strong allegiance with antislavery leaders.

—Christine Miner Minderovic

DOWELL, John (Edward, Jr.)

American printmaker

Born: Philadelphia, 25 March, 1941. **Education:** Tyler School of Art, Temple University, Rome, B.F.A. 1963; John Herron Art Institute, Indianapolis, 1963; Tamarind Lithography Workshop, Los Angeles, 1963 and 1966; University of Washington, Seattle, M.F.A. 1966. **Career:** Associate professor of art and printmaking, Tyler School of Art, Temple University, Rome, 1971-74, Philadelphia, 1974-76; professor of art and printmaking, Temple University, Philadelphia, 1976-82. **Awards:** Fellowship, University of Illinois, Champaign, 1970; National Endowment for the Arts Fellowship, 1974-75; Temple University resident grant, 1975-77. **Address:** 1516 North Fifteenth Street, Philadelphia, Pennsylvania 19121, U.S.A.

Individual Exhibitions:

1968	Swope Art Gallery, Terre Haute, Indiana
	University of Illinois, Champaign
	Print Club, Philadelphia
1969	Western College for Women, Oxford, Ohio
	Bradley University, Peoria, Illinois
	Fisk University, Nashville
1970	*35th Venice Biennale,* Venice
	Western Illinois University, Macomb

1971   Corcoran Gallery of Art, Washington, D.C.
        University of Kentucky, Lexington
1972   Fort Worth Art Center Museum, Texas
1973   Galleria Swartz, Milan, Italy
        Lunn Gallery, Graphics International, Washington, D.C.
1974   Galleria Massimo, Valsecchia, Milan, Italy
        Gallery of the Tyler School of Art, Temple University,
            Rome, Italy
1975   Carl Solway Gallery, Cincinnati, Ohio
1976   Dart Gallery, Chicago
1977   Arnold Gallery, Atlanta, Georgia
        Print Club, Philadelphia (retrospective)
1978   Galerie Haus 11, Karlsruhe, Germany
        Dorsky Galleries, New York
        Pennsylvania Academy of Fine Arts, Philadelphia
1979   Galerie Art in Progress, Munich
        Barbara Fiedler Gallery, Washington, D.C.
1980   Diane Gilson Gallery, Seattle
        A. J. Wood Galleries, Philadelphia
1981   Offset Lithographs, Lehigh University, Bethlehem, Penn-
            sylvania
        Chi-Wara Gallery, Atlanta, Georgia
1982   Metropolitan Museum of Art, New York
        Rosemont College, Rosemont, Pennsylvania
1983   Institute of Contemporary Art, University of Pennsyl-
            vania, Philadelphia
        Benjamin Mangel Galleries, Philadelphia
        Siegfred Gallery, Ohio University, Athens
1986   American College, Bryn Mawr, Pennsylvania
1987   Marianne Deson Gallery, Chicago
1989   Simms Fine Art Gallery, New Orleans
1990   Hughley Gallery, Atlanta, Georgia
1994   Print Club, Philadelphia

Selected Group Exhibitions:

1993   Afro-American Historical and Cultural Museum,
            Wilberforce, Ohio
        National Afro-American Museum and Cultural Center,
            Wilberforce, Ohio
        Parish Gallery, Washington, D.C.
        Wichita Art Museum, Wichita, Kansas
        Yale University, New Haven, Connecticut
        Paine Webber Art Gallery, New York/Montclair Art
            Museum, Montclair, New York (traveling)
        Diverse Works from the Brandywine Graphic Workshop
            (sponsored by the United States Information Agency),
            Brazil, El Salvador, and Peru (traveling)
1994   Brandywine Graphic Workshop, Philadelphia
        American Craft Museum, New York
        *Sign and Symbols: Works from the Brandywine Graphic
            Workshop* (sponsored by the United States Informa-
            tion Agency), Egypt, India, Pakistan, Turkey, Saudi
            Arabia (traveling)

Collections:

Afro-American Historical and Cultural Museum, Philadelphia; Amon Carter Museum of Western Art, Los Angeles; Anacortes Museum, Anacortes, Washington; Alabama A & M University, Normal; Baltimore Museum, Maryland; Ben R. Smith Collection, Los Angeles;

Biblioteque Nationale, Paris; Boston Museum of Fine Art; Brooklyn Museum of Art, New York; Bradley University, Peoria, Illinois; Art Institute of Chicago; Cincinnati Art Museum, Ohio; City Museum of St. Louis, Missouri; Colgate University, Hamilton, New York; Corcoran Gallery of Art, Washington, D.C.; Fisk University, Nashville; Fogg Museum of Harvard University, Cambridge, Massachusetts; Fort Worth Art Center Museum, Texas; Grunwald Graphic Art Foundation, University of California at Los Angeles; Haverford College, Haverford, Pennsylvania; Henry Gallery of the University of Washington, Seattle; Krannert Art Museum, University of Illinois, Champaign; La Jolla Art Museum, La Jolla, California; Lessing J. Rosenwald Foundation, Washington, D.C.; Los Angeles County Museum of Art, Los Angeles; Metropolitan Museum of Art, New York; Miami University, Oxford, Ohio; Mills College, Oakland, California; Museum of Modern Art, New York; Library of Congress, Washington, D.C.; National Collection, Washington, D.C.; New York Public Library; New York City Library Collection of Contemporary Prints; New York State Government Collection; Oklahoma Art Center, Oklahoma City; Pasadena Art Museum, Pasadena, California; Pennsylvania Academy of Fine Arts, Philadelphia; Philadelphia Museum of Art; Philadelphia Public Library; Rhode Island School of Design, Providence; San Francisco Museum of Modern Art; Schomburg Center, New York; Smithsonian Institution, Washington, D.C.; Studio Museum in Harlem, New York; University of Delaware, Newark, Delaware; University of North Dakota, Grand Forks; University of Western Michigan, Kalamazoo; Wichita Museum of Art, Kansas; Worchester Art Museum, Worchester, Massachusetts.

Publications:

On DOWELL: Articles—"Scribble" by Henry Martin, in *Art International*, March 1973; "Musicianly Painting" by Donna Stein, in *Art News*, November 1973; "John Dowell's Sound Perspective," in *Arts Exchange*, May 1977.

*   *   *

John Dowell is best known for his innovative printmaking and for his conceptual works keyed to music. He has spent most of his years living, creating, and teaching in Philadelphia. He grew up in a Philadelphia housing project, and his earliest art-making occurred when he began emulating his older brother by copying Lone Ranger comic books. He volunteered to draw a backdrop for a second-grade class play and has been drawing and painting ever since. His school mentor was the ceramist Rudy Staffel, and Dowell has said that he learned more about drawing and space representation from Staffel than from any of his other teachers. In developing his aesthetic he was influenced by Willem de Kooning, Jackson Pollock, and Philip Guston.

Dowell's music series lasted about twenty years and included a ten-year period (1973-83) of concerts with the quartet Visual Music Ensemble, which he founded. The ensemble, with Dowell at the piano, played in the United States and other countries. He developed drawing as a form of musical notation and emphasized structure in the way that John Cage rejected structure, but similarities to Cage's compositions were evident. Dowell's visual art simulated the rhythms and excursions in improvisation of musical performance. The feel of music was captured in color painted in kitelike shapes, most often on white fields. His prints from 1970 to 1984 represented his use of abstraction to create balance and sensuousness in a visual and auditory way.

Dowell's large, white abstract paintings and white ceramic fountains attracted considerable attention and became a signature of his work. The surfaces of his canvases danced with fragments of color. The canvases became the foundation that inspired ceramic fountains. By adjusting the flow of water through channels at various levels, Dowell created harmonic water sounds. His fountains later served to promote his theories about African and African American passages by abstraction and music in three-dimensional forms.

Dowell's spiritual encounters with Oshun, the Yoruba deity, returned him to his African roots. He began to explore the concept of ancestor worship visually. The connection between Oshun and Dowell's art can be seen in the white spaces, white being the color of Oshun. A trip to Bahia, Brazil, in 1988 climaxed his years of probing and research into space.

In the 1990s Dowell has put aside ceramics and concentrated on his paintings. The paintings have heavily textured surfaces containing shapes that change to figures. The colors have become the brightest of his career, and he has reversed the dominance of white. Intense colors and figurative images such as the heart now dominate his work. Where he once used color to create space, he now works for psychological effects. By using a variety of techniques, including wash and crayon drawings, Dowell has come to focus on images such as lace, fire, and the sea—all inspired by spiritual forces and surrounded by metaphysical auras.

In explaining the heart in his later work, Dowell has said, "In using the heart I am attempting to stop, look, listen, and feel the levels and layers of love, respect, and just being. The heart's spiritual overtones generate reflections on life, bringing me closer to my internal world, my humanity, my peace. These forms and objects, along with light and sounds, act as stimuli and provoke my inner discovery."

—Louise Davis Stone

DRISKELL, David (C.)
American painter, printmaker, and sculptor

Born: Eatonton, Georgia, 7 June 1931. **Education:** Skowhegan School of Painting and Sculpture, Skowhegan, Maine, certificate 1953; Howard University, Washington, D.C., B.A.. 1955; Catholic University of America, Washington, D.C., M.F.A. 1962; Rijksbureau voor Kunsthistorisches Documentatie, Den Hague, Netherlands, Study Certificate in Art History 1964. **Military service:** United States Army, 1957-65: first lieutenant. **Family:** Married Thelma G. Deloatch in 1952. **Career:** Professor, Talladega College, 1955-62, Howard University, Washington, D.C., 1962-66, Fisk University, Nashville, 1966-77, University of Ife, Nigeria, 1970; chair, Department of Art, University of Maryland, College Park, 1978-83. Since 1977, professor of art, University of Maryland, curator, Aaron Douglas collection, Amistad Research Center, curator, Cosby Collection of Fine Arts. Acting chairman and director, Gallery of Art, Howard University, Washington, D.C., 1963-64 and 1965-66; associate director, Barnett Aden Gallery, 1962-66; visiting scholar and lecturer, Talladega College, 1987, Queens College, Flushing, New York, 1989, University of Michigan, Ann Arbor, 1990; visiting professor, Obafemi Awolowo University, Ile-Ife, Nigeria, 1969-70, Bowdoin College, 1973, Bates College, 1973; visiting artist, Haystack Mountain School of Crafts, Deer Isle, Maine, 1975, Skowhegan School of Painting and Sculpture, Maine, 1976 and

1978, Haystack Mountain School of the Crafts, Deer Isle, Maine, 1992. **Awards:** Rockefellow Foundation Fellowship for Museum Study in Greece, Italy, Spain, France, Holland, Denmark and England, 1964; Netherlands Institute for the History of Art Fellowship, The Hague, 1964; Rockefeller Foundation Faculty Fellowship, Fisk University, Nashville, 1967 and 1970; National Endowment for the Arts grants, 1969 and 1975; American Film Institute grant, 1969; Purchase awards, Birmingham Museum of Art, 1972. Honorary doctorates: Daniel Payne College, Tougaloo College, 1977; Bowdoin College, 1989; State University of New York, Old Westburg, 1989; Rust College, 1991. President's Achievement Award, 1991; Model of Excellence Award in Art, Colgate-Palmolive Company, Washington, D.C., 1993; Art Service citation, National Association of Schools of Art and Design, 1993; Amistad Research Center Creative Award, 1993. **Address:** University of Maryland, College Park, Maryland 20742, U.S.A.

Individual Exhibitions:

1956   Savery Art Gallery, Talladega, Alabama
1957   Barnett Aden Gallery, Washington, D.C.

David Driskell, 1995.

1961	Barnett Aden Gallery, Washington, D.C.
1966	Carl Van Vechten Art Gallery, Fisk University, Nashville
1968	Tennessee Fine Arts Center, Nashville
1973	Bowdoin College Museum of Art, Brunswick, Maine
1980	Collectors Gallery New York
	Foundry Gallery, Washington, D.C.
	University of Maryland Art Gallery, College Park, Maryland
1981	Middlebury College, Vermont
	Johnson Gallery, North Carolina State University
1987	Goodwin Art Gallery, Talladega, Alabama
	Fisk University Museum, Nashville
1989	Amelia Wallace Gallery, SUNY, College at Old Westbury, New York
	Colby College Museum of Art, Waterville, Maine
1992	Sherry Washington Gallery, Detroit
1993	Midtown Payson Galleries, New York
	Cleveland Community College, Shelby, North Carolina
	Bomani Gallery, San Francisco

Selected Group Exhibitions:

Baltimore Museum of Art, Maryland; Birmingham Museum of Art, Alabama; High Museum of Art, Atlanta, Georgia; Howard University Gallery of Art, Washington, D.C.; L.B.J. Memorial Library Museum, Austin, Texas; Corcoran Gallery of Art, Washington, D.C.; National Museum, Santiago, Chile; Oakland Museum of Art, California; Portland Museum of Art, Maine; Studio Museum of Harlem, New York; Terra Museum, Chicago, Illinois; The White House, Washington, D.C.; Whitney Museum of American Art, New York.

Publications:

By DRISKELL: Books—*Modern Masters from the Guggenheim Museum,* exhibition catalog, Alabama, Talladega College, 1956; *Klee, Kandinsky and Other Modern Masters from the Guggenheim Museum,* exhibition catalog, Alabama, Talladega College, 1958; *Eight Young Printmakers,* exhibition catalog, Tennessee, Fisk University, 1966; *Contemporary Trends in African Art,* exhibition catalog, Tennessee, Fisk University Art Gallery, 1968; *The Fisk University African Collection,* exhibition catalog, Tennessee, Fisk University Art Gallery, 1970; *The Rites of Color and Form,* exhibition catalog, Tennessee, Fisk University, 1974; *Harlem Renaissance Art of Black America,* New York, Abrams, 1987; *Introspectives: Contemporary Art by Americans and Brazilians of African Descent,* California Afro-American Museum Association, 1989. **Articles**—"Black American Artists, 1750-1950," in *Smithsonian Magazine,* September 1976; "The Legacy of Afro-American Art," in *New Art Examiner,* June 1980; "Black Artists and Craftsmen," in *Portland Review of the Arts,* Spring 1982; "Art of Charles White," in *Christian Science Monitor,* January 1988; "Elizabeth Catlett, Black American Artist in Mexico," *Christian Science Monitor,* March 1988; "Denying Credit, an Incomplete Arts Curriculum," in *New Art Examiner,* February 1991.

*

David Driskell comments:

(1976) Art for me is a way of life. It is as much a vital part of my lifestyle as all of the other experiences that have helped to make me

David Driskell: *Yaddo Circle,* 1980.

a particular individual. I try to exercise certain value judgments each time I choose one subject over another when painting. Yet, somehow, these choices of rendering form, regardless of how abbreviated they may seem, always tell the viewer something about my experiences and the culture out of which I have come.

My art allows me to be a free soul no longer bound by the physical toils of the natural order. This freedom of expression I seek through art is no illusion. It is a deeply spiritual experience, one which elevates the mind beyond seeing only that which exists in the natural order. With art I shall always be able to see a second time more than I saw when I first glanced the physical shape or form. This is why time and space can be as one in the lively sight of art. I want to share these experiences in my art.

(1980) My decision to become an artist came through many stages, but I knew from the very beginning that I wanted to paint. I wanted to put a graphic image on paper. I didn't stop to think of it as a two-dimensional surface. My desire to paint may also have been based on my need to communicate something. I don't mean communication in the literal sense of language, semantics, or the spoken word. I wanted to share images that were of my own personal making.

*   *   *

David Driskell, by his own definition, believes that "art is a special calling, even priestly in function," as he states in the catalog for *Contemporary Visual Expressions*, an exhibition he curated in 1987 for the Anacostia Museum of the Smithsonian Institution. Driskell holds a unique position in American art history, both as a scholar and as an artist. His career as an expressive abstract painter, printmaker, and sculptor has addressed issues of the human spirit and ways in which spirituality can transcend physical matter.

Driskell's work since the early 1960s has sought to use Western models to interpret in abstract motifs the nature of the environment, the social and political condition of African American humanity, and the traditional aesthetics of African culture. Through his passionate love of color and form, these issues have become the fundamental core of his artistic impulse to investigate the inherent powers of the spiritual energy evoked by the creative process and the emotional response to that imagery.

Driskell's aesthetic has been critically informed by the enormity of his contributions as an intellectual and a scholar in the field of American and African American art history and criticism. His achievements as an artist, his primary career objective, have on occasion been eclipsed by his curatorial successes, not unlike the experience of other artist-scholars such as James Porter, Floyd Coleman, Deborah Willis, Keith Morrison, and Joe E. Lewis. Given the sheer paucity of critics willing to address African American contributions to the visual arts, Driskell has assumed the largest burden of this responsibility with meritorious distinction.

His early training in the 1950s was greatly influenced and encouraged by the abstract color-field painter Morris Louis, who taught Driskell while he was studying at Howard University. Contrary to the trend for large-scale works among the 1960s post-abstract expressionist and color-field painters, Driskell's works remained moderate- to small-scale compositions worked in the acrylic medium. Paintings from the early 1960s and the 1970s reflected the gestural indulgences of the abstract expressionist era, with references to cubism and a decided preoccupation with the functional, creative processes of traditional African imagery that gained critical attention among African American artists of the civil rights and black nationalist era.

Color in Driskell's work increasingly became more bold in intensity in the 1970s and 1980s, resulting in compositions that enhanced the range of atmosphere, emotions, and spiritual tension in his studies. During this period Driskell began to incorporate more mixed-media materials into his composition. He had aesthetic inquiries similar to those of Howardena Pindell, Alvin Loving, Sam Gilliam, and William T. Williams, making him a member of that group of African American artists who grew dissatisfied with the structural limits of abstraction and who sought to discover new forms of imagery through investigations of the spiritual and transformative properties of the creative process. This philosophical and technical approach was inspired through each of these artist's individual studies of African culture, religion, and aesthetics.

Driskell's drawings, prints, and sculptures from the mid-1980s to the 1990s became increasingly concerned with minimalism. In contrast, his paintings increased in scale, with densely layered surfaces worked into complexly structured compositional studies. The challenge for Driskell is a deep and personal commitment to develop a visual voice to complement his scholarly contribution to the legacy of American and African American art as well as to participate in the experience of being an artist in twentieth-century America.

—Leslie King-Hammond

DUNCANSON, Robert S.
American painter

Born: Cincinnati, Ohio, 1817. **Education:** Studied art in Italy, c.1853, and in Glasgow, Scotland, c.1840-43. **Family:** One son from first marriage. Married second wife, Phoebe Duncanson, in 1857, one son and one daughter. **Career:** Commissioned portrait, mural, and landscape artist, Cincinnati, c.1847-1860s. Suffered mental breakdown, September 1872. **Died:** 21 December 1872 (suicide).

Selected Exhibitions:

1842	*Annual Exhibition of Paintings and Statuary,* Western Art Union, Cincinnati
1843	*Annual Exhibition of Paintings and Statuary,* Western Art Union, Cincinnati
1865	Art Association of Montreal, Canada
	Dublin Exhibition, Ireland
1871	Western Art Gallery, Detroit

Collections:

Cincinnati Art Museum; Detroit Institute of Arts; Taft Museum, Cincinnati; University of Cincinnati.

Publications:

On DUNCANSON: Books—*Six Black Masters of American Art* by Romare Bearden and Harry Henderson, Doubleday and Company, Garden City, New York, 1972; *Robert S. Duncanson: 19th Century Black Romantic Painter* by J.D. Parks, Associated Publishers, Washington, D.C., 1980; *The Emergence of the African-American Artist Robert A. Duncanson, 1821-1872* by Joseph D. Ketner, University of Missouri Press, Columbia, 1993. **Articles**—"Duncanson: An American Artist Whose Color was Forgotten" by Wendell Dabney, in *Ebony and Collectanea* (New York), 1927, pp. 128-29; "Robert S. Duncanson—Midwestern Romantic-Realist" by James A. Porter, in *Art in America,* 39, October 1951, pp. 99-154; "Robert S. Duncanson" by James A. Porter, in *Art in America,* 42, October 1954, pp. 220-21, 235; "Robert S. Duncanson in Montreal, 1863-1865" by Allan Pringle, in *The American Art Journal,* Autumn 1985, pp. 28-50; "Robert S. Duncanson," in *A History of African-American Artists, from 1792 to the Present* by Romare Bearden and Harry Henderson, Pantheon Books, New York, 1993, pp. 19-39.

*   *   *

The work of Robert S. Duncanson, created during a time when many African descendants in the Americas were living in forced bondage, survives to tell a story of courage, commitment, and determination. Though his imagery did not generally reflect his personal struggles with the issue of race, his life's work is honored as a significant milestone in the artistic achievements of African Americans during the mid-1800s.

In Michigan Duncanson apprenticed in his family's prosperous house painting and decorating business, and by the middle to late 1840s the skilled artisan began to realize his ambition to become a fine artist. He received several commissions for portraits, but the critical determinant in Duncanson's beginnings was in gaining members of the Michigan and Ohio elite as clients. Abolitionist patronage was also a crucial factor in Duncanson's successes.

Early in his career as a painter of portraits, fancy pictures, historical paintings, and landscapes, Duncanson became familiar with—and eventually the student of—several enormously popular painters of the Ohio River valley. T. Worthington Whittredge and William Sonntag introduced Duncanson to the Hudson River school style of painting that was adaptive of an English landscape tradition. During this period the primary American landscape painters were Thomas Cole, considered by many art historians to be the father of American landscape painting, and Asher Durand. These individuals significantly influenced Duncanson's aesthetic sensibilities as well as his overall painting style, which was attracting considerable attention from the area press, art critics, and influential benefactors.

In spite of not having a formal education, Duncanson was quite knowledgeable of the popular literary works of the period. He sensitively rendered much of the romantic literature with a distinctively picturesque and pastoral vision. It was the paradisiacal and sublime qualities of Duncanson's imagery that eventually raised him to a level of international acclaim.

A noteworthy accomplishment that established Duncanson as a highly skilled landscape painter and decorator were his *Belmont Murals,* commissioned by noted Cincinnati philanthropist and abolitionist Nicholas Longworth. These eight, nine-by-seven-feet murals were the largest undertaking in the artist's career. The paintings depict floral vignettes, patriotic eagles, and rustic scenes reminiscent of the Ohio River valley. The high level of craftsmanship involved in this project is evidenced by the wallpaper scheme that Duncanson creatively adapted from French and English designs. Each scene was painted with an elaborate border that mimicked a picture frame, creating the effect of a gallery with monumental landscape paintings in ornate frames.

Some of Duncanson's finest technical achievements occurred late in his life and career. A self-imposed exile from the United States in the early 1860s provided an opportunity for him to tour some of his paintings for a broader audience and to escape the escalating racial tensions compounded by war in the States. He did, however, eventually dominate the art world of the Midwest and became a distinguished painter known throughout Canada and Europe.

Two of his most significant works are *Land of the Lotus Eaters* and *Ellen's Isle, Loch Katrine,* both inspired by literary classics. The lush and tropical landscape of *Land of the Lotus Eaters,* with its quiet streams, snowcapped mountains, and brown-skinned natives, is rendered precisely as Alfred, Lord Tennyson describes in his poem "The Lotus Eaters." This "great picture" is one that established Duncanson among the artistic community, patrons, and critics as the best landscape painter in the West. *Ellen's Isle* was painted a decade later in 1871 from another epic poem, "The Lady of the Lake" by Sir Walter Scott. Duncanson masterfully portrays an isolated island in the Scottish Highlands with the golden glow of sunset dramatically reflected off of the lake, detailing trees, ferns, and moss in the foreground and mountains and horizon in the distance.

The oeuvre of Robert Duncanson remains a treasure in the legacy of American landscape painting and holds a permanent place in this transcontinental artistic tradition. Although Duncanson's work fell into obscurity for close to eighty years after his death, it has come to serve as a major source of inspiration for generations of African American artists.

—Regina Holden Jennings

DUNKLEY, John
Jamaican painter and sculptor

Born: Sav-la-mar, Jamaica, 11 December 1891. **Family:** Married Cassie Fraser, one daughter and two sons. **Career:** Barber, 1930-47. **Awards:** Saint George's Exhibition Prize, Kingston, Jamaica, 1938; honorary award, San Francisco Golden Gate Exposition, 1939; Gold Musgrave Medal (posthumous), Institute of Jamaica, 1991. **Died:** 17 February 1947.

Individual Exhibitions:

1947 *John Dunkley Memorial Exhibition,* Institute of Jamaica, Kingston
1977 National Gallery of Jamaica, Kingston (retrospective)

Selected Group Exhibitions:

1938 *All Island Exhibition,* Saint George's Hall, Government of Jamaica, Kingston
1945 *Survey of West Indian Painting,* Institute of Jamaica, Kingston (traveling)
1951 *First Caribbean Exhibition,* San Juan, Puerto Rico
1960 Institute of Jamaica, Kingston
1969 *Art in Jamaica Since the Thirties,* Spelman College, Atlanta
1971 Commonwealth Institute Art Gallery, London

John Dunkley: *Woodland,* c.1945. Photo courtesy of the National Gallery of Jamaica.

John Dunkley: *Diamond Wedding,* 1939. Photo courtesy of the National Gallery of Jamaica.

Collections:

National Gallery of Jamaica.

Publications:

On DUNKLEY: Book—*John Dunkley Memorial Exhibition,* exhibition catalog, Kingston, Institute of Jamaica and Cassie Dunkley, 1948; *John Dunkley,* exhibition catalog, Kingston, National Gallery of Jamaica, 1976. **Article**—"Dunkley" by Edwin Todd, in *Jamaica Journal,* 2(3), September 1968.

*   *   *

John Dunkley's output as a painter was small. His oeuvre spanned little more than a decade, and because he kept most of his works and continued to refine or repaint them, there is no clearly discernible development. Less than fifty paintings are known, but they suffice to demonstrate a unique and compelling aesthetic, allowing Dunkley to assume the rank of Jamaica's greatest painter. He was essentially self-taught.

Most of Dunkley's paintings are imagined landscapes that seem full of a decidedly hidden symbolism. Typically, the vegetation seems fantastic, with trees or shrubs having overblown inflorescences that are counterpointed by bare truncated branches, often depicted in a manner that encourages their being read as phallic symbols. Small animals—crabs, birds, a mongoose, a rabbit, and often spiders negotiating complex webs—frequent these dark, disturbing woodlands. Only rarely does a human figure intrude. Man is implied, however, in the occasional house seen in the distance or at the edge of the woods but even more so in what is surely Dunkley's most persistent motif—the path or road that pushes through the vegetation to suggest great depth. In his *Back to Nature* (c.1939) the path divides in the foreground to encircle a heart-shaped grave. Footprints of the departed hauntingly trod the path.

There is a distinct group of Dunkley's works, which may have been his last, that seem more expansive. They include *Lonely Road, Springboard, Woman Feeding Fish,* and *Footbridge,* in which the usual claustrophobia, imparted by dense, bracketing vegetation, gives way to clearer skies, white rather than gray, and with far fewer elements in the landscape. In some of these works the black outlines of a spare vegetation are silhouetted against the sky. The haunting quality of the classic Dunkley, in the works that were inevitably compared to the jungle paintings of Henri Rousseau, is replaced here by a decided unease akin to that suggested by many of the piazza paintings of the young Giorgio de Chirico. Unrealistic touches like the isolated springboard that seems out of context in *Springboard,* the leaves pushing up between the cracks in *Woman Feeding Fish*, and the unstable support of the bridge in *Footbridge* contribute to the disquiet of the woods in these works.

Parade with Tram Cars (c.1940), which is Dunkley's only known cityscape, lovingly depicts a landmark edifice, the Coke Methodist Church in Kingston. The building is flanked by a street given directional force by tramlines that support two approaching cars emerging from an indistinct gloom and by a tangle of overhead wires that perhaps are meant to evoke the customary spiderwebs. A jaunty suspended gentleman on the right is balanced by a black cyclist, a servant, at the left who carries a small white boy as his passenger.

Contemporary events occasionally inspired Dunkley. There is a painting-collage of Joe Louis, and in the *Good Shepherd* (c.1938) Dunkley painted the tall gangly figure of the populist politician Alexander Bustamante gathering flocks of sheep, while in the distance a few straggly goats run away. In *President Roosevelt Gazed at Portland Bight* (1940) Dunkley painted the U.S. politician as a looming presence on the horizon as he contemplated the establishment of an American base on Jamaican soil.

Dunkley also produced a small body of sculptures, mostly wood carvings. Few, however, are as accomplished as his paintings. Perhaps his finest works in this medium are *Old Joe*, a small but intense portrait of a black man clasping his knees and bent in prayer, and *Sandy Gully* (1940), a seated portrait of a proud Jamaican man carved from the first lignum vitae tree cut down in preparation for the building of the U.S. air base in Jamaica. His *Dray with Two Men* is a charming genre work, with a witty characterization of the two draymen.

After a memorial exhibition in 1947 and a joint exhibition with Daley in 1960, Dunkley was virtually forgotten. With the resurrection of a fair percentage of his oeuvre in the National Gallery's retrospective in 1977, its accompanying illustrated catalog, and the subsequent permanent display of a representative collection of his work, Dunkley has regained his position in the public's eye as a true Jamaican master.

—David Boxer

DUVAL-CARRIÉ, Édouard
Haitian painter

Born: Haiti, 1954. **Awards:** South Florida Cultural Consortium Art Award, 1995; commission, Jefferson Reeves Rehabilitative and Health Center in Overtown, Miami. **Agent:** Porter Troupe Gallery, 301 Spruce Streeet, San Diego, California 92103-5626, U.S.A.

Individual Exhibitions:

1980	Art Center, Port-au-Prince, Haiti
1982	Franz Bader Gallery, Washington, D.C.
1983	Paul Waggoner Gallery, Chicago
1986	Commonwealth University, Richmond, Virginia
	Anderson Gallery, Virginia
1987	Nicole Gallery, Chicago
	Brent Gallery, Houston
1991	Armand Gallery, Paris
	Malraux Gallery, Los Angeles
1992	Museo de Arte Contemporaneo de Monterrey, Mexico (retrospective)
1994	Porter Randall Gallery, San Diego
	Lakaye Gallery, Los Angeles
	Galeria Fernando Quintana, Bogota, Colombia
	Gutierrez Fine Arts, Miami Beach
1995	Gutierrez Fine Arts, Miami Beach
1996	Musée du College Saint Pierre, Port au Prince, Haiti

Selected Group Exhibitions:

1982	Davenport Municipal Art Gallery, Iowa
1983	Art Institute of Detroit
1985	Municipal Art Gallery, Davenport, Iowa
1989	*French Revolution in the Tropical Area,* National Museum of African and Oceanic Arts, Paris
1993	Center of Contemporary Art, North Miami
1994	South Florida Art Center, Miami Beach
1995	Fowler Museum, University of California, Los Angeles (traveling)
	Davenport Museum of Art, Iowa
	October Gallery, London
1996	Nexus Contemporary Art Center, Atlanta, Georgia

Collections:

College for Human Services, New York; Davenport Municipal Art Museum, Iowa; Detroit Institute of Art, Detroit; Musée des Arts Africains et Oceaniens, Paris; Museo de Arte Contemporaneo de Monterrey, Mexico; Musée du Pantheon National Haitian, Port au Prince, Haiti.

Publications:

On DUVAL-CARRIÉ: Articles—"Latin American Art: Global Outreach" by Paulo Herkenhoff and Geri Smith, in *ArtNews,* October 1991; "Haitian Painting: Painful History" by Michael Gibson, in *International Herald Tribune,* 26 September 1992; "Paris Connections: African and Caribbean Artists in Paris" by Asake Bomani and Belvie Rooks, in *Q.E.D. Press* (San Francisco), 1992; "Édouard Duval Carrié" by Charles Merewether, in *Ediciones Marco* (Monterrey), 1992; "Haiti's Hellish Landscape: Édouard Duval Carrié" by Robert L. Pincus, in *San Diego Union-Tribune,* 25 August 1994; "Painting the Body Politic: Édouard Duval Carrié" by Judy Cantor, in *New Times,* 21-27 July 1994; "Art Shows Have Pent-Up Power" by Sue Keller, in *La Jolla Light* (California), 30

June 1994; "Matters of Spirit: Édouard Duval Carrié" by Carol E. Damian, in *Latin American Art,* 5(4), 1994; "Interview with Édouard Duval-Carrié" by Karen McCarthy Brown, in *Tracing the Spirit: Ethnographic Essays on Haitian Art ,* Iowa, Davenport Museum of Art, 1995 (illustrated); "If You Knew Vodou Like They Know Vodou" by Lucille Renwick, in *Los Angeles Times,* 3 November 1995.

*   *   *

Édouard Duval-Carrié's work has an otherworldliness, a magical quality. His large Haitian family encouraged a respect for the rituals of his ancestors. Leaving Haiti with his family as a young adult, he lived in Puerto Rico, Canada, and France before settling in the Haitian community of Miami, Florida.

One can see the influence that Haitian naïf paintings, promoted and partially constructed by non-Haitians, has had on the work of Duval-Carrié. The outlook he shares with the culture of these artists is evident in his choice of subject matter. Nonetheless, he ex-

Edouard Duval-Carrié: *Trois Petits Anges,* 1991. Photo courtesy of Porter Troupe Gallery.

tracts elements of the tradition, such as color and ritual, to synthesize them into a language that has contemporary and international implications. While he responds to the paintings of Haitian artists such as Hector Hyppolyte, Robert St. Brice, and Bazile, he also incorporates elements of cubism, surrealism, and expressionism as well as traditional carving styles of West African wood sculpture into his work. In doing so he often explores the imagery of peasants, dressing his figures in robes of vegetation and his plants in fabrics. More specifically, as in his *La 7eme division des Loas Congo* (c. 1991), his often fantastic forms of realism possess a liberating force that is a result of a magical universe inspired by the observation of voodoo.

Duval-Carrié's work has succulent bright colors with an abundance of blues, hot pinks, and greens. Aqueous shapes based on Haitian mythology interact with one another on canvas. Luxurious vegetation cools his paintings, opening a window into a utopian landscape, yet the hot violence of his colors give his work a sense of foreboding danger. Some works have political overtones, derived from his experiences with the repressive Haitian government police and with military infractions against the people of Haiti, but he often views the gravity of political and social life in Haiti with humor. His political cynicism, however, is not restricted to Haitian subjects. In his mixed-media "Aesthete" series (c. 1989) he created several portraits of essentially the same man with a cigarette in his hand but with different skin colors and clothing to signify different cultural backgrounds. The suggestion is that, although the outward appearances are different, smug authoritarianism is the same in Germany, Norway, Saudi Arabia, or Senegal.

In addition, Duval-Carrié carves and paints the frames that border his paintings and in doing so acknowledges preexisting forms of African sculpture and mythology. Snakes and toads often share residence with people in the painted compositions. Frames with crescent moons, suns, hearts, lizards, sabers, devil-like masks, fishes, leaves, and medallions all work like Mexican *milagras*. The combination of genres suggests a modernized baroque decorativeness, as in *L'Arbre Habille* (c. 1991), in which a tree's trunk and branches are tied with red bows and pierced with small spikes that cause blood to pour from its wounds. The tree is shown in its fruit-bearing cycle against a backdrop of vegetation and of clouds drifting in a blue sky. Nothing seems amiss, yet the piercings will surely kill the tree. Such contradictions are frequently presented in Duval-Carrié's work.

In the 1980s and 1990s Duval-Carrié has participated in exhibitions in France, the United States, Colombia, Mexico, and Haiti that focus on Haitian art or contemporary art from African and Caribbean nations. Duval-Carrié sees himself as an individual who contributes to the cultural well-being of his nation rather than being bound by its sense of communal authority. Toward that end he consistently refers to traditional forms but does not replicate them.

—Lizzetta LeFalle-Collins

EBOIGBE, Felix
Nigerian sculptor

Became American citizen in 1991. **Born:** Lagos, Nigeria, 28 July 1944. **Education:** Apprenticeship with Mr. Ben Aye, Lagos, Nigeria, 1964-1967. **Family:** Married Delphia Robinson in 1972 (divorced 1983), one son and one daughter. **Career:** Instructor, Yarba Technology School, Lagos, Nigeria, 1969-70; associate professor, Indiana University, Bloomington, Indiana, 1970-83. Distinguished professor, University of Cincinnati, Ohio, 1983-91. Lecturer in Denmark, Canada, Switzerland. Artistic advisor, Sabo Museum, Chicago, Illinois; Museum of Connecticut, Hartford; Eli Lilly Museum, Indiana; Children's Museum, Indianapolis; Indianapolis Museum of Fine Art; Museum of Nigeria, Lagos. **Awards:** Ohio First Scholar, Ohio Board of Regents, Cincinnati, 1983. **Address:** Post Office Box 9466, Cincinnati, Ohio 45209, U.S.A.

Individual Exhibitions:

1971	Matrix Gallery, Indiana University, Bloomington
	Cleo Rogers Memorial County Library, Columbus, Indiana
1972	North Shore Art League, North Shore, Illinois
	Clafin College, Orangeburg, South Carolina
1973	Franklin College, Franklin, Indiana
	Thor Gallery, Louisville, Kentucky
1974	South Bend Art Center, South Bend, Indiana
	Commons Art Center, Columbus, Indiana
1975	Floria International University, Miami
1976	Arts Exclusive Inc., Watch Hill, Rhode Island
	Vincennes University, Vincennes, Indiana
	Oak Park River Forest School, Oak Park, Illinois
	Deligny Galleries, Fort Lauderdale, Florida
1977	Boone Grove School, Boone Grove, Indiana
	First National Bank, Elkhart, Indiana
	Afro-American Arts Institute, Bloomington, Indiana
1978	African American Institute, United Nations Plaza, New York
	Smithsonian Institution Traveling Exhibition, Washington, D.C.
	Jasper Art Center, Jasper, Indiana
	Wise Middle School Art Gallery, Wise, Virginia
	Space Gallery, Western Michigan University, Kalamazoo
1979	Indianapolis Childrens' Art Museum, Indiana
	Art Gallery of Ball State University, Muncie, Indiana
1981	University of Houston, Texas
1982	Ohio State University, Columbus
	Western Inn, Cincinnati, Ohio
	Graphic Glass Gallery, Bloomington, Indiana
	Art Link Gallery, Fort Wayne, Indiana
1984	Tangeman Fine Arts Gallery, University of Cincinnati, Ohio

Felix Eboigbe: *A Bust of an African Native Doctor.*

	Purdue Union Gallery, West Lafayette, Indiana
1985	Hiesland Fine Arts Gallery, Miami, Ohio
1986	The Loft, Cincinnati, Ohio
	The Atrium, Indianapolis, Indiana
1988	*Felix Eboigbe: Contemporary African Sculpture,* Lexington, Kentucky
1989	Gardner Student Center, University of Akron, Ohio
1990	Cincinnati Museum of Natural History, Ohio
1992	National Afro-American Museum and Cultural Center, Wilberforce, Ohio
1993	Purdue Union Gallery, Indiana
1994	Kathy McCoy Design Services, Inc., Batavia, Ohio
	Madison House, Cincinnati, Ohio
1996	Alzheimer's Association Fund Raiser Dinner, Cincinnati, Ohio

Selected Group Exhibitions:

Art Education Association of Indiana, French Lick; Arts Exclusive

Felix Eboigbe (self-portrait with *Fulani Mother and Child*).

Gallery, Simsbury, Connecticut; Black Fine Arts Festival, Illinois State University, Bloomington; Indianapolis Museum of Art, Indiana; Jacques Baruch Gallery, Chicago; Matrix Gallery, Bloomington, Indiana; Midwest Museum of Art, Elkhart, Indiana; South Vermont Arts Center, Manchester; Southside Community Art Center, Chicago; Wooster College Exhibition, Wooster, Ohio.

*   *   *

Pictures of marble and wood sculptures so impressed Felix Eboigbe that he decided to become an artist, to "create art with his own hands." Instead of training to become a doctor as his parents desired, Eboigbe, who was born in Lagos, Nigeria, in 1944, dropped out of school and returned to Lagos to study art. He was sixteen years old when he began a seven-year apprenticeship under Ben Aye, a prominent Nigerian artist. After only three years of the apprenticeship, however, Eboigbe left Aye and established his own studio in Lagos in 1967. He carved wood into full figures or busts depicting culture heroes, dancing girls, and animals celebrated in the oral history of the ancient Kingdom of Benin.

Eboigbe was a successful artist with an international clientele. His work became known abroad, and eventually he was invited to demonstrate his carving technique in the United States. Through the efforts of the Ford Foundation, the United States Information Agency, and the American Embassy, Eboigbe went to Bloomington, Indiana, as an artist in residence, teaching sculpture in the School of Art Education at Indiana University. Thereafter, for the past thirty years, Eboigbe has enjoyed a successful career in art. He has had numerous solo and group exhibitions, taught sculpture at the University of Cincinnati since 1983, and demonstrated his carving technique at numerous colleges and museums in the United States and abroad.

Eboigbe carves in both representational and abstract styles. The "feeling" he gets from the wood—its size, its texture, and its grain—determines the style in which he carves. His sculptures embody the essence of the people and countries of Africa, from which he captures moments and moods, preserving them forever.

—Roslyn Adele Walker

EDMONDSON, William
American sculptor

Born: Davidson County, Tennessee, c.1870. **Career:** Worked as a farmhand, as a groom, and in railway shops until 1907; orderly, fireman, and handyman, Woman's Hospital, 1907-1931; painter, Works Progress Administration, 1939-41. From c.1932 tombstone carver, Nashville. **Died:** 7 February 1951.

Individual Exhibitions:

1937	Museum of Modern Art, New York
1951	Nashville Artist Guild
1964	Cheekwood Fine Arts Center, Nashville
1975	Montclair Art Museum, New Jersey
1981	Tennessee State Museum, Nashville (retrospective)

Selected Group Exhibitions:

1938	Musée du Jeu de Paume, Paris
1940	Spelman College, Atlanta, Georgia
1964	Lyzon Galleries, Nashville
	Tennessee Fine Arts Center, Nashville
1967	City College, City University of New York
1970	La Jolla Museum of Contemporary Art, La Jolla, California
1975	Carl Van Vechten Gallery of Fine Arts, Fisk University, Nashville
1976	Los Angeles County Museum of Art (traveling)
1982	Corcoran Gallery of Art, Washington, D.C. (traveling)

Collections:

Abby Aldrich Rockefeller Folk Art Center, Williamsburg, Virginia; Cheekwood Fine Arts Center, Nashville; Columbus Museum of Arts and Crafts, Columbus, Ohio; Hirshhorn Museum and Sculpture Garden, Washington, D.C.; Memorial Art Gallery, University of Rochester, New York; Montclair Art Museum, Montclair, New Jersey; National Museum of American Art, Washington, D.C.; Newark Museum, New Jersey; San Francisco Museum of Modern Art.

Publications:

On EDMONDSON: Book—*Visions in Stone: The Sculpture of William Edmondson* by Edmund L. Fuller, Pittsburgh, Pennsylvania, University of Pittsburgh Press, 1973. **Articles**—Interview by John Thompson, in *Nashville Tennessean,* 9 February 1941; "'Jesus Has Planted the Seed of Carvin' in Me': The Impact of Afro-American Folk Religion on the Limestone Sculpture of William Edmondson" by William H. Higgins, Jr., in *William Edmondson: A Retrospective,* Nashville, Tennessee State Museum, 1981; "Edmondson's Art reflects his Faith, Strong and Pure" by Louise LeQuire, in *Smithsonian* (Washington, D.C.), 12, August 1981, pp. 50-55; "William Edmonson," in *A History of African American Artists, from 1792 to the Present* by Romare Bearden and Harry Henderson, Pantheon Books, New York, 1993, pp. 349-355.

*   *   *

The limestone carvings of William Edmondson were unknown outside his suburban neighborhood in Nashville until they were seen and photographed by a New York photographer for *Harper's Bazaar* who visited Tennessee in 1936. She showed the photographs to the director of the Museum of Modern Art in New York City, and during the following year the museum arranged an exhibition of Edmondson's works. Although no catalog was published, Edmondson became the first African American to have a solo exhibition at the Museum of Modern Art.

Following his retirement after almost twenty-five years as an orderly in a Nashville hospital, Edmondson had a religious conversion and was called to preach and cut tombstones according to God's command. Concurrently, when Edmondson discovered a pile of limestone that had been accidentally dumped on his property, he considered it a "gift from heaven."

Edmondson began his sculptural career as a tombstone carver, working in limestone, and later progressed to carving figures. His tools consisted of several chisels of different sizes, hand-fashioned from old spikes, a short wood-handled hammer, a heavy rope, and a file for smoothing surfaces. Edmondson worked primarily in lime-stone that varied greatly in color and texture, from a porous, granular variety to a type almost as smooth as marble. The majority of the stones he obtained were rectangular blocks that had been used as sills, lintels, steps, building foundations, and curbs, and his finished sculptures generally retained their original shapes.

Sculptures by Edmondson are simple, rotund, emphatic forms that range from one to three feet in height. His figures are roughly carved directly into the stone, and forms are frequently suggested rather than articulated. Human faces are usually curved forms, with a few simple indentations denoting features. Feet are sometimes without toes, arms without wrists, and legs without ankles. Textures in Edmondson's sculptures are usually reserved for hair and animal fur. Anatomical proportions are usually distorted in a manner that gives a vigorous and expressive effect to the pieces. His female figures are almost invariably rotund, with large busts, broad hips, and round buttocks that are ably suggested beneath their simple garments. Doves constitute another interesting subject in Edmondson's works. They were carved singly, in pairs, and in arrangements of threes and as finials for his birdbaths and tombstones. Many of Edmondson's tombstones reveal his lack of literacy or concern with formal spacing. He sometimes completed a word or date on the edge of the stone or corrected a misspelled word by placing an omitted letter below.

Edmondson's career spanned a period of some fifteen years, part of which was under the auspices of the Works Progress Administration, from which he received several brief assignments that were free of stipulations. He created noncommissioned works, and his yard was filled with old stones and the images he created from them: tombstones; a menagerie of recognizable beasts that he called "critters" and fantastic "varmints"; and a proliferation of preachers, angels, choir girls, nurses, teachers, and figures from popular culture such as Jack Johnson and Eleanor Roosevelt.

Employing only a few unsophisticated tools and a myriad forest of stone that ranged from Bedford limestone to common fieldstone, Edmondson lived in harmony with a dream. During the last several years of his life he was in poor health and worked with small blocks of limestone and carved only a few tombstones. Edmondson was buried in an unmarked grave in a cemetery near his home. The cemetery records were later destroyed by fire, and the exact location of Edmondson's grave is unknown. The stone carver who devoted years of labor to carving tombstones for others does not have one marking his own plot. The sculptures of Edmondson, however, are at the forefront of the vast arena of African American art.

—Regenia A. Perry

EDWARDS, Melvin

American sculptor

Born: 4 May 1937. **Education:** Los Angeles County Art Institute; Los Angeles City College, University of Southern California, B.F.A. **Career:** Instructor, San Bernardino Valley College, California, 1964-65, California Institute of Arts, Valencia, 1965-67, Orange County Community College, California, 1967-79; assistant professor, University of Connecticut, Storrs, 1970-72. Since 1972 assistant professor, Rutgers University, New Brunswick, New Jersey. Guest-

Melvin Edwards. Photo courtesy of G.R. N'Namdi Gallery.

lecturer, Howard University, Washington, D.C., 1976, University of Connecticut, Storrs, 1980 and 1982, Bloomsburg State College, Pennsylvania, 1983. Has served as panelist, Massachusetts Commission on Arts, 1976, New Jersey Arts Council Public Art Program, 1980 and 1985, Ohio State Individual Grant panel, 1982, National Endowment for the Arts, 1983 **Awards:** John Hay Whitney Fellowship, 1964; Los Angeles Contemporary Art Council, 1965; Long Beach Museum of Arts awards, 1965, 1967; Santa Barbara Art Association Award, California, 1969; Cassandra Foundation Award, 1969; National Endowment for the Arts Fellowship, 1970; CAPS sculpture award, New York, 1973; Guggenheim Foundation Fellowship, 1975; National Endowment for the Arts Fellowship, 1984; New Jersey State Arts Council Award, 1984; Fulbright Fellowship to Zimbabwe, 1988,1989; Fujisankei Bienale Grand Prize, Utsukushi-ga-hara Open Air Museum, 1993.

Individual Exhibitions:

1965	Santa Barbara Museum of Art, California
1968	Barndsdall Art Center, Los Angeles
	Walker Art Center, Minneapolis, Minnesota
1970	Whitney Museum of American Art, New York
1972	Wright State University, Dayton, Ohio
1978	Studio Museum of Harlem, New York
1980	YM-YMHA Greene Lane, Union, New Jersey
	55 Mercer, New York
1981	New Jersey State Museum, Trenton, New Jersey
1982	Sculpture Center, New York

1983	Winston-Salem State University, North Carolina
1984	UNESCO, Paris
1985	Jersey City Museum, New Jersey
	Atrium Gallery, University of Connecticut
	Robeson Center Gallery, Newark, New Jersey
1986	Atrium Gallery, University, Connecticut
1989	Extension Gallery, Johnson Atelier, New Jersey
	Colgate University, Hamilton, New York
	Korn Gallery, Madison College, New Jersey
1990	Montclair State College Art Gallery, New Jersey
	DeLuce Gallery, Northwest Missouri State University, Maryville
	Franklin Marshall College Art Gallery, Lancaster, Pennsylvania
1992	Cedar Rapids Museum of Art, Iowa
1993	Museum of Fine Arts, Springfield, Massachusetts
	Neuberger Museum (thirty year retrospective)

Selected Group Exhibitions:

1962	La Jolla Museum of Art, California
1975	Cinque Gallery, New York
1979	Bronx Museum, New York
1983	*Young Talent Awards, 1963-1983,* Los Angeles County Museum of Art, California
1984	Kenkeleba Gallery, New York
1986	Alternative Museum, New York

Melvin Edwards: *Lucky You,* **1990. Photo courtesy of G.R. N'Namdi Gallery.**

1988	*The Law and Order Show,* Gladstone Gallery, New York
1990	Whitney Museum of Art at Philip Morris, New York
1991	Sewall Art Gallery, Rice University, Houston, Texas
1992	*Bridges and Boundaries,* Jewish Museum, New York (traveling)

Collections:

Bronx Museum of Art, New York; Brooklyn Museum of Art, New York; Center for the Arts, Vero Beach, Florida; Herbert Johnson Museum, Cornell University, Ithaca, New York; Kingsborough Community College, Brooklyn, New York; Lafayette Gardens, Jersey City, New Jersey; Livingston College, Rutgers, New Jersey; Long Beach California Museum, California; Los Angeles County Museum, California; Metropolitan Museum of Art; Montclair Museum, New Jersey; Morgan State University, Baltimore, Maryland; Museum of Modern Art, New York; New Jersey State Museum, Trenton; Newark Museum, New Jersey; Schomburg Center, Harlem, New York; Studio Museum in Harlem, New York; Wadsworth Atheneum, Hartford, Connecticut; Winston-Salem State University, North Carolina.

Publications:

On EDWARDS: Book—*Melvin Edwards Sculpture: A Thirty-Year Retrospective, 1963-1993* by Lucinda H. Gedeon, University of Washington Press, Seattle, 1993. **Articles—**"New Surge in the Arts" by Allan Morrison, in *Ebony,* August 1967; "Exhibition at the Whitney Museum" by Robert Pincus-Witten, in *Art Forum,* May 1970; "It's Not Enough to Say Black Is Beautiful" by Frank Bowling, in *Art News,* April 1971.

*   *   *

Melvin Edwards is unquestionably the most prolific African American sculptor working today. When he is not teaching in a classroom, his work environment is charged with smoke, fire, sparks, and the clanging of metal, with strains of jazz often forming a musical background.

Although he was born and raised in Texas and studied art at the University of Southern California in Los Angeles, Edwards has spent most of his active career in New York and New Jersey. This national background has brought him into contact with many African American artists across the continent. He is politically active and has been in the forefront of progressive causes. He has given support to scholars, to other artists, and to institutions that have been formed to enhance the study of African American art. For many years he has been on the faculty of Rutgers University, first at Livingston College and then at the Mason Gross School of Art.

Edwards is among the generation of artists who create works from found objects. He welds scraps of metal into assemblages that explore the possibilities of sculptural form and that are loaded with meaning. In this way he is like African artists who have a long tradition of reusing materials in the hope that out of discarded items something new and different can emerge.

The scale and breadth of Edwards's works differ widely. Some are quite large and are designed for placement in a public, outdoor setting. Most of the large works have a stability that one would expect from large pieces of iron and steel. Edwards also has experimented with kinetic sculpture, however, large works that can be moved with a gentle touch. He has created a group of barbed wire and chain works (1969-70) that bear the titles *Pyramid Up, Pyramid Down* and *Curtain for William and Peter.* Most people think of sculpture in terms of volume and form, but in these innovative sculptures Edwards used the linear qualities of the materials to create drawings in space. Other works, like the extensive series "Lynch Fragments," are small, only a foot or so in height, and are intended for interior spaces. Each item in this series, which evolved and grew in three different periods (1963-67, 1972-73, and 1978-96), is a work of high relief, exploits line and volume, and has its own inherent architectonic logic. As a group the works exude compact, concentrated energy and power. Edwards also has done elegant lyrical works in the minimalist mode, and in addition to sculpture he has made prints.

Although Edwards is associated with the abstract sculpture that dominated the art world of the 1970s, he has also used recognizable images in his assemblages, chains and tools, for example. Edwards selects objects for their inherently appropriate sculptural properties. Thus, they help to solve purely formal problems in his work, but they also have symbolic value. The repeated use of chains, for example, is an important symbol in the history of the African and African American experience. The chain symbolizes slavery and the unleashing of African American energy. Among the Yoruba the chain is used prominently as an emblem of membership in the Osugbo (Ogboni) society. Chains are used to link male and female images together, and the chain can indicate connection to ones roots, Americans to Africa.

Edwards sees himself as the descendant of a long line of African metalworkers. To this end he has been to Africa many times, especially to Nigeria, where he became familiar with the work of the brass casters of the kingdom of Benin. Some of Edwards's large works now grace the African continent. The continuity with West Africa has thus come full circle, for examples of his work are now in African collections, including those of the Asantehene of Ghana and the oba of Benin.

—Thomas M. Shaw

EGONU, Uzo

Nigerian graphic artist, illustrator, painter, and printmaker

Born: Onitsha, Anambra State, Nigeria, 25 December 1931. **Education:** Teachers Training College, Onitsha, Nigeria; Camberwell School of Art and Design, London, 1949-52. Traveled and studied in Europe, 1952-60; studied with Italian painter in Rome. **Family:** Married Hildred Egonu in 1971, nine children. **Career:** Freelance artist; licentiate, Society of Industrial Artists and Designers, London, 1968-79; illustrator, Ginn and Company, Heinemann Educational Books, Oxford University Press. Member, Royal Society of Arts, London. **Awards:** First Prize, Junior All-Nigeria School Art Competition, 1944; First Prize, oil painting, BBC Morning Show Art Competition, 1970; Bronze Medal, graphics, *Les Arts en Europe,* Brussels, 1971; Cup of the City of Caserta for oil painting, Naples, Italy, 1972; Second Prize for oil painting, University of California at Los Angeles, 1972; UNESCO Prize, 1976; Purchase Prize, *13th International Biennial of Graphic Art,* Ljubljana, Yugoslavia, 1979; honorary counsellor-for-life, International Association of Art, UNESCO, 1983; medal, *Tenth International Print Biennial,* Krakow, Poland, 1984; fellow, Asele Institute, 1985. **Died:** 14 August 1996.

Individual Exhibitions:

1964	Woodstock Gallery, London
1966	Atelier Vincitore, Brighton, England
1967	Phoenix Theatre, Leicester, England
1968	Upper Grosvenor Galleries, London
	Commonwealth Institute, Edinburgh, Scotland
1970	George Room Gallery, Stroud, England
1971	Gallery Africa, Nairobi, Kenya
1972	Afro-Centrum Agisymba, Berlin, Germany
1973	Commonwealth Institute Art Gallery, London
1974	University of Lancaster, England
1979	St. Paul's School Art Gallery, London
1980	Liberales Zentrum Art Gallery, Cologne, Gemany
1982	Bhownagree Gallery, Commonwealth Institute, London
1983	Westbourne Gallery, London
1985	Galerie Neue Horizonte, Frankfurt, Germany
	Ana Gallery, University of Nigeria, Nsukka
1986	Royal Festival Hall, London (traveling)
	Civic Centre, Exhibition Area, Harrow, England

Selected Group Exhibitions:

1984	*Inter-Grafik 84,* Berlin, Germany
	Museum of Modern Art, Rijeka, Yugoslavia
	Norwegian International Print Biennial, Fredrikstad, Norway
	Tenth International Print Biennial, Krakow, Poland
1985	National Theatre, Lagos
1986	National Theatre, Lagos
	Black-Art Gallery, London
	Royal Festival Hall, London
1990	Hayward Gallery, London (traveling)
	Herbert Art Gallery and Museum, Coventry, England (traveling)

Collections:

Africa Centre, London; Arts Council of Great Britain; Bradford City Art Gallery and Museum, Bradford, England; Centre for Black and African Arts and Civilization, Lagos; Commonwealth Institute, Edinburgh, Scotland; Fylde Arts Association, Modern British Prints, Blackpool, England; Gorner and Millard Gallery, London; Inner London Education Authority, London; International Centre for Public-Owned Enterprises in Developing Countries, Ljubljana, Yugoslavia; Jacob Kramer College, Leeds, England; Muszeum Narodowe w Poznaniu Poznan, Poland; National Council for Arts and Culture, Lagos; National Gallery of Modern Art, Lagos; National Museum of Modern Art, Baghdad; Nigerian High Commission, London; Overseas Newspapers (Daily Mirror Group), London; Spencer, Stuart and Associates, London; United Africa Company International, London; Victoria and Albert Museum, London.

Publications:

By EGONU: Books—*Lithographs: Once Upon a Time in Ibo-Land: Original Short Story,* London, Uzo Egonu, 1971; *Photocopies of exhibition catalogs, newspaper clippings and 50 color slides of paintings and prints,* Wembley, England, 1984 (illustrated; copy available in National Museum of African Art Library). **Articles**—"The Culture of Nri and Igbo-Ukwu," in *West Africa* (London), 3403, 25 October 1982, pp. 2786-87; "African Art: Its Impact on the West," in *Arts Review* (London), 36(21), 9 November 1984, pp. 558 (illustrated).

On EGONU: Book—*Let the Canvas Come to Life with Dark Faces,* exhibition catalog, London, Herbert Art Gallery and Museum and Eddie Chambers, 1990 (illustrated). **Articles**—"Artist from Onitsha," in *West African Review* (London), April 1960, pp. 21-24 (illustrated); "Painting: Uzo Egonu" by Ronald Moody, in *Magnet News* 5, 10-23 April 1965 (illustrated); "The Vision of Egonu," in *West Africa* (London), 2922, 11 June 1973; "The Modern African Artist Who is Still Loyal to Tradition" by Emmanuel Jegede, in *West Indian World* (London), 15 June 1973; "Uzo Egonu of Nigeria" by Adeyemi Adekeye, in *African Arts* (Los Angeles), 7(1), Autumn 1973, pp. 34-37 (illustrated; some color); "1972 Prizewinners: Uzo Egonu," in *African Arts* (Los Angeles), 6(2), Winter 1973 (illustrated; color); "How Uzo Egonu, Nigeria's Best Known Artist in Europe, Earns His Living" by Gordon Tialobi, in *Punch* (Lagos), 13 May 1978; "Black Living Picasso" by Alex Ebele, in *West Africa* (London), 3391, 2 August 1982, p. 1988 (illustrated; color); "Reflections of Uzo Egonu," in *Third Text* (London), 8-9, Autumn-Winter 1989, pp. 173-82; "Our Nigerian: Uzo Egonu—Painting the Soul" by Omotayo Afolabi, in *Homenews* (London), 22-28 February 1990, p.3 (illustrated).

*   *   *

Some critics and a few admirers regard Uzo Egonu as one of the greatest modern British artists, but the general British art world knew nothing of his consuming passion for making art and would hardly recognize his work. The Nigerian-born Egonu was, however, a hardworking artist and a man of magnificent vision. Although throughout his youth and adult life he lived and practiced art in England, the formal basis of his work went beyond European modernism. He was a rigorous printmaker and painter whose accomplishments helped extend the discourse on the polarities of both contemporary British and African art. The reclamation and manipulation of traditional forms eventually came to characterize his figurative art.

A cursory view of the art of Egonu reveals an interplay of foreign and indigenous modalities within a setting in which non-European art is an object of half-mocking admiration. Egonu's forms are spread over the picture surface, demarcated by bold lines, and embellished with allover patterns similar to those found on textiles. The motifs are often repeated to reinforce the design and proportion. In his works are found the themes of reorientation, strife, the tragedy of war, and desperation, as well as their weight upon the artist. These internal and external preoccupations were obviously brought about by his alienation. Displacement from his culture, the exclusive structure of the British art establishment, and the rejection by the Nigerian government of applications for jobs or scholarships for graduate study were the anvils upon which Egonu's art was forged.

By 1942, while he was still a child, Egonu was taking watercolor, still life, and clay-modeling classes from a local self-taught teacher, John Okechukwu. Winning the top prize at the first all-Nigerian junior art contest made it possible for Egonu to go to England in 1945 for further training. It was customary among the Nigerian elite during this period to send their prodigies to the West, where it was thought they could realize their full potentials.

At the Camberwell College of Art and Crafts, where he majored

in painting and printing, Egonu was steeped in the traditional European style. Upon graduation he visited various museums and galleries in Europe to study traditional African art and works of European masters. He was able to make a livelihood through genre watercolors and drawings, and in 1954 he met a Gambian businessman whose fascination with his work increased sales and commissions and eventually brought gallery exhibitions.

In 1960 Egonu received a public commission and the press attention that came with it. The brewing firm Whitbread and Company commissioned him to paint a market scene for Nigerian House in London, but the portrait of Kwame Nkrumah he produced in a neoclassical style was rejected. Although Egonu became dissatisfied with his work, a visit to Nigeria kept him from losing faith in his art.

Between 1962 and 1965 Egonu transformed his technique and the style of his art. Formal devices became his primary interest. He evolved a unique visual perspective, with preeminent borders, a disregard for anatomy, consummate use of texture, and an austere palette. *Nude Combing Her Hair, Woman with Umbrella, Woman before a Mirror,* and *A Dog Named Lost,* all produced during this period, seem European on the surface.

The late 1960s were a period of political crisis in Nigeria, and the cruelties of war inspired a body of works Egonu called the "Protection" series. In the 1970s he turned to etching, lithography, and serigraphy. His use of flat color and his emphasis on line and distinct shapes made his switch to printmaking effortless.

By 1971 themes of Igbo rituals and cosmology had become prominent in his work. He hoped to revive Igbo cultural values, and his artistic stamp, well established by this time, resulted in numerous commissions for book illustrations. After 1979 the emphasis of his work shifted from a broad humanistic commitment to introspective visions of the potency of painting. Although fumes from etching caused his eyesight to fail and he suffered other health problems, he continued to work until his death.

—Barthosa Nkurumeh

EL ANATSUI
Ghanaian sculptor, ceramist, and mixed-media artist

Born: Anyako, Ghana, 4 February 1944. **Education:** University of Science and Technology, Kumasi, Ghana, 1964-69, B.A. 1968, post graduate diploma (art education), 1969. **Career:** Lecturer, Art Education Department, Specialist Training College, Winneba, Ghana (now University of Winneba), 1969-75; lecturer, 1975-82, and senior lecturer since 1982, University of Nigeria, Nsukka. Visiting artist, Cornwall College, Redruth, England, 1985, International People College, Helsingor, Denmark, 1997. **Awards:** Honorable Mention, First Ghana National Art Competition, 1968; Best Student of the Year, College of Art, University of Science and Technology, Kumasi, Ghana, 1969; honorable mention (joint), Venice *Biennale,* Italy, 1990; Kansai Telecasting Corporation Prize, Osaka Triennale, Japan, 1995. **Agent:** Artists Alliance Gallery, Monaye House, P.O. Box 718, Teshie-Nungua, Accra, Ghana; October Gallery, 24 Old Gloucester Street, London WCIN3AL, England; Signature Gallery, 107 Awolowo Road, Ikoyi, Lagos, Nigeria. **Address:** P.O. Box 3059, University of Nigeria, Nsukka, Enugu State, Nigeria.

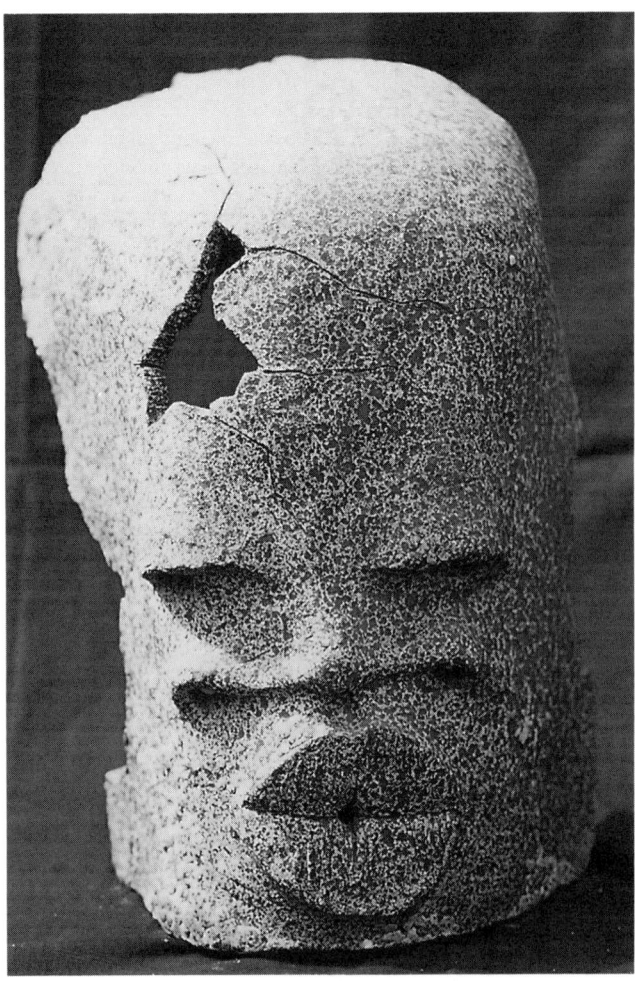

El Anatsui: *Chambers of Memory,* 1977.

Individual Exhibitions:

1976	Asele Gallery, University of Nigeria, Nsukka
1979	British Council Hall, Enugu, Nigeria
1980	Community of the Arts, Cummington, Massachusetts
1982	Goethe Institute, Lagos, Nigeria
1987	Franco-German Auditorium, Lagos, Nigeria
	Faculty of Arts and Design, Cornwall College, Redruth, England
1991	*Old and New: Mural Sculptures,* National Museum, Lagos, Nigeria
1995	October Gallery, London
1996	*Images of Africa,* Torpedo Hall, Copenhagen, Denmark

Selected Group Exhibitions:

1990	*Five Contemporary African Artists,* Venice *Biennale,* Italy
	Contemporary African Artists: Changing Tradition, Studio Museum in Harlem (traveling)
1992	Modern Art Museum, Rio de Janeiro, Brazil (traveling)
1994	*Fifth Havana Biennale,* Cuba
1995	*Africus: First Johannesburg Biennale,* South Africa
	Setagaya Museum, Tokyo, Japan
	Whitechapel Art Gallery, London

Osaka Triennale (Sculpture), Osaka, Japan
1996   Sala 1, Rome
        Container '96: Art Across Oceans, Lagelinie, Copenhagen, Denmark

Collections:

African Studies Gallery, University of Nigeria, Nsukka; Asele Institute, Nimo, Nigeria; Diamond Bank, Victoria Island, Lagos, Nigeria; Embassy of Ghana, Copenhagen, Denmark; Ghana National Art Collection, Accra; Hamburgishes Museum fur Volkerkunde Hamburg, Germany; Hammermill, Hellebaek/Helsingor, Denmark; International People's College, Helsingor, Denmark; Iwalewa-Haus, University of Bayreuth, Germany; National Gallery of Contemporary Art, Lagos, Nigeria; National Museum of African Art, Washington, D.C.; Osaka Foundation of Culture, Japan; Setagaya Museum, Tokyo, Japan; Volkerkunde Museum, Frankfurt, Germany; World Bank, Washington, D.C.

Publications:

On EL ANATSUI: Articles—"Anatsui's Pieces of Wood" by Chinye Nwosu, in *Lagos Life* (Lagos), 26 February 1987, p. 11; "El Anatsui: Visual Incantations" by C.C. Aniakor, in *International Review of African American Art* (Hollywood and Los Angeles), 9(3); "El Anatsui and Sol" by Holland Cotter, in *New York Times,* 5 July 1996. **Video**— *Contemporary Nigerian Artists: Kindred Spirits,* Smithsonian World, 1990.

*   *   *

The distinguished award-winning sculptor and ceramist El Anatsui has participated in a series of major international exhibitions and exchange workshops. Born in Ghana, he moved to Nigeria in 1975, where he has since taught at the University of Nigeria, Nsukka. A founding member of the Aka Circle of exhibiting artists and now the chair of the department of sculpture, Anatsui attained national prominence after he pioneered a new sculptural language with the power saw and blowtorch. His awards have included the Kansai Telecasting Corporation's prize for sculpture in 1995, in Osaka, Japan, and a joint honorable mention at the forty-fourth Venice Biennale in 1990. His works are in public collections in Nigeria, Ghana, Germany, Denmark, the United States, and Japan.

Anatsui's use of the power saw as a creative tool began in 1980 when, as an artist in residence in the Cummington (Massachusetts) Community of Arts in the United States, he set out to log a tree for a composite sculpture to be produced with chisels, gouges, and mallets. A few inches into the cut, he recounts, he struck a chord that heightened his sensibilities and enabled him to see the evocative character of the rough, fuzzy incision created by the power saw. Though he had used the saw before for cutting logs, he had never recognized the sculptural potential of the tool. Notwithstanding the definite limitations of the raw power, devastating speed, and clumsy maneuverability of the power saw, the creative process of the tool recalled for him the historical trauma of colonization. Since the slashing process of the power saw invoked a not-too-distant experience in which African peoples, nations, and cultures were brutally cut up into separate parts and redistributed across national boundaries, he appropriated the equipment as his signature tool. With this sculptural tool Anatsui has produced hauntingly beautiful two-dimensional forms that are metaphors of a tur-

El Anatsui: *Akua's Surviving Children,* 1996. Photo courtesy of Garba Diallo.

bulent colonial past as well as the equally turbulent postcolonial experiences of contemporary times.

Since 1981 Anatsui has concentrated on wood as an expressive medium of creativity, achieving in the process an intimate relationship with the medium that has led him to speculate that it must have a soul or resident spirit. The idea of working with the resident soul of his chosen material has galvanized him into producing visually compelling works, sometimes with narrative titles like *When I last wrote to you about Africa, I used a letterheaded parchment paper, There were many blank slots in the letter . . . I can now fill some of these slots because . . . I've grown older* (1986); *They made it happen, watched it happen but now, with battered bodies, wonder what happened* (1986); and *They came at dawn, a crowd of unusually identical people. They bought four little pots which they said are from each of the four corners of the earth* (1987). At other times the titles of Anatsui's works are short and succinct and point to selected events and ideas that he wants his audience to dwell on. For example, the titles of his sculptures-in-the-round—such as *Human Wall* (1988), *Group Photographs* (1987-88), and *Pillars* (1988)—and of relief plaques—such as *Migration and Illusion* (1995), *Old Towel* (1995), and *Fragments of History* (1995)—allude to the harrowing realities of the postcolonial condition.

Reflecting on the creative process, Anatsui has asserted that the opening of his inner vision has facilitated his move beyond preoc-

cupation with the ordinary surfaces of events, objects, people, and experiences to see their deeper constitutive essence. In his view it was this same spirit that led both the *adinkra* symbolists (the Akan originators of the symbols he uses profusely) to contrive a visual sign for the abstract concept of seriousness and that led the female *uli* artists to capture the visual essence of the in-between spaces of organic and vegetal forms. He rejects the idea that the novelty and difference of the blowtorch and power saw are what make his sculptures art. Rather, what commands attention is the combination of the strong technical skill he brings to the work and the eloquent expressiveness of his forms.

Since 1990 Anatsui has been meticulously perfecting his sculptural language, systematically eliminating flowery expressions that clutter up the substantive statement of his message. Although this approach may sound highly restrained and controlled, Anatsui's works attain a measure of conceptual fluidity by avoiding designs that prescribe relational and spatial fixity. The pieces of wood that make up each of Anatsui's two-dimensional relief plaques and three-dimensional sculptures do not have fixed relationships or positions. Hence, they can easily be moved around to create new compositional designs and effects.

—Nkiru Nzegwu

EL SALAHI, Ibrahim

Sudanese painter

Born: Omdurman, Sudan, 1930. **Education:** School of Design, Gordon Memorial College, and Khartoum Technical Institute, 1948-51; Slade School, University College, London, 1954-57. **Awards:** UNESCO Fellowship, 1962; Rockefeller Foundation Fellowship, 1964-65.

Individual Exhibitions:

1960	Grand Hotel Exhibition Hall, Khartoum, Sudan
1961	Mbari Gallery, Ibudan, Nigeria
1962	American Cultural Centre, Khartoum
	Gallery Lambert, Paris
1963	ICA Gallery, London
	Murphy Gallery, Baltimore, Maryland
	Middle East House, Washington, D.C.
1964	Irvington-on-Hudson, New York
	Daberkow Gallery, Frankfurt, Germany
1967	Gallery Lambert, Paris
	Traverse Gallery, Edinburgh
	French Cultural Centre, Khartoum
1969	French Cultural Centre, Khartoum
1972	Agisymba Gallery, Berlin
1974	Art Gallery, N.C.C.A.L., Kuwait
1984	Iwalewa Haus, Bayreuth
1990	Iwalewa Haus, Bayreuth

Selected Group Exhibitions:

1963	Academy of Fine Art, Calcutta
1964	Sudan Pavilion, New York World's Fair
1965	Museum of Modern Art, New York
1966	Museum of Philadelphia—Civic Center
1967	ICA, London
1969	Mommo Gallery, Kampala
1975	Royal Commonwealth Society, London
1977	FESTAC, Lagos
1978	Maison de la Culture, Rheims
1992	Laing Art Gallery, Newcastle upon Tyne

Collections:

Metropolitan Museum of Art, New York; Museum of Modern Art, New York; National Gallery, Berlin; National Gallery of Victoria, Sydney, Australia; Newcastle Art Gallery, Australia; Betty Parsons Gallery, New York.

*   *   *

Ibrahim El Salahi's drawings and paintings span a period of forty years. Line is preeminent in his work and functions as a methodical device of elemental form and, inextricably, as spontaneous expression of a primeval unconscious. Though modernism presumes a contradiction between reason and intuition, El Salahi, who is a modernist, shifted with fluidity between the two. This negotiation of objectivity and subjectivity is a significant continuum in the artist's oeuvre, which manifests a bold, calculated, linear style wherein symbolic iconography is intuitively imbued with a compassionate concern for humanity.

El Salahi's work constitutes a stylistic rupture in the art of Sudan and Africa in general. At the same time it marks a departure from modernist styles of the Slade School of Art (London), where he studied from 1954 to 1957. He observes in an interview published in *Arab World*, "I was in a great turmoil. I felt that I had things to say that were beyond the representation of portraiture and scenery from nature. It was difficult for me to work for awhile. Then I began to feel the pull of the Islamic symbolism that I had known all of my life. And I broke away, finally, to express life as I felt it." It was a quest fulfilled by his discovery of "treasures of wonderful Islamic art" at the Victoria and Albert Museum and in the manuscript and nature section of the British Museum, along with African art at the latter. El Salahi's first and second stylistic periods are characterized by figurative subject matter organized by expressionist line and subdued color. Emblematic icons of the human figure, Islamic script and design, the cosmos, masks, animals, and mathematical shapes permeate the works of these periods. From this time on, elemental form gains increasing importance in successive phases of Salahi's paintings and drawings. By the second period, precedence is given to the square and circle, and by the third period, color disappears as line takes over to produce subject matter in complex, interpenetrating shape-spatial relationships with emotional content that extends the artist's iconic mysticism and social criticism.

Funeral and Crescent (1963), an oil painting on board, is a signature painting of this first phase, typically depicting the human figure in a specific drama. Death is the subject in this painting of a skeletonized funeral procession with hoisted deceased. Confrontational gazes of elongated, emaciated pallbearers prophetically summon the spectator into the macabre reality of her/his own mortality in earthly spaces beneath heavenly bodies. The calligraphic outlines and interior patterns of the figures, juxtaposed with crescent shapes, circles, spirals, and lines, epitomize Islamic influence. Their rhythmic patterns instill passionate drama, welding the human and the spiritual, subject and spectator. Forms and iconography, utilizing Islamic, African, and modernist elements, are laden with mysticism and nostalgia, suggesting Salahi's psychological return "home" from the cosmopolitanism of London and from the urban regions of British colonialism in Sudan.

The second phase (c.1970-c.mid-1970s) consists primarily of compositions in watercolor that range from warm, brilliant abstract shapes contained by line to subdued palettes expressively delineating human figures or geometrical design. These compositions are largely coloristic studies or abstract patterns inspired by Islamic tantra and mandala designs that El Salahi rendered optically and subjectively as he improvised, split, opened, closed, and fragmented them to explore their unlimited potential. They were an intimate part of Salahi's meditation as he escaped into the desert, away from the urban life of Khartoum or the European, African, and American cities, where he exhibited. During his second period the circle and square dominated the structure of his compositions. Their appearance, according to El Salahi, corresponds to meditation which functioned for him as direct communication with God, a form of comfort and a way to peace of mind or "tama'nin."

It was during the second period that El Salahi's work was interrupted. He was Undersecretary for Culture and Information when, as he observes, he went from a real circle (government) into a real square (jail); he spent six months and three days in jail in 1975 without trial, "because he was falsely suspected of anti-government activities." Subsequently El Salahi left Sudan and began to spend much of his life between Qatar and Britain.

The third phase (late 1970s-1990s) began after El Salahi expatriated to Qatar. The circle and square are revised in this period to construct formalist, interpenetrating organic and mechanized form. The compositions display affinities with elements of cubism, expressionism, surrealism, and constructivism, yet they resist each of these categories. The subjects and media of this period were stimulated by El Salahi's deep reflections on the cycle of life, initiated by a gaze at elderly Qatar women who were fully clothed and masked, "walking by the sea." The idea of drawing in ink, rather than color, was impressed by the dark masks that covered their faces from the top of the forehead to the nose; it was a striking contrast between the internal human and the external container. The black dress psychologically translated into pen and ink, extending an optical reality and a theoretical content about the social condition of confinement in the cycle of life. The images of those women expanded in El Salahi's ink drawings/paintings to engage the tyranny which subjects humanity to systematized rituals of subjugation, including his own imprisonment. Salahi's persistent formal interest, the balance of human, cosmological, and biological elements that he chose in the works of the 1960s, expands into a concern to balance interpenetrating, organic-mechanical form in the 1980s and 1990s. Many works in this period consist of multiple panels that constitute a monumental unit, as in a conceptualized triptych or improvisational patchwork quilt. They are often produced spontaneously, panel by panel, growing with the artist's processual conceptualization. Other works are individual ink drawings on paper of various subjects, including portraits (frontal and profile) that are imbued with psychological intensity. Of these works El Salahi has observed, "I am more concerned now with the internal structure of the work, which I prefer to express in black and white . . . in the end all images can be reduced to lines."

—Freida High

EMOKPAE, Erhabor Ogieva

Nigerian muralist, painter, sculptor, and graphic artist

Born: Benin City, Edo State, Nigeria, 4 May 1934. **Education:** Yaba Technical Institute, two years; studied art in England, 1963. **Career:** Graphic artist, Eastern Nigeria Information Service, Engugu, 1965; visualizer, Lintas, Nigeria, 1959; Lintas, London, 1963-65; creative director, Lintas, Nigeria, 1973; chair/managing director, Asa Productions Nigeria. Co-founder, Nigerian Arts Council, c.1963. Design brochures and murals for FESTAC '77. Founding member, Society of Nigerian Artists. **Awards:** Prize in carving, Festival of Arts, Lagos, 1950; Officer of the Order of the Niger; fellowship (posthumous), Asele Institute, Nimo, Nigeria, 1985. **Died:** 16 February 1984.

Individual Exhibitions:

1966   Goethe Institute, Lagos
1972   Goethe Institute, Lagos

Selected Group Exhibitions:

1977   FESTAC '77, Lagos
         National Theatre, Lagos
1978   National Theatre, Lagos
         Exhibition of Nigerian Traditional and Contemporary Art,
            Lagos
1980   National Theatre, Lagos
         Exhibition of Contemporary Nigerian Art, Dakar, Senegal
1985   National Theatre, Lagos
         Silver Jubilee National Art Exhibition, National Theatre,
            Lagos, Federal University of Technology, Owerri, Nigeria
1986   National Theatre, Lagos
1987   Continental Merchant Bank, Lagos

Collections:

Didi Museum, Lagos; Lagos University Library, University of Lagos; National Gallery of Modern Art, Lagos.

Publications:

On EMOKPAE: Articles—"Emokpae Dies," in *West Africa* (London), 3472, 5 March 1984, p. 528; "Adieu Erhabor Emokpae," in *Nigeria* (Lagos), 148, 1984, pp. 73-75; "Dualism and Expressive Dynamism in the Sculpture of Erhabor Emokpae" by Agbo Folarin, *Kurio Africana: Journal of Art and Criticism* (Ile-Ife, Nigeria), 1(2), 1989, pp. 61-67.

*   *   *

The murals, paintings, sculptures, and graphic designs of Erhabor Ogieva Emokpae range in style from abstraction to photo-realism. Like the work of his contemporaries Yusuf Grillo, Demas Nwoko, and Bruce Onabrakpeya, Emokpae's work led developments in modern Nigerian art that mapped endless possibilities for art and artists in an early postcolonial epoch and earned him a preeminent place in the history of modern Nigerian and African art. (Nigeria gained its independence from Britain in 1960.) Emokpae's range of materials and styles disallows any narrow stylistic categorization, yet the work displays an internal unity in the preeminence of the human figure and/or theme and the pervasive modernist mode. Whether monumental murals or oil paintings, the works are largely formulated on principles of elemental form, truth to material, and the resolve of an objective-subjective dialectic.

Emokpae's art evinces his vision of a postcolonial hybridity and reveals an orientation that corresponds to that of Valente Malangatana of Mozambique, Afewerk Tekle of Ethiopia, and Charles White of the United States, all of whom utilized muralism to aestheticize the world with humanitarian subject matter. In his compositions, man and woman, materially and spiritually, are constituted as subject matter framed by such contingencies as colonialism and nationalism, traditionalism and modernism, and individualism and communitarianism. Subject matter and meanings transcend the internal unity of form to engage transcendental questions of life and death, love and hate, and materiality and spirituality. Emokpae's commanding public works in Nigeria earned him a global historical presence. Located in government buildings, banks, an airport, and national collections, his works are daily seen by an international public.

One of Emokpae's most compelling works is the *Mural of Understanding* (1964-65), a wall structured in concrete and mosaic materials that measures 12' x 60'. Dynamically geometricized, the mural displays an internal unity, yet bespeaks a utopian internationalism. Located on the exterior of the Nigerian Institute of International Affairs on Victoria Island, Lagos, Nigeria, this mixed-media work is arguably Emokpae's greatest. The mural is on an extended wall that foregrounds the architectural structure of the building, which is a severe rectangular International style. The light concrete sculptural figures dramatically contrast with the dark-blue mosaic background. Their high-relief, individuated, geometricized forms move rhythmically against a monochromatic, luminous surface with subtly integrated geometric patterns. Mass and spatial relationships are symmetrically arranged in diagonal movements on both sides of an agitated spherical center. The human figures move dynamically toward the center and are flanked on both sides by frontal Africanesque forms that reiterate the unified symmetry of the mural. Emokpae observed of the mural that its iconography has a double meaning—1) an "international cooperation through understanding" as people around the world work together to overcome obstacles and 2) "a movement from the old into the new," that is, "Africa is moving away from Africa into the world."

The human figure, the conventional universal subject of sculpture, is prominent in Emokpae's sculpture and painting, too. Like his murals, the sculptures and paintings enact a dialogue that engages the duality of the material and the spiritual. *Iya Abiku* (1970), a sculpture of wood that is in the collection of the National Gallery in Nigeria, is such a work. An abstract human figure of wood, it consists of a dynamic interpenetration of geometricized form, pierced voids, and open negative areas, displaying a modernism influenced by conventional African sculpture and bearing affinities to the modernism of Ben Osawe (Nigerian), Henry Moore (British), Amedeo Modigliani (Italian), and other modernists influenced by African and Oceanic art. Vertically organized in organically fluid lines, the frontality and symmetry of the stylized human figure elegantly depicts the mother-and-child theme in simplified disc shapes and an extremely attenuated neck. The negative void within the figure structurally inflects Emokpae's conceptual dualism; the child is present and absent, material and spiritual. It also manifests his dialectal resolve of modernism and traditionalism. In general Emokpae's sculpture is characterized by highly geometricized forms with smooth luminous surfaces indicative of his remarkable respect for the natural wood grain and process of production. His extensive "Dialogue" series of the 1970s consists of frontal and rounded forms, always abstracted in duality of mass and space and themes of opposition.

Some works, however, depart from the smooth surfaces in their conception of accumulation processes and surface collage. An example of this is *Olokun* (1962), a monumental carving of iroko wood (approximately twelve feet high) that is covered with coins from various parts of the world. It is in the collection of the United Bank of Africa in Lagos.

As the philosophical Emokpae produced monumental murals, sculptures, and paintings for public metropolitan sites, primarily in Lagos, he simultaneously produced mass culture graphics as a graphic artist with the Federal Ministry of Information from 1953 to 1958. This was followed by positions as creative visualizer, then creative director, of Lintas W.A. Ltd. (formerly West African Publicity Limited) and as chairman/managing director of Asaproductions Nigeria Ltd. His graphic designs achieved international stature during Festac '77, the Second World Black and African Festival of Arts and Culture.

From his first professional position as graphic artist for the Ministry of Information in Lagos to his recognition by the Nigerian national government, Emokpae was prolific in his production, and his work sustained a critical public eye. The culmination of recognition was on 16 February 1984, just prior to his death, when he was awarded the Officer of the Order of the Niger, one of three artists to achieve this pinnacle of honor.

Emokpae's oeuvre was central to the origin of modern art in Nigeria. It addressed the necessity of monumental modernist production for contemplation and identity-formation and of an art for mass cultural consumption in a cosmopolitan consumer society. It charted a balance in artistic production for both elite and mass culture by appealing to an audience that required both private contemplation and mass dissemination. Emokpae's work was a modernism that intervened in the world as a modernist dialogue, reinventing the cosmopolitan site of a postcolonial Africa and thus reinventing "African art." He continuously announced his intention in the following statement, "The important thing for me is symbolization, the expression of an inner feeling, the experience." His works manifest his emancipatory vision, which resonates in posterity as a vision that influenced developments in Nigeria and extended internationally with his exhibitions in Germany, England, Poland, Russia, Brazil, India, Canada, Ghana, Senegal, the Republic of Benin, and the United States.

—Freida High

ENWONWU, Ben(edict Chukwukadibia)
Nigerian sculptor and painter

Born: Onitsha, Anambra State, Nigeria, 14 July 1921. **Education:** Learned carving from father, a sculptor. Ibadan and Umuahia Universities, Nigeria, 1934-37; Goldsmith College, London, 1944; Ruskin College, Oxford, 1944-46; Slade School of Fine Arts, London, 1946-48, graduate (first class honors); University of California; Louisiana State College, Baton Rouge. **Career:** Art teacher in various schools, including Government College, Umuahia, and mission schools in Calabar Province, 1940-41, Edo College, Benin City, 1941-43; art adviser to the Nigerian government, from 1948; cultural advisor to the Nigerian government, 1968-71. Traveled and lectured in United States, 1950. Editor *Nigeria* Magazine, 1966. Visiting artist, Institute of African Studies, Howard University, Washington, D.C. First professor of fine arts, University of Ife, Ile-Ife, Nigeria, 1971-75. Fellow, Royal Anthropological Institute, London; member, Royal Academy of Art, London. **Awards:** IBM Bronze Medal and Prize, 1939; scholarship, Shell Company of West Africa, 1944; Medal of the British Empire, 1954; R.B. Bennett Empire Art Prize, Royal Society of British Artists, 1957; Commonwealth Certificate, Royal Institute of Art, Commerce and Agriculture; National Order of Merit, 1980; Fellow, Lagos University, Nigeria, 1966-68, Asele Institute, Nimo. Honorary doctorate: Ahamdu Bello University, 1969. **Died:** February 1994.

Individual Exhibitions:

1942	Exhibition Centre, Marina, Lagos
1947	Berkeley Galleries, London
1948	Berkeley Galleries, London

1950   Berkeley Galleries, London
        Howard University, Washington, D.C.
        Galerie Apollinaire, London
1952   Berkeley Galleries, London
1955   Berkeley Galleries, London
1973   USIS, Lagos
1976   Goethe Institute, Lagos
1985   Mall Galleries, London
1987   Salon Exhibition, Lagos

Selected Group Exhibitions:

1980   National Theatre, Lagos
        Exhibition of Nigerian Contemporary Art, Dakar, Senegal
1982   *Ausstellung Nigerianishe Kunst der Gegenward,* Bonn
        Exhibition of Nigerian Contemporary Art, Islamabad, Pakistan
1984   *Evolution in Nigerian Art,* Lagos
1985   Gatwick Airport, London
        National Theatre, Lagos
1986   National Theatre, Lagos
1988   Salon Exhibition, Lagos
1990   Quintessence, Lagos

Collections:

Carl Van Vechten Gallery of Fine Arts, Fisk University, Nashville; Federal Ministry of Information, Cultural Division, Lagos; Hampton University Museum, Hampton, Virginia; Lagos University Library, University of Lagos; National Gallery of Modern Art, Lagos; National Museum, Lagos; Tate Gallery, London; United Nations, New York.

Publications:

By ENWONWU: Articles—"Problems of the African Artist Today," in *Présence Africain* (Paris), 8-10, June-November 1956, pp. 174-178; "African Art in Danger," in *The Times* (London), 29 September 1960; "Into the Abstract Jungle: A Criticism of the New Trend in Nigerian Art," in *Drum* (Lagos), June 1963, pp. 25-29 (illustrated; color); "Africanists Must Take Blame, Too," in *Drum* (Lagos), July 1963, pp. 27-28 (color illustrations); "The African View of Art and Some Problems Facing the African Artist," in *Function and Significance of African Negro Art in the Life of the People and for the People, March 30-April 8, 1966, [the] Colloquium on Negro Art, Dakar, 1966* (Paris), *Présence Africain,* 1968, pp. 417-426.

On ENWONWU: Articles—"Africa's Greatest Artist," in *Ebony* (Chicago), 4, March 1949, pp. 27-29; "Masterpiece in Bronze, Ben Enwonwu," in *Drum* (Johannesburg), January 1955, pp. 65-67 (illustrated); "Portrait of an Artist," in *West African Review* (London), 28(352), 1957, pp. 2-7 (illustrated); "Lonely Boy is Becoming a Fine Sculptor," in *Drum* (Johannesburg), April 1958, pp. 35-37 (illustrated); "Ben Enwonwu, Pentre et Sculpteur Nigerian," in *Jeune Afrique* (Paris), (16), September 1962, pp. 36-38 (illustrated); "Artists are Born , Not Made" (interview) by Willy Bozimo, in *Daily Times* (Lagos), 3 April 1975; "Ben Enwonwu Speaks with *Ophelia* Magazine," in *Ophelia* (London), 1(2), pp. 45, 55, 1982; "Enwonwu's Dry Run," in *West African Review* (London), 3555, 14 October 1985, p. 2146 (color illustrations).

Ben Enwonwu: *Agbogo Mmuo,* 1978. Photo courtesy of Nkiru Nzegwu.

An internationally renowned sculptor and painter, Ben Enwonwu was initiated by his father into the mysteries of *nka* (the Igbo conception of creativity). For more than sixty years, Enwonwu practiced as a professional artist, while working intermittently as an administrator and educator. In 1956 Enwonwu produced a bronze bust and a full-figure portrait of Queen Elizabeth II. He also executed a number of major commissions, including *Four Winged Evangelists* (1959), at All Saints Anglican Cathedral in Onitsha; *The Risen Christ* (1961), at the Chapel of the Resurrection at the University of Ibadan; and *Anyanwu* (1961), at the National Museum in Lagos and at the United Nations in New York City. As the first black artist ever to sculpt a European monarch, his much-sought-after works are in prestigious public and private collections worldwide.

Between 1945 and 1960 Enwonwu entered an extremely important creative period. Defining himself as an anticolonial, pan-African activist, he unapologetically injected his politics into his art. As his art became a tool to be deployed in the political struggle for cultural affirmation and independence, paintings like *Evolution* and *Black World* became visual metaphors. They represented images of Africa's cultural life and extolled the redemptive qualities of its cultural heritage. "Negritude" was the conceptual term for this artistic goal focused on culture. As Enwonwu put it, "Negritude meant everything. It meant the revitalization of African force, both in art and in all forms of creativity. It crystallized a particular age or period of artistic expression and we [the artists] were motivated by its political impetus."

There was nothing propagandistic in the evocative forms of Enwonwu's culturally centered drawings and imaginative composi-

Ben Enwonwu: *Ogolo (Metamorphosis),* **1991. Photo courtesy of Nkiru Nzegwu.**

(1990). To unleash the polyrhythmic essence of different dances, he juxtaposed pulsating bodies at different angles in his paintings, while using scattered patches of colors to amplify the vigor of the dance and to invoke the restless chatter of rattles and *ishaka* (a calabash percussion instrument). The interminable crisscrossing lines found in *Obitan I* (1989), *The Glory of Ancient Benin* (1942-89), and *Purakapali*, a dance drama staged by Peggy Harper in Ife and which Enwonwu saw, amplify the crescendo and weave together the many disparate parts of the paintings.

Along with dance forms *agbogo mmuo* (maiden spirits), erroneously known in the West as masks, also fascinated Enwonwu. For almost four decades, between 1951 and 1989, he celebrated elegance in his *agbogo mmuo* paintings. The fluid moves of *ayolugbe,* variants of *agbogo mmuo*, are captured in a painting titled *Nne Mmuo* (1987). Created immediately after the funeral ceremony of his elder brother, *Nne Mmuo* is an exhortatory reminder of the mutability of life. The appearance of this and other spirits at funerals reminds people that earthly life is not the only expression of the life force. Death is not the cessation of life but its transformation to other phases and modes. The central figure in *Nne Mmuo* is captured in a tight, crouching dance movement that choreographs the grand drama of life and death. The dramatic intensity, color, and emotional style of the dancing spirits are captured in the movement of the spirit's hands, in the intense facial concentration, and in the suggested ripple of muscles in the thighs. Displaying human skills, the spirit reenacts the Igbo metaphysical maxim "As it is above, so it is below; as it is in humans, so is it in spirits."

Toward the last decade of his life, from 1984 to 1994, Enwonwu entered a profoundly philosophical creative cycle in which questions about the metaphysical transformations of life predominated. He defined this period, in which he saw carved spirit images in the shrine as living objects, as taking him back to his father. Focusing on another spirit form, the *ogolo* (runner spirits) that are closely related to the *agbogo mmuo*, he reconciled his concept of art with intrinsic values, deep truths, and mysteries. The paintings in the "Ogolo" series, namely, *Ogolo Adonis* (1989), *Ogolo* (1989), *Ogolo in Motion* (1989), *Ogolo Emerging* (1989), and *Ogolo Metamorphosis* (1991), capture the transformational essence of life through the spirits. The linear shape of the canvases Enwonwu chose to capture the lithe, skittish spirits wonderfully accentuates the vertical, elongated forms of the *ogolo* and their long heads. They are beautiful to behold in their multicolored, appliquéd fabric, or skin, which is intersected by the black lines and geometric patterns of *uli,* or body markings.

—Nkiru Nzegwu

tions, however. His creations were largely poetic and visionary. A central issue of interest in Enwonwu's artistic goal was his elaboration of the dynamics of bodies in dance. For the better part of his sixty-year career, he prodded and pushed the tensile shape of pliant dancing forms to the limit. Dances inspired and excited him, and he produced endless sketches, paintings in oil and gouache, and sculptural forms that captured motion, rhythm, and the choreographic movements of specific African dances.

From the 1950s onward, Enwonwu recurrently explored the gestural patterns of traditional dance forms in paintings such as *Olokun, Obitan, Otu Odu*, and *Kano Dances*. His paintings, some of which are detailed studies and others of which are in semirepresentational style, explore the effect of the force of motion coursing through the entire muscular system. In the large triptych *Obitan* he attended as well to the dynamics of the relation of the virtuosic principal dancer to others in the group. His perspective reveals the processes by which the rigid volume of bodies is melted by the complex resonance and dissonance of generated rhythms. Using clean, curving lines, Enwonwu captured the melodic fluidity of principal dancers in *Obitan* and *Negritude* and in ebony sculptures like *Snake Dance*

ESSON, Tomás
Cuban painter and sculptor

Born: Juan Tomás Esson Reid, Marianao, Havana, Cuba, 8 February 1963. **Education:** Academia de Artes Plásticas San Alejandro, Havana, Cuba, 1982; Instituto Superior de Arte, Havana, Cuba, 1987. **Family:** Married Katja Kümmerle in 1994. **Address:** 120 West 25th Street, Apartment 4e, New York, New York 10001, U.S.A. **Online Address:** http://www.articons.com/ebony2/e5.html.

Individual Exhibitions:

1987   Museo Provincial de Villa Clara, Santa Clara, Cuba
1988   Centro de Arte 23 y 12, Havana, Cuba
1991   Fredric Snitzer Gallery, Miami
1993   Galeria Ramis Barquet, Art Cologne/Internationaler
           Kunstmarkt, Cologne, Germany
1995   Vrej Baghoomian Gallery, Soho, New York

Selected Group Exhibitions:

1993   Porter Troupe Gallery, Las Jolla, California
1995   Santa Barbara Museum of Art, California
           Centre de Culture Contemporánia de Barcelona, Spain
           Museo do Arte Contemporaneo de Monterrey, Mexico
           Center for the Fine Arts, Miami (traveling)
1996   Centro Atlántico de Arte Moderno, Las Palmas de Gran
           Canaria, Spain (traveling)
           Museo Contemporaneo de Monterrey, Mexico
           Drawing Center, New York
           Cambridge Multicultural Arts Center, Massachusetts
           Brewster Art, New York

Collections:

Museo de Arte Contemporaneo, Monterrey, Mexico; Museo Nacional de Bellas Artes, Havana, Cuba; Museum of Art, Fort Lauderdale, Florida; Museum of Contemporary Art, San Diego, California; John D. and Catherine T. MacArthur Foundation, Chicago; Ludwig Forum für Internationale Kunst, Aachen, Germany; Whitney Museum of American Art, New York.

Publications:

On ESSON: Articles—"A Tarro Partido, Pinturas de Tomás Esson," in *Cartelera/Revolución,* January 1988, pp. 7-13 (illustration p. 3); "Tomás Esson Confeso Delito de Alzar la Voz" by Nelson Llanes, in *Exito,* 18 December 1991, p. 58; "Tomás Esson: Sexo, Censura y Disidencia" by Diana Montanè, in *Exito,* 14 October 1992, pp. 60-61 (illustrated); "Dissident Cuban Artists Seek a New Vision in a New World" by Gonzelez Márques, in *Miami Herald,* 13 July 1992, p. 3C (illustrated); "Cuban Expatriate Artist Paints Another View of Castro Revolution" by Nancy Kaptanof, in *Los Angeles Times,* 14 February 1993, p. 85.

*

Tomás Esson comments:
Talisman will be of meat one day, fucking you and flying among us like flies.

*　　*　　*

The painter Tomás Esson is an important exponent of what has been termed "new Cuban art," the work of the iconoclastic generation of Cuban artists that emerged in the 1980s. As a postgraduate student he caused consternation with his grotesque sexual and scatological imagery. When he introduced national icons such as Fidel Castro, Ché Guevara, and the Cuban flag into his paintings, he was set on a collision course with the conservative elements within Cuba's cultural and political establishment. In his notorious *My*

Homage to Ché (1987), for instance, he challenged deeply entrenched political, sexual, and racial taboos by representing two monstrous copulating creatures in front of a portrait of Guevara as a black man.

Esson's 1988 solo exhibition at a prestigious Havana gallery, which included *My Homage to Ché,* caused major controversy and was closed within hours. After several other incidents of censorship and interference with his work, he applied for political asylum in the United States in 1991 and now lives in New York City. Several other Cuban artists of his generation have, for similar reasons, moved to Mexico, the United States, or Europe. The recent economic difficulties in Cuba and the international interest in Cuban art have contributed to this phenomenon.

Esson has stated that he wants to "represent all aspects of life through the prism of the sexual and the grotesque." He is particularly interested in the relationship between sexuality, aggression, and power, which he explores with a subversive, hyperbolic machismo that flies in the face of intolerance and hypocritical political correctness. His paintings are disturbing and provocative, although their satirical overtones should not be overlooked.

Although Esson's works defy description, they are easily recognizable. Many paintings represent bloated, often cruelly mutilated bestial figures with liquid or gaseous substances spurting from various orifices. Inanimate objects and vegetal forms receive similar treatment and assume grotesque sexual characteristics. One recurrent motif, which Esson calls his talisman, has obvious personal significance and is often used in combination with recognizable self-images. It is a red-and-black, horned, kidney-shaped object that comes in male and female variants. Although usually found in compromising situations (Kellie Jones has described it as a "scatological anti-hero"), the talisman occasionally appears on its own surrounded by a halo of light, a surprising token of the transcendental in Esson's profane iconography.

No matter how raw and repulsive certain images are, Esson's paintings are strangely seductive as they explore our often unacknowledged fascination with the grotesque. His imposing canvases also seduce the viewer with their sensual painterliness. Such ambivalence is found in the work of James Ensor, an artist Esson greatly admires. Esson is also an accomplished draftsman, and the same contradictions apply to his drawings.

Moving to the United States inevitably affected Esson's work, although his general interests have not changed significantly. While he could have exploited his status as a Cuban defector, especially when he lived in Miami, Florida, the political references soon vanished from his work, although only after a few punches at the American flag. With the exception of ironic, "exotic" titles like *Chá-chá-chá* (1993) and *Chiribamba* (1992), explicit references to his Cuban background have also largely disappeared.

For a while the theme of violence became more prominent in Esson's work, and violent acts such as whipping the canvas became part of the creative process, as in *Riding Crop* (1993). In his recent "wet" paintings and drawings, his attention has again shifted to the erotic and the representation of liquidity and wetness, which has always fascinated him. These works also epitomize Esson's remarkable mastery of the painting medium, now enhanced by his access to good art materials.

—Veerle Poupeye

EVANS, Minnie

American painter

Born: Long Creek (Pender County), North Carolina, 1890. **Family:** Married Julius Evans in 1908, three sons. **Career:** Gate attendant, Airlie Gardens, Wilmington, North Carolina. **Died:** 19 December 1987.

Individual Exhibitions:

1966	Church of the Epiphany, New York (retrospective)
1970	Portal Gallery, London
1975	Whitney Museum of American Art, New York
1977	Roko Gallery, New York
1980	St. John's Museum of Art, Wilmington, North Carolina
1981	Wake Forest University Fine Arts Gallery, Winston-Salem, North Carolina
1986	North Carolina Museum of Art, Raleigh

Selected Group Exhibitions:

1976	Los Angeles County Museum of Art (traveling)
1981	Southern Arts Federation, Atlanta, Georgia (traveling)
	Center for the Visual Arts Gallery, Illinois State University, Normal (traveling)
1982	Anderson Gallery, Virginia Commonwealth University, Richmond
1983	Museum of American Folk Art, New York
	IBM Gallery of Science and Art, New York
1985	Hickory Museum of Art, North Carolina
1988	High Museum of Art at Georgia-Pacific Center, Atlanta, Georgia
1989	New Visions Gallery of Contemporary Art, Atlanta, Georgia
	African-American Museum, Hempstead, Long Island, New York

Collections:

Ackland Art Museum, University of North Carolina at Chapel Hill; High Museum of Art, Atlanta, Georgia; Museum of American Folk Art, New York; National Museum of American Art, Washington, D.C.; Newark Museum, Newark, New Jersey; North Carolina Museum of History, Raleigh; Schomburg Center, New York; Weatherspoon Art Gallery, University of North Carolina, Greensboro; Whitney Museum of American Art, New York.

Publications:

On EVANS: Book—*Minnie Evans: Artist,* exhibition catalog, North Carolina, Wellington Gray Gallery, East Carolina University, 1993. **Film**—*The Angel That Stands By Me: Minnie Evans Paintings,* San Francisco, 1983.

*   *   *

The paintings of Minnie Evans represent scenes from a private dreamworld envisioned by, but not entirely comprehensible to, only the artist herself. Through oral tradition Evans traced her ancestry to a female slave taken to Wilmington, North Carolina, from Trinidad. Although Evans never traveled to the island (she never left North Carolina before 1966, when she went to New York City for the opening of her first solo exhibition), there are elements in her art that invite comparison with Caribbean folk art forms.

Evans's complex designs reveal the unaccountable presence of Caribbean, East Indian, Chinese, and Western elements in color and subject matter. Her own explanation of the basis for her work was that her art came from nations that were destroyed before the Flood of the Old Testament and that God gave it to her to return to the world.

Always a dreamer, Evans stated that the origins of her paintings were in her subconscious state of mind. The dreamworld of Evans produced its earliest visual manifestations on Good Friday 1925, when she completed her first two drawings. These two small pen-and-ink drawings are dominated by numerous curvilinear rhythms and overall surface patterns. Evans always placed a great deal of significance on these drawings without understanding why they were important.

Evans's earliest paintings were executed entirely in wax crayons, and they resemble an exercise employing every color in a gigantic box of Crayolas. The colors include greens shaded from light to medium to deep; purples from mauve to pink, rose, and royal; and full ranges of reds, blues, and yellows, with only a sparing use of black and white. She also produced a small number of oil paintings that used more subdued colors than the better-known wax crayon designs.

For many years Evans worked as the attendant at the admission gate at Airlie Gardens near Wilmington. Her close proximity to the botanical specimens in the gardens was undoubtedly reflected in the bright colors and numerous floral motifs that appear in many of her paintings.

The genesis for a number of Evans's paintings is a human face surrounded by curvilinear and spiral plant and animal forms. The ubiquitous eyes in Evans's paintings, which merge with foliate patterns, are equated with the omniscience of God and with the concept of the eye as the window of the soul. The figures in the paintings are portraits of ancient wise men and women who peopled her visions, ancestral visitors from a spiritual order, or angels, demons, and chimerical creatures. Her paintings are essentially religious in inspiration and represent a world in which God, man, and nature are synonymous. In Evans's works God is frequently represented as a winged figure with a wide multicolored collar and a rainbow halo. He is surrounded by a proliferation of eyes, butterflies, trees, other plants, and floral forms in a paradisiacal garden of brilliant colors, all contained within a cartouchelike frame of curvilinear rhythms.

Evans also completed a small group of crayon drawings that she called the "funny animal" series. The soft tones used in these drawings, as well as the sensitive modeling of the animal figures and the simplicity of the compositions, place them in a unique category among her works.

Around 1966 Evans began creating collage paintings by cutting out her earlier wax crayon designs, pasting then to a canvas board or cardboard background, and using them in combination with oils and watercolors. Some of Evans's earliest collage paintings feature a single crayon design in the center of the composition. This central motif is flanked by similar symmetrical, curvilinear, foliated, and ocular forms executed in watercolors, which creates a more expansive mixed-media design. Evans's later collage paintings incorporate as many as three wax crayon designs in an approximately pyramidal grouping on a rectangular background. The remaining space is filled with colorful floral, plant, and hybrid forms of the artist's dreamworld, which does not exist in the objective realm.

The paintings and colored drawing of Evans are surrealistic without intellectualism or a conscious aesthetic. They are the works of a talented naive artist and a visionary who equated God with nature, color with his divine presence, and dreams and visions with reality. The world as depicted in Evans's psychic revelations is a sacred province of complex visionary forms: angels, demons, hybrid plants, animals, Christ's face surrounded by rainbows, his crucifixion against a background of shooting comets and falling stars, walled temples on the shores of restless seas, and the all-seeing eyes of God.

There are no parallels in the history of art for Evans's personal images. While her paintings initially appear to be entirely whimsical, the majority of them express the omnipotence of God and were the results of visions that allowed her to transcend the barrier between reality and fantasy.

—Regenia A. Perry

EVERSLEY, Frederick

American sculptor

Born: Brooklyn, New York, 28 August 1941. **Education:** Carnegie-Mellon University, Pittsburgh, Pennsylvania, 1959-63, B.S.E.E. 1963. **Career:** Project engineer, WYCE Labs, El Segundo, California, 1993-67. Since 1967 freelance artist. **Awards:** First Purchase Prize, Fourth Annual California Small Images Exhibition, California State College at Los Angeles, 1970; Purchase Prize, Tenth Annual Southern California Exhibition, Long Beach Museum of Art, 1972; National Endowment for the Arts Fellowship, Washington, D.C., 1972; First Artist in Residence, Smithsonian Institution, Washington, D.C. **Address:** 29 Mercer Street, New York, New York 10013, U.S.A. **Online Address:** fredever@bigfoot.com.

Individual Exhibitions:

1970   Phyllis Kind Gallery, Chicago
   Whitney Museum of American Art, New York
   O.K. Harris Gallery, New York
   Jack Glenn Gallery, Corona Del Mar, California
1971   Morgan Gallery, Kansas City, Missouri
   Quay Gallery, San Francisco
1973   J.L. Hudson Gallery, Detroit
1975   Andrew Crispo Gallery, New York
1976   National Academy of Science, Washington, D.C.
   Los Angeles Institute of Contemporary Art, Los Angeles
   Santa Barbara Museum, California
   Newport Harbor Art Museum, Newport Beach, California
1977   Oakland Museum of Art, California
   Quay Gallery, San Francisco
1978   Palm Springs Desert Museum, California
1981   National Academy of Science, Washington, D.C.
   American Institute of Architects, Washington, D.C.
1982   Pepperdine University Art Gallery, Malibu, California

Frederick Eversley: *Parabolic Flight,* 1980.

1983   Braunstein Gallery, San Francisco
1984   Bacardi Art Gallery, Miami
1985   Loyola Marymount University, Los Angeles
1988   Hokin Gallery, Palm Beach and Bal Harbor, Florida
1991   Eve Cohon Gallery, Chicago
1992   Lorenzelli Arte, Milan, Italy

Selected Group Exhibitions:

1969   Limited Editions Gallery, California State College of Los Angeles
1970   Milwaukee Art Museum, Wisconsin
1971   Aldrich Museum of Contemporary Art, Ridgefield, Connecticut
   Rath Museum, Geneva, Switzerland
1972   Richmond Art Center, California
   Whitney Museum of American Art, New York
1976   San Francisco Museum of Art
1978   Solomon R. Guggenheim Museum, New York
1987   Merging One Gallery, Santa Monica, California
1995   National Museum of American Art, Smithsonian Institution, Washington, D.C.

Frederick Eversley.

Collections:

California State College at Los Angeles; Cranbrook Art Gallery, Bloomfield Hills, Michigan; Currier Gallery of Art, Manchester, New Hampshire; Fisher Gallery, University of Southern California, Los Angeles; Guggenheim Museum, New York; Laguna Art Museum, Laguna Beach, California; Long Beach Museum of Art, California; Massachusetts Institute of Technology, Cambridge; Milwaukee Art Museum, Wisconsin; Museum of Contemporary Art, Los Angeles; National Academy of Science, Washington, D.C.; National Museum of American Art, Washington, D.C.; Neuberger Museum of Art, Purchase, New York; Newport Harbor Art Museum, Newport Beach, California; Oakland Art Museum, California; Palm Springs Desert Museum, California; Rose Museum of Art, Brandeis University, Boston; Smith College Museum of Art, Northhampton, Massachusetts; Smithsonian Institution, Washington, D.C.; Taft Museum of Art, Cincinnati, Ohio; University of Kansas Art Gallery, Lawrence; Whitney Museum of American Art, New York.

Publications:

On EVERSLEY: Articles—"Eversley Show in New York" by Henry J. Seldis, in *Los Angeles Times,* 8 June 1970; "Fred Eversley Retrospective" by Laurie H. Glass, in *Artweek,* 26 March 1977, p. 16; "Interview Frederick Eversley" by Peggy Loar, in *Ocular,* 5(2), Summer Quarter, 1980; "Eversley Revives the Finish Fetish Mode" by Kristine McKenna, in *Los Angeles Time,* 2 October 1985.

*

Frederick Eversley comments:

Art to me should ideally be universal in content, understanding, and appeal, self-contained in the sense of not requiring external explanation or interpretation, and it should actively interact with and involve the spectator and his environment. It should ideally cause the spectator to transcend the intrinsic nature of the object itself and combine with memories of past experiences to create a new subjective perceptual act. Thus the perceptual act becomes a self-referential subjective experience with the spectator's perceptual cognition being energized by the object of art.

My early works were involved with using art as a phenomenon as opposed to using art as a language, and as such I am dealing with real energies, forces, space, time, and matter. I am attempting to use phenomena as a means of focusing the spectator into perceiving the complex nature of reality, both physical and social, and through these perceptions, forming new kinds of subjective meanings and higher awareness. My current works combine phenomena with language to focus the spectator towards specific social topics.

An important aesthetic criteria is for the art object to be so immediately engaging for the spectator that it demands instant and close attention and study. I try to achieve this goal by making the object obviously beautiful and seductive, an instant eye-catcher, and by creating an instant interaction between the object, the spectator, and the surrounding environment. If the spectator is drawn into contemplating the obvious aspects of the object, it is hoped this involvement will cause perception of the more subtle and mystical elements and their interaction with the viewer and surroundings. The goal of my early pieces of sculpture was to create kinetic art without using kinetic elements such as mechanical movement or artificial light changes. I preferred to employ natural changes in light, the environment, and the spectator to create the kinetic effects. Energy concerns, both physical and metaphysical, formed the intellectual and aesthetics basis for these artworks. Since the original and ultimate source of all energy on earth is that derived from the sun, my sculpture efforts were directly influenced by the concepts of this energy source but are representative of the broad sense of energies. A study of energy naturally leads one to consider the creation of, the transcendental nature of, and the eventual transformation of the universe. My current works utilize my classic sculpture forms as control devices for multi-media computer systems to interactively introduce direct language and images of socially relevant subjects.

*   *   *

Frederick Eversley's work is a blend of several abstractionist styles of the 1960s. His sculptures are created from cast, color-tinted polyester resin that is then carved and polished into sleek spherical and concave shapes of varying sizes. For example, *Untitled* (1970), which resembles a large cushion, is four feet in diameter. *Oblique Prism II* (1977), a much smaller piece (only six inches in diameter), is a hollowed-out cylinder cut at an angle. Polyester resin is a relatively unexplored medium in which the artist can control the intensity of color, degree of opacity or transparency, and shape.

Eversley's sculptures change their appearance as the viewer moves around them or changes the viewing angle. Although his works resemble kinetic sculpture, the movement is made by the viewer, not the sculpture. A sense of movement is also created by the interaction between the amount and type of light (factors determined by the environment in which the sculpture rests) and the particular physical structure of the piece. In addition, the appearance of the environment can be altered by the way in which the viewer interacts with the sculpture. The sculpture also can act as a lens or a mirror, and it can impart color to its surroundings.

Eversley typically uses three colors—violet, amber, and blue. The intensity of the color is determined by the thickness of the resin, and the hue is controlled by the color or combination of colors the viewer peers through. One cylindrically shaped sculpture, also called *Untitled* (1970), appears to have numerous shapes contained within it. The sculpture, whose base is round, tapers off at the top to create a four-sided figure; two sides are flat, while the others appear as points and the very top edge is notched. These seemingly simple physical features control the reflection of the light and, along with the internal arrangement of color, create a complex and intriguing effect.

One modern artist who has influenced Eversley is Larry Bell, whose vacuum-plated glass cubes—for example, *Memories of Mike* (1967)—reflect continuously changing light and color. Nonetheless, in form Eversley's sculptures are an expression of the pure representation of the basic shapes used in classical art: sphere, cone, and cylinder. Similar to the hard-edge paintings of Kenneth Noland, in which the painting is the form, Eversley's works use form as an entity for its own sake. In Noland's art, however, the form sometimes extends beyond the canvas, there is no background or foreground, and different perspective illusions are created.

Eversley has worked extensively with plastics, and his pieces reflect his background in engineering and photography. Many of his sculptures have been included in exhibitions focusing on the connection between art and technology. His sculptures often provoke the viewer to think of science fiction, something otherworldly, art as it might be found in outer space.

—Christine Miner Minderovic

FAKEYE, Lamidi (Olonade)
Nigerian sculptor

Born: Ila-Orangun, Oyo State, Nigeria, 1928. **Education:** Began carving under father's tutelage; apprenticed for three years to sculptor George Bandele (Bamidele, son of Areogun); attended Father Kevin Carroll's sculpture workshop, Oye-Ekiti, Nigeria, 1947-51; studied stone carving, École des Beaux Arts, Paris, 1962-63. **Career:** Lecturer, United States, 1963-66. Artist-in-residence/visiting international scholar, Western Michigan University, Kalamazoo, 1966, 1983, Obafemi Awolowo University, Ile-Ife, Nigeria; visiting art fellow, Department of Fine Arts, University of Ife, Ile-Ife, Nigeria, 1978. Worked for University of Ibadan, Western House of Assembly, and numerous European and American Galleries. **Awards:** Order of the Federal Republic of Nigeria, 1960. **Address:** Department of Fine Arts, Obafemi Awolowo University, Ile-Ife, Oshun State, Nigeria.

Individual Exhibitions:

1949   British Council, Lagos and Ibadan, Nigeria
1961   British Council, Ibadan, Nigeria
1986   American Cultural Center, Ibadan, Nigeria
1987   Western Michigan University, Kalamazoo (retrospective)

Selected Group Exhibitions:

1965   *Commonwealth Arts Festival,* Royal Festival Hall, London
1966   *First World Festival of Negro Arts,* Dakar, Senegal
1969   Camden Arts Centre, London
1973   University of Ife, Ile-Ife, Nigeria
1974   University of Lagos
        Field Museum of Natural History, Chicago
1977   FESTAC '77, Lagos
1980   Tropenmuseum, Amsterdam
1982   Ohio State University, Columbus
1990   Kauffman Museum, Bethel College, North Newton, Kansas

Collections:

Carl Van Vechten Gallery of Fine Arts, Fisk University, Nashville; Federal Ministry of Information, Cultural Division, Lagos; Hampton University Museum, Hampton, Virginia; National Museum of African Art, Washington, D.C.; Oxford University, England; Seattle Art Museum; Studio Museum in Harlem, New York.

Publications:

By FAKEYE: Books—*Lamidi Olonade Fakeye: African Sculptor of the Twentieth Century* and *Recent Works by Lamidi O. Fakeye* (with Bruce Haight), exhibition catalogs, Kalamazoo, Michigan, Western Michigan University, 1987 (illustrated; some color).

On FAKEYE: Books—*American Cultural Center Presents Lamidi Fakeye,* exhibition catalog, Ibadan, Nigeria, American Cultural Center, 1986; *Yoruba Images: Essays in Honour of Lamidi Fakeye,* Ile-Ife, Nigeria, Ife Humanities Society (Ife Humanities Monograph Series, no. 3), 1988. **Articles**—"Complicated Carver: Lamidi Fakeye Exhibition in Ibadan," in *West African Review* (London), 31, June 1960, p. 30-37; "Portrait—Fakeye, Lamidi," in *West Africa* (London), 53, 1969, p. 551 (illustrated); "Lamidi Fakeye: Nigerian Traditional Sculptor" by Titus A. Ogunwale, in *African Arts* (Los Angeles), 4(2), Winter 1971, pp. 66-67; "An African Sculptor at Work" by Frank Willett, in *African Arts* (Los Angeles), 11(2), January 1978, pp. 28-33, 96 (illustrated; bibliography).

*   *   *

A descendant of five generations of woodcarvers, Lamidi Olanade Fakeye employs the forms, themes, and idioms of traditional Yoruba culture in his architectural and freestanding sculptures. He was born around 1928 and came of age at a time in Nigerian history when, much despised because of their associations with non-Christian beliefs, traditional art objects were burned and destroyed by colonial missionaries and zealous Nigerian converts to Christianity. Conversely, in the decades that immediately preceded and followed Nigerian independence, intellectuals, politicians, and artists preoccupied themselves with rediscovering and perpetuating Nigeria's past cultural heritage and discussing how it could be synthesized with their modern circumstances. Many of Fakeye's academically trained peers working in a variety of media focused heavily on this synthesis of the past with the present, the African with the Western. Fakeye chose to adhere strictly to traditional Yoruba models.

Both his great-grandfather Gbongunjoko and his father, Akobi Ogun Fakeye, were noted woodcarvers from Ila-Orangun near Oshogbo. Under the tutelage of his father and older brother, Fakeye was carving toys and small household utensils in the family style by age ten. He was later inspired by the carvings at the palace of the Oloja of Oro by the late Aerogun (Arowogun), a renowned Yoruba carver from Osi-ILorin. In 1948, shortly following his discovery of these works, Fakeye met and later apprenticed for Aerogun's son David Ole Bandele (Bamidele), a woodcarver for the Catholic mission workshop in Oye-Ekiti. Frank Willet wrote in *African Art* that Aerogun's style is characterized by smoothly carved low-relief figures with large eyes and ears that dominate their faces. At the end of Fakeye's three-year apprenticeship, his style had changed, and his works no longer resembled his earlier family style but reflected the Osi style of his master, whose relief sculptures are noted for their boldness and depth.

The cultural rediscovery that was building during the 1950s blossomed into a Nigerian renaissance in the 1960s and 1970s. Modern architecture played an important role in this renaissance by revitalizing and sustaining traditional architectural woodcarving. During the fifteen years of Fakeye's association with the mission workshops in Oye-Ekiti and later as a master carver in Ondo, he worked on numerous public commissions ranging from doors, portals, veranda posts, and furniture carved with depictions of religious and secular folklore for Catholic churches, hospitals, Nigerian royalty, governmental edifices, and universities to smaller sculptures of the *orisha* for private patrons.

Although the majority of his public projects during the mission years were doors and portals for churches, his first major commission was two large veranda posts and tow doors for the Edena gatehouse at the Oni's palace in Ife, carved in 1953. On the doors he depicted scenes from Yoruba folklore, one of which is a warrior on horseback escorting a prisoner, a popular image in traditional Yoruba carving. Four years later he completed a series of door panels and portal for a church in Oke-Padi, Ibadan. It is interesting to compare Fakeye's different manners for composing and rendering the figures in these Yoruba and Christian scenes. In the panel *Christ among the Elders* from Oke-Padi, the figures, carved in low relief, are rigid with mechanically synchronized poses and awkwardly outstretched hands. Although their faces and Mary's hair exhibit some of the classic Yoruba traits (e.g., prominent ears and bulging eyes), they are more naturalistic in appearance. In contrast, the figures from the Edena panel are voluminous; they seem almost carved in the round. And though their features and stances are iconic, there is a more fluid movement across the panel. In this panel the most important figures are large, and as is characteristic of traditional Yoruba carving, the least important are dwarfed—in this case it is the prisoner. The figures from Oke-Padi have more or less natural proportions and relationships to each other.

By the 1980s the era of large public commissions had waned, and Fakeye started working primarily on small sculptures and freestanding panel reliefs of the *orisha* and folklore for private collectors and gallery exhibitions. By this time he had studied rock-carving at the Cité Université in Besancon and the L'École des Beaux Arts in Paris, traveled and had exhibitions and important commissions in the United States and Europe, and become a staff member in the Department of Fine Arts at Obafemi Awolowo University. Even with his mission training, travel to Europe and the United States, and conversion to Islam, Fakeye's subject matter, forms, and themes remained consistent with the classic Yoruba idioms of his ancestors. He continued innovating tradition in his highly finished, adeptly carved original compositions.

—Regina L. Woods

FAVORITE, Malaika
American painter and printmaker

Work also appeared under the names Barbara Ann Favorite, Bobbie Malaika Favorite, Barbara Favorite Kellman. **Born:** Barbara Ann Favorite, Geismar, Louisiana, 7 February 1949. **Education:** Louisiana State University, Baton Rouge, Louisiana, 1967-73, B.F.A. 1971, M.F.A. 1973. **Family:** Married 1) Wellington J. Walker in 1972 (divorced 1973); 2) Lewen Anthony Kellman in 1988 (divorced 1993, remarried in 1995). **Career:** Instructor of art, Grambling State University,

Grambling, Louisiana, 1973-75, 1976-78, Louisiana State University, Baton Rouge, Louisiana, 1987-89, Augusta College, Augusta, Georgia, 1989-93. Artist-in-residence, Assumption Parish Schools, Napoleonville, Louisiana, 1975-76, Episcopal High School, Baton Rouge, Louisiana, 1978-84, Baton Rouge Arts Council, Louisiana, 1993-95. **Awards:** Grant, African American Institute, 1975; Fulbright-Hays Award, 1978; painting grant, Georgia Council for the Arts, 1992. **Agent:** Camille Love Gallery, 309 East Paces Ferry Road, Suite 120, Atlanta, Georgia 30305.

Individual Exhibitions:

1984	Posselt Baker Gallery, New Orleans
1985	Posselt Baker Gallery, New Orleans
1986	Posselt Baker Gallery, New Orleans
1988	Zigler Museum, Jennings, Louisiana
	Baton Rouge Gallery, Louisiana
1989	Posselt Baker Gallery, New Orleans
1990	Galerie Melancon, Lake Charles, Louisiana
1993	Paine College Library Gallery, Augusta, Georgia
	Augusta College Gallery, Augusta, Georgia
	Davis Art Gallery, Stephens College, Columbia, Missouri
1996	Camille Love Gallery, Atlanta, Georgia

Selected Group Exhibitions:

1984	Contemporary Arts Center, New Orleans
	Southeastern Louisiana University Gallery, Hammond
1985	Contemporary Arts Center, New Orleans
1986	Contemporary Arts Center, New Orleans
	Arnold Blackmon Hales, Houston
	Scripps College Gallery, Claremont, California
	Museum of African American Art, Los Angeles

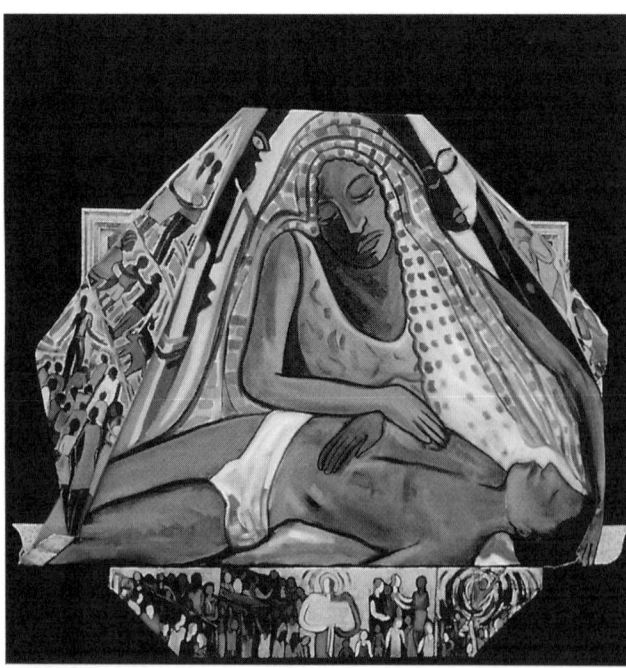

Malaika Favorite: *Pieta of South Africa,* **1991.**

1987   Contemporary Arts Center, New Orleans
1992   International Marian Research Institute, University of
        Dayton, Ohio
1996   Georgia Southern University Gallery, Statesboro
        150 Franklin Street Gallery, Harrisonburg, Virginia

Collections:

Alexandria Museum of Art, Louisiana; Louisiana State University
Print Collection, Baton Rouge, Louisiana; Lucey Laney Walker
Museum, Augusta, Georgia; Morris Museum of Art, Augusta,
Georgia; National Ecumenical Museum of Art, St. Louis, Missouri;
River Road African American Museum, Burnside, Louisiana; St.
Margaret's Catholic Church, Lake Charles, Louisiana.

Publications:

By FAVORITE: Books—*Illuminated Manuscript,* (poetry and
prints), New Orleans Poetry Journal Press, 1991. **Articles**—"Portrait of Self Contemplating Self," in *Sage* (Atlanta, Georgia), 1987;
"Tempting the Muse," "Black Women Artists in the American
South," both in *Gallerie* (Vancouver, Canada), 1990; "A Colored
Name, " in *New Orleans Review,* 1994. **Stories**—Two short stories, *African American Review* (Indiana), 1993.

On FAVORITE: Articles—"Malaika Favorite" by Karla Heusner,
in *International Review of African American Art* (Los Angeles),
1987; "Malaika Favorite: The Search for God" by Jim Grissom, in
Rouge (Baton Rouge), October/November 1988.

*

Malaika Favorite comments:

   My work is presently a journey between two and three dimensional surfaces. Though I consider myself a painter, I often explore
painting on relief and three dimensional surfaces. I suppose that
deep down I wanted to be a sculptor, but I could never find the
medium that was right for me. My first experiment in this form was
to attach cloth to washboards and build a painting around that
structure. The results were exciting and pushed me in a whole new
direction. In 1985, I started painting on folded canvas surfaces.
What I mean is I started creasing and folding planes in the unprimed
canvas, and then primed it with gesso, thus sealing the creases in
place. This became a predefined surface that limited but structured
what I could say in the space provided. It became a challenge to me
to work with this structured form and dare myself to create within
and around it. I then started working with the idea that if I could
fasten canvas to frame or stretcher then I could also decide what
other surfaces I could tack it to, such as chairs and found objects. I
had a good idea of the possibilities available to me and started
exploring.
   Right now, I continue my journey of exploration and investigation. While I use the same story ideas in paint the kind of surface
helps me to give a greater depth to the story I am trying to tell. This
exploration has led me to consider working with a variety of objects
such as plastic bottles, coffee pots, dress forms, and whatever else
excites me. The pallet is limitless. My best inspiration in this search
is the work of self-taught artists. They never seem to have a limit in
terms of what they can use to create with. I remember seeing bottles
painted by Clementine Hunter that made me laugh but also gave me

Malaika Favorite: *Mother & Child* **from "The People of Color"
series, 1995.**

a tinge of envy. From viewing works by many self-taught artists, I
saw that they, like our African ancestors never asked, "Will this
last forever? Will the art critics approve? Is this really art?" They
instead worked with a passion that consumed whatever their hands
touched, and made it into a statement that reflects and transcends
our times.

*   *   *

   The art of Malaika Favorite is as imaginative as it is grounded in
the reality of the everyday lives of African American women. In
many of her pieces she abandons such traditional tools of artists as
the paintbrush and canvas in favor of unconventional materials like
washboards, fabric, metal, and remnants of wood, turning this
mélange into sculptures that reveal her concerns about the world.
   Favorite's formal training took place in her home state of Louisiana, where she earned bachelor's and master's degrees in fine arts at
Louisiana State University in Baton Rouge. Now based in Atlanta,
Georgia, Favorite has exhibited her work throughout the South, and
her paintings and sculptures are held in private collections in the
United States and Europe.
   Favorite began using unconventional materials in the early and
lean years of her career, when she first struck out on her own as an
artist, and they soon became her trademark. "I went through a
period when all I wanted to do was create art. I began draping cloth
on things like washboards," Favorite has said. "It opened my eyes
to other possibilities. And when I was able to buy supplies again,
there was no turning back." She created the work *The Flag Needs a
Washing,* for example, by stitching bits of canvas together and
applying paint over a washboard. The work speaks to her views on
social and political matters related to African Americans and women
in particular.
   Women are a recurring theme in Favorite's work, although she
says that this is not a "conscious choice." A recent body of work,
"Women's Group," also referred to as "A Quilt Study of Women of

Color," consists of a series of ten oil paintings on wood panels. The works are rich in color, and some of them feature triangular shapes with a three-dimensional quality. She often uses extended hands in the paintings to show the strength of women and their role as the backbone of family life. The painting *Women of Color,* for example, shows hands holding a paint pan, and in *Mother of Color* she accentuates the hands of a figure holding a child. "My paintings reflect the nurturing quality of women, their sensitivity to the needs of the family and in the community," Favorite once said of her work.

In "Homebody" women in different stages of life are featured in a series of similar, connected houses that seem to suggest a oneness and sisterhood shared by African American women. Each of the pieces in the series tells a women's story in vibrant, intricately crafted images.

Favorite said in the beginning of her career that she would do battle with her work. But after more than twenty years as an artist, the paintbrush has taken the lead. "I learned that the painting had the right to lead me. It is very exciting and it shows my maturity as an artist," she has said. Favorite has continued to evolve as an artist as she moves from one medium to the next. Whether it is a painting, a sculpture, or a work crafted from conventional art supplies or nontraditional materials, all of her pieces speak of her life and of the lives of other African American women.

—Coria Holland

FENI, Mhlaba Zwelidumile Mgxaji
South African sculptor

Also known as Dumile. **Born:** Worcester, Cape Province, South Africa. **Family:** Married Fazile, two children. **Died:** 16 October 1991.

Individual Exhibition:

1966   Gallery 101, Johannesburg

Collection:

Voices from Exile, Washington, D.C.

Feni in his studio, c. 1989. Photo courtesy of Carole Storch-Dladla and Edward Dladla.

Mhlaba Zwelidumile Mgxaji Feni, known widely among friends and colleagues as Dumile, was born in Worcester, a town in Cape Province in South Africa. (Dumile's first name appears in some records as Mslaba, a variant transliteration from the Xhosa.) He later lived as a political refugee in England and the United States, and he died in New York City. His wife, Fazile, and two children remained in South Africa.

Dumile was a member of the large community of exiles from South Africa who, during the decades of the 1970s and 1980s, looked forward to the time they could safely return home. Many of those living in New York gravitated to the residence of Carole Storch-Dladla and Edward Dladla, where they found a home in the intervening time. It is unfortunate that Dumile died prematurely and did not live to enjoy the opportunity of returning to his native South Africa.

Dumile studied art and developed his skills in South Africa. He became adept in sculpture and pottery, and, more important, he learned to work in metal at the foundry of Block and Leo Wald in Jeppe in the Transvaal.

Dumile's work, which consists largely of line drawings and sculptures, is distinctive in style and content. Among the images that commonly appear are humans, some with multiple heads, fantastic animals, and creatures that combine both animal and human features. The humans are rendered in a cubist style. One of his two-dimensional works became the cover for the Hugh Masekela album *Home Is Where the Music Is*.

The art of Dumile stands as a political and humanistic statement. He created many of his works as pointed protests against apartheid, the system that led to his exile. He was a member of and activist in the African National Congress (A.N.C.). One important work, *The Pathfinder Mural,* a large public mural (now destroyed) in the West Village in New York, was the product of a collaborative effort. His art is in many private and public collections in Europe, Africa, and North America.

Dumile struggled to survive as an artist in exile. He worked briefly in academic settings as a teacher of art. He was, for example, associated with the African Humanities Institute at the University of California at Los Angeles, and he became a visiting lecturer at the Massachusetts College of Art. In addition, many people generously supplemented Dumile's own efforts. One of the people who was especially helpful was Sir Granville Gray, a patron at the United Nations.

Dumile is remembered as being constantly at work on his art. He was also an avid and animated storyteller. He was extroverted and gregarious, at ease with many different groups of people. The image one has of Dumile is of a man with pen and pad in hand, surrounded by a group of people, telling an animated story, his long dreadlocks swinging as he made a dramatic point.

The memorial service for Dumile was held at New York's Schomburg Center for Research in Black Culture. Among those who officiated were his fellow sculptor Mel Edwards, represented by wife Jayne Cortez, and the printmaker Bob Blackburn. True his given name—Zwelidumile, which in Xhosa means "known all over the world"—Dumile had acquired international fame at the time of his death.

—Thomas M. Shaw

FERGUSON, Amos

Bahamian painter

Born: Exuma, Bahamas, 1920. **Career:** Sign and house painter.

Individual Exhibitions:

1985	Wadsworth Atheneum, Hartford, Connecticut (traveling)
	Alexander Gallery, Atlanta, Georgia
1988	Ute Stebich Gallery, Lenox, Massachusetts
1989	Popularis Gallery, San Antonio, Texas

Collections:

Brooklyn Children's Museum, Brooklyn, New York; DuSable Museum of African-American History, Chicago; Museum of International Folk Art, Museum of New Mexico, Santa Fe; Studio Museum in Harlem, New York; Wadsworth Atheneum, Hartford, Connecticut; Waterloo Municipal Galleries, Waterloo, Iowa.

Publications:

On FERGUSON: Book—*Paint by Mr. Amos Ferguson* by Ute Stebich, Hartford, Connecticut, Wadsworth Atheneum, 1984.

*   *   *

The Bahamian painter Amos Ferguson fits squarely into the group sometimes called visionary artists. Their inspiration comes from their deeply held religious beliefs, and because they have no formal training, their work is highly individualistic. Like his counterparts in the United States—Minnie Evans, Howard Finster, and Sister Gertrude Morgan—Ferguson paints what and when God tells him to.

Ferguson, a Baptist, received a call from God, albeit in a nephew's dream and not in his own. How painting pictures can show God to viewers is made clear by the dream content, Ferguson says: "He's trying to let people know to live by what He gives them, like what he give me"—the ability to paint. Harry Bober of the Institute of Fine Arts at New York University places Ferguson in the tradition of the Middle Ages. Bober has compared Ferguson to the medieval legend of the juggler who worshiped the Virgin with his only talent, juggling. God sends Ferguson a vision, complete with colors and subject. If this occurs during a dream, he may get up and "do a little mark, a little scribble." In the morning he then works from the scribble. "I just cherish what the Lord can do. You don't know how I feel when something like that comes to me and I can paint. I say: 'Thank you Jesus.' "

Ferguson, a retired sign and house painter, at first painted scenes of the flowers and birds of the Bahamas as souvenirs for tourists. He still uses the flat opaque paint of his former profession for his larger works, which include stories from the Bible, landscapes with flora and fauna, street scenes, and people at work and play. Fantasy, in the form of mermaids, also sometimes enters his work. His brush strokes are broad and flat, and he uses unmixed colors. For the most part Ferguson paints large flat shapes, omitting perspective and texture, as in *Nativity* and *Jesus and Peter Walking on the Sea of Gaillee* [sic] *and Peter*

Amos Ferguson: *Girl in Garden Yellow*. Photo by Manu Sassoonian; courtesy of the Schomburg Center for Research in Black Culture.

FLEET, Thomas, slave of

American printmaker

Active during the 1720s.

*   *   *

Commonly overlooked in the art world are the slave artisans and craftspeople. Slaves were often trained as blacksmiths, printers, potters, seamstresses, carpenters, and weavers. Most of these "artists" were anonymous and rarely, if ever, received credit for their accomplishments. In many cases the slave and master maintained a working relationship in which the master profited from the slave's products. In other instances the master hired the slave out for a fee or the slave was allowed to work elsewhere with a portion of his salary given to the master. The work of the slave artisans was an important part of the colonial economy. Although people who became slaves were stripped of their culture, their sense of design and use of certain colors and motifs reveal their heritage.

Thomas Fleet, a printer who came to Boston from England in 1721, obtained three slaves (possibly in 1724), a father and two sons, to work in his printing establishment. The father, who was unnamed, and his sons, Pompey and Caesar, were taught to engrave wood blocks and set type. According to Isaiah Thomas, who wrote a book entitled *History of Printing in America* (1810), the father was exceptionally skillful, and his work adorned numerous books and ballads composed by Fleet. Though little is known about the father, his work is an important reminder that many of the artifacts from the pre-Civil War era were made by anonymous slaves.

—Christine Miner Minderovic

FLEMING, Sherman

American performance artist and painter

Also performed under the name RodForce and Generator Exchange. **Born:** Sherman I. Fleming, Jr., Hampton, Virginia, 13 September 1953. **Education:** Virginia Commonwealth University, Richmond, 1971-75, B.F.A. 1975; Hartford Art School, Connecticut, 1975-77, M.F.A. 1977. **Career:** Assistant director, Montpelier Cultural Art Center, Laurel, Maryland, 1982-87. Since 1987 art teacher, Washington International School, Washington, D.C. **Address:** 2400 Sixteenth Street, N.W., #439, Washington, D.C. 20009, U.S.A.

Individual Performances:

1978	*Shavesharp,* National Gallery of Art, Washington, D.C.
1980	*Cold Sweat,* Washington Project for the Arts, Washington, D.C.
1989	*AXVAPOR,* Duke University, Durham, North Carolina
1983	*Something Akin to Living,* J. Wayne Higgs Studio Gallery, Washington, D.C.
1983	*Mammoth Time,* Washington Project for the Arts, Washington, D.C.
1984	*Tonto Beaver,* WYCB-AM Radio, Washington, D.C.

Lose Faith in God and He Begain [sic] *Sinking.* But he can also be delicate as he paints plants and birds, as in *Scottle Leaves* (1983). Through the repetitive designs or allover patterns that Ferguson sometimes employs, the elements of the paintings seem to vibrate in their space, as in the imaginative and more subtly colored works like *Date Tree with Nest* and *Jackfish.*

Of special interest are the paintings of the John Canoe dancers, variously written as Junkanoo in the Bahamas and as Jonkonnu in Jamaica. These festivals, which are held throughout the West Indies, may have roots in Africa. Ferguson's *Pineapple Hat* (1983), *King and Queen of the Joungle* [sic] (1983), and *Polka Dot Junkanoo* (1984) all capture the dance rhythms of the celebration. Although the figures are still and frontally posed, the intricate patterns and colors of the filled spaces set up a lively exchange with the empty ones. But Ferguson expresses surprise that these paintings are popular. His preference is for his sacred paintings, based on his dreams and on Bible reading. Bible reading, Ferguson believes, lends greater experience to his work and brings him "more advances." He is sure that his gift has come from God and that it is his mission to show people that God is in all things.

—Betty Kaplan Gubert

Tonto Beaver, Maryland Art Place, Baltimore City, Maryland

1985   *City of Monuments,* Corcoran Gallery of Art, Washington, D.C.

   City of Monuments, Martin Luther King Library, Washington, D.C.

1988   *AXVAPOR, Equestrian and Other Stories,* Area Cooperative Educational Services, Hamden, Connecticut

1989   *Underground Structures,* George Mason University, Fairfax, Virginia

1993   *Pretending to Be Rock,* City Gallery, Raleigh, North Carolina

1995   *The Making of Steam,* Philadelphia Museum of Art

1996   *Pretending to Be Rock,* Real Art Ways, Hartford, Connecticut

Individual Exhibitions:

1989   Gallery IPOMAL, Landgraaf, Netherlands
   Louise Jones Brown Gallery, Duke University, Durham, North Carolina

1990   Nexus Gallery, Atlanta, Georgia

Selected Group Exhibitions:

1980   Washington Project for the Arts, Washington, D.C.
   Jamaica Arts Center, New York

1984   Maryland Art Place, Baltimore City, Maryland

1988   Washington Project for the Arts

1990   Intermedia Arts, Minneapolis, Minnesota
   Andrea Ruggieri Gallery, Washington, D.C.

1995   Arti et Amicitiae, Amsterdam, Netherlands

1996   Real Art Ways, Hartford, Connecticut
   Colorado Springs Fine Arts Center
   Painted Bride Art Center, Philadelphia

Collections:

Arti et Amicitiae, Amsterdam, Netherlands; Duke University, Durham, North Carolina; Video Data Bank, Chicago, Illinois.

Publications:

By FLEMING: Articles—"The Power to Define/Control," in *National Association of Artists' Organizations' Bulletin,* Fall 1988; "The Function of Art in Culture Today," in *High Performance* 41/42, Spring/Summer 1988; "Nigger as AntiBody," in *WhiteWalls Magazine,* Spring 1990; "Living in a City of Monuments or Why I No Longer Walk with an Erection," in *Washington Review* 16(5), February/March 1991; "Vectors, Ciphers and Rewrites," in *Washington Review* 20(4), December/January 1995.

*

Sherman Fleming comments:

My performance work employs childhood games and ritual dance actions as derived from vodun spectacle and African and pre-Columbian cultures. I use traditional artistic methods and nontraditional and utilitarian resources, in concert with quotidian gesture. I believe that I employ uniquely male body-actions that exhibit elements of balance, instability, duration, and stamina. The action to achieve and maintain balance, over time, is a metaphor for the maintenance of a position within culture that may be described as "impeccable"—meaning the ability to remain self-possessed and authentic within the social and institutionalized construct of racism and sexism. This bodily behavior, which I have defined as "psychophysical behavior," operates through the act of repetition, and its duration is determined by my body's stamina. My objective is to maintain the quality of stability through the behavioral constructions of rotation, suspension, inversion, and inertia.

*   *   *

Working in diverse mediums, Sherman Fleming excels in the arena of performance. He is also a painter and arts educator, however, and his endeavors in these areas are noteworthy. The crux of his lifework is art, and through all aspects of its varied manifestations he strives to convey the complex matrix existing within the African American experience. He celebrates his personage as a black male by challenging and confronting stereotypical concepts prevalent in Western society. In his performance works and rebus paintings he intends to expose the psyche of man as a sexual being.

Sherman Fleming: *Pretending to Be Rock.* **Photo courtesy of David Simonton.**

Fleming uses his body in all of his performance works as the principal vehicle for enacting real and theatrical time. Working in this mode for more than fifteen years, Fleming conducts feats of endurance that allude simultaneously to the body's fragility and strength. At intervals he courts the realm of danger, like the acrobat and daredevil traversing its parameters. Fleming's mimetic feats of aerial dynamism, flirtations with near suffocation, and use of dangerous paraphernalia such as propane torches evoke excursions into kaleidoscopic collision courses. The feats, however, are carefully orchestrated to avoid actual harm, although the risks are taken and openly solicited. The evocation of awe and the focus on process, as his activities are brought to a climax through the engagement of spectacle, are significant.

For Fleming there is syncretism between ritual and process. Throughout his work complexities in gesture as sign and symbol are explored, yet the symbolism inherent in his performance activities may be ambiguous or left unresolved. Exploits such as sustaining a stationary pose for minutes or hours without flinching or of being buried in hundreds of pounds of brown sugar all signify the transformation of the body as object.

Greatly influenced by the conceptualists of the 1970s, Fleming concluded early on in his career that he would do anything he pleased. Conceptualism provided a springboard into an acceptance of the idea that the means of expression are boundless. His iconographic mechanisms are multivalent and are based on diverse aesthetic precepts from the West as well as from Africa and Australia. The key to Fleming's performances is to understand that rituals governed by symbolic and expressive features, whether based on simplistic repetitious movements or spectacle, have the propensity to alter one's perception of reality.

Fleming's work is part of the continuum of the investigations of the art from the African continent that have informed twentieth-century movements in Europe and America. Alluded to in his performances are cross-cultural insignia, coded and abstracted, as means to convey complex modalities of the psyche. The psychological data encoded in his work is pronounced and mirrors life's traumas, dichotomies, and states of consciousness. Fleming is in search of vehicles to articulate the inner sanctums of the black man's mind. By electing to use his body as form and subject, he directly confronts cultural, historical, and racial issues as they pertain to interpretations of the black body on view. Through the conscious process of analysis that encompasses the stylizations and stamina of the vocalist James Brown, the myth of John Henry, and the persecution of Jack Johnson, Fleming claims his legacy. An analogy can be forged between his work, cathartic and laden with paradigms, and the double entendres and meanings expressed in black dialect.

—A. M. Weaver

FLEMISTER, Frederick (C.)

American painter

Work also appeared under the names Fred Flemister and Fred C. Flemister. **Born:** Atlanta, Georgia, 1916. **Education:** Morehouse College, Atlanta, Georgia, 1935-39; John Herron Art Institute, Indianapolis, Indiana, 1940-41. **Military Service:** United States Army. **Career:** Instructor, Atlanta University, Georgia, c.1941-1942. **Awards:** First Prize in oils, *American Negro Exhibition,* Chi-

cago, 1940; Purchase Prize, *Atlanta University Annual,* Georgia, 1942; Third Prize, High Museum of Art, 1941; Second Prize, *Atlanta University Annual,* Georgia, 1945. **Died.**

Selected Group Exhibitions:

1936   Atlanta University, Georgia
1937   Atlanta University, Georgia
1939   High Museum of Art, Atlanta, Georgia
1940   *American Negro Exhibition,* Chicago
1941   High Museum of Art, Atlanta, Georgia
1942   Atlanta University, Georgia
1945   *The Negro Comes of Age,* Albany Institute of History and Art, New York
1967   *The Evolution of the Afro-American Artist,* City University of New York

Collections:

Atlanta University, Georgia; Barnet-Aden Collection, Washington, D.C.

Publications:

On FLEMISTER: Book—*Evolution of Afro-American Artists,* exhibition catalog by Romare Bearden, City University of New York, 1967.

*   *   *

The content and settings of Frederick Flemister's paintings of the 1940s are decidedly pre-twentieth century: medieval Madonnas, Old Testament characters, and self-portraits of the artist in Italian Renaissance garb. Yet Flemister was an undeniable modernist who in his brief career introduced an adapted visual canon to his audiences.

An Atlanta native, Flemister attended Morehouse College and studied art with Hale Woodruff from 1935 to 1939. Flemister, Wilmer Jennings, Robert Neal, and Vernon Winslow were Woodruff's most successful protégés, with Flemister winning the first prize in oil painting at the *American Negro Exhibition* in Chicago in 1940. That Flemister also studied for a year (1940-41) at Woodruff's alma mater, the John Herron Art Institute in Indianapolis, is further measure of Woodruff's influence on the younger man's career. Following his training, Flemister taught art at Atlanta University, although his appointment was interrupted by military service.

Flemister was most active as a professional artist from 1939 to 1945, when he exhibited in Atlanta University's annual exhibitions and in other all-Negro shows. Critics' knowledge of his work is limited to the extant paintings and reproductions of paintings produced during this period.

Samson and Delilah (1939) depicts the biblical story of betrayal. While the protagonists and the two onlookers in the background of the painting bare their upper bodies—and in that sense are classical nudes—their forms are massively muscular and sculptural and their faces heavy and masklike. Furthermore, Flemister crowds the small cast of actors into a compressed space, and he places some elements at the front of the picture plane. Delilah's cramped hand and the anachronistic scissors seem to lie closer to the viewer than to the head of the sleeping Samson, which draws attention to the key moment of the narrative. By distorting forms and the pictorial space, Flemister tells the ancient story anew.

For reasons unknown Flemister was fascinated by the period of the European Renaissance. Perhaps he sought to liken the situation of the Negro artist in the 1940s with the Renaissance period of artistic *flourit*. Flemister sometimes even pictured himself in a historical role. *Man with a Brush* (1940) and *Self-Portrait* (1941) are two remarkable paintings of the black artist in Renaissance costume and setting.

Man with a Brush is painted in oil and tempera, a combination used by fifteenth-century artists for the burgeoning mode of easel painting. The artist is presented in his studio, stiffly holding a modern-looking brush and flanked by a blank canvas. The vista behind him is the Italian *campagna*, executed according to the standards of perspective followed by Renaissance artists. Severe lines and dramatic chiaroscuro characterize the representation of the stiff and broad-shouldered figure and the surrounding drapery, however. It is for reasons such as these that critics conclude that Flemister's paintings were not meant to be read as mere imitations. In their self-conscious executions and referential look to the past, the works deliberately startle audiences with their clever irony.

In *The Mourners* (1942) Flemister adapted the Renaissance presentation of the pietà to depict the aftermath of a lynching. Like a Christ figure brought down from the cross, a partly clad black man slumps against a female figure in a cowl and shawl. Another nearby female figure raises her elongated arms in lamentation, with her left hand directing attention to the cut noose hanging from a framing tree limb. If the dress of the assembly of onlookers—straw hats and cottons shifts—and the horse-drawn wagon and driver crossing the field in the painting's background place the scene in rural America in the nineteenth or early twentieth century, the emotional gestures and positions of the figures effectively link it with a pivotal moment of Christian history. The artist is undeniably drawing a parallel between these grievous episodes of human sacrifice.

—Jacqueline Francis

FOLARIN, Agboola
Nigerian muralist, painter, sculptor, and graphic artist

Born: Ibadan, Oyo State, Nigeria, 20 March 1936. **Education:** Yaba College of Technology, 1955-58; Regent Street Polytechnic, London, 1961-62; Central School of Art and Design, London, B.A. 1967; Howard University, Washington, D.C., M.F.A. in sculpture 1980; School of Architecture, Howard University, M.A. 1984. **Career:** Graphic artist, Federal Ministry of Information, Lagos, 1959-60; graphic artist/scenographer, Western Nigerian Television, 1960-61; set designer, Nottingham Playhouse, England, 1966-67. Since 1968 junior research fellow/research fellow/senior art fellow, Institute of African Studies and Department of Fine Arts, University of Ife, Ile-Ife, Nigeria. Since 1979, professor, sculpture and architectural design, University of Ife, Ile-Ife, Nigeria. Member, Society of Nigerian Artists. **Awards:** Award for theatre design, Arts Council of Great Britain, 1966; design award, Arts Council of Great Britain, 1967-68; award (Murtala Mohammed International Airport mural), National Art Competition, Lagos, 1978. **Address:** Department of Fine Arts, Obafemi Awolowo University, Ile-Ife, Oyo State, Nigeria.

Individual Exhibitions:

1967	Africa Centre, London
	Central School of Art, London
1968	University of Ife, Ile-Ife, Nigeria
1969	Ori-Olokun Cultural Centre, Ile-Ife, Nigeria
1971	University of Ife, Ile-Ife, Nigeria
1972	Haus Dakunst, Munich, Germany
	University of Ibadan, Nigeria
1973	*Exhibition of Graphic Paintings,* Zurich, Switzerland
1974	Goethe Institute, Lagos
1975	British Council, Ibadan, Nigeria

Selected Group Exhibitions:

1978	National Theatre, Lagos
1980	Mayor's Office, Washington, D.C.
	Howard University, Washington, D.C.
1985	*Silver Jubilee National Art Exhibition,* National Theatre, Lagos
1987	Oyo Trade Fair Textile Designs, Ibadan, Nigeria
1988	Italian Cultural Institute, Lagos
1989	Hodson Gallery, Hood College, Frederick, Maryland
	Obafemi Awolowo University, Ile-Ife, Nigeria
	National Theatre, Lagos
1990	School of Architecture, Obafemi Awolowo University, Ile-Ife, Nigeria

Collections:

Asele Institute, Nimo, Nigeria; Iwalewa Haus, Bayreuth, Germany; Lagos University Library, University of Lagos, Nigeria.

Publications:

By FOLARIN: Articles—"Relating Sculpture to a Modern Nigerian Environment," in *Black Orpheus* (Lagos), 4(1), 1981, pp. 28-31 (also published in *Stone 10* [Washington, D.C., Howard University], October 1982); "Modern Scenography in Western Nigeria," in *Nigeria* (Lagos), 53(2), April-June 1985, pp. 14-24 (illustrated); "Notes on Creative Experimentation: Nigerian Contemporary Arts Example," in *Nigeria* (Lagos), 55(3), July-September 1987, pp. 66-68 (bibliography); "The Role of Public Sculpture in Nigeria," in *Artist* (London), September 1987, pp. 40-48; "Scenographic Art in Nigerian Dance and Some Suggestions Concerning its Revitalization," in *Society of Theatre Arts*, 2(1), 1988, pp. 25-29; "Imaginative Image in Modern Nigerian Contemporary Art," in *Kurio Africana; Journal of Art and Criticism* (Ile-Ife, Nigeria), 1(1), 1989, pp. 38-56 (bibliography); "Dualism and Expressive Dynamism in the Sculpture of Erhabor Emokpae," in *Kurio Africana; Journal of Art and Criticism* (Ile-Ife, Nigeria), 1(2), 1989, pp. 61-67.

On FOLARIN: Article—"Money Doesn't Make a Man, Says Agbo Folarin, Veteran Professor of Fine Arts" by Dele Momodu, in *National Concord* (Lagos), 31 March 1989, p. 5.

*   *   *

Agboola Folarin is primarily a muralist and sculptor, but his work might also be considered architecture. He has graduate degrees in both fine arts and architecture and has studied at Yaba College of Technology in Lagos; the Regent Street Polytechnic; Hammersmith College of Art in London; the Central School of Art and Design in London; and Howard University in Washington, D.C. Folarin has said that, "No culture can exist without taking ideas from the outside, but selectivity is my watchword." Regardless of his influences, he believes art is about discovering yourself and becoming "a pathfinder, a prime mover of the society of its time . . . and a communicator."

"I first thought of being a scientist or a doctor," he has said, "but one's talent is one's destiny.'" He has followed both his talent and his destiny and now produces large wall murals using materials such as cast fiberglass, cut-and-welded copper, aluminum, and steel. These sculpted murals are fully integrated into the structure of the associated buildings. Using modern, polished materials and established African forms to depict modern activities, these murals connect past to future and architecture to art. His work appears in the Obafemi Awolowo University, the National Theatre in Lagos, and the Murtala Mohammed Airport in Ikeja.

In addition to his mural/sculpture work, Agboola is also an accomplished costume maker and has designed costumes for films, for the Olympic Games, for musical compositions, and for play productions. Folarin is also principal art fellow at Obafemi Awolowo University in the department of fine arts.

—Terry Bain

FRAZIER, L'Merchie

American performance artist, jewelry designer, and fiber artist

Born: Jacksonville, Florida. **Education:** City College of New York; University of Hartford, B.A. in political science, philosophy; Hartford Technical College; Research Institute of African and African Diaspora Arts, Boston; Chinese Cultural Institute, Boston; School of the Museum of Fine Arts. **Career:** Artist-in-Residence, TPS, Hartford, Connecticut, 1989-90, Boston Public Schools, 1992-94, Walker Home School for the Mentally Challenged, Newton, Massachusetts, 1993, Curley School, Jamaica Plain, Massachusetts, 1993, English High School, Jamaica Plain, Massachusetts, 1993, Dorchester Drug and Alcohol Substance Abuse Prevention Project, Boston, 1994, Kennedy School, Mashpee, Massachusetts, 1994, Lawerence High School, Massachusetts, 1996, Museum of the National Center of Afro-American Artists, 1996. Lecturer, Frederick Douglass Gallery, Hartford, Connecticut, 1993, Watertown, Massachusetts, 1993, Emerging Artists Gallery, Jamaica Plain, Massachusetts, 1994, Harriet Tubman Gallery, Boston, 1994, Museum of the National Center of Afro-American Artists, Boston, 1996. **Awards:** ICCD Mentor Award, Institute for Community Research, Hartford, Connecticut, 1993-94; Kentucky Art and Craft Foundation Merit Award, African-American Craft National, 1994; Lila-Wallace International Artist Fellowship to Brazil, 1994-95; Francis S. Merritt/Mary B. Bishop grant, 1996. **Address:** 12 Morley Street, Roxbury, Massachusetts 02119, U.S.A.

L'Merchie Frazier: *Casa da Transformacao (House of Transformation): Save the Children,* 1996. Photo courtesy of Chee Heng Yeong.

Individual Exhibitions:

1993   Crystal Blue Bead, Watertown, Massachusetts
        Dillaway-Thomas House Gallery, Roxbury, Massachusetts
1994   Harriet Tubman Gallery, Boston
        Jamaica Plain, Massachusetts
1995   B. Dalton Books, New York
1996   Museum of the National Center of Afro-American Artists, Boston

Selected Performances:

1989   Sankofa Dance Troupe, Hartford, Connecticut
1993   PENC and Sistren Theater Collective, Roxbury Community College, Massachusetts
1994   *A Tribute to Langston Hughes,* Grand Amphitheatre Institut du Monde Anglophone, Paris
1996   *The River Is Still Flowing,* United South End Settlements, Boston

Dance of the Orixas, Museum of the National Center of Afro-American Artists, Boston

Four Rivers, Museum of the National Center of Afro-American Artists, Boston

Mothers of the Diaspora, Save Me from My Amnesia, University of Vermont, Burlington

Poetry Slam, National Black Arts Festival, Atlanta, Georgia

Selected Group Exhibitions:

1990   CRT Craftery Gallery, Hartford
1992   Museum of the National Center of African American Artists, Boston
        Matrix Gallery, Sacramento
        Concord Art Association Gallery, Massachusetts
1993   National Civil Rights Museum, Memphis
        Gallery 788, Toronto, Canada
1994   Learning Resource Center Gallery, Dayton, Ohio
1995   Daryl Reich Rubenstein Gallery, Washington, D.C.
1996   Boston Center for the Arts
        American Craft Museum, New York

Collections:

Afro American Museum, Dallas; American Craft Museum, New York; University of Vermont, Burlington.

Publications:

On FRAZIER: Articles—*Bay State Banner,* November 1992; *Art News,* 11 February 1993; *The Watertown Sun,* April 1993; *Art New England,* August and September 1994; *Jamaica Plain Gazette* (Massachusetts), January 1994; *The Women's Forum,* June 1994; *Bay State Banner,* August 1996.

*

L'Merchie Frazier comments:

Textile designs emit a presence, a spirit, an energy, a vitality connecting us with our ancestors and other human beings unlike any other medium. As a result of the function and fancy, we embellish the human form, ornament decor, raise ancestral spirits, and worship deities through the cloth and beads. Imbued with icons and images linked to cultural heritage, social status, and expression, i.e., language in coded form, we experience different hues and textures. Textile design captures my focus as a visual artist to express the patterns of life, myth, magic, and supreme rhythm in exaggerated symbolic form.

*   *   *

L'Merchie Frazier studied at the City College of New York, the University of Hartford, and the School of the Museum of Fine Arts in Boston. She works in Boston as a fabric and performance artist as well as a jewelry maker. An activist in spirit, she is the founder of the African American Bead Society International, a board member of Many Colors of a Woman, Inc., a teacher at the Boston Community Academy, and a member of the educational staff at the museum of the National Center of Afro-American Artists.

L'Merchie Frazier: *Orixa Oxumare: Joseph's Coat of Many Colors,* 1996. Photo courtesy of Chee Heng Yeong.

Frazier has an intense interest in themes of black experience, often framed through Yoruba cultural and religious practices as they exist throughout the Americas. She has undertaken extensive study of *orisha* art in Brazil, including a period of fieldwork and research pertaining to Candomblé, the Brazilian Christian-African sect. Based on her study, she has produced a series of individual works and installations under the theme "Houses of Transformation." At the same time she has continued a series of works on the theme "Save Me from My Amnesia," in which she probes the role of memory in the African diaspora. As part of the latter series she comments on a wide range of issues, ranging from poverty to sexual abuse, that affect the lives of women and children. She situates her art in the context of wider social and cultural concerns, thereby aligning herself with African (masks as judges) and Caribbean (calypso) traditions in which the artist comments on the fabric of the sociocultural matrix of society.

Frazier's work, even though it embodies common themes and aesthetic approaches, expresses itself in several forms. In jewelry she produces small but exquisitely detailed pins, brooches, necklaces, and earrings assembled from beads, cowrie shells, wire, and other materials. These sometimes resemble masks or pendants. In her sculpture she often integrates built structures with highly embellished, often movable attachments and beaded centerpieces, as, for example, small wooden houses with enamel on copper doors and beaded configurations inside. Other sculptures use fabric panels and attachments in the manner of African masquerade dancers. In both her fabric sculptures and hangings Frazier demonstrates her mastery of tie-dyeing. She gives additional interest to her works in fabric by overprinting through the use of either stamps or photo transfers. Silk, her preferred material, lends both transparency and elegance to her work. As a performance artist Frazier dances, acts, writes and reads her own poetry, and in general animates her works, many of which take their inspiration from a setting rich in dance and theater.

—Edmund Barry Gaither

FREELON, Allan (Randall)

American painter and printmaker

Born: Philadelphia, 2 September 1895. **Education:** Pennsylvania School of Industrial Art; University of Pennsylvania, Philadelphia; Tyler School of Fine Art, Elkins Park, Pennsylvania. **Awards:** Four-year scholarship, Pennsylvania Museum School of Art; First Prize, Art League of Germantown, Pennsylvania, and Racial Commission of Philadelphia, 1935. **Died:** 1960.

Exhibitions:

1922	Tanner Art League
	Harmon Foundation, Tuskegee, Alabama (through 1931)
1929	National Gallery of Art, Washington, D.C.
1930	National Gallery of Art, Washington D.C.
1933	Smithsonian Institution, Washington, D.C.
	National Gallery of Art, Washington, D.C.
1934	Whitney Museum of American Art, New York
	Gimball Galleries
	Moorestown High School, New Jersey
1935	Newton Galleries, New York
	New Jersey State Museum, Trenton
	Warwick Gallery, Philadelphia
	College Art Association
1936	Texas Centenary
1937	Howard University, Washington, D.C.
	Lincoln University, Pennsylvania
1939	Howard University, Washington, D.C.
1940	*American Negro Exposition,* Chicago

Collections:

Jay Cooke High School, Philadelphia; Gloucester High School, New Jersey; Lincoln University, Lincoln University, Pennsylvania; South Philadelphia Boys School; Vineland Museum of Art, New Jersey.

Publications:

On FREELON: Articles—"Allan Randall Freelon: Artist-Teacher" by Francis Holbrook, in *Southern Workman,* 53, April 1924, pp. 225-26.

*   *   *

The painter and printmaker Allan Randall Freelon was one of a large number of artists-explorers whose works served as a gateway to their identities. While some artists were drifting toward a modernist style that incorporated aspects of an African aesthetic allowing for the expression of their own identities, others, like Freelon, were firmly grounded in a European sensibility. Artists of the period, however, were all challenged by the subtext of the new Negro movement.

During the time Freelon served as editor for the short-lived *Black Opal,* he was concerned with painting issues and what happened at the nexus of medium and surface. Along with William Farrow, Laura Wheeler Waring, and Edwin A. Harleston, among others, Freelon was thought of as a traditionalist. These artists' work focused on technique and avoided interpreting social issues, which at the time helped define the African American artist's presence. Freelon's prints, however, sometimes gave precise and impeccable renderings of issues affecting African Americans.

Freelon was very much influenced by Hugh Breckenridge, one of his instructors who maintained an art school in Gloucester, Massachusetts, on the New England coast, where Freelon spent his summers. It is not surprising therefore that his work embraced an impressionistic style echoing Breckenridge's influence. Freelon's voice, however, was clearly his own, as demonstrated by his bright palette and his use of separate hues of blue, gray, and brown to describe New England's coastal landscape.

With its endless possibilities for color and action, nature was a seductive siren tempting Freelon. Even though he may have been working out complex color and compositional problems, the viewer senses a certain spontaneity that energizes surface movement. Freelon's impressionistic style—small touches of pure color to represent tonal qualities—became his means of problem solving, as did his repetitive paintings, which emphasized technique. He often painted the same scene over and over again from different perspectives and under varying light conditions. His interest in technique can be seen, for example, in the work *Glouscester Harbor, Boat at Harbor, Late Afternoon,* in which he built up "blocks of color to create flickering light effects that underscore his interest in technical problems."

There is a certain abstract relationship between Freelon's impressionistic paintings and his printed works. The precision required in the print mediums can be directly linked to Freelon's use of pure color to define the shapes and forms in his impressionistic paintings. In *Modern Negro Art,* James A. Porter highly praised Freelon and his consistent quality, whether he was working in drypoint, soft-ground etchings, or aquatints.

—Crystal Britton

FREEMAN, Robert (T.)

American painter

Born: Brooklyn, New York, 8 May 1946. **Education:** Howard University, Washington, D.C., 1965-67; Boston University, 1967-71, 1980-81, B.F.A. 1971, M.F.A. 1981. **Family:** Married Bettye C. Freeman, three daughters. **Career:** Director of art, Weston Public Schools, Massachusetts, 1974-82; visiting lecturer, Harvard University, Cambridge, Massachusetts, 1988-93. Since 1982 artist-in-residence, Noble and Greenough School, Dedham, Massa-

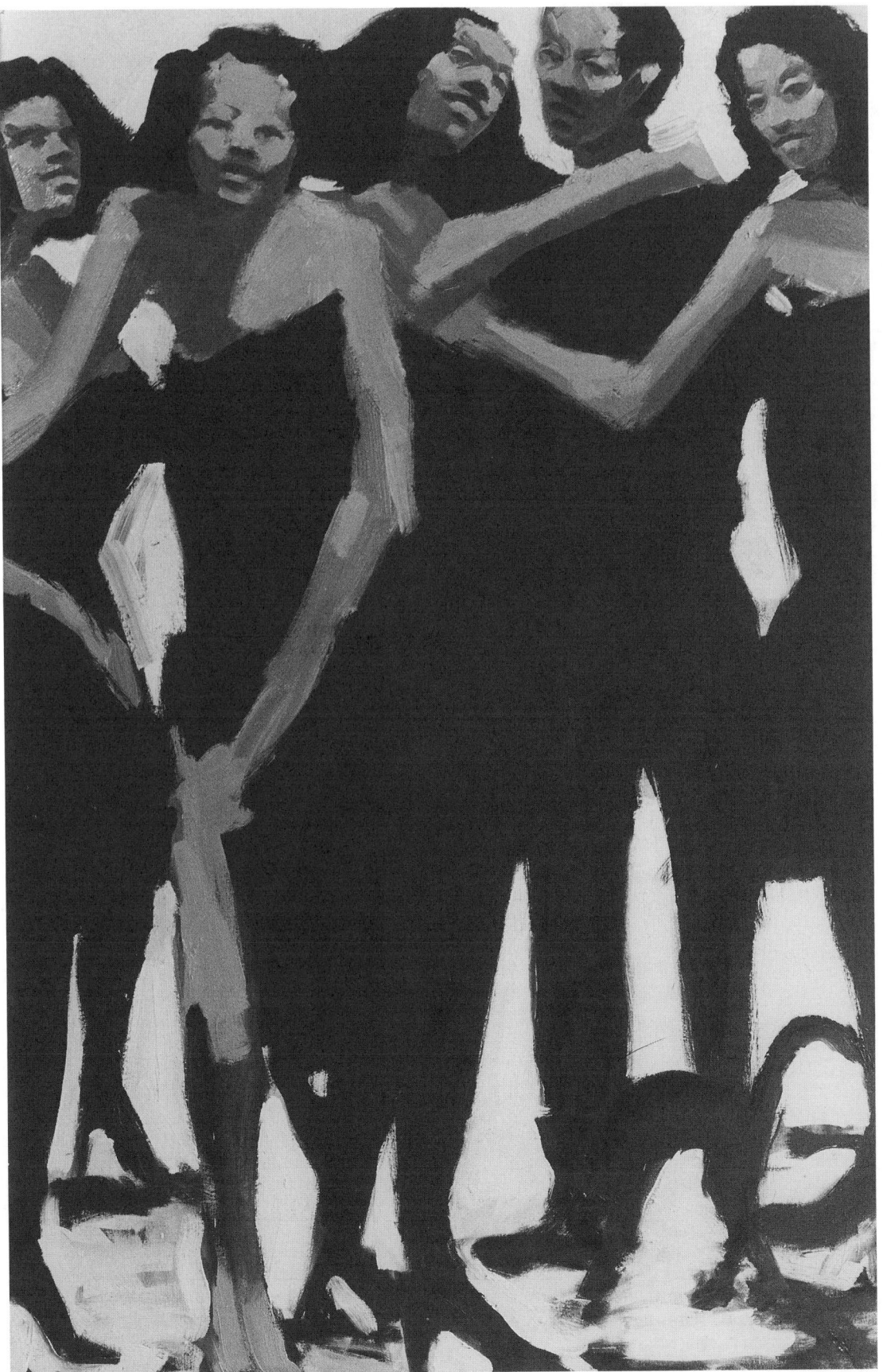

Robert Freeman: *Trysting Place.*

Robert Freeman: *10,000 Shields and Spears,* **1989.**

chusetts. Traveled in Ghana, Nigeria, Egypt, Morocco, France, Germany, Switzerland, England, Italy, Greece, Spain, Finland, Sweden, Russia, Canada, Puerto Rico, Bermuda, Belize. **Agent:** Clark Gallery, Lincoln Station, Lincoln, Massachusetts 01773, U.S.A.; Wendell Street, 17 Wendell Street, Cambridge, Massachusetts 02138, U.S.A. **Address:** 36 Crescent Street, Weston, Massachusetts 02193, U.S.A.

Individual Exhibitions:

1970	Smith and Mason Gallery, Washington, D.C.
1981	National Center of Afro-American Artists, Roxbury, Massachusetts
1982	Addison Gallery of American Art, Andover, Massachusetts
1983	Clark Gallery, Lincoln, Massachusetts
	Wendell Street, Cambridge, Massachusetts
1984	Zenith Gallery, Washington, D.C.
1986	Clark Gallery, Lincoln, Massachusetts
	Wendell Street, Cambridge, Massachusetts
1987	Wendell Street, Cambridge, Massachusetts
1988	Clark Gallery, Lincoln, Massachusetts
1989	June Kelly Gallery, New York
	Isobel Neal Gallery, Chicago
1990	Clark Gallery, Lincoln, Massachusetts
1992	Wendell Street, Cambridge, Massachusetts
	Zenith Gallery, Washington, D.C.
1994	Wendell Street, Cambridge, Massachusetts
1995	Wendell Street, Cambridge, Massachusetts
1996	Boston University Gallery of Art

Selected Group Exhibitions:

1985	Crystal Britton Gallery, Atlanta, Georgia
1986	Museum of Fine Arts, Boston
	Clark Gallery, Lincoln, Massachusetts
1988	Carpenter Center for Visual Arts, Harvard University, Cambridge, Massachusetts
	Clark Gallery, Lincoln, Massachusetts
	Museum of Fine Arts, Boston
1989	Williams College Museum of Art, Williamstown, Massachusetts
1990	Artists Foundation Gallery, Boston
	Newport Art Museum, Newport, Rhode Island
1993	Rose Art Museum, Brandeis University, Waltham, Massachusetts

Collections:

DeCordova Museum, Lincoln, Massachusetts; National Center of African-American Artists, Roxbury, Massachusetts.

Publications:

On FREEMAN: Articles—"Freeman Takes a Satirical Look at Social Life" by Christine Temin, in *Boston Globe,* May 1983; "Artist's Images of Greece Highlight Gallery Exhibit" by Nancy Stapen, in *Lincoln Journal,* September 1986; "French Travels Yield Harvest of Work" by Edward Strickland, in *Bay State Banner,* November 1987; "Freeman's Art Chronicles Black Middle Class" by Christine Temin, in *Boston Globe,* January 1988.

*   *   *

Robert Freeman is a painter who has succeeded in capturing the attitudes at a high society party, the tranquility and profound silence of a moonlit lagoon, and the vibrancy of a sun-splashed hillside. He is a highly skilled artist whose works resonate with the intensity of his impassioned study of everyday sights and events.

Born in Brooklyn, New York, Freeman moved to Ghana at the age of eleven with his family and then returned to the United States for his secondary school and college studies. He is now based in Massachusetts and travels extensively in France, Spain, Morocco, and Greece. Creating in a style derived from the impressionist aesthetic, Freeman is often compared to Cézanne and cites Edvard Munch, Max Beckmann, and James Van Der Zee as some of his influences.

In the realm of figurative painting, Freeman has become a master of documenting the political, interpersonal, and power relations between people in an array of social situations. Several series of his work have dealt with these subjects, including "Black Tie" (1981-89), "Electric Lady Land" (late 1980s to early 1990s), and "Adam, Eve and the Serpent" (early 1990s). In the "Black Tie" series Freeman recounts the dynamics of many a wealthy dinner and dance party. As in all his work, the majority of the figures are African American or of African descent. He shows us people strutting, gossiping, and dining and has an uncanny ability to capture the furtive glance, the shy smile, and the inquiring stare. While he clearly illustrates facial expression on some individuals, many others have little to no expression or facial features. This lack of emotion, together with their uniform black-and-white formal dress, is the artist's way of critiquing the lack of individuality in some social groupings. The tight composition of these works reinforces this sense of identity. The figures overlap and intertwine, and because of the flatness of the painting and the solid black of the dress, it is sometimes impossible to distinguish one form from another; they have become one mass. Another interesting and effective element of Freeman's composition is the way in which many of the figures are cut off, extending their actions beyond the canvas.

The palette in this series is dominated by black and white, with striking accents of bright red in the fingernails, jewelry, and boutonnieres of the social folk. The artist has said of this work that "the black and white color drama that goes on is one tension. And I think that seeing blacks in roles that are not in paintings or art is another tension...It's a very real portrait of black social life."

Robert Freeman's extensive travels have become another central subject matter for his paintings. Freeman's works are studies in color, light, texture, and shadow using oils and gouache. He is able to convey the living energy of a landscape with his deft application of warm oranges, lush greens, and vivid blues in bold, quick brush strokes. In *Wheatfields at Les Milles* (1987), the painting seems to jump off the canvas and beckon you to explore the sunny, golden fields or sit under a large shade tree and contemplate the boundless countryside. Freeman achieves a wonderful sense of depth in this piece by alternating between long and blunt brush strokes and by composing a careful interplay between complimentary and contrasting colors. But beyond his expertise with color, the artist proves his mastery of the landscape genre by infusing his work with emotion and temporality. One critic has observed that "Freeman's series cease to be about the facts that identify a spot and instead become studies of change—in mood, weather, light and, above all, paint's possibilities."

Freeman explores themes of theater and scenes of backstage life in his most current work. He sees theater as a metaphor for public and private life. He has also investigated the world of jazz and the relationship between the feelings and sounds of music and the colors and brush strokes they represent. A fascinating element in this body of work, as evidenced in the piece *Show Time* (1995-96), is the sense of mystery, secrecy, and the unknown. In this painting the viewer is privy to seeing the scene of what is going on backstage just as the curtain is opening and revealing a sliver of the audience beyond. The performers are turned toward the viewer, and one is struck by the feeling of impending change and the transformation that will come over these expressionless figures when they turn to face the other audience.

Robert Freeman's rendering of these scenes from our daily lives continues to produce compelling works that are widely collected and exhibited. He will long be remembered as one of the most skillful chroniclers of his time.

—Monique G. Curnen

FREEMAN, Roland (Leeon)

American photographer

Born: Baltimore, Maryland, 27 July 1936. **Military Service:** United States Air Force, 1954-58: airman third class; Good Conduct medal. **Family:** Married Marcia Felton Freeman in 1968. **Career:** Director, First National Survey of African-American Quilters, Washington, D.C., 1974-96, Philadelphia Folklife Project, 1988-90, Mississippi Folklife Project (in conjunction with Center for Southern Folklore), Memphis, Tennessee, 1975-78. Since 1967 freelance photographer, Washington, D.C. Since 1972 field research photographer in folklore, Center for Folklife Programs and Cultural Studies, Smithsonian Institution, Washington, D.C. Photographer-in-residence/research associate, Howard University, Washington, D.C., 1971-72. **Address:** 117 Ingraham Street NW, Washington, D.C. 20011, U.S.A.

Individual Exhibitions:

1969	Gallery de Gaines, Washington, D.C.
1972	Goddard College, Plainfield, Vermont
1973	Mind's Eye Gallery, Vancouver, British Columbia
	Shado' Gallery, Oregon City, Oregon
1975	Massachusetts Institute of Technology Creative Photography Gallery, Boston
1977	Mississippi State Historical Museum, Jackson
1978	Antioch University/Maryland and Antioch University, Philadelphia
1979	University of Maryland, Baltimore
	County Library, Baltimore, Maryland
1981	International Center of Photography, New York
1982	World's Fair, Knoxville, Tennessee
1984	Smithsonian Institution, Washington, D.C.
1985	Smithsonian Institution, Washington, D.C.
1986	Smithsonian Institution, Washington, D.C.
	California Afro-American Museum, Los Angeles
	National Mall, Washington, D.C.
	Alabama State Council on the Arts and Humanities Gallery, Montgomery
1987	King-Tisdell Cottage, Savannah, Georgia
	Smithsonian Institution, Washington, D.C.
1988	Bergen Museum of Art and Science, Paramus, New Jersey
	Detroit Historical Museum
	African American Museum, Cleveland, Ohio
	National Black Arts Festival, Atlanta, Georgia (retrospective)
1989	Museum of Contemporary Photography, Columbia College, Chicago
1990	Banneker-Douglass Museum, Annapolis, Maryland, and Apex Museum, Atlanta, Georgia
	Academy of the Arts, Easton, Maryland
	Baltimore Museum of Art (traveling)
1991	National Afro-American Museum and Cultural Center, Wilberforce, Ohio
1992	National Civil Rights Museum, Memphis, Tennessee
	Jackson State University, Jackson, Mississippi

Selected Group Exhibitions:

1972	National Collection of Fine Arts, Smithsonian Institution, Washington, D.C.
1980	National Museum of History and Technology, Smithsonian Institution, Washington, D.C.
	National Portrait Gallery, Smithsonian Institution, Washington, D.C.

1984   *Soundings: Traditions in Maryland Life,* Denton, Baltimore, Salisbury, Frostburg, and La Plata, Maryland (traveling exhibition sponsored by Maryland State Arts Council)

1987   National Museum of American History, Smithsonian Institution, Washington, D.C.

Burden Gallery of the Aperture Foundation for Photography and the Visual Arts, New York

1990   Mitchell Museum, Mount Vernon, Illinois (with Nigerian photographer Jide Adeniyi-Jones)

1992   Eubie Blake National Museum and Cultural Center, Baltimore, Maryland

Corcoran Gallery of Art, Washington, D.C. (traveling)

APEX Museum, Atlanta, Georgia

Collections:

Auburn Avenue Research Library on African American Culture and History, Atlanta, Georgia; Baltimore Museum of Art, Maryland; Beach Institute of African American Art and Culture, Savannah, Georgia; Center for Southern Culture, University of Mississippi, Oxford; Corcoran Gallery, Washington, D.C.; High Museum of Art, Atlanta, Georgia; International Center of Photography, New York; Mississippi Department of Archives and History, Jackson; Mississippi State Historical Museum, Jackson; Penn Center Museum of Gulliculture, St. Helena Island, South Carolina; Smith-Robinson African American Museum, Jackson, Mississippi; Smithsonian Institution, Washington, D.C.; Studio Museum in Harlem, New York; University of Maryland, Catonsville, Maryland.

Publications:

By FREEMAN: Books—*Something to Keep You Warm: The Roland Freeman Collection of Black American Quilts from the Mississippi Heartland,* Jackson, Mississippi, Mississippi Department of Archives and History, 1979; *Southern Roads/City Pavements: Photographs of Black Americans,* New York, International Center of Photography, 1981; *Stand by Me: African American Expressive Culture in Philadelphia,* Washington, D.C., Smithsonian Institution, 1989; *The Arabbers of Baltimore,* Centreville, Maryland, Tidewater, 1989; *Margaret Walker's For My People: A Tribute: Photographs by Roland Freeman,* Jackson, University of Mississippi Press, 1992; *A Communion of the Spirits: African-American Quilters, Preservers, and Their Stories,* Nashville, Rutledge Hill, 1996. **Articles**—"Folkroots, Images of Mississippi Black Folklife (1974-1976)," in *Long Journey Home,* (Chapel Hill), North Carolina, Southern Exposure, 1977; "The Black Church: A Photo Essay," in *Sagala: A Journal of Art and Ideas,* (Washington, D.C.), Howard University Press, 1981; "Folkroots," in *Afro-American Folk Arts and Crafts,* (Boston), G.K. Hall, 1983; "Women of West Africa," in *Ritual and Dissent: A Journal of Afro-American Arts and Letters,* (New Haven), Connecticut, 1984; "Families: Making the Rounds," in *American Visions,* (Washington, D.C.), Smithsonian Institution, 1986; "An African American Celebration of Life," in *National Geographic,* (Washington, D.C.), National Geographic Society, 1990.

On FREEMAN: Articles—"Roland Freeman Preserves Naturally" by M. Denise Dennis, in *Village Voice* (New York), 6 May 1981; "Photographer Roland Freeman Mirrors His Heritage Along 'Southern Roads'" by Marcia Robertson, in *Atlanta Constitution,* 12 July 1988; "Common Lives, Uncommon Photos" by Alexis Moore, in *Philadelphia Enquirer,* 27 August 1990; "Arabbers: Preserving the Image of a Baltimore Institution, the Horse Cart Vendors" by Stephanie Shapiro, in *Sun* (Baltimore, Maryland), 20 January 1990.

*   *   *

Roland L. Freeman's formal career in 35mm photography started in 1963, when he began making photographs as a form of creative expression. He was later inspired by the documentary styles of Gordon Parks and Roy De Carava and the social movement of the 1960s. He identified with the black art movement that followed. "I champion the working class of the black community," he said. Freeman has dedicated his art to sharing in pictures his passion for social justice and human rights for all. His photographs depict ordinary struggles in everyday life, shot with dignity and simplicity—street vendors in his urban hometown, Baltimore, Maryland; quilters in rural Mississippi; black extended families like his own at work, at play, at rest, or in silent supplication—and depicted always as rising, striving, and moving to higher ground.

Freeman also used the art of photography as a way of seeing and sharing. While his camera focuses and then rests, he allows the self-conscious subject an opportunity to confront the waiting lens with a selective self-image that presents either the outer self or the inner self. Freeman's consistent conquest of the inner selves of his subjects makes him a truly great American photographer.

"Each day," he said, "on television and in print, millions of people see African American communities represented as drug-infested areas of inner city ghettos, spewing bullet-ridden black bodies across the urban landscape . . . . Ignored are the masses of people in these same communities who are religious and hard working, who love and care for their families and society." In his solo man exhibit *Stand by Me: African American Expressive Culture in Philadelphia, the Davis Family at Home* is an open-door photographic metaphor for the sustainability of African American family life. Maceo Davis, Sr., and his son Maceo, Jr., are shown exploring a textbook, as the father rocks and rests in a chair in the child's bedroom. In an adjoining room, divided symbolically by a wall bearing a dual electric light switch, Rita Davis and her daughter, Paige, enact the ritual of hair combing, as mother combs and daughter squirms. In one wide-angle shutter click, Freeman has plumbed the depths of African American family life to its rock-bottom floor.

Roland L. Freeman's career is not limited to photography. He has directed the Mississippi Folklife Project and is president of the Group for Cultural Documentation, a project based in Washington, DC. His work in ethnography as a field researcher for the Smithsonian Institution has helped him move beyond photodocumentation to visual storytelling and allowed his photographs to master the social and cultural landscape. "Freeman regards the camera as a research tool," says Cornell Capa, executive director of the International Center of Photography. "He was a witness documentarian, and to a large extent that is what he has remained."

His most recent triumph is *A Communion of the Spirits: African American Quilters and Their Quilts,* Rutledge House Press, Nashville, Tennessee (1996). The book features African American quilters he photographed from across the nation, sharing their stories.

Freeman's own sixty years of warmth and sharing are reflected in the faces of the people he has photographed. If he has any faults at all, it is his tendency to include too many photographs in his studies, although he seldom sacrifices quality for quantity.

—Worth W. Long

FULLER, Meta Vaux Warrick

American sculptor

Work also appeared under the name Meta Vaux Warrick. **Born:** Philadelphia, 9 June 1877. **Education:** Pennsylvania Museum School for the Industrial Arts, 1894-97; Academie Colarossi, Paris; École des Beaux Arts, Paris, 1899. Studied drawing and sculpture in Paris under Henry Ossawa Tanner, c.1900; student of Auguste Rodin. Pennsylvania Academy of Fine Arts, 1907. **Family:** Married Dr. Solomon C. Fuller in 1909 (died 1953), three sons. **Career:** Self-supporting sculptor with commissions from W.E.B. Du Bois, City of New York, National Council of Negro Women in Washington, D.C., Framingham (Massachusetts) Union Hospital, and Framingham Center Library. Warehouse fire in 1910 destroyed works created in Paris and in Philadelphia since 1894. Contracted and suffered from tuberculosis, c.1950-56. **Awards:** Metalwork Prize, 1889; First Prize, George K. Crozier; First Prize, pottery, 1904; Gold Medal, Jamestown Tercentennial, 1907; Second Prize, Massachusetts Branch of Women's Peace Party, 1915; Silver Medal, New Vistas in American Art Exhibition, Howard University, 1961; honorary degree of letters, Livingston College, 1962; scholarship, Pennsylvania School of Industrial Art (now Philadelphia College of Industrial Art). **Died:** 18 March 1968.

Selected Exhibitions:

1898	Paris Salon
1899	Paris Salon
1903	Paris Salon
1907	Jamestown Tercentennial Exposition
1921	New York Public Library
1922	Making of America Exhibit, New York
	Boston Public Library
1927	Art Institute of Chicago
1931	Emancipation Exhibit, New York
	Harmon Foundation
1939	Augusta Savage Studios, New York
1940	*American Negro Exhibition,* Chicago
1961	Guild of Arts and Crafts
	Howard University, Washington, D.C.
1967	City College of New York

Collections:

Atlanta YMCA; Cleveland Museum, Ohio; Framingham Center Library, Massachusetts; Framingham Union Hospital, Massachusetts; Garfield School, Detroit; Howard University, Washington, D.C.; Livingston College, Salisbury, North Carolina; 135th Street Branch, New York Public Library; Palmer Memorial Institute; Saint Andrews Episcopal Church, Framingham, Massachusetts; San Francisco Museum of Fine Arts; Schomburg Center, New York.

Publications:

On FULLER: Book—*God-Given Work: The Life and Times of Meta Vaux Warrick Fuller* (dissertation) by Judith N. Kerr (includes interviews with Solomon C. Fuller, Jr., and Harriet Fuller), 1986. **Articles**—"Meta Warrick, Sculptor of Horrors" by W. F. O'Donnell, in *World Today,* November 1907, pp. 1139-45; "Meta

Meta Warrick Fuller: *The Awakening of Ethiopia,* c. 1910. Photo courtesy of the Schomburg Center for Research in Black Culture.

Warrick Fuller," in *Southern Woman,* January 1918; "Meta Warrick, a Promising Sculptor" by Florence Lewis Bently, in *Negro History Bulletin,* March 1939, p. 56; "The Negro Sculptor" by James V. Herring, in *Crisis,* August 1942; "Meta Fuller Warrick: The Sculptor Rodin Admired," in *Encore,* 6, 3 January 1977, p. 3; "The Genius of Meta Warrick Fuller" by Kathy Perkins, in *Negro American Literature Forum,* 24, September 1990, pp. 65-72.

*   *   *

Meta Vaux Warrick Fuller was one of the first renowned African American women sculptors in America. Her work is considered a precursor to the Harlem Renaissance in that it reflects a serious exploration of the African heritage. Fuller was most known for dealing with African American subjects and experience in her work at a time when most artists of African descent shied away from confronting such matters. She was born during the post-Civil War Reconstruction period into a middle-class black Philadelphia family. With an older sister who was an art student and a father who took her to the Pennsylvania Academy of Fine Arts and other artistic venues in Philadelphia, Fuller grew up in an environment that sparked and nurtured in her an interest in the arts. Fuller studied first at the Pennsylvania Museum School for the Industrial Arts in Philadelphia (now the University of the Arts) between 1894 to 1897, before traveling to Europe to further her art training and education. Between 1899 and 1902 Fuller lived in Paris, where she studied drawing and sculpture at the Académie des Beaux Arts and the Académie Colarossi.

While a student at the School for Industrial Arts, Fuller won a prize for creating a bas-relief composed of thirty-seven medieval figures entitled *Procession of the Arts and Crafts.* In Paris, Fuller came in contact with African American artists and other important figures who played a significant role in shaping her intellectual and artistic concerns. Such figures included the painter Henry Ossawa Tanner, and W. E. B. DuBois who described her in *Crisis* (1926) as a genius whom "accidents of education and opportunity had raised . . . on a tidal wave of chance." Most importantly, while living in France, Fuller became acquainted with Auguste Rodin to whom she was first introduced through a fellow student at the Colarossi. It was with Rodin that Fuller shared her interest in the psychology of human emotions as a function of art. Upon seeing her clay model of *Man Eating His Heart,* Rodin was quoted to have said to her, "My child, you are a sculptor, you have a sense of form!" Under Rodin's tutelage, Fuller's work grew daring in concept and execution. As Judith Kerr, the scholar and biographer of Fuller, has explained, Fuller "refused to limit herself to subjects that were merely aesthetically pleasing, never avoiding portrayals because they were ugly or abhorrent." Through creation of positive images that comment on the complexity of the African American experience, Fuller indirectly protested the negative stereotypes that were common in the representation of African Americans in mainstream popular culture and fine art during the post-Reconstruction era.

Upon her return to the United States in 1902, Fuller set up a studio in Philadelphia but soon faced the racial barrier in marketing her art. She gradually became more involved in black social and political life, with more African American themes and concerns entering her work.

Works such as *Comedian,* a seated figure of the black performer George Walker, are exemplary of this transitional period. In 1907 she became the first black woman artist to receive a federal commission when asked to produce a set of tableaux for the Negro Pavilion at the Jamestown Tercentennial Exposition. She produced an award-winning diorama of 150 figures, representing black progress since the arrival of the first slave cargo in 1619.

Her marriage in 1906 to Dr. Solomon C. Fuller, a Liberian-born neurologist at Massachusetts Hospital, resulted in her relocation to Framingham, Massachusetts, where she continued to work on her art. In 1910 sixteen years worth of her work, stored in a Philadelphia warehouse, was destroyed in a disastrous fire. This tragic incident caused a lapse in her career during which she concentrated more on her role as a mother of three children. She resumed her

career in 1913 when requested by DuBois to reproduce for the fiftieth anniversary of the Emancipation Proclamation an earlier work, *Man Eating His Heart,* which was lost in the fire.

Instead of replicating this work, Fuller decided to produce a new sculpture, *The Spirit of Emancipation,* which ushered in a new productive period in her art career that was characterized by a change in style but continued her focus on earlier themes and concerns. A three-figure group standing eight feet high, *The Spirit of Emancipation* differs from other works in this genre in being free of any paternalistic representation and in offering a more realistic depiction of African American features absent in earlier works. Fuller's heightened racial consciousness grew more clear in later works, such as in *A Silent Protest against Mob Violence,* produced in 1919 to commemorate the tragic Mary Turner case.

Fuller's most significant work, *The Awakening of Ethiopia,* considered a powerful symbol of the spirit of the Harlem Renaissance, has been dated by most scholars to 1914 or 1917. Judith Kerr disagrees and instead suggests that it was created in response to James Weldon Johnson's request for a work for the New York City "Making of America" Festival, which dates it to 1921. The original version, which was twelve inches high with the left hand open and pointed outward, was changed in the enlarged bronze cast version (housed in the Schomburg Center for Research in Black Culture in New York), in which the left hand is depicted resting on the thigh. The figure represents a partially wrapped mummy bound from the waist down but reveals a head and shoulders of an African woman with the headdress of an ancient Egyptian queen. As the title reveals, Fuller used the Egyptian motifs to symbolize the African American's awakening and gradual unwrapping of bandages from an oppressive past. Fuller continued to be productive through the 1930s and into the 1940s, producing sculpture more rooted in the African American experience. The *Talking Skull* and the *Water Boy* were among many appealing figures inspired by African American folklore and popular culture.

The long illness and eventual death of Fuller's husband in 1953 and her own bout with tuberculosis, which confined her to a sanitarium, caused a lapse in her work. In 1957 she finally recovered and resumed working on more commissions. In the 1960s Fuller became more involved in the civil rights movement by donating proceeds of her artwork in support of the cause. At the same time she produced works inspired by the African American struggle. *Crucifixion,* for example, was a commemoration of the death of the four young girls in the infamous bombing of the church in Birmingham, Alabama, in 1963. Meta Vaux Warrick Fuller died on 18 March 1968 in Framingham, Massachusetts, at the age of ninety after a productive career that spanned more than seventy years.

—Salah Hassan

GAMMON, Reginald (A.)
American painter and printmaker

Born: Philadelphia, Pennsylvania, 31 March 1921. **Education:** Philadelphia Museum School of the Industrial Arts, 1941, 1946-49, certificate; Tyler School of Fine Art, Temple University, Philadelphia, 1950-51. **Military Service:** U.S. Navy, 1944-46: 3rd class shipfitter. **Family:** Married Janice Goldberger in 1974; one daughter and one son. **Career:** Visiting artist, assistant professor, full professor, Western Michigan University, Kalamazoo, 1970-91. Clerk, U.S. Post Office #1, New York, 1952-55; artist, Lifton, Gold and Ashen Advertising Agency, New York 1955-62; artist expert, board of education, New York, 1962-69. **Address:** 1511 Aragon Road S.W., Albuquerque, New Mexico 87105, U.S.A.

Individual Exhibitions:

1983   Kalamazoo Institute of the Arts, Kalamazoo, Michigan
1986   Wayne State University, Detroit (retrospective)
1987   Light Fine Arts Building Gallery, Kalamazoo College, Michigan (retrospective)
1990   Governor State University, University Park, Illinois
1995   Visiones Gallery, Albuquerque, New Mexico (retrospective)
        Santa Fe Contemporary Art, Santa Fe, New Mexico
1996   African American Museum, Dallas

Selected Group Exhibitions:

1994   State Fair Fine Arts Gallery, Santa Fe, New Mexico
        Sharing the Dream, College of Santa Fe, New Mexico (traveling)
1995   South Broadway Cultural Center, Albuquerque, New Mexico
        Horwitch Lewallen Gallery, Santa Fe, New Mexico
1996   Center for Southwest Research, Zimmerman Library University, Albuquerque, New Mexico

Collections:

Battle Creek Fine Arts Permanent Collection, Battle Creek, Michigan; Kalamazoo College Permanent Fine Art Collection, Kalamazoo, Michigan; National Afro-American Museum and Cultural Center at Wilberforce, Ohio; Permanent Collection of the Board of Education, Endicott Johnson Public Schools, New York.

*

Reginald A. Gammon comments:

My paintings depict a continued interest in rendering the human presence in all its variety, dignity, and sometime depravity or grandeur. Although the figure has been the predominant subject of my work, landscape and still life have also been important aspects, too, since they help place the subject in context and add interest and excitement to my compositions.

Choosing to use the figure as a visual metaphor and having a background in humanistic studies, I can in more universal terms communicate my ideas and attitudes concerning the human condition.

*   *   *

For Reginald Gammon the road to becoming a celebrated African American artist has been long and at times bumpy. Born to a family of modest means in Philadelphia, Gammon would regularly draw and paint pictures as a child, but it wasn't until he reached high school and was eventually offered a scholarship to the Philadelphia Museum School of the Industrial Arts in the early 1940s that his

Reginald Gammon. Photo courtesy of Janice Gammon.

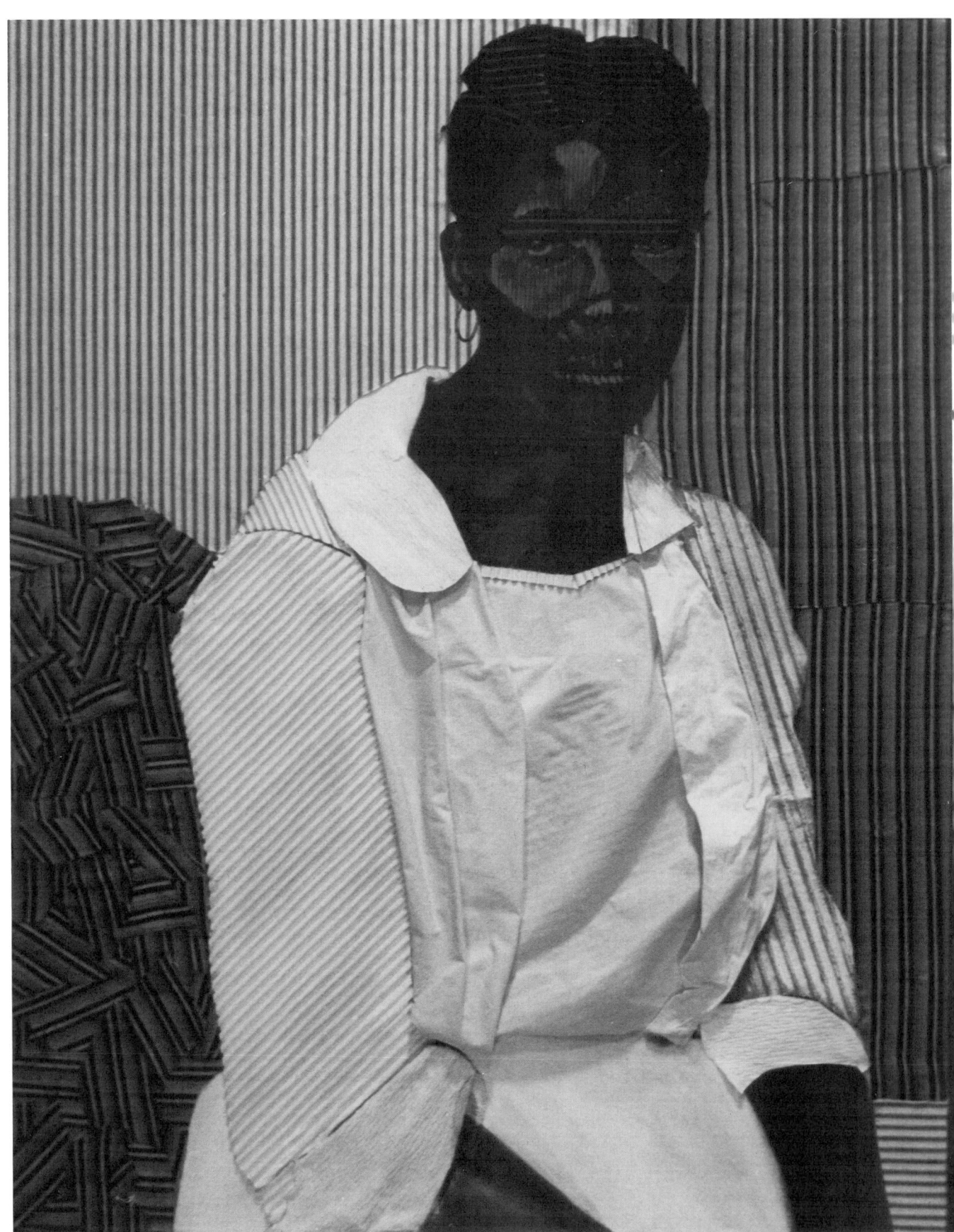

Reginald Gammon: *Gullah Woman.*

talent began to fully emerge. Role models, particularly African Americans in the art world, were scarce at that time. In addition the idea of actually making a living drawing and painting pictures seemed remote and far-fetched to many, including Gammon. It was this notion that led him to his first job at the New York City Post Office, one of the few places in the country that employed a substantial number of African Americans.

Gammon's desire to view his work on a canvas in a public gallery was something that would not go away, however. He finally landed a job at Lifton Gold & Asher in New York City as a paste-up artist. Between the mid 1950s and late 1960s, Gammon continued to develop his artistic style, his paintings depicting his vivid and creative interest in rendering the human presence. These images reflected the human condition through Gammon's eyes. During this period of racial unrest and injustice in America, pain, suffering, and depravity, as well as dignity, hope, and grandeur were the predominant subjects of his work. Although the figure has always been his prevailing subject, Gammon maintains that landscape and still lifes are essential aspects of his work, too.

One of his first individual exhibitions was in 1983 at the Kalamazoo Institute of the Arts in Michigan. A few years later his paintings were displayed at museums and galleries across the country, including the Santa Fe Contemporary Art Museum and the prominent African American Museum in Dallas. During this period Gammon worked as a visiting artist, assistant professor, and then full professor of art at Western Michigan University. One of the most revered contemporary African American artists in America, Gammon has continued to work since retiring from teaching and is regularly invited to speak to art students and young art hopefuls.

—Glenn Townes

GENTRY, Herbert
American painter and graphic artist

Born: Pittsburgh, Pennsylvania, 17 July 1921. **Education:** New York University, 1940-42; Académie de la Grande Chaumiere, Paris, 1946-49; École des Hautes Études, Paris, 1947-49. **Career:** Visiting instructor, Montclair State College, 1980 and 1982; visiting professor, Rutgers University, Newark, New Jersey, 1986. **Address:** Alitash Kebede Gallery, 964 North LaBrea Avenue, Los Angeles, California 90038, U.S.A.

Individual Exhibitions:

1949	Galerie de Seine, Paris
1974	Galerie Andre Zarre, New York
1975	Royal Art Academy, Stockholm, Sweden
1976	Amos Anderson Museum, Helsinki, Finland
	Gallery Glaub, Cologne, Germany
1985	Gallery Goovier Fine Arts, Amsterdam
1986	New York University

Selected Group Exhibitions:

1957	Burr Gallery, New York
1959	Galerie Suzanne, Bollage, Zurich
1960	Galerie Aesthetica, Stockholm
1961	Galerie Passepartout, Copenhagen
	Galerie Perron, Geneva
1962	Galerie Rudolf Meier, Davos, Switzerland
1963	Galerie Moderne, Silkeborg
1965	American Center for Students and Artists, Paris
1966	Lorensbergs Konstalong, Goteborg
1970	Art Museum, University of Texas, Austin

Collections:

Harmon Foundation, New York; Moderna Museet, Stockholm; Museum of African-American History, Chicago; National Museum, Stockholm; Riverside Museum, New York; Stedilijk Museum, Amsterdam; UNESCO, Paris.

Publications:

On GENTRY: Articles— "Elma Lewis: A New Show, a New Showplace," in *Boston After Dark,* 16 August 1970; "Herbert Gentry" by Jacqueline Spaulding, in *Black Art Quarterly,* 3, April 1979, pp. 4-11.

*   *   *

Initially a product of art instruction at the Works Progress Administration center in Harlem, Herbert Gentry was encouraged by his mother, one of the few black Ziegfeld showgirls, to travel to Europe if he wanted to become an artist. After being stationed in Paris from 1942 to 1945, during World War II, Gentry returned in 1946 to study at the École des Beaux-Arts. Leaving there, he then enrolled in the Académie de la Grande Chaumiere, where he studied with the Russian-born sculptor Ossip Zadkine and the French painter Yves Brailler. As a part of his art training, he was encouraged to view art outside the classroom environment, to visit museums, and to discuss art with other artists and art appreciators in cafés and restaurants. His teachers felt that the classroom was too limiting and that such social experiences helped to created a better-rounded artist. Consequently, it was in France that Gentry, visiting the Musée de l'Homme and other museums, first became familiar with traditional African sculpture.

By the early 1950s Gentry had met several modernists, including Alberto Giacometti, Constantin Brancusi, and Georges Braque (who gave him six lessons in painting). All were working in Paris at the time, and all were looking at African art for its abstract structural qualities. Gentry also became intrigued with the work of the German expressionists, saying that "a lot of the Germans went to Africa and because of that [experience] their work was less calculating and nearer to African art than any other group of artists." He found their work, especially that of Ernst Ludwig Kirchner, to be direct, truthful, and consistent.

Gentry also became associated with the influential group Cobra. He was in Paris when this group of northern European artists began to focus on intense, spontaneous color evoked by the subconscious. These artists also focused on African art, and Gentry said that most of them visited countries in Africa as part of their attempt to capture the energy and light of the sun in their compositions.

Gentry has made many trips back and forth between Europe and New York City, and he continues to maintain homes both in New York and in Malmö, Sweden. His experience as a bicontinental artist has informed his work in such a way that investigations of the

Herbert Gentry: *Meeting Series A,* 1987. Photo by Manu Sassoonian; courtesy of the Schomburg Center for Research in Black Culture.

subconscious, rather than subject matter, take precedence in his often surreal paintings. Gentry has focused on dreamworld imagery, including totems and emblems of magic and of the supernatural found in prehistoric art, African art, and early Christian calligraphy, as well as the art of the Middle Ages. By the mid-1950s, as a result of the supportive environment for abstraction in both Paris and the United States, his work had become more abstract. By then New York was viewed as the center for abstract expressionism, and, through an aggressive exhibition and promotional campaign supported by the U.S. government and New York's Museum of Modern Art, artists such as Jackson Pollock, Willem de Kooning, Robert Motherwell, and Clyfford Still were becoming known throughout Europe and the rest of the world. One of Gentry's best-known works from this period, *The Claw,* is still one of his favorite pieces. In *The Claw* (1958) a person from another world extends his hand to an unsuspecting receiver, who realizes that it is not a hand at all but rather a claw, an oppressive force, with ulterior motives.

Even as his mature work has become more abstract, Gentry has returned to the concept of the family of man, something that he was exposed to early on in Paris at the Musée de l'Homme. This can be explained by his feeling that the figure "gives more of a life to the composition than pure abstraction." In *Mes Aime* (1987) the blues cool and quiet the composition of three figures. The man has a dark blue face, and the family unit is completed with an animal and a woman.

Gentry continues to exhibit in the United States and Europe. As he reflects on his thirty-year career, however, he is grateful for his mother's having urged him to find himself in Europe, for it was there that he "felt free . . . like almost every foreigner who has lived there."

—Lizzetta LeFalle-Collins

GEORGE, Milton
Jamaican painter

Born: Manchester, Jamaica, 1939. **Education:** Jamaica School of Art. **Awards:** National Gallery of Jamaica Fellowship, 1978; Festival Exhibition Silver Medal, 1981; Silver Musgrave Medal, 1987; Gold Medal, *Santo Domingo Biennial,* Dominican Republic, 1994.

Individual Exhibitions:

1970	The Gallery, Kingston, Jamaica
1976	John Pear Tree Gallery, Kingston, Jamaica
1978	John Pear Tree Gallery, Kingston, Jamaica
1981	John Pear Tree Gallery, Kingston, Jamaica
1982	Frame Centre Gallery, Kingston, Jamaica
1987	Frame Centre Gallery, Kingston, Jamaica

Selected Group Exhibitions:

1971	Commonwealth Art Gallery, London
1974	*Three Decades of Jamaican Paintings,* Jamaican High Commission, Ottawa (through 1981)
1976	Pegasus Hotel Gallery, Kingston, Jamaica
1977	Gallery on the Hill, Jamaica
1983	National Gallery of Jamaica, Kingston
1986	Commonwealth Institute, London
1988	Frame Centre Gallery, Kingston, Jamaica
1991	Gallery Malraux, Los Angeles
	Jamaica to Brooklyn, Salena Gallery, New York

Collections:

Frame Centre Gallery, Kingston, Jamaica; National Gallery of Jamaica, Kingston.

Publications:

On GEORGE: Articles—"Milton" by Laurie Mahfood, in *Arts Jamaica,* 2(4), May 1984; "The Intimate World of Milton George" by Gloria Escoffery, in *Jamaica Journal,* 19(2), 1986, pp. 28-37; "Milton George" by Ricky D'Oyen, in *The Art of Living: The Jamaican,* August-September 1987; "Milton George's Nostalgia" by Ann Buttrick, in *The Jamaica Herald,* 1 April 1996, p. 3B; "Many Rivers Crossed" by Petrine Archer-Straw, in *New World Imagery: Contemporary Jamaican Art, National Touring Exhibition,* 1996.

*   *   *

Born in a rural community in Manchester parish in Jamaica, Milton George was enamored from an early age with the idea of being a painter. He entered the Jamaica School of Art in the early 1960s, but, ever suspicious of the academic approach, he had an irregular stay there and eventually abandoned school. Thus, George is essentially self-taught.

George has painted seriously and exhibited since the 1960s, and he had modest early successes, as with the much-publicized *Mother and Child* (1967) that was used on the cover of a booklet produced for distribution in West Africa by the British Family Planning Association. His art, however, remained marginal to the development of modernism in Jamaica until well into the 1970s, when his lyrical brand of expressionism began to change. An ensuing intensification and more complex involvement with subject matter can be linked to the social tensions that enveloped Jamaica in the late 1970s. Developments in Jamaican art in the 1970s—in particular the works of Karl Parboosingh, the late works of Eugene Hyde, and my own Francis Bacon-inspired expressionism—as well as more careful study of artists like Pablo Picasso, Chaim Soutine, and the German expressionists also played a part in releasing the deeper, darker side of George's nature. By the early 1980s a profound change was seen in his work.

George's mature paintings are marked by a highly personal approach to color and an idiosyncratic caricatural drawing style. In sharp contrast to his earlier works, these paintings are saturated with strident, intense color, although he went through a short phase in which the works were restricted largely to grays and blacks. One such monochromatic painting is *Judgement* (1985), in which the unrelieved blackness of what was his largest painting to date, was linked to a pan-African statement of outrage against the seeming endlessness of South African apartheid. His approach to space has become psychologically determined, and the paintings can alternately exhibit an almost Mark Rothko-like sparseness or the dense *horror vacuii* of a Pierre Alechinsky.

George's later paintings are deeply rooted in personal experience and are essentially autobiographical. Images of the self and of women dominate. He sometimes presents himself in the guise of the suffering Christ, as in the *Mocking of Christ* (1983), in which it is the artist himself who is mocked by comedic stand-ins for taunting, jeering society types, and in *Crucifixion* (1984), in which the artist replaces Christ on the cross. The three women who accompany him in this diptych are archetypes (bride, harlot, mother) representative of his varied and complex relationships with women.

George's fourteen-paneled *Pages from My Diary* (1983) comments on the man-woman relationship and shows the artist accompanied by woman in a variety of guises. She is seen as the painter's muse guiding him as he portrays her on canvas. In other guises she is a dance hall companion or a sexual toy, and in others a taunting harpy. Whatever her guise, woman is omnipresent, the essential other.

Politics also provided themes in the 1980s, and Jamaican political leaders have suffered at the hands of George's sharp and concise wit. In *The PM Speaks at 8 P.M.* (1986), the artist derides the autocratic style of Edward Seaga, then prime minister, while in the five-paneled *Searching for the Right Head* (1988) George wickedly pillories Michael Manley's restructuring of his political persona as he faced the 1989 elections.

George's magisterial output of the 1980s and the early 1990s has elevated him to prominence as one of Jamaica's premier painters. He also has been an important influence on younger artists such as Omari Ra, Douglas Wallace, and Stanford Watson.

—David Boxer

GILLIAM, Sam
American painter

Born: Tupelo, Mississippi, 30 November, 1933. **Education:** University of Louisville, 1952-55, 1958-61, B.A. 1955, M.A. 1961, L.H.D. 1980; Northwestern University, L.H.D. 1990. **Military Service:** United States Army, 1956-58. **Family:** Married Dorothy Buller in 1962, three daughters. **Awards:** National Endowment for the Arts grants, 1967, 1973, 1974, 1989; Washington Gallery of Modern Art Fellowship, 1968; Norman B. Harris Prize, Art Institute of Chicago, 1969; Longview Foundation Award, 1970; Guggenheim Memorial Foundation Fellowship, 1971; National Endowment for the Arts activities grant, 1973-75; Order of Merit Award, University of Louisville Alumni Association, 1987. Honorary doctorates: University of Louisville; Memphis College of Art and Design; Corcoran Gallery and School of Art; Northwestern University. **Agent:** Annie Gawlak, 1750 Lamont St. N.W., Washington, D.C. 20010, U.S.A. **Address:** c/o Middendorf/Lane Gallery, 2009 Columbia Road N.W., Washington, D.C. 20010, U.S.A.

Individual Exhibitions:

1956	University of Louisville, Kentucky
1963	Frame House Gallery, Louisville, Kentucky
	Adam Morgan Gallery, Washington, D.C.
1964	Adam Morgan Gallery, Washington, D.C.
1965	Jefferson Place Gallery, Washington, D.C.
1966	Jefferson Place Gallery, Washington, D.C.
1967	Jefferson Place Gallery, Washington, D.C.
	Phillips Collection, Washington, D.C.
1968	Jefferson Place Gallery Washington, D.C.
	Byron Gallery, New York
1969	*Gilliam/Krebs/McGowin,* Corcoran Gallery of Art, Washington, D.C.
1970	Jefferson Place Gallery, Washington, D.C.
	Galerie Darthea Speyer, Paris
1971	Museum of Modern Art, New York
1972	Jefferson Place Gallery, Washington, D.C.
1973	Jefferson Place Gallery, Washington, D.C.
	New Gallery, Cleveland
	Greenburg Gallery, St. Louis
	Howard University, Washington, D.C.
	University of California at Irvine
	Maison de la Culture, Rennes, France
	Fendrick Gallery, Washington, D.C.
	Galerie Darthea Speyer, Paris
1974	Fendrick Gallery, Washington, D.C.
	Linda Farris Gallery, Seattle
	Gilliam/Edwards/Williams: Extensions, Wadsworth Atheneum, Hartford, Connecticut
	Phoenix Gallery, Seattle
	Carl Solway Gallery, Cincinnati, Ohio
1975	Fendrick Gallery, Washington, D.C.
	Linda Farris Gallery, Seattle
	Philadelphia Museum of Art
	Collectors Gallery, Baltimore
1976	J.B. Speed Art Museum, Louisville, Kentucky
	Nina Freudenheim Gallery, Buffalo, New York

Rutgers University Art Gallery, New Brunswick, New Jersey
Fendrick Gallery, Washington, D.C.
1977   Pennsylvania State University, University Park
        Artpark, Lewiston, New York
1978   Fendrick Gallery, Washington, D.C.
        University of Kentucky, Lexington
        Virginia Commonwealth University, Richmond
        University of Massachusetts, Amherst
        Galerie Darthea Speyer, Paris
        Solway Gallery, New York
1979   Nina Freudenheim Gallery, Buffalo, New York
        Middendorf/Lane Gallery, Washington, D.C.
        Hamilton Gallery, New York
1980   Middendorf/Lane Gallery, Washington, D.C.
        Hamilton Gallery, New York
1981   Nina Freudenheim Gallery, Buffalo, New York
        Middendorf/Lane Gallery, Washington, D.C.
        Nexus Galleries, Atlanta
        Hamilton Gallery, New York
        Carl Solway Gallery, Cincinnati, Ohio
1982   Dart Gallery, Chicago
1983   Galerie Darthea Speyer, Paris
        Modern Painters at the Corcoran: Sam Gilliam, Corcoran
            Gallery of Art, Washington, D.C.
1984   Middendorf/Lane Gallery, Washington, D.C.
1985   Monique Knowlton Gallery, New York
        Seuferer Chosy Gallery, Madison, Wisconsin
1986   Davis/McClain Gallery, Houston, Texas
        Alice Simsar Gallery, Ann Arbor, Michigan
        Dalsheimer Gallery, Baltimore, Maryland
1987   Klein Gallery, Chicago
        Robert Kidd Gallery, Birmingham, Michigan
        Carl Solway Gallery, Cincinnati, Ohio
1988   Iannetti-Lanzone Gallery, San Francisco
        Klein Gallery, Chicago
        Birmingham Museum of Art, Alabama
1989   Middendorf Gallery, Washington, D.C.
        Fendrick Gallery, New York
1990   Koplin Gallery, Los Angeles
        Middendorf Gallery, Washington, D.C.
        Philadelphia Museum of Art
1991   Gallery Simone Stern, New Orleans
        Gallery Darthea Speyer, Paris
        Nancy Drysdale Gallery/de Andino Fine Arts, Washington, D.C.
        Walker Hill Arts Center, Seoul, Korea
        American Craft Museum, New York
1992   Smith Anderson Gallery, Palo Alto
        Michael H. Lord Gallery, Milwaukee, Wisconsin
1993   Nancy Drysdale Gallery, Washington, D.C.
        Brandywine Workshop, Philadelphia, Pennsylvania
        Golden Windows Inside Gold (installation through 1995),
            Whitney Museum of American Art at Philip Morris,
            New York
1994   Galerie Simmone Stern, New Orleans, Louisiana
        Baumgartner Galleries, Washington, D.C.
1995   Imago Gallery, Palm Desert, California
        44th Biennial Exhibition of Contemporary American
            Painting, Corcoran Gallery of Art, Washington,
            D.C.

Selected Group Exhibitions:

1964   9 Contemporary Painters U.S.A., Pan-American Union,
            Washington, D.C.
1970   Works on Paper, Museum of Modern Art, New York
1971   Works for New Spaces, Walker Art Center, Minneapolis
1972   Biennale, Venice
1973   Works for Spaces, San Francisco Museum of Art
1986   Abstraction-Abstraction, Carnegie-Mellon University,
            Pittsburgh
1987   The Afro-American Artist in the Age of Cultural Plural-
            ism, Anacostia Museum of the Smithsonian, Washing-
            ton, D.C.
1988   Prints: Washington, Phillips Collection, Washington, D.C.
1989   Looking South Continual, Memphis Brooks Museum,
            Memphis
        The Blues Aesthetic, Washington Project for the Arts,
            Washington, D.C.
1990   African American Art from the Collection, Philadelphia
            Museum of Art
1994   New Acquisitions, Studio Museum in Harlem, New York
        Tandem Press: Five Years of Collaboration and Experi-
            mentation, Elvejhem Museum of Art at the University
            of Wisconsin, Madison

Collections:

Baltimore Museum of Art; Carnegie Institute, Corcoran Gallery of
Art, Washington, D.C.; Howard University, Washington, D.C.;
Phillips Collection, Washington, D.C.; Museum of African Art,
Washington, D.C.; Museum of Modern Art, New York; National
Gallery of Art, Washington, D.C.; Art Institute of Chicago; Walker
Art Center, Minneapolis; Boymans van Beuningen Museum,
Rotterdam; Tate Gallery, London; University of Iowa Museum;
Washington Gallery of Modern Art, Washington, D.C.; George
Washington University; Washington, D.C.; Whitney Museum of
American Art, New York.

Publications:

By GILLIAM: Article—"Solids and Veils," in *Art Journal*, 50,
Spring 1991, pp. 10-11.

On GILLIAM: Books—*Art in Washington* by Leslie Judd Ahlander,
Washington, D.C. 1968; *Art and Ideas* by William Fleming, New
York, 1973; *The Great American Salt Works* by Jack Burnham,
New York 1974; *Gilliam/Edwards/Williams: Extensions*, exhibition
catalog, Hartford, Connecticut, 1974; *Sam Gilliam*, exhibition cata-
log, Louisville, Kentucky 1976; *Modern Painters at the Corcoran:
Sam Gilliam* by John Beardsley, Washington, D.C. 1983. **Articles**—
"Meet the Artist: Sam Gilliam" by Cornelia Noland, in *Washingto-
nian*, October 1965; "A Gallery without Walls" by Barbara Rose,
in *Art in America* (New York), March/April 1968; "Painting Is
Alive and Well" by Barbara Rose, in *Vogue* (New York), November
1969; "3 Washington Artists" by Walter Hopps and Nina Felshin
Osnos, in *Art International* (Lugano, Switzerland), May 1970; "En-
ergy Is the Catalyst in Sam Gilliam's Formula," in the *Washington
Star*, 19 October 1975; "Sam Gilliam: Recent Black Paintings" by
Jay Kloner in *Arts* (New York), February 1978; "Skin Deep" by
Kay Larson, in *New York*, 23 March 1981; "Amplifications" by
Marjorie Welish, in *Art in America* (New York), November 1981;

"A Metaphor for Human Being: New Paintings by Sam Gilliam" by Gerrit Henry, in *Arts Magazine,* February 1985; "Letting Go" by Jane Addams Allen, in *Art in America,* 74, January 1986, pp. 98-105 (illustrated); review (Klein Gallery, Chicago) by Andy Argy, in *New Art Examiner,* 14, Summer 1987, p. 48; review (Middendorf Gallery, Washington, D.C.) by Florence Rubenfeld, in *Arts Magazine,* 63, Summer 1989, p. 79; "Gaining Self-Confidence and Patience" by Daniel Grant, in *American Artist,* 54, November 1990, p. 12.

*   *   *

Sam Gilliam first rose to prominence in the late 1960s with his "drape paintings," large-scale, unstretched canvases suspended from the wall or ceiling, on which the artist had variously soaked, stained, and splattered luminous layers of bright color. Extending the spontaneity and process orientation of the Washington Color school to encompass the flexibility of the painted support itself, Gilliam achieved a sculptural projection of color into three-dimensional space, allowing light to play over his richly hued surfaces from within and without. These works did not so much literalize the color "field" as collapse the notion of the painted ground.

In *A and the Carpenter II* (1973), Gilliam went so far as to lose even the vertical orientation of the support by draping the canvas over low wooden sawhorses and the floor. The drape paintings could be reconfigured spatially for each new installation, allowing for continuous change and adaptation. Underlying these works—which draw upon what artist and historian David C. Driskell has identified as "ancestral forms such as the tie-dye process" and "the improvisational character of African textiles as well as the encrusted surfaces of African sculpture"—is a dialogue between improvisation and order that has informed Gilliam's formalist oeuvre for the ensuing three decades.

In paintings from the mid-1970s, such as *Darted Again* (1974-75), Gilliam began cutting up his stained canvas and rearranging the shapes into precise forms so that the flux of their painterly surfaces appeared sectioned into neat geometric divisions of the circle or rectangle. Soon after, Gilliam abandoned the staining process altogether and began to apply acrylic paint in thick layers to his canvases, working it over with combs, rakes, and brooms to create turbulent, heavily textured surfaces grooved with lush color. Once again the paintings were sliced apart and reconstructed, resulting in rich juxtapositions of texture and hue. At first simple geometric forms prevailed—circles, square, triangles—but in time Gilliam was freely cutting irregular shapes, slathering them with more color, exchanging them in unexpected ways with other paintings. The resulting pieces were dissonant patchworks of color and shape, reminiscent of the crazy quilts of the artist's rural Southern childhood. Permutations of certain shapes or elements, such as a single arching form, might constitute one series of paintings; in another, such as the elegant red-and-black *Arc Maker I* and *II* from 1981, the series might be built on limited chromatic means. In these paintings structural relationships based on texture and shape seem to rival coloristic effects for compositional dominance.

In the wall construction *Someplace to Someplace Else* (1989), aluminum arcs loaded with turgid swatches of enamel and acrylic paint literally explode off the surface of the painting to reach into three-dimensional space. Here the contradictory impulses of Gilliam's art towards freedom and restraint recall jazz, with its hot and cool tonalities, its complex harmonic and percussive structures overlaid with surging improvisational melodies.

Gilliam's later works, like *Minor Key* (1992), return to a flat rectangular format with panels of acrylic-painted fabric sewn and mounted into broad strips. Bold, clashing colors are combed on in trademark Gilliam fashion. The varied scale of the interlocking, raked strokes form rhythmic intervals that suggest speed and weight: they are rolled or blocked, delicately stained or built up like hefty bricks; here they frame a glimpse of deep space, there they sit insistently on the surface.

Even as Gilliam's painted stroke becomes increasingly reductive, a signature device, he endeavors to remain deeply engaged in the physicality of his medium, distancing himself from post-formalist abstractionists for whom the stroke functions more or less self-consciously as a painterly sign. In less successful pieces, Gilliam's technical accomplishment and bright chromatic palette combine to make the paintings look facile or contrived. At their best, however, his visceral surfaces and colliding shapes convey a vitality and presence that pulsate convincingly between painterly spontaneity and formalist rigor.

—Dorothy Valakos

GLOVER, Ablade
Ghanaian painter and fiber artist

Born: Labadl, Accra, 1 August 1934. **Education:** University of Science and Technology, Kumasi, Art teachers certificate, 1958; Central School of Art and Design, London, N.D.D. (diploma in art) 1962; University of Newcastle-Upon Tyne, England, A.T.D. 1965; Kent State University, Ohio, M.Ed. 1972; Ohio State University, Columbus, Ph.D. 1974. **Career:** Teacher, Adaabraka Middle School, Accra, 1956-57; art instructor, Akodze Middle School, Tema, 1958-59; art tutor, Winneba Training College, Winneba, 1962-63; poster artist/exhibitions officer, Ghana Information Services, Accra, 1963-64; lecturer, College of Art, University of Science and Technology, Kumasi, 1965-75; senior lecturer, University of Science and Technology, Kumasi, 1975-82. Head, Department of Art Education and dean of College of Art, University of Science and Technology, Kumasi, 1982-94. Retired 1994 to paint full-time. Member, Arts Council of Ghana, Ghana Museums and Monuments Board, International Society for Education Through Art; life fellow, Royal Society of Arts, London; vice-president, Ghana Association of Artists, 1978; fellow, International Biographical Centre, Cambridge, England. **Awards:** Academician of Italy Gold Medal, Academia Italia, 1980; Artist of the Year Award, Entertainment, Critics and Writers Association of Ghana; Leisure Special Award, Rex-Image Foundation, Accra, 1989. **Address:** Department of Art Education, College of Art, University of Science and Technology, Kumasi, Ghana.

Individual Exhibitions:

1963	Arts Centre, Accra
1964	Arts Centre, Accra
1967	Arts Centre, Accra
1970	Arts Centre, Accra
1975	Arts Centre, Accra
1976	Asele Gallery, Nsukka, Nigeria
	Arts Centre, Accra

1978   Arts Centre, Accra
1979   British Council, Enugu, Nigeria
1980   National Theatre, Lagos, Nigeria
        Community of Arts, Cummington, Massachusetts
1981   Arts Centre, Accra
        National Gallery of Modern Art, Lagos, Nigeria
1982   Goethe Institute, Lagos, Nigeria
        Africa Centre, London
        October Gallery, London
        Arts Council of Ghana, Accra
1983   International Student Center, University of California,
            Los Angeles
        Commonwealth Institute, London
1984   October Gallery, London
        Arts Centre, Accra
        International Student Center, University of California,
            Los Angeles
1985   IFA Gallery, Bonn, Germany
        University of Science and Technology, Kumasi
1987   October Gallery, London
        Cornwall College, Redruth, England
        National Gallery of Zimbabwe
1988   British Council, Accra
1989   BIZ Art Gallery, Geneva, Switzerland
1995   October Gallery, London

Selected Group Exhibitions:

1962   *Young Commonwealth Artists,* Edinburgh Festival, London
1969   Smithsonian Institution, Washington, D.C.
1977   FESTAC, Lagos, Nigeria
        Howard University, Washington, D.C.
1983   *Ghanaian Contemporary Artists,* African-American Mu-
        seum of Arts and Culture, Dallas
1985   Westbourne Gallery, London
1987   IFA Gallery, Bonn, Germany
1988   Goethe Institute, Accra
1994   TreasureHouse, A Gallery of African Art, Lagos, Nigeria
1995   October Gallery, London

Collections:

Africa Centre, London; Embassy of Ghana, Washington, D.C.; French Embassy, Accra; Ghana Arts Council, Accra; Ghana Embassy, Bonn, Germany; Ghana Museums and Monuments Board, Accra; International House, Ohio State University, Columbus; Kent State University, Ohio; National Gallery of Modern Art, Lagos, Nigeria; National Gallery of Zimbabwe, Harare; United States Embassy, Accra; Visiting Arts Unit of Great Britain, London.

Publications:

By GLOVER: Article—"Art Is a Very Creative Institution that Plays a Dominant Role in Nation Building," in *P and P,* 12-19 May 1994, p. 7.

On GLOVER: Books—*Exhibition of Oil Paintings by Ablade Glover,* exhibition catalog, Accra, Ghana Arts Council, 1981 (illustrated); *Ablade Glover,* exhibition catalog, Accra, British Council, 1988 (illustrated); *Ablade Glover: New Works,"* exhibition catalog, London, October Gallery, 1995. Articles—"Art for Today" by Nadir

Thirani, in *West Africa* (London), 9 April 1984; "Ablade Glover in Perspective" by John Duke, in *West Africa* (London), 23 January 1989 (illustrated).

*   *   *

Ablade Glover is a tireless observer of human activities. A passive viewer may describe Glover's painting style as impressionism because he portrays rural life and forest scenes, but the possibility of external influences on his art cannot be ruled out given that he received his formal education in Ghana, Britain, and the United States. Throughout the history of African art, artists have been preoccupied with scenic views of everyday local life and the natural world. Rock engravings and paintings in South Africa and Sahara cave sites are reminiscent of the peoples' everyday activities and principal animals in the areas. Bronze plaques of the ancient Benin Kingdom recast scenes of court life. In the Owerri region of Nigeria, Mbari house is, in part, a gallery of scenes from the everyday life of the Igbo.

In contemporary Ghana, Kofi Antobam, Ato Delaquis, and Ben Offei-Nyarko have produced genre paintings that are as charming as Glover's. Glover's unique artistic style, prolific exhibition record, early research on the Adinkra symbols, and indulgence in international critical dialogues in the arts have brought him to the foreground of Ghanaian art and, in fact, the contemporary African art field.

Ablade Glover is of the Ga tribe. He trained in Ghana as a textile artist but during his education overseas, he was drawn to painting, which has become his tongue. He has produced some works in acrylic, but oil on canvas is his primary medium. His undergraduate thesis in Adinkra motifs was a pioneer study of the importance of these pictographs in the daily lives of the people. It had a measurable impact on most of the artists who trained at the University of Science and Technology, Kumasi.

In formal context Glover's work defies easy classification. His work has a touch of poetic warmth. No grand political, satirical, or mimetic overtones are conveyed here. Earlier paintings of this artist are mostly expressive poses of Ghanaian women, especially as seen in the market culture. He paints the intensity of the marketplace as a way of stressing its economic and social roles in contemporary Africa. In *Fishy Scene* and *Mothers* the women were selected from the crowd, and Glover uses the technique of overpainting to leave a relief effect. The artist faced the challenges of how to communicate the complexities of the shapes, colors, textures, and rhythms of his subjects to the viewer. Thus, his painting process was a responsive act.

A close encounter with later canvases reveals a loose field of colors—broken areas of bright hues thickly applied directly from the tube with the palette knife. As one retreats from his canvas, crowd behavior begins to merge with urban and pastoral environments. This use of optical color mixing is an important painting technique in traditional African societies. A broad area of a color is often hemmed and filled with lines or dots of different colors. As these colors mix in the viewer's eyes, they offset the work from the two-dimensional surface. Paintings such as *Pilgrimage, Every Knee Shall Bow, Call for Prayer, Prayer for Allah,* and *Sabbath Inspiration* focus on crowd behavior. They are records of his people's religious concerns. Although titles such as *My Enemy's Enemy; When Rivals Meet, Where Rivals Meet; Two Trouble, One God, Two Husband, One Wife; Orderly Disorder, Disordered Order;* and

Redeployment Deployment are heightened expressions, their formal bases are certainly not in the abstract vein.

After retiring from teaching to work as a full-time artist, Dr. Glover opened an art gallery in his hometown, Labadi, near Accra. The subjects of his art, when viewed with his three decades of educating Ghanaian artists, tell us that he was not far from his people. His varied contributions, no matter how controversial or heraldic, will be spoken of by many generations to come.

—Barthosa Nkurumeh

GONZALEZ, Christopher (Francis)
Jamaican painter and sculptor

Born: Kingston, Jamaica, 15 March 1943. **Education:** Jamaica School of Art, Kingston, Jamaica, diploma 1963. **Family:** California College of Arts and Crafts, Oakland, M.F.A. 1972. **Awards:** Artist-in-residence, Denmark, 1965; tuition scholarship, Jamaica Government, 1971; Silver Musgrave Medal for sculpture, 1974.

Individual Exhibitions:

1975	Olympia Center, Kingston, Jamaica
1980	RJK Gallery, Atlanta, Georgia
1983	Mutual Life Center, Kingston, Jamaica
1984	Frame Centre Gallery, Kingston, Jamaica
	Makonde Gallery, Kingston, Jamaica
1986	Mutual Life Gallery, Kingston, Jamaica
1988	Frame Centre Gallery, Kingston, Jamaica
1989	Mutual Life Gallery, Kingston, Jamaica
1995	*Creations,* Mutual Life Gallery, Kingston, Jamaica

Selected Group Exhibitions:

1970	Pacific Grove Art Center, California
1972	Richmond Art Center, California
1975	*Ten Jamaican Sculptors,* Commonwealth Institute Art Gallery, London
1976	Gallery Barrington, Kingston, Jamaica
1977	National Gallery of Jamaica, Kingston
1979	Spelman College, Atlanta, Georgia
1980	Chi-Wara Gallery, Atlanta, Georgia
1985	Upstairs Downstairs Gallery, Kingston, Jamaica
1986	Commonwealth Institute, London
1996	Victoria Mutual Building Society, Kingston, Jamaica

Collections:

National Gallery of Jamaica, Kingston.

Publications:

On GONZALEZ: Articles—"The Gonzalez-Kayiga Exhibition" by John Maxwell, in *Jamaica Journal* 7(4), 1973, pp. 54-56; "Gonzalez Carvings: Birth of a Nation" by Andrew Hope, in *The Sunday Gleaner,* 7 December 1975; "Gonzalez Display Opens," in *The Daily Gleaner,* 16 April 1975; "Christopher Gonzalez" by

Gloria Escoffery, in *Jamaica Journal,* 20(2), 1987, pp. 55-64; "Regrets, No Bitterness," in *The Sunday Gleaner,* 4 December 1994.

*   *   *

Despite the heightened symbolism of Christopher Gonzales's sculpture and paintings, there is a literalness to their composition that makes them easy to read. Within the context of Caribbean religious and spiritual beliefs, the significance of Gonzales's forms is barely allegorical or hidden. For those who know their Bible, his sculpted forms are transparent. All are archetypal: a tree, for example, is the tree of life; its roots, the roots of a culture; its fruit, the fruit of mankind.

Most of Gonzales's work has been informed by his early exposure to Roman Catholicism and by his later interest in Buddhism, Rosicrucianism, and Rastafarianism and a greater appreciation of the Bible. In this realm of the spiritual, Afro-Caribbean and European artistic forms fuse. What once might have been a fairly transparent borrowing from Pre-Raphaelite imagery, West African masks, and biblical icons has been synthesized into an artistic style perfectly at ease within an eclectic Caribbean aesthetic.

Although Gonzales received postgraduate training at several institutions abroad, including the California College of Arts and Crafts and Spelman College in Atlanta, Georgia, he can claim a Caribbean historical lineage. His art refers to the work of the Jamaican sculpture Edna Manley, the paintings of Barrington Watson, his tutor at the Jamaica School of Art, and the ceramics of his colleague Gene Pearson.

Yet, for all his suitability, his commitment to a developing black aesthetic, his grasp of Jamaica's social concerns, and his ability to convert religious and political conviction into visual form, Gonzales has often found himself at odds with his viewing public. His sculpture, and in particular his publicly commissioned sculpture, has regularly fallen afoul of popular taste in Jamaica. The commanding scale and distinctive style of Gonzales's work has meant that he has often been selected to execute images of religious, political, or national significance, but sometimes with controversial effect.

Certainly Gonzales's most provocative work to date is that of the life-size figure of Bob Marley commissioned by the Jamaican government to commemorate the reggae singer's death in 1982. Of this piece, which never reached its intended podium but instead came to stand in the lower hall of the National Gallery of Jamaica, Gonzales was to say that "my real intention . . . [was] to get something beyond the person, to capture a spirit and a time."

Cast in a dark bronze, the anthropomorphic form, half-man, half-tree, is conceptually more akin to Marley than the waxworklike replacement that now stands outside the National Stadium. It is strongly rigid, phallic, and arresting in its blackness, a piece convincingly committed to the precepts of Marley's beliefs, which in their most naked form the public found disturbing.

The rejection of the statue was received philosophically by Gonzales, who in other works, such as his self-portraits, has often represented himself as a suffering messianic figure, a prophet in the wilderness. Such images, along with their nymphlike female counterparts, figure prominently in Gonzales's paintings. Normally executed in watercolor, the paintings are less strident than the sculpture, which employs bold and incisive lines. The paintings are, nevertheless, compelling evocations of a mythical or spirit world; in contrast to the women, whose faces echo Baule and Fang ancestry, the men are sagelike and Orientalized. The figures sometimes fuse in art nouveau swirls and erotic passion. At other times they are distinctly individualized, scarified, and patterned. The colors of the images are integrated and easy on the eye, sometimes to the point of prettiness. Yet this surface distraction should not deter the viewer from the underlying strength of Gonzales's compositional style and the even deeper significance of his meditated religious symbolism.

—Petrine Archer-Straw

GOODNIGHT, Paul T.

American painter

Born: Chicago, Illinois, 31 December 1946. **Education:** Vesper College, Boston, 1969-71; Roxbury Community College, Massachusetts, 1972-73; Massachusetts College of Art, 1972-75, B.A., 1975. **Military Service:** U.S. Army, 1967-69. **Family:** Lives with Bernice Robinson, one daughter. **Career:** Since 1975 free lance artist. Drawing instructor, Charlestown Middle School, Boston, 1975-78, Bridgewater State Prison, Massachusetts, 1977-78; environmental art instructor, Lincoln-Sudbury High School, Sudbury, Massachusetts 1982-83, Wyland High School, Wyland, Massachusetts, 1984-85. Album cover artist, Kool and the Gang, Boston, 1995. **Awards**: Award Fellow, Artist's Foundation, Boston, 1971; National Conference of Artists Award, 1979; Ten Artists at Their Best, Gallery of the Martin Luther King Library, Washington, D.C., 1984; Unsung Heroes Award, Museum of Afro-American History, Boston, 1988; Governor of Massachusetts proclamation, 1991; Paige Academy Award, 1994. **Address:** 791 Tremont, Boston, Massachusetts 02118, U.S.A. **Online Address:** http://www.afrinet.net-gallery.

Individual Exhibitions:

1981	Cousen Rose Gallery, Martha's Vineyard, Massachusetts
	Piano Craft Gallery, Boston
	Arthur D. Little, Inc., Cambridge, Massachusetts
	Bentley College, Waltham, Massachusetts
	Gutman Library, Harvard University, Cambridge, Massachusetts
	New Muse Museum, Brooklyn, New York
	Triangle Gallery, Washington, D. C.
	U.S. Coast Guard Academy, Connecticut
1983	Nyamgoma's Gallery, Washington, D. C.
1985	*Southern Exposure, One-Man Travelling Show,* Amber Gallery, Hampton, Virginia (traveling)
	Frames and Fine Arts Gallery, Richmond, Virginia
1987	CRT Craftery Gallery, Hartford, Connecticut
1990	Copley Historical Society, Boston
1991	Clinton Hill Simply Art, Brooklyn, New York
1993	Colours Art Decor, Gary Indiana
	Annie Lee and Friend Gallery, Chicago, Illinois
1994	Blackberries Gallery, Washington, D.C.
	Tina's Gallery, Silver Spring, Maryland
	M'Print Gallery, Atlanta, Georgia
	Pyramid Gallery, Little Rock, Arkansas
	Galerie 500, Washington, D. C.

Paul Goodnight.

Selected Group Exhibitions:

1981	Gallery Papyrus, Petionville, Haiti
1983	Nyamgoma's Gallery, Washington, D. C.
	Black Cultural Center, Halifax, Nova Scotia
1985	*Vietnam Veteran's Show,* Chicago, Illinois
1989	Impressive of Brasil, Colorlines Tenth Annual Exhibition
1990	Milton Museum of Art, Milton, Massachusetts
	Black Arts Festival, London, England
1994	Piano Craft Guild, Boston
	Bahia Music and Arts Festival, Bahia, Brazil
1995	*Artists Salute to Black History Month,* Los Angeles

Collections:

Atlanta Life Insurance Company, Georgia; Hampton Institute, Hampton, Virginia; Howard University, Washington, D.C.; Museum of the National Center of Afro-American Artists, Boston; National Gallery of Art, Washington, D.C.

Publications:

On GOODNIGHT: Articles—"Faces to Watch," *Boston Magazine,* 1987; "Artist to Watch," in *Black Enterprise,* December, 1988; "The Prime-Time Painter" by Sandy Coleman, in *The Boston Globe,* Living Arts section, 27 August 1996.

*

Paul Goodnight comments:

Art creates an avenue for me, an avenue I would like to travel. I want to play a part in helping build the road, but in reality, it's helping to build me. I'm starting to believe in things that I've always heard about but never paid any attention to. Things like God; "being human" as opposed to the human being; prejudice, paranoia, and abstinence.

I find myself anxiously looking forward to discovering new ways of drawing and painting by simply doing what we all do from time to time: observe, practice, and document. The trick is being patient enough to allow this process of creating to grow and manifest itself in me.

I think that mental and physical agility are necessary to endure, for they provide a balance and demonstrate the unlimited energy or potential within us. I strive to endure because I know it is hard to maintain consistency. Sometimes I welcome it.

*   *   *

After military service Paul Goodnight studied at the Vesper George School of Art, Roxbury Community College, and the Massachusetts College of Art. His extensive travels and his close relationships with other artists throughout the Americas, Africa, Europe, and Asia have been as important as his art training, however. From these he has drawn inspiration, perspectives, themes, and endless subject matter as seen through the prism of his experiences as an African American.

In addition to teaching art at several Boston-area institutions, Goodnight has received commissions for murals, such as that in the Ruggles Station of Boston's transit system, and for illustrations from the publishers Harper and Row, Houghton Mifflin, and Blackside and from television station WGBH. Among the most highly visible commissions executed by Goodnight was his poster for the 1996 Olympic Games in Atlanta. His works have also appeared in a number of contemporary television programs, including *The Cosby Show* and *Fresh Prince of Bel-Air,* and in the movie *Ghosts.* Goodnight operates his own publishing business, and prints of his works are widely available.

Goodnight originated the concept of the middle passage project titled "Mural Masters." He is at the center of this international endeavor to create a monument to the triumphant spirit of those who survived the middle passage to become the African Americans of the New World. The project underscores the extent to which Goodnight is an informal ambassador within the black world.

Goodnight's paintings are in the tradition of such African American masters as John Biggers. Goodnight remains committed to figuration as it is filtered through formal elaborations such as colorfields rendered in broken patches of paint and the use of unusual hues in warm tones. He is also fond of literary titles that push the interpretation of his works toward ideas captured in vernacular speech and proverbs. Through the creation of works set in several countries of the Americas as well as in Africa and Asia, Goodnight expresses a unified vision of black people as a global population with shared manners and behaviors, while at the same time offering his viewers wit and universal humanism.

—Edmund Barry Gaither

GORDON, Russell
American painter and printmaker

Born: Philadelphia, Pennsylvania, 3 July 1936. **Education:** Temple University, Philadelphia, B.F.A. 1962; University of Wisconsin,

M.S. 1966; University of Wisconsin, M.F.A. 1967. **Career:** Assistant professor, University of California, Berkeley, 1969-70; associate professor, Mills College, Oakland, California, 1974-75. Since 1975 associate professor, Concordia University, Montreal, Quebec. Visiting lecturer, San Francisco Art Institute, 1969-70; artist-in-residence, 3-EP Press, Palo Alto, California, 1981, University of Saskatchewan, Saskatoon, 1984, Lakeside Studio, Michigan, 1986, 1988, East Carolina University, North Carolina, 1989. **Awards:** George C. Marshall Fellowship, Denmark, 1972; McDowell Fellowship, McDowell Colony, New Hampshire, 1975; National Endowment for the Arts grant, 1981; Award of Excellence, Museum of Science and Industry, Chicago, 1986. **Agents:** Renata Hochelbert, Hochelbert Fine Art, 3445 Avenue Ridgewood, PH 500, Montreal, Quebec H3V 1B7, Canada; Kraushaar Gallery, 724 Fifth Avenue, New York, New York 10019, U.S.A.; Simon Lowinsky, Lowinsky Gallery, 568 Broadway, New York, New York 10012, U.S.A.

Individual Exhibitions:

1969	University of Utah, Salt Lake City, Utah
	Berkeley Art Center, California
	San Francisco Art Institute, California
	Eastern Oregon College, La Grande
1972	Ars Studio, Arhus, Denmark
	På Trudstolpegard, Kunst Hallen, Sakskøbing, Denmark
	Vikingsberg Kunst Museum, Helsingborg, Sweden
1973	Gallery Alliance, Copenhagen, Denmark
1974	Quay Gallery, San Francisco
1975	Quay Gallery, San Francisco
1976	Waddington Galleries, Montreal
	Memorial Union Gallery, Arizona State University, Tempe (traveling)
1977	Braunstein Gallery, New York
	Braunstein Gallery, San Francisco
1978	Quay Gallery, San Francisco
1979	Waddington Gallery, Toronto
1980	Braunstein Gallery, San Francisco
1982	Los Angeles Municipal Art Gallery, Los Angeles (traveling)
1983	Utah Museum of Fine Arts, Salt Lake City
	University of Utah, Museum of Fine Arts
	Miami-Dade Public Library
	Theo Waddington and Company, Montreal
1985	Moosart Gallery, Miami
	Waddington and Shiell, Toronto
	Gallerie Convergence, *Petits formats*, Montreal
1986	Waddington and Gorce, Montreal
	Allrich Gallery, San Francisco
1987	Joy Moos Gallery, Miami
1988	Chicago International Arts Exposition
1989	Alan Short Gallery, Stockton, California
1990	Waddington and Gorce, Montreal
1991	Musée Régional de Rimouski, Rimouski, Quebec
1992	Waddington and Gorce, Montreal

Selected Group Exhibitions:

1973	Cincinnati Art Museum, Ohio
1974	Mills College Art Gallery, Oakland, California
1975	*Waterworks: Painting and Sculpture,* Berkeley Art Center, California

1984   Lill Street Gallery, Chicago
1985   San Jose Art League Center and Gallery, San Jose, California
1986   Walnut Creek Art Center, California
1987   Weissman Gallery, Concordia University, Montreal
1992   *Professor's Choice Exhibition,* Gallery Barbara Silverberg,
        Montreal
1995   Louis Stern Fine Arts, San Diego
        Kraushaar Galleries, New York

Collections:

Achenbach Foundation, San Francisco; British Museum, London; Canada Council Art Bank, Ottawa; Carnegie Corporation of New York; Duke University, Durham, North Carolina; Honolulu Academy of Arts, Hawaii; Museum of Fine Arts, University of Utah; Library of Congress, Washington, D.C.; New Jersey State Museum, Trenton; Mills College, Oakland, California; Minneapolis Institute of Art; Oakland Museum, California; Musée d'Art Contemporain, Montreal; Musée du Québec, Quebec City; Museum of Fine Arts, Springfield, Massachusetts; Philadelphia Museum of Art; Ringling Museum, Sarasota, Florida; Rosenwald Collection, Philadelphia; San Francisco Museum; Smithsonian Institution, Washington, D.C.; University of New Hampshire; University of Wisconsin; Walker Art Center, Minneapolis.

Publications:

On GORDON: Articles—"Gumball Machine," in *San Francisco Examiner and Chronicle,* 23 December 1973, p. 21 (illustrated); "Russell Gordon's Egging On" by Mimi Jacobs, in *Black Times,* August 1974, pp. 8-9 (illustrated); "Russell Gordon Colorful Ideas," in *Art Week,* 20 December 1975, p. 16 (illustrated); "The Art of Slashing and Slashing" by Gary Michael Dault, in *The Toronto Star* (Canada), 13 October 1979 (illustrated); "The Pictorial Existentialism of Russell Gordon" by Serge Jongué, in *Vie des Arts,* 27(107), Summer 1982, pp. 36-39 (illustrated); "Regard, Image, Masques" by Serge Jonqué, in *Vie des Arts* 30(120), Fall 1985, p. 64-65; "Big Man Gordon Displays Impeccable Craftsmanship" by Stuart Wilson, in *The Montreal Downtowner* (Canada), March 1990, p. 17 (illustrated).

*

Russell Gordon Comments:

I've had a career of observing human behavior and asking questions about that behavior . . . often humorously, sometimes politically, sometimes formally, and more recently through the exploration of beauty and spirituality.

Russell Gordon, c. 1986. Photo courtesy of Louise Allrich.

Russell Gordon: *Guardian Angel,* **1991.**

Beauty is an experience, not a quality. It is what happens when what I behold simultaneously attracts and awes me, stopping me dead in a standoff of desire and reverence. The experience may be mild, a pleasant ripple of consciousness, or convulsive, changing my life. In every case, it merges my mind and body in a rush of praise. Each part of me contributes a note to beauty's choral sensation, which reconciles me to existence. The event enters my memory whole and is retrievable in detail ever after. . . Beauty is about securing conviction with things that can have no reasonable cause to exist apart from somebody's need to look at them . . . Besides essentialism, relativism stands in the way. A hateful cliché is true as far as it goes: beauty is indeed in the eye (and brain, heart, gut and genitals) of the viewer. Where else would it be? But it sure doesn't *feel* relative. It feels like what it is, a conviction about one's relation to the universe.*

Most of my work is generally a combination of all of these as content . . . I see myself as representing the mix of these elements in my character/personality/sensibility. On top of this, I love to do! To create! I feel that I am my best self when I am creating, and many things prompt me to do so.

*From Peter Schjeldahl, "Beauty Is Back," *New York Times Magazine,* September 29, 1996, p. 161.

*   *   *

To experience Russell Gordon's work is to be lured into and enveloped by fields of richly textured, interacting planes of color. Perhaps the most striking characteristic of his enormous nonrepre-

sentational collages and paintings is their energy and physicality. The works possess evidence of his consummate mastery of the media and an inherent understanding of the basic principles of composition and design.

Gordon became an artist in a rather roundabout way. As a student in the late 1950s and early 1960s his plans were to study math and play basketball. After changing his major to art, he eventually graduated, had a brief career as a professional basketball player, and then decided to pursue his interest in the art field. Gordon went on to earn an M.F.A. in printmaking but discovered his love for acrylic paint after a fellowship in Denmark. It was there that he produced some of his first major paintings.

In the 1970s, after living in California, Gordon moved to Montreal, Canada. This change in milieu made a considerable difference in his work. Most of the representational imagery he produced while on the West Coast referenced external light and depicted events that took place outdoors. His move to Montreal triggered changes in his thinking about the process of making art, thus affecting his palette and paintings.

Gordon's work contains a rhythmic quality directly influenced by the complex jazz idioms of some of the musicians of the 1950s, 1960s, and 1970s. His *Straight No Chaser* is a visual counterpart to Thelonious Monk's jazz composition of the same title. On the largest field in the collage is a gridwork containing two distinct crossing lines. Superimposed upon this plane are random blotches of paint, rectangles, and other geometric shapes in varying colors echoing the phrases of the musical composition.

Many of the artist's collages and paintings are quite theatrical and reveal a wry sense of humor through his often absurd juxtapositions of disparate elements. His hilarious titles are derived from an affinity for alliteration. *Simple Simon Stumbles Over Piaget* and *Fashion Freak Fedora*, two large mixed-media collages, are generated from his personal experiences of imagining ridiculous incidents.

Gordon's "Masks" series, a synthesis of abstraction and realism, explores questions of the potential spiritual and transformative impact of paintings. In them, he attempts to recreate the mysterious and supernatural characteristics that make masks important objects in tribal societies. The paper fragments, torn edges, scribbles, splatters, dots, dashes, stripes, and linear forms with drypainted shadows create texture and depth in these images bearing a striking resemblance to assemblages.

The artist's most recent work comes out of a representational and spiritual frame of reference and has become more of an investigation of cultural dilemma. In this aesthetic shift, Gordon associates dissimilar imagery by juxtaposing standard still lifes of flowers with figures of ceramic Aunt Jemimas or plastic lawn jockeys. This visual activity of combining comfort with angst speaks to Gordon's interest in challenging and reconstructing the conventional ideas of beauty and the compartmentalization of art.

Though Russell Gordon's ethnicity is not readily identifiable in all of his works, he nonetheless brings to us a distilled and transposed essence of his cultural heritage. This orientation in his vision can be seen as part of a larger, more universal search in twentieth-century art for ways of directing our attention to or reconnecting us with our primal culture.

—Regina Holden Jennings

GORLEIGH, Rex

American painter and printmaker

Born: Penllyn, Pennsylvania, 2 September 1902. **Education:** Private study with Xavier J. Barile, New York; Art Institute of Chicago; André Lhote Académie, Paris; sculpture with Leo Z. Moll, Berlin, Germany; University of Chicago. **Career:** Teacher, Harlem Art Center, New York, 1936-37; associate director, Community Center, Greensboro, North Carolina, 1938-39; director, South Side Community Art Center, Chicago, 1942-44; director, Princeton Group Arts, New Jersey, 1947-53. From 1955 director/owner, Studio-on-the-Canal, Princeton, New Jersey. **Awards:** Afro-American Award, 1955; Certificate Award, New Jersey State Council on the Arts, 1971; New Jersey State Council on the Arts Award and grant, 1973. **Died:** 1987.

Individual Exhibitions:

1935	Strindberg Gallery, Helsinki, Finland
1940	Greensboro Public Library, North Carolina
1961	Lambertville House, New Jersey
1968	Westtown School Pennsylvania

Selected Group Exhibitions:

1931	Anderson Gallery, New York
1932	Atlanta University, Georgia
1936	Anderson Gallery, New York
	Harmon Foundation
	Atlanta University, Georgia

1939	Baltimore Museum, Maryland
1940	Negro Exposition, Chicago
1942	Atlanta University, Georgia
	Pyramid Club, Philadelphia
1943	American Artist Gallery, Chicago
1950	Watercolor Exhibition, Trenton Museum, New Jersey
1953	Montclair Art Museum, New Jersey
1968	Newark Museum, New Jersey
1971	Renaissance Gallery, Washington, D.C.
1973	National Center for Afro-American Artists, Boston
	Studio Museum in Harlem, New York

Collections:

First Baptist Church, Princeton, New Jersey; Schomburg Center, New York.

Publication:

On GORELEIGH: Book—*Seventeen Black Artists* by Elton C. Fax, New York, Dodd, Mead, and Company, 1971.

*   *   *

A teacher can be pivotal and even crucial in the life of an artist. Besides offering points in sharpening technique, the teacher provides inspiration and serves as a role model for success. In turn a good student builds upon what is learned from a good teacher. Rex Goreleigh was such a teacher.

Goreleigh received his own training at the Art Students League in New York City and in France with André Lhote. He was perhaps one of the lesser-known artists of the generation of the Harlem Renaissance. He lived and worked in Harlem at a critical time, however, and was active as an artist and teacher. In fact, he taught at the Harlem Community Art Center, then located at Lenox Avenue and 125th Street. The center was an outgrowth of the Works Progress Administration, the federal program that supported artists during the Great Depression. Among the students who were nurtured by Goreleigh's instruction and who rose to prominence in the art world were Jacob Lawrence and Robert Blackburn.

Although he lived in the center of the cultural efflorescence known as the Harlem Renaissance, perhaps more accurately the Harlem golden age, Goreleigh eventually left New York for a more comfortable and idyllic life in Princeton, New Jersey. He lived there in a restored mill, which he called Studio-on-the-Canal and in which he taught.

Goreleigh was known largely as a painter and printmaker. The style of his work was consistently realistic. Among the many interests reflected in his subject matter were rural blacks, especially the status of the black farmer. In considering his art in 1960, Cedric Dover wrote that Goreleigh was as "fresh and youthful as . . . thirty years ago."

As a septuagenarian Goreleigh reentered the student-teacher world to study art as an undergraduate at Livingston College at Rutgers University. Among his teachers was the sculptor Mel Edwards. While a student there, he created a mural for the college that depicted black workers engaged in tasks such as tilling, planting, and harvesting. He then made prints based on this monumental figurative work. The specific imagery is based on one of his lifelong interests, but the metaphor in the educational setting is stunning—that of a generation of blacks planting seeds in the earth for future harvest. In 1976 he achieved his long-desired goal of earning a baccalaureate degree.

—Thomas M. Shaw

GRAUER, Gladys Barker
American painter

Born: Cincinnati, Ohio, 15 August 1923. **Education:** Art Institute of Chicago, 1941-45; Rutgers University, New Brunswick, New Jersey, 1980-84. **Family:** Married Solomon Grauer, two daughters and two sons. **Career:** Instructor of advertising design, Essex County Vocational and Technical College, Newark, New Jersey; instructor of painting, Newark Museum, New Jersey. Artist-in-residence, Newark Museum, New Jersey, 1991. Established the AARD Studio Gallery, Newark, New Jersey. Creator and cofounder, *Black Woman in Visual Perspective,* Newark, New Jersey. President, National Conference of Artists, New Jersey, 1982-85. **Awards:** First prize for watercolor, James Street Commons, 1983; fellowship, New Jersey State Council of Arts, 1985; fellowship, Rutgers University, New Brunswick, New Jersey, 1992. **Address:** 352 Seymour Avenue, Newark, New Jersey 07112, U.S.A.

Selected Exhibitions:

Clocktower Gallery, New York; Courtney Gallery, Jersey City, New Jersey (1985); Essex County College, New Jersey; Jersey City Museum, New Jersey (1981); Morristown Atrium, New Jersey (1992-94); Morristown Museum, New Jersey (1986); National Art Gallery, Senegal (1985); Newark Museum, New Jersey (1981, 1992); Newark Public Library, New Jersey; Passaic County College, New Jersey; Pavilion Gallery, Mount Holly, New Jersey (1986); Southside Community Art Center, Chicago; Studio Museum in Harlem, New York.

Publications:

On GRAUER: Articles—"Black Women Artists: Images in the River" by Deborah Stapleton, in *Graphica,* 18 April 1982; "Artists Paintings a Depiction of Blacks" by Edna Bailey, in *Newark Star Ledger,* 13 January 1986.

*   *   *

Gladys Barker Grauer grew up in Chicago during the Great Depression. Her mother worked and didn't want Gladys to waste her free time on the city's streets. So instead Gladys spent her time in the city's museums, some of which were within walking distance of her home. Grauer credits the early experience of an art supervisor who visited her public school and singled out her work for praise as important in her becoming an artist. "Until then I never thought what I was doing was particularly important," says Grauer, "not until that teacher said it was. A skinny little black kid was never given much consideration by those teachers, so when they took my drawing, I was impressed."

Later Grauer was able to attend the Art Institute of Chicago, where she studied with and was influenced by artists such as Rex

Gorley, Jacob Lawrence, and Charles White. After the Art Institute she moved to New York, which she found a disappointment. The art circle's "intellectual approach to art" was incompatible with Grauer's attitude toward creating art, selling art, and being an artist. Grauer's paintings tell stories. Her media vary—whatever best allows the story to shine through loads her brush. Her colors are bold and applied intuitively, and her paintings are multifaceted with well-defined messages. In New York she painted on items such as shoes, nightgowns, shower curtains, and combs to earn a living.

After she and her husband moved to Newark, New Jersey, in 1952 and she had brought up her four children, she began to have a significant influence on her community as well as her artistic community. She opened the AARD Studio Gallery, which was named for one of her favorite animals, the aardvark. It was a neighborhood gallery, where black people could see the work of black artists, and where someone who may not otherwise consider themselves able to buy a work of art could pay installments of as little as a dollar a week until a piece was theirs to take home. "They say people don't appreciate art," says Grauer, "but no one ever brings art to the people so they can enjoy it."

—Terry Bain

GREEN, Renée
American installation artist

Born: Cleveland, Ohio, 1959. **Education:** Wesleyan University, Middle Town, Connecticut, B.A. 1981; Whitney Museum Independent Study Program, New York, 1990; Radcliffe College, Cambridge, Massachusetts, M.A. 1991. **Career:** Instructor, University of the South Pacific—Suva, Fiji, and Veti Levu; University of Benin, Nigeria; Makala University, Kampala, Uganda. Artist-in-residence, Tamarind Institute, New Mexico, 1977. **Awards:** Ford Foundation Fellowship, 1981; National Endowment for the Arts Fellowship, 1988; Tiffany Foundation grant, 1988.

Selected Exhibitions:

Brody's Gallery, Washington, D.C. (1992); *Herstory,* Oakland Museum, California (1991); Christian Nagel Gallery, Cologne (1992); *Through Sister' Eyes: Children's Books Illustrated by African-American Artists,* National Museum of Women in the Arts Library and Research Center, Washington, D.C. (1992); Pat Hearn Gallery, New York (1992); San Francisco Museum of Modern Art; University of California, Davis; University of Miami, Ohio; University of New Mexico Fine Arts Center, Albuquerque.

Collections:

Los Angeles County Museum; Museum of Contemporary Art, Rio de Janeiro, Brazil; National Gallery, Lagos, Nigeria; Philadelphia Museum; United States Information Service, Washington, D.C.

Publications:

On GREEN: Articles—"Social Studies: 4+4 Young Americans" (interview) by Elizabeth A. Brown, in *Bulletin* (Oberlin College,

Ohio), 44(1), 1990, pp. 6-57 (illustrated); "A Genealogy of Desire: Renee Green Explores the Continent of Power" by G. Roger Denson, in *Flash Art* (International Edition), 160, October 1991, pp. 125-27; review (Pat Hearn Gallery, New York) by Yasmin Ramirez, in *Art in America,* 79, October 1991, pp. 148-49; review (Christian Nagel Gallery, Cologne) by Manfred Hermes, in *Flash Art* (International Edition), 166, October 1992, p. 94; review (Brody's Gallery, Washington, D.C.) by James Curtia, in *New Art Examiner* (Washington, D.C.), 19, February/March 1992, pp. 34-35; "Visiting Artist" by Suvan Geer, in *Artweek,* 24, 6 May 1993, p. 20 (illustrated); "Beyond the Pale: Art in the Age of Multicultural Translation" by Homi K. Bhabha, in *Kunst and Museum Journal,* 5(4), 1994, pp. 15-23 (illustration); "Installing History (Artist Created Museological Installations)" by Lisa G. Corrin, in *Art Papers,* 18, July/August 1994, pp. 6-14.

*   *   *

Renée Green is one of a group of young artists who have benefited from the refusal of people like David Hammons, Adrian Piper, and Jean-Michel Basquiat to be pigeonholed as artists of color. This antiessentialism does not conform to the philosophy of, say, the Studio Museum in Harlem, whose foremost concern is the African diaspora, a seeming umbrella of blackness. Yet Green, who has exhibited widely, both internationally and at major venues in the United States (including, early in her career, the Studio Museum in Harlem), has demonstrated more than most of those in her group the desire to cross racial and sociological boundaries in the creation of her artwork. She did this earlier in her career more so than in the recent past, but, with influences as diverse as Michel Foucault and Bill Gates, she infuses her work with a complex and challenging wit for the contemplative viewer. Her large-scale traveling exhibition *World Tour* (1993), which was organized by the Museum of Contemporary Art in Los Angeles and which included installations in Worcester, Massachusetts; Clisson, France; Caracas, Venezuela; New York City; Cologne, Germany; and Los Angeles, hinted at the range and depth of her work.

Formally, Green is of a generation of installation artists who came of age in the early 1990s but whose work is firmly rooted in the conceptualism of the 1960s and, in the case of Green perhaps, in a little too much theory, particularly French deconstructionism. Although her work shows an obvious debt to the dual philosophical and artistic strategies of Piper, Green's approaches are more akin to those of Lawrence Weiner, Fred Wilson, Marcel Broodthaers, and Joseph Kosuth, who seek to overturn the aura of the space in which they exhibit and treat the museum or gallery as metaphor. As with Weiner and Kosuth, who were greatly influenced by Ludwig Wittgenstein's philosophy of language, Green has shown a predilection for linguistics and multiplicity of meaning. And, like Wilson, her work often takes on an anthropological conception as it dabbles with the objets d'art of pop culture and history and their lopsided representation in what purport to be inclusive spaces of display.

In her installation *Import/Export Funk Office*, which was included in *World Tour,* Green collaborated with the German cultural critic Diedrich Diederichsen. In an intriguing play on the commodification of hip-hop music, Green, an African American female, followed hip-hop through the eyes of the white male critic in Cologne. Creating an interesting dual take on the idea of importing and exporting, the artist and critic both embodied each side of the equation. Not only does the title imply the difficult questions surrounding "the

body as commodity," but it also asks who the commodity is in this cross-cultural exchange. The installation included elements of video, audio, and text, and it not only directed the viewer's attention to the actual content of Green's directive but also, in terms of art history, to the formal play of sculpture and architecture. Like her contemporary Ann Hamilton, Green wants the viewer to experience her work on a gestural and visceral level. What you see is not necessarily what you get. As Green has said, "You have to look, listen, and move through the parts to figure out what's going on."

—M. Franklin Sirmans

GRIGSBY, J(efferson) Eugene, Jr.
American painter and printmaker

Born: Greensboro, North Carolina, 17 October 1918. **Education:** Johnson C. Smith University, Charlotte, North Carolina, 1934-35; Morehouse College, Atlanta, Georgia, 1935-38, B.A.; American Artists School, New York, 1938-39; Ohio State University, Columbus, 1939-40, M.A.; Ecole des Beaux Arts, Marseilles, France, 1945 (six weeks); Arizona State University, Tempe, summers 1947

J. Eugene Grigsby: *Desert Madonna, 1958.* Photo courtesy Eugene and Thomasena Grigsby.

and 1949; Columbia University, New York, summers 1950-52; New York University, summers 1953-63, Ph.D. **Military Service:** United States Army, 1942-45: master sergeant; ETO medals for service in the European Theater of Operations with five battle stars. **Family:** Married Rosalyn Thomasena Marshall in 1943; two sons. **Career:** Head of art department, Phoenix Union High School, Phoenix, Arizona, 1954-66; professor of art, Arizona State University, Tempe, 1966-88. Artist-in-residence, Johnson C. Smith University, Charlotte, North Carolina, 1940-41; art teacher, Elizabeth City Teachers College, Elizabeth City, North Carolina, summer 1941; art instructor, Bethune-Cookman College, Daytona Beach, Florida, 1941-42, Barber-Scotia College, Concord, North Carolina, 1946; art teacher and head of art department, Carver High School, Phoenix, Arizona, 1946-54. **Awards:** 75th Anniversary Medallion of Merit, University of Arizona, 1960; 25th Anniversary Medallion, National Gallery, 1966; Danforth fellowship, 1974; Meritorious Service Award, National Art Education Association's Affiliate Committee on Minority Concerns (now the J. Eugene Grigsby, Jr. Award for Service to Art Education), 1980; Distinguished Research Scholar Award, Arizona State University Graduate College, 1983; Four Corner's Art Education Award for Service to Art Education, 1984; Outstanding Contributions to the Arts Award, Consortium of Black Organizations and Others for the Arts (COBA), 1985; National Art Education Distinguished fellow, 1985; Art Educator of the Year, National Art Education Association, 1988; Arizona Governor's Tostenrud Art Award to an Individual for Contributions to the Arts of Arizona, 1989; Award for Distinguished Service to Education, Arizona Alliance of Black School Educators, 1994; Bennie Trailblazer Award, Morehouse College, 1995; Kappa Alpha Psi Achievement Award, 1996. Honorary Doctor of Fine Arts, Philadelphia University of the Arts, 1965. **Agent:** Eugene Foney, Artcetera, P.O. Box 131914, Houston, Texas 77219, U.S.A. **Address:** 1117 North 9th Street, Phoenix, Arizona 85006-2734, U.S.A.

J. Eugene Grigsby: *The Family,* **1963. Photo courtesy of Eugene and Thomasena Grigsby.**

Individual Exhibitions:

1945	Wirsham Gallery, Luxemborg
1952	Phoenix Art Center, Phoenix, Arizona
1965	Texas Southern University, Houston, Texas (retrospective)
1966	Johnson C. Smith University, Charlotte, North Carolina
1967	Morehouse College, Atlanta
	Northern Colorado College, Greely
	Central State University, Wilberforce, Ohio
1971	Winston-Salem State University, North Carolina
1988	Hewitt Gallery, New York
1992	Delta Fine Arts Center, Winston-Salem, North Carolina
1994	Phoenix Unitarian Universalist Church, Paradise Valley, Arizona (retrospective)

Selected Group Exhibitions:

1938	*Annual Exhibit of Negro Artists*, Dillard University, New Orleans, Louisiana
1940	*Art of the American Negro,* Tanner Art Galleries, Chicago
1970	*Dimensions of Black,* La Jolla Art Museum, University of California, San Diego
1972	*Delta Sigma Theta Exhibit,* Bemton Convention Center, Winston-Salem, North Carolina
	Negro Artists, Duke University, Durham, North Carolina
	Negro Artists, Jersey State Museum, Trenton, New Jersey
1978	*Arizona State University Faculty,* Tehran University, Iran
1979	*Black Artists/South,* Huntsville Museum, Huntsville, Alabama
1980	*Atlanta Life Juried Exhibit,* Atlanta Life Insurance Company, Atlanta
1989	*African-American Artists in the Southwest,* Udinotti Gallery, Scottsdale, Arizona

Collections:

Arizona State University Art Museum, Tempe; Bank America, Phoenix, Arizona; Bank One, Phoenix, Arizona; Children's Art Carnival, New York; Delta Art Center, Winston-Salem, North Carolina; Glendale Community College, Glendale, Arizona; Hampton University, Hampton, Virginia; Howard University, Washington, D.C.; Johnson C. Smith University, Charlotte, North Carolina; Malcolm X College, Chicago; Milwaukee Art Museum, Wisconsin; National Art Education Association, Reston, Virginia; Ohio State University, Frank Hale Cultural Center, Columbus, Ohio; Phoenix Opportunities Industrialization Center, Phoenix, Arizona; Phoenix Unitarian Universalist Church, Paradise Valley, Arizona; Printmaking Workshop, New York; Richmond Art Center, Richmond Public Schools, Richmond, Virginia; Texas Southern University, Houston; United Presbyterian Archives, Charlotte, North Carolina; U.S.West—Phoenix, Arizona.

Publications:

By GRIGSBY: Book—*Art and Ethnics,* Dubuque, Iowa, William C. Brown, 1977. **Articles**—"Why Art," in *The Phoenix* (Phoenix, Arizona), Phoenix Union High School District, 1950; "Art Education at Carver High School," in *National Art Education Association Journal* (Washington, D.C.), February 1954; "Partners in Art," in *School Arts* (Massachusetts), February 1955; "BaKuba Art at the Brussels International Exposition," in *Presence Africain* (Paris), 1958; "Teaching Children at the Brussels World Fair," in *Pacific Arts Association Bulletin* (Tempe, Arizona), 1958; "Art Education," in *Black Arts Quarterly* (Los Angeles), 1976; "The Black Artist in America," in *The Humanities: A Quest for Meaning in Twentieth-Century America,* edited by Frazier, Horowitch, and Marquardt, Dubuque, Iowa, Kendall Hunt, 1982; "Unfolding a Hidden Rainbow of Cultures," in *Arts and Activities* (San Diego), February 1991; "MLK at the Heard Museum," in *Arts and Activities* (San Diego), April 1993.

On GRIGSBY: Articles—"Two Young Interviewers Get a Sense of Heritage from African-American Artist and Educator Dr. J. Eugene Grigsby, Jr.," in *Art Education* (Reston, Virginia), March 1955; "Leading Negro Artists" by Samella Lewis, in *Ebony* (Chicago), February 1972; "Outstanding Educators of America," in *Outstanding Educators of America* (Washington, D.C.), 1974.

*

J. Eugene Grigsby comments:

My work has had many influences. The first was from a wonderful artist whose contribution to me was to instill a sense of enthusiasms. Walker Foster, a self-taught artist, was in demand throughout the South as a stone mason. Although his formal education was no more than the fourth grade, he introduced me to the wonders of painting. The next influence came from Hale Woodruff, who was my first formal art teacher. Before meeting Woodruff at an exhibit in Atlanta, I didn't realize that art was taught in schools. This accidental meeting led to my transfer from Johnson C. Smith University to Morehouse College to study art with Hale Woodruff. In addition to the classics in art history with an emphasis on modern art, Woodruff introduced me to African art, an influence that became major in my approach to style and design.

One body of content in my art comes from a concern for conditions found among the least of us, especially the ones considered minority—blacks, Hispanics, Native Americans (Indians).

Another body of content concerns African mythology and imagery. The story of Yemenja, protector of all living things in the waters and queen mother of all the *orishas,* has been a fascinating subject for me.

My work is not limited to these two themes, as it sometimes takes directions that surprise even me.

*   *   *

Some of the most remarkable figures in African American art history—including Romare Bearden, Hughie Lee-Smith, Charles White, Elizabeth Catlett, Reginald Gammon, John Biggers, Betye Saar, and William Pajaud—were born in the early decades of the twentieth century. One key representative of that generation, J. Eugene Grigsby, has contributed powerfully to the tradition through his inseparable roles as artist and art educator. From the 1940s to the present, he has produced scores of paintings and prints focusing on African American, African, and other themes that appeal to diverse audiences.

Grigsby's mature artistic development began at Morehouse College in Atlanta, Georgia, where he studied under Hale Woodruff from 1935 to 1938, and Woodruff's mentorship has remained the major artistic influence throughout Grigsby's career. After graduating from Morehouse, Grigsby continued his association with Woodruff and later, while completing work for a Ph.D. in art education at New York University from 1952 to 1963, resumed formal studies with him.

In painting Grigsby began with oils but eventually moved to acrylics. In printmaking he has produced woodcuts, lithographs, and serigraphs. Many of his efforts in both mediums express his interest in the beauty and dignity of ordinary scenes of black life, strongly reflecting the influence of Woodruff's early visual realism. Such works as *Carolina Shack, Girl in Green,* and *Two Girls* are typical of Grigsby's skill and effectiveness in capturing the essence of black people's emotional lives and of their physical surroundings.

Like many other African American visual artists, Grigsby was deeply moved in the 1960s by the momentous events of the civil rights movement. Many of his works of the era add further luster to the rich legacy of socially conscious art that has chronicled the struggles and triumphs of the African American people in resisting racism and oppression during the twentieth century. *Freedom Now, Freedom March, Poverty Playground,* and *Drop Outs* are representative of Grigsby's powerful additions to this major theme. One of his most widely known and reproduced works in this vein, *No Vacancy,* compares the exclusion of African Americans from hotels and other public accommodations with the biblical exclusion of Jesus from the inn. This highly charged woodcut shows a black couple and their child along with the Ku Klux Klan, thus making a deeper visual comment about racism and injustice.

Grigsby's travels as a visiting lecturer throughout Africa in 1972 gave rise to another major focus of his artwork, and his paintings and prints with African themes have added luster to a central dimension of African American art since the Harlem Renaissance. Like many of his artistic contemporaries and descendants, Grigsby has found the African motherland a fruitful source for his personal visual creativity. Such striking efforts as *African Genesis, Kuba Warrior, Mothers of Somalia,* and *The Mask Speaks* complement his major series paying homage to Bolongongo, the Kuba patron saint. Consisting of several paintings and lithographs, this series provides a compelling vision of African history and culture for people of African descent and for others seeking appreciation of the heritage.

Beyond his exemplary artistic record Grigsby has also been a seminal force in art education for several decades. His teaching and his published writings in the field are internationally recognized and appreciated. Most significantly, he had pioneered and advanced the area of multicultural art long before the art world in the late 1980s and early 1990s truly discovered the visual products of various ethnic groups. His 1977 book *Art and Ethnics* is deservedly regarded by artists and scholars alike as a definitive work of the late twentieth century. Featuring the artistic contributions of African Americans, American Indians, and Latinos, it achieved a stature that led the African American Studies Center at the University of California in Los Angeles to schedule a revised edition for 1997. By including Asian American visual art, the revised edition will reinforce its central commitment to the diverse U.S. population on the threshold of the next millennium.

Grigsby has followed many of his generational peers—including Jacob Lawrence, Saar, Pajaud, Catlett, and Biggers—in remaining artistically and intellectually active in his senior years. His continuing efforts have solidified his reputation as a worthy successor to Woodruff, his distinguished teacher and mentor.

—Paul Von Blum

HAMMONS, David

American painter, printmaker, and mixed-media artist

Born: Springfield, Illinois, 24 July 1943. **Education:** Los Angeles Trade Technical City College, 1964-65; Chouinard Art Institute, Los Angeles, 1966-68; Otis Art Institute of the Parson's School of Design, Los Angeles, 1968-72. **Awards:** Guggenheim Memorial Foundation Award, 1983-84; National Endowment for the Arts Fellowship, 1983-84; New York State Council on the Arts Award, 1983-84; Art Matters Award, New York Foundation for the Arts, 1987; Rome Prize for Sculpture, American Academy of Rome, Italy, 1989; Tiffany grant, 1990; Brendan Gill Award, Municipal Art Society, 1991; MacArthur Foundation Fellowship, 1991; D.A.A.D. Award, Berlin, 1992. **Agent:** Jack Tilton Gallery, 49 Greene Street, New York, New York 10013, U.S.A.

Individual Exhibitions:

1971	Brockman Gallery, Los Angeles
1974	Fine Arts Gallery, Los Angeles
1975	*Greasy Bags and Barbecue Bones,* Just above Midtown Gallery, New York
1976	Just above Midtown Gallery, New York
1977	Neighborhood Art Center, Atlanta, Georgia
1980	New Museum of Contemporary Art, New York
1982	*Higher Goals* (public installation), Harlem, New York
1986	Just above Midtown Gallery, New York
1989	Exit Art, New York
1990	P.S. 1 Museum, Long Island City, New York (traveling retrospective)
	Jack Tilton Gallery, New York
1991	Museum of Contemporary Art, La Jolla, California
1992	American Academy in Rome
1993	Williams College Art Center, Williamstown, Massachusetts (traveling)
	Illinois State Museum, Springfield, Illinois
1994	*VERAVITAGIOIA,* Milan, Italy
	Sara Penn/Knobkerry, New York
1995	Salzberger Kunstverein, Austria

Selected Group Exhibitions:

1970	La Jolla Museum of Art, California
1976	*Printmaking New Forms,* Whitney Museum of American Art, New York
1985	Ronald Feldman Fine Arts, New York
1990	*The Decade Show,* Studio Museum in Harlem, New York
	MOCA, New York
1991	Museum of Modern Art, New York

1992	Carnegie Institute, Pittsburgh, Pennsylvania
1994	Cleveland Contemporary Arts Center, Ohio
1995	*Ripple across the Water,* Watari Museum of Contemporary Art, Tokyo, Japan
1996	Tribes Gallery, New York
	Art at the End of the 20th Century: Selections from the Whitney Museum of American Art (traveling)

Publications:

On HAMMONS: Books— *Dislocations,* exhibition catalog, New York, Museum of Modern Art and Robert Storr, 1990; *David Hammons: Rousing the Rubble,* Cambridge, Massachusetts, MIT Press, 1991; *David Hammons in the Hood,* exhibition catalog, Illinois State Museum and Robert Sill, 1994. **Articles—** "Interview with David Hammons" by Kellie Jones, in *Real Life Magazine,* Autumn 1986, pp. 2-9; "David Hammons" by Kay Larson, in *Galleries Magazine,* February/March, 1991, pp. 99-103; "Dirt Rich" by Kay Larson, in *New York Magazine,* 14 January 1991; "David Hammons" by Patricia Phillips, in *Artforum,* April 1991, p. 126; "David Hammons: Nobody's Champion" by Lois E. Nesbitt, in *Artscribe,* Summer 1991, pp. 39-43; "Man of the Street" by S. Wiggins, in *Artweek,* October 1991, pp. 11-12; "Art in Your Face" by Phil Patton, in *Esquire,* December 1991, p. 64; "Kinky Black Hair and Barbeque Bones: Street Life, Social History and David Hammons" by Calvin Reid, in *Arts Magazine,* April 1991, p. 59; "David Hammons in Life in Art" by Steve Cannon, in *The International Review of African-American Art,* 1992, p. 16; "David Hammons: Art Alchemist" by Samella Lewis, in *The International Review of African-American Art,* April 1992, p. 14; "David Hammons: Coming in From the Cold" by Dan Cameron, in *Flash Art,* January 1993, pp. 68-71; "Interview with David Hammons" by Robert Storr, in *Artpress,* September 1993; "'Will/Power' at the Wexner Center" by Brian Wallis, in *Art in America,* February 1993; "David Hammons' Secret Magic Show" by Amel Wallach, in *New York Newsday,* 23 December 1994; "Wreaking Havoc on the Signified: The Art of David Hammons" by Coco Fusco and Christian Haye, in *Freize,* May 1995, pp. 34-41.

*   *   *

David Hammons became known in the late 1970s for developing a graphics technique called "body printing." The procedure involved applying grease to his body and clothing, pressing himself against illustration board, and then fixing the image by sifting powdered paint onto the surface. The results were dramatic expressions of textural contrasts that he sometimes combined with silk screen designs and three-dimensional materials. Hammons's body prints were produced during the height of the civil rights movement, and he frequently incorporated the American flag as a symbol of the country's violence against and unfulfilled promises to African

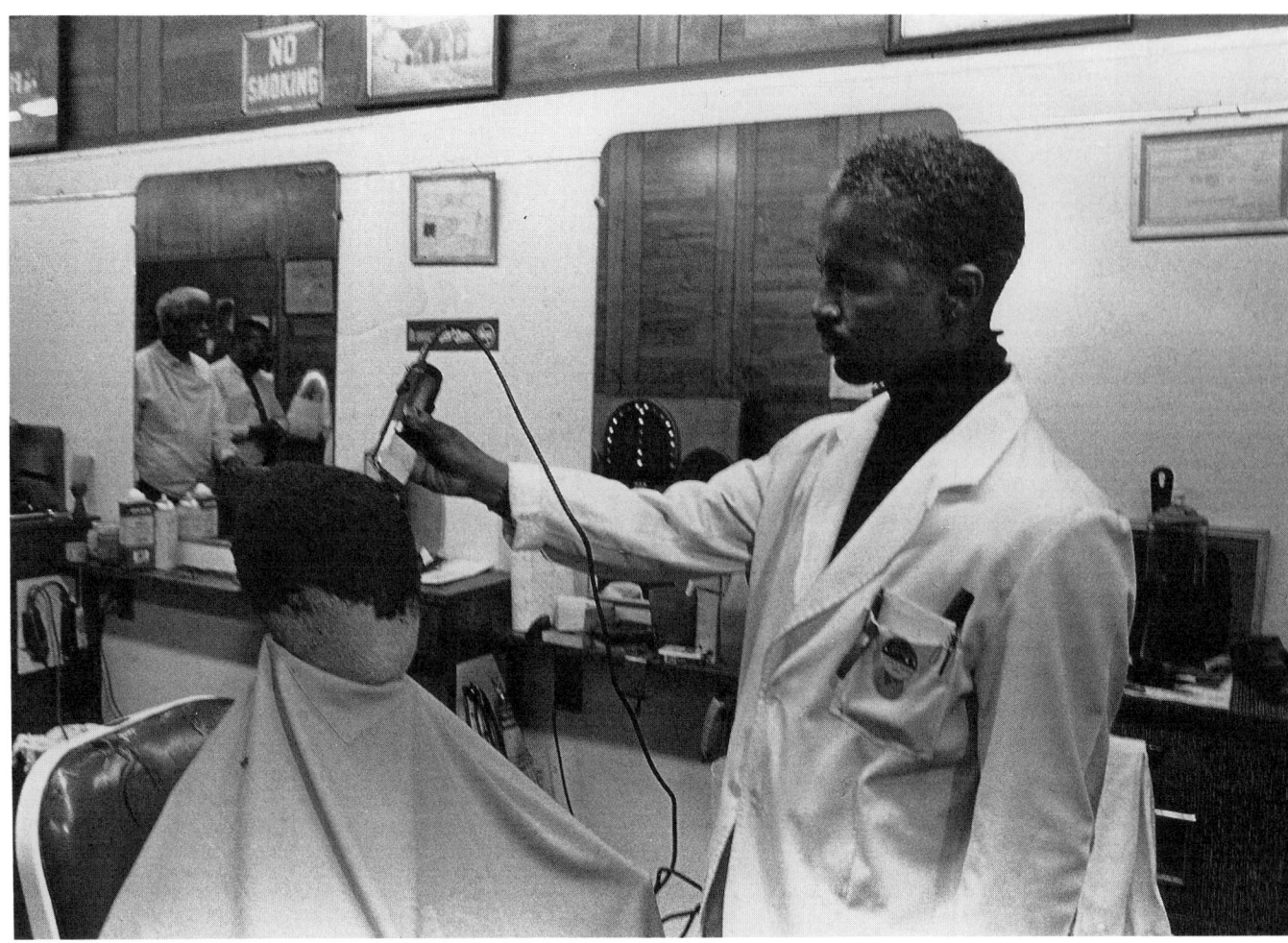

David Hammons: *Stone Getting a Hair Cut,* **1992. Photo courtesy of Coreen Simpson.**

Americans. Since then, however, he has come to employ his own trademark that uses the red, green, and black of Marcus Garvey's Universal Negro Improvement Association and of the pan-African and black nationalist movements.

In about 1973 Hammons began his "Spade" series, based on the derogatory reference to African Americans as being "black as the ace of spades." He explored the spade, or shovel, in numerous variations: masks, spades run over by Volkswagens, spades under sand, spades with chains, and spades in combination with body prints. The symbolism recalled African battle shields and ritual objects as well as the burden of slavery in the United States.

In 1976 Hammons moved from Los Angeles to Harlem, which he considers the spiritual center of African American culture. There he continued to create three-dimensional mixed-media works employing found objects. As can be seen in *Night Train* and *Thunderbird,* for example, Hammons's materials are almost always cast-off objects from African American neighborhoods, including empty wine bottles, greasy paper, shopping bags, fried chicken wings, gnawed barbecue ribs, bottle caps, and nappy hair. He also has worked with objects such as dolls, crosses, miniature heads, and candles. Hammons possesses the uncanny ability to combine and convert such objects into profound, and often provocative, social statements.

For example, Hammons arranges wine bottles, some of which are still in their brown paper bags, into open-ended or closed wheel-like compositions. He emphasizes the fact that every one of the bottles has been touched by black lips. He also has used wine bottles to create bottle trees. Perhaps Hammons's best-known productions, however, are his works that incorporate African American hair collected from local barbershops. He weaves the hair into tapestry-like designs, delicately threading or winding it around slender wire rods and attaching it to stone heads that he then takes back to barbershops for haircuts. In emphasizing hair as a material, Hammons wants African Americans to view themselves naturally.

Hammons has engaged in several unconventional commercial activities, including *Blizzard Ball Sale* in front of Cooper Union during a blizzard in 1983, when he sold snowballs. He later sold doll shoes for fifty cents each at the same location. Both activities were intended as a spoof on the venerable art school. In 1988 Hammons created a billboard featuring Jesse Jackson with blond hair and blue eyes, entitled in graffiti letters *How Ya Like Me Now?* The billboard appeared along a commuter route in Washington, D.C., and although it was directed at white audiences, a group of enraged African American youth attempted to destroy it with sledgehammers. Hammons later repaired the work and displayed it in a gallery, with a cordon of sledgehammers in front. In a provocative installation at Williams College in 1993 entitled *Yardbird Suite* (a tribute to Charlie Parker), Hammons created a forest of barren trees on whose limbs were perched boom boxes playing music by Parker, Billie Holiday, Miles Davis, and Thelonious Monk.

Perhaps the two most important influences shaping the art of Hammons are his love of jazz and of basketball. He has produced a number of works on basketball themes. His most celebrated basketball works use goals attached twenty to fifty feet above the ground on telephone poles decorated with bottle caps in geometric patterns. Installed in outdoor spaces in Harlem and Brooklyn, the works symbolize the unattainable goals of African American adolescents to become superstars and also remind them that their goals should be higher than playing basketball. Another aspect of Hammons's basketball series is his mysterious ability to place basketballs in vessels with small openings. He also has devised an unusual drawing technique in which he bounces a chalk-coated basketball off gallery walls.

While serving as a fellow at the American Academy in Rome, Hammons fell in love with the city, and since 1989 he has divided his time between Rome and New York. The time spent in Rome has had an impact on Hammons's series "Spitting Images." Inspired by the desire to maintain an African aesthetic, he has created installations employing African masks that spout water from their mouths in a manner reminiscent of fountains in Rome. In 1995 Hammons participated in the summer festival in Salzburg, Austria, where he displayed his trademark black nationalist flag on the facade of the late-nineteenth-century Kunstlerhaus. For the same exhibition he created the provocative *Freudian Slip*, in which an African mask was placed under a woman's see-through slip. For the counterexhibition at the Venice Biennale of 1990, Hammons draped a venerable marble sculpture of Venus with faux designer handbags and gold chains as a pun on the ever present street vendors. While his work has been compared to Marcel Duchamp, dadaist art, outsider art, and Arte Povera, Hammons's compelling conversions of cast-off debris and thrift-shop items into thought-provoking artifacts are unique.

—Regenia Perry

HAMPTON, James

American sculptor

Born: Elloree, South Carolina, 1909. **Military Service:** United States Army, 1942-1945. **Career:** Janitor, General Services Administration, Washington, D.C. **Online Address:** http://www.nursery.com/~dkossy/hampton.html. **Died:** 1964.

Selected Group Exhibitions:

1972   Abby Aldrich Rockefeller Folk Art Center, Williamsburg
1974   Walker Art Center, Minneapolis, Minnesota
1976   Whitney Museum of American Art, New York
        Museum of Fine Arts, Boston
1977   Montgomery Museum of Fine Arts, Alabama

Collection:

National Museum of American Art, Washington, D.C.

Publication:

On HAMPTON: Book—*The Throne of the Third Heaven of the Nations Millennium General Assembly*, exhibition catalog, by Lynda Hartigan, Montgomery, Alabama, Montgomery Museum of Fine Arts, 1977.

*   *   *

If modernist enterprises have a credo of continual change, with the unexpected emblazoned upon it—"going where no one has gone before"—they are also defined by a critical model that presumes to account for all the mysteries of the unknown. When a new mystery appears, it can rattle the cage and disrupt the flow of modernist preconceptions and assumptions. Such is the case with James Hampton, the son of an itinerant preacher and gospel singer from rural South Carolina.

Hampton moved to Washington, D.C., at the age of nineteen, where he worked as a cook in local cafés. He was drafted into the army in 1942 as a noncombatant. Upon his discharge in 1945, Hampton returned to Washington and took a job as a janitor for the General Services Administration, which he held until his death. In 1950 he rented a garage and began work on his *Throne of the Third Heaven of the Nations Millennium General Assembly,* which was discovered after his death. The work is a collection of 180 handmade ornate ecclesiastical objects—an altar, a winged throne, chairs, vases and stands, offertories, crowns, plaques with scripture, and a pulpit— all fashioned from cast-off furniture, found objects, toys, and cutout cardboard and covered in silver and gold aluminum foil. Hampton's endeavor was driven by a profound religious belief, most likely based on the visions in the Book of Revelation that tell of the Second Coming and the Last Judgment. Indeed, Hampton christened himself Saint James and may have considered himself a latter-day prophet.

In contrast to most contemporary folk or outsider art, there is nothing anecdotal or biographical in Hampton's work and approach. Nor is there the stylistic charm of the self-taught. While it has been suggested that he may have offered *Throne* for installation in nearby churches, there is no indication that he sought to exhibit the work in public. Hampton's work has the quality of the transcendental state as well as that of the loner, the hand and mind directed by a higher authority than the vanity of originality, the cherished hallmark of the modernist age. This is a quality that can also be seen in the work of visionary artists such as the British poet and painter William Blake or the American painter Elihu Vedder. Compare this to the penultimate modernist visionary, Marcel Duchamp, who renounced the conventions of painting and sculpture to posit meaning in the readymade. Duchamp did not produce art objects for much of his adult life, but he elevated his nonactivity to a high art.

Hampton's adult life, on the other hand, was spent working on one thing in private. If he operated outside the accepted market economies for art, Hampton was conscious of his organization of ideas and had a sense of purpose, as evidenced by the notebooks he inscribed in an indecipherable script. This, too, is a hallmark of the devoted keeper of faith, as with isolated religious orders.

Hampton's *Throne* thus stands as an achievement comparable to Antonio Gaudi's church Sagrada Familia in Barcelona, Spain, for one must accept Gaudi's unfinished vision as transcending the practical concerns of architecture. As the critic Robert Hughes wrote in

Time magazine in 1976, Hampton's *Throne* "may well be the finest work of visionary religious art produced by an American." Comparisons may also be made with the humanist paintings of the Canadian artist William Kurelek, which often include warnings of a final reckoning, and even with the public shamanistic activity of the German artist Joseph Beuys, a life's work that serves to enlighten and heal in an age of mistrust and of a profound loss of faith.

The words "Where there is no vision the People Perish" are inscribed on Hampton's *Throne*. The power of these objects is no less significant than the centuries-old search for the Holy Grail and the Ark of the Covenant—man-made objects that stand as a sign for the salvation of humankind. Hampton left a remarkable twentieth-century spectacle that continues to elicit a sense of awe and wonder about the mysteries of the mind and the indefatigable spirit of human endeavors.

—Ihor Holubizky

HARDEN, Marvin
American draftsman and painter

Born: Austin, Texas, 1935. **Education:** University of California at Los Angeles, B.A. in fine arts 1959, M.A. in creative painting 1963. **Career:** Since 1968 professor of art, California State University at Northridge. Instructor, University of California at Los Angeles, 1964-68, Los Angeles Harbor College, University High Adult School, 1965-68, Santa Monica City College, 1968. Co-founder, Los Angeles Institute for Contemporary Art, 1973. **Awards:** First Prize, University of Judaism Invitational Art Exhibition, Los Angeles, 1969; First Purchase Prize, San Diego Jewish Community Center, 1966; Purchase Prize, Westside Jewish Community Center, 1964; Annual All University of California Art Exhibit Prize, 1964; National Endowment for the Arts Fellowship, 1972; Awards in the Visual Arts Fellowship, 1983; Guggenheim Memorial Foundation Fellowship, 1983; Distinguished Professor Award, Exceptional Merit Service Award, California State University at Northridge, 1984. **Address:** California State University at Northridge, 18111 Nordhoff Street, Northridge, California 91330, U.S.A.

Individual Exhibitions:

1968	Occidental College, Los Angeles
1971	Rath Museum, Geneva, Switzerland
	Whitney Museum of American Art, New York
	Eugenia Butler Galleries, Los Angeles
	Los Angeles Harbor College
	Brand Library Art Center, Glendale, California
	Whitney Museum of American Art, New York
1978	Corcoran Gallery of Art, Washington, D.C.
1979	Newport Harbor Art Museum
1982	Los Angeles Municipal Art Gallery

Selected Group Exhibitions:

1965	Los Angeles County Museum of Art
	Western Washington State College, Bellingham

1966	Oakland Museum of Art, California
	High Museum of Art, Atlanta, Georgia
1969	Los Angeles County Museum of Art
	La Jolla Museum, California
	Fort Worth Art Center, Texas
1977	Brooklyn Museum, New York
1983	Chicago Museum of Contemporary Art
	Mint Museum of Art, Charlotte, North Carolina

Collections:

Berkeley Museum, California; Metromedia, Inc., Los Angeles; Museum of Modern Art, New York; San Diego Jewish Community Center; Whitney Museum of American Art, New York.

*   *   *

An exceptional draftsman, Marvin Harden is best known for his intricate pencil drawings. Harden possesses the complex and carefully applied technique of a Renaissance master, but his subject matter is not at all traditional. His pencil drawings consist of multiple shades of gray, and the negative space within the format is essential.

Harden received his training in the fine arts during the late 1950s and the early 1960s, a time when social equality for African Americans was a major political issue, and he began his career during a period when many black artists represented a militant perspective. Harden's work, however, reflects a personal, not an obviously political, consciousness. His work is conceptual, and as an artist he is more concerned with ideas than with objects.

The titles of Harden's drawings are highly provocative and poetic and seem to be as important as the compositions themselves. He also has developed a highly personal iconography that often uses images of plants and animals as symbols. For example, Harden often uses the image of a tree to represent himself. His tree images also resemble orifices—a mysterious opening to another reality. Many of the drawings consist of one or two such icons, usually located off-center, with an obvious framelike border. The drawing *What Can One Say about a Life So Suddenly Rushed, Soonly Hushed* (1970) was produced several years after the tragic death of Harden's younger sister. There is a figure of a cow in the bottom right corner, and in the upper right corner, within the center expanse of negative space, there is a complicated branching object. The border is a patchwork of pencil strokes. Another drawing, *ritual of consumption, illusion, share and salient flaw* (1971), also depicts a cow and has a similar border.

Little Boys Are Very Impressionable (1967) and *A Fine and Secret Place* (1967) are drawings with a perplexing and obscure arrangement of shapes; the curious tree form, representing an orifice, is also present. The penciled-in areas are enhanced by the magnitude of negative space. The viewer can either try to extract meaning from the titles or simply rely on a visceral reaction to the subtle shadings and linear abstractions. The viewer may not be able to decipher Harden's drawings, but he or she will definitely respond to Harden's expert control of his chosen media. Even though the shapes and symbols may not be recognized or understood, they appear quite convincing, almost photographic.

—Christine Miner Minderovic

HARDISON, Inge (Ruth)

American sculptor and photographer

Born: Portsmouth, Virginia, 3 February 1914. **Education:** Tennessee State A & I, 1935-36; Art Students League, New York, 1937-37; Vassar College, Poughkeepsie, New York, 1942-44. **Career:** Actor, from Massachusetts to California, 1936-46; artists' model, 1940-50, teacher, Hampton Instutute, Virginia, 1944-45, Hunter College, New York, 1961-63; guest teacher, CBS-TV, New York, 1969-71; teacher and artist-in-residence, Wyandanch High School, Long Island, 1977-78; Dialogue House counsellor, Isabella Geriatric Center, New York, 1971-73. Created sculpture of Sojourner Truth presented by New York governor Mario Cuomo to Nelson Mandela, 1990. **Awards:** Harlem Cultural Council grant, 1975; Cottonwood Foundation grant, 1980; Cultural Achievement Award, Riverside Club of the National Business and Professional Women's Clubs, 1987. **Agent:** Margaret McCaden, 444 Central Park West #4B, New York, New York 10025, U.S.A.

Individual Exhibitions:

1981	Counterpoints Guild Lever House, New York
1986	Interchurch Center, New York
1987	Bergen County Museum of Arts and Sciences, Paramus, New Jersey
1988	Cathedral of Saint John the Divine, New York
	Community Gallery of Portsmouth Museum, Virginia
1992	Occidental College, Los Angeles
1994	Virginia Tech, Blacksburg, Virginia
	MTA Transit Authority Building, Brooklyn, New York

Selected Group Exhibitions:

1990	Nikon House, New York
	Konica Plaza, Japan
	Port Authority Exhibit, New York
1992	Hudson Guild Art Gallery, New York
	Mayor's Gallery, Stamford Governor's Center, Connecticut
1993	Hilton Hotel, New York
1996	Savacou Gallery, New York

Publications:

On HARDISON: Book—*Illustrated Bio-Bibliography of Black Photographers, 1940-1988* by Deborah Willis Thomas, New York, Garland Publishing Company, 1989. **Articles**—"The Lady Who Builds Giants," in *Call Them Heroes,* New York, Silver Burdett, 1965; "The Lady Who Builds Giants," in *Handstands,* Boston, Allyn and Bacon, 1978.

*

Inge Hardison comments:

When my brother and I were children, parents taught us that we should try to live in such a way as to make the world a better place for having lived in it. During my long life I have enjoyed using different ways to distill the essences of my experiences so as to share them for the good they might do in the lives of others.

Inge Hardison, 1989. Photo courtesy of Lynn Wozniak.

In the early days I studied to be a singer—but I didn't become a professional. I did some acting on Broadway. I was a photographer for a number of years. I write poetry, but my major form of expression is sculpture. I have created an ongoing series of sculptured portraits I call, "Negro Giants in History." I started this work in 1963.

By memorializing such great, selfless people as Harriet Tubman, Frederick Douglass, Sojourner Truth, Paul Robeson, and others, I have been able to put within the experience of many schoolchildren, college students, and adults these much-needed models of inspiration, and many of those who read the biographies of these sculptured heroes are encouraged to try to make their own lives more meaningful.

*   *   *

A life devoted to creativity and art speaks of a certain nobility. When such a life shines with many facets, it also speaks of commitment and determination. Such is the case with Inge Hardison.

Hardison is a sculptor whose major interest is portraiture, both contemporary and historical. She molds images in wax, clay, and plaster. The sculptures are sometimes done at the request of clients and then cast in other materials, such as bonded bronze. She signs her works as Inge.

Inge Hardison: *Sojourner Truth* from "Negro Giants in History" series, 1990. Photo courtesy of Anthony Abercrombie.

Hardison's work is closely attached to her heritage as a woman of African descent. She has created a series of busts of African American heroes that she has called "Negro Giants in History." The series is ongoing and was created in part to make sculpture readily available to a wide range of people. The series also has preserved for a younger generation the memory of people who made important contributions to the advancement of African Americans.

Three of Hardison's sculptures are in academic settings and thus are for the direct benefit of students. One of these, a portrait of Frederick Douglass, was commissioned by the black alumni of Princeton University. Another, a bust of Martin Luther King, Jr., as a young man, is in a serene garden in the courtyard of the former student center at Kean College of New Jersey. The third sculpture was commissioned to commemorate the twenty-fifth anniversary of the founding of Medgar Evers College in Brooklyn. The work, an abstract seven-foot sculpture called *Jubilee,* was installed in the college amphitheater on 28 September 1995.

Hardison is sometimes seen wearing a small work of her own creation. It is a two-inch lapel pin that depicts the abolitionist and prototypical feminist Sojourner Truth as a lean figure with long arms and legs. Honoring an eloquent African American woman of the nineteenth century, the pin also speaks of the strides made by all women, including Hardison, in working and competing in realms

dominated by men. The original work, of which the lapel pin is a replica, was a two-foot work given to Nelson Mandela by New York Governor Mario Cuomo in 1990 on behalf of the people of the state. The specific occasion was Mandela's triumphant visit to the United States shortly after his release from prison and before he became the first black president of South Africa.

In addition to being a sculptor, Hardison is interested in other arts. She is an accomplished photographer, and an exhibition of her work was mounted at the Portsmouth Museum in Virginia, the city where she was born. She has had an interest in dance, and she particularly enjoys watching performances of the Alvin Ailey dancers. Her observations of dancers, whose bodies are in constant motion, has translated into a quality of fluidity in her sculptures. Her interest in the arts was also manifested in her involvement as a founding member of the Black Academy of Arts and Letters. She was the only woman among the six artists who were founding members.

Margaret McCaden, Hardison's longtime friend and business associate, has been an important advocate for her work. Together they have collaborated in many adventures. Both, for example, participated in the experimental Life Enrichment Program of the psychologist Ira Progroff. One important aim of the dynamic workshops of Dialogue House, which were his creation, was to tap into and release one's creativity. Both McCaden and Hardison were leaders of the workshops. For Hardison a life given to creativity is evidence of the success of the experience.

—Thomas M. Shaw

HARDRICK, John Wesley
American painter

Born: Indianapolis, Indiana, 21 September 1891. **Education:** Studied at John Herron School of Art. **Awards:** Bronze Medal (second place), Harmon Foundation, 1927; Outstanding Work and Outstanding Portrait Size Awards, Indiana State Exhibition, 1933. **Died:** 1968.

Exhibitions:

1927	Harmon Foundation, New York (through 1931)
1929	Smithsonian Institution, Washington, D.C.
1932	Chicago Art Institute
1933	Harmon Foundation, Tuskegee, Alabama
1940	American Negro Exposition, Chicago

*   *   *

John Wesley Hardrick, born in 1891 in Indianapolis, Indiana, was a person who labored in the shadows of artistic greatness. He was known for his portraits and his landscapes. His portraits were studies that gave insight into the personalities of the subjects. His landscapes were made up of actual and imagined elements; he seldom did on-site sketching but rather absorbed a scene that he then put onto canvas, seemingly with little effort.

Experiencing segregated schools, Hardrick found an island of creativity in the Herron School of Art, where he was embraced for his ability notwithstanding the color of his skin. Although he had a natural ability for painting, his skills and techniques were developed through the efforts of a high school teacher, Otto Stark, and of John Forsythe of the Herron School of Art. The influence of these teachers can be seen in his early works, even though critics also have noted the development of an individualistic signature. His primary tool of creativity was the palette knife, which he used to create textures in his landscapes.

Hardrick was recognized in and out of the state of Indiana. He won a number of awards in the Hoosier Salon Exhibit at the Marshall Field's Gallery in Chicago, and his painting *Little Brown Girl* won a second-place bronze medal and $100 in the 1927 Harmon Foundation competition in New York. The same portrait had been shown in the Hoosier Salon exhibition, and in 1929 it became only the second painting by an African American to be accepted into the Herron School of Art's permanent collection. A Works Progress Administration (WPA) painter, Hardrick exhibited in the 1940 *American Negro Exposition: Celebrating 75 Years of Negro Achievement,* held in Chicago.

In his portraiture Hardrick was able to capture the essence of the individual he was painting. In the painting of children, for example, the innocence and shyness of each child is present in the portrait. In the painting of adults Hardrick's touch induces viewers to perceive a sense of the subject's personality. He was a master of the painting of subjects' eyes. Hardrick was in demand by people in both the black and white communities.

The influence of Forsythe can be seen in Hardrick's landscape compositions. The tops of the trees are cut off, and Hardrick sometimes divides a forest with a dissecting path, balanced with tree trunks on either side. If the trees are not divided by a path, Hardrick uses a stream to interrupt the viewer's eye. In many compositions the viewer is led from the bottom left, with the journey continuing through the painting, up and out of the right side of the composition, with no obvious horizon. In later years Hardrick experimented with slightly different coloring, but his impressionistic technique with textures basically remained the same. The textures he created with the palette knife simply increased the illusion of the woodiness of the landscapes. The viewer becomes a part of the work, expecting to hear the rustle of the leaves or the running of the water.

Although Hardrick did not do sketches for his landscapes, he enjoyed painting on the street in downtown Indianapolis in the summertime. He sometimes sold a painting on the spot, still wet. At other times, coming upon someone who he felt would appreciate his work but was short of money, he would simply give the painting away in the hope that it would bring happiness into others' lives.

While a number of African American artists who received monetary awards from the Harmon Foundation went on to study in Europe, Hardrick chose to stay in Indiana, mainly because of family obligations. His choice did not inhibit his artistic maturity, however, and the proof of his worth as an artist is reflected in the number of his paintings found in private and public collections.

—William Edward Taylor

HARLESTON, Edwin (Augustus)
American painter and muralist

Born: Charleston, South Carolina, 1882. **Education:** Atlanta University, A.B. 1904; Boston Museum of Fine Arts School, 1906-12;

Harvard University, Cambridge, Massachusetts. **Awards:** Amy E. Spingarn Prize, *Crisis;* Harmon Foundation, 1931. **Died:** 5 May 1931.

Exhibitions:

1928	Harmon Foundation, Tuskegee, Alabama
1930	National Gallery of Art
1931	Harmon Foundation, Tuskegee, Alabama
1933	National Gallery of Art
1935	Howard University, Washington, D.C.
1936	Harmon Foundation, Tuskegee, Alabama
	Texas Centennial
1937	Howard University, Washington, D.C.
1941	South Side Community Art Center, Chicago
1942	Downtown Gallery, New York
1945	South Side Community Art Center, Chicago
1967	City College of New York

Collections:

Fisk University, Nashville; Howard University, Washington, D.C.; National Archives, Washington, D.C.

Publication:

On HARLESTON: Article—"Harleston: Who is E.A. Harleston?" by Madeline G. Allison, in *Opportunity,* January 1924.

*   *   *

Historians of black art have not been kind to Edwin Harleston, and an account of his work has been left out of several publications. He was a victim of the time in which he lived, for his life spanned two radically different periods in American creative consciousness. He was eighteen years old at the turn of the century, growing up in segregated Charleston, South Carolina, where he had no opportunity to visit a museum or receive training in the visual arts. Harleston left Charleston to attend Atlanta University, but there, too, he had few opportunities to study art. Atlanta's connection to black art was through Henry O. Tanner, who had earlier taught in the city. Although Tanner's art was anchored more in the past than in the changes taking place in the United States, his legendary reputation had an impact on the young Harleston.

In 1905, when Harleston arrived in Boston to attend its museum school, the changes taking place in New York City had had little impact there. Boston, like Charleston, retained English traditions. Its artists, too, nurtured connections to the past rather than to the new ideas coming out of New York. Harleston was thirty-one years old in 1913, the year of New York's revolutionary Armory Show, an exhibit of some 1,600 works by American artists and by celebrated European modernists such as Georges Braque, Pablo Picasso, and Henri Matisse. By the time the show arrived in Boston later that year, Harleston had returned to Charleston. As fate would have it, Harleston seemed always to be in the wrong place at the wrong time, through no fault of his own.

In spite of these circumstances, Harleston made a significant contribution to the evolution of black art. No one can deny that the radical and revolutionary changes in the American art scene sparked by the Armory Show influenced the new Negro movement that came a decade later. There was a prevailing mood of experimentation and a desire for something new that fueled black aspirations. Some called the Negro movement a renaissance, a reevaluation of the contributions and mores of the African homeland and of the impact of those values on black life in the United States. Just as the Italian Renaissance had sought values in the arts of antiquity, the artists of the Harlem Renaissance, for example, sought similar connections to their African past.

Thus, just as Duccio and Giotto, through changes in their work, signaled the beginning of the Renaissance in Italy, Harleston's elegant, dignified images of blacks, painted in Charleston between 1913 and 1920, foretold the coming changes in blacks' awareness of their rich, dignified heritage. Many important figures of the period, including W. E. B. Du Bois, recognized Harleston's important contributions. Although his gift was one of interpretation rather than of style, Harleston's portraits countered the negative stereotyped images depicted in the Currier & Ives prints and the other illustrations of blacks that had been circulated during Reconstruction.

Aaron Douglas's account of his collaboration with Harleston on murals at Fisk University indicates that he was highly impressed with Harleston's skill and knowledge. Douglas was the principal artist of the Negro movement, and Harleston was invigorated by the association with him. Afterward, Harleston's work changed markedly. His portrait of Douglas, completed in 1930, shows the artist against the muted colors of the mural in the background. The colors of Harleston's warmer palette interact gently with the figure, adding a subtle movement that gives the painting a life unlike anything he had done earlier. One can only imagine what direction Harleston's work might have taken if he could have pursued this new direction, which so exhilarated him. A year later, however, after a brief illness he died.

—Leo Twiggs

HARPER, William A.

American painter

Born: Cayuga, Canada, 27 December 1873. **Education:** School of Art Institute of Chicago, 1895-1901, B.F.A. 1901. **Career:** Teacher, Houston Public School System, 1901-03. **Awards:** Second Honors, School of Art Institute of Chicago, 1901; First Prize, Fortnightly Club Exhibition, 1908; Municipal Art League Prize, 1905. **Died:** 27 March 1910.

Individual Exhibition:

1910   Art Institute of Chicago

Selected Group Exhibitions:

1903   Art Institute of Chicago
1904   Art Institute of Chicago
1905   Art Institute of Chicago
1906   Art Institute of Chicago
1907   Art Institute of Chicago
1908   Art Institute of Chicago
1909   Art Institute of Chicago

1940   Tanner Galleries, Chicago
1967   Howard University, Washington, D.C.
1989   Smithsonian Institution, Washington, D.C.

Collections:

Carver Museum, Tuskegee Institute, Tuskegee, Alabama; Oregon Public Library, Oregon, Illinois; Provident Hospital, Chicago.

Publications:

On HARPER: Articles—"William A. Harper" by Florence L. Bentley, in *Voice of the Negro* (Atlanta, Georgia), February 1906; "William A. Harper" by Florence L. Bentley, in *Voice of the Negro* (Atlanta, Georgia), February 1908; "William A. Harper," in *Bulletin of the Art Institute of Chicago,* July 1910; "Four Problems in the History of Negro Art" by James Porter, in *Journal of Negro History* (Washington, D.C.), January 1942.

*   *   *

Much like English painter John Constable and members of the French Barbizon school, William A. Harper, too, was fascinated by nature: his idyllic paintings depict riverbanks, trees, vegetable fields, and cottages in American, English, French, and Mexican locales. Harper is said to have advanced modernist strategies of generalizing and simplifying form for pictorial unity and design. His lively brushwork is a twentieth-century hallmark, a rejection of the staid and finished surfaces of academic art.

Harper's strong compositional sense likely developed at the Art Institute of Chicago, where he studied from 1895 to 1901 and graduated with honors. As a trained artist, he may have produced portraiture, a viable manner of making an artistic living in his time. Yet his known surviving works are almost exclusively landscapes, and this is a measure of the genre's suitability for creative experimentation. In this manner, Harper was akin to the French impressionists and turn-of-the-century artists struggling to find avenues of originality.

Harper was nonetheless more of an "impressionizer" than an impressionist, an observation that has been made by art historians regarding many American painters who took up the French practice. Although he did picture after picture of calm, pastoral spaces, he did not paint versions of the same subject in order to capture temporal changes in light and color as did Claude Monet. Nor did Harper depict the public spaces of leisure for the working- and middle-classes. Like the impressionists, though, he was dedicated to evoking the sensations that the natural world provoked. In marked contrast to the type of landscapes that attempt to flawlessly represent the visual fact, his are moody interpretations of what he observed and recalled.

For several years in the early 1900s Harper lived in Europe. In Paris, he and William E. Scott, a black painter and an Art Institute graduate, worked with expatriate Henry Ossawa Tanner. A painter who increasingly affected a freer, more active style for his religious paintings in his mature years, Tanner may have influenced and been influenced by the younger artists; the work of all three is characterized by heavy impasto and summarized forms.

Harper chose the country geography as his subject matter, emotionally rendered in *Landscape with Poplars,* also known as *Afternoon at Montigny* (1905); *Eventide, Cornwall* (not dated); *Provincial Landscape* (1908); and *The Banks of the Laing* (not dated). He studied the look of natural light striking form and expressed the feel of its shimmering and dissolving effects. His method apparently was to make field sketches in front of his chosen motif and then return to the studio to paint canvases based on these images and his memories.

The artist relied on a free application of bright color to circumvent a static look, and both the rare human figure and the more common object are conveyed with a few swipes of the brush or palette knife. Still, he never relinquished the academician's concern for the balanced composition. Contrasts in scale, texture, and volume are rendered by rhythmic changes in the direction of the brushstroke, skillful arrangement of masses and voids, and perspectival conventions. Significantly, Harper imposed calm and order on nature, but he also sought to invigorate the representation of it with formal tensions and dynamism.

—Jacqueline Francis

HARRIS, Michael D(eHart)

American painter, printmaker, fiber artist, and mixed-media artist

Born: Cleveland, Ohio, 14 July 1948. **Education:** Bowling Green State University, Bowling Green, Ohio, B.S. in education 1971; Howard University, Washington, D.C., M.F.A. in painting 1979; Yale University, New Haven, Connecticut, M.A. (distinction) in African and African-American Studies 1989, M.A. in history of art 1990, M. Phil. in history of art 1991, Ph.D. 1996. **Career:** Assistant professor, Morehouse College, Atlanta, Georgia, 1981-93, Georgia State University, 1993-95. Since 1995 assistant professor, University of North Carolina at Chapel Hill. Art teacher, Cleveland Public Schools, 1971-73; artist-in-residence, Georgia Council for the Arts and Humanities, Dougherty County public schools, 1977, Atlanta public schools, 1978, Neighborhood Arts Center, Atlanta, Georgia, 1980-81; adjunct professor, Atlanta Junior College, 1980-82, Georgia State University, 1984-85, Wellesley College, Wellesley, Massachusetts, 1992; technical services editor, Frederick Douglas Papers, Yale University, 1988-90; curriculum consultant, Portland, Oregon Public Schools, 1982-92. **Awards:** Georgia Council for the Arts and Humanities grants, 1981, 1983; Bronze Jubilee Award in Visual Arts, Atlanta, Georgia, 1985; Mayor's Fellowship, City of Atlanta, 1987; Charles Dana Faculty Improvement Fellowship, United Negro College Fund, 1988-89; Foreign Language Area Studies Fellowship (to study Yoruba), Yale University, 1989-92; Patricia Roberts Harris Fellowship, U.S. Department of Education and Yale University, 1989-92; Yale Center for International and Area Studies foreign research grant, 1991-92; National Endowment for the Humanities Graduate Study Fellowship, 1992; Andrew W. Mellon Pre-Dissertation Fellowship, Yale University, 1993; Hartsfield International Airport Purchase Award, Atlanta, Georgia, 1995. **Address:** 905 Harrier Court, Durham, North Carolina 27713, U.S.A. **Online Address:** Olushina@aol.com.

Individual Exhibitions:

1973   Karamu House, Cleveland, Ohio
1975   Karamu House, Cleveland, Ohio

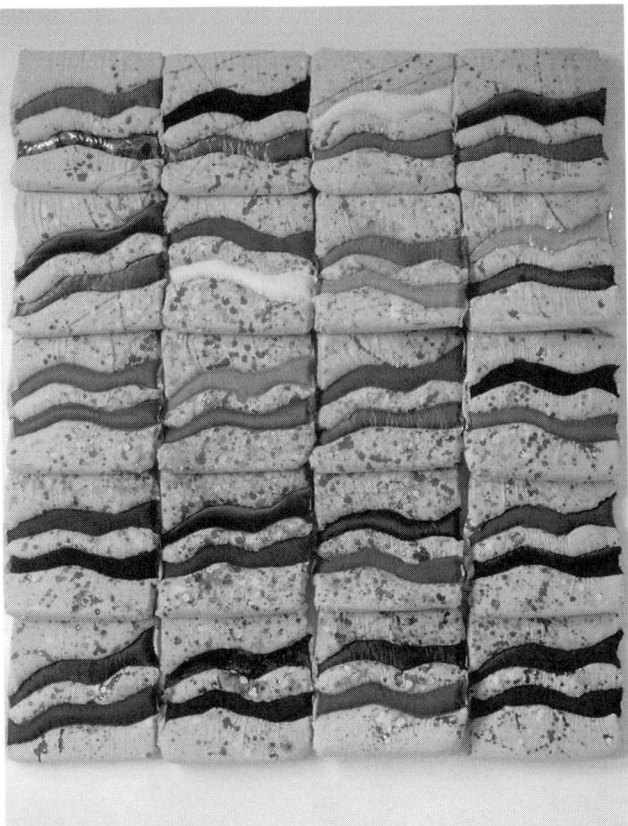

Michael Harris: *After the Rain,* 1995.

1977   Banks Haley Gallery, Albany, Georgia
1978   Walks of Peachtree Gallery, Atlanta, Georgia
1979   Norfolk State University, Virginia
        Cleveland State University, Ohio
        Howard University, Washington, D.C.
1980   Neighborhood Arts Center, Atlanta, Georgia
1982   Wesleyan College, Macon, Georgia
1983   Highland Gallery, Atlanta, Georgia
1984   Miles College, Birmingham, Alabama
1991   Kent State University, Kent, Ohio

Selected Group Exhibitions:

1988   National Black Arts Festival, Atlanta, Georgia
1989   Atlanta Life Insurance Company National Exhibition, Atlanta, Georgia
1990   *Africobra: The First Twenty Years,* Southern Arts Federation (traveling)
1991   University of Massachusetts at Boston
        Pennsylvania State University
1992   Museum of Science and Industry, Chicago
1993   University of Cincinnati, Ohio
        City Gallery, Chastain Park, Atlanta
1994   Nexus Gallery, Atlanta, Georgia

Michael Harris: *Dear Granddaddy*, 1996.

Publications:

By HARRIS: Books—*Atlantis,* 1977, and *Oms and Okra,* 1978, Cleveland, Ohio, Sun People Press; *Astonishment and Power: Kongo Minkisi/The Art of Renee Stout* (with Wyatt MacGaffey), Washington, D.C., Smithsonian Institution Press for the National Museum of African Art, 1993; *African Art: An Essay for Teachers,* Atlanta, Georgia, High Museum of Art and Atlanta Public Schools, 1994; *Hand Me Downs: Innovation within a Tradition,* Charlotte, North Carolina, Afro-American Cultural Center, 1995. **Articles**—"Ritual Bodies - Sexual Bodies: The Role and Presentation of the Body in African-American Art," in *Third Text* (London), 12, 1990; "Toward 'Object and Verb': History, Dualities, and the African-American Artist," in *C Magazine* (Toronto), 33, Spring 1992; "Africentrism and Curriculum: Concepts, Issues and Prospects," in *Journal of Negro Education,* 61(3), Summer 1992; "From Double Consciousness to Double Vision: The Africentric Artist," in *African Arts,* 27(2), 1994; "Beyond Aesthetics: Visual Activism in Ile-Ife," in *The Yoruba Artist: New Theoretical Perspectives on African Arts,* edited by Rowland Abiodun, Henry Drewal, and John Pemberton, Washington, D.C., Smithsonian Institution Press, 1994.

*

Michael D. Harris comments:

My belief is that art is best as the articulation of spiritual ideas or transformative intention. It can be an agent of spiritual inspiration or personal and social transformation. My conviction is that the best expression presents individual creativity within a collective context or awareness; form represents a means or an aid to an end rather than an end in itself.

For the past fourteen years the forms I have used have been based upon the rhythmic, organized grid of African American quilts. To this now has been added a series quoting from and inspired by shrine paintings done by Yoruba women. I have improvised in ways that reflect an attempt to discover a symbiotic relationship between African American musical expression and the visual organization of the works based in quilting. The shrine works deal with the sense of ritual performance and family tribute and the sense of sacred space. The process of creating art represents a path of discovery rather than a state of mastery, and the work at any point provides a glimpse of an act of becoming.

It is my desire to work in a way that is in harmony with a great deal of traditional African expression—the work should be an expression of affirmation, not that seeking to destroy canons, conventions, or definitions. I want to talk about who we are, who we were, and who we can be.

*   *   *

As a painter and tapestry designer, Michael Harris has always been concerned with designs formed by textures. His designs are based on his study of African symbols and spirituality, and he is ever conscious of the ways in which they conflate with his identification with Africa. In the 1980s he explored the rhythmic patterns of African American quilts, incorporating much of their energy into his paintings. Most of these works show a predominance of reddish hues. Incorporated among the horizontal fluid, wavelike movements are text and portraits of African Americans. In one silk screen from 1980 the text reads, "For All Black Daddies," which is also the title of the work. In this monochromatic work the portraits, text, and wave patterns are compressed onto one plane so that all share the same space and must be read at once. Harris believes that the present must be connected with the past so that contemporary African American realities do not lose sight of traditional African expressions. Avoiding the element of depth places the past and present in his compositions on the same plane and calls ancestors into the present dimension.

Harris has also adopted the patterns of African American quilters in his artwork. These literal works possess the same asymmetrical patterns as the quilts, uniform but quite suddenly taking another course before returning to the established pattern. Among African American quilters this departure has been explained as "making something of my own." The tradition among these quilters is to personalize an established pattern, seen at work in Harris's derivative works such as *Spirit Quilt* (1992).

As Harris has continued to explore West African cultures and their cosmology, his work has taken a decidedly different turn in the 1990s. The horizontal movement and the decorative quality of his marks and brush strokes are gone, replaced with often dark surface colors and with symbols based on autobiography that employs, as Harris says, "historic script by African peoples." These provocative works seem more thoughtful and also ask more of the viewer. In attempting to decipher the symbols and marks, viewers must read beyond the surfaces into the deep tonal recesses to understand what Harris has laid before them.

Mixed-media works such as *Soul Chart* (1996) and *Family Shrine* (1996) share the sense of mysticism and spirituality that is a part of the work of the Cuban artist Wifredo Lam. In his own works

Lam refers to Santeria worship ceremonies that he and his family participated in. Harris shares with Lam a sense of spirituality and memory that was lost, but Harris finds it again through the study of African art and culture.

Harris has been a member of Africobra (African Commune of Bad Relevant Artists) since 1979. The principal aim of their work has been to articulate and pursue a black aesthetic in the visual arts through the use of what they call Kool-Aid colors, lost and found lines, text, and the black figure. Harris's study of African art and life has clearly affected and changed his style of work, to the point that little of his earlier style is recognizable. Some elements, like the use of the figure and text in the form of pictographs, remain, but his palette and the linear quality of his later work are more closely associated with African textiles and even the deep, dense quality of central African sculptural forms.

—Lizzetta LeFalle-Collins

HARVEY, Bessie
American sculptor

Born: Dallas, Georgia, 11 October 1929. **Family:** Married 1) Charles Harvey in 1944 (divorced 1968), four sons and seven daughters; 2) Carl Henry in 1989. **Career:** Housekeeper's Aide, Block Memorial Hospital, Alcoa, Tennessee, late 1960s-1983. Various service and industrial jobs, Alcoa, Tennessee, 1940s-1960s. **Agent:** Shari Cavin and Randall Morris, Cavin-Morris Gallery, 560 Broadway, Suite 405B, New York, New York 10012, U.S.A. **Died:** 12 August 1994.

Individual Exhibitions:

1987	Cavin-Morris Gallery, New York
1989	East Tennessee State University Museum, Johnson City, Tennessee
1991	Blue Spiral One Gallery, Asheville, North Carolina
1993	Fisk University Galleries, Nashville
	Community College of Philadelphia
1995	Jazzberry General, Maryville, Tennessee
	Cavin-Morris Gallery, New York

Selected Group Exhibitions:

1991	Artist Space, New York
	Alternative Museum, New York
1993	Sidney Kiskin Gallery, Baruch College, New York
	Diggs Gallery, Winston-Salem State University, Winston-Salem, North Carolina
	New Orleans Museum of Art (traveling through 1995)
1995	Whitney Museum of American Art, New York (traveling)
	Center for Cultural Studies Museum, Bard College, Annandale-on-Hudson, New York
	Inaugural Exhibition of the American Visionary Art Museum, Baltimore, Maryland
1996	New Museum, New York
	Florida State University Museum of Fine Arts, Tallahassee

Collections:

Carroll Reece Museum, East Tennessee State University, Johnson City, Tennessee; Dallas Museum of Art; Museum of the National Center of Afro-American Artists, Boston; National Museum of American Art, Smithsonian Institution, Washington, D.C.; University of Tennessee, Knoxville; Whitney Museum of American Art, New York.

Publications:

On HARVEY: Articles—"Bessie Harvey: The Spirit in the Wood" by Shari Cavin-Morris, in *Clarion,* 12(2/3), Spring-Summer 1987, pp. 44-49; "Bessie Harvey at Cavin-Morris" by Carlo McCormick, in *ArtForum,* January 1988 (illustrated); "God Blessed a Stick" by Amy Thomas, in *Touching Life,* 1(1), Fall 1989, pp. 8-10; "Two Tennessee Visionaries: Bessie Harvey and Homer Green" by Robert Cogswell, in *Folk Art Messenger,* 4(4), Summer 1991, pp. 1, 3-4; "God is the Artist: Thoughts from a So-Called Folk Artist" (interview), in *New Art Examiner,* September 1994; "Sculptor Bessie Harvey Dies at Sixty-Four" by Robert Cogswell, in *Folk Art Messenger,* 8(1), Fall 1994, p. 9.

*   *   *

During her lifetime self-taught folk artist Bessie Harvey was many things to many people. A deeply religious woman with tremendous pride in her African American heritage, she married at age fourteen, had eleven children, was the grandmother of twenty-eight, and the great-grandmother of three. The last twenty years of her life were spent creating vigorous, evocative figurative sculpture, and her work was exhibited posthumously in the 1995 Whitney Biennial. Harvey's life had always been a struggle, as she recalled in a 1987 interview in *Clarion* magazine: "I really didn't become truly human until my youngest was half grown. I was a little better than an animal trying to scrape together food and shelter for them. Later, that's when I began to develop my mind and question the spiritual nature of my life."

Harvey fashioned wild, grinning, benevolent characters from tree roots and branches she gleaned from nature. She described her working method as a process in which she saw souls among the twigs and roots, then worked to free them. Her involvement with wood echoes traditional African folk beliefs that trees have a spiritual life. The artist encrusted each organic form with glitter, beads, artificial flowers, shells, feathers, hair, and acrylic paint to draw out the personality that had initially attracted her. Harvey's inspiration came from within as well, as she explained in *Clarion:* "I see this vision of one of these dolls ... and I can't sleep. I even have to get up and draw it out the best I can on a piece of paper, or take a piece of wood and do it before I can even go to sleep. It's something like a torment."

Harvey's sculptures first gained attention in 1974, when she was working as a housekeeper's aid at Block Memorial Hospital in Tennessee. She entered a piece in the hospital's annual art show. Her work interested one of the staff doctors, who in turn introduced her to the directors of the Cavin-Morris Gallery in New York City. Harvey sold her work exclusively through this gallery for the next several years.

The themes of Harvey's pieces reach beyond individual character studies to embrace the spiritual aspects of life. Although not conventionally religious, she communicated her spiritual feelings

articulates the bridge between her rich African roots and the bleak world of racial oppression that surrounded her.

—Laurie Fitzpatrick

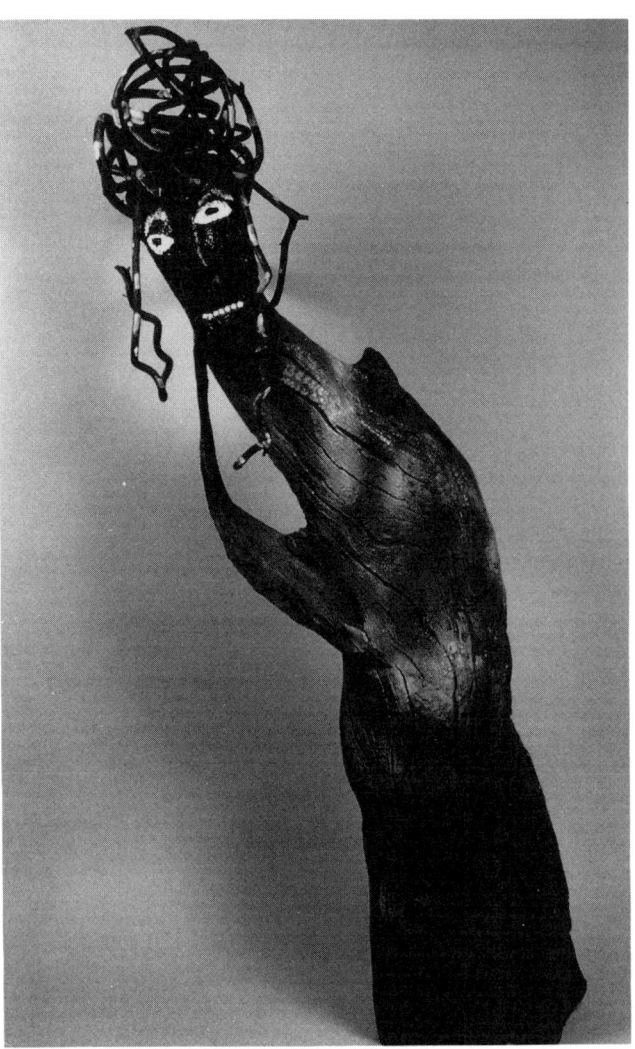

Bessie Harvey: *Sha-Cha,* 1987.

HASSINGER, Maren

American sculptor, performance artist, and printmaker

Born: Los Angeles, 1947. **Education:** Bennington College, Vermont, B.A. 1969; University of California, Los Angeles, M.F.A. 1973. **Career:** Instructor, Los Angeles County Museum of Art, 1977-78, California State University, Los Angeles, 1979, Otis/Parsons Institute, Los Angeles, 1980-81, Pasadena Art Workshop, California, 1981, University of California, Los Angeles, 1983-84, Parsons Art Institute, New York, 1985, Art Partners, New York, 1985-88. Adjunct professor, School of Visual Art, New York, 1990, Hunter College, New York, 1988-91; associate adjunct professor, Long Island University, Southampton Campus, New York, 1992. Lecturer, State University of New York, Stony Brook, 1992-94. Artist-in-residence, Studio Museum in Harlem, New York, 1984-85, The Printmaking Workshop, New York, 1990. Visiting artist, Southern Illinois University, Carbondale, 1991, University of Iowa, Iowa City, 1991. **Awards:** Commission Award, City of Los Angeles, 1977; Special Projects grant, California Arts Council, 1977; National Endowment for the Arts fellowships, 1980, 1984; Betty Brazil Memorial Fund Prize in Sculpture, 1983; Studio Award, P.S. 1, Long Island City, New York, 1986-87; Artist's Space grant, New York, 1988; New York Foundation for the Arts Fellowship, 1988-89. **Address:** 9 Rowman Court, East Hampton, New York 11937, U.S.A.

Individual Exhibitions:

1980   Just above Midtown/Downtown Gallery, New York
1981   Los Angeles County Museum of Art
1985   Los Angeles City College
        Art Gallery, California State University, Northridge
1986   Contemporary Arts Forum, Santa Barbara, California
1989   Soho 20 Gallery, New York
1991   Gracie Mansion Gallery, New York
1992   Fine Arts Gallery, Long Island University, Southampton, New York
1993   Benton Gallery, Southampton, New York

Selected Group Exhibitions:

1975   *Artists Choose Artists,* Los Angeles County Museum of Art
1977   Otis Art Institute, Los Angeles
1981   California Museum of Science and Industry, Los Angeles
1983   Long Beach Museum of Art, California
1984   Kenkeleba Gallery, New York
1986   Chicago Museum of Science and Industry
1990   New Museum of Contemporary Art, New York
1994   Neuberger Museum of Art, Purchase, New York
1995   Cinque Gallery, New York
        Studio Museum in Harlem, New York

through a vibrant blend of Baptist faith and voodoo beliefs. Harvey saw voodoo as a life-affirming, strongly African religious system that acknowledged and respected natural forces. She denounced any negative associations or misinformation about the religion. In addition, Harvey expressed her deeply felt connection to "Old Africa" through imagining it as an Eden where all black people lived together in harmony a long time ago. She often used an African-English dictionary to name her pieces, using the language as a simple and direct tribute to African culture.

The characters Harvey sculpted represent a visual record of black involvement in the building of America. They also recall her rural upbringing of tending livestock, sowing and harvesting crops, dancing and socializing, raising children, and attending church. Harvey was as much the master of restraint as she was of accretion: knowing when one eye was enough, she did not need to add a second. This lent a disarming gaiety to her works, despite all hints of otherworldly ghosts, ancestors, and wild things flying through the night.

The strong presence of Harvey's figures is primal and can sometimes be frightening. Although thickly coated with paint and objects, the artist's works skillfully capture life's earthiness and rawness. This power, heightened by Harvey's magical imagination,

Selected Performances:

1977	Studio Z, Los Angeles
1982	Barnes Municipal Gallery, Los Angeles
1983	Long Beach Museum of Art, California
1993	Whitney Museum at Philip Morris, New York
1994	Victor D'Amico Institute of Art, Amagansett, New York
1995	Studio Museum in Harlem, New York

Collections:

California Afro-American Museum, Los Angeles; California State University, Long Beach; Studio Museum in Harlem, New York.

Publications:

On HASSINGER: Articles—"Hassinger and Mahan: Works in Transition" by Sandy Ballatore, in *Artweek,* 4 September 1976, p. 4; "Steel Trees Grow Along Freeways" by Mark Stein, in *Los Angeles Times,* 22 November 1979; "An Artist Looking for Dangerous Ground" by Judith Hart-Sonte, *Museum of California,* November/December 1982; "Sticks and Stones at Kenkeleba" by Amy Slaton, in *East Village Eye,* November 1984, p. 35; "Bold Sculpture for Wide Open Space" by Michael Brenson, in *The New York Times,* 21 July 1989, pp. C1, C24; "Maren Hassinger at Soho 20" by Ken Johnson, in *Art in America,* May 1990, pp. 244-45; "Maren Hassinger" by Michael Brenson, in *The New York Times,* 29 March 1991, p. C19; "Airport Art for Pittsburgh" by Mary Jean Kenton, in *Art in America,* October 1992; "Interview" by Becky Godwin, in *Quadrille,* Spring 1993, p. 39; "Interview with Maren Hassinger" by Curtia James, in *Artpapers* (Georgia), January and February 1994, pp. 6-8.

*   *   *

Maren Hassinger creates organic, living articles from inorganic, industrial materials. When she set out for her undergraduate degree at Bennington College in the mid-1960s, she intended to study dance. The school steered her toward sculpture, and later, as a graduate student at the University of California, Los Angeles, she became a fiber sculptor, eventually choosing wire rope as a favorite material.

With wire rope Hassinger could "create a semblance of growing things," and the mass of the subject could be created entirely from the "line" of the wire rope. She says her sculptures are "three dimensional drawings . . . pseudovolumes . . . they occupy space and are concerned with volume, like sculpture, yet their fundamental elements being line, they recall drawing." Her history of dance also remained in her work, and there often seems to be a sense of movement suggested in these "pseudovolumes."

There is also movement, of course, in her performance work. She says, "Performance helps me to get away from traditional aesthetic notions . . . from the aesthetic frame [of mind] and the work, the artifice that prevents me from communicating directly with the spectator." Furthermore, Hassinger has been more recently working on video and multimedia works. Though Hassinger is not interested in the "commodity" nature of some art, she is interested in the more popular aspect of film. "I have a new appetite now not for the quiet, but for 'remembering' and 'speaking.' The quiet stuff is egoless . . . the new stuff is about experience and has to have ego in it. I like the idea that film is seen by more people."

Hassinger remembers a particular art exhibit, of the sculpture of Eva Hesse, that especially influenced her work. "After seeing a major show of [Hesse's] work at the Pasadena Museum—particularly a piece called *Seven Poles,* an incredible experience—I felt she was looking at someone's spirit made manifest. The sculpture was like flesh, luminous and transparent as though Hesse had put all the experience of her life into it." Seeing Hesse's work was like a confirmation to Hassinger that she was headed in the right direction, as Hassinger puts her life into her work and makes her work out of her life.

—Terry Bain

HAWKINS, Cynthia

American painter

Born: New York, 1950. **Education:** Queens College, City University of New York, B.F.A. 1977; Maryland Institute College of Art, Baltimore, M.F.A. 1992; Brooklyn Museum Art School, New York. **Family:** Married, two children. **Awards:** Award, Provincetown Workshop, Brooklyn Museum Art School, New York, 1985; fellowship, Studio Museum in Harlem, 1987; Patricia Roberts Harris Fellowship, 1990-91, 1991-92.

Individual Exhibitions:

1974	Queens College, New York
1981	Midtown/Downtown Gallery, New York
1986	Francis Wolfson Art Center, Miami-Dade Community College, Florida
1989	Cinque Gallery, New York

Selected Group Exhibitions:

1979	Emily Lowe Gallery, Hempstead, New York
1980	Jamaica Art Center, New York
	Bronx Museum, New York
1984	James Szoke Gallery, New York
	Mississippi Museum of Art, Jackson
	Augusta Savage Gallery, University of Massachusetts, Amherst
1986	Grace Borgenicht Gallery, New York
	Kenkeleba Gallery, New York
1988	Studio Museum in Harlem, New York
1990	Dome Gallery, New York
1991	Decker Art Gallery, Baltimore, Maryland

Publications:

On HAWKINS: Book—*Cynthia Hawkins,* exhibition catalog, Miami, Francis Wolfson Art Center and Judith Wilson, 1986. **Articles**—"Cynthia Hawkins" by Judith Wilson, in *Art in America,* October 1980; "Cynthia Hawkins" by Vivian Raynor, in *New York Times,* 20 July 1984; "African-American Women Artists: Another Generation, Cynthia Hawkins" by Thelma Golden, in *International Review of African American Art,* 9(2), January 1991.

*   *   *

Cynthia Hawkins has said that, about the time when she was in high school, "for some reason there were two Jackson Pollocks on exhibit behind glass. . . . I wondered where this work came from, where in him did it come from, how could this be. I was enthralled, amazed. I think that is what finally gripped me about art, that it has so many faces, so many forms, and it is up to the artist which way to go."

Hawkins's exploration of "which way to go" has led her to an abstract expressionist style of painting. In her early work she combined painting with sculpture, covering all sides of an object so that it would seem a different work from every angle. Later her work began to investigate the geometry of two dimensions as she began painting mostly on canvas. In her two-dimensional works, Hawkins uses a mature and highly developed vocabulary of abstraction. Symbols and signs, calligraphic and static marks, choice of color and layering of brush stroke divide, unite, and move across the face of her canvases.

In her "Currency of Meaning" series, Hawkins divides space into separate areas that are sometimes referred to as habitats, environments, or fields. The "inhabitants" of Hawkins's environments differ and sometimes contrast enough that it might seem each environment is its own painting, related to other environments perhaps only by being a part of the same painting. Parts of a painting may touch on familiar territory for Hawkins, as in *Currency of Meaning #5* and *#6* (1989), where the bottom field in each is a grid of squares; other fields may be more intuitive and abstract and perhaps difficult to interpret without close examination. Hawkins says this is a compositional device to indicate motion, something like that occurring on a television screen, which offers a continuous stream of images that combine to form the illusion of motion. Even the lines separating environment in her paintings include motion, as in *Currency of Meaning #9*, where the lines do not just divide but incorporate symbols (arrows) leading the eye toward the center field of the painting.

Cynthia Hawkins is not concerned much with interpretations of her paintings. As with most abstract expression, there is room for levels of interpretation and meaning not intended by the artist but observed by the viewer. In any case, it is not necessarily the product of painting to which Cynthia Hawkins devotes her energy but the painting itself. "I am in love with the very act of painting," she says, "the magic, mystery, and meaning. It is about the self, and the world, and vision. Anyone who says painting is dead has no vision."

—Terry Bain

HAYDEN, Palmer

American painter

Born: Peyton Cole Hedgeman, Wide Water, Virginia, 15 January 1890 (1893 in some sources). **Education:** Studied under Victor Perard, Cooper Union, New York, 1919; Boothbay Art Colony, Maine, beginning 1925; studied with M. Clivette LeFevre, École des Beaux-Arts, Paris, 1927-32. **Military Service:** U.S. Army, 1914. **Family:** Married Miriam Hoffman, a schoolteacher. **Career:** House cleaner, postal clerk, and porter, 1919. Easel painter, Division of Public Works, 1934-40. **Awards:** Harmon Gold Award in Fine Arts, Harmon Foundation, 1926; Rockefeller Prize, 1933;

American Veteran's Society of Artists honorable mention, 1965; CAPS Fellowship, 1973. **Died:** 18 February 1973.

Individual Exhibitions:

1935	New Jersey State Museum, Trenton
1937	Bernheim-Jeune Gallery, Paris
1939	Baltimore Museum of Art, Maryland
1947	Argent Gallery, New York
1954	New York Public Library
1974	Studio Museum in Harlem, New York

Selected Group Exhibitions:

1928	Harmon Foundation, Tuskegee, Alabama
1930	Salon des Tuileries, Paris
1933	Smithsonian Institution, Washington, D.C.
1940	Rockefeller Center Galleries, New York
	Tanner Art Galleries, Chicago
1945	Albany Institute of History and Art, New York
1968	Studio Museum in Harlem, New York
1970	Newark Museum, New Jersey
1976	Los Angeles County Museum of Art, California
1985	Bellevue Art Museum, Washington (traveling)

Collections:

Atlanta University, Georgia; Fisk University, Nashville; Oakland Museum, California; Smithsonian Museum, Washington, D.C.

Publications:

On HAYDEN: Book—*Echoes of Our Past: The Narrative Artistry of Palmer C. Hayden* by Allan M. Gordon, Los Angeles, Museum of African-American Art, 1988.

*   *   *

Palmer Hayden, named Peyton Cole Hedgemen at birth, is best known for his paintings of rural and urban black folk. The circumstances under which his name was changed are unclear, but it is known that he was a laborer and U. S. soldier for many years before giving his full time to painting. Mostly self-taught, he was well into adulthood before receiving any academic art training. At one time Hayden studied to be a commercial artist but realized that his desire to be a fine artist was stronger, and he consequently pursued formal training.

A turning point in the fledgling artist's life came when he joined the Boothbay Harbor art colony in Maine, where, exchanging labor for instruction, he learned more about composition and color. Later, after winning first prize in the Harmon Foundation's first exhibit in 1926 for one of his Boothbay Harbor paintings, Hayden moved to Paris and connected with established artists who offered their criticism and taught him technique. Although he developed as an artist during the Harlem Renaissance, he did not completely fit into the movement's ideological mold. Hayden was not compelled to paint in abstract form or to paint with African themes, although *Fétiche et fleurs* (1928-32), which includes an African fetish and weaving, closely resembles the African-cubist style that was popular at the time.

Hayden's paintings exhibit varying styles. His early works were mostly of the waterfront and scenes of Paris. *Boothbay Harbor,*

Palmer Hayden: *Harbor Traffic.* **Photo by Manu Sassoonian; courtesy of the Schomburg Center for Research in Black Culture.**

Maine (1926) and *St. Servan, France* (1927-32), both waterfront scenes, are impressionistic in technique. *Old Military Prison-Paris,* (1927-32) shows that while the artist received formal art training, his paintings retained the flat, naive style that would be seen throughout his career.

Café l'avenue (1932), a sarcastic look at cafe society, is somewhat expressionist in technique. Many of Hayden's paintings are full of irony and satire, elements that sometimes led people to malign and misunderstand them. Some thought his paintings were a mockery of African Americans painted to suit white viewers. *Midsummer Night in Harlem* (1938) is a satiric portrayal of a crowded Harlem neighborhood on a hot night, complete with all the characters and personalities of the milieu; the figures appear almost minstrel-like. The subject of *The Janitor Who Paints a Picture* (1936) is an artist/janitor—a situation with which Hayden could well identify. The setting is a basement studio apartment. The janitor is wearing a beret and holding a palette, and the room is complete with

tools of both trades: brushes, easel, and the models—a mother with her child; other objects depicted include a feather duster, trash can, and clock. This piece is thought to have been painted in protest, as Hayden was often identified as a laborer who dabbled in the arts rather than as a black artist. Recent X rays of the painting revealed an underpainting in which the subjects were originally portrayed as unflattering caricatures of African Americans. Curiously, a cat was painted over a portrait of Abraham Lincoln.

Hayden usually painted from memory, using dreams, folktales, and legends for inspiration. After 1940 he painted many scenes from the events and rituals of everyday life, and while his works focus on African Americans they also portray several other ethnic and racial groups. Hayden's best known works are twelve paintings called the "John Henry" series that were produced over a ten-year period. They are based on a ballad about a true story of the birth, life, and death of an African American male who leaves his agricultural existence to enter the industrial sphere of life.

During the 1970s Hayden worked on a series of paintings depicting the lives of African American soldiers from the era between World War I to the end of segregated military units. Many of his other paintings are autobiographical in nature. *Moonlight at the Crossroads* is a painting of a small boy holding a fiddle, standing in the moonlight at a crossroads. Hayden always wanted a fiddle as a boy and often wondered what turns his life would have taken had he owned one.

—Christine Miner Minderovic

HAYES, Vertis (C.)

American painter, muralist, and sculptor

Born: Atlanta, Georgia, 20 May 1911. **Education:** National Academy of Design, Florence Kane School of Art, Art Students League, New York. **Family:** Married Florence Alexander, one son. **Career:** Art teacher, Lemoyne College, Tennessee, 1938-49; head of Federal Art Center, Memphis, Tennessee, 1938-39; teacher, Le Moyne College, Memphis, Tennessee, 1939-40; founder/director, Hayes Academy of Art, 1947-52; lecturer, California State College Immaculate Heart College, 1971-74. Mural painter, Federal Art Project, New York, 1934-38; founding fellow, Black Academy of Art and Letters, 1969. **Awards:** Carter Foundation grant, 1965; Creative Commission Award, Art Institute of Boston, 1971. Honorary doctorate: Art Institute of Boston, 1971. **Address:** 118 Nottingham Way, Windsor, California 95492, U.S.A.

Selected Exhibitions:

1931	Atlanta University, Georgia
1936	Harmon Foundation, New York
	Federal Artists Project, Mural Division
1938	Fisk University, Nashville, Tennessee
	Artists School, New York
1939	Baltimore Museum, Maryland
1940	*American Negro Exhibition,* Chicago
1941	Dillard University, New Orleans, Louisiana
1942	Atlanta University, Georgia
1944	Atlanta University, Georgia

Collection:

Harlem Hospital, New York.

Publications:

On HAYES: Articles—"Advance on the Art Front" by Alain Locke, in *Opportunity,* May 1939; "A Checklist of Afro-American Art and Artists" by Ralph L. Harley, Jr., in *The Serif,* December 1970.

*   *   *

The work of Vertis C. Hayes, painter and muralist, is distinguished by its subtle symbolism. Hayes's images narrate: his stories are about segregation, agrarian life, and black history stretching from the African village to the American city. Figures are central in his strong, energetic compositions as his consistent objective is to picture episodes of black experience.

Having studied with the Mexican muralist Jean Charlot in Chicago before traveling to New York City in the 1930s, Hayes earned early recognition for his Federal Art Project (FAP) murals. He made *Pursuit of Happiness,* an Africa-to-America chronology at Harlem Hospital, for an FAP project involving Charles Alston, Sara Murrell, Elba Lightfoot, and Georgette (Seabrooke) Powell. In *Pursuit of Happiness,* African hunters are juxtaposed with renderings of Southerners picking cotton and of the "Great Migration" to Northern factory jobs and professional opportunities. Each panel significantly depicts the moral and physical efforts of industrious blacks, and resultingly, the viewer makes positive associations about the work ethic in Old and New World societies—rural and agrarian, industrial and urban. Hayes's other mural commissions of the 1930s and 1940s were also narrative: *The Chelsea Story* (1934) for a New York City high school and *The Carver Mural* (1942) for Jackson State University.

An early painting, *Bus Stop* (1946), offers commentary on the machinations of Jim Crow laws in the South. Hayes employed the frame-within-a-frame device: a wintry, nighttime view is offered through a bus's rear window. Positioned as a back-of-the-bus passenger, the audience sees a white traveler entering the warmth of a diner through its front door, while a black patron picks up his order from an exterior, side window. The separation of two worlds, one black and the other white, is effected by the darkness of the former section of the painting and the warm coloration of the latter, particularly, the yellow glow of the diner's lights. Still, Hayes underscores the irony of their proximity as the lengthy shadows cast by these individuals threaten to cross one another.

Hayes's work consistently focuses on the ordinary and everyday. *Landscape: The Scales* (1939), *Harvesters* (1945), and *Single Track* (1946) eloquently bespeak simple farm life. In characteristic fashion, Hayes exaggerates the pictorial forms: clapboard houses, wagons, and laborers alike are animated. *Here I Come, Ready or Not* (1982) is a watercolor of a girl shielding her eyes as her unseen playmates scurry for a game of "hide-and-go-seek." With economy, Hayes communicates the innocence of the girl's youth. She wears a simple frock and ankle socks; her hair is combed into two flyaway pigtails, and the lankiness of her frame is echoed in the verticality of a centralized tree. Less literally read, the young protagonist may be a symbol of school desegregation, integration, and affirmative action. Indeed, the title's announcement proclaims determination in response to inertial resistance to change and progress.

Hayes's portraiture includes studies of the black middle class in Memphis, Tennessee, where he was the director of a Federal Art Center and the art department at LeMoyne College in the 1940s, and in Los Angeles, where he moved in 1951. His late career work includes a mural on a favored theme of African traditions, namely the *Roots*-inspired *Naming the Baby* (1974), and religious sculpture and statuary design.

—Jacqueline Francis

HAZARD, Benjamin (W.)

American painter, sculptor, and graphic artist

Born: 1940. **Education:** California College of Arts and Crafts, Oakland, California, B.F.A. 1968; University of California, Berkeley, M.A. 1969; California Community College, Sacramento, teaching credential 1986. **Career:** Curator, Oakland Museum, California, 1970-81; director, Creative Concepts Design, Incorporated, Oakland, California, 1984-91. Since 1981 director, Benjamin Hazard Associates, Oakland, California. Art instructor, Berkeley High School, 1968-69, University of Nevada, Reno, 1969-70, Stanford University, California, 1970-72, Laney College, Oakland, California, 1987-88. Since 1994 art history instructor, Laney College, Oakland, California. Served as panelist, National Science Foundation, Washington, D.C., National Endowment for the Humanities, Washington, D.C., National Endowment for the Arts, Washington, D.C. Appointed by President Jimmy Carter to the National Institute of Museum Service Board. **Awards:** Proclamation, "Benjamin W. Hazard Day," Oakland, California, 18 December 1985; commencement speaker, Holy Names College, Oakland, California, 1979. **Address:** 3528 Bowman Court, Alameda, California 94502, U.S.A.

Selected Exhibitions:

1967	Alamo Gallery, Benicia, California
	Lowell Colbus Gallery, Sausalito, California
1968	California State University, Hayward
	Cohtra Costa College, San Pablo, California
	Oakland Museum, California
	Berkeley Art Center, California
1969	Lobby Gallery, Chicago
	Carl Van Der Voort Galleries, San Francisco
	Saint Mary College, Morago, California
	Oakland Museum, California
	Worth Ryder Gallery, University of California, Berkeley
	Walnut Creek Art Center, California
	University of Nevada, Reno
	Nevada Art Gallery, Reno
	California College of Arts and Crafts, Oakland
	San Francisco Art Festival Invitational
	Palace of Fine Arts, San Francisco
1970	University of Nevada, Reno
	World's Fair, EXPO 70, Osaka, Japan
	University of California, San Diego
	Quay Gallery, San Francisco
	Oakland Museum, California
1972	Richmond Art Center, California
	Stanford University Museum, California
1989	Security Pacific Bank, Los Angeles
1992	Ebony Museum of Arts, Oakland, California
1994	Ebony Museum of Arts, Oakland, California
	Ohlone College, Fremont, California
	San Francisco State University
	Grand Oak Gallery, Oakland, California
1995	Laney College, Oakland, California
1996	Bomani Gallery, San Francisco
	Triton Museum, Santa Clara, California
	Oakland Museum, California

Collections:

Ebony Museum of Art, Oakland, California; Exploratorium, Palace of Fine Art, San Francisco; Oakland Museum, California; San Fran-

cisco Arts Commission; University of California, Berkeley; University of Nevada, Reno.

*   *   *

Benjamin Hazard is a sculptor, graphic artist, portraitist, and printer whose career began in the late 1960s. His early works, including *Medal of Honor* and *The Struggle,* reveal his concern for social issues related to the civil rights movement and U.S. involvement in the Vietnam War. Throughout his career Hazard's paintings, drawings, and installations have exhibited a characteristic emotional intensity and colorful vibrancy.

Hazard has produced a number of works in plastics. *Sweet Dreams,* from his "Modular Series II," is an acrylic work suggesting harmony between what is created and the natural environment. Composed of interconnected shapes, *Sweet Dreams* uses a high-gloss surface and burnished metallic colors to make it serve as a kaleidoscope of reflected light and adjacent forms.

In recent years Hazard has turned to charcoal as his primary medium. He credits his preference for charcoal to the ease with which he can use it to seize the emotional quality of his subjects. The bulk of his later works are life-size charcoal renderings of children. In drawings entitled *Danny and Me* and *Girl with Flower,* for example, Hazard displays the emotional range and complexity of children. He captures their innocence as it is tempered by frustration and shyness or coupled with joy.

Although he is a native of Providence, Rhode Island, Hazard has lived in Alameda County, California, for more than two decades. He has served as a curator for the Oakland Museum of Art and the Bomani Gallery in San Francisco. He also directs a design and exhibits consulting firm.

—Deirdre Cross

HENDRICKS, Barkley (L.)

American painter, assemblage artist, and photographer

Born: Philadelphia, 16 April 1945. **Education:** Pennsylvania Academy of the Fine Arts, 1963-67, certificate; Yale University School of Art, 1972, B.F.A., M.F.A. 1972. **Career:** Professor of art, Connecticut College, New London. **Awards:** Thouron Prize, Cecilia Beaux Portrait Prize, William E. Cresson Memorial Traveling Scholarship, Pennsylvania Academy of Fine Arts, 1966; J. Henry Scheidt Memorial Traveling Scholarship, Pennsylvania Academy of Fine Arts, 1967; Childe Hassam Purchase Award, American Academy of Arts and Letters, 1971 and 1977; Richard and Hinda Rosenthal Award, National Academy of Arts and Letters, 1972; First Prize, Connecticut Artist Annual, Slater Memorial Museum, 1974, 1976; Purchase Award, Connecticut Commission on the Arts, 1991. **Address:** 22 Addison Street, New London, Connecticut 06320, U.S.A.

Individual Exhibitions:

1980	Studio Museum in Harlem, New York
1982	A.C.A. Galleries, New York
1983	Walnut Street Theater, Philadelphia
1984	Brattleboro Museum and Art Center, Vermont

1985   Pennsylvania Academy of Fine Arts, Peale House Gallery, Philadelphia
1988   Housatonic Museum of Art, Bridgeport, Connecticut
1992   Cap May County Art Gallery, Cape May, New Jersey
        Manchester Community College, Connecticut
1993   Norwalk Community College, Connecticut
        Connecticut College, New London, Connecticut
        Benjamin Mangel Gallery, Philadelphia

Selected Group Exhibitions:

1988   Fine Arts Museum of Long Island, New York
1992   Central Connecticut State University, New Britain
        Philadelphia Art Alliance
1993   Hera Art Gallery, Wakefield, Rhode Island
        Benjamin Mangel Gallery, Philadelphia
        Laura Knott Gallery, Bradford College, Bradford, Massachusetts
1994   Connecticut College, New London
        Whitney Museum of American Art, New York
1995   Discovery Museum, Bridgeport, Connecticut
        Armand Hammer Museum, Los Angeles

Collections:

Afro-American Historical and Cultural Museum, Philadelphia; Butler Instate of American Art, Youngstown, Ohio; Chrysler Museum, Norfolk, Virginia; Connecticut Commission on the Arts Collection, Hartford; Cornell University, Ithaca, New York; Pennsylvania Academy of Fine Arts, Philadelphia; Philadelphia Museum of Art; National Afro-American Museum and Cultural Center, Wilberforce, Ohio; National Center of Afro-American Artists, Boston; National Gallery of Art, Washington, D.C.; Studio Museum in Harlem, New York; Ulrich Museum, Wichita State University, Kansas.

*

Barkley L. Hendricks comments:

In 1968 I was asked to make a statement concerning my art. At that time I quoted these words by Charles Mingus: "My music is as varied as my feelings are, or the world is, and one composition or one kind of composition expresses only part of the total world of my music." If you substitute music for art (painting, drawing, photography, and assemblage), you will have an honest assessment of my art—then and now. Mr. Mingus goes on to say: "Each composition builds from the previous one and the succession of compositions creates the statement I'm trying to make at that moment."

Having a variety of media in my arsenal allows me various formats to explore and address the struggles and joys of being an artist. Although no pencil, paint, film, etc., will adequately describe certain feelings and desires, the variety makes it more compelling, thus more comprehensive and encompassing.

*   *   *

Sharply dressed young urban men and women populate Barkley L. Hendricks's world on canvas. In full-length and life-size portraits, they gaze at the viewer, perhaps about to speak or, as is more likely, skeptical of what they are going to hear. Hendricks pays great attention to the clothing, shoes, jewelry, and sunglasses worn by his subjects, and he paints them with a heightened realism, usually against backgrounds of pure, shimmering color. There is no attempt to give more information by placing the figures in a room, in a park, or on a neighborhood street. The paintings are stark encounters between the subjects and the viewer, and the viewer's knowledge of the subjects is derived from the facial expressions and fashion statements that Hendricks paints. He has written, "There's a lot told in what one wears," and of his subjects, "some are from photographs, some from life, some come right out of the ol' noggin."

Although young African Americans and the raiment they wear to present or disguise themselves interest Hendricks, his main concern is with a more painterly tradition. He paints the effects of light and the relations of colors and their tones. Light, as it plays upon the range of black skin shades and as it strikes the glitter of jewelry and the colors of the clothing, is his real subject. In *North Philly Nigger* (1975), for example, a man in a pink coat is set against a gray pink background, and in *Tuff Tony* (1978) a man in white pants and with a sun visor is set against gray white. Hendricks makes these realistic figures emerge from a glow of light, their posture charged and their faces filled with vivid, if mysterious, emotion.

Although *Sweet Thang* (1974) shows the usual solitary figure, it differs from most of Hendricks's other paintings in that the young woman portrayed is set in a room with a couch, rug, and wallpaper. The woman's detailed, relaxed body and the bubble of pink gum at her mouth contrast starkly with the expanse of smooth, empty couch on which she slouches. The bubble and the roundness of her breasts and her earrings and bracelets emphasize her vitality against the inert material objects.

Mary Schmidt Campbell has written, "Because Hendricks's art matured during the mid-70s, . . . it is tempting to place him in the tradition of photo or super realism which emerged in 1970 [with such artists as] Robert Bechtle, Robert Cottingham, Richard Estes, and Chuck Close." Hendricks's paintings share with these artists a large scale, tight brush strokes, and a photograph-like appearance. But Campbell goes on to note that Hendricks's subjects have a high energy level and a feeling of drama that is missing in the work of the superrealists: "The single most obvious difference . . . is that Hendricks' men and women are most often black." In choosing to treat this urban ethnic group, Hendricks presents a community with common beliefs and values.

Hendricks's earliest works were in watercolor, but he changed to oil while at the Pennsylvania Academy of Fine Arts. While there, he absorbed traditional knowledge of artistic materials, techniques, and scholarship. Hendricks also creates collages and assemblages, many of the latter from shoes found at yard sales. These works, which sometimes include chains, "underscore a notion of slave-to-fashion that seems fresh, funny and disturbing all at once," he says. Hendricks began to photograph his work as a means of documentation and so ventured into another artistic medium. Working in a number of media, he aims to get his students to see correctly and to do work himself that will last.

—Betty Kaplan Gubert

HENRY, Janet Oliva
American assemblage artist and painter

Born: New York, 1947. **Education:** Haryou-Act Graphics and Plastics Workshop, New York; School of Visual Arts, New York,

1964-66; Art Student's League, New York; Fashion Institute of Technology, New York, 1967-69. **Career:** Co-director, Jamaica Art Mobilization, 1974-77; coordinator of artists programs, Just above Midtown Gallery, New York; program auditor, Department of Cultural Affairs, New York; field representative, New York State Council on the Arts, 1980-92. Visiting teacher, New Museum of Contemporary Art, New York, and Children's Art Carnival.

Selected Exhibitions:

Basement Workshop; Exhibitionists Gallery; Just above Midtown Gallery, New York; Snug Harbor Cultural Center; Studio Museum in Harlem, New York.

Publications:

On HENRY: Article—"... she is talking unruly curls not peppercorns..." by Susan Y. Dyer, in *Women's Art Magazine,* 67, November/December 1995, p. 28 (illustrated).

*   *   *

Janet Oliva Henry is primarily known as an assemblage artist who tells stories with her work. Henry says that the narratives of her pieces develop at the same time as the composition, often heavily influenced by the storytelling traditions of Antigua, where she grew up. In some of her early assemblages—six-inch-square boxes containing dolls and miniature accoutrements—she allowed the owner of the piece to arrange the objects. In this way Henry encouraged the sort of natural "play" or do-it-yourself storytelling that often accompanies these objects in the hands of children. In these "hands-on" compositions the objects themselves would only suggest a subject, and it was up to the viewer to actually tell the story.

Henry began to regain creative control of her work in a series in which she placed the individual objects into plastic bags that would later be hung on a wall. In *Anthropology 101* (1982) she presents characters dressed in gold lamé as participants of a West Indian carnival parade. Depending upon her exhibition space and preference, Henry could make the parade as large or as small as she liked.

The most narrative of Henry's work consists of series of photographs. Dolls are used again but are arranged in scenes and then photographed and displayed in narrative sequence. In *The Life of Assimilata Lefkowitz* Henry exhibits her fascination with middle- and upper-class African American woman. She presents the several stages of Assimilata's life through marriage and children and eventually crisis and maturity.

In her "Tree Apron" series (in which narratives were placed in clear plastic envelopes and displayed outside on trees) Henry recognized "gossip," or perhaps more accurately public storytelling, as a source of power for women in many societies. By displaying narratives outside, the stories became more available to the general public—to be observed, interpreted, and retold by whomever might pass by. In this type of public art, the story and the storyteller become more powerful with each retelling.

—Terry Bain

HICKS, Leon (Nathaniel)
American printmaker

Born: Deerfield, Florida, 25 December 1933. **Education:** Kansas State University, Manhattan, B.S; Iowa State University, Ames, M.A. and M.F.A.; Stanford University, California; La Romita School of Art, Italy; Atlanta University, Georgia. **Career:** Art instructor, Concord College, Athens, West Virginia, 1965-67; assistant professor of art, Lincoln University, Jefferson City, Missouri, 1967; assistant professor of printmaking, drawing and history, Lehigh University, Bethlehem, Pennsylvania, 1970-74. Beginning 1974 associate professor of printmaking, drawing and history, Webster University, St. Louis, Missouri. Chairman of the board and executive vice president, Hicks Etchprint, Inc., Philadelphia, Pennsylvania. **Awards:** Second Prize, Atlanta University, Georgia, 1965; First Prize, *Tuskegee Institute's Ninth Annual Beaux Arts Guild Exhibition,* 1968; commission winner, Arts and Humanities, St. Louis Edition Portfolio, 1981. **Address:** 7791 Charing Square Lane, St. Louis, Missouri 63119.

Selected Exhibitions:

Academy of Design, New York; Cincinnati Art Museum; Des Moines Annual Exhibition, Iowa; Midwest Museum of American Art, Elkhart, Indiana (1981); National Conference of Artists; Northwest Printmakers International Exhibition, Seattle; Saint Mary's College, Notre Dame, Indiana (1980); Smithsonian Institution (1980-83, traveling); Studio Museum in Harlem, New York (1980); Tuskegee Institute, Alabama.

Collections:

Oakland Museum, California.

Publications:

On HICKS: Article—Review (exhibit, St. Louis, Missouri), in *New Art Examiner,* 16, November 1988, p. 46.

*   *   *

Leon Hicks is a master of line and form. He is known primarily for his intaglio prints, which are often made up of a myriad of lines. Some areas appear soft, delicate, and carefully rendered, while others are bold and obvious. This approach gives his prints the appearance of having a great range of depth. The overall effect is complex, which gives the viewer a lot to absorb.

Printed with black ink, *Black Boy* (1961) is a profile of a boy that is, at first, disturbing to view. Hicks uses small vertical and diagonal lines for the hair, but, strangely, the density of the lines is uneven. The hair is dense toward the forehead, but the viewer notices a sparse patch at the top, giving the illusion of, perhaps, a lump. The texture on the rest of the head is fairly uniform except for an obvious bald patch at the back. Why does the boy's hair look like this? No one would get his hair cut like this on purpose. Another disturbing detail is the curved line that seems to separate the boy's face from the rest of his head. One of the heaviest lines on the print, it starts at the bridge of the boy's nose, continues up to outline his forehead, and then angles off to the right to continue down across his temple, cheek, and jaw. The line makes the boy look as if he were wearing a mask. Created during the civil rights era, *Black Boy* may represent the life of an African American male during turbulent times.

Without making obvious political statements, Hicks uses contrasting textures and tones, along with subtle implications, to convey social commentary in his images. In *New Faces* (1969), one of a series, Hicks covers the entire printing surface with monochromatic colors. *New Faces* is dark, and the viewer's eye is drawn to a nose, the lightest area. The emergent image is the frontal view of a haunting and beautiful face. When looking at *Apogee* (1962), a black and white intaglio print, the viewer first notices hands and a bird of prey resting on an arm. One hand is very light toned, while the other hand is medium toned. A black face looms in the recesses of the print. The obvious and the ambiguous structures are united by cubist forms.

Hicks's *Appalachian Sequela #6* (1967) is a more abstract work. The entire image consists of square and triangular shapes that create the appearance of several overlying picture planes depicting what seem to be pine needles, perhaps seen at different magnifications. In the center of one plane, amid a multitude of tiny branches and needles, rests an enigmatic structure. There seems to be something vaguely fetal about the image.

—Christine Miner Minderovic

HIGH, Freida

American painter and installation artist

Also wrote under the names Freida High-Wasikhongo and Freida High W. Tesfagiorgis. **Education:** Graceland College, Lamoni, Iowa, A.A. 1966; Northern Illinois University, DeKalb, B.S. 1968; University of Wisconsin, Madison, M.A. 1970; University of Wisconsin, Madison, M.F.A. 1971; University of Chicago, Ph.D. program in art history and visual culture, beginning 1994. **Family:** Married 1) Joab Njekho Meshak Wasikhongo (from Kenya, died 1979), two sons; 2) Gebre Hewit Tesfagiorgis (from Eritrea, Ethiopia) in 1985, one son and one daughter. **Career:** Assistant professor, Department of Afro-American Studies, University of Wisconsin, Madison, 1972-77; associate professor, University of Wisconsin, Madison, 1977-86. Since 1986 professor, University of Wisconsin, Madison. Chair, Department of Afro-American Studies, University of Wisconsin, Madison, 1990-93. Artist-in-residence, University of Wisconsin, Madison, 1971-72; visiting research associate, University of Ibadan, Nigeria, 1973 and 1974. Served as chair, 2nd and 3rd National Africatown Folk Festival, Prichard, Alabama, 1982 and 1983. **Awards:** CIC Scholar, Indiana University, Bloomington, 1970; Ford Foundation Fellowship, University of Wisconsin, Madison, 1971; field work fellowships, University of Wisconsin, Madison, 1973 and 1974; Knapp Bequest, 1975; Wisconsin Arts Board grant, 1977; Madison City Arts grant, 1981; Chancellor's Award in the Creative Arts, 1983-88; Vilas Award, University of Wisconsin, Madison, 1989 and 1990; William S. Noland Award, University of Wisconsin, Madison, 1991; Teaching Excellence Award, University of Wisconsin, Madison, 1992; AAUW Retraining grant, 1994; University of Chicago Special Trustee Fellowship, 1994-97; Ford Foundation grant, 1995. **Address:** Department of Afro-American Studies, Room 4141, Helen C. White Hall,

University of Wisconsin, 600 North Park Street, Madison, Wisconsin 57306, U.S.A. **Online address:** high@facstaff.wisc.edu.

Individual Exhibitions:

1973   Cartwright Center, University of Wisconsin, LaCrosse
        Afro-American Cultural Center, Purdue University, Lafayette, Indiana
        Wisconsin Academy of Arts, Letters and Science, Madison
1975   Kentucky State University Art Gallery, Frankfort
1976   Studio Museum in Harlem, New York
1986   Rosenthal Gallery, Fayetteville State University, North Carolina
        Fine Arts Museum of the South, Mobile, Alabama
1988   Grand Rapids Art Museum, Michigan

Selected Group Exhibitions:

1972   Museum of Science and Industry, Chicago
1973   *Four Black Women,* DePauw University, Greencastle, Indiana
1985   National Conference of Artists, Dakar, Senegal
1988   Diverse Works Gallery, Houston (traveling)
1990   Milwaukee Art Museum, Wisconsin
1993   Chicago South Side Community Art Center
        Madison Art Center, Wisconsin
1994   National Arts Club, New York
1995   Montgomery Art Gallery, Scripps College, Claremont, California
1996   *Bearing Witness: Contemporary Works by African American Women Artists,* Spelman College Museum of Fine Art, Atlanta (traveling)

Publications:

By HIGH: Articles—"Afrofemcentrism: The Work of Elizabeth Catlett and Faith Ringgold," in *Sage: A Scholarly Journal for Black Women,* 4(1), Spring 1987; "In Search of a Discourse and Critique/s That Center the Art of Black Women Artists," in *Theorizing Black Feminisms: The Visionary Pragmatism of Black Women* edited by Stanlie M. James and Abena P.A. Busia, Routledge Press, 1993; "Chiasmus—Art in Politics/Politics in Art: Chicano/a and African American Image, Text and Activism of the 1960s and 1970s," in *Voices of Color in the Americas* edited by Phoebe Dufrene, New York, Humanities Press, 1997.

On HIGH: Article— "Freida High W. Tesfagiorgis" by Robert Henke, in *The Art of Black American Women: Works of Twenty-Four Artists of the Twentieth Century,* Jefferson, North Carolina, McFarland and Company, 1993; "Freida High," in *Bearing Witness: Contemporary Works by African American Women Artists* by Jontyle Theresa Robinson, New York, Rizzoli International Publications, Inc., 1996.

*   *   *

Known for her exceptional feminist art historical writings and for her artworks, Freida High is a multitalented warrior woman. Her widely acclaimed "In Search of a Discourse and Critique/s That Center the Art of Black Women Artists" was a groundbreaking essay in the feminist art movement. In the essay, which was published in 1993 in *Theorizing Black Feminisms: The Visionary Pragmatism of Black Women,* edited by Stanlie M. James and Abena P. A. Busia, High sets forth her *afrofemcentrist* theory, which examines African American women artists depicting and exploring the African American woman and her realities as subjects. The afrofemcentrist construct is powerful, provocative, and timely.

High's theories, writings, and creations and fabrications are congruent. The large mixed-media work *Homage to Ida B. Wells* (1990), which is ninety-six by eighty-nine inches, is instructive. To come into the presence of this enormous bigger-than-life image and installation is to hear High proclaim, "Do you get my point?" Wells, known for her political savvy, ideas, strategies, tactics, and analyses, was also a warrior woman, but her importance is often subordinated to the masculinist tradition in civil rights activism. She will be remembered for her willingness to fight a train conductor who tried to eject her when she refused to leave the women's car and sit in the smoking car with the men. She was known for refusing to be silent and compromising in the face of injustice and oppression, as women were expected to be. In her book *When and Where I Enter,* the journalist Paula Giddings suggests that Wells's "analysis of the relationship among political terrorism, economic oppression, and conventional codes of sexuality and morality . . . has still to be surpassed in its incisive condemnation of the patriarchal manipulation of race and gender." In the High installation viewers come face-to-face with Wells so that they will never forget how important her deeds and beliefs were. A tree with a hangman's noose is on her right, reminding the viewer of the many essays, articles, and editorials Wells wrote against the lynching of African American men. High also reminds the viewer that Wells was often alone, depending on nothing save her sheer determination to effect change and reform for black people. According to Giddings, "what was and has remained unique about Wells's theorizing is its dissection of sexual ideologies and mores." High's installation complements the writings of Giddings, for both acknowledge that history asserts a male prerogative to ignore, devalue, or interpret women's experience, thus ensuring women's conformity to a male hegemonic worldview. Afrofemcentrism militates against this gender asymmetry.

Returning to the Door of No Return (1995) is an acrylic and sand work on canvas that gives a personal account of an African American woman's herstory. In this respect it is related to the Wells installation. Another similarity is the size of the painting, which is a monumental eight by five feet. As in *Homage to Ida B. Wells,* High makes the statement loom so large that it is difficult not to read clearly the meaning she wants to convey. *Returning to the Door of No Return* is a personal account of the artist's 1993 sojourn on Gorée Island, a transshipment point in the slave trade off the coast of Senegal in West Africa. High makes what happened during her visit literal and gritty through the use of sand. She brings viewers up to the door so that they are able to see through and beyond it. Millions of African men, women, and children passed through the ancient door, and the viewer's gaze through it conjures up both hopeful and hopeless memories that are related to the fate of those who passed through. Their lives and the lives of High and of all who come within the presence of the door are connected, continuous, and palpable. People of African descent looking at the door feel what their African ancestors must have felt. By creating such a work and remembering what happened to her ancestors, the artist explains, "I pay homage, seek comfort, and experience rage."

—Jontyle Theresa Robinson

HIMID, Lubaina

Tanzanian painter

Born: Zanzibar, Tanzania, 1954. **Education:** Wimbledon School of Art, London, 1973-76, B.A. in theatre design 1976; Royal College of Art, London, 1982-84, M.A. in cultural history, 1984; University of East Anglia. **Career:** Teacher, South Thames College, London, 1980; youth worker, London, 1982. Since 1990 senior lecturer in fine art, University of Central Lancashire.

Individual Exhibitions:

1986	Pentonville Gallery, London
1987	Rochdale Art Gallery
1989	Chisenhale Gallery, London
1992	Rochdale Art Gallery
1993	Black Art Gallery, London
1994	*Fifth Havana Biennale,* Cuba
1995	Peg Alston Fine Art, New York

Selected Group Exhibitions:

1983	Africa Center, London
1984	Mappin Art Gallery, Sheffield
1985	*The Thin Black Line,* Institute of Contemporary Arts, London
1986	Whitechapel Art Gallery, London
1987	Stoke-on-Trent Art Gallery (traveling)
1988	Tom Allen Center, London
1989	*The Other Story,* Hayward Gallery, London (traveling)
1993	Steinbaum Kraus Gallery, New York
1994	*Seen Unseen,* Bluecoat Gallery, Liverpool
1995	Streetlevel Gallery, Glasgow (traveling)

Collections:

Arts Council of Great Britain; Elbow Room, London; Rochdale Art Gallery; Tate Gallery, London.

*   *   *

Lubaina Himid is one of the most important and accomplished women to be identified with the emergence and development of black artists in Britain in the 1980s. Alongside her studio practice as a painter and creator of mixed-media pieces, she also has established a reputation as a curator of exhibitions of black artists.

Himid was born in Zanzibar but was taken to Britain shortly after her birth. She received a degree in theater design in 1976 from the Wimbledon School of Art. In 1979 she began to organize exhibitions. Himid started by establishing a gallery in a central London restaurant, and in 1983 she organized the first of several widely respected exhibitions of work by black women artists. The first such exhibition was *Five Black Women,* at the Africa Centre. Others followed, including *Black Woman Time Now,* at the Battersea Arts Centre, and *The Thin Black Line,* at the Institute of Contemporary Visual Arts in London. Himid has also been involved in numerous other initiatives and projects involving black artists. In 1984, for example, she was one of two curators responsible for *Into the Open,* an exhibition at the Mappin Art Gallery in Sheffield that was widely regarded as the first major exposure of the new generation of black British artists. From 1990 Himid has been on the staff of the University of Central Lancashire.

Himid is a wide-ranging artist whose work embraces many themes. It has been observed, however, that her work falls into three basic areas: satires of white society, satires of white and European cultural orthodoxies, and celebrations of the creativity and resourcefulness of black people. But Himid's work does more than simply satirize and celebrate. Through her paintings she challenges dominant and oppressive versions of history, and in so doing she continually seeks to rescue black historical figures from an ever-threatening obscurity. Typical in this regard is her 1987 work "Scenes from the Life of Toussaint L'Ouverture," a watercolor and pencil series in which she depicts scenes from the life and legend of the eighteenth-century military commander and revolutionary, known as the "Gilded African," who occupies a respected position in black history.

Himid's work also has the aim of challenging and undermining patriarchal systems and modes of thought and behavior. To this end she regularly employs humor, often producing caustic renderings of her tormentors in the form of cutout wooden figures. One such figure depicts a white man as a facile clown, with a carrot on a stick, chasing a black woman. Another piece shows a white man, with an enormous penis, masturbating. Out of his penis comes the filth of the world: warfare, destruction, pornography, and exploitation.

Perhaps some of Himid's strongest work is that which celebrates the resilience and determination of black women. Her *We Will Be* (1983) consists of a wooden cutout figure—perhaps Harriet Tubman. The lower part of the woman's dress is a visual cacophony of defiance and black pride. Central to the piece is the text "We will be who we want where we want with whom we want in the way that we want when we want and the time is now and the place is here + there."

Himid later produced series of paintings under titles such as "Revenge" (1992) and "Beach House" (1995). These acrylics on canvas are multifaceted bodies of work that have many points of reference and often distinctive starting points. "Beach House," for example, is a series in which the artist uses the beach house as a means of giving expression to reflections on history and identity.

For much of the past decade Himid has worked closely with the Glasgow-born artist Maud Sulter. Together they are responsible for *Passion: Discourses on Blackwomen's Creativity* (1990), the only British book dedicated to examining and celebrating the work of black women artists.

—Eddie Chambers

HOARD, Adrienne (W.)

American painter

Education: Northwestern University, Evanston, Illinois, 1966-68; Lincoln University, Jefferson City, Missouri, B.S. 1970; University of Michigan, Ann Arbor, M.F.A. 1972; University of Illinois, Urbana-Champaign, Ed.D. 1986. **Career:** Assistant professor, University of Arkansas, Pine Bluff, 1972-73; instructor, New York-Phoenix School of Design, New York, 1973-74; instructor, Brooklyn Museum, New York, 1973-75; assistant professor, Ohio State University, Columbus, 1975-81; art teacher, University of Illinois, Urbana-Champaign, 1982-85; visiting associate professor, North-

western University, Evanston, Illinois, 1985-86; associate professor, college coordinator, Louisiana State University, Baton Rouge, 1985-88. Since 1988 professor, University of Missouri, Columbia. Visiting professor, Hong-Ik University, Seoul, Korea, 1980-81, Ewha Women's University, Seoul, Korea, 1981; visiting artist, Korean Educational Development Institute, Seoul, Korea, 1980-81; graduate teaching associate, University of Illinois, Urbana-Champaign, 1981-82. Traveled to Georgia, South Carolina and the Sea Islands, 1978, and Italy, 1993-94, under faculty research leave grants. **Awards:** CAPS grant in painting, New York Council on the Arts, 1974-75; Outstanding Young Women in America Award, 1976; International Who's Who of Women Award, Cambridge, England, 1978; Fulbright-Hays Scholar, 1980-81; Who's Who in the Midwest Award, 1983; Kappa Delta Pi Award, 1983; Ford Foundation Postdoctoral Fellowship, Northwestern University, Illinois, 1985-86; Atlanta Arts Festival Juror Award, Georgia, 1988; Lake Mary/Heathrow Festival of the Arts Juror Award, Florida, 1988; Very Special Arts grant, 1987 and 1988. Since 1985 chairperson, executive boardmember, and scholarship chairperson, Committee on Multiethnic Concerns. Since 1985 state representative and member, International Society on Education through the Arts, Missouri Art Education Association. Served on the editorial board, *Journal of Multi-cultural and Cross-cultural Research in Art Education,* 1992-93. Board member, Heart of Missouri Girl Scout Council, 1995-98. **Address:** 815 E. Dunklin Street, Jefferson City, Missouri 65101, U.S.A. **Online Address:** ciawh@mizzou1.missouri.edu.

Individual Exhibitions:

1976	Artforce Gallery, Columbus, Ohio
1977	Studio Museum in Harlem, New York
1980	Shelton Gallery, New York
1981	American Embassy, Seoul, Korea
1991	Fontbonne College Gallery, Saint Louis, Missouri
1994	Hotel Park Palace, Florence, Italy
1996	Lincoln University, Jefferson City, Missouri

Selected Group Exhibitions:

1971	Detroit Institute of Arts
1974	Brooklyn Museum, New York
1977	Rockefeller Center, New York
1982	Schomburg Center, New York
1984	Nexus Galleries, Atlanta
1985	Cinque Gallery, New York
1987	Southern University, Baton Rouge
1988	Dillard University, New Orleans
1992	Portfolio Gallery, St. Louis, Missouri
1997	Margaret Harwell Museum, Poplar Bluff, Missouri

Collections:

Columbus Museum, Ohio; Korea National Museum of Modern Art, Seoul; Korean Educational Development Institute, Seoul, Korea; Schomburg Center, New York; University of Arkansas, Pine Bluff.

Publications:

By HOARD: Articles—"Frederick D. Bell, Black Classical Composer," in *Black Creation Magazine* (New York), 6(4), December

1974, pp. 42-43; "The Vision That Was Once a Reality: The Art of Brenda Lynn Robinson," in *Mahogany Magazine,* 2(25), 6 May 1979, p. 16; "Treatise on Creativity," in *Gifted and Talented Digest,* 15(1), January-March 1988, pp. 14-15; "The Black Aesthetic: An Empirical Feeling," in *Art, Culture and Ethnicity: An Anthology* edited by B. Young, Reston, Virginia, National Art Education, 1990, pp. 155-68.

On HOARD: Articles—"On Art in Detroit: Hoard-Taylor Exhibition" by Joy Hakanson, in *The Detroit News,* 25 June 1972, p. 4E; "Adrienne Hoard's Splashes of Paint Create a Flowing Visual Experience" by Mary Bridgman, in *The Columbus Dispatch,* May 14, 1978, p. 10K; "Adrienne W. Hoard, Artist/Teacher" by June Kelly, in *Black Art: An International Quarterly,* 2(2), Winter 1978, p. 48-53; "Hoard Exhibit at Xavier" by Anne Price, in *Sunday Advocate Magazine* (Baton Rouge, Louisiana), 19 February 1989, p. 25.

*

Adrienne Hoard comments:

The life of an artist is lived on the edge. The edge of creativity, the edge of a new color mixture, the edge of a new culture uncovered through direct experience. There is always the thrill of risk, the invitation of the *feeling* of the next unknown adventure, waiting to be accomplished, then brought from artistic subconscious into tangible form for the emotive pleasure of the artist and the viewing pleasure of an audience.

As artists we *feel* all the passions of humanity, not spared the pain or ecstasy, but the EXPRESSION of it all, in form and substance, creates the balance we desire, we need, to live in the fullness of Light and Oneness.

Abstraction allows me the freedom of total emotional expression but keeps my secrets. Only the colors, authentic and bold, give any indication of the depth of my feelings, the intensity of my Truth.

I have lived as a visitor in Asia, Africa, Europe, and throughout the Americas, and people reached out to me and allowed me to reach back with heart and film to record the moment.

Gratefully I present my images; they are the proof that I have lived. Thank you, Father Mother God.

*   *   *

Adrienne Hoard is a paradox in the discourse on contemporary American art. Already located on the fringes of mainstream art history as a woman and African American, she mocks such categorizations in her works with an unrelenting focus on abstraction in the tradition of Kandinsky and Klee. As a challenge to prejudices entrenched in contemporary perceptions of otherness, her practice provides a fine example of contrarian aesthetics.

Hoard works in multimedia, using oil painting as her technical base, while expanding her reach to include many related materials and grounds. Her works include oil on shaped canvas, oils on paper, oil pastels, watercolors, mixed-media paintings, collage, and silkscreen printing, among others. In these works organic and rhythmic forms combine with nonobjective forms or, in later works, stylized images of birds in flight to create richly textured forms and nuanced juxtapositions of analogous colors.

Her themes are inclined to cosmological and spiritual phenomena, which reflect the influence on her work of Kandinsky and early

Adrienne Hoard (with *Woman of the Ouled Nail*), 1980. Photo courtesy of Roy Lewis.

modern abstract art's preoccupation with the spiritual. Some of her paintings are also prompted by deeply felt personal issues. For example, the exhibition *Cosmic Moments* resulted from the deaths of her parents in 1991. In the paintings she produced for this exhibition, Hoard sublimates grief, subjecting the chaos of her emotions to a rigid screen of shaped canvases. Hoard's paintings are also influenced by Eastern philosophy, which she studied in Seoul as a Fulbright scholar in 1975 and later as a visiting scholar to several Korean institutions of higher learning. Her sojourn in Korea generated a concern with texture and expressionist colors, which replaced an earlier focus on carefully modulated analogous colors in her paintings.

At the beginning of her career as an artist in the 1960s, Hoard was involved in the black struggle for political and cultural emancipation, which instituted formalistic and conceptual directions for African American art and culture. Her art was at this time heavily invested in figuration. She produced several drawings and painted portraits of African Americans, including those of members of radical groups like the Black Panthers. One of her portraits, *Lady in Waiting,* won a state contest in Missouri in 1974.

Her involvement with black radicalism was soured by its attempts to institute an official aesthetics, which prescribed figuration as the only relevant form of artistic expression for the black community. Hoard, who was experimenting with abstract art as a valid form of social commentary on issues of color and race, found herself faced with the problem of politics and representation. With the descent of black art into essentialism in the highly charged period of the early 1970s, the great reconfiguration of African

American art and culture, which began with the collective ideals of Chicago's 1969 *Wall of Respect,* became mired in an Orwellian dichotomy. Hoard broke with black radicalism, withdrew further from figuration, and began to explore a contrarian aesthetics, which came to fruition with the "Tribal Bird" series (1984-85).

Hoard's travels in Korea were pivotal to her development as an individual and an artist, since they provided her with a chance to encounter notions of difference that were not tied to value judgments about superiority or inferiority. Growing up black in America, Hoard had encountered racism in the form of segregated institutions and later in the more insidious form of social and cultural invisibility. It is thus not surprising that her works explore the idea of color as values, those implied codes of difference whose effect on individuals is relative to their location on a scale that equates black skin with negative values. In her work abstraction based on color proves to be the archetypal American art form, a distinct mode of commentary on the narratives of dispossession inherent in racial discrimination and the contemporary attempt in American society to deny such discrimination by postulating an evasive neutrality for abstract art. Hoard subverts that attempt; her abstract paintings confront a reluctant audience with its untenable myths. They utilize color as a means of exploring entrenched codes of difference in American society and the resulting effects of racism on the African American psyche.

Hoard's sojourn in Asia helped her confront the paradox of life in America and enabled her to overcome some of the psychological complexes that she unwittingly inherited from growing up in a society that perceived otherness as a sign of lack. In the paintings she produced in Korea, Hoard adopted the image of birds as a symbol of freedom, a code for her own freedom from the shackles of prejudice. This new direction in Hoard's paintings brought a greater understanding of the role of color in nonfigurative expression and a broader philosophical attitude, which stressed the universal nature of humanity's quest for harmony.

Throughout her career Hoard's paintings were subjected to an outsider status, exacerbated by a demand to justify her practice within the mainstream art establishment *and* within her own African American community. In the context of reversals of the notion of a monolithic "black identity," Hoard's insistence on her abstract forms has come to be seen as the audacity of a true visionary.

—Sylvester Okwunodu Ogbechie

HOLDER, Geoffrey

Trinidadian painter and performance artist

Born: Port-of-Spain, Trinidad and Tobago, 1 August 1930. **Education:** Queens Royal College, West Indies, 1948. **Family:** Married Carmen deLavaliade in 1953. **Career:** Company member, Roscoe Holder's Dance O Trinidad, 1942; formed dance troupe and toured Puerto Rico and Caribbean, 1950-53; United States debut, 1953, Broadway debut, 1954; solo dancer, Metropolitan Opera, New York, 1956-57, *Showboat,* 1957; dancer, Kaufmann Auditorium, 1956-60; performer, Geoffrey Holder Dance Company, 1956-60. Choreographer, *Bele,* 1955; *To the Divine Horsemen,* 1956; *Dance for Two,* 1957; *Prodigal Prince,* 1957; *PaPa Clown,* 1959; *African Suite,* 1959; *Brouhaha,* 1960; *Mhil Daiim,* 1964; *I Got a Song,* 1964; *Sybarites,* 1968; *Pas de Deux,* 1968. **Awards:** Guggenheim

Fellowship in painting, 1957; United Caribbean Youth Award, 1962; Drama Desk Award, 1975; Tony Award, Best Director of a Musical, Best Costumes for *The Wiz,* 1975; Monarch Award, National Council of Culture and Art, 1982; Harold Jackman Memorial Award, 1982. **Address:** Donald Buchwald Associates, 10E 44th Street, New York, New York 10017, U.S.A.

Individual Exhibitions:

1955	Barone Gallery, New York
1956	Barone Gallery, New York
1957	Barone Gallery, New York
1958	Barone Gallery, New York
1959	Barone Gallery, New York
1960	Barone Gallery, New York
1963	Griffin Gallery, New York
1960	Barone Gallery, New York
1968	FAR Gallery
1969	Barone Gallery, New York

Selected Theater Works:

1951	*Ballet Congo*
1952	*Bal Negre*
1957	*Rosalie*
1978	*Timbuktu*

Publications:

On HOLDER: Articles—"One Man Shows: Geoffrey Holder" by James R. Mellow, in *Arts,* 30, February 1956, p. 58; "People in the Arts: Guggenheim Fellowship to Holder," in *Arts,* 30, June 1956; "Reviews and Previews: Geoffrey Holder, On Solo at Griffin Gallery" by Lawrence Campbell, in *Art News,* 62, December 1963, p. 52; "Reviews and Previews: Geoffrey Holder, on Solo at FAR Gallery" by Kim Levin, in *Art News,* 67, November 1968, p. 14; "The Wiz's Wizzes" by Maurice Peterson, in *Essence,* 6, September 1975; "The Whiz Behind 'The Wiz'" (interview) by Carlyle C. Douglas, in *Ebony,* 31, October 1975, pp. 114-16 (illustrated).

*   *   *

Although Geoffrey Holder is best known as a performing artist, he is also a visual artist. He first came to wide public notice as the dry-witted "Un-Cola Man" in Seven-Up commercials, and because of this he has a signature voice. While Holder shies away from being called a Renaissance man, his kaleidoscope of talents has allowed him artistic expression in dance, acting, writing, directing, photography, set design, sketching, and painting. He first found encouragement to pursue painting in imitating his older brother, and the general theme of his drawings and paintings is the Caribbean. His choices of subjects, scale, and colors all reflect his native Trinidad.

Everything about Holder's work suggests his native land. His subjects are blacks, portrayed with enough fluidity to suggest the Caribbean attitude of "no problem, mon." In his colored pencil work *Man in Water* (1985), for example, a man's head rises out of rippling water. The man's head is like an island, as is Trinidad. The piece offers a worrisome yet serene appearance. Holder's still lifes are exotic, featuring plants with large flowers and unusual leaves.

Scale is the most consistent element in Holder's artwork. His works are big, as is almost everything in an area where the growing season knows no end. (At six feet six inches, Holder himself is a towering man, and his physical presence has no doubt been responsible in part for his success in the performing arts.) Even though he has spent more than three decades in New York City, size remains a dominant feature of his artwork. *Man in Water*, for example, which is just a head shot, is more than a foot in either direction (eighteen by fifteen inches). *Flowers* (1986) is three feet by four feet, and *Woman in a Yellow Dress* (1981) is nearly four feet square. The woman in this last work, like those in many of his paintings, is large and voluptuous. Imitating his own body, Holder elongates figures so that they tower with gentle lyricism over colorful scenery.

As in the tropics, where the hot weather allows plants to grow far into maturity, Holder's subjects take nearly all the space available. For the Broadway show *The Wiz* (1975), a black adaptation of the classic film *The Wizard of Oz*, Holder dressed most of the female cast members in large hoopskirts. His work netted Holder a 1975 Tony award for costume design. Later, after the award of a Guggenheim Foundation fellowship, he painted a thirty-foot mural on the Trinidad Hilton Hotel.

The tropical influence is also apparent in the vibrant colors of Holder's works. The sun-drenched simplicity of his paintings offers an array of color harmonies common to his native land. This can be seen, for example, in *Flowers* and in *Woman in the Yellow Dress*, in which the clothing is almost fluorescent. Holder has achieved his lustrous palette by working through mediums to find those that allow him to control intensity. He has progressed from oil to using a combination of oil, wax, and grease-based colored pencils and sticks.

Simple, yet full of personality, Holder invests a focused isolation in his art. As he does personally, his artistic forms need their own space. This is the feeling that underlies Holder's art.

—Neale A. Shultz

HOLLINGSWORTH, Alvin (C.)

American painter

Born: New York, c.1928. **Education:** High School of Music and Art, graduated 1946; Art Students' League, New York; City College, New York, B.A. (phi beta kappa) 1956, M.A. 1959. **Career:** Teacher, High School of Art and Design, New York, 1969; professor, Hostos Community College, Bronx, New York, 1980, City University of New York. Creator, *Scorchy Smith* comic strip, 1950s. Writer and host of television series, *You're Part of Art*, 1971, *You've Gotta Have Art*, 1977, *The Creative Years of the Child*, 1980. **Awards:** Emily Lowe National Competition Prize, 1963; Whitney Fellowship, New York, 1964; Artist of the Year Award, New York, 1967; Outstanding Graduate in Art, High School of Music and Art Alumni Association, 1975; Show Man of the Year Award, NAACP, 1979; Artist of the Year, Bronx Museum of the Arts, 1981.

Selected Individual Exhibitions:

1961	Ward Eggeston Gallery
1968	Harbor Gallery, New York

1970	Studio Museum, Staten Island, New York
1971	Harbor Gallery, New York
1973	Saint John's University, Jamaica, New York
	Lee Nordess Gallery
1975	Harbor Gallery, New York
	Eyes of the City, Borough of Manhattan Community College, New York (retrospective)
1977	Afro-American Museum, Los Angeles
	Space Time Infinity, Allan Stone Gallery, New York
1980	Noa Gallery, Washington, D.C.
1981	NBC Gallery, New York
1983	*Graphic Grandeur,* Cellar Gallery, South Nyack, New York
1987	*Prevailing Women,* Northern Lights Gallery
	Aspects of Women, Noel Fine Art, Bronxville, New York
1989	Westchester College, Valhalla, New York
	Elaine Benson Gallery, Bridgehampton, New York
1991	James E. Lewis Museum of Art, Morgan State University, Maryland
1993	*A. C. Hollingsworth: Revisioning of Life,* Episcopal Social Services, New York
1995	*Paintings of JAZZ and the Feminine Mystique,* Aaron Faber Gallery, New York

Selected Group Exhibitions:

1957	City Center, New York
1959	Gallery Herve, New York
1960	Gallery Herve, New York
1962	Spiral Gallery, New York
1965	Terry Dintenfass Gallery, New York
1966	University of California, Berkeley (traveling)
1967	Koltnow Gallery, New York
	ANTA Theater
1968	Harbor Gallery, New York
1975	Afro-American Museum, Los Angeles
1976	Randall Galleries, Limited
1980	Gallery 306, Balacynwyd, Pennsylvania
	San Antonio Cultural Center, Texas
1981	Howard University, Washington, D.C.
1983	Automation House, New York

Collections:

Brooklyn Museum, New York; African Museum, Washington, D.C.

Publications:

On HOLLINGSWORTH: Articles—"Seeing the Light," in *Jet,* 19, 30 March 1961; "Why Spiral" by Jeanne Siegel, in *Art News,* 65, September 1966, p. 48; "New York Letter" by Peter Schjeldahl, in *Art International,* 13, October 1969, pp. 74-79; "Al Hollingsworth: Portrait of the Artist as a Believer" by Orde Coombs, in *Essence,* 1, February 1971, pp. 50-51, 70-71; "Artists Portray a Black Christ," in *Ebony,* 26, April 1979, pp. 176-78, 180; "An Exhibit of Two Artists: Different . . . Vital and Inspiring" by Romare Bearden, in *New York Amsterdam News,* 8 January 1983, p. 38.

*   *   *

Active as a painter, designer, lecturer, and teacher, Alvin Hollingsworth can be described as an expressionist. He is noted for his ability to use fine lines and forms with an exact symmetry to illustrate simple expressions. In his mixed-media painting *Mulligan's Mood* (16" x 20"), Hollingsworth uses simple lines to show a figurative form, as if in deep thought. His use of cool colors such as purples and blues sets the mood for the whole painting, which is soft and flowing.

In many of his works his earlier training in graphics and commercial art is apparent. *Cry City,* for example, is much more than advertisement. The human figure is surrounded by letters that have been incorporated around the figure. Hollingsworth puts a great deal of emphasis on facial and human expression.

A minimal amount of realistic qualities are embodied in Hollingsworth's forms. His "Dream" series deals with light and sensuousness. *Golden Dreamscape 11* and *Dream Frieze* both contain a suggestive flow that lends an airy feel. The focus on women is sensuous and provocative.

As a commercial artist, he studied the use of florescent materials which produce different effects under ultraviolet light. In the late 1960s he collaborated with the late Edgard Varese, pioneer of electronic music, to create a large multi-media work that would provide sensory experience for the spectators. Hollingsworth, like other black artists, also made collages with objects such as wire hangers, fish bones, teeth, clotheslines, wood, and cloth. Raised in New York, he sometimes described these collages as symbols of urban crisis.

Hollingsworth is also a translator of the black experience. He said some time ago that "if anybody is going to translate the black experience, it's got to be the black artist." The blackness in his paintings is vivid. In his famous "Visions of Visionaries" series of paintings and prints shown at Morgan State University in 1991, the religious images are all characters with black features. At this exhibition Hollingsworth illustrated the courage of African American males, their dreams and religion, and their often deep interest in jazz music and poetry. *The Leaders All,* for example, is a monument to the civil and spiritual leaders among African Americans throughout the world.

—Gabriel Tenabe

HOLLOWAY, Charnelle D.

American sculptor and jewelry designer

Education: Spelman College, Atlanta, Georgia, 1975-79, B.A. 1979 (cum laude); Georgia State University, Atlanta, 1980-83; Georgia State University, School of Art and Design, Atlanta, 1983-86, M.F.A. 1986. **Career:** Instructor of art, Spelman College, Atlanta, Georgia, 1988-90; lecturer on art, Spelman College, 1990-92. Since 1992 assistant professor of art, Spelman College. Juror, National Black Arts Festival Artists Market, 1994; Society of North American Goldsmiths Minority Fellowship Program, 1994-95, Atlanta Arts Festival, Artists Market, 1995. Participant, inaugural meeting, Organization of Black Designers Conference, Chicago, 1994. **Awards:** Felicia B. Hurd Art Award, Spelman College, 1978; Alumni Association Merit Award, Georgia State University, Atlanta, 1986; Third Prize in sculpture, *Eighth Annual National Art Competition,* Atlanta Life Insurance Company, Georgia, 1988; Medal for Distinguished Services, Spelman College, 1988; Second Prize in sculpture, *Ninth Annual National Art Competition,* Atlanta Life Insur-

ance Company, 1989; Presidential Inaugural Medal, Spelman College, 1990; Medal for Distinguished Community Service, Spelman College, 1993; Coretta Scott King Award, Martin Luther King Center for Nonviolence, 1993; Who's Who Among American Teachers Award, 1994.

Selected Exhibitions:

1986   Georgia State University, Atlanta
        Georgia State Annual Juried Student Show
1987   Spelman College, Atlanta
        McIntosh Gallery, Atlanta
1988   *Eighth Annual National Art Competition,* Atlanta Life Insurance Company
        National Black Arts Festival, Spelman College, Atlanta
        Swanston Fine Arts Gallery, Atlanta
1989   North Arts Center, Atlanta
        Nexus Contemporary Art Gallery, Atlanta
        Ninth Annual National Art Competition, Atlanta Life Insurance Company
1990   Spelman College, Atlanta
        Tenth Annual National Art Competition, Atlanta Life Insurance Company
        Trinity School, Atlanta
        National Black Arts Festival, Atlanta
1991   Spelman College, Atlanta
        New Visions Gallery, Atlanta
1992   Atlanta Life Insurance Company Invitational Exhibition
        National Black Arts Festival, Atlanta
1993   Chastain Art Gallery, Atlanta
        Afro-American Museum and Cultural Center, Wilberforce, Ohio (traveling)

*   *   *

To understand Charnelle Holloway's choice to be an artist and why she sculpts, depicts, and fabricates certain subjects, one must go back several generations in her family to the artists Henry O. Tanner and Jenelsie Walden Holloway. Charnelle Holloway is a product of a long family tradition of artists. Her mother, Jenelsie Holloway, served for almost twenty years as the chairperson of the department of art at Spelman College, an institution which was founded in 1881 to train African American women. Along with her sister artist Varnette Honeywood, Charnelle Holloway grew up in the thick of Spelman's century-old museum tradition and its fine arts collection, which included works by African and African American women. She graduated from Spelman in 1979, and her woman-centered art is part of the Spelman heritage.

Fertility Belt for the Career Woman (1995) and *Woman's Ark* are examples of the effects of Holloway's training on her creative work. Spelman College affords a unique opportunity for rethinking the place of African Americans in American art history and for reconsidering the role of historically black colleges and universities in the formation of that history. The place of African Americans in American art history has been fraught with racial oppression. Moreover, African American art, circumscribed within the racial oppression of American art, carries an oppression of its own, for both American and African American art carry the banner of patriarchy and its attendant gender asymmetry. Throughout its history, however,

Spelman has sought to decenter this masculine tradition, and Holloway's art is heiress to and a reflection of this decentering.

Fertility Belt for the Career Woman is an 8-by-3½-inch repoussé *akua-ba* (an Ashanti doll) with sterling silver and bronze *adinkra* symbols, chimes, braided silk rope, and cowrie shells. It is a personal vision of the kind of sexual gear that is required for a woman who makes the decision early in her life to focus on her career without offspring or to delay the process. Later, after childbearing has been delayed and the woman's career is in place, a fertility belt may be needed, since by then the most fertile years may have passed. By creating such a work Holloway suggests several things. She acknowledges that artists can also be women and that women artists may wish to have a family. She also suggests that decisions made early in life can have far-reaching implications. Cowrie shells are symbols of fertility, and they also ward off the evil eye. Chimes give the belt an interactive quality; they conjure up energy and are used in meditation. The chimes also are placid and serene, creating a quiescent ambiance.

Fertility Belt for the Career Woman is a testimony to Holloway's consummate skill as a metalsmith. She fabricates exquisitely rendered jewelry creations that reveal her deeply rooted knowledge of traditional African art.

—Jontyle Theresa Robinson

HONEYWOOD, Varnette (P.)

American painter

Born: Los Angeles, 1950. **Education:** University of Southern California, Los Angeles, M.S. and State Teaching Credentials, 1974; Spelman College, Atlanta, Georgia, B.A. 1974. **Career:** Intern, Teacher Corps-Urban Corrections, University of Southern California, Los Angeles, 1972-74; art instructor, Los Angeles County Special Schools, Downy, 1974; program coordinator, Education Department, Los Angeles County Museum of Art and the Joint Educational Project, 1975; director of art programs, Joint Educational Project, Los Angeles Unified School District and the University of Southern California, 1975-79. Since 1975 owner, Black Lifestyles, Los Angeles. Artist-in-residence, the Woman's Building, Los Angeles, 1981, Spelman College, Atlanta, Georgia, 1992. **Awards:** Silver Medal for Campus Graphics, Council for Advancement and Support of Education, 1986; Detroit Alumnae Association of Spelman College Achievement Award, 1986; Virginia Kiah Service Award, National Conference of Artists, Los Angeles, 1987; Founders Day Citation, Spelman College 106th Anniversary, Atlanta, Georgia, 1987; Women of Achievement Award, Crenshaw LaTijera Business and Professional Women, 1988; Silver Achievement Award, YWCA, Los Angeles; Artists' Salute to Black History Month Award, Los Angeles, 1992; Los Angeles Howard University Club Award, 1993; Alpha Kappa Alpha Sorority Award, Los Angeles, 1994; Sisters Award, Los Angeles Alumnae Association of Spelman College, 1995. **Address:** 1185 South Victoria Avenue, Los Angeles, California 90019, U.S.A.

Individual Exhibitions:

1981   Gallery Tanner, Los Angeles
           Bakersfield College, California

1982   Compton College, California
           Alabama State University Gallery, Montgomery
1984   Brockman Gallery, Los Angeles
1987   Spelman College, Atlanta, Georgia
1990   Hampton University Museum, Virginia
1992   Spelman College, Atlanta, Georgia
           Southern Bell Center
           Greensboro Cultural Center, North Carolina
1993   National Conference of Artists Gallery, Detroit
1994   Museum of African American Art, Los Angeles

Selected Group Exhibitions:

1981   *Forever Free: Art by African-American Women 1862-1980,* Center for the Visual Arts Gallery, Illinois State University, Normal (traveling)
1982   William Grant Still Community Arts Center, Los Angeles
1984   Art Gallery, Office of the Mayor, Washington, D.C.
1985   National Gallery of Art, Dakar, Senegal
1989   *Six African American Artists,* University Art Gallery, California State University, Dominguez Hills
1990   National Afro-American Museum, Wilberforce, Ohio
           William Grant Still Community Arts Center, Los Angeles
1991   Howard University Art Gallery, Washington, D.C.
1992   Santa Monica Museum of Art, California
1995   Watts Towers Arts Center, Los Angeles

Publications:

On HONEYWOOD: Books—*Black Women: Achievement against the Odds,* exhibition catalog, Washington, D.C., Smithsonian Institution Traveling Exhibition Service, 1983; *Notes on the Changing Same: Varnette's Got a Brand New Roots Bag in the Mix,* exhibition catalog, Los Angeles, Museum of African American Art and Greg Angaza Pitts, 1984. **Articles**—"Varnette's World: A Study of a Young Artist," in *Black Art: An International Quarterly,* 3(4), 1979; "Black Lifestyles: Stroked by the Brush of Varnette P. Honeywood" by Rita Williamson, in *Sepia,* September 1981, pp. 42-45; "Varnette Honeywood: A Woman to Learn From" by Guy Hubbard, in *Arts and Activities,* June 1983, pp. 29-31; "Art That Hits Home" by Stephanie Honeywood, in *Essence Magazine,* August 1983, pp. 97-100.

*   *   *

Varnette Honeywood comes from a close-knit family that has been exceedingly influential on her life and work. Honeywood's mother is from Mississippi; her father is from Louisiana. Her mother, Lovie, moved to Los Angeles in 1945 and married Stepney Honeywood in 1946. Varnette was born in 1950. Both parents were elementary school teachers, who tested the art projects to be used at school on Varnette and her sister, Stephanie. As a child Varnette loved to draw, and her first art lessons were at the Chouinard Art Institute, where she had to draw from an almost nude figure. She may have been the youngest person in the class.

Honeywood's earliest works reveal a merging of scenes from rural Mississippi and Louisiana with the orange and lemon trees that dotted the southern California landscape, which the artist saw on family car trips. The early works suggest that the artist was already interested, though in a very tentative way, in color, texture, pattern, and light, which became hallmarks of her later work.

Varnette Honeywood attended Spelman College in Atlanta, Georgia. The choice of Spelman, an institution for black women, was important because at this institution the artist met an uncommon group of artists and art educators. Originally she intended to major in history but changed to art at the prompting of her drawing instructor, Joe Ross. Nevertheless, history and art meld in the work of this talented artist. She visited Africa in 1977 on the occasion of her work being exhibited at FESTAC, and in the late 1970s she began publishing her first note cards and prints from her original acrylic paintings.

In the 1980s two important events occurred in the artist's life. She became an honorary member of Delta Sigma Theta, Inc., the national service sorority for women, and she met Bill and Camille Cosby. A reproduction of Ms. Honeywood's painting *Birthday* (1974) appeared in the living room on the set of the Cosby show across from *Senegalese Boy* by Archibald John Motley, Jr. (1891-1981). Samella Lewis suggests in *Art: African American* that Honeywood's works are reminiscent of Motley's paintings that deal with African American urban life.

In the 1990s the artist turned towards media that will give her immediate results, such as monoprinting and painting. An acrylic on canvas painting that dates from this period, *The Caregiver* (1995, 37" x 52"), details information about the family of the artist and the love and care that they need. Honeywood allows her audience to glimpse this very personal moment in the lives of the warm, close family that has roots in the deep South. The preliminary work for *The Caregiver* was generated on a computer, and Honeywood aspires for opportunities in the electronic market.

Lifelong Learning (1996, collage, 36" x 17") was created by Honeywood for the invitation and program of the Camille Olivia Hanks Cosby Academic Center dedication and celebration at Spelman College. The featured figures in this collage are philanthropist Camille Olivia Hanks Cosby, Spelman President Johnnetta Betsch Cole, a prototype of a 1996 Spelman College student, early scholar and educator Anna Julia Cooper, historic poet Phyllis Wheatley, and an African woman. Superimposed over the figures of these six is the following: "It is the wise who untie the wisdom knot. A map of lifelong learning. Celebrating the Humanities. The Talking Drum."

—Jontyle Theresa Robinson

Earl Hooks. Photo courtesy of Gil Williams Productions.

west Campus, 1954-61. **Awards:** Second Prize, John Herron Art School, 1959; First Prize, Indiana University, 1960; Third Prize, De Pauw University, 1960; Purchase Prize, South Bend Art Center; James D. Parks Award, National Conference of Artists; certificate of recognition, FESTAC 77, Lagos, Nigeria; Colonel Aide de Camp, Governor's Staff Award, State of Tennessee, 1977. **Address:** 2733 Buena Vista Pike, Nashville, Tennessee 37218, U.S.A.

HOOKS, Earl J.

American ceramist, sculptor, and photographer

Born: 2 August 1927. **Education:** Howard University, Washington, D.C., 1945-49, B.A. 1949; Catholic University, Washington, D.C., 1949-51; Rochester Institute of Technology, Rochester, New York, 1954, graduate certificate 1954; School of American Craftsman, New York, 1954-55, certificate in ceramics. **Military Service:** United States Coast Guard, 1946-47: first class seaman. **Family:** Married Juanita Hooks in 1950, two daughters and one son. **Career:** Professor of art and chair of art department, Fisk University, Nashville, 1961-67. Art instructor, District of Columbia Adult Recreational Program, Washington, D.C., 1951-53, Shaw University, Raleigh, North Carolina, 1953-54, Indiana University North-

Individual Exhibitions:

1954	Howard University Gallery of Art, Washington, D.C.
1966	Fisk University, Nashville
1981	Pickering Galleries, Nashville
1985	Carl Van Vechten Gallery of Fine Arts, Fisk University, Nashville
	South Side Community Center, Chicago

Selected Group Exhibitions:

1954	Smithsonian Institution, Washington, D.C.
1957	Smithsonian Institution, Washington, D.C.
1963	Smithsonian Institution, Washington, D.C.
1967	Art Institute of Chicago

1976   Los Angeles County Museum of Art
        Dallas Museum
        Brooklyn Museum, New York
1977   Lagos, Nigeria
1996   National Center for African-American Artists, Roxbury,
            Massachusetts
        James-Ben Studio and Gallery, Franklin, Tennessee
        Actors Theatre of Louisville, Kentucky

Collections:

Barnett-Aden Gallery, Washington, D.C.; Cheekwood Museum of
Art, Nashville; De Pauw University, Greencastle, Indiana; Fisk
University Art Galleries, Nashville; Howard University, Washing-
ton, D.C.; Illinois State University, Normal; Milliken University,
Decatur, Illinois; Rochester Institute of Technology, Rochester,
New York; Speed Museum, Louisville, Kentucky; Talladega Col-
lege, Alabama; Tennessee Art Commission, Nashville; University
of Alabama, Montibello.

Publications:

On HOOKS: Book—*Recent Works by Arthur Orr, Carl Van
Vechten, and Earl J. Hooks,* exhibition catalog, by Stephanie Pogue
and Robert Hall, Nashville, Fisk University, 1981; *Hooks at the
Pickering,* exhibition catalog, by Bronislaw M. Bak, Nashville, 1981.

*

Earl J. Hooks comments:
(1996) Remembering yesterday influences today's condition. Our
remembering of those past experiences which have survived in names,
stones, steel, wood, and film is the gathering of the icons of our
individual and collective humanity which provides the sustenance
for a more sane tomorrow. This celebration will continue until the
automatic "on-button" of human insensitivity toward one another
and Mother Earth will no longer function.

LEAVES

There Exists No Exclusion
In Life's Grand Inclusion—For
Living And Giving—Growing
And Knowing That Life Is All
Will Insure You A Ticket To A
Great Regal Ball

(Earl J. Hooks, 1981)

*   *   *

As a child Earl Hooks always knew that he would someday
become an artist. He managed to carve out a niche for himself in a
field that at the time provided few role models. With just a few
strokes of a pencil or a dash of color and with a flair for tapping into
the subliminal yet abstract, he learned to produce works that are
creative yet subdued, sometimes humorous yet at other times mo-
rose. He has shown a preference for the unusual and the daring,
executed with a sense of individuality and independence. Some of
his work has been controversial and seen as sarcastic because it

challenges nature or the accepted way of thinking. For Hooks an
artist must be capable of offending the masses.

When the Chicago-born sculptor and ceramist commenced his
extraordinary career in the early 1950s, his obstacles were plenti-
ful. Hooks began modestly as an instructor in crafts and ceramics in
a Washington, D.C., adult recreational program. He often encouraged his students to explore their innermost feelings and eccentrici-
ties when creating a work of art. He also inspired them to take risks
and to remember that in the universe one thing is related to everything else and that the past is related to the present and the future.

Hooks views unity and life as a gift. For him interrelationships
among nature and humanity are a given, and true artists must show
this vital component in every piece of their work. The wholeness of
a painting, sculpture, or ceramic work in its form, style, and texture
is the element, Hooks believes, that makes artwork truly authentic
and not specious.

In many ways Hooks's work has not changed over the years. To
at least some degree he has also tried to avoid the advances of
technology. He prefers to rely on the traditional methods of creating works that have enabled him to become a revered artist.

Hooks has exhibited widely. His unique sketchings and ceramic
pieces have been shown at the Smithsonian Institution, Howard
University, Art Institute of Chicago, Los Angeles County Museum
of Art, National Center for African-American Artists, and Actors
Theatre of Louisville, Kentucky. His work *Syracuse Biennial* was
displayed at the Everson Museum of Art in Syracuse, New York, in
1961. After more than thirty years of teaching, Hooks retired from
the faculty of the art department at Fisk University in 1996.

—Glenn Townes

HOWARD, Humbert (Lincoln)
American painter

Born: Philadelphia, 12 July 1915. **Education:** Howard University,
Washington, D.C., 1934; University of Pennsylvania, 1935; Barnes
Foundation, 1961. **Family:** Married Beatrice Wood, two sons.
Career: Instructor, Cheltonham Art Center, 1962-66, Allens Lane
Art Center, Philadelphia, 1967-71. **Awards:** Purchase Prize, Penn-
sylvania Academy of Fine Arts, 1951; Outstanding Achievement
in Art Award, American Exhibiting Artists, 1965; Woodmere Van
Scriver Memorial Prize, 1968; Silver Medal for painting, Interna-
tional Academy of Arts and Letters, Rome, 1970; honorary degree,
International Academy of Arts and Letters, Rome. **Died.**

Individual Exhibitions:

1956   Philadelphia Art Alliance
1958   Pyramid Club
1959   Howard University, Washington, D.C.
1962   Newman Gallery, Philadelphia
1968   Grabar Gallery

Selected Group Exhibitions:

1951   Pennsylvania Academy of Fine Arts, Philadelphia
1961   Pennsylvania Academy of Fine Arts, Philadelphia

1969   Pennsylvania Academy of Fine Arts, Philadelphia
         Living Philadelphia Museum of Art
         Arts Festival, Green Hill
1970   McCleaf Gallery

Collections:

Howard University, Washington, D.C.; Pennsylvania Academy of
Fine Arts, Philadelphia; Philadelphia Civic Museum; Sterne School.

*   *   *

Humbert Howard gained his first real recognition in the art world
in 1950 when he showed *The Yellow Cup* (1949-50) at the 146th
annual exhibition of the Pennsylvania Academy of the Fine Arts.
But he had been positioning himself and his art for that moment
since 1937.

Howard showed flexibility in his work as in his life. His ascension and recognition in the art world was closely tied to his position
and membership in the Pyramid Club, founded in 1937, whose
stated purpose was "to create a place of good fellowship as well as
develop better civic life" among the black elite of Philadelphia. The
annual art exhibition Howard organized for the club was always one
of its most important and memorable events. When he was appointed promotional chairman of the club's exhibition committee in
1940, Howard used the opportunity to cement important contacts
among black and white artists, while at the same time propelling his
own career in both black and white circles. By the time the club had
declined, two decades later, Howard had established himself as one
of the leading African American, if not American, artists among the
old guard of Philadelphia. Leslie King-Hammond has written that
"Howard's philosophy of integration, and the level at which he
appeared to ingratiate himself to whites, who could further his
prominence and career, permeated—and, perhaps, for some, became glaring— in—the annual art-program presentations of the late
fifties."

Howard had attended the art school of the Barnes Foundation.
Albert Barnes, who had one of the earliest and largest collections of
African art in the United States, exhibited traditional African sculpture next to works of cubism so that students could see how artists
such as Pablo Picasso had borrowed ideas on form. This experience
may have had an effect on Howard's earlier work.

In the still life *The Yellow Cup* Howard shows the clarity of light
by using the ultrawhite of a label on a wine bottle, the top fold of an
envelope, a pane in a window as well as the windowsill, and the
belly of a fish. The white shapes leap from the solid forms of the
still life. He has lifted the table at one end in a cubist style so that it
is no longer resting squarely on all four legs and so that he can
expose all of the objects making up the montage. By the mid-1950s
the solidity and the heavy impasto quality of his paintings were
replaced with a less heavy-handed application of oil paint that he
thinned to create, even in its opaqueness, a more transparent feeling.

Howard was also concerned with the depth of the field. In *Girl
with Mynah Bird* (1956) he painted the background in complementary colors of blues mixed with orange tones, evoking colors found
in the tropics. The mynah bird and the edge of a floral carpet
complement the warm tones seen through a window. The mood of
the painting is also suggested by the orange and gold stripes on the
blouse of the woman. The treatment of the figure and bird in their
environment recall the work of Ben Shahn in line quality, but the

subject and warm environment is far from Shahn's often desolate
scenes.

By the 1970s Howard's figurative style had changed once more,
with the gazes of his figures becoming more mysterious than earlier.
Even his early portraits, however, suggest that Howard was not
just after likenesses in his sitters but that he was also attempting to
penetrate their emotions and gain access to their psyches. As black
art exhibitions proliferated in the early to mid-1970s, Howard's
interpretation of Africanized subjects, as in *Janiform* (1972), showed
his sense of survival in the art world. His work of the time likely
was a response from a member of Philadelphia's old guard to the
tide of interest in African themes rather than an identification with
African or pan-African experiences.

It remains clear that Howard lived and wanted to function in a
narrowly defined world in which money and skin tone were factors
in inclusion in or exclusion from the tightly knit Pyramid Club and
the social class that supported it. This is borne out by his figurative
studies and his life.

—Lizzetta LeFalle-Collins

HOWARD, Mildred
American installation and mixed-media artist

Born: San Francisco, 26 August 1945. **Education:** College of
Alameda, California, A.A. (Fashion certificate) 1977; John F.
Kennedy University, Orinda, California , M.F.A. (Fiberworks) 1985.
Career: Coordinator, Art Programs for Children and Resource and
Referral Program, Fiberworks, Center for the Textile Arts, Berke-
ley, California, 1977-79; art instructor, Berkeley Alternative School,
California, 1978-82, Alameda County Juvenile Hall, Oakland, Cali-
fornia, 1978-82; Institute for Clinical Developmental Psychology,
Berkeley, California, 1979-81; program coordinator, Pro Arts, Oak-
land, California, 1981-84; program coordinator, Youth Develop-
ment Center, Oakland, California, 1981-87; program administrator,
California Arts Council, Sacramento, California, 1987-89; consulting professor, California College of Arts and Crafts, Oakland, California, 1991. Since 1991 consulting adjunct professor, Stanford
University, California. Since 1991 teacher/artist coordinator, School
in the Exploratorium, San Francisco. Artist-in-residence, Mount
Zion Hospital, San Francisco, 1985-86; visiting professor, Espacio
Ciencie Viva, Rio de Janeiro, Brazil, 1991.

Individual Exhibitions:

1984   Mill Valley Old Post Office, California
1985   Dade County Library, Miami
1987   California State University, Hayward
1991   Headlands Center for the Arts, Sausalito, California
         San Francisco Art Institute
         Gallery Paule Anglim, San Francisco
         INTAR, New York
1992   University Art Gallery, Sonoma State University, Rohnert
             Park, California
1993   Gallery Paule Anglim, San Francisco
1994   Hammonds House Galleries, Atlanta, Georgia
         Capp Street Project, San Francisco

San Jose Museum of Art, California
Nielsen Gallery, Boston
1996   Ohlone College, Freemont, California
Horwitch Lew Allen Gallery, Santa Fe, New Mexico
Nielsen Gallery, Boston
Porter Troupe Gallery, San Diego
1997   Gallery Paule Anglim, San Francisco

Selected Group Exhibitions:

1994   *Contemporary Collage/Assemblage,* University of Maine,
          Augusta
          California Crafts Museum, San Francisco
          Sharing the Dream, Hampton University Museum, Vir-
          ginia (traveling)
          California African American Museum, Los Angeles
1995   *A Late-Twentieth-Century Perspective/American Color,*
          Porter Troupe Gallery, San Diego
          Horwitch LewAllen Gallery, Santa Fe, New Mexico
          Nielsen Gallery, Boston
1996   Bedford Gallery, Walnut Creek, California
          Atrium Gallery, University of Connecticut, Storrs
1997   San Jose Museum of Art, California

Publications:

On HOWARD: Books—*Ten Little Children Standing in a Line
(one got shot and then there were nine): Mildred Howard,* exhibition catalog, San Francisco Art Institute, 1991; *Fragile Power:
Explorations of Memory,* exhibition catalog, Massachusetts, New-
ton Arts Center and Daniel L. Schacter, 1993. **Articles**—"Deifying
Personal Trivia" by Cathy Curtis, in *ArtWeek,* 17 October 1981, p.
6; "Threads of Line, Form and Meaning" by Cathy Curtis, in
ArtWeek, 2 February 1980; "She Made a Performance Installation"
by Phyllis Bragdon, in *Marin Independent Journal* (California), 30
August 1984; "Mildred Howard, Memory Garden Phase: II" by
Miyoshi Barosh, in *Now Time,* 2, 1992; "Remarkable Opening for
Capp Street" by David Bonetti, in *San Francisco Chronicle,* 2
February 1994.

*   *   *

With a sensitivity to an array of cultural nuances, the theme of
congregation is presented through multiple repetitive images in
Mildred Howard's work as she investigates memory and remembrance in her own life. She associates the act of congregating with
her personal family history. Encounters with the supernatural are
suggested in her bottle gardens that have been explored in installations from the late 1980s to the present; these resulted from real-
life experiences in both San Francisco and East Texas.

Howard uses materials that reference African American folk culture,
but she reinterprets them in a contemporary art language. Fragments of
memory and history, architectural elements, and found and purchased
objects are employed to create a visual language that is both personal
and communal. In the early 1980s her architectural reconstructions
began as manipulated windows from storefronts and churches; they
later evolved into constructed environments that not only recall real-
life structures but provide walk-in environments.

Howard was trained technically as a textile artist to combine
different threads and fibers, often from disparate sources. She studies cultures as she had studied fibers, weaving stories together that

speak of their simultaneous separateness and unity. The materials
themselves—metal taps, glass bottles, black painted chicken egg
shells—are all elements of her culture, a culture that she knows she
shares with others who may be worlds away.

As a young art student Howard was attracted to the work of
fellow artist and friend Betye Saar. Saar influenced the fledgling
artist's collecting sensibilities and style of arrangement. Unlike
Saar, though, Howard minimizes her chosen motifs into one or
two primary objects that are multiplied hundreds and even thousands of times in her installations. By focusing on a singular shape,
she explores all of the connotations of that shape in the context of
her personal and communal experiences, thereby requiring the viewer
to dissect the meaning of that shape and the context in which she
has placed it.

The feelings of loss caused by the displacement of people and
cultures led Howard to explore the impact of the African diaspora
on other cultures. Her later works explore issues of cultural contact
and impact, confronting the question of assimilation and the importance of community in the midst of conflicts and fear as diverse
groups search for a common ground.

In one installation, the presence of eggs give the notion of something that is not yet in the world. This congregation of eggs, with
the embryos growing within the shells, suggests a potential birth of
a people or birth of an idea confronting the issues of cultural contact, including ethnicity and religion. Individual eggs in the group
will surely develop on their own, but each egg will eventually serve
the life of the congregation.

While the simulated yokeless eggs form the core of the installation, the extant work includes projected images as in an earlier
piece, *Last Train from Caney Creek to 16th and Wood,* in which
Howard recalls leaving a small, close-knit semirural community in
East Texas for the metropolitan city of San Francisco, a journey
made by her family. Her work is engaging for its folk expressions of
African American life and ways, yet she has consistently created
conceptual works that speak to a wide audience. Howard shares her
personal experiences and interpretations of her culture with all
viewers, regardless of race or degree of artistic sophistication.

—Lizzetta LeFalle-Collins

HUDSON, Julien
American painter

Work may also appear under the names Julian Hudson, Jules Hudson,
Pickhil Hudson, or Alexandre Pickhil. **Born:** New Orleans, 9 January 1811. **Education:** Tailor's apprentice, 1926-27. Studied under
A. Abel de Pujol, Paris, 1837. **Career:** Art teacher, New Orleans,
1831; portrait painter, New Orleans, 1937-44. **Died:** 1844.

Exhibitions:

1967   Howard University, Washington, D.C.
1976   Metropolitan Museum of Art, New York

Collections:

Louisiana State University, New Orleans; Zigler Museum, Jennings,
Louisiana.

Publications:

On Hudson: Articles—"Black Artists in Antebellum New Orleans" by Patricia Brady, in *Louisiana History* (Lafayette, Louisiana), Winter 1991; "A Mixed Palette: Free Artists of Color of New Orleans" by Patricia Brady, in *International Review of African American Art* (Hampton, Virginia), Fall 1995.

*   *   *

Although Julien Hudson was a professional portraitist in New Orleans for nearly thirteen years, his extant body of work is quite small. Only four paintings, all portraits in oil and dated and signed "J. Hudson," are known to survive.

Hudson's earliest work, which is dated 1834 and which surfaced at an auction in New Orleans in 1983, is a three-quarter-length depiction of a blue-eyed young girl with light brown hair. Dressed in white and holding a full-blown pink rose, she stands daintily lifting a corner of her skirt. The background is a vividly colored, featureless landscape. The blue sky overcast with pinkish clouds is separated from the green field by a horizontal streak of pink light, suggesting sunset. The work is naive and flat, and the rather two-dimensional girl, with crudely modeled chubby hands, appears almost generic rather than a fully realized likeness. Overall, however, the painting is pleasing, suffused with cheerfulness and a springlike charm.

In 1993 a New Orleans antique dealer offered for sale a powerful half-length portrait, dated 1835, of a black man with a gray beard and dressed in a black coat, white waistcoat, soft-collar shirt, and loosely knotted black tie. The sitter also wears a red turban with a madras scarf tied around it, as well as a gold earring, attire carrying a suggestion of Africa. He sits in an upholstered chair against a background of hazy blue. One can see that Hudson's technique had improved dramatically between the 1834 and 1835 portraits. The dignity and introspection of the subject in the individualistic portrait of 1835 would have made the man instantly recognizable.

An 1838 half-length portrait of Jean Michel Fortier III, a white Creole merchant, represents the only fully documented subject among Hudson's works. It was given to the Louisiana State Museum in New Orleans in 1934 by a member of the Fortier family. In the work Hudson began to approach the smoothly finished, detailed, and realistic European high-style portraiture that he had studied in Paris with Abel de Pujol. The dapper Fortier is shown seated, wearing an elegant dark coat with fashionably stiff collar points and an elaborately tied cravat. His curly, slightly graying dark hair, long sideburns, quizzical brows, and intense dark eyes are emblematic of Creole style. The background is a rich dark brown, suggesting a gentleman's study, and Fortier sits in a chair with his left arm resting on its straight back, a roll of sheet music in his hand. Only the clumsy treatment of the hand, awkward in position and execution, betrays an artist who is not quite the master of his craft.

The fourth painting, dated 1839, is a miniature portrait of a young man and is usually referred to in twentieth-century sources as a self-portrait. There is, however, no documentary evidence to support this attribution. Purchased by the Louisiana State Museum in 1920 from a local collector, the painting was first labeled a self-portrait in the 1930s by the Works Progress Administration. Whether or not this rather formal miniature depicts Hudson, the image within the painted oval is of a thin young man with a long

nose, blue eyes, and thinning reddish brown hair and sideburns. His complexion is high-colored, with pink lips and cheeks vividly flushed with pink. He is fashionably dressed in a black frock coat, high black cravat, and white and red plaid waistcoat. The sitter looks at the world with an intent, serious gaze. The painter has returned to the pastoral, sunset background of the young girl painted five years earlier.

According to at least one secondary source, Hudson despaired of the racism in Louisiana that impeded his career and destroyed the many works he had painted. There is certainly something mysterious about the paucity of works by Hudson in New Orleans and about his death at age thirty-three, the precise details of which have not been discovered.

—Patricia Brady

HUGHES, Manuel
American painter

Born: Arkansas, 1938. **Education:** University of Missouri, Columbia, B.A., M.A. **Career:** Adjunct instructor, Pratt Institute, Brooklyn, New York, 1972-75; adjunct associate professor, Baruch College, New York, 1989-91; associate professor, Parsons School of Design, New York, 1992-94. Since 1972 adjunct professor, Pratt Institute, Brooklyn. **Awards:** CAPS grant, New York, 1977. **Agent:** O.K. Harris Works of Art, 383 West Broadway, New York, New York 10012, U.S.A.

Individual Exhibitions:

1976	Everson Museum, Syracuse, New York
	Kornblee Gallery, New York
1980	Getler Pall Gallery, New York
1981	Massachusetts College of Art, Boston
1985	Marris Brown Gallery, Boston
1987	Liz Harris Gallery, Boston
1989	Liz Harris Gallery, Boston
1992	O.K. Harris Works of Art, New York
1993	Locus Gallery, St. Louis, Missouri
1995	O.K. Harris Works of Art, New York
1996	Hubert Gallery, New York
	Locus Gallery, St. Louis, Missouri

Selected Group Exhibitions:

1971	Whitney Museum of American Art, New York
1984	High Museum of Art, Atlanta
1985	Getler-Pall-Saper Gallery, New York
1987	Kenkeleba Gallery, New York
1994	Hans and Walter Bechtler Gallery, Charlotte, North Carolina
	Nevada Institute for Contemporary Art, Las Vegas
1995	Pratt Manhattan Gallery, New York
	Rubelle and Norman Schafler Gallery, Pratt Institute, Brooklyn, New York
1996	Posco Gallery, Seoul, South Korea
	J.J. Brookings Gallery, San Francisco

Manuel Hughes: *Le Soleil,* 1996. Photo courtesy of O.K. Harris Works of Art, New York.

Collections:

M. C. Carlos Museum, Atlanta, Georgia; Delaware University Gallery, Newark; Everson Museum, Syracuse, New York; High Museum of Art, Atlanta, Georgia; New Jersey State Museum, Trenton; Newark Museum, New Jersey; Port Authority of New York and New Jersey; Saint Louis City Museum, Missouri; Whitney Museum of American Art, New York.

Publications:

On HUGHES: Book—*Recent Works by Manuel Hughes,* exhibition catalog, New York, Alternative Museum, William T. Williams and Jack Whitten, 1979. **Articles**—"Manuel Hughes," in *Arts Magazine,* February 1977; "Manuel Hughes Paints the Subtleties" by Benny Andrews, in *Encore American,* February 1977; "Fabrics Drape over Works of Hughes at Harris Brown" by Kay Boume, in *Bay State Banner* (Boston), 18 April, 1985; "Manuel Hughes" by Deborah C. Phillips, in *ArtNews,* October 1980.

*   *   *

Manuel Hughes has been propelled throughout his life to assuage his curiosity about art of diverse forms. Of his own volition, at the early age of eight, he enrolled himself in a local art center in the city of St. Louis. This marked the beginning of a lifetime commitment to the visual arts. His pursuit of formal training continued, resulting in a B.A. and M.A. in painting from the University of Missouri. Making the transition from abstraction, shortly after college, to realism was the route through which Hughes arrived at the realistic renderings of his mature work.

Exposure to the wealth of art and art objects existent in America and Europe has been paramount to his development. His travels have supplied preeminent source material for all the directives pursued in his career. Splitting his time between New York and Paris haunting flea markets, Hughes collects numerous types of antique objects. The accumulation of objects, such as vessels, toys, furniture, and tools, is an integral part of his present aesthetic. He renders these diverse entities in orderly clusters, engaging a formalist approach to painting.

Although a contemporary painter, his aesthetic has been informed by the Baroque era. Seventeenth-century still life painters from Holland and Spain, along with works by French painter Jean-Baptiste-Simeon Chardin, were of particular significance. Hughes treats his objects with a heightened sense of reverence, as did Chardin. His recent paintings of boxes and containers can on some level be compared with the work of installation artist Haim Steinbach; however, Hughes's sensibilities are at odds with those of Steinbach. His relationship to the objects conveyed in his paintings is akin to a reflective romanticism that cajoles and titillates the viewer, while Steinbach's satirical displays, full of wit and humor, coerce an acceptance as "high art" the most pedestrian displays of utilitarian items readily available on the shelf of any supermarket.

Hughes selects antiques rather than new items for his subject matter because they have been used and allegedly lost their usefulness. He resurrects worn and discolored objects through a type of realism that evokes an animated presence, infusing the presence of a renewed life force. Light, through the use of color, is a vehicle to heighten the dramatic effect of the appearance of objects that comprise his cluttered compositions. The theatrical quality of his paintings are enhanced at intervals through the use of stark black backgrounds.

Hughes's work does not fit comfortably within the confines of established categories of contemporary representation paintings. His pieces are not infused with references alluding to social themes, nor do they exist as cultural indicators of American society; conversely, he embraces concepts of spiritualism. Although removed from literal interpretations of spirituality, Hughes tries to imbue his work with a vital life force. Vacillating between ephemeral contemplations of life and death, his work is a contextualization of these states. He refers to the French translation of still life, "nature morte," which literally means "dead nature," as a point of departure for configuring a philosophical base for his creations. His interest is to capture something eternal.

—A. M. Weaver

HUMPHREY, Margo
American printmaker, sculptor, and installation artist

Born: Oakland, California 1942. **Education:** California College of Arts and Crafts, Oakland, B.F.A. 1972; Stanford University, Palo Alto, California, M.F.A. 1974. **Career:** Teacher, University of the South Pacific—Suva, Fiji, and Veti Levu; University of Benin, Nigeria; Tamarind Institute of New Mexico, 1977; island nation of Senegal; Makala University, Kampala, Uganda. **Awards:** First Prize, Berkeley Post, 1965; Purchase Prize, Golden State Insurance Company, 1968; Circle-Lets Award, 1968; Ford Foundation Fellowship, 1981; National Endowment for the Arts Fellowship, 1988; Tiffany Foundation grant, 1988.

Individual Exhibitions:

Brody's Gallery, Washington, D.C. (1992); Casa de Ena Gallery (1965); San Francisco Museum of Modern Art; University of California, Davis; University of Miami, Ohio; University of New Mexico Fine Arts Center, Albuquerque.

Selected Group Exhibitions:

1964   Oakland Flower Show, California
1968   Western Addition Library, San Francisco
        Lytton Savings and Loan Association

        New Perspectives, Oakland Museum, California
        Western Addition Art West Associated North Exhibit
1990   *Herstory,* Oakland Museum, California
1992   *Through Sisters' Eyes: Children's Books Illustrated by African-American Artists,* National Museum of Women in the Arts Library and Research Center, Washington, D.C.

Collections:

Los Angeles County Museum; National Gallery in Lagos, Nigeria; Philadelphia Museum; Rio de Janeiro, Brazil; United States Information Service, Washington, D.C.

Publications:

By HUMPHREY: Book—*The River That Gave Gifts,* 1992.

On HUMPHREY: Articles—"Kate Delos and Margo Humphrey" by Lydia Matthews, in *Artweek,* 22, 14 February 1991, pp. 16-17; review (Brody's Gallery, Washington, D.C.) by Curtia James, in *New Art Examiner,* 19, February/March 1992, pp. 34-35.

*   *   *

Margo Humphrey takes her place in a long line of distinguished African American printmakers, beginning with Grafton Tyler Brown, Robert Blackburn, James L. Wells, and Lou Stovall. In describing her own artistic identity, Humphrey says, "I think as a printmaker . . . When I have ideas, I see them as prints." She has been creating prints for more than thirty years. It is important to point out that Margo Humphrey is among the first, if not the first, African American female printmakers to achieve national as well as international acclaim. Her prints are found in major collections in the United States and abroad, and in 1974 she was the first African American female to have her prints published by the internationally renowned atelier, the Tamarind Institute in Albuquerque, New Mexico.

Humphrey's works are essentially autobiographical and deeply rooted in the imagery and folk traditions of her family, within the context of the African diaspora. She was raised in Oakland, California, and has grandparents from the deep South (New Orleans, Louisiana) and relatives from Port-au-prince, Haiti. Her autobiographical emphasis is combined with an approach to printmaking that Humphrey calls "narrative symbolism." The confluence of these various influences on her work is revealed in an interview with Clinton Adam published in *The Tamarind Papers.* Her grandmother's gift of a record player provided the stimulus for a print called *James Brown's Sounds of Escapism.* She comments:

> My work may have been more difficult to categorize because I didn't want to be blatant about my subject. I felt that if the symbolism was too pronounced, the time would come when the work would be rejected because it would only fit a certain period. The symbolism would not be profound or lasting enough. In my print of the record player, *James Brown's Sounds of Escapism,* I was talking about blacks escaping not just from the physical bonds of jail but from prejudice and all the other things that come with it. This print established for me the fact that narrative symbolism was the direction I wanted to take.

The major influences on Humphrey's prints are African American cultural traditions reflected in the spirituals and the blues, Haitian paintings, the mystical realism of Brazil, and Western artists such as Gauguin and Rousseau. Humphrey is a cultural and artistic citizen of the world. She has traveled extensively around the globe.

To understand and to appreciate Humphrey's prints is to see the interrelationships among the title, the imagery, and the use of color. Humphrey comments in the interview from *The Tamarind Papers* that "it is when all three elements are in sync that my work functions at its highest level." Art critic Robert L. Hall made a similar observation about her work in *Gathered Visions: Selected Works by African American Women Artists*: "Typically found in Margo Humphrey's color lithographs are energized elements that comment on contemporary living. The artist combines fantasy images, bold color, and memorable titles to narrate her social tales."

These three elements are exemplified in two of Humphrey's most masterfully executed and celebrated prints—*The History of Her Life Written across Her Face* and *The Last Bar-B-Que*. The inspiration for *History of Her Face* is fascinating. Humphrey recalled the image of her mother wearing hats with veils. Then she saw a photograph in *National Geographic* (October 1971) of a woman with a Sanskrit prayer tattooed on her face. Next she did a print which was a self-portrait from a picture made when she was four years old. These sources combined to yield the beautiful, multilayered, textured print. The bold use of black for the background with primary colors in the foreground and the lettering in white across the face are striking. As Humphrey would say, the title, the imagery, and the color are in sync.

My first reaction to *The Last Bar-B-Que* was laughter from pure delight, and I am smiling as I write about it now. As one continues to observe the print, one realizes the profundity of its meaning. Humphrey has liberated and transformed the symbols of watermelon, fried chicken, and barbecued ribs, which have been used to debase and devalue African Americans in this society. Her use of color is absolutely astonishing. In an interview with bell hooks, she commented, "I use color to provoke, to startle, to engage the viewer in a particular narrative process." For Humphrey color is a tool of power. Color symbolizes life, energy, empowerment, and liberation.

—Robert Steele

HUNT, Richard (Howard)

American sculptor, painter, and printmaker

Born: Chicago, Illinois, 12 September 1935. **Education:** School of the Art Institute of Chicago, 1953-57, B.A.E. **Military Service:** United States Army, 1958-60. **Career:** Sculptor; lives and works in Chicago. Instructor, School of the Art Institute of Chicago, 1960-61, University of Illinois at Chicago, 1960-62; visiting professor, Chouinard Art School, Los Angeles, 1964; visiting artist, Yale University, New Haven, Connecticut, 1964, Purdue University, Indiana, 1965; visiting professor, Northern Illinois University, De Kalb, summer 1968, Northwestern University, Evanston, Illinois, 1968-69; artist consultant, Hobart Welding School, Troy, Ohio, 1969; visiting artist, Wisconsin State University, Oshkosh, 1969, Southern Illinois University, Carbondale, 1969, and Washington University, St. Louis, Missouri, 1977-78. Artist-in-residence, Eastern

Michigan University, Ypsilanti, 1988, Harvard University 1989-90. Member, National Council on the Arts, 1968-74, Illinois Arts Council, 1970-75, Board of Directors, College Art Association, 1972-76, Board of Trustees, Museum of Contemporary Art, Chicago, 1975-79, Board of Directors, American Council for the Arts, Board of Trustees, American Academy in Rome, 1980-82. **Awards:** Logan Prize, 1956, 1961, 1962; Palmer Prize, 1957; James Nelson Raymond Travel Fellowship, 1957; Campana Prize, 1962; Guggenheim Fellowship, 1962; Tamarind Fellowship, Ford Foundation, 1965; Cassandra Foundation Fellowship, 1970; Outstanding Chicagoan in the Arts Award, Chicago Junior Chamber of Commerce, 1971. **Agent:** Terry Dintenfass Gallery, 50 West 57th Street, New York, New York 10019, U.S.A. **Address:** 1017 West Lill Avenue, Chicago, Illinois 60614, U.S.A.

Individual Exhibitions:

1958	Alan Gallery, New York
1959	Stewart Rickard Gallery, San Antonio, Texas
1960	Alan Gallery, New York
1962	Alan Gallery, New York
1963	B. C. Holland Gallery, Chicago
	Alan Gallery, New York
1964	Wesleyan College, Macon, Georgia
	University of Tulsa, Oklahoma
1965	Felix Landau Gallery, Los Angeles
	Occidental College, Los Angeles
1966	University of Notre Dame, Indiana
	B. C. Holland Gallery, Chicago
	Ohio State University, Columbus
1967	Cleveland Museum of Art
	Milwaukee Art Center (retrospective)
1968	B. C. Holland Gallery, Chicago
	Dorsky Gallery, New York
	Fisk University, Nashville, Tennessee
1969	David Strawn Art Gallery, Jacksonville, Illinois
	Dorsky Gallery, New York
	Kendall College, Evanston, Illinois
	Wisconsin State University, Oshkosh
1970	Southern Illinois University, Carbondale
	Dorsky Gallery, New York
	Living Art Center, Dayton, Ohio
	Southern Illinois University, Carbondale
	Macalester College, St. Paul, Minnesota
	B.C. Holland Gallery, Chicago
	Carleton College, Northfield, Minnesota
	St. Olaf College, Northfield, Minnesota
1971	Museum of Modern Art, New York (retrospective)
	Dorsky Gallery, New York
	Art Institute of Chicago (retrospective)
1973	Dorsky Gallery, New York
1975	Dorsky Gallery, New York
	University of Iowa, Iowa City
1976	Dorsky Gallery, New York
	Sears Bank & Trust Co., Chicago
1977	Dorsky Gallery, New York
1979	Dorsky Gallery, New York
1980	*Prints by a Sculptor: Richard Hunt*, Baltimore Museum of Art
1981	Dorsky Gallery, New York

St. Joseph Art Association, Michigan
Springfield Art Museum, Missouri
Columbia University, New York
Westbeth Art Gallery, New York
Fordham University, New York
1982   Brooklyn Artists Cultural Association, New York
1983   Terry Dintenfass Gallery, New York
1984   Terry Dintenfass Gallery, New York
1985   Martin Gallery, Washington, D.C.
1986   Terry Dintenfass Gallery, New York
1991   Gwenda Jay Gallery, Chicago
Louis Newman Gallery, Los Angeles
Shiduni Gallery, Sante Fe, New Mexico
1994   Woolot Gallery, Sheboygan, Wisconsin

Selected Group Exhibitions:

1961   Cincinnati Art Museum, Ohio
1962   *World's Fair,* Seattle
1965   Arkansas Arts Center, Little Rock
1966   *World Festival of Negro Art,* Dakar, Senegal
University of Notre Dame Art Gallery, Indiana
1967   Milwaukee Art Center, Wisconsin
1968   Fisk University, Nashville
Museum of Contemporary Art, Chicago
1970   Museum of Modern Art, New York (traveling)
1979   *100 Artists, 100 Years: Alumni of the School of the Art
Institute of Chicago,* Art Institute of Chicago

Collections:

Albright-Knox Art Gallery, Buffalo, New York; Art Institute of
Chicago; Chicago Circle Campus, University of Illinois; Cleveland
Museum of Art, Ohio; Dorsky Galleries, Limited, New York;
Guggenheim Museum, New York; Israel Museum, Jerusalem; Loui-
siana State University, Baton Rouge; Metropolitan Museum of
Art, New York; Milwaukee Art Center, Wisconsin; Museum of
Modern Art, New York; Nelson Atkins Museum, Kansas City,
Missouri; New Jersey State Museum, Trenton; Oakland Museum,
California; Ridgewood High School, Norridge, Illinois; Whitney
Museum of American Art, New York.

Publications:

On HUNT: Book—*The Sculpture of Richard Hunt* by Lieberman,
New York 1971. **Articles**—"Art: Welding New Forms" by Dore
Ashton, in *New York Times,* 30 September 1958; "Richard Hunt"
by Edith Burckhardt, in *Art News* (New York), November 1958;
"Richard Hunt, Yutaka Ohashi, and Nathan Oliveira" by Jill
Johnston, in *Art News,* April 1962; "Yutaka Ohashi, Richard Hunt,
Nathan Oliveira" by Vivian Raynor, in *Arts Magazine,* April 1962;
"Richard Hunt," in *Art News,* April 1963; "In Pursuit of Content"
by Edward B. Henning, in *Cleveland Museum of Art Bulletin,* Octo-
ber 1963; "Portrait of the Artist as a Lonely Man" by Donald M.
Schwartz, in *Chicago Sun-Times Magazine,* 14 August 1966; "Ri-
chard Hunt" by Donald Key, in *Art Scene,* November 1967; "Sculpture above the Fashions" by Hilton Kramer, in *New York Times,* 18
May 1968; "Richard Hunt" by Lawrence Campbell, in *Art News,*
Summer 1969; "Richard Hunt" by Anita Feldman, in *Arts Magazine,* Summer 1969; "He Seeks the Soul in Metal," in *Ebony,* April
1969; "Dewar's Profiles: Richard Hunt," in *Boston Globe,* 12 No-

vember 1970; "The Sculptor Who Draws in Space with Steel" by
Leonard Sykes, in *Sepia,* 28, July 1979, pp. 58-61; review (Anacostia
Museum, Washington, D.C.) by Curtia James, in *Art News,* 93,
March 1994, pp. 146-47; review (Printworks Limited, Chicago) by
Teresa Buczinsky, in *New Art Examiner,* 18, December 1990, p. 41;
review (Anacostia Museum, Washington, D.C.) by David Ebony,
in *Art in America,* 81, July 1993, p. 109; "Interview: Richard Hunt
Talks with Paul Cummings," in *Drawing,* 16, November/December
1994, pp. 78-81 (illustrated).

*   *   *

Born and raised in Chicago, the sculptor Richard Hunt studied at
the School of the Art Institute of Chicago. Revolutionary developments in the black experience of the time did not overwhelm his
aesthetic values, however, and he has always shied away from
being typecast as a black artist and has avoided giving a polemic
edge to his work. Most of his work is abstract, with allusions to
recognizable human and natural forms.

By age fifteen Hunt was modeling in clay and carving in his
bedroom at home. He later created a studio in the basement of his
father's barbershop. He was intrigued by metalworks that were
part of the African collection at Chicago's Field Museum of Natural
History, where his mother, a librarian, frequently took him. Working in a zoological lab at the University of Chicago contributed to
his fascination with animal and insect forms and helped spawn
sculpture that is menacing, elegant, organic, and sometimes extra-
terrestrial. Both his parents and others recognized his exceptional
abilities, and they created a web of support that eventually enabled
him to pursue his work as a private, independent, studio-based
artist.

At the Art Institute, Hunt was exposed to the work of the sculptors Julio González and David Smith, to whom he has attributed his
inspiration to use direct-metal techniques to transform steel, aluminum, copper, and bronze into sculpture. The welding torch became
his mallet and chisel, and his materials mostly junked auto parts.
Unlike González, who used raw materials, Hunt employed the
garbage of industrial sites. Critics have referred to his work as
sculptural calligraphy or, as González called his own work, "drawing in space."

Hunt won his first award in 1959 at an annual show for artists in
the Chicago area. One of the jurors was highly impressed with
Arachne, the work he had submitted, and urged New York's Museum of Modern Art to purchase it. After college Hunt traveled to
Europe on a fellowship. Examining Etruscan and Renaissance sculpture reinforced his feeling that metal was the medium of the twentieth century: "Metal is a dominant and omnipresent material in
twentieth-century use. We know the feel of it, we know the look of
it—so anything made of iron, steel, or aluminum has an immediacy
in this environment. Therefore in our industrial society, the use of
metal is a way of developing both an individual identity—in the
way you use it as a sculptor—and, at the same time, having a direct
link with everybody else who uses metal in the industrial culture."

Hunt has gradually moved away from his early calligraphic style
to closed contours and solid shapes. As commissions have been
bestowed upon him, the scale of his sculpture has grown. He has
produced more than fifty-five public-site sculptures, thirty-four of
them in his home state of Illinois alone. Although his success as a
large-scale public art sculptor has taken him out of the exhibition
circuit, Hunt has become interested in color lithographs, which
have a graphic interest distinct from his three-dimensional work.

In 1971 Richard Hunt became the first black American accorded a retrospective at the Museum of Modern Art. Throughout the years he has received Guggenheim, Ford, and Tamarind fellowships, awards from the Art Institute of Chicago, and Logan, Palmer, and Compana prizes. Hunt holds eight honorary degrees, and his work is represented in major museums and collections. His background includes professorships and residencies in art, and his work includes drawings and lithographs as well as sculpture. He has served on the National Council of the Arts and as a commissioner of the Smithsonian Institution's National Museum of American Art. Scholars and critics have hailed Hunt as one of the most gifted artists working in the direct-metal, open-form medium in the United States and elsewhere.

Hunt has characterized his art in this way: "One of the central themes in my work . . . is the reconciliation of the organic and the industrial. I see my work as forming a kind of bridge between what we experience in nature and what we experience in the urban, industrial technology-driven society we live in."

—Louise Davis Stone

HUNTER, Clementine

American painter

Born: Hidden Hill Plantation, Cloutierville, Louisiana, December 1886 or January 1887. **Family:** Lived with Charlie Dupree (died 1914), one son and one daughter; 2) Emanuel Hunter in 1924, five children (two deceased). **Career:** Farm laborer, c.1903-1925, Melrose Plantation. From 1925 domestic servant, Melrose Plantation. **Awards:** Grant, 1945. Honorary doctorate, Northwestern Louisiana State University. **Died:** 1 January 1988.

Individual Exhibitions:

1955   *Clementine Hunter: Primitive Painter,* Northwestern State University, Natchitoches, Louisiana
1970   Louisiana State University, Baton Rouge
        Grambling College, Louisiana
1974   Fisk University, Nashville
        Security National Bank, Alexandria, Louisiana
        Bank of New Orleans
1975   Louisiana Bank and Trust Company, Shreveport
        Barnwell Center, Shreveport, Louisiana
1976   Sister's Gallery, Memphis, Tennessee
1977   Lauren Rogers Library and Museum of Art, Hattiesburg, Mississippi
1979   Exchange Bank and Trust Company, Natchitoches, Louisiana
1980   *A Black Woman on the Move,* Barksdale Air Force Library, Barksdale Air Force Base, Louisiana
        University of Texas at Arlington
1981   Grambling College, Louisiana
        Gasperi Folk Art Gallery, New Orleans
1982   Gilley's Gallery, Baton Rouge
1984   Saint Olaf College, Northfield, Minnesota
        Louisiana State University, Shreveport
        Bossier Bank and Trust Company, Louisiana
        Louisiana Arts and Science Center, Baton Rouge

1985   Dillard University, New Orleans
        A Centennial Salute to Clementine Hunter, New Orleans Museum of Art
1987   South Arkansas Arts Center, El Dorado
        Alexandria Museum Visual Art Center, Louisiana

Selected Group Exhibitions:

1955   Delgado Museum, New Orleans
1970   La Jolla Museum of Contemporary Art, San Diego
1976   Los Angeles County Museum of Art (traveling)
1978   Cleveland Museum of Art, Cleveland, Ohio
1981   *Forever Free: An Exhibit of Art by African American Women, 1862-1980,* Illinois State University, Normal (traveling)
1983   University of Texas at Arlington
        Fennimore House Gallery, New York State Historical Association, Cooperstown, New York
1984   Anacostia Neighborhood Museum, Smithsonian Institution, Washington, D.C.
1985   deSaisset Museum, University of Santa Clara, California
1987   *Two Black Fold Artists,* Miami University Art Museum, Oxford, Ohio

Collections:

African House, Melrose Plantation, Natchitoches, Louisiana; Birmingham Museum of Art, Alabama; Capital Children's Museum, Washington, D.C.; Dallas Museum of Fine Arts; Fisk University, Nashville; High Museum, Atlanta, Georgia; Illinois State University, Normal; Louisiana Arts and Science Center, Baton Rouge; Louisiana State University, Baton Rouge, Louisiana; New Orleans Museum of Art; New York Historical Association; Northwestern State University, Natchitoches, Louisiana; Old State Capitol Gallery, Baton Rouge, Louisiana; Radcliffe College, Cambridge, Massachusetts; Rural Life Museum, Baton Rouge, Louisiana; Trafton Academy, Baton Rouge, Louisiana; University of Texas, Arlington; Vassar College, Poughkeepsie, New York.

Publications:

On HUNTER: Book—*Clementine Hunter: American Folk Artist* by James L. Wilson, Pelican Publishing, 1988. **Articles**— "Clementine Hunter—American Primitive" by Herschel Miller, in *New Orleans,* December 1968, pp. 6-11; "The Primitive Art of Clementine Hunter" by Steven Morris, in *Ebony,* May 1969, pp. 144-48; "The Fame of Clementine's Primitives" by Verdis Dowdy, in *Centre Magazine* (Louisiana), 1972; "Living with Art— Clementine Hunter: First Look for Memphis" by Gary Northrop, in *Commercial Appeal* (Memphis), 23 May 1976; "Clementine Hunter" by Mildred Hart Bailey, in *Four Women of Cane River: Their Contributions to the Cultural Life of the Area,* 1980; "Hunter's Folk Art: Rockmore's Invention" by Juliana Harris-Livingston, in *Gambit* (New Orleans), 4 April 1981; "Clementine Hunter: A Personal Story" by Bob Ryan and Yvonne Ryan, in *Louisiana Life,* September/October 1981; "Painted Memories of a Slave's Daughter" by Mildred Hart Bailey, in *Modern Maturity,* October/November 1981, pp. 42-44; "NOMA Exhibit to Honor Clementine Hunter's 100th," in *River Parishes Guide* (Boutte, Louisiana), 10 February 1985; "Clementine Hunter: A New Orleans Salute" by Bob and Yvonne Ryan, in *Arts Quarterly,* New Orleans Museum of

Art, January/February/March 1985, pp. 14-15; "Clementine Hunter: Visions from the Heart" by Mimi Read, in *Dixie Times Picayune* (New Orleans), 14 April 1985; "A Visit With Clementine Hunter: Painter of Visions and Dreams" by Eva Lamothe, in *Arts Quarterly,* New Orleans Museum of Art, April/May/June 1985, pp. 32-34; "The Centennial of Clementine Hunter" by Anne Hudson Jones, in *Women's Art Journal,* Spring/Summer 1987. **Audiocassette**—"Interview with Clementine Hunter," in *Black Women Oral History Project* (Cambridge, Massachusetts), Schlesinger Library, Radcliffe College, 1980. **Video**—"Clementine Hunter and the Cane River Country" produced by WDSU-TV, New Orleans, 10 February 1974; "Miss Clemmie" produced by KSLA-TV, Shreveport, Louisiana, 9 March 1984.

*   *   *

Clementine Hunter's first painting is thought to have been completed in 1940, when she was fifty-five years old and already a grandmother. This work, depicting a baptism at Cane River, was painted on a window shade. (Hunter used paints left from a visiting guest at the Melrose Plantation, where she worked as a domestic.) Though she started her artistic career late in life, Hunter created thousands of artworks. She also sold or gave away everything she ever painted. In her lifetime she saw her works sell for twenty-five cents to thousands of dollars. Before she started to paint, Hunter's artistic talents were expressed in many ways—she sewed clothes, made quilts, wove baskets, made hand-tied lace. She also enjoyed a reputation as a creative cook.

Hunter's desire to paint could be described as a compulsion. During the first years of her career she waited until the end of her workday, both on the plantation and in her own home, to work on her art. She would get a picture in her head and have to paint it, or "mark" it, often going without sleep until the painting was finished. At this time paints were hard for Hunter to procure, so her palette was limited; many of her early paintings were so thinned out with turpentine that they had a transparent, almost watercolorlike quality, as seen in *Madam Carencrow Sitting upon Her Nest* (c. 1944). Hunter would paint on anything she could find—canvas, wood, gourds, paper, snuff and wine bottles, iron pots, cutting boards, and plastic milk jugs.

Accepted in the art world as both folk and primitive art, Hunter's paintings and artifacts are a record of her everyday life. They reflect a slice of Southern American culture that has received little attention and, consequently, has practically disappeared. The artist's fundamental beliefs and activities are reflected in her paintings. The viewer sees everyday situations, such as picking cotton, fishing, doing the laundry, and attending funerals, weddings, and dances, along with the usual painterly subjects such as portraits, flowers, and landscapes.

Hunter's works fall into four categories: work, religion, play, and "other." Within each category there are several themes and variations. Even though she painted the same themes many times over, no two paintings are quite alike. As primitive art typically disregards perspective, Hunter's paintings pay no attention to spatial reasoning or reality. Often the most significant object in a painting is the largest. Some of Hunter's works are on the verge of being surreal—*Chicken Hauling Flowers* (1980) shows a young girl leading a giant chicken pulling a cart full of flowers. In *Trying to Keep the Baby Happy* (1944), a large adult is holding up a large baby. On the same plane is a relatively small tree and a car with a person holding either a rattle or lollipop.

Hunter usually painted people in the side view and without facial expression. Most of these people, and most of her figures representing the spiritual world, are black. Another common feature of Hunter's paintings is the use of a single, double, or sometimes even triple baseline on which her figures are anchored. In *Plantation Harvest* (1979), a painting in which several plantation chores are crammed onto one canvas, as many as ten baselines are used.

During the mid-1950s, when she was in her late sixties, Hunter painted a series of murals consisting of nine large panels and several small connecting panels. The murals depict plantation life in Cane River country and encircle one room in a building on Melrose Plantation called the African House.

In the early 1960s Hunter was introduced to the art form of montage. During a period of two years she produced hundreds of paintings, many of which reflect a montagelike composition. In *Alice in Wonderland* (1962), *Flowers* (1962), *Flower Garden* (1963), and *Abstract* (1963), the artist clearly shows an abstract approach. Hunter returned to her distinctive primitive style, but her "abstract period" seems to have influenced her subsequent works, such as *Washday* (1987) and *Uncle Tom in the Garden* (1975), which appear to be a blend of the two styles.

Hunter's use of bright colors and her childlike portrayals of common everyday activities offer the viewer a sense of contentment. While her paintings serve as a cultural and historical reminder of the past, there is no militant political message. Clementine Hunter simply painted her world as she saw and felt it.

—Christine Miner Minderovic

HYPPOLITE, Hector
Haitian painter

Born: St. Marc, Haiti, 16 September 1894. **Education:** Apprenticed to shoemaker. **Career:** Voodoo *hougan* (priest). Worked as a cobbler, housepainter, innkeeper, furniture decorator, and shipbuilder. Made and sold postcards to United States Marines. Traveled to Cuba, New York, French equatorial Africa. Member Centre d'Art, Port-au-Prince, Haiti. **Died:** 1948.

Individual Exhibition:

1947   *UNESCO Exhibition,* Paris

Publication:

On HYPPOLITE: Article—"The Discovery of Hector Hyppolite," in *Where Art Is Joy—Haitian Art: The First Forty Years* by Selden Rodman, Ruggles de Latour, New York, 1988.

*   *   *

A seminal figure in modern Haitian art, Hector Hyppolite is generally considered to be the most important of the untrained painters to emerge at midcentury. Details of his life are sparse, although it is known that he was a *houngan,* or voodoo priest. In an often cited, although probably apocryphal, account of his early

Hector Hyppolite: *Le President Florvil Hyppolite*, c. 1945-47. Photo courtesy of Davenport Museum of Art.

life, the artist is reported to have traveled to Africa as part of a five-year trip. Whether this is true or not, Ginen, or Africa, had spiritual resonance for Hyppolite as the home of ancestors and of voodoo spirits, or *lwas*. The voodoo pantheon of deities was central to Hyppolite's artistic expression.

Following his early trip, the artist was an itinerant housepainter until he began his association with Le Centre d'Art in Port-au-Prince in 1945. What followed was a brief but prolific period of creation that lasted until the artist's death in 1948. Although the quality of his output was somewhat uneven, at his best Hyppolite's bold, simplified forms, embellished with complex decorative patterns and high-keyed yet harmonious color combinations, formed works of powerful and direct spirituality. The artist worked primarily on Masonite or paperboard, beginning his paintings with a rough preliminary drawing directly on the support in order to block out the basic forms. He then painted spontaneously, working on

several different panels at any given time. He is reported to have painted between 250 and 600 paintings during this three-year period.

The subject matter of Hyppolite's mature paintings ranges from Christian themes based on chromolithographs to genre scenes, still life paintings, and more overtly recognizable voodoo imagery. Several of Hyppolite's finest works portray Ezili Freda, the voodoo *lwa* of sensual love, whose corollary in classical mythology would be Aphrodite or Venus. His painting *Maitresse Ezili* (1948) is a tour de force of abstract surface patterning, with delicately scumbled surfaces, brilliant areas of color, and graceful arabesques that weave together an intuitively cohesive composition. The goddess figure fills the central section against a contrasting white background, which in turn is surrounded by a black border that creates a field of alternating dark and light. Lyrical lines describe tree branches with pink, white, and orange leaves and with yellow, red, and blue flowers that decorate and unify the surface of the background planes. Perched on the flower branches are pink birds, suggesting the luxurious and exotic nature of Ezili. The intricate design of the linear branches, in particular the heart-shaped *veve* of Ezili, recall the *veve* of voodoo ceremonies. These ephemeral symbols, drawn on the ground with cornmeal in the *houmfor* (temple), are used to call forth particular spirits during ceremonies. Thus, in Hyppolite's seemingly secular works like the still life *Birds, Flowers and Pink Basket* (1947) the pink birds and *veve*-like branches invoke the goddess Ezili.

In a historical portrait from c.1945-47, *Le President Florvil Hyppolite,* Hyppolite represented the man who was the Haitian leader from 1889 to 1896. The format of the portrait alludes to nineteenth-century French academic portraiture, which was also practiced in Haiti. The elegant *veve*-like lines of the floral wreath and the characteristically rich blushes of color in the flowers, however, recall the artist's representation of the voodoo *lwas* and essentially deify the president. Hyppolite portrayed the difficult and brutal president with a *terribilita* that Robert Farris Thompson has attributed to a voodoo spirit.

During the final phase of his career Hyppolite's highly imaginative and spontaneous paintings attracted international attention, including that of the surrealist spokesman André Breton and the philosopher Jean-Paul Sartre. Moreover, his works were widely collected, both privately and by museums, including the Museum of Modern Art in New York City. Hyppolite's spiritually and aesthetically complex yet intuitive paintings have made him a figure of almost legendary stature in Haitian art. He has influenced virtually every subsequent generation of Haitian artists, including important contemporary artists like Édouard Duval-Carrié, as well as contemporary non-Haitian artists such as Alison Saar.

—Brady Roberts

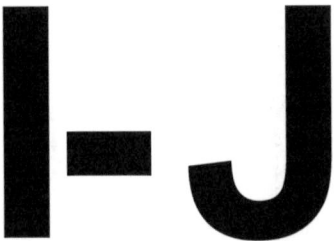

IDAH, Ovia
Nigerian sculptor

Work also might have appeared under the names Igbolovia (Igbinovia) Ida and Ovidah Ida. **Born:** Oria, Nigeria, 1908. **Education:** Learned Benin-style wood carving while serving as a page under Oba Eweka II of Benin. **Career:** Carpenter/Designer, Public Works Department, Lagos, 1923-47; teacher, King's College, Lagos; art instructor, Benin Divisional Council Secondary Modern School, Benin City, Nigeria, 1947-50; head, carving section, arts and crafts school, Benin Divisional Council until 1967. Operated Olokun Gallery, Benin City, Nigeria. Organized ebony carvers into Carvers Cooperative, Ministry of Trade and Industry, Benin City, Nigeria. **Died:** 1968.

Selected Group Exhibitions:

1938	Empire Exhibition, Glasgow, Scotland
1962	Harmon Foundation, New York
1963	Harmon Foundation, New York
1964	Harmon Foundation, New York
1969	Camden Art Centre, London

Publications:

On IDAH: Articles—"Idah: An Original Bini Artist" by Ulli Beier, in *Nigeria* (Lagos), 14, June 1938, pp. 146-48; reproductions of terracotta reliefs, in *Black Orpheus* (Ibadan, Nigeria), 17, June 1965 (plates 1-8); "Benin Artist Idah, Court Art and Personal Style" by Sara Jane Hollis Dickerson, in *Interdisciplinary Studies* (New Orleans), 2(2), March 1979, pp. 1-98 (special issue; illustrated; bibliography); "Ovia Idah and Eture Egbede: Traditional Nigerian Artists" by Philip Peek, in *African Arts* (Los Angeles), 18(2), February 1985, pp. 54-59, 102 (illustrated; some color); "The House That Idah Built" by Joseph Nevadmonsky, in *African Arts* (Los Angeles), 19(2) February 1986, p. 8; "Oba's Portraits in Benin" by Barbara Winston Blackmun, in *African Arts* (Los Angeles), 23(3), July 1990, pp. 61-69, 102-04 (illustrated; notes; bibliography).

*   *   *

Nigerian sculptor Ovia Idah began his training when he was seven years old and was taken to work for the oba (king) of Benin's court. The reigning oba, Eweka, was also a carver and passed his craft on to the young Idah. The palace environment also provided Idah with access to the vast resources of Benin's traditional artwork, knowledge of which he would later use in his own work.

While still a youth, Idah moved to Lagos. There he studied carpentry and taught wood carving at King's College; he didn't return to Benin for twenty-seven years. When he did return, Oba Akenzua, a childhood friend of Idah, recognized his talent and skill and appointed him court sculptor. Idah produced many commissioned works, including wall reliefs, door carvings, and other sculpted items, and he used the traditional materials of ivory, ebony, and bronze. But in many of his sculptures, including the building that he lived in, he also used nontraditional materials such as cement and terra-cotta, creating work that mirrored the colors and contents of the more common structures of Benin. Idah's house/sculpture was originally conceived as a huge elephant (elephants are a recurring subject in Idah's work), with the entrance hall in the shape of an elephant's head. He used found items, including crockery and movie seats, alongside his and other artists' work to decorate and construct the house. He was granted a variance on the structure (it violated city ordinance) only because of his reputation.

Idah gives credit for the inspiration of one of his most famous statues, that of Oba Ozolua, a late fifteenth-century warrior, to the subject himself. He said that Ozolua ordered him in a dream to create the statue, telling him how it should look and that it would be bestowed with a force to keep anyone from taking a good picture of it.

As director of the Benin Crafts Workshop, Idah had a profound influence on the work of numerous young carvers and other artists. Upon Idah's death in 1968, a chief in Benin is quoted as saying, "Idah's name will be remembered a thousand years in Benin." As interest in African and Nigerian art continues to grow, and as Idah's influence on contemporary artists becomes more apparent, perhaps his name, and his work, will be remembered just as long in the rest of the world.

—Terry Bain

JACKSON, Harlan
American painter

Born: Cleburne, Texas, 21 April 1918. **Education:** California School of Fine Art, 1945-48; Hans Hoffman School of Fine Art, 1950-51. **Awards:** Abraham Rosenberg Traveling Fellowship, 1948; Special Projects grant, New York State Council on the Arts, 1975. **Died.**

Individual Exhibitions:

1947	Artist Guild Gallery, San Francisco
1949	Centre D'Art, Port-au-Prince, Haiti

1950   International Exposition, Palais des Beaux Arts, Haiti
        Barnett-Aden Gallery, Washington, D.C.
1955   Panoras Gallery, New York
1964   Parrish Art Museum, Southampton, New York
1965   African Trader Gallery, New York
1969   Guild Hall, East Hampton, New York
1970   Nassau County Black Museum, Hempstead, New York
        Howard University College of Art, Washington, D.C.
1971   Southampton College, New York
1975   Acts of Art Gallery, New York
        Nassau County Black Museum, Hempstead, New York

Selected Group Exhibitions:

Cincinnati Art Museum, Ohio; California Palace of Legion of Honor;
Oakland Museum, California; Riverside Museum, New York; San
Francisco Art Institute.

Collections:

Guild Hall, East Hampton, New York; Howard University, Washington, D.C.; Southampton College, New York.

*   *   *

Between 1945 and 1975, the years of his active career, the painter
Harlan Jackson was primarily concerned with issues of modernism
and the nature of abstraction. His placement in art history locates
Jackson as one of the critical African American artists to explore
questions of abstraction by way of inquiries into the interpretation
of the figure through his studies of Western, African, and Haitian
aesthetics.

In the mid- to late 1940s Jackson's education led him to study at
the California School of Fine Art. His presence on the West Coast
was important since he was one of the few artists of African descent to be represented, in 1946, 1948, and 1954, in the annual
exhibitions sponsored by the San Francisco Art Association at the
city's art museum. This was a significant period of history, one of
great transition and change, in which the development of abstract
expressionism and the American response to modernism were primary issues of concern for African American artists in search of
their own authentic imagery and identity.

Jackson's works in oil on canvas in the late 1940s were heavily
influenced by his travel to Haiti, which resulted in works focusing
on the structural interpretation of the mask with strong cubist
influences. His work later came under the influence of the Hans
Hofmann School of Fine Art, where he studied from 1950 to 1951.
Hofmann, one of the foremost teachers of abstraction and modernism, stressed the concept of "no perspective but plastic depth."
Jackson sought to experiment on his canvases with these issues for
the remainder of his painting career.

Jackson began painting at the age of two and by the age of six
knew that he was going to become an artist. Yet by the mid-1970s
Jackson's convictions had radically changed, and, given the strong
fundamentalist religious beliefs he had adopted, he refused to paint.
Jackson died in near obscurity, having left a legacy of aesthetic
questioning and artistic risk in his innovative quest to discover his
own personal voice in the rising tide of the American modernist
tradition.

—Leslie King-Hammond

JACKSON, May Howard

American sculptor

Born: May Howard, Philadelphia, Pennsylvania, 12 May 1877.
Education: Pennsylvania Academy of Fine Arts, 1895-99. **Family:** Married Sherman William Jackson in 1902(?). **Career:** Educator. **Awards:** Scholarship, Pennsylvania Academy of Fine Arts,
1895-99; Bronze Medal, Harmon Foundation Awards in Fine Arts,
1928. **Died:** 12 July 1931.

Individual Exhibition:

1916   Veerhoff's Galleries, Washington, D.C.

Selected Group Exhibitions:

1913   National Association for the Advancement of Colored
        People, New York
1915   Corcoran Gallery of Art, Washington, D.C.
1916   National Academy of Design, New York
1919   Veerhoff's Gallery, Washington, D.C.
        Tanner Art Students Society, Washington, D.C.
        Dunbar High School, Washington, D.C.
1928   National Academy of Design, New York
1929   Harmon Foundation, New York

Collection:

Howard University, Washington, D.C..

*   *   *

May Howard Jackson is an example of the need to reexamine the
canon of African American art as well as its relationship to American art history. Typically described as a conservative, competent,
but not inspired artist, she is usually compared unfavorably to
Meta Vaux Warrick Fuller, her exact contemporary. Both were born
to middle-class families in Philadelphia in 1877, yet while Fuller
has risen in esteem, Jackson has not. The reasons reveal as much
about the criteria used to judge black artists as about the quality of
the work itself.

Jackson studied at J. Liberty-Tadd's Art School in Philadelphia,
followed by four years at the Pennsylvania Academy of Fine Arts,
where she was the first African American woman to receive a scholarship. After graduating in 1899, she did not pursue further education in Paris, as did many Americans of all ethnicities, including
Fuller. Her decision not to travel to Europe seems to have been
counted against her by many critics, who suggest that this was a
deprivation that sustained the conservatism of her style. Yet she
produced highly crafted, perceptive, reflective portraits that are no
less capable than those of other artists trained in the beaux arts
style. That such a style seemed anachronistic by the second decade
of the twentieth century should not diminish the accomplishment
of her skills in conception and technique.

In 1902 she married Sherman William Jackson, a mathematics
teacher and principal in the Washington, D.C., public schools, and
the city provided several of the black leaders, including Kelly Miller
of Howard University and the Reverend Francis J. Grimké, who
became her subjects. The Dunbar High School Alumni Association

commissioned her to create a bust of the poet Paul Laurence Dunbar. As a fair-skinned woman herself, she pursued mulatto subject matter, as in *Mulatto Mother and Her Child*. The subject was not only of pertinence to her own life, but it also paralleled a theme popular at the time in literature and the performing arts. But the unique social situation of those of mixed-race ancestry may have seemed less consequential to critics and scholars writing later in the century.

Jackson's diligent attempts to represent the African American society she knew stood in sharp contrast to the virulent stereotyping prevalent at the time. She was not unrewarded for these efforts. She exhibited at the National Emancipation Proclamation Exposition and the NAACP national convention in New York City in 1913. She received a bronze medal in fine arts from the Harmon Foundation in 1928 for the body of her work. She was also frequently mentioned in *Crisis,* the journal of the NAACP. Her works were exhibited in several mainstream galleries, including the Corcoran Gallery of Art in Washington, D.C., and the National Academy of Design in New York City. As an academic sculptor she was one of the few black artists of the period to receive notice in the largely conservative general art press. One of her designs was reproduced by the Gorham Company, a retailer of mass-market objets d'art. Yet in his eulogy of her, W. E. B. Du Bois, another of her subjects, wrote of her continual doubts and sense of isolation as an artist within both the black and the American communities.

The teaching and mentoring Jackson offered were also significant. As an established artist she was asked to judge the second round of the Harmon Foundation exhibitions in 1927. She taught sculpture occasionally at Howard University, where her students included James A. Porter, the art historian. She also provided inspiration to her nephew, the sculptor Sargent Claude Johnson, who as a child lived with her and her husband, his mother's brother, during his own family's difficulties.

—Helen M. Shannon

JACKSON, Oliver L(ee)

American painter, sculptor, and printmaker

Work also appeared under the name OLJ. **Born:** St. Louis, Missouri, 23 June 1935. **Education:** Illinois Wesleyan University, Bloomington, 1954-58, B.F.A.; University of Iowa, Iowa City, 1961-63. **Military Service:** United States Army; honorable discharge, 1961. **Career:** Professor of art, Washington University, St. Louis, Missouri, 1967-69, Oberlin College, Oberlin, Ohio, 1969-70. Since 1971 professor of art, California State University, Sacramento. **Awards:** National Endowment for the Arts Award, 1980-81; Nettie Marie Jones Fellowship in the Visual Arts, Lake Placid, New York, 1984; Yaddo residency, 1984; Art Matters Award, 1988; Fleishhacker Foundation Eureka Fellowship Award, 1993. **Agent:** Anne Kohs, 251 Post Street, Suite 425, San Francisco, California 94108, U.S.A.

Individual Exhibitions:

1964   Downstairs Gallery, St. Louis, Missouri
1967   Red Balloon Gallery, St. Louis, Missouri

Oliver Jackson: *Untitled,* 1984. Photo courtesy of M. Lee Fatherree.

1968   South County Bank, St. Louis, Missouri
1969   Contra Costa College, San Pablo, California
1970   Compton College, California
        Richmond Art Center, California
1973   Gallery of the Loretto-Hilton Center, Webster College, Webster, Missouri
1977   Crocker Art Museum, Sacramento, California
        Artspace, Sacramento, California
        Florida Technical College, Orlando
1979   Bixby Gallery, Washington University School of Fine Art, St. Louis, Missouri
1980   Allan Stone Gallery, New York
        Artists Contemporary Gallery, Sacramento, California
        Southeastern Center for Contemporary Art, Winston-Salem, North Carolina
1981   C.N. Gorman Museum, University of California, Davis
1982   Kirk deGooyer Gallery, Los Angeles, California
        Seattle Art Museum, Seattle
        Quay Gallery, San Francisco
1983   Matrix Gallery, University Art Museum, Berkeley, California
1984   Reed College Art Gallery, Portland, Oregon
        Quay Gallery, San Francisco
        Crocker Art Museum, Sacramento, California
        Arthur Roger Gallery, New Orleans
1985   Harris-Brown Gallery, Boston
        University Art Museum, University of California, Santa Barbara
        Rene Bransten Quay Gallery, San Francisco
1987   De Saisset Museum, Santa Clara University, California
        Liz Harris Gallery, Boston

Oliver Jackson: *Untitled No. 1,* 1988. Photo courtesy of M. Lee Fatherree.

1988	Gallery Nine, University of Illinois, Champaign
	Iannette-Lanzone Gallery, San Francisco
1989	Iannette-Lanzone Gallery, San Francisco
1990	St. Louis Art Museum, St. Louis, Missouri
1991	J. Noblett Gallery, Boyes Hot Springs, California
	Porter Randall Gallery, La Jolla, California
1992	Bomani Gallery, San Francisco
1993	Triton Museum of Art, Santa Clara, California
	Crocker Art Museum, Sacramento, California
	Newport Harbor Art Museum, Newport Beach, California

Selected Group Exhibitions:

1971	Oakland Museum, Oakland, California
1974	Los Angeles County Museum of Art
1975	San Francisco Museum of Modern Art (traveling)
1982	San Francisco Museum of Modern Art
1983	Whitney Museum of American Art, New York
1984	Museum of Modern Art, New York
1985	Seattle Art Museum

1989	Albright-Knox Art Gallery, Buffalo, New York (traveling)
1990	Museum of Contemporary Art, Chicago
1994	Newport Harbor Art Museum, Newport Beach, California

Collections:

Crocker Art Museum, Sacramento, California; Fine Arts Museums of San Francisco; High Museum of Art, Atlanta, Georgia; Metropolitan Museum of Art, New York; Museum of Contemporary Art, Chicago; Museum of Contemporary Art, San Diego; Museum of Fine Arts, Boston; Museum of Modern Art, New York; New Orleans Museum of Art; Newport Harbor Art Museum, Newport Beach, California; Oakland Museum, California; Phoenix Art Museum, Arizona; San Jose Museum of Art, California; San Francisco Museum of Modern Art.

Publications:

On JACKSON: Books—*Oliver Jackson: Works on Paper,* exhibition catalog, by Allan M. Gordon, Sacramento, California, Crocker Art Museum; *Oliver Jackson,* exhibition catalog, by Bruce Guenther, Newport Beach, California, Newport Harbor Art Museum; *Oliver Jackson,* exhibition catalog with interview by Thomas Albright, Seattle, Seattle Art Museum, 1982; *Oliver Jackson,* exhibition catalog, by George Rivera, Santa Clara, California, Triton Museum, 1993. **Articles**—"Oliver Lee Jackson: Forms That Feeling Takes" by Regina Hackett, in *Artforum,* Summer 1979; "St. Louis—Oliver Jackson at Bixby Gallery" by Sidra Stich, in *Art in America,* October 1979; "Jackson's Exhibit Is Cohesive, Bold" by Lee Montgomery, in *South End News,* (Boston), 31 January 1985; "Oliver Jackson" by Alfred Jan, in *FlashArt* (New York), December 1985/January 1986; "Oliver Jackson's Fierce Passion for Painting" by Robert L. Pincus, in *San Diego Union Tribune,* January 16, 1994, pp. E1, E3.

*   *   *

Form, an essential element of life and of all art, is at the heart of Oliver Jackson's work, but the most riveting thing about his art is the nervous energy created by his brushwork. Figuration is critical to his work, but the viewer must search out the "paint people," as he calls them, in their terrain, where the paint moves in an expressionistic flurry in spaces that seem to deny control. Jackson, however, is in control of his compositions, making his figures and the surfaces and spaces they occupy run together into one seamless stream of color. The figures and surfaces can also trade places, figures becoming the ground and the ground the figures. This happens, for example, in an untitled work from 1983 in which the figures appear at first to rest in their landscape of blues, greens, and beiges but, as the viewer's eyes bring them into focus, then meld into the "hills," making them a part of the environment.

Jackson's figures react and collaborate with the world around them. It seems that their collaboration is often a spontaneous act that is not restricted to a static set of rules but rather enlivened with the freedom of improvisation. His work is clearly influenced by his presence in the San Francisco Bay Area, where figuration refused to take a back seat to the pure painting of abstract expressionism. Influenced by the Willem de Kooning school of figuration, such artists felt that art need not be totally abstract to be modern or contemporary. These artists felt that they could explore the figure and nature itself under the umbrella of abstraction and abstract expressionism. Jackson has developed a sensuousness of form similar to that of de Kooning, in which sensuous shapes trigger spontaneous energy.

For many African American artists in the 1960s and 1970s the black figure became a signifier for so-called black art, and it has always occupied a politicized position in American art. But rather than limit himself to literal translations in his compositions, Jackson has identified a series of specific gestures and figurative forms that often congregate in small groups to create a sense of community and collaboration in a sacred ceremony or circle of play. The posture of many of his figures recall the self-contained stance and economy of design found in much West African wood sculpture. Jackson collects African art, and his visual investment in African figurative iconography in his paintings parallels his overall concern for the recognition of the language of form. He refers to these forms not as a reflective measure but to bring a sense of clarity about the spiritual state and to suggest a direction in which the spirit should move. He sometimes leaves the figure out, creating densely painted canvases that have the same quality, the openness and breath, of those with figures. His compositions often have an airy and linear quality, as in many of his works from the 1980s. But Jackson's way is to swing from dense to sparse, impasto paint to watercolor, familiar to unfamiliar.

The large size of Jackson's canvases requires that he paint flat so that the enamels do not run or drip. As he walks around the canvas on the floor, the visual and verbal suggestions contained within one image begin to suggest the nature and placement of an adjacent image. The images thus derive power from one another.

The dense quality of Jackson's paintings is also evident in his marble and wood sculpted figures that grow out of their block of matter. *Untitled No. 4,* for example, cannot seem to shake itself free of its marble block, or perhaps it does not want to. Again, the figurative form grows out of the landscape, the marble block, insisting that the viewer read the background and foreground, the block and the figure, that are in the stage of becoming or transcending the definition of figure.

—Lizzetta LeFalle-Collins

JACKSON, Suzanne (Fitzallen)

American painter, mixed-media artist, and scenographer

Work also appeared under the name Suzanne Jackson Odùsolú. **Born:** St. Louis, Missouri, 30 January 1944. **Education:** San Francisco State College (now University), 1962-66, B.A. 1966; Otis Art Institute, Los Angeles, 1967; School of Drama, Yale University, 1987-90, M.F.A.D. 1990. **Family:** Married 1) Pete Muriaki Mhunzi in 1970 (divorced 1972), one son; 2) Wayne Leonard in 1976 (divorced 1978); 3) Funmi Dominu Odùsolú in 1986 (divorced 1987). **Career:** Chair, Department of Fine and Performing Arts, Elliot-Pope Preparatory School, Idylwild, California, 1982-85; assistant professor, scenographer, Department of Dramatic Arts, St. Mary's College of Maryland, 1994-96. Since 1996 professor of art and design, Savannah College of Art and Design, Georgia. Instructor, Academy of Dance, Fairbanks, Alaska, 1961, Watts Towers Art Center, Los Angeles, 1967-68. **Awards:** Associate fellowships for etching, bookmaking and dance, Idylwild School of Music

and the Arts, 1982, 1983, 1984; Grand Prize, Eyes and Ears Foundation, 1979. **Address:** 121-e, West Hall Street, Savannah, Georgia 31401, U.S.A.

Individual Exhibitions:

1972	San Jose Art League, San Jose, California
	University of the Pacific, Stockton, California
	Fresno Art Center, California
	Ankrum Gallery, Los Angeles
1974	Ankrum Gallery, Los Angeles
1976	Ankrum Gallery, Los Angeles
1978	Ankrum Gallery, Los Angeles
1979	Robert's, Venice, California
1981	Savannah College of Art and Design, Georgia
1983	Multi-Cultural Art Institute, San Diego
1984	Fashion Moda, New York
	Ingber Gallery, New York
	Mitzi Landau 20th Century Art, Los Angeles
1985	Sargent Johnson Gallery, San Francisco
1986	Black Like Me Gallery, San Francisco

Selected Group Exhibitions:

1973	Santa Barbara Museum of Art, California
	New York Cultural Center
1974	Herbert F. Johnson Museum of Art, Ithaca, New York
1975	University of the Pacific, Stockton, California
	University of Illinois, Normal
1977	Studio Museum in Harlem, New York
	Hirshhorn Museum, Washington, D.C.
1981	California Museum of African-American History and Culture, Los Angeles
1985	Museum of African American Art, Los Angeles

Collections:

Ankrum Gallery, Los Angeles; Crenshaw Wall (mural), Los Angeles; Indianapolis Museum of Art, Indiana; Monroe High School, Fairbanks, Alaska; Museum of African American Art, Los Angeles; University of California at Los Angeles, African American Studies collection.

Publications:

By JACKSON: Books—*What I Love,* San Francisco, Contemporary Crafts, 1972; *Animal,* Los Angeles, Continuity Transcripts and Features, 1978.

On JACKSON: Articles—"Creating Her Own World" by Gordon Hazlitt, in *ArtNews,* November 1974; "Suzanne Jackson," in *Black Art, An International Quarterly,* 3(4); "Artists and the 'Fine Art' of Survival" by Diane Weathers, in *Black Enterprise,* 6, December 1975.

*

Suzanne Jackson comments:

My early work was an attempt to reinterpret images and symbols that implied visual impressions of thoughts, environments, or existences from other times and other places, particularly investigations of abstractions from various ancestral traditions. From 1968 development of a series of paintings based upon dreams and fantasy versus reality evolved into the next series, which was more concerned with dreams and mysticism as examined through the use of color as aura surrounding objects. Continued refining of acrylic wash techniques contributed to more articulated color, space, and kinetic relationships juxtaposing implied real and nonreal images with their auras. From 1983 to 1986 my works reflected responses or reactions to the "rhythm rituals" that exist in nature, thus evolving into the most recent *Yemenji-water spirit* series, works as drawn and painted responses to urban environments—mythical city spirits, real night and daytime "ghosts"—the polluted interaction of these peculiarities in opposition to deceptively poetic rural environments.

The spirits that speak to me at this time are those which emanate from woman's nature of space and time: reused materials, canvas hung off-stretcher, extending the picture beyond the limits of the surface, pushing paint to extreme edges of the canvas or paper, forcing energy to move across the wall resonate within and without the painted shape. My new work examines textures over textures, paint translucent, and paint opaque as sensuous-spiritual ritual movement across, up, out, and off the canvas, not forgetting, still reaching for truth.

* * *

Suzanne Jackson is best known for her paintings, but she is also a poet and an accomplished scenographer. She has created costumes, lighting, and scenic designs for the theater, as have such artists as Meta Vaux Warrick Fuller, Lois Mailou Jones, and Betye Saar, to name but a few.

Jackson was born in St. Louis, Missouri, and raised in Fairbanks, Alaska. The topographical palette of Alaska and the totems and hand-painted houses of the native Inuit have significantly influenced the content and colors of her artwork. She attributes her attraction to earth tones to her love of the land and her African and Native American ancestry. Whether realistically or abstractly rendered, the figurative form is at the center of Jackson's work. It is often accompanied by such natural elements as birds, rocks, feathers, plants, and shells, along with spiritual ideas and notions—all of which create the layers and textures shaping her paintings.

Jackson has explored several themes and approaches in her paintings. During the late 1960s—the period between abstract expressionism and pop art—Jackson's art was based on dream content. At the same time she began experimenting with space and color while painting with inks and washes on canvas. Although Jackson also worked with the possibilities that existed with white paint, she used its varying layers to delineate objects, shapes, forms, and figures on the surface of the canvas. At the metaphysical level Jackson's use of white referred to protection, which she later realized in a group of paintings of African imagery called the "Rah" series. Directly or indirectly, the viewer is left with an impression of an object or idea—a shadow—that Jackson is exploring.

Linda Goode-Bryant has commented that, by controlling and restricting the stain within delineated boundaries, Jackson confined her images to certain sections of the surface rather than to the overall working space. As a result a good deal of negative space occupies Jackson's canvases: "Color ceases to define form but acts as an element which enhances the character and emotive qualities of her imagery when contained within the structural boundaries."

When Jackson experimented with space and bold color, her brush strokes became fuller, and the energy of her forms was propelled across the surface by an abstract expressionist movement. Jackson created a number of color figures and groups of figures that she referred to as "spirit ghosts." She took her canvases off the stretchers. These paintings, with much darker colors—deep browns and ochers—were Jackson's angry paintings. Included in the series were works with surfaces primed with black gesso, upon which she placed forms and figures. In a series on fantasy versus reality, Jackson dealt with real and nonreal images. As with her use of paint, whether by creating black gesso surfaces and then painting on them to seek out the truth of an image or object or by using white and subtle shadows as a means of dealing with fantasy and reality, Jackson considered esoteric questions of truth and illusion.

Works such as *Grandparents* and *Escaped* (both 1970) were peopled by figurative and natural elements rendered in rich but soft colors. Hands, hearts, birds, and plants appeared in these and later works. By combining natural and figurative elements, Jackson alluded to humanity's relationship to and role in the natural environment. It was after this period that the artist felt that her painting style really began to change and mature.

Jackson says that she feels as if she is just beginning to paint. She continues to use color as an esoteric element—as in color-field painting—and color very much meets the painterly and contextual dilemmas Jackson conceptually explores in her paintings. Jackson's recent work—the "Yemenji" water spirit series and drawn and painted responses to urban environments—incorporates early elements. Canvases hang off the stretcher, expanding the surfaces' boundaries, color continues to be layered and textured, brush strokes are thicker and fuller, and mixed media—including recycled materials and objects—are incorporated, but the large expanses of negative space—white backgrounds—have disappeared.

—Crystal Britton

JACKSON-JARVIS, Martha

American sculptor and ceramist

Born: 1952. **Education:** Howard University, Washington, D.C., 1970-71; Temple University, Philadelphia, 1971-75, B.F.A. 1975; Antioch University, Columbia, Maryland, 1978-81, M.F.A. 1981. **Career:** Ceramics instructor, University of the District of Columbia, Washington, D.C., 1986-89, Corcoran School of Art, Washington, D.C., 1986-91, Maryland Institute College of Art, Baltimore, 1992-94. Presently sculptor, Jackson-Jarvis Studio, Washington, D.C. Artist-in-residence, Howard University, Washington, D.C., 1979-81, University of Delaware, Newark, 1988, Guilford College, Greensboro, North Carolina. Served as art designer for film production, *Daughters of the Dust,* 1989. Panelist, Pennsylvania Council on the Arts, 1986, National Endowment for the Arts, 1989, GSA National Design Award in Arts and Architecture, 1990, Southgate Public Art Project, Dayton, Ohio, 1994, Glenwynn Fall Greenway Public Art, Baltimore, Maryland, 1994. **Awards:** Crafts Artist grant, 1977-78; individual artist grant in sculpture, D.C. Commission on the Arts and Humanities, 1979, 1980 and 1986; Mayor's Art Award, Washington, D.C. Emerging Artist Award, 1982; National Endowment for the Arts grant, 1986; Penny McCall Foundation grant award in sculpture, 1988; Virginia Groot Fellowship, 1992; Arts

International Lila Wallace-Readers Digest grant, 1992; Pilchuck Glass School study grant, Seattle, 1994. **Address:** 1215 Lawrence Street, N.E., Washington, D.C. 20017, U.S.A.

Individual Exhibitions:

1977	African American Historical Museum, Philadelphia, Pennsylvania
1980	Washington Project for the Arts (WPA), Washington, D.C.
1981	Howard University Gallery of Art, Washington, D.C.
1983	Franz Bader Gallery, Washington, D.C.
1988	Museum Gallery, University of Delaware, Newark
1989	Kornblatt Gallery, Washington, D.C.
1990	SUNY College at Brockport Tower Fine Arts Gallery, New York
1991	Kornblatt Gallery, Washington, D.C.
1996	Swarthmore College, Pennsylvania
	Structuring Energy, Corcoran Gallery of Art, Washington, D.C.
	Maryland Art Place, Baltimore

Selected Group Exhibitions:

1979	Brooks Memorial Museum, Memphis
1983	Maryland Art Place, Baltimore, Maryland
1986	Chicago Museum of Science and Industry
1987	Anacostia Museum, Smithsonian Institution, Washington, D.C.
1991	National Museum of Women in the Arts, Washington, D.C.
1992	Fernbank Museum of Natural History, Atlanta, Georgia
1993	Studio Museum in Harlem, New York
1995	Snug Harbor Cultural Center, Staten Island, New York
1996	African-American Museum, Dallas
	Museum of Fine Arts, Florida State University, Tampa

Collections:

LaGuardia Community College; New York Transit Authority.

Publications:

On JACKSON-JARVIS: Books—*Contemporary Visual Expressions: The Art of Sam Gilliam, Martha Jackson-Jarvis, Keith Morrison, William T. Williams* by David C. Driskell, Smithsonian Institution Press, Washington, D.C., 1987; *Martha Jackson-Jarvis: Structuring Energy,* exhibition catalog, Washington, D.C., Corcoran Gallery, John Beardsley and Nancy Grove, 1995. **Articles**— "Sculptor's Work Reflects Early Experience" by Anita Blackburn, in *The News and Daily Advance,* 21 June 1987; "Local Artist Shines in Second Solo Show" by Eric Gibson, in *Washington Times,* 27 June 1991.

*   *   *

For more than fifteen years Martha Jackson-Jarvis, an accomplished ceramist and sculptor, has been involved in representing varied aspects of abstraction. In her work, dominated by sensibilities that could be labeled a part of the modernist tradition, there are resolute concerns with symbolism. Her work ranges from organically derived forms to installations that are axiomatic assemblages of disparate fragments, illustrative visual narratives that symbolize cogitations of ancestral and personal memories.

Because nonrepresentational modes of art making are deeply steeped within the constructs of twentieth-century modernism, the temptation to place Jackson-Jarvis solely within this context is tempting. Her work, however, embraces a timelessness that transcends Western-based precepts. She is a modern-day mythmaker, articulating through a complex language of symbols, materials, and forms the principles inherent in mythology, collective memory, and history. She creates vehicles of passage, translating indigenous African cosmological beliefs and concepts into structures and environments that are related to their retention within the African diaspora. Jackson-Jarvis reclaims her ancestry, reveals an awareness of vast forces existing in the universe, and acknowledges the complexity of nature and man's relationship to it. Her work concretizes man's need to invoke, placate, and accept the presence of forces beyond the empirical realm. She does not attempt to provide naturalistic representations of the divine but pursues giving presence to the metaphysical attributes of life and nature.

Time and the process of accumulation are a part of Jackson-Jarvis's aesthetic. Power and the supplication of spirits are implied through her dense assemblages of diverse materials and symbols, such as Kissi votive figures of the Kongo. Jackson-Jarvis's approach is mimetic of African visual traditions, in which abstraction, accumulation, obscurity, omission, and containment serve significant functions. The tendency to create through aggregate processes serves as notations of experiences from Jackson-Jarvis's past. Her abstract vocabulary alludes to the preponderance of mysteries existing within the temporal and spiritual realms, creating symbolic links between conscious and unconscious states. This system precludes linear intellectual thought processes attributed to reason and logic and evokes a holistic matrix that engages mind, body, and spirit.

Jackson-Jarvis began creating subterranean-like terra-cotta forms in the early 1980s. Her later investigations with clay as a sculptural medium resulted in mosaic-styled installations that incorporated ceramic elements, tiles, and shards of wooden tablets. Moving from environmental installations in the 1990s back to constructing singular power objects, Jackson-Jarvis introduced the process of terrasae to her repertoire of mosaic and construction techniques. Her newer works contain multimedia elements that range from wall-dependent sculptural containers to bas-relief paintings. Within these works her densely manipulated surfaces allude to states in which elements contained within a vortex appear to implode. Also significant to this period is a series of sarcophagi and table structures. The "Sarcophagi" series, which are related to environmental issues, address in vibrant visceral form the need for reverence toward natural forces and elements. Constantly evolving, this series has shifted into horizontally stacked layers of materials, shapes, and objects, marking a transition into the series "Tables of Plenty." Central to these works are symbols and elements, previously amorphous and primordial, that emerge as recognizable life-forms and vegetal matter.

Jackson-Jarvis's vast vocabulary converges into a comprehensive system that reflects her many-sided investigations in sculpture, ceramics, painting, and assemblage. As an artist she exists in an irony of her own making. Although marginally influenced by outsider art and architecture, she constructs a clear path through a postmodern landscape laden with ambiguity. She has manufactured a complete narrative visual scheme that allows for conversant tools in which to translate autobiographical and universal data. Working through the confines of a Western-based aesthetics, Jackson-Jarvis has produced work that reflects lessons from antiquity that are still revered within many indigenous cultures throughout the world and that need to be resuscitated. As sound, music, and language are synthesized into the composition of a song, Jackson-Jarvis's distinct voice resonates as polyphonic, ululating cadences.

—A. M. Weaver

JARRELL, Wadsworth A.

American painter

Born: Albany, Georgia, 1931. **Education:** Studied at Art Institute of Chicago. **Family:** Married Elaine Johnson. **Career:** Formerly professor, Howard University, Washington, D.C., and University of Georgia.

Selected Exhibitions:

1970   Howard University, Washington, D.C.
       National Center of Afro-American Artists, Washington, D.C.
       Studio Museum in Harlem
1972   Howard University, Washington, D.C.
       National Center of Afro-American Artists, Washington, D.C.

Publications:

On JARRELL: Book—*Wadsworth Jarrell: The Artist as Revolutionary* by Robert L. Douglas, San Francisco, Pomegranate, 1996. **Articles**—"Where Down Home Meets Back Home," in *Boston after Dark,* September 1970.

*   *   *

Wadsworth Jarrell was born in Georgia to creative, independent parents of modest means. He indicates that art was all he ever wanted to do, something he realized as a young boy. His father was an outstanding furniture craftsman who had his own shop. This independent spirit would serve Jarrell well in his career, for, as one of the founders of Africobra in 1967 and a participant in painting the famed *Wall of Respect* in Chicago, he was one of the artists in the forefront of the black arts movement in the 1960s and 1970s. Jarrell's interest in art persisted through stints as a photographer and graphic artist and through a long career as a professor at Howard University and then at the University of Georgia, in the same town where he had grown up. After retiring from teaching, Jarrell and his wife worked independently in Atlanta before moving to New York in 1993.

After a stint in the military, Jarrell settled in Chicago, where he studied at the art institute and developed the technical prowess and theories that he later applied to his socially conscious work. Jarrell's early work explored formal questions and drew upon his interest in social settings, musical performances, and horse racing. Among those who influenced him early in his career were the Chicago artists Archibald Motley, for his social scenes, and Eldzier Cortor, for his elongated figures. He also admired the work of Paul Cézanne.

After his marriage to Elaine "Jae" Johnson, who also was a member of Africobra for a time in its early years, Jarrell was inspired by the brilliant colors he discovered on their Caribbean honeymoon, and he began to incorporate intense colors in his paintings. His involvement with OBAC (Organization of Black American Culture) in the 1960s allowed a close collaboration with Jeff Donaldson, another cofounder of Africobra, and the development of the aesthetic at the center of Africobra's efforts. Bright, so-called Kool-Aid, colors became one of the first tenets of the approach they developed.

In the late 1960s and early 1970s Jarrell began to paint vibrant works filled with bursts of color, many of which included words and messages tied to his social consciousness. Well-known personalities like Martin Luther King, Jr., Malcolm X, and Angela Davis were often the subjects of his paintings. The letter *B*, signifying the theme "Black Is Beautiful," became a component of his imagery. During the 1970s, however, after he attended Festac in Nigeria, Jarrell's style evolved toward the use of complex patterns that were a simulacrum of those found on African textiles and carvings. He elongated human figures in the style of Senufo sculpture (and of Cortor), and his imagery returned to the subjects most comfortable for him: urban street scenes, musical performances by jazz and blues musicians, and horse racing. His works on horse racing celebrated particularly the many black jockeys of the nineteenth century, many of whom were Kentucky Derby riders and winners.

In the 1980s Jarrell involved his children in his work, incorporating their imagery by peopling his scenes with playful figures with large heads. He experimented with patterns, often creating them by repeating the shapes of everyday objects like leaves and aluminum can tabs on the canvas. Jarrell also began creating sculptural forms that employed some of the same patterns and colors found in his paintings, although the sculptures often drew their shapes from African objects. At other times he formed completely new and surprising configurations.

Through the years Jarrell has remained committed to socially conscious, color-filled, vibrant art based in African and African American culture and history. While he has kept his philosophical and political center, his style has evolved greatly during his long and productive career.

—Michael D. Harris

JENNINGS, Wilmer (Angier)

American painter and printmaker

Born: Atlanta, Georgia, 13 November 1910. **Education:** Morehouse College, Atlanta, Georgia, B.S. 1933; Rhode Island School of Design, Providence. **Family:** Married Mary C. Howard, one son and two daughters. Daughter Corrine Jennings is director, Kenkeleba Gallery, New York. **Career:** Worked for Imperial Pearl, 1948-79. **Awards:** Second Atlanta University Purchase Award for Graphics, 1946. **Agent:** Corrine Jennings, Kenkeleba Gallery, New York, New York 10009, U.S.A. **Died:** 25 June 1990.

Selected Group Exhibitions:

1971   Newark Museum, New Jersey
1976   Los Angeles County Museum of Art

1978   Bannister Gallery, Rhode Island College, Black Heritage
        Society
1980   Studio Museum in Harlem, New York
1986   Museum of Art, Rhode Island School of Design, Providence
1989   Newark Museum, New Jersey
        Lehman College Art Gallery, City University of New
        York, Bronx
1992   Newark Museum, New Jersey
1996   Georgia Museum of Art, University of Georgia

Collections:

Amistad Research Center at Tulane University, New Orleans; Clark College-Atlanta University, Georgia; Fisk University, Nashville; Howard University, Washington, D.C.; Kenkeleba Gallery, New York; Museum of the National Center of Afro-American Artists, Boston; Newark Museum, New Jersey; Rhode Island School of Design, Providence.

*   *   *

Wilmer Angier Jennings, a painter and printmaker, was among the third generation of African American artists to work in Rhode Island. He followed in the footsteps of the painter Edward Bannister, one of the founders of the Providence Art Club, and the sculptor Nancy Elizabeth Prophet. Under the tutelage of Hale Woodruff, Jennings designed, cut, and printed his own linocuts and woodcuts. In 1934 he worked as a muralist for the WPA in Atlanta, Georgia, and in 1935 he worked in the graphics division of the WPA in Providence.

Jennings, best known for his black-and-white prints, was inspired by the so-called outhouse school of Woodruff. Jennings's images of the vernacular architecture of the South—dilapidated shacks and abandoned farms—and of the eroded red clay specific to the region reflected the national mood during the Great Depression. He showed the African American laborer isolated within a stark, distressed landscape. A natural storyteller, Jennings also captured the humor of African American folktales, and he protested social injustice. A dramatic wood engraving of 1935 commented on the brutality of lynching. He conscientiously placed himself and family members in the crowd scene in the print *Sanctuary* (1946).

After Jennings moved to New England in the mid-1930s, his subjects and themes broadened in scope. His prints document the greater Providence area, its old boat station, the fishing industry, an oil refinery, horse racing, and urban street scenes. Jennings had a studio in the Fox Point neighborhood, near India Point, a former port for slave ships. His work commented on the African American presence in New England and also provided a historical backdrop for urban development. Like his contemporaries Aaron Douglas, Palmer Hayden, and Charles Alston, to name only a few, Jennings was influenced by the new Negro movement to incorporate African artifacts and symbolism into his art. His still lifes were detailed renderings of vases, urns, baskets, playing cards, textiles, and African sculpture.

Jennings's wood engravings are comparable to those of his contemporary James Lesesne Wells. They are technically different from Wells's works of flowing linear movements and complex patterns, however, for Jennings preferred simple and jewel-like compositions. Jennings was an innovator and fashioned his own carving tools. Although he is best known for wood engravings, he explored the nuances of light and shadow in linocuts, woodcuts, mezzotints,

and lithographs. His interest in dramatic light led to a passion for photography, which he pursued by using a camera he made himself. He experimented with a broad range of graphic media, papers, and inks and consciously adapted printing techniques that best suited his subjects, themes, and artistic ideas.

What makes Jennings's prints distinctive are the compositional structures and spatial designs attributed to his training in jewelry design at the Rhode Island School of Design and his experience with theatrical set designs at Morehouse College in Atlanta. In addition, Jennings earned a degree in mathematics in 1933, and his compositions are based on mathematical systems.

Like many artists, Jennings was not able to earn a living from his artwork, and from 1948 until his death he was employed by the Imperial Pearl Company in Providence as its head jewelry designer and chief model maker. He achieved recognition in the field and won several awards, including a National Silversmith Award and a bronze medal for jewelry design. In 1981 he received an honorary doctorate in fine arts from Rhode Island College.

Jennings maintained a printing press at home, and, beginning in the 1930s, he produced art on a consistent basis. In the late 1950s Jennings injured his right hand, which ultimately made it difficult for him to manipulate engraving tools and to carve the surface of hard wood. He then trained himself to draw and to paint with his left hand. He continued to paint until his death, working from nature with his wife, the artist Mary Howard Jennings. His paintings reflected a shift from portraiture, academic landscapes, and social realism to abstraction. Jennings's observations speak to the cultural experience of African Americans who migrated from the South to the North, and he remains important because he expanded the repertoire of images of the American scene, particularly of the South and of New England.

—Claude L. Elliott

JOAQUIM, Leandro

Brazilian painter

Born: Rio de Janeiro, c.1738. **Died:** 1798.

Publications:

On JOAQUIM: *A Mao Afro-Brasileria: Significado da Contribucao Artistica e Historica* by Emanoel Arajo, Tenege, Sao Paulo, 1988. **Articles**—"Leandro Joaquim" by Doria Escragnolle, in *Revista da Semana,* 24 December 1938; "Os Panéis de Leandro Joaquim" by Gustavo Barroso, in *O Cruzeiro,* 26 February 1949; "Leandro Joaquim e os Paneis do Museu Historico Nacional" by Oliva de Menezes, in *A Santa do Pau. Oco* (Rio de Janeiro), 1957, pp. 57-73; "As Primeiras Telas Paisigisticas da Cidade" by Gilberto Ferrez, in *Revista do APHAN,* 17, 1969, pp. 219-37; "Negros Pardos e Mulatos na Pintura e na Escultura" by José Roberto and Teixera Leite, in *Brasileira do Séd,* 18.

*   *   *

Leandro Joaquim secured his place in Brazilian art history by producing a series of six elliptical paintings that are considered among the finest paintings of the colonial epoch. These works, the first land and seascapes painted in Brazil, now hang in the National Historical Museum in Rio de Janeiro.

The paintings include *Seasape, Military Parade in the Palace Square, Whale Fishing in Guanabara Bay, Procession by the Sea from the Lepers Hospital, View of the Gloria Church,* and *View of the Lagoon from the Mouth with the Carioca Archways.* Each of these paintings shows tremendous attention to details, bright color, and a sense of movement. The boats on the bay at Rio de Janeiro, the precision of the buildings, and the depiction of people at work on the shore are evident in several of these paintings.

Joaquim also painted religious paintings and portraits, including several works for the São Sebastião Church on Castelo Hill. Three of these paintings, *Senhora de Belém, São João,* and *São Januario* now hang in the São Sebastião Church on Rua Haddock Lobo. Other works attributed to Joaquim are the *Painel da Boa Morte* (*The Panel of the Good Death*) in the Church of Nossa Senhora da Conceição e Boa Morte. Joaquim produced portraits of Luiz de Vasconcelos, the Count of Bobadela, and Captain Gregório Francico de Miranda, also in the National Historical Museum. His portraits are said both to portray the subject and to signify the age of which they were a part.

—Carolyn Richardson Durham

JOHNSON, Malvin Gray

American painter

Born: Greensboro, North Carolina, 1896. **Education:** National Academy of Design, New York. **Career:** Commercial artist; worked for Public Works of Art Project (P.W.A.P.), 1934. Associated with members of the Harlem Renaissance, including Aaron Douglas, Palmer Hayden, and Archibald Motley, Jr. Member, Society of Independent Artists. **Award:** Otto H. Kahn Prize, Harmon Foundation, 1928. **Died:** 1934.

Selected Exhibitions:

1928	Harmon Foundation, New York
1929	Harmon Foundation, New York
	Smithsonian Institution, Washington, D.C.
1930	Harmon Foundation, New York
1931	Harmon Foundation, New York
1933	Harmon Foundation, New York
1934	Nicholas Roerich Museum, New York
	Corcoran Gallery of Art, Washington, D.C.
1935	Harmon Foundation, New York
	New Jersey State Museum, Trenton
1936	Hall of Negro Life, Texas Centennial, Dallas
1939	Baltimore Museum of Art, Maryland
1940	Library of Congress, Washington, D.C.
1971	Newark Museum, New Jersey
1976	Los Angeles County Museum of Art (traveling)
1984	Center Gallery of Bucknell University, Lewisburg, Pennsylvania (traveling)
1985	Art Museum Association of America (traveling)

Collections:

Aaron Douglas Collection, Amistad Research Center, New Orleans; Atlanta University, Georgia; Fisk University, Nashville; Gallery of Art, Howard University, Washington, D.C.; National Museum of American Art, Washington, D.C.; Schomburg Center, New York.

Publications:

On JOHNSON: Book—*Negro Artists: An Illustrated Review of Their Achievements,* Harmon Foundation, Inc., New York, 1935. **Articles**—"Along the Color Line—The Middle States," in *Crisis,* 36, February 1929, pp. 53-54; "Malvin Gray Johnson, Artist" by James A. Porter, in *Opportunity,* April 1935, pp. 117-18; "Negroes Exhibit Their Art," in *Pictures On Exhibit,* 2, February 1939, pp. 8-9; "Malvin Gray Johnson," in *A History of African American Artists, from 1792 to the Present* by Romare Bearden and Harry Henderson, Pantheon Books, New York, 1993, pp. 181-84.

*　　*　　*

Malvin Gray Johnson died at an early age, and not much is known about him. What is clear is that Gray Johnson, as he was called, was attracted to abstraction and cubistic compositional structures. He worked as a commercial artist after studying with Francis Coates Jones at the National Academy of Design in New York City, and his first recognition came in 1929 when he won the Otto H. Kahn prize for the best painting in the Harmon Foundation exhibition. *Swing Low, Sweet Chariot,* an interpretative piece, pictures a group of African Americans, with their backs to the viewer, gazing upward at a white cloud formation of a chariot pulled by horses. The painting, which was reproduced in the February 1929 issue of *Crisis,* reflected his preference for themes on Negro spirituals and other aspects of life in Harlem. Such themes can also be seen in the paintings *Roll, Jordan, Roll* (c.1930) and *The Elks* (c.1933). Johnson was celebrated and encouraged for his use of African American subjects in his work. Alain Locke wrote that his work was an "object lesson in direct and sincere approach and convincing evidence of what contemporary Negro art lost in the premature death of this young genius." Others, however, criticized him for his style of painting, saying that it showed a lack of finish and was too abstract.

Johnson had but five short years between the Harmon Foundation award for *Swing Low, Sweet Chariot* and his death in 1934 to decide whether he would follow the prescription for American art laid out by the social realists or pursue his tendencies toward abstraction. He chose his own road. *Self-Portrait* (1934) clearly shows Johnson's tendencies toward abstraction and African-inspired cubism. Angles rise up and around the figure, and they conjoin with the angles of his shoulders and elbow. While Johnson did not travel to Paris, it appears that he shared stylistic sensibilities with artists there and that he also adopted their persona. In his self-portrait Johnson is wearing a striped, long-sleeved turtleneck, a sign of the Parisian artist at the time. (There is also a well-known photograph of Johnson, pipe in mouth, sitting at his easel, painting, and wearing the same striped shirt, with *Self-Portrait* hanging in the background.) He also states his alliances visually with the oil painting in the rear of him of the masklike, African-derived heads. Realistic representations of African American experience in the United States have been replaced by Parisian cubism informed by African sculp-

Malvin Gray Johnson: *Negro Soldier*, **1934. Photo by Manu Sassoonian; courtesy of the Schomburg Center for Research in Black Culture.**

Malvin Gray Johnson: *Postman,* 1934. Photo by Manu Sassoonian; courtesy of the Schomburg Center for Research in Black Culture.

tural traditions. This, it seems, might have been the foundation of his future works.

After a painting trip to Virginia, Johnson unexpectedly died. He had been preparing for an exhibition planned by the Harmon Foundation. In April 1935 a memorial exhibition of fifty-three watercolors and oil paintings, along with the work of sculptors Richmond Barthé and Sargent Claude Johnson, was held at the Delphic Studios in New York City. Johnson was lauded for his genre scenes, as he had been during his life. Most reviewers felt that the scenes possessed the "real Negro spirit." Because so much emphasis was placed on the subject matter, Johnson's interpretation of cubistic conventions was virtually ignored.

Lizzetta LeFalle-Collins

JOHNSON, Marie E.
American painter and installation artist

Name also appears as Marie Johnson-Callaway. **Born:** Baltimore, Maryland, 10 April 1920. **Education:** Coppin Teachers' College, Baltimore, Maryland, elementary school teaching certificate, 1939; Morgan State College, Baltimore, Maryland, B.A. in art education, 1952; San Jose State University, California, M.A. in painting, 1968; San Francisco State University, 1976. President, NAACP chapter,

San Jose, California. **Family:** Married, one son and one daughter. **Career:** Teacher, California College of Arts and Crafts, Oakland, California, San Jose State University, California, San Francisco State University. Assistant professor in art and black studies, San Jose State College, California, until retirement, 1983. Member, San Jose Urban Coalition, California, Board of Directors, San Jose Civic Art Gallery, California; organizer and teacher, *Self Image Art,* San Jose, California.

Selected Exhibitions:

Brockman Gallery, Los Angeles; Cornell University, Ithaca, New York; Expo '70, Osaka, Japan; Los Angeles County Museum of Art; Lucien Labaudt Gallery, San Francisco (1964, solo); New York Cultural Center; Oakland Museum, California; William Sawyer Gallery, San Francisco; Womanspace, Los Angeles.

Publications:

On JOHNSON: Book—*Directions in Afro-American Art,* exhibition catalog, New York, Herbert F. Johnson Museum of Art and the Africana Studies and Research Center, Office of University Publications, 1974. **Articles**—"Marie Johnson," in *San Francisco Examiner Chronicle,* 14 June 1970; *Black World,* 22, December 1972; *Christian Science Monitor,* 13 October 1973, p. 16; "Why, in 1973, a 'Black Art' Show" by Henri Ghent, in *New York Times,* 14 October 1973; *Ebony,* 29, December 1973; "Scene," in *Art Gallery,* 20, May 1977; *American Quarterly,* 30(3), 1978, p. 384.

*   *   *

To see Marie E. Johnson's artwork is to know her values. Johnson's art form of choice is three-dimensional iconography. She goes beyond the icon as an image painted on wood panels, however. Her icons, done in the images of African American people, are cut from wood. She dresses them with various materials, including hair, cloth, and glass, that help project the art into the viewer's reality. Hence, her works are most often described as mixed media. It is thus that Johnson re-creates the people she loves.

Johnson's icons are large, life-size in some cases but at least three feet tall, and are appointed with recognizably human characteristics. She puts human hair on their heads. They wear real clothes, and if the icon is in a setting, the environment contains appropriate objects. *Hope Street* (1971), for example, features a man leaning out of his window. On the window ledge is his canary in a cage, and the canary is alive.

Johnson's work is often compared to the collages of Romare Bearden. Johnson's attitude, however, is thoroughly of her era, the late 1960s and the 1970s. She is militant in her commitment to the idea that community and relationships are art. Such an uncomplicated, comforting attitude can easily be interpreted as folksy and lacking in strong emotion. In the late 1960s and the 1970s, however, her wholesome understatement was refreshing amid the black protest art of her peers and may have helped her work gain attention.

Johnson's experience with protest included being jailed herself during a civil rights march. The experience led to an icon described by San Francisco art critic Walter Blum as "a young black peering forlornly from behind the bars of a jail cell." Blum, who viewed the work in Johnson's home, said that it was "so arresting that visitors invariably stop and stare in shocked silence."

Johnson's work primarily emphasizes the communal nature of African American existence in the United States. Groupings of two or more figures constitute much of her work, communicating her value of organic community. Where a single figure is involved, the icon's title points to a community beyond the immediate vision. Hence, the work *Mrs. Jackson* (1968) refers to a woman who has a significant other. *Papa, the Reverend* (1968) refers to a man with children who recognize him and to a man following a calling to establish or maintain a community through God.

Johnson's work is humanistic, with representations reminiscent of black life. She is quoted in *The Afro-American Artist: A Search for Identity* as saying that "It is important to me that blacks understand and identify with my work. When a black person looks at one of my pieces and says, 'Yeah, that's mama, that's grandmama, that's sister, that's me,' I am gratified." She adds, "Blacks are a family bound and unified by common experiences in a hostile land. I aim to speak to, of and for 'my family.' "

—Dedria A. Humphries Barker

JOHNSON, Sargent Claude
American sculptor, printmaker, and ceramist

Born: Boston, 7 October 1887. **Education:** A. W. Best School of Fine Arts, San Francisco; California School of Fine Arts, 1919-23, 1940-42; Boston School of Fine Arts; California School of Fine Arts. **Career:** Worked for Federal Art Project, Works Progress Administration; sculpture instructor, Mills College, Oakland, California, summer 1947; Junior Workshop program, San Francisco Housing Authority, 1947. Numerous trips to Mexico between 1945-65; traveled to Japan in 1958. Important artist of the Harlem Renaissance. **Awards:** Medals for sculpture, San Francisco Art Association, 1925, 1931, 1935; Otto H. Kahn Prize, Harmon Foundation, 1927; Harmon Bronze Medal, Harmon Foundation, 1929; California Legion of Honor, 1931; Robert C. Ogden Prize, Harmon Foundation, 1933; prize for lithograph, San Francisco Art Association, 1938; Third Prize, sculpture, American Negro Exposition, Chicago, 1940; Abraham Rosenberg Scholarship, 1944, 1949. **Died:** 10 October 1967.

Individual Exhibitions:

1971   Oakland Museum, California (retrospective)
1987   Richmond Art Center, Richmond, California

Selected Group Exhibitions:

1936   *Annual Exhibition,* San Francisco Art Association
1938   *Annual Exhibition,* San Francisco Art Association
1939   Harmon Foundation, New York (traveling)
1945   San Francisco Museum of Art
1952   *Annual Exhibition,* San Francisco Art Association
1966   University of California at Los Angeles
1970   La Jolla Museum of Contemporary Art, La Jolla, California
1976   Los Angeles County Museum of Art (traveling)

1984   Center Gallery of Bucknell University, Lewisburg, Pennsylvania (traveling)
1985   Bellevue Art Museum, Bellevue, Washington (traveling)
1989   Smithsonian Institution, Washington, D.C. (traveling)

Collections:

Aaron Douglas Collection, Amistad Research Center, New Orleans; Evans-Tibbs Collection, Washington, D.C.; Fine Arts Museum of San Francisco; Fisk University, Nashville; Gallery of Art, Howard University, Washington, D.C.; National Museum of American Art, Washington, D.C.; Newark Museum, New Jersey; Oakland Museum, California; San Diego Museum of Art; San Francisco African American Historical and Cultural Society; San Francisco Museum of Modern Art; Schomburg Center, New York; Whitney Museum of American Art, New York.

Publications:

On JOHNSON: Book—*Sargent Johnson: Retrospective* by Evangeline J. Montgomery, Oakland, California, Oakland Museum, 1971, pp. 17-18. **Articles**—Interview in *San Francisco Chronicle,* 6 October 1935, p. D3; "Sargent Johnson," in *Opportunity,* July 1939; "Sargent Johnson Sculptor," in *Our World,* July 1946; "Sargent Johnson: We Call Him Ours" by Jehanne Bietry Salinger, in *Opera and Concert,* January 1949; "Sculptor in Touch with the People," in *People's World* (San Francisco), 2 February 1950; "Sculptor at 2 Cardell Place," in *The Post* (Berkeley, California), 6 November 1965; "Sargent Johnson," in *A History of African American Artists, from 1792 to the Present* by Romare Bearden and Harry Henderson, Pantheon Books, New York, 1993, pp. 216-26.

*   *   *

Throughout his career Sargent Claude Johnson grappled with the issue of modernity and figuration in the context of African American characterizations. Works such as the terra cotta *Standing Figure* (1934), the chalk drawing *Mother and Child* (1934), and the polychrome *Forever Free* (1935) are prime examples of the self-contained, cylindrical forms that characterize his sculpture. They further represent an archetype for black motherhood that continued to inform Johnson's work and the works other of African American artists through the 1960s and 1970s.

Various movements contributed to the development of Johnson's style, including American Regionalism, the Mexican Muralists, the North Beach arts movements, and philosopher Alain Locke's strategies to define and promote African American culture. Johnson attempted to follow a mandate articulated by Locke—that African American artists create artworks informed by their African heritage. Much of Johnson's early imagery recalls the literature of the day as well, by writers and poets such as Langston Hughes who referred to the African American folk population as the "low down folk." Johnson, like other artists in the 1930s, however, sought to define Americanisms and to project a sense of America—the place in his art. Lithographic works such as *Singing Saints* (1940) and *Lenox Avenue* (c.1940) document cultural contributions of African Americans in music (the spiritual and jazz respectively), employing the contrast of curvilinear and angular lines that characterized modernist figurative styles influenced by traditional African sculpture. These "American" works also reflect Johnson's growing sense of modernism in linear contours, shapes, and content.

In addition, Johnson was influenced by his teacher/colleagues such as Benjamino Bufano and Ralph Stackpole in developing his modernist style. Bufano's self-contained, solid, orblike figures of Bufano's—with a minimal amount of line delineation to indicate the extremities of his figures—are also shared by Johnson. The massive angularities in Johnson's cast stone *Incas,* commissioned for the Court of Pacifica at the 1939 Golden Gate International Exposition, also recall the work by Stackpole for the same exposition.

As late as 1948 Johnson continued to receive public commissions, mainly for figurative friezes on exterior and interior walls such as the green *Vermont* slate incised relief on the exterior of the Maritime Museum in the Aquatic Park at San Francisco's Fisherman's Wharf (1939). From the 1940s and into the 1960s Johnson experimented with techniques more closely associated with the California arts and crafts movement in works such as *Tea Pot* (1941). He created a number of small painted terra cotta pieces and over ten polychrome, porcelain-enamel, two-dimensional works. He was also greatly influenced by the work of pre-Hispanic civilizations in Mexico as well as the murals of Diego Rivera, the leader of a major movement in figuration in the Bay Area during the 1930s. From 1945 to 1965 Johnson made frequent visits to southern Mexico to work in Oaxacan black clay. These trips resulted in a series of small animal and figurative forms. Johnson's Mexican figures show the same concern for racially specific representations that informed his early sculptures of African Americans.

Johnson's strongest work, however, was in the era of the 1930s and 1940, when he participated in the Bohemian artist community in San Francisco's North Beach. It was the context of the North Beach crowd of culturalists and artists in which he may have moved most freely. During these prolific years he seemed to welcome and enjoy affiliations with all contexts equally. This period also paralleled a window of opportunity for financial support from private and public agencies like the WPA, FAP, and the Harmon Foundation. Like Charles Alston in New York, Johnson was a supervisor for the FAP in San Francisco. But as public and private support declined in the 1950s and ended in the 1960s, so did Johnson's ability to create major works.

—Lizzetta LeFalle-Collins

JOHNSON, Stephanie A.
American mixed-media artist

Born: 1952. **Education:** Emerson College, Boston, B.F.A. in theater, 1974; San Francisco State University, M.A. in interdisciplinary art, 1994. **Career:** Since 1974 freelance lighting designer. Since 1983 freelance gaffer, electrician. Guest lecturer, Melkweg, Amsterdam, 1984-85, San Francisco State University, 1991, California College of Arts and Crafts, 1992, University of California, Berkeley, 1992-1993, University of San Francisco, 1994-95; California College of Arts and Crafts, Oakland, 1995. **Awards:** National Endowment Fellowship in Design, 1982; grant, New Langton Arts, San Francisco, 1992. **Address:** 2740 Mabel Street, Berkeley, California 94702, U.S.A.

Individual Exhibitions:

1991	Southern Pacific Railroad Station, Oakland, California
1992	Bayview Opera House, San Francisco
1993	Ohana Gallery, Oakland, California
	I.D.E.A. Artspace, Sacramento, California
1994	San Francisco African American Historical and Cultural Society
1996	Oakland Cemetery, Atlanta

Selected Group Exhibitions:

1983	Studio W, San Francisco
1985	Rietveld Academie, Amsterdam, Holland
1989	Sargent Johnson Gallery, San Francisco
1990	Skylight Studio, Berkeley, California
1991	I.D.E.A./Brockman Gallery, Sacramento, California
1993	Richmond Art Center, California
	San Francisco Arts Commission Gallery
	Yerba Buena Center for the Arts, San Francisco
	ProArts Gallery, Oakland, California
1994	Berkeley Art Center, California

Publications:

On JOHNSON: Articles—"Flickering Lights and a Lonesome Whistle" by Steve Rubenstein, in *The San Francisco Chronicle,* November 1991; "Rail Art Show Plays Old Depot" by Bill O'Brien, in *The Express,* December 1991; "We Built the Pyramids" by Sheila Moody, in *Mahogany,* June 1992; "Johnson's Art Binds Ties at 16th Street," in *Architectural Lighting Magazine,* April 1992; "Advanced Placements" by Terry Cohn, in *Visions,* Summer 1992; "Telling the Tale of a City" by Jacqueline Ginley, in *The Contra Costa Times,* January 1993; "Main Street" by Santiago Chiori, in *Main Street,* January 1993; "Black Artist Bridges a Gap with Asians" by Sheila Buto, in *Asianweek,* April 1993; "On Death, Friends, and a Child's Sorrow" by Victoria Dalkey, in *The Sacramento Bee,* October 1993; "A Show of Qualities" by Jeff Kelly, in *Artweek,* November 1993; "East Meets West" by Chiori Santiago, in *The Express,* December 1993; "A Conversation with Ann Chamberlain and Stephanie Johnson, Artists" by Meredith Tromble, in *Artweek,* July 1994; "Stephanie Johnson's *Underground Railroad* at Intersection for the Arts," *Artweek,* January 1995.

*   *   *

A special light emerges from Stephanie Johnson's compelling artworks. The light is double-edged, and she uses it to dispel the darkness. She also uses light to transform and augur the future. Light in Johnson's artworks comes from her training as a lighting designer and from her having grown up in a home where the parents were educated and artistic. Her mother was involved in the theater, and Stephanie developed her own skills by watching her mother.

A Bouquet (1995), for example, reveals theatricality, transformation, and auguring. The theatricality of the work—which is seven by six by two feet and which is made of lightbulbs, steel tubes, and steel boxes—is expressed by the use of multiple and interactive aspects of sound, light, and image. Johnson used steel tubes from a junkyard but transformed them by changing their purpose. At the ends of the tubes she placed lights designed to capture the essential glowing nature of children. All children are included, especially those who are differently abled. Johnson augurs the future by reminding the viewer that children are the future and that their voices, which can be heard as part of the artwork, must not be silenced.

Johnson's *The Glass Ceiling,* also created in 1995, is another study in light. Here the artist makes a provocative statement regarding the United States and its unwillingness to allow people to move beyond a certain level. Through the use of gloves of varying sizes—and of different gloves for different genders—the artist develops her theme that the system holds individuals down. Without warning or forethought people attempt to climb the ladder of success, only to have their progress thwarted. Johnson uses horizontal bands of light for each of the rungs of the ladder. A steel bar is a metaphor for the end of the climb. Her use of light in this work, which is ten by two by three feet, is captivating and powerful.

Johnson is best known for her dramatic outdoor productions, which include video or slide projections of individuals and subjects onto a large panoramic backdrop. The productions often take place at night, and they include lights, voices, and music. In 1996 Johnson created such a production in the Oakland Cemetery in Atlanta, Georgia. Largely set aside for Atlanta's white population, the historic cemetery contains exquisite marble statuary and gravestones. In one corner of the segregated cemetery are grave sites for African American Atlantans who worked for whites interred there. The voices used in the production came from interviews conducted by the artist herself with some of Atlanta's citizens, who recounted important events from the city's history and the impact of the events on their lives.

Johnson has garnered a widespread reputation for such productions. She has held them throughout the United States and has incorporated a wide variety of historical and cultural material, including immigration, oppression, slavery, gender discrimination, and Native American issues. What is so critical about the works is that she has employed the productions, which spring from training Johnson first received within her family circle, to benefit so many others.

—Jontyle Theresa Robinson

JOHNSON, William H(enry)

American painter and graphic artist

Born: Florence, South Carolina, 18 March 1901. **Education:** National Academy of Design, New York, 1921-26, under Charles L. Hinton; Cape Cod School of Art, Provincetown, Massachusetts, summers 1923-26; studied with Chaim Soutine and Paul Cezanne, Paris, 1926-29. **Family:** Married Holcha Krake (ceramist and weaver) in 1930 (died 1943). **Career:** Worked as hotel porter, cook, stevedore, New York, c.1918-25. Lived in Denmark, Norway, and Sweden, 1930-38, 1946. Diagnosed with paresis in Oslo, Norway, 1947; confined to Islip State Hospital, New York, until his death. **Awards:** Canon Prize, 1924, Hallgarten Prize, 1925-26, School Prize, 1925-26, all from National Academy of Design; Gold Medal, Harmon Foundation, 1929. **Died:** 13 April 1970.

Individual Exhibitions:

1927	Students and Artists Club, Paris
1928	Nice, France
1929	Harmon Foundation, New York
1939	Artists Gallery, New York
1971	Smithsonian Institution, Washington, D.C. (retrospective)
1982	Smithsonian Institution, Washington, D.C.

Selected Group Exhibitions:

1940	Harlem Art Center, New York
	American Negro Art, Chicago
1941	Alma Reed Gallery, New York
1943	Wakefield Gallery, New York
1944	Marquette Gallery, New York
1970	James A. Porter Gallery
1971	State Armory, Wilmington, Delaware
	Newark Museum, New Jersey
	Tuskegee Institute, Alabama
1987	Studio Museum in Harlem, New York (traveling)

Collections:

National Collection of Fine Arts, Smithsonian Institution, Washington, D.C.; Oakland Museum, California.

Publications:

On JOHNSON: Books—*William H. Johnson, 1901-1970* by Adelyn Breeskin, Smithsonian Institution Press, 1971; *Harlem Renaissance: Art of Black America* edited by Harry N. Abrams, Studio Museum in Harlem, 1987; *Against the Odds: African-American Artists and the Harmon Foundation* edited by Gary A. Reynolds and Beryl J. Wright, Newark Museum, 1989; *Novae: William H. Johnson and Bob Thompson,* exhibition catalog, Los Angeles, California Afro-American Museum Foundation, 1990; *Homecoming: The Art and life of William H. Johnson* by Richard J. Powell, New York, Rizzoli, 1991. **Articles**—"Is William H. Johnson, Negro Prize Winner, Blazing a New Trail?" in *Art digest,* January 1930, p. 13; "Johnson One-Man Show Opens in New York May 4," in *Crisis,* April 1941; "Tempera Paintings by Johnson Shown in New York," in *Opportunity,* 1943; "William H. Johnson: Expressionist Turned Primitive" by Jacob Landy, in *Journal of the American Association of University Women,* March 1958; "William H. Johnson, An Artist of the World Scene" (New York), Harmon Foundation, n.d. (available from Materials on Negro Artists, Art Department, Fisk University, Nashville); articles in *Smithsonian,* November 1971, *Black American Literature Forum,* Winter 1986, and *People Weekly,* 25 May 1987. **Video**—*The Life and Art of William H. Johnson,* Reading and O'Reilly, 1992.

*   *   *

William H. Johnson was a favorite artist of the Harmon Foundation exhibitions, participating in many and winning a number of prizes. A prolific painter, he seemed to churn out works as if trying to hold onto his sense of self even as his mental state was rapidly diminishing. His most prolific years were between 1929 and 1943. At first he adopted a painting style that had influenced American artists in the early twentieth century, the school of Paris. Johnson was particularly taken with the work of Vincent van Gogh, paying close attention to his brush work, and of Paul Cézanne, for his use of pictorial space and skewed treatment of elements in the landscape. The agitated and swirling movement of the paint added to the meandering roads, as in *Street Scene in Florence, S. C.* (c.1930), bears witness to this influence.

Johnson, however, was affected by the modernist thoughts of those around him. In a reversal from the late nineteenth century, artists increasingly came to believe that so-called primitive peoples lived more harmoniously with the world around them and therefore were much closer to their own emotions. Artists in Europe as well as the United States began to study the social patterns of indigenous peoples and also became intrigued with African American life. Living in France in the mid- to late 1920s and in Denmark and Sweden in the 1930 into the 1940s, Johnson was in an atmosphere that believed greater emotionalism to equal a closer connection with a primitive past.

Johnson abandoned his earlier style for one in which he could better convey the human drama and emotions of his people. His more personal explorations turned toward naivelike renderings of the lives of African Americans in rural and urban settings. The rural Southern farm and urban Northern street corner signified a sense of place for his African American subjects. The idyllic family unit of mother, father, and child in *Farm Family* (c.1939) stands in front of a modest farmhouse as animals surround them in a nativity-like tableau. The flat colored shapes give no hints of Johnson's former explorations with textural brush strokes and tonal gradations to achieve depth. The space is now shallow and direct, stating in simple forms the complex place this family occupies in the American landscape. Remaining on the farm became more and more difficult, and families left the farm for the rewards of jobs, for better educational opportunities for their children, and to avoid racial oppression and violence in the South. But many of the same difficulties awaited those who migrated to the North. This family finds itself somewhere in between, the mother and child firmly on the farm but the father gazing into the distance.

It seems that Johnson was attempting to place many of his characters in a particular and oftentimes intimate cultural context away from the American mainstream. Johnson said of himself that he was "no ordinary American Negro painter, or no ordinary American painter" and said that he was devoted to seeing the primitive ways of people. In an interview in Copenhagen, Johnson said, "I myself feel like a primitive man, like one who is at the same time both a primitive and a cultured painter." In another interview he said that "with me, being primitive is something inborn. I just cannot be otherwise." Johnson therefore felt that he was in a position to speak from the inner spirit of primitive man, which he felt was embodied in him, and that the European and American painters who sought the primitive in their work could not come closer than he could.

By 1939 Johnson had fully adopted a naive style and iconography. This suited the Harmon Foundation, which encouraged African American artists to look to their own people for inspiration. One wonders if his search for the primitive led to his increasing mental instability or if he was allowed to diminish further into mental discord because his problems were confused with the emotional state of a primitive man. Whatever the case, he left behind a provocative body of work that in its sheer power is a testament to his embrace of European and American modernist ideals.

Lizzetta LeFalle-Collins

JOHNSTON, Joshua

American painter

Name sometimes listed as Joshua Johnson. **Born:** Baltimore, Maryland, c.1765. **Career:** Portrait painter, c.1796-1824. **Died:** c.1830.

Selected Exhibitions:

1948	Peale Museum, Baltimore
1961	Metropolitan Museum, New York
1962	Walker Art Center, Minneapolis, Minnesota
	City Art Museum of St. Louis, Missouri
	Municipal Art Gallery, Los Angeles
	de Young Museum, San Francisco
	Atlanta Art Association Galleries, Georgia
1963	Virginia Museum of Fine Arts, Richmond
	Art Institute of Chicago
	Dallas Museum of Fine Arts
	Milwaukee Art Center, Wisconsin
	Isaac Delgado Museum, New Orleans
	Baltimore Museum, Maryland
1964	Museum of Fine Arts, Boston
	Detroit Institute of Arts

Collections:

Bowdoin College, Brunswick, Maine; Frick Gallery, New York; Metropolitan Museum of Art, New York; Museum of Early Southern Decorative Arts, Winston-Salem, North Carolina; Smithsonian Institution, Washington, D.C.

Publications:

On JOHNSTON: Book—*Joshua Johnson, Freeman and Early American Portrait Painter* by Carolyn J. Weekley and Stiles Tuttle Colwill (with Leroy Graham and Mary Ellen Hayward), Williamsburg and Baltimore, Abby Aldrich Rockefeller Folk Art Center, Colonial Williamsburg Foundation, and Maryland Historical Society, 1987. **Articles**—"Joshua Johnston, the First Negro Portrait Painter" by J. Hall Pleasants, in *Maryland Historical,* June 1942; "Joshua Johnston: Eighteenth Century Negro Artist" by Wilbur Harvey Hunter, Jr., in *American Collector,* February 1948; "An Early Negro Portrait Artist" by Katherine Scarborough, in *Negro History Bulletin,* February 1968; "The Question of Joshua Johnston," in *A History of African-American Artists, from 1792 to the Present* by Romare Bearden and Harry Henderson, Pantheon Books, New York, 1993.

*   *   *

Joshua Johnston (also known as Johnson) was one of the earliest African American artists who can be identified by name. A freeman, he operated a successful portrait painting business in Baltimore from 1796 until 1824, producing a body of over eighty surviving paintings of that city's most prominent families. An advertisement taken out in the *Baltimore Intelligencer* of 1798 attests to Johnston's ability to paint a dignified and formal portrait in the style of the day, which was derived from eighteenth-century European conventions and widely adopted by early American artists. It reads in part, "As a self-taught genius deriving from nature and industry his knowledge of the Art and having experienced many insuperable obstacles in the pursuit of his studies, it is highly gratifying to him to make assurances of his ability to execute all commands, with an effect, and in a style, which must give satisfaction."

The "insuperable obstacles" mentioned by Johnston probably refer to a childhood of slavery. Evidence suggests that Johnston was born in the West Indies and may have been brought to Baltimore while still a boy by Robert Polk, the brother-in-law of Charles Wilson Peale, the head of a family of renowned American artists. Johnston most likely learned to paint while working as a valet for Peale or Charles Peale Polk, both prominent artists who, along with Rembrandt Peale, were active in Baltimore during the early 1790s. Johnston somehow gained or purchased his freedom at the age of twenty-five or so, probably around 1790, and by 1796 he had established himself in his profession as a limner. He probably did not maintain his own studio but worked in his sitters' homes. In addition, Johnston may have supported his family by working as a varnisher, sign painter, or carriage or house painter.

Johnston's paintings share many stylistic affinities with those of the Peales and Charles Peale Polk. His figures sit or stand stiffly, slightly turned to one side. Their set lips, inflexible hands, and eyes that stare directly forward reveal no inner psychology or emotion. In group portraits there is little hint of the relationship between sitters. Johnston's palette tends to be more subdued than that of the Peales, and the modeling of his figures less plastic. His mature style, which he attained around 1805, evinces an increasing repetition of pose, background, and rendering of facial types, but he supplied his sitters with a distinctive array of studio props, including sprigs or baskets of berries, small dogs, and interestingly, large fanciful moths.

Nearly half of the paintings attributed to Johnston feature full-length standing portraits of children, a subject in which the artist seems to have specialized. *Charles John Stricker Wilmans* (1803-05), typifies Johnston's mature style, with its precise, linear quality and smooth finish. The subject of the painting stands motionless in three-quarters view, his left hand resting on the barrel of a rifle; to his right, a little white dog raises one paw and gazes up at his master inquiringly. The vermilion of the boy's slippers enlivens an otherwise restrained color scheme of warm whites, grays, and muted olive greens. The swagged curtain with gold tassel that acts as an asymmetrical backdrop is a typical Johnston device. Here it is balanced by a view opposite through an ivy-trimmed stone archway to two distant rowhouses, the portrait thus distinguished by its combination of exterior and interior settings. The overall effect is one of balance and stillness, with the underlying geometry of the drawn forms creating a subtle compositional interplay.

Somewhat less formal and to modern eyes peculiarly charming is Johnston's portrait of Emma Van Name (c.1805). With a toy whistle around her neck and a strawberry in one hand, the round little girl reaches towards a glass compote dish nearly half her size filled with berries. The precise symbolic significance of the glass vessel is unknown, but it allows Johnston to demonstrate his ability to render complex materials with confidence, as does his deft handling of the diaphanous fabric of Emma's overdress and lace cap.

Johnston's most frequent subjects were members of white aristocratic families, many of whom were likely slaveholders. An exception is a portrait from c.1805-10 that has been tentatively identified as that of Daniel Coker, a prominent African American Methodist bishop, community leader, and abolitionist. The small painting depicts the sitter with great sympathy and dignity. Dressed in a high white collar and vest with a black overjacket, Coker gazes out at the viewer with benevolent composure, the red-brown tones of his skin complemented by the olive green spandrels that feign the oval format of the composition. The painting is one of two known portraits by Johnston of stately, well-dressed black men; together they form a matching pair. Though individual portraits of blacks by other artists of the period do exist, Johnston's companion portraits are unique.

Another subject of Johnston's for which there was limited precedence is the large scale family portrait. *Mrs. Thomas Everette and Her Children* (c.1818) is a particularly ambitious composition for a "self-taught" artist, with its grouping of six variously seated and standing figures. With the two full-length portraits of children at either end of the family grouping acting as "bookends" for the composition, the oval shapes of the sitters' heads create a rhythmic repetition across the canvas. The textured white of lace collars and the creamy pages of open books punctuate the smooth, dark tones of the overall composition, while the small boy in a bright red suit and a baby girl in white draw the eye towards the center. Here again, the small children hold fruit and flowers, emblems of fertility, while the older boys hold the books that proclaim their imminent social standing as educated men of the world.

As Beatrix Rumford wrote in *Joshua Johnson: Freeman and Portrait Painter,* "Johnston typifies the situation of a number of freemen of color in Baltimore during the early National Period. . . . He was neither unique in his racial situation or the manner in which he conducted his life. However, his chosen profession of painting portraits, and possibly other types of ornamental painting, was not common among men of his racial background anywhere in America during those years." As such, Johnston's body of work is as fascinating and valuable as a document of extraordinary individual achievement, and the social context in which it took place, as it is for its considerable aesthetic merit.

—Dorothy Valakos

JOLIMEAU, Serge

Haitian sculptor

Born: Croix-des-Bouquets, 1952. **Education:** Charlotin Marcadieux and Lycée Jacques, Croix des Bouquets. Joined Centre d'Art, Haiti, 1972.

Selected Exhibitions:

1975	Contemporary Crafts of the Americas
1976	Primitivo y Moderno de Haiti, Mexico
1977	Festival Organization of the American State, Jamaica
1978	Brooklyn Museum, New York
1982	Davenport Museum of Art, Iowa

Publications:

On JOLIMEAU: Books—*Haitian Art* by Ute Stebich, Abrams Publishers and Brooklyn Museum, New York, 1978; *Where Art Is Joy, Haitian Art: The First Forty Years* by Selden Rodman, Ruggles de Latour, New York, 1988; *A Haitian Celebration: Art and Culture* by Ute Stebich, Milwaukee Art Museum, 1992; *Tracing the Spirit: Ethnographic Essays on Haitian Art* by Karen McCarthy Brown, University of Washington Press, Seattle and Davenport Museum of Art, Iowa, 1995.

*   *   *

Serge Jolimeau was born and raised in Croix des Bouquets, a village thirty miles east of Port-au-Prince and the locus of the origin

Serge Jolimeau: *Le Demon Aile,* **1982. Photo courtesy of the Davenport Museum of Art.**

of Haitian metal sculpture. It was there at midcentury that Georges Liautaud, a blacksmith who forged iron crosses as grave markers, began the remarkable tradition of metal sculpting. His decorative crosses evolved into whimsical figurative sculptures based on everyday life and the pantheon of voodoo deities. From the simple forms of his forged works, Liautaud developed more complex two-dimensional sculptures cut from oil drums. His wonderful innovations spawned subsequent generations of Haitian metal sculptors. Among the most elegant and complex of the contemporary sculptures are those done by Serge Jolimeau.

Jolimeau began sculpting in the early 1970s under the tutelage of Seresier Louisjuste, who was creating large-scale cutout iron sculptures depicting many figures organically interconnected with the indigenous jungle flora of Haiti. Thus, it is not surprising that Jolimeau's early sculptures were ambitious in their compositions. By the late 1970s he had developed a distinctive style of large-scale works characterized by fluid designs. The elegance of his sculptures seems to run contrary to the simple forms and sometimes crude techniques associated with the native tradition of self-taught artists from Haiti. A parallel approach in painting would be the meticulous work of Rigaud Benoit, reportedly one of Jolimeau's favorite artists.

Le Demon aile (1982; "Winged Demon"), a work 5½ by 6 feet, is typical of the intricate design and scale of Jolimeau's mature sculpture. Using two flattened oil drums joined by a folded seam, Jolimeau began the work by drawing the outline of the forms and the intricate patterns of the negative spaces directly on the metal with chalk. The lines were then incised with a razor and cut by hand with a hammer and a chisel or large nail. The result of this seemingly primitive process of manipulating industrial refuse yielded an unusually refined and elegant sculpture. Its sensuality, however, has an edge, typical of Jolimeau's subjects. He frequently depicts voodoo spirits imbued with a sexual malevolence and represented in a state of metamorphosis. Imaginative variations on this theme have provided Jolimeau with an ongoing subject.

Jolimeau, whose works are collected in Haiti, the United States, and Europe, now heads an atelier, with assistants to do the rough cutting for his works, which are often on a monumental scale. *Turtle Woman* (1990), for example, combines the lacelike design of *Le Demon aile* with a pounded variegated surface that is almost eight feet long. The snake coils coming from the Medusa-like head are completed with rings from the spout of the oil drum that are attached by a thick wire loop.

Jolimeau's assemblage technique and fiercely sensual imagery done on a grand scale have pushed the expressive boundaries of Haitian metal sculpture. Although he has influenced a number of artists from his own generation, notably his peer Gabriel Bien-Aime, and many younger artists, few posses his natural ability as a draftsman or his endlessly inventive imagination.

—Brady Roberts

JONES, Ben (Franklin)

American painter, sculptor, and mixed-media artist

Born: Benjamin Franklin Jones Paterson, New Jersey, 26 May 1942. **Education:** William Paterson College, Wayne, New Jersey, B.A. 1963; New York University, M.A. 1966; University of Kumasi, Ghana, postgraduate study, 1970; Pratt Institute, M.F.A. 1983. **Career:** Art teacher, Passaic Senior High School, New Jersey, 1963-67. Since 1967 professor of art, Jersey City State College, Jersey City, New Jersey. Traveled in Spain, Soviet Union, Cuba, Haiti, Martinique, Guadeloupe, France, Mauritania, Senegal, Mali, Niger, Guinea, Ghana, Ivory Coast, Togo, Nigeria, Canada, Brazil. Chair, Board of Sulaimoan Dance Company, 1981-83; president/vice president, National Conference of Artists; member, World Print Council. **Awards:** National Endowment for the Arts Fellowship, 1974-75; New Jersey State Council for the Arts Fellowship, 1977-78; Purchase Award, National Afro-American Art Exhibition, Atlanta, Georgia, 1980-83; Career Development grant, Jersey City State College, 1980-81 and 1982-83; first and second place awards, Atlanta Life Insurance Competition, 1982-83; Award of Excellence, Passaic County College, 1984; Excellence in the Arts Award, Delta Sigma Theta Sorority, 1985. **Address:** 117 Kensington Avenue, Apartment 206, Jersey City, New Jersey 07304, U.S.A.

Individual Exhibitions:

1969   Studio Museum in Harlem, New York
1973   Studio Museum in Harlem, New York
1974   Brooklyn Children's Museum, New York

Ben Jones: *Shango/Chango,* 1995. Photo courtesy of Mansa Mussa.

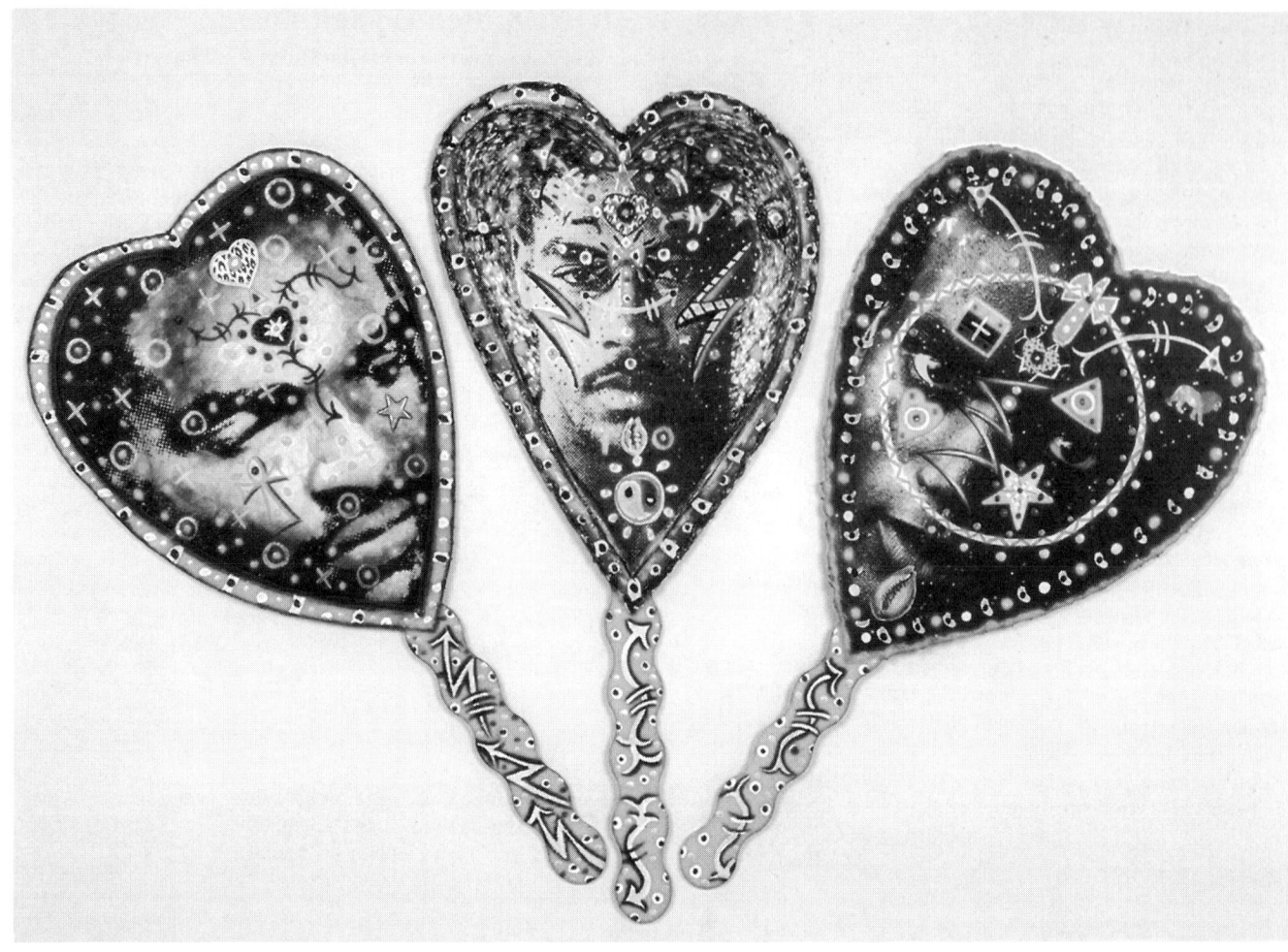

Ben Jones: *Shango/Chango Fans,* 1995. Photo courtesy of Mansa Mussa.

1975	Howard University, Washington, D.C.
	Acts of Art Gallery, New York
1982	Jersey City Museum, New Jersey
1984	Newark Museum, New Jersey
1986	New Jersey State Museum, Trenton, New Jersey
1989	William Center, Rutherford, New Jersey
1992	Centro Provincial de Artes Plasticas, Santiago de Cuba
	Centro Provincial de Artes Plasticas, Havana, Cuba
	Broadway Gallery, Passaic County College, Paterson, New Jersey
	Courtney Gallery, Jersey City State College, New Jersey
1993	Rene Portocarrero Gallery, Havana, Cuba
1994	198 Gallery, London
	Bratton Gallery, New York
	Jersey City Museum, New Jersey
1995	Bratton Gallery, New York
1996	Jadite Gallery, New York
	Espace Gaite, Paris, France
1997	Avery Museum, Charleston, South Carolina
	Jadite Gallery, New York

Selected Group Exhibitions:

1982	Studio Museum in Harlem, New York
1984	Center Gallery, Bucknell University, Lewisburg, Pennsylvania (traveling)

1986	Pennsylvania Academy of Art, Philadelphia
1987	Kenkeleba Gallery, New York
	Terada Warehouse, Tokyo, Japan
1989	Afro-American Historical and Cultural Museum, Philadelphia
1993	Paine Weber Gallery, New York
1995	Modern Art Museum of Fort Worth, Texas
1996	Cinque Gallery, New York
	Henry Street Settlement, New York

Collections:

Howard University, Washington, D.C.; Jersey City State College, New Jersey; Musée Dynamique, Dakar, Senegal, West Africa; Museo Nacional de Bellas Artes, Havana, Cuba; New Jersey State Museum, Trenton; Newark Museum, New Jersey; Studio Museum in Harlem, New York; Terakada Gallery, Tokyo, Japan.

*

Ben Jones comments:
    Africa, spirituality, politics, religion, and sexual issues have been a major aspect of the content of my work. Experimentation with various media in both two and three dimensions has been the form.

I use symbols, both representational and iconographic, to illustrate my ideas.

My visits to Africa, the Caribbean, Latin America, and Europe, along with my travels throughout the United States and Canada, have enabled me to study the philosophical, spiritual, political, social, and artistic connections of the African Diaspora.

My art does not attempt to superficially imitate decorative connections with the African Diaspora but is one that is searching for authenticity and validity of various African belief systems and lifestyles. Also, I'm trying to understand their relationship to today's and tomorrow's living.

One of the spiritual influences in my art is the Yoruba culture in Africa, Cuba, and Brazil. In these countries I have observed and participated in African-influenced rituals, religions, culture, and art. Another influence is the Black Church—its rituals and their similarities to some of the ritual traditions in African societies. Faith, spiritual healing, renewal, and hope are the force. The heart and the mind as one.

*   *   *

Benjamin Jones first became well known as an artist during the 1960s. Although much of his art is of mixed media, with a strong sculptural presence, he considers himself to be primarily a painter. The lively painted surfaces of his works attest to this focus.

Jones studied art at William Paterson State College and at New York University. He has been on the faculty of Jersey City State College for many years, where he has made his home. Because of his extensive travels, his exhibitions (including London), and the popularity of his art, he is a New Jersey artist with a firmly established national and international reputation.

One of Jones's multimedia sculptures, titled *Five Black-Face Images* (1970) and consisting of a series of painted masks, became familiar to scholars and artists when it appeared on the cover of Elsa Fine's book *The Afro-American Artist*. The images of this and similar works spoke to the heart of many of the issues of the late 1960s. The mask is one of the distinctive art forms of Africa, and it was clear from the forms of *Five Black-Face Images* that the person whose face was used for the plaster casts had been of African descent. Too, in many parts of Africa the painting of the face for both ritual and decorative purposes is important. The underlying mass of the faces and the disjointed limbs in other works also spoke to the violence of two decades in which bombings left African American victims torn apart, the victims literally and their families emotionally.

The human figure, both bodies and faces, appears in much of Jones's art. Some of the faces are those of well-known people, and some of the subjects are people close to Jones. Other works are inspired by photographs. In many of his works the black male body and face are prominent. Although he experimented with abstraction during the period of about 1981 to 1986, he has since returned to figurative art.

Jones has a strong interest in the African diaspora, and he has been to Africa many times. He also has traveled to Brazil and to the Caribbean, especially Haiti and Cuba. In addition, he travels frequently to Europe in search of African cultural objects.

Among Jones's more recent works are several brightly painted fans, part of the "Shango Fan" ("Hearts of Love") series. Most of the fans contain faces, and the bright painting indirectly recalls the *vehveh*s, or designs that refer to the spirits in Haitian voodoo.

Their underlying aesthetic recalls the early work for which Jones received so much acclaim.

Jones's interest in the god Shango is both aesthetic and political. As the god of thunder and lightning for the Yoruba people, Shango is honored wherever descendants of the Yoruba live in the African diaspora. The colors red and white are closely associated with the deity, and these colors appear frequently in Jones's works. For Jones, Shango is not just an element in the content of his art but also a metaphor for the empowerment of African peoples.

—Thomas M. Shaw

JONES, Loïs Mailou

American painter and illustrator

Work also appeared under the name Loïs Jones Pierre-Noël. **Born:** Boston, Massachusetts, 3 November 1905. **Education:** Boston Museum School of Fine Arts, 1923-27, diploma; Boston Normal Art School (now Massachusetts College of Art), 1926-27, certificate; Designers Art School of Boston, 1927-28, diploma; Académie Julian, Paris, 1937-38, certificate; Howard University, Washington, D.C., 1945, A.B. (magna cum laude) 1945; Académie de la Grande Chaumiére, Paris, 1962, certificate. **Family:** Married Vergniaud Pierre-Noël in 1953. **Career:** Professor of design and watercolor, Howard University, 1930-77. Chair, Department of Art, Palmer Memorial Institute, Sedalia, North Carolina, 1928-30; professor of art, A & T College, Greensboro, North Carolina, summers of 1928, 30. **Awards:** Nathaniel Thayer Prize for Excellence in Design, 1923, 28, 29; General Education Board Fellowship for Study in France and Italy, 1937-38; Second Annual Edward Mitchell Bannister Award for Contribution to American and Afro-American Art, Boston, 1976; Living Legend Award, National Black Arts Festival, Atlanta Arts Festival, 1990. **Address:** 4706 17th Street, N.W., Washington, D.C. 20011, U.S.A.

Individual Exhibitions:

1948	Whyte Gallery and Howard University Gallery of Art, Washington, D.C.
1954	Centre d'Art, Port-au-Prince, Haiti
1961	Galerie Internationale, New York
1966	Galerie Soulanges, Paris, 1966
1972	Howard University, Washington, D.C. (retrospective)
1973	Boston Museum of Fine Arts (retrospective)
1979	Phillips Collection, Washington, D.C.
1990	Meridian House International (retrospective)
1992	California Museum of African-American Art, Los Angeles
1993	Schomburg Center for Research in Black Culture, New York
1994	Terra Museum of American Art, Chicago
	Corcoran Gallery of Art, Washington, D.C.

Selected Group Exhibitions:

1941	National Academy of Design, New York
1949	Atlanta University Annual Exhibition, Georgia
1950	ACA Gallery, New York

Loïs Mailou Jones. Photo courtesy of Scurlock Studio.

1951	*Biennial Exhibition,* Corcoran Gallery of Art, Washington, D.C.
1963	Boston Museum School of Fine Arts
1966	Societé des Artistes Français, Grand-Palais, France
1967	City University of New York
1976	Los Angeles County Museum (traveling)
1985	Studio Museum in Harlem
1988	Hong Kong Museum of Art, Sogetsuu Kaikan, Tokyo

Collections:

American Embassy, Luxemborg; Andrew Rankin Chapel, Howard University, Washington, D.C.; Atlanta University, Georgia; Brooklyn Museum of Art, New York; Corcoran Gallery of Art, Washington, D.C.; Carl Van Vechten Gallery of Art, Washington, D.C.; Galerie Internationale, New York; Hirshhorn Museum and Sculpture Garden, Washington, D.C.; Howard University Gallery of Art, Washington, D.C.; International Fair Gallery, Ismir, Turkey; Johnson Publishing Art Collection, Chicago; Metropolitan Museum of Art, New York; Milwaukee Art Museum, Wisconsin; Le Musée d'Art Haitien, Port-au-Prince, Haiti; Museum of African-American Art, Tampa, Florida; Museum of Fine Arts, Boston; Museum of the National Center of Afro-American Artists, Boston; National Museum of American Art, Washington, D.C.; National Museum of Women in the Arts, Washington, D.C.; Phillips Collection, Washington, D.C.; Rosenwald Foundation, Chicago; Schomburg Center for Research in Black Culture, New York Public Library; Studio Museum in Harlem, New York; Taylor Gallery, North Carolina Agricultural and Technical State University, Greensboro; University of the District of Columbia; University of Panjab, Pakistan; Wadsworth Atheneum, Hartford, Connecticut; Walker Art Museum, Bowdoin College, Brunswick, Maine; Walter Reed Army Medical Center Museum, Washington, D.C.

Publications:

By JONES: Book—*Peintures—1937-1951,* Tourconing, France, Presses Georges Frere, 1952. **Article**—"Black Women in the Visual Arts," in *New Directions* (Washington, D.C.), 1976.

On JONES: Book—*The Life and Art of Loïs Mailou Jones* by Tritobia Hayse Benjamin, Pomegranate Books, 1994.

*

Loïs Mailou Jones comments:

I was inspired by Meta Warwick Fuller, Henry O. Tanner, and Harry T. Bunleigh to have an art career. Meta Fuller encouraged me to study in Paris as she had. I set my goal to study at the Académie Julian in Paris. This dream was realized when I received a General Education Board fellowship on my first sabbatical leave as a young teacher of design and watercolor painting at Howard University in 1937.

*   *   *

Loïs Mailou Jones has participated in the art world as a painter, book illustrator, textile and costume designer, and art teacher. In her career Jones overcame the prevalent gender and racial barriers, and through her continual development as an artist and her extraordinary teaching talent she became a prominent and influential advocate of African American art and artists. Many of her students have become major contemporary African American artists and art teachers. Jones's career as an artist spans nearly seven decades, and her paintings display several artistic styles, techniques, and types of subject matter, reflecting the various cultures she has encountered. While holding a teaching position at Howard University, Jones managed to produce a wide array of paintings and maintain an active career as a book illustrator. Her work has won dozens of prizes, and her paintings hang in major museums.

Jones's early works, such as *Young Girl (Rodin)* (1923) and *Nude* (1927), show an academic, carefully rendered approach to her subjects. *Negro Youth* (1927) won honorable mention in the Harmon Foundation exhibition in 1930. Jones's work during the early 1930s, like that of many African American artists at the time, was influenced by the exciting political and artistic arena of the Harlem Renaissance. During this time Jones expressed the black experience in her abstract symbolist painting *The Ascent of Ethiopia* (1932), inspired by a sculpture by Meta Vaux Warrick Fuller entitled *The Awakening of Ethiopia*. Much of the art in Europe and the United States at the time was influenced by the popularity of African art, and, similarly, many of Jones's paintings contained African themes. She was, in fact, one of the first African American women to include African themes in her work. One of Jones's best-known works is *Les Fétiches* (1938), a montage painting of African masks from five different regions. The masks, painted in subdued hues, are on a dark background and appear to be floating toward the viewer.

In 1937 Jones spent a sabbatical in Paris, where she painted landscapes, still lifes, and street scenes. *Déjeuner, Place du Tertre, Montmartre* (1937) and *African Bathers* (1937) are paintings done in the postimpressionist tradition of Paul Cézanne. For several decades Jones spent many summers in Paris, often painting on location. Even her late paintings of the French countryside, such as *La Route à Spéracédès* (1989), reflect the styles that Jones experimented with during her first years in Paris. During the 1940s Jones's palette became brighter and more colorful, and perhaps as a response to the influence of Alain Locke she painted subjects that reflected the personal circumstances of black people. *Jennie* (1943), *The Banjo Player* (1944), and *Mob Victim (Meditation),* also from 1944, are all emotionally provocative paintings.

Jones's work changed considerably after she married the Haitian artist Vergniaud Pierre-Noël and made Haiti her second home. While in Haiti, she painted the traditions, landscapes, and people in a postimpressionist style. Her style gradually became more modern and abstract, however, her palette became even brighter, and her work showed new themes, such as voodoo and spirits. *Cockfight* (1960) and *Vévé Voudou II* (1963) resemble the Russian abstract style, while *Mardi Gras, Haiti* (1961) is an abstract expressionist work. Other paintings from this period are cubist in their approach. Jones later added an obvious political content. *Haiti Demain?* (1987) portrays a nation in crisis, the dilemma of a race of people living among political corruption, starvation, a population explosion, and critical challenges to religious faith. In 1970 Jones visited several African countries, and she put her experiences on canvas. These paintings reflect regional African motifs, costumes, hairstyles, textiles, color combinations, and symbols. During this period Jones painted *Ubi Girl from Tai Region* (1972), one of her best-known works. The painting is of a Nigerian girl in ceremonial makeup along with two masks from Zaire and a fetish from the Ivory Coast.

All of Jones's work shows a strong sense of design. Her artistic styles show a progressive evolution, and throughout her career she has managed to experiment with and master a myriad of techniques. In the 1980s, toward the end of her career, she again painted in the impressionistic style she had put aside several decades earlier and produced several landscapes. Jones also produced *We Shall Overcome* (1988), a powerful montage painting of contemporary African American themes and topics in which images of prominent

Loïs Mailou Jones: *Petite Ballerina,* **1982. Photo courtesy of Marvin Jones.**

politicians, sports figures, and various celebrities are painted along with images of destruction—the KKK, drugs, and apartheid.

—Christine Miner Minderovic

JONES-HENDERSON, Napoleon
American weaver, printmaker, and quiltmaker

Born: Chicago, 23 November 1943. **Education:** American Artist Student Center, Paris, 1963, certificate 1963; Art Institute of Chicago, 1967-70, B.F.A. 1970; Northern Illinois University, Dekalb, 1972-74, M.A. 1974. **Career:** Art instructor, Malcolm X Community College, Chicago, 1970-72; professor, Massachusetts College of Art, Boston, 1974-78, Roxbury Community College, Massachusetts, 1984-87, Emerson College, Boston, 1986-89. Director of education, Museum of National Center of Afro-American Artists, Boston, 1975-76. Since 1978 executive director, Research Institute of African and African Diaspora Arts, Roxbury, Massachusetts. Artist-in-residence, Northeastern University, Chicago, 1978. Traveled in Haiti, 1981, and Barbados, 1982. **Awards:** Traveling Fellowship, School of the Art Institute of Chicago, 1971; Excellence Award, National Conference of Artists, 1982. **Address:** 12 Morley Street, Roxbury, Massachusetts 02119, U.S.A.

Exhibitions:

1980	South Side Community Art Center, Chicago
	United Nations, New York
	Third Floor Gallery, Atlanta, Georgia
1981	Museum of the National Center of Afro-American Artists, Boston
	Zenzele House Gallery, Chicago
1982	Tennessee State University, Nashville
1983	Boston Gallery, University of Massachusetts
	Carolyn Adams and Associates Gallery, Richmond, Virginia
	Zenzele House Gallery, Chicago
1984	Augusta Savage Gallery, University of Massachusetts, Amherst
	Mt. Holyoke College, North Hadley, Massachusetts
1988	Museum of Fine Arts, Boston
1990	Brandies University, Waltham, Massachusetts

* * *

Napoleon Jones-Henderson studied at the School of the Art Institute of Chicago and at Northern Illinois University. He has continued his education through a number of international residencies and fellowships. They have taken him to Africa and to countries in the Americas and have afforded him a rich grasp of the various roles played by the arts in other black societies. Through the Research Institute of African and African Diaspora Art, which he founded, he conducts research on and documents the black visual arts heritage.

Since the mid-1970s Jones-Henderson has been active in Boston as a textile and enamel artist, printmaker, and leather artisan. In addition to his activity as an artist, he has taught at several New

Napoleon Jones-Henderson.

England colleges and community-based institutions, including the Massachusetts College of Art, Roxbury Community College, and the Elma Lewis School of Fine Arts. Jones-Henderson is an activist who has played a leading role in the National Conference of Artists, one of the nation's oldest organizations of artists and art educators.

One of the original members of Africobra, Jones-Henderson has rooted his work in the aesthetic developed by that Chicago-based group, which in the late 1960s sought to find a visual language with the intensity and power of black soul music. Embracing artists working in media that ranged from textiles to photography, Africobra displayed a preference for bright colors, African and African American iconography, metallic paints, threads and foil, integration of text into the pictorial frame, and a nationalist cultural perspective. Since leaving Chicago, Jones-Henderson has remained a part of Africobra. The group's tenets may be seen in his work, although his expansive artistic development has come to be independent of it.

As a printmaker Jones-Henderson produces serigraphs, often in series. These works frequently share motifs with his textile and fabric art. In both media he commonly repeats images, thereby establishing strong rhythmic movements that he counterbalances with arcs of African zigzags and pyramidal and circular forms. The overall effect is highly patterned and improvisational in feeling. Through the use of metallic paints, inks, and threads in combination with bright colors, his works exude vitality and energy.

Since the mid-1980s Jones-Henderson has executed several ambitious, dramatic large-scale commissions. A series of huge highly patterned fans "à la Japan" (1988) are installed in the grand concourse of Boston's Black Falcon Passenger Ship Terminal. The fans are both imaginative and elegant in their presence. For the entrance to the library of Roxbury Community College, Jones-Henderson in 1987 executed a pair of eight-foot mahogany doors faced with enamel on copper images that interpret the theme "God, There Is Something in Heaven." The first of his grand works employing the delicate medium of enamel on copper, the doors anticipated his *Procession of the Ancients,* created in 1996 for the Providence Convention Center Authority in Rhode Island.

—Edmund Barry Gaither

JONES-HOGU, Barbara (J.)
American painter, printmaker, and sculptor

Work also appeared under the name Barbara Jones. **Born:** Chicago, 17 April 1938. **Education:** Howard University, Washington, D.C., B.A. 1959; Chicago Art Institute, B.F.A.; Illinois Institute of Technology, M.S.; Governor State University, Park Forest South, Illinois, 1992-93. **Family:** Married Jean-Claude Hogu, one child. **Career:** Clerk, Chicago Post Office, 1961-64. Teacher, Chicago Public High Schools, Art Institute High Schools, 1964-70. Currently professor, Malcolm X College, Chicago. Member, AFRICOBRA. **Awards:** Art history honor, Art Institute of Chicago, 1962; Art Institute of Chicago Scholarship, 1962-64; Malcolm X Umoja Award, 1973. **Address:** Malcolm X College, Humanities Department, 1900 West Van Buren, Chicago 60612, U.S.A.

Selected Exhibitions:

Howard University, Washington, D.C. (1970, 1972); Lakeside Gallery; Chicago; Malcolm X College Gallery, Chicago; National Center of Afro-American Artists, Boston (1970, 1972); Southside Community Art Center, Chicago; Studio Museum in Harlem, New York (1970, 1972); 353 East Gallery, Chicago; The Wall of Respect, Chicago.

Publications:

On JONES-HOGU: Articles—"Where Down Home Meets Back Home" by Jean B. Grillo, in *Boston after Dark,* September 1970; *Art Journal,* 33, Winter 1973/74, p. 139; *Art News,* 73, December 1974, p. 63; *Artforum,* 13, January 1975, p. 65; *Black Dimensions,* 1971, pp. 72-73; *Black Art: An International Quarterly,* 2(3), 1978, p. 19; *Black Creation,* 6, 1974/75, p. 20; "News," in *Black Shades,* 1, October 1970; "News," in *Black Shades,* 2(4), 1972; "News," in *Black World,* 19, October 1970, p. 82; *Essence,* 2, December 1971, p. 12; *Ms. Magazine,* 2, September 1973, p. 24; *National Conference of Artists Newsletter,* 3(2), 1977, p. 2.

*   *   *

Of the black protest artists, Barbara Jones-Hogu is one of the most outspoken. Her work shouts: *Unite; Black Men We Need You;*

Nation Time; Rise and Take Control; I'm Better Than You, M.F. A black nationalist, Jones-Hogu is an artisan of silk screening and printmaking. In the late 1960s and the 1970s she used her considerable skill to produce some of the most politically explicit message art done by a woman. Her more recent works, for example, *Love Is Unconditional—In All Forces of Nature There Is Love* (1993), continue to showcase her artistic skills, although she has come to make more subtle statements in her compositions. Jones-Hogu's control of her art comes through academic degrees in printmaking. Her skill as a printmaker is evident in her success with intricate designs, and she won a first prize in 1969 for her work.

During the black protest era the design of Jones-Hogu's lettered messages dominated all other graphic elements in her art. Many times Jones-Hogu overprinted the message throughout the entire composition. In *Rise and Take Control,* for example, the faces of three black men are covered with words. The positioning of the words in *I'm Better Than You, M.F.* (1970) clarifies the objects. In this serigraph a black woman and a blond woman are sitting opposite each other. The words "I'm better" are near the black woman, while the letters "M.F." surround the blond woman. The total printed message is "I'm better than these motherfuckers and they know it."

Jones-Hogu embraced the aesthetic standards of Africobra, the African Commune of Bad Relevant Artists, of which she was one of five founders in 1968. Africobra based its standards on connection with the black community. Jones-Hogu herself shocked the American art establishment and captured the attention of the black community. Her colorful, didactic poster art decorated college dormitory walls with instructions on how individuals should act to benefit African Americans. One such work was *Unite* (1970), which featured a group of black people with natural hairstyles, their arms and fists uplifted. The background consists of the word "unite" shaped like baseball team pennants. The overriding theme is blackness, and among the group of blacks there is no obvious distinction between men and women. The smooth color overlays and posterlike colors of *Unite* were noted in *Black Art: An International Quarterly.*

Criticism of Jones-Hogu's work takes issue with her message exclusively, never her technique. The message is integral to the design, but not as an exploration of typography. Rather, the lettering is stylized. She shows a decided preference for the curve of the circle, which is the symbol of community.

Jones-Hogu's work is informed by the political correctness of the late 1960s. Her nation-building activities knew few bounds. She could be found helping to paint the *Wall of Respect* mural on the South Side of her native Chicago, donating the proceeds from the sale of her art to the Union of Black Artists, working as an illustrator at the Third World Press, or teaching humanities at Malcolm X College in Chicago.

—Dedria A. Humphries Barker

JOSEPH, Tam
Dominican painter, sculptor, and graphic artist

Born: Thomas Helaire, Dominica, West Indies, 3 December 1947. **Education:** Central School of Art and Design, London, 1967; Slade School of Art, London, 1968, B.A. 1972; London College of Printing, 1973, DIPAD (diploma in typographical design) 1976. **Family:** Mar-

Tam Joseph.

Museum of Bastia, Corsica
Minories, Colchester, England
1994   Lancaster City Art Galleries, England
1996   Arts Factory, Islington, London

Collections:

Art Council of Great Britain; Bradford City Museum, England; Camden Library, England; Contemporary Art Society, London.

Publications:

On JOSEPH: Book—*Twentieth Century Painters and Sculptors* by Andrew Spalding, London, Thames and Hudson, 1989. **Article**—"Graphic Agitation" by Liz McQuistan, in *Phaidon Press,* London, 1994.

*

Tam Joseph comments:
     " . . . Thy will be done on Earth
     As it is in heaven . . ."

ried 1) Elizabeth Kayode in 1972 (divorced 1978), one son; 2) Francoise Christophe, one daughter. **Career:** Production manager, *Africa Journal,* London, 1976-84. Since 1994 social worker, Stamford House Security Unit, London. **Address:** 8 Burghley Road, London, N8 OQE, England; 6 boulevarde Talabot, Nimes 30000, France.

Individual Exhibitions:

1984   Barbican Centre, London
1986   Camden Town Hall and Library, London
1988   Newlyn Orion, Penzance, Cornwall
          Bedford Hill Gallery, London
1989   Showroom, London
          Smith Art Gallery, Sterling, Scotland
          Minories, Cochester, England
          Royal Festival Hall, London
1991   Greenwich Citizen's Art Gallery, England

Selected Group Exhibitions:

1986   Whitechapel Art Gallery, London
          Cartwright Hall, Bradford, England
1987   Prema Art Gallery, Old Mill Uley, Gloucestershire, England
          Bedford Hill Gallery, London
1988   Usher Art Gallery, Lincolnshire, England
1992   Glasgow Art Museum, Scotland
          Savannah Art Gallery, London

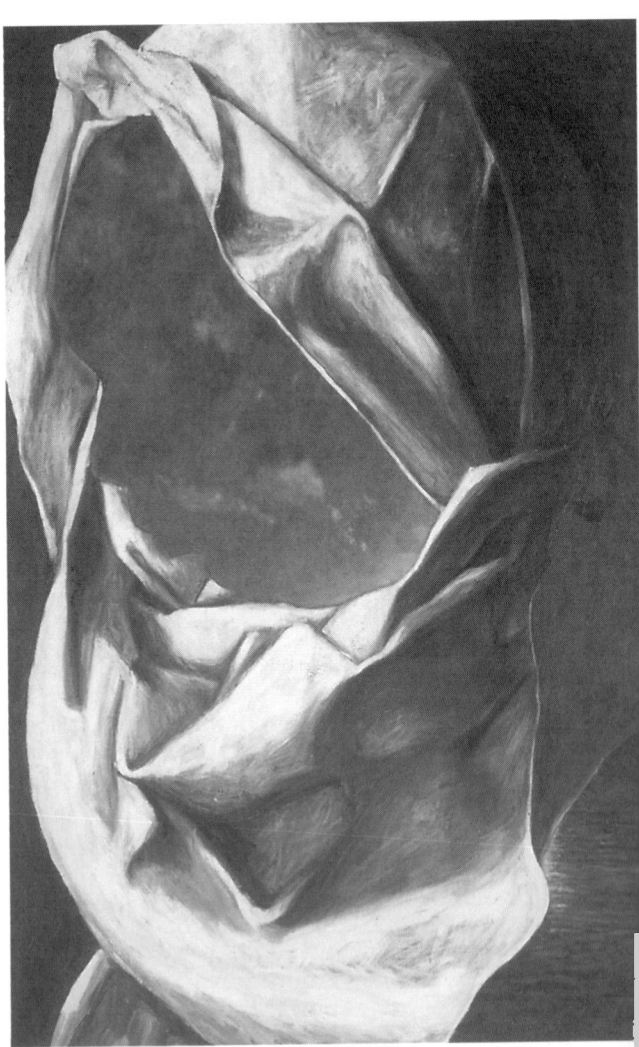

Tam Joseph: *Aqba,* 1993.

I'll go along with that.

*   *   *

Tam Joseph is a uniquely talented multidimensional artist. There are two primary reasons why, within the context of black artists in Britain, he is such a fascinating individual: his age and his distinctive style.

Joseph was born in Dominica in the Caribbean in 1947. He moved to London at the age of eight, eventually going on to fractious, unsatisfactory periods of study at London art colleges in the late 1960s. He has, since the end of that decade, maintained and developed his practice as a visual artist and sometime sculptor.

This makes him, on the one hand, too young to be linked to major figures in Caribbean and African art who made London their home in the decades immediately following the end of World War II. But Joseph is too old to be properly linked to the fiery, boisterous, young black artists typified by Keith Piper (born 1960) and Donald Rodney (born 1961), whose brand of "Black Art" descended like a whirlwind on Britain in the early 1980s. Quite possibly, it is for this reason that Joseph is very much his own man, his own painter.

The other reason for Joseph's uniqueness is that he stubbornly refuses to be typecast or pigeonholed. He considers nothing to be above or beyond his cutting, witty, and sometimes cynical observation. Once a subject has caught his eye, it cannot escape his canvas. Attempts have been made to link him to the 1980s Black Art movement, but Joseph calmly distances himself and his work from such a neatly identifiable arena. Joseph's position on himself and his practice can be summed up by his insistence that "I wasn't trying to develop a distinctly Black art. I was trying to develop myself as a person, through my art, and that's what I've been trying to do all the time." As an artist Joseph does not limit or restrict himself. He refuses to be perceived solely as a social commentator or political representative of his race. He draws his subject matter from wherever he chooses and executes his ideas in whatever medium seems appropriate.

At the same time, however, Joseph has contributed a number of memorable paintings that locate themselves at the center of sociopolitical commentary, often making work that shocks as it amuses, amuses as it shocks. Typical in this regard are paintings for which he is universally loved and respected, such as *Spirit of the Carnival* and *UK School Report.* The latter piece, subdivided into three portraits, shows the passage of a black youngster through the British educational system. In the first portrait the neat and tidy lad is "good at sports." In the second portrait the best that his teachers can say about him is that he "likes music." The third is inevitable: a few years of underachievement at school have put him on the "other" side of society and he "needs surveillance."

A more recent body of Joseph's work indicates another one of his unpredictable shifts in artistic direction. The work in question, collectively titled *Great White,* was described by Hiroko Hagiwara as "a series of picturesque and illusory landscapes, which induce us to quiet reflection" and signal a "move towards a more contemplative body of work." Hagiwara noted that "it may seem odd ... that an artist of Afro-Caribbean origin, should paint [sea]scapes of blue water and white shining icebergs." In truth, Joseph has *always* struck out on his own course. But witty takes on black "problems" or black "issues" continue to be the most engaging aspect of his practice. *White House Killings* is a recent painting that recasts the traditional tourists' map of Washington, D.C. Peppered throughout the northwest, northeast, southeast, and southwest quarters of the capital, literally surrounding the White House, are dozens of tiny figure motifs. It is only when we look closer and reference the figure motifs that we realize each one represents the "location of killings in 1991."

Joseph, though a champion of artistic independence, never forgets his African heritage. His Africanness is the starting point for his work; from there he can move in any direction he wants. As Joseph himself was quoted as saying: "I use total experience. I use every bit of what I see; almost every bit of what I know, to bring out something, but it's not coming from just one experience."

—Eddie Chambers

K

KAPO
Jamaican painter and sculptor

Born: Mallica Reynolds, Bynloss, Saint Catherine, Jamaica, 10 February 1911. **Family:** Married 1) Norma Atkinson in 1977, one daughter; 2) Sheila Tucker in 1978, one son and one daughter. **Awards:** Gold Medal, presented by Emperor Haile Selassie, 1966; Silver Musgrave Medal, Institute of Jamaica, 1969; Silver Medal, Jamaica Festival Exhibition, 1970; Gold Medal, Jamaica Festival Exhibition, 1972; Order of Distinction, National Honors, 1977; Norman Manley Award of Excellence, 1986; Gold Musgrave Medal, Institute of Jamaica, 1986. **Died:** 1989.

Individual Exhibitions:

1959	Juster Galleries, New York
1962	Hills Galleries, Kingston, Jamaica
1968	Kingston and Saint Andrew Parish Library, Kingston, Jamaica
1970	Institute of Jamaica, Kingston
1975	Just above Midtown Gallery, New York
	Stony Hill Hotel, Kingston, Jamaica
1980	Giammaca Gallery, Los Angeles
1982	National Gallery of Jamaica, Kingston

Kapo (Mallica Reynolds), c.1980. Photo courtesy of National Gallery of Jamaica.

Kapo (Mallica Reynolds): *Queen I Ras,* 1978. Photo courtesy of National Gallery of Jamaica.

Selected Group Exhibitions:

1968	Hills Galleries, Kingston, Jamaica
1975	*Ten Jamaican Sculptors,* Commonwealth Institute, London
1977	*Annual National Exhibition,* National Gallery of Jamaica, Kingston (and annually through 1989)
1978	*Four Jamaican Primitives,* Museum of Modern Art of Latin America, Washington, D.C.
1979	National Gallery of Jamaica, Kingston
1980	Museum of Modern Art of Latin America, Washington, D.C.
1982	Smithsonian Institution Traveling Exhibition Service (traveling through 1985)
1986	Commonwealth Institute and Wolverhampton Art Gallery, England
1987	National Gallery of Jamaica, Kingston

Collections:

Museum of the Americas, Washington, D.C.; National Gallery of Jamaica, Kingston; Stedelijk Museum, Amsterdam.

Publications:

On KAPO: Books— *The Intuitive Eye,* exhibition catalog by David Boxer and Rex Nettleford, Kingston, Jamaica, National Gallery, 1979; *Kapo: The Larry Wirth Collection,* exhibition catalog by Rodman Selden, Kingston, Jamaica, National Gallery, 1982; *Fifteen*

Intuitives, exhibition catalog by David Boxer, Kingston, Jamaica, National Gallery, 1987. **Articles—**"Kapo: Cult Leader, Sculptor, Painter" by Alex Gradussov, in *Jamaica Journal* (Kingston), 3(2), 1969; "Kapo" by Jean Small, in *Jamaica Daily News,* 23 May 1970.

*   *   *

Born Mallica Reynolds in Bynloss in Saint Catherine parish in Jamaica, Kapo, as he called himself, was totally self-taught as an artist. His highly intuitive art was an extension of his spiritual development, which led him into a life of service to his people as a religious leader.

Kapo's first paintings, done in the mid-1940s, were of traditional religious symbols depicted in a straightforward manner. In 1947, however, he was inspired by God in a dream to depict a scene from the Bible, and he produced his first important painting, a black Christ seated and reading the Scriptures by the Sea of Galilee. This and another important early painting demonstrate Kapo's attitude toward race. In *Two Angels,* the two figures face each other in a gesture of comradeship. One is painted white and the other black. On the reverse is inscribed the legend "If there are white angels in Heaven then there are black angels too." He soon abandoned painting for carving, primarily in wood but also in alabaster, producing for the next twenty years a remarkable oeuvre in sculpture that has few equals in Caribbean art.

Many of Kapo's sculptures—such as *Three Sisters* (c.1963), *Revival Goddess Dina* (1968), *The Flame* (1971)—draw on the intense emotionalism and the rhythms and gestures of Revivalism, a hybrid Afro-Christian religion. Kapo himself was a Revivalist shepherd and was eventually ordained as the patriarch bishop of the Saint Michael Revival Tabernacle. Other sculptures are simple portraits of acquaintances and members of his flock or of figures from African and Jamaican history—*Queen Candace* (c.1952), *Paul Bogle* (1952), *Paul Bogle and His Followers* (1966)—while still others depict family relationships and family loyalty—*Trouble Not* (1964), *Sisters in Love* (c.1964), *Obedience Covers All* (c.1965), *The Family* (c.1965). In their hierarchical, frontal presentation and in their proportions, many of his earliest sculptures recall traditional African carving.

Kapo began to paint again in the 1960s, and as his powers as a painter increased, his work in sculpture gradually diminished. As a painter he is best known for vibrant depictions of the Jamaican landscape—*Sweet Oranges* (1969), *Sunny Hill* (1971), *Orange Paradise* (1975)—in which houses and vegetation, with trees often bursting with ripe fruit, are arranged in splendid contrapuntal rhythms across backdrops of verdant fields and hills. It is in his figurative paintings, however, that his extraordinary inventiveness is best experienced. Again, Revivalism and his own role as a shepherd in the faith provided the inspiration for many of his best works. In *Revivalists* (1969) the viewer is swept up into the movement and sway of Kapo and his practitioners in the throes of a Revivalist ceremony, with many of the worshipers already "in the spirit." *There She Go Satan* (1974) is a virtual sermon on good and evil, in which Kapo himself, supported by subordinate shepherds, does battle with the forces of evil led by a beautiful bird-woman sorceress. In *Move Satan Move* (1974) the artist-shepherd battles for the soul of his estranged wife and takes on the devil himself. Formal, almost minimal portraits of women, usually members of his flock, exhibit a quiet dignity that is particularly moving, as in *Elena Ball* (1970).

Kapo also painted traditional Christian themes. Foremost among these is the moving *Crucifixion* (1967), in which Christ on the cross is isolated in a desolate, barren landscape; the solemn, highly formal *Dark Madonna* (1978); and the superb *Silent Night* (1979), in which the stacked dwellings of an imagined Bethlehem threaten to overwhelm the tiny Nativity scene. In all of these works the subjects are consistently portrayed as black people.

—David Boxer

KAYIGA, Kofi
Jamaican painter

Born: Ricardo Wilkins, Kingston, Jamaica, 1943. **Education:** Jamaica School of Art, Kingston, diploma 1966; Royal College of Art, London, M.F.A. 1971; Makerere University, Kampala, Uganda, 1971-73. **Career:** Assistant professor, Makerere University, Kampala, Uganda, 1971-73; chairperson, painting department, Jamaica School of Art, Kingston, Jamaica, 1973-81. Since 1981 professor, Massachusetts College of Art. Artist-in-residence, College of the Holy Cross, Worcester, Massachusetts, 1980-83; guest lecturer, University of Costa Rica, 1981, Institute of Contemporary Art, Boston, 1988. Since 1985 artist-in-residence, Northeastern University, AAMARP Department, Boston. Since 1985 artistic director and curator, Gallery Light Center, Cambridge, Massachusetts. Since 1993 commissioner, City of Cambridge Commission for the Arts for the Twenty-First Century. Co-founder, JUKA Arts, Inc. **Awards:** Graduate Scholarship Award (Royal College of Art, London), Government of Jamaica, 1968; Silver Medal, Festival Commission of Jamaica, 1969; Film Award for *Kayiga, the Artist in his Studio,* Jamaica Broadcasting Corporation, 1974; Second Prize for *Festival Costume Queen,* Festival Commission of Jamaica, 1975; College of the Holy Cross Travel and Research Fellowship, Worcester, Massachusetts, 1981; Massachusetts College of Art professional grant, Boston, 1982; grant for senior citizen murals, Massachusetts Council for the Arts, 1986; grant for publication, Massachusetts Council for the Arts, 1988; New England Foundation/National Endowment for the Arts Fellowship, 1991. **Address:** 197 Fayerweather Street, Cambridge, Massachusetts 02138, U.S.A.

Individual Exhibitions:

1967   Contemporary Art Gallery, Kingston, Jamaica
1969   Contemporary Art Gallery, Kingston, Jamaica

Kofi Kayiga. Photo courtesy of Tina Giannakopoulos.

Kofi Kayiga: *Vision Upwards,* 1990. Photo courtesy of Hakim Raquib.

1970	Kingston Parish Library, Jamaica
1971	Nomo Gallery, Kampala, Uganda
1972	West Indian Student Center, London
1973	Tom Redcam Library, Kingston, Jamaica
1974	Jamaica High Commission, Port of Spain, Trinidad
1975	Olympia International Art Center, Kingston, Jamaica (retrospective)
1976	Goblin Hill Hotel, Port Antonio, Jamaica
1977	Mutual Life, Kingston, Jamaica
1978	Bolivar Gallery, Kingston
1979	Mercer Arts Salon, New York
1980	Cinque Gallery, New York
1981	*Major Works,* Museum of the National Center of Afro American Artists, Boston
1982	Sala de Exposiciones, San Jose, Costa Rica, California
1983	Brownagree Gallery, Commonwealth Institute, London
1984	Museum of the National Center of Afro American Artists, Boston
1986	Frame Center Gallery, Kingston, Jamaica
1987	Gallery Light Center, Brookline, Massachusetts
1988	Mante Contemporary Arts, London
1989	Frame Center Gallery, Kingston, Jamaica
1990	Museum of African American Life and Culture, Dallas
1991	AAMARP Gallery, Northeastern University, Boston
1993	Blake Industries Gallery, Port of Spain, Trinidad
1994	Mutual Life Gallery, Kingston, Jamaica
1995	Julian Art Gallery, Mass Bay Community College, Wellesley
	Miller Gallery, Jamaica Art Center, New York
1996	Gateway 4, Newark, New Jersey

Selected Group Exhibitions:

1971	Sussex University, England
1982	Stores Gallery, Stanford, Connecticut
1983	Museum of the National Center of Afro American Artists, Boston
1988	Institute of Contemporary Art, Boston
1991	Virginia Museum of Fine Arts, Richmond
	Bromfield Gallery, Boston
1993	Cavin Morris Gallery, New York
1995	Cinque Gallery, New York
	Attleboro Museum, Massachusetts
1996	City without Walls, Newark, New Jersey

Collections:

College of the Holy Cross; Consulate of Jamaica; Makerere University, Kampala, Uganda; Museum of the National Center of Afro American Artists, Boston; National Bank of Jamaica; National Gallery of Jamaica; Olympia Hotel, Jamaica; Royal College of Art, London.

Publications:

On KAYIGA: Articles—"Kofi Kayiga's Rasta Rhythm" by Julie Kitchener, in *New Africa's London,* February 1983, p. 50; "Midsummer Delights and Ordeals" by Gloria Escoffrey, in *Jamaican Journal,* 1987, pp. 57-61. **Video**—"Kayiga: The Artist in His Studio," Jamaica Broadcast Service.

*   *   *

As a young art student in Europe during the 1960s, Kofi Kayiga refused to give in to his instructors when they attempted to discourage him from using bright primary colors in his paintings. When pushed to adopt the standard European style of color, Kayiga told one teacher, "I carry the colors of Africa and the Caribbean." Thirty years later, Kayiga is still carrying his banner of bright colors. In fact, the use of such colors has become his distinct trademark.

Born and reared in Kingston, Jamaica, Kayiga creates paintings that are a marriage of his Caribbean heritage and the strong spirituality he has developed as a student and teacher of African-inspired religion. This spirituality is evident in every painting he creates.

An artist whose style is abstract, Kayiga produces paintings that are surprisingly direct. His work is also so simplistic at times that it can be considered almost childlike in nature. Coupled with this simplicity are an energy and a vibrancy of color similar to a Fourth of July display, and his work sometimes appears to explode off the canvas into real life. His extensive travels throughout Uganda and Tanzania are a major presence in his work, and Kayiga's study of the teachings of the classical religions influences the figurative nature of his work.

Kayiga's work also tends to the sublime. In one particular painting, *Aunt May,* Kayiga shows a favorite relative. The piece is an abstract portrait of a woman in a contemplative pose who represents the power of the woman in African society. The shoulders of the woman are shown to be drawn inward by nature and old age, but her head is held high and she sits proudly erect. The green background represents her long life and the leaves of a tree that disappear each winter to reappear later with the first sign of spring. Many of Kayiga's pieces center around women and their influence in both African and American society.

Kayiga's lifelong study of spirituality and religion, particularly the tribal religions of West Africa, is a major focus in his work. In a stunning piece titled *Mask Anancy,* Kayiga explores the spirituality and passion of Africa. Named for the Ghanaian god Anancy, the work deals with the concealing and imbuing powers of another dimension. It symbolizes both the complexities of the sexual passion of lovers and the absence of beauty in a loving relationship.

In Ghanaian folklore Anancy is viewed as a trickster and spoiler of love. According to West African myth Anancy creates discord in the relationship of a husband and wife and pits brother against brother. With its uneven lines and wild eyes, this passionate painting does more than simply suggest these emotions. *Mask Anancy* screams the warning loud and clear in mysteriously light, confining colors that create a mysticism.

This journey into mysticism and the metaphysical concern and search for reality are what personify Kayiga's art. His gift for transforming these concerns on canvas makes him one of the most exciting and enigmatic Jamaican artists of his generation.

—Coria Holland

KEENE, Paul (F., Jr.)
American painter

Work appeared under the names Paul Keene and Paul F. Keene, Jr. **Born:** Philadelphia, 24 August 1920. **Education:** Philadelphia Museum School, 1939-41, certificate; Tyler School of Fine Arts, Temple University, Philadelphia, 1945-48, B.F.A., B. Sc. Ed. 1947, M.F.A. 1948; Academie Julian, Paris, 1948-52, certificate 1951. **Military Service:** United States Army Air Corp, 1941-45: second lieutenant. **Family:** Married Laura M. Keene in 1944, one son and one daughter. **Career:** Professor of art, Philadelphia College of Art, 1954-68, Bucks County Community College, Newtown, Pennsylvania, 1968-85. Graduate instructor, Tyler School of Fine Arts, Philadelphia, 1947-48; Director of Courses, Centre d'Art, Port-au-Prince, Haiti 1952-54. **Awards:** John H. Whitney Fellow, 1952-54; Temple University Award, Philadelphia, 1967; Alumni Award, Philadelphia College of Art, 1972. **Agent:** Sande Webster Gallery, 2018 Locust Street, Philadelphia, Pennsylvania 19103, U.S.A.

Individual Exhibitions:

1970	Wells College, Aurora, New York (retrospective)
	Montclair State College, Montclair, New Jersey (retrospective)
1974	Langman Gallery, Jenkintown, Pennsylvania (retrospective)
1976	Langman Gallery, Jenkintown, Pennsylvania (retrospective)
1980	Rosenfield Gallery, Philadelphia (retrospective)
1984	Bloomsberg University, Bloomsberg, Pennsylvania (retrospective)
1985	Buck County Community College, Newtown, Pennsylvania (retrospective)

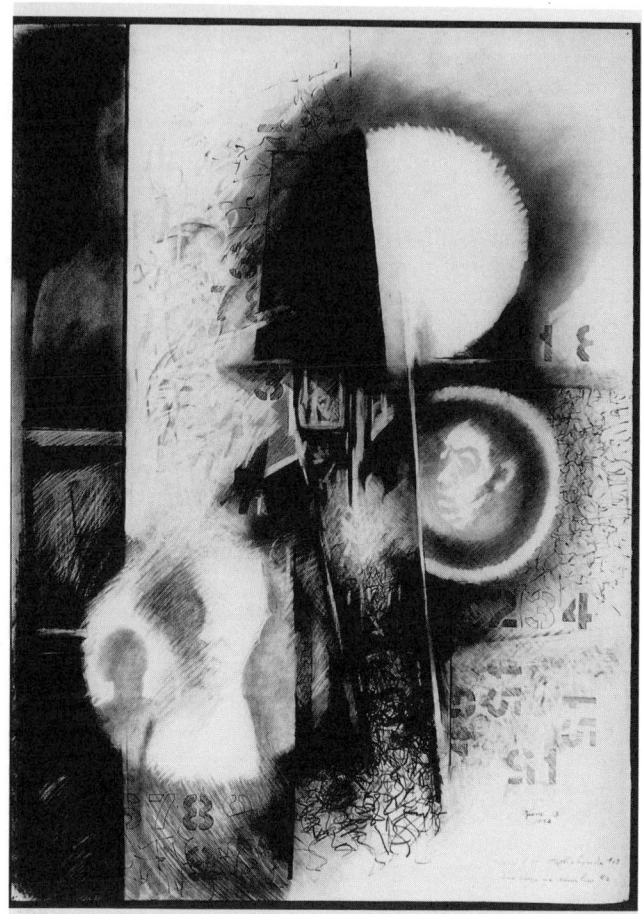

Paul Keene: from "Keepers of the Myths & Legends" series.

Paul Keene: from "Keepers of the Myths & Legends" series.

1990	Hahn Gallery, Philadelphia (retrospective)
	Afro-American History and Culture Museum, Philadelphia (retrospective)
1991	Michner Museum, Doylestown, Pennsylvania
1995	Ryder University, Lawrenceville, New Jersey

Selected Group Exhibitions:

1960	Roko Gallery, New York
1971	Carnegie Library, Pittsburgh, Pennsylvania
1972	Carnegie Library, Pittsburgh, Pennsylvania
1974	University of Pennsylvania, Philadelphia
1976	Harrisburg, Pennsylvania
1992	J. Bloch College, Philadelphia
	Philadelphia Art Alliance
1993	J.A. Michner Museum, Doylestown, Pennsylvania

Collections:

Afro-American History and Culture Museum, Philadelphia; Bowdoin College, Brunswick, Maine; Brandywine Workshop, Philadelphia; Centre d'Art, Port-au-Prince, Haiti; Dallas Museum; Delaware Museum, Wilmington, Delaware; Federal Reserve Bank, Philadelphia; Howard University, Washington, D.C.; J.A. Michner Museum, Doylestown, Pennsylvania; J.C. Smith University, Charlotte, North Carolina; Morgan State University, Baltimore, Maryland; Nigerian National Museum, Lagos; Pennsylvania Academy of Art, Philadelphia; Philadelphia Museum of Art; Tucson Museum, Arizona; Tyler School of Fine Arts, Temple University, Philadelphia.

*

Paul Keene comments:

Speculation is the only way possible for me to indicate why I follow one direction or another. Happenings on paper or canvas are predictable up to a critical point for me. Beyond this, intuition and instinct take over. I only know that any verbal statement can only give vague clues as to why I pursue a certain direction in working and thinking.

For me the subject matter simply becomes a vehicle used to help discover the mystery. Then the idea becomes the mystery that must be made real; it is the means by which I render some of what I assume I know with the unknown. I hang on and take the wild ride.

*　　*　　*

Paul Keene can be described as a strong abstract colorist and expressionist painter. Keene is known for both his abstract and realistic work, and at times he has managed to combine both. He has worked in both oil and watercolor. His teachings on art exemplify the concept of man's inhumanity to man. His numerous paintings can be divided into the following categories or periods: the Haitian period (1952-1954), the figurative period (1939-1949), the abstract period (1949-1958), the "Root-Man/Shango" series (1977-1978), and also the "Watercolor" series. The abstract painter will always have to dig deeper into his creative capabilities. Keene, however, has always provided the art world with pieces that show visions of sacrifice and movement towards a better experience. He leaves the viewer in deep thought. He was once quoted as saying that "the subject matter simply becomes a vehicle used to discover the mystery."

The Barrier, done in the early 1960s, is a portrayal of the time when civil rights activities intensified in the South and throughout the United States. Protesters marched and committed civil disobedience in the fight for equality for all people. In the painting one can see the weapons of oppression—the water cannon, the police barricades, and the beatings. This nonfigurative piece of social commentary uses a vast range of both warm and cool colors and shapes such as circles, squares, and rectangles to suggest a gathering of people. Keene often distorted figures for representation because he wanted the viewer to appreciate his work from a different angle. Many have questioned Keene's frequent use of circular shapes in his artwork, and he once stated, "I like circles." Keene wanted to avoid the oil paint medium because it irritated his skin, so he changed to watercolor, which became his preferred medium.

In his "Keeper of Myths and Legends" series, Paul Keene moved away from total social commentary and into mythology. He added faces of black men and also incorporated circles, which he maintained as a kind of signature. The faces are within circles and squares. He also combined the piece with the abstract theme of little shapes and combined elements, which can also be seen in *The Barrier.* Keene has stated that "Speculation is the way possible for me to indicate why I follow one direction or another. Happenings on paper or canvas are predictable up to a certain point for me." So it is easy for him to move in any direction in style and composition, and the viewer at one of his exhibitions does indeed see variety in Keene's paintings and prints.

Keene has exhibited in the United States and abroad and is represented in numerous collections. An abstract artist who continues to maintain his love for painting and expression, Keene acknowledges the social and economic barriers that are sometimes left untold and puts them down distinctively on paper.

—Gabriel Tenabe

KEITA, Souleymane

Senegalese painter, printmaker, and ceramist

Born: Gorée Island, Senegal, 17 April 1947. **Education:** École des Beaux Arts, Dakar, 1960-64; Atélier de Caramique, Dakar, 1964-67. **Career:** Tapestry designer, La Manufacture Nationale des Tapisserie, Thiès, 1963; director, Atélier de Ceramique, Dakar, 1964-67; professor ceramics and painting, Jamaica Arts Center, New York, 1984-85. Lives and works on Gorée Island. **Award:** Jerome Foundation Award.

Individual Exhibitions:

1969	Hall B.I.A.O., Banque, Dakar
	Centre Culturel Français, Dakar
1971	Centre Culturel Français, Nouachott, Mauritania
1972	Centre Culturel Français, Dakar
	Centre Culturel Français, Saint Louis, Senegal
	Maison du Parti, Libreville, Gabon
	Centre Culturel Français, Ouagdougou, Burkina Faso
1973	Maison du Parti, Libreville, Gabon
	Centre Culturel des USA, Dakar
1974	Maison des Arts et Loisirs Creusot, Loire
1975	Centre Culturel Français, Dakar
	Best of Africa Gallery, Toronto
1976	Centre Culturel Français, Saint Louis, Senegal
	Best of Africa Gallery, Toronto
	Phelps-Stokes Fund, New York
	Randall Gallery, New York
1978	Uptown Gallery, New York
	Jane Woodland, New York
	Spectrum IV Gallery, New Rochelle, New York
1979	Centre Culturel Français, Dakar
	Best of Africa Gallery, Toronto
	Spectrum IV Gallery, New Rochelle, New York
1981	Centre Culturel Français, Dakar
1982	Clorles Gallery, Brooklyn, New York
	Spectrum IV Gallery, New Rochelle, New York
1983	Kenkeleba Gallery, New York
	Diane Brewer Gallery, New York
	Colleen Goldberg Gallery, New York
	Robonart Gallery, New York
1984	Art Society of the International Monetary Fund, Washington, D.C.
1985	Exposition Prive Voyage au Mali, Gorée Island, Senegal
1987	Exposition Prive Aquarelle Centre Cultural, Senegal
1988	Souvenirs du Cap-Vert, Gorée Island, Senegal
1989	National Gallery of Art, Dakar
	Souvenirs du Cap-Vert, Gorée Island
1990	Gallery of Art, Gorée Island
1991	Espace d'Art, Paris

Selected Group Exhibitions:

1969	Semaine Senegalaise a Rabat, Morocco
1970	Nigeria Festival, Lagos
1974	Salon des Artistes du Senegal, Dakar
1976	Salon des Artistes du Senegal, Dakar
1977	Howard University, Washington, D.C.
1980	Spectrum IV Gallery, New Rochelle, New York
1982	Jazzonia Gallery, Detroit
1985	Schomburg Center for Research in Black Culture, New York
1987	Exposition Ceramique Almadies, Paris
1988	Musée National des Art Africains et Oceaniens, Paris

Collections:

Bellevue Hospital, New York; Centre Culturel Italien, Dakar; Citibank, Dakar; Museum of Art, Buffalo, New York; Schomburg Center for Research in Black Culture, New York; World Bank, Washington, D.C.

Publications:

On KEITA: Articles—"Souley Keita of Senegal" by Bob Barde, in *African Arts* (Los Angeles), 10(3), April 1977, p. 76; "Souleymane Keita, Senegalese Artist" by Faye Rice, in *Black Art: International Quarterly* (Jamaica, New York), 3(2), pp. 49-55 (illustrated); "Souleymane Keita, La representation de l'absolu" by Sankalé Sylvain, in SÉPIA-NEAS, France, 1994.

*   *   *

Souleymane Keita is an abstract painter who translates his vision of the landscape of his home, Gorée Island, Senegal, into a vibrant language of colors, symbols, and patterns. According to Grace Stanislaus, Keita takes "nature, music, and spiritualism" as his primary subject matter, and in his paintings he captures a life force of movement, growth, and activity surrounding him in the skies, waters, plants, and marine life of his island. There are a unique spontaneity and vitality in his use of multiple layers of curvilinear lines, spring-shaped forms, spirit writing, abstracted stars, fish, and leaves. These shapes, laid in a labyrinth of pattern and color, seem at once to emerge and disappear into the depths of the canvas.

A master of color, Keita works primarily with watercolor and oil paint. He uses both subtle tones and striking contrasts to achieve a finely tuned tension and balance in his compositions. Keita's expansive color palette ranges from varying shades of brown, burnt orange, saffron, evergreen, and cobalt blue to deep black, indigo, saturated red, and bright white. His remarkable manipulation of light and color gives his canvases tremendous depth, which in turn conveys a sense of a profoundly intimate expression of interior thoughts and spaces. As evident in the painting *Full Moon* (1989), Keita creates the sensation of an almost telescopic view of the expanse of the skies. Within this work he captures the elements of a universe remaking itself through the dynamics of a black hole, the lyrical dancing paths of the stars, and explosions of blinding white light and fiery orange red that leave behind remnants that become the new fabric of the cosmos. The painting is an excellent example of Stanislaus's observation that many of his works "are not considered abstract art but abstractions or close-up views of elements in nature." In addition, the writings of Amadou Hampaté Ba aptly describe Keita's artistic vision: "Synthesis of the universe and crossroads of vital energies, man is therefore called upon to be a point of balance, where, through him, all of the different dimensions he represents may flow. Then he will deserve the name of Mea-Kumanyon, the interlocutor of Maa-Ngala (the supreme being), and defender of creation's harmony."

Full Moon is also among Keita's large body of signature rondelle paintings. These round canvases are, as Ousmane Sow Huchard has said, symbolic of "the artist's preoccupation with infinity and the essence of the life-cycle." The shape of the canvases can also be interpreted as a metaphor for an island's contour and isolation. Clémentine Deliss has described Keita's circular paintings as "deep black holes into the sea off Gorée Island" that reveal "the tails of organisms flitting across space and the fishhook hieroglyphics of cultural memories, African memories buried deep in the sea-bed of this ex-slave-trading island off Dakar's shores." At the same time the circular shape is far more charged when used for the painting *Le Massacre des Tutsi* (1991). The presentation of ethnic conflict, death, and destruction as an ongoing cycle is a pointed critique of the long-standing history of violence that has formed and transformed contemporary African geography and identity. While it is not his most common choice of subject matter, Keita has been known to comment on social and intertribal conflict in other paintings, such as *Bougonn Boura* (1988).

Keita's work with abstraction and his extensive travels and exhibitions throughout the United States and Europe have played an important part in the worldwide recognition of contemporary African art. Following in the footsteps of other postindependence Senegalese masters such as Iba N'Diaye and Papa Ibra Tall, Keita and his contemporaries have been instrumental in adjusting the Western art world's perception that the only authentic African art is traditional and "tribal."

—Monique G. Curnen

KHALIL, Mohammad Omer

Sudanese printmaker and painter

Born: Burri, Republic of the Sudan, 1936. **Education:** School of Fine and Applied Art, Khartoum, Sudan, diploma in painting 1959; Academy of Fine Arts, Florence, Italy, 1963-66. **Career:** Instructor, Pratt Institute, Brooklyn, New York, 1971-83, Cultural Moussem, Asilah, Morocco, 1978-80, 1983-84, 1994. Since 1971 instructor, New School for Social Research, New York. Since 1991 instructor, New York University. **Awards:** Scholarship, Ministry of Education, Sudan, 1963-66; Society of American Graphic Artists Award, New York, 1979; Bronze Prize, *Osaka Triennial,* Japan, 1991.

Individual Exhibitions:

1987   Bronx Museum of the Arts, New York
1991   Galerie Teinturerie, Paris
1992   Institut du Monde Arabe, Paris
        Galerie Teinturerie, Paris

Selected Group Exhibitions:

1984   El Paso Museum of Art, Texas
        Tacoma Art Museum, Washington
1985   Toledo Museum of Art, Ohio
        Columbia Museum, South Carolina
1986   Alif Gallery, Washington, D.C.
1987   June Kelly Gallery, New York
1988   El Wasiti Gallery, Amman, Jordan
1992   Alif Gallery, Washington, D.C.
1993   Herbert F. Johnson Museum of Art, Cornell University, Ithaca, New York

Collections:

Bronx Museum of the Arts, New York; Chamaliers Museum, France; Grenoble Museum, France; Jordanian National Museum, Amman; Library of Congress, Washington, D.C.; Metropolitan Museum of Art, New York; Museum of History, Taipei; National Museum of African Art, Washington, D.C.

Publications:

On KHALIL: Book—*Mohammad Omer Khalil, Etchings and Amir I.M. Nour, Sculpture,* exhibition catalog, Washington, D.C., National Museum of African Art, Smithsonian Institution and Sylvia H. Williams, 1995. **Article—**"Skunder Boghassian and Mohammed Omer Khalil at the Contemporary African Art Gallery" by Calvin Reid, in *Art in America,* 82(3), March 1994.

* * *

Mohammad Omer Khalil began his career as a painter and still paints from time to time. His primary medium and passion, however, is printmaking. For the past twenty years he has concentrated on the art of etching, or intaglio. Although he has worked in a variety of print mediums, including silkscreen, wood and linocut, as well as lithography, none of them satisfies him like etching does. Khalil feels that etching is the closest creative process to painting. He loves the medium because of its qualities—the tactility, the textures, and the fact that color, especially the color black, seems to penetrate the surface of an etching. He feels that in etching one seems to be able to control the degree of blackness and thereby the sensuousness and mystery of the color and its darkness. He feels that the blacks in lithography are too flat and don't adequately penetrate the surface of the print.

Khalil explores the medium as one would an obscure landscape. His work has been inspired by the dramatic landscape forms and architectural structures of his native Sudan, as well as other exotic, beautiful places that are rich in history. His "Petra" series, executed between 1989 and 1990, was inspired by an ancient site in Jordan. The abstractions in this series evoke the natural forms and hint at the historical structures and desert vistas he encountered there. There are multicolored sandstone cliffs, rock formations, and an eclectic mixture of architectural styles. All of these elements seem to come together in the delicate poetic statements Khalil has rendered using the technique of chine colle, which is a method of attaching thin pieces of colored paper, lace, etc. to layers of paper as the inked image is being printed. In the "Petra" series he adheres thin sheets of rose-colored paper to the richly etched prints and uses black and white both for the strength of the composition and to reference the dark, the light, and the sense of antiquity he felt in the caves of Petra. This seems to be an expression of his personal philosophy—the ambiguity of life, the positives and negatives, the high and low points, and the brief seasons of balance between them. The processes involved in printmaking can also be applied to the way one lives life—a combination of experience, trial and error, and maneuvering and surviving through change. About the medium of etching, Khalil says, "The parameters of etching are limitless, endless."

Etching is a very involved process that marries the scientific process to the artistic. There is an element of experimentation, anticipation, and therefore excitement about what the outcome will be. All of this is based on how long the acid is allowed to bite into the plate and what specific processes of intaglio are employed, since each process produces its own unique visual quality.

The printmaking process of intaglio involves the artist's design being drawn, engraved, or cut into a an acid resistant substance known as "ground" on a metal plate made of either zinc or copper. The "bite" is caused by acid incising the exposed metal. The ground can be either hard or soft depending on which process the artist wishes to employ. According to Khalil, technique is the basis of printmaking.

Khalil executes every stage of his own etchings and combines a variety of processes, such as aquatint, which produces rich dark tones and other subtleties; soft ground, which allows the artist to impress a variety of materials to the plate and achieve different patterns and textures; and hard ground, into which linear shapes are drawn or scratched onto the surface of the plate. Lift ground, spit biting, and photoengraving are also used, and the chine colle technique provides varied surfaces.

Khalil has worked primarily with zinc plates, which bite quickly and are good for experimental effects but says he is considering working exclusively with copper plate because it is a harder metal with a more even texture and the potential for making larger editions.

Characteristics of his compositions include representation combined with nonrepresentation, creating mystery and ambiguity. His abstractions are grounded in reality and are emotions made visible. An analogy would be to compare these works to music, which is often inspired by and evocative of an emotional response. In his "Dylan" series, for example, his compositions include his emotional responses while listening to the music of Bob Dylan. He combines his technical and conceptual ideas to create these provocative works.

The "Dylan" series is not, as Khalil says, "an illustration of Bob Dylan's lyrics." But rather it represents "my feelings of the music while I was working. All the pieces that you see here, they do not represent Dylan; they represent me." There are seven prints in the series. *Dirge* and *It Ain't Me Babe* are both compositions in which his intent is to convey strong emotional feelings.

Dirge was Khalil's artistic reaction to his father's death. The composition is built around the calligraphic representation of the Arabic word for "father." Khalil remarked that he used the written image in his composition as an abstract visual symbol, as much for its meaning as for its design qualities. He then executed the composition using color plates and collage to create *The Jack of Heart*.

It Ain't Me, Babe is the first print for which Khalil used two plates and two sheets of paper to create one image. Again his reasoning is both technical and conceptual. Graded tonalities, pattern, and texture provide a rich subtext for the unfolding story,

which has to do with the end of a complex relationship. The vertical composition seems to symbolize the lowering of a portiere and thus the ending of a season of experiences for the artist and for the viewer. Yet one eagerly awaits the next sojourn in the boundless horizons of Mohammad Khalil's art.

—Nashormah N.R. Lindo

KINGELEZ, Bodys Isek
Zairian sculptor

Born: Kimbenbele-Ihunga, Zaire, 27 August 1948. **Career:** Professional art restorer, Institut des Musées Nationaux du Zaire. **Address:** Institut des Musées Nationaux B.P. 4249, Kinshasa II, Zaire.

Individual Exhibitions:

1991   Jean-Marc Patras Galerie, Paris
1992   *Bodys Isek Kingelez: Architekturvisionen aus Zaire,* Haus der Kulturen der Welt, Berlin

Selected Group Exhibitions:

1989   *Magiciens de la Terre,* Centre Georges Pompidou, Paris
1991   Centro Atlantico de Arte Moderna, Las Palmas de Gran Canaria, Spain (traveling)
1993   Museum for African Art, New York

Collections:

Institut des Musées Nationaux du Zaire.

Publications:

On KINGELEZ: Books— *Home and the World: Architectural Sculpture by Two Contemporary African Artists,* exhibition catalog, New York, Museum for African Art, 1993.

*   *   *

The Zairean sculptor Bodys Isek Kingelez is a self-trained artist with a singularly distinctive vision. His work is best described as architectural sculpture. Employing materials such as paper, card stock, polystyrene, and plastic, he produces sculpture that resembles architectural models. The inclusion of a presentational base underscores their reading as architectural proposals. Kingelez's works bear a strong visual relationship to the appearance of postmodern architecture. The unusual geometric forms, curvilinear and baroque details, and use of color and surface design all parallel the whimsical play of a postmodern vocabulary. Collectively his models are also reminiscent of early to mid-twentieth-century modernist architecture constructed for world fairs and international expositions. Works such as *Mongolique Sovietique* (1989) and *Palais Hiroshima* (1991) suggest the context of a pavilion at an exposition, while *Kimbembele City* (1993) and *Kimbembele-Ihunga (Kimbéville)* (1993-94) present modernist utopian re-creations named after the town where the artist was born.

Although Kingelez's models resemble a number of architectural styles, closer scrutiny reveals that they are purely fictive structures—technical impossibilities. The models form an architecture of the artist's own invention, closely allied to a personal vision and ideology. His work can be seen as purely imaginative—architectural fantasies bordering on the naive. His choice of materials, technical skill in execution, and formal presentational style, however, mitigate the distance between a fantasy construction and the reality of a model for a proposed structure. Kingelez calls his works *les extrêmes maquettes* (extreme, or final, models). Each model is signed, dated, and titled, often with the title in the form of an emblem or logotype affixed to the building's spire, facade, or rectangular base. An accompanying narrative written by Kingelez is also included with each model. For example, *Stars Palme Bouygues* (1989) was created as a challenge to the French architect Francis Bouygues. Many of Kingelez's models display witty and playful references to the exterior world. *Papillon de Mer* (1990-91), for example, resembles two intersecting butterflies with a central projecting spire, and *Etoile Rouge* (1990) is a fanciful monument dedicated to the city of Brazzaville, Congo. While his works borrow from a number of modern and postmodern sources as well as from Asian and non-Western styles, they do not incorporate indigenous Central African architectural forms.

In the 1980s Kingelez was employed in the objects restoration department of Zaire's national art museum (Institut des Musées Nationaux). He refined his technical skills in order to make the restoration of masks and other objects of traditional Zairean art invisible to a discerning eye. His mastery and command of fragile materials is evident in his own works.

Kingelez's work first came to prominence in the 1980s, especially with the international exhibition *Magiciens de la Terre,* held in Paris in 1989. The artist has created well over three hundred models. The examples dating from the late 1980s and early 1990s, which are the best known of his works, are largely held in private collections.

—Patricia J. Darish

KNIGHT, Gwen

American painter and printmaker

Work also appeared under the names Gwendolyn Knight, G. Knight L., and Gwendolyn Lawrence. **Born:** Gwendolyn Clarine Knight, Bridgetown, Barbados, West Indies, 26 May 1913. **Education:** Howard University School of Fine Arts, Washington, D.C., 1931-33; New School for Social Research, New York, 1960-66; Skowhegan School of Painting and Sculpture, 1968-70. **Family:** Married Jacob Lawrence in 1941. **Awards:** Caucus Centennial Medallion, Black Caucus, Centennial Award of Merit, Arizona State University, 1984; National Honor Award, Women's Caucus for Art; Pioneer Award, Twelfth Annual Artists' Salute to Black History Month, 1994. Honorary doctorates: University of Minnesota, Seattle University, 1996. **Agent:** Francine Seders Gallery, 6701 Greenwood Avenue, North, Seattle, Washington 98103, U.S.A.

Individual Exhibitions:

1976	Seattle Art Museum
1988	Virginia Lacy Jones Gallery, Atlanta University Center, Atlanta, Georgia (retrospective)
1994	Francine Seders Gallery, Seattle

Selected Group Exhibitions:

1994	St. Paul Companies, St. Paul, Minnesota
1995	SAFECO, Seattle
	Washington State Convention and Trade Center, Seattle
	Florence Valore Miller Arts Center, Atlantic City, New Jersey
	Pacific Arts Center's Anne Gould Jauberg Gallery, Seattle
	North Seattle Community College
	Painted Table, Seattle
	Bellevue Art Museum, Bellevue, Washington
	Sande Webster Gallery, Gettysburg College, Pennsylvania
	Howard University Gallery of Art and Fondo del Sol Visual Arts Center, Washington, D.C.
	Bellevue Art Museum, Bellevue, Washington
	Center for the Fine Arts in Miami, Florida
1996	Plaza Pasadena, Pasadena, California

Collections:

Atlanta University, Georgia; Hampton University, Virginia; Hawthorne Elementary School, Seattle; King County Art Commission, Seattle; Microsoft, Redmond, Washington; Museum of Modern Art, New York; North Sound Evaluation and Treatment Center, Sedro Woolley, Washington; SAFECO, Seattle; St. Louis Art Museum, Missouri; St. Paul Companies, St. Paul, Minne-

Gwen Knight, 1992. Photo courtesy of Spike Mafford.

It is not so much "who has influenced one" as what kinds of art have intrigued and given pleasure and inspiration. For myself I would say West African sculpture because it is powerful and mystical; Asian drawings for their linear beauty and economy of means; and the impressionist school for its use of color and subtlety.

*　　*　　*

Evolving from a creative temperament that was carefully nurtured at a tender age, Gwen Knight presents her imagery in a way that reflects imaginative thinking and a unique vision. She is not a storyteller, yet her work communicates an interest in the mundane and the extraordinary events of everyday life. Her engaging visual interpretations pay close attention to her personal experiences and, in viewing them, translate into our own.

Knight's formal training began in the 1920s at Howard University where she encountered Lois Mailou Jones and James Lesesne Wells, both of whom encouraged and supported her desire to become a painter. After her sophomore year Knight had to leave Howard and return home to Harlem. Though a disappointment, an extremely significant turning point in Knight's life was taking place. Despite the country's tremendous economic depression, Harlem was still a place where art and creativity flourished. There, at a WPA artists' workshop, Knight would meet two of the most important individuals in her life and career: Augusta Savage, her teacher and mentor, and Jacob Lawrence, her artist-husband of over forty years.

Since the beginning of her career Knight has been interested in line and movement, gaining most of her inspiration from African sculpture, the impressionists, dance, and theater. She studied dance and has experimented with other media including clay and printmaking. Her main body of work, however, consists of portraits and still lifes in oil. In the portrait *Augusta Savage,* Knight conveys her continued reverence for her mentor, lovingly capturing Savage in a contemplative gaze. Knight's painting portrays a nobility in Savage's expression that articulates her triumphs and failures. With warm colors and long, careful brush strokes, Knight describes Savage on canvas in a manner that comes from knowing and admiring her at a deeply personal level.

Knight has lived and worked during two distinctive periods in the history of African American art: the Harlem Renaissance and that more recent surge of activity in the 1960s and 1970s expressive of a social, political, and cultural awareness. Sometime during the 1960s Knight became considerably intrigued with the work of West African sculptors. During an extended stay in Africa, Knight had the opportunity to meet African artisans and actually witness works of art being made. In *African Memories* she incorporates stylization reminiscent of Yoruba sculpture of Nigeria. The male and female figures in this composition are painted in a manner that demonstrates Knight's ability to capture the essence of the African people. The geometric shapes and grayish brown tones of *Mask IV* incorporate the abstractionism of traditional African aesthetic forms that created the foundation for the development of Cubism. This painting deftly fuses her African and impressionist influences.

Her preoccupation with movement and line are evident in her drawings, figure studies, and monoprints done between 1992 and 1994. In *Dancer with Drapery,* Knight's experimentation with line and movement is articulated in sharp and forceful diagonals sweeping across the picture plane, defining the draped body of the dancer. In *Two Dancers,* Knight explores printmaking as an alternative medium. This monoprint depicts two leaping female figures. The

Gwen Knight: *Dancers I,* 1992. Photo courtesy of Chris Eden.

sota; Seattle Art Museum; Seattle Arts Commission; Seahurst Elementary School, Seattle; Sunrise Elementary School, Kent, Washington; Weisman Art Museum, University of Minnesota, Minneapolis.

Publications:

On KNIGHT: Books—*Gwendolyn Knight,* exhibition catalog, Atlanta, Georgia, Virginia Lacy Jones Gallery, 1988; *Significant Others: Artist Wives of Artists* by Amy Wolf, New York, Kraushaar Galleries, 1993. **Articles**—"Notes on Gwen Knight: A Painter" by Barbara E. Thomas, in *Francine Seders Gallery Quarterly Newsletter,* Fall 1987; "Knight Is Content with Artistic-Shadow Role" by Deloris Tarzan Ament, in *Seattle Times/Seattle Post-Intelligencer,* 18 October 1987; "Gwendolyn Knight Stands on Her Own with Retrospective" by Catherine Fox, in *Atlanta Journal,* 19 January 1988; "Gwendolyn Knight: A Portfolio and Conversation" by Charles H. Rowell, in *Callaloo,* 37(11/4), 1989.

*

Gwen Knight comments:

Follow your vision and observe, observe, observe. Do works about the things you have experienced and your feelings about them; use your strengths. If you draw well, use drawing. If you are a colorist, use that skill. Whatever you do best, use that, then work on your weaknesses.

agile, acrobatic forms illustrate her fascination with motion and convey the pleasure she derives from observation.

The visual diary of Gwen Knight is a lyrical documentary of her interests in life's ephemeral moments. It is difficult to look at her paintings and not be affected by their bold colors and arousing figures. For more than forty years Knight has painted from her experiences and has developed an idiom that subtlely reflects themes that are familiar to all.

—Regina Holden Jennings

KODI, Khalid (Ibrahim)

Sudanese painter, illustrator, graphic artist, and installation artist

Born: Sudan, Jazira, City of Wadmadni, 1 January 1962. **Education:** Khartoum Polytechnic College of Fine and Applied Art, Khartoum, Sudan, 1982-87, B.F.A. 1987; Massachusetts College of Art, Boston, 1991-93, M.F.A. 1993. **Career:** Since 1992 Art educator, Museum of the National Center of Afro-American Artists, Boston. Since 1995 adjunct professor, Boston College.

Art instructor, Art Institute of Boston, 1995. **Awards:** Sudanese Cultural Foundation Festival Award, 1985; Seventh Arab Youth Festival Award, Khartoum, Sudan, 1989; General Exhibition Award, Abudhabi, United Arab Emirates, 1990; First Place Award in Creativity, First Annual African American Show at New England School of Art and Design, 1992; Fine Art Graduate Book Award, Massachusetts College of Art, Boston, 1993; Liquitex Excellence in Art Award, Massachusetts College of Art, Boston, 1993. **Address:** Post Office Box 1683, Jamaica Plain, Massachusetts 02130, U.S.A.

Individual Exhibitions:

1986	Tehraga Hall, Alexandria, Egypt
1987	Gazira University, Wad Madui, Sudan
1988	Goethe Institute, Khartoum, Sudan
1990	The Cultural Foundation, Abudhabi, United Arab Emerites
1992	Museum of the National Center of Afro-American Artists, Boston
1994	Medani Estudio, Galleria de Arte, Madrid, Spain
1995	Renaissance Art and Design Gallery, Boston
1996	AAMARP Gallery, Boston

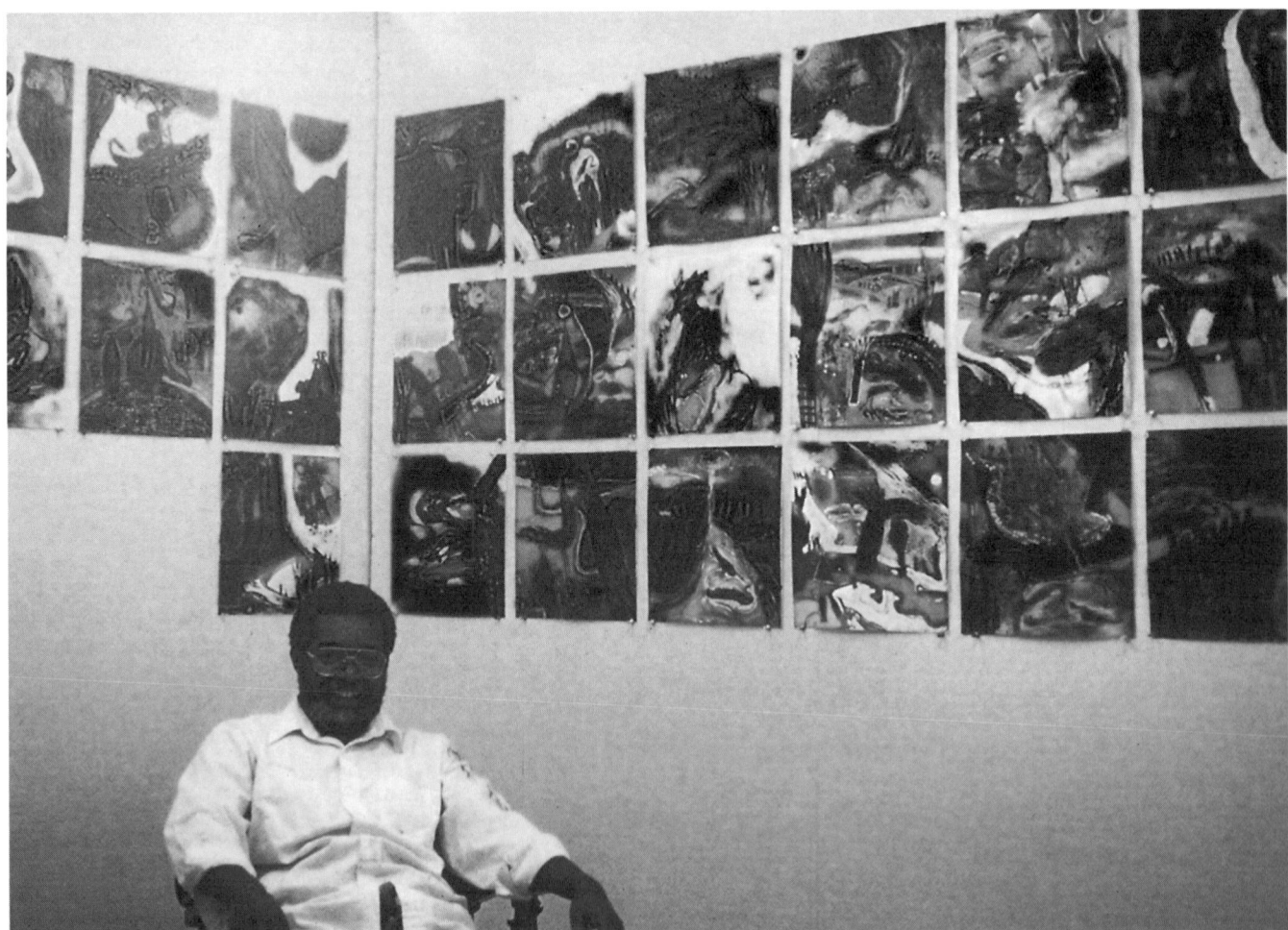

Khalid Kodi, 1993. Photo courtesy of Rashed Ranna.

Selected Group Exhibitions:

1990   Cultural Foundation, Sharjah, United Arab Emirates
        India Center for the Arts, Bombay
1994   Boston Public Library
        Centro de Informacion y Documentatcion, Madrid, Spain
        AAMARP Gallery, Boston
1995   Attleboro Museum, Massachusetts
        Cinque Gallery, New York
        McCrorey Gallery, University of Vermont, Burlington

Collections:

Cultural Foundation, Abudhabi, United Arab Emerites; Goethe Institute, Khartoum, Sudan; Howe Library, University of Vermont, Burlington; Massachusetts College of Art, Boston; Museum of the National Center for African-American Artists, Boston; National Center for Art and Letters, Khartoum, Sudan; Renaissance Art and Design Gallery, Boston; School of Fine Art, Khartoum, Sudan; Tehraga Hall, Alexandria, Egypt; United Arab Emerites Art Society, Sharjah.

Publications:

On KODI: Articles—"Sudanese Artist Fuses Ancient with Modern" by Edward Stricland, in *Bay State Banner* (Boston), 2 July 1992; "Artist's Work is Proof of 'Nubian Legacy'" by Joanne Silver, in *Bay State Banner* (Boston), 2 July 1992; "A Triangle of Abstractions" by Edward Stricland, in *Jamaica Plain Gazette* (Boston), 8 April 1994; "Khalil and Khalid" by Stash Horowitz, in *The Back Bay Courant* (Boston), 23 July 1996; "Artist Gives Arabian Theme" by Kay Bourne, in *Bay State Banner* (Boston), 7 March 1996.

*

Khalid Kodi comments:

I choose to be a painter because it is the best way to express myself. My work reflects my visual history and education—a marriage of African imagery, tradition, and concepts with my western knowledge of art. The beauty of natural creation which I see with my eyes is the language of reality. Yet the oral tradition of my grandmother's tales fills my mind with images of ancient kingdoms and long past Nubian ways. From foreign places and spaces, I add new tradition, philosophies, and arts . . . dance, music, and crafts. From inner spaces I construct a worldview molded by philosophy, metaphysics, spirituality, and my own consciousness of being.

All of this converges as I find my true language to be that of the visual artist. Art thus transcends all other languages as I create my visions in the "magical" realism of my own space. In the process I destroy old space and translate/integrate others' visions of nature into my own. I freely play with colors, shapes, textures, and spaces until my inner vision fills its own space. My art is therefore the documentation of my inner vision revealed for all to see; it is my own version of nature in its space.

*   *   *

Khalid Kodi is a Boston-based Sudanese painter, illustrator, and graphic designer whose works have graced magazines and newspapers in the Sudan, the Persian Gulf states, and the United States. He is representative of a younger generation of Sudanese artists whose work continues to broaden the scope of the Sudanese contemporary art movement while enriching and bringing a fresh perspective to the international art scene. The major corpus of Kodi's works, as he himself asserts, are explorations of his artistic legacy, cultural heritage, and oral traditions as a Sudanese. Executed in an abstract expressionist style, his work represents an infusion of Western modernist conventions and the visual vocabulary of colors, symbols, and calligraphic motifs developed by the pioneers of the Sudanese modern art movement known as the Khartoum school. As with other Sudanese artists, Kodi's works are full of multiple references that range from ancient Nubian architectural designs, calligraphic motifs, and urban and rural Sudanese landscapes to African masklike figures, and hence they invite multiple interpretations. Kodi is also a musician who tries his hand at the lute, an instrument he often plays at openings.

Kodi was born into a family of prominent musicians and artists in the city of Wad Madani, a provincial capital. He decided at an early age upon a career as an artist, and he studied painting at the College of Fine and Applied Arts in Khartoum, where he graduated in 1987. After a short period of travel, exploration, and work in Egypt, Saudi Arabia, and the United Arab Emirates, Kodi emigrated to the United States in the early 1990s and continued his studies at the Massachusetts College of Art in Boston, where he earned a master's degree. Since then he has continued to live in Boston, and he teaches at Boston College.

As Kodi himself has asserted, the influences in his work come from whatever he can see and observe. His work brings disparate elements together. At the same time one can easily see and sense the magical vision that gives his work a distinct style characterized by a dreamlike world of colors, forms, and textures. Of his work Kodi observes, "My visions begin and end in magical realism." Space for him is where the miracles of nature have materialized, from which he draws his visions. The works included in his early solo exhibition at the National Museum of Afro-American Artists in Boston in 1992, entitled *The Nubian Legacy in Contemporary Art,* is an example of his creative synthesis. Dedicated to the exploration of his Nubian heritage, the exhibition included a group of mixed-media paintings with heavily textured surfaces created by the innovative use of collages of paint, paper, and built-up areas of modeling compound and sand. The reference to Nubia evoked loss, memory, and dreams, but it also emphasized the artist's desire to assert his present identity. The series of drawings entitled "Sheba" demonstrate Kodi's preoccupation with space in formal, psychic, and spiritual senses. Using a linear perspective, these drawings show Sudanese town spaces with intricate architectural and masonry details. Although the drawings are articulated in a descriptive physical manner, they also convey the memories that haunt the imagination of a child listening to stories of times gone by. In contrast, the space in the painting *Queen of Sheba* turns into something spiritual and fantastic, with objects and human figures floating in a Chagall-like manner, in which things merge and move about without the limitation and fixity of physical space.

Kodi continued to explore the magical world of ancient stories in his series entitled "A Thousand and One Nights," exhibited at the Art Gallery of Northeastern University in Boston in May 1996. The paintings included in the exhibition represented his continued interest in old stories, with images gleaned from the well-known tales invoking the magical atmosphere of the Arabic-Persian medieval world. Since then Kodi has begun to explore the genre of con-

Khalid Kodi: black-and-white drawing on paper, 1993.

ceptual art in a series of installations that combine paintings, sculpture, music, and live performances and that are dedicated to Sudanese and African refugees. This development has seemed to usher in a new direction in Kodi's artistic career, one in which he is clearly influenced by contemporary trends in the international art world, with which he keeps in close touch.

—Salah Hassan

KOFI, Vincent (Akwete)

Ghanaian sculptor

Born: Odumasi-Krobo, Ghana, 1923. **Education:** Achimota College, graduated 1951; Royal College of Art, London, 1952-55; Columbia University, New York, 1959; Sculpture Center and Ceramics Workshop, New York. **Career:** Art teacher, Prempeh College, Kumasi, Winneba Teacher Training College, 1961-69. Department head, College of Art, University of Science and Technology, Kumasi, Ghana. Commissioned sculptor for two fountains, State House, Accra. **Awards:** Study grant to Columbia University, United States Government, 1959; Hammond Foundation grant. **Died:** 1974.

Individual Exhibition:

1963   *Vincent Kofi Sculpture,* Mbari, Ibadan, Nigeria

Selected Group Exhibitions:

Accra, Ghana (1964); Akuafo Hall, University of Ghana, Legon; Camden Arts Center, London; *Contemporary African Art,* London (1969); Festival of Negro Arts, Dakar, Senegal; First International Congress of African Culture, National Gallery, Salisbury, Rhodesia (1962); Hampton Institute, Virginia; Lagos, Nigeria; Phelps-Stokes Fund, New York (1961-62); University College, Ibadan; University of Ghana, Legon; World Festival of Negro Arts, Dakar, Senegal (1968).

Collections:

Akuafo Hall, University of Ghana, Legon; Harmon Foundation Collection, Hampton University Museum, Virginia; Parliament House, Accra; School of Administration, University of Ghana, Legon; State House, Accra.

Publications:

By KOFI: Book—*Sculpture in Ghana,* Ghana Information Services, 1964.

On KOFI: Books—*Traditional Background of Contemporary African Art: A Study in Detail of Ghana's Vincent Kofi* by Marilyn E. Thornton, 1973; *Vincent Kofi, 1923-1974: A Critical Biography of an African Artist* (masters thesis) by Gilbert Amegatcher, Indiana University, 1992 (illustrated). **Articles**—"Vincent Akwete Kofi: A Sculptor from Ghana" by Ulli Beier, in *Black Orpheus* (Ibadan), 9, June 1961, pp. 35-36 (illustrated); "Mbari Exhibitions: Vincent Kofi, Sculpture, Mbari, Ibadan" by Denis Williams, in *Black Orpheus* (Ibadan), 13, November 1963, pp. 61-62; "Ghana's Vincent Kofi" by Lawrence Grobel, in *African Arts* (Los Angeles), 3(4), Summer 1970, pp. 8ff; "Vincent Kofi" by Lawrence Grobel, in *African Arts* (Los Angeles), 8(3), Spring 1975, p. 8 (illustrated); "For Kofi (1923-1974): To Weep without Eyes" by Roy Watts and Peggy Watts, in *Transition* (Accra), October 1975, March 1976; "Samtal med Vincent Kofi" by Maxine Lautre, in *Modern Konst I Afrika: Modern Art in Africa*, Lund, Kalejdoscop, 1978 (illustrated); "Vincent Kofi (1927-1974)" by Kojo Fosu, in *20th Century Art of Africa*, Zaria, Gaskiya, 1986, 106-08 (illustrated).

*   *   *

Within the short span of his life, Vincent Kofi produced a body of work that solidified his place in history as the preeminent sculptor of Ghana. As Lawrence Grobel noted, Kofi sculpted through the conceptualization of four guiding principles—inspiration, conceptualization of form, application of technique, and the factor of recognizability. Using those principles, he worked with sculptural processes in carving, casting, and molding that brought pure plasticity to life. But it was the medium of wood that Kofi preferred, and it was wood in which he produced his most monumental and vital forms. Those works are characterized by what Charles Harrison calls a "three-dimensionalness" and "immanent vitality" that are recognized as proscriptions for modernism. Such qualities, however, coincide with those of African sculpture. Modernist sculptors and traditional African sculptors, the former influenced by the latter, meet at this confluence. Kofi, the modernist and Ghanaian/African, drew upon the plastic structures of both to affect an original style. This style emerges from his search for the inner life of form, which is found primarily through external observation of the natural environment, internal reflection, and the enactment of his guiding principles.

Kofi's process of sculpting wood began with the examination of the structure and mass of his selected material and concluded with the resolve of the potentiality of his struggle. His forms consistently display an organic quality that is balanced by volumetric weight and linear delicacy. The human figure, in its generalizable form and recognizable themes, constitutes the fundamental continuity in his work. Formulated on ideals of resemblance to the natural body, each work is abstracted to an organic, elemental form. The most well-known works, outside of the bronze *Awakening Africa* (1959-60), are massive sculptures that consist of a contained energy, intensity, and fluidity, displaying an organic power enhanced by accentuating surface textures. *Awakening Africa*, though small in scale, also has those qualities.

Resulting from Kofi's balance of visual and conceptual experience, the forms are solidified in a massive verticality, revealing both a formalist truth to materials and emotional elements in themes of religion (as in *Christ*), love (as in *Mother and Child*), nationalism (as in *Awakening Africa*), and genre (as in *Drummer*). Massive figures are conceived in symbolic exaggerations that produce an expressive dynamic within the structure. Feet and hands, in particular, are enlarged to emphasize their importance. Exaggerated feet, literally and metaphorically, produce an unwavering stability in form and content.

While studying at the Kumasi College of Technology with Kofi Antubam, then the leading sculptor in Ghana, Vincent Kofi was introduced to art through Antubam's Asante-British aesthetics and the vibrant, multimedia artistic environment at the school. The forms in sculpture, textiles, architecture, and pottery contributed to his way of seeing sculpture. He also learned approaches to form at the Royal College of Art in London (1952-55), where Henry Moore's modernism had been instituted. In addition he studied African and Oceanic Art at Columbia University in 1959. It was in New York that he learned casting. In general Kofi moved though the world of art in search of knowledge and techniques to enhance his own creative vision. As he derived pleasure from the formalism of the Akuaba in its geometric, columnar structure, he also found pleasure in Moore's *Reclining Figure* and other works. The freedom he located in Moore's grace and bulk and Barbara Hepworth's massive folded/clasped hands can be seen in his own work. But his style is neither conventional Asante, Moore, nor Hepworth. Rather it is the resolve of the tensions between the eye and the hand of this imaginative artist.

Mother and Child (1957-58), *Christ* (c.1960), and *Dancer* (1962) are several of Kofi's massive works that reveal his interest in the materiality of sculptured form in wood. Each is an impressive, commanding figure with a rounded, compact form that is volumetric and accentuated by exaggerated hands and feet. Volumetric and textural variation produce a harmonious effect and a balance of raw force and refinement. The massive, columnar form of *Christ* stands eight feet, displaying a generalized masculine form and the theme of suffering, but this sculpture constitutes an original approach to the universal Christian theme.

The figure stands firmly anchored by enormous, organic feet. Its compact, columnar structure is extended by the two vertically raised arms and exaggerated hands that stabilize the symmetry of the piece. The gesture is dynamic, making sweeping movements upward and centering the protruding, ovoid head. The play of light on its luminous surface accentuates the linear clarity of form and the expressive textures. The subject matter of the universal suffering Christ who carries the burdens of man's sins is transformed sculpturally into a metaphor for strength and the material man—African, suffering, yet strong. This work, like others, engages themes of the human condition, revealing the artist's attitudes regarding life, plastic form, and the embodiment of the former in the latter.

Awakening Africa (1959-60) is a much celebrated piece. It contains the volumetric interest of Kofi and addresses the theme of nationalism in a seemingly reclining nude. This work epitomizes the conceptualization of Kofi's critical eye, which engages, resists, and subverts canonicity according to his individual persuasion. Kofi's nude resists the classical iconographic associations with passivity. It also resists the conventional, columnar frontality of African conventions. The highly textural surfaces, including bas-relief facial features, ringed neck, and exaggerated appendages, unite fluidly within the form's own plasticity. Yet its formalism suggests a continent processing liberation, in the act of getting on her feet. This seminal work, stimulated by the independence of Ghana from Britain in 1957, reveals Kofi's interest in the immediacy of symbolic representation. *Awakening Africa*, like Kofi's monumental wood sculptures, consists of counterbalances of volume, mass, and line unified in expressive harmonies. Kofi's oeuvre signifies its own modernism in its truth to materials and to the artist's didactic vision.

—Freida High

L

LACY, Laura Jean
American sculptor, painter, and mixed-media artist

Born: Washington, D.C., 10 December 1932. **Education:** Southern University, Baton Rouge, Louisiana, B.A. in Art Education 1956; Art Students League, New York; Otis Art Institute, Los Angeles; Southern Methodist University, Dallas; North Texas State University, Denton. **Career:** Art instructor, Walnut Hill High School, Shreveport, Louisiana, 1956-59; docent, Dallas Museum of Fine Arts, Dallas, 1971-76; curator/director, Museum of African-American Life and Culture, Dallas, 1975-76, African-American Cultural Heritage Center, Dallas Independent School District, 1977-88, Visual Arts Gallery, South Dallas Cultural Center, 1989-90. Artist/consultant and education specialist, *Ramses II Exhibition*, Dallas Natural History Museum Association, 1989; exhibition curator, *Black Dallas Remembered*, South Dallas Cultural Center, 1994. Designer, stained glass windows, Saint Luke Community Methodist Church, Dallas, 1994-95. **Awards:** Wesley Foundation Award, Houston, Texas, 1977; United for Action Award, Dallas, 1977; Rockefeller Award, 1979; Southwest Black Artist Guild Award, Dallas, 1980; Black Dallas Remembered Award, Dallas, 1987; Dallas County Heritage Society Award, 1989; Carter G. Woodson Award, 1989; Afro-American History Award, United States Department of Labor, Dallas, 1989; Living Legend Honoree, Junior Black Academy of Arts and Letters, Dallas, 1994; Artistic Achievements in the Preservation of African American Heritage Award, Black Dallas Remembered, 1994.

Individual Exhibitions:

1990	Barnes Blackmen Gallery, Houston, Texas
1993	D'Art Visual Art Center, Dallas
	Corcoran Gallery of Art, Washington, D.C. (traveling)
1994	Blaffer Gallery, University of Houston, Texas

Selected Group Exhibitions:

1978	*Dallas Art,* City Hall
	Birdwell Library, Southern Methodist University, Dallas
1979	Huntsville Art Museum, Alabama
1980	Barnwell Art Center, Shreveport, Louisiana
1983	Longview Museum of Art, Texas
1987	National Urban Art League Exposition, Houston, Texas
1988	Hughes-Trigg Gallery, Southern Methodist University, Dallas
1989	Dallas Museum of Art
1991	Laguna Gloria Art Museum, Austin, Texas
1992	*Black Creativity in Texas,* Lubbock Fine Arts Center, Texas

Collections:

First Federal Bank of Dallas; Dallas Museum of Art.

Publications:

On LACY: Book—*Ancestral Legacy: The African Impulse in African American Art,* exhibition catalog, Dallas Museum of Art, 1989. **Articles**—"Call and Response: The Art of Jean Lacy" by Alvia J. Wardlaw, in *American Visions,* 8(6), December/January 1994; "Jean Lacy: Art and Soul" by Cecelia Field, in *Masterpieces: The Associates Newsletter* (Dallas Museum of Art), Fall/Winter 1991.

*   *   *

Whether she is creating reliquaries, mosaics, stained glass windows, sculptures, or paintings, Laura Jean Lacy's work reveals her profound interest in the religion, history, and sociopolitical development of her people. For several decades these subjects have consistently been incorporated into her art. A look at three successive decades—from the 1970s through the 1990s—is instructive.

During the 1970s Lacy received commissions from the United Methodist Church to complete a narrative of thirty-five Old and New Testament stories with black Christian images for use in church school curricula in the inner cities of southern California and Arizona. Lacy agreed that creating images of black individuals in biblical stories was critical in developing self-esteem in black children. She created works about Jacob wrestling with the angel, Passover, the Creation, the golden calf, Moses and the pharaoh, Joseph, Abraham, and Solomon. The first images in the series were collages in bold colors made from dramatic shapes cut from paper.

In *Little Egypt Condo/New York City* (1987), a 10½-by-13½-inch mixed-media work on museum board, Lacy used paper cutouts to create a collagelike effect. In this work the mixed media include xerography, which enhances the narrative drawing. The artist's sense of the history of black people bridges the gap between Africa and the African presence in America. She starts first with a tenement building and the suggestions of such a reference. Then, instead of calling the building exactly what it is, in the title of the work she turns the idea on its head by referring to it as a condo, a habitat for the prosperous. Graffiti and hieroglyphics accentuate the scene, creating an aesthetic counterpoint. Lacy transforms the tenement into an Egyptian temple resplendent with hieroglyphics, or *medu neter* ("the word of God"), inhabited by an assortment of Egyptianized people involved in various pursuits. On the first floor a man is grooming his hair, and a centrally placed woman stands in the door of the edifice while she converses energetically with everyone in the building. She and the sphinx above her are strategically placed. On the second floor two men affirm each other's place in African American life by slapping their palms, while another solitary male figure sits by the window, lost in his own thoughts. Denizens of the third floor work and communicate with one another. A cosmic timekeeper reiterates the notion of the rhythm and flow of life. Everyone in this setting knows, communicates, and is connected. Architectural restrictions and barriers dissolve and disappear. Nevertheless, Lacy reminds us that danger is afoot with the presence of two rodents that attempt to eat away at, or erode, the bonds and connections of the past and present. The rodents are metaphors for destruction, disease, and death for a people who do not remain vigilant and discerning. Still employing the collage technique, the artist sensitively places xerographic paper cutouts of certain images and details of importance.

A stained glass commission in the 1990s is reminiscent of the collage paper cutouts of the 1970s and of *Little Egypt Condo/New York City* in the 1980s. The work was created for Trinity United Methodist Church, the oldest African American church in Houston, Texas. Led by historian Berniece W. McBeth, a retired teacher in Houston, the church worked in concert with the artist to develop a series that would depict ethnic religious and historical images, the only example of its genre in the city. Fabricated by Robert Foster, the pieces of glass recall the cutouts and stories presented in *Little Egypt Condo/New York City*. Lacy's work is a tour de force. There are eleven windows: *Old Testament Window, New Testament Window, Crucifixion Scene, Black Women* (expressly significant in the patriarchal United Methodist Church), *Black Methodist Window, Early Trinity Churches Window, Ancestor Quilt Window, 1917 24th Infantry Commemorative Window, Civil Rights Window, Two Choir Window,* and *Stair Window*. The commission demonstrates what can transpire when a church has progressive parishioners.

Lacy has enjoyed a groundswell of national support for her work. It is important that the artist continue doing commissions such as these so that her phenomenal talents reach and inspire generations yet unborn.

—Jontyle Theresa Robinson

LAM, Wifredo

Cuban painter

Born: Wifredo Oscar de la Concepcion Lam y Castilla, Sagua la Grande, 2 December 1902. **Education:** Academia San Alejandra, Havana, 1920-23; Free Academy, Madrid; studio of Fernando Alvarez di Sotomayor (director of the Prado), Madrid, 1924-28. **Military Service:** Fought with the Republicans in the Spanish Civil War. **Family:** Married 1) Eva Piris in 1929 (died 1931); 2) Elena Holzer in 1944 (separated 1950); 3) Lou Laurin in 1959, 3 children. **Career:** Painter, Academia de Quatre Gates, Barcelona, 1936-37. Moved to Paris, 1938. Associated with Surrealists, especially André Breton and Max Ernst, Paris, 1938. Traveled to New York, Cuba, and Paris, 1946-52. **Awards:** First Prize, Salone Nacionale, Havana, 1951; Gold Medal for foreign painters, Premio Lissone, Rome, 1953; Guggenheim Award, 1964; Premio Marzotto, Milan, 1965. **Died:** Paris, 11 September 1982.

Individual Exhibitions:

1928	Galerie Vilches, Madrid
1939	Galerie Pierre, Paris

	Peris Gallery, New York (with Pablo Picasso)
1942	Pierre Matisse Gallery, New York
1944	Pierre Matisse Gallery, New York
1945	Galerie Pierre, Paris
	Pierre Matisse Gallery, New York
1946	Centre d'Art, Port-au-Prince, Haiti
1948	Pierre Matisse Gallery, New York
1950	Pierre Matisse Gallery, New York
1951	Ministry of Education, Havana
1952	Institute of Contemporary Arts, London
1953	Galerie Maeght, Paris
1955	Galerie Colibri, Malmo, Sweden
	University of Havana
	Museo de Bellas Artes, Caracas
	Instituto Venezuela-Francia, Caracas
1957	Palacio de Bellas Artes, Marcaibo, Venezuela
	Galerie Cahiers d'Art, Paris
1959	Galleria Grattacielo, Milan
1961	University of Notre Dame, Indiana
	Galerie La Cour d'Ingres, Paris
	Galleria del Canale, Venice
	Galleria del Obelisco, Rome
	Albert Loeb Gallery, New York
1962	Salone Annunciata, Milan
1963	Galerie Krugier, Geneva
	Galeria de la Habana, Havana
	La Bibliteca Nacional, Havana
1964	Galleria Notizie, Turin
1965	Museo de Arte Moderna, Havana
	Galerie Anderson, Malmo, Sweden
	Galerie Christine, Aubry, Paris
1966	Kestner-Gesellschaft, Hannover
1967	Galerie Albert Loeb, Paris
	Stedelijk Museum, Amsterdam
	Moderna Museet, Stockholm
	Palais des Beaux-Arts, Brussels
1968	Galerie Villand et Galanis, Paris
1969	Kunstkabinett, Frankfurt
	Galleria Bergamini, Milan
1970	Galleria Arte Borgogna, Milan
	Galerie Krugier, Geneva
	Gimpel Fils, London
	Gimpel and Weitzenhoffer, New York
1971	Galerie Gimpel und Hanover, Zurich
1972	Galerie Tronche, Paris
	Studio Bellini, Milan
1978	Ordrupgaard Samlingen, Copenhagen
1979	Artcurial, Paris
1982	Pierre Matisse Gallery, New York
1987	Galerie Maeght Lelong, Zurich

Selected Group Exhibitions:

1947	*Exposition Internationale du Surrealisme,* Galerie Maeght, Paris
1958	*50 Ans d'Art Moderne,* Palais des Beaux-Arts, Brussels
1959	Kassel, West Germany
1963	*Zeugnisse der Angst in der Modernen Kunst,* Darmstadt
1966	Musée d'Art Moderne de la Ville, Paris
	Kunsthalle, Basel (with Vic Gentils)

1968   *Painting in France, 1900-1967,* National Gallery, Washington, D.C. (traveling)
        Musée d'Art Moderne de la Ville, Paris (with Matta and Alicia Penalba)
1978   *Cuba: Peintres d'Aujourd hui,* Musée d'Art Moderne de la Ville, Paris

Collections:

Art Institute of Chicago; Centre Georges Pompidou, Paris; Centro Medico, Havana; Moderna Museet, Stockholm; Musée d'Art Moderne de la Ville, Paris; Museum Boymans-van-Beuningen, Rotterdam; Museum of Modern Art, New York; Nationalgalerie, Berlin; Stedelijk van Abbemuseum, Eindhoven, Netherlands; Tate Gallery, London.

Publications:

By LAM: Articles—"Lettre de Wifredo Lam," in *Opus International* (Paris), September 1971; "Lam della Giungla" (interview), in *Bolaffiarte* (Turin), April 1974.

On LAM: Books—*Lam,* exhibition catalog, Port-au-Prince, Haiti, André Breton, 1946; *Wifredo Lam y su Obra Vista a traves de Significados Criticos* by Fernando Ortiz, Havana, 1950; *Lam* by Jacques Charpier, Paris, 1960; *Lam* by Hubert Juin, Paris, 1964; *Wifredo Lam* edited by Alex Grall, Paris, 1970; *Servizi in Porcellana Decorati da Wifredo Lam* by M. V. Ferrero, Turin, 1970; *Wifredo Lam* by Michel Leiris, Milan, 1970; *Lam* by Alain Jouffroy, Paris, 1972; *Wifredo Lam,* exhibition catalog, Paris, Anne Tronche, 1972; *Wifredo Lam,* exhibition catalog, Zurich, Per Kirkeby, 1987. **Articles**—"Oiseau d'eau, ou, Oiseau de feu," in *Art in America,* 72, December 1984; "Wifredo Lam," in *Siecle,* 52, July 1979, pp. 5-124 (illustrated); "Wifredo Lam: s'aboucher a l'invisible" by Lucien Curzi, in *L'Oeil* (Lausanne, Switzerland), 363, October 1985, pp. 42-45 (illustrated); "Wifredo Lam: Transpositions of the Surrealist Proposition in the Post-World War II Era" by Lowery Stokes Sims, in *Arts Magazine,* 60, December 1985, pp. 21-25 (illustrated); "Please Wait by the Coatroom" in *Arts Magazine,* 63, December 1988, pp. 56-59; "In Search of Wifredo Lam" by Lowery Stokes Sims, in *Arts Magazine,* 63, December 1988, pp. 50-55; "The Insights of Cubism Seen through Afro-Cuban Eyes" by Andrew Patner, in *Art and Antiques,* 15, May 1993, p. 85; "The Engravings" by Martine Arnault, in *Cimaise,* 41, January/March 1994, pp. 69-70; "Lam and His Contemporaries" by Juan A. Martinez, in *Art Nexus,* 11, January/March 1994, pp. 208-09; "Wifredo Lam—Oeuvre Grave et Lithographie" by Laurence Pythoud, in *L'O'eil* (Lausanne, Switzerland), 459, March 1994; "Dancing in the Dark" by Susana Torruella Leval, in *Art News,* 93, Summer 1994, p. 153; "Wifredo Lam" by Gerardo Mosquera, in *Art Nexus,* 15, January/March 1995, pp. 72-79.

*   *   *

After leaving his homeland, Havana, Cuba, where he concentrated on painting still lifes and landscapes, Wifredo Lam traveled to Spain where he thought that his work could be freed from its academic constraints. He became familiar with the work of Pablo Picasso and equally with the Republican cause, which he supported in the Spanish Civil War. He did not actually meet Picasso until 1938 in Paris, but much speculation and myth has grown around the supposed influence that this looming figure had on Lam's

work, almost ignoring the impact that Henri Matisse's decorative style had on Lam's compositions.

By 1936 Lam's paintings had become increasingly influenced by cubism, but with a more ritualistically "Africanized" character. His subjects were more structural, connecting them to traditional African sculpture from Zaire and other West African cultures. The spirit of African mythology and ritualism is evidenced in the accentuated breasts and genitalia, elongated limbs, and pronounced masklike facial features on figures often placed in a surreal lush environment of leaves and other foliage. Attention to ritualized forms came not from European artists' explorations of Cubism—although it may have provided a catalyst—but because Lam's life in Cuba had been grounded in the Africanized religion of Santeria. (Santeria is actually a Cuban-based religion that relates Yoruba deity worship with the Roman Catholic tradition of prayer to saints.)

After the civil war escalated in Spain, Lam left for Paris with a letter of introduction to Picasso. Although he was only in Paris for two years, he continued to be influenced by the avant-garde school there and by his comrades. (Together they had fled Paris for Marseilles when it was invaded in 1940 and subsequently occupied during World War II.) He was later forced to flee Marseilles for Martinique, where he met Aime Cesaire, a disciple of Negritude, whose influence of Africanized themes and philosophy affected Lam's own investigations of his Afro-Cuban culture for the remainder of his life. As Lam himself said: "I . . . wanted to paint the drama of the Negro spirit, the beauty of the plastic art of the blacks. In this way I could act as a Trojan horse that would spew forth hallucinating figures with the power to surprise, to disturb the dreams of the exploiters. I knew I was running the risk of not being understood either by the man in the street or by the others [the art world]. But a true picture has the power to set the imagination to work even if it takes time."

Lam's interest in African-derived spirituality and mythology was further reinforced by a visit to Haiti in 1945 in which he witnessed a voodoo ceremony and found similarities in worship and a belief system among Afro-Cubans in his own country. He thus took the techniques of synthetic Cubism, which were based on forms of traditional African sculpture, and reinterpreted them through what he knew and experienced from his own Afro-Cuban heritage. What resulted were lush, enigmatic, and ritualized works in which shapes were often outlined in black line, no doubt initially influenced by the linear outlines of Matisse, Joan Miro, Fernand Leger (with whom he had worked in Paris), and Max Ernst (one of his colleagues in Marseilles). Lam developed a personal vision of Cubism, unlike Picasso and others who appropriated structural elements of traditional African sculpture and design. Lam concerned himself not only with the structure of the forms but with the myth and authority that empowered them. His greatest achievement was the manner in which he fused modernist ideals of abstraction with his knowledge, as an insider, of African-derived forms and the context in which they were used in the sacred arena.

—Lizzetta LeFalle-Collins

LANE, Artis
Canadian sculptor, painter, and printmaker

Born: Artis Marie Shreve, North Buxton, Ontario, Canada, 14 May 1927. **Education:** Ontario College of Art, Toronto; Cranbrook

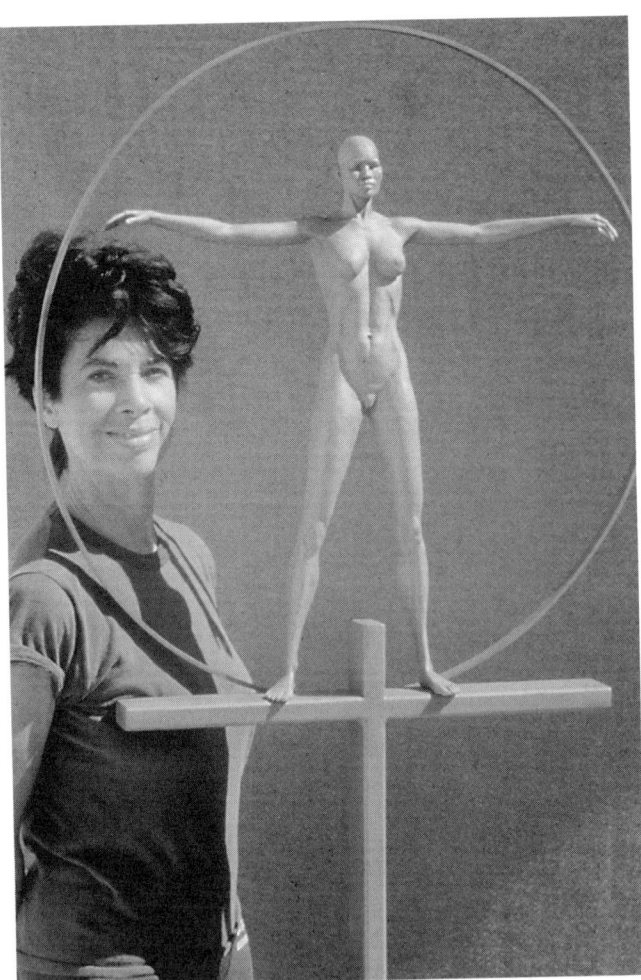

Artis Lane (with *New Woman* sculpture), 1989. Photo courtesy of Vince Cannon.

Art Academy, Bloomfield Hills, Michigan; University of California, Los Angeles. **Family:** Married (1 Bill Lane in 1949 (divorced 1958), one daughter; 2) Vince Cannon, 1974. **Career:** Visiting lecturer, Dillard University, New Orleans, Southern University, Baton Rouge, Louisiana, Exceptional Children's Foundation, Los Angeles, Duke Ellington School for the Arts, Washington, D. C., Charles Drew Medical Center, Los Angeles, California Correctional Institute for Women, Chino, California. Artist-in-residence, National Art Association, Los Angeles; guest lecturer, Phys-Art-Lit-Mor-, Los Angeles. Served as juror for NAACP ACT-SO Art Program, Los Angeles; designer, Nelson Mandela Courage Award, Trans-Africa, Kwanza Foundation award, United Negro College Fund award, Dance Theatre of Harlem Original Logo and Brass Ring award, Carousel Fall, Children's Diabetes Foundation. **Awards:** Dominion of Canada Award; O'Keefe Fellowship Award, Canada; Medgar Evers Community Service Award, Hollywood, California; Museum of African American Art Award, Los Angeles; YMCA Silver Achievement Award; State of Louisiana Award. **Agent:** Vince Cannon, Box 4948 Ruidoso, New Mexico 88345, U.S.A. **Address:** P.O. Box 4948, Ruidoso, New Mexico 88345, U.S.A.

Individual Exhibitions:

1987	G.R. N'Namdi Gallery, Detroit
1989	Isobel Neal Gallery Limited, Chicago
	M. Hanks Gallery, Santa Monica, California
1990	G.R. N'Namdi Gallery, Detroit
1993	Sherry Frumkin Gallery, Santa Monica, California
	Hammonds House Museum, Atlanta
	Southern University, Baton Rouge, Louisiana
	Pyramid Gallery, Little Rock, Arkansas
1995	Dillard University, New Orleans
1996	Junior Black Academy of Arts and Letters, Dallas

Selected Group Exhibitions:

1985	Museum of African American Art, Los Angeles
1989	Bernice Steinbaum Gallery, New York
1992	Santa Monica Museum of Art
1993	Pauline Hersch Gallery, Los Angeles
1994	Bomani Gallery, San Francisco
	Margulies-Taplin Gallery, Miami
1995	Horwitch Lew Allen Gallery, Santa Fe
1996	New Mexico State Capitol Building, Santa Fe
	Horwitch Lew Allen Gallery, Santa Fe
	Center for Contemporary Arts, Santa Fe

Collections:

Smithsonian Institution, Washington, D.C.; Howard University; Dillard University, New Orleans; National Council of Negro Women; United Negro College Fund.

Publications:

On LANE: Articles—"Emergence," in *The Georgia Review,* Winter 1991, p. 695; "Profile: Artis Lane" by Marlena Doktorczyk-Donohue, in *Visions Art Quarterly,* Winter 1993, p. 44; "Bronze Sculptures Carve a Metaphor from Human Spirit" by Catherine Fox, in *The Atlanta Journal/Atlanta Constitution,* 28 May 1993; "Artis Lane, in Possession of Souls" by J.A. Jahannes, in *Upscale,* January 1994, p. 70.

*

Artis Lane comments:

My latest body of work is called *Emerging into Spirit.* I am leaving the workings of the foundry (the gating material, ceramic shell mold, etc.), the "birthing" materials, in the foundry to symbolize Generic Man emerging out of material thinking into spiritual consciousness. I then show most of the work in pairs, the traditional black patina bronze, with the ceramic shell pieces as a metaphor for the moralistic/materialistic conversations that mankind has wrestled with throughout eternity. Fragments of these completed pieces are often used, suggesting "life cut off too soon," "journeys cut short," or "mental searching distracted," etc.

Born and educated in Canada, my basic art training was Eurocentric in its limited sense of "classic." But through the years of study in metaphysics, the influence of Egyptian art and African sculpture has surfaced in my work. Combined with my African heritage, this evolution in metaphysics has transcended ethnicity, leading to my use of African and African American models to symbolize Universal Man, forcing the definition of "classic" to be all-inclusive.

For the future I am enlarging my images to life-size and moving them into installations that more clearly express this human journey out of darkness (ignorance) into the light (understanding) of man's spiritual reality.

*   *   *

The sculptor Artis Lane is primarily concerned with portraying what she sees as enduring spiritual truths. These truths are that the growth of spiritual awareness is continuous and that nobody ever arrives at perfection. In addition, spiritual awareness connects humans with a universal force.

Because Lane sees the physical body as a vehicle for a spiritual journey, the best way to illustrate such truths is to use the human figure cast in bronze. Her technique is to mold male and female nudes and to cast them in bronze but to leave the ceramic casing, wire, and tubing used in the casting process to show that the figure has not attained perfection.

An example can be seen in *New Waiting,* a standing female nude

Artis Lane: *New Man Dialogue,* **1993. Photo courtesy of Bruce Wright.**

with her hand on her hip. She has bits of the ceramic casting material on various parts of her body, and the tubing used to channel the molten bronze is still attached. She is like a butterfly that has not completely emerged from its cocoon. The look symbolizes the continuous spiritual journey and transformation that every person must undertake.

Another example of Lane's technique is *Emerging New Man.* The figure here is also partially covered with ceramic casting material; he has not yet been fully formed. But the figure looks as if he were dancing. A nude dancing figure in some cultures represents a relationship between the figure and the universe, and perhaps Lane intends for this pose to reinforce the idea of spiritual transcendence and to show a connection with universal force.

Not all of Lane's work employs the technique of leaving casting material on the figure. In fact, many of her pieces have dual or companion versions that are traditionally cast bronzes. *Emerging New Man,* for example, has a companion piece titled *New Man.* The traditionally cast bronze figure presumably represents perfection, perhaps a deity. It cannot be a mere mortal since humans never achieve perfection. Lane sometimes places the two versions face-to-face, engaging them in a dialogue. Such is the case with *Emerging New Man* and *New Man.*

Leaving remnants of the casting process is not the only way Lane shows spiritual truths. In *Release,* for example, a woman is stepping forward, away from a man behind her, as if he were releasing her. Lane says that this work is less about female liberation than about the expression of the universal law that growth occurs by letting go.

There are other things to consider when viewing Lane's work. First, generally speaking, different patinas symbolize various races. Black represents persons of African descent, white symbolizes Caucasians, and bronze stands for all races. Second, texture has special significance. For the most part roughness shows motion or struggle, while smoothness indicates thought.

Finally, Lane is concerned about the dignity of persons of African descent. The figure in *Adam,* for example, clearly has African features, demonstrating to the world that humanity originated in Africa. *Classic Head* depicts a woman of African descent in a classic pose, as in an ancient Greek sculpture. The woman looks dignified, and Lane has elevated her to the same level as, or even higher than, Eurocentric figures of the past.

—Eric Hanks

LANE, Doyle

American ceramist

Born: New Orleans, 1925. **Education:** Los Angeles City College, A.A. 1953; East Los Angeles City College; University of Southern California. **Career:** Glaze technician, L.H. Butcher Company; studio craftsman.

Selected Exhibitions:

Ankrum Gallery (1967, 1968); Brockman Gallery (1968); Mills College, Oakland, California; Oakland Museum, California; Pasadena Art Museum, California (1956, 1957).

Collections:

Lutheran Nursing Home and Health Center, Alhambra, California; Oakland Museum, California; Temple B'Nai David, Southfield, Michigan.

* * *

A longtime Los Angeles resident, Doyle Lane studied ceramics at Los Angeles City College, where he received an associate of arts degree in 1953. He studied further at East Los Angeles College and at the University of Southern California. He is best known for the glazed clay paintings he did from the 1960s into the 1980s.

Lane developed a method of painting glazes onto flat, circular pieces of clay that he then fired so as to create textures approximating color-field explosions on painted canvas. The glazes separated from the surfaces, thereby creating beaded and streaking textures and effects. He also dripped glazes onto fired surfaces that he then refired. Using the drip-and-splatter techniques employed by abstract expressionists to create push-and-pull elements on the clay, he then mounted the works on white wooden surfaces, giving them a feeling of suspension. The finished clay paintings, as Lane refers to them, resemble exploding orbs and recall the cosmic landscapes of color-field painters such as Robert Motherwell and Adolph Gottlieb.

The separation of glazes was also a technique Lane used in making earthenware pots. In the pots he experimented with running colored glazes into one another. He also created the effects of crackling by firing the pots at high temperatures so that weblike textures formed. The influences of Japanese glazing techniques and of minimalist form are also evident in his pots and vases. Their round, small-necked shapes recall modest forms that exhibit a truth to materials and whose beauty comes from their unadorned nature. Lane's most successful pots have glazes that resemble natural formations such as cracks and fissures in rocks, water in streams, and gently blowing grasses in fields. Their small necks can hold only a few blades of grass or a few dried flowers, the spiny verticals of the plant material forming a contrast with the pregnant shapes of the vases.

The same economy of form is found in Lane's beadwork. His work with beads began when he welcomed visitors, including groups of children, to his studio. (Making beads was also an alternative for Lane to the often difficult processes of working with clay and to the heavy labor associated with loading and unloading large clay pieces into and out of kilns.) When he had visitors, he would teach them to make beads that could be strung into necklaces, bracelets, or key chains. Lane later became interested in the commercial possibilities for his beads, and he now creates beads for fine jewelry that is sold in hotel boutiques and other one-of-a-kind jewelry stores. His mastery of glazes is also apparent in his beads, which range from iridescent swirls reminiscent of celestial bodies to items with the textures of speckled bird eggs. In designing beads, he continues to take his clues from nature. Many, for example, resemble the kind of small stones that would be overlooked by the casual observer but that in Lane's hands become jewels. Because of their use, the beads must be lightweight enough to be strung together. Lane's truth to materials, an integral part of all of his art processes, thus continues in his work with beads, and he makes their small shapes as dynamic as his clay paintings and glazed pots.

—Lizzetta LeFalle-Collins

LASEKAN, Akinola
Nigerian painter and illustrator

Born: S.A. Oladetimi, Owo, Nigeria, June 1916. Changed his name to Akinola Lasekan in 1941. **Education:** Correspondence through Hammersmith School of Art, London, 1945. **Career:** Textile designer, 1935-?; illustrated Bible stories and calendars, Church Missionary Society Bookshop, Lagos; cartoonist, *West African Pilot*, Lagos, 1944-66; lecturer, University of Nigeria, Nsukka, 1961-66. Founded art correspondence school, Lash Studio, 38 Forsyth Street, Lagos, 1944. **Awards:** First Prize, All-Nigeria Book Cover Design Competition, Nigerian government, 1944. Associate fellow/fellow, Institute of African Studies, University of Ife, Ile-Ife, Nigeria, 1966-74, Royal Society of Art, London, Asele Institute, Nimo, 1985 (posthumous). **Died:** 1974.

Individual Exhibitions:

1968   Goethe Institute, Lagos

Selected Group Exhibitions:

1955   Carnegie Center, New York
1956   Boston University
1959   Fisk University, Nashville
1962   NAACP, New York
1968   University of Ife, Ile-Ife, Nigeria
1971   Gallery of the University Library, University of Ife, Ile-Ife, Nigeria
1977   FESTAC '77, Lagos
              National Theatre, Lagos
1978   *Exhibition of Nigerian Traditional and Contemporary Art*, Lagos
1985   National Theatre, Lagos
1986   National Theatre, Lagos

Collections:

Carl Van Vechten Gallery of Fine Arts, Fisk University, Nashville; Federal Ministry of Information, Cultural Division, Lagos; Lagos University Library, University of Ife, Ile-Ife, Nigeria; Hampton University Museum, Hampton, Virginia; National Gallery of Modern Art, Lagos.

Publications:

By LASEKAN: Books—*Drawing and Paintings Simplified,* Lagos, c.1940; *Drawing Made Easy,* Lagos, African Art and Craft Studio, 1942; *Nigeria in Cartoons,* Lagos, 1944; *Nigeria in 1945,* Lagos, 1946; *Paintings and Cartoons on the Life of Herbert MacCauley 1944-1947,* n.d. **Articles**—"Wanted: Sublime Art," in *West African Pilot* (Lagos), 22 August 1962; "Authenticity of Ife Art," in *Yoruba Images: Essays in Honour of Lamidi Fakeye* (Ile-Ife, Nigeria), Humanities Society, 1988 (reprint); "Problems of Contemporary African Artists," in *Kurio Africana: Journal of Art and Criticism* (Ile-Ife, Nigeria), 1(1), 1989, pp. 25-37 (notes; reprint).

On LASEKAN: Article—"Nigerian Political Cartoonists in 1970s," in *New Culture* (Ibaden), 1(10), September 1979, pp. 13-20, 25.

* * *

A painter, draftsman, and political satirist, Akinola Lasekan gained national prominence when he became the official cartoonist for the *West African Pilot,* an anticolonialist newspaper owned by Nnamdi Azikiwe, the first president of Nigeria. Between 1944 and 1959 Lasekan's cartoons provided a commentary on colonialism in Nigeria. They emphasized the attitudes, worldview, and behind-the-scenes machinations of colonial officials from an African nationalist's perspective. By 1946, when his cartoon regularly appeared as the visual complement of the day's editorial opinion, strips like "Modern Partnership," "Eternal Servitude?," and "For Immediate Action" were presented as editorials in their own right.

Lasekan's satirical gaze constantly excoriated the colonial administration for its indifference on matters affecting the welfare of Nigeria, a debilitating lethargy that vanished once the issues at stake impinged on the welfare of Europeans. In *The Rent Assessment Board,* for instance, Lasekan portrayed the enervation of a potbellied, cigar-chomping white man, a visual metaphor for the colonial administration, in curbing unscrupulous landlords. The stupor vanishes in "The Beast of Burden," however, as the same official darts nimbly about in self-interested glee while piling debt on the proverbial Nigerian donkey. Just as the reader is about to cheer the newfound energy of this bureaucrat, he drops off in a doze in "Wanted a Nigerian Art Museum."

Lasekan also addressed issues of ethnicity, class, and culture within the complex dynamics of the colonial-colonized relationship. His astute analyses indicated that it was the convergence of exploitative foreign and local interests that ensured the success of colonialism in Africa. Most of his works were at pains to show that colonialism thrived by setting up parasitic structures with unscrupulous locals. In cartoons like "For Immediate Action," Lasekan regularly pilloried landlords. In "Hates Independence in His Life-Time," he showed a pathetic-looking Uncle Tom in pin-striped pants caught groveling under his master's dinner table for scraps. He also viewed divisive politicians like T. Odutola, in "Modern Deification," and the leadership of the trade unions, in "The Fateful Meal," as belonging to the class of subservient Uncle Toms.

In the *West African Pilot,* Lasekan regularly parodied imperialism. In "The Scramblers" he depicted white imperialists as a pack of ravenous dogs aggressively fighting over a bone in the shape of Africa. In another cartoon Lasekan explored the metaphor of food by portraying a group of European men with mean-looking knives hungrily carving up the contents of an Africa-shaped dish. Two bored men representing the United States and the Soviet Union observe the feeding frenzy, and their disinterest appears to be as damaging as the Europeans' gluttony.

Lasekan's commentary on world politics continued in cartoons like "The Pilgrim's Progress" and "Poor African, Poorer UNO." Playing off John Bunyan's *The Pilgrim's Progress,* Lasekan likened the politics of the Cold War to the folly of a blindfolded traveler heading into a pit in the middle of the road. "Poor African, Poorer UNO" depicted the consequences of Western nations' abdication of their moral responsibility. The cartoon shows the United Nations lying prostrate as a rambunctious white South African, aided by the prevailing moral malaise of the superpowers, stomps on the organization. In "Comrade in War, Vassals in Peace," Lasekan poked fun at the contradiction at the core of racism when superficial biological differences in color are assigned normative ethical values.

Lasekan has also produced an extensive array of oil paintings focusing on the everyday realities of Nigeria's cultural life. Working in a photo-realist style, he has captured a well-defined spatial stillness in paintings such as *Moremi* and *University of Ife Moving to Its Present Site.* Spatial stillness is achieved with the static artificial poses of flat figures that are designed to convey dignity and good breeding. He pays meticulous attention to hair, hairstyles, and fabric designs in *Yoruba Girl, Market Scene,* and *Nigerian Constable under Colonial Rule,* all at the National Gallery of Modern Art in Lagos. The contrived nature of some of the poses suggests that Lasekan is not engaged in an ordinary documentary project. Rather, his project is a calculated visual rebuttal of racist commentaries and images that have portrayed Africans and African life as barbaric. As a product of a definite sociohistorical time, Lasekan's creative work has mostly been concerned with presenting a positive picture of Nigerian cultural life.

—Nkiru Nzegwu

LATTIER, Christian
Ivory Coaster sculptor and muralist

Born: Grande Lahou, Ivory Coast, 25 December 1925. **Education:** École des Beaux-Arts, Paris, 1947-54. **Career:** Professor of sculpture, National School of Beaux-Arts of Abidjan, 1962. **Awards:** Grand Prize, Dakar World Festival of Negro Art, 1966. **Died:** 23 April 1978.

Individual Exhibitions:

1959	Beaux-Arts Gallery, Paris
1963	Hotel de Ville, Ivory Coast

Selected Group Exhibitions:

1958	Sorbonne, Paris
1959	Musée Rodin, Paris
1961	Salon de Comparaison, Paris

Selected Public Works:

Abidjan Airport; City Hall, Abidjan; Caisse de Stabilisation, Abidjan; Maison des Ingenieurs, Treichville.

Publications:

On LATTIER: Books—*Twentieth Century Art of Africa* by Kojo Fosn, Zaria, Nigeria, Gaskiya Publishing, 1986; *New Currents, Ancient Rivers: Contemporary African Artists in a Generation of Change,* by Jean Kennedy, Washington, D.C., Smithsonian Institution Press, 1992; *Christian Lattier: Le sculpteur aux main nue,* Saint-Maur, Édition SÉPIA, 1993.

*   *   *

Christian Lattier belongs to the group of African artists who came to prominence in the first decades of the postcolonial era. His art was steeped in the nationalist struggles of the colonial period and in the social, political, and epistemological concerns of African societies in the wake of political independence. Lattier was the first internationally recognized modern artist from the Ivory Coast (Côte d'Ivoire), and his unique fiber sculptures established formalistic and conceptual directions for modern art in his country. Lattier's art also revealed a romantic attitude, stemming from his identification with Negritude ideology and an awareness of his pioneering role in the emergent context of modern art practice in Africa.

Lattier's techniques were derived in part from an adaptation of the fiberwork found in traditional textiles and masking forms among the Baule of the Ivory Coast and their Senufo neighbors to the north and west. He was also influenced by the formalistic experiments of European constructivists such as Naum Gabo, whose works Lattier knew from his training and a period of professional practice in France. As a young artist he worked on the restoration of the cathedral at Chartres, and his later works were influenced by the attenuated Romanesque and Gothic forms he came in contact with during this period. Lattier combined these experiences with an earlier knowledge of basket weaving, studies of prehistoric art and architectural forms, and several years of experimentation to create his sculptural techniques.

Lattier produced his first fiber sculptures between 1950 and 1952, after he became dissatisfied with the limitations of his earlier works in wood. In his new works he wove fiber around aluminum armatures to create fluid dynamic forms whose multiple lines injected an airiness into rather massive volumes yet enabled the forms to retain the solidity of sculptures in wood. Lattier focused on the physical properties of space, and he developed negative space as an essential component of form. Although his open forms emphasized the linear qualities of the subjects, Lattier's sculptures showed a keen appreciation of mass and volumes. He cited architecture and jazz among his major thematic influences, and his metal armatures and fiber constructions evoked Paris's most famous visual landmark—the Eiffel Tower.

Lattier's fiber sculptures progressed from individual pieces and stylized images of masks to complicated tableaux featuring several figures. His representation of figures ranged from naturalism in the aggressive stance of *Panther* (1954), through stylized human and animal forms whose proportions reproduced the ideals of classical African sculpture, to the architectonic volumes of late works like *Les Trois Ages de la Côte d'Ivoire* (1972). In this last sculpture several figures are superimposed on other figures, and the entire structure rises more than twenty-five feet in the shape of a Gothic-style cathedral.

Lattier had a wide range of themes and subjects. He drew inspiration equally from Christian religious imagery and from indigenous religious and secular ideas. In his renditions of old people and of beggars and others less privileged, he showed an awareness of the social contradictions of postcolonial Ivorian society. His works also revealed a romantic vision of technological development, a wry humor, and occasional flights of fancy, as in *La Côte d'Ivoire en l'an 3000* (c.1976?), with its nonrepresentational metal form and muted tones achieved through fibers of contrasting colors.

In addition to fiber sculptures Lattier produced bas-relief wood murals, low-relief metal sculptures, and sculptures in concrete, especially in works done as public commissions. Although his early works were received with ambivalence by the Ivorian art establishment, who rejected the early masterpiece *Panther*, a sculpture that subsequently won the artist much acclaim, Lattier was later embraced as an important presence and influence on contemporary art in the Ivory Coast.

Lattier's adaptation of fiberwork and European constructivism revealed a judicious synthesis, for it redirected modernism's notion of art for art's sake toward an African interpretation of art as so-cially oriented material production. His sculptures were rendered more enigmatic by the fact that he usually destroyed his sketches after each work was completed. Lattier planned to enhance his technique further by substituting plants for the fibers he used in his sculptures, thus enabling him to create living, growing pieces. He felt that this kind of work would be less intrusive on the environment while providing a cogent example of the artwork as process rather than as product, a central concern of what he considered indigenous African creativity. It is unfortunate that he died before he could realize this objective.

—Sylvester Okwunodu Ogbechie

LAWRENCE, Jacob

American painter

Born: Atlantic City, New Jersey, 1917. **Education:** Harlem Art Workshop, New York, 1932-39; American Artists School, New York 1937-39. **Family:** Gwendolyn Knight in 1941. **Awards:** Julius Rosenwald Foundation fellowships, 1940, 1941, 1942; Guggenheim Post Service Fellowship, 1946; Norman Wait Harris Medal, Art Institute of Chicago, 1948; National Institute of Arts and Letters grant, 1953; Chapelbrook Foundation Fellowship, 1954; First Prize (shared with Stuart Davis), mural competition, United Nations Building, 1955; Springarn Medal, National Association for the Advancement of Colored People, 1970; Brooklyn Arts Book for Children citation, Brooklyn Museum and Brooklyn Public Library, 1973; National Association of Schools of Art citation, 1973; Washington State Governor's Award of Special Commendation, 1981; Images Award for Outstanding Achievement in Art, University of Pittsburgh, 1988; National Medal of Arts, President George Bush, 1990; National Arts Award, The Links, 1992; National Arts Club Medal of Honor, New York, 1993; Charles White Lifetime Achievement Award, Los Angeles, 1994; Skowhegan Medal for Painting, Skowhegan School of Painting and Sculpture, New York, 1995; Algur H. Meadows Award for Excellence in the Arts, Meadows School of the Arts, Southern Methodist University, Dallas, 1996. Honorary doctorates: Denison University, 1970; Pratt Institute, 1972; Colby College, 1976; Maryland Institute of Art, 1979; Carnegie-Mellon University, 1981; State University of New York, 1984; Howard University, 1985; Yale University, 1986; Spelman College, 1987; Rutgers University, 1988; Tulane University, 1989; New York University, 1992; Harvard University, 1995; Amherst College, 1996; Seattle University, 1996. **Agent:** Francine Seders Gallery, 6701 Greenwood Avenue North, Seattle, Washington 98103-5294, U.S.A.

Individual Exhibitions:

1974   Whitney Museum of American Art, New York (retrospective)

1991   New Orleans Contemporary Art Center
     Hampton University Museum, Hampton, Virginia (traveling through 1994)

1992   Katonah Museum of Art, Katonah, New York
     Wellington B. Gray Gallery, Greenville, North Carolina (traveling through 1993)

Jacob Lawrence, 1994. Photo by Spike Mafford; courtesy of the artist and Francine Seders Gallery, Seattle, Washington.

1993	Midtown Payson Galleries, New York
	Phillips Collection, Washington, D.C. (traveling through 1995)
1994	Jacob Lawrence Gallery, University of Washington, Seattle (retrospective)
	Francine Seders Gallery, Seattle
1996	DC Moore Gallery, New York
	Dixon Gallery and Gardens, Memphis, Tennessee (traveling through 1997)

Selected Group Exhibitions:

1995	Rubelle and Norman Schafler Gallery, Pratt Institute, Brooklyn, New York
	Bellevue Art Museum, Washington
	Art Institute of Chicago
	Tulane University, New Orleans
	Boise Art Museum, Boise, Idaho (traveling through 1997)
1996	Salander-O'Reilly Galleries, New York
	Pace Wildenstein Gallery, New York
	Whitney Museum of American Art, New York
	National Academy of Design, New York

Collections:

Addison Gallery of American Art, Andover, Massachusetts; Albright-Knox Art Gallery, Buffalo, New York; American Academy and Institute of Arts and Letters, New York; Atlanta University, Georgia; Baltimore Museum of Art, Maryland; Birmingham Museum of Art, Birmingham, Alabama; Benedict College, Columbia, South Carolina; Bennet College, Greensboro, North Carolina; Brooklyn Museum, New York; Carolina Art Association/Gibbes Art Gallery, Charleston, South Carolina; Dallas Museum of Art; Detroit Institute of Arts; Evansville Museum of Arts and Science, Indiana; Fisk University, Nashville; Flint Institute of Art, Michigan; George Washington Carver Museum, Tuskegee, Alabama; Hampton University Museum, Virginia; High Museum of Art, Atlanta; Hirshhorn Museum and Sculpture Garden, Washington, D.C.; Howard University, Washington, D.C.; Library of Congress, Permanent Collection, Washington, D.C.; Metropolitan Museum of Art, New York; Museum of Fine Arts, Boston; Museum of Modern Art, New York; National Collection of Fine Arts, Washington, D.C.; National Gallery of Art, Washington, D.C.; Philadelphia Museum of Art; Phillips Collection, Washington, D.C.; Schomburg Center, New York; Spelman College, Atlanta; University Art Museum, Berkeley College, California; Vatican Gallery of Modern Art, Vatican Museum, Vatican City, Italy; Walker Art Center, Minneapolis, Minnesota; Weisman Art Museum, University of Minnesota, Minneapolis; Whitney Museum of American Art, New York.

Publications:

By LAWRENCE: Book—*The Great Migration: An American Story,* Harper Collins, New York, 1992.

On LAWRENCE: Books—*Jacob Lawrence,* exhibition catalog, by Milton W. Brown, New York, Dodd, Mead, 1974; *Jacob Lawrence American Painter,* exhibition catalog, Seattle, University of Washington Press and Ellen Harkins Wheat, 1986; *Jacob Lawrence: The Frederick Douglass and Harriet Tubman Series of 1938-40,* exhibition catalog, Seattle, University of Washington Press and Ellen Harkins Wheat, 1991; *Jacob Lawrence* by Richard J. Powell, New York, Rizzoli International, 1992; *Jacob Lawrence: The Migration Series* by Elizabeth Hutton Turner, Washington, D.C., Rappahannock Press, 1993; *Jacob Lawrence: Thirty Years of Prints (1963-1993) A Catalogue Raisonné* by Patricia Hills, University of Washington Press, Seattle, 1994. **Articles**—"Jacob Lawrence and the Legacy of Harlem" by Ellen Harkins Wheat, in *Archives of American Art Journal,* 26(1), 1986, pp. 18-25; "The World of Jacob Lawrence" by Liz M. Weiman, in *Southwest Art,* 16, July 1986, p. 80; review (Seattle Art Museum), in *American Artist,* 50, August 1986, p. 15 (illustrated); "Jacob Lawrence: A Living History" by Ron Glowen, in *Artweek,* 17, 23 August 1986, p. 1; "Jacob Lawrence: American Painter" by Fridolf Johnson, in *American Artist,* 51, September 1987, p. 28; "Jacob Lawrence: Art Builder" by Amy Fine Collins, in *Art in America,* 76, February 1988, pp. 130-45 (illustrated); "Labors of Love" by Sheila Farr, in *Artweek,* 23, 26 March 1992; "Jacob Lawrence: The Migration Series," in *Museum News,* 72, September/October 1993, pp. 16-17; review (Phillips Collection, Washington, D.C., traveling) by Eric Gibson, in *The New Criterion,* 12, December 1993, p. 51; "The Saga of American Blacks According to Jacob Lawrence" by Jason Edward Kaufman, in *Art Newspaper,* 4, December 1993, p. 14; "Jacob Lawrence: Chronicles of Color" by Elizabeth Hutton Turner, in *Southwest Art,* 23, April 1994, pp. 72-75 (illustrated); "Common Directions, Epic Dimensions: Jacob Lawrence's Murals at Howard University" by Michelle Lee White, in *International Review of African American Art,* 12(4), 1995, pp. 30-37; "Jacob Lawrence" by Glenn C. Tomlinson, in *Bulletin* (Philadelphia Museum of Art), 90, Winter 1995, p. 18-19 (illustrated); "The Naive and the Modern: Horace Pippin and Jacob Lawrence" by Karen Wilkin, in *The New Criterion,* 13, March 1995, pp. 33-38; "Jacob Lawrence" by Jenifer

Jacob Lawrence, *Other Rooms,* 1975, unframed serigraph. Photo by Spike Mafford; courtesy of Francine Seders Gallery, Seattle, Washington.

Borum, in *Artforum,* 33, May 1995, pp. 101-02; "Jacob Lawrence: Full Circle" by Roger Green, in *Art News,* 95, March 1996, p. 67 (illustrated); "Black Exodus" by Barry Schwabsky, in *Art in America,* 84, March 1996, pp. 88-93; "The Artist's Eye: Jacob Lawrence" by Carey Lovelace, in *Art News,* 95, December 1996, pp. 79-80 (illustrated). **Videos**—*Jacob Lawrence: The Glory of Expression* by Linda Freeman, Chappaqua, New York, L & S Video, 1992; *Jacob Lawrence, An Intimate Portrait,* Los Angeles, Los Angeles County Museum of Art, 1993.

*   *   *

Jacob Lawrence is the most celebrated living African American artist and the most widely acclaimed of this century. He is the only African American whose works have consistently been included in textbooks on American art. He is one of the few African American painters of his generation who was taught and influenced primarily by blacks. His paintings, which often portray the lives and struggles of African Americans, are noted for their abstract, colorful style. Lawrence works almost exclusively in gouache.

When Lawrence was twelve years old, he moved with his mother and siblings from Philadelphia to New York City. His arrival in Harlem in 1924 put him in the middle of the Harlem Renaissance. He attended public schools and enrolled in the Utopia Children's Center, an after-school program in arts and crafts. The center was operated at the time by the painter Charles Alston, who immediately recognized young Lawrence's talents. The boy showed a particular interest in drawing simple geometric patterns, which laid the foundation for the style he developed during the next decade.

Lawrence dropped out of high school during the Great Depression and, to help support his family, enrolled in the Civilian Conservation Corps, a jobs program. He was sent to upstate New York, where he planted trees, drained swamps, and built dams. When he returned, he became associated with the Harlem Community Art Center, directed by the sculptor Augusta Savage, and began painting his earliest scenes.

Lawrence immersed himself in Harlem's cultural activities. He met the self-styled "Professor" Seifert, a lecturer and historian with a large collection of African and African American literature. Seifert encouraged Lawrence to use his own personal library, to visit the Schomburg Library, and to see the Museum of Modern Art's 1935 exhibition of African art. It was this extensive exposure to African American and pan-African literature that provided the historical background for the series of panels Lawrence later painted.

During the Depression, Lawrence was assigned to an easel project with the Works Progress Administration, and under Seifert's influence he became interested in the life of Toussaint-Louverture, leader of the Haitian independence movement. Lawrence felt that he could not depict Toussaint-Louverture's achievements in a single painting, however, and so he produced a series—"The Life of Toussaint L'Ouverture" (1937)—of forty-one panels. Lawrence came to be known primarily for such series, many of them on the lives of prominent African Americans and scenes of African American life. Frederick Douglass, Harriet Tubman, and John Brown were among his subjects. Other series included those on World War II, the South, a history of the struggles of the American people, supermarkets, Genesis, and Hiroshima.

Lawrence's best-known series is "The Migration of the Negro" (1940-41), sixty panels portraying the migration of more than a million African Americans from the South to industrial cities in the North between 1910 and 1940. As in other series, the panels are linked together by color, design, and descriptive phrases. In November 1941 Lawrence's "Migration" series was exhibited at the prestigious Downtown Gallery in New York to wide acclaim. At the age of twenty-four Lawrence thus became the first African American artist to be represented by a mainstream downtown gallery. During the same month *Fortune* magazine published an article on Lawrence that included illustrations of twenty-six of the panels. In 1943 the Downtown Gallery exhibited Lawrence's "Harlem" series (1942), thirty panels that were lauded by some critics as being even more successful than those of "Migration."

In 1937 Lawrence was awarded a scholarship to the American Artists School in New York, and at about the same time he received a Rosenwald grant for three consecutive years. In 1943 Lawrence joined the U.S. Coast Guard. Following his discharge in 1945, he resumed painting. By the late 1940s he had become the most prominent African American painter in the United States. Young, gifted, and personable, he presented the image of the black artist who had truly arrived. Lawrence was, however, overwhelmed by his success, and he was deeply concerned that most of his equally talented African American peers had not fared as well. In July 1949 he voluntarily entered Hillside Hospital in Queens for treatment of depression. While he was there, he completed the remarkable "Hospital" series (1949-50) of thirty panels.

Following his discharge in 1950, Lawrence resumed painting with renewed enthusiasm, and he has continued to do so ever since. Teaching has also been an important part of his career. In 1947 he taught at Black Mountain College in North Carolina, and for a number of years he taught at the Art Students League in New York. In addition he has served on the faculties of Brandeis University, the New School for Social Research, California State College at Hayward, the Pratt Institute, and the University of Washington, where is professor emeritus of art. In 1974 the Whitney Museum of American Art in New York held a retrospective of Lawrence's work that toured nationally, and in December 1983 Lawrence was elected to the American Academy of Arts and Letters. A retrospective of Lawrence's paintings organized by the Seattle Art Museum in 1986 was accompanied by a major catalog.

Lawrence lives in Seattle with his wife, the artist Gwendolyn Knight. They were married in 1941, and their close and mutually supportive relationship has been an important factor in Lawrence's career.

—Regenia Perry

LEE-SMITH, Hughie

American painter

Born: Eustis, Florida, 20 September 1915. **Education:** Cleveland Institute of Art, Ohio, certificate of graduation, 1938; Wayne State University, Detroit, Michigan, B.S. in art education, 1953. **Military Service:** United States Navy, 1943-45: seaman first class; certificate of commendation, 1974. **Family:** Married Patricia Ann Thomas. **Career:** Instructor of painting, Art Students League, New York, Grosse Point War Memorial Association, Grosse Point Farms, Michigan, 1955-66; instructor of painting and drawing, Princeton Country Day School, New Jersey, 1963-65; adjunct professor of history, Trenton State College, New Jersey, 1972; instructor, Art Student's League, New York, 1972-84. Artist-in-residence,

Hughie Lee-Smith: *Big Brother,* 1970. Photo by Manu Sassoonian; courtesy of the Schomburg Center for Research in Black Culture.

Howard University, Washington, D.C., 1969-71. President, Audubon Artists, 1980-82. **Awards:** Clarke Prize, National Academy of Design, 1958; Allied Artists American Prize, 1958; Bronze Plaque, Maryland Commission on Afro-American History and Culture, 1981; Ralph Fabri Award, Audubon Artists, 1982; Binny and Smith Award, Audubon Artists, 1983; Art Achievement Award, Wayne State University, 1983; Key to the City of Hartford, 1984; Hughie Lee-Smith Day proclaimed, Cleveland, Ohio, 19 October 1984; Emily Lowe Award, 1985; Len Everette Memorial Prize, Audubon Artists, 1986. **Address:** 152-a Chatham Drive, Cranbury, New Jersey 08512, U.S.A.

Individual Exhibitions:

1945	Snowden Gallery, Chicago
1960	Janet Nessler Gallery, New York
1962	Janet Nessler Gallery, New York
1964	Janet Nessler Gallery, New York
1977	Western Michigan University, Kalamazoo
1984	CRT's Craftery Gallery, Hartford, Connecticut

	Century Association of New York
	Malcolm Brown Gallery, Cleveland, Ohio (through 1988)
1988	New Jersey State Museum, Trenton (traveling retrospective)
1989	Butler Institute of American Art, Youngstown, Ohio

Collections:

Alain Locke Society, Princeton University; Barnet-Aden Collection, Washington, D.C.; Howard University, Washington, D.C.; National Museum of American Art, Washington, D.C.; Schomburg Center, New York; United States Post Office, New York; University of Michigan, Ann Arbor.

Publications:

On LEE-SMITH: Articles—"The Metaphysical World of Hughie Lee-Smith," in *American Artist,* October 1978; *Link* (Cleveland Institute of Art), 1981; *Art News,* October 1994.

*   *   *

Themes of alienation and loneliness are hardly strangers in the art world, but Hughie Lee-Smith stands out as a champion of these human quandaries. His art mixes fantasy and realism in surrealistic scenarios. His ribbons, balloons, and blue skies speak of good things just beyond arm's reach and promises and poetry. His work nearly always portrays people in the throes of desolation and confusion, their feet planted in barren, crumbling environments. His attachment to piers, shorelines, vacant lots, tenement buildings, and walls is apparent in paintings done after he moved to Detroit, where city decay was abundant, and he uses the city as a metaphor for isolation. He has traced his personal alienation and pessimism to racial prejudice: "In my case, aloneness, I think, has stemmed from the fact that I'm black. Unconsciously it has a lot to do with a sense of alienation."

Lee-Smith credits his success to the influence of his mother and extended family, who recognized his art leanings at an early age and nurtured his talent. During World War II he worked in a Detroit factory making parts for airplane engines, and he served in the U.S. Navy. After the war he concentrated on painting. His education outfitted him with the techniques of classical art, and he relied on teaching and fellowships to support himself. He also studied acting and dance and has performed professionally. Lee-Smith's recognition as a professional, technically effective artist came only after fifty years of painting when a traveling retrospective of his art opened at the New Jersey State Museum in 1988. Up to that time, for the most part his work had been seen only in galleries or in survey exhibitions of African American art.

Lee-Smith once said, "My whole orientation from the beginning was towards [a] solid Renaissance kind of drawing and painting. I was very much taken with chiaroscuro at the beginning and that has carried through all my work." Growing up during the period of the Great Depression, when social realism flourished among artists, Lee-Smith admired and was influenced by Edward Hopper, Albert Pinkham Ryder, and Giorgio de Chirico. He first won accolades for his prints and etchings as a Works Progress Administration artist. In them he depicted reality but used symbols to comment on social values.

Walls have a special meaning and fascination for Lee-Smith. Their meaning is not always accessible to the viewer, however. Incongruous architectural components in controlled clutter speak of social contradictions. Lee-Smith may paint an immobile figure with his back turned or a hat hiding the face of a person contemplating an uncertain future, a man standing on his head with his mouth open as if he were screaming, or a young actress poised to speak but with questions in her eyes. These are the people in Lee-Smith's riddles. Children's play as a compositional device is also prevalent in his art and can be interpreted as an allegorical way of causing disquietude by placing social issues in the viewer's lap.

In Lee-Smith's art time has stopped. His figures have lost their bearings. Mysteries and puzzles are presented by ordinary people who have been stopped in their tracks by invisible impediments. The people are more often than not African Americans, but they sometimes are whites—simply people isolated from one another as well as from their personal worlds. Although his images often address an African American sensitivity and a concern for common people in commonplace circumstances, they have an appeal to all cultures.

As Lee-Smith has matured, his art has became lighter. Paintings in the 1980s and 1990s reflect his theatrical orientation and the mystery of the stage. Cautious optimism appears in his timeless settings, along with an element of anticipation and with ambiguous exits and entrances.

—Louise Davis Stone

LEWIS, James (Edward)
American sculptor and painter

Born: Phenix, Virginia, 4 August 1923. **Education:** Philadelphia College of Art, B.F.A.E. 1949; Temple University, Philadelphia, M.F.A. 1950; Temple University (Ford Foundation faculty fellow), Philadelphia, 1954; Syracuse University (Ford Foundation faculty fellow), 1954; Yale University (Ford Foundation faculty fellow), New Haven, Connecticut, 1955. **Military Service:** United States Marine Corps: corporal, 51st Defense Battalion's Operations and Intelligence Headquarters Company. **Family:** Married Jacqueline L. Adams in 1946, one son and one daughter. **Career:** Professor of art, chairman of the art department, and director of the Gallery of Art, Morgan State University, Baltimore, Maryland, 1950-73. Lecturer and coordinator-in-residence, Haystack Mountain School of Crafts, Deer Isle, Maine, 1974-75. Member, Owo archaeological research team, Nigeria, 1971-72. Consultant, U.S.I.A. State Department Tour to Senegal, Gambia, Nigeria, Zambia, Kenya and the Sudan, 1978. Guest curator, *Afro-American Artists Abroad,* University of Texas, 1969, *Traditional and Contemporary African Art,* Baltimore Museum of Art, Maryland, 1973, *Monumentality of Miniature African Sculpture,* Baltimore Museum of Art, Maryland, 1973. Treasurer, Maryland Art Association, 1972. **Awards:** Carnegie Grant in Art, 1939-41; Ford Foundation Fellowship, 1954-55; Anonymous Donor Award, American Federation of Arts, 1964; Outstanding Baltimore Artist, Fairmount Hill High School, Maryland; Distinguished Achievement Award, National Conference of Artists, Howard University, Washington, D.C., 1973; citation for *Black American Soldier* sculpture, U.S. Congress, 1972, Maryland State Legislature, 1973; American Cultural Scholar grant, State Department, Washington, D.C., 1974; Outstanding Educators of America Award, 1974, 1975; Personality of the South Award, American Biographical Institute, 1975-76; Outstanding Person in the Field of Art Award, Baltimore Chapter of the National Arts Equity Association, Inc., Maryland, 1978; James E. Lewis Museum of Art dedication, University of Maryland, College Park, 9 December 1990. **Address:** 5001 Herrind Run Drive, Baltimore, Maryland 21214, U.S.A.

Selected Exhibitions:

Art Alliance of Philadelphia; Atlanta University, Georgia; Baltimore Arts Festival (1972); Baltimore Museum of Art; Britain Salutes Baltimore at Stewarts, Maryland (1975); Britain Salutes Baltimore Artists, London (1976); Enoch Pratt Free Library, Baltimore (solo); Federal Plaza, Baltimore; Fellowship House, Philadelphia; Gallery I, Baltimore; Goucher College Gallery, Baltimore; Howard University, Washington, D.C.; Johns Hopkins University, Baltimore; Loyola College, Baltimore; Morgan State University, Baltimore; Peale Museum of Art, Baltimore; Philadelphia Academy of Art; Philadelphia College of Art; Phoenix Galleries, Baltimore; Print Club of Philadelphia; Pyramid Club, Philadelphia; Towson State College, Baltimore; Wharton Center, Philadelphia.

Collections:

Atlanta University, Georgia; Baltimore Museum of Art; Battle Monument Square, Baltimore; Berean School, Philadelphia; W. P. Carter Elementary School, Baltimore; Cherry Hill Junior High

School, Baltimore; Douglass High School, Baltimore; Howard University, Washington, D.C.; King Memorial Park, Baltimore; Morgan State University, Baltimore; Philadelphia College of Art; Southwestern High School, Baltimore; Tyler School of Art, Temple University, Philadelphia; U.S.I.A. Library, Lusaka, Gambia; Wharton Center, Philadelphia.

Publications:

By LEWIS: Book—*Ethiopian Artists in America,* exhibition catalog, Baltimore, Morgan State University, 1973. **Articles**—"Traditional African Art and Its Influence," in *Baltimore Bulletin of Education,* 55(203), 1968-69; "Senoufo Firespitter Masks," in *African Forum: Journal of the American Association of African Culture,* December 1969; "Highlights from the Atlanta University Collection of Afro-American Art," in *Afro-American Newspaper* (Baltimore Museum of Art), 1974.

On LEWIS: Articles—"The Owo Dig: A New Dimension on West Africa Age" by James H. Bready, in *Baltimore Evening Sun,* 10 May 1971; "Two Blacks Discover Lost African World," in *Ebony,* November 1971; "James E. Lewis: Making Visible the Invisible Artist," in *Sunday Sun,* 19 March 1972; "Treasures of Ancient Nigeria," in *Philadelphia Tribune,* 17 March 1982; "Sculpting a Legend: A Bust of Dr. King," in *Sunday Sun,* 16 May 1982; "MSU Renames Gallery," in *Baltimore Afro-American,* 12 January 1991.

*   *   *

James Lewis is best known for his bronze statues of Frederick Douglass, which were completed in 1956 at Morgan State University in Baltimore. These classic sculptures were rendered in a dignified style, with Douglass's head held high. The stride with the cane depicts the intellectual and statesmanly character of the subject. Lewis also treated the black soldier in elegant, heroic posture in his nine-and-a-half-foot *Salute to the Black Soldier,* which is located in downtown Baltimore. The soldier raises high a wreath and medal of honor to show the pride and dignity with which the black soldier performed his duties. Other heroic pieces done by the artist include the bust of Martin Luther King, Jr., for the King Memorial Park in Baltimore and a felicitous figure of Clarence Mitchell, former president of the NAACP.

In the mid-1950s Lewis had an opportunity to work with Josef Albers of Yale University, who greatly influenced his later style. Albers, a leading figure in the German Bauhaus movement, helped Lewis to expand his art beyond his earlier academic forms and to reach out to the traditional African art forms for inspiration. Albers also helped Lewis to develop his awareness of modern art movements. Lewis once said, "with Albers, my previous concepts were completely shaken up and I had to begin to think of art in a much broader sense than I had ever done before. And on the heels of that was a new awareness and interest in traditional African Art."

In 1958 Lewis mounted an exhibition entitled *Calculated Image,* which was one of the most significant influences on his later work of that period. Lewis said, "we need to look at the image created and calculated, planning to get certain kinds of response. It involves optics and seeing, both physical and psychological phenomena."

Both the *Cherry Hill Relief* and the *Broadway Fountain* in Baltimore were total departures from his early works, as he made use of the geometric forms found in Ashanti art. Lewis explained that he did not copy the Ashanti designs but adapted them to his own

works. A combination of the hard-edge, calculated abstract expressionist forms with Ashanti motifs enabled Lewis to create his own black aesthetic. The lines and shapes of the *Broadway Fountain,* for example, are repetitious, yet elegant and rhythmical with the rise and fall of water from the fountain.

Lewis's works are not political statements, but they did help to create a new movement in the African American art world. Like Picasso, Derain, Matisse, and other famous painters, who made use of traditional African art to create new movements at the turn of the twentieth century, so James Lewis and other African American artists have created the unofficial movement known as Afro-centric abstract expressionism.

—Gabriel Tenabe

LEWIS, Joseph (S., III)
American painter and sculptor

Born: New York, 22 February 1953. **Education:** Hamilton College, New York, B.A. 1975; Brooklyn College, New York; Maryland Institute College of Art, Baltimore, Maryland, M.F.A. 1989. **Career:** Administrator, Public Art Program, Cultural Affairs Department, City of Los Angeles, 1992-94; project manager, Art for Rail Program, Metropolitan Transportation Authority, Los Angeles, 1994-95. Since 1995 chair, Department of Art, California State University, Los Angeles. Founding trustee and vice president of the board, Museum for Contemporary Art, 1990-92; board president, Side Street Projects, Santa Monica, California, 1992-95. **Agent:** Robert Berman Gallery, 2525 Michigan Avenue, #C2, Santa Monica, California 90404, U.S.A. **Address:** 4350 Beverly Boulevard, Los Angeles, California 90004, U.S.A.

Selected Exhibitions:

1978	*Chant Acapella,* Museum of Modern Art, New York
1980	New Museum, New York
1985	P.S. 1, New York
1990	*The Decade Show,* Studio Museum in Harlem, New York
1992	California Afro-American Museum, Los Angeles
1993	*Primary Peoples Colleges and Shapes,* University Gallery, Illinois State University, Normal
1994	San Antonio Museum of Art, Texas
	High Museum, Atlanta, Georgia
1995	Los Angeles County Museum of Art
	Smithsonian Institution, Washington, D.C.
1996	*Disciples of the Hood: Joe Lewis and the Neo-Ancestralist,* Contemporary Arts Center, Cincinnati, Ohio

Collections:

Experimental Print Workshop, New York; University of New York, Potsdam; Studio Museum in Harlem, New York; University of Colorado, Boulder.

Publications:

By LEWIS: Articles—"How to Commit Suicide in South Africa: The Work of Sue Coe," in *Artforum,* April 1982; "Jean Michel

Basquiat," in *Contemporanea*, July-August 1988; "Soul Shadows: Urban Warrior Myths: The Work of Dawn Dedeaux," in *Artspace*, March/April 1993; "Radcliffe Bailey at Fay Gold," in *Art in America*, March 1995; "Jim McHugh at the High Museum," in *Art in America*, June 1996.

*   *   *

It is not enough for Joe Lewis to create art that addresses problems of technique or other compositional dynamics of space and form. Rather, his art is inclusive of his life's experiences, which he does not separate from his artistic processes. Because his life was affected by poverty and prejudice in his youth, resulting in a keen recognition of injustices on personal, community, and institutional levels, his artwork is not only influenced by these experiences but is also of them.

Much of Lewis's work is concerned with the inner strength needed to move through life. Most of his works therefore make reference to life-giving organisms themselves. In *D.N.A. Black and Blue* (1989) the enzymatic sweetness, or even preciousness, of life is represented by Tootsie Roll Pops. The chain saw that intrudes upon the DNA loop has the neon letters *CIA* and *DOD* (Department of Defense) above it, signifying these agencies' involvement in and experimentation with human lives for political gain. *The First Time I Saw a Radio like This Was the Day after I Heard That White People Could Get Sickle Cell Too* (1989) also addresses the core of human existence, cell structure. In this work a large boom box is held in the arms of white blood cells with a red neon sign that reads "SICKLE CELL" suspended in the back corner of the gallery wall, which is bathed in red light. A digital display sign rests at the bottom of the monsterlike cells and continually runs the complete title of the work, signifying that "what goes around comes around." Both of these works attempt to level the playing field among the races by going to the biological components that all humans share. If one group is going to be denied access to insurance because of sickle cell anemia, AIDS, or other diseases or denied immigration because of strains of disease in their native country, as in Haiti, all must be denied.

Lewis also creates works as reminders of how communities have been "ripped apart by false prophets, fear and misunderstanding." In his installation *Circle the Mules* (1993), which refers to the promise of forty acres and a mule that many African Americans consider one of the first promises denied after emancipation, Lewis's mules are painted with the seven principles of Kwanza: unity, self-determination, collective work and responsibility, faith, creativity, purpose, and cooperative economics. The work is about reclaiming space, dignity, artifacts, and pride in communities. In the work he also addresses the humanity of people rather than their biological makeup and maintains a positive outlook that eventually the personal humanistic commitment represented by the mules will be embraced.

In *I'm on My Way* (1994) Lewis refers to his work as an undergraduate at Hamilton College. There he concentrated on the work of fourteenth-century Italian painters who depicted the deeds of martyrs and saints and the obstacles they had to confront as they sought to enter the kingdom of God. Lewis found parallels in other cultures to their persisting fortitude and strength. In *I'm on My Way*, therefore, he has painted photographically assisted murals of components of Italian and Middle Eastern landscapes. The image in the work is a sultan's palace in Canaan, referring to the text of the song ("I'm on my way to Canaan land [modern-day Palestine]") and signifying the continuing struggle for self-determination by African Americans. The juxtaposition of paintings by Titian and Rembrandt and of sculpture by Michelangelo with freedom songs that were appropriated from Negro folk songs or spirituals of the nineteenth century consciously meshes Western concepts of fine art with the vernacular art forms of African Americans. This denies the whole premise of modern thinking on art that was fostered by critics such as Clement Greenberg as he successfully articulated a distinction between fine and folk, refined and unrefined, literate and illiterate, and academic and self-taught art, creating biases against one and establishing privilege for the other.

While not shying away from the political messages inherent in his work, Lewis is cautious not to be heavy-handed and to forsake the objects that he has assembled and recontextualized. He says that he remains "interested in the beauty of objects. People who do political art tend to focus more on propaganda, and consequently then can miss more interior, intuitive stuff."

—Lizzetta LeFalle-Collins

LEWIS, (Mary) Edmonia

American sculptor

Also used the name Wildfire. **Born:** Greenbush, New York, 14 July 1845(?). **Education:** Oberlin College, 1859-63; studied with Edmund Brackett, Boston, c.1863-65; traveled to Italy in 1865. **Family:** Married D.J. (or D.G.) Peck c.1869. **Career:** Supported herself through commissions and private patronage. Lived and worked in Rome, where she might have died. **Award:** Gold Medal, Naples Academy of Art and Science, c.1876. **Died:** Date unrecorded.

Selected Exhibitions:

1862	Centennial Exhibition, London
1870	Farwell Hall Exhibit, Chicago
1873	San Francisco Art Association
1876	Philadelphia Semi-Centennial
1878	Chicago Exposition
1940	American Negro Exhibition, Chicago
1945	South Side Community Art Center, Chicago
1967	Howard University, Washington, D.C.
1969	City College of New York
1972	Vassar College, Poughkeepsie, New York

Collections:

Frederick Douglass Institute of Negro Arts and History, Washington, D.C.; Harvard College Library, Cambridge, Massachusetts; Kennedy Gallery, New York; National Museum of American Art, Washington, D.C.; San Jose Public Library, California.

Publications:

On LEWIS: Books—*How Edmonia Lewis Became an Artist,* Cambridge Massachusetts, Harvard Library, 1870; *The Centennial Exposition* by J.S. Ingram, Philadelphia, Hubbard Brothers, 1876; *Ten*

Afro-American Artists of the Nineteenth Century, exhibition catalog, Washington, D.C., Howard University and James A. Porter, 1967. **Articles**—"Edmonia Lewis" by Laura Bullard, in *Revolution* (New York), 20 April 1871; article, in *Pacific Appeal,* 16 August 1873; "Race Prejudice and the Negro Artist" by James Weldon Johnson, in *Harper's Magazine,* 157, November 1928, pp. 769-76; "John Mercer Langston and the Case of Edmonia Lewis: Oberlin, 1862" by Geoffrey Blodgett, in *Journal of Negro History,* July 1968, p. 201; "Edmonia Lewis" by James A. Porter, in *NAW,* 2, 1971, pp. 397-99; "Edmonia Lewis," in *A History of African-American Artists, from 1792 to the Present* by Romare Bearden and Harry Henderson, Pantheon Books, New York, 1993, pp. 54-77; "Edmonia Lewis' *The Death of Cleopatra: Myth and Identity*" by Marilyn Richardson, in *The International Review of African American Art,* Hampton University Museum, Virginia, 1995.

*   *   *

Edmonia Lewis achieved a high degree of fame, independence, and wealth as a neoclassical sculptor in the late nineteenth century. Both Lewis and her best-known work, *Cleopatra,* came to the attention of the world at the 1876 Philadelphia Centennial Exhibition. Although she lived much of her life in Europe, Lewis's sculptures celebrate both her Native American and African American heritages, while reflecting her feminist ideals.

Lewis created more than sixty marble sculptures during the course of a career that spanned five decades. Her sculpture, termed ideal because her imagery was often based on narratives from literature, mythology, and the Bible, depicted abolitionist themes and openly discussed the precarious social position of newly freed blacks. Later sculptures celebrated Lewis's Ojibwa heritage through illustrations of episodes from *The Song of Hiawatha,* the popular poem by Henry Wadsworth Longfellow. Despite the commercial nature of her sculpture, Lewis subverted Victorian stereotypes of Native and African American peoples that were negative, sexually exploitative, and inaccurate.

Forever Free (1867), for example, depicts a black man standing next to a kneeling black woman, both of whom have just been freed from the bonds of slavery. The title was inspired by a line of text from the Emancipation Proclamation. In Lewis's bust *Minnehaha* (1868) she sculpted the princess with perceptible Native American facial features—high cheekbones and a bump on the bridge of her nose. In *Old Arrow Maker and His Daughter* (1872) the girl's nose is straight, while her father's is not, and he also has high and prominent cheekbones. The narrative behind Lewis's *Hagar in the Wilderness* (1875), which was based on the biblical story, became an allegorical statement about the abuses suffered by black women when a black patriarchy is not in place to protect them. Speaking in reference to an earlier version of *Hagar* that is now lost, Lewis was widely quoted as saying, "I have a strong sympathy for all women who have suffered."

Cleopatra is an exalted image of black identity. In the late nineteenth century Egypt was a code name for black Africa. Contemporaries of Lewis used the Egyptian queen to illustrate themes of lust, greed, violence, and decadence. Lewis countered these fantasies by making her Cleopatra a noble queen, thus restoring the historical reality of a remarkable woman while elevating ideals about African and African American people as a whole.

Lewis has been criticized and dismissed for depicting her ethnic subjects with Caucasian facial features. While her men look specifically ethnic—her black men have curly hair and thick lips and her Native American men high cheekbones and pronounced noses—the majority of Lewis's women appear distinctly Caucasian. What is ethnic about them, however, is their costuming. Her black women wear chains, manacles, and iron balls, while her Indian women wear animal skins, beads, and feathers. Of greater significance is what Lewis chose not to sculpt: half-naked black or Indian women representing the erotic exploitation of the nonwhite female body as the exotic other, which was the stock-in-trade of her neoclassical contemporaries.

Lewis walked a fine line with her sculpture. Her content was an assertion of ethnic truth within the bounds of what white patrons would allow. The Western, European faces of her women were modeled on the classical Roman busts she had studied, while safely conforming to prescriptions defining the cult of womanhood found throughout Victorian literature. Unable to move boldly forward, Lewis moved sideways and eliminated ethnic identity in order to eliminate negative stereotypes. Mediating the experience of her racial heritages through sympathetic models sanctioned by the dominant culture, Lewis recast images of Native and African American women in European discourse. Her work is thus that of the quiet revolutionary. In the context of modern strong ethnic identification, however, Lewis's intent may be difficult to believe in and may also seem naive.

Lewis returned to the United States from time to time to show her sculptures. In later years her fame was eclipsed by the rise of the impressionists, and her sculptural style fell out of vogue.

—Laurie Fitzpatrick

LEWIS, Norman
American painter, printmaker, and muralist

Born: New York, 23 July 1909. **Education:** Columbia University, New York, John Reed Club Art School, New York, c.1933-35. **Family:** Married Ouida Lewis. **Career:** Instructor, Savage Studio, New York, 1935-37, Harlem Art Center, Federal Art Project, New York, 1936-39, George Washington Carver School, New York, 1943-44, Thomas Jefferson School of Social Science, New York, 1944-49, Indian Hill Music School, Stockbridge, Massachusetts, 1954, Harlem Youth in Action (HARYOU-ACT), New York, 1965-71, Art Students League, New York, 1972-77. Seaman, South America, c.1929-31. **Awards:** Popularity Prize, Carnegie International Exhibition, 1955; American Academy of Arts and Letters, 1970; National Institute of Arts and Letters, 1971; National Endowment for the Arts grant, 1972; Guggenheim Memorial Foundation Fellowship, 1975. **Died:** 27 August 1979.

Individual Exhibitions:

1949	Willard Gallery, New York
1950	Willard Gallery, New York
1951	Willard Gallery, New York
1952	Willard Gallery, New York
1953	Willard Gallery, New York
1954	Willard Gallery, New York
1957	Willard Gallery, New York
1976	Graduate Center, City University of New York (retrospective)

Norman Lewis: *Street Music (Jenkins Band)*, 1944. Photo by Manu Sassoonian; courtesy of the Schomburg Center for Research in Black Culture.

| 1985 | Robeson Center Gallery, Newark, New Jersey |
| 1989 | Kenkeleba Gallery, New York (retrospective) |

Selected Group Exhibitions:

1940	Tanner Galleries, Chicago
1941	Downtown Gallery, New York
1944	Carnegie Institute, Pittsburgh
1945	Albany Institute of History and Art, New York
1951	Museum of Modern Art, New York
1955	Carnegie Institute, New York
1956	Art Institute of Chicago
1958	Whitney Museum of American Art, New York
1967	City College of New York

Collections:

Addison Gallery of American Art, Andover, Massachusetts; Art Institute of Chicago; Barnett-Aden Collection, Washington, D.C.; Evan-Tibbs Collection, Washington, D.C.; Munson-Williams-Proctor Institute, Utica, New York; New Jersey State Museum, Trenton.

Publications:

On LEWIS: Books—*Norman Lewis: A Retrospective,* exhibition catalog, by Tom Lawson, New York, City University of New York, 1976; *Norman Lewis: The Black Paintings,* exhibition catalog, by Kellie Jones, Newark, New Jersey, Rutgers University, 1985; *Norman Lewis: From the Harlem Renaissance to Abstraction,* exhibition catalog, by Ann Gibson, New York, Kenkeleba Gallery, 1989. **Articles**—"Fifty-Seventh Street in Review: Abstractions by Norman Lewis" by Marynell Sharp, in *Art Digest* (New York), 1 April 1950; "Fifty-Seventh Street in Review: Norman Lewis" by Dore Ashton, in *Art Digest* (New York), 15 November 1951; "Reviews and Previews: Norman Lewis" by Irving Sandler, in *Art News* (New York), January 1962; "Recasting the Canon: Norman Lewis and Jackson Pollock" by Ann Gibson, in *Artforum* (New York), March 1992.

*   *   *

Norman Lewis tested the limits of abstraction, and his artistic journey is a record of the evolution of the New York avant-garde. His early work in the social realist mode often featured strong icons, and their elegant lines and color schemes bore the portent of his talent. In his mature years the artist worked representation in

325

and out of his canvases, creatively exploring the concepts of abstract expressionism.

Sculpture was a formative influence in Lewis's training. The New York-born artist studied with the sculptor Augusta Savage at her Harlem school in the 1930s, and he later taught there as well. He was a keen student of African sculpture, then on display at the Museum of Modern Art, and his pastel drawings of busts and masks illuminate his efforts to give two-dimensional art the power of sculpture. The genre portraits *Washerwoman* and *The Yellow Hat* (both 1936) and *Madonna* (1939) succeed in doing so. In his depiction of these female subjects, the artist transformed them into sturdy volumetric forms and put their body designs in play with the geometry of the setting.

In the following decade Lewis's interests moved from abstract figuration toward inventive pastiches of European modernism. Key paintings of the 1940s—*Untitled 5* (1945), *Composition Number One* (1945), and *Fantasy* (1946)—were influenced by the cubism of Pablo Picasso and Georges Braque, by the organic forms of Wassily Kandinsky and Joan Miró, by the grids of Piet Mondrian, and by the indeterminate pictorial spaces of Arshile Gorky. Early in the decade Lewis painted eerie, liquid figures. Figuralism then gave way to abstract masses, confluent lines, and color-fields. His nonobjective paintings frequently referred to black settings and culture, as in *Harlem Courtyard* (1954) and *Players Four* (1966). Other works were less referentially titled, as Lewis attempted to develop a visual language that depended on the strength of an idea-driven structure. Describing his efforts, Lewis wrote that he was trying to shed the particularity of realist imagery in favor of more conceptual expression. His sentiments were the objectives voiced by Jackson Pollock, Robert Motherwell, and Ad Reinhardt, with whom Lewis socialized and debated in the group known as Studio 35. An exhibitor at the influential Marion Willard Gallery in Manhattan from 1946 to 1964, Lewis knew intimately and was influenced by the work of fellow Willard artists Mark Tobey, Lyonel Feininger, and David Smith. These artistic exchanges, like those Lewis had had at the Savage Studio, in the Harlem Art Guild, and at the Art Union, stimulated his imagination.

Lewis's visual language of the 1950s and 1960s was alternately fragmentary and suggestive (*Ovum,* 1961), improvisational and decorative (*Kites,* 1962), and occasionally restrained (*Mumbo Jumbo,* 1950). Many paintings were large in scale, in the grand mode of abstract expressionism, and their titles reflected the movement's lofty themes. Exemplary of this is *Arrival and Departure* (1963), a stately work whose monochromatic surface appears torn by jags of color, creating a shifting and unpredictable pictorial space.

The 1965 work *Processional* is a unique composition done at Lewis's creative peak. A black, horizontally expanding field is interrupted by a narrow band of graceful white swaths. The image resembles moving figures, and the painting, done in the era of civil rights protests, seems to be a dynamic frieze of marching demonstrators. A founding member of SPIRAL, a black artists group established to make visual contributions to the civil rights struggle, Lewis was a lifetime political activist. *Processional* is a document not only of the movement and of racial advancement but also of its maker's triumphant artistry.

—Jacqueline Francis

LEWIS, Samella (Sanders)
American painter and mixed-media artist

Born: Greater New Orleans, 27 February 1924. **Education:** Hampton University, Virginia, B.S. 1945; Ohio State University, M.A. 1948, Ph.D. 1951. **Family:** Married Paul G. Lewis in 1948, two sons. **Career:** Instructor, Hampton Institute, 1946-47; associate professor, Morgan State University, 1948-53; professor and chair, Florida A & M University, 1953-58; professor, University of the State of New York, 1958-68; associate professor, California State University, Long Beach, 1966-67; coordinator of education, Los Angeles County Museum of Art, 1968-69; professor, Scripps College (Claremont Colleges), California, 1970-84. National cochairperson, National Conference of Artists, 1972-74; director, Clark Humanities Museum (Scripps College), 1976-84; administrator, College Art Association of America, 1990-94. Beginning in 1976 editor, *International Review of African American Art.* Since 1980 project director, National Endowment for the Arts. Founder, Museum of African American Art, 1976, Museum of African American Art, 1976; member, national screening committee Fulbright Fellowship Awards, 1977-80. **Awards:** Fulbright Fellowship, 1962; National Defense Education Act Fellow, 1964; Ford Foundation Fellow, New York, 1965; National Research Council/Ford Foundation Fellow, 1981; honorary doctorate, Chapman College, 1976; Who's Who in Black America Award, 1982; Senate of California Special Award, 1983; Vesta Award, 1984; Scripps College Faculty Recognition Award, 1984; Professor Emerita, Scripps College 1984; Los Angeles Achievement in the Visual Arts Award, 1985; Citation for Distinguished Alumnae, Ohio State University, 1986; National Conference of Artist Achievement Award, 1988; Outstanding Achievement in Visual Arts, Women's Caucus for the Arts Honor Award, 1989; Legends in Our Time Tribute, Essence Magazine, 1990; honorary doctorate, Hampton University, 1990; Lifetime Achievement Award, Brandywine Workshop, 1992; Charles White Lifetime Achievement Award, 1993; honorary doctorate, University of Cincinnati, 1993; UNICEF Award, 1995; honorary doctorate, Bennett College, 1996; Getty Center for the History of Art and the Humanities Distinguished Scholar Award, 1996-97. **Agent:** Claude Lewis, Art Traditions, 14565 Ogden Drive, Los Angeles, California 90019, U.S.A.

Individual Exhibitions:

1972	Rainbow Sign Gallery, Berkeley, California
1981	Pasadena City College, California
	University of California, San Diego
1984	Museum of African Art, Los Angeles
1986	West Dade Regional Library, Miami
1990	Hampton University, Virginia
	Delta Art Center, Winston Salem, North Carolina
1993	*The Evolution of an Artist,* Morehouse College
	Robert Joseph Gallery, Cincinnati, Ohio
1994	Bennett College, Greensboro, North Carolina
1995	Junior Black Academy of Arts and Letters, Dallas
	N.C.A. Gallery, Detroit
1996	Bill Hodges Gallery, New York
1997	Hampton University Museum, Virginia
	Norman Parish Gallery, Georgetown

Selected Group Exhibitions:

1981	*Impressions/Expressions: Black American Graphics*
	Mandeville Gallery, University of California, San Diego
1984	African American Art in Atlanta, Georgia

Samella Lewis. Photo courtesy of Sid Fridkin.

1987 *Reality, Myth and Ritual,* California State University, Long
       Beach
1992 Newark Museum, New Jersey
1993 Bomani Gallery, San Francisco
1995 Studio Museum in Harlem, New York (traveling)
       Montgomery Art Gallery, Pomona College, Claremont,
         California
       Baltimore Museum of Art, Maryland
1996 Satori Fine Art Gallery, Chicago
       Stella Jones Gallery, New Orleans

Collections:

Atlanta University Gallery of Contemporary Art, Georgia; Baltimore Museum of Fine Arts, Maryland; Hampton University Collection, Virginia; High Museum, Atlanta, Georgia; Howard University Museum, Washington, D.C.; Johnson Publications Collections; Oakland Museum, California; Ohio State University; Viktor Lowenfeld Memorial Gallery; Virginia Museum of Fine Art, Richmond.

Publications:

By LEWIS: Books—*Black Artists on Art,* 2 volumes, Hancraft Studios, Los Angeles, 1969 (revised 1976); *Art: African American,* Harcourt, Brace, Jovanovich, New York, 1978, revised 1990; *The Art of Elizabeth Catlett,* Museum of African American Art and Hancraft Studios, Los Angeles, 1984; *African American Art for Young People,* Hancraft Studios, Los Angeles, 1991; *African American Art and Artists,* University of California Press, Berkeley, 1994. **Articles**—"Cuba," in *Black Scholar,* Summer 1977; "Black America," in *Centro de Estudio Economicos 7 Sociales del Tercer Mundo AC.,* Mexico, 1982; "Elizabeth Catlett," in *Journal of Paint World,* 16(4), Fall 1993.

On LEWIS: Article—"Dealers," in *Black Enterprise,* Volume 6, December 1975, pp. 43-45.

*

Samella Lewis comments:
   My art evolves out of the need to communicate ideas and expe-

riences that have influenced my life and the lives of those of my culture and my community.

I am motivated to express myself primarily through two- and three-dimensional forms and to structure my content in a concise manner so as to be understood by ordinary people. Further, my wish is to express some of what history has taught me and use it to better understand what life will bring.

My study at Hampton (Institute) University brought about the turning point in my development as an individual and as an artist. The Hampton experience reinforced my belief in self and, through a strong academic program and an enriched system, enhanced my cultural and creative values.

*   *   *

Variety and experimentation characterize the oeuvre of Samella Lewis. Prominent among her works—from her student days in the early 1940s to the 1990s—are paintings on canvas, most executed in oil though some in acrylic. But she has also produced ink paintings, woodcuts, and linocuts; drawings in graphite, charcoal, or litho crayon; watercolors, serigraphs, lithographs, and pieces in mixed media; and, recently, prismacolor computer prints. The style of the work is also wide ranging, from realistic portraiture to abstract landscapes. What is common throughout her work is the inspiration of African American culture and a strong ability to convey emotion through color.

While still a high school student, Lewis studied portraiture. Her 1940 painting *Portrait of Warren Kenner* (oil on canvas), among the earliest of her work that is extant, is remarkably realistic and powerful. Recognized by her fellow Hampton Institute classmates as one of the most talented of the group in the early 1940s, Lewis in this painting demonstrates her skill, even at the beginning of her career, as a draftswoman. It is also an early suggestion of her preference for the use of strong color, such as ocher, reds, and blues, which is evident throughout her work.

While a student at Hampton, Lewis produced a group of genre paintings, capturing scenes from family life on large canvases or boards. While several appear to be inspired directly by her Louisiana childhood (*Sharecropper Family*, 1944, and *Waterboy*, 1944), others are drawn from the everyday experience of ordinary people (*Stimulant*, 1943, *The Preacher*, 1943, and *Home from Boot Camp*, 1943). In each of these paintings the forms fill the space. Individual bodies and closely clustered groups of people extend from the top to the bottom and one side to the other of the canvas, frequently pushing beyond the edges. The result pulls the viewer into the scene as a participant in a very forceful way.

During the late 1940s and well into the 1950s, Lewis largely turned to producing smaller works on paper. Colorful, engaging watercolors include portraits (*Aunt Laura*, 1949), landscapes (*Plantation House*, 1949), and genre scenes (*Prayer Meeting*, 1951). During the same time, she created portraits in charcoal, graphite, or wax crayon and a group of ink paintings with strong social messages (*Social Commentary*, 1949, *Three Shades of Blackness*, 1951, and *Church Scene*, 1951). A 1951 acrylic painting, *Southern Expose*, is perhaps one of her strongest and most immediate political statements; with a dark canvas, crowded with bodies, it is an effective comment on the American South.

A renowned art historian, teacher, and arts administrator, Lewis has said that African American art should be understandable to the community and should use symbols familiar to "black lives." Her black and white prints and graphite drawings of the 1960s, 1970s,

and 1980s are an important subcollection of her work. They demonstrate as well as any of her work that as an artist she successfully achieved the standards that she set for others. Her graphite pieces are very able examples of technique reinforcing subject matter and are often characterized by strong black areas in the image. Although the content of Lewis's work has continued to be drawn from African American experience, by the 1970s and 1980s it was also inspired by her research into Afro-Caribbean and Afro-Brazilian culture and by her travels to those regions.

In the 1990s Lewis was still producing work in a variety of media: serigraphs, lithographs, computer art, graphite drawings, and mixed media. She has returned, however, to creating paintings on large canvases. These are expressive, bright, and strongly colored works that include both human figures and landscapes. Infrequently an abstract painting also emerges, demonstrating this versatile artist's comfort with experimentation and variety. She has commented that with this body of work she has finally been able to "produce work from beautiful things."

—Jeanne Zeidler

LIAUTAUD, Georges
Haitian sculptor

Born: Croix-des-Bouquets, Haiti, 1899. **Career:** Railroad repairman and blacksmith. Joined Centre d'Art in 1953. **Died.**

Individual Exhibitions:

1960   Port-au-Prince, Haiti
        Pan American Union, Washington, D.C.

Selected Group Exhibitions:

1968   Center for Inter-American Relations, New York
1969   Davenport Art Gallery, Davenport, Iowa
1973   Fabian Gallery, New York
1974   Davenport Art Gallery, Davenport, Iowa
1978   Brooklyn Museum, New York (traveling)
1982   Studio Museum in Harlem, New York
1983   Chicago Public Library Cultural Center
        Davenport Art Gallery, Davenport, Iowa
1985   Yale University Art Gallery, New Haven, Connecticut
        Davenport Art Gallery, Davenport, Iowa
1987   Musée du Panthéon National, Port-au-Prince, Haiti
        Cavin Morris Gallery, New York
1988   Galleries Nationales d'Exposition du Grand Palais, Paris
1989   Museum of Art, Fort Lauderdale, Florida
        Musée National d'Art Moderne, Paris

Collections:

Centre d'Art, Port-au-Prince, Haiti; Davenport Museum of Art, Iowa; Flagg Collection, Milwaukee, Wisconsin; Musée d'Art Haitien du Collège St. Pierre, Port-au-Prince, Haiti; Museum Boymans-van Beuningen, Rotterdam; Museum of Modern Art, New York; Museum of Modern Art of Latin America, Washington, D.C.; New

George Liautaud, c.1980. Photo courtesy of Thomas M. Shaw.

Orleans Museum of Art, Perry E.H. Smith Collection; Pan American Union, Washington, D.C.; Studio Museum in Harlem, New York; Yale University Art Gallery, New Haven, Connecticut.

Publications:

On LIAUTAUD: Book—*Tracing the Spirit: Ethnographic Essays on Haitian Art, from the Collection of the Davenport Museum of Art,* by Karen McCarthy Brown, Davenport Museum of Art, Iowa, 1995, pp. 3, 10, 12. **Article**—"Georges Liautaud" by Randall Morris, in *Black Art,* 4(4), 1981, p. 35.

*   *   *

The genre of Haitian metal sculpture had its inventor and great master in the person of Georges Liautaud. He has had many imitators and followers, both in his hometown of Croix-des-Bouquets and in Port-au-Prince. Although few of these men have attained his prominence and stature, all of them owe their ultimate inspiration to him.

Liautaud's characteristic work consisted of monochromatic images cut out of flat metal, often pieces of oil drums. The figures

were distinctive, and there was often one major image, a humanlike figure with wispy or understated appendages for arms and legs. Occasionally one large figure was surrounded by smaller subsidiary figures. Details such as breasts stood out from the surface in subtle raised relief. Liautaud created such details by hammering the figure from the reverse side.

Liautaud typically worked by planning out a sculpture on paper. He first drew the outline of his intended work and then cut out a silhouette from the drawing. He used this silhouette as a kind of pattern for the image in metal.

Most of Liautaud's sculptures were small, but others, like the great figure in the Musée d'Art Haitien, were monumental in scale. He did not paint the surfaces, but he often enhanced them by rubbing them with oil. The painting of metal sculptures was a later development that took the form into a different aesthetic realm.

Liautaud created his sculptures at a hearth located next to his home. In later years he worked there with assistants. Overshadowing the hearth was a mountainous heap of scrap metal, a testament to his long life of work at the forge. Perhaps the metallic mound also symbolically honored the voodoo spirits of metalwork.

The link between Liautaud's work and the African past was strong. Haiti is perhaps the most West African society in the New World, and many visitors say that it is as if part of the African continent had drifted westward into the Caribbean Sea. Too, the town of Croix-des-Bouquets, just outside Port-au-Prince, is a major center for the practice of voodoo, the African-based religion of Haiti. The vivid imagery of the Liautaud's figures hinted at the richness of voodoo as a source for his art. Of the many *lwa*s, or spirits, associated with voodoo metalwork, Ogou Feray and Bawon Samdi are especially strong. Liautaud began his work with metal by making iron crosses for a cemetery, which is the realm of Bawon Samdi. His metal sculpture was thus an outgrowth of his early work on iron crosses. Ogou Feray is the *lwa* equivalent of Sen Jak (Saint-Jacques or Saint James). In the Middle Ages, Saint James intervened on the side of the Christians against the Muslims, his military assistance ensuring that Europe would become Christianized.

In the 1980s Liautaud was at the apex of a Haitian cultural triad, the other two men being Pierre Monosiet, the director of the Musée d'Art Haitien and a patron of young artists, and Max Beauvoir, a voodoo *houngan*, or priest, and an entrepreneur and interpreter of voodoo to foreigners. Liautaud was a gracious, patient, and unpretentious man, and he grew accustomed to receiving a stream of art scholars and art lovers from Europe and the United States who made the trek to Croix-des-Bouquets.

—Thomas M. Shaw

LIGON, Glenn

American painter, printmaker, and installation artist

Born: 20 April 1960. **Education:** Rhode Island School of Design, Providence, 1980; Wesleyan University, Middletown Connecticut, 1978-82, B.A. 1982; Whitney Museum Independent Study Program, 1985. **Career:** Administrative assistant, Boys' Harbor, New York, 1982-83; proofreader, Skadder Arps, New York, 1983-91. **Awards:** National Endowment for the Arts internship, 1982; P.S. 1 National Studio Program, The Clocktower, New York, 1989-90; National Endowment for the Arts Fellowship (drawing), 1989; Dewar's Young Artist Recognition Award, 1990; Art Matters, Inc., Fellowship, 1990; National Endowment for the Arts Fellowship (painting), 1991; Rockefeller Foundation, Bellagio Study Center, Italy, 1994; Joan Mitchell Award, 1996; ArtPace International Artist-in-Residence Program, San Antonio, Texas, 1997-98. **Agent:** Max Protetch, 560 Broadway, New York, New York 10012, U.S.A. **Address:** 168 Prospect Place, Brooklyn, New York 11238, U.S.A.

Individual Exhibitions:

1982	Davison Art Center, Wesleyan University, Middletown, Connecticut
1990	BACA Downtown, Brooklyn, New York
	P.S. 1 Museum, Long Island City, New York
1991	Project Room, Jack Tilton Gallery, New York
1992	Whitney Museum of American Art at Philip Morris, New York (traveling)
1993	Max Protetch Gallery, New York
1994	Ruth Bloom Gallery, Santa Monica, California
1995	Des Moines Art Center, Iowa
	MIT List Visual Arts Center, Cambridge, Massachusetts

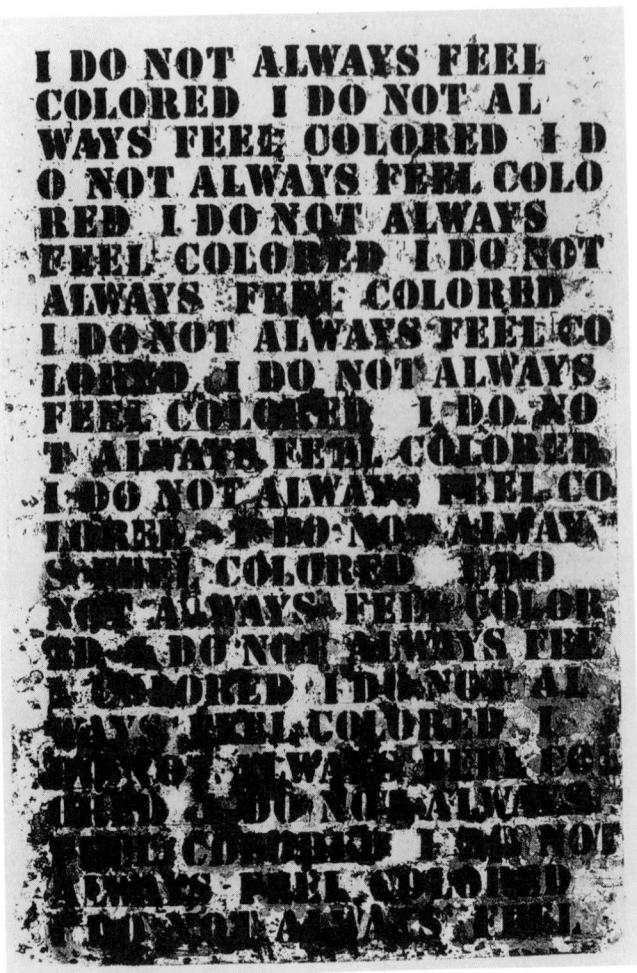

Glenn Ligon: untitled, 1992. Photo courtesy of Max Protetch Gallery.

	Max Protetch Gallery, New York
1996	San Francisco Museum of Modern Art, California
	Brooklyn Museum, New York

Selected Group Exhibitions:

1991	Grey Art Gallery, New York (traveling)
	Whitney Museum of American Art, New York
1995	Fabric Workshop, Philadelphia and Beaver College, Glenside, Pennsylvania
	Twenty-Five Americans: Paintings in the 90s, Milwaukee Art Museum, Wisconsin
1996	Frankfurt Kunstverein, Germany
	Maison des Arts et de la Culture, Paris-Creteil
	Fogg Art Museum, Cambridge, Massachusetts
	Art Gallery of New South Wales, Sydney, Australia
	Museum of Modern Art, New York
	Steirischer Herbst 96, Graz, Austria

Collections:

Baltimore Museum of Art, Maryland; Boston Museum of Fine Art; Eli Broad Family Foundation, Santa Monica, California; Fisher

Landau Center, New York; Carnegie Museum of Art, Pittsburgh; Des Moines Museum, Iowa; Detroit Institute of Arts; High Museum, Atlanta, Georgia; Hirshhorn Museum and Sculpture Garden, Washington, D.C.; List Art Gallery, MIT, Boston; Museum of Modern Art, New York; Norton Family Foundation, Santa Monica, California; Philadelphia Museum of Art; San Francisco Museum of Modern Art; Walker Art Center, Minneapolis, Minnesota; Whitney Museum of American Art, New York.

Publications:

By LIGON: Articles—"Artist Page," in *Documents,* Summer 1994; "Narratives," in *Yale Journal of Criticism,* Summer 1994; "Memorial," in *New York Times Magazine,* 9 April 1995.

On LIGON: Books—*The Pressure of Voices,* exhibition catalog, New Jersey, State Museum at Trenton and Michael Brenson, 1992; *Glenn Ligon/Matrix 120,* exhibition catalog, Connecticut, Wadsworth Atheneum and Andrea Miller-Keller, 1992. **Articles**—"The Art of Questioning Identity" by Christine Temin, in *The Boston Globe,* 4 August 1991; "Review" by Yoshi Suznobu, in *The New Yorker,* 31 July 1995; "Lack of Location Is My Location" by Roberta Smith, in *New York Times,* 16 June 1991; "Review" by Lois Nesbitt, in *Artforum,* Summer 1991; "Glenn Ligon at Max Protetch Gallery" by Ken Johnson, in *Art in America,* November 1992, p. 131; "Body Politic" by Sarah Kent, in *Time Out, London,* 24 May 1995, p. 49; "Skin Pigmentation as a Determinant of Attitudes" by Helen Harrison, in *New York Times,* 1 December 1991; "To Disembark: The Slave Narrative Tradition" by Kimberly Rae Conner, in *African American Review,* 30(1), May 1996, pp. 35-57.

*   *   *

Glenn Ligon's aesthetic articulations are infused with modernist sensibilities. His vocabulary is minimalistic and abbreviated, leaving great latitude for interpretation. He is efficacious, however, in creating a visual system of communication that is vigorous. His works encompass site-specific installations, paintings, works on paper, and photo-stenciled prints. Over the past decade he has produced a body of work that includes a breadth of concerns surrounding issues pertaining to identity. His official version of the black experience, if one can derive such a voice through his collective body of works, consists of snapshots laden with data and implications about reality.

Glenn Ligon: installation view, 1993. Photo courtesy of Max Protetch Gallery.

Ligon's recent works include self-portraits, paintings and photo-stenciled images of his head, both front and back, indicating the private versus the public connotations evident in his earlier work. Although they are mimetic of the coolness of mug shots, the stark presentation of these works perpetuates the image of the black male beyond the packaging of stereotypes or neutered persona evident in the media and popular culture. As Ligon moves toward an autobiographic stance in these portraits, he opts for the elusive and clinical. They raise numerous questions about his process of introspection rather than provide declarative insight into his psyche. The works are evidence of a life bound to experiences both black and gay with their dichotomies and complexities. In his austere fashion Ligon illuminates the fragmentation of such an existence, coercing the art world to make room for discourse on race and sexuality at the same time.

As a young artist Ligon's orientation was based on explorations in the tradition of abstract expressionism. Eventually reaching an impasse, he turned to text-based works as a means to incorporate ideas generated through language in graphic terms. The works initially approximated human proportions, eighty by thirty inches, the size of a door, alluding to the dimensions intended to accommodate the human form. Their verticality referred to the proportions of the printed page, with his linear recording of repeated text read from left to right an attempt to transfigure the printed page into a monumental icon. A confrontational stance was evident in this body of work, but the comprehensive interfacing of meaning was obfuscated by the fact that the repeated phrases or quotes became blurred as the painted text was stenciled over the working surface. The paints and oil sticks that he used caked the stencil as he worked across and down the surface of the work, eventually rendering the information illegible. The attempt to communicate became an abstracted interplay of form, paint, and surface. The text broke down into pieces, referring to aesthetic and conceptual associations outside its meaning. His process became a deconstructivist device; moving from the state of lucidity to the bemasked in form and content, it implied derivations of abstraction and minimalism. Clarity of interpretation rested within the domain of the viewer.

Starting with his "Dream Book" series, Ligon made a transition from total abstraction to the literal use of text and numbers as subject and image. The principle source material for these stenciled expressions and numerical configurations stemmed from popular tracts used heavily in the black community to interpret dream images. The interpretations were translated into numerical combinations that gave the user insight into playing the numbers, a form of illegal street gambling. The works earmarked Ligon's expedition into the domain of identity and cultural experiences particular to the black Americans.

As Ligon continues in his linguistic-based exploits, he extracts quotes from numerous literary sources by authors such as Zora Neale Hurston, Jean Genet, Percy Bysshe Shelley, Mary Shelley, and James Baldwin. The texts, which he alters at times, are heavily laden with historical overtones, observations particular to the black experience, both confessional and exponential, and philosophical idioms that illuminate the complexities of relationships between the oppressed and the oppressor. Based on his astute linguistic renditions, Ligon gives voice to the outsider's purview of social interactions. Continuously involved in the struggle with imagery and signs that are related to the history of blacks and their contemporary circumstances, Ligon traverses the terrain of self-exploration and autobiography.

—A.M. Weaver

LINDSAY, Arturo

American installation artist, painter, sculptor, and performance artist

Born: Colon, Republic of Panama, 29 September 1946. **Education:** Central Connecticut State University, New Britain, 1965-70, B.A. 1970; University of Massachusetts at Amherst, 1973-76, M.F.A. 1976; New York University, 1985-90, D.A. 1990. **Family:** Married 1) Diane Freeman in 1968 (divorced 1983), three sons; 2) Melanie Pavich in 1985. **Career:** Assistant director, Royal Athena Galleries, New York, 1984-89. Since 1990 associate professor, Spelman College, Atlanta, Georgia. Scholar-in-residence, Franklin and Marshall College, Lancaster, Pennsylvania, 1989-90. **Address:** 4026 Birchwood Dove, Decatur, Georgia 30034, U.S.A. **Online Address:** alindsay@spelman.edu.

Individual Exhibitions:

1971	Central Connecticut State University, New Britain
1972	Bridgewater State College, Bridgewater, Massachusetts
1977	Craftery Gallery, Hartford, Connecticut
1981	Trinity College, Hartford, Connecticut
	Old State House Gallery, Hartford, Connecticut
1982	Mona Berman Gallery, New Haven, Connecticut
1983	Augusta Savage Gallery, Amherst, Massachusetts
1984	Sutton Gallery, Houston
1986	Gallery 69, South Bronx, New York
1988	Hammonds Gallery, Atlanta
1992	Chastain Gallery, Atlanta
1993	Franklin Furnace, New York
1994	Museo de Arte Contemporaneo, Panama
1996	Chassie Post Gallery, Atlanta, Georgia
	Nexus Contemporary Art Center, Atlanta

Selected Group Exhibitions:

1991	High Museum of Art, Atlanta
1992	Museo de Arte Contemporaneo, Panama
1993	Branau University, Gainesville, Georgia
	University of Cincinnati, Ohio
	Mexican Museum, San Francisco (traveling through 1996)
1994	International Museum of Art and Design, Atlanta
	Telfair Museum, Savannah, Georgia
1996	Artist-in-Residence International (traveling)
	Palazzo del Esposizioni, Rome

Collections:

Amistad Cultural Resource Center, Hartford, Connecticut; Barnett-Aden Collection, Washington, D.C.; Royal-Athena Galleries, New York/Beverly Hills, California; Slater Memorial Museum, Norwich, Connecticut; University of Massachusetts, Amherst.

Publications:

By LINDSAY: Books—*Santería Aesthetics in Contemporary Latin American Art,* Washington, D.C., Smithsonian Institution Press, 1996. **Articles**—"Mestizaje and the Postmodern Aesthetic," in *Ceremony of Spirit, Nature and Memory in Contemporary Latino*

Arturo Lindsay: *Ancestral Fathers Known and Unknown,* **1995.**

Arturo Lindsay: *Ancestral Mothers Known and Unknown*, 1996.

Art edited by Amalia Mesa-Bains (San Francisco), Mexican Museum, 1993.

On LINDSAY: Articles—"Arturo Lindsay at Chastain Gallery," in *Art in America* 81(4), April 1993, p.136; "Conversation with Geoff Weston and Arturo Lindsay," in *Redefining the Nineties* (Atlanta), Art Papers, 20(5), September/October 1996, pp. 30-35.

*

Arturo Lindsay comments:

My interest in African retentions in the Americas has brought me to a crossroads where the paths of my spiritual, scholarly, and aesthetic pilgrimages meet. As an artist-scholar, I use ethnographic research methods to uncover information people utilize to order their lives and construct their cultures. My research findings are presented in works of art, scholarly articles, essays, and lectures. In recent years I have been particularly interested in observing the presence of African spiritual and aesthetic retentions grounded in the concept of cultural *mestizaje* (cross-cultural mixing in Cuba and Panama).

Recently I began pouring libations in my installations in veneration of my ancestors. With this act, the installations ceased to exist solely as works of art in a Western European aesthetic frame and emerged as sacro-secular objects. This fusion was solidified in 1994 when I established a studio in Portobelo Panama, a 16th century Spanish colonial village steeped in magic, myth, mystery, and miracles. This experience gave me an insider's understanding of the ways peoples of African descent in Panama tell their stories through art. In Portobelo I became interested in telling the stories of the *cimarrones* (runaway slaves) and their descendants, the Congos. My residency in Portobelo has also afforded me an opportunity to reacquaint myself with the reverence Latin Americans have for the spirit world.

* * *

The decades marked by the verve and vitality of the civil rights movement (1970s) and of the so-called generation Xers (1990s) are also the decades in which the individual elements shaping Arturo Lindsay's art—theater arts, sculpture, and painting—merge into a larger landscape whose subtext and symbols inform both the past and the present. His work eclipses traditional boundaries and emerges as the artistic expression called performance art. Thus, individual elements, although able to stand alone, are unified and made much more powerful as part of a whole, stressing the importance of the group aesthetic over that of the individual.

Lindsay was initially introduced to the arts through his involvement in a Brooklyn-based traveling theater company. Along with other artists of the 1970s, he was caught in the ontological throes of self-discovery. Although Lindsay, of black and Latino heritage, had few if any role models, he was no less compelled to seek out who he was and the way in which he could express his discovery.

"When I first went to the paint store," Lindsay recalled, "I didn't really know what to buy—a lot of it was teaching myself." While this may have been the case early on, Lindsay's graduate school experience later provided him the opportunity to develop as a painter. There is an immediacy to Lindsay's mature work. He speaks bilingually, in the language of his ancestors, and brings a type of primitive and spontaneous sensibility to his work.

As Lindsay's paintings began to explore metaphysical questions,

he found himself creating the "Guardian Angel" series, dealing with spiritual phenomena in the physical world. Lindsay's work then came increasingly to explore spiritual phenomena. In doing so, he began to see how art could be and was used as a tool for healing. What is referred to as art in Western cultures is referred to as ritual performance in African and Latino cultures. "I wanted to depict some of this on a two-dimensional plane," he has said.

Lindsay entered the door to this other reality through altars. They addressed his ancestral duality, and through them Lindsay was able to refer to the African presence in the Americas. Although that experience was individually different, the *orisha*s or the cosmology of which they are a part is the same.

Lindsay recently completed a residency in his native Panama. There he lived in Portobelo, where he researched the history of Africans. He also has edited *Santeria Aesthetics in Contemporary Latin American Art* (1996).

—Crystal Britton

LION, Jules
French printmaker, photographer, and painter

Born: Paris, France, c.1809-10. **Education:** Studied daguerreotype in Paris. **Family:** Married Maria Ana Muñoz in 1957, one son. **Career:** Lithographer, *The Bee,* New Orleans, Louisiana, 1837. Daguerreotypist and portrait painter, New Orleans, 1837-66. Professor of drawing, Louisiana Academy, New Orleans, 1865-66. Founded art school, New Orleans, 1841. Painted portrait of John James Audubon. **Awards:** Honorable mention for lithograph "Affut Aux Canards," 1833. **Died:** 9 January 1866.

Selected Exhibitions:

1831(?) *Paris Salon,* Paris (through 1833)
1840 *Daguerreotypes,* Saint Charles Museum, New Orleans
1976 *Selections of 19th Century Afro-American Art,* Metropolitan Museum of Art, New York

Collections:

Historic New Orleans, Louisiana; Louisiana State Museum, New Orleans; National Museum of American Art, Washington, D.C.

Publications:

On LION: Articles—"Jules Lion's New Orleans" by Charles East, in *Georgia Review,* Winter 1986; "Black Artists in Antebellum New Orleans" by Patricia Brady, in *Louisiana History,* Lafayette, Louisiana, Winter 1991; "A Mixed Palette: Free Artists of Color of New Orleans" by Patricia Brady, in *International Review of African American Art,* Hampton, Virginia, Fall 1995.

* * *

Jules Lion reversed the pattern for people of color in Louisiana, for he went from France to New Orleans rather than the reverse. When he arrived in Louisiana, he was already a highly skilled lithographer and a talented portraitist. Shortly before Lion sailed for the United States, the first volume of Germain Sarrut's *Biographie des hommes illustres du jour* (1836) was published, including lithographic portraits by the artist. These and other lithographs Lion had executed in France set the standard for the hundreds of works he would produce in Louisiana (more than two hundred of which are extant), distinguished by highly realistic representations and a mastery of lithographic technique.

The sitters in Lion's French work appear in the pose he almost invariably employed throughout his American career—bust portraits of a seated subject, generally a man, in a three-quarter view, facing slightly right, without a background. Every detail of the sitter's person and dress was rendered in meticulous detail, and the composition was finished with a crosshatched nimbus at the level of the upper arms. Lion's portrait of Andrew Jackson was an exception, however. The artist's forte was capturing a sitter from life, and his attempt to portray a subject he had never seen produced an unusually stiff, poor likeness.

In 1837, his first year in New Orleans, Lion was employed by the lithographic office of the *Bee*, a bilingual newspaper, and he produced a spate of lithographed portraits. Throughout his career the artist typically signed his work on the stone on the lower left of the image. He also frequently added the date and indicated the city where the portrait was done beneath his flowing script "J. Lion." During 1937 he sometimes added "lith. of the Bee" or "lith. de l'Abeille" to the lower right of the image. Although most of the early portraits were done in New Orleans, the place names Baton Rouge, Donaldsonville, Saint James, and Assumption appear on some, suggesting that he made a circuit as a traveling artist throughout southern Louisiana. After 1837, with the end of Lion's employment there, the *Bee* designation disappeared.

Most of Lion's lithographic portraits fall into two distinct periods—1837-39 and 1845-47—with scattered examples in the intervening years. There are a considerable number of undated portraits that cannot be dated stylistically since Lion's style of portraiture and lithography remained unchanged from his arrival in New Orleans until his death. Because they are formulaic repetitions of the artistic conventions Lion had adopted in Paris, his lithographic portraits at first glance appear boringly similar. Yet within the formula the individuality of each sitter is fully realized. The faces are expressive and lifelike, meticulously represented down to the last wart. Hairstyles (some of them singular indeed), attire, and jewelry are also extremely realistic. The portraits are by far the best images of nineteenth-century Louisianians available. Among the exceptions to Lion's formula are a small number of portraits of women and children, including those of a Mrs. Luzenberg (1837) and of Mme Duplessis and her daughters (1839), and full-length studies, including those of John Brownson (undated) and of William Freret (1839). These last portraits are among his least successful, marked by a lack of technical proficiency in rendering body proportions, especially hands, and background perspective.

In 1841 the signatures of the sitters began to appear beneath their portraits. The practice was in preparation for Lion's plans for a bound volume of portraits of famous Louisianians to be financed by subscription. His plans never came to pass, but there are two extant bound copies of Lion's lithographs that were gathered and bound later, and each is unique.

Architectural scenes were a minor part of Lion's work, but their precision and accuracy make them important for historical research. Known images are the Saint Louis Cathedral before its reconstruction (1842) and a Canal Street block (1846). At the beginning of the

Civil War, before New Orleans was captured, Lion lithographed sheet music covers for several publishers in the city. Ironically, all showed Confederate subjects, including a portrait of Jefferson Davis.

An undated pastel portrait on canvas of a middle-aged white man and a mulatto youth, both well dressed and posing arm-in-arm with clasped hands, is an anomaly in Lion's work. The subjects are said to be Asher Moses Nathan and his son, Achile Leon Lion. The highly detailed, realistic portrayal of the two men was typical of the artist's favored pose and style. The medium and the signature ("JLion" in block caps) were, however, unique.

During his lifetime Lion was best known for introducing the daguerreotype process to New Orleans. In 1839 he began making daguerrean views of the city's landmarks for an exhibition that opened in 1840. Newspapers raved over the revolutionary new process and the silvery beauty of the images. None of Lion's daguerrean images is known to be extant.

—Patricia Brady

LLOYD, Thomas
American sculptor

Born: 13 January 1929. **Education:** Pratt Institute, Brooklyn, New York, 1952-56, B.F.A. 1956; Brooklyn Museum, private study with Peter Agostini, 1961-63; New York University, 1964-66. **Career:** Art instructor, New Lincoln School, New York, Community Mental Health Workers, Einstein College of Medicine, New York, Group Service Agencies, Lincoln Hospital, New York, 1960-66; director, Adult Creative Arts Workshop, Department of Parks/Office of Cultural Affairs, New York, 1967-69; faculty member, Sarah Lawrence College, and Cooper Union for the Advancement of Science and Art, New York, 1968-71; founding board member, Queens Museum, Flushing, New York, 1971-76; director and founder, Store Front Museum/Paul Robeson Theatre, Jamaica, New York, 1971-86. Founding member, National Association of Black Museums and Cultural Organizations, Jamaica, New York, 1973-82. Founding member and chairman, Artworker's Coalition, 1969-70. Founder and coordinator, Community Artists Cultural Survey Committee, Jamaica, New York, 1970. Producer and director, *African Liberation Day: Washington, D.C.,* May 1973. Founding member, Queens Inner City Arts Council, Jamaica, New York, 1974-83. Traveled in Caribbean and Africa 1977-84. Founder, *Save the Lewis H. Latimer House,* Flushing, New York, 1989. **Died:** 20 August 1996.

Individual Exhibitions:

1965   Amel Gallery, New York
1968   Studio Museum in Harlem, New York (inaugural exhibition)
1969   Howard Wise Gallery, New York
1972   Howard Wise Gallery, New York

Selected Group Exhibitions:

1964   Amel Gallery, New York
1966   Walker Art Center, Minneapolis

1968	Museum of Modern Art, New York
1970	Studio Museum in Harlem, New York
1972	Newark Museum, New Jersey
1973	Hudson River Museum, Yonkers, New York
1977	Schenectady Museum, New York
1979	La Jolla Museum of Art, California
1980	Emory University, Atlanta, Georgia
1993	55 Mercer Street Gallery, New York

Collections:

Chrysler Art Museum, Provincetown, Massachusetts; Museum of Modern Art, New York; New York University; Phillip Morris International, New York; Studio Museum in Harlem, New York.

Publications:

By LLOYD: Article—"Museums and the Ghetto," in *Newsweek,* 76, 17 August 1970.

*   *   *

Although he was a leading exponent of the black art movement of the late 1960s and 1970s, Tom Lloyd's light constructions and wall sculptures differed radically from the politically and socially charged works by many of his peers. The technological revolution and not the cultural revolution motivated Lloyd's works. He explored the aesthetic possibilities that resulted when coupling science with art. His nonrepresentational abstract light sculptures are devoid of specific meanings and reflect Lloyd's interest in found objects, his fascination with technology, and his grounding in abstract expressionist idioms.

Lloyd experimented with myriad artistic media, including painting, collage, drawing, photography, plaster work, and film, but his forays in electric light represent his most enduring work. He was part of the burgeoning art of light and motion movement that exploded in the mid-1960s. Utilizing incandescent, florescent, and neon light as both medium and subject, Tom Lloyd, Dan Flavin, Chryssa, and others associated with this movement, privileged effect over meaning in a variety of kinetic sculptures, projections, and installations. These artists strove to expand artistic expression by employing electric light in the service of fine art.

Fundamental to Lloyd's philosophy was the desire to create art from everyday life. He often used cast-off machine and car parts in his earlier works. Flashing traffic signals, theater marquees and automobile lights encountered on busy New York City streets inspired him. He found beauty in the high-tech urban landscape. In 1964 after meeting Al Sussman, an engineer with whom he collaborated on several light sculptures, Lloyd built his first light works. These were Christmas tree lamps underneath transparent, refracting cover lenses from car back-up lights, attached to found object assemblages. To activate the works, Sussman devised a simple six-channel electrical controller in which each channel operated one light. They flashed on and off in staccato patterns that Lloyd "programmed" by interrupting the electrical contact with insulating tape. Like Lloyd, many light-and-motion artists formed collaborations with engineers and scientists to explore the possibilities electronic technology offered.

As Lloyd became more familiar with the medium's expressive qualities, his appetite grew for more complex structures. He hoped ultimately to create "active pure light" sculptures, not simply light appendages. In response to Lloyd's expanding needs, Sussman devised a ten-channel controller that could operate groups of lights per channel. The resulting works, which he called *Electronic Refractions,* consisted of several rows of light units (a trio of programmed colored lights encased in metal cylinders and covered with plastic refracting lens) contained within simple geometric sculptural forms, usually variations on X and diamond shapes. Some critics called these sculptures the stained glass of the electronic age.

By 1968 Lloyd's *Refractions* had grown in size, as well as in technical and structural complexity. Some of his free-standing light tables allowed for viewers to program light patterns themselves. The wall sculptures included more closely packed colored light units within larger detachable chevron, and pentagonal modules that he would rearrange to create new composite forms. The lights created vibrant air paintings as they flashed and faded and the afterimage intermingled with new color displays.

In the mid 1980s, after more than a decade of not exhibiting or making art, Lloyd reengaged his earlier light and technology explorations in *Prismatic Transformations.* They are a series of large computer-programmed multicomponent modular LED units that were intended to exhibit a variety of high-resolution changing abstract digital images. He and Sussman began developing a program that could be modified by audience interaction. Although they were not completed before his death in 1996, full-scale mock-ups of these do exist.

Tom Lloyd believed that artists should use the new materials that science had to offer. Throughout his career he embraced the instruments of technology to expand his artistic vision, and in turn his light sculptures championed their practical and aesthetic possibilities.

—Regina L. Woods

LOCKARD, Jon (Onye)
American painter, muralist, and illustrator

Born: Detroit, 25 January 1932. **Education:** Wayne State University, Detroit, 1949-50; Fields School of Art, 1951-52; Meinzinger Art School, Detroit, 1951-52; Chicago Institute of Art, 1952; University of Washington, Seattle, 1953; University of Toronto, Canada, 1954. **Career:** Proprietor, Studio 21, Detroit, 1960-64, Ann Arbor Art Center, Ltd., Michigan, 1965-75. Since 1969 professor, Department of Humanities, Washtenaw Community College, Ann Arbor, Michigan. Since 1970 adjunct lecturer, Center for Afro-American and African Studies, University of Michigan, Ann Arbor, Michigan. Since 1973 president, Academy of Creative Thought, Inc., Ann Arbor, Michigan. Served as executive vice president, National Conference of Artists, 1972-83. Served as International Coordinator, First World Cultural Festival, Bahia, Brazil, 1980. Served as consultant, Ohio Commission for the Arts, National Black Arts Festival (NBAF), Michigan Council for the Arts and Cultural Affairs, New Initiatives for the Arts (NIFTA). Assistant director, National Association for the Study of African and Afro-American Culture and the Arts. **Awards:** Merit Award, Afro-American Cultural Lounge Committee, University of Michigan, Ann Arbor, 1972; citation, *Black Journal,* New York, 1977; citation, Kuumba Workshop, Chicago, 1979; testimonial resolution, Detroit City Council,

1981; tribute, State of Michigan, Lansing, 1981; citation, Institute of Positive Education, Chicago, 1983; citation, Huron Valley Women's Facility, Ypsilanti, Michigan, 1983; citation, Afro-American Museum of Detroit, 1983; Medallion for Distinguished Service, National Conference of Artists, 1985; Center for Afro-American and African Studies Service Citation, University of Michigan; Artistic Merit Award, *Ebony* Magazine, 1993; Meritorious Service Award, Washtenaw Community College, 1993. **Address:** 2649 Wayside Drive, Ann Arbor, Michigan 48103, U.S.A.

Selected Exhibitions:

African World Festival, Detroit; Anacortes Art Association, Guemes Island, Washington; Canbahia, Toronto; Center for Afroamerican and African Studies, University of Michigan, Ann Arbor; Central State University, Wilberforce, Ohio; Dayton Black Arts Festival, Ohio; DePauw University, Greencastle, Indiana; Expo '74 World Fair, Spokane, Washington; Flint Art Institute, Michigan; Grand Rapids Art Institute, Michigan; Indianapolis Art Institute, Indiana; Lincoln Center Exhibition, New York; Malcolm X College, Chicago; Museum of African American History, Detroit; National Afro-American Museum and Cultural Center, Wilberforce, Ohio; National Black Arts Festival, Atlanta, Georgia; National Conference of Artists, Detroit; National Gallery of Arts, Dakar Senegal, West Africa; New York University; Pontiac Art Center, Michigan; Purdue University, West Lafayette, Indiana; Schomburg Center, New York; Seattle World's Fair; Selma Burke Art Center, Pittsburgh; Shrine of the Black Madonna, Detroit; Southside Community Center, Chicago; University of Chicago; University of Cincinnati, Ohio; University of Michigan Museum of Art, Ann Arbor; University of Wisconsin, Madison; Washtenaw Community College, Ann Arbor, Michigan; Your Heritage House, Detroit.

Collections:

Black Journal, New York; Central State University, Wilberforce, Ohio; Ferris State Community College, Big Rapids, Michigan; Howard University, Washington, D.C.; Institute for Positive Education, Chicago; Kuumba Workshop, Chicago; National Afro-American Museum and Cultural Center, Wilberforce, Ohio; Oakland County Community College, Michigan; Ohio State University, Columbus; Schomburg Center, New York; Shrine of the Black Madonna, Detroit; Southside Community Center, Chicago; University of Michigan, Ann Arbor; Wayne State University, Detroit.

Publications:

By LOCKARD: Article—"An Ideology for Black Artists," in *First World,* 2, Spring 1978, pp. 42-44.

*   *   *

Detroit native Jon Onye Lockard has been a fixture in Ann Arbor, Michigan, since moving there in 1965. The powerful, heroic figures in his paintings are instantly recognizable and in some ways reflect the early influence of Charles White. Nothing in Lockard's youth, however, gave an indication that he would become a politically conscious artist.

Lockard took a different path to becoming an artist, something he never considered in his early life. For two years during high school,

Jon Lockard.

in the postwar 1940s, he worked as an apprentice in the only black sign-painting shop in Detroit for a dollar a day. He learned discipline and how to work on scaffolding, skills that would later serve him well. Around 1948 he saw the work of White and began a lifelong admiration. White was the first black artist Lockard knew about, and his heroic figures celebrated the common, everyday people Lockard knew from his own community. White made their everyday survival seem to be acts of heroism, something that Lockard had never seen before. Lockard later came to admire the work of Hughie Lee-Smith, who was well regarded in Detroit in the 1950s and 1960s, and he was befriended by John Biggers, whom he met in Texas at the end of the 1950s. Biggers was the first artist Lockard knew who had traveled to Africa.

In the early 1960s Lockard began traveling throughout the United States, Canada, Mexico, and even overseas to do pastel portraits. He opened a studio in Detroit and earned a living from the work. He also began to apply the disciplines of his sign-painting days by creating murals in bars and nightclubs and decorating the interiors of homes in the black community with unique pictoral environments. An incident involving the murder of three black men by the Detroit police at a motel across the street from Lockard's studio, along with the fact that many of his clients traveled to his studio from Ann Arbor and outlying communities, convinced him to relocate. He did so despite his own comfort on the urban streets of Detroit. Lockard soon was teaching classes at the University of Michigan, and his art began to move in a different direction, away from portraiture and commercial projects toward the expression of the volatile times and the growth of black consciousness.

When in 1969 Lockard attended the Conference of Functional Black Artists (CONFABA) meeting in Evanston, Illinois, organized by Jeff Donaldson, he became aware of other black artists with the same political consciousness and commitment to the black community. Lockard emerged from CONFABA with a new clarity and sense of mission. Instead of portraits he began to produce politically charged art dealing with the struggles of black people. His commitment had evolved from making a living to making a difference.

When he was younger, Lockard had identified with the remnants of Marcus Garvey's Universal Negro Improvement Association, but he now formulated his own social action through works like the charcoal drawing *A Dream Deferred* and *No More,* an image of Aunt Jemima thrusting a black power fist through a pancake box. In the 1972 he became actively involved with the National Conference of Artists as a way of maintaining contact with other black artists across the nation. Around this same time Lockard began creating public murals with inspirational and political content. He had studied Mexican murals and particularly admired the work of Diego Rivera, David Siqueiros, and José Clemente Orozco, and his outdoor advertising experience gave him a special aptitude for work on murals. He also saw public murals as a means of bringing positive images and messages to people who might not otherwise have access to such ideas or images of such dimension.

Trips to Africa and to South America beginning in the 1980s caused Lockard to recognize color in new ways, which affected his paintings and murals. His ideas became more sophisticated, and by the 1990s his work began to incorporate symbols from Africa and the African diaspora along with his narrative figurative imagery. Lockard's work has remained figurative, however, and the portrait work of his early years has yielded outstanding draftsmanship and techniques for rendering the human form. As often as not, his powerful figures now appear in compositions filled with vibrant color, African symbols, and complex meanings. Lockard has mastered a visual language that he employs in the service of his people.

—Michael D. Harris

LOGAN, Juan (Leon)

American painter, sculptor, printmaker, and installation artist

Born: Nashville, 16 August 1946. **Education:** Howard University, Washington, D.C., 1964-65; Clark College, Atlanta, Georgia, 1965-67; Maryland Institute, Baltimore, 1996-. **Military Service:** United States Air Force, 1967-69. **Family:** Married 1) Lorna Hosein in 1967 (divorced 1970), one daughter; 2) Geraldine Johnson in 1974, one daughter and one son. **Career:** Color chemist, Burlington Industries, McAdenville, North Carolina, 1970-75; consumer affairs representative, Eastern Airlines, Charlotte, North Carolina, 1976-87. Since 1985 free-lance artist, Belmont, North Carolina. **Awards:** Romare Bearden Award for Creativity/Innovation of Medium, Carnegie Institute, 1972; first place award, Louisiana Watercolor Society's 14th Annual International Exhibition, 1984; North Carolina Arts Council Artists Fellowship, 1991-92. **Agent:** June Kelly, June Kelly Gallery, 591 Broadway, New York, New York 10012, U.S.A.

Individual Exhibitions:

1969   Jefferson Gallery, Denver

1971   Sacred Heart College, Belmont, North Carolina
1972   Barber-Scotia College, Concord, North Carolina
1973   Mint Museum of Art, Charlotte, North Carolina
        Davidson College, North Carolina
        North Carolina A & T State University, Greensboro
1974   Queens College Art Gallery, Charlotte, North Carolina
        Winthrop Gallery, Winthrop College, Rock Hill, South Carolina
1976   South Carolina State University, Orangeburg
1979   Winston-Salem State University, North Carolina
1980   Frederick Douglass Institute, Washington, D.C.
1983   Rowe Gallery, University of North Carolina at Charlotte
1985   Deborah Peverall Gallery, Charlotte, North Carolina
        Somerhill Gallery, Durham, North Carolina
        North Carolina Central University, Durham
        Gaston College, Dallas, North Carolina
1986   Gaston County Museum of Art and History, North Carolina
        Afro-American Cultural Center, Charlotte, North Carolina
1987   Gallery Two Nine One, Atlanta, Georgia
        Lucien Crump Gallery, Philadelphia
        Green Hill Center for North Carolina Art, Greensboro
1988   McIntosh Gallery, Atlanta, Georgia
1989   Theatre Arts Galleries, High Point, North Carolina
1990   Marita Gilliam Gallery, Raleigh, North Carolina
        School of Design Gallery, North Carolina State University, Raleigh
        Jerald Melberg Gallery, Charlotte, North Carolina

Selected Group Exhibitions:

1967   Atlanta University, Georgia
1971   Carnegie Institute, Pittsburgh
1974   *Directions in Afro-American Art,* Herbert F. Johnson Museum of Art, Cornell University, Ithaca, New York
1984   *Louisiana Watercolor Society's 14th Annual International Exhibit,* New Orleans
1986   *Choosing: An Exhibit of Changing Perspectives in Modern Art and Art Criticism by Black Americans, 1925-1985,* Museum of Science and Industry, Chicago (traveling)
1990   *Sign, Symbol and Spirit,* Lawton Gallery, University of Wisconsin, Green Bay
1992   *Elizabeth Catlett and Juan Logan: Visual Narratives,* A. Montgomery Ward Gallery, University of Illinois, Chicago
1994   McIntosh Gallery, Atlanta, Georgia
        National Afro-American Cultural Center, Wilberforce, Ohio
        Montgomery Museum of Art, Alabama
1995   Southeastern Center for Contemporary Art, Winston-Salem, North Carolina
        Hammonds House Galleries, Atlanta, Georgia
1996   Spirit Square Center for Arts and Education, Middleton McMillian and First Union Galleries, Charlotte, North Carolina

Collections:

Art in Embassies Program, Pretoria, South Africa; Asheville Art

Museum, North Carolina; Blue Cross of Greater Philadelphia; Davidson College, North Carolina; Hammonds House Galleries, Atlanta, Georgia; Mint Museum of Art, Charlotte, North Carolina; Museum of African-American Art, Los Angeles; National Museum of African Art, Washington, D.C.; Northwestern University, Mary and Leigh Block Gallery, Evanston, Illinois; Saint John's Museum of Art, Wilmington, North Carolina; Tubman African American Museum, Macon, Georgia.

Publications:

On LOGAN: **Book**—*North Carolina Artists and Craftsmen,* North Carolina, Wilkes Art Guild, 1974. **Articles**—"Artist's Cool Approach to Life Reflected in His Works" by Harriet Doar, in *The Charlotte Observer* (North Carolina), February 1971; "Struggle of Black Man Finds Way Onto Canvas" by Ed Book, in *The Gastonia Gazette* (North Carolina), February 1971; "I - Says Juan Logan," in *Twin Cities Weekly* (North Carolina), 13 July 1972; "Juan Logan Uses His Talents for Art and Business," in *Winston-Salem Journal* (North Carolina), 3 June 1973; "Logan Art Exhibit Has Humorous Titles" by Bud Newcomb, in *The Evening Herald* (South Carolina), 4 October 1974; "Juan Logan, Painter/Sculpture" by T.J. Reddy, in *Emergence* (North Carolina), 1 April 1978; "Juan Logan's Ethereal Art" by Jalyne Strong, in *Charlotte,* 16(4), 1983; "Juan Logan, Artist" by Edward Waddell, in *Black American Literature Forum* (Indiana), 19(1), Spring 1985; "Interviews: Clarence Morgan, Juan Logan, James and Earnestine Huff" by Christopher Redd, in *Art Papers* (Georgia), 22 December 1988; "The Paintings of Juan Logan" by Ken Bloom, in *Charlotte* (North Carolina), March/April 1989; "Juan Logan/McIntosh Gallery" by J. W. Cullum, in *Art Papers* (Georgia), March/April 1989; "Juan Logan/Isobel Neal Gallery" by Allen Gamble, in *New Art Examiner* (Illinois), November 1989; "Juan Logan's Show Offers Power Images" by Sandy Seawright, in *Break Magazine* (North Carolina), 12 December 1990; "Exhibit Gives Voice to the Black Experience," in *The State Journal-Register* (Illinois), 9 January 1992; "Juan Logan, Painting His Mind" by Hunter Bretzus, in *The Gastonia Gazette* (North Carolina), 25 April 1992; "N.C. Artist Gets Views From News" by Dan Maley, in *The Macon Telegraph* (Georgia), 27 November 1992; "Juan Logan: New Small Scale Paintings" by Linda L. Brown, in *Art Papers* (Georgia), March/April 1993; "Three Exhibits Show the Breadth, Variety of Juan Logan's Work" by Tom Patterson, in *The Charlotte Observer* (North Carolina), 22 May 1994; "Juan Logan: Not Separate and Apart From" by Linda L. Brown, in *Art Papers* (Georgia), July/August 1994; "Juan Logan's Sculpture: Facing Problems Common To Us All" by Margaret Shearin, in *Triad* (North Carolina), 6 December 1995; "Juan Logan" by Max Halperen, in *Art Papers* (Georgia), 20(2), March/April 1996.

*

Juan Logan comments:

When we look at who we have been as Americans, we have at times been a very cruel people. Much of that exists today, perhaps in a more refined manner, but it is still there. Traditionally as a culture we talk about the things we believe in rather than practice those things. Again that is part of who we are. Even when it is necessary to deal with minor things, when we see wrongs that someone should do something about, we often say that someone *should* do something about that—let's write our congressmen— instead of opting to become actively involved ourselves. Simply because of our inability to do something or to be able to do it, we tend to invalidate those things that we simply can't relate to. And even when we deal with other cultures, of course, we will just go in and appropriate what we want and invalidate the remainder. This is how we do things. Faith is about those things not seen, not necessarily made evident, but things that should be believed in. It is necessary to ask, are we trying to evaluate who we are, and what are we asking about those virtues? What are the virtues of the sane and civilized?

*   *   *

Juan Logan's visual language is concerned with the contradictions of human relationships, which act as inspirational catalysts for his art. The essentialness of humanity remains a constant source of fascination and the primary impetus for his aesthetic interpretation. Logan is a multifaceted artist who fuses the poetics of a bard with the oral tradition of the African griot, a sacred raconteur and genealogist. Since the early 1970s his professional career has been spent investigating a broad range of abstract imagery, trying to find "symbolic ways of saying things" in minimalist fields of color, line, texture, and iconographs through the mediums of painting, sculpture, printmaking, drawing, installations, and mixed media.

Logan is part of a long legacy of artists—including Thomas Day, Charles Alston, Malvin Gray Johnson, Richard Lindsay, Selma Burke, Thomas Sills, John Biggers, David Driskell, William T. Williams, Beverly Buchanan, Minnie Evans, and Romare Bearden— who have their origins in North Carolina. The regional development of the African American artistic evolution in North Carolina is essential to bridging a critical void in our understanding of the aesthetic development of American art and of the contributions of these individuals to the cultural heritage.

In the early stage of Logan's artistic development, his ambitions were inspired by the intensity of the civil rights movement and his need to create an imagery in a quick medium to address the urgency of those issues. While studying at Clark University, he created his first linocut, and he experimented with other print mediums for the next five years in screen prints, embossings, and etchings. During the 1970s his interests centered on steel sculpture but by the late 1970s shifted back to acrylic painting. In 1990-91 printmaking captured his imagination again in a series of glass plate prints, called vitrographs, dealing with relationships of conflict and contradiction.

Manipulating surface textures and abstract symbols such as hooded masklike images in the 1980s, Logan created works that went beyond the need for traditional figurative representation. Until the 1930s, with the introduction of modernism and abstraction, the stylistic concerns for African American artists had been grounded in traditional academic figuration. Logan felt the need "to go beyond the figure and simplify the form in an effort to more fully define the essence of that expression." Abstraction became for Logan—as in the work of Sam Gilliam, William T. Williams, Clarence Morgan, Alvin Loving, Mel Edwards, Barbara Chase-Riboud, David Hammons, Richard Hunt, Senga Nengudi, Maren Hassenger, Martin Puryear, and Jack Whitten—a force of liberation creating a climate of intellectual freedom, unrestrained creativity, and individualistic modalities of style, process, and media.

In the 1960s and the early 1970s, Logan's first artistic experience with sculpture began with clay pottery. He then began a foray of experimentation with found objects, painted television screens, carved toilet seats, and, finally, hard-edged, abstracted, galvanized steel sculptures that were influenced by artists like Marcel Duchamp, Pablo Picasso, and Louise Nevelson, whose works became popular in the American art scene of the 1950s and 1960s. In the mid-1990s Logan returned to sculpture, creating monumental structures in painted black fabricated steel or mirrored stainless steel. These minimalist works were like ominous totems that used provocative social themes to address issues of gender, teenage pregnancy, AIDS, and abuses of sex, drugs, and humanity.

Logan creates symbolic icons that address the inner and outer conflicts of the relationships of humanity as inspired by his concern for growing acts of irresponsibility. His imagery appears to be apocalyptic. It is his intent, through his love of texture, color, and line, to create an image that is haunting and memorable yet beautiful. His aesthetic is structured on visual signifiers that he transforms into poetics of line and form. The moral imperatives confronting the artist and society as we approach the coming millennium are central to Logan's artistic raison d'être.

—Leslie King-Hammond

LOVE, Ed

American sculptor and installation artist

Born: Los Angeles, California, 21 September 1936. **Education:** California State University, Los Angeles, B.F.A. 1966, M.F.A. 1967; University of Uppsala, Sweden, 1967-68 (postgraduate fellowship in humanities and fine arts). **Military Service:** United States Air Force, 1954-58: airman first class. **Family:** Married Monifa A. Love, two daughters and one son. **Career:** Professor of art, Howard University, Washington, D.C., 1968-87; founding dean, New World School of the Arts Visual Art Division, Miami, 1987-90. Since 1990 professor of art, Florida State University, Tallahassee. Senior engineering draftsman, North American Aviation, Downey, California; architectural designer, Interim Assistance Project Design of Park/Outdoor Recreation Centers, Washington, D.C.; associate fellow, Institute for Pan-African Culture, University of Massachusetts, Amherst, 1972. Artist-in-residence, Workshops for Careers in the Arts, Washington, D.C., 1973-74. Board of advisors, Washington Project for the Arts, Washington, D.C., 1981-82, National Foundation for the Advancement of the Arts, Miami, 1988-90. **Awards:** District of Columbia Commission on the Arts Fellowship, 1986-87; District of Columbia Award in the Arts, 1987; Guggenheim Memorial Foundation Fellowship, 1987-88; Arts Educator Award, National Foundation for Advancement in the Arts, 1990; Art Educator Recognition Award, Pratt Institute, 1990; Distinguished Alumni Award, California State University, 1991; Council on Research and Creativity Award, 1996. **Agents:** Kathleen Coleman, c/o Art Ventures, 3350 Rosedale, #2, Houston, Texas 77004, U.S.A.; Caleb A. Davis, c/o Gallery Antigua, 5138 Biscayne Boulevard, Miami, Florida 33137, U.S.A.; Monifa A. Love, Free Zone Productions, 2920 Parrish Drive, Tallahassee, Florida 32308, U.S.A. **Address:** Florida State University School of Visual Arts and Dance, Department of Art, Tallahassee, Florida, U.S.A. **Online Address:** Ealsilver@aol.com; http://www.fsu.edu/~svad/Art DepartFaculty/FacultyLove/Love.html.

Individual Exhibitions:

1975   Corcoran Gallery of Art, Washington, D.C.
1986   Howard University, Washington, D.C. (retrospective)
1987   Montpelier Arts Center, Laurel, Maryland

1988   Miami-Dade Community College, Miami
1989   Miami-Dade Public Library, Miami
        One Brickell Square, Miami
1990   Florida State University, Miami
1991   The Forum, St. Louis, Missouri
1993   South Dallas Cultural Center, Dallas
1994   Yale University Gallery, New Haven, Connecticut
        Valdosta State University Gallery, Valdosta, Georgia
        Haas Gallery of Art, Bloomsburg University, Bloomsburg, Pennsylvania
1995   Gallery of Art, University of Central Arkansas, Conway

Selected Group Exhibitions:

1990   Southeastern Center for Contemporary Art, Winston-Salem, North Carolina (traveling through 1992)
1991   High Museum of Art, Atlanta, Georgia
        United States Information Agency, Washington, D.C. (traveling)
        Quinlan Art Gallery, Gainesville, Georgia
        Florida State University Museum of Art, Tallahassee, Florida (through 1997)
1992   AFRAM 2, Tallahassee City Hall, Florida
        Nexus Contemporary Art Center, Atlanta, Georgia
1993   University of South Florida and Museum of African-American Art, Tampa, Florida
        Art Festival of Atlanta, Georgia
        Visual Arts Center, Panama City, Florida

Collections:

Golden State Life Insurance, Los Angeles; Goucher College, Baltimore, Maryland; Howard University, Washington, D.C.; Nyangoma's Gallery, New York; Robert W. Woodruff Arts Center, High Museum of Art, Atlanta, Georgia; University of the District of Columbia, Washington, D.C.; Yale university Gallery, New Haven, Connecticut.

Publications:

On LOVE: Book—*Soundings: An Exhibition of Sculpture by Ed Love,* exhibition catalog, Washington, D.C., Howard University, 1986. **Articles**—"Ed Love," in *Miami Herald* (Miami), 23 August 1987, "A Sculptor to Know," in *Miami Herald* (Miami), 4 August 1988, both by Helen Kohen; "One Love!" by Faith Atlass, in *Southern Dawn,* Winter 1989; "Common Ground, Separate Choices" by Matthew Kangas, in *Art in America* (New York), March 1992. **Video**—*Kindred Spirits* (Dallas), KERA, 25 March 1992; *Ed Love on Fire* (Washington, D.C.), WETA, March 1986.

*   *   *

How does one gain access to a culture or heritage through its iconography? This is the question Edward Love must answer since he has committed himself to explorations of African and African American culture in his artwork. In doing so, he pays homage to the cultures and uses them as guideposts for his own life. For Love a sense of grounding in African and African American culture is an essential part of his life and work, and he seeks to reclaim his personal sense of an Africanness through his art.

Ed Love: *Sweet Jessye.* **Photo courtesy of Deborah Simpson.**

African culture was an early source of influence on Love's sculpture. He remembers being aware of Africa from the time of his youth in Los Angeles, when his father and uncle discussed Marcus Garvey's Back to Africa movement. Love also studied Egyptian art and became aware of African sculpture. This led him to explore the various art forms of Africa as inspiration for his own works. He was drawn not only to the formal structures of African artworks but also to the meanings behind them. He did not therefore separate the forms from the people who had created them, and when he reinterpreted the African forms in new materials, he kept this idea uppermost in his mind.

Love has often explored the idea of totems, as in *Totem for Senufo* (1974). This tall welded-steel piece is based on the large hornbill bird sculptures of the Senufo of the Ivory Coast. It stands full-bellied and erect. Like its carved wooden counterparts, which for Ivorians are symbols of fertility, Love's totem has markings that may suggest an identification with a specific family or community.

It was Africa that actually led Love back into African American culture, specifically music, where he developed imagery that evoked jazz and its rhythms, riffs, and improvisatory spontaneity. *Mask for Mingus* (1974) can alternatively be read as a face or torso mask. As a face mask large slits represent the eyes, while pursed, flattened lips protrude from the beardlike shape below. As a torso the work recalls Noah Purifoy's *Sir Watts* (1965), which was made of various metals assembled from the Watts riots. Beginning in the mid-1960s, Purifoy had great influence on the work of African American sculptors and assemblage artists living in Los Angeles.

In the mid-1980s Love created a series of sculptures, entitled "Arkestra," as a tribute to African American musicians. In works such as *Song Lines* (1989) he assembled multicolored steel rods to evoke the musical sounds of specific musicians. Like the music itself, the painted rods seemed to move in collaborative, yet improvisational, gestures. In works such as *Music from the Wailers* (Bob Marley and the Wailers) and in a series that included *Trane's Bird, Rahsaan's Trane,* and *Thread's Rahsaan,* Love tried to arrive at a visual representation of the music he was hearing.

His welded steel pieces, such as *Bird XI* (1994) and *Sphere Marker* (1994), like his earlier works, stretch through space, seeming to capture it in their forms while remaining indebted to African sculptural forms.

Love constructed a site-specific installation entitled *Goree Harvest: Angels and Jewels* at Florida State University, where he is on the faculty. The installation includes a circle of black images with targets on their chest. The figures are rendered unable to think (or inhuman) since the word "void" fills the halos around the backs of their heads. The work is made more powerful by a wall of bodies, as if they were bound in slavery. The bodies are wrapped in plastic, like cargo ready for removal by a forklift. Although the bodies look like tangible goods to be sold on the open market, Love reminds us through the sound track of a murmuring heartbeat in the background that they are human cargo.

—Lizzetta LeFalle-Collins

LOVING, Al(vin)

American painter

Born: Detroit, Michigan, 19 September 1935. **Education:** University of Illinois, Normal, B.F.A. 1963; University of Michigan, Ann

Al Loving. Photo courtesy of G.R. N'Namdi Gallery.

Arbor, M.F.A. 1965. **Career:** Since 1988 associate professor, City College of New York. Artist-in-residence, University of California, San Diego, 1970, Ohio University, Athens, 1974, Skowhegan School of Painting and Sculpture, 1981, Maryland Institute, Baltimore, 1981, University of Kansas, Lawrence, 1981, Virginia Commonwealth University, 1985-86, Notre Dame University, South Bend, Indiana, 1986, University of Vermont, Johnson, 1987, Cornell University, Ithaca, New York, 1990. Visiting artist, The Print Making Workshop, New York, 1984, Brandywine Printmaking Workshop, Philadelphia, 1987, International Art Workshop, Ka Mahi a Rika No Te Ao Ni, Dunedin, New Zealand, 1991, The Cooper Union, New York, 1994. **Awards:** Rakham Memorial Fellowship, University of Michigan, 1964; teaching fellowship, University of Michigan, 1965; National Endowment for the Arts Award, 1970-71; CAPS grant, New York State Council of the Arts, 1975; National Endowment for the Arts collaboration grant, 1975-76; Guggenheim Fellowship for painting, 1986; National Endowment for the Arts grant, 1985; Pollock-Krasner Foundation grant, 1996.

Individual Exhibitions:

1969   Gertrude Kasle Gallery, Detroit
1970   Gertrude Kasle Gallery, Detroit

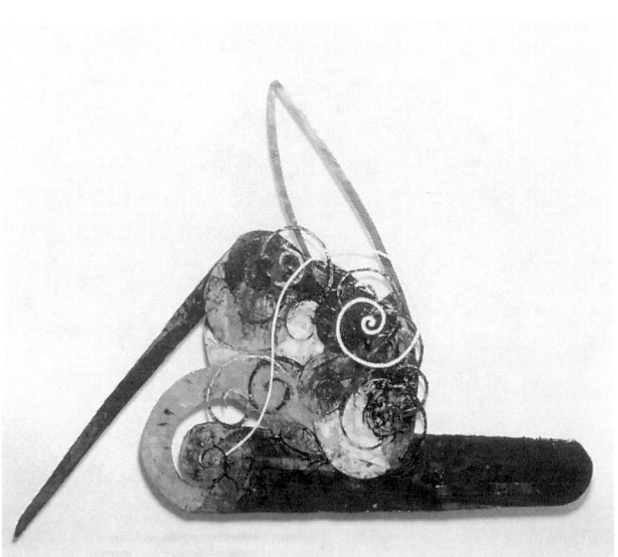

Al Loving: *Power & Love #2*, 1996. Photo courtesy of G.R.
N'Namdi Gallery.

1971	William Zierler, Inc., New York
1972	William Zierler, Inc., New York
1973	Tylor School of Art, Philadelphia
	William Zierler, Inc., New York
1974	Fishbach Gallery, New York
	University of Ohio, Athens
1975	Notre Dame University, South Bend, Indiana
1976	Fishbach Gallery, New York
1977	Studio Museum in Harlem, New York
1978	University of Wisconsin, Oshkosh
1979	Grippi-Zivian Gallery, New York
1983	Andrea Olitzky Gallery, New York
	N'Namdi Reid Gallery, Detroit
	Diane Brewer Gallery, New York
1984	Onyx Gallery, New York
	University of Vermont, Johnson
1986	Studio Museum in Harlem, New York
1987	Harris Brown Gallery, Boston
	University of Vermont, Johnson
	University of Tennessee, Knoxville
1988	Liz Harris Gallery, Boston
	G.R. N'Namdi Gallery, Detroit
	June Kelly Gallery, New York
1989	Harlem School of the Arts, New York
	Bronx Museum of the Arts, New York
1990	June Kelly Gallery, New York
	Franklin and Marshall College, Lancaster, Pennsylvania
	G. R. N'Namdi Gallery, Birmingham
1991	Galbreath Gallery, Lexington, Kentucky
	Birmingham Bloomfield Arts Association, Michigan
	National Academy of Arts and Sciences, Washington, D.C.
1992	Kreft Center for the Arts, Concordia College, Ann Arbor, Michigan
	Pace University, New York
	June Kelly Gallery, New York
1993	Alitash Kebede Gallery, Los Angeles
	Sande Webster Gallery, Philadelphia
	G. R. N'Namdi Gallery, Detroit

1994	Long Island University, Southhampton, New York
1995	The Ice House Gallery, Telluride, Colorado
	Sande Webster Gallery, Philadelphia
1996	G. R. N'Namdi Gallery, Detroit
	University of Rhode Island, Providence
1997	Elaine Benson Gallery, Bridgehampton, New York

Selected Group Exhibitions:

1970	Gallery Maeght, Paris
1973	Whitney Museum of American Art, New York
1981	Everson Museum, Syracuse, New York
1983	Cleveland Museum of Art, Ohio
1987	Montclair Museum, New Jersey
1990	Speed Museum, Louisville, Kentucky
1991	Kenkeleba Gallery, New York (traveling)
1992	Smithsonian Institute of Art, Detroit
1993	U. B. Blake Museum, Baltimore, Maryland
1996	James Howe Fine Arts Gallery, Kean College, Union, New Jersey

Collections:

Akron Art Museum, Ohio; Currier Gallery, Manchester, New Hampshire; Detroit Institute of Art; Detroit Library; Everson Museum, Syracuse, New York; Franklyn and Marshall College, Lancaster, Pennsylvania; Johnson Museum, Ithaca, New York; Kenkeleba Gallery, New York; Metropolitan Museum of Art, New York; Montclair Museum, New Jersey; Museum of Art, Durham, North Carolina; New Jersey Library, Newark; New Jersey State Museum, Trenton; Newark Museum, New Jersey; Renaissance Center, Detroit; Studio Museum in Harlem, New York; Toledo Museum of Art, Ohio; University of Michigan, Kalamazoo; Vassar College, Poukeepsy, New York; Whitney Museum of American Art, New York.

Publications:

On LOVING: Articles— Review (June Kelly Gallery) by Terry R. Myers, in *Arts Magazine,* September 1990; review (National Academy of Arts and Sciences) by Michael Welzenbach, in *Washington Post,* 11 May 1991; review (June Kelly Gallery) by Eleanor Hartney, in *Art in America,* June 1993.

*   *   *

While remaining focused on exploring color as a language to describe space and to manipulate spatial perception, Alvin Loving's painting style has evolved greatly over the years. Beginning his career as an abstract expressionist, Loving then streamlined his ideas into geometric abstractions. In the early 1970s he began chafing against the constraints of the picture plane, and he broke out by turning gallery spaces into environments. He gradually retreated from this radical stance, and by the mid-1980s he had returned to something similar to his abstract expressionist beginnings. Because they have shared similar pictorial concerns, Loving has long been compared to Frank Stella. Loving's approach, however, is considered more introspective and personal and less detached and cool.

Loving's first recognized work of the late 1960s drew from Hans Hofmann's experiments with squares, while incorporating the ideas of Josef Albers, who placed rectangles within rectangles. Loving's introduction to the New York art world came through his one-man show at the Whitney Museum of American Art in 1969. Considered color geometry, these canvases were built in the shapes of his forms—interlocking cubes that were painted illusionistically. The modulations of tone and juxtapositions of hue within the forms (in the edges and planes of the cubes) created interiors that optically pushed and pulled, alternating their structures between foreground and background. Loving used color as a bold, simple language that discussed issues of the perception of space and color relationships. The large size of some of the canvasses drew the blank area of the wall into the composition as well, lending an environmental feel to the work.

In 1972 Loving broke radically away from the picture plane, illusionistic painting, and the use of fine materials by filling entire gallery rooms with long strips of hand-dyed canvas. The strips were sewed into various configurations, then tacked to the wall and draped from the ceiling. The effect was pictorial (strips on the wall), sculptural (strips hanging from the ceiling and brushing the floor), and confounding. In subsequent work Loving withdrew back into the picture plane, this time sewing the strips of cloth into colorful woven fabric paintings that countered traditional picture making by confounding, and therefore questioning, the normal visual cues people rely upon when they perceive space.

Loving's next phase became more structured as he took up the ideas of Stella in works that recalled Henri Matisse's late cutout collages. Both Loving and Stella were concerned with finding a literal equivalent for the traditional illusionism found in many forms of painting. While Stella worked in aluminum, Loving worked in layers of corrugated cardboard and acrylic paint. Both artists created objects that were offset slightly from the wall. Loving's images lacked a traditional pictorial order as they coalesced with a serpentine rhythm around a center with either a vertical or horizontal axis. His colors were generally hot, but he used cool accents to maintain a sense of visual balance. It was at this point that Loving's work attained the label "painterly sculpture."

During the early 1980s Loving learned papermaking, and he immediately incorporated the medium into his art. What had before been jaggedly torn strips of cardboard now became shapes (torn or cut) of stripes, arcs, spirals, and crisscrosses. His colors remained similarly hot and cool, and they were arranged in seemingly infinite, random combinations. The works hearkened back to Loving's abstract expressionist beginnings, while they maintained a preoccupation with disturbing the normal perceptions of space. Loving's inventive, painterly approach to paper as a medium subverted the meaning of papermaking as craft.

Loving has termed his next formal development "material abstraction." These works are often compared to the large aluminum wall constructions of Stella, whose colors and forms, in contrast, celebrate artifice. Loving's colors are warmer and more intimate. His compositions of shapes and lines suggest natural forces such as wind, air, fire, and water. Overall, Loving's material abstractions breathe with the energy and sheer joy of life.

—Laurie Fitzpatrick

MAGLIANI, Maria (Lidia Dos Santos)

Brazilian painter

Born: Pelotas, Rio Grande do Sul, 1946. **Education:** Art Institute, Federal University of Rio Grande do Sul, graduated 1967. **Career:** Teacher of drawing, Santa Marcelina Arts College, Center for the Arts and Culture, Federal University of Sergipe, Aracaju, 1989. President, Association of the Plastic Artists, Tiradentes, Minas Gerais, c.1990. Address: Rua Jaguaribe 768/11, 01224-001 Sao Paulo, Brazil.

Individual Exhibitions:

1966	Galeria Espaço, Porto Alegre, Rio Grande do Sul
1967	Galeria Leopoldina, Porto Alegre, Rio Grande do Sul
1976	Art Museum, Rio Grande do Sul
1977	Galeria do Instituto dos Arquitetos do Brasil
1979	Galeria Independencia, Porto Alegre, Rio Grande do Sul
1980	Spazio Pirandello, Sao Paulo
1981	Galeria de Arte do Centro Comerical, Porto Alegre, Rio Grande do Sul
	Pinacoteca do Estado de Sao Paulo
1983	Centro de Estudos Brasileiros
	Sala de Esposicoes da Universidade Federal
1984	Galeria Tina Presser, Porto Alegre, Rio Grande do Sul
1987	Art Museum, Rio Grande do Sul, Porto Alegre (retrospective)
	Galeria Tina Presser, Porto Alegre, Rio Grande do Sul
	Galeria Espaco Capital, Brasilia
	Paulo Figueiredo, Sao Paulo
1990	Galeria Tina Zappoli

Maria Magliani, self-portrait. Photo courtesy of the Sao Paulo State Museum.

Selected Group Exhibitions:

1977   Salao de Desenho, Margs, Porto Alegre, Rio Grande do Sul
1978   Projeto Arco Iris
1979   *Panorama da Arte Atual Brasileira,* Sao Paulo
1980   *Panorama da Arte Atual Brasileira, Desenho,* Sao Paulo
1981   Desenho e Gravura no Rio Grande do Sul
1984   Salao Nacional de Artes Plasticas de Goias
1985   *Bienal Internacional de Sao Paulo*
1986   *Bienal Latino-Americana de Arte Sobre Papel,* Argentina
1987   Co-Nexus Project, Museum of Spanish Art, New York
1989   *Introspectives: Contemporary Art by Americans and Bra-
        zilians of African Descent* (traveling)

*

Maria Magliani comments:

I was born in Pelotas, Rio Grande do Sul, in 1946. As a child I was rather indifferent to playing: I preferred to read, to observe, and to draw the adults around me. They seemed to be always hiding emotions that they were unwilling to show. When I was nine years old I saw some reproductions of works by Van Gogh in a magazine, and I realized there was a way of depicting what I perceived behind those adult body masks. Eleven years later, while I was still a student of Arts at the Federal University of Rio Grande do Sul, I exhibited my work for the first time. In the next thirty years I took part in various collective exhibitions and salons—in Brazil and abroad—and I showed my work in more than fifteen individual exhibitions. I was awarded some prizes, illustrated some books and newspapers, designed stage settings and fashion plates, and acted in plays.

I lived in Sao Paulo for ten years. I took part in the 18th International Biennial Art Exhibition, taught drawing both privately and, in 1985, at the Santa Marcelina Arts College. In 1989 I also taught drawing at the Center for the Arts and Culture at the Federal University of Sergipe in Aracaju.

I lived for six years at the historical town of Tiradentes, in Minas Gerais, where I was president of the local Association of the Plastic Artists. At the time I started to work with sculptures with papier-maché. Since December 1995 I have been living in Sao Paulo, where I carry on my work on human gestures and attitudes which I had started in 1993.

*   *   *

Stacks of canvases fill Maria Magliani's tiny apartment, so many that the visitor must move sideways through the space. This creative energy shows in the artist. She is as animated as her images, quick to laugh, playful, bubbling with enthusiasm. At the same time one senses a deep loneliness and hidden sadness.

Bold and colorful human figures populate Magliani's canvases. Swirls of color and active lines and shapes fill the spaces. The energy of her creative actions dominates the works. Strongly expressive, blurred forms move before the viewer's eyes, their explosive power heightened by their monumentality. The viewer confronts parts of torsos, heads, and limbs from positions too close for comfort. Many are rippled, some are lumpy, and others are sinewy. There are volumes of flesh, clinging garments, and sparse interior spaces. The expressive power of her lines and shapes of color remind one of Francis Bacon's canvases, but Magliani's are brighter and more animated.

Magliani began her career in the 1960s with powerful political cartoons. Since then her central theme has become identity, more precisely identity of sex and gender rather than color. She explains, "I do a lot of masked figures of women from all over the planet. Friends ask me why I don't paint black figures, and I reply that I paint them in *color,* in the color of no person, not racial color, but color, not an African woman, not a Brazilian woman, but a woman—WONDERWOMAN!" When, on looking at her voluminous female figures, one critic remarked, "I see mother Africa," Magliani replied by saying, "You don't know anything about my work."

Magliani struggles to go beyond the boundaries others want to impose upon her. That is probably why she has come to work on the theme of femaleness and maleness. It is an issue that concerns her for both ideological and personal reasons. It transcends racial and national boundaries, and it affects her friends, many of whom are transvestites.

Magliani wrestles with her own identity as well. "Some blacks criticize me, saying my work is not black. But I don't know how to paint *blackly.* I have seen African art—masks, clothes, jewelry—and it's different. I am not an African. It is difficult here because some black Brazilian artists feel that they must paint in a way that can be identified as 'black art' and that others [must] do the same in order to be considered black." At the same time she supports aspects of the black-consciousness movement and the celebration of Zumbi, a seventeenth-century Afro-Brazilian freedom fighter.

Magliani explains further that "everything in Brazil is so mixed up. How does one choose? Depending upon the circumstances or opportunities, I can choose to be black, Italian, Spanish, German, Catholic, or Jewish—all are part of my heritage. It is very difficult in Brazil, unlike in the United States, where you were separated. All Brazilians have a mixture of races; there weren't the conditions to separate us. It is difficult to expose racism here; it exists, but it is very subtle."

Class is also an issue in Brazil, Magliani explains. She does not often experience racism because she is well educated, in contrast to many blacks. This, she believes, has caused resentment and misunderstanding since blacks expect her to be the way they imagine her, not the way she is. As a result she often feels isolated and lonely—"all that I am is in my painting; it must show."

—Henry John Drewal

MALOBA, Gregory

Kenyan sculptor

Born: Mumias, Kenya, 1922. **Education:** Saint Mary's College, Kisubi, Kenya, 1940-41; Makerere University College School of Fine Arts, Kampala, 1941-45; Bath Academy of Art, England, 1948-50; Camberwell School of Arts and Crafts, London, 1956-59; Royal College of Art, London, 1956-57; Corsham Court, Wiltshire, England. **Career:** Instructor, Makerere University College, Kampala, 1945-66. From 1966 department head, University of Nairobi, Department of Fine Arts. President, Uganda Arts Club, 1956-62, and 1964; member, Kenya College of Arms.

Selected Exhibitions:

1949   Imperial Institute, London
1950   British Council, Bristol (solo)

1961 Sorsbie Gallery
Independence Day, Dar es Salaam
1962 Commonwealth Institute, London
1965 Munich, Germany

Collections:

Bank of India, Kampala; City Hall, Nairobi; Commonwealth Institute, London; Imperial Institute, London; Jinja Town Hall, Uganda; Masulita Secondary School, Uganda; Safari Parks Hotel, Ruaraka, Kenya; Saint Francis Chapel, Makerere University; Uganda Banquet Hall; Uganda Embassies; Uganda Growers Cooperative Society; Uganda Independence Monument; Uganda Museum; Uganda Boy Scout's Association.

*   *   *

As one of the first students at Makerere University College of Fine Arts in Kampala, the sculptor Gregory Maloba successfully displayed sufficient talent and energy to quickly become an instructor at the school. Maloba spent much of his career encouraging and influencing emerging African artists. He taught at Makerere University College from 1945 to 1966 and served as head of the Department of Design at the University of Nairobi from 1966 until his retirement.

Maloba's most formal and traditional training came from his studies at four different schools in England: Bath Academy of Art, Corsham Court, Camberwell School of Arts and Crafts, and the Royal College of Art. He began his career producing Western-style portraiture and later moved to massive, contemporary, angular forms that have been compared to those of Henry Moore and Jacob Epstein. Maloba's academic background loosened its hold on his more recent work, and he became more grounded in the African tradition. His work acts as a bond between foreign, indigenous, and modern cultures, and he has been commissioned numerous times for public works in countries outside his native Kenya, including his sculpture *Independence Monument* which is located in Uganda.

Though Kenya has produced a relatively small art movement compared to Nigeria, Senegal, Ethiopia, Sudan, Zimbabwe, and South Africa, Gregory Maloba has managed to break free of the rather sentimental tourist art and Western academic painting that represents the dominant art climate in much of East and Central Africa. Maloba's sculptures are formed with stone, wood, bronze, cement fondue (a luminous cement used for casting), and terra-cotta. His work is giant, and though influenced by European and academic artistic ideals, he also manages to produce sculpture that is wholly his own, thus retaining a powerful African/Kenyan voice.

—Terry Bain

MANLEY, Edna

Jamaican sculptor, painter, and printmaker

Born: Edna Swithenbank, Bournemouth, England, 1 March 1900. **Education:** Regent Street Polytechnic, London, 1918-20; St. Martin's School of Art, London, 1920-22; Royal Academy, London, 1920-22. **Family:** Married Norman Washington Manley (first prime minister of Jamaica), in 1921 (died 1969), two sons (Michael Manley, Prime Minister of Jamaica, 1972-80 and Douglas Manley, cabinet member, 1972-80). **Career:** Teacher, Jamaica. Co-founder, Jamaica Art School, 1950. Member, London Group, beginning 1930. **Awards:** Silver Musgrave Medal, Institute of Jamaica, Kingston, 1929; Gold Musgrave Medal, Institute of Jamaica, Kingston, 1943; honorary degree, University of the West Indies, 1975; Order of Merit, National Awards, 1980; Fellow, Institute of Jamaica, Kingston, 1980. **Died:** 6 February 1987.

Individual Exhibitions:

1937 Jamaica Mutual Life Assurance Building, Kingston
French Gallery, London
1948 Doorly Memorial Hall, Kingston, Jamaica
1960 *Edna Manley: Drawings,* Hills Galleries, Kingston, Jamaica
1970 Bolivar Gallery

Edna Manley: *The Diggers,* 1936. Photo courtesy of Maria La Yacona.

1971   *Edna Manley: Fifty Years a Sculptor,* Bolivar Gallery, Kingston, Jamaica

1973   Spelman College, Atlanta

1976   *Sculptures and Drawings: 1922-1973,* Mutual Life Center, Kingston, Jamaica

1980   National Gallery of Jamaica, Kingston

1981   Queen's Park House, Bridgetown, Barbados

1990   *Edna Manley: A Retrospective,* National Gallery of Jamaica, Kingston

Selected Group Exhibitions:

1928   Burlington Galleries, London

1930   New Burlington Galleries, London

1932   French Galleries, London
        New Burlington Galleries, London

1962   Institute of Jamaica, Kingston

1964   Kaiser Center Gallery, Oakland, California

1973   O.A.S. Gallery, Washington, D.C.

1975   *Ten Jamaican Sculptors,* Commonwealth Institute, London

1976   National Gallery of Jamaica, Kingston

1983   Commonwealth Institute, London

Collections:

Commonwealth Institute, London; National Gallery of Jamaica, Kingston; Sheffield Art Gallery, England; Spelman College, Atlanta, Georgia; Wadsworth Athaneum, Hartford, Connecticut.

Publications:

On MANLEY: Books—*Edna Manley: The Private Years, 1900-1938* by Wayne Brown, London, Andre Deutsch, 1975; *Edna Manley: Selected Sculpture and Drawings,* exhibition catalog, Kingston, National Gallery and Mutual Life Society and M.G. Smith, 1976; *Edna Manley, The Seventies,* exhibition catalog, Kingston, National Gallery and David Boxer, 1980; *Edna Manley, Sculptor* by David Boxer, Kingston, Edna Manley Foundation and National Gallery, 1990. **Articles**—"The Wood Carvings of Edna Manley" by Madeline Kerr, in *The Studio* (London), June 1950; "Edna Manley Retrospective: An Interview with the Artist" by

Edna Manley: *Generations,* 1943. Photo courtesy of Maria La Yacona.

Basid McFarlane, in *Jamaica Journal,* 4(1), March 1970; "Edna Manley, Sculptor" by David Boxer, in *Americas* (Washington, D.C.), 32, 1980; "Edna Manley: A Legend in Her Own Time" by Mae Tate, in, *International Review of African American Art* (Los Angeles), 7(4), 1987. **Films**—*Edna Manley: Sculptor* by David Boxer, Kingston, Jamaica Broadcasting Corporation, 1970; *Edna Manley: A Retrospective* by David Boxer, Kingston, Jamaica Broadcasting Corporation, 1990.

*   *   *

Edna Manley was a seminal figure in the development of twentieth-century Jamaican art. As an artist and as a cultural activist and educator, her influence spanned her entire career, from 1922 when she first arrived in Jamaica until her death in 1987. Her sociopolitical carvings of the mid- and late 1930s—especially her renowned *Negro Aroused* (1935), *Diggers* (1936), *Strike* (1938), and *Tomorrow* (1939)—operated beyond the realm of art, becoming virtual political icons that helped shape the national consciousness. They were a key ingredient of the political activism of her husband, the national hero Norman Manley.

Manley was trained in England at various art schools, notably Saint Martin's and the Royal Academy, and her strong romantic bent and love of animals caused her to seek out the private tutorship of the animal sculptor Maurice Harding. Her first works in England were dominated by romantic animal studies in a style reminiscent of Antoine-Louis Barye. In 1992 she married her Jamaican cousin and moved with him to Jamaica. Her earliest works in Jamaica, notably *Beadseller* (1922) and *Ape* (1923), revealed a willingness to experiment with contemporary formal ideas, especially cubism, while the neoclassicism of Pablo Picasso and of contemporary British sculptors such as Frank Dobson pushed her in the direction of classicism in the later 1920s. Cubism and classicism were reconciled in Manley's works of the 1930s, which were marked by a highly elegant, refined figurative style and with elements akin to manifestations of art deco. It was the heightened social content of her art after 1935, however, and the manner in which content and form were so carefully matched that allowed her works to transcend the decorativeness associated with art deco.

In the 1940s Manley retreated from the pungent declamatory works of the late 1930s and developed a highly romantic style that emulated the paintings of William Blake. His poetry was also an influence in her development of a personal mythology based on the landscape and skyscape of the mystical environs of the Blue Mountains, where she built the retreat Nomdmi. The central motifs of the "Nomdmi" carvings and drawings are the energetic masculine sun and the nurturing female earth. The motifs are presented in a variety of guises, but most persistently the sun is seen rising and setting in poignant symbols of rebirth and renewal, as in *New World, Old World* (1942) and *Generations* (1943). The sun, however, received its most eloquent representation in the famous *Horse of the Morning* (1943), a spirited image of a rearing horse, its eyes and mane blazing with the intensity of the sun's light.

The 1950s and 1960s were marked by a series of public commissions for churches and for a national monument to Paul Bogle, the hero of the Morant Bay rebellion. This last work, the first public statue of a black man in Jamaica, was the subject of much outcry, especially over the black material chosen for the cast. In 1962, the year of Jamaica's independence, Manley carved *He Cometh Forth,* a large bas-relief for the Sheraton Hotel in Kingston as a poetic homage to Jamaican life.

Outstanding among Manley's later works is a series of wood carvings in which the artist attempted to come to terms with the death of her lifelong companion and husband. The most profound of the group, *Mountain Women* (1971), abandons the themes of death and the grieving woman, however, to present the age-old theme of the three ages of man, cast here as a succession of generations of women. The emphasis is thrown on the oldest head, which is seen as a grand climax to the group, a culmination of three generations of experiences. Two late works, *The Voice* (1980) and *Ghetto Mother* (1981), are given over to contemporary themes. *The Voice* celebrates the potent social force of Rastafarianism, while *Ghetto Mother* is an indictment of the political system that has fostered political tribalism and violence in Jamaica's urban areas.

Manley's influence on successive generations of Jamaican artists was profound. In the 1930s and 1940s her essential, symbolist figurative mode informed much of the work of Koren der Harootian, Albert Huie, and others, yet it could still be discerned in the 1960s and 1970s in artists as disparate as Colin Garland, Christopher Gonzalez, and Fitzroy Harrack.

—David Boxer

MARSHALL, Kerry James

American painter

Born: Birmingham, Alabama, 1955. **Education:** Otis Art Institute, Los Angeles, B.F.A. 1978. **Career:** Since 1993 associate professor of art, University of Illinois, Chicago. Production designer, *Daughters of the Dust,* directed by Julie Dash, 1989, *SANKOFA,* directed by Haile Gerima, 1990, *Praise House,* directed by Julie Dash, 1991. **Awards:** Resident Fellowship, Studio Museum in Harlem, New York, 1985; Art Matters, Inc., painting grant, 1990; National Endowment for the Arts Visual Arts Fellowship, 1991; Illinois Arts Council Fellowship, 1992; Louis Comfort Tiffany Foundation grant, 1993; American Academy of Arts and Letters Award, 1996.

Individual Exhibitions:

1981	Southwest College Art Gallery, Los Angeles
1983	James Turcotte Gallery, Los Angeles
1984	Pepperdine University Art Gallery, Malibu, California
1985	Koplin Gallery, Los Angeles
1986	Studio Museum in Harlem, New York
1991	Koplin Gallery, Los Angeles
1992	*Terra Incognita,* Chicago Cultural Center
1993	Koplin Gallery, Santa Monica, California
	Jack Shainman Gallery, New York
1994	*Telling Stories,* Cleveland Center for Contemporary Art, Ohio (traveling through 1995)
1995	Greg Kuchera Gallery, Seattle
	Jack Shainman Gallery, New York
1997	Addison Gallery of American Art, Phillips Academy, Andover, Massachusetts

Selected Group Exhibitions:

1995	*Korrespondenzen/Correspondences,* Berlinische Galerie, Berlin, and Chicago Cultural Center

Kerry James Marshall: *Many Mansions,* 1994-95.

High Museum of Art, Atlanta, Georgia
Mary Leigh Block Gallery, Northwestern University, Evanston, Illinois
Kemper Museum of Contemporary Art and Design, Kansas
Columbia College Art Gallery, Chicago
Bass Museum of Art, Miami
Aldrich Museum of Contemporary Art, Ridgefield, Connecticut
Museum of Contemporary Art, Chicago
Museum of Art, Fort Lauderdale, Florida
1997   Kassel, Germany

Collections:

Art Bank, Santa Monica, California; Art Institute of Chicago; Corcoran Gallery of Art, Washington, D.C.; Denver Art Museum, Colorado; Johnson County Community College, Overland Park, Kansas; Laguna Art Museum, Laguna Beach, California; Legler Branch Public Library, Chicago; Los Angeles County Museum of Art; Loyola Law School, Los Angeles; Museum of Art, University of Arizona, Tucson; Northwestern University, Evanston, Illinois; St. Louis Art Museum, Missouri; Studio Museum in Harlem, New York; Wadsworth Atheneum, Boston.

*

Kerry James Marshall comments:

My paintings are an attempt at representing the existential complexities of the black cultural body. The images are rhetorical and unequivocal, the context manifestly pictorial.

An artist's responsibility is to manufacture surprise. I take the challenge to do so very seriously. What is art anyway, if not the construction of synthetic phenomena from the raw material of life.

*   *   *

Kerry James Marshall embarked on the endeavor of making art at an early age. From kindergarten on he diligently searched for stimuli to feed his creative instincts. He combed libraries to copy images from art history books, and youthful cult heroes from comic books served as studies in anatomy, form, and drama. As a young artist pursuing formal studies, he expressed enthusiasm for Giotto and for neoclassical and romantic painters such as Théodore Géricault. The draftsmanship of Charles White and the erudite compositions, narrative subject matter, and geometrically articulated forms of Jacob Lawrence also deeply inspired Marshall. The works of these artists fostered his thirst for making art.

Marshall's style of painting large-scale narrative works is a compilation of diverse techniques. Although he is basically a figurative painter, his excursions into abstraction emerge in his works on multiple levels. His figures, often flat and rendered in hues related to the darkest color spectrum, are designed to effect compelling and powerful representations of black people. He places the human form in a context with references to everyday existence, giving insight to activities conducted in the home. At intervals he plays the role of voyeur, exposing private life within the confines of interior spaces. The complexities of romantic encounters are rendered in a boudoir scene, for example, and lovers dance a slow drag in a living room in which proportions between human forms and furnishings are slightly askew. He also assumes the role of social advocate with bravura and force. Marshall's narrative approach approximates the insider's view of the variants of the black experience placed within sociological constructs.

His housing project paintings are a *Better Homes and Gardens* for many black urban dwellers. His depictions of these environments are compositionally rich, and he collages highly stylized renditions of figures and architectural structures with incongruently encoded metaphorical devices. Letters and numbers appear along with blue birds and decorative banners bearing text or slogans. Infused in the idyllic pastoral of *Garden Project* is an ironic note in contrast to its planned obsolescence. Most housing projects are designed to last only twenty-five years or less.

As a representational painter Marshall is aware that he is a part of an extensive legacy that places great burdens on him to portray an idea or concept effectively. The freshness of his style is indicative of the infusion of multiple tendencies. Of significance to the structural underpinning of his compositions are lessons learned from the Renaissance. His decorative sensibilities and palette pay homage to Henri Matisse and folk art, while notes of the expressionistic application of strategically placed paint create a cohesion of design and syncopated moments on his planar surfaces. The term "bricolage"—used in reference to literature, anthropology, and the combination of disparate elements in sculpture—is appropriate in describing the many-sided visual motifs that comprise Marshall's style. He has mastered the ability to articulate social issues, create scenes that touch the heart, and affect speculative thinking.

—A.M. Weaver

MAYHEW, Richard

American painter

Born: Amityville, New York, 3 April 1924. **Education:** Art Students League, New York; Brooklyn Museum Art School, 1951; Columbia University, New York; Pratt Institute. **Career:** Freelance medical illustrator and professional singer, c.1945-50. Instructor of art, Brooklyn Museum Art School, 1963-68, Art Students League, New York, 1965-71; instructor, Smith College, Northampton, Massachusetts, 1971-75. Beginning 1977 professor, Pennsylvania State University, University Park. Beginning 1963 member, Spiral (dis-

cussion group). **Awards:** MacDowell Colony Fellowship, 1958; John Hay Whitney Fellowship, 1959; Ingram Merrill Foundation Award, 1960; Ford Foundation Purchase Award, 1962; Tiffany Foundation Award, 1963; National Institute of Arts and Letters grant, 1965; Childe Hassam Purchase Award, 1963-64; Henry Ward Ranger Purchase Prize, 1964; Benjamin Altman Award, 1970; National Academy of Design Merit Award, 1977; Grumbacher Gold Medal, 1983. **Address:** c/o Alitash Kebede Gallery, 964 North LaBrea Avenue, Los Angeles, California 90038, U.S.A.

Individual Exhibitions:

1955	Brooklyn Museum, New York
1957	Morris Gallery, New York
1963	Sutherland Gallery, Boston
1964	Durlacher Brothers Gallery, New York
1966	Durlacher Brothers Gallery, New York
1967	The Contemporaries, New York
1978	Studio Museum in Harlem, New York
1980	San Jose Museum of Art, California
1983	Pennsylvania State University, University Park
1985	Young Gallery, San Jose, California

Selected Group Exhibitions:

1961	Butler Institute of American, Youngstown, Ohio
1963	University of Illinois (retrospective)
1968	Minneapolis Institute of Arts
1969	Everson Museum of Art, Syracuse, New York
	Flint Institute of Arts, Michigan
	High Museum of Art, Atlanta, Georgia
1970	Contemporary Art Museum, Houston, Texas
	Boston Museum of Fine Arts
1971	Newark Museum, New Jersey

Collections:

Albion College, Michigan; Ball State Teachers College, Indiana; Brooklyn Museum, New York; Evansville Museum, Indiana; Midtown Galleries, New York; Whitney Museum of American Art, New York.

Publications:

On MAYHEW: Book—*Richard Mayhew: An American Abstractionist,* exhibition catalog by Mary Schmidt-Campbell, New York, Studio Museum in Harlem, 1978. **Articles**—Review, in *Arts,* March 1957; review by Stuart Preston, in *New York Times,* 6 May 1961; article by Emily Genauer, in *New York Herald-Tribune,* 5 October 1963; "The Ax Hits Richard Mayhew" by Benny Andrews, in *Encore,* 8 March 1976, pp. 34-5; review (Midtown Gallery, New York) by Amy Fine Collins, in *Art in America,* 76, February 1988, p. 141; "Alchemists" by Clarissa J. Welsh, in *Artweek,* 23 September 1993, pp. 18-19 (illustrated); "Richard Mayhew," in *A History of African-American Artists, from 1792 to the Present* by Romare Bearden and Harry Henderson, Pantheon Books, New York, 1993, pp. 470-77.

*   *   *

Because Richard Mayhew paints landscapes, observers have compared his work to nineteenth-century art, notably to the Barbizon school, impressionism, and tonalism. Mayhew's work is not entirely derived from any one of these styles, however. Yet he, like the artists associated with these movements, has chosen the landscape genre for intimate, gestural expression. His paintings are evocations of what he remembers seeing, and understanding that he resurrects memory and feeling is critical to the appreciation of his art.

Born in Long Island and raised there and in New York City, Mayhew attended the area's prestigious art schools, where he was trained by the surrealist Edwin Dickinson, the abstractionists Reuben Tam and Hans Hofmann, and the expressionist Max Beckmann. He was also well trained in drawing the human figure, having apprenticed as a medical illustrator, and people are evident in his early paintings. He gradually eliminated the human presence from his work, however, because he believed that it brought unwanted specificity and interfered with his aim of making universal statements. Instead, he began to use stands of trees, meadow grasses, and meandering paths to communicate vital life forces in hazy spaces. There are almost no hard shapes and few distinct lines and contours in his paintings, and details are kept to a minimum. Exquisitely balanced forms, often general and summary, are suggested rather than delineated.

Like abstract expressionist paintings, Mayhew's work is usually on a large scale. Moreover, like the 1968 paintings *Birth* and *Counterpoint,* some are either square or almost so, and the regularity focuses the viewer's attention on the content. Nature is the star of these paintings, and the dynamism of nature parallels the artist's fluid manner of painting. He does not paint in front of his subject, *en plein air,* but rather composes pictures in his studio. He uses a palette knife to apply pigment to the canvas in layers, and as a result colors are often unexpectedly revealed and the viewing experience heightened by the element of surprise.

The restrained values of Mayhew's work in the early 1960s gave way by mid-decade to brighter and more intense hues. *The Gorge* (1965), for example, is a sensuous expanse of mingling purples, greens, and yellows. Standing before the canvas and reflecting on a scene already viewed, Mayhew sought not to record but rather to respond. In this sense his creative process seems more like an abstractionist's.

Since the 1980s representational elements have turned up more frequently in Mayhew's paintings, although he remains an artist committed to demonstrating the emotive capacity of color. The "Santa Cruz" series (1991) boasts fiery oranges and deep greens rendered in liquid pastels and watercolors. The move to iridescent chroma was appropriate to the California subject, which he had treated in his "Big Sur" paintings of the late 1980s. In content his oeuvre is distinguished by its topographic diversity, from Western deserts to forests and shores of the Northeast.

Music also has been a source of inspiration for Mayhew. He is a lifelong jazz aficionado, and for a period in the 1940s he performed as an actor and singer. *Vibrato* (1974), *Sonata in G Major* (1987), and *Mood Indigo* (1990) allude both to his passion for music and to his belief in the close relationship of the expressive arts.

—Jacqueline Francis

MAYNARD, Valerie (J.)

American sculptor

Born: New York, 22 August 1937. **Education:** Museum of Modern Art, New York, 1954-55; Elaine Journey Art School, New Roch-

elle, New York, 1955-60; New School, New York, 1968-69; Goddard College, Plainsfield, Vermont, M.F.A. 1977. **Career:** Instructor, Studio Museum in Harlem, New York, 1969-74, Langston Hughes Library, 1971-72, Howard University, Washington, D.C., 1974-76, Jersey City State College, 1977-78, Baltimore School for the Arts, Maryland, 1980-81, College of the Virgin Islands, St. Thomas, 1984-88; visiting professor/artist-in-residence/Rockefeller Humanities fellow, Susan B. Anthony Center for Women's Studies, University of Rochester, New York, 1992-94. Artist-in-residence, Blue Mountain Center, New York, 1987-91, MacDowell Colony, Peterborough, New Hampshire, 1991-92, Massachusetts Institute of Technology, Cambridge, 1992, Brandywine Graphic Workshop, Philadelphia, 1992, Bob Blackburn Print Workshop, New York, 1992-93; printmaker-in-residence, Women's Studio Workshop, Rosendale, New York, 1989. Lecturer, Northeastern University, Boston, Goddard College, Plainfield, Vermont, Rutgers University, New Jersey, Harlem State Office Building, New York, College of the Virgin Islands, St. Thomas, 1979-85. **Awards:** Riksututallningar National Museum purchase/travel/lecture grant, Stockholm, Sweden, 1975; Virgin Islands Humanities Council research grant, 1986-87; Sculpture Award, Atlanta Life Insurance, Georgia, 1990; New York Foundation for the Arts grant for printmaking, 1990; New Forms Regional Initiative grant, New England Foundation for the Visual Arts, 1992; Artist of the Year, MacDowell Colony, Peterborough, New Hampshire, 1992; MacDowell Colony Fellowship, 1992-93; Rockefeller Humanities Fellowship, 1992-94.

Individual Exhibitions:

1971	American International College, Springfield, Massachusetts
1973	Howard University, Washington, D.C.
1974	University of Massachusetts, Amherst
1975	Riksutstallnlngar National Museum, Stockholm, Sweden (traveling)
1983	Reichhold Center for the Arts, University of the Virgin Islands, Saint Thomas
1988	New Visions Gallery, Millersville University, Lancaster, Pennsylvania
	Caribbean Cultural Center, New York
1989	Hammonds House Gallery, Atlanta, Georgia
1990	*Roadworks,* Dorsey Gallery, Brooklyn, New York
1991	Towne Art Gallery, Wheelock College, Boston
1992	Compton Gallery, Massachusetts Institute of Technology, Cambridge
1994	*Roots Through the Heart,* Hartnett Gallery, University of Rochester, New York

Selected Group Exhibitions:

1979	Black American Graphics Studio Museum, New York (traveling through 1984)
1985	Studio Museum in Harlem, New York (traveling through 1987)
1989	Caribbean Center, New York (traveling)
	New York Community College

Collections:

Brooklyn Museum, New York; Memorial Art Gallery, University of Rochester, New York; National African American Museum,

Wilberforce, Ohio; National Museum of Mozambique; National Museum of Nigeria, Lagos; Rlksutstallningar National Museum, Stockholm, Sweden; Studio Museum in Harlem, New York.

Publications:

On MAYNARD: Article—"Inner City Beat," in *Christian Science Monitor,* February/March 1992.

*   *   *

According to Alexis De Veaux, Valerie Maynard makes the viewer aware of what a black woman sees when the world is shaped by her hands. Maynard seeks to suffuse her art with emblems, signs, and symbols that are related to the multivalent realities of African Americans. Her forty-year legacy of work gives visual form to the African American experience by encompassing sculptural renditions of everything from the music of Lester Young to the social and political struggles of blacks. Maynard embraces an aesthetic informed by an African-derived sensibility to create revelatory works that are vehicles for discourse. Her world is holistic, embodying representations of symbiotic relationships and vacillating between the spiritual and temporal realms. Rather than following a linear path of reason and separating ethics from values, Maynard identifies and amalgamates the spiritual with ethical and political concerns, thus placing it definitively within an expanded ontological context. As an activist she uses the arts as a tool to bring to consciousness issues of global proportions such as apartheid, rites of passage, and AIDS. She is sincerely committed to chronicling the history of Africans and African Americans by using a visual language.

Maynard uses a profuse array of materials to interpret an African American reality that spans thousands of years. In each material used she invokes a specific language system that articulates meaning, power, and force. Recurring throughout her works is the significance of gesture captured in motion or as suspended metaphors. In her sculpture there is always the implication of movement. The incorporation of multiple figures in varied animated poses and of solitary carvings using diverse techniques and configurations recalls the versatility required of African dancers, who have to move different parts of their body in response to different rhythms. For Maynard it is the gesture that consummates the meaning and power of the African American presence on a universal scale.

The narrative quality evident in many of Maynard's series of works clearly serves as a means to articulate her theme or idea. Although working serially is an approach she constantly revisits, Maynard does not adhere to one style. Depending on the medium used, she consciously alters her approach to subjects. For Maynard the creative process is an evolutionary one. Functioning as a spiritualist or diviner, the message is derived from the material used or extracted from the varied sources and researched. Maynard serves as a medium through which messages pertinent to a heightened understanding of the human condition are broached. In traditional African culture the medium and diviner are often embodied in different individuals with specialized skills. The former links human beings with the spirit world, and the latter interprets the information gleaned; it is the diviner's role to serve as an intermediary between the physical, human, and spiritual realms. Maynard, however, performs both of the functions as a contemporary African American artist. She shapes impulses into visual dictums that range from the documentation of dwelling places of blacks through the

centuries to a figurative wooden rendition of the Twenty-third Psalm. These exemplify explications of nuances pertaining to a universal quest for knowledge and understanding. Without being blatantly didactic, Maynard is a woman on a mission. Her works are visual proverbs, short stories, and epic narratives designed to convey principles and states of being.

Maynard embraces a wide range of mediums and exhibits exceptional proficiency in each. Her works range from the miniature to the monumental, as is evident in her public art ventures. Accomplished in a variety of sculptural materials, including stone, wood, metal, and ceramics, Maynard also commands mastery in painting, printmaking, and set and costume design.

—A.M. Weaver

MENDIVE, Manuel
Cuban painter

Manuel Mendive is a painter of imaginative, mythologizing images. His life and work are steeped in the traditions of the Yoruba as preserved in Cuba's Creole culture by descendants of African slaves. His paintings and prints are notable for their use of myths and related imagery. With its pantheon of several hundred *orishas*—among whom are Chango, Eleggúa, and Yemayá—Yoruba mythology is especially suited to this kind of appropriation. The *orishas* serve as intermediaries between supernatural and human entities, and in contemporary Cuban art they are a constant source of themes and images. Mendive harnesses the structural and narrative traits of this African element in his representation of the hybridity that defines contemporary Afro-Cuban culture.

Mendive's early adult life coincided with the revolution in Cuba, and his art has unfolded parallel to this. With the postrevolutionary focus on indigenous traditions as a basis for modern Cuban culture, in the wake of fierce pressure from external, imperialist sources, Cuba's Yoruba and Creole cultures came to be invested with new forms and meanings. The conceptual possibilities inherent in an adaptation of these heritages were first explored in the paintings of Wifredo Lam, whose career proved important to the subsequent development of contemporary Cuban art. Like other contemporary artists, Mendive was aware of this tradition, but he also was aware of the dangers inherent in the canonical Lam-derived style, which had become schematized into a stultifying mannerism in the socalled school of Havana.

In his earlier period Mendive produced carved monochrome reliefs, with themes focusing on Yoruba gods and runaway slaves, on trunks of the ceiba tree, regarded by Cubans of West African descent as the god-tree, and the palm tree, the national symbol of Cuba. He often painted these carved tree trunks in earth tones. In the 1960s, however, Mendive's work took a surprising turn. According to the artist the sight of blood from an injured foot radically changed his concept of color, and his works became more poetic and sensual. The bright colors of neoexpressionist figuration that dominated the works of many Cuban artists during the 1970s also found their way into Mendive's compositions. In addition to many paintings in which he explored an idiosyncratic notion of figuration, he also experimented with diverse media.

In the early 1980s Mendive produced a series of intimate, vibrantly colored gouaches of landscapes outlined in black and bounded by fierce yet controlled lines, some with strange figures looking wistfully through open windows. The landscapes celebrate an intertwined organic nature in which vegetal life assumes the attributes of animal life and vice versa; trees, for example, take on human faces, feet, and reproductive organs. Many of Mendive's paintings allude to themes of fertility, and his images replicate these allusions through their references to human anatomical and reproductive features. Some of his images combine characteristics of animal and plant life into complex, indeterminate creatures. Imprinted within a vortex of biological allusions, the images seem capable of multiplying on their own. In other paintings and prints recognizably human figures are adorned with multiple breasts and genital organs. The solar images that appear in several of the compositions lend an elemental aspect to his work.

By the time of the first Havana *Bienale,* in 1984, Mendive was producing large oil paintings rendered in fluid strokes. The fluidity of his *Bienale* exhibits signified the beginning of an involvement with images of aquatic life and a renewed commitment to the transformative powers of art and myth. He also branched out into stained glass compositions and further developed his lithographic techniques, and he took up textile design. Not surprisingly, Mendive's projects for textile design led to performance art in collaboration with dancers who replicated his ritual motifs. In his collaboration with these other artists, Mendive focused on history, specifically on slavery and on the African diaspora.

Mendive's imaginative, mythologizing images emphasize the role of hybridity and myths in the formation of Cuba's national identity. They also point to the transformative power conferred on artists within the ritual and cultural practices of the worship of *orisha*s. Within his canvases forms are fluid, and human subjects are invited to integrate themselves into the larger cycle of natural and supernatural occurrences. In this larger context Mendive's art makes no promises of certainty but instead offers up experience as a possibility.

—Sylvester Okwunodu Ogbechie

MEO, Yvonne Cole

American painter and printmaker

Born: Seattle, Washington, 1923. **Education:** University of California, Los Angeles, B.A. 1948; California State University, Los Angeles, M.A. 1960, M.F.A. 1988; Union Institute, Cincinnati, Ohio, Ph.D. 1977. **Career:** Teacher, Los Angeles Public Schools, Fisk University, Nashville. Studied in Mexico, 1950s. Researched art and symbolism, Africa, 1969. **Awards:** Honorary Doctor of Art for Exploratory and Innovative Painting Techniques, World University, Hong Kong, Sweden, and Italy, 1973.

Publications:

By COLE: Book—*Survey on Traditional Arts of West Africa and Contemporary Black American Arty: A Study of Symbolic Parallels and Cultural Transfer,* dissertation, Cincinnati, Ohio: Union Institute, 1977. **Article**—"Ritual as Art: The Work of Houston Conwill," in *Black Art Quarterly,* 3, Fall 1979.

*   *   *

In *Spirit Tree,* the first painting by Yvonne Cole Meo containing a self-portrait, she represents herself as walking out from a Baobab tree. Meo learned of the legend of the Baobab tree when she traveled to Africa in 1969. There, she said, "I ate as they ate . . . dressed as they dressed . . . lived as they lived. . . . I am always studying life . . . because I love art and life is art." The legend of the Baobab tree says that the tree never dies. The heart of the tree can be cut out, or it can be burned to the ground, but the tree will still grow.

The metaphor of the Baobab is appropriate for Meo's life, which is carried on through her paintings and the acts and knowledge of many thousands of students that she came in contact with during nearly a half century of teaching. "My job as an artist," Meo said, "is to carry forth the principle of light which is the invisible made visible through the symbol or 'the force,' for it is through the symbol that one learns to understand and thus becomes knowledgeable of the language of art."

Though Meo experienced little overt discrimination during her career as an artist and teacher, she did have trouble during the 1960s and 1970s convincing people to buy her work—figural paintings focusing on black subject matter. At the time, the trend was to paint abstract art, but Meo said, "I'm African American and these are my experiences. I paint about my people." When the artist Charles White encouraged Meo to show her paintings to Los Angeles galleries in the 1960s, he told her she was fifty years ahead of her time. If the growing interest in "ethnic art" is any indication, then the times may be catching up to Yvonne Cole Meo.

—Terry Bain

MILLER, Tom

American painter and sculptor

Born: Thomas Patton Miller, Baltimore, Maryland, 13 October 1945. **Education:** Maryland Institute College of Art, 1963-67, 1985-87, B.F.A. 1967, M.F.A. 1987. **Career:** Art resource teacher, Department of Education, Baltimore, Maryland, 1967-87. **Awards:** Merit Work Scholarship, Baltimore City Public School System, Maryland, 1963; Ford Foundation grant, 1986; Purchase Award, St. Joseph's Hospital, Baltimore, Maryland, 1986; Maryland State Arts Council grant-in-aid, 1987, individual artist grant, 1990; citation for artistic excellence, Governor William Donald Schaefer, Maryland, 1990; Purchase Award, Louisville Visual Art Association, Kentucky, 1991; mural commission, Mayor's Advisory Committee on Arts and Culture, Baltimore, Maryland. **Agent:** Steven Scott Gallery, 515 North Charles Street, Baltimore, Maryland 21201, U.S.A. **Address:** 2010 McCulloh Street, Baltimore, Maryland 21217, U.S.A.

Individual Exhibitions:

1986   Lafayette College, Easton, Pennsylvania
1988   Columbia Center for the Arts, Columbia, Maryland
1990   G.H. Dalsheimer Gallery, Baltimore, Maryland
       Lew Allen/Butler Gallery, Santa Fe, New Mexico
1992   Steven Scott Gallery, Baltimore, Maryland
1993   Steven Scott Gallery, Baltimore, Maryland
       Hammond House, Atlanta, Georgia
       Williams Gallery, Princeton, New Jersey

Tom Miller: *Summer in Baltimore,* 1994. Photo courtesy of the artist and Steven Scott Gallery.

1995   Baltimore Museum of Art and Maryland Art Place, Baltimore, Maryland (retrospective)

Selected Group Exhibitions:

1991   University of California, San Diego
        Southeastern Center for Contemporary Art, Winston-Salem, North Carolina (traveling)
1992   Baltimore Museum of Art, Maryland
1993   Steven Scott Gallery, Baltimore, Maryland
        Eubie Blake Cultural Center, Baltimore, Maryland
1994   Steven Scott Gallery, Baltimore, Maryland
1995   National Afro-American Museum and Cultural Center, Wilberforce, Ohio (traveling)
        Steven Scott Gallery, Baltimore, Maryland
1996   Mainline Art Center, Haversford, Pennsylvania
        Artscape '96, Baltimore, Maryland

Publications:

On MILLER: Books—*Tom Miller's Afro-Deco,* exhibition catalog, by Lowery S. Sims, New York, Steven Scott Gallery, January 1992; *Most Definitely!* exhibition catalog, Baltimore, Maryland, Baltimore Museum of Art and Maryland Art Place, 1995. **Articles**—"Two Artists Graft Worlds of Africa, Route 66" by David Bell, in *Journal South* (Santa Fe, New Mexico), 12 April 1990; "Southern Art with a Sense of Mission" by Michael Brenson, in *New York Times,* 3 June 1990; "Southern Art with a Sense of Mission" by Michael Brenson, in *The New York Times,* 3 June 1990; "Exhibit Bequeaths African Tradition" by Catherine Fox, in *Atlanta Journal,* 29 July 1990; "Neo-Romanticism on Display at Steven Scott" by Eric Adams, in *The Sun,* Baltimore, Maryland, 24 May 1991; "African American Presence at Artscape" by Camay Murphy, in *Baltimore Times,* 7 May 1991; "Miller's Crossing" by Jim Duffy, in *Baltimore Magazine,* February 1995; "New Found Furniture" by Jene Stonesifer, in *The Washington Post,* February 1995.

*

Tom Miller comments:
    I use objects as my canvas. I only record what I see and feel based on my experiences as an African American living in Baltimore, Maryland, in the United States of America. All of my influences are by no means artistic. The people around me, the community I live in, provide a great deal. Artistically I'm influenced by the greats—Romare Bearden, Jacob Lawrence, and Henri Mattise.

*   *   *

Tom Miller: *Pretty, Pretty,* 1994. Photo courtesy of Carl Clark.

Tom Miller is a critical voice in the contemporary generation of postmodernist artists who have reevaluated and deconstructed the traditional formal assumptions about how art functions, the intent of its meaning and symbolism, and the materials used in the construction of its imagery. He was born in Maryland and educated in the Baltimore public schools and at the Maryland Institute, College of Art. This is particularly important to his brightly painted furniture, which finds its reference and context directly in his keen response to the lifestyle of Baltimore's urban neighborhoods and the specific cultural characteristics observed within the African American community in which he lives.

There exists a significant history of painted furniture in the United States and among its regional styles. Within the confines of plantation slave life or as with freedmen like Thomas Day in North Carolina, black craftsmen in the early years of the country found their skills essential to the construction of utilitarian objects required by residential, public, and sacred architecture. Miller uses found objects that he then reconfigures into new functions. In the mid-1980s many of his works were derived from boxes, cabinets, large chests, and wardrobes found in thrift shops and flea markets or as castoffs from friends.

From the 1970s until 1985 Miller largely concentrated on figurative paintings conceived in his characteristic "bold, graphic style."

Entering graduate school in 1985, he began to refine his style, adding complex patterns and bright colors and experimenting with visual puns, whimsy, political commentary, gender issues, and kinetic art. In the 1990s Miller's work became more sculptured, with assembled units that took on anthropomorphic form. Printmaking, street murals, and illustrated children's books increased his repertoire and popularity among patrons and museums. The city of Baltimore incorporated Miller's aesthetic designs in a commissioned mural and in illustrated pages for its successful application for a $100 million empowerment zone grant from the U.S. government.

The subversive nature of Miller's socially confrontational subjects has often confused critics. Fond of using black stereotypical, minstrel-inspired imagery, Miller often reverses and satirizes society's preoccupation with the horrors, atrocities, classical race conflicts, personal insecurities, and shortcomings of the human condition. This is further challenged by his blurring the thin line between the "fine" and "decorative" elements of his art.

Miller is distinguished by his innate, traditional African yet African American aesthetic sensibilities in the animated conceptualizations of his sculptural compositions. Contrary to assumptions about the viability of what constitutes an authentic African American artistry, Miller has noted that "it should not be surprising that I, a black man, would choose to paint doors, floors, tables, cabinets, etc., with my own aesthetic." Miller uses humor and history to reinvent the experience of the common man through the use of ordinary materials, thus elevating the object and the experience of art to a higher level of understanding in what he perceives to be the remarkable experience of being an African American.

—Leslie King-Hammond

MILLS, Lev (T.)

American printmaker and assemblage artist

Education: Florida A & M University, Tallahassee, B.A. 1962; University of Wisconsin, Madison, M.A. 1968, M.F.A. 1970; Slade School of Fine Art, University College, London, diploma, 1972; Atelier 17 Workshop, Paris, 1972; School of Visual Arts, New York, 1986. **Career:** Art teacher, Boward County Public School System, Fort Lauderdale, Florida, 1962-68; assistant professor of art, Clark College, Atlanta, Georgia, 1973-78, Spelman College, Atlanta, Georgia, 1978-85; associate professor of art, Spelman College, Atlanta, Georgia, 1985-88. Since 1988 chair and associate professor, Spelman College, Atlanta, Georgia. Designed Seal for the National Coretta Scott King Book Award, American Library Association, Chicago, 1974, "First Mayor's Day for the Arts" poster, Atlanta, Georgia, 1975, logo and brochure, Division of Science, Spelman College, Atlanta, Georgia, 1986, Morehouse College Candle Award, Atlanta, Georgia, 1989. **Awards:** Most Creative Development Award, Florida A & M University, Tallahassee, 1962; Teacher of the Year, Everglades Junior High School, Fort Lauderdale, Florida, 1966; Outstanding Postgraduate Fellowship, University of Wisconsin, Madison, 1969; Ford Foundation European Study and Travel Fellowship, 1970; Bronze Jubilee Award for Cultural Achievement, Atlanta, Georgia, 1978; Department of Cultural Affairs grants, Atlanta, Georgia, 1982, 1986; Mayor's Fellowship in the Arts, Atlanta, Georgia, 1984; Spelman College Sloan grant, Atlanta, Georgia, 1986; James D. Parks Special Award, Los Angeles, 1986; Gal lery of Distinction, Florida A & M University, Tallahassee, Florida, 1987; Jubilee Southern Festival of the Arts Citation, 1987; Special Congressional Recognition Certificate, Atlanta, Georgia, 1987; Fulton County for the Arts grant, 1988; Bush Faculty Development grant, Spelman College, Atlanta, Georgia, 1988; Presidential Award for Scholarly Achievement, Spelman College, Atlanta, Georgia, 1988. **Address:** 3378 Ardley Road Southwest, Atlanta, Georgia 30311, U.S.A.

Individual Exhibitions:

1968	Board of Public Instruction, Fort Lauderdale, Florida
1969	Lewis State Bank, Tallahassee, Florida
	First National Bank, Miami Beach, Florida
1970	International Student House, London
	University of Bristol, England
	Saint Olaf College, Northfield, Minnesota
	Press House, Madison, Wisconsin
	University of Manchester, England
1971	York Art Festival, England
	American Embassy, London
1972	The Africa Center, London
	Dar es Salaam Library, Tanzania
	American Cultural Center, Nairobi, Kenya
	Makere University, Kampala, Uganda
	Kunsthandel K276 Gallery, Amsterdam
	American Cultural Center, Paris
	Amwell Gallery, London
1973	Creative Cancer Gallery, Atlanta, Georgia
	American Cultural Center, Abidjan, Ivory Coast
	American Cultural Center, Beruit, Lebanon
	American Cultural Center, Rabat, Morocco
	American Cultural Center, Tananarive, Madagascar
1975	Studio Museum, New York
1978	Fisk University, Nashville
	Galerie Kloster-Muble, Hude-Oldenburg, West Germany
	Callanwolde Arts Center, Atlanta, Georgia
	South Carolina State University, Orangeburg, South Carolina
1980	Florida A & M University, Tallahassee, Florida
1981	Nexus Gallery, Atlanta, Georgia
1982	Gulf Coast Community College, Panama City, Florida
	Western Michigan University, Kalamazoo
1983	University of Alabama, Birmingham
1984	Evans-Tibbs Collection Gallery, Washington, D.C.
	Alabama State University, Montgomery
1986	Florida A & M University, Tallahassee, Florida
1987	Spelman College, Atlanta, Georgia
	Albany State College, Georgia

Selected Group Exhibitions:

1971	Royal College of Art, London
1978	Galeria Kloster-Muble, Hude-Oldeburg, West Germany
1980	High Museum of Art, Atlanta, Georgia
	Smithsonian Institution Traveling Exhibition, Washington, D.C. (through 1984)
1982	Columbia Museum of Art, South Carolina
1985	American Center, Helsinki, Finland
1987	Studio Museum in Harlem, New York
1989	Nexus Gallery, Atlanta, Georgia

	Carl Van Vechten Gallery of Fine Arts, Fisk University, Nashville
1990	Spelman College, Atlanta

Collections:

Ackland Museum, Chapel Hill, North Carolina; Bibliotheque National, Paris; British Museum, London; Evans-Tibbs Collection, Washington, D.C. Flint Community Schools Collection, Michigan; Florida A & M University, Tallahassee; High Museum of Art, Atlanta, Georgia; Library of Congress, Washington, D.C.; Museum of Modern Art, New York; National Center of Afro-American Artists, Inc., Boston; National Library of Scotland, Edinburg; North Carolina A & T State University, Greensboro; Victoria and Albert Museum, London; Western Michigan University, Kalamazoo.

Publications:

By MILLS: Books—*I Do,* London, Cut-Chain Press, 1971. **Articles**—"Intaglio Printmaking," in *Florida A Education Magazine,* (Fort Lauderdale), 1968.

On MILLS: Articles—"Lev Mills" by Pat Gilmour, in *Arts Review London,* 1972; "Printmakers" by Samella Lewis, in *International Review of African American Art,* 1985; "Nine Afro-Americans Put Their Ideas into Print," in *Detroit News,* 1988; "Tallahassee's Lev Mills Art Show Opens at GCCC," in *Panama City Florida News-Herald,* 1982.

*   *   *

Florida-born Lev Mills is an artist who takes great pride in his independence, and he cherishes having the freedom to grow. He names few artistic influences, but he admires Pablo Picasso as an unstructured person who always wanted his art to be fresh. In his early years Mills also admired the work of Charles White.

Mills grew up in a small northern Florida community as the only child of confident, independent parents who did not feel the brunt of Southern segregation. His father had his own store, and Mills always had constructive contacts with whites, facts that have affected him throughout his career in art. Encouraged by a high school teacher and by Howard Lewis, his instructor at Florida A&M University, Mills, who had earlier expressed an interest in mathematics, pursued art through graduate school at the University of Wisconsin, where he studied with Dean Meeker, one of the leading printmakers in the United States.

During the 1970s Mills's work involved socially relevant images reflecting the activities of the era, but he did not create protest or didactic art, preferring instead to maintain a level of ambiguity open to interpretation. For him artistic issues took precedence over social narrative and political statements. When Mills completed graduate study, he received a fellowship to study at the Slade School of Art in London. He remained in Europe for three years, receiving a diploma from the Slade School and exhibiting his work in Paris, where it was picked up by the United States Information Agency for touring in Africa. Mills himself periodically accompanied the exhibition and made stops in the East African countries of Uganda, Tanzania, and Kenya and in Madagascar. He also visited Ghana, Ivory Coast, Benin (Dahomey), and Morocco.

After his European study Mills moved to Atlanta, Georgia, to teach printmaking at Clark College and later at Spelman College.

His work during this period consisted primarily of intaglio and silk screen prints. At the end of the decade, with the award of a commission for a tile mural in a Metro Atlanta Regional Transit Authority (MARTA) subway station, he began the first of many public installations. Installations and sculpture dominated his expression during the 1980s, and to this he added computer graphics in the 1990s.

Mills's work always has been precise and well designed, and his images have been more graphic than expressionistic. His attention to detail is consistent with his early propensity for mathematics. Mills's sculptural forms have a clean, linear, almost minimalist quality, and they often contain vertical forms and surprising textures or colors. His tile designs are more complex visually, but they also have a geometric organization and precision consistent with his other work. Mills's skills were showcased when he was commissioned to design the tile floor for the first-floor main concourse in Atlanta's new City Hall, and his stylistic touch was evident in the three-story sculpture he and fellow Spelman faculty member Charnelle Holloway executed in the new international concourse of the Hartsfield-Atlanta International Airport in 1994-95.

Mills has stated that his interests lie in the creation of compelling, moving art, not in the creation of social or political statements. His childhood experiences have influenced his sense of independence and individuality, and his attention to detail and ability to control every element in a project have led to works that are elegant and well thought out. These qualities have shown themselves throughout his entire career in prints, sculptural installations, and computer graphics.

—Michael D. Harris

MILLS, Priscilla

American painter and sculptor

Born: Connersville, Indiana, 1918. **Education:** Art Institute of Chicago; studied with Carolton Ball, University of Southern California. **Family:** Married Tommie Mills, Jr. **Died:** 1964.

Publications:

On MILLS: Articles—"The Negro Woman" by Lerone Bennet, Jr., in *Ebony,* September 1963; "The Black Artist" by Harry Ploski and Ernest Kaiser, in *Afro USA,* 1971; "The Black Artist" by Harry Ploski, Ernest Kaiser, and Otto Lindenmeyer, in *Reference Library of Black America,* Book IV, 1971.

*   *   *

Priscilla, or P'lla (pronounced Pela), Mills, who studied at the Art Institute of Chicago and lived in Los Angeles, died at age forty-three, and little has been published on her life or work. The available publications, however, are significant. Most informative is a several-page article, "The Negro Woman," in the September 1963 edition of *Ebony* magazine, which appeared just a year before her death. Commentary from Mills, several photographs of the artist and her family, photographs of several pieces of her work, and a powerful photograph of the artist creating a piece of sculpture with a blowtorch suggest much about the artist and what she believed.

The *Ebony* issue is particularly revealing about her home life. In the poignant photograph of Mills with a blowtorch/welding tool in hand and protective covers over her eyes, she is accompanied by her husband, Tommie Mills, Jr., who in the 1960s worked for the Los Angeles Maintenance Department. Mills explains in commentary next to the photograph that she spent most of her days sculpting and painting and that she stopped only to prepare dinner for her husband. She said, "I'm not a very good housekeeper so I try to make everything bright and unusual, then my husband doesn't notice the dust and mess." Her son, then twenty-one and in the army, was quoted as saying, "If there are no children to consider, a woman should do what she wants to do and is capable of doing, as long as she doesn't hurt anyone or herself by doing it." The magazine also includes a photograph of Mills showing clients her painting and sculpture. Another photograph shows the artist painting on the patio at her home.

Artist and scholar Samella Lewis, also from Los Angeles, included Mills in her book *African American Art and Artists* and discussed Mills's welded-metal construction *Star of Bethlehem.* Dr. Lewis explained that Mills's constructions were made of welding rods and sometimes sheet metal and that the material was cut and shaped using an oxyacetylene torch. An example of this method is *Star of Bethlehem,* a representation of Mary sitting on a donkey, which is marked by rough surfaces and curved and joined welding rods. Another sculpture—a beautiful, unidentified work photographed in the *Ebony* issue—is of a man pushing a woman up in the air in a swing. The works photographed in *Ebony* and elsewhere suggest a painter and sculptor of considerable talent who deserves greater study.

—Jontyle Theresa Robinson

MOKE

Zairian painter

Work also appeared under the names Mbao, Art P. Moke, and Peintre Moke. **Born:** Ibe, Bandundu, Zaire, 1950.

Individual Exhibition:

1981   Colloque National sur l'Authenticité

Selected Group Exhibitions:

1978   Exposition du CIAF, Foire Nationale de Kinshash
1979   Berlin
1982   Musée des Arts Décoratifs, Paris
1991   Center for African Art, New York
          Maison de la Culture de la Province de Namur
1992   Hotel Maastricht
1995   *An Inside Story: African Art of Our Time,* Setagaya Art
          Museum, Tokyo (traveling)

Collections:

CICIBS, Libreville, Gabon; Institute des Musées Nationaux du Zaire.

*   *   *

The painter Moke is recognized as one of the most successful self-taught artists of Zaire. His desire to become a painter stems from his experiences as a young orphan on the streets of Kinshasa. After he saw displays of paintings for sale by popular artists at the tourist art market (Place du 27 Octobre) in 1963, he started painting on pieces of cardboard, using his fingers as paintbrushes. As he achieved success, the added income provided him with the means to acquire more conventional painting materials.

Early in his career Moke distinguished himself from numerous other popular artists who were painting clichéd and stereotypical views of idyllic settings—villages, rivers, and sunsets. Moke's themes are drawn from the social milieu and bustling ambiance of Kinshasa. His choice of subjects demonstrates that he loves the spectacle of daily life, and he casts an ironic eye upon the familiar urban landscape as his compositions are inspired by the pulse and routines of life in the capital city. This is clear in such paintings as *Le Marche* (1982), on the mixing of social classes at the market; *Matanga* (1981), a funeral scene; and *Pas de chance* (1979), on an accident caused by an overcrowded city bus.

As is characteristic of Zairean popular artists, Moke produces compositions that are often variations upon successful themes. In his works of the late 1970s and the 1980s, he often rendered the social life of nightclubs, cafés, bars, and restaurants. Such paintings as *Zeka Bar* (1979), *Nganda* (1982), and *Tutex Africa Oye* (1989) repeat the same compositional device: cabaret scenes populated by couples or groups of figures seated at tables starkly illuminated by bare lights suspended from the ceiling. But through variations in the number of figures and in their brightly colored clothing, Moke makes these crowded interior and exterior night scenes demonstrate the mastery of his figural compositions within a shallow pictorial space. An emphasis on idiosyncratic physical features and hairstyles often suggests the character of portraiture. Nonetheless, because the size of his subjects' heads is often proportionally enlarged, Moke's figures also suggest caricature.

Narrative content emerges from reading the incidental elements within Moke's compositions. He often varies these elements from composition to composition. *Le Photographe* (1982), of an itinerant photographer shooting a family portrait in front of their house, and *Photographing a Veteran* (1984) are almost identical paintings, but in the latter composition the inclusion of a photograph of the elderly soldier as a young member of the army (La Force Publique) particularizes the painting and adds a biographical note to the image.

Moke's astute observations of the Kinshasa scene also extend to his portrayal of political and military events. Paintings such as *Mobutu in Bandundu* (1977) and *Motorcade with Mitterrand and Mobutu* (1990) suggest a form of reportage. In such paintings the serious or joyous facial expressions make any political criticism ambiguous.

The satiric and often humorous side of urban life in Kinshasa is also an important element of Moke's paintings. *La Course de pousse-pousseurs* (1979) presents a parade of pushcart laborers escorted by a police car. The repeated images of men with their pushcarts crowded across the canvas underscore the visual wit. The name of a local beer (Skol) is emblazoned across the front of each uniform. Each man is dressed in the official state party colors and wears the official state emblem, a raised arm holding a flaming torch. The composition clearly suggests the nature of the political and economic control of all organized events in the capital.

More recent paintings—*Autoportrait* (1990) and *Moke n'a pas de l'argent* (1991)—are autobiographical and suggest Moke's in-creasing interest in the art-making process and in his own place in the art world. In *Untitled* (1991) he depicts himself seated dejectedly in the corner as Chéri Samba, his more famous contemporary, gives a thumbs-up salute while crushing Moke's painting under his foot.

Moke's work was first recognized at the 1978 exhibition *Art Partout* in Kinshasa. Since that time he has been featured in many international group exhibitions, and today he is recognized as one of the most successful nonacademic painters of Zaire.

—Patricia J. Darish

MONTGOMERY, Evangeline (Juliet)

American sculptor, jewelry designer, printmaker, photographer, and mixed-media artist

Work also appeared under the names E.J. Montgomery and E.J.M. **Born:** Evangeline Thompson, New York, 2 May 1933. **Education:** Los Angeles City College, 1955-58, A.A. 1958; California State University, Los Angeles, 1958-62; University of California at Berkeley, 1968-70; California College of Arts and Crafts, Oakland, 1967-69, B.F.A. 1969. **Career:** Since 1960 freelance artist; since 1983 program development officer, Arts America Program, United States Information Agency. Consultant, Rainbow Sign Gallery, 1971-77; curator, Oakland Museum, California, 1968-74, Mills College, Oakland, California, 1971-72, Western Association of Art Museums, Oakland, California, 1972-74; workshop coordinator, American Association for State and Local History, Nashville, 1979-80, African American Museums Association, Washington, D.C., 1981-82. Administrator and Vice President, ARK Urban System, 1973-78. National Regional Coordinator, Washington, D.C., 1973-81; art commissioner, City of San Francisco, 1976-79; National Director of Fine Arts Culture, Washington, D.C., 1976-79; director of Community Affairs, Washington, D.C., 1980-81. **Awards:** National Program Award, NANB and PW Clubs, 1977; National Conference of Artists service awards, 1970, 1974, 1976; National Endowment for the Arts museum grant, 1973; Smithsonian Professional Fellowship, 1973; Third World Fund grant, 1974; Arts America Special Achievement Award, 1989. **Agent:** Norman Parish Gallery, 1054 31st Street NW, Washington, D.C. 20007, U.S.A.

Individual Exhibitions:

1973   Bowie State College Art Gallery, Maryland
1993   H.C. Taylor Gallery, Greensboro, North Carolina
        Savannah State College, Georgia
1994   Hampton Institute Art Gallery, Virginia
        DePaul University Art Gallery, Indiana

Selected Group Exhibitions:

1971   Mills College Art Gallery, Oakland, California (traveling)
1972   University of Southern Illinois, Edwardsville
        San Francisco Annual Art Festival
1973   University of West Florida
1974   Black Pavilion, Seattle World's Fair
        Berkeley Art Center, California

1975   Governor's Gallery, Sacramento, California
1979   Brook Memorial Gallery, Memphis, Tennessee
1992   A Space, Toronto, Canada
1996   NCA Gallery, Detroit

Collections:

Board of Education, Los Angeles; Illinois State College, Normal; Museum of the National Center for African American Artists, Boston; Oakland Museum, California.

*

Evageline Montgomery comments:

My inspirations come from nature, daily events, and ancestral recall. All trigger an emotional journey, a symbol or motif that later appears in some form in the art I create. My palette is generally earth tones, no matter what materials are used to create the art (metals, fibers, paint, printer's ink, glass enamels, etc.). The surface is often heavily textural, like the bark of the tree, crusty rocks, and rusty metals. The photographs I take provide glimpses of both urban and rural landscapes, daily events I've witnessed by people of color. Shorelines of California, taken at Big Sur, Carmel, and Point Lobos are the most recurring themes in my photographs. The metal and sculpture are inspired by my mother's ceremonial incense burner and African ceremonial objects of several ethnic groups. My themes are ancestral boxes and spirit sculptures, landscapes, festivals, and motion, and the titles are taken from these ideas and subjects. The two-dimensional work is usually in the abstract mode.

*   *   *

In the work of Evangeline Montgomery, as in that of many others of the diaspora, memories of the African heritage are contemporized and preserved. She is a sculptor, jeweler, printmaker, photographer, and mixed-media artist, and her aesthetics have been influenced by a combination of three factors: residency in Nigeria from 1962 to 1965, the U.S. civil rights movement, and discussions of Africa's creative traditions with artist-friends Arthur Carraway and Arthur Monroe.

Artists like Montgomery have invested their works with symbols of racial and cultural identity. Not only do their creations assert black identity and consciousness, but they also ameliorate the force of the afflictions the artists have experienced. For Montgomery art is not just a physical object produced for the aesthetic delight of its exterior; its function and its symbolic meaning are also important dimensions that allow histories to be affirmed and the traumas of life to be assuaged. Art constitutes one means of defining and nurturing identities outside institutionalized structures.

On the occasion of the death of her mother, for example, Montgomery came to terms with the loss by using the ancient symbols of her ancestral heritage. She created *Spirit Mother* (1978), a *bwiiti* constructed of fabric strips. *Spirit Mother* affirms a history and heritage that the racial environment of the United States negates. The hybrid nature of life in the diaspora is indicated through the white feathers at the top of the *bwiiti*. Sprouting from the apex, the feathers make reference to many cultures, but they allude specifically to eagle feathers, which Native Americans and some ethnic groups in Africa treat as a symbol of prestige, spiritual triumph, and purity. The seven-beaded hearts stitched to the central stem of *Spirit Mother* honor the seven daughters borne by Montgomery's biological mother, including the six sisters she never met. The layers of white binding strips covering the inner semioval core form parallel lines that evoke the process of creating an identity, and the wrapping process re-creates the lifeline in which personal experiences are wound into a personality. Montgomery's reinterpreted sculpture thus becomes an icon of the inner self that chronicles the spiritual death of an old self and the resurrection of a new, purified self. Linking her biological mother to the woman who had been her mother by adoption and whose death she was then mourning, Montgomery drew together the loose, uncommemorated strands in her life in a rite that fused the present with the past in order to usher in the future.

Montgomery also uses art to subvert official histories that seek to erase counterhistories. The uncommon becomes historical text, avoiding the elisions of official history. Her diminutive mojo boxes, for example, most of which were created in the mid- to the late 1970s to preserve elements of African American history and identity, contest the dominant narratives of official history. Constructed of bronze or sterling silver, the richly textured, meticulously crafted, and polished boxes are set off to perfection with tasteful patterns of geometric decorations. One of these mojo boxes, *Ancestor Box 1,*

Evangeline Montgomery: *Duality Principle I,* 1992. Photo courtesy of Sharon Farmer.

Evangeline Montgomery: *Justice Ancestral Box,* 1973. Photo courtesy of Jonathan Eubanks.

Justice for Angela (1973), is a two-inch cube made of sterling silver that preserves the memory of women's participation in the civil rights struggle. The public and memorial role of such mojo boxes transforms them into mnemonic devices. Each box codes memories, each boxful of memories is a historical text, and each historical text is a rite of remembrance.

In 1992, after ten years in arts administration, Montgomery resumed her work with the creation of *Duality Principle I & II,* multi-media objects fabricated of cardboard cores and using cotton yarns, bone and glass beads, and fiber. Since 1993 she has expanded her repertoire while working with the Detroit, Michigan, chapter of the National Conference of Artists. In her new creative cycle she is exploring the memorializing and remembering processes in abstract, color-saturated offset lithographs. *Autumn Breeze* (1996), for example, has yielded three variations: *Autumn Night, Night Gardens,* and *Warm Breeze* (all 1996).

—Nkiru Nzegwu

MOODY, Ronald (Clive)

Jamaican/British sculptor and painter

Born: Kingston, Jamaica, August 12, 1900. **Education:** Calabar College Kingston, Jamaica ?-c.1918; Kings College, London University, 1923-30, L.D.S. R.C.S. 1930. **Family:** Married Helene in

1938. **Awards:** Musgrave Gold Medal, 1977; Centenary Medal, Jamaica Institute, 1980; M.A.A.S. Award, London, 1981. **Died:** 6 February 1984.

Individual Exhibitions:

1937	Galerie Billiet-Worms, Paris
1938	Kunstzaal van Lier, Amsterdam
1946	Arcade Gallery, London
1950	Galerie Apollinaire, London
1960	Woodstock Gallery, London
1961	Woodstock Gallery, London
1969	Hove Museums and Libraries, England

Selected Group Exhibitions:

1935	New Burlington Galleries, London
1938	Palais de Chaillot, Paris
1939	Baltimore Museum of Art, Maryland
1953	Society of Portrait Sculptors, London (through 1971)
1956	Burlington House, London
1971	Caribbean Artists Movement at the Commonwealth Institute, London
1977	Comonwealth Institute, London
1989	Hayward Gallery, London
1993	Tate Gallery, London
1995	Center for Fine Arts, Miami

Ronald Moody, 1977. Photo courtesy of David Sharkey.

Ronald Moody: *Johanaan*, 1936. Photo courtesy of Cynthia Moody.

Collections:

Center for Black and African Arts and Civilization, Lagos; Government Art collection, London; Leicestershire Museums and Art Gallery, Leicester; National Gallery of Jamaica, Kingston; Nehru Memorial Museum, New Delhi; Tate Gallery, London; University of the West Indies, Jamaica.

Publications:

By MOODY: Articles—"Parboo Singh, an appreciation," in *Corona* (London), 1951; "The Colonial Spectator," in *Corona* (London), 1951; "A Way of Life," in *West Indian Gazette,* 1961; "Art in the Caribbean," in *Flamingo,* 1962; "Uzo Egono: An Appreciation," in *Magnet News*, 1965.

On MOODY: Articles—"Traditie Zonder Traditie: Beeldhouwkunst van Ronald C. Moody" by Max Osborne, in *De Telegraaf* (Amsterdam), 31 January 1940; "A Visit to Ronald Moody" by Denys Sutton, in *France Libre* (London), December 1946; "Prophet of Man's Hope" by Marie Seton, in *Studio* (Lon-

don), January 1950; "Sculpture by Ronald Moody" by Jessica Young, in *Corona* (London), August 1950; "Ronald Moody: Man with a Vision," in *Tropic* (Jamaica), August 1960; "Ronald Moody—Sculptor of Distinction" by Rudolph Dunbar, in *Daily Gleaner* (Jamaica), 17 September 1961; "An Evening with Ronald Moody" by Dawn Ritch, in *Jamaica Journal* (Jamaica), September 1972; "Ronald Moody" by Cynthia Moody, in *Third Text* (London), Autumn 1989.

* * *

Although Ronald Moody lived in England for most of his life, he is regarded as a Jamaican sculptor. Born in Jamaica, he went to London in 1923 to study dentistry. Visits to the British Museum left him deeply impressed by the art of ancient Egypt and motivated him to start sculpting in his free time. His interest in philosophy led him to study Chinese and Indian metaphysics, which provided an enduring conceptual basis for his art.

In 1934 Moody turned to wood carving and produced his first major work, a head entitled *Wohin,* after the song by Franz Schubert. In the following years he made some of his most memorable wood carvings, including *Johanaan (Peace),* a half-figure done in 1936, and *Tacet* (1938), a colossal head. The hieratic monumentality, frontal emphasis, and silent inwardness of these early carvings reflect Moody's interest in Egyptian and Buddhist sculpture. They also illustrate his exceptional mastery of wood carving, especially his ingenious use of the natural veining of wood.

Although his brother Harold was active as the head of the League of Coloured Peoples, Moody's artistic interests were metaphysical rather than political. This separates him from the early Jamaican school and its nation-building aspirations. There is, nonetheless, a notable stylistic kinship between Moody's early work and that of Jamaican-based contemporaries such as Edna Manley and Alvin Marriott, both of whom were accomplished wood sculptors. This points toward the still largely unexamined place these artists hold in the broader contexts of modernist sculpture and black art of the interwar period.

In 1938 Moody moved to Paris to devote himself fully to art. His work attracted attention in Europe and the United States, and it was included in various exhibitions, including several specialized exhibits of black art. At the beginning of World War II, Moody fled to Marseilles, from where he made it back to England. Despite health problems he soon resumed sculpting and overcame wartime shortages by recycling materials. *Sleeper Mask* (1943), for instance, was carved from a railway sleeper.

Moody's later work was profoundly affected by the war and its aftermath and, no doubt, by his own struggle with tuberculosis in the late 1940s. The creative and destructive duality of human nature became a central theme in his increasingly complex symbolical explorations. He also started using modern man-made materials such as concrete, fiberglass, and resins. This, in turn, led him to produce more intricate, dynamic forms and allowed him to freely juxtapose organic with geometric elements and smooth areas with heavily textured ones. One such example is the glass resin sculpture *Man . . . His Universe* (1969), a fanciful hybrid figure now at the Leicester (England) Museum and Art Gallery. Moody was also a noted portraitist, and he joined the Society of Portrait Sculptors in 1954. His portraits include *Head of Paul Robeson* (1968), made from copper resin.

In the 1960s Moody became more actively interested in his Caribbean background. His best-known work of the period, *Savacou*

(1964), represents a stylized, emblematic parrot figure inspired by the mythical bird deity of the Carib Indians. The cast aluminum sculpture, a commission, is now a landmark on the Jamaican campus of the University of the West Indies. Moody went to Jamaica for the unveiling, his first visit in forty-one years. In 1967 he joined the Caribbean Artists Movement, which was then the focus of cultural and intellectual activity within the growing West Indian community in England. Moody was an active participant in the organization's debates and exhibitions, although he continued to maintain his apolitical, individualist perspective.

Moody's involvement in Caribbean affairs contributed to his growing recognition in Jamaica, where he received, among other honors, the Institute of Jamaica's prestigious Gold Musgrave medal in 1978. In the mid-1970s *Tacet* was acquired by the National Gallery of Jamaica, and several other works have since been bought by local private collectors. In England it is only in recent years that his work has been rediscovered by the mainstream, most notably when the Tate Gallery acquired *Johanaan* in 1992.

—Veerle Poupeye

MOORE, Philip

Guyanese painter and sculptor

Name also sometimes spelled Phillip Moore. **Born:** Manchester Village, Corentyne, Guyana, October 1921. **Education:** Studied painting and drawing with Wilfred Patterson, 1936. **Career:** Beginning in 1947 professional carver; woodcarving tutor, Government Technical Institute, Georgetown, 1955-56; pattern maker, Government Pottery Factory, 1957; art and craft officer and wood-carving tutor, National History and Arts Council, 1964-70; woodcarving tutor, New Jersey Department of Education, 1975, Burrowes School of Art in Guyana, 1978-82. Artist-in-residence and tutor in wood sculpture, black studies program, Princeton University, New Jersey and Rutgers University, New Jersey, 1971-74. Owner and director, Moore's Methodical Meditation Museum, New Brunswick, New Jersey, 1972-77. Produced the model for *The 1763 Monument* erected in Georgetown, 1976. Associated with the Jordanites (Afro-Guyanese religion). **Award:** National Honours, 1981.

Selected Exhibitions:

1953	*National Annual Exhibition,* Guyana (through 1969)
1972	Baltimore Museum, Maryland
	Studio Museum in Harlem, New York
	Caribbean Festival of the Arts, Guyana
1973	University of Maryland, Baltimore
1976	Caribbean Festival of the Arts, Jamaica
1977	*Second World Black Arts Festival of the Arts,* Lagos, Nigeria
1979	Caribbean Festival of the Arts, Cuba
1991	Caribbean Festival of the Arts, Barbados
1992	*First Biennial of Painting,* Santo Domingo, Dominican Republic
1996	*Third Biennial of Painting,* Santo Domingo, Dominican Republic

Collections:

Guyanese National Collection, Georgetown; Dorothy Taitt Foundation, Georgetown, Guyana.

* * *

The Guyanese painter and sculptor Philip Moore is one of the great visionary artists of the Caribbean. In spite of the current interest in Caribbean art, however, he is scarcely known outside Guyana, due in part to his reluctance to let his work leave his home country.

Moore comes from the Corentyne coast of Guyana, an agricultural area with a rich popular culture. He is associated with the Jordanites, an inspirational Afro-Guyanese religion, although his work is primarily the expression of a personal utopian vision. His belief in the supreme importance of community, inspired by the tightly knit village-based society in which he came of age, is a recurrent theme in his work. He places great emphasis on what he calls "Godmanliness"—humanity's ability to transcend its limitations by means of spiritual self-actualization and to act as God's cocreator. Moore views himself as a spiritual teacher, and he would like to exhibit his major works in a permanent didactic display that he has named *Moore's Methodical Meditation Museum,* as he did while living in New Jersey.

Moore started carving in the late 1940s after receiving visionary instruction, and he defines himself as "spirit-taught" rather than self-taught. By the 1960s he was producing major sculptures such as *Watamama* (1962), a hybrid aquatic creature from Guyana's Afro-Amerindian folklore, and the relief carving *Ball and Bat Fantasy* (1965), a whimsical ode to cricket. The central figure in *Ball and Bat Fantasy* is made up of an intricate pattern of cricket paraphernalia in a manner reminiscent of the Italian mannerist Archimboldo. This metaphoric use of polymorphic imagery is a typical characteristic of Moore's mature work.

In the early 1970s Moore traveled to the United States and visited several universities and cultural institutions, including Princeton University, where he was artist in residence. He started painting during this period and soon produced major works such as *Brooklyn Bridge of Stars and Stripes.*

Shortly before Moore returned to Guyana, he produced his most ambitious sculpture, *The 1763 Monument* (1976), a Guyanese government commission in commemoration of the 1763 slave rebellion against the Dutch settlers of Berbice. The central element of the monument is a colossal bronze figure covered with emblems of strength and resistance. With its striated surfaces and clutching stance, the figure brings to mind certain Benin bronzes. The monument caused major controversy when it was unveiled in Georgetown, mainly because it deviates from the entrenched Caribbean tradition of academic monumental sculpture. Although Moore had wanted the work mounted at street level, close to the people, it was placed on a high, incongruously modernist fountain base, another source of controversy.

Whereas Moore pursues the same interests in carving and painting, it is in his larger paintings that he gives his unique visionary imagination full reign. The flexibility of the painting medium allows him to take his brilliantly colored, intricate pattern structures to such extremes that it becomes nearly impossible to reproduce the works adequately. Yet even the most minute detail is significant and contributes to the complex symbolism of the compositions.

Moore is an accomplished storyteller, and many of his works are parables of unity and reconciliation created in a country with a history of political and racial divisiveness. The painting *Canje Bridge* (1978) is a good example of his utopian vision of community and fascination with man-made structures. The work depicts the festive opening of a bridge built in record time by the people of the Corentyne. In Moore's version of the story, the pylons supporting the bridge are represented as stylized human figures, a reference to the communal effort that made its construction possible, while the crowd of minute faces on the bridge represents the many who benefit. In the heavens above, multiple, swirling suns look like cosmic fireworks and affirm the spiritual importance of the event.

In spite of his limited international reputation, Philip Moore is highly regarded in Guyana. The Guyanese National Collection has accumulated some 140 of his works, including masterpieces like *Canje Bridge*, *Ball and Bat Fantasy,* and *Watamama*.

—Veerle Poupeye

MOORHEAD, Scipio
American painter

Active in Boston, c.1773. **Career:** Slave of Reverend John Moorhead, Boston. Friend of Phillis Wheatley, who wrote and dedicated a poem entitled "To S.M., a Young African Painter, on Seeing His Works." **Died.**

*   *   *

Details about the life and art of Scipio Moorhead, who is said to have painted and engraved figurative works in Boston during the late eighteenth century, are sketchy at best. Only one work attributed to Moorhead has survived, a painted portrait of the black colonial poet Phillis Wheatley. An anonymously engraved reproduction of the image was published with her *Poems on Various Subjects, Religious and Moral*. Although little is known about Moorhead, he is recognized as one of the many enslaved and obscure black artists and artisans who contributed a unique and significant sense of style and utility to colonial American art.

Moorhead was owned by the Reverend John Moorhead of Boston's Presbyterian church on Long Lane. Although a slave, Moorhead enjoyed some of the rights granted to free workers, as was customary in more liberal colonies such as Massachusetts. His artistic talents were recognized and developed by the minister's wife, Sarah, who was a painter and art instructor. In colonial America there were four distinct relationships between the slave and the free man or woman—black or white—who exploited his labor. First were the artisan slaves whose goods and services profited the people who owned, housed, and fed them. Second were the slaves apprenticed to the artisans, who produced goods that likewise profited the owner. In the third type of relationship the slave owner rented an artisan slave to another owner. In the fourth, and most liberal, relationship a slave worked where he found employment, agreeing to turn over all or a portion of his earnings. Moorhead most likely fell into the fourth category. An advertisement in the 7 January 1773 edition of the *Boston News Letter,* which some writers have conjectured was for Moorhead's services, illustrates his social position in colonial Boston as a black artist: "Negro artist. At McLean's Watch-Maker, near Town Hall, is a Negro Man whose extraordinary Genius has been assisted by one of the best Masters in Lon-

don; he takes faces at the lowest Rates. Specimens of his performance may be seen at said Place."

Because of his formal education with Sarah Moorhead, who had trained as an artist in Europe, Scipio Moorhead was not a folk artist, and he most probably painted in the European tradition. A direct reference to Moorhead's painting exists in the form of a poem by Wheatley titled "To S.M., a Young African Painter, on Seeing His Works." In a penciled note on a 1773 edition of *Poems on Various Subjects,* Wheatley identified "S.M." as "Scipio Moorhead, Negro servant to the Rev. John Moorhead of Boston whose genius inclined him that way." The language of her tribute to Moorhead's painting is soaring and highly subjective, along the lines of Biblical verse and classical mythology. Wheatley contemplated the nature of creativity more than any specific image Moorhead had created: "When first thy pencil did those beauties give, And breathing figures learnt from thee to live. . . ." It has been inferred from the poem that two of Moorhead's works may have depicted the Greek myths of Damon and Pythias and of Aurora.

—Laurie Fitzpatrick

MORGAN, Clarence (Edward)
American painter

Born: Philadelphia, 21 May 1950. **Education:** Pennsylvania Academy of Fine Arts, certificate 1975; University of Pennsylvania School of Fine Arts, M.F.A. 1978; Temple University, Philadelphia, 1978. **Career:** Since 1978 associate professor of painting and drawing, East Carolina University, Greenville. Artist-in-residence, Minneapolis College of Art and Design, 1984-85. **Awards:** Faculty research grant, East Carolina University, Greenville, 1979; merit award in painting, Fayetteville Museum of Art, 1982; visual arts fellowship, North Carolina Arts Council, 1982. **Address:** Marita Gilliam Gallery, 126 Glenwood Avenue, Raleigh, North Carolina 27603-1704, U.S.A.

Individual Exhibitions:

1986   Harris Brown Gallery, Boston

Selected Group Exhibitions:

1983   *Seven Contemporary American Artists,* Cleveland Museum of Art, Ohio
1984   Palazzo Venezia, Rome
         Wake Forest University, Winston-Salem, North Carolina
1985   Hodges Taylor Gallery, Charlotte, North Carolina
         Carleton College, Northfield, Minnesota
         Alternative Museum, New York

Publications:

On MORGAN: Articles—"Abstractionist Uses Religious Imagery" by Richard Maschal, in *Charlotte Observer* (North Carolina), 1985; review (Hodges/Taylor Gallery, Charlotte, North Carolina) by Shaw Smith, in *New Art Examiner,* 16, June 1989, pp. 50-51; "Southern Arts Federation, National Endowment for the Arts Regional Visual Arts Fellowships" by Jon Meyer, in *New Art Exam-*

iner, 17, October 1989; review (Second Street Gallery, Charlottesville, Virginia) by Stephen Margulies, in *New Art Examiner,* 19, June/Summer 1992, p. 43.

*   *   *

Clarence Morgan is clear-sighted, as articulated through his evolution as a painter. For over twenty years his innovations in concepts and the medium of painting have embodied the broad spectrum of varied explorations in abstraction. He is tenacious in his willingness to engage in discourse on the diverse aspects of his life through introspective reconnaissance within the discipline of painting. Through constant processes of discovery from the 1980s to the present, Morgan has been immersed in his work and has celebrated the materiality and physicality of painting.

Early in his career Morgan's commitment to the purity and expressive qualities of abstraction, whether intelligible or unintelligible, became evident. Following directives in painting reminiscent of Raymond Saunders, Morgan superimposes a geometric mark-making matrix over gestural applications of paint. Interwoven within a rich color-field are variegated intersections of the aggressive marks and derivations of geometric forms. His visual language is comprised of elements existing in the context of modernist movements such as abstract expressionism and minimalism. At times he captures still, poignant moments in time, akin to the spontaneity of the snapshot, while conversely creating explosive surfaces that exude the lyricism of ambient sound. Morgan proves himself to be in full command of a medium and a stylistic thrust that continue to exist as conundrums for the modernist and the postmodernist theorist.

Morgan has stated that "the intelligence of painting does not manifest itself in words, but rather in material and how that material is manipulated to evoke a broad range of sensibilities and forces." What has become important in Morgan's work during recent years are its visceral quality and muscularity. He is completely immersed in the sheer essence of paint as substance. Although he professes to demystify process, it is his application of paint and impasto and his surface treatments that place his paintings definitively within the sphere of mysticism. His works demand a response that transcends intellectual and emotional analysis. Morgan coerces a rendezvous with the unconscious and provokes confrontation with its disparate elements.

—A. M. Weaver

MORGAN, Norma (Gloria)

American painter and printmaker

Born: New Haven, Connecticut, 1928. **Education:** Art Students League, New York; Hans Hofmann School, New York; Atelier 17, New York. **Career:** Since 1949 freelance artist. **Awards:** John Hay Whitney Fellowship, 1941; Louis Comfort Tiffany Fellowship, 1954; John and Ann Lee Stacey Fellowship, 1960. **Agent:** Bertina C. Hunter, 501 LaGuardia, New York, New York 10012, U.S.A.

Individual Exhibitions:

1960   Bodley Gallery, New York
        Howard University, Washington, D.C.
1964   Woodstock Gallery, London

Norma Gloria Morgan: *Three Musicians,* 1982.

1965	Keighley Museum and Art Gallery, Yorkshire, England
1966	Bondgate Gallery, Northumberland, England
1970	Huntington Hartford Museum, New York
1972	Kenosha Public Museum, Wisconsin
1974	Central Wyoming Museum of Art, Casper
1979	Petrucci Gallery, Saugerties, New York
1980	Capitol East Graphics Gallery, Washington, D.C.
1989	Watermark/Cargo, Kingston, New York

Selected Group Exhibitions:

1959	New York Coliseum, New York
1964	Den Frie Gallery, Copenhagen, Denmark
1965	New York World's Fair, New York
1971	Whitney Museum, New York
1987	Association of American Artists Gallery, New York
1989	State Museum of Albany, New York
1991	Woodstock Artists Association, New York
1993	Federal Plaza Galleries, New York
1995	National Arts Club, New York

Collections:

Art Institute of Chicago; Boston Museum; Cliffe Castle Art Gallery and Museum, Keighley, Yorkshire, England; City Art Museum, St. Louis, Missouri; Glasgow Museum, Scotland; Howard University, Washington, D.C.; Leeds Museum, England; Lessing Rosenwald College, Pennsylvania; Library of Congress, Washington, D. C.; Metropolitan Museum of Art, New York; Museum of Modern Art, New York; National Gallery of Art, Washington, D. C.; Portland Art Museum, Oregon; Philadelphia Museum, Pennsylvania; Schomburg Center, New York; Victoria and Albert Museum, London; Walker Art Center, Minneapolis.

Publications:

By MORGAN: Articles—"Engraving," in *The Artist* (New York and London), 1963; "Imaginative Painting," in *The Artist* (New York and London), 1964.

On MORGAN: Book—*The Art of the Print* by Fritz Eichenberg, New York, Abrams, 1976. Articles—"The Engravings of Norma Morgan" by Bernard Bovasso, in *Woodstock Times* (New York), 1979; "Some Moors" by Dakota Lane, in *Woodstock Times* (New York), 1989; "Norman Morgan—Romanticism and Printmaking" by E. Exler, in *Journal of the Printed Word* (New Hampshire), 1990.

*

Norma Morgan comments:

Nothing makes me happier or more inspired than to sit out in the wilderness and work on my art. It is getting increasingly more difficult to find unspoiled, undeveloped areas that I can walk to (or in winter with snow—I don't have a car—to ski to, as I am sports-minded). There are many untapped resources in nature, without always trodding the well-worn artistic paths, and I try to seek out the wilder, eroded, weathered, rocky gorges, ancient woodlands, and I would like to revisit the Utah-Arizona deserts again.

I work in the Catskill Mountain area of New York State some of the time. Hopefully, I would like to visit England and Scotland again. I am also inspired by faces and persons where lifestyles have fashioned them into interesting characters.

Rembrandt (art), Romanticism in literature, and biographies of interesting composers of music keep me reading. My friends and family inspire my paintbrush and engraving tools.

*   *   *

Norma Gloria Morgan is known for her intricate and meticulously done ethereal etchings and engravings. Yet she describes herself as a painter, engraver, and etcher, and she is particularly intrigued by unusual landforms.

Norma Gloria Morgan: untitled (acrylic of two overlapping scenes: Artists Gorge, Pottersville, New York, and Central Highlands, Scotland), 1995.

Morgan's first painting of note, *Reflections,* was executed when she was just seventeen years old, yet the sophistication apparent in her use of silver on silver was a precursor of her fascination with and use of the subtle relationships of form and tonality. She studied privately with Hans Hofmann, who taught her about color and pictorial structure. She also studied with Stanley William Hayter, who taught her engraving and graphics. It was at his print shop in Paris that she perfected her printing technique.

While on a fellowship in the early 1950s, Morgan discovered the English countryside and the Scottish moors. She seems to have developed an insatiable love affair with the craggy, windswept terrain of the British Isles. She explored the land, sketching and committing to memory the feeling the environment evoked in her. Morgan transmitted her images and feelings to her prints, and she has returned to the landscape often as a theme for her work.

Morgan has occasionally incorporated the human figure into her compositions. One of her personal favorites is the figure of a friend, Alfred Holdsworth, sitting on a rock. Entitled *Alf of the Moors,* the work is a rhythmic series of geometric shapes and planes. Morgan achieves a chiaroscuro effect through thousands of tiny cuts in the copper plate. The man stares calmly out of the composition as if he were a part of the rock. Another composition in which Morgan uses the figure is *David in the Wilderness.* The compositional format in this work is reminiscent of Chinese landscape painting, with asymmetrically placed rocks delicately and precariously balanced with a spherical sun or moon and the light of the sky. The human figure is almost camouflaged by the profusion of color values, textures, and shapes of the hill, and the organic and inorganic forms meld one into the other in a confusing jumble of bushes and rocks. Yet the figure sits meditatively facing the sky, totally at the mercy of the wilderness but seemingly at peace. Morgan's engraving *Portrait of My Grandfather* is in the collection of the Metropolitan Museum of Art in New York City.

Copper engraving requires a great deal of skill and patience, and Morgan is a meticulous craftsperson. She works with relatively large plates to produce powerful works. The engraving *Castle Maol, Isle of the Sky, Scotland,* for example, is 17½ by 33½ inches. The work is a wonderful example of the skilled use of the burin to achieve subtle atmospheric shading, the clouds in stark contrast to the isolated monument that seems to float in space with the soaring birds. The engraving *Dark Height* is a masterful study of light and line. It seems to be showing a treacherous mountain path of light that leads the viewer into an otherworldly land of adventure. The intricate forms and shapes suggest unseen entitles, and there are spirits present. The shapes are so complex that the composition takes on an abstract mystical quality.

Morgan has continued to paint as well as make prints. Her massive paintings are executed in Woodstock. One painting, *Fawn's Leap,* is a large, vivid acrylic depicting her mother and friends in the middle of a rocky wooded area playing music and singing. For Morgan, who plays several instruments, music is an important influence.

Much of Morgan's work displays a lyrical romanticism, with subtle shifts of light and a delicate translucent quality. She balances her work by combining these elements with sharp geometric planes and contrasting dark solid shapes. Her compositions elicit abstract, symbolic meanings. The landscapes become slightly threatening, inhospitable, ominous, even a bit turbulent, yet they remain serenely beautiful. Morgan feels that these conflicting elements in her work speak to the ultimate struggle of men and women against nature. It is the statement she wishes to make with her art.

—Nashormeh N. R. Lindo

MORRISON, Keith (Anthony)

Jamaican painter and printmaker

Born: Linstead, Jamaica, 20 May 1942. **Education:** School of Art Institute of Chicago, B.F.A. 1963, M.F.A. 1965. **Family:** Married Alexandra in 1989. **Career:** Professor of art, Fisk University, Nashville, 1967-68; chairman, art department, DePaul University, Chicago, 1969-71; associate dean, College of Art and Architecture, University of Illinois, Chicago, 1971-75; professor and then chairman, art department, University of Maryland, College Park, 1979-92; dean, College of Creative Arts, San Francisco Art Institute, 1993-96. **Awards:** Prize, Jamaica Institute, 1959; Bicentennial Award for Painting, City of Chicago, 1976; International Award for Painting, OAU Monrovia, Liberia, 1978; Organization for African Unity Painting Award, Liberia, 1979; National Association for Equal Opportunity in Education Painting Award, 1984. **Agent:** Jan Cicero Gallery, 437 North Clark Street, Chicago, Illinois, U.S.A. **Address:** San Francisco Art Institute, 800 Chestnut Street, San Francisco, California 94133-2299, U.S.A.

Selected Exhibitions:

1971	Art Institute of Chicago
1983	Corcoran Gallery, Washington, D.C.
1987	Brody's Gallery, Washington, D.C.
1989	African American Museum, Los Angeles
1990	Bronx Museum, New York
	Alternative Museum, New York
1992	Cavin Morris Gallery, New York
1996	Bomani Gallery, San Francisco (solo)
1997	*New Jamaican Painting,* Smithsonian Institution, Washington, D.C. (traveling)

Collections:

Art Institute of Chicago; Corcoran Gallery of Art, Washington, D.C.; National Museum of American Art; Schomburg Center, New York.

*   *   *

Born in Jamaica, Keith Morrison studied art in Chicago and began his teaching career there at De Paul and Loyola universities. Like many other students and painters in the mid-1960s, he followed the legacy of abstract expressionism, but with the ensuing turmoil over basic civil liberties for African Americans, abstraction became too limiting for Morrison. He thus returned to the figure, which offered a means of expressing visually his concerns for justice and an improved quality of life, especially in the cramped urban ghettos of northern U.S. cities. As Morrison sought ways to delimit his artwork, thematic figurative paintings proved as limiting as abstract expressionism, however. He then moved back into abstraction but with a renewed sense of how he could employ concepts from both abstraction and figuration. He arrived at something that had always been with him, a recognition of the abstract thoughts that created fanciful images of African legends and mythologies, something that had informed his days as a youth in the Caribbean. His concentration on specific colors is thus related to tangible references to the religion, family life, and community of his childhood.

This is something far removed from abstract expressionism and the urban-inspired protest art of the 1960s and the early 1970s.

Other artists have spoken of dreamworld experiences based on stories that were told to them by family or community members. The stories of Morrison's youth have clearly found their way into his artwork. Of Morrison's work the artist and art historian David Driskell has written, "The world of myth and legends becomes a part of the real world in his painterly approach. The viewer is drawn to the edge of his paintings by the continuing drama of real-life experiences." In many of his compositions from the 1980s and 1990s, for example, Morrison seems preoccupied with death. He has said that as a child in Jamaica he was told of an African legend of death rituals that took place at ponds. As the legend goes, for a brief moment every evening at dusk a table drawn by bulls and laden with gold was lifted from the depths of a pond in the woods. If a person witnessed the event, he would be drawn into the pond and carried down into its waters. The legend frightened Morrison as a child, but as an adult it has provided him with many images he has used to re-create and reinterpret the story. The story also has very personal meanings for Morrison, for a childhood friend drowned in a pond at dusk, leaving questions in the minds of those who firmly believed in the power of the legend. *Zombie Jamboree* (1988), with its fanciful Africanized animals of the desert inserted into a tropical beachlike atmosphere of palms, banana trees, and flowers, is a homage to the friend and the legend.

Most of Morrison's paintings are based on elaborate narratives, as, for example, *Chariot* (1988), which shows a chariot of death and destruction flying over a wasteland being left behind. An open coffin, filled with bones and skulls but also with puppetlike merrymakers, teeters on the edge of the chariot as if ready to fall. In an open window an African statue stands poised watching the flagellation of Christ, which symbolizes human savagery. Later works such as *A Night in Tunisia* (1991), based on the Dizzy Gillespie composition, and *Crabs in a Pot* (1994) were exhibited at the Bomani Gallery in San Francisco in April 1996. The works are tongue-in-cheek commentaries that are at once both humorous and serious, referring back to principles of abstraction that were always a part of Morrison's Caribbean heritage in myth and legend.

In recent years Morrison has divided his time between his art making and academic appointments. He has served as a dean at the San Francisco Art Institute and at San Francisco State University, as well as at the University of Maryland.

—Lizzetta LeFalle-Collins

MORRISON, Petrona
Jamaican sculptor and assemblage artist

Born: Manchester, Jamaica, 20 August 1954. **Education:** McMaster University, Hamilton, Ontario, 1973-76, B.F.A. 1976; Howard University, Washington, D.C., 1983-86, M.F.A. 1986. **Career:** Art teacher, Wolmers Girls School, Kingston, Jamaica, 1976-77; scriptwriter and producer, Agency for Public Information, Kingston, Jamaica, 1978-83; acting registrar, National Gallery of Jamaica, Kingston, Jamaica, 1988-94. Since 1988 lecturer, Edna Manley School for the Visual Arts, Kingston, Jamaica. Artist-in-residence, Burchfield Art Center, University of New York, Buffalo, 1991, Studio Museum of Harlem, New York, 1994-95. Participated

in exchange programs to Kenyatta University, Nairobi, Kenya, 1984-85, and to Thapong International Artists Workshop, Mahalapye, Botsuana, 1996. **Awards:** International Student Exchange Program Fellowship, 1984; Yamagata Fellowship, Suffern, New York, 1992. **Address:** Abbey Court, Apartment 32A, 44 Trafalgar Road, Kingston 10, Jamaica West Indies.

Individual Exhibitions:

1981   John Peartree Gallery, Kingston, Jamaica
1983   Upstairs Downstairs Gallery, Kingston, Jamaica
1989   Babylon Gallery, Kingston, Jamaica
1991   Makonde Gallery, Kingston, Jamaica

Selected Group Exhibitions:

1982   *Six Artists,* Gallery Four, Washington, D.C.
1984   *Artists of the Diaspora,* Pan-Africa Forum, Washington, D.C.
1985   Hood College, Maryland
1988   Frame Centre Gallery, Kingston, Jamaica
        Annual National Exhibition, National Gallery of Jamaica, Kingston (and annually through 1993)
1992   Salena Gallery, Long Island University, Brooklyn, New York
1994   October Gallery, London
        Frame Centre Gallery, Kingston, Jamaica
1995   Studio Museum in Harlem, New York
1996   *Petrona Morrison and Veronica Ryan: Sculptural Works,* Bronx Museum of the Arts, New York

Collections:

National Gallery of Jamaica, Kingston; Studio Museum in Harlem, New York.

Publications:

On MORRISON: Books—*The Fire Next Time,* exhibition catalog by Daniel Veneciano, New York, Studio Museum in Harlem, 1995; *Petrona Morrison and Veronica Ryan,* exhibition catalog, New York, Bronx Museum of the Arts and Mora J. Beauchamp-Byrd, 1996. **Articles**—"Jamaica to Brooklyn 1992" by Valerie Gladstone, in *ARTnews* (New York), Summer 1992; "Artists in Residence" by Geoffrey Jacques, in *Journal of Contemporary African Art* (New York), Fall/Winter 1995.

*

Petrona Morrison comments:

My work is about transformation—transformation of self. I choose to use old discarded materials from our environment that have a sense of history but that may be considered useless by some. I am interested in changing their context—in "transforming" them and, in so doing, presenting a metaphor for self. The process of making objects, sculptures, from these materials becomes a personal ritual for healing and renewal.

Traditional African art has been the central and enduring influence on my work, and it is that aesthetic that informs the form of much of my work. I see myself as Afro-centric but also hybrid, a

Petrona Morrison: *Survivors,* **1995.**

product of the complex and often contradictory environment that is the Caribbean.

*   *   *

Petrona Morrison started her artistic career in the 1970s, a period of intense cultural and political activism in Jamaica. While her work has always been devoid of dogmatic political statements, its underlying philosophy has been shaped by the prevailing debates on race, the social order, and postcolonial culture.

Most of Morrison's early works are paintings, drawings, and prints done in a figurative expressionist style. With their emphasis on the human face and, more specifically, the self-image, these works may seem dramatically different from her mature work. Yet they contain the rudiments of her later thematic and formal concerns. The elongation of the forms and the use of gridlike designs, for instance, prefigure the vertical, rectilinear structure of her later work. Similarly, the autobiographical connotations in her later work can be traced back to the early images.

Morrison's postgraduate studies at Howard University were a turning point in her artistic development. She studied assemblage sculpture with Edgar Sorrels Adewale, who greatly influenced her artistic development, and she went to Kenya for a year on an exchange program with Kenyatta University. Her early assemblages were box structures, painted with figurative scenes inspired by fieldwork in Kenya.

After her return to Jamaica in 1988, Morrison abandoned the representational and the narrative in favor of the abstract and the metaphorical. She started producing relief assemblages on plywood by combining small found objects—such as pieces of wood, rusted metal, and stones—with malleable materials such as celluclay. Although she still used pigment occasionally, she began to rely more on the natural colors and textures of her materials. This resulted in a reduction of color mainly to earth tones. It also introduced an ephemeral element into her work, as some materials she used were bound to corrode further.

The direction Morrison's work took at the time was profoundly influenced by her experience in Kenya and her study of African art history. The carved doors she saw in Mombasa, for instance, influenced the color scheme and panel structure of her assemblage reliefs. Their verticality and frontal emphasis are suggestive of Dogon art, and the accumulation of found objects, held together by nails and wires, reminds one of Kongo power objects, two lasting formal and conceptual influences on her work.

Morrison has stated that her work evolves around the general themes of transformation, renewal, and healing, which have personal and broader social significance. She explores these themes by means of an informal, evolving system of signs and symbols, which also documents her interest in the processes of signification. The recurrent symbol of the vessel or bowl, for instance, denotes wholeness, the body as a protective shell, and the performance of ritual, but it is also suggestive of a begging cup.

Although Morrison's first assemblages were relatively small, they gradually became larger. She also moved off the wall and started making freestanding objects and installations. By 1992 she was making towering totem structures from scrap wood and corroded metal. Although highly abstract, these totem forms are usually suggestive of the body, as in *Sentinel* (1993), one of her largest sculptures to date. The silent, powerful monumentality of these constructions belies the frailty and ephemeral nature of the materials, which reinforce their symbolic meaning.

Morrison was artist in residence at the Studio Museum in Harlem in 1994-95, which placed her work on its current course. She found inspiration in the urban environment of Harlem and started using elements from derelict buildings, which gave her work a constructed, architectonic quality. Although there was already a ritualistic element in Morrison's assemblages of the late 1980s, she pursued this approach further in altarlike installations such as *Remembrance (124th Street),* a moving 1995 memorial to a woman who died in a fire that destroyed a derelict building behind the museum. She used fragments from the burned-out building in its construction.

The transformation of discarded objects and materials into tokens of the transcendental has become a fundamental characteristic of Morrison's work. The structural emphasis of her recent installations is accompanied by a renewed interest in the ephemeral. In some works she has used wood fragments strewed in geometric patterns reminiscent of Afro-Caribbean signs.

—Veerle Poupeye

MOTELY, Archibald (Jr.)

American painter

Born: New Orleans, 7 October 1891. **Education:** Art Institute of Chicago, 1914-18. **Career:** Painter, Mural Division of the Illinois Federal Arts Project, 1935-39. **Awards:** Harmon Collection Gold Medal, 1928; Frank J. Logan Medal, 1925; J.N. Eisendrath Prize, 1925; Newark Museum Prize, 1927; Guggenheim Fellowship, 1929. **Died:** 1981.

Exhibitions:

1928	New Galleries, New York
1929	Harmon Foundation, New York

1931	Harmon Foundation, New York
	Guggenheim Fellows Exhibition, New York
	American Scandinavian Exhibition
	Illinois Academy of Fine Art
	Chicago Women's Club
1932	Art Institute of Chicago
1933	Guggenheim Fellows Exhibition, New York
	Smithsonian Institution, Washington, D.C.
	Chicago Women's Club
1934	Art Institute of Chicago
	Toledo Museum, Ohio
	Corcoran Gallery, Washington, D.C.
1936	Dallas Exposition
	Texas Centennial
1937	Howard University, Washington, D.C.
1938	Howard University, Washington, D.C.
1939	Baltimore Museum, Maryland
1940	American Negro Exposition, Chicago
	South Side Community Art Center, Chicago
	Library of Congress, Washington, D.C.
1941	South Side Community Art Center, Chicago
1942	College Art Traveling Exhibition
1945	Howard University, Washington, D.C.
1967	City College of New York
1970	La Jolla Art Museum, California

Collections:

Chicago National Archive; Chicago Public Library; Doolittle School, Chicago; Evansville State Hospital; Harmon Collection, New York;

Archibald Motley, Jr.: *Woman Peeling Apples,* **1924. Photo by Manu Sassoonian; courtesy of the Schomburg Center for Research in Black Culture.**

Archibald Motley, Jr.: *Dans la Rue, Paris,* **1929. Photo by Manu Sassoonian; courtesy of the Schomburg Center for Research in Black Culture.**

Howard University, Washington, D.C.; National Archives, Washington, D.C.; Nichols School, Evanston, Illinois; Ryerson School, Chicago; Schomburg Center for Research in Black Culture, New York Public Library; Wood River Post Office.

Publications:

On MOTLEY: Book—*The Art of Archibald Motley, Jr.* by Jontyle Theresa Robinson and Wendy Greenhouse, Chicago Historical Society, 1991. **Articles**—"Mr. and Mrs. Frank C. Logan Medal to Motley for 'A Mulattress'" and "Joseph N. Eisendroth Prize to Motley for 'Syncopation'," both in *Chicago Art Institute Bulletin,* XIX, March 1925, p. 36; "Archibald J. Motley," in *Opportunity,* April 1928; "Top Negro Artist Works in Factory Job," in *Scrapbook of Art and Artists of Chicago,* 1956, p. 121.

* * *

One of the most important artists of his generation, Archibald Motley is best known for his stylized paintings of urban street scenes. He liked to use the activities and social lives of African Americans as his subject matter. He favored lively, although sometimes disreputable, activities, but he did not paint African Americans as caricatures. His images were optimistic, engaging, and sensual, as, for example, in the paintings *Chicken Shack* and *Liar* (both 1936). Motley was influenced by the painter George Bellows, who shared his appreciation for the inherent humanity and dignity in everyday life.

Motley, whose family wanted him to study architecture, received his formal training at the Art Institute of Chicago. He worked his way through school and met several other artists there who would remain close friends throughout his life. After finishing school Motley worked as a laborer. Within the next decade, however, he produced several of his best-known paintings, and in 1928 he had a one-man show at the New Galleries in New York City. Works of the period included *Mending Socks* (1923), *Woman Peeling Apples* (1924), and *Old Snuff Dipper* (1928), produced in a classical, carefully rendered realistic style.

Motley particularly liked to paint nighttime themes, not only because of the activities that take place at night but also because he was fascinated with the interplay of moonlight and artificial light and their effect on color. Motley developed a distinct technique that he used throughout his career. His images appear soft, almost glowing, and some paintings have an airbrushed quality.

Motley also liked to portray the various colors and shades of skin found within the African American community, and he sometimes painted scenes with an interracial theme, as in *Black and Tan Cabaret* (1923), *Blues* (1929), and *Stomp* (1927), all set in nightclubs. Motley loved jazz, and some of his paintings appear to have a noisy, jazzy rhythm in their design. In 1929 Motley spent a year in Paris, where he painted *Jockey Club, Paris* (1929), one of his best-known works. It is interesting to note that Motley married a Caucasian woman and lived mostly in white neighborhoods and that, while he was in Paris, he did not associate with other African American artists living there.

Like many other artists Motley was subsidized by the Works Progress Administration during the Great Depression, and during this time he was chosen to paint a panel of a stagecoach, *U.S. Mail* (1936), for an Illinois post office. By 1940 Motley was the best-known African American artist in Chicago. In 1945, when his wife died, Motley stopped painting for eight years. With the help and support of his nephew, the writer Willard Motley, who took him to Mexico, he gradually began working again. During the 1950s African American artists such as Hughie Lee-Smith and Walter H. Williams produced paintings showing the despair and alienation of people who had migrated from rural life in the South to the promised prosperity of the industrial areas of the North. *After Fiesta, Remorse, Siesta* (1959-60) resembles Motley's earlier works in terms of style, technique, and color, but it lacks the crowded, festive atmosphere and instead expresses a feeling of isolation, abandonment, and sadness. The setting is a nightclub, and while the tables hold bottles and cocktail glasses, they are empty of people except for one patron, who is resting his head on the tabletop. Sitting at a piano is a nude Hispanic woman who is surrounded by other instruments without musicians. Outside, through a doorway, stands an embracing couple.

In 1963 Motley began a painting, which he intended to finish within the year, to honor the 100th anniversary of the Emancipation Proclamation. Although he did not stop working on it until nearly a decade later, he felt that the work was essentially unfinished. What he did produce was an allegorical work addressing the assassinations of President John F. Kennedy and the Reverend Martin Luther King, Jr., the revival of the KKK, the bombing of a church in Birmingham, Alabama, and other important historical events. Motley used a great deal of blue in the painting to convey sadness.

African American artists of the 1960s and 1970s, who focused on the victimization and worsening conditions of their people, were critical of Motley and the images he portrayed. Motley's work, however, reflected an earlier, more optimistic era, and, most important, he helped create the African American identity.

—Christine Miner Minderovic

MUKAROBGWA, Thomas
Zimbabwean painter and sculptor

Born: Nyanga, Zimbabwe, 1942. **Education:** National Gallery Workshop School, 1958 (informal). **Career:** Worked in domestic service as a waiter and for a bakery. Since 1957 assistant marketing officer, Rhodes National Gallery. First member of the National Gallery Workshop School. **Awards:** First Prize, Annual Nedlaw Exhibition, National Gallery of Zimbabwe, 1983; Third Prize, Annual Nedlaw Exhibition, National Gallery of Zimbabwe, 1984; Annual Nedlaw Exhibition, National Gallery of Zimbabwe, 1986; Award of Merit, Zimbabwe Heritage Exhibition, National Gallery of Zimbabwe, 1989; Award of Merit and Certificate of Excellence, Zimbabwe Heritage Exhibition, National Gallery of Zimbabwe, 1990.

Selected Exhibitions:

1962	*New African Talent,* National Gallery of Zimbabwe
1963	Commonwealth Institute, London
1966	*Ninth Annual Exhibition,* National Gallery of Zimbabwe
1967	*Tenth Annual Exhibition,* National Gallery of Zimbabwe
1968	*Eleventh Annual Exhibition,* National Gallery of Zimbabwe
	Museum of Modern Art, New York
1969	*Twelfth Annual Exhibition,* National Gallery of Zimbabwe
	Contemporary African Arts, Camden Arts Center, London
1970	*Thirteenth Annual Exhibition,* National Gallery of Zimbabwe
1971	*Fourteenth Annual Exhibition,* National Gallery of Zimbabwe
	Sculpture Contemporaine des Shonas d'Afrique, Musée Rodin, Paris
1972	*Fifteenth Annual Exhibition,* National Gallery of Zimbabwe
1973	*Sixteenth Annual Exhibition,* National Gallery of Zimbabwe
1974	Shona Art International, Rhodes National Gallery, Salisbury
1975	*Eighteenth Annual Exhibition,* National Gallery of Zimbabwe
1976	*Nineteenth Annual Exhibition,* National Gallery of Zimbabwe
1977	*Twentieth Annual Exhibition,* National Gallery of Zimbabwe
1978	*Twenty-First Annual Exhibition,* National Gallery of Zimbabwe
1979	*Twenty-Second Annual Exhibition,* National Gallery of Zimbabwe
1980	*Twenty-Third Annual Exhibition,* National Gallery of Zimbabwe
1981	*Art from Africa,* Commonwealth Institute, London
1985	PG Gallery, National Gallery of Zimbabwe
1989	*Zimbabwe Heritage Exhibition,* National Gallery of Zimbabwe
1990	National Gallery of Zimbabwe
	Contemporary Stone Carvings from Zimbabwe, Yorkshire Sculpture Pary, England

Collections:

Museum of Modern Art, New York; National Gallery of Zimbabwe.

Publications:

On MUKAROBGWA: Books—*Life in Stone: Zimbabwean Sculpture—Birth of a Contemporary Art Form* by Olivier Sultan, Baobab Books, 1992. **Articles**—"Sky and Land in Zimbabwe" by Jean Kennedy, in *New Currents, Ancient Rivers: Contemporary African Artists in a Generation of Change,* Washington and London, Smithsonian Institution Press, 1991.

*   *   *

As the first member of the National Gallery Workshop School (originally the Workshop School) in Zimbabwe, Thomas Mukarobgwa was encouraged and influenced by Frank McKewen, who was both the founder of the school and the first director of the Rhodes National Gallery. Mukarobgwa first became a painter in the school, as well as an employee of the National Gallery, with strong ties to the natural world. Even the titles of many of his paintings invoke the bush landscape: *The Old Man Afraid to Cross, The Tree and the Sky in the Middle, Very Important Bush, Beautiful Crossed Tree,* and *River Coming in the Middle of the Bush.*

Mukarobgwa later began to sculpt, and he became a part of what is known as the Shona sculpture movement, based on the Shona culture and mythology. Mukarobgwa is sometimes credited with introducing McKewen to Shona culture (as McKewen is credited with introducing Mukarobgwa to classical art forms through the National Gallery), thus becoming a major influence on the origins of the Shona movement as it emerged from the Workshop School. The Shona movement emphasizes the culture and mythology of the individual artist rather than a particular style of work. McKewen asked the artists at the Workshop School not to mass-produce or plagiarize work for tourists or for placement in airports but to "imagine shapes that could please" those far more important to the Shona—"their ancestors or the spirits." The effort to do so is evident in Mukarobgwa's paintings and sculptures.

For Mukarobgwa and the Shona, people are a part of nature. People do not live in or around the bush but within it, as naturally as does a tree or a river. Thus, much of his sculpture resembles both man and nature. Humans emerge from stone, landscape resembles the body, and animals take the shape of rock formations. Since both the stone and the artist are a part of the bush, the art itself is an elemental expression of nature, as important to the Shona people perhaps as the path the river takes as it comes through the middle of the bush.

—Terry Bain

NASCIMENTO, Abdias do
Brazilian painter

Career: Professor, New York State University, Buffalo. Director, Center of Puerto-Rican Research and Study, Buffalo, New York. Professor, Catholic University of São Paulo. Founder, Afro-Brazilian Institute of Research and Study. Founder, Black Experimental Theater (TEN), 1944. Editor, *Dramas Para Negros e Prology Para Brancos* (anthology of dramatic Afro-Brazilian literature), 1961. Organized the First Congress of African Brazilians, Rio, 1950. Author, *Sortilégo* and various other critical studies on the African experience in Brazil. Vice-President and coordinator, Third Congress of African Americans, São Paulo, 1982.

Individual Exhibitions:

1969	Harlem Art Gallery, New York
	Yale University, New Haven, Connecticut
	Crypt Gallery, Columbia University, New York
	Wesleyan University, Middletown, Connecticut
1970	Gallery of African Art, Washington, D.C.
1971	Museum of Afro-American Art, Boston
1972	Harvard University, Boston
1973	Langston Hughes Center, Buffalo, New York
1975	Banco Nacional, São Paulo
	Galeria, Rio Grande do Sul
	Inner City Cultural Center, Los Angeles
	Howard University, Washington, D.C.
	Afro-American Historical and Cultural Museum, Philadelphia
1977	Museum of African-American Art
1980	Spanish Harlem, New York

Selected Group Exhibitions:

1972	Everson Museum of Art, Syracuse, New York
1973	Gallery Salomé, New Orleans
1975	Rainbow Signs Gallery, Berkeley, California
1977	Museum of Art, Buffalo, New York
1979	United Nations, New York

Collections:

Museum of Art, Buffalo, New York.

*   *   *

Abdias do Nascimento, the Brazilian painter, actor, dramatist, poet, essayist, musician, historian, professor, and politician, has devoted his many talents to recovering and affirming African cultural values. The inspiration for his painting is the Afro-Brazilian religion Candomblé. He has written that Candomblé's public ceremonies "evoke the collective past and the Orishas' history through spoken and staged myth." Candomblé has survived despite a concerted effort to suppress it or to supplant it with values from Europe and Roman Catholicism. Nascimento's art is a testimony to the continued viability of African beliefs.

Nascimento's paintings represent the cosmology of Candomblé, which encompasses a universe composed of four parts. There are both visible and invisible realms, and Nascimento's paintings make the invisible realms visible. The Candomblé universe consists of the world of the *orisha*s, or gods, the realm of pharmacology and plant life, the world of human beings, and the realm of the spirits of ancestors. The *orisha*s, which represent cosmic forces and energy in its many forms, are objects of worship. The *orisha*s in Nascimento's work include Eshu, the emissary between the divine and the human realms; Oshún, the goddess of beauty, love, and money; Ogún, the warrior; Oshossí, the god of the hunt; Ossaim, the god of plant life; Shangó, the god of thunder and lightning; Yansã, the goddess of storms; Iemanjá, the goddess of the sea; and Obatalá, the god of creation. The attributes and deeds of each of the *orisha*s are contained in a body of myths that have been passed down for centuries through an oral tradition. Each *orisha* is associated with symbolic implements and colors that, in essence, form part of a visual tradition. Nascimento seizes on this corpus of beliefs as the thematic substance of his work.

The myths, colors, and symbols that represent the *orisha*s constitute part of an unchanging Candomblé tradition, comparable to the theology and iconography of other religions. This recognizable core is a constant in Nascimento's work. These traditional elements are sometimes combined with people and events of the twentieth century, thus making it evident that ancient religious values are applicable to the status of people of African descent today. Even when he makes occasional forays into Catholic religious symbols, Nascimento portrays them within an Afrocentric context. An example of this approach can be found in his painting of the Crucifixion, with Malcolm X as the crucified figure. Guerreiro Ramos writes that Nascimento expresses the alienation of people of African descent in his work when he "brings African motives and issues into the mainstream of twentieth century ideals."

Nascimento's art does not represent a particular school or movement. He decries the tendency by some critics to place works derived from African cultural values into the category of folk art. The eclectic nature of his work, which is derived from many sources and is fully conscious of the constructs of so-called erudite art, precludes its being dismissed or relegated to the category of folklore. Nevertheless, Nascimento has made a conscious decision to perpetuate traditional sources of inspiration from daily life.

Behind the brilliance of color, geometrical form, and religious symbols characteristic of Nascimento's art is an ideological stance that is typical of many of his endeavors regardless of the field. The art historian Joel Rufino dos Santos refers to this stance as that of the "breacher of limits." He notes that Nascimento has battled for equality as a public figure on many fronts, using the weapons in his arsenal of talents to fight for access to rights not only in Brazil but also throughout the world. Nascimento has written that he views his art as the "pictorial result of a life's attempt to rescue and restore African cultural values, free of exoticism, folklorism and cultural domestication." The perspective he brings to his work has led scholars such as Molefi Asante to proclaim him to be one of the preeminent exponents of pan-African thought of contemporary times.

—Carolyn Richardson Durham

NASH, Teixeira
American painter, photographer, and weaver

Work also appeared under the names Teixeira and Mildred L. Teixeira. **Born:** Mildred Lucille Teixeira, Quincy, Massachusetts, 9 September 1931. **Education:** Howard University, Washington, D.C., B.A. in philosophy 1966, M.F.A. in graphics and painting 1970; George Washington University, Washington, D.C., 1957-58; Howard University, Washington, D.C., 1978; American University, Washington, D.C., 1985. **Family:** Married 1) Robert J. Nash in 1952 (divorced 1979), two daughters and one son; 2) Jerome E. Keith in 1981. **Career:** Policy and program director, Computer Center, Washington, D.C., 1974-79; researcher and program writer and analyzer, National Endowment for the Arts, 1978-79; management specialist, A.L. Nellum and Associates, 1983; curriculum designer and developer for public housing staff, MATCH Institute, 1983-84; economic development designer, Goodwill Industries, 1983-84; television producer, WHMM, 1983-90; economic and management development executive, Minority Business Enterprises, Legal Defense Fund, 1984. Since 1985 public affairs manager and media producer, African Development Foundation, Washington, D.C. Editor, *Beyond Relief,* 1985-88, *Advance,* 1986-93. Speechwriter, ADF Board and Office of the President. **Awards:** Outstanding Woman in Education Award, National Endowment for the Arts, 1967; Teixeira Nash Day, Mayor's Proclamation, 11 January 1981; Outstanding Achievement awards, African Development Foundation, 1986-96; Commemorative Poster Award, National African Festival, Smithsonian Institution, Washington, D.C., 1988, 1989; Silver Star Plus Award, Alpha Kappa Alpha Sorority, Inc., 1997; Outstanding Achievement Award, Washington, D.C. Teachers' Association; Outstanding Achievement Award, Metropolitan Women's Democratic Club. **Agent:** Robyn Bandele Nash Esquire, Post Office Box 1061, Oak Bluffs, Massachusetts 02557, U.S.A.

Individual Exhibitions:

1966	The Studio, Washington, D.C.
1967	The Studio, Washington, D.C.
1969	Martha's Vineyard, Massachusetts
1971	New Thing Art Gallery
1975	Holston Gallery

Teixeira Nash, 1995. Photo courtesy of Katherine Pryor.

1977	Miya Gallery
1979	Women's National Bank
1980	Martha's Vineyard, Massachusetts
1981	District Building
	National Public Radio, Washington, D.C.
1982	Nyangoma's Gallery

Selected Group Exhibitions:

1958	Corcoran Gallery, Washington, D.C.
1968	Smithsonian Institution, Washington, D.C.
1970	Howard University, Washington, D.C.
1972	Mrs. Powell's Gallery
1974	*Jazz,* Franz Bader Gallery, Washington, D.C.
1975	Philadelphia Museum
1982	Last Stop Gallery, Richmond, Virginia
1994	Tabernacle Gallery, Martha's Vineyard, Massachusetts
1995	Grand Gallery, Washington, D.C.
1997	Ascension Gallery, Washington, D.C.

Collection:

Executive Office, The White House, Washington, D.C.

Publications:

By TEIXEIRA: Books— *ART, A Teacher's Handbook,* Friends of the Arts in Public Schools, 1965; *Round and Round What Mulberry Bush?* Black Child Development Institute, 1970; *Open Schools,* Portal Schools Project, Howard University, Washington, D.C., 1978; *Grassroots and Pavement,* National Endowment for the Arts, Washington, D.C., 1978; *Minority Report,* National Endowment for the Arts, Washington, D.C., 1980; *STYLUS: An Anthology of Writings of Black Authors,* Howard University, Washington, D.C., 1994.

*

Teixeira Nash comments:

I look upon myself as a translator of essences—both physical and spiritual essences. God or the "Force" has given artists the capacity to be sensitive and aware of those things and spirits that surround us, and he has given us the means by which we can translate those "essences" so that others can share in the experience. African people have had the fortune of integrating these essences into their lives in a very fundamental way—integrating the intellect and emotional soul, unlike the Platonic model followed in other groups. All art is political in that it involves the body politic—the people. I have translated many things in my life, the greatest of which was love.

* * *

With an extensive background in philosophy, politics, African culture, and arts administration, Teixeira Nash has always seen herself as a translator, believing that curiosity is the one significant trait of artists. "They are incurably inquisitive," she has said. Her artistic curiosity was aroused early on, in the 1940s, by an entrepreneurial father from the Cape Verde Islands and an artistic African American mother who had married after their spouses had both died in the influenza epidemic.

Teixeira's impressionistic paintings and tapestries, which celebrate her African and American heritages, use vivid color schemes and bold juxtapositions to intensify their impact. Her focus on racial unrest, African culture, and landscapes points generally to a concern for society but specifically to the importance of interpreting the black experience for blacks. Her concern is that too many blacks are not accustomed to evaluating themselves artistically.

Teixeira studied at Howard University in the 1950s, at a time when its art department included James Porter, Lois Mailou Jones, and James Wells. They helped her build the foundation that has enabled her to make art a lifetime pursuit.

Teixeira continued to develop her talents when she and her husband moved to Nigeria to start an architectural and engineering company. While there, she worked in oils and began using the palette knife. In 1958 her painting *Hausa Trader* (1956) was included in the prestigious area show at the Corcoran Gallery of Art in Washington, D.C. The work had been selected by the renowned artist Andrew Wyeth. With the self-assurance of one who had been accepted by the mainstream, Teixeira went on to earn her master's degree in fine arts from Howard University.

In the 1960s Teixeira was caught up in the civil rights and black arts movements, and she responded by mixing water-based with oil-based paint as a strike against tradition. Finding that painting on white canvases had a negative effect on her, she began painting a black background on her canvases before creating works of art on them, a practice she continued for ten years. She then came to feel that she had the freedom to move in other directions. She also began painting in series, sticking with a theme for anywhere from five to twelve years. Her first series, "Black on Black" (1968-73), reflected her spirit of rebellion and conveyed the impact of suffering.

In her second series, "Spirits" (1975-80), Teixeira moved away from a literal depiction of blacks in their environment but continued to use the human figure to contemplate relationships—in this case the relationship of mind and spirit. In *Genesis* (1976) the spiritual world is presented in black, beige, and white, with chiaroscuro lending an ethereal, or ghostlike, quality to the two white bodies emerging from a dark body. All of this is outlined in black against a bold geometric pattern. The only elements of color come from the

Teixeira Nash: *Sunset through the Trees,* 1995. Photo courtesy of Harlee Little.

earth—sun, flowers, trees, birds, fruit, and fish—allusions to the cycle of life.

Influenced by the environmental movement, Teixeira's third series, "Scapes" (1976-88), shows the beauty and serenity of landscapes. The brilliant yellows, blues, and greens of *Scape—Beyond a Gichi Memory* (1980) bleed into one another to create a harmonious blend of nature and a reminder that humans must take care of natural resources. Since then Teixeira's work has grown more personal. The introspective multimedia series "Back in Sinus Rhythm," begun in 1992 as a response to open-heart surgery, turns her world in upon itself and culminates in a celebration of life.

Teixeira is an important member of a movement that included Charles Young and Robert Thompson and that broadened the scope of expressionist experimentation in figurative painting. Her body of work, spanning almost half a century, expresses the dynamics of humanity.

—Joanne Harris

N'DIAYE, Iba

Senegalese painter

Born: Saint Louis, Senegal, 1928. **Education:** École des Beaux-Arts de Montpellier (architecture); École des Beaux-Arts de Paris (Atelier Pingusson); Académie de la Grande Chaumière (painting), Paris. **Career:** Founder, 1959, and head, until 1967, Plastic Arts Department, L'École Nationale des Arts, Senegal.

Individual Exhibitions:

1962	Maison des Artes, Dakar
1970	Annual Festival, Sarlat, Ancien Eveche
1971	Maison des Arts et Loisirs
1972	*Festival du jazz,* Chateauvallon

1974   Maison de la Culture, Amiens
1975   Comite d'Etablissement de Renault, Sandouville
1976   Office Communal des Loisirs et de la Culture, Dugny
1977   Musée Dynamique, Dakar (retrospective)
1978   Palais des Arts et de la Culture, Brest
1979   Maison de la Culture, Vannes
1980   Galerie des Cheminées de Paris
        Spelman College, Atlanta, Georgia
        Maison de la Culture, Bobigny
1981   Galerie Artes, Oslo
        Galerie 39 et Centre Culturel Gaston-Berger, Dakar
1982   Centre Georges Pompidou, Paris
        Centre Culturel Paul Paillart, Massy
        Comité d'Enterprise du Journal, Paris
        Galerie Café Mozart, Salzburg (retrospective)
        Foundation Bawag, Vienna (retrospective)
        African American Institute, New York
1983   Kulturhauset, Stockholm
        Maison pour Tous, Elancourt
        National de Musique, Angouléme
        Centre Culture Gerard Philipe, Plessis
1984   Musée Municipal, Brive (retrospective)
        UNESCO, Paris
1986   Musée des Beaux-Arts, Saintes

Selected Group Exhibitions:

1962   Musée d'Art Moderne, Paris
1963   Betrand Russell Foundation, London
1966   Palais de Justice, Dakar
1969   Camden Art Center, London
1971   Musée Marmottan, Paris
1974   Musée Municipal, Stockholm
1978   Maison de la Culture André Malraux, Reims
1980   UNESCO, Paris
1983   Grand Palais, Paris
1985   Grande Halle de la Villette, Paris

Collections:

Africain Center, Oslo; Bibliotheque Nationale, Paris; Centre National d'Art Contemporain, Paris; Foundation Bawag, Vienne; Albert Gordon Gallery, New York; Morgan State University, Baltimore, Maryland; Musée d'Art Moderne de la Ville de Paris; Spelman College, Atlanta, Georgia; United African Corporation, London; University of Dakar.

Publications:

By N'DIAYE: Article—"A propos des arts plastiques dans l'Afrique Contemporaine," in *Cathiers de la Maison de la Culture de Reims,* February 1978.

On N'DIAYE: Books—*L'Univers Passionné d'Iba N'Diaye,* exhibition catalog, Paris, International Art Organization, 1979; *Iba N'Diaye, Evolution of a Style,* exhibition catalog, New York, African American Institute and Lowery S. Sims, 1982; *The Double Vision of Iba N'Diaye* by J. Wilson, Department of Art and Architecture, Yale University, New Haven, Connecticut, 1983. **Articles**—"Iba N'Diaye, Peintre Senegalais, Chef de la Section Arts Plastiques a la Maison des Arts de Dakar" by C. O. Stern, in *Bingo* (Paris), June 1962; "Entretien Avec Iba N'Diaye" by C. Joliot, in *L'Afrique Litteraire et Artistique* (Paris), 1969; "Iba N'Diaye ou une Dynamique de la Lumiere" by J. Nothines, in *Express Afrique* (Bruxelles), 239, February 1972; "Iba N'Diaye" by C. Sokolsky, in *Jeune Afrique* (Paris), 805, June 1976; "Iba N'Diaye a Royan" by P. Paret, in *Sud Ouest* (Bordeaux), 23, March 1977; "Iba N'Diaye's Exhibition at the Musée Dynamique of Dakar" by C. Polakoff, in *African Arts* Los Angeles, 10(3), 1977, pp. 72-75; "Senegalese Artist Conveys Rhythms of Jazz in Paintings" by W. C. Burnett, in *The Atlanta Journal,* 24 September 1980; "African Touch" by R. F. Shepard, in *New York Times,* 15 March 1982. **Video**—"Entretien Avec Iba N'Diaye" produced by R. J. Moulin, International Art Organization, Paris, 1980.

*   *   *

Iba N'Diaye produces sonorous compositions that are structured by painterly, improvisational surfaces and emotional content. Though his oeuvre is often laden with a critique of human existence, it also includes abstract formats of French informalism that excite the contemplative imagination. Whether representational or abstract, the paintings reveal a consistency in their flat structures, luminous color-contrasts, and muted atmospheric spatial qualities accentuated by spontaneous lines and variegated textures. N'Diaye's drawings, in their black-and-white contrast, similarly insist on a calculated spontaneity.

Since 1955, when N'Diaye studied fine arts at the Grand Chaumiere of Paris, he has maintained a colloquy on themes of existential freedom. His oeuvre consists primarily of figurative imagery that expressively depicts scenes of landscapes, jazz performances, animals of sacrifice, the Senegalese marketplace, transfigurations of classical European paintings and African sculpture, and human subjects of divergent temperaments. The figures are not delineated in a technique of objective realism but in conceptual two-dimensional representation consisting of planar contours, polyrhythmic lines, and poetic atmospheric spaces that effect an evocative mood. N'Diaye's signature style interlaces figuration and abstraction in a harmonious blend of structural and gestural qualities. Its command of line and structure suggests the artist's architectural background (École Nationale des Beaux-Arts), and its improvisational rhythms and schematic contrasts evince an emotional automatism coherent with the artist's individualism. In general, N'Diaye's dramatic, representational style displays his resolution of a structural-spontaneous dialectic derived from his inventiveness and deep introspection.

N'Diaye's style evolved through a number of influences, including the artist's persistent questioning of human existence, his critical eye on European "masterpieces," his recognition of the pure plasticity of African art, and the insight derived from the personal experience of traveling, sketching, listening to jazz, and consciously negotiating human freedom. In the artistic community of La Ruche, where N'Diaye lived periodically when he first arrived in Paris from Senegal (his birthplace) in 1948, the artist was stimulated by the cosmopolitanism and intellectual/artistic life. Within that Parisian scene, N'Diaye's imagination engaged the philosophical discourse of Jean-Paul Sartre's existentialism, the styles of the Jeune Peintures of La Ruche, the creative tenor of jazz overlaid by the discourse of jazz musicians, the international exchanges of French, Cuban, Japanese, and other artists, the literary and philosophical thought of Negritude, colonial and anticolonial discourse, the dialectics of Negritude and creative expression as discussed at the Congress of African Writers and Artists of Paris-Sorbonne (1955) and Rome (1959).

The early foundation of N'Diaye's study of painting and sculpture included many visits to the Louvre, where he encountered and sketched paintings of Goya, Rembrandt, Valesquez, and other European masters. Paintings such as *Juan de Pereja agressé par les chiens* (Juan de Pereja Attacked by Dogs, 1985-86), *Femmes a la Fontaine, hommage a Poussin* (Women at the Fountain, Homage to Poussin, 1979), and *Dessin d'apres Picasso* (Design after Picasso, 1985) are a few of the works that are set up a dialogue with those masterpieces of modernism. The first of the three works politically speaks to Valesquez's portrait of Juan de Pereja (Valesquez's slave), adhering to a diffused painterly surface with evocative mysterious effect. The latter two works improvise on the works of Poussin (painting) and Picasso (drawing); the former displays a raw unfinished linear spontaneity and the latter, a geometric parody. N'Diaye extends this interest into African art, producing works such as *Pilier anthropomorphe Dogon* (Dogon Anthropomorphic Pillar, 1980), *Tete Bamoun* (Bamoun Head, 1982), and *La Femme-anteloppe* (The Antelope Woman, 1986).

Paintings and drawings such as *Big Band* (1984-85), *Blues a Manhattan* (Blues in Manhattan, 1984), *Le Trompettiste* (The Trumpet Player, 1986), and *Homage a Bessie Smith* (Homage to Bessie Smith, 1986) emerged from the artist's love of jazz. N'Diaye has said that "jazz doesn't have just a musical value for me: it has always been an aspect of the struggle that the blacks were leading in the U.S.A. against racism. I am sensitive to all problems of oppression and more especially to those in Africa. I consider that it is my duty." This didactic quality within aesthetic form critically signifies N'Diaye' orientation. It appears consistently over the years in works that engage the problem of colonialism, slavery, and various forms of oppression. *Soweto* (1979) is a singular composition, oil on canvas, that dramatically depicts the "bloody" horror of life under the firm power of apartheid. The subjects of oppression are graphically delineated in repetitive drippings, contained within swift regimented brush strokes in the lower half of the composition, below a ghostly impression of an invisible human power.

"Le Cri d'un Continent" (The Shout/Cry of a Continent), an oil on canvas series dated 1982-86, displays the artist's inventiveness in the dynamic reversal of space and form. The warm sienna-and-white high contrast schema, balanced by complementary, transparent green and red tonalities and spontaneous dark, contrasting lines, reveals traces of a Rembrandtesque glow. Like many of his works, it addresses the problematic history of domination that plagued his ancestors on the African continent. The painting addresses the futility of slavery and the divisiveness of racism. Stylistically, its gestural quality recalls the drama of Goya and the expressionist qualities of the Jeune Peintures and European informalists .

As N'Diaye paved a way through the currents of modernism and colonialism, he reinvented his life, constructing an individualism with which he could take control of his thought, life, and creative production. With a free imagination, he rejected exotica and chose from an international vocabulary, the essential in artistic expression, translating expressive dribbles, restrained yet sonorous color, and muted scumbling, into intense emotional design and subject matter that resonates in existential consciousness.

—Freida High

NEFERTITI
American printmaker

Born: Cynthia Freeman, Albany, New York, 1949. **Education:** Massachusetts College of Art, B.F.A. 1974; Rhode Island School of Design, M.F.A. 1977. **Awards:** First Prize, Catskill Art Society, Monticello, New York, 1973; First Prize, City Art Festival, Boston.

Individual Exhibition:

1974   Overland Gallery, Boston

Selected Group Exhibitions:

1972   Empire State Invitational Exhibition, Albany
1973   Roger Williams College, Providence, Rhode Island
        Catskill Art Society, Monticello, New York
1974   State Street Bank, Boston
        Museum of Fine Arts, Boston
1975   Regis College, Weston, Massachusetts
        Mabel Colgate Gallery, Cambridge Art Association, Massachusetts
        Jubilee: Afro-American Artists on Afro-America, Museum of Fine Arts, Boston, and Museum of the National Center of Afro-American Artists
        Boston Symphony Hall
1976   Nasrudin Gallery, Boston
        Smith-Mason Gallery, Washington, D.C.
        El Museo de Arte Moderno, La Fertulia, Colombia

*   *   *

Nefertiti, who was born Cynthia Freeman, studied at the Rhode Island School of Design in Providence and at the Massachusetts College of Art. She then taught at the Elma Lewis School of Fine Arts before leaving Boston for Nutley, New Jersey. She received a fellowship in printmaking from the New Jersey State Council on the Arts and has had commissions from the Philadelphia Percent for the Arts Program. She is widely regarded as one of the foremost printmakers working in the United States.

Nefertiti has distinguished herself for her exquisitely produced relief prints that use highly decorative patterning. In her work *Radiant Heliconia,* for example, she formed the essential elements by establishing the image and composition through a dense network of black lines arranged in careful patterns. She used solid black forms to create the shapes of the central image of a potted plant, thus resolving the design order of the pictorial surface. She then enlivened the print with the addition of a few carefully chosen colors—blue, red, yellow, and purple—and by exploiting the white ground of the paper. She created a repeating pattern of blue triangles along the vertical axis, offsetting their regularity with three bright red and yellow irregularly placed blossoms and with three somewhat fluid tall leaves with an inner fringe of purple.

This approach to printmaking is recurrent in Nefertiti's work. She uses her imaginative and technical powers to produce magnificent large-scale color relief prints.

—Edmund Barry Gaither

Nefertiti: *Getting Fixed to Look Pretty,* **1978. Photo by Manu Sassoonian; courtesy of the Schomburg Center for Research in Black Culture.**

NENGUDI, Senga

American sculptor, installation artist, and performance artist

Work also appeared under the name Senga Nengudi Fittz. **Born:** Sue Ellen Irons, Chicago, 18 September 1943. **Education:** Pasadena City College; California State University at Los Angeles, 1962-66, B.A. 1966; Waseda University, Tokyo, 1966-67; California State University at Los Angeles, 1969-71, M.A. in sculpture 1971. **Family:** Married Elliout Fittz in 1975, two sons. **Career:** Arts programs coordinator/developer, Friendship Day Camp, Los Angeles, Children's Art Carnival, New York, Community School, Los Angeles, Fairburn Elementary School (self-employed), Los Angeles. Since 1991 self-employed cultural program developer/arts program coordinator, Colorado Springs, Colorado. **Agent:** Thomas Erben Gallery, 476 Broome Street, New York, New York 10013, U.S.A.

Individual Exhibitions:

1971	California State University at Los Angeles
1977	Woods Gallery, Los Angeles
	Just above Midtown Gallery, New York
1978	Woods Gallery, Los Angeles
1981	Just above Midtown Gallery, New York
1996	Thomas Erben Gallery, New York

Selected Group Exhibitions:

1971	Musée Rath, Geneva, Switzerland
1977	Just above Midtown Gallery, New York
1978	Just above Midtown Gallery, New York
1980	Bronx Museum of the Arts, New York
	A.I.R. Gallery, New York
1984	Everson Museum of Art, Syracuse, New York
1989	Studio Museum in Harlem, New York
1990	Capp Street Project, San Francisco
1993	Artists Space, New York
1996	Louisiana Museum of Modern Art, Humlebaek, Denmark

Publication:

On NENGUDI: Article—"The Unseen, Inside Out: The Life and Art of Senga Nengudi" by Donald Odita (New York), Thomas Erben Gallery, New York, 1996.

*

Senga Nengudi comments:
CRYING ACROSS THE
WAVES
I SEE MY SIGHT
COMING AT ME
DESPERATE TO SEEK
THE TRUTH
I BRACE MYSELF FOR
THE EMBRACE

HEAD BACK AND HIGH
I HOWL AT THE MOON

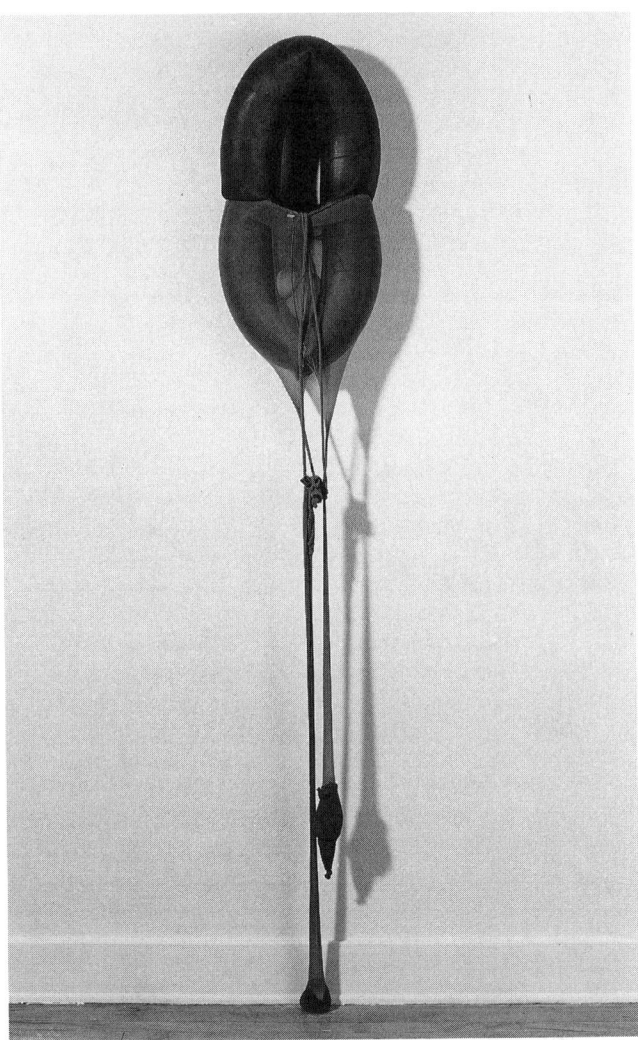

Senga Nengudi: *R.S.V.P. XI,* 1977. Photo courtesy of Thomas Erben Gallery, New York.

THE JOURNEY BACK TO
YOU
IS LONG AND TRICKY
MUD COATS MY FEET
THE MORNING TIDE
WASHES THEM CLEAN
DELIGHTED I MOVE
QUICKLY ON
LOOKING BACK OVER
MY SHOULDER LESS AND
LESS

THE NOON-DAY SUN
DRIES MY FEET
I GO FORWARD
GATHERING FLOWERS
AND SUNBEAMS
ALONG THE WAY
I ENTHUSIASTICALLY
EMBRACE THE MOMENT
IMPOSSIBLE TO HOLD
I LET IT GO

Senga Nengudi: *Rapunzel,* **1980. Photo courtesy of Thomas Erben Gallery, New York.**

AND REMEMBER IT IN
SONG AND DANCE

I GO FORWARD
LETTING THE AIR
I PENETRATE
CARESS MY FACE—MY
LIPS, MY BROW
I BREATHE DEEPLY
I EXHALE
I GO ON

*   *   *

The aesthetic pursuits of Senga Nengudi (Sue Irons) chronicle her life experiences. She was introduced to performance art and happenings in the 1960s during her studies in art and dance at Pasadena City College and California State University. The work of Allan Kaprow, Claes Oldenberg, and Jim Dine served as an impetus for her subsequent explorations in synthesizing movement with visual concepts. Nengudi spent 1966 in Japan studying Gutai, a movement whose genesis paralleled abstract expressionism in the United States. The Japanese movement was a process-based art form in which activities and performances often resulted in the creation of paintings and residual artifacts. The events were usually staged in the open in rural areas. The contextualization of process and spirit captured in this approach to making art expanded on aesthetic qualities deeply established in Japanese traditions. Nengudi's immersion in Japanese culture and aesthetic movements was pivotal in shaping the sensibilities that have come to permeate her work.

In 1971 Nengudi became associated with the Weusi-Nyumba Ya Sanaa Academy of Fine Arts Studies and the Studio Museum in Harlem. It was in this environment that Nengudi identified formal and informal relationships between African and Asian cultures. Her cross-cultural analyses fostered the recognition of similarities among diverse cultural groups that approached life through holistic modalities. Her conclusion was that art and life are integrally intertwined.

During the 1970s Nengudi used discarded materials, accepting their transient qualities without transforming or distorting their meaning. Rather than isolating found materials, like the contextualists she tried to infuse her works with an understanding of their original functions or ephemeral properties. She shared with the minimalists a concern with perceptual and experiential conditions beyond formal essence and the confines of categories. Her concerns were broader, however, for she was also interested in process and materials and in anthropomorphic and metaphysical terms. She finds joy in using materials such as nylon, mesh, sand, dirt, wood, lint, and paper. Her choice of material is often based on emotional and psychological states.

Never interested in realism, Nengudi moved comfortably from performance-based works in the late 1960s to highly abstract explorations with anthropomorphic associations and then to the body itself as subject. Her constructions of stretched and contorted multihued nylons, for example, were derived from their resilient and elastic capacity. While Nengudi allowed the natural properties of the stockings to define the form, she used sand to weigh down certain areas, formulating pockets to suggest flesh and genitalia. She has stretched flexible materials taut along various axes to articulate linear architectonic spatial relationships. Her environmental works allude to the transitory qualities of nomads' abodes. Pieces of strategically draped fabric, affected by the slightest circulation of air,

hover in space, while the properties of materials used in her rooms of piled wood and stacked papers effectively convey the transcendence of the temporal. A construction of wooden slates is reminiscent of the unstable dwellings found in Harlem and many other areas and serves as a metaphor for surviving against all odds.

Nengudi's experiences as a woman inform her works and foster a feminist aesthetic as she synthesizes art and politics. Her interpretation of descending, pendulous, and bulbous forms, for example, not only refers to her instinct to nurture, experienced through the breast feeding of her son, but also to the servitude and exploitation of black wet nurses. Suckling child after child exhausted the energies and life forces of these women, leaving them disfigured and worn. Nengudi's associations thus extend from the personal to sociopolitical implications and embrace many concerns addressed in feminist art criticism. Her ideas, however, do not comfortably fit all of the categories delineated within its discourse. Hers is a transcendent aesthetic, with the female body existing in an expanded field. She implies an activist posture, documenting and at the same time challenging the prevailing attitudes toward being female within a patriarchal society.

Nengudi captures the sensual and the ephemeral in her work. Subtle color combinations enhance these qualities. She possesses a quiet poetic vision that taps into the multiple areas of the feminine psyche and beyond. Her resolve emanates from a quest for the spiritual in art, transcending the empirical to reach enlightened dimensions of consciousness.

—A. M. Weaver

NGWENYA, Valente Malangatana
Mozambican painter

Born: Matalana, Marracuene, Mozambique, 6 June 1936. **Education:** Swiss Mission School of Matalana, 1945-47; Catholic Mission Ntsindya, graduated 1948; Art Nucleus, 1958. **Career:** Basket weaver, servant. Since 1960 professional painter. Refused to allow his art to be shown in South Africa following the arrest of Nelson Mandela, 1963. Refused participation in *Bienal*, São Paulo, 1962. Imprisoned for eighteen months for suspected alliance with FRELIMO, 1965-67. Organizer, Festival de Arte de Matalana, 1968. Travels in Europe, 1973-74. Mobilizer, Labor Institute, 1973-74. Curator, Galeria de Artesanato (National Museum of Art), 1977. Established colonial villages throughout Mozambique. Director, Department of Art, Maputo, 1980-85. **Awards:** Honorable mention for *Woman in the City*, Concurso de Artes Plasticas de Mozambique, 1959; Painting Prize for *Humanity*, Commemorative of Lorenco Marques, 1962; Second Prize for *Last Supper,* Commemorative of Lorenco Marquese; Silver Medal, Tomase Campanella Academy of Art, 1970; Gulbenkian Foundation Scholarship, Portugal, 1971; guest artist designation, Artists Against Apartheid, das Nacoes Unidas, 1982; guest artist designation, Jury of Annual National Art, Zimbabwe, 1985.

Individual Exhibitions:

1961   Lourenco Marques, Mozambique
1970   Lourenco Marques, Mozambique

Selected Group Exhibitions:

1959   Lourenco Marques, Mozambique
1972   Conferencia Dramatica Sobre o Lobolo
1977   Festival of Black and African Art, Nigeria

Collections:

Cabo Verde a Nigeria; Centro de Arte Moderna da Fundacao Gulbenkian; Mbari de Oshagbo, Nigeria; Museu de Arte Contemporanea de Lisboa; Museu Nacional de Arte de Mozambique; Musea Nacional de Luanda; National Art Gallery of Harare; National Gallery of Contemporary Art of New Delhi; Partido Comunista Portugues.

*   *   *

Valente Malangatana Ngwenya is recognized as the most notable Mozambican artist to date. Since the 1950s, when he began to draw and paint, his work has consistently projected his imagination in mystical forms imbued with harmonious colors that are evocative of symbolic emotional content. His paintings dramatically critique the daily trauma of colonial and postcolonial society, something Malangatana witnessed growing up in Mozambique during its domination by Portuguese colonialism. But rather than depicting the optical world, their subject matter implies the artist's inner experience and sensitivity to a materiality and spirituality that he negotiates.

The human figure is preeminent in Malangatana's compositions. It is not a figure that imitates nature but often multiple figures that represent mystical distortions and organic fragments, interspersed with fantastic animal motifs and symbolic patterns. They are images of the subconscious and conscious, shifting chiasmatically between the psychic experience of dreams and reality. He works intuitively and improvisationally, constructing recognizable imagery in flat, abstracted representation. Given the intuitive method and form, the compositions display affinity to the surrealists in their grotesque and fantastical qualities. But they differ significantly from the surrealism of Salvador Dali's irrational superreality or Paul Klee's automatism. Malangatana's paintings are expressive symbols that convey common experiences to those familiar with life and mythology in Mozambique.

The combination of human mask forms with birds, chameleons, and other abstracted animal motifs corresponds to the unity of human and animal forms in the Shetani carvings of northern Mozambique and Tanzania. Popular genre figures and animal spirits in those forms are sculpted to signify oral narratives pertaining to indigenous cosmologies. Icons of the forest, rivers, villages, and spirit world are interpreted in styles of naturalistic and highly abstract figures, evoking collective identity and power in the face of oppression. Ujaama style forms also correspond to those works but are more figurative and ideologically convey principles of social cooperation. They extend into liturgical Catholic symbols, recalling images seen during his youth in school and elsewhere.

Through the particular in Malangatana's paintings, one experiences the universal. Works such as *Mondhojo* (the medicine man) (1961), *Don't Strike Down Birds That Fly Free-Once They've Learnt to Spread Their Wings!* (1978), and *People's Struggle in the Context of Nature* (an external mural painted for the Natural History Museum) exhibit pervasive human themes such as healing, freedom, optimism, domination, rape, revolution, self-determination, work, identity, environment, etc.

Malangatana's paintings are clearly modernist given their flat surfaces, geometricized forms, and painterly qualities. His style is similar to that of Mankeu Mahumana, Samate, Agostino Mutemba, and other figurative artists who paint didactic themes in linear styles. Although Malangatana had no formal training, except fellowship study in Portugal in 1971 and travels in Europe during 1973-74, his informal training began as a young child when he began to draw from books. He essentially educated himself through studying, reading, and experimenting, and his work exhibits an academic maturity that comes with professional development.

In 1958 Malangatana joined the Nucleo de Art, an art association in Laurenco Marque (now Maputo). By 1960 a studio donated to him by "Pancho" Miranda Guedes, a Portuguese architect, facilitated his ability to work full-time on his paintings. In 1961, at his first one-man show, his paintings exhibited surreal figures delineated in heavy dark lines that contained flat areas of bold colors. This show marked his emergence as a professional artist. During the colonial period, his works, including *Violence, Madmen! Don't Touch Me,* and *In Spite of Everything There is Love Around Us* were overtly politically charged. The titles speak to a range of themes from anti-colonialism to familial bonding. As the struggle for independence intensified between 1974 and 1981, Malangatana did not paint. He engaged in divergent forms of struggle, including theater. He was also imprisoned for eighteen months; an event that had a profound impact on his way of seeing, living, and painting. It affected, for example, his decision about where he would exhibit. When Nelson Mandela was imprisoned at Robben Island, he refused to exhibit in South Africa. When Malangatana returned to painting, he painted larger compositions, in a more painterly style, and with an ambivalent surface that gave the illusion of both depth and flatness. Whereas the earlier paintings were stark contrast, the later paintings have more subtle gradations of color and greater variation in surface design. Dark areas of color are more pronounced, and forms show more variety in scale and proportion. Dark lines (brown and black) are also more variable and lyrical. The surfaces and individual figures are more organic and display greater detail within more complex compositions, though the linear style dominates.

Malangatana is often called an artist of revolution because of the political themes of his work. Involved in collective self-help developments, particularly for educational and economic opportunities in southern Mozambique where he was born, Malangatana engaged the passion of that involvement in his paintings. Among that generation of African artists who came of age during the 1960s, the decade of independence for many African countries, Malangatana was involved in Mozambique's political struggles even after independence in 1975.

His paintings deploy memories, nightmares, and a passion for human relief. Foreboding figures stare at each other and out at the audience, heightening the sense of drama with their directional movement. The crowded surreal scenes produce the psychological effect of pain and anguish under forced crowded conditions that are perhaps not unlike the South African mines to which his father and many other Mozambicans were forced to work. There are also allusions to mystical powers, not only in animal and mask motifs but also in curvilinear and spherical, cosmological forms that vibrate in light and dark contrasts. His drawings have changed, too, displaying an elegiac quality. He was familiar with cultural practices of witch-herbalism and indigenous beliefs derived from Ronga mythology, which was taught to him by his grandmother. That cultural continuum frames his evolution and has been seen in exhibitions of his works in many countries, including Nigeria, Portugal, Sweden, Norway, Bulgaria, Germany, Cuba, and Austria. Whether evoking a mood of folk tradition, revolution, or some abstract passion, Malangatana's paintings synthesize subconscious and conscious experiences to stimulate an emotional content that has a deep psychological effect on the viewer.

—Freida High

NORMAN, Joseph (E.)

American printmaker and painter

Born: Chicago, 9 March 1957. **Education:** Central State University, Wilberforce, Ohio, 1975; University of Arkansas, Fayetteville, 1976-79, 1980, B.S. 1980; University of Illinois, Urbana, 1985, M.A. 1985; University of Cincinnati, Ohio, 1986, M.F.A. 1986. **Career:** Lecturer/instructor, Cincinnati Arts Consortium, 1985-86, Museum School, Newport Art Museum, Rhode Island, 1986, Newport School of Department, Rhode Island, 1986-87, Salve Regina College, Newport, Rhode Island, 1987-88, Rhode Island College, Providence, 1987-89. Since 1991 instructor, Rhode Island School of Design, Providence. Program coordinator (Art in Public Places), Rhode Island State Council on the Arts, 1988-89. Visiting artist, University of Rhode Island, Kingston, 1989-91. **Awards:** Jurors Award, Newport Art Museum, 1989; Tamarind Institute Fellowship, 1993. **Agent:** Virginia Lynch, Virginia Lynch Gallery, 3883 Main Road, Route 77, Four Corners, Tiverton, Rhode Island 02878, U.S.A. **Address:** 1151 Aquidneck Avenue, Suite 426, Middletown, Rhode Island 02840, U.S.A.

Individual Exhibitions:

1988	Virginia Lynch Gallery, Tiverton, Rhode Island
	DeBlois Street Gallery, Newport, Rhode Island
1989	University of Rhode Island, Kingston
	Museum/National Center of Afro-American Artists, Boston
1990	DeBlois Street Gallery, Newport, Rhode Island
1991	Harrington Galleries, Vancouver, British Columbia
	Hunt-Cavanaugh Gallery, Providence, Rhode Island
1992	Museum of Art, Rhode Island School of Design, Providence
	Museo de Art, San Jose, Costa Rica
	Art Chicago International, Harrington Galleries
	Virginia Lynch Gallery, Tiverton, Rhode Island
1993	Miller Gallery, Cincinnati, Ohio
	Virginia Lynch Gallery, Tiverton, Rhode Island
	DeBlois Gallery, Newport, Rhode Island
1995	Museum of Fine Arts, Boston
	Virginia Lynch Gallery, Tiverton, Rhode Island

Selected Group Exhibitions:

1992	*Biennial,* Rhode Island State Arts Council
	Warwick Museum, Warwick, Rhode Island

Joseph Norman: #3, "Dangerous Garden" series.

1993	Rose Art Museum, Waltham, Massachusetts
	World Gallery, South Beach Miami, Florida
	Tamarind Institute, Albuquerque, New Mexico
1994	University of Connecticut, Storrs
	National Museum of American Art, Washington, D.C.
	Museum of Art, Rhode Island School of Design, Providence
	David Winton Bell Gallery, Brown University, Providence
1995	National Museum of American Art, Washington, D.C.
	Miller Gallery, Cincinnati, Ohio

Collections:

Cincinnati Art Museum; David Winton Bell Gallery, Brown University, Providence, Rhode Island; Museum and National Center of Afro-American Artists, Boston; Museum of Art, Rhode Island School of Design, Providence, Rhode Island; Museum of Fine Arts, Boston; Museum of Modern Art, New York; National Gallery of Art, Washington, D.C.; National Museum of American Art, Smithsonian Institution, Washington, D.C.; Newport Art Museum, Newport, Rhode Island; New York Public Library; Peat Marwick Main, Providence, Rhode Island.

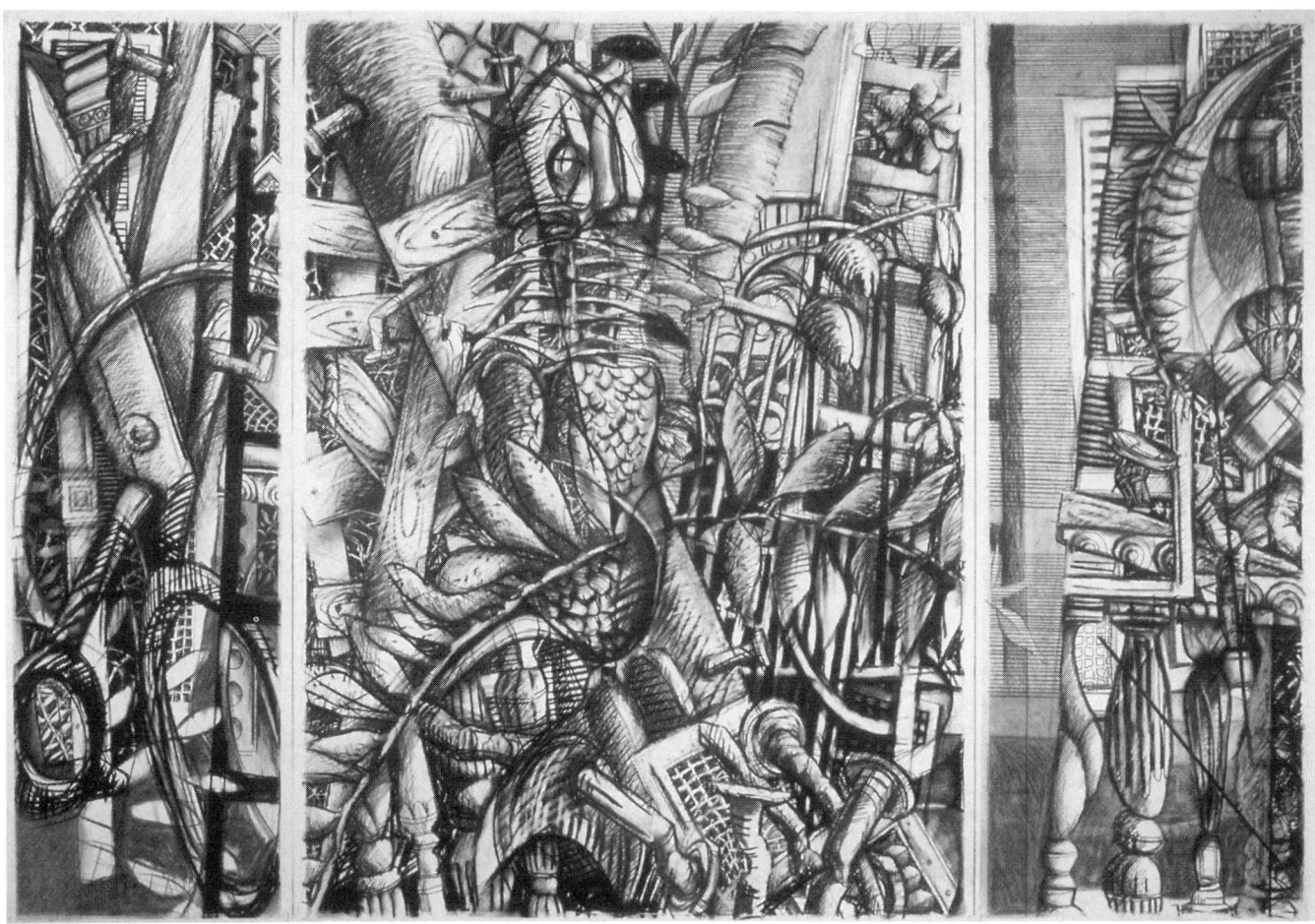

Joseph Norman: #4, "Dangerous Garden" series.

Publications:

On NORMAN: Books—*Joseph Norman: 39 Trey Nine Persian Rd Suite, Chicago,* exhibition catalog, by Deborah Johnson, Newport, Rhode Island, DeBlois Gallery, 1989; *Joseph Norman—"Monologue" Paintings, Drawings, Prints on Paper: 1984-1989,* exhibition catalog, by Deborah Johnson and John Pantalone, Boston, Museum of the National Center for Afro-American Artists, 1989; *Slum Fantasies: Latin American Portfolio Drawings and Prints,* exhibition catalog, by Deborah Johnson, Providence, Rhode Island, Hunt-Cavanaugh Gallery, 1991; *Joseph Norman: Reality. Fantasy. Dream. Nightmare,* exhibition catalog by Deborah Johnson, Vancouver, British Columbia, Harrington Galleries, 1992; *Joseph Norman: Works on Paper,* exhibition catalog, by Maureen C. O'Brien, Providence, Rhode Island School of Design, 1992; *Dialogue, John Wilson/Joseph Norman,* Boston, Museum of the National Center of Afro-American Artists and the Museum of Fine Arts, 1995. **Articles**—"Virginia Lynch Gallery/ Tiverton: Joseph Norman: Paintings, Lithographs, and Drawings" by John Pantalone, in *Art New England,* February 1989, p.29; "Directions: African American Artists Now" by John Pantalone, in *Art New England,* December/January 1990/91, p. 35; "Dialogue: John Wilson/ Joseph Norman" by Shelley Langdale, in *Preview: Museum of Fine Arts, Boston,* July/August 1995, p.3.

*

Norman Joseph comments:

Wherever I am, I am a Chicago artist, an inner-city cactus planted in a bed of daffodils with no illusions about ever being mistaken for a rose. Chicago's grand scale, its architecture, sights, sounds, the smells of its industry, its many different faces, both positive and negative—these are all things I carry with me, and so they inform my work no matter where I am. But I've also learned to let my experience of other places, such as my stays in Cost Rica and Spain, flow into the work, inflecting it with my memories of discoveries made in other countries. That's why, for example, tropical flora or forms inspired by Arabic calligraphy may appear admidst images that in other respects spring from my origins in Chicago.

Of course I have been influenced, too, by other artists. Some whose work I especially admire are Picasso, Matisse, Max Beckmann. I try to find something of each of them in myself. With Max Beckmann I love the way he composed with such great force. He had a very classical, stoic approach to things. I have a love for structure, drawing, and composition, therefore I love Beckmann. With Matisse I share a love for color, and I greatly respect the fearlessness with which he reworked his subjects, spinning variations on each single theme, something that is very important to me in my own work. And Picasso gives me hope because he is so versatile, his vision is so powerful and convincing. I like to think that the playfulness in my work is something I absorbed from him.

Within the scope of my major themes—portraiture and land-scape—I probe, mix, and experiment with my experiences of reality, fantasy, dream, and nightmare in ways that I hope ultimately transcend the personal to speak clearly and universally to the beholder.

*   *   *

Joseph Norman studied at Central State University and at the universities of Arkansas, Illinois, and Cincinnati. He did additional study at the Malespina Print Workshop in Vancouver, British Columbia, and at the Tamarind Institute in Albuquerque, New Mexico. While taking a respite from college, Norman worked as a technical illustrator for the U.S. Department of Defense. In 1991 he begin teaching at the Rhode Island School of Design in Providence.

Norman has used his travels to Costa Rica, Spain, Morocco, Italy, and France for inspiration in his drawings, paintings, and prints, although he has always counterbalanced such influences with memories of his early life in Chicago. Norman tends to create works in series, often exploring a theme exhaustively, as in his "Strange Fruit," "Invictus," and "Notorious" series. Almost without exception Norman's art is autobiographical. Series such as "Patty's Little White Lies" (1986) directly interpret events from his life, and other works, such as the "Trey Nine, Persian Road Suite" (1990), use a more allegorical approach to visualize and comment on the areas of Chicago in which he spent his childhood. Still other works, for example, the "Torch for Heather" series, are highly symbolic confessions based on his intimate life.

Norman's most compelling works are the drawings and lithographs in which he exhibits a total mastery of composition by using dark, sometimes brooding tonalities and silvery graphic strokes on densely rendered grounds. Whether in diptych or triptych format, his large-scale graphic works attain dramatic expressive power, and

they have brought him wide critical attention as a draftsman and printmaker. A number of influences are evident in Norman's work, reflecting his interest in Pablo Picasso, Philip Guston, Max Beckmann, and midcentury surrealists.

—Edmund Barry Gaither

NOUR, Amir (I. M.)
Sudanese sculptor

Born: Shendi, Sudan, 1939. **Education:** Khartoum School of Fine Art; Slade School of Fine Arts, London University; Royal College of Art; Yale School of Art and Architecture, B.F.A. and M.F.A. (late 1960s). **Career:** Head, department of sculpture, School of Fine and Applied Arts, Khartoum, 1963-65; associate professor of art, Truman College, Chicago. Speaker, International Sculpture Conference, Washington, D.C., 1980. **Awards:** Prize for *Ancestor, African Arts Magazine,* 1968; New Haven Festival of Art Prize, 1969.

Individual Exhibitions:

African-American Institute, New York; Carnegie Museum of Art, Pittsburgh; International Monetary Fund (IMF), Washington, D.C.

Collections:

Fisk University, Nashville; Morocco Ministry of Culture; Smithsonian Institution, Washington, D.C.

Amir Nour: *Calabash 4,* **1983.**

Amir Nour: *Expanded Gourd,* 1991.

Publications:

On NOUR: Book—*New Currents, Ancient Rivers: Contemporary African Artists in a Generation of Change* by Jean Kennedy, Smithsonian Institution Press, Washington, D.C., 1992. **Articles**—"Sculpture Reviewed," in *African Arts Magazine,* Autumn 1974, p. 61; interview, in *Africa Report,* 20(3), May/June 1974; "Sculpture Review," in *Pittsburgh Press,* 22 April 1976; "Sculpture Review," in *Post-Gazette,* 5 May 1976; article, in *Arts in Illinois,* September/October, 1978; "The Making of the Modern Sudanese Art Movement" by Salah Hassan and Acha Debela, in *Seven Stories about Modern Art in Africa,* Whitechapel and Flammarion, London and New York, 1995.

*

Amir Nour comments:

In my hometown . . . all the houses had doors and windows painted green—all except one house. It was painted red—sort of an earthy crimson color—and I always admired that house. I can't tell you why, but I always thought I would buy it when I grew up and became a man. There was a very old man standing in front of the house. I used to dream about the shadows of that house. I used to love the fact that it had a veranda with an arch and this tree next to it.

Well, getting up early in the morning and seeing people at dawn going to the mosque . . . . There's some mysterious quality about that. And also when you go to the river at night, you see the moonlight and you hear the silence of the place. There's nothing but insects and frogs and the sound of waterwheels turning. That kind of atmosphere sticks with you.

(From *New Currents, Ancient Rivers* by Jean Kennedy, Washington and London, Smithsonian Institution Press, 1992.)

*   *   *

Amir Nour is a Sudanese-born, Chicago-based sculptor who employs a variety of media, including bronze, stainless steel, cement fondu, plaster, wood, and molded plastic. His sculpture reflects his ability to integrate techniques, forms, and ideas drawn from his dual experience as an African living in the West. Nour asserts that the artist should feel free to employ whatever is available to him to make his aesthetic statement. This attitude is a reflection of his long journey of training and work from his home country into Western centers of modernism.

Born in the historic city of Shendi, Nour studied at the Khartoum School of Fine Art in the late 1950s, then at the Slade School and Royal College of Art in London, and, finally, at the Yale University School of Art and Architecture, where he graduated with B.A. and M.F.A. degrees in the late 1960s. His training introduced him to the different media of painting, printmaking, and sculpture, but he has focused his efforts for the past two decades on sculpture. From 1963 to 1965 he taught and served as the head of the department of sculpture at the College of Fine and Applied Arts in Khartoum, one of the most active centers of modern African art. He has lived in Chicago since 1974, and he is now an associate professor of art at Truman College.

To the uncritical eye Nour's work may appear nonfigurative and highly abstract. Yet it consists of geometric forms drawn from the images of his childhood in the Sudan. These images—including domes and arches, cattle horns, calabashes, and sand hills—are all part of the landscape of his homeland and have become part of his aesthetic concern. The forms are recognizable in Nour's work, especially if one is familiar with the architecture of northern Sudan. The form of his sculpture *House,* for example, is derived directly from that of adobe architecture. In other works the shapes are more formalized and highly abstracted. Such is the case with Nour's masterpiece, *Grazing at Shendi,* a stainless steel sculpture that is composed of 202 semicircles of varying sizes. The piece was inspired by childhood memories of watching goats grazing on the outskirts of his hometown. Nour's arrangement of the repetitive units suggests the sloping hills and the animals' backs, and the variations in their sizes suggest a sense of distance. The polished surfaces of the units reflect Nour's concern with light in relation to form.

One dominant object in Nour's work has been that of the calabash, or gourd, which he has abstracted to simple hemi-spheres. Examples of such works are *Expanded Gourd* and *Split Gourd,* which were inspired by his watching calabash artisans in village marketplaces "shining their domed-shaped gourds with animal fat." Domes and spheres are also visible in works showing mosques and shrines of Muslim saints. Nour also uses strong geometric forms molded in the cubist style and easily recognizable in African sculpture, as, for example, in the sculpture *Melancholy Portrait.*

Nour's sculpture has been exhibited internationally and in the United States. He has held several one-man shows at the African-American Institute in New York City, at the Carnegie Museum of Art in Pittsburgh, Pennsylvania, and at the headquarters of the International Monetary Fund in Washington, D.C. Nour has won several awards, among them the 1968 *African Arts* magazine prize for graphic and plastic arts for his sculpture *Ancestor* and the New Haven (Connecticut) Festival of Art prize in 1969. His work is included in several museums and private collections, among them the Smithsonian Institution, Fisk University, and the Moroccan Ministry of Culture. In 1983 Nour completed a large commissioned sculpture, *Calabash 4,* under Chicago's Percent-for-Art Program. Composed of five cold-rolled steel hemispheres, *Calabash 4* is installed in a public square next to the police station for the city's Fourth District. Nour has recently completed a concrete sculpture for Asilah, Morocco, commissioned by UNESCO and the Moroccan Ministry of Culture.

—Salah Hassan

OBIN, Philomé
Haitian painter

Born: Leimbe, Haiti, 1892. **Career:** Barber; coffee bean trader; clerk, city of Cap Haitien finance department. Organized and directed Branche Capoise, Centre d'Art, Cap Hatien, Haiti, beginning c1944. **Died:** 6 August 1986.

Collections:

Cathédrale de la Sainte Trinité, Port-au-Prince; Davenport Museum of Art, Iowa; Museum of Modern Art, New York.

Publications:

On OBIN: Book—*The Miracle of Haitian Art,* 1974. **Articles**—"Philomé Obin" by Michel Philippe Lerebours, in *Haiti et ses*

Philomé Obin: *U.S. Marines versus the Cacos,* 1949. Photo courtesy of Davenport Museum of Art.

Peintres, Volume I; "Hector Hyppolite and Philomé Obin," in *Haitian Painting: Art and Kitsch* by Eva Pataki, Chicago, Adams Press, 1986; "Philomé Obin: From Popular Realism to Abstraction," in *Where Art Is Joy* by Selden Rodman, Ruggles de Latour, New York, 1988.

* * *

As the founder of the Cap Haitien school of history painting, Philomé Obin is a figure of central importance in twentieth-century Haitian art. Although Obin painted in the early part of the twentieth century, his art flourished at midcentury, around the time of the founding of the Centre d'Art in Port-au-Prince. Established by the American DeWitt Peters, the Centre d'Art provided a communal meeting place for artists and a venue for exhibiting and selling works and for obtaining supplies. Obin received encouragement from Peters, but he then established his own branch of the Centre d'Art in the northern city of Cap Haitien, the region where Haiti's revolutionary war against France began. It may have been this connection with the history of Haiti, the first independent black nation in the Western Hemisphere, that led Obin to concentrate on political subjects in a seemingly objective, documentary style.

In contrast to Hector Hyppolite, his illustrious contemporary working in Port-au-Prince whose voodoo-inspired scenes were painted with brilliant spontaneity, Obin painted secular scenes with calculated clarity. His subjects were frequently related to Haiti's ongoing struggle for independence, and he focused mostly on events that occurred during his lifetime. Although his subjects were emotionally charged, Obin attempted to be objective and typically recounted the specific event portrayed in a brief caption at the bottom of the painting, adding to the journalistic approach. Yet in a letter to Peters the artist elucidated a higher purpose for art: "As I see it, painting should be considered in part like the Holy Book . . . with paint one can have documents for future generations that writing alone would not provide."

Obin's figurative scenes can be quite complex, with a tendency toward geometric reduction that borders on abstraction. His painting *U.S. Marines versus the Cacos* (1949) depicts one of the many skirmishes between Haitian resistance fighters and the U.S. Marines during their nineteen-year occupation of the country from 1915 to 1934. The central stage of the scene is a dirt road rendered as a flat tan area that divides the composition and recedes into space. Columnar trees with meticulously rendered decorative leaves line the sides of the road and serve as a screen for the mountainous landscape. The carefully composed scene is divided into areas of broad planes that are unified with finely painted decorative elements. The guerrilla (*caco*) fighters are shown defeating the Marines, and the particular unit of guerrillas, place, and date (September 1915) are recorded at the bottom of the painting.

On at least one occasion Obin worked from a photograph to record an important episode of Haitian history. The event was the slaying of Charlamegne Perrault, a *caco* leader, by the U.S. Marines. In an effort to document the event and deter further resistance, the Marines tied the slain leader to a door and photographed him, circulating the image throughout the countryside. Perrault's martyrdom was assured, and his Christlike pose in the photograph served as the starting point for Obin's portraits, which he created in two versions. With simplified planes of color and spare means, Obin rendered the leader with subtle pathos in one of his most popular paintings.

Obin's style of history painting would become widely practiced in Cap Haitien and elsewhere in the country. His brother Seneque and his sons, grandsons, and nephews, in addition to other followers, continue to paint scenes of Haitian history in Obin's precise, geometrically mannered style. Unlike Obin, however, many of his followers depict revolutionary subjects from the early nineteenth century. And although he is widely emulated, virtually none of his followers possess Obin's intuitive sophistication of design, august purpose, and understated poignancy.

—Brady Roberts

OKEKE, C(hristopher) Uche(funa)
Nigerian illustrator, painter, and sculptor

Born: Nimo, Anambra State, Nigeria, 30 April 1933. **Education:** Correspondence course in taxidermy, Omaha, Nebraska; Nigerian College of Arts, Science and Technology, Zaria, diploma in fine arts (painting), 1961; University of Ibadan, 1959, (seminar on West African religion); studied stained glass and mosaic techniques, Munich, Germany, 1962-63. **Family:** Married Eunice Uche-Okeke. **Career:** Visual aids designer, St. Peter Claver College, College of Mary Immaculate, Kafanchan, 1954-55; organizing assistant, Jos Museum, Jos, 1956; Franz Mayer Company, Munich, 1962-63; director, Mbari Art Centre Workshop, Engugu, Nigeria, 1964-67; head, visual arts section, Refugee Affairs Committee, Aba and Umuahia, Nigeria, 1967-70; acting head, Department of Fine Arts, University of Nigeria, Nsukka, 1970-71; chair, cultural sector, Nigerian National UNESCO Commission, 1971-86; lecturer, various United States colleges and universities, 1974; head, Department of Fine and Applied Arts, University of Nigeria, Nsukka, 1976; dean, Faculty of Arts, University of Nigeria, Nsukka, 1979-81; director, Institute of African Studies, University of Nigeria, Nsukka, 1984. Visiting scholar, University of Minnesota, 1981-82; visiting lecturer, Department of Creative Arts, University of Port Harcourt, 1986-87. Founded Cultural Centre, Kafanchan, 1958 (now Asele Institute). Freelance artist, poet, playwright beginning 1961. Member, Arts Council of the African Studies Association, International Association of Artists, International Bibliophile Association, Paris, Society of Nigerian Artists. **Awards:** First Prize, Nigerian College of Arts, Science and Technology, 1957; First Prize, Esso Calendar Competition for Nigeria's Independence; Illustrator of the Year, Nigerian National Commission for UNESCO, 1971; certificate of honour, Society of Nigerian Artists, 1989.

Individual Exhibitions:

1956	*Life in Northern Nigeria,* Jos and Kaduna, Nigeria
1958	British Council, Kano, Nigeria
	Anglo-Nigerian Art Centre, Lagos
1962	Rott am Inn, Wasserburg, Germany
1963	Franz Mayer Company, Munich, Germany
1965	Geothe Institute, Lagos
	Hotel Presidential, Enugu, Nigeria
	British Council, Port Harcourt, Nigeria
1966	Mbari Gallery, Ibadan, Nigeria
1967	British Council, Enugu, Nigeria

1972   University of Nigeria, Nsukka
1978   Goethe Institute, Lagos
1982   African-American Center, Minneapolis, Minnesota
        Dolly Fitterman Gallery, Minneapolis, Minnesota
1983   Goethe Institute, Lagos

Selected Group Exhibitions:

1980   National Theatre, Lagos
1982   University of Nigeria, Nsukka
1983   Mintec Galleries, Port Harcourt, Nigeria
1984   *Evolution in Nigerian Art,* Lagos
1985   Kashim Ibrahim Library, Ahmadu Bellow University,
            Zaria, Nigeria
        Iwalewa-Haus, Beyreuth, Germany
        Silver Jubilee National Art Exhibition, National Theatre, Lagos
1988   Italian Cultural Institute, Lagos
1989   Asele Gallery, Nimo, Nigeria
1990   University of Nigeria, Nsukka

Collections:

African Studies Center, University of California, Los Angeles; Academie der Kunst, Berlin; Asele Institute, Nimo, Nigeria; Broadcasting House, Radio Nigeria, Kaduna; Gong Gallery, Lagos; Hampton University Museum, Hampton, Virginia; Iwalewa-Haus, Beyreuth, Germany; Lagos State Council for Arts and Culture; Lagos University Library, University of Lagos; National Gallery of Modern Art, Lagos; New Culture Studios, Ibadan; Ovuomaroro Gallery, Lagos; Staatliche Graphische Sammlung, Munich, Germany; State House, Enugu, Nigeria; University Gallery, University of Minnesota, Minneapolis.

Publications:

By OKEKE: Books—*Drawings by Uche Okeke,* Ibadan, Nigeria, Mbari (New African Artists Series, 1), 1961 (illustrated); *Tales of the Land of Death: Igbo Folk* Tales (New York), Zenith Books, Doubleday, 1971; *Natural Synthesis: Collected Notes 1959-1970,* Nimo, Nigeria, Asele Institute, n.d.; *A Retrospective Exhibition of Uche Okeke Drawing [sic] 1957-58* with Ego Uche-Okeke, Nsukka, Nigeria, Uche Okeke, 1978; *Art Culture of Anambra State: The Eri Inheritance,* Nimo, Nigeria, Asele Institute, 1985 (bibliography); *Uche Okeke, A Retrospective,* Minneapolis, Minnesota, The Gallery, 1982. **Articles**—"We Can Learn from Germany," in *Nigerian Outlook* (Enugu, Nigeria), 27 January 1964; "Ekeama" (dance drama), in *African Arts* (Los Angeles), 5(2), Winter 1972, pp. 50-51; "Igbo Drawing and Painting," in *Ufahamu* (Los Angeles), 6(2), 1976, pp. 76-115 (bibliography); "The Search for a Theoretical Basis for Contemporary Nigerian Art," in *Nigerian Journal of the Humanities* (Benin City, Nigeria), 1(1), 1977; "The Place of Art in the Traditional Culture of Nigeria," in *Ugo* (Enugu, Nigeria), 1, October-December 1977; "Igbo Art and Culture" (with C.U.V. Okechukwu), in *Nsukka Environment 1978* edited by G.E.K. Ofomata, Enugu, Nigeria, Fourth Dimension Press, 1978, pp. 307-14; "An Introduction to Contemporary Nigerian Art," in *New Culture* (Ibadan, Nigeria), 1(1), 14-23, November 1978 (illustrated); "African Traditions of Drawing," pp. 19-20 and "Compiling and Keeping Reference Materials," pp. 20-21, both in *Illustrating for Children,* Ibadan, Nigeria, Children's Literature Association of Nigeria, 1988.

On OKEKE: Books—*Uche Okeke Drawings and Prints, 1954-1972,* exhibition catalog, Nsukka, Nigeria, Institute of African Studies, University of Nigeria, 1972; *Art in Development: A Nigerian Perspective* edited by Uche Okeke, Nimo, Nigeria, Documentation Centre, Asele Institute; Minneapolis, Minnesota, African American Cultural Center, 1982. **Article**—"Artist Uche Okeke" by Emmanuel Umegakwe, in *Catholic Life* (Calabar, Nigeria), September 1967.

*   *   *

In a 1965 interview with the *Lagos Morning Post,* C. Uche Okeke admitted his frustration with the tourist/collector who expects African and Nigerian art to be a re-creation of art made by his predecessors. He said, "the world of the new artists is the great wide world, not the narrow world of his ancestors, peopled as it were by mysterious beings, living and dead." Okeke describes an approach to the artist's past as one that "re-educat[es], to disabuse his mind of stories of the glories of Europe." Never able to reverse the effects of colonialism, perhaps the artist can reverse at least the perceived flow of influence. The work of many modern European masters such as Picasso was heavily influenced by African art, but it has sometimes been assumed by critics in Europe that the reverse was true. "In his quest for truth," said Okeke, "[the artist] has accepted the synthesis as a means of resolving the crisis—he must know his past, he must live in the present and face the future with confidence. . . . He employs new materials and techniques to express or interpret his African soul." Such a view seems to ignore the critics altogether, a seemingly healthy stance for any artist to take.

The world that Okeke depicts with modern techniques is the world of mythic stories of his Igbo people. In his book *Tales of Life and Death,* Okeke describes people "who grew roots where they should have had legs; some had no heads at all while others had as many as ten heads!" Okeke has done a great deal of research on traditional Igbo art forms, including wall and body decoration that his mother practiced. The lines of these traditional forms seem to travel directly into his drawings, taking the shape of flowing, almost grotesque figures. "The notion that spirits have fantastic forms," says Okeke, "is evident from the masks and the symbols of the nature spirits, or Alusi." Patterns in his drawings derive from the feathers, shells, and scales of supernatural beings, and their organic familiarity connects them to a world to which we're more accustomed.

Okeke says the tradition in his art is "a religion, a way of worship; it is a social system, a way of protecting or strengthening the moral code of a dynamic human group with common ancestry and destiny." The context of Okeke's art, the stories provided to him by his culture, is in the work itself, and his work, in turn, attempts to restore his Nigerian context in the world.

—Terry Bain

OLATUNDE, Asiru

Nigerian sculptor

Work also appears under the name Asiru. **Born:** Oshogbo, Oshun State, Nigeria, 1918. **Education:** Attended Oshogbo art workshops, Oshogbo, Nigeria. **Career:** First president, Oshogbo Artists As-

Asiru Olatunde. *Oshayko*. Photo by Dawoub Bey; courtesy of the Schomburg Center for Research in Black Culture.

sociation, 1967. **Address:** 38 Kajola Street, P.O. Box 247, Oshogbo, Oshun State, Nigeria.

Individual Exhibitions:

1964   Mbari Mbayo, Oshogbo, Nigeria
1967   Goethe Institute, Lagos
1975   Goethe Institute, Lagos
1976   Portfolio, Dusseldorf-Urdenbach, Germany
1981   Goethe Institute, Lagos

Selected Group Exhibitions:

1984   National Center of Afro-American Artists, Boston

1985   Städtische Galerie, Regensburg, Germany
        Myth and Image: An Exhibition of Works by 14 Nigerian Artists, Denton, Texas
1988   Aljira, Newark, New Jersey
1989   Zamana Gallery, London
1990   Kauffman Museum, Bethel College, North Newton, Kansas
        National Museum of African Art
        Onira Arts Africa, Ottawa
        National Museum, Lagos
        Africa Centre, London

Collections:

Cleveland State University, Afro-American Cultural Center, Ohio; Council House, Johnson Wax, Racine, Wisconsin; Iwalewa-Haus, Bayreuth, Germany; Mbari Art, Washington, D.C.; Studio Museum in Harlem, New York; Institute of African Studies, University of Ibadan, Nigeria.

Publications:

By OLATUNDE: Book—*Asiru, a New Yoruba Artist,* Oshogbo, Nigeria, Mbari Mbayo, 1965.

On OLATUNDE: Book—*The Art Society of the International Monetary Fund Presents Works by Asiru Olatunde, Bruce Onobrakpaya, Muraina Oyelami, September 19-October 19, 1972,* Washington, D.C., Art Society of the International Monetary Fund, 1972. **Articles**—"Nigerian Folk Art" by Ulli Beier, in *Nigeria* (Lagos), 75, December 1962, pp. 26-32; plates, in *Black Orpheus* (Ibadan, Nigeria), 16, October 1964, pp. 32-33; "Asiru Olatunde" by Ulli Beier, in *Modern Kunst i Africa: Modern Art in Africa* (Lund, Sweden), Kalejdoskop, 1978, p. 58; "Kuntu Sculpture from the 1950s to 1982," in *Perspectives in the Study of Nigerian Kuntu Art: A Traditionalist Style in Contemporary African Visual Expression* (Ph.D. dissertation, Ohio State University, 1985), Ann Arbor, Michigan, University Microfilms International, 1985, pp. 66-119 (see pp. 556-64 for interview); "A Betrayed and Neglected Pioneer Artist: Ashiru Olatunde" by Hakeem O. Shitta, in *Arts Illustrated Weekly* (Lagos), 37, 20-26 December, 1990.

*   *   *

Forced by ill health to abandon the blacksmith's trade for which he was originally trained, Asiru Olatunde began producing metal jewelry in the early 1960s to make ends meet. Shortly afterward, his artistic talents were discovered by the German art critic Ulli Beier and his former artist-wife, Susanne Wenger, who were then living in Nigeria and who encouraged him to create freestanding sculptures and decorative panels in copper and aluminum. Olatunde quickly mastered the technique of hammering designs and figures on sheet metal, and his conceptual style and compositions captured the pulse and spirit of Oshogbo, a Yoruba town unique for its admirable synthesis of African, Western, Islamic, and Christian values. The town has also produced other renowned contemporary Nigerian artists, including Twins Seven-Seven, Jimoh Buraimoh, Muraina Oyelami, Rufus Ogundele, Adebisi Fabunmi, Yinka Adeyemi, and Jacob Afolabi.

Olatunde's works are characterized by a simplification of form and disregard for human anatomy and mathematical perspective. He is wont to arrange forms across the picture plane, either in rows or one on top of the other, so that his compositions have a decorative and otherworldly aspect at the same time. In *Cocoa Picking* (1964), for example, a woman and her dog walk past two males harvesting cocoa pods from a tree. The composition is casual and vibrates with life, yet there is a certain uncanniness about the figures that suggests a reality different from the visible one. Olatunde often combines side and frontal views of the same figure, sometimes using size to denote importance. Thus, in *Homage to the King* (1962) the king (*oba*) is larger than his subjects. A fish motif dominates the panel titled *Ohsun River Legend* (n.d.), which refers to Ohsun, the tutelary river goddess of Oshogbo and the focus of the town's most important annual festival, which Olatunde also celebrates in many of his works. In a panel titled *Oba in Festival* (1981) the preeminence of the king in Yoruba society is indicated not only by size but also through a tripartite arrangement. The king, flanked by his wives, occupies the top register, emphasizing his position as the head of a given community. The middle register features a dancing and elaborately costumed priest of Shango (the Yoruba thunder deity) surrounded by attendants, while the bottom register shows a drummer in front of two dancers.

A majority of the figures in Olatunde's works stare blankly into space, ignoring the viewer and transforming the composition into an enigmatic sheet of silence. Some panels resonate with celebrations, with scenes of drummers, singers, and dancers inviting the viewer to participate in the joy of living. Apart from narrating the story or folktale that inspired a given panel, the artist rarely interprets his works, leaving the viewer to react to each scene in his or her own way. As he once told me, "Each panel is self-explanatory, because it is filled with figures and objects from our daily experience and imagination." Thus, in order to fully appreciate the artist's works, one must be aware of his background. One must understand the Yoruba religious and cultural traditions that inspired him as well as the social milieu of and the artistic metamorphosis taking place in Oshogbo.

—Babatunde Lawal

OLUGEBEFOLA, Ademola
American painter and printmaker

Work also appeared under the name Bedwick. **Born:** Bedwick Lyola Thomas, Charlotte Amalie, St. Thomas, U.S. Virgin Islands, 2 October 1941. **Education:** Fashion Institute of Technology, New York, 1958-59; African Theological Archministry, New York, 1966-67; Weusi Academy of Arts and Studies, Harlem, New York, 1968-76; Printmaking Workshop, New York, 1970-72. **Career:** Program coordinator, New York Urban Coalition, 1983-93. Since 1977 co-director, Grinnell Gallery, New York. Since 1983, vice president, Gumbs and Thomas Publishers, New York. Instructor, Wesleyan University, Middletown, Connecticut, 1970-72, City College of New York. **Awards:** Frederick Douglas Award, 1965; Lois Noel Award, 1974. **Agent:** Banks Enterprises, Triangle Fine Arts, International. **Address:** 800 Riverside Drive, #5e, New York, New York 10032, U.S.A. **Online Address:** http://www.harlem.nyc.ny.us.

Individual Exhibitions:

1979   Phoenix Gallery, Atlanta, Georgia
1981   Benin Gallery, New York

1982   Folk Art Gallery, Syracuse University, New York
1986   Claremont Resort, Oakland, California
1987   Harlem Renaissance Gallery, Soho, New York
1988   Grinnell Gallery, New York
1989   Design Master Intergroup Galleries, New York
1991   Edith Barrett Gallery, Syracuse University, Syracuse, New York
        Hamilton Hill Art Center, Schenectady, New York
        Fort Frederik Museum, Frederiksted, St. Croix, U.S. Virgin Islands (retrospective)
1994   873 Broadway Gallery, New York (retrospective)
        Yale University, New Haven, Connecticut

Selected Group Exhibitions:

1987   Museum of Art Archeology, University of Missouri, Columbus, Missouri
1988   Jamaica Art Center, Queens, New York
1989   Folk Art Gallery, Syracuse University, Syracuse, New York
1990   Westbeth Gallery, New York
        High Museum of Art, Atlanta, Georgia
1991   Virginia Museum of Fine Art, Richmond
        Bronx River Art Center Gallery, Bronx, New York

Ademola Olugebefola. Photo courtesy of Saffirah Rabb.

Ademola Olugebefola: *Gateway to Atlantis,* c.1976-78. Photo courtesy of Pat Davis.

1992	Weusi Academy Center for Art and Culture, Brooklyn, New York
1995	Center for Fine Arts, Miami (traveling)
1996	New Harlem Gallery, New York

Collections:

African American Museum, Dallas; Afro-American Cultural Center, Yale University, New Haven, Connecticut; Brandywine Gallery, Philadelphia; Banks Enterprise Collection, New York; DuSable Museum, Chicago; Grinnell Gallery, New York; Hatch Billops Gallery, New York; Howard University, Washington, D.C.; Library for the Performing Arts, New York; Museum of African American Art and History, Detroit; Museum of the National Center of African American Art, Boston; National Afro-American Museum and Cultural Center, Wilberforce, Ohio; Printmaking Workshop, New York; Schomburg Center, New York; Studio Museum in Harlem, New York.

Publications:

On OLUGEBEFOLA: Book—*Ademola Olugebefola: A Twenty-Five Year Legacy of Classics in American Art,* by Harold A. Thomas III (New York), Gumbs and Thomas, 1993.

*

Ademola Olugebefola comments:
My art is laying a foundation for future rituals which will begin to unite people. Also I hope that it is preparing the mind for some of the future directions that are going to be necessary for our people.

God has endowed me with the task to redefine, update, and reorganize ancient concepts and bring them into contemporary, modern realities.

*   *   *

The painter and printmaker Ademola Olugebefola believes that he is a conduit for the expression of ancestral power and metaphysical energy, that his mind and hands are but instruments of higher forces in the universe, and that the purpose of his art is to engage the human senses in the discovery of the oneness of humanity. Whether creating paintings or prints, Olugebefola is guided by his understanding of spiritual and metaphysical aspects of ancient Egyptian and African traditions. His work is an ongoing exploration and celebration of creativity, beauty, and the power of unity.

Born in the U.S. Virgin Islands, Olugebefola became a central figure of the Uptown New York arts scene in the late 1960s and a major figure in the black arts movement. His neo-African works of this period were compelling expressions of a new black aesthetic. Works such as *Shango* (1969) and *Emerging Spirit* (1970-71) not only celebrated an African heritage and traditional art but were also intended to evoke much of the same psychological engagement. The use of African symbolism, brilliant colors, and cowrie shells, inspired in part by the artist's Caribbean roots and by the rich mix of African and Caribbean peoples living in New York City, greatly influenced Olugebefola's imagery of the diaspora.

The very principles that direct Olugebefola's life as an artist led to his involvement and association with several community-based organizations. He is one of the founding members of Weusi, an important Harlem-based visual arts academy. Weusi, whose name means "black" or "blackness" in Swahili, was established in 1965. As an organization Weusi sought to preserve, develop, promote, and advance African and African American culture through the visual arts. Like other organizations of artists, such as Africobra, which was founded in Chicago during the same period, Weusi artists are committed to making their work available to ordinary people at affordable prices.

Writers and musicians such as Sonia Sanchez, Ed Bullins, and Amiri Baraka were early influences and figured substantially in Olugebefola's work in the theater. He served as resident designer and associate art director for the New Lafayette Theater and was a consultant on several projects for the National Black Theater. He is also a prolific graphic designer and printmaker as well as an illustrator, and he has the ability to use bold calligraphic lines to convey complicated themes in a highly simplified, stylized manner.

Olugebefola has received several commissions to produce cover designs and illustrations for prominent book publishers and authors, and he has been engaged to design promotional materials for a variety of cultural organizations and businesses.

Olugebefola studied at the Fashion Institute of Technology, the Printmaking Workshop, and the Weusi Academy of Arts and Studies. Weusi awarded him an honorary doctorate in 1970.

—Deirdre Bibby

OMARI RA
Jamaican painter

Work also appeared under the name African. **Born:** Robert Cookhorne, Kingston, Jamaica, 1960. **Education:** Jamaica School of Art (changed in 1987 to Edna Manley School for the Visual Arts), graduated 1983. **Career:** Instructor, Edna Manley School for the Visual Arts. **Awards:** Honorable mention, *Second Biennial of Caribbean and Central American Painting,* Santo Domingo, Dominican Republic, 1994.

Individual Exhibitions:

1985	Suti Galerie, Bern, Switzerland
1990	Suti Galerie, Bern, Switzerland
1994	Suti Galerie, Bern, Switzerland

Selected Group Exhibitions:

1983	*Annual National Exhibition,* National Gallery of Jamaica, Kingston (through 1994)
1985	*Young Talent '85,* National Gallery of Jamaica, Kingston
1986	*Caribbean Art Now,* Commonwealth Institute, London (traveling)
	Havana Biennale, Wifredo Lam Center, Cuba
1987	Mutual Life Gallery, Kingston, Jamaica
	O.A.S. Gallery, Washington, D.C.
1991	*Aspects III: Eight Jamaican Avant Garde Artists,* National Gallery of Jamaica, Kingston
1992	Espace Carpeaux, Courbevoie, France (traveling)
	Museum of Contemporary Art, Caracas, Venezuela
1994	*Biennial of Caribbean and Central American Painting,* Museum of Modern Art, Santo Domingo, Dominican Republic
	October Gallery, London
1995	*First Johannesburg Biennale,* Museum Africa, Johannesburg, South Africa

*   *   *

As a student the young Robert Cookhorne adopted the name African as a means of identifying with his black heritage. He later officially changed his name to Omari Ra, although he is still affectionately called African by many people who know him.

Omari Ra graduated from the Jamaica School of Art in the early 1980s and quickly established himself as a leading figure of the so-called neoexpressionists. This generation of young artists came to the fore in Jamaica in the mid-1980s. With artists like Douglas Wallace and Stanford Watson, Omari Ra developed a strident new imagery that spoke to issues of black consciousness, ghetto violence, and post- and neocolonialism without resorting to the social realism of the 1970s. For many in this group art was seen as the visual equivalent of the reggae and dance hall music that were an essential part of Jamaica's ghetto culture. In their formative years they drew inspiration from earlier Jamaican expressionists like Parboosingh and Milton George, as well as from contemporary international neoexpressionists such as Jean-Michel Basquiat, who because of his black Caribbean roots was particularly influential. The Jamaican painter and sculptor Osmond Watson, with his strong affirmation of self and of his blackness, has been a special source of inspiration.

A deliberate crudeness, reflecting the harsh ugliness of the urban ghetto where Omari Ra lives and where his works are created, has been a hallmark of his painting from the very beginning. An early series of aggressive masklike heads were drawn with oil pastels on brown torn paper bags taken from the refuse of the streets, while later canvases are unstretched with irregularly torn edges. The surfaces are also highly evocative of ghetto aesthetics, using caked raw soil and with an abundance of scratched, torn, and pitted surfaces. Yet all is essentially controlled by an aesthetic of spare, limited color.

The year 1987 was pivotal for Omari Ra. Although it had always been an important part of his palette, the color black became an essential element, with clear psychological meanings that spoke to an intensifying black consciousness. The key works of 1987 were his black South African landscapes and the first of his works acquired by the National Gallery of Jamaica, the powerful triptych *Three Black Heads for Marcus Garvey*. Indeed, there are many subsequent works that are painted in a virtually single, unmodulated shade of flat black acrylic that is relieved only by the varied textures of the elements attached to the canvas or paper. Collage has become of increasing importance, whether in the form of images torn from magazines and newspapers or with objects such as feathers, safety pins, and accretions of plastic integrated into the painted surfaces.

An avid reader, Omari Ra has steeped himself in Caribbean and world literature. A persistent recent theme is that of the white whale from Herman Melville's *Moby Dick*, which becomes a stand-in for white neocolonialist aggression. The counterpoint to the whale is a black penis, symbolic of the virility (or, depending on its state, lack of it) of blacks in the evolving new world order.

Haitian voodoo, popularly categorized as "black magic," has been an area of special study for Omari Ra, as has Jamaican obeah. These elements have informed works like the six-paneled "Dambala" series, in which a mysterious linkage of black painted ritualized heads, black penises, and images of blacks torn from magazines hint at a personal exorcism. In 1993 Omari Ra visited Zimbabwe, and while there he produced a small series of inspired landscapes depicting the Matopo Hills, which continue the black phallus theme in subjugated form.

Omari Ra is a popular tutor at the Edna Manley School for the Visual Arts. His dynamic approach to both the content and act of painting has had a deep effect on a new generation of Jamaican painters.

—David Boxer

ONABOLU, Aina

Nigerian painter

Born: Ijebu Ode, Nigeria, 13 September 1882. **Education:** St. John's Wood Art School, 1922, diploma; Académie Julien, Paris, Certificate of Proficiency in oil painting and fine arts. **Career:** Portrait painter, Nigeria, 1910-15; art teacher, Methodist Boys' High School, Lagos, Kings College, St. Gregory's College, Lagos Baptist Academy, and other Lagos schools. Art teacher, primary schools, 1915-20. Sometimes known as the "father of modern Nigerian art." Namesake of the Chief Aina Onabolu Art Prizes, established by Society of Nigerian Artists, 1965. **Awards:** Medal of the British Empire, 1957, for fine arts education in Nigeria; fellow (posthumous), Asele Institute, Nimo, 1985. **Died:** 1963.

Individual Exhibitions:

1919   Lagos
1920   Lagos
1954   At artist's residence, Osholake Street, Ebutte-Metta

Selected Group Exhibitions:

1925   Glover Memorial Hall, Lagos
1950   *First Art Exhibition of the Nigerian Arts Centre,* Tom Jones Hall, Lagos

1977   FESTAC 77
1978   *Exhibition of Nigerian Traditional and Contemporary Art,* Lagos

Publications:

By ONABOLU: Book—*A Short Discourse on Art,* Lagos, 1920.

On ONABOLU: Article—"Aina Onabolu" by Dapo Onabolu, in *Nigeria Magazine* (Lagos), (79), December 1963, pp. 295-98.

*   *   *

The rise of modern art in Nigeria at the beginning of the twentieth century was largely the result of the emergence of an influential class of educated Africans in Lagos. After the restoration of oba Akitoye to the throne in 1852 and before the British annexation of Lagos in 1861, a burgeoning cultural center began to develop with the influx of Christian missionary groups, immigrants from other parts of Nigeria and Africa, and European merchants on trading missions. The presence of this diverse, multiethnic population gave the city a cosmopolitan air. This was the Lagos of Aina Onabolu.

While still a primary school student in Ijebu-Ode, Onabolu began designing charts and other aids for the teachers. Following the completion of his elementary education he moved to Lagos, where he attended secondary school. He lived in the home of his guardian and mentor, J.K. Randle, a medical practitioner and friend of his father. Proximity to this well-connected political activist and nationalist placed Onabolu at the hub of the upper echelon of society in Lagos, where he established ties with the families of future clients. At his first salon in 1901, at the home of Randle, his drawings, still lifes, landscapes, and portraits were favorably received. After secondary school he worked as a marine clerk in the customs department while practicing art on the side. The most memorable of his early works were the portraits *Mrs. Spencer-Savage* (1906) and *Dr. Randle* (1910). Between 1915 and 1920 Onabolu taught part-time at primary schools while perfecting his skill in portraiture. In 1920 he held a solo exhibition of two hundred works to show the public "some of the pictures he had been able to paint without the aid of an Art master, and thereby . . . prove that God is impartial in his endowment of various talents to mankind."

On the completion of a two-year art program at Saint John's Wood Art School in London and at the Julien Académie in Paris, in 1922 Onabolu opened a studio in Lagos, where he established a reputation for artistic excellence and innovation. He was particularly drawn to portraiture, and his preference for the genre coincided with his audience's interest in self- and family portraits. In Onabolu's view portrait painting was "the highest and the most difficult of pictorial art." His portraits are distinguished by the dignified countenances of the sitters and by the rich, subtly contrasting coloration of the overall works, as in *Rt. Rev. I. Oluwole, Rev. J. Johnson,* and *The Barrister.* He created skillfully structured moods, as in *Man with a Beret,* that evoked a romantic atmosphere and fascinating tales, a technique that is strongly suggestive of Rembrandt. Onabolu's professionalism and artistic excellence attracted a clientele of Nigerian luminaries belonging to affluent circles of businessmen, lawyers, doctors, and clergy. As with photography, his pictorial style allowed the elite to capture their self-images and their status, the difference being that Onabolu could render his clients' images in color.

As the demand for Onabolu's services increased, he was commissioned by the Lagos Town Council in 1923 to design a poster for the sale of new buildings that were then under construction. The public's response to the poster was overwhelming. Taken in by the illusionistic effects of the painting, some believed the houses to have been completed and came to pay for a unit. In 1924 Onabolu's gouache painting *Nigerian Weaver* was selected in a worldwide competition as a poster for the British Empire Art Exhibition in Wembley. In the same year *The Trumpeters* (1924) was commissioned by the colonial government for presentation to the Prince of Wales. Another well-known oil painting, *The Village Belle* (1924), a portrait of his wife, Mabel, done in *aso oke* (a richly woven cloth), also dates to this period.

Onabolu did not limit himself to portraiture. When the opportunity presented, he explored new media and different techniques. In 1932, for example, he designed the pews of the Cathedral Church of Christ in Lagos. Between 1940 and 1950 he produced a number of pastel compositions and studies. In 1954 he completed the construction of his home in Ebute-Metta, with a permanent gallery that was open to the public. Onabolu's self-taught naturalistic style and his skillful use of European materials subverted Western claims of supremacy. Of far greater importance, however, was that his artistic achievement exposed the falsity of racist claims that Africans were incapable of drawing realistically.

—Nkiru Nzegwu

O'NEAL, Mary Lovelace

American painter and printmaker

Born: Jackson, Mississippi, 10 February 1942. **Education:** Tougaloo College, Tougaloo, Mississippi, 1959; Howard University, Washington, D.C., 1960-64, B.F.A 1964; Columbia University, New York, 1967-79, M.F.A. 1969. **Career:** Instructor, San Francisco Art Institute, 1970-76; lecturer, University of California, Berkeley, 1976-78, California College of Arts and Crafts, Oakland, California, Humboldt State University, Arcata, California, 1978-79. Assistant professor, University of California, Berkeley, 1979-85; associate professor, University of California, Berkeley, 1985-1993. Since 1993 professor, University of California, Berkeley. **Awards:** Skowhegan School of Painting and Sculpture Scholastic Scholarship Award, 1963; Best Performing Student Award, Howard University, Washington, D.C., 1964; Columbia University Scholarship, 1964-69; Regents' Junior Faculty Fellowship, University of California, Berkeley, 1980; Development Program summer research grant, University of California, Berkeley, 1981, 1982; Black Women's Conference Honoree, University of California, Berkeley, 1988; Humanities Research Fellowship, University of California, Berkeley, 1989-90; "Mary Lovelace O'Neal Day" proclamation, Office of the Mayor, Oakland, California, 1993; Artiste en

Mary Lovelace O'Neal, 1994. Photo courtesy of Patricio Moreno Toro.

Mary Lovelace O'Neal: *Running Freed More Slaves Than Lincoln Ever Did,* **1995.**

France Award, French Government, 1993-94; Biennale Internationale des Arts Award, Dakar, Senegal, 1993-94; Troisieme Triennale Mondiale D'Estampes Petit Format Prize, 1994-97; Berkeley Convocation Honoree, University of California, Berkeley, 1994.

Individual Exhibitions:

1973	Main Art Gallery, California State University, Sacramento
1977	Isabelle Percy West Gallery, California College of Arts and Crafts, Oakland
	California State University, Sacramento
1979	San Francisco Museum of Modern Art
	Foyer Gallery, Humboldt State University, Arcata, California
1982	Gallery of Art, Howard University, Washington, D.C.
	Pro Arts Gallery, Oakland, California
1983	Miami Lakes/Palm Springs North Branch Library, Miami, Florida
1984	Jeremy Stone Gallery, San Francisco
1987	Jackson State University, Mississippi
	Tougaloo College, Mississippi
	Rolando Castellon Gallery, San Francisco

1988	Rolando Castellon Contemporary Art Gallery, San Francisco
1989	Zimmerman/Saturn Gallery, Nashville
1990	de Saisset Museum, Santa Clara University, California
	Floyd Huddleston Gallery, New York
1991	Instituto Chileño Norte Americano de Cultura, Santiago, Chile
	Dominican College, San Rafael, California
1992	Porter Randall Gallery, La Jolla, California
	Theresa Mullen Gallery, San Francisco
1993	French Cultural Services, French Embassy, New York
1994	Cité International des Arts, Paris
	Instituto Chileño Norte Americano de Cultura, Santiago, Chile
	Alliance Francaise de San Francisco
	Longwood Center for the Visual Arts, Farmville, Virginia
	Bedford Gallery, Longwood College, Farmville, Virginia
	Alliance Francaise Galerie, San Francisco
	Cité International des Arts, Paris
1995	Tougaloo College, Mississippi
	Berkeley Art Center, California
	Instituto Chileño Norte Americano de Cultura, Santiago, Chile

Selected Group Exhibitions:

1985	Museum of African American Art, Los Angeles
1986	Leonarda Di Mauro Gallery, New York
1989	Museum of Asilah, Morocco
1990	Kenkeleba Gallery, New York
	Albuquerque Museum of Art, New Mexico
1992	San Jose Museum of Art, California
	John Natsoulas Gallery, Davis, California
1995	Arizona State University, Tempe
	Horwitch Lewallen Gallery, Sante Fe, New Mexico
	Howard University, Washington, D.C.

Collections:

Al Kasabah Art Gallery, Morocco; Art in Embassies Program, Washington, D.C.; California Afro-American Museum Foundation, Los Angeles; Columbia University, New York; Fisk University, Nashville; Howard University, Washington, D.C.; Kenkeleba Gallery, New York; National Museum of Fine Arts, Santiago, Chile; Oakland Museum, California; San Francisco Museum of Modern Art; Smith Robertson Museum, Jackson, Mississippi.

Publications:

On O'NEAL: Books—*Events: Artists Invite Artists,* exhibition catalog, New York, New Museum and Lynn Gumpert, 1981; *Connecting Conversations: Interviews with Twenty-Eight Bay Area Women Artists,* edited by Moira Roth, California, Mills College, 1988, pp. 153-59 (interview by Mia Carenya Seabrooks); *Yesterday and Tomorrow: California Women Artists,* edited by Sylvia Moore, New York, Middlemarch Arts Press, 1989, p. 197, 200. **Articles**—"Five Oakland Artists" by Charles Shere, in *Oakland Tribune* (California), 5 May 1974; "Nommo Muse: Black Improvisation in California" by Allan M. Gordon, in *New Art Examiner* 7(9), June 1980, pp. 6-7; "She Likes Stuff that Shines" by Melinda Levine, in *The Berkeley Gazette* (California), 1 May 1983; "Whales and Pirates on a Grey City Day: Painter Mary O'Neal's Life Is as Vivid as Her Art" by Alyce Miller, in *The Berkeley Gazette* (California), 25 January 1984; "Mary Lovelace O'Neal" by A. Baba, in *Al Mithaq al Watani,* 22 August 1984; "Wrestling with Abstraction" by Leonard Michael, in *Artweek* 21(18), 10 May 1990; "Mary O'Neal: Una Pintora Afro-Americana," in *El Mercurio* (Chile), 18 November 1991, p. 8; "Artis Latinos y Afro Americanos Invaden Museode Bellas Artes," in *Las Ultimas Noticias* (Chile), 23 November 1991, p. 31; "Mary O'Neal—Painting on the Edges of a Black and White World" by David Driskell, in *New Observations Magazine,* Fall, 1993, pp. 30-34; "Mary Lovelace O'Neal: Art Teacher, Painter" by Jolene Thym, in *Oakland Tribune* (California), 5 October 1993, p. c2; "O'Neal is Artiste en France," in *Berkeleyan* (California), 22-28 September 1993, p. 3.

* * *

Mary Lovelace O'Neal's aggressive style of painting inspired one reviewer to say that "she paints like a man," intended as a compliment. She controls the paint and makes it explode into abstract shapes on her monumental canvases. When she interprets a representational form in paint, it is often barely, if at all, recognizable. All the viewer sees are exploding colored shapes that resemble paint hurled onto a surface. O'Neal also creates works on paper with the same energy but on a smaller scale. In either case her sensuous manipulation of paint makes the viewer want to slide in its slippery surfaces.

O'Neal's paintings also include loosely structured shapes resembling inkblot designs in which the viewer's responses can be analyzed and interpreted. In the 1970s and 1980s she worked with lamp black pigment (a powdery construction material) in an attempt to solve problems of flatness and depth. She was trying to arrive at a more lyrical quality in her work through spatial manipulations. The lamp black also focused on a more literal view of blackness as related to the consciousness of African Americans. Working on the floor with this medium, she learned to make space concessions, consciously resisting the hard floor surface and thereby creating paintings with a more fluid form of abstract expressionism. She strove for fluid shapes rather than the more reductive forms in which she felt her passion was compromised.

In 1970 O'Neal settled in California. She noticed that she experienced discernible changes in light there, suggesting a freedom that she had not had in New York City, where all things were stacked on top of one another in confined canyons of concrete. Her paintings of whales evolved from her encounter with light on the Pacific Ocean, where she saw whales for the first time, and in subsequent trips to Bay Area aquariums. The imagery of these works show her interest in how the whales displace water and their powerful yet gentle quality. To see them in nature or in a nature park led her back to something primal, an element that has remained in her paintings.

In the mid-1980s, in what O'Neal termed a "hot period of paint," her works included whales, still lifes, and desert scenes based on travels to Africa (Morocco and Egypt) and South America (Chile) contrasted with areas of greenness, fruits, and flowers. She invoked a more fleshy treatment of paint, which was a return to the work of her undergraduate years at Howard University. During those earlier years, influenced by the work of Willem de Kooning and Franz Kline, she had been interested in color and brushy painted areas. In graduate school at Columbia University she became fascinated with the "coolness" evoked by the paintings of Kenneth Nolan, Frank Stella, and Barnett Newman. O'Neal began to pursue the same kind

of reductive painting in her work, moving away from the brushiness of de Kooning. She always maintained a mathematical approach to her paintings, however, with geometry being an important facet of work that centered on her concern with space, whether flat or three-dimensional.

Figuration has also been a part of O'Neal's paintings, and she has been interested in movement. She is, for example, interested in the way the wind moves through and around objects or the way clothing moves around women's bodies. This has heightened her consciousness of women in Islamic cultures. She is particularly interested in how the women of restrictive cultures have fused their indigenous customs of dress with an imposed external custom. The women of Senegal, for example, wear cloth of bright, complicated designs that is wrapped around their bodies, with elaborate headdresses adorning their often ornate coiffures, even as they practice Islam. O'Neal's interest in the African synthesis of tradition and modernity in dress has encouraged her to explore the same phenomenon in the vernacular Islamic architecture of West and North Africa, which is infused with indigenous forms of shelter.

O'Neal has always been concerned with traditional formal elements, questioning how she will use them, reinventing them for herself, and renewing herself as an artist. She also realizes that she is a witness to many changes that have taken place in the second part of the twentieth century and that it is important for her to acknowledge these developments but not to fasten onto any given one. For her it is more important to transform traditions by making changes.

—Lizzetta LeFalle-Collins

ONOBRAKPEYA, Bruce
Nigerian printmaker, painter, sculptor, and graphic artist

Born: Agbarha-Otor near Ughelli, Delta State, Nigeria, 30 August 1932. **Education:** Nigerian College of Arts, Science and Technology, Zaria, fine arts diploma in painting and art history, 1961, art teacher's certificate, 1962; Department of Extra Mural Studies, University of Ibadan, Nigeria, and Writers' Club, Ibadan, 1961; apprenticed to Ben Enwonwu, 1962; studied printmaking with Dutch graphic artist Ru van rossem, Mbari Artists' and Writers' Club, Ibadan, August 1963; participated in workshop directed by Jacob Lawrence, Lagos, 1964; attended printmaking workshop, Mbari Mbayo, Oshogbo, 1964; studied in print section, London Museum, 1969. **Career:** Art teacher, Western Boys High School, Benin City, 1953-57; Ondo Boys' High School, 1957; St. Gregory's College, Lagos, 1963-c.1980. Guest instructor/teacher, printmaking, Haystack Mountain School of Crafts, Deer Isle, Maine, July 1975, Tacoma Public Schools, Tacoma, Washington, 1989; artist-in-residence, Elizabeth City State University, North Carolina, August 1979, Institute of African Studies, University of Ibadan, Nigeria, 1984. Traveled in Italy 1968, London, 1969, United States, 1970. Member, Zaria Art Society. Founding member, Society of Nigerian Artists. **Awards:** Third Prize, Gottschalk Textile Competition, Nigerian College for Arts, Science and Technology, Zaria, 1959; Pope Paul VI Gold Medal, 1977; Fulbright-Hays Award, American Council for International Exchange of Scholars, 1979; Ciba Geigy Travel and Exhibition Award, 1980; Silver Medal and twenty thousand rupees, *Fifth Triennial,* New Delhi, India, 1982; Solidra Circle Award, Lagos, 1985; fellow, Asele Institute, 1985; British Council Award, 1989; Merit Award, Bendel State, 1990. Honorary Doctorate: University of Ibadan, 1989 **Address:** Obuomaroro Gallery, 39 Oloje Street, Papa Ajao, Mushin, Lagos, Nigeria.

Individual Exhibitions:

1959	Ughelli, Nigeria
1961	Nigerian Art Council Exhibition Centre, Lagos
1962	Exhibition Centre, Marina, Lagos
1964	Mbari Club, Ibadan, Nigeria
	Nigerian Museum, Lagos
1966	Mbari Club, Ibadan
	Nigerian Art Council Exhibition Centre, Lagos
1968	University of Ife, Ile-Ife, Nigeria
1969	USIS, Lagos
1970	Howard University, Washington, D.C.
1975	Martin Luther King Memorial Library, Washington, D.C.
1978	Goethe Institute, Lagos
1979	Best of Africa Art Gallery, Toronto
	Walter N. Ridley University Center, Elizabeth City State University, North Carolina
1984	Institute of African Studies, University of Ibadan, Nigeria (retrospective)
1986	Whitney Young Resource Center, USIS, Lagos
1989	Greenwich Citizen Gallery, Woolwich, England
1990	Galerie Wolfgang Riegelsberger, Mannheim, Germany

Selected Group Exhibitions:

1989	Tudor Hall, Montreal
	Home Design Centre, Lagos
1990	Onira Arts Africa, Ottawa
	Biennale, Venice, Italy
	Watermark/Cargo Gallery, Kingston, New York
	National Museum, Lagos
	National Theatre, Lagos
	Contemporary African Art Gallery, New York
	Galerie Wolfgang Riegelsberger, Mannheim, Germany
	Studio Museum in Harlem, New York (traveling through 1991)

Collections:

Asele Institute, Nimo, Nigeria; Carl Van Vechten Gallery of Fine Arts, Fisk University, Nashville; Cleveland State University, Afro-American Cultural Center; Didi Museum, Lagos; Hampton University Museum, Hampton, Virginia; Iwalewa-Haus, Bayreuth, Germany; Lagos University Library, University of Lagos; Mbari Art, Washington, D.C.; Museum of African and African-American Art and Antiquities, Buffalo, New York; Museum für Völkerkunde, Frankfurt, Germany; National Gallery of Modern Art, Lagos; National Museum of African Art, Smithsonian Institute, Washington, D.C.; Tropenmuseum, Amsterdam; University of Alberta, Edmonton, Alberta, Canada; University of Ibadan, Ibadan, Nigeria; University of Lagos, Centre for Cultural Studies, Lagos; University of Nigeria, Ana Gallery, Nsukka; University of Redlands, Eda Lord Demarest Memorial African Art Collection, Redlands, California; Vatican Museum, Rome.

Publications:

By ONOBRAKPEYA: Books—*Bruce Onobrakpeya: Twenty-Five Years of Creative Search,* exhibition catalog, Agbarha-Otor, Bendel State, Nigeria, Institute of African Studies, University of Ibadan, 1984; *Symbols of Ancestral Groves: A Monograph of Prints and Paintings, 1978-1985,* Lagos, Bruce Onobrakpeya, 1985 (illustrated; some color; bibliography); *Sahelian Masquerades: Artistic Experiments: November 1985-August 1988* edited by Safy Quel, Lagos, Ovuomaroro Gallery, 1988 (illustrated; some color); *Poems and Lithographs,* Lagos, Bruce Onobrakpeya, 1989. **Article**—"African Art and the American Collections," in *Interlink* (Lagos), January-March 1971.

On ONOBRAKPEYA: Books—*The Art Society of the International Monetary Fund Presents Works by Asiru Olatunde, Bruce Onobrakpeya, Muraina Oyelami, September 19-October 19, 1972,* Washington, D.C., Art Society of the International Monetary Fund, 1972; *Bruce Onobrakpeya: Nigeria's Master Printmaker,* Toronto, Best of Africa, 1978 (illustrated); *Reconstruction of Bruce Onobrakpeya* by Paul Jacob, Bornor Regis, Sussex, New Horizon, 1982. **Articles**—"Bruce Onobrakpeya" by Jean Kennedy, in *African Arts* (Los Angeles), 5(2), Winter 1972, pp. 48-49 (illustrated; some color); "The Mythical Realism of Bruce Onobrakpeya" by Babatunde Lawal, in *Nigeria* (Lagos), 120, 1976, pp. 50-59 (illustrated); "Bruce Onobrakpeya: Nigeria's Master Printmaker" by John Povey, in *African Arts* (Los Angeles), 13(4), August 1980, pp. 9-12; "Bruce Onobrakpeya" by Robert Barde, in *Black Art* (Jamaica, New York), 4(3), 1981, pp. 49-58 (illustrated; some color); "An Interview with Onobrakpeya" by Oboira Udechukwu, in *Okike* (Nsukka, Nigeria), 21, July 1982, pp. 61-66 (illustrated); "Bruce Onobrakpeya: An Art of Synthesis" by Jean Kennedy, in *Print News* (World Print Council), 6(5), September-October 1984, pp. 8-9, 11 (illustrated); "Bruce Onobrakpeya: Artist from Nigeria" by Jean Kennedy, in *Topic* (Washington, D.C.), 161, October 1984, pp. 43-46 (illustrated); "Synthesized Mannerisms in Onobrakpeya's Art" by Dele Jegede, in *Nigeria* (Lagos), 53, July-September, 1985, pp. 17-23 (illustrated; bibliography); "Bruce Onobrakpeya and the American Connection" by Toyin Akinosho, in *Guardian Express* (Lagos), 6 March 1986.

*   *   *

Though primarily known as a printmaker and painter, Bruce Onobrakpeya is heavily influenced by the sculptural and textile traditions of his ancestors and specifically of his father, who was a sculptor. His best-known works are probably his "deep-etchings." In this technique a plate is built up with other materials and then carved into before the print is made.

Many of the techniques he uses he has invented. He described one of these techniques as follows: "I use wood panels and I build up the surface with a plastic glue compound. Then I carve into the surface. Over it I pour plaster of Paris, creating a negative image. From the negative I can make limited editions of positive, low relief sculptured panes by pouring plastic resin into the negative mold." About his experiments he says, "Concepts are sometimes enriched by accidental results. Printmaking should not be dull routine. I like to improvise, to leave room for discoveries."

His techniques are both classic and modern, both traditional sculpture and experimental printmaking, and his subjects and approach could also be described as classic and modern. One of his purposes, he says, is "making meaning out of landscape." He seeks out patterns and textures for his work. "Ant hills have interesting sculptural forms, especially when they become old or slightly eroded by the rain. If an ant hill is still active, that is if the ants still live in it, you can always find new layers of earth growing around the old one thereby forming contrast in colour, texture, and form."

Further permutations of Onobrakpeya's work are as a teacher (though he retired after seventeen years to work on his art full-time) and as a book illustrator. Even as an illustrator he is concerned with sculpture. In 1979 he illustrated a German prayer book that included seven pictures aligned in an unusual vertical formation inspired by the book's format. He said of the illustrations: "all the forms were held together like a piece of sculpture." He says further of illustrating books, "The task of the illustrator . . . is to create illustrations which are very alive, suitable for any age . . . that invite children to read and develop their critical sense and love for beauty." Though no longer a teacher by trade, he remains a teacher as long as his work remains.

—Terry Bain

OUATTARA

Ivory Coaster painter

Born: Abidjan, Ivory Coast, 1957. **Agent:** Gagosian Gallery, 980 Madison Avenue, New York, New York 10021, U.S.A.

Individual Exhibitions:

1986	Centre Culturel de la Rochelle, La Rochelle, France
1989	Marilyn Butler Gallery, Los Angeles
	Vrej Baghoomian Gallery, New York
1990	Galerie Philippe Boulakia, Paris
	Akira Ikeda Gallery, Nagoya, Japan
	Vrej Baghoomian Gallery, New York
1992	Vrej Baghoomian Gallery, New York
1993	Galerie Boulakia, Paris
1994	University Art Museum, Berkeley
1995	Gagosian Gallery, New York

Selected Group Exhibitions:

1985	Musée National des Arts Africains et Oceaniens, Paris
1986	Galerie Georges Lavrov, Paris
1988	Vrej Baghoomian Gallery, New York
1990	Museum of Art, Milwaukee
1991	Alternative Museum, New York
	New Museum of Contemporary Art, New York (traveling)
1992	Cavin-Morris Gallery, New York
1994	Museum of Contemporary African Art, New York
1995	Vrej Baghoomian Gallery, New York
	La Virreina Exposicions Barcelona

Publications:

On OUATTARA: Books—*Ouattara* by Ben Michel Warren, Kyoto, Art RANDOM, 1989; *Ouattara,* exhibition catalog, by Frederick Castle, (New York) Vrej Baghoomian Gallery, 1990; *Ouattara,* exhibition catalog, by Gerard Barrier, Paris, Galerie Boulakia, 1990; *Ouattara: Dark Star,* exhibition catalog, Missouri, Kemper Museum and Dana Self, September 1996. **Articles**— "Ouattara Ritualistic Paintings" by Margot Mifflin, in *Elle* (New York), March 1989; "Ouattara" interview by Mantegna Gianfranco, in *Journal of Contemporary Art,* New York, Fall/Winter, 1990, pp. 26-33; "Ouattara" by Kim Levin, in *Village Voice,* New York, 13-19 June 1990; "Ouattara, Magic Man," interview by Konan Vanance, in *Ivoir Soir,* Abidjan, 11 February 1991; "Ouattara" by Sylvie Last, in *Africa International,* January 1991; "Ouattara" by Henri-Francois Debailleux, in *New Art International Reviews,* February 1991; "Ouattara, Magic Man" by Sydney Picasso, in *Contemporaine,* February 1992; "Ouattara: Beyond Shamanism" by Okwui Enwezor, *Nka Journal of Contemporary Art,* Spring/Summer 1995; "Mix of Cultures, Politics and Bravado" by Holland Cotter, in *New York Times,* 19 May 1995, p. C30.

*   *   *

Ouattara arrived in New York City in 1988 at the urging of the painter Jean-Michel Basquiat. Although Ouattara had already worked in Paris for a decade, no other city so aptly represents his work as does New York. Spilling across his canvases are the inscriptions of his eccentric mind: snapshots of preexisting portraits, album covers, shards of mirrors, and bottles on tree branches—the last evoking the religion of voodoo and the historical transplantation of Africa to the New World (a symbol of Ouattara's own expatriate status from the Ivory Coast). The detritus of life initially seems to be haphazardly placed on his canvases, but after inspection there is no doubt that every part is integral to the whole.

Born and raised in Abidjan, Ivory Coast, Ouattara now divides his time between New York, Paris, and Abidjan. His work has been shown in New York, Paris, and Tokyo and at the museum of the University of California, Berkeley, among other places. His paintings are large and colorful, based on neoexpressionism but open to contemporary readings. Like Julian Schnabel and David Salle, Ouattara has used neoexpressionism as a means to an end. And as with the Zairean painter Chéri Samba, his paintings tell stories. This can be seen in the abundance of written words and printed matter found on the works. Words in Arabic, German, English, French, and other languages cut swaths in open fields of blue, yellow, and red.

Found materials and artifacts of popular culture work like objets d'art on the surfaces of Ouattara's paintings. Although in painting nothing is new, his works are marked by the recycling of such materials on their surfaces, which creates a daunting ambiguity. This apparently awkward quality turns into a simple matter, however, after the viewer has taken in the composition. On the one hand it simply makes visual sense, yet on the other there is a somewhat unrelaxed cosmology of floating symbols, all personal to their creator but all asking the viewer to make something of them. Ouattara describes his paintings as "personal and spiritual documents filled with inscriptions for the world to discern. . . ." There are a lot of things going on in them. The narrative qualities offered by the parts of the paintings, for example, break down into the neosurreal interpolations of male/female, life/death, and all things elemental. The difficulty with this vocabulary is that it seems to be handled so loosely. Because Ouattara's work is so heavy with symbolism, it cultivates an enigma. Nonetheless, his work is visually seductive.

In *Untitled* (1995) Ouattara has paid homage to Kwame Nkrumah. In another work a Fela Kuti album cover is coupled with that of the hip-hop group EPMD, juxtaposed on a bed of color. Although Ouattara treads in pop cultural products, the paintings, with their constant references to Dakar (Senegal), Paris, and New York, embrace and redistribute his own international spirit and ideology toward art that creates a natural synthesis between Africa and the West. In the process Ouattara has created documents on the fin de siècle globalism of the world's metropolises.

—M. Franklin Sirmans

OUBRE, Hayward (Louis)

American painter and sculptor

Born: New Orleans, 17 September 1916. **Education:** Dillard University, New Orleans, B.A. 1939; University of Iowa, Iowa City, M.F.A. 1948. **Military Service:** United States Army, 1941-43: master-sergeant; American Defense Ribbon, 1942, North American Service Ribbon, 1943, Asiatic Pacific Ribbon, 1943, Alcan Highway citation, 1943, Sharp Shooter Medal (Rifle). **Family:** Married Juanita Hurel in 1945 (died), one daughter. **Career:** Associate professor of art, Florida A & M College, Tallahasse, 1949-50; professor of art, Alabama State College, 1950-65, Winston-Salem University, North Carolina, 1965-81; curator, Selma Burke Art Gallery, 1984-90. **Awards:** First Prize, Iowa State Fair, 1947; Atlanta University Annual prizes, 1947-49, 1955, 1957, 1962, 1964, 1968; Third Prize in sculpture, Emancipation Proclamation Centennial, 1963. **Address:** 2422 Pickford Court, Winston-Salem, North Carolina 27101, U.S.A.

Individual Exhibitions:

Florida A & M University, Tallahassee; Fort Valley State College, Fort Valley, Georgia; James G. Hanes Community Center, Winston-Salem, North Carolina; Lincoln University, Jefferson City, Missouri; Savannah State College, Savannah, Georgia; Southern Illinois University, Carbondale; Southern University Branch, New Orleans; Winston-Salem State University, Winston-Salem, North Carolina.

Selected Group Exhibitions:

Baltimore Museum of Art, Maryland; High Museum of Art, Atlanta, Georgia; Jacksonville Art Museum, Jacksonville, Florida; Minnesota Museum of Art, St. Paul, Minnesota; Museum of the National Center of Afro-American Artists, Dorchester, Massachusetts; Southeastern Center of Contemporary Art; Studio Museum in Harlem, New York; Winston-Salem Delta Fine Arts, Winston-Salem, North Carolina.

Publication:

On Oubre: Book—*Alone in a Crowd: Prints of the 1930-40s by African-American Artists,* exhibition catalog, from the Collection of Reba and Dave Williams, New York, Metropolitan Museum of Art.

*   *   *

To satisfy the human impulse to classify, scholars create pathways out of the tumult of history by inventing ages and eras. Nowhere is this desire to create a sense of order more rampant than in the art world, especially for artists of color. Historically, black artists were seen as a collective phenomenon. Some black artists, however, have fought to be viewed individually and have resisted being categorized, boxed, and tied for posterity. Hayward Oubre is one such artist.

Nurtured with pride and security in a family of black and French ancestry in cosmopolitan New Orleans, Oubre was prepared to enter the larger society as an equal and with a keen sense of identity. He refused to be ghettoized and pursued all avenues of artistic expression—drawing, painting, etching, sculpture, construction (or assemblage), and research in color—while maintaining a distinguished career as an arts educator. He challenged convention when he corrected the color triangle devised by Johann Wolfgang von Goethe. Oubre designed a three-intensity color wheel, thereby proving Goethe's color triangle to be mathematically incorrect. He received a copyright for his color wheel in 1975. In addition, in 1966 Oubre prepared *A Concise Study of Color Mixing and Color Relationships.* His artwork is held in important collections, and he has received dozens of honors, among them the Order of the Long Leaf Pine given by the governor of North Carolina.

Oubre's elementary school teachers recognized his talent and pulled him aside to draw murals for classroom walls. He initially thought that drawing was copying, but then he saw a cast of a Michelangelo sculpture and was transformed: "I was never the same after that." Art and athletics consumed him at Dillard University. Following graduation in 1939, he continued to study at Atlanta University under Elizabeth Prophet and Hale Woodruff, and he earned a master's degree at the University of Iowa. He was drafted during World War II and was one of the three thousand black Americans sent to build the Alaska Highway, which gave him the opportunity to use his engineering skills.

Oubre is a master of linear emphasis. His wire sculptures possess anthropomorphic qualities. His life-size *The Prophet,* at five feet eleven inches, and his sculptures of horses are spectacular examples of imagination and resourcefulness. His handling of line ranges from realistic to abstract. In 1966 Oubre wrote, "Some degree of abstraction must be dealt with in order to produce art; in other words, all art automatically falls somewhere within the field of abstraction. The act of abstraction is nothing more or less than the artist's way of revealing a facet or facets of the cosmic order inherent in nature." He is equally comfortable in wood and stone, and his powerful *Stevedore* demonstrates his skill with solid figures.

Oubre was on the faculties and served as the chair of the art departments at Florida A&M University, Winston-Salem State University, and Alabama State University, and he was curator of the Selma Burke Art Gallery at Winston-Salem State University. Under Oubre's leadership the department of art at Alabama State, established in 1941, came to be distinguished for its full program of study leading to the baccalaureate degree, with concentrations in either studio art or art education. In retirement Oubre has continued to create sculpture.

—Louise Davis Stone

OUTTERBRIDGE, John (Wilfred)
American sculptor, painter, and installation artist

Born: Greenville, North Carolina, 12 March 1933. **Education:** A & T University, Greensboro, North Carolina, 1952-53; American Academy of Art, Chicago, 1956-59; State of California, teaching credential 1970. **Military Service:** United States Army, three years: corporal; Foreign Service, Good Conduct medal. **Family:** Married Beverly Marie Outterbridge in 1960 (divorced 1990), one daughter. **Career:** Artist/designer, Artcraft, Los Angeles, 1964-68; artistic director, Communicative Arts Academy, Compton, California, 1969-75; director, Watts Towers Arts Center, Los Angeles, 1975-92. Art instructor/fine arts installer, Pasadena Museum of Art, California, 1967-72; lecturer, Arts and Humanities Department, California State University, Carson, 1970-73. Founder, GOCART (Gallery of Children's Art), City of Los Angeles, 1978. **Awards:** National Conference of Arts Educators Award, 1987; Fulbright Fellowship, 1988; J.R. Hyde Visiting Artist Fellowship, Memphis Institute of the Arts, 1994; J. Paul Getty Fellowship for the Visual Arts, 1994; National Endowment for the Arts Fellowship, 1994. Honorary doctorate: Otis College of Art and Design, 1994. **Address:** 5838 South Woodlawn Avenue, Los Angeles, California 90003, U.S.A.

Individual Exhibitions:

1972	Brockman Gallery, Los Angeles
1992	Rancho Santiago College, Orange, California
1994	California Afro-American Museum, Los Angeles (retrospective)
1996	Artcore Cultural Center, Los Angeles

Selected Group Exhibitions:

1968	Long Beach Museum of Art, California
1970	La Jolla Museum of Art, California
1972	Los Angeles County Museum of Art, California
1984	California Afro-American Museum, Los Angeles
1986	Everson Museum, Newark, New Jersey
1989	Wight Art Gallery, University of California, Los Angeles
1994	*Bienal of São Paulo,* Brazil
	Johannesburg Biennale, Transitional Metropolitan Council, South Africa
	INSITE 94, United States/Mexico: Installation and Site Specific Art, San Diego, California
1995	Studio Museum in Harlem, New York

Collections:

California African American Museum, Los Angeles; Mills College, Oakland, California; Oakland Museum of Art, California; San Jose State University, California.

Publications:

On OUTTERBRIDGE: Books—*Artists Select: Contemporary Perspectives by Afro-American Artists,* Arizona State University, 1986; *John Outterbridge: Sculptor of Oppositions,* exhibition catalog, California, Rancho Santiago College and Dr. Shifra M. Goldman, 1992. **Articles**—"Community Carver" by Ayofemi Folayan, in

John Outterbridge (with *Window with Ball*), 1991. Photo courtesy of Willie Middlebrook.

John Outterbridge: *First Poet, Olivia,* 1993. Photo courtesy of Sammy Davis.

High Performance (Los Angeles), 1992; "Outterbridge: Assembling Stories" by Christopher Knight, in *Los Angeles Times,* 1993; "John Outterbridge in Retrospect: From Carolina to Watts," in *Los Angeles Sentinel,* 1993; "Conversation with John Outterbridge" by Kay Mills, in *Los Angeles Times,* 1994; "Report from São Paulo" by Ed Leffingwell, in *Art in America,* 1995.

*

John Outterbridge comments:

(1988) Deep within the spirit and flesh of my being, the fretting breadth of ancestors guides the burning faith. Sacred are the visions ingrained like gleaming sermons preached far beyond the face of my nights. Give me the courage to know the things of life that I may be worthy of my place. Above all, teach me to share the gifts.

I was born in North Carolina during the Depression era. Art making was prevalent in my family and community as far back as I can recall. After a European tour of duty (U.S. Army), I returned to the States and lived in Chicago, where I studied at the American Academy of Art. Chicago was brimming with creative energy, and here I met the dean of African American painters, Archibald Motley, and Margaret Burroughs, artist and founder of the DuSable African American Museum of History and Culture. I moved to Los Angeles in 1963 and began making art during the emergent civil rights movement, working in collaboration with such positive influences as Noah Purifoy, Judson Powell, Dan Concholar, John Riddle, Alonzo and Dale Davis, Mel Edwards, David Hammons, Dr. Samella

Lewis, Ruth Waddy, Betye Saar, Stanley Wilson, William Pajaud, Charles White, Debbie Brewer, and many others. This group of artists evolved a distinct Afro-centric, Beat-styled aesthetic that transformed the debris of the after-period of the 1965 Watts revolt environment into an abstract visual language that continues to resonate. My art is layered with political, historical, and very personal meanings, registered in a minimalist fashion, reshaping and assembling a great variety of materials.

*   *   *

John Outterbridge works with recycled materials, refabricating and reinterpreting them into artworks that address social and political ills while they retain their character. He credits his knowledge of refurbishing to his father, who collected castaway objects as a profession. Outterbridge was thus taught to value found and discarded materials for their potential for reconditioning. His philosophy toward such materials intersects with his views on human potential, that is, that society's castaways—specifically homeless men, women, and children—have the potential to be reinterpreted, refurbished, and restored.

Outterbridge was first active in the art scene after returning to Chicago from the army in 1955, but he did not find his own voice in art until he relocated to Los Angeles in 1963. He witnessed the riots in Watts in 1965, an event that was critical in helping African American artists in the area find a niche for addressing their social and artistic concerns. Artists such as Noah Purifoy, John Riddle, David Hammons, and Outterbridge collected charred debris from Watts and refashioned it into art objects. At the same time Outterbridge's sense of sculpture was heightened through his employment as an art preparator at the Pasadena (California) Art Museum, where exhibitions featuring the works of Mark Di Suvero, Robert Rauschenberg, and Andy Warhol were installed. Outterbridge's study of these artists was helpful in solving some of the technical problems he faced with assemblage. He was most influenced, however, by Purifoy, in ways of using discarded objects to address social ills, and by Di Suvero, in art processes and the use of tools and technology. Nonetheless, Outterbridge always credits his father for first instilling in him the belief that he could in fact make something out of nothing—art from debris.

Outterbridge was working in Los Angeles at a time when Charles White, who encouraged artists to work in a serial format, was influential. Outterbridge created several dynamic series, beginning with "Containment" (1968), which addressed feelings of entrapment, "Rag Man" (1970-78), which addressed the notion of collecting other people's discards as a means of survival, "Ethnic Heritage Group" (1978-82), which was concerned with the historical restrictions on access to the American dream that had been the legacy for African Americans as well as the notion of display and power, and "Aesthetics of Urban Blight" (1989-1990s), which contrasted rusted and highly polished surfaces, the old and the new, the rich and the poor that often rest side by side in the urban landscape and, depending upon the eyes of the beholder, can be viewed as beautiful in their own right.

More recently Outterbridge has explored site-specific installations. One such work, *Window with Wall* (1994), was based on the window as an invitation for dialogue and a pathway for spiritual communication. The work was made of rusted and polished steel and of rope and small tufts of colored string. It was first exhibited at the Centro Cultural in Tijuana, Mexico, so that those outside the building could view the piece through large walls of glass. When viewers stood inside the gallery, however, the parklike landscape on the outside created a pastoral background for the installation. This double way of looking at the work served as a metaphor for two-way seeing and understanding and for binational interaction. Outterbridge said of the work that it was a way to "peer past surface windows of opposition, to open up spaces for the flight of vision." The work created "crevices, holes, and possibilities to channel one's vision," with "vision" not restricted to the eye but also encompassing aspirations. *Window with Wall* has become the beginning of a new series.

The work *Lye Lye Soap Factory and Seven Scarecrows* (1994) was created for the twenty-second São Paulo Bienal in Brazil. It was also installed in 1995 at the first Johannesburg Biennale in South Africa, where Outterbridge and Betye Saar were the official artists representing the United States.

—Lizzetta LeFalle-Collins

OVERSTREET, Joe (Wesley)

American painter

Born: Conehatta, Mississippi, 20 June 1933. **Education:** San Francisco Arts Institute; San Francisco State University; California School of Fine Arts, 1953; California School of Arts and Crafts, 1954; Contra Costa College, 1951-52; studied with Sargent Johnson. **Military Service:** Merchant Seaman, 1951-58. **Family:** One daughter and three sons. **Career:** Founder (with Corrine Jennings and Samuel C. Floyd), 1974, and since 1974 artistic director, Kenkeleba House, New York. Animation artist, Walt Disney Studios, 1953; lecturer, California State University at Heyward, 1971-73. Print artist-in-residence, Brandywine Workshop, 1988-89. **Address:** c/o Kenkeleba Gallery, 214 East Second Street, New York, New York 10009, U.S.A.

Individual Exhibitions:

1954	The District, Oakland, California
1955	Vesuvio's, San Francisco
1956	Cousin Jimbo's Bop City, San Francisco
1958	International Gallery, New York
	Tea Gallery, San Francisco
1961	Spengerman Gallery Atlanta, Georgia, New York
1965	Hugo Gallery, New York
1969	Studio Museum in Harlem, New York
1970	Berkeley Rotary Art Center, California
1971	De Luxe Black Art Center
	Rice University, Houston, Texas
	Living Art Center, Dayton, Ohio
	Ankrum Gallery, Los Angeles
	Dorsky Gallery, New York
1976	Kenkeleba House, New York
1988	Kenkeleba Gallery, New York
1990	Vaughan Cultural Center, St. Louis, Missouri
1991	Wilmer Jennings Gallery, New York
1992	Montclair State College Art Gallery, Upper Montclair, New Jersey
	G.R. N'Namdi Gallery, Birmingham, Michigan

Joe Overstreet: *Black Star Line,* 1990. Photo courtesy of Kenkeleba House, Inc., New York.

1993	Kenkeleba Gallery, New York
1996	Everson Museum, Syracuse, New York
	New Jersey State Museum, Trenton (retrospective)
	Aljira Contemporary Art Center, Newark, New Jersey

Selected Group Exhibitions:

1984	Bucknell University, Lewisberg, Pennsylvania (traveling)
1986	Pennsylvania Academy of Fine Arts, Philadelphia
	Bergen County Museum, New Jersey
	Hampton Institute, Virginia (traveling)
	Newark Museum, New Jersey
	Studio Museum in Harlem, New York
1989	Washington Project for the Arts (traveling)
1991	Museo Nacional des Bellas Artes, Santiago, Chile
1992	New Jersey State Museum, Trenton (traveling through 1994)
	A/CROSS CURRENTS: Synthesis in African American Abstract Painting, Dakar Biennale, Senegal (traveling through 1993)
1995	Anita Shapolsky Gallery, New York
1996	Kenkeleba Gallery, New York

Collections:

Atlantic Richfield Corporation, Philadelphia; Brooklyn Museum, New York; Carillon Corporation, Fort Lee, New Jersey; Chase Manhattan Bank, New York; Chicago Bank for Savings; Cochran Collection of Works on Paper, Stone Mountain, Georgia; Colgate-Palmolive Corporation, New York; Crockett Museum, Sacramento, California; John de Menil Collection, Houston, Texas; Living Art Center, Dayton, Ohio; Menil Foundation, Houston, Texas; New York Health and Hospital Corporation, New York; New York Urban Coalition; Newark Museum, New Jersey; Oakland Museum, California; Port Authority of New York and New Jersey; Sam Dorsky Gallery, New York; University of California at Berkeley Museum.

Publications:

On OVERSTREET: Books—*Joe Overstreet: (Re)call and Response,* exhibition catalog, Syracuse, New York, Everson Museum of Art, 1996; *Joe Overstreet: Works from 1957 to 1993,* exhibition catalog, Trenton, New Jersey State Museum, 1996. **Articles**—*Arts,* 44, December 1969; *Time,* 6 April 1970; *Art Forum,* September 1970; "Joe Overstreet: Work in Progress" by C. L. Jennings, in *Black American Literary Forum,* 19(1), Spring 1985; "Seedbeds of Jazz Captured on Canvas" by Vivien Raynor, in *New York Times,* 16 February 1992; "Joe Overstreet" by Tom McEvilley, in *Art Forum,* April 1994 (illustration); "Getting a Feel for Joe Overstreet" by Janet Purcell, in *Trenton Times,* 2 February 1996.

*   *   *

The versatility of Joe Overstreet's artistry is measured by its breadth and its contribution to postmodernism. He has worked in figuralism, geometric abstraction, process art, and mixed-media construction. He is an engaged artist who has successfully balanced the demands of addressing visual and cultural histories while remaining attuned to the contemporary and relevant.

Overstreet's straightforward figural expressionism burgeoned into his earliest examples of cultural criticism and satire in the 1960s. In 1963 the Mississippi-born artist offered *Strange Fruit,* a painting that takes its title from the blues dirge about lynching. Its disturbing imagery includes contorted, masklike faces and, most strikingly, the sneaker-clad feet and legs of a boy, who is the "strange fruit" hanging from an unseen tree. This sobering commentary on racist violence and terror was followed by the radical black power statement of *The New Jemima* (1964). Like his peers Murry DePillars, Jeff Donaldson, and Betye Saar, Overstreet subverted the commercial and cultural icons of pop art by transforming this symbol of black servility into a gun-toting, pancake-blasting militant. This revised Aunt Jemima is painted on a larger-than-life box construc-

tion and introduced for consumption as fine art. Overstreet's brash move matched the innovation of Andy Warhol's Brillo boxes and Roy Lichtenstein's comic strip paintings.

In the late 1960s Overstreet made geometric abstractions inspired by African, Native American, and Asian iconography. He began making wall-size paintings and then developed the strategy of lashing canvases with ropes and battening them to gallery walls, ceilings, and floors. In design these colorful cloths resembled flags, sails, pinwheels, coats of arms, shields, canopies, kites, and targets. Variably taut, slack, and airy, they existed dynamically within exhibition spaces and surprised audiences with their playful, antiprecious, and ritual appearances. This sizable body of work, along with contemporaneous innovations by Sam Gilliam, challenged the parameters of painting and sculpture. In addition, it made for readable symbolism. The color selection and titles were suggestive of the hues of the black liberation flag (red, black, and green), as in *Power Flight* (1971); *Hoo Doo Mandala* (1970), alludes to the ritual art of the East and black folk tradition.

The human figure, which had appeared in some of Overstreet's abstractions, such as *Gemini* (1971), reemerged again in his "Storyville" series of paintings and prints (1988). Inspired by New Orleans jazz, these works use raw silhouettes to represent musical trailblazers, among them Buddy Bolden. The works are rendered in impastoed high-key values of yellow, red, and orange. The faces are indiscernible and the pictorial space deliberately sketchy, but the instruments depicted and the body language of performance convincingly set the scene for Overstreet's tribute.

After a trip to Senegal in 1992, Overstreet created a series of large paintings centered on the history of the slave trade and on African culture and geography. Metaphors operate in brilliant and dark passages that perhaps represent, respectively, African fields and marketplaces, slave prison dungeons and ship holds.

—Jacqueline Francis

PAJAUD, William (E., Jr.)
American painter

Born: New Orleans, Louisiana, 3 August 1925. **Education:** Xavier University, New Orleans, 1942-46, B.A. 1946; Chouinard Art Institute, Los Angeles, 1952-55, M.A. 1955. **Family:** Married 1) Harriette Pajaud in 1946 (divorced 1952), three sons; 2) Donla Pajaud in 1970, two daughters; 3) June M. Pajaud in 1996. **Career:** Sign Artist, F. W. Woolworth, Chicago, 1946-48; designer (freelance), Los Angeles, 1949-51; postal clerk, United States Post Office, Los Angeles, 1951-53; artist, Los Angeles County, Los Angeles, 1953-57; art director, Golden State Mutual Life, Los Angeles, 1957-88. Served as president of the National Watercolor Society. **Awards:** Paul Robeson Award; Angeles Plaza Senior Center Award; *Legends of Black Art* Award, Artists Salute to Black History Month, 1996 and 1997. **Agent:** Eric Hanks, M. Hanks Gallery, 3008 Main Street, Santa Monica, California 90405, U.S.A.; Bernard Basley, Third World Art Exchange, 2016 Hillhurst, Los Angeles, California 90027, U.S.A. **Address:** 4428 Circleview Drive, Los Angeles, California 90043, U.S.A. **Online Address:** PajArt@aol.com.

Individual Exhibitions:

1966	Brockman Gallery, Los Angeles
1987	Harris-Brown Gallery, Boston
1988	Alitash Kabede Fine Arts, Los Angeles
1992	Left of Center Art Gallery, Las Vegas
1995	Bomani Gallery, San Francisco
	Angeles Plaza Senior Center, Los Angeles
1996	Angeles Plaza Senior Center, Los Angeles

Selected Group Exhibitions:

1981	Afro-American Museum, Los Angeles
1996	Satori Fine Arts, Chicago
	Stella Jones Gallery, New Orleans

Collections:

Amistad Research Center, New Orleans; Las Vegas Art Museum, Nevada; Pushkin Museum, Leningrad; Smithsonian Institution, Washington, D.C.

Publications:

On PAJAUD: Articles—"The Life and Art of William Pajaud" by Paul Von Blum, in *American Visions,* December 1995.

*

William Pajaud comments:
Both my ethnic and cultural backgrounds serve as root sources of my work. The awareness and acceptance of humankind—universal, following life's awesome rhythms with dignity and pain, joy, poverty, and often jubilation—cause me to paint. My primary need is to show my "gut reaction" to our efforts to cope with the cycles of life and death. The aesthetic results of attempting to communicate these universal concepts is to me almost coincidental.

* * *

William Pajaud's prolific contributions in producing a body of work and in fostering community awareness of African American art have made him a powerful presence in the vibrant community of African American artists in southern California. From the early 1950s through the 1990s he has produced scores of engaging paintings and prints highlighting the triumphs and chronicling the problems of his fellow African Americans. Combining stylistic innovation with diverse themes, he has augmented the distinguished stature of his contemporaries, including Jacob Lawrence, John Biggers, Elizabeth Catlett, Betye Saar, Samella Lewis, and J. Eugene Grigsby.

Pajaud's memories of his Southern childhood and youth have deeply informed his artwork. The rich experiences of the renowned musical accomplishments of African Americans, for example, find vivid expression in Pajaud's watercolors and other efforts. His personal encounters with the overt racism of the era have similarly influenced his visual work, providing a powerful social undercurrent throughout his career.

For more than thirty years Pajaud worked full-time while producing his paintings, drawings, and prints at night and during weekends. While he was the art director at the Golden State Mutual Life Insurance Company in Los Angeles, he developed one of the most striking collections of African American art in the country. With a minuscule budget he acquired works from a stunning array of artistic luminaries. His curatorial vision has enabled viewers of all ethnicities to augment their knowledge of black culture and history.

Pajaud has articulated a strong vision of his artistic objectives. He paints and draws in response to white society's continuing propensity to tell African Americans that they have little or no worth. He proudly revels in his own heritage, using his art to tell a more positive story to his audience. Specifically eschewing the overt social protest of many black artists, he prefers a less obvious but no less effective form of artistic communication. His works routinely provide an affectionate glimpse into the daily lives of his fellow African Americans. His numerous paintings about ordinary existence reveal a deeper social truth. Pajaud's sympathetic depictions join a long tradition of twentieth-century black artists who create positive imagery to repudiate harmful and inaccurate stereotypes of African Americans in the media and elsewhere.

An especially gifted watercolorist, Pajaud uses the medium regularly to highlight the vitality of black musical history. His vivid

William Pajaud. Photo courtesy of Howard Morehead.

recollections of his father's renowned musical performances in New Orleans inform his own artistic production. His efforts contribute to the extensive musical motif among notable twentieth-century black masters such as Archibald Motley, Romare Bearden, William H. Johnson, and Charles White. Like Bearden in particular, he celebrates jazz as the embodiment of African American culture.

Pajaud has also used his work to honor African American women for their strength and perseverance. Several major paintings express affection and respect for women's devotion to their children and families. These artworks also repudiate insensitive images of black women as being callous and unconcerned about the present activities and future lives of their children.

Despite his discomfort with trenchant protest art, Pajaud has nevertheless created some works that call explicit attention to various social problems in the United States. These efforts are rooted in the deeper humanist strain of Western art. His socially oriented paintings and prints follow in the figurative tradition of such major figures as Francisco Goya, Honoré Daumier, Georges Rouault, Käthe Kollwitz, Diego Rivera, and Ben Shahn as well as twentieth-century African American figures that include Lawrence, Catlett, and White. His works over the years have focused, for example, on poverty and homelessness, the bleak prospects for African American children, and the sexual abuse of African American women.

Pajaud's curatorial energies and artworks have documented and celebrated the experiences and accomplishments of his people. His efforts for more than forty years add depth and distinction to a visual tradition whose origins derive from the Harlem Renaissance, and he has proved himself an accomplished successor to the major African American artistic figures of that era. He has authentically

established himself as a genuine legend, a title appropriately bestowed on him when he was honored at the fourteenth annual artists' salute to Black History Month in Los Angeles in 1996.

—Paul Von Blum

PARKS, Gordon (Alexander Buchanan)
American photographer

Born: Fort Scott, Kansas, 30 November 1912. **Education:** Self-taught in photography. **Military Service:** Office of War Information: photographer, 1943-45. **Family:** Married 1) Sally Alvis in 1933 (divorced 1961); 2) Elizabeth Campbell in 1962 (divorced 1973); 3) Genevieve Young in 1973, four children. **Career:** Worked as busboy, piano-player, lumberjack, dining-car waiter and professional basketball player, St. Paul, Minnesota, 1928-37; freelance fashion photographer, Minneapolis, 1937-42; staff photographer, Farm Security Administration, Washington, D.C., and throughout the United States, 1942-43; photographer and documentary filmmaker, Standard Oil Company, New Jersey, throughout the United States and in Saudi Arabia, 1945-48; staff photographer, *Life* magazine, New York, 1948-61; independent photographer, film writer and director, working for *Show, Vogue, Venture,* and Warner Brothers/Seven Arts film companies, Metro-Goldwyn-Mayer and Paramount Pictures, 1962-71; editorial director, *Essence* magazine, New York, 1970-73. **Awards:** Julius Rosenwald Fellowship in photography, 1942; Frederic W. Brehm Award, 1962; School of Journalism Prize, Syracuse University, New York, 1963; National Council for Christians and Jews Award, 1964; Philadelphia Museum of Art Award, 1964; Art Directors Club of New York Award, 1964, 1968; Carr Van Anda Journalism Award, Ohio University, 1970; Springarn Award, National Association for the Advancement of Colored People, 1972. Honorary doctorates: Maryland Institute of Fine Arts, Baltimore, 1968, Boston University, 1969, University of Connecticut, Storrs, 1969, Kansas State University, Manhattan, 1970, Saint Olaf College, Northfield, Minnesota, 1973. **Address:** 860 United Nations Plaza, New York, New York 10017, U.S.A.

Individual Exhibitions:

1953	Art Institute of Chicago
1960	Limelight Gallery, New York
1966	Time-Life Gallery, New York
1979	Alex Rosenberg Gallery, New York
1981	Alex Rosenberg Gallery, New York
1984	Baltimore Museum of Art, Maryland
1985	Laguna Gloria Art Museum, Austin, Texas
	Chrysler Museum, Norfolk, Virginia
1986	Union National Bank and Trust Company, Manhattan, Kansas

Selected Group Exhibitions:

1951	*Memorable Life Photographs,* Museum of Modern Art, New York
1964	*World Exhibition of Photography: What is Man?,* Pressehaus Stern, Hamburg (traveling)

1967 National Gallery of Canada, Ottawa (traveling)
1973 *The Concerned Photographer 2,* Israel Museum, Jerusalem (traveling)
1977 Museum Friedericianum, Kassel, West Germany
1979 Centre Georges Pompidou, Paris
1980 *The Imaginary Photo Museum,* Kunsthalle, Cologne
1983 International Center of Photography, New York
1984 Museum Ludwig, Cologne
1985 *American Images 1945-80,* Barbican Art Gallery, London (traveling)

Collections:

Art Institute of Chicago; International Center of Photography, New York; International Museum of Photography, George Eastman House, Rochester, New York; Library of Congress, Washington, D.C.; Museum Ludwig, Cologne; Museum of Modern Art, New York; Wichita State University, Kansas.

Publications:

By PARKS: Books—*Flash Photography,* New York, 1947; *Camera Portraits,* New York, 1948; *The Learning Tree,* New York, 1963, London, 1964; *A Choice of Weapons,* New York, 1966; *A Poet and His Camera,* New York and London, 1968; *Whispers of Intimate Things,* New York, 1971; *Born Black,* New York, 1971; *In Love,* New York, 1971; *Moments without Proper Names,* London, 1975; *Flavio,* New York, 1978; *To Smile in Autumn: A Memoir,* New York and London, 1979; *Shannon,* Boston, 1981; *Voices in the Mirror,* 1990. **Music—***Piano Concerto,* 1953; *3 Piano Sonatas,* 1956, 1958, 1960; *Tree Symphony,* 1967. **Films—***Flavio,* 1962; *The Learning Tree,* 1969; *Shaft,* 1972; *Shaft's Big Score,* 1972; *The Super Cops,* 1974; *Leadbelly,* 1976.

On PARKS: Books—*Gordon Parks* by Midge Turk, New York, 1971; *Gordon Parks: Black Photographer and Film Maker* by Terry Harnan, Champaign, Illinois, 1972. **Articles—**"The Concerned Photographer" by Cornell Capa, in *Zoom* (Paris), 16, 1973; "Le Dossier de la misere," in *Photo* (Paris), February 1980; "A Gordon Parks Retrospective" by Jim Jordan, in *Artweek,* 30 March 1985, p. 12; review (Union National Bank and Trust Company, Manhattan, Kansas) by Angel Kwolek-Folland, in *New Art Examiner,* 13, Summer 1986, p. 54; "Six Stories That Made a Difference" by Vicki Goldberg, in *American Photo,* 2, September/October 1991, pp. 80-88 (illustrated); "Parks' Department (Gordon Parks)" by Caroline Smith, in *British Journal of Photography,* 21 October 1993, pp. 10-11 (illustrated).

* * *

The related fields of photography and motion pictures have been the vehicle through which many African Americans have risen to prominence. Gordon Parks is one who has made such a mark, and he was a first in many of his achievements.

Parks was born in Fort Scott, Kansas, a part of America's heartland that is tinged with a Southern flavor. His hometown was not a place he particularly liked. In his autobiography, *Voices in the Mirror,* he mentions that the town made him aware of the tremendous barriers he faced because of his race. His other formative years were spent in Minnesota, on the northern edge of the heartland.

Parks is multitalented, and his creativity manifests itself in such a wide variety of ways that one has to strain to find someone his equal. He could have had a career in many fields, including writing, painting, or composing. In addition to being a photographer, Parks turned his trained eye to motion pictures. He was a pioneer as the first black Hollywood director, and his film *Shaft* was a great commercial success. His entry into mainstream Hollywood, however, was the success of a work he produced called *The Learning Tree,* which was based on a book he had written.

Shaft has become somewhat controversial, for it was the seminal work in a genre of films that, rightly or wrongly, have been called blaxploitation. The films had flashy antiheroes from the black ghetto as principal figures and graphically depicted violence. On a positive note Parks has remarked that *Shaft* gave many black people, including himself, experience behind the camera. Too, the theme song for *Shaft,* written by Isaac Hayes, received an Academy award, a first for a black composer. The film thus opened doors in Hollywood for numerous black professionals.

Parks has achieved commercial success in other areas. His work has appeared in such national magazines as *Life,* where he was the first black staff photographer. His earliest assignments suggest the breadth of his creativity as artist. For example, he produced a photoessay on the underbelly of Harlem and immediately following that was sent to Paris to photograph the latest French fashions. He has not only documented African American life but also focused his trained eye on the world at large. He is, for example, well known for his work on Flavio, a waif in Brazil. His images reveal a distinctive exploitation of chiaroscuro, the dramatic use of light and dark contrasts to enhance visual effect.

Parks seems to have moved effortlessly through the social world and transcended the racial divide. And yet the candor of his autobiography reveals complexities, as when, even though he had become a famous and successful photographer and filmmaker, he encountered slights and difficulties when he returned to his hometown to make a film. Above all, however, in both photography and motion pictures Parks succeeded where other African Americans had not.

—Thomas M. Shaw

PERKINS, Marion

American sculptor

Born: Marche, Arkansas, 1908. **Education:** Informal training at South Side Community Art Center, Chicago. **Family:** Married Eve Perkins, three sons. **Career:** Worked as janitor, dishwasher, postal worker, newspaper seller, and freight handler. **Awards:** Robert Rice Jenkins Prize, 1948; Julius Rosenwald Fellowship, 1948; Pauline Palmer Purchase Prize, 1951; purchase prize, Art Institute of Chicago, 1951. **Died:** 17 December 1961.

Selected Exhibitions:

American Negro Exposition (1940); Art Institute of Chicago; DuSable Museum of African American History, Chicago; Howard University, Washington, D.C.; Hull House, Chicago; Rockford College, Illinois (1960); Xavier University, New Orleans (1960).

Collections:

Jackson State College, Mississippi.

Publications:

On PERKINS: Article—"Marion Perkins," in *Ebony,* 6, October 1951, pp. 107-13; "Marion Perkins—Worker-Artist" by Victoria Steele, in *Masses and Mainstream,* August 1952, p.17.

*   *   *

During the Great Depression, Marion Perkins sold newspapers on Chicago's South Side and carved likenesses of friends and relatives out of soap. Though primarily self-taught, his sculpting talent was noticed by Community Arts Center director Peter Pollack during a Works Progress Administration playwright workshop. Pollack introduced him to Simon ("Sy") Gordon, who was teaching at the South Side Community Art Center. Gordon befriended Marion Perkins and later acquainted him with the methods of clay models, molds, and the mallet and chisel.

Though Perkins received many awards (including the Robert Rice Jenkins Prize, the Julius Rosenwald Fellowship, and the Pauline Palmer Purchase Prize) and a good deal of notoriety, he was never able to support himself by proceeds from his art alone. Prize money allowed him to go to New York, where he visited museums and discussed art with other artists. But he continued working as a freight handler long after becoming a successful sculptor, and he often sought out buildings that were being demolished so he could salvage the limestone and other materials necessary to his sculpture.

An art critic at the *Chicago Daily News* said Marion Perkins was "an artist of great integrity," particularly "noted for his expressive portraits." Also proclaimed one of "the more conscious social realists" by art historian Cedric Dover, Perkins, though exposed to European-influenced art, was more affected by the art and history of Africa and African Americans. Some of his more famous sculptures are *John Henry (1943), Ethiopia Awakening (1948),* and *Man of Sorrows* (1950), the last being a commanding bust of a black, unshaven Christ.

Throughout his life, Perkins devoted part of his time to encouraging art in Chicago's black communities. He was one of the promoters of the South Side Community Art Center, and he was a founder of the Lake Meadows Art Fair, a street fair in Chicago displaying the work of black artists. The Marion Perkins Memorial Foundation exists at Jackson State College in Mississippi (where much of his sculpture resides) to encourage art education.

—Terry Bain

PHILLIPS, (Charles) James

American painter and muralist

Born: Brooklyn, New York, 1945. **Education:** Philadelphia College of Art, 1964-65. **Career:** Artist-in-residence, Studio Museum in Harlem, New York, 1971-72, Howard University, Washington, D.C., 1973-77, San Francisco County Jail, San Bruno, California, 1988-89. **Awards:** Creative Artists Public Service Award, New York, 1971; National Endowment for the Arts Exchange Fellowship, 1980.

Individual Exhibitions:

1968	Children's Museum, New York
1970	Weusi Numba Ya Sanaa Gallery, New York
1972	Pennsylvania Academy of Fine Arts, Philadelphia
	Howard University, Washington, D.C.
1981	American Center, Tokyo
1987	Sargent Johnson Gallery, San Francisco

Selected Group Exhibitions:

1972	Wesleyan University, Middletown, Connecticut
1973	Corcoran Gallery of Art, Washington, D.C.
	Selma Burke Center, Pittsburgh, Pennsylvania
1979	*Second New World Festival of the African Diaspora,* Port-au-Prince, Haiti
1983	Kenkeleba House, New York
1984	Center Gallery, Bucknell University, Lewisburg, Pennsylvania (traveling)
1985	Studio Museum in Harlem, New York (traveling)
	University of Maryland Eastern Shore, Princess Anne, Maryland
1987	Fort de France, Martinique
1988	Fay Gold Gallery, Atlanta, Georgia

Collections:

Adam Clayton Powell, Jr. State office Collection, New York; Hall of Justice, City of San Francisco; Fisk University Museum of Art, Nashville; Gallery of Art, Howard University, Washington, D.C.; Schomburg Center, New York.

*   *   *

The paintings of James Phillips offer a unique visual interpretation of sound and movement. In them he demonstrates a vast knowledge of color and an exhaustive mastery of his medium. Much of what he conveys through his imagery is informed by his early arts education and an intrinsic understanding of rhythm and its various applications.

After formal training in the 1960s, Phillips spent time in New York City, where he became acquainted with several popular jazz musicians of the time. Contact with musicians like John Coltrane and with visual artists like Romare Bearden in the late 1960s had a lasting affect on Phillips's aesthetic sensibilities. With this innovative music and art as a source of inspiration, he began incorporating large shapes, zigzags, and strong color opposites in his work.

Phillips revealed an investigation of his African heritage in *JuJu.* This large-scale, square-shaped mixed-media painting is energized by the irregular patches of color that move freely throughout the composition. Pairs of eyes belonging to masks dance and bounce in synchroneity with dots and zigzags that are dispersed over the ground of the painting. The work is emblazoned with contrasting colors and abstracted masks, creating improvisational rhythmic statements in some ways analogous to the music Phillips was hearing.

During the 1960s and 1970s Phillips's association with two artists' groups, Weusi and Africobra, added a significant dimension to his art and profoundly affected the development of his artistic vision. Phillips's expanded vocabulary of African icons was consistent with the prevailing sentiments of the African American scholarly and artistic communities that espoused an identification with African culture.

The decade of the 1970s became a defining moment in the evolution of Phillips's signature style. During this time he encountered a number of African artists, including Skunder Boghossian and Twins Seven-Seven, from whom he drew considerable influence. He would later come to know the work of John Biggers, who incorporated in his own imagery an unmistakably African and African American iconography. Phillips was also affected by a multitude of other cultural influences, including West African sculpture and fabrics, Egyptian mythology and iconography, Native American cosmograms, African American quilts of the nineteenth and twentieth centuries, and *veves,* the complex designs that represent specific deities in the voodoo religion of Haiti. In 1980 Phillips spent a year in Japan studying painting techniques and Buddhist symbols.

In *Ancestral Dream,* Phillips united African and Asian influences. A large red circle in the left middle ground of the painting is the fusion of the Kongo cosmogram and Japanese mandala. This image and others like it are encircled by a snake figure from Ghanaian and Haitian mythology, and throughout the composition are stars and crescent moons, referring to the galaxy. Translucent Janus-faced profiles and the heads of Ashante fertility figures float on the currents created by the zigzags and patterns of colored squares and triangles taken from African textile designs.

It was in the late 1970s and the early 1980s that Phillips's paintings became architectonic and grid based. In these hard-edged, geometric compositions his African signs and symbols remain intact, and his painting style and technique are more calculated. The grids on the paintings are obvious. At first glance shapes and patterns that are arranged asymmetrically appear to be random and nonrepeating, but further examination reveals a deliberate, conscious, and well-balanced configuration.

In his later works Phillips speaks a more elaborate visual language that reflects his experiences abroad as well as in different areas of the United States. Today he makes sociopolitical statements such as those found in *No Justice Then, No Justice Now,* and *The Positive Aspects of Huey P. Newton,* with many of the same symbols continuing to occur in opaque and translucent forms. More important, however, is his adeptness at painting images that impart universal messages of heaven and earth, positive and negative, and life and death. It is in addressing these concepts that Phillips has secured his position among contemporary urban shamans.

—Regina Holden Jennings

PIERCE, Delilah
American painter

Born: Delilah Williams, Washington, D.C., 3 March 1904. **Education:** Howard University, Washington, D.C., B.S.; Columbia University, New York, M.A. **Career:** Traveled in Africa, Europe, and Middle East in 1962. **Awards:** Agnes Meyer Summer Fellowship, 1962; American Federation of Arts Award, 1964; Delilah Pierce Day for Cultural Contributions, 1980; National Conference of Artists Award, 1981; Washington, D.C., Federation of Civic Associa-

tion, Inc., Award, 1983; Washington, D.C., AAUW Professional Achievement Award, 1984; Howard University Art Department Alumni Award, 1989; Honorary doctorate: University of Columbia, 1992. **Died:** 1992.

Selected Exhibitions:

1952	Atlanta University, Georgia
	Smithsonian Institution, Washington, D.C.
1955	Smithsonian Institution, Washington, D.C.
1957	Corcoran Gallery of Art, Washington, D.C.
1958	Corcoran Gallery of Art, Washington, D.C.
	Barnett Aden Gallery, Washington, D.C.
1959	Corcoran Gallery of Art, Washington, D.C.
	Barnett Aden Gallery, Washington, D.C.
	Baltimore Museum of Art, Maryland
1960	Barnett Aden Gallery, Washington, D.C.
	Howard University, Washington, D.C.
	Georgetown University, Washington, D.C.
1963	Howard University, Washington, D.C.
1964	Howard University, Washington, D.C.
	20th Century Gallery, Williamsburg, Virginia
1966	Howard University, Washington, D.C.
1968	Hampton Institute, Virginia
1969	Catholic University, Washington, D.C.
1970	New Jersey State Museum, Trenton
1972	University of Pennsylvania
1973	United States Embassy in Cairo, Egypt and Zaire
1976	Howard University, Washington, D.C. (through 1980)
1982	National Museum of American Art, Washington, D.C.
	Montpelier Cultural Arts Center, Vermont
1983	Schenectady Museum, New York
	Evans-Tibbs Gallery, Washington, D.C.
1985	United Nations Conference on Women, Nairobi, Kenya, Africa
1986	Kenkeleba Gallery, New York
1989	Anacostia Museum, Smithsonian Institution, Washington, D.C.

Collections:

Barnet-Aden Collection, Museum of African American Art, Tampa, Florida; Howard University, Washington, D.C.; University of the District of Columbia.

Publications:

On PIERCE: Book—*The Barnett-Aden Collection* by John Kinard, Washington, D.C., Smithsonian, 1974. **Articles**—"The Negro Artist and the Racial Mountain" by Langston Hughes, in *Black Expression,*1969; "Delilah W. Pierce" by Judith Means, in *Art Voices/ South,* May-June 1980.

*   *   *

Delilah Pierce was a contributor to the American art scene as both teacher and painter. She mastered painting media and explored various techniques, and her paintings cannot be categorized as belonging to one predominant style. Pierce's paintings reflected the influences of both the evolution of the abstract expressionist movement and the post-World War II African American consciousness. Other early influences included Loïs Mailou Jones, who was Pierce's teacher at Howard University, and the Washington Workshop Center, where Pierce experimented with color-field painting.

Many of Pierce's early paintings were of humans, and although the people appear peaceful, the paintings impart an attitude suggesting a desire for change. *Supplication (*1960), for example, shows a young woman in a blue dress standing in what appears to be an American city street and looking toward heaven. The woman's hands, which have long and graceful fingers, are held palm up in a pleading manner. The buildings in the background are tilted, suggesting unsteadiness. The paintings *Sudanese Tradesmen* (1962) and *On the River Niger* (1963) are of black people living in another culture, but they also, perhaps in a less obvious way, suggest the desire for change. Along with the human subjects in *Sudanese Tradesmen* are a camel, sheep, a mask, and drums—items indicative of both mobility and tradition. In *On the River Niger* only the backs of the heads can be seen. The subjects are turned away from the viewer and are looking at the river, a symbol of movement, life, change, and the irreversible passage of time. The brush strokes and the acrylic washes in the painting create the illusion of movement. *Tradermen-Khartoum, Sudan* (1962) shows a close grouping of men, perhaps in a crowded marketplace. In these so-called Sudanese paintings Pierce uses groups of people to suggest strength. Other devices for conveying the feeling of strength are the use of vertical structures such as trees or pillars and the vertical composition of the subjects.

Pierce often used conspicuous vertical images in her paintings. In 1980 she finished a triptych entitled *Nature's Legacy/Symphony* that is reminiscent of Gustav Klimt's early symbolist landscapes. Each panel depicts tall tree trunks, highly contrasted against the background, and the trees in the center panel are separated by a path, making the viewer wonder where it leads. Other examples of prominent vertical images are seen in the paintings *Vineyard Haven Harbor* (1957), *Waterfront* (1958), and *Daffodils* (1958). These paintings also reflect the influence of cubism and impressionism; the images are angular and highly textured, with strong contrasts achieved by shadowing through the application of paint rather than through the use of color.

Abstract expressionist in style, *Nebulae* (1982) and *Jazz Vibrations* (1988-89) use color as a structural form and were painted to create a mosaic effect. *Harborside Mosaic* (1979) is a circular image of a coastal village painted on a rectangular canvas. The ocean and sky appear as a smooth expanse, while the village, beach, and trees are done in vertical and horizontal brush strokes. As a result the viewer may feel that the village is seen through a circular window. As with other black artists influenced by what was known in the 1950s and 1960s as the Washington color school, Pierce explored the connection between nature, color, and sound and emphasized form over content.

—Christine Miner Minderovic

PIERCE, Elijah
American wood-carver

Born: Near Baldwin, Mississippi, 5 March 1892. **Family:** Lived with Carrie Beene, one son. Married 1) ZeHa Palm, one son; 2)

Cornelia Hoeston; 3) Estelle Green. **Career:** Self-employed barber, Pierce's Barber Shop and Art Gallery. **Awards:** Honorary doctorate of fine arts, Franklin University, Columbus, Ohio, 1980; Columbus Art League Distinguished Service Award, 1983. **Died:** 7 May 1984.

Individual Exhibitions:

1971   Hopkins Hall Gallery, Ohio State University, Columbus
1993   Columbus Museum of Art, Ohio (retrospective)

Group Exhibitions:

1968   *Columbus Folk Art,* Y.W.C.A., Columbus, Ohio
1971   Ohio State University, Columbus
        Bernard Danenberg Galleries, New York
1972   University of Illinois, Urbana
        Museum of Modern Art, New York
1982   Corcoran Gallery of Art, Washington, D.C.

Collections:

Columbus Museum of Art, Ohio; National Museum of American Art, Washington, D.C.

Publications:

On PIERCE: Books—*Elijah Pierce Carvings,* exhibition catalog, Columbus, Ohio, Ohio State University, 1971; *Elijah Pierce: Painted Carvings,* exhibition catalog, New York, Bernard Danenberg Galleries, 1972; *Carvings,* exhibition catalog, Urbana, Illinois, Krannert Art Museum, University of Illinois, 1972; *Untitled III,* exhibition catalog, New York, Museum of Modern Art, 1972; *Elijah Pierce: Woodcarver,* exhibition catalog, University of Washington Press and Columbus Museum of Art, 1992. **Articles**—"Elijah Pierce: Preacher in Wood," in *American Collector,* 42(6/7), pp. 24-25; "Elijah Pierce: Sculptor, Preacher, Barber" by Betty Garrett, in *Art News,* 73, March 1974, pp. 114-15; "Sermons in Wood," in *Ebony,* 29, July 1974, pp. 67-69+; "Pierce at Phyllis Kind Gallery" by Jeff Perrone, in *Artforum,* 15, January 1977, pp. 60-61.

*   *   *

Elijah Pierce practiced the professions of barbering, preaching, and wood carving in Columbus, Ohio, for sixty years. His interest in wood carving, however, began during his childhood in rural Mississippi, where he often carved on trees in the woods near his home. After he settled in Columbus, Pierce's wood-carving instincts were rekindled when he made a small animal as an anniversary gift for his second wife. At the time of his death, at the age of 92, he was the most celebrated African American wood-carver of his generation. He was also the first of his generation to perceive the significance of this work and to present it to the public in a gallery setting.

Pierce's work may be divided into three periods. The early works were created during the 1930s, the middle works during the 1940s and the early 1950s, and the late works during the early 1970s and the 1980s. Pierce's style, method of working, and iconographic content were clearly different during the three periods. Although Pierce's primary profession was barbering, he was called to preach during the early 1920s, and many of his early- and middle-period works were carved as teaching tools to be used in his itinerant ministerial activities, including revivals and tent meetings.

Pierce's early wood carvings were characterized by a marked flatness of outline and detail and a lack of three-dimensionality. As his skills grew, Pierce's figures emerged from their backgrounds in low bas-relief, and he sometimes carved entirely through the wood to create three-dimensional cutouts. During the 1930s he also began combining cutouts and small reliefs into larger assemblages. He mounted some of these on paper or cardboard, others in large vertical frames that he then hinged together to create freestanding screens. The majority of Pierce's three-dimensional tableaux were created during this early period. The two works generally considered to be his masterpieces, *The Crucifixion* and *The Book of Wood*, were both produced in the 1930s.

Pierce's middle-period works exemplified a more accomplished carving technique as well as a more sophisticated design. The panels and three-dimensional figures of this period displayed softer contours and various levels of relief, and he also began introducing textural contrasts. Unlike his early period, which consisted primarily of religious works, his middle period showed a dramatic increase in secular scenes. Pierce portrayed sports heroes, popular entertainers, and other public figures, including those from his immediate surroundings in Columbus.

For reasons that are still not explained, Pierce discontinued his wood-carving activities from the mid-1950s to the early 1970s. A dormant period of almost twenty years is unusual for a folk artist. During this time, however, Pierce organized a gallery in one room of his barbershop and filled it with his panels and three-dimensional figures.

By 1972 Pierce's works had come to the attention of numerous folk art collectors, and he began carving again to meet the demands of a new audience. His barbershop and gallery were deluged with visitors, and Pierce received more commissions than he could complete. The subject matter of his late panels included new heroes, such as the Reverend Martin Luther King, Jr., and President John F. Kennedy, as well as numerous animals. In their flat, abbreviated modeling, the late works were stylistically more like the early panels. They were also painted in brighter colors and were less subtly carved than the middle-period works. During this time Pierce created second versions of some earlier works, for example, remounting *The Crucifixion*. He also cannibalized earlier works to create new pieces, employed vertical perspective, and used scale as a symbol of importance.

Many of Pierce's works were autobiographical in content. He was a masterful storyteller and depicted scenes of slavery, his early life in the South, and artifacts associated with membership in the Freemasons. Nonetheless, religious relief panels, which have been called "sermons in wood," make up the largest body of Pierce's works. His religious works were not visionary but were often drawn from biblical stories and his own experiences. Other works included freestanding animals and human figures, message signs, and moral lessons.

In 1979 Pierce accepted the young African American Leroy Almon as his aide, establishing the only known master-apprentice relationship between a contemporary African American folk artist and a nonfamily member. Almon assisted Pierce in his work, even executing some works in full partnership, and he helped Pierce incorporate the Elijah Pierce Art Gallery. Almon has continued the carving traditions of his mentor and today is a recognized folk artist in his own right.

—Regenia Perry

PIGATT, Anderson J.

American sculptor

Born: Baltimore, Maryland, 30 October 1928. **Education:** Studied woodworking and carpentry on the G.I. Bill; apprentice to furniture craftsman James Leach. **Career:** Gallery owner in Baltimore, Maryland.

Individual Exhibitions:

1973   Museum of the National Center of Afro-American Artists, Boston
        Anderson Pigatt Gallery, Baltimore, Maryland

Selected Group Exhibitions:

1967   Empire State Building, New York
1968   Pan Am Building, New York
1969   Brooklyn Museum, New York (traveling)
1971   Illinois Bell Telephone (traveling)
1974   Boston Museum of Fine Arts
1989   Meyerhoff Gallery, Maryland Institute College of Art, Baltimore

Collections:

Schomburg Center, New York.

Publications:

On PIGATT: Article—"Art: Anderson J. Pigatt" by Joyce Griffens, in *Unique New York,* October 1976.

*   *   *

The wood sculptor Anderson J. Pigatt infuses his works with symbols of Africa and African American spirituality. He began his career in the late 1960s and the early 1970s, at the height of the black arts movement. A great deal of African American writing and visual art from this period mirrored the social and political upheaval occurring in the country. While Pigatt's work is not without evidence of social protest (*Nigger Chained,* for example, is in the permanent collection of the Schomburg Center for Research in Black Culture at the New York Public Library), he also presents his appreciation of an African and African American artistic sensibility.

Pigatt's heavy, roughly carved sculptures are often grounded in large wooden platforms. Through his works the artist speaks eloquently about principles such as reciprocity and balance. These ideals can be clearly seen in *One*, a large lacquered carving. With *One*, Pigatt orchestrates a complicated communion of human and spirit worlds. The work is topped by a disk-shaped beatific figure. Suspended from the sculpture by a thin rod, the disk seems to float above the other more terrestrial elements of the work. Opposing the benevolent character of the disk is a dark amorphous shape imprisoned by several surrounding columns at the base of the sculpture. Between these two extremes Pigatt asserts his ideas concerning spiritual equilibrium, for at the sculpture's center is a singular human form protected by symbols derived from the artist's understanding of West African religions.

Pigatt continues his representation of religion and morality in the African diaspora in two other works—*The Prophet* and *Red Stick*. In *The Prophet* he comments on Christianity. He places a black Christ figure against a carving of the Ten Commandments, comparing the pronouncement of an arbitrary jealous God against his empathetic and forgiving Son. *Red Stick* is Pigatt's interpretation of the evolution of American Indian cultures under the dominance of European settlers. The sculpture is also the result of his urge to replicate balance in his art. A series of totemic symbols, the work shows tribal life in harmony with nature, an existence destroyed by the encroachment of the United States.

A native of Baltimore, Maryland, Pigatt began his training in woodworking at George Washington Carver High School. In 1955, following five years of military service, Pigatt began an apprenticeship in cabinetmaking. In the early 1960s he moved to New York City to do freelance work restoring furnishings by Thomas Chippendale, Thomas Sheraton, and Duncan Phyfe. It was also during this time that Pigatt launched his career as an artist. After living in New York for nearly twenty years, Pigatt then returned to Baltimore, where he continues to sculpt and operates his own gallery.

—Deirdre Cross

PINDELL, Howardena (Doreen)

American painter

Born: Philadelphia, 14 April 1943. **Education:** Boston University School of Fine and Applied Art, 1961-65, B.F.A. (cum laude) 1965; Yale University, New Haven, Connecticut, 1965-67, M.F.A. 1967. **Career:** Exhibition assistant, curatorial assistant, assistant curator, associate curator, Museum of Modern Art, New York, 1967-1979. Since 1979 professor of art, State University of New York at Stony Brook. Since 1995, visiting professor, Yale University, New Haven, Connecticut. Visiting faculty member, Skowhegan School of Painting and Sculpture, Maine, Vermont Studio School, Johnson, summer 1980. **Awards:** Creative Arts Fellowship, U.S./Japan Friendship Commission, 1981-82; National Endowment for the Arts grants, 1972-73; 1983-84; Ariana Foundation, 1984-85; Guggenheim Memorial Foundation Fellowship, 1987-88; Joan Mitchell Painting Award, 1994; Rockefeller Mentor Grant for College Art Association Conference, 1995; Boston University Alumni Award, 1983; award for distinguished body of work, College Art Association, 1990; Studio Museum in Harlem Artist Award, New York, 1994. **Agent:** George N'Namdi, G.R. N'Namdi Gallery, 161 Townsend, Birmingham, Michigan 48009, U.S.A. **Address:** 1793 Riverside Drive, #1H, New York, New York 10034, U.S.A.

Howardena Pindell: *Slavery: Memorial,* 1993.

Individual Exhibitions:

1992   Grove Gallery, State University of New York, Albany
       David Heath Gallery, Atlanta, Georgia
       G.R. N'Namdi Gallery, Birmingham, Michigan
       Brandeis University (traveling retrospective through 1995)
1995   G.R. N'Namdi Gallery, Birmingham, Michigan
       Arting Gallery, Cologne, Germany
1996   Bethel College, St. Paul, Minnesota
       Charter Oak Cultural Center, Hartford, Connecticut
       G.R. N'Namdi Gallery, Birmingham, Michigan

Selected Group Exhibitions:

1990   New Museum, Museum of Contemporary Hispanic Art,
       Studio Museum in Harlem, New York
1991   Kenkeleba House Gallery (traveling through 1992)
1992   Boston Museum of Fine Arts
       High Museum of Art, Atlanta, Georgia (traveling through
       1993)
1994   Munson Williams Proctor Museum, Atlanta, Georgia
1995   Yale University Art Museum, New Haven, Connecticut
1996   Spelman College Art Museum, Atlanta, Georgia
       Louisiana Museum, Copenhagen, Denmark
       Museum of Modern Art, New York

Collections:

African Historical and Cultural Museum, Philadelphia; Afro-American Museum, Los Angeles; Brooklyn Museum, New York; City University of New York; Corcoran Gallery of Art, Washington, D.C.; Davison Art Center, Wesleyan University, Middleton, Connecticut; Everson Museum, Everson, New York; New York Public Library; Fogg Art Museum, Harvard University, Cambridge, Massachusetts; High Museum, Atlanta, Georgia; Jane Voorhees Zimmeril Art Museum, Rutgers University, New Brunswick, New Jersey; Maryland Art Institute, Baltimore, Maryland; Metropolitan Museum of Art, New York; Mount Holyoke College Museum, South Hadley, Massachusetts; Museum of Contemporary Art, Chicago; Museum of Fine Arts, Houston; Museum of Modern Art, New York; National Gallery (Vogel Collection), Washington, D.C.; New Museum of Art, New York; Newark Museum, New Jersey; Philadelphia Museum of Art; Rockefeller University, New York; Roy Neuberger Museum, Purchase, New York; Snug Harbor Cultural Center, Staten Island, New York; Studio Museum in Harlem, New York; Toledo Museum of Art, Ohio; University of California at Los Angeles; University of Iowa, Iowa City; Wadsworth Atheneum, Hartford, Connecticut; Walker Art Center, Minneapolis, Minnesota; Wayne State University, Detroit; Whitney Museum of American Art, New York; Yale University Art Gallery, New Haven, Connecticut.

Publications:

By PINDELL: Articles—"Mandaleo Yaa Wanawake, The Progress of Women," in *Feminist Art Journal,* Winter 1973-74, p. 17; "Collette Omagvai, Nigerian Printmaker," in *Women Studies Journal* (United Kingdom), 1979; "Criticism or Between the Lines," in *Heresies #8,* 2(4), January 1980, pp. 2-4; "Artists' Periodicals: An Event for 1984 or page 2001," in *Art Journal,* 39(4), Summer 1980, pp. 282-83; "An American Black Woman in a Japanese Garden," in *Her-*

Howardena Pindell: *Slavery Memorial: Naratives,* 1993.

esies #15, 4(3), February 1983, 54-55; "Cultural Colonialism," in *Lies of Our Times,* December 1990, pp. 4-5; "Some Reminiscences," in *Kaleidoscope,* Winter/Spring 1996, pp. 12-16.

On PINDELL: Book— *Howardena Pindell, Paintings and Drawings: A Retrospective Exhibition 1972-1992,* New York, Potsdam College, SUNY, 1992. **Articles**—"Howardena Pindell/Cyrus Gallery" by Ruth Bass, in *Art News,* March 1990, p. 162; "Long Island Q & A: Howardena Pindell, The Subtle and Not-So-Subtle Politics Inside the Artworld" by Sandra Weber, in *New York Times,* 21 October 1990, Long Island section, p. 2; "Howardena Pindell: The Culture Wars Continue," in *Sink,* Cleveland Institute of Art, pp. 6-7.

*   *   *

Howardena Pindell, born in Philadelphia in 1943, decided to become an artist when she was twelve years old. Encouraged by her parents, she undertook formal instruction in art, earning a B.A. from Boston University School of Fine and Applied Art and an M.F.A. at Yale University. She has been a practicing artist since 1967, when she began working at New York's Museum of Modern Art.

Beginning as a painter of urban scenes, Pindell became an abstract painter, initially less interested in color than in texture. In the 1970s her pale canvases supported richly textured surfaces. She applied paper dots dipped in paint and layered them on the canvas. She also sewed strips of canvas, which she embellished with such materials as paper, fiber, sequins, and even talcum powder.

An automobile accident in 1979 resulted in partial memory loss. To regain her memory, Pindell collected postcards depicting familiar places. She later used these postcards, and others from later journeys, to create new compositions on irregular canvases and boards. She cut the postcards—sometimes several of the same image—into strips to extend the icon and glued them onto the board. She painted the spaces between the postcard strips.

Pindell has often been the token African American in group shows, and the strong political content in her work has been attacked by both conservatives and radicals. This has been a source of pain and anger that she has channeled into stunning works of art and videos. For example, in *Autobiography: Air/CS 560* (1988), a painting on an oversized, irregular canvas, she painted silhouettes of her prone body on which words such as "assassination," "buried alive," "censorship," and "slave market" and questions such as "How dare you question" are superimposed. Other materials such as art and photography supplies and her own blood are embedded in the piece. Lowery S. Sims has said that "Pindell has managed to combine that exquisite sense of beauty and craft with a content that speaks to the arduousness of her journey and her confidence at its progress."

—Roslyn Adele Walker

PIPER, Adrian (Margaret Smith)
American conceptual, installation, and performance artist

Born: New York City, 1948. **Education:** School of Visual Arts, New York, 1966-69, A.A.; City College of New York, 1970-74, B.A. in philosophy; Harvard University, Cambridge, Massachusetts, 1974-77, M.A. in philosophy; University of Heidleberg, Germany, 1977-78; Harvard University, Cambridge, Massachusetts, 1981, Ph.D. in philosophy. **Awards:** First Prize in Drawing, School of Visual Arts, New York 1968; National Endowment for the Arts fellowships, 1979,1982; National Endowment for the Arts artists forums grant, 1987; Guggenheim Memorial Foundation Fellowship, 1989; Skowhegan School of Painting and Sculpture Medal, 1995. **Agent:** John Weber Gallery, 142 Greene Street, New York, New York 10012, U.S.A.; Paula Cooper Gallery, 155 Wooster Street, New York, New York, 10012, U.S.A. **Address:** Wellesley College, 106 Central Street, Wellesley, Massachusetts 02181, U.S.A.

Individual Exhibitions:

1987   Alternative Museum, New York (retrospective)
        Nexus Contemporary Art Center, Atlanta, Georgia (retrospective)
1989   Goldie Paley Gallery, Philadelphia (retrospective)
        John Weber Gallery, New York
1990   University of Colorado Art Gallery, Boulder (retrospective)
        Power Plant Gallery, Toronto (retrospective)
        Wooster Art Museum, Ohio (retrospective)
        Whitney Museum of American Art, New York (retrospective)
        Lowe Art Museum, Coral Gables, Florida (retrospective)

1991   Santa Monica Art Museum of Contemporary Art, California (retrospective)
        Washington Project for the Arts, Washington, D.C. (retrospective)
        Ikon Gallery, Birmingham, England (retrospective)

Selected Group Exhibitions:

1994   Whitney Museum of American Art, New York
1995   Southeastern Center for Contemporary Art, Winston-Salem, North Carolina
        Castle Gallery, College of New Rochelle, New York
        Forum for Contemporary Art, St. Louis, Missouri
        Cleveland Center for Contemporary Art, Ohio
        Stanton Gallery, Denver Art Museum
        Paula Cooper Gallery, New York
        Newark Art Museum, New Jersey
1996   Louisiana Museum of Modern Art, Humlebaek, Denmark
        Museum of Modern Art, New York

Collections:

American Academy of Art and Letters, New York; Art Institute of Chicago; Baltimore Museum of Art, Maryland; Brooklyn Museum, New York; Denver Art Museum; High Museum of Art, Atlanta; Musée d'Art Moderne, Paris; Museum of Contemporary Art, Chicago; Museum of Fine Arts, Houston; Ohio State University Museum of Fine Art, Dayton, Ohio; Williams College Art Museum, Williamstown, Massachusetts.

Publications:

By PIPER: Books—*Talking to Myself: The Ongoing Autobiography of an Art Object,* Bari, Italy, Marilena Bonomo, 1974; *Colored People,* London, Bookworks, 1991; *Decide Who You Are,* New York, Paula Cooper Gallery, 1992; *Out of Order, Out of Sight,* 2 volumes, Cambridge, Massachusetts, Massachusetts Institute of Technology Press, 1996. **Articles**—"Three Models of Art Productions Systems," in *Information* (New York), 1970; "The Mythic Being: I/You (Her)," in *Individuals: Post-Movement Art* edited by Alan Sondheim, New York, E.P. Dutton, 1976; "I Embody," in *From the Center: Feminist Essays on Women's Art* by Lucy Lippard, New York, E.P. Dutton, 1976; "Political Self-Reflections, (July 1980)," in *Issue* (London), November 1980; "Untitled Art-Political Meditation," in *Village Voice* (New York), 4 February 1981, p. 62; "Critical Hegemony and the Division of Labor in Art," in *Position Paper for the Visual Arts Seminar on Art Criticism* (Washington, D.C.), 19-20 September 1983; "Two Kinds of Discrimination," in *Yale Journal of Criticism,* (New Haven), 6(1), 1993, p. 25-74.

On PIPER: Articles—"Catalysis: An Interview with Adrian Piper" by Lucy Lippard, in *NYU Drama Review,* March 1972, pp. 76-78; "The Funk Lessons of Adrian Piper" by Irene Borger, in *Helicon Nine,* 14-15, 1986, pp. 150-53; "Adrian Piper," in *New Yorker,* (New York), 29 October 1990; "The Critique of Pure Racisim" (interview), by Maurice Berger, in *Afterimage,* 18(3), October 1990, pp. 5-9; "Choices: The Political Arm" by Vince Aletti, in *Village Voice* (New York), 19 February 1991; "Shedding Her Male Identity" by Lita Barrie, in *Artweek,* 14 March 1991; "The Indexical

Adrian Piper, 1996. Photo courtesy of Maurice Berger.

Present: A Conversation with Adrian Piper" by Elizabeth Hayt-Atkins, in *Arts Magazine,* March 1991, pp. 48-51; "Seville: Carmen on a Motorcycle" by Judy Cantor, in *ArtNews,* 91(2), February 1992, pp. 32-33; "Adrian Piper" by Eddie Chambers, in *Art Monthly,* 1991, pp. 13-15.

*   *   *

Adrian Piper's artistic development and expression have evolved from a self-referential impetus that over time converged into an activist stance. With her friend and mentor Sol de Wit, Piper was at the forefront of the conceptualist movement in the late 1960s. Indicative of the philosophical thrust of this movement were Piper's early forays into concept-focused work that contextualized intellectual ideals while making process and product clearly secondary. Her map works and geometric drawings from this period were abstract ideations of finite systems. She engaged in the construction of graphic renderings while alluding to thought processes and the documentation of her own creative impulses. She used her body and image within the context of multiple persona to explore onto-

logical issues as they pertained to discourse on reason, logic, and autobiographic data. Eventually earning a degree in philosophy, she formalized a disposition she had made evident in her work by synthesizing her predilections for rationalism, ethics, politics, and art.

Piper's development has not followed modernist tendencies toward serial stylizations. She has often used means that are easily transferable and commodified, manipulating modes of creation based on her response to the medium used. Piper disavows the capitalist concept of an investment value attached to the production of art. She remains free of the dictates of the marketplace and chooses her direction and content outside its accepted parameters, which often results in her being marginalized.

Piper conveys dynamism within the context of her performances. Over the years she has shifted from the formats of spectacle and street performance to carefully orchestrated environments using technology and minimalist spatial treatment. These works engage videos of staged images and text, both written and spoken. Static modes of working include posters, digitally manipulated flat works, and photography. Often incorporating text that is politically charged, she is among the precursors of postmodernist theories and practices by artists immersed in activism, including Barbara Krueger, Edgar Heap of Birds, and Jenny Holtzer. The driving impetus behind all of her work is to galvanize viewers, transforming their position from voyeurs to subjects. She speaks directly to the audience, abrasively and on a cerebral level, challenging them to confront irrational perspectives.

Particularly on issues of race Pipers assumes the stance of protagonist. She is the informant, projecting images and data that are intended to divulge internalized impulses, attitudes, and behaviors that pertain to otherness and coerce contemplation. Her personal conundrum on race was shaped by early experiences of ambivalence about her identity. Although she was raised in Harlem, she lived in a world willing to accept her as white, or exoticize her as other, until she informed people otherwise. Caught within this matrix, she chose to claim herself as black. Autobiographical data infused with dialectic analysis have provided her with a great deal of source material for investigating the formulaic underpinnings of racism and xenophobia.

Piper's work addresses audiences that are diverse in ethnicity and gender. Because of the demographics of the United States, however, a great number of those in her audience are white. Whites' reactions to Piper's work vary. Some align themselves with her values and epithets, and others identify themselves as targets of her critiques. The black viewer often finds her work cathartic in nature. Blacks identify with her antithetical presentations of racial stereotypes and her attempts to address frustrations endemic in black experience.

Piper's antiracist campaign—executed in performance works, installations, and collages—epitomizes the transformation of consciousness as a concept of struggle that necessitates a collective effort to change the system. She professes that her work courts interpersonal manifestations of racism because institutions are comprised of such dynamics. Piper has an expanded audience, one that has been growing for generations. Her appeal is to bring the viewer into the present by creating an experience that can be immediately digested. She is one of many intellectuals and artists who struggle continuously through various means to challenge racist concepts, however subtle they have become.

—A. M. Weaver

PIPER, Keith

British sculptor

Born: Birmingham, England, 1960. **Education:** Lanchester Polytechnic Coventry, England, 1979-80; Trent Polytechnic Nottingham, England, 1980-83, B.A. 1983; Royal College of Art, London, 1984-86, M.A. 1986. **Career:** Co-organized the exhibition, "Black Art an done," Wolverhampton Art Gallery, 1982; staged "The First National Black Art Convention," Wolverhampton Polytechnic, 1982; organized Pan-Afrikan Connection.

Individual Exhibitions:

1984	Black Art Gallery, London
1987	Battersea Arts Centre, London

1988	Cutty Sark Gardens, London (traveling)
	Woolwich Town Centre, London
	Telemann Square, London
	The Albany Empire, London
	The Piazza, Huddersfield
	Mandela Centre, Leeds
	Leeds City Art Gallery
	The Bullring, Wakefield
	Provincial House, Bradford
	Forest Fields, Nottingham
	Nottingham Castle Grounds
	Leicester City Centre
	Moss Side, Manchester
	Saint Peter's Square, Manchester
	Sainsbury's, Oldham
	High Street, Oldham
	Town Centre, Rochdale
1989	Bedford Hill Gallery, London
1991	Ikon Gallery, Birmingham

Selected Group Exhibitions:

1982	Africa Centre, London
	38 King Street Gallery, Bristol
1983	Herbert Art Gallery, Coventry
1984	Mappin Art Gallery, Sheffield
1985	Bluecoat Gallery, Liverpool
1986	ICA, London
	Whitechapel Gallery, London
1987	Chelsea School of Art, London
	Hayward Gallery, London
1988	Westham Town Hall, London

Collections:

Manchester City Art Galleries; Sheffield City Art Galleries.

*   *   *

In the latter half of the 1980s critics and artists such as Maurice Berger, Sunil Gupta, Paul Smith, Isaac Julien, and Kobena Mercer began to question the image and presentation of black males in popular culture and imagination. In a 1992 article in *Artforum*, Mercer stated that "black masculinity is not merely a social identity in crisis. It is also a key site of ideological representation, a site upon which the nation's crisis comes to be dramatized, demonized, and dealt with—enter Willie Horton as apogee of the most unAmerican Otherness imaginable." From Willie Horton to Rodney King, Marion Barry, and O.J. Simpson, the ten years between 1985 and 1995 saw the body, mind, and soul of stereotypical black masculinity constantly displayed on the universal television screen. The writings of Mercer and other critics on black masculinity culminated in the exhibition *Black Male,* organized by Thelma Golden at the Whitney Museum of American Art in 1994.

Though Keith Piper's work of the past twenty years has been occupied by strident investigations of race and representation—mainly black and British—in various media, he has centered much of his subject matter around the cloak of black masculinity. Works like *Go West Young Man* (1988), *Father I have done questionable things* (1989), and *Step into the Arena: Notes on Black Masculinity and the Contest of Territory* (1991)—the title of the last taken from a song by the hip-hop duo Gang Starr—have demonstrated Piper's interests in reimagining the fallacies of popular representations of black masculinity. Many of his strongest works are created via the techniques of high-tech installations. Video monitors, projectors, and speakers are integral pieces of the installation *Father I have done questionable things*. Images of riot police in blue and gray were projected on one wall at its original presentation at the Bedford Hill Gallery in London. As the viewer approached the work, his or her silhouette became a part of the action on the wall. The conceptual basis of the project could be no less direct than to announce Piper's view that, in an oppressive state, anyone can be caught up in the forces of violence. Supplementing the visual action was a droning sound track, synchronized with the projections, that quietly created an audible assault upon the viewer.

In *Go West Young Man,* Piper uses text to draw parallels between his own personal history as a so-called first-generation black in Britain and the history of the slave trade—" 'Go West young man.' I first heard that joke as they loaded us into the hold of the ship. . . . Yes I first heard that joke 400 years ago." *Step into the Arena* demonstrates Piper's tactic of using the metaphor of popular sports in his work. Whereas Matthew Barney employs sports to examine male behavior, Piper's work is also filled with the history of the black athlete, often both idolized and demonized. Yet Piper is keen enough and feminist enough to admit the similarity to Barney's critique of masculinity: "As a heterosexual Black man, I suspect that one of the reasons for this relative absence of an introspective voice is that, like heterosexual white men, we have been raised upon the assumption that somewhere along the line it is our job to 'manage' the planet."

It is this understanding of antiessentialism that makes Piper's work so important. Piper is from a generation of politically conscious black British artists who came up in the 1980s around an activist movement comparable to that of American artists in the 1970s, when museums in New York City were picketed for their discriminatory curatorial efforts. His peers include Sonia Boyce, Eddie Chambers, and Lubaina Himid in Britain and artists like Jean-Michel Basquiat, Glenn Ligon, and Lorna Simpson in the United States. (The last three, with Chambers, were all born in 1960, the same year as Piper.) And he has cited London-based reggae groups such as Aswad, Steel Pulse, and Burning Spear as early influences on his work, more so than visual art. Although he is still young, Piper's powerful artistic output places him at the vanguard of art history, and his use of new technologies makes him of seminal importance in the history of late twentieth-century art.

—M. Franklin Sirmans

PIPER, Rose

American painter

Owned greeting card company and designed textiles under the name Rose Ransier. **Born:** Rose Theodosia Sams, New York, 7 October 1917. **Education:** Hunter College, New York, 1936-40, B.A. 1940; Art Students League, New York, 1943-46; Beaux Arts (not registered), Paris, 1947-48. **Family:** Married 1) William Ashby Piper in 1943 (divorced 1946), one son; 2) Glenn Ransier in 1947 (divorced 1959), one daughter; 3) George Edward Wheeler in 1959 (died 1990). **Career:** Owner, Ransier Studio Cards, New York, 1949-53; print

Rose Piper. Photo courtesy of Rob Klein.

designer and colorist, Studio Fred Levi, New York, 1953-56; knit director of styling and design, Alamac Knitting Mills, New York, 1956-59, G & G Knitting Mills, New York, 1959-62, Sesom Knitting Mills, New York, 1962-64, Inwood Knitting Mills, New York, 1964-65; executive director of styling and design, Spring Mills-Knit Division, New York, 1965-68, Lebanon Knitting Mills, New York, 1968-71; executive vice president, styling and design, Jarmel Knitting Mills, New York, 1971-73; executive director of retail division of styling and design, Heller Knitting Mills, New York, 1973-75; executive director of styling and design, Lively Knits Division, Tex-Fi Knitting Mills, New York, 1975-78; consultant, Barrington Mills, New York, 1978-80. **Awards:** Rosenwald Foundation grant, 1946 and 1947; First Prize, Seventh Annual Exhibition of Contemporary Negro Art, Atlanta University, Georgia, 1948. **Agents:** Asake Bomani, The Bomani Gallery, 251 Post Street, San Francisco, California 94108, U.S.A.; Charlotte Sherman, The Heritage Gallery, North La Cienega Boulevard, Los Angeles, California 90069, U.S.A.; Corrine Jennings, Kenkeleba House, 214-16 East 2nd Street, New York, New York 10025, U.S.A. **Address:** 250 West 94th Street, Apt. 7g, New York , New York 10025, U.S.A.

Individual Exhibitions:

1947   Roko Gallery, New York

Rose Piper: *Go Down Death, Easy,* **1988. Photo courtesy of James Dee.**

1989   Phelps Stokes Fund, New York
1993   Bomani Gallery, San Francisco
1995   Bomani Gallery, San Francisco

Selected Group Exhibitions:

1948   *Seventh Annual Exhibition of Contemporary Negro Art-
        ists,* Atlanta University, Georgia
1949   *Exhibition of Negro Artists,* Roko Gallery, New York
1963   *National Art Exhibition,* Xavier University, New Orleans,
        Louisiana
1988   *New Images,* Hudson Guild Art Gallery, New York
1991   *The Search For Freedom: African-American Abstraction,*
        Kenkeleba Gallery, New York
1994   *Contemporary African-American Artists,* National Arts
        Club, New York
1995   *The Fine Art of Textile Design,* Cinque Gallery, New York

Collections:

Ackland Museum, Chapel Hill, North Carolina; High Museum of
Art, Atlanta, Georgia; Kenkeleba Gallery, New York.

Publications:

On PIPER: Books—*The Search for Freedom: African-American
Abstract Painting, 1945-1975* edited by Ann Gibson, et al., New
York, Kenkeleba Gallery, 1991; *Gumbo Ya Ya: Anthology of Con-
temporary African-American Women Artists* edited by Sylvia
Moore, New York, Midmarch Arts Press, 1995; *Black Culture of
the Twentieth Century* by Joan Marsh, London, Thames Publishing
Company, 1996. **Articles**—"The Arts," in *New York Voice,* New
York, 1989; "Rose Piper" by Alexandra Shaw, in *Manhattan Arts*
(New York), 1989; "See a World of Art in the Heart of North
Carolina" by Ray Williams, in Ackland Museum brochure (Chapel
Hill, North Carolina), 1991; "Seven Artists Speak" by Ray Will-
iams, in Ackland Museum brochure (Chapel Hill, North Carolina),
1991; "Search For Freedom" by George Silva, in *Kingston Daily
Freeman* and the *Beacon Journal,* 1992. **Video**—*Textiles Design-
ers* by Michelle Hill, New York, Cinque Gallery, 1995.

*

Rose Piper comments:

My early paintings in the 1940s were inspired by the so-called
"race records." They were work songs and blues recorded by African Americans in the 1920s and sold exclusively in Harlem to black
audiences. I drew on the powerful passions and the anguished recollections of that black experience.

Most of my paintings were abstractions—moments of heightened
expression. Some titles, for instance, were *The Death of Bessie Smith;
Long, Long Time to Freedom; Slow Down Freight Train; Grievin'
Hearted; Empty Bed Blues; I Been to the City;* and *Backwater Blues.*

Circumstances forced me to give up painting. After twenty-five
years, I returned to my painting but with a completely different
style—no longer abstract or expressionist. I now, because of my
long experience in designing knit fabrics on 20 x 20 squares-to-the-
inch graph paper, have a more "controlled" approach. My color is
brighter by far, and I use acrylics rather than oils.

I began painting again by doing still life studies and then discovered John Lowell, Jr.'s book, *Black Song: The Forge and the Flame.*

The "slave songs" were so inspiring that I did a series of ten paintings. They are small (9" x 12") and are painted on masonite. My
favorite is *I Want You fo' to Go Down Death, an' Bring My Servant
Home.*

*   *   *

Rose Piper's career as an artist, which has spanned five decades,
can be neatly divided into three parts. From 1946 to 1949 she
painted in the abstract expressionist style. Her ability was recognized even though at the time the art world, and particularly that
style, was dominated by white men. Piper's first solo show was
held at the Roko Gallery in 1947. The owner, Michael Freilich, was
unusual in that he represented more than one Negro artist at a time,
the others being Beauford Delaney and Claude Clark. In 1950 family considerations (two young children and an ailing husband) took
precedence over the creativity of painting, and Piper took her artistic talents to the garment industry, where she worked for the next
thirty years. She embarked on a career as director of styling and
design for various knitting mills, and she won several awards for her
designs. When she retired in 1980, Piper again took up her brushes.
Painting still lifes to get her hand going again, Piper discarded her
former style. Her work became more realistic, her palette was
brighter, and she used rich details, especially in drapery and in
architectural elements.

With her first Rosenwald fellowship Piper traveled to both Paris
and the U.S. South in 1946 to research family stories and to hear
work songs, blues, and spirituals. For Piper, Bessie Smith ("raun-
chy, funny, earthy") symbolized "an emancipated woman." Smith
and other blues singers inspired the content of her series "Negro
Folk Songs and Blues," also the title of her first solo exhibition.
Piper noted that the paintings were "impressions of the imaginative
experiences evoked by the world of Negro folks songs, and are not
illustrative works or accompaniments." In October 1947 *Art News*
wrote, "Early luminous, romantic canvases bring to mind her studies with Kuniyoshi at the Art Students League. The recent pictures
are strong, flat, semi-abstract compositions. . . . Miss Piper gets a
lot of pathos and drama through stylized postures, as in the most
effective *Empty Bed Blues.*" The painting forcefully displays longing in its juxtaposition of a woman's bulky, elongated figure against
the linear elements of bed, table, and chair. Also in the exhibition
was *Slow Down Freight Train,* a painting in which bright and dark
flat shapes alternate. The rounded, elongated male figure is offset
by the geometrical walls and floorboards of the boxcar, showing a
deep yearning for home or stability. "Briefly, this show is a success," declared *Art Digest* in its October 1947 review. Indeed, twelve
of the fourteen paintings shown were sold, and one, *Grievin'
Hearted,* won the top prize in 1948 in the seventh annual competition for contemporary Negro art at Atlanta University. Other entrants included Jacob Lawrence, Richmond Barthé, and Robert
Blackburn.

Piper's series "Slave Songs," a group of ten 9" x 12" paintings,
was inspired by John Lovell's *Black Song: The Forge and the
Flame.* In these paintings Piper's poetic, surreal imagination and
her finely honed technical skills create searing images of urban poverty and the loss of dignity that results from it. The words of the
spirituals, or slave songs, combine with radiant colors and musical
sweeps of fabric to offer images of hope and courage. Piper's paintings also are reminders of her own strength as she has re-created her
life several times out of hardship, drive, and innate ability.

Charles Alston was an early mentor of Piper. Artists she has admired include Jan Vermeer, Ben Shahn, Robert Gwathmey, and Rufino Tamayo. She also has admired the modern realists Claudio Bravo and Chuck Close, along with Romare Bearden and Jacob Lawrence for their deft handling of color and design.

—Betty Kaplan Gubert

PIPPIN, Horace
American painter

Born: West Chester, Pennsylvania, 22 February 1888. **Family:** Married Jennie Ora Featherstone Wade in 1920. **Military Service:** United States Army, 1917-19: corporal; Croix de Guerre (wounded in action). **Career:** Painter, 1931-46. Worked as farm hand, coal unloader, feed store assistant, hotel porter, furniture loader. **Awards:** Purchase Prize, Pennsylvania Academy of Fine Arts, 1943; First Prize, Pyramid Club exhibition, 1943; honorable mention, Carnegie Institute, 1944; J. Henry Schiedt Memorial Prize, Pennsylvania Academy of Fine Arts, 1946. **Died:** 6 July 1946.

Selected Exhibitions:

1937	West Chester Community Center, Pennsylvania
1938	Museum of Modern Art, New York
1940	American Negro Exposition, Chicago
	Carlen Galleries, Philadelphia
	Bignou Gallery, New York
1941	Arts Club of Chicago
	Carlen Galleries, Philadelphia
	Downtown Gallery, New York
	Southside Community Art Center, Chicago
1942	San Francisco Museum of Art
1944	Carnegie Institute
	Atlanta University, Georgia
1945	Howard University, Washington, D.C.
1946	Phillips Memorial Gallery, Washington, D.C.
1947	Knoedler Galleries
c.1950	Walker Art Center
1967	City College of New York
1971	Newark Museum, New Jersey

Collections:

Albright-Knox Art Gallery, Buffalo, New York; Barnes Foundation, Philadelphia; Boston Museum of Fine Arts; Metropolitan Museum of Art, New York; Museum of Modern Art, New York; National Archives, Washington, D.C.; Phillips Collection, Washington, D.C.; Rhode Island Museum; Whitney Museum of American Art, New York; Wichita Museum, Kansas.

Publications:

By PIPPIN: Article—"My Life Story," in *Horace Pippin: A Negro Painter in America* by Selden Rodman, Quadrangle Press, New York, 1947.

On PIPPIN: Books—*Three Negro Artists,* exhibition catalog, Washington, D.C., Phillips Memorial Gallery, 1946; *Horace Pippin: A*

Horace Pippin: *Portrait of Marian Anderson II.* Photo by Manu Sassoonian; courtesy of the Schomburg Center for Research in Black Culture.

Negro Painter in America by Selden Rodman, Quadrangle, 1947; *Four American Primitives: Edward Hicks, John Kane, Anna Mary Robertson Moses, Horace Pippin, February 22-March 11, 1972,* exhibition catalog, ACA Galleries, 1972; *I Tell My Heart: The Art of Horace Pippin* by Judith E. Stein, Philadelphia, Pennsylvania Academy of Fine Art/Universe Publishing, 1993. **Articles**—"Primitive Pippin," in *Time Magazine,* 29 January 1940; "Art the Hard Way" by Jerome Klein, in *Friday Magazine,* 17 January 1941, pp. 22-23; "Modern Primitive: Horace Pippin," in *Crisis,* June 1946, pp. 178-79; "Pippin, Negro Primitive, Given Memorial Show at Knoedler Galleries," in *Art Digest,* 1 October 1947, p. 16; "Horace Pippin, A Negro Painter in America" by S. Rodman, in *Magazine of Art,* May 1948, p. 202; "Negro Primitive Finds Peace After War," in *Art Digest,* 1 October 1947, p. 16; "Horace Pippin," in *A History of African-American Artists, from 1792 to the Present* by Romare Bearden and Harry Henderson, Pantheon Books, 1993, pp. 356-370.

*   *   *

The paintings of the self-taught artist Horace Pippin record with great directness and depth of feeling his responses to events both historical and personal. Realized in vibrant colors, flattened shapes, and rich patterns, they constitute a uniquely eloquent portrayal of black life in the United States at the mid-twentieth century.

Perhaps the defining event in Pippin's life was the experience of fighting in World War I with the heroic all-black 369th Infantry.

Although he earned the Croix de Guerre, Pippin returned in 1919 to an America indifferent to the courage and sacrifices of its black soldiers, who were still denied full rights as equal citizens in peacetime society. Pippin married and settled in West Chester, Pennsylvania, but he was in anguish from his memories of the war and in physical discomfort from his right arm, which had been shattered by a bullet and now lay useless, bound to his side.

Seeking to recover the pleasure he had always found in drawing, Pippin discovered in 1925 that he could use a hot poker to draw by burning lines into wood. Seventeen of these burnt-wood panels followed before Pippin attempted to paint by clasping a brush in his deadened right hand and then pushing it across the canvas with his left arm. It was in this painstaking fashion that in 1930, after three years of effort, Pippin completed his great antiwar painting *The End of War: Starting Home*. The painting is impastoed so heavily that many of its forms appear in low relief, and its sculptural quality is echoed by the wooden frame, on which the artist hand-carved grenades, tanks, rifles, and bombs. The composition of muted greens, grays, browns, and blacks is punctuated by fiery bursts of red from exploding shells and human blood. A diagonal array of fence posts at the bottom directs the eye to a central German soldier, with arms outstretched in a gesture of surrender. Overhead, burning planes spiral and dive from a leaden sky. The dark-skinned U.S. regiment grimly picks it way over the carnage and detritus of destruction. There is no glory in victory, only a terrible emptiness, the desolation of both land and human spirit.

After completing a series of paintings on the war, Pippin expanded his subject matter to include landscapes, still lifes, and portraits. By the early 1940s he was recollecting the world of his childhood in paint. The resulting works, such as *Domino Players* (1943) or *Saturday Night Bath* (1945), are suffused with a sense of domestic tranquillity, their simple, cozy interiors filled with human warmth and activity. Women figure strongly in these works as monumentalized, nurturing figures who bathe, feed, and care for children, and brightly patterned rugs and quilts often enliven the scenes, attesting to the artist's respect for the creative labors of women.

Also dating from the early 1940s are a series of paintings treating historical themes of slavery and emancipation, specifically scenes from the lives of Abraham Lincoln and the abolitionist John Brown. In *John Brown Going to His Hanging* (1942) a crowd of somberly dressed white men face Brown as he is carried to his death. A lone black woman stands in the lower left of the picture, facing the viewer, a scowl of rage on her face. This moral presence is in fact Pippin's mother, Harriet, who witnessed Brown's hanging as a girl in Virginia and recalled the event many times. In contrast to Pippin's personal identification with the figure of Brown, *Mr. Prejudice* (1943) deals with the theme of racial injustice in symbolic terms— its *V* for the Allied victory cleft in two by the opposing forces of liberty and racial intolerance before a contingent of black and white soldiers and laborers.

Pippin's late works express his deeply felt longing for peace and racial harmony in the face of World War II. *The Holy Mountain III* (1945), for example, depicts a black shepherd who stands in a brightly flowered field with a peaceable kingdom of lion and lamb who lie down together. In the dark woods behind them lurk the muted silhouettes of soldiers.

An untrained artist whose work garnered the respect and support of prominent figures in the art world of his day, Pippin remained at the end of his life undaunted by success, visited by feelings of isolation and loneliness, and preoccupied by a driving need to realize his personal vision. He produced more than seventy-five paintings in the last six years of his life. In his own way Pippin was to arrive, through intuition and necessity, at many of the formal devices ascribed to modernist painting—brilliant color and the interplay of flattened shapes and patterned textures. But it is Pippen's emotional urgency, honesty, and wholeness of vision that make his unique record of the African American experience so compelling and moving.

—Dorothy Valakos

PLATT, Michael B(ernard)

American painter and printmaker

Born: Washington, D.C., April 1948. **Education:** Columbus College of Art and Design, Ohio, B.F.A. 1970; Howard University, Washington, D.C., M.F.A. 1973; George Washington University, Washington, D.C., 1976; Hartford University, Connecticut, 1977; Howard University, Washington, D.C., 1993; Rutgers' Center for Innovative Printmakers Workshop, 1993. **Family:** 1) Married Linda Thomas in 1972 (divorced 1980); 2) lived with Rhonda Hobday in the early 1980s, one son; 3) married Carol Anne Beane in 1991. **Career:** Drawing instructor, Duke Ellington School of the Arts, Washington, D.C., 1981-82, Corcoran School of Art, Washington, D.C., 1982-84. Since 1973 Assistant Professor of Fine Arts, Northern Virginia Community College, Alexandria, Virginia. Visiting professor, Maryland College of Art, Baltimore, 1991; printmaking instructor, Howard University, Washington, D.C., 1994. Artist-in-residence, Bob Blackburn's Printmaking Workshop, 1993, Pyramid Atlantic Center for Hand Papermaking, 1994. Founding member, W.D. Printmaking Workshop, Washington, D.C., 1971; advisor, Congressional Awards Initiative Achievement Service, 1993. Served as an advisor for the Congressional Awards Initiative Achievement Service, 1993; member, Community Advisory Board, Corcoran Museum, 1993-94; member, Board of Directors, Washington Projects for the Arts, 1992-96; artist, Artist-Mentor program, Corcoran Museum, 1993. **Awards:** George Bellows Scholarship, Columbus, Ohio, 1966; Howard University Trustee Fellowship, Washington, D.C., 1971; Washington D.C. Artist of the Year, 1982; Blue Mountain Center Fellowship Award, New York, 1988, 1986; Washington Projects for the Arts grant, 1989; Washington, D.C. Commission on the Arts and Humanities grant, 1999, 1990, 1991; Brandywine Workshop Fellowship grant, Philadelphia, 1991; finalist, Washington D.C. Mayor's Award for Excellence in the Arts, 1991; Washington Project for the Arts Exhibition grant, 1992; Rutgers' Center for Creative Printmakers Fellowship grant, 1992; National Cultural Arts Alliance Arts Educator of the Year Award, 1994. **Address:** 1362 Perry Place N.W., Washington, D.C. 20010-1317, U.S.A.

Individual Exhibitions:

1973	Howard University, Washington, D.C.
1975	Franz Bader Gallery, Washington, D.C.
1977	Franz Bader Gallery, Washington, D.C.
1979	Franz Bader Gallery, Washington, D.C.
1981	Franz Bader Gallery, Washington, D.C.
1983	Franz Bader Gallery, Washington, D.C.

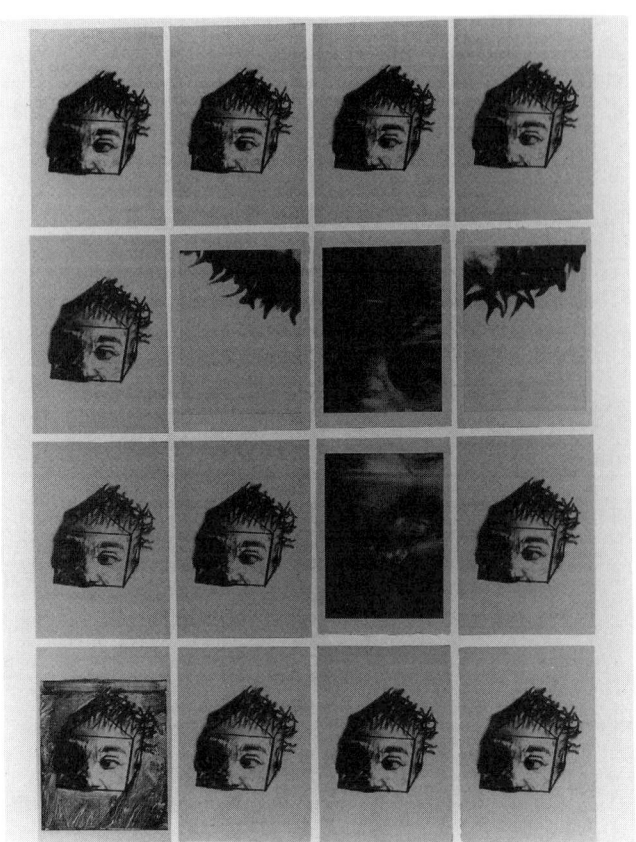

Michael Platt: *They Woke Up One Morning and Said the Issue Was Race,* 1996. Photo courtesy of Harlee H. Little.

1985	Franz Bader Gallery, Washington, D.C.
1987	Franz Bader Gallery, Washington, D.C.
1989	Franz Bader Gallery, Washington, D.C.
1991	Franz Bader Gallery, Washington, D.C.
1994	Arnolfini Arts Center, Bristol, England
	City Gallery, Leicester, England
	Oldham Art Gallery, England
1995	Franz Bader Gallery, Washington, D.C.

Selected Group Exhibitions:

1979	Howard University, Washington, D.C.
1985	Dade County Library, Miami
1987	George Washington University, Washington, D.C.
1989	*Blues Aesthetics,* Washington Project for the Arts, Washington, D.C.
1991	Franz Bader Gallery, Washington, D.C.
1993	Susquehannah Museum, Harrisburg, Pennsylvania
	Maryland Art Place, Baltimore
1995	Tivoli Gallery, Ljubljana, Slovenia
	Center of African American History and Culture, Smithsonian Institution
1996	Numark Gallery, Washington, D.C.

Collections:

Brandywine Print Workshop, Philadelphia, Pennsylvania; Corcoran Gallery of Art, Washington, D.C.; Rutger's Center for Innovative Printmaking, New Brunswick, New Jersey; Smithsonian Institution, Washington, D.C.

Publications:

On PLATT: Book—*Other Gods: Containers of Belief,* Washington, D.C., Fondo del Sol—F.U.N.K. Humanifesto, 1986, p. 64. **Articles**—"Art: Harris and Platt" by Benjamin Forgey, in *Washington Post,* 25 August 1975, p. C5; "Interview with Michael Platt" by Mary Swift, in *Washington Review,* XII(6), April/May 1987, pp. 3-6; "Galleries: Michael Platt's Sordid Realism" by Michael Welzenbach, in *The Washington Post,* 25 March 1989, p. D2; "Galleries: Platt's Work Confronts Violence Head-on" by Alice Thorson, in *Washington Times,* 30 March 1989, p. E2; "Michael Platt: New York" by Rex Weil, in *Washington Review,* XVI(2), December/January 1992, pp. 21-22; "Interview with Michael Platt" by Charles H. Rowell, in *Callaloo,* 17(4), 1994, pp. 1105-18.

*

Michael Platt comments:

I tend to draw, paint, and print about people, the abuse of power, and its effect on us all. These effects are more obvious on certain people than on others and are like the events you may see from the window of the bus you ride to work, when you can't get off the bus to fully check out what caught your eye. But from riding the same route daily, these fragments, like newspaper articles and TV news, come together to form a particular image of what kind of people we are.

*   *   *

Michael Platt's early works were more abstract than those done since about 1980. In the moody and atmospheric prints and drawings of his earlier period, the viewer experiences constructs of ominous cosmologies. Subdued and brooding backgrounds are combined with overlays of strategic mark-making systems in which submerged figures reveal themselves slowly to the conscious viewer. The works imply an introspective journey as vast as a view of the constellations in a blackened sky. Platt creates high drama through the infusion of an amalgam of varied techniques.

Since 1979 Platt has been engaged in recording incidents of social and political importance. His prints and drawings are populated with frames from life's movie. They celebrate black heroines, depict the tragedies of civil strife, such as the Rwandan civil war, and convey the ephemeral dreams of children who want to fly. Platt's prints function as windows for passengers on a moving vehicle in which fleeting and fragmented events in life are the scenery that passes by. He constructs a mirror through which the viewers are able to see what kind of people they really are.

The act of observation is key to Platt. Whether in drawing, painting, or printmaking, he functions as a visual journalist. His works range from the disclosure of varied aspects of the human struggle to effective recollections of childhood. He is particularly concerned with the effects of oppression and with the abuse of power that exists within the human community. Each piece, whether a print or monumental installation, recounts experiences and realities indicating the condition of man and the persuasions of the collective soul.

Since the early 1990s Platt has constructed works in large cutout formats that symbolically allude to states of being that reflect the black experience in America. The African American as target and victim and the cartoonlike forms refer to familiar physiological stereotypes existing inside the black community and within the context of a racist society. Endangered black men are represented by the figurative renditions and portraits that grace the walls of an installation trimmed with life-sized gun targets. As if bearing witness, targeted pickaninnies, caricatured by toothy grins and large buttocks, are wedged between male and female constructions, with concentric marks in the area of the chest, poised to withstand lethal attacks. The black community is portrayed as being in a state of siege both internally and within a broader social context.

Platt's work vacillates between the African American as object of attack and the age of innocence in his constructions of children at play. In these latter works Platt interweaves remembrances of childhood—including trips to New Orleans from Washington, D.C., and poetic portraits of family members and shotgun houses indigenous to the rural South—with graphic renditions of atrocities on a global scale. These photomontages are explications on the narrative. Akin to casting a spell, Platt's prints are glimpses into events and memories that transcend the ordinary and give voice to tragedy and lyricism to memory.

Platt is the embodiment of power, engaging all aspects of his being in the creation of his work. His work is infused with his presence. The works are intense, with irrefutable emotion that defies clear articulation via intellectual rhetoric directed toward the soul. He is a present-day shaman, blessed or cursed with vision into worlds beyond the temporal realm. His vision encompasses the personal and universal. His is a roving eye that attempts to portray reality and the metaphysics of existence on a multiplicity of levels.

—A.M. Weaver

Michael Platt: *Little Plattman,* 1996. Photo courtesy of Harlee H. Little.

POGUE, Stephanie (Elaine)
American printmaker and graphic artist

Born: Shelby, North Carolina, 1944. **Education:** Syracuse University, New York, 1962-63; Howard University, Washington, D.C., 1963-66, B.F.A. 1966; Cranbrook Academy of Art, Bloomfield Hills, Michigan, 1966-68, M.F.A. 1968; Studio 22, Chicago, 1969; Printmaking Workshop, New York, 1976; Vanderbilt University, Nashville, 1979-80. **Career:** Assistant professor, Fisk University, Nashville, 1968-77; associate professor, Fisk University, Nashville, 1977-81; associate professor, chair and gallery director, Fisk University, Nashville, 1980-81; associate professor, University of Maryland, College Park, 1981-92; associate professor and acting assistant dean, University of Maryland, College Park, 1991; professor of art and acting assistant dean, University of Maryland, College Park, 1992-93. Since 1993 professor and chair, University of Maryland, College Park. Visiting artist, Xavier University, New Orleans, 1971, Alabama A & M State University, Normal, 1974, Clark College, Atlanta, Georgia, 1974, Winston-Salem Delta Fine Arts, North Carolina, 1982. **Awards:** Cecil Billington Scholarship for Advanced Study in Graphics, Cranbrook Academy of Art, Bloomfield Hills, Michigan, 1967-68; research grant, Fisk University, Nashville, 1969; teaching fellowship, Vanderbilt University, Nashville, 1979-80; Fulbright Hays Cross Cultural Fellowship, 1981; Creative and Performing Arts Award, University of Maryland, College Park, 1982, 1985 and 1989; Fulbright Hays Fellowship, 1986; travel award, University of Maryland, 1991. **Address:** Department of Art, Art/Sociology Building, Room 1211E, University of Maryland, College Park, Maryland 20742, U.S.A.

Individual Exhibitions:

1971   Xavier University, New Orleans
1974   Virginia State University, Petersburg
        Alabama A & M State University, Normal
1976   El Museo de Arte Moderna La Tertulia, Cali, Columbia
        (traveling)
1977   Cinque Gallery, New York
1982   Montgomery Bell Academy, Nashville
        Clark College, Atlanta, Georgia
        University of North Alabama, Florence
1983   City Museum of Fine Arts, Taipei, Taiwan
        Gallery 409, Baltimore, Maryland
        Delta Arts Center, Winston-Salem, North Carolina
1985   Sam Houston State University, Huntsville, Texas
        City Museum, Arondelovac, Yugoslavia
1987   *The Art of Black America in Japan, Afro-American Modernism: 1937-1987,* Tokyo and Chiba, Japan
        Gallery International, Washington, D.C.
1988   Centre d'Art du Rouge-Cloitre, Brussels, Belgium
        IBM Education Center Art Gallery, Mainz, West Germany
1989   Castle Gallery, Hyattsville, Maryland
1991   Museo do Gravura, Curitiba, Brazil
        University of the State of Rio de Janeiro, Brazil
        Galleria Test, Warsaw, Poland (traveling through 1995)

Selected Group Exhibitions:

1966   Fisk University, Nashville
1971   *Five Afro-American Printmakers,* Kansas State College, Pittsburgh

1975   Metropolitan Museum of Art, New York
1982   Nyangoma's Gallery, Washington, D.C.
1985   Fonda del Sol Gallery, Washington, D.C.
1989   National Academy of Sciences, Washington, D.C.
1990   Museum of Science and Industry, Chicago (traveling)
1991   Art Gallery, Howard University, Washington, D.C.
1992   James V. Herring Art Gallery, Howard University, Washington, D.C.
1995   University Art Gallery, University of Maryland, College Park

Collections:

Alabama A & I State University, Normal; Arkansas Arts Center, Little Rock; Century III Collection, Nashville; Cinque Gallery, New York; Clark College, Atlanta University, Georgia; Cranbrook Academy of Art, Bloomfield Hills, Michigan; Fisk University, Nashville; Maryland Printmakers, Baltimore; Saint Mary's College of Maryland; Southern Graphics Art Council, Baltimore, Maryland; Southern University, Baton Rouge, Louisiana; Spelman College, Atlanta, Georgia; Studio Museum in Harlem, New York; Tennessee Arts Commission, Nashville; Tennessee Museums Collection, Nashville; University of Maryland, College Park; University of North Dakota, Grand Forks; University of the South, Sewanee, Tennessee; Vanderbilt University, Nashville; Virginia State University, Petersburg; Wabash College, Crawfordsville, Indiana; Whitney Museum of American Art, New York; Winston-Salem University, North Carolina; Xavier University, New Orleans; Xian College of Art, China.

Publications:

On POGUE: Books—*Stephanie E. Pogue, Color Prints, 1972-1991*, exhibition catalog, Warsaw, Galeria Test, 1991; *Pogue Graphic Work 1985*, exhibition catalog, Yugoslavia, City Museum, 1985. **Articles**—"Art Exhibit Features Ms. Pogue," in *Mid-State Observer* (Nashville), 2(18), 6 November 1979, p. 6; "Artist Intrigued with Larger-Than-Life Model" by Julie Pursell, in *Nashville Banner*, 31 October 1979, p. 82; "Portrait of Artist-Professor: Stephanie Pogue," in *Afro-American* (Maryland), 23 January 1982; "Art Exhibit Features Stephanie Pogue," in *The Chronicle* (North Carolina), 6 October 1983, p. 20; "Artist Finds a Paradise in India" by Janet Fox, in *The Sentinel*, (North Carolina), 12 October 1983, p. 17; "Stephanie Pogue, Joyce, Wellman" by Curtia James, in *New Art Examiner* (Washington, D.C.), Summer 1992, pp. 41-42.

*   *   *

Stephanie Pogue believes in the ability of the individual to create concrete expressions that can speak a universal language. Universality has been at odds with the concept of difference, which rose to prominence in the 1980s, and difference continues to be the banner under which many artists create, especially those working on the margins. But Pogue believes that people share sensibilities, and she tries to speak to these commonalities through her art.

Pogue was at first distinguished by her landscapes and figurative graphic works, in which she used curvilinear lines that stretched and swept across the surfaces. As a graphic artist she concentrates on line as it shapes and forms objects in the environment, and she relates line to its use in other cultures. Her investigation of linear

movement is clarified in the powerful swirl and force of waves in *Sea Storm*, a color viscosity etching of 1977. In this monochromatic composition the flamelike waves rise on either side, pulled toward each other with a viscose energy. In other works, like the color viscosity etching *Deep Dream* (1978), she inserts a reclining body facedown. The torso acts like a grainy rock in a landscape of a terrain of individually drawn leaves.

In her more mature work Pogue's concentration on line has been replaced with emphasis on color. Her colors are muted, influenced by her travels in India. Her monotypes are most engaging for their restrictive palette and the sensuous fluidity of the ink, and her love of landscape and its elements have drawn her to an introspective investigation of herself. In *Woman on a Pedestal* (1989) a form that resembles a fifty-pound clay block before it has been shaped rests atop an Ionic column, like a fine sculpted work. It reminds the viewer of the degree to which the female form has been vulnerable since antiquity, displayed as a symbol of beauty and procreation rather than of intellect. Although unmolded by the sculptor's hand, the block also reminds the viewer of the relationship of the female form to art itself, as being central in the development of many studio artists. Could the artist, who until the twentieth century was by and large male, divorce himself and his eye from sexual fantasies while following the sensuous lines of the female body? This is the issue that is at the heart of *Woman on a Pedestal*.

The pliable-looking form has no identifying characteristics to suggest that it is a female. It is as if the figure wants to enfold itself, hiding its naked body from the spectator's gaze while all others around it are clothed. The piece speaks of vulnerability, as does a similar work from the same year entitled *Self-Portrait: Vulnerable*. A form slightly resembling a seated nude female is crouched on the floor with nothing revealed but her back. She seems to be totally alone in the midst of a black void, although three faintly discernible shadowy shapes intrude into the darkness of her private space. Pogue presents her own personal vulnerability in this autobiographical work.

This series of self-reflective works also ponders Pogue's place in the world as an artist and educator. She has had to endure male colleagues lamenting an accomplished work by a female artist with the comment "Too bad she's a woman," and she has had her work virtually ignored by critics. *Balancing Act* (1989) shows how she has come to confront these issues in her work. In this piece Pogue's enigmatic torso teeters on the edge of a sharply defined cube, suggesting that her life as an artist calls for constant adjustments and a recognition that hovering on the edge may not be such a bad place after all.

—Lizzetta LeFalle-Collins

POLK, Prentice Herman
American photographer

Born: Bessemer, Alabama, 25 November 1898. **Education:** Tuskegee Institute, Alabama, 1916-20. Apprenticed with Fred Jensen, 1924-26. **Family:** Married Margaret Blanche Thompson in 1926, one son. **Career:** Worked in shipyards, Chickasaw, Alabama, 1920-22; instructor of photography, Tuskegee Institute, Alabama, 1928-38; department head, Tuskegee Institute, Alabama, 1933-39. From 1939 official university photographer, Tuskegee Institute, Alabama. Owned and operated a private portrait studio in Tuskegee, Alabama, 1927, and in Atlanta, Georgia, 1938. Photographed the progress of the Tuskegee Airmen in the 1940s. **Awards:** Zeta Phi Beta award, Alpha XI Chapter, 1975; National Conference of Artists award, 1979; Black Photographers Annual Testimonial award, 1980; National Endowment for the Arts fellowship, 1981. **Died:** 29 December 1984.

Selected Exhibitions:

Art Institute of Pittsburgh; P.H. Polk, Corcoran Gallery of Art, Washington, D.C. (1981); New York Museum of Natural History; Washington Gallery of Photography.

Collection:

P. H. Polk Room, Tuskegee Institute Archives, Alabama.

Publications:

On POLK: Books—*P. H. Polk,* exhibition catalog, Washington, D.C., Corcoran Gallery of Art, 21 March 1981; *P. H. Polk: Southern Photographer* by Louise E. Shaw, Atlanta, Nexus Press, 1986. **Articles**—"P. H. Polk. . . A Kind of General Practitioner" by Joe Crawford, in *The Black Photographers Annual, Volume 2,* New York, Rapoport Printing Corporation, 1974; "Portraits of P. H. Polk Emerge From 'the Space Behind the Eye.'," in *Voices South,* November/December 1980; "P. H. Polk" by Deborah Willis-Thomas, in *Black Photographers: 1840-1940,* New York, 1985; "Noted Black Photographer of Rural South Dies at 86, in *The Tuskegee News,* 3 January 1985, p. A-7.

*   *   *

Prentice Herman Polk was a commercial photographer and witness documentarian of twentieth-century African American life in rural Tuskegee, Alabama. Growing up, Polk witnessed poverty and prejudice in the rural mill town of Bessemer, Alabama, where the steel mill dominated the environment and affected almost everyone, including his father, mother, and four siblings.

Polk survived the town's segregated school system and went on to attend Tuskegee Normal Sand Industrial Institution, now Tuskegee University. There he studied with black photographer C. M. Battey, who headed the photography department. Battey viewed photography as an art and specialized in portraiture, photographing the black heroes of his era. He taught Polk the rudiments of portrait photography but found him an undisciplined student. Dissatisfied, Polk left Tuskegee and enrolled in a correspondence course in photography.

Through this study Polk was able to learn his craft and discover new photo techniques. He was obsessed with the artistic use of light and shadow in photography. "In my correspondence course I came across an article . . . talking about Rembrandt. When Rembrandt came along everybody painted their pictures from the highlight side. But Rembrandt went to the shadow side . . . . If you look at my pictures, you'll see most of them are from the shadow side." His course also taught him photomontage, mise-en-scène, dramatic lighting, and retouching techniques, which he used to raise his status as a commercial photographer. Although most of Polk's studies are tripod studio shots, he also became proficient with handheld news cameras.

After opening his first studio, Polk was hired by the now struggling Tuskegee Institute photography department. Within five years he was appointed head of the department. Polk witnessed the Great Depression and its sweeping devastation of black sharecroppers and farmers. His quiet portraits during this time of squalid rural conditions belie the deep scars cut into the hopes of his people. Polk's studies seemed to suggest, as did his earlier portraits, that the poverty and denial visiting the nation were accepted as a constant reality for rural African American people.

In 1938 Polk sojourned to Atlanta, Georgia, to start a commercial studio that was short-lived due to hard times. He returned to Tuskegee within a year and brought with him additional skills and the honor of having some of his work selected by the Southeastern Photographers Convention. Moving back to Tuskegee Institute, he was designated official photographer, a title he held until retirement.

The body of work Polk left to us is essentially the legacy of a twentieth-century commercial photographer. As a small town campus photographer, he showed how his popular craft could serve his community. He photographed weddings, funerals, graduations, proms, and annual yearbook rituals. His most sensitive studies are of Dr. George Washington Carver of Tuskegee in his lab, his flower garden, and at rest at home. Carver advised Polk to take a lot of pictures of him. "They will make you famous some day," he predicted.

Another special series Polk photographed was of black folklife in rural Macon County, Alabama—dirt-floor cabins with their tenants posed or settled outside. *The Boss* is a study of a strong black woman, steadfast like a rock, costumed in a bandanna headdress and servant's apron and dress. Polk also shot a portrait that resembles the work of his early mentors. In *Portrait Of An Ex-Slave* Polk lavishes soft light on his subject's beautifully black-bearded face.

Polk's studies of rural folks rank him with his contemporary James Van DerZee. Both men sold photographs to an all-black clientele. Both grew in craftsmanship as they grew in age. Polk was a master of small-town rural simplicities; Van DerZee was a master of big-city urban complexities. Both were prime witnesses to the cultural changes of their time and will become photographic heroes of destiny.

—Worth W. Long

PORTER, Charles Ethan
American painter

Born: Hartford, East Hartford, or Rockville, Connecticut, 1847 or 1848. **Education:** National Academy of Design, New York, 1869. **Career:** Studio owner, Hartford, Connecticut, Rockville, Connecticut, and New York, 1869-c.1896. Traveled and studied in London and Paris, 1881-84. Charter member, Connecticut Academy of Fine Arts. **Died:** 6 March 1923.

Selected Exhibitions:

1871   National Academy of Design, New York
1873   American Society of Painters in Watercolor

1875   American Society of Painters in Watercolor
1876   National Academy of Design, New York
1885   National Academy of Design, New York
1889   Vorce's Gallery, Hartford, Connecticut

*   *   *

Charles Ethan Porter was a still life painter who worked for most of his life in Hartford, Connecticut. His still lifes were modest and unembellished, showing the simple pleasures of nature. Because Porter became quickly known as an accomplished still life painter, even a genius at what he did, his patrons always steered his efforts in that direction. He was a fellow student with William Merritt Chase at the National Academy of Design in New York City, and both Porter and Chase developed their still lifes beyond simple flower and fruit arrangements to encompass an array of subjects. Porter also painted landscapes, nudes, interiors, and portraits, as well as dead game or strings of trout in the tradition of William Harnett, another fellow student. Nevertheless, still life painting provided success and a steady income for artists like Porter, and few of his other works remain.

After Porter moved back to Hartford from New York, he quickly won praise for his oil paintings, especially his paintings of apples that captured the essence of the color and shape of the fruit in a natural environment. *Still Life: Apples* (c.1877), for example, shows six apples, three green and three red, resting on a surface of wheat straw. The background is painted in a dark umber, with slight variations in light that echo the highlights at the edge of the straw. The apples are not perfect, the green ones, for example, showing imperfections that may have been caused by the pecks of birds. A branch of leaves rises from the back to the apex of the painting, showing Porter's experimentation with spatial perspective. The straw is draped over its ledge, covering any hint of an edge to the surface. That the apples are placed in a natural setting along with other plants that grow from the earth shows that Porter was aware of the philosophy of John Ruskin and the Pre-Raphaelites, which dominated American thinking in still life painting at the time. According to this view artists should be inspired by nature, and they should study and paint objects in their natural contexts.

In *Still Life: Two Baskets of Strawberries* (c.1878) Porter's brush strokes create a rough, dry surface texture, with the berries tumbling out of their baskets onto an ocher-colored dirt surface and with a canopy of leaves forming the backdrop. The berry plants range from those with small white flower blooms that are not quite open to those with fully ripe red berries that are ready to eat, as if Porter were attempting to reveal the life cycle of the berry itself. It has been suggested that Porter mixed sand into the ocher to give the dirt-colored paint a gritty texture, approximating a trompe l'oeil effect.

Porter went to Paris in November 1881 with a letter of introduction from Mark Twain giving him access to the American art community there. Few paintings can be identified from his Paris years, but *Still Life of Flowers* (c.1881) gives a sense of his work at the time. In the painting (where, below his signature, Porter inscribed the word "Paris") he lightened the background so that the flowers, while separate, fuse with it. While the conservative Porter did not adopt the invisible brush stroke method of the Salon painters, his work was informed by French techniques. The casual and fluid treatment of the rose petals and the vase, painted impressionistically rather than being a carefully rendered shape, for example, all suggest the influence of French painting.

Before he returned from Paris in 1884, Porter studied the Barbizon painters and did landscape sketches in the French countryside. Upon returning to Hartford he painted two landscapes that clearly show French influence. Both employ broad strokes of the brush, give few details, and use light that illuminates from within the natural shapes. Porter's patrons and the critics, however, were not interested in his landscapes or other works. Although in his mature style he became an accomplished still life painter, he was the product of a conservative age that tried to retain the values of earlier times—purity and beauty in everyday things. Porter could not escape this confinement, and thus he succumbed to it as an artist.

—Lizzetta LeFalle-Collins

PORTER, James (Amos)
American painter

Born: Baltimore, Maryland, 22 December 1905. **Education:** Howard University, Washington, D.C., B.A. (honors) 1927; Institute of Art and Archeology, University of Paris, Certificat de Presence 1935; New York University, M.A. in art history 1937. **Family:** Married Dorothy Burnett in 1929. **Career:** Beginning 1953 department head, Howard University, Washington, D.C. **Awards:** Honorable mention, Harmon Foundation Exhibition, 1929; Arthur Schomburg Portrait Prize, 1933; stipendiary, Rockefeller Foundation, 1935, 1945; research grant, *Washington Evening Star*; Achievement in Art Award, Pyramid Club; Distinguished Achievement in Art Education medal and honorarium, National Gallery of Art, 1965. **Online Address:** http://www.artnoir.com. **Died:** 28 February 1970.

Exhibitions:

1928   Harmon Foundation
1929   Smithsonian Institution, Washington, D.C.
1932   American Watercolor Society
1933   Harmon Foundation
        Smithsonian Institution, Washington, D.C.
        Philadelphia Watercolor Society
1935   New Jersey State Museum, Trenton
1937   Howard University, Washington, D.C.
1939   Howard University, Washington, D.C.
1940   American Negro Exposition, Chicago
1942   Atlanta University, Georgia
1944   Atlanta University, Georgia
1945   Howard University, Washington, D.C.
1965   *James A. Porter, Retrospective Exhibition,* Howard University Gallery of Art, Washington, D.C.
1970   James A. Porter Gallery
1971   Smith-Mason Gallery

Collections:

Howard University, Washington, D.C.; Lincoln University, Jefferson City, Missouri; Hampton Institute, Hampton, Virginia.

Publications:

By PORTER: **Book**—*Modern Negro Art,* Washington, D.C., Howard University Press, 1943. **Articles**—"Negro Art in Review," in *American Magazine of Art,* 27, January 1934, pp. 16-27; "Versatile Interests of the Early Negro Artist: A Neglected Chapter of American Art History," in *Art in America,* 24, January 1936, pp. 16-27; "Four Problems in the History of Negro Art," in *Journal of Negro History,* 27, January 1942, pp. 9-36; "Robert S. Duncanson: Midwestern Romantic-Realist," in *Art in America* (New York), 39(3), October 1951, pp. 99-154; "A Further Note on Robert S. Duncanson," in *Art in America* (New York), 42(3), October 1954, pp. 220-21, 235; "Afro-American Art at Floodtide," in *Arts in Society,* 5, Summer/Fall 1968, p. 264.

On PORTER: Book—*James A. Porter, Artist and Art Historian: The Memory of the Legacy,* exhibition catalog, Washington, D.C., Howard University Gallery of Art, 1992. **Article**—"James A. Porter," in *A History of African-American Artists, from 1792 to the Present* by Romare Bearden and Harry Henderson, Pantheon Books, New York, 1993, pp. 373-80.

* * *

James Amos Porter was an artist, art historian, and educator who was dedicated to research on African American art and artists, and he was a pioneer who opened the door for other African American art historians. Starmanda Bullock Featherstone called Porter the "father of African American art history."

Porter's own success in painting and drawing helped him understand other artists and their work. His ability as an exceptional historian stemmed in part from his understanding of the thought, emotion, and technique that had gone into a particular artwork. He was the author of many books and essays. His book *Modern Negro Art,* published in 1943 and reprinted with a new preface in 1969, was an in-depth account of African American artists and their contributions to the arts and humanities.

As a complete creative artist Porter himself produced many paintings, drawings, and illustrations that were later shown in exhibitions and held in private and public collections. As early as 1928 Porter had become known as an interpreter of human feelings. The details of his portraits of family members and friends revealed the emotions of his subjects. In 1945 Porter traveled to the Caribbean, where he studied, photographed, and painted the people of African decent. In the 1960s he traveled to Egypt and West Africa, where he painted in Lagos, Nigeria. Porter was quoted as saying, "My paintings reflect the enthusiasm and the understanding admiration which I have felt for Africa and the Africans, even though, admittedly, the most skillful expatriate artist may utterly fail to capture those ineffable traits in the African people which we believe are made visible to us in their arts." His later works were based on his visits to Haiti, Cuba, and West Africa and included local scenes and paintings of the residents.

Porter used a combination of techniques from fauvism and expressionism. His portraits were colorful, bold, and three-dimensional. Well-known paintings included *Woman Holding a Jug* (c.1932-33), an oil on canvas that won him the Harmon Foundation's 1933 portrait award; *In a Cuban Bus* (1946), also called *On a Cuban Bus*; and *The Colonial Soldier* (c.1937). His *Vendors at Bar Beach* (1963-64) and *Eyo Masquerade* (1964), both painted in Lagos, were from the period when he had moved into a combination of late fauvism and pure expressionism. The two paintings were scenes of day-to-day life in Lagos.

One of Porter's accomplishments was his ability to combine teaching and writing with the production of art. He was enthusiastic about his paintings, he loved to take part in exhibitions, and he was always willing to discuss his works with viewers. He expressed his feelings to his viewers by saying: "From me to you. . . . As long as I am alive and able to give expression to my experiences and ideas, I shall deem it a privilege as well as an obligation to show the concrete results of my efforts with all others. That for this purpose I have not chosen to rely upon the services of a dealer or agent is explained by the fact that I am more interested in a personal confrontation with my viewers than I am in such impersonal services as may hinder the disclosure of my message as an artist. In other words, I believe that my whole enthusiasm for this opportunity of showing my work is personal, my acceptance of it could not possibly be selfish."

During his lifetime Porter nurtured many minds through his teaching, writing, and painting. He was a crusader who brought African American artists and their contributions into the limelight. In 1992 Howard University held a memorial exhibition, for which many people wrote tributes. In her tribute Tritobia Benjamin said: "He honed his skill as a draftsman rendering fine portraits and figure studies with the precision of a surgeon. His drawings particularly revealed an affinity with the academic tradition, and a patient capacity for detail."

—Gabriel Tenabe

POWELL, Georgette
American painter

Work also appeared under the name Georgette Seabrooke and Georgette Seabrooke Powell. **Born:** Charleston, South Carolina, 2 August 1916. **Education:** Cooper Union Art School, New York, 1933-37, certificate 1937; ; Fordham University, New York, 1950; Washington School of Psychiatry, 1970-72; Howard University, Washington, D.C., B.F.A. 1973; **Family:** Married George W. Powell 1936 (died 1982), one daughter and two sons. **Career:** Master artist, Federal Art Project, W.P.A., New York, 1935-39; art therapist, D.C. General Hospital, 1963-67; therapeutic recreation specialist, D.C. General Hospital, 1969-78. Since 1972 registered art therapist. Since 1970 founder-director, Tomorrow's World Art Center, Washington, D.C. Since 1967, inceptor, Community Art Happening, Washington, D.C., "Annual Arts Festival." Designed and painted murals, Harlem Hospital and Queens General Hospital, Federal Arts Project, New York, 1936-39. Since 1967 inceptor, Community Art Happening, Washington, D.C. "Annual Arts Festival". **Awards:** Cooper Union Art School silver medal, 1935; Outstanding Performance award, D.C. General Hospital, Washington, D.C., 1964; Mental Health Program award, D.C. Department of Recreation, Washington, D.C., 1974; American Art League award, 1967, 1972, 1976; Outstanding Service award, D.C. Art Association, Washington, D.C., 1977; National Achievement Certificate award, National Conference of Artists award, 1977; FESTAC certificate of recognition, 1977; James D. Parks special award, 1978; Howard University "Salute to Black Women award, Washington, D.C., 1978; Institute for Urban Affairs and Research Certificate award, 1978; certificate award, Ukrainian National Auditorium, 1984; special recognition, Saint Patrick's Senior Award, 1986; Salute to Georgette Powell, 1987; Inspirations/Anacostia Neighborhood Museum award, D.C. Art Association award, Washington, D.C., 1989; National Conference of Artists Life Achievement award,

Georgette Powell: *Girl by a Window.* **Photo by Manu Sassoonian; courtesy of the Schomburg Center for Research in Black Culture.**

1989. Address: 5203 New Hampshire Avenue NW, Washington, D.C. 20011, U.S.A.

Selected Exhibitions:

1982	*Heritage Awareness Through the Arts—One Woman Exhibit,* YMCA, Palm Coast, Florida
	George Meany Center, Silver Spring, Maryland
1984	*Florida Artists,* Palm Coast Art Festival
1982	Museum of African American Life and Culture, Dallas
1983	Museum of African American Life and Culture, Dallas
	Market Five Gallery, Washington, D.C.
1984	Carnegie Library, Washington, D.C.
1985	*International Afro-American Senegalese Artist Exhibition,* National Conference of Artists, Dakar, Senegal
	Arts Club, Washington, D.C.
1985	Evan Tibbs Collection, Washington, D.C.
1986	Kenkeleba Gallery, New York, 1986
1988	Tweedy Gallery, New York
	Schomburg Center, New York
1989	Anacostia Museum, Washington, D.C.

*   *   *

Georgette (Seabrooke) Powell gained distinction early in her career as a muralist commissioned to decorate the walls of New York's Harlem Hospital. She was barely out of her teens at the time of her appointment and was among the prodigies of the black art circles around Charles Alston, Augusta Savage, and James Wells. A painter, decorator, art therapist, and collagist, she has been involved in creative endeavors throughout her life.

Powell actively exhibited in the major black shows of the 1930s and 1940s, earning prizes for her work even while she was still in art school. At Cooper Union she studied with the regionalist John Steuart Curry, and she won a first prize for her social realist scene of black worship, *Church Scene* (1935). She also studied printmaking with Wells at the Harlem Arts Workshop, and the linocut *Young Girl of African Descent* (1933) is a surviving work that demonstrates her graphic skills and her interest in depicting black lives.

With the help of Savage, who actively sought government patronage for black artists during the Great Depression, Powell joined the Works Progress Administration's Federal Art Project (FAP) in 1936 and completed murals at Harlem (1936-37) and Queens General (1937-38) hospitals. She was joined on the Harlem Hospital murals by Alston, Selma Day, Vertis Hayes, Elba Lightfoot, Sara Murrell, and the white artist Alfred Crimi. Powell, designated a "master artist," supervised assistants Beauford Delaney and Louis Vaughan and painted a recreation room for nurses in the hospital's penthouse. She used the natural light of the setting to accentuate the small and narrow space for the oil mural, which was painted directly on the walls. Entitled *Recreation in Harlem*, it included imagery of interracial groups engaged in leisure activities at the beach, on picnics, at the theater, and elsewhere.

Because of its progressive nature, Powell's mural, along with Alston's and Hayes's, was controversial. Although it was initially accepted by the FAP administration, preparatory sketches by the three artists were subsequently rejected by the hospital officials, who felt that black imagery was not appropriate for Harlem. A firestorm of protest by the Harlem Artists Guild and the interracial Artists Union ultimately brought about the reversal of the decision, and the project was completed as planned. Sadly, Powell's *Recreation in Harlem,* like her Queens General Hospital mural, fell into ruin over the years.

A self-described "people person," Powell employed more realistic modes in her easel paintings. *Emilie* (1938), a genre portrait of a black woman at her toilette, derives its strength from the economic use of contour lines. Taking a close-up view of the subject's face and torso, Powell communicated the woman's concentration on her task and directed the viewer's attention to it. The picture's compact space is divided by stabilizing shapes and angles: the nearly square mirror sitting on the woman's vanity table in the foreground, the angles formed by her arms as she holds her hair between the tongs of a curling iron, and the diagonal of her bare shoulder. Powell's skillful use of such geometries is offset by delicate details like the slack strap of the woman's chemise.

Marrying, raising a family, and pursuing a career in art therapy after 1940, Powell took up assemblage in the 1960s. *Tropical Motif* (1968), a mixed-media collage, is a cacophony of patterns, some geometric and some inspired by flora and fauna. The piece exemplifies her move from realism and representationalism to symbolic abstraction that employs the very fabric of African and other non-Western art materials. Emblematic of the decades of black power and black nationalist activism, this imagery invoking Africa was hardly new to Powell, who had come of age in the Harlem Arts Workshop, the Harlem Artists Guild, the Artists Union, and the studio of Alston and Savage, and continues to work in this vein.

—Jacqueline Francis

POWERS, Harriet

American quiltmaker

Born: Georgia, 29 October 1837. **Family:** Married Armstead Powers, six children. **Career:** Self-employed seamstress. **Died:** 1911.

Group Exhibitions:

1886 Athens Cotton Fairs, Georgia
1895 Cotton States Exposition, Atlanta, Georgia

Collections:

Museum of Fine Arts, Boston; National Museum of American History, Washington, D.C.

Publications:

On POWERS: Book—*Harriet Powers' Bible Quilts* by R. Perry, Rizzoli, 1993. **Articles**—"The Harriet Powers Pictorial Quilts" by Marie Jeanne Adams, in *Black Art,* 1979; "Harriet Powers: Portrait of a Black Quilter" by Gladys-Marie Fry, in *Sage,* Spring 1987; "Black Women: Making Quilts of Their Own" by M. Acua McDaniel, in *Art Papers,* September/October 1987.

*   *   *

Most of the information about the quilt artist Harriet Powers must be gleaned from her two known works, tax and census records, and a tiny photograph. After emancipation Powers became the wife of an independent farmer who lived on the outskirts of Athens, Georgia, where she helped farm, raised chickens, and sewed for the black and white members of the community. Between 1886 and 1895 Powers completed two unusual quilts that departed from the geometric patterns and strips typically used by African Americans. Called the Harriet Powers Bible quilts, they are in the collections of the Smithsonian Institution's National Museum of American History and of Boston's Museum of Fine Arts.

The pieces for the quilts were cut from colored scraps of fabric and appliquéd using a sewing machine, with the three layers of the quilts then being joined by hand. The earlier of Powers's quilts is the one in the Smithsonian collection. A vivid interpretation of biblical scenes from both the Old and the New Testaments, the quilt is divided into eleven scenes, beginning with the Garden of Eden and ending with the Nativity. When the quilt was originally purchased from Powers, she explained its iconography, which was recorded by the buyer. The quilt in the Boston collection has fifteen rather than eleven squares. Unlike the Smithsonian quilt the Boston quilt offers a combination of biblical symbolism and astronomical and climatological events. The iconography of this quilt was also apparently explained by Powers, but the explanation has been lost. In both quilts each square attempts to tell a complete story. The squares read horizontally, from left to right, rather than vertically, which is unusual for story quilts.

Powers's style probably did not develop in isolation. The technique of using appliquéd designs to tell a story and the depiction of numerous birds and animals are similar to practices in Benin (formerly Dahomey). It is possible that some of Powers's African-born ancestors were Dahoman and that they made appliquéd de-

signs that inspired her. It is more plausible, however, that Powers's quilts were conceived and executed within the context of the appliqué quilt-making techniques that flourished in Southern regions of the United States from about 1775 to 1875. The proportions of her figures are Western.

There has been considerable speculation over the sources for Powers's unusual iconography. Given the literal depiction of biblical themes, it must be assumed that Powers was deeply religious and familiar with the Bible and that she had committed to memory the fiery sermons she heard at church. Powers's interest in celestial phenomena appears to have been extraordinary, however. She represented numerous versions of the sun, moon, and stars in both quilts. The appearance of astronomical and climatological events—"dark days," "red-light nights," "falling stars," and extreme temperatures—in the Boston quilt is difficult to explain, but she may have seen them as lessons of the power of God. Although Powers was apparently unable to read or write and some of the climatological events depicted occurred before her birth, she recorded their exact date and time. She was probably apprised of the astronomical and climatological events by an older relative, a remarkable testimony to the power and persistence of the oral tradition among African Americans.

Neither of Powers's quilts conforms to standard sizes or shapes for use as bed covers. The Smithsonian quilt is smaller than the standard, and the Boston quilt is larger. Neither is rectangular. The extraordinary amount of attention given to detail in both quilts also indicates that they were probably not made to be used on beds. Supporting this theory are Powers's designation of the Smithsonian quilt as a "Sermon in Patchwork" and her statement that she wanted to "preach the gospel in patchwork, to show my Lord my humility . . . and to show where sin originated, out of the beginning of things." Since Powers and most of the African American members of her community could not read or write, she may have used the quilts to teach Bible stories.

Powers's quilts not only informed the faithful of familiar stories from the Old and New Testaments, but they also recorded and preserved important and complex astronomical and climatological events for members of her generation and beyond. The Harriet Powers Bible quilts are without parallel in the history of American quilt art.

—Regenia A. Perry

PRIESTLY, Debra

American painter

Born: Springfield, Ohio. **Education:** Ohio State University, Columbus, B.F.A. 1983; Pratt Institute, Brooklyn, New York, M.F.A. 1986. **Awards:** Purchase Award, *Sixth Annual Art Exhibition and Competition,* Atlanta Life Insurance Company, Georgia, 1986; fellowship, Printmaking Workshop, New York, 1988-89.

Individual Exhibitions:

1983 Model Neighborhood Facility, Columbus, Ohio
    Drake Union, Ohio State University, Columbus
1986 Pratt Institute, Brooklyn, New York

1987   Ollantay Center for the Arts, Jackson Heights, New York
        Springfield Museum of Art, Ohio
1988   Cinque Gallery, New York
1989   The Print Studio, Wellington City Art Gallery, New
        Zealand
1990   Beaux Arts Collectors Gallery, Columbus Museum of
        Art, Ohio
1994   June Kelly Gallery, New York

Selected Group Exhibitions:

1982   Battelle Memorial Institute, Columbus, Ohio
1983   Hoyt L. Sherman Gallery, Ohio State University, Colum-
        bus
1985   State Office Tower, Columbus, Ohio
1987   *Autobiography: Herstory,* Woman's Caucus for Art,
        Castillo Gallery, New York
1988   J.B. Speed Museum, Louisville, Kentucky
        Schomburg Center, New York
1989   *Contemporary Works by African-American Artists and
        Traditional African Art,* Christie's, New York
1990   Dowd Fine Arts Gallery of SUNY, Cortland, New York
1992   Hopkins Hall Gallery, Ohio State University, Columbus
        Columbus Museum of Art, Ohio

Collection:

Ohio State University, Columbus.

*   *   *

When Debra Priestly was a child, she often visited Patoka, Indiana, with her parents. "Patoka Series" chronicles these childhood
visits to the town where her father was born. The series is in two
parts and includes a 22" x 22" x 6½" box format and a 38" x 42" x
4" format. There is a great deal of difference between the two
Patoka formats. In terms of imagery and physicality, the box form
projects from the wall. The other is a horizontal format. Priestly
did not realize she was "keeper of the memories" until she was on
the other side of the world. From such a distant vista as New
Zealand, the artist's memories of Patoka began to crystallize and
distill. Visions, incidents, and people returned. In connecting to
these memories from the other side of the world, Priestly felt a
heightened sense of location and presence. Working primarily in
acrylic, she painted the "Patoka Series" on birch plywood because
a richer surface results. In two works from the series, Priestly
recalls the mystical farm where her father matured.

Using sparse details in *Patoka #11 Boat* (1994, acrylic, canvas,
pine on birch, 32" x 48" x 4"), Priestly reveals through color that
there must have been a lake or some body of water on or near her
father's farm. We connect the artist with this place because she
includes a boat on which is superimposed two frames side by side.
In one of the frames her face is observed. The other frame is blank.
Above the frames are what appear to be two oars. Priestly is not
narrating or storytelling in this series. She is not giving us literal
information but a subtitle that assists in guiding the viewer through
this mystical return to her past. Explanation takes away the mystery, as she moves us between abstraction and illusion.

Patoka #3 Lightning (1992, acrylic, charcoal, pastel, paper,
feather on birch, 22" x 22" x 6½") is one of the box forms in the
series that project from the wall. Priestly's box forms create am-

biguous space and break the continuum of conventional space. An
unsuspecting viewer is not certain whether what she is perceiving is
actually on the surface or inside the box. This format is supremely
successful in Priestly's series. What occurs in *Lightning* is noteworthy. The artist moves us around this dizzying panoramic vista.
Although we see over in the left-hand corner what appears to be a
lightning flash and then a felled tree, apparently struck by this bolt
of light, the very vigilant Priestly is careful not to give us clear facts.
There is yet another lightning flash seen in the right-hand corner of
this projected-box format. Nearby another felled tree is observed,
or is it the shadow of the tree that is upright? Color is not used
naturalistically, so the observer must find her way in Priestly's
world. Indeed, these intense hues distance the painter from the
subject matter. Such a choice of color distances her viewers, too.

Priestly's visit to New Zealand unleashed in her memories what
she did not know that she had kept. As "keeper of the memories,"
Priestly confidently reminds us about her celebration of life and the
connections she has with distant places and distant people.

—Jontyle Theresa Robinson

PRIMUS, Nelson (A.)

American painter

Born: Hartford, Connecticut, 1843. **Family:** Married Ret sometime before 1865, one daughter. **Career:** Self-employed carriage
and sign painter, Boston, 1865-90; counterman, Turk and Divisidero
streets delicatessen, by 1907 and until c.1915. **Died:** c.1916.

Group Exhibition:

1989   *African-American Artists, 1880-1987: Selections from the
        Evans-Tibbs Collection,* Smithsonian Institution, Wash-
        ington, D.C. (traveling)

Collections:

Connecticut Historical Society, Hartford; Oakland Museum of California.

*   *   *

Nelson Primus's extant work is a testament to the struggle of the
African American painter to acquire skills in easel painting, to join
the ranks of professional artists, and to participate in the aesthetic
discussion regarding the character and form of an evolving American art. Toward these ends Primus, a Connecticut-born artist, studied and apprenticed with the regionally prominent teachers George
Francis and Elizabeth Jerome. Highly motivated, he often reinterpreted popularly acclaimed compositions of his day that were reproduced in newspapers and magazines. Most of these canvases
have been lost, however.

Portraiture, a genre that afforded many American artists of the
time their daily bread, accounts for important surviving works by
Primus: *Lizzie May Ulmer* (1876), *Portrait of an Unknown Woman*
(1881), and *Portrait of a Lady (Lady with Golden Hair)* (1907). The
earliest, *Lizzie May Ulmer,* shows the white subject posed in a

three-quarter view and painted against a sepia background. Ulmer was an actress in Boston, where Primus lived from 1865 to 1894. A variety of reddish tones color her hair and enliven the solidly depicted form. The painting demonstrates its maker's ability to handle details: a convincing delicacy characterizes the lacy collar of Ulmer's dress, and a bejeweled earring dangles from her prominently executed ear. Primus's color choices for her clothing are relatively bright, with the powder blue dress she is wearing upstaged by a central pink ribbon. The portrait is without props, and it focuses attention on a subject whose gaze avert the viewer's.

Portrait of an Unknown Woman and *Portrait of a Lady* are also distinguished by the artist's interest in tonal harmonies and depiction of costume. The reddish highlights of the latter subject's long tresses are especially brilliant and eye-catching. The subject was the daughter of a San Francisco delicatessen owner who employed Primus as a counterman sometime during the early twentieth century.

Throughout his career Primus maintained his predilection for gathering subjects from close at hand, from the civic community of personal acquaintances and local notables to people from popular culture. In California his oeuvre came to include paintings of members of San Francisco's Chinatown community, a new subject in the catalog of American genre painting. A resident of the Bay Area from 1895 until his death in 1916, he was likely familiar with the Chinatown neighborhood and with Arnold Genthe's photojournalistic studies of it.

The Fortune Teller (1898) and *The Oriental Child* (1900) are compositions that may have been inspired by Genthe photographs. In both the subjects are clothed in loose-fitting jackets, silky pants, and soft slippers, and they have facial features that make them recognizably Chinese. While the paintings are small—about 8 1/2 by 11 inches—the protagonists are fully articulated pictorial elements.

The Chinatown subjects stand toward the middle ground of their respective paintings. The fortune teller is a calm, pipe-smoking figure who sits at his desk—a small folding table—with his right hand gripping a writing instrument and propped on a stack of paper. Behind him is the clutter of his shop; tables and boards are stacked on end, and a calligraphic wall sign welcomes passersby. The subject of *The Oriental Child* is a crying boy standing on a cobbled street, his face contorted with emotion not evident in the placid adult portraits. Yet like all of Primus's known paintings, *The Oriental Child* shows the artist's serious commitment to the study of human form and character.

—Jacqueline Francis

PROPHET, Nancy Elizabeth

American sculptor

Born: Warwick, Rhode Island, 19 March 1890. **Education:** Rhode Island School of Design, diploma in drawing and painting, 1918; École des Beaux Arts, Paris. **Family:** Married Francis Ford, 1915 (separated 1932). **Career:** Art instructor, Spelman College, Atlanta, Georgia, 1934-44. Also worked at a ceramics factory, Rhode Island, 1940-1950, and as a domestic after 1944. **Awards:** Harmon Prize for Best Sculpture, Harmon Foundation, 1929; Richard Greenough Prize, Art Association of Newport, 1932. **Died:** December 1960.

Individual Exhibitions:

1945	Providence Public Library

Selected Group Exhibitions:

1924	Salon d'Automne, Paris
1927	Salon d'Automne, Paris
1928	Boston Independent Exposition
1929	Societé des Artistes Français, Paris
1930	Harmon Foundation, New York
1931	Harmon Foundation, New York
	Societé des Artistes Français, Paris
1932	Boston Independent Exposition
	Societé des Artistes Français, Paris
1935	Whitney Sculpture Biennial, New York
1936	Harmon Foundation, New York
1937	Whitney Sculpture Biennial, New York
1978	Bannister Gallery, Rhode Island College, Providence
1985	Bellevue Art Museum, Bellevue, Washington (traveling)

Collections:

Black Heritage Society of Rhode Island, Providence; Rhode Island School of Design; Whitney Museum of American Art, New York.

Publications:

On PROPHET: Articles—"Beth Prophet Is Hailed in Paris as Real Artist," in *The Afro-American*, Baltimore, 3 August 1929, p. 8; "Elizabeth Prophet: Sculptress" by Countee Cullen, in *Opportunity*, July 1930, pp. 204-05; "Can I Become a Sculptor? The Story of Elizabeth Prophet," in the *Crisis*, October 1932, p. 315; "Anne Elizabeth Prophet Wins R.S. Greenough Prize," in *New York Times*, 8(1), 9 July 1932; "Art and Life," in *Atlanta University Review of Race and Culture*, Georgia, 1940; "Four from Providence: Bannister, Prophet, Alston, Jennings," in *Providence: Rhode Island Black Heritage Society and Rhode Island College*, 1978; "Nancy Elizabeth Prophet, Sculptor" by Blossom S. Kirschenbaum, in *SAGE IV*, Spring 1987, pp. 45-52; "Elizabeth Prophet (1890-1960)" by Theresa Leininger, in *Notable Black American Women*, edited by Jessie Carney Smith, Detroit, Gale Research, Inc., 1992.

*   *   *

Nancy Elizabeth Prophet was a fiercely independent woman and a sculptor of exceptional talent and vision. Most of her work—figures, busts, and heads produced in France from 1922 to 1934—represents emotional states of mind.

After Prophet graduated in 1918 from the Rhode Island School of Design with a degree in painting and freehand drawing, she tried to make a living doing portraits. Frustrated by the lack of opportunity in Providence, she went to Paris in 1922. There she began to sculpt again, and she took classes with the noted sculptor Victor Segoffin at the École des Beaux-Arts. She completed at least two busts in 1923, one of which (an untitled work in wood) was included in a salon in the following year. In 1924 Prophet earned her living by making and selling batik. She also began her first life-size statue, *Volonté*. Later, believing it to be mediocre, she smashed the work. Plagued by self-doubt and loneliness, Prophet filled her diary with melancholic outpourings.

In June 1926 the destitute Prophet moved into cramped quarters in Montparnasse, where she lived for the next seven years. The first work she created there was *Poverty* (also called *Prayer*), a life-size plaster female nude in a *contrapposto* pose with upraised head and a snake curling about her ankles. Other untitled statues and busts from this time reflect the sensibility of French sculpture in the 1920s. Like the work of Antoine Bourdelle, a student of Auguste Rodin, they have an androgynous quality, with close-cropped or covered hair, heavy-lidded eyes, enigmatic smiles, and small breasts and hips. Prophet's clay and plaster masks, with their broad, calm foreheads and archaic smiles, recall ancient Etruscan statues. Often ethnically ambiguous, her works may reflect Prophet's ambivalence about her mixed African American and Narragansett-Pequot heritage.

Prophet sculpted from life whenever models, sometimes people she met in cafés, would pose cheaply for her. These works are usually types rather than portraits of individuals, such as *Head of a Cossack* (with a tall, columnar hat) and *Reptile Woman* (executed perhaps after a circus performer). The latter work depicts the bust of a woman with a pageboy hairstyle, mysterious eyes, and crossed arms. Prophet mostly worked from imagination, however, producing pieces in marble and wood (cherry, sycamore, ebony, and pear) and also in bronze, alabaster, granite, terra-cotta, plaster, and clay. She lightly painted some of her bas-relief carvings—for example, *Facing the Light* (c.1928-31), showing two women shielding themselves from the sun's rays—and occasionally added gold highlights.

The titles of some of Prophet's works—including *Bitter Laughter* (or *Laughing Man*), *Violence*, *Discontent* (a gaunt head wearing a cowl, done in painted pear wood), and *Silence* (a subtly modeled marble head with small eyes without pupils, thin lips, and bobbed hair)—reflect her continuing physical and emotional discomfort. Yet in other works—*Poise* (a male head in marble, with squared chin and tensed throat muscles), *Peace*, *Confidence*, and *Le Pélerin* (a sorrowful robed figure)—Prophet seems to have expressed her ambition to obtain what she called the "abstract qualities" of poise and courage.

In the late 1920s Prophet produced a striking series of heads of people of African descent, including *Head of a Negro*, *Buste d'homme*, *Buste ébène*, and *Negro Head* (also called *Head of Roland Hayes*). Her most notable work is *Congolais* (c.1931), a cherry-wood head with a smooth, expansive brow, half-closed eyes, hollow cheeks, sensual lips, and a Masai warrior's single plait of beaded hair on the forehead. It is not known why she called her depiction of an East African a Congolese, that is, a person from the Congo region of Central Africa, but Prophet may have done so in ignorance, for few people knew much about Africa at the time.

Little is known about Prophet's art after her return to the United States in 1934. While teaching at Spelman College in Atlanta, Georgia, she maintained a studio, but she reportedly covered her sculptures with cloths so that no one could see them. She worked at a commercial ceramics factory in Rhode Island in the late 1940s and early 1950s, and she converted to Roman Catholicism in 1951. Only a handful of her pieces are in collections, and the whereabouts of most of her sculpture is unknown. Yet Prophet is remembered as one of the leading sculptors of the new Negro movement.

—Theresa Leininger-Miller

PURIFOY, Noah

American assemblage artist

Born: Snowhill, Alabama, 17 August 1917. **Education:** Alabama State Teachers College, Montgomery, B.S.; Chouinard Art Institute, Los Angeles, B.F.A.; Atlanta University, Georgia, M.S.S. **Military Service:** United States Navy, 1941-45: 3rd Class Petty Officer. **Career:** Teacher, Tuscaloosa, Alabama, 1940-44; social worker, Los Angeles, 1959-75; member, State Arts Council, Sacramento, California, 1975-86. Founder, Watts Towers Art Center, Los Angeles, 1964. **Awards:** Krasner Pollock Foundation Award, 1993. **Agent:** Sue Welsh, 354 South Harvard Boulevard, Los Angeles, California 90020, U.S.A. **Address:** P.O. Box 1036, Joshua Tree, California 92252, U.S.A.

Individual Exhibitions:

1971   Brockman Gallery, Los Angeles
1988   Old Masonic Lodge Gallery, Los Angeles
1989   Museum of African American Art, Los Angeles
1993   *As Is in Joshua Tree,* Tara's Hall, Los Angeles
1995   Mountainview Memorial Gallery, Altadena, California
1997   *Purifoy: Outside and in the Open,* African American Museum, Los Angeles (traveling through 1999)

Selected Group Exhibitions:

1966   Dickson Center, University of California, Los Angeles
1968   Washington Gallery of Modern Art, Washington, D.C.
1970   Huntington Galleries, Knoxville, Tennessee
1971   Chicago Bell Galleries
        Whitney Museum of American Art, New York
        Kalamazoo Institute of Art, Michigan
1972   *Garbage Needs Recycle Exhibition,* U.S. Office of Information, Berlin
1977   African Festival of the Arts and Culture, Lagos, Nigeria
1993   *I Remember: Thirty Years after the March on Washington—Images of the Civil Rights Movement, 1963-93,* Corcoran Gallery of Art, Washington, D.C.
1994   Getty Center for the History of Art and Humanities, Santa Monica, California

Collections:

California Afro-American Museum, Los Angeles; Corcoran Gallery of Art, Washington, D.C.; Illinois Bell Telephone Company, Chicago; Oakland Museum, California; Oran Belgrave Museum, Omaha, Nebraska; Whitney Museum, New York.

Publications:

On PURIFOY: Book—*Nineteen-Sixties: A Cultural Awakening Reevaluated 1965-1975,* edited by Nancy McKinney, California Afro-American Museum Foundation, 1989. **Articles**— "Noah Purifoy and Edward Kienholz," in *Cirrus Editions Limited* (Los Angeles), November 1972; "Black Improvisation in California" by Alan Gordon, in *New Art Examiner,* 1980; "Southern California Assemblage Past and Present" by Elena Siff, in *Santa Barbara Contemporary Arts Forum,* 1986; "Artist Makes Unusual Medium Talk" by Su-

Noah Purifoy: *White House,* **1992.**

san L. Chaney, in *Hi-Desert Star,* 19 August 1994; "The L.A. Connection in African American Art," in *International Review of African American Art,* 10(4), (Virginia) Hampton University Museum, 1994.

*   *   *

Noah Purifoy is considered by African American artists to be the father of the black assemblage movement in southern California. He came to art from a career in social work but with a firm grasp of how objects could be reconditioned, redefined, and reinterpreted. In works such as *Watts Riot* (1965) he collected and reinterpreted debris from the Watts section of Los Angeles as a comment on the deterioration of the quality of life for many African Americans. He also created a series of black paintings, including *Six Birds* (1967), with a small caged area, that suggested the feeling of entrapment of many African Americans.

As a sensitive and patient teacher and listener, Purifoy has encouraged artists to look at the essential qualities embodied in materials and to question and explore them. He has taught or influenced many artists—including John Outterbridge, David Hammons, and Betye Saar—to tell their stories with common objects, showing them that they do not have to use the traditional materials of painting and sculpture but can define their artwork on their own terms with any materials they chose. He is also a testament to the concept

of community-based art centers and what they can offer to those who have been underserved by the larger establishment. One of the founders of the Watts Towers Art Center just prior to the Watts riots, he provided guidance for the novice and the academically trained who wanted a voice in expressing their cultural identity in art. He provided the catalyst for those artists who wanted to explore abstract forms but who were hesitant to depart from the figural representations that were their connection with the African American communities of their youth. Purifoy showed them how to use symbols to replace figurative representations, while preserving the essence and presence of the figures. His work opened the door for many artists to develop a contemporary language that satisfied their investigations into conceptual works and yet maintain their connections to their African American heritage.

Purifoy left art-making for over ten years to work as an arts administrator for the state of California. He returned to art in the mid-1980s, exploring further his forms and themes of the 1960s but also branching out into larger and more complex works. During this period, as a backdrop for rusted and denigrated materials, he experimented with bright colors that suggested a polished newness. As his works grew larger, his studio in the cramped urban environment of Los Angeles grew too small. Relocating to the semirural desert community of Joshua Tree, California, allowed him the space and a safer environment in which to create. The effect of the desert can be seen in his installations in the 1990s. Many works, for example,

Noah Purifoy: *Collage,* **1996.**

Untitled (1995), are made of welded steel and aluminum and rise like steles in the desert. The materials of the sculptures and assemblages are those used in various forms of construction, giving his works an architectural quality. In some works Purifoy has built actual environments—encampments for the homeless, spiritual dwellings, motel-like stalls painted in pastel colors, and a desert igloo.

In *Environment #2* the viewer must walk down into a dug-out path to enter a partially subterranean enclosure. Light filters in from the aboveground openings and from a conical ceiling at the top of the shelter. Fabrics are attached to the walls, creating color and movement as the wind passes under them, and debris is strewn on the floor. The earthen walls, natural light, and wood armature construction create an environment that protects against the harsh sunlight outside. *Surrealistic Piece* (1991) is reminiscent of Marcel Duchamp's use of bicycles. Two bicycles, their wheels propelled by the desert wind, rest on a slanted roof. The structure below, with a window in the center, encloses found objects from the desert. This and other works are perforated structures that allow the viewer to see through to the landscape on the other side, perhaps suggesting a breaking down of the barriers that enclose and separate in the city. Purifoy's structures in the country stretch and reach to pierce the high desert air, and as they weather and collect sand particles from the sudden storms or sink into the sand from the drenching rains, they become a part of the desert environment.

Purifoy's abstract assemblages represent a counterforce within a countermovement. By creating sociopolitical sculptures, architectural in form and scale, he demonstrates the power of abstract art to make statements about the adverse social conditions which we all often experience.

—Lizzetta LeFalle-Collins

PURYEAR, Martin

American sculptor

Born: Washington, D.C., 23 May 1941. **Education:** Catholic University of America, Washington D.C., 1959-63, B.A. 1963; Swedish Royal Academy of Art, Stockholm, 1966-68; traveled and studied in Lapland and Scandinavia, 1967-68; Yale University, New Haven, Connecticut, 1969-71, M.F.A. 1971. **Family:** Married Jeanne Gordon in 1986, one daughter. **Career:** Teacher, Peace Corps, Sierra Leone, West Africa, 1964-66; assistant professor of art, Fisk University, Nashville, 1971-73; teacher, University of Illinois, Chicago, 1978. Designer, SCAN, Scandinavia, 1968. Artist-in-residence, Yaddo, Saratoga Springs, New York, 1979; visiting artist, American Academy, Rome, 1986. **Awards:** Scandinavian-American Foundation Study grant, Stockholm, 1966; Creative and Performing Artists grants, University of Maryland, 1975, 1978; Creative Artists Public Service grant, New York Creative Artists Public Service Program, 1976; Robert Rauschenberg Foundation grant, 1977; National Endowment for the Arts Fellowship, 1978; National Endowment of the Arts Planning Grant for Art in Public Places, 1979; Louis Comfort Tiffany grant, 1984; Guggenheim Memorial Foundation grant, 1984; Greenburger Foundation Award, 1988; Grand Prize, São Paulo Bienal, 1989; MacArthur Foundation Fellowship, 1989; Skowhegan Prize, 1990. **Agents**: Margo Leavin Gallery, 812 North Robertson Boulevard, Los Angeles, California 90069, U.S.A.; Donald Young Gallery, 2107 3rd Avenue, Seattle, Washington 98121, U.S.A.; McKee Gallery, 745 Fifth Avenue, New York, New York 10151, U.S.A. **Address:** c/o McKee Gallery, 745 Fifth Avenue, New York, New York 10151, U.S.A.

Individual Exhibitions:

1968	Grona Palletten Gallery, Stockholm
1972	Henri 2 Gallery, Washington, D. C.
1977	Corcoran Gallery of Art, Washington, D. C.
	Artpark, Lewiston, New York
1980	Museum of Contemporary Art, Chicago
	Young Hoffman Gallery, Chicago
	Joslyn Art Museum, Omaha, Nebraska
1984	University Gallery, University of Massachusetts, Amherst (traveling)
1985	Margo Leavin Gallery, Los Angeles
1987	David McKee Gallery, New York
	Chicago Public Library Cultural Center
1988	McIntosh/Drysdale Gallery, Washington, D.C.
	Brooklyn Museum, New York
1989	Margo Leavin Gallery, Los Angeles
	São Paulo Bienal, Brazil
1990	Museum of Fine Arts, Boston

1991   Art Institute of Chicago (traveling retrospective)
1992   Hirshhorn Museum and Sculpture Garden, Washington, D.C.
        Museum of Contemporary Art, Los Angeles (traveling
            retrospective)
        Philadelphia Museum of Art (traveling retrospective)
1993   Cleveland Center for Contemporary Art, Ohio (traveling
            retrospective through 1994)
1995   McKee Gallery, New York

Selected Group Exhibitions:

1963   Baltimore Museum of Art, Maryland
1968   Swedish Royal Academy of Art
        Stockholm Biennial
1978   Solomon R. Guggenheim Museum, New York
1979   Protetch-McIntosh Gallery, Washington, D. C.
        Whitney Museum of American Art, New York
        National Oceanic and Atmospheric Administration, Seattle
1981   and/or Gallery, Seattle
        Whitney Museum of American Art, New York
1985   Guggenheim Museum, New York

Collections:

Addison Gallery of American Art, Andover, Massachusetts; Art
Institute of Chicago; Centro Cultural Arte Contemporaneo, Mexico
City; Corcoran Gallery of Art, Washington, D.C.; Dallas Museum
of Art; Solomon R. Guggenheim Museum, New York; High Museum of Art, Atlanta, Georgia; Hirshhorn Museum and Sculpture
Garden, Washington, D.C.; Indianapolis Museum of Art, Indiana;
Joslyn Art Museum, Omaha, Nebraska; Los Angeles County Museum of Art; Metropolitan Museum of Art, New York; Milwaukee
Art Museum, Wisconsin; Museum of Contemporary Art, Chicago;
Museum of Modern Art, New York; National Gallery of Art, Washington, D.C.; Nelson-Atkins Museum of Art, Kansas City, Missouri; Philadelphia Museum of Art; St. Louis Art Museum, Missouri; San Diego Museum of Contemporary Art, California; Seattle
Art Museum, Washington; Walker Art Center, Minneapolis, Minnesota; Whitney Museum of American Art, New York.

Publications:

On PURYEAR : Books—*Maryland Regional Exhibition,* Maryland, Baltimore Museum of Art and Charles Parkhurst, 1963; *Young
American Artists, 1978 Exxon National Exhibition,* exhibition catalog, New York, Solomon R. Guggenheim Museum and Linda Shearer,
1978; *Options 2: Martin Puryear,* exhibition catalog, Chicago,
Museum of Contemporary Art, and Judith Russi Kirshner, 1980;
1-80 Series: Martin Puryear, exhibition catalog, Omaha, Nebraska,
Joslyn Art Museum and Holliday T. Day, 1980; *Martin Puryear,*
exhibition catalog, Amherst, Massachusetts, University Gallery,
Hugh Davies and Helaine Posner, 1984; *Martin Puryear: Matrix/
Berkely 86,* exhibition catalog, Berkeley, California, University Art
Museum and Constance Lewallen, 1985; *Martin Puryear: Public
and Personal,* exhibition catalog, Chicago, Public Library Cultural
Center and Deven K. Golden, 1987; *Martin Puryear: Sculpture and
Works on Paper,* exhibition catalog, Pittsburgh, Carnegie Mellon
University and Elaine King, 1987; *Edelson, Puryear, Scanga,
Stackhouse,* exhibition catalog, Washington, D. C., Corcoran Gal-
lery of Art and Christopher French, 1988; *I Martin Puryear,* exhibi-
tion catalog, New York, Jamaica Arts Center and Kellie Jones,

1989; *Connections: Martin Puryear,* exhibition catalog, Boston,
Museum of Fine Arts, Vishakha Desai and Kathy Halbreich, 1990.
Articles—"An Interview with Martin Puryear" by Mary Swift
and Clarissa Wittenberg, in *Washington Review* (Washington, D.
C.), 4(3), October/November 1978, p. 33. **Videos**—*Profile: Martin
Puryear* edited by Kate Horsfield and Lyn Blumenthal, Chicago,
School of the Art Institute of Chicago, 1977; *Bodark Ark* (video
document of Martin Puryear's installation at Nathan Manilow Sculp-
ture Park), Art Institute of Chicago, 1991; *Pavilion in the Trees,*
Fairmount Park Arts Association and WHYY, 1994.

*   *   *

Martin Puryear is a sculptor of great imagination and restraint
whose uncanny, elegant forms achieve a highly nuanced presence.
A self-described "worker," "maker," and "builder," Puryear has
married his abiding commitment to hands-on processes and technical virtuosity with materials, especially wood, with the modernist
legacy of Constantin Brancusi and minimalism and a fascination
with cultures ranging from the Native American to the Japanese.
The result is a body of work that quietly erodes such received artworld oppositions as high art/craft, subject/object, Western/other,
and black/white.

A consummate craftsman, Puryear has studied woodworking
using traditional hand tools with carpenters in Sierra Leone and
with highly technical cabinetmakers in Sweden. Adopting the techniques of the joiner, wheelwright, shipbuilder, cooper, and pattern
maker, Puryear fashions an array of unexpected forms that are

**Martin Puryear: *Alien Huddle,* 1993-95. Photo courtesy of Mckee
Gallery, New York.**

subtly charged with multiple meanings and associations. Some of his organic abstractions allude to human figures and animals, especially birds; others seem endowed with an artifactual quality and refer to vessels, to vernacular architectural forms such as the yurt, to traps and nets, and to tools, caskets, and decoys. Some seem to hint at a nascent animation. *Empire's Lurch* (1987), of painted ponderosa pine, for example, suggests a strangely truncated beast of burden. The elegance of the sculpture's laminated bottle green surface is belied by the suggestion of awkward locomotion conveyed by the title. Built to human scale like much of his work, it appeals directly to the emotional and physical levels of experience.

Puryear's work often engages an equilibrium of oppositions. *Thicket* (1990), a basswood and cypress tangle of intersecting wooden studs attached to a narrow base, is simultaneously open and closed, shallow and dense. The sculpture functions like an animated fence sprung to life before one's eyes, its character at once prohibitive and playful. A formidable barrier made up of a rhythmic interplay of boards and pegs, it encloses the overgrown space of its own interior so that inside and outside are wholly inextricable. *Lever #3* (1989), of painted ponderosa pine, plays on the form of a conventional lever. A gracefully curling outstretched tendril, tail, or tongue displaces the visual attention of the work to its extremity, creating a tension with the main bulk of the sculpture, a shallow upright box with an undulating, faceted upper spine. The projecting limb seems to have been thrust out by the main body at the same time that it appears to pull the body forward. The balance that results is one of charming dexterity and willful unease.

Wire, steel mesh, and tar are exploited for their properties of enclosure, disclosure, concealment, and revealment in *Greed's Trophy* (1984). The work consists of an oblong wire relief sculpture that extends vertically twelve feet from floor to ceiling to form a large net or cage. A small wooden flap hangs open near the floor, suggesting escape from a trap or the futility of containment. The lack of a complete segregation of inner and outer space is further manifested by the sculpture's dependency for closure upon the wall on which it is hung and its mesh skin, a crude sieve. With its raw ends and deliberate lack of finish, *Greed's Trophy* contrasts with the refinement of many of Puryear's wood sculptures, although the artist has increasingly let the staples and clamp marks of his wood-joining and laminating processes show, as if to offset their exquisite facture.

Puryear's time-consuming method of sculpting engages both memory and tradition, allowing him to draw upon diverse artistic and cultural sources for his work's meaning and to subsume himself in the process of making it. In doing so, Puryear, a highly educated artist of broad knowledge and experience, aligns himself with the anonymous makers of traditional art forms who work with reverence but do not deem themselves artists in the modern sense. But Puryear has not allowed a romantic or simplistic notion of traditional and non-Western approaches to diminish his intellectual or creative engagement. It is precisely the refinement and sophistication of these forms that Puryear seeks to emulate without disavowing his own sophistication or history. In this way Puryear seeks a new kind of synthesis. His art clearly draws upon the deepest part of himself. In his hands materials and forms become imbued with a palpable presence, at once understated and richly evocative. In this way Puryear has infused the formalism and economy of means of the late modernist sculptural tradition with a new beauty, integrity, and associative power.

—Dorothy Valakos

PURYEAR, Rachelle

American printmaker

Born: Washington, D.C., 1947. **Education:** Trinity College, Washington, D.C., 1965-69, B.A. 1969; Indiana University at Bloomington, 1969-71, M.A. 1971; Royal College of Art, Stockholm, 1974-76. **Career:** Associate professor, printmaking department, Royal College of Art, Stockholm, Sweden. Resident of Sweden since 1974. **Awards:** National Endowment for the Arts Fellowship, 1973; Swedish Art Council grants, 1977-93; Swedish Art Council grant for research, 1990; BUF grant, 1994.

Individual Exhibitions:

1977	Gallery Kallsprang, Linkoping
1980	Gallery Bildhornan, Umeå
1985	Grafiska Sallskapet Gallery, Stockholm
1986	Gallery Skånes Knost, Malmo, Joar Blå, Enkoping
1987	Gamla Rådhuset, Sodertalje
1992	Gallery Skånes Konst, Malmo
1994	FGK Gallery, Visby

Selected Group Exhibitions:

1980	*Miami Print Biennale,* Grafiska Sallskapet Gallery, Stockholm
1984	Grafiska Sallskapet Gallery, Stockholm
1986	Gallery Grona Paletten, Stockholm
1987	Japan Artists Association, Tokyo
1989	*First International East-West Arts Exhibition,* Hanoi, Viet Nam
1990	*Mini Print International,* Cadaques, Spain
	Sixth International Print Triennale, Jyvaskyla, Finland
1991	University of Barcelona, Spain
1994	Trinity College Gallery, Washington, D.C.
	Terry Dintenfass Gallery, New York

Collections:

Museum of the National Center of Afro-American Artists, Boston; National Museum, Stockholm; Swedish Art Board, Statenskonstrad.

* * *

Born in Washington, D.C., the artist Rachelle Puryear lives with her husband in Sweden. She joins a long line of African American artists who live abroad but who maintain close ties with family and events in the United States, where she often visits. She earned a master's degree in art history from Indiana University, where her major focus was the study of African art, and in the 1970s she did fieldwork in Africa. Puryear is both an art historian and a studio artist who specializes in printmaking, photography, weaving, papermaking, collage, and mixed-media works combined with texts. Her palette is known for being placid and subdued.

Puryear's work reflects the many years that she has lived outside the United States. Her inclination toward abstraction, however, began during her undergraduate years at Trinity College in Washington, D.C. First, abstracted photographic images appeared in her work. Later, after she had moved to Sweden, her use of abstracted photographic images was heightened by exposure to the urban environment there. In Sweden, which is noted for its pristine natural areas, even urban locations offer wonderful vistas of woods, forests, and the sea, as well as of rocks that were scarred by glacial movements during the Ice Age.

There are two works that especially reflect the natural habitat in which Puryear lives. In *Bladverket* (1995; "Leafwork"), a silk screen 31½ by 22½ inches, the artist assists the viewer in inspecting and enjoying all of the details the leaves have to offer. Puryear revels in such exploration as she moves from detail to detail with proficient precision. In the silk screen *Crevice*, showing Sweden's rocky terrain, the artist's analysis helps the viewer understand the ruggedness of the terrain and how water has perhaps created a small crevice in the rock. The work is on an intimate scale, but it shows Puryear's ability to inspect and then express to her audience the distillation of her ideas.

A colony of African American visual artists, dramaturges, musicians, and dancers live in Scandinavia, and most of them know one other. Travel between the countries is easy and inexpensive. Visual artists enjoy the respect and faithful support of their compatriots, and Puryear is no exception. Her work is well known in countries of Europe and Asia as well as in the United States, and she has been involved in innumerable international traveling exhibitions. Puryear was designated chair of printmaking at the Royal College in Stockholm in 1988. In 1994 Puryear and three other African American artists who live abroad—Clifford Jackson, Herbert Gentry, and Ronald Burns—exhibited together at the Terry Dintenfass Gallery in New York City.

—Jontyle Theresa Robinson

RAMOS-BLANCO, Teodoro

Cuban sculptor

Born: Havana, Cuba, 1901. **Education:** Art Academy, San Alejandro; Rome, 1927-30. **Awards:** Gold Medal, Seville, Spain, 1939; prize awards, National Cuban Shows, 1938-39; prize, *American Negro Exposition,* Chicago, 1940. **Died.**

Selected Exhibitions:

Collections:

Harmon Foundation; Howard University, Washington, D.C.; Riverside Museum, New York; Schomburg Center, New York.

Publication:

On RAMOS-BLANCO: Article—"Blanco, A Colored Sculptor in Cuba," in *Crisis,* September 1931, p. 299.

*   *   *

Although he did not make exceptional stylistic innovations, the works of the Cuban-born sculptor Teodoro Ramos-Blanco offer penetrating insight into his subjects, as, for example, in *Portrait of Langston Hughes*. His oeuvre consists primarily of strongly felt and compellingly rendered representations of anonymous figures, portraitures, maternal and family motifs, and allegorical and thematic images. His works embody the ideas of the new Negro movement and the sophistication and aesthetic ideas of his historical moment. During a period of study in Europe after he had participated in a national competition in Cuba, Ramos-Blanco seems to have absorbed the stylistic influence of Auguste Rodin and French modernism. In general, however, Ramos-Blanco's production cannot be construed as a rebellion against or as an innovation in the academy-based realist tradition. Yet his expressive power and authoritative command of materials, particularly his sculptures in rare native woods, lend his images a unique quality that substantiates his position as the foremost Cuban sculptor of the 1930s and 1940s.

Familiarity with the artists of the Harlem Renaissance, including a friendship with the poet Langston Hughes and correspondence

Teodoro Ramos Blanco: *Head of Langston Hughes,* c. 1930s. Photo by **Manu Sassoonian.**

with Arturo Schomburg, indicates that the aesthetic values and ideals of the movement infused Ramos-Blanco's works. Many of his works were featured in *Crisis* magazine. Thus, his employment of Afro-Cuban and black themes may be construed as self-consciously political. Indeed, a number of Ramos-Blanco's most significant works center on Antonio Maceo, the Afro-Cuban hero of the island's war of independence, and he was often engaged in memorial commissions designed to celebrate figures of political significance within the African diaspora, including Henry Christophe and Alexandre Sabès Pétion of Haiti.

Always profoundly expressive, Ramos-Blanco's works occasionally lapse into somewhat sentimental representationalism, but the sentimentality appears with artistic restraint and a true, forthright, and sensual tenderness. An example of this is his *Country People,* in which a simple worker, perhaps a farmer, is shown embracing his wife or lover in a well-planned composition of pleasing, interlacing forms. Especially poignant is the loving support given to the female figure by the man. The roughly textured surface of the work may be intended to reflect the country or day laborer's hard existence, yet an inner strength and intelligence permeate the sentimental configuration of the composition.

Ramos-Blanco is perhaps at his best in allegorical works such as *Inner Life*, a marble sculpture in which the mystery of being is addressed by his sensuous rendition of a woman of African descent who epitomizes reverie. Her circular, placid features lend a disconcerting serenity to a thoroughly provocative and seductive aesthetic presence.

Ramos-Blanco's stylistic variations, different treatments of subject matter, and choice of medium (including marble, stone, and wood) inevitably affect the perception of his images. Yet his communicative power and sense of the inner strength of his subjects are extraordinarily consistent. Ramos-Blanco's art has endured beyond his sociocultural moment because of its aesthetic and ideological significance. His works will continue to translate his conception of the essential nature of the human condition to future generations with meaning and sensitivity.

—Frank Martin

RAMSARAN, Helen (Evans)

American sculptor

Born: Helen Beatrice Evans, Bryan, Texas, 11 May 1943. **Education:** Ohio State University, Columbus, 1961-65, 1966-68, B.S. 1965, M.F.A. 1968; New School for Social Research, New York, 1973-74; Art Students League, New York, 1995-96. **Family:** Married Raj Ramsaran in 1973. **Career:** Instructor, Florida A & M University, Tallahassee, 1968-69; professor, Bowie State College, Bowie, Maryland, 1970-73. Since 1974 professor, City University of New York. Artist-in-residence, Palm Beach High School, West Palm Beach, Florida, 1969-70, San Jose Foundry, California, 1995, I.S.P., 1995; exhibits coordinator, Studio Museum in Harlem, New York, 1973-74. **Awards:** City University of New York Research grant, 1985; Elizabeth Foundation grant, 1993; City University of New York Research grant, 1994. **Address:** 30 West 13th Street, New York, New York 10011, U.S.A. **Online Address:** hramasaran@aol.com.

Individual Exhibitions:

1984   Kenkeleba Gallery, New York
1989   La Fourmi Ailee, Galerie-Libraire, Paris
1992   Hughley Gallery, Atlanta, Georgia
1994   Chysler Museum, Norfolk, Virginia
        Studio Museum in Harlem, New York

Selected Group Exhibitions:

1994   Art in General Gallery, New York
1995   City without Walls Gallery, Newark, New Jersey
        City Gallery, San Jose College, California
        Norman Schafler Gallery, New York
        Pratt Manhattan Gallery, New York
        Harbor Cultural Center, Staten Island, New York
        Sculpture Garden, Studio Museum in Harlem, New York

Helen E. Ramsaran. Photo courtesy of Frank Gimpaya.

1996   National Civil Rights Museum, Memphis, Tennessee
        Gallery 121 Henry, New York
        Atagoyama Gallery, Ginza, Tokyo

Collections:

College of Staten Island, City University of New York; Harlem School of the Arts, New York; John Jay College, City University of New York; Johnson Publishing, Chicago; Ohio State University, Columbus.

*

Helen Ramsaran comments:

In recent years in my work, I have been exploring issues concerning house, home, and community. This has led me to do some research on African cosmology, particularly as it relates to house construction and familial organization. In my research I have discovered the unique architecture of the Batammaliba people who reside in northern Ghana, Togo, and Benin. What captured my imagination about this marvelous architecture was the symbolism in the forms, both exterior and interior, which is the cohesive force in the lives of the residents, the community, and the entire village. I also learned of the overwhelming importance of the "path" in the life and culture of the Batammaliba people. In fact, one cannot fully comprehend the symbolic aspects of the architecture without recognizing the important role that "paths" play in organizing basic architectural features, i.e., the orientation of the doorway, the placement of the house shrine, and the placement of facade ornamentation. Thus paths may be definite or simply implied.

During the past two years, I have been exploring the idea of the "path" as a metaphor in sculpture. Sometimes the forms that I use suggest the house itself on which I have applied symbols that appear, disappear, and reappear. Often this is achieved through the repetition of forms with subtle variations. At other times I have created the path itself by using symbolic forms, such as forked trees and shapes that suggest fire or arrows. This idea of the "path" has proved to be a real breakthrough in my work, and I am looking forward to creating more of the small bronze sculptures, translating some of the ideas to other materials, and creating large-scale public works. In fact, one of my large-scale bronze works, entitled *Kuca— A Well-Worn Path,* is a work in progress that will be installed at Battery Park City (New York) in the spring of 1997. This will remain on view for one year.

*   *   *

There is a paradoxical quality to the work of Helen Ramsaran. Although she uses heavy metals that are typically associated with male artists, her work has a quiet and delicate strength, which she often achieves by the repetition of forms. Her compositions of handmade paper, the other medium in which she works, are often

massive yet gentle and also communicate a hushed resilience that is timeless.

While she was in college during the 1960s, Ramsaran's aesthetic sensibilities were informed in part by her interactions with African students. In 1981, after her first visit to the African continent, her work changed significantly. Her focus became her own Africanness, and her mission became not to duplicate the works of master African sculptors but to move toward birthing the African essence in her own visual expressions.

Ramsaran's interest in early history is due partly to her considerable world travel and contact with other cultures. The motifs that abound in her work are anthropological and explore the phenomenon of fossilization and the prevalence of ancient ritual. Her linear abstractions are derived from a profound interest in initiation societies and a thorough analysis of the traditional arts and religions of Africa, Latin America, China, and Japan. Architectural and spiritual elements are intended to convey the idea that belief systems are the foundations that hold the family and community intact.

A Cosmic Shelter is a small hutlike structure that, like many of her works, fuses skeletal and architectural forms. In the composition there are two rows of four slender vertical constructions that resemble tree branches or bones. Each branch has several other twiglike extensions that support two longer branches connected by horizontal appendages to form a crest. The short corridor formed

Helen E. Ramsaran: *Houses of Refuge,* **1993. Photo courtesy of Frank Gimpaya.**

by these hovering, intertwining limbs recalls the sacred groves where ceremonies and rituals take place. The base resembles a crude frame of a hut, and resting there, quiet and still, is an egg. The structure is a protective space for the life that incubates within its sanctuary.

Other works by Ramsaran contain winglike elements that evoke a sense of transcendental flight. *A Women's Shrine* and *Shrine with Flaming Windows* are small bronze enclosures that show a likeness to cages. The former is a diamond-shaped sculpture with open wings on one side and a delicate birdlike figure perched on top. The base resembles a flame or perhaps suggests the footprint of a bird. The latter also includes forms that combine bone and wing configurations, which bring dancing flames to mind. The elaborately etched textures she creates on the external surfaces of these and other works are evidence of her interest in body scarification as practiced in several parts of Africa during rituals. On some sculptures these designs refer more to the natural environment: the scattered fragile bones of a bird or the bleached skeleton of a giraffe, the bark of large trees, or bits of fragmented rock. Even her use of earthy patinas produces a weathered artifact-like quality that lures the viewer into a primal and enigmatic world.

The looming and monolithic elements of Ramsaran's larger sculptures demonstrate her reverence for physical and metaphysical environments. These works arouse contemplation of and prompt reflection on one's personal history and specific cultural experiences and are a testimony to the artist's sensitive probing of the collective search for life's meaning.

In work that is as fluid and rhythmic as Richmond Barthé's *Feral Benga* and as organic and natural as Richard Hunt's *Hybrid Figures,* Ramsaran demonstrates an inherent understanding of the development of modern sculpture as attributed to Pablo Picasso, Alberto Giacometti, Constantin Brancusi, and others. Nevertheless, the sublime property in the sculpture of Ramsaran suggests a heritage that is distinct and unique yet tends toward being transculturally universal.

—Regina Holden Jennings

RAVARRA, Patricia

American sculptor and installation artist

Born: San Francisco, California, 19 August 1947. **Education:** San Francisco State University, B.A. 1971, M.A. 1976; State College of Art, Poznan, Poland (Fulbright Fellow), 1979. **Career:** Instructor of fiber art, Apprentice Alliance, San Francisco, 1985-94; instructor of visual arts, San Jose State University, California, 1990. Board member, California Crafts Museum, California Confederation of the Arts, Artists' Equity Association, San Francisco. Participant, *Frontiers in Fiber,* USIA, 1988-1990. **Awards:** Fulbright Hays Travel Study grant, 1977-79. **Address:** 1045 Leavenworth Street, Apartment 5, San Francisco, California 94109, U.S.A.

Selected Exhibitions:

1985   Richmond Art Center, Virginia
        Fifth International Triennale and Textiles, Textiles Museum, Lodz, Poland
1988   *Eighth Annual National Black Art Exhibition,* National Black Arts Festival, Atlanta, Georgia

1990   *Color and Light,* Danish Museum of Applied Arts, Wroclaw, Poland
        Aarhus Academy of Art, Denmark
1991   Meridian Gallery, San Francisco

Publications:

On RAVARRA: Articles—"African American Imagery Enjoying a Renaissance" by Marcia Tanner, in *San Francisco Chronicle,* 19 August 1992; "Contradictory Natures" by Salli McQuaid, in *Artweek,* 23(22), 20 August 1992.

*   *   *

While still completing her master of fine arts degree at San Francisco State University, Patricia Ravarra began to teach weaving at Laney College. There she met Ted Odza, who had worked in Poland as a sculptor. His influence eventually led Ravarra to a Fulbright scholarship in Poland, where she studied for two years with master weaver Magdalena Abakanowicz at the State College of Art in Poznan. Though Ravarra's work is very different from her teacher's, her time with Abakanowicz changed the way she approached her art, the way she worked with fiber, and the way she lived her life.

Ravarra is primarily interested in the interaction of color with the surrounding space. Her primary material is monofilament nylon line, which is sometimes referred to as "fishline." Often her installations take place in large spaces, hanging from ceilings or even stretched across rooftops. Carolyn Ramsey described one of her installations (at San Francisco's Meridian Gallery, 1991) in *California Home and Garden*: "she twisted a handful of fibers together and ran them between points in the perimeter of the rooftop. The lines of the building, the changing sun, the color of the sky—all add to the final visual effect." Ravarra herself further described the piece: "Fishline has wonderful qualities of reflection and refraction which natural materials lack. But the results you can achieve outdoors would be impossible inside without theatrical lighting." Some of these effects seem supernatural, as if they don't exactly reflect natural objects but enhance them. Much of her work is reminiscent of water, or extremely long and colorful manes of hair.

Ravarra has served on the board of directors at the California Crafts Museum, the California Confederations of the Arts, and the Artists' Equity Association. She also served as the copresident of the Northern California Chapter of the Artists' Equity Association.

—Terry Bain

REASON, Patrick Henry

American printmaker, painter, engraver, and draftsman

Born: c.1817. **Education:** African Free School, New York, late 1820s to early 1830s. **Family:** Married Esther Cunningham in 1862, one son. **Career:** Printmaker, New York, c.1830-40, Philadelphia, c.1839-50. **Awards:** First Premium, Mechanics Institute Fair, 1838. **Died.**

Exhibition:

1967   Howard University, Washington, D.C.

Collections:

Howard University Gallery of Art, Washington, D.C.; Schomburg Center, New York.

Publications:

On REASON: Books—*Ten Afro-American Artists of the Nineteenth Century* by James A. Porter, Washington, D.C., Howard University, 1967; *Two Centuries of Black American Art* by David Driskell, Los Angeles County of Art and Alfred A. Knopf, 1976. **Article**—"Patrick Reason," in *Negro Genius,* 1937, p. 90.

*   *   *

Patrick Henry Reason was noted for his engravings, lithographs, and pencil and wash drawings of abolitionists and escaped slaves. He was a child prodigy who attended the African Free School in New York City. His first engraving, the frontispiece for Charles C. Andrews's *The History of the African Free School* (1830), was published when he was just thirteen. The work is a rather stiff, geometric rendering of the two-story brick building surrounded by a white picket fence and flanked by shorter cropped buildings. A simple cloudy sky somewhat enlivens the piece.

After serving as an apprentice to a white printmaker, Reason maintained a studio in New York, where he advertised himself in the *Colored American* newspaper in the spring of 1838 as "Historical, Portrait and Landscape Engraver, Draughtsman & Lithographer . . . Address, Visiting and Business Cards, Certificates, Jewelry &c., neatly engraved." Sometime after 1839 the artist moved to Philadelphia, where he had a successful business.

Reason received wide acclaim for his copper engravings of chained slaves, possibly based on earlier Wedgwood relief prototypes. The first featured a female with the caption "Am I not a woman and a sister?" It was commonly used as a letterhead by abolitionists from the mid-1830s and was reproduced on both British and American antislavery plaques, publications, and medals. Another version, "Am I not a man and a brother?" (1839), depicted a male slave in tattered clothing, kneeling among low bushes, his enchained arms clasped in prayer. This image adorned membership certificates of Philadelphia's Vigilant Committee, a group of young African American activists who aided escaped slaves. The names of the committee's secretary, Jacob C. White, and of its president, Robert Purvis, are on the certificate, and they may have commissioned the piece.

As a freelance printmaker Reason received portrait commissions from several important abolitionists, including the British reformer Granville Sharp (1835); Governor De Witt Clinton of New York (1835), and James McCune Smith (n.d.), an African American physician. The portraits were typically profiles or three-quarter or bust-length images of stoic men in coat and tie against a blank background. Reason's portrait of James Williams (c.1838), after a painting by a white artist, is stylistically similar. It was used as the frontispiece for the escaped slave's autobiography, *Narrative of James Williams, an American Slave: Who Was for Several Years a Driver on a Cotton Plantation in Alabama* (1838). Here, however, the subject is imbued with more warmth and expression, as Williams's large, dark eyes look slightly off to the side in this frontal portrayal.

Reason also completed two portraits of Henry Bibb. A lithograph (1840) depicts the African American antislavery lecturer standing rigidly before a draped window in the manner of conventional British portraiture. A copper engraving, used as the frontispiece for *The Narrative of the Life and Adventures of Henry Bibb* (1848), is a much more relaxed and realistic image, with Bibb, posed against a dark background, holding a book in his right hand. The work is likely based on a daguerreotype.

Among Reason's other works was a certificate of membership for the Freemasons. He also did the frontispiece for Lydia Maria Child's *The Fountain for Every Day in the Year* (1836) and a copper nameplate for Daniel Webster's coffin.

An ardent speaker and abolitionist, Reason was involved with a number of educational, cultural, and antislavery groups. On 4 July 1847, he delivered a speech, "Philosophy of the Fine Arts," to the Phoenixonian Literary Society in New York, which the *Colored American* reported to be "ably written, well delivered, and indicative of talent and research." He may have taught in the New York schools after 1850; Public School No. 1 was associated with the American and Foreign Anti-Slavery Society, an organization with which Reason had close ties.

—Theresa Leininger-Miller

REID, Robert (Dennis)
American painter

Born: Atlanta, Georgia, 9 November 1924. **Education:** Clark University, Atlanta, Georgia, 1941-43; Art Institute of Chicago, 1946-48; Parsons School of Design, New York, 1948-50, diploma 1950. **Military Service:** United States Navy, 1943-46: Hospital Corpsman, 1st Class. **Career:** Instructor, Summit Art Center, New Jersey, 1970-74, State University of New York, Purchase, 1975, Drew University, Madison, New Jersey, 1978, Parsons School of Design, New York, 1978-83; associate professor, Rhode Island School of Design, Providence, Rhode Island, 1970-88. Lecturer, Drew University, Madison, New Jersey, 1969, Dordogne College, Mussidan, France, 1978. Artist-in-residence, MacDowell Colony, 1988 and 1990. **Awards:** Childe Hassam Purchase Award, American Academy and Institute of Arts and Letters, New York, 1969; Third Annual Celebration of Black Scholarship in New England Award, University of Massachusetts, Boston, 1993; professor emeritus, Rhode Island School of Design, 1995. **Agent:** June Kelly Gallery, 591 Broadway, New York, New York 10012, U.S.A.

Individual Exhibitions:

1965	Grand Central Moderns, New York
1968	Baruch College, New York
1969	Lehigh University, Bethlehem, Pennsylvania
1970	Summit Art Center, New Jersey
	Drew University, Madison, New Jersey
	Benson Gallery, Bridgehampton, New York
	Alonzo Gallery, New York
1971	Alonzo Gallery, New York
1972	North Carolina Central University, Durham, North Carolina
1973	Benson Gallery, Bridgehampton, New York
1974	ADI South Gallery, Campbell, California
	Leslie Rankow Gallery, New York

1976   Leslie Rankow Gallery, New York
        Benson Gallery, Bridgehampton, New York
1977   Grand Central Moderns, New York
        Lenore Gray Gallery, Providence, Rhode Island
1979   Alonzo Gallery, New York
1987   George Ciscle Gallery, Baltimore, Maryland
1988   George Ciscle Gallery, Baltimore, Maryland
1991   Bill Bace Gallery, New York
1992   Nye-Gomez Gallery, Baltimore, Maryland
1993   June Kelly Gallery, New York
1995   June Kelly Gallery, New York
1996   June Kelly Gallery, New York

Selected Group Exhibitions:

1962   *Young Artists of Promise,* Mortimer Brandt Gallery, New
        York
1968   American Academy and Institute of Arts and Letters,
        New York
1968   *Thirty Contemporary Black Artists,* Minneapolis Insti-
        tute of Art, Minnesota
1969   Museum of Art, Rhode Island School of Design, Provi-
        dence
1971   Whitney Museum of American Art, New York
1973   Musée et Galerie des Beaux-Arts, Bordeaux, France
1974   Montclair Art Museum, New Jersey
        Fairweather-Hardin Gallery, Chicago
1981   Alternative Museum, New York
1993   Albright-Knox Members Gallery, Buffalo, New York
1996   Arkansas Art Center, Little Rock

Collections:

Baruch College, New York; Cornell University, Ithaca, New York; Drew University, Madison, New Jersey; Lehigh University, Bethlehem, Pennsylvania; Meyers College, Birmingham, Alabama; Montclair Art Museum, New Jersey; Musée et Galerie des Beaux Arts, Bordeaux, France; Museum of African Art, Washington, D.C.; Newark Museum, New Jersey; New York University, New York; Notre Dame University, South Bend, Indiana; Studio Museum in Harlem, New York; Syracuse University, New York; University of Pennsylvania, Altoona.

Publications:

On REID: Articles—"Reviews and Previews: Robert Reid and James Russell" by Jill Johnston, in *ARTnews,* 60, April 1961; "Solo at Grand Central Moderns" by Kim Levin, in *ARTnews,* 65, March 1966; "Solo at Grand Central Moderns" by Marcia Tucker, in *ARTnews,* 66, December 1967; "Solo at Alonzo Gallery" by Charlotte Lichtblau, in *Arts Magazine,* 45, November 1970; "Reid at Alonzo" by Dorothy Hall, in *Park East,* 19 November 1970; "Robert Reid" by John Canaday, in *New York Times,* 4 March 1972; "Solo at Alonzo Gallery" by Jane Gollin, in *ARTnews,* 70, February 1972; "Reid's Newer Landscapes Display Greater Complexities" by John Dorsey, in *Baltimore Sun,* 7 October 1988.

*   *   *

The innovative work of Robert Reid is disciplined but endlessly searching, with the result that he has virtually rewritten the book on watercolor. He has created a new vision of landscape that is both representational and abstract. His work is a tower of aesthetic qualities that reveal the banality of much American painting regardless of race. Reid's work is analytic, precise, and cool, free of the emotionalism so often palmed off as meaningful art.

Reid, who initially planned to be a librarian, became a fashion illustrator and for many years taught the subject, along with drawing and watercolor, at the Rhode Island School of Design. He first won attention with a series of beach paintings that treated the vast spaces of the sky, sea, and sand as the basic elements of life, emphasizing their greatness and the insignificance of man. Prompted by a headline that read "12,000 AT BEACHES," Reid painted scenes in which Arabic numbers or Roman numerals stood like ancient monuments or fell sideways on the sand. These subtle and poetic statements reflected Reid's singular vision and his need to follow it. His imaginative and mysterious work won the 1969 Childe Hassam purchase award of the American Academy of Arts and Sciences.

Reid's work as an illustrator required intensive study and practice in washes, which led to his approach to watercolor. He was still teaching at the Rhode Island School of Design when he lost his Manhattan studio. Only his small apartment was then available for painting, which prompted him to concentrate on watercolor. Even earlier he had discovered that the quality of the paper determined what could be done with watercolor, and he turned to a 400-pound stiff Japanese paper. "You learn what the paper can do and what it cannot do," he has said. Reid proceeded by experiment to saturate the paper with color, usually applying three coats so that it was permeated.

A trip into the countryside of France, a symbol of freedom since childhood for Reid, proved inspirational. He was attracted by the orderliness of the fields and the plantings, the way the houses were arranged, and the trees that lined the roads. Everything seemed planned and harmonious. Reid's paintings came to seek this same harmonious serenity, and French farms, houses, and trees inform his paintings in many subtle ways. He shuffles landscape sketches made in France among various trial compositions until he is satisfied. The final painting, which is based on these sketches, then follows.

Many elements contribute to the effect of Reid's paintings. The works are painted on vertical sheets of very heavy paper with ragged edges, twenty-eight by twenty-two inches in size. They have an overall tone, often a purplish gray, and at the top and bottom there appear the silhouettes of houses or French poplar trees in deeper muted tones. But the central focus is a rectangular area that may feature a tree or a scene in brilliant color, contrasting with the overall tone. There may be two or even three such areas in a painting. Everything is meticulously painted, and the rectangular areas are razorlike in their sharpness. The result is that the viewer looks through the large area into several other scenes—of fields, crops, or distant vistas—which creates a collagelike effect. A glowing orangish daub offsets the vast warm grays. No one else paints like this.

Despite disparate elements, Reid achieves an acute sense of balance that is both vertical and horizontal. Color is the critical element he uses to achieve this balance, and he is very sensitive to the order in which each color is laid down. Reid credits Byzantine art and the book of hours with influencing his concept of balance.

Ralph Ellison noted that the greatest difficulty of the African American writer was to reveal what he truly felt rather "than serving what Negroes were supposed to feel and were encouraged to feel." Although African American artists may feel these same pressures today, Reid has ignored them to follow his own vision. He is a singular artist who has made significant contributions to American art.

—Harry Henderson

RHODEN, John (W.)

American sculptor

Born: Birmingham, Alabama, 13 March 1918. **Education:** Talladega College, Birmingham, Alabama; School of Painting and Sculpture, Columbia University, New York. **Career:** Member artist, delegation to the Soviet Union, U.S. Department of State, Washington, D.C., 1959; commissioned sculptor, Harlem Hospital, New York, 1966, Metropolitan Hospital, New York, 1968, Clifton Senior High School, Baltimore, 1971, Bellevue Hospital, New York, 1975, Lincoln University, Pennsylvania, 1989, Birmingham Civil Rights Museum, Alabama, 1991. **Military Service:** U.S. Armed Services 1942-45. **Awards:** Rosenwald Fellowship, 1947-48; First Prize in Sculpture, Columbia University, New York, 1947, 1948 and 1950; Tiffany Award in sculpture, 1950; Skowhegan School Scholarship, 1950; honorable mention, Painters and Sculptors Society, New Jersey, 1950; Fulbright Fellowship, 1951-52; Prix de Rome Fellowship, 1952-54; First Prize in sculpture, Atlanta University, Georgia, 1955; Rockefeller grant, 1959; First Prize in sculpture, University of Atlanta, Georgia; honorarium and Medal Pro Sculpture Egregia, Howard University, Washington, D.C., 1961; Guggenheim Fellowship, 1961; Humanitarian Award, Harlem School of the Arts, New York, 1990. **Address:** 23 Cranberry Street, Brooklyn, New York 11202, U.S.A.

Selected Exhibitions:

American Academy, Rome; Art Institute of Chicago; Atlanta University, Georgia; Birmingham Museum of Art, Alabama; Boston Museum of Fine Arts; Brooklyn College, New York; Camino Gallery, Rome; Fairweather-Harden Gallery, Chicago; Fisk University, Nashville; Frick Museum, New York; Howard University, Washington, D.C.; Metropolitan Museum of Art, New York; Museum of Fine Arts, Boston; National Academy of Art, New York; Pennsylvania Academy of the Fine Arts, Philadelphia; Saidenberg Gallery, New York; Schneider Galleria, Rome; University of Pittsburgh, Pennsylvania; Whitney Museum of American Art, New York.

Collections:

Delaware Museum; Heinz Collection, Pittsburgh, Pennsylvania; Steinberg Collection, St. Louis, Missouri; Stockholm Museum, Germany.

Publications:

On RHODEN: Article— "Leading Negro Artists," in *Ebony,* September, 1963.

*   *   *

The master sculptor John Rhoden began his lifework early and with humble materials. He and his brothers and sisters (he was the second of eight children) often played with the red clay found near their home, filling sardine cans with it, which they then tied together as trains, or using it to model figures. "It seemed a wonderful thing to take huge handfuls and shape it into different forms. Even then it was exciting, and even I think I knew it was sculpture. . . . I am still excited by pure form, and shaping it is an act of love. Treat any material with love and I think you can almost make it come alive."

A Scottish artisan who worked in plaster and was so impressed with Rhoden's talent that he gave him the key to his studio was an early mentor. Rhoden began modeling heads, and, on the strength of the portrait head he made of the principal of his junior high school, he received a scholarship to Talladega College. When Rhoden moved to New York City in 1938, he studied briefly with Richmond Barthé. Studying archaic sculpture in Rome in 1952-53, Rhoden worked in marble, sculpting both humans and animals such as horses and lions.

Although Rhoden also works with wood, his favored medium has been bronze. Exploring the possibilities of the metal, Rhoden has created monumental works such as *The Family* (1966), commissioned for the front of Harlem Hospital in New York, and such delicate, airy works as *Acrobats* (1966), reminiscent of Makonde sculpture, and *Sumo Wrestlers* (1980). The elongated, ribbonlike form of this last work is due to Rhoden's ignoring the wrestlers' bulk and abstracting the skeleton of their dancelike movements.

Rhoden invests his sculpture, whether figurative or abstract, with great sensuality, as, for example, in *Woman in Orbit* and *Richanda* (1975). Inspired by the legends and mythology of America (his grandfather was Choctaw), Africa, and Asia, Rhoden has created works, such as *Potlatch* and *African King and Queen* (1968), of bronze inlaid with jewel glass. The extraordinary contrast of the roughened dark bronze with the smooth jewel glass makes Rhoden's constructions look like altar pieces in a cathedral. Eight or nine feet high, the linear bronze elements interlock in a variety of patterns. They seem to form small rooms, or chapels, in which the brightly colored glass glows, recalling stained glass windows. In *Priest of the Borealis* (1980) Rhoden employs the curved shapes used in his sculptures of nudes, but in flattening them he makes the piece one of stark ritual.

Rhoden received commissions to create sculptures of the abolitionist Frederick Douglass (1989) and the civil rights activist Fred L. Shuttlesworth (1991) for Lincoln University in Pennsylvania and the Birmingham (Alabama) Civil Rights Museum, respectively. *Slave Ship,* a sculpture that refers to the grim struggle of African Americans, is made up of a rocking oval boat filled with stacked bodies, both dead and alive. In the center is a figure hanging from a scaffold. As the boat rocks, the movement plays against the heaviness of the piece, expressing great power and emotion.

In over sixty years of work Rhoden has created an enormous body of sculpture. He believes in discipline and is not comfortable unless he does a certain amount of sculpting each day. By working each day he believes that he can bring a mellowness and understanding to his art that would otherwise be missing: "Art . . . must be constantly lived."

—Betty Kaplan Gubert

RICKSON, Gary (Ames)

American painter and muralist

Born: Boston, Massachusetts, 12 August 1942. **Education:** Boston University, Massachusetts, 1961-62; Moorish Science Temple, Baltimore, Maryland, 1962-64, Ministry Degree, 1964; Roxbury Community College, Massachusetts, 1985-86. **Family:** Married 1) Karen Fox in 1965 (divorced 1972); 2) Rosa Underwood in 1974 (divorced 1995), three children. **Career:** Tutorial director, Cooper Community Center, Massachusetts, 1967-1969; producer, *Artistically Revealing Truth,* Harvard Radio WHRB, 1974-84; instructor, Roxbury Community College, Massachusetts, 1981-82; head groundskeeper, Roxbury Community College, Massachusetts, 1987-88; project manager, Roxbury Multi-Service Center, Massachusetts, 1992-94. Since 1967 private consultant to various organizations, including Institute of Contemporary Art, Boston Foundation, New England Conservatory, and Boston Afro-American Artist Association. Since 1968 residential and commercial paint contractor, Massachusetts. Founder, Camden African American Artists Association, New Jersey; began mural movement in Boston, 1968. **Awards:** Outstanding Roxbury Citizens Award, Black Brothers Association, 1970; Champ of Black Youth Award, Roxbury Boys Club, 1970; National Endowment for the Arts grant, 1970.

Address: 107 DeWitt Drive, Roxbury, Massachusetts 02120, U.S.A.

* * *

Gary Rickson perceives himself to be a public artist and communicator. As such it is not surprising that his artistic and community activities evolved from and overlapped with the issues of the 1960s. In 1962 he cofounded the Boston Afro-American Artist Association, and he was later an organizer of Boston's annual outdoor arts festival. Along with Dana Chandler and Adelle Seatounde, in the late 1960s Rickson gained recognition as one of the black art movement's muralist painters. Their murals paid homage to Africa or celebrated the identity of African Americans and encouraged their continued struggle. The murals were most often rendered in primary colors and used representational imagery. Rickson's, however, also embraced a universal cosmology that addressed the consequences of inhumanity. The visual language of his murals relied upon spiritual and metaphysical elements that produced a decidedly surrealistic iconography.

Rickson grew up in an environment in which the arts were highly respected. His grandfather, George Rickson, Sr., had taught George Gershwin. Rickson's mother was a costume designer, and the boy was exposed to and trained in the dramatic and theater arts. At the

Gary Rickson (in front of *Africa Is the Beginning*), 1994. Photo courtesy of Eugene Busby.

age of nine he was playing the piano and writing and performing his own works. As a teenager Rickson frequented Boston's coffeehouses, playing his music and reciting his poetry. After a bout with tuberculosis diminished his physical stamina, his interests turned toward the visual arts.

Rickson's development was influenced by two community-based artists, Winston Alves and Don Berry. In 1961 Rickson met Alves, an artist who did abstracts and representational portraits. As a result of their association Rickson began drawing, and his initial works were patterned after Alves's realistic style. His realistic approach to drawing continued as he met artists such as John Wilson, Calvin Burnett, and Marcus Mitchell, who were also cofounders and members of the Boston Afro-American Artist Association.

Rickson then sought out Don Berry, a master portrait painter living in the community. Although Berry wanted him to explore anatomy, Rickson's interest was in mastering the basic elements that would improve his rendering of the human face. He wanted to represent human phenomena without showing the human figure, to go inside the head and show what the mind could do. Berry helped Rickson with contour, light and shadow, and form. Starting him off in charcoals, Berry continued working with Rickson until he graduated to oils. Over time Rickson's once representational and abstract imagery metamorphosed into a surrealistic style. He refers to his style as "organic symbolism—having an ideology and foundation where you can create symbols from a bank of information significant and important to self."

Rickson's organic symbolism can be seen in his first mural, *Segregation: BC (Before Christ)/AC (After Christ),* a widely acclaimed 1968 work that combines spiritual and political elements to predict the consequences of racist behavior. The mural's content is articulated through the third eye, the door to enlightenment. A straight line, the path to enlightenment, is done in yellow and brown, representing the people of the world. The road leads from the eye to a man dressed in red, white, and blue and hanging from a scaffold. Along with many other black artists of the period, Rickson used the American flag as a symbol of the nation's double standards, dishonesty, and inhumanity. He has suggested that the mural speaks to the adage that what goes around comes around.

The same style is apparent in Rickson's Roxbury YMCA mural, *Africa Is the Beginning,* painted in 1969 and restored in 1996. The mural uses symbols such as the sun and the moon, lightning, comets, and a pyramid to make a statement about the nature of the universe and the relationship of men and women. Against a deep blue night Rickson has painted a pyramid that symbolizes Africa as the place of humanity's origin and as the source of wisdom, knowledge, and understanding. A streak of lightning separates night from day and the sun from the moon. Men and women are represented by comets that are aimed at the pyramid's apex, which stands for sanity. An eclipse prophesies that women's nonviolent nature will replace men's violence.

Between 1968 and 1976 Rickson produced eight outdoor murals, four of which are still intact. Later works include *Day of Atonement* and *Crackdom,* the latter a painting representing a crack user trying to climb out of a glass pipe. He has assisted African American artists living in Camden, New Jersey, in organizing their own association with the aim of working with them on a mural. Rickson has also written a manifesto for the twenty-first-century artist entitled *A.R.T.: Artistically Revealing Truth.*

—Crystal Britton

RIDDLE, John (Thomas, Jr.)

American sculptor and painter

Born: 1933. **Education:** Los Angeles City College, A.A. 1960; California State College, Los Angeles, B.A. 1966; California State University, Los Angeles, M.A. 1973. **Military Service:** United States Air Force, 1953-57: Airman, 2nd Class. **Career:** Teacher, Los Angeles High School, 1966-70, Beverly Hills High School, California, 1970-73; freelance artist, 1973-74; veteran's counselor, Economic Opportunity Atlanta, Georgia, 1974-76; executive director, Neighborhood Art Center, Atlanta, Georgia, 1976-81. Since 1984 assistant director, Atlanta Civic Center, Georgia. Artist and owner, Carcinto, Limited, Atlanta, Georgia, 1981-84. **Awards:** New Teacher of the Year Award, Los Angeles High School, 1967; Emmy Awards (2) for *Renaissance in Black,* 1971; Governors Award for Visual Arts, Atlanta, Georgia, 1981; Fulton County Visual Artist of the Year, Atlanta, Georgia, 1987. **Address:** 3034 Rebecca Drive S.W., Atlanta, Georgia 30311, U.S.A.

Selected Exhibitions:

Albany Museum, Georgia; California Afro-American Museum, Los Angeles; California Black Printmakers, Los Angeles; Eighth Annual Art Festival, Martinique, West Indies; High Museum of Art, At-

John Riddle: *The Umbrella of Culture,* 1994.

John Riddle.

lanta, Georgia; Huntsville Museum of Art, Alabama; Los Angeles County Museum; Minneapolis School of Art and Design, Minnesota; Oakland Museum of Art, California.

*   *   *

A native of Los Angeles, John Riddle attended Los Angeles City College and received B.A. and M.A. degrees from California State College (now University) in the city. He was initially influenced by the figurative work and color of Paul Gauguin, but with the eruption of the Watts riots in 1965 his concept of what art should do changed. He became aware of the realities that led people to destroy their neighborhoods in an effort to have a voice, and he felt that his work should engage the struggle of black people in America. He thus began to search for avenues in art that he could use to expose the harsh conditions under which many black people lived and labored in South-Central Los Angeles. Initially he concentrated on working in welded steel by combining pieces of debris from the Watts riots into forms that would poignantly speak to the concerns of his people.

Much of Riddle's early work was highly political and addressed the restraints that black people faced within and outside their communities. *There's More at Stake Than Just Attica* (c.1972) had a simulated white jail cell (symbolizing white America) in which a black metal figure fell through the bars (the cracks). Black people were not only falling through the cracks of the judicial system, the work said, but on the whole they also were far from achieving the basic American dream, as evidenced by the civil disobedience in Los Angeles, Chicago, Detroit, and other major cities in the 1960s and 1970s. In the series "Made in Mississippi," Riddle took empty ammunition boxes as icons of American defense and in each one assembled objects that represented aspects of popular culture. In *Made in Mississippi: Ken and Barbie* (1973), for example, the ideal couple appeared disheveled as they rested atop a heap of rubble rather than sand on a beach. Riddle suggested in *Made in Missis-*

sippi: Bird and Diz (1973) that, even in the context of despair, African American people were resilient enough to produce great musicians like Charlie "Bird" Parker and Dizzy Gillespie. In *Ghetto Merchant* (1975) he used an adding machine collected from the debris of the Watts riots to signify the merchants who entered the ghettos to do business because it required little investment and who took their earnings with them as they returned to their affluent communities. The work also attacked the high prices that ghetto dwellers often paid for basic services.

After relocating to Atlanta, Georgia, Riddle began to work on low-relief assemblages and paintings. With their solid-color angular shapes and shallow pictorial spaces, these animated figurative works recall the paintings of Jacob Lawrence. The often vertical format encourages a narrative reading of the figures, who give glimpses of African American culture from musicians to men playing dominoes or cards. In *Clubs Is Trumps* (1987), for example, all of the black figures are pictured with spades, an obvious play on the term "spade" as used to make disparaging reference to black people. The only trump card stands alone, out of the reach of the black figures. In addition to creating these colorful hard-edged figurative paintings, Riddle also has reproduced them and other compositions in a large color serigraph format. His later work has become more decorative than the biting metal works from the 1960s and 1970s.

—Lizzetta LeFalle-Collins

RINGGOLD, Faith

American painter, sculptor, quiltmaker, performance artist, and printmaker

Born: New York, 8 October 1930. **Education:** City College of

New York, B.S. 1955, M.A. 1959. **Family:** Married 1) Earl Wallace in 1950 (divorced 1956), 2 daughters; 2) Birdette Ringgold in 1962. **Career:** Art instructor, New York Public Schools, 1955-73; lecturer, part-time, Pratt Institute, Brooklyn, New York, 1970, Wagner College, Staten Island, New York, 1970-78, Banks Street College, New York, 1970-80; visiting lecturer, University of California, San Diego, 1983-85. Since 1985 professor of art, University of California at San Diego. Artist-in-residence Syracuse Public Schools, New York, 1973, University of Delaware, Newark, 1974, Wilson College, Chambersberg, Pennsylvania, 1976, Purdue University, Indianapolis, 1977, Pima College, Tucson, Arizona, 1978, Burlington City Schools, New Jersey, 1982, Paris, France, 1990, Atlantic Center for the Arts, New Smyrna Beach, Florida, 1992. Has conducted workshops since 1972 throughout the United States. **Awards:** Creative Artists Public Service Award, New York, 1971; Found Woman Award, *Ms. Magazine*, New York, 1973; National Endowment for the Arts Award, 1978; Dreyfus/MacDowell Fellowship, 1982; Wonder Woman Award, Warner Communications, New York, 1983; Candace Award, New York, 1984; Women's Caucus for Art Award, New York, 1986; Guggenheim Fellowship, New York, 1987; New Foundation for the Arts Award, 1988; National Endowment for the Arts Award, 1988 and 1989; Mid-Atlantic Arts Foundation Award, Baltimore, Maryland, 1989; Annual Youth Friends Award, School Arts League, New York, 1990; LaNapoule Foundation Award, France, 1990; "Faith Ringgold Day" proclamation, Nassau County, 1990; "Faith Ringgold Day" proclamation, Hempstead, New York, 1990; ALA Notable Children's Book Award, 1991; Booklet Editors Choice Award, 1991; Hungry Mind Children's Book Award, 1991; Best Book of the Year Award, 1991; California Children's Book, Video and Software Award, 1991; Parents Choice Gold Award, 1991; Artist of the Year Award, Studio Museum in Harlem, New York, 1991; Ten Best Illustrated Books Award, New York Times, 1991; Artist of the Year Award, School of Art League of New York, 1991; Coretta Scott King Award, 1992; Caldecott Honor Book, 1992; Distinguished Artist Award, National Council of Art Administrators, Sarasota, Florida, 1992; "Faith Ringgold Day" proclamation, City of Oakland, California, 1992; Jane Addam's Peace Association Picture Book Award, 1993; Booklist Editors' Choice Award, 1993; Womens Caucus for Art Honor Award, Queens Museum of Art, Flushing, New York, 1994; Womens Caucus for the Arts Honors Award for Outstanding Achievement in the Visual Arts, Queens Museum, New York, 1994; Art Start for Children Award, Guggenheim Museum Children's Program, 1994; Key to the City, Mayor's proclamation, Lake Charles, Louisiana, 1995. **Agent:** Jeff Bergen, ACA Gallery, 41 East 57th Street, New York, New York 10022, U.S.A. **Online Address:** any1canfly@aol.com; Fringgold@aol.com.

Individual Exhibitions:

1967	Spectrum Gallery, New York
1970	Spectrum Gallery, New York
1972	Louisiana State University, Baton Rouge
1973	Wellesley College, Massachusetts
	Faith Ringgold: Ten Year Retrospective, Voorhees Gallery, Rutgers University, New Brunswick, New Jersey
1974	University of Wisconsin, Stevens Point
	Lamar University, Beaumont, Texas
	University of Tennessee, Chattanooga
	University of Northern Iowa, Cedar Falls
1975	Southeastern Missouri State College, Springfield

	University of Wisconsin, Superior
	University of Wisconsin, Whitewater
1976	Bowdoin College, Maine
	Polk Community College, Winterhaven, Florida
	Wilson College, Chambersberg, Pennsylvania
1977	Hamilton-Kirkland College, Clinton, New York
	William Smith College, Geneva, New York
1978	Hampton Institute, Virginia
	Edwards University, Austin, Texas
	University of Minnesota, Minneapolis
	Pima Community College, Tucson, Arizona
	Rutgers University, New Brunswick, New Jersey
1979	Texas Technical University, Lubbock
	Brookdale Community College, Lincraft, New Jersey
	Summit Gallery, New York
1980	Museum of African and African-American Art, Buffalo, New York
	University of Massachusetts, Amherst
	Middlesex County College, Edison, New Jersey
1981	Trinity College, Hartford, Connecticut
	Earlham College, University of Richmond, Virginia
	Old Dominion University, Norfolk, Virginia
1982	Youngstown State University, Ohio
1983	San Antonio College, Texas
	Lehigh University, Bethlehem, Pennsylvania
1984	Appalachian State University, Boone, North Carolina
	Rutgers University, New Brunswick, New Jersey
	Faith Ringgold: Twenty Years of Painting, Sculpture and Performance, (1963-1984), Studio Museum in Harlem, New York
1985	College of Wooster Art Museum, Ohio
1987	Bernice Steinbaum Gallery, New York
	Real Art Ways, Hartford, Connecticut
	DeLand Museum of Art, Florida
	Baltimore Museum of Art, Baltimore, Maryland
	Contemporary American Artists Series, Sag Harbor, Long Island, New York
1988	Sims Gallery, New Orleans
	Vaughn Cultural Center, St. Louis, Missouri
	Thomas Center Gallery, Gainesville, Florida
	Educational Testing Service, Princeton, New Jersey
	Bernice Steinbaum Gallery, New York
1989	Simms Fine Art, New Orleans
	Henry Art Gallery, University of Washington, Seattle
	University Gallery, Fine Arts Center, University of Massachusetts, Amherst
1990	Sawhill Art Gallery, James Madison University, Harrisonburg, Virginia
	Faith Ringgold: A Twenty-Five Year Survey, Fine Arts Museum of Long Island, Hempstead, New York (traveling)
	Southwest Craft Center, San Antonio, Texas
	Community Gallery, Lancaster, Pennsylvania
	Grove Gallery, University of California, San Diego
1991	DuPont Gallery, Washington and Lee University, Lexington, Virginia
	Greenville County Museum, South Carolina
1992	Bernice Steinbaum Gallery, New York
1993	Textile Museum, Washington, D.C.
	Children's Museum of Manhattan, New York
	Hewlett-Woodmere Public Library, Hewlett, New York
1994	St. Louis Art Museum, Missouri

1995   Athenaeum: Music and Arts Library, La Jolla, California

         Faith Ringgold: Paintings and Drawings Spanning Four Decades, ACA Gallery, New York

         Indiana University of Pennsylvania

1996   Bowling Green State University, Indiana

Selected Performances:

1976   *The Wake and Resurrection of the Bicentennial Negro,* Women's Inter Art Center, New York

1981   *Being My Own Woman,* Niagara County Community College, Sanborn, New York

1985   *Once Upon a Time Story Telling Performance Series,* Newark Museum Sculpture Garden, New Jersey

1987   *Change: Faith Ringgold's Over 100 Pounds Weight Loss Performance Story Quilt 1987,* Bernice Steinbaum Gallery, New York

1993   *Aunt Harriet's Underground Railroad in the Sky,* Queens Borough Public Library, Jamaica, New York

         You Were Too Young to Remember What You Must Never Forget, Isabella Stewart Gardner Museum, Boston

         Dinner at Aunt Connie's House, Studio Museum in Harlem, New York

1995   *My Dream of Martin Luther King,* Katonah Museum of New York

Selected Group Exhibitions:

1968   Carroll Reese Museum, East Tennessee State University, Johnson City

         Museum of Modern Art, New York

1972   Gedok, Kunstalle, Hamburg, Germany

1975   Bronx Museum, New York

1981   Whitney Museum of American Art, New York

1985   *Tradition and Conflict: Images of a Turbulent Decade 1963-1973,* Studio Museum in Harlem, New York (traveling)

1986   Clock Tower, New York

1987   Rockland Center for the Arts, West Nyack, New York

1990   *Definitive Contemporary American Quilt,* Bernice Steinbaum Gallery (traveling)

1996   New Museum of Contemporary Art, New York

Collections:

American Craft Museum, New York; Boston Museum of Fine Art; Brooklyn Children's Museum, New York; Clark Museum, Williamstown, Massachusetts; Fort Wayne Museum of Fine Art, Indiana; Solomon R. Guggenheim Museum, New York; High Museum, Atlanta, Georgia; Metropolitan Museum of Art, New York; Metropolitan Transit Authority, New York; Museum of Modern Art, New York; Newark Museum, New Jersey; Philadelphia Museum of Art; St. Louis Museum of Art, Missouri; Spencer Museum, Lawrence, Kansas; Studio Museum in Harlem, New York; Harold Washington Library Center, Chicago; Williams College Museum of Art, Williamstown, Massachusetts.

Publications:

By RINGGOLD: Books—*Tar Beach,* Crown, 1991 (illustrated by author); *Aunt Harriet's Underground Railroad in the Sky,* Crown,

1992; *We Flew Over the Bridge: Memoirs of Faith Ringgold,* Little Brown and Company, Boston, 1995; *Talking to Faith Ringgold,* by Faith Ringgold, Linda Freeman, and Nancy Roucher, New York, Crown Books for Young Readers, 1995. **Articles**—"Black Art: What Is It?" in *The Art Gallery Guide,* April 1970, pp. 35-36; "Women's Traditional Arts," in *Heresies: A Feminist Publication on Art and Politics,* Winter 1978, p. 84; "Being My Own Woman," in *Confirmation: An Anthology of African American Women* edited by Amiri Baraka and Amina Baraka, New York, Morrow, 1983.

On RINGGOLD: Books—*Faith Ringgold: Twenty Years of Painting, Sculpture, Performance (1963-1983),* by Michele Wallace, New York, Studio Museum in Harlem, 1984; *Faith Ringgold: Painting, Sculpture, Performance,* exhibition catalog, New York, Bernice Steinbaum Gallery, Thalia Gouma-Peterson and Kathleen McManus Zurko, 1987; *Stitched Memories: African-American Story Quilts,* exhibition catalog, Williamstown, Massachusetts, College Museum of Art, 1989; *Faith Ringgold: A Twenty-Five Year Survey,* exhibition catalog, Hempstead, New York, Fine Arts Museum of Long Island, 1990; *Paris Connections, African American Artists in Paris,* exhibition catalog, San Francisco, Bomani Gallery, 1992. **Articles**—"Images Truths Drama on Ringgold Canvases," in *Amsterdam News,* New York, 16 December 1967, p. 9; "Faith Ringgold Flying Her Own Flag" by Lucy R. Lippard, in *Ms. Magazine,* July 1976, pp. 34-39; "Faith Ringgold Makes Dolls an Art" by Stephanie Stokes, in *Essence Magazine,* New York, July 1979; "Faith Ringgold" by Thalia Gouma-Peterson, in *Dialogue: An Art Journal,* (Columbus, Ohio), 1985, p. 75; "Aspects of Performance in the Work of Black American Women Artists" by Lowery Stokes Sims, in *Feminist Art Criticism, An Anthology* edited by Arlene Raven, Cassandra Langer and Frueh Joanna, Ann Arbor, Michigan, University of Michigan Research Press, 1988 (illustrated); "Faith Ringgold and Her Escapes" by Susan Snead, in *Sage, A Scholarly Journal on Black Women,* 1988, pp. 19-22; "Interview," in *Baltimore Evening Sun,* Maryland, January 10, 1988; "Faith's Hopes: An Interview with Performance Artist Faith Ringgold" by Christy Sheffield Sanford, in *Zelo,* 3(5), 1989, pp. 20-21, 40-41; "Women on Bridges, Faith Ringgold in Conversation with Claire Rubach," in *Gallerie Women's Art, 1989 Annual,* pp. 42-43; "Ringgold Retrospective," in *Art Academy Notes,* 9(5), 4 January 1991; "The Freedom to Say What She Pleases: A Conversation with Faith Ringgold" by Melody Graulich and Mara Witzling, in *NWSA Journal: A Publication of the National Women's Studies Association* (Norwood, New Jersey), 6(1), Spring 1994, pp. 1-27; "An Artist Traces Her Life on Quilts" by Betty Freudenheim, in *The New York Times,* 27 May 1995; "Faith Ringgold Works Shown at Museum," in *The Atlanta Journal and Constitution,* 23 July/5 August 1995; "Faith Ringgold: A Twenty-Five Year Survey" by Eleanor Flomenhaft, in *Surface Design Journal* (Oakland, California), 15(1), Fall 1995, pp. 22-23. **Videos**—*Faith Ringgold,* Random House, 1990; *Portrait of an Artist: Faith Ringgold, The Last Story Quilt* produced by Linda Freeman, for *Home Visions,* Chappaqua, New York, L & S Video Enterprises, 1991; *Faith Ringgold Paints Crown Heights,* produced by Linda Freeman, Chappaqua, New York, L & S Video Enterprises, 1991.

*   *   *

Faith Ringgold has enjoyed a thirty-year career as a painter, sculptor, writer, and performance artist. Her work has redefined and enriched black and feminist cultural ideals through themes of African American culture, family, mother-daughter relations, marriage, sexuality, and female self-expression. Ringgold's painting style mimics folk art, providing images of black people that were unavailable to her during her formal art education but that originate comfortably within the context of the African American art that has developed throughout the twentieth century.

Ringgold's mother was the well-known fashion designer Willi Posey, and she learned quilting from her grandmother (a former teacher who became a dressmaker), who in turn had learned the art from her mother, a former slave. Her family had a strong storytelling tradition that empowered Ringgold to say what she chose while affirming the continuity of black culture through the teaching of moral codes. Her family's stories were grounded in the lives of real people who had experienced real events, and thus the stories dispelled negative stereotypes about African Americans.

Ringgold's first recognized works were politically strident and vaguely resembled pop art. *Die* and *U.S. Postage Stamp Commemorating the Advent of Black Power* openly expressed anger with the marginalization of blacks in America. Her 1969 painting *Flag for the Moon: Die Nigger* reflected deep resentment toward a government that spent billions of dollars to put one man on the moon while millions of blacks lived in poverty.

During the 1970s Ringgold refocused her vision to celebrate contemporary black culture in America. Eschewing the materials of the fine arts, such as canvas and oil paint, Ringgold used craft materials as a feminist statement, recognizing otherwise dismissed or overlooked forms that women traditionally practiced in the home. Her mother sewed costumes that hung from Ringgold's needlepoint masks of black cultural heroes such as Martin Luther King, Jr., and Adam Clayton Powell, works that had an amusing yet powerful presence.

In the late 1970s Ringgold redirected her attention to celebrating the lives of common people. Likewise, she reduced her larger than life-size sculptures to the scale of dolls. Ringgold's portraits of neighbors from her Harlem community, consisting of blacks, Hispanics, and Asians, included the churchgoing *Miss Martha*; *Little Joe*, who carried a large radio-tape player; *Momma*, in curlers; and *Daddy*, in boxer shorts. Ringgold also explored performance art, using her life-size sculptures as costumes in *The Wake and the Resurrection of the Bicentennial Negro*. This fable about black cultural rejuvenation began as a Romeo and Juliet death scenario, but it concluded as a rebirth that was not Christian in origin but rather inspired by matriarchal power.

In 1980 Ringgold collaborated with her mother to create their first quilt, *Echoes of Harlem*, which recorded the faces of people they had known throughout the years. Ringgold employed quilting as a metaphor to commemorate one of the few art forms that enslaved American blacks had been allowed to indulge in and by which they had surreptitiously developed and preserved African culture. After experiencing difficulty in getting her autobiography published, Ringgold understood how editors and publishers controlled what black women wrote. To ensure the freedom of her voice, she began imbedding the text of her writings into her quilts, thus realizing the natural synthesis between narrative and image that would characterize her mature work.

Using acrylic paint, Ringgold illustrates her stories with a picture in the center panel, surrounded by text written on strips of cloth that most often frame the piece. Her stories are generally based on the lives of people she knew while growing up. As a grandmother she made the easy transition to writing and illustrating award-winning children's books centered on black themes that were not available to her or her daughters while they were growing up. She has written three such books—*Tar Beach, Aunt Harriet's Underground Railroad in the Sky*, and *Dinner at Aunt Connie's House.*

Ringgold's series "The French Collection" questions the verity of Western art history through an examination of the predominantly white male artistic hegemony. Her protagonist, Willa (evoking the presence of her mother Willi, to whom the work is a tribute), is Ringgold's alter ego embarking on a surrealistic journey through the history of art. Each panel gathers a cast of black women around a "masterpiece" of the Eurocentric art tradition. With great humor and humanity Ringgold presents an affirmative vision of women realizing and then assuming their own power to create art within the context of an African American and feminist culture.

—Laurie Fitzpatrick

RIVERS, Haywood ("Bill")

American painter

Born: Morven, North Carolina, 8 May 1922. **Education:** Art Students' League, New York, 1946-49; École du Musée du Louvre, Paris, 1945-52. **Awards:** Maryland State Scholarship, 1946-49; Gretchen H. Hutzler Award, 1948; John Hay Whitney Fellowship, 1952; Baltimore Museum Annual Prize, 1948; Julius Rosenwald Fellowship, 1948.

Selected Exhibitions:

1948	Baltimore Museum, Maryland (solo)
	Baltimore Museum Annual
1949	*Carnegie International,* Carnegie Museum of Art, Philadelphia
1950	*Le Salon d'Hiver,* Paris
	Le Salon de Mai, Paris
	Le Salon de l'Art Libre, Paris
	Embassy Show, Paris
1967	City College of New York
1970	Stout State University, Wisconsin
	Boston Museum of Fine Arts
1971	*Rebuttal to the Whitney Museum Exhibition*
	Newark Museum, New Jersey

Collections:

Baltimore Museum, Maryland; Musée d'Art Moderne, Paris; Schomburg Center, New York.

Publications:

On RIVERS: Articles—"Black Art" by Caron LeBrun, in *Herald Traveler* (Boston), 24 May 1970; "Trying to Define 'Black Art': Must We Go Back to Social Realism" by Hilton Kramer, in *New York Times,* 31 May 1970; "Is Politics Submerging Black Art" by Hilton Kramer, in *Courier-Journal and Times* (Louisville, Kentucky), 7 June 1970; "The Rupture," in *Arts,* Summer 1970; "Ellsworth Ausby and Bill Rivers: Artists of the Soul" by Randy Williams, in *Black Creation,* 3, Spring 1972, pp. 40-42.

*   *   *

A source of inspiration and a guide to black abstractionists, Haywood "Bill" Rivers is a painter who has also been a teacher and gallery director. His style, at first figurative and then nonobjective, has always involved heavy and vigorous applications of pigment and formidable displays of color.

Rivers studied at the Art Students League from 1946 to 1948 and at the École Musée du Louvre in Paris from 1949 to 1952. In New York he saw the figurative modernism of Jacob Lawrence and Horace Pippin, and both made strong impressions on the young artist. His early work also demonstrated a familiarity with the modernism of the school of Paris and its general tendencies toward figural simplification, planarity, and nonillusionism.

The surface of Rivers's *Untitled* (1952) is thick and textured like Jean Dubuffet's canvases, and yet the picture is without the anguish and irony of the Frenchman's work. Instead, *Untitled* resembles a Kandinsky tableau of summarized figures in a gaily colored landscape. Considering the unfashionability of both Wassily Kandinsky's modernism and Dubuffet's avant-gardism in post-World War II Paris, *Untitled* was a bold gesture of Rivers's artistic independence and willingness to experiment.

With backing from the Rosenwald Foundation, in 1950 Rivers opened Galerie Huit, an exhibition space for American artists in Paris. His partners in the venture included the artists Al Held and Jules Olitski, and over a five-year period the gallery's exhibitors included the black American painters Edward Clark, Herbert Gentry, and Paul Keene.

Rivers's paintings are markers of the 1960s avant-garde. *Op* (1965) is a playful suprarealist composition that depicts three zebras at a railroad crossing. An exaggeratedly large stop sign looms above them, and the design of the sign's concentric circle and triangle visually echoes the animals' patterned stripes. Flanking this assembly are two smaller signs bearing the words "and" and "look," entreaties and warnings to human viewers. In the spirit of the op art movement, Rivers sought to focus viewers' attention on the elements of expression that make every painting.

As the decade progressed, Rivers's art moved decidedly toward nonobjectivity. His "Eclipse" paintings belong to the mode of geometric abstraction. In *Eclipse I* (1970) a scheme of concentric circles is complicated by its central petal design and by intersections with bands of color and pyramidal volumes. *Eclipse I* firmly establishes its grounds: color changes and dramatic shading heighten the illusions of depth and spatial perspective. This brash canvas issues a challenge to the viewer to follow the uncountable, expressive movements of color as they assert themselves in the environment, beyond the confines of easel painting.

Although he has traveled widely and in diverse art circles, Rivers has also stated that his North Carolina roots were formative in his artistic development. The daisy fields of the state are among his treasured memories, and the flower's petals are often design motifs for the artist. In *North Carolina As I Remember It* (1977) these organic forms join a quilt of colored squares, diamonds, and circles. In fact, Rivers has likened his painting to quilt making, which more than any art movement or style has grounded his practices. "I just can't work by theories," he once explained in an interview. "Why not be simple about it?"

—Jacqueline Francis

ROBERTS, (Lucille) Malkia

American painter

Born: Lucille E. Davis, Washington, D.C., 2 February 1917. **Education:** Howard University, Washington, D.C., 1932-36, B.F.A.

1936; University of Michigan, Ann Arbor, 1936-39, M.F.A. 1939. **Family:** Married Dr. A.K. Roberts in 1942 (separated). **Career:** Visiting Associate Professor, African Art, State University of New York, College at Oswego, New York, 1970-71, Duke Ellington High School for the Fine Arts, Washington, D.C., 1974-1975; assistant professor, Washington Technical Institute, Washington, D.C., 1972-74; comoderator and studio teacher, Division of Instructional Television, Maryland Center for Public Broadcasting, 1973-75. Professorial Lecturer, American University, Washington, D.C., 1972-77; associate professor, Howard University, Washington, D.C., 1976-79. Professor, Howard University, Washington, D.C., 1979-85. Artist-in-residence, Fairfax County Public Schools, 1975-76; visiting artist, Arlington Virginia Public Schools Art in Non-Western Cultures Program, 1976-77. Since 1968 volunteer lecturer, Anacostia Museum, Smithsonian Institution, Washington, D.C.; since 1987 volunteer lecturer, Museum of African Art, Washington, D.C.; since 1989 volunteer lecturer,National Gallery of Art, Washington, D.C. **Awards:** Agnes Meyer Fellowship, 1963; Twenty-Sixth Annual Atlanta University Show Painting Award, 1969; James A. Porter Special Award in Painting, Cleveland State University, 1972; Who's Who in American Art Award, 1973; Outstanding Service Award, D.C. Chapter, National Conference of Artists, 1977; Saint Patrick's Episcopal Church Senior Center Award, Washington D.C., 1986. Honorary doctorate, Elizabethtown College, Pennsylvania, 1993. **Address:** 2445 Lyttonsville Road, Silver Spring, Maryland 20910.

Individual Exhibitions:

1969	Salve Regina Gallery of Art, Washington, D.C.
1970	Florida Memorial College Library, Miami
1971	Howard University Gallery of Art, Washington, D.C.
	College Museum, Hampton Institute, Virginia
	Smith-Mason Gallery, Washington, D.C.
1974	Watkins Gallery, American University, Washington, D.C.
1976	Lincoln University, Pennsylvania
1978	W.E.B. DuBois Institute, Harvard University, Cambridge, Massachusetts
1980	Paul Robeson Cultural Center, Pennsylvania State University, University Park
1984	Bethune Museum and Archives, Washington, D.C.
1987	Kings-Tisdell Cottage, Savannah, Georgia
1988	Gallery Antigua, Miami

Selected Group Exhibitions:

1966	Museum of Fine Art, Florida State University
1972	Acts of Art Gallery, New York
1980	Washington Women's Art Center, Washington, D.C.
	Library Gallery, University of Maryland at Baltimore County
1981	D.C. Armory, Washington, D.C.
1983	Nyangoma's Gallery, Washington, D.C.
	Volta Place Gallery, Washington, D.C.
1986	Evans-Tibbs Collection, Washington, D.C.
	Bethune Museum Archives, Washington, D.C.
1989	Tatum Art Center, Hood College, Frederick, Maryland

Collections:

Atlanta University; Evans-Tibbs Collection, Washington D.C.; Greensboro Agricultural and Technical University; King-Tisdell

Cottage Museum; Spelman College, Atlanta; West Virginia State College.

Publications:

On ROBERTS: Book—*Black Dimensions in Contemporary American Art* by J. Edward Atkinson, New York, New American Library, 1971.

*

Malkia Roberts comments:

Art educators concede that the appreciation of a work of art must be on two levels: (1) an understanding of the elements and principles of aesthetic structure and (2) an appreciation of the context from which it springs. Context here implies the geographical, historical, social, and spiritual climate that nurtures it.

It is also generally conceded that the black African people who were brought to the shores of the "New World" came from a variety of ethnic backgrounds which had produced, as part of their lifestyle, religious sculptures and objects recognized today not only as significant works but also as an influence on "Modern World Art."

These Africans carried in their memories the rhythm of their chants and drum beats and the natural gifts of those who feel with their hearts and shape with their hands what glows in the imagination. Sculptors in bronze and carvers in wood, workers in clay and fabric and a variety of materials made works to honor ancestors, spirits, or for daily use.

Today this African traditional art is celebrated in the world's great museums as a link in the chain of world art history.

Yet it has only been in comparatively recent years that the art of African Americans has begun to be recognized as a powerful nexus to the motherland. An explosion of exhibitions, showcasing a variety of thematic approaches, media, and techniques, has made a strong impact in the last thirty years.

Space permits this article to list but a few of these giants. Our aim is to whet your curiosity about African American artists, so you will seek them out in reputable galleries, books, and reproductions.

Recall the rise of black consciousness in the 1960s with its slogans, "Black is beautiful," "I'm black and I'm proud," etc.? Many jests and jibes poked satirical fun at African Americans rushing to Africa to discover their "Roots" after the advent of Alex Haley's searing novel.

In April of 1966, I, too, became open to the recognition of the spiritual legacy which was to permeate the course of the remainder of my life. I traveled to Dakar, Senegal, as part of the group AMSAC, attending the *First World Festival of African Arts*. With our group came writers, musicians, artists, and dancers, who had previously been only legends to me. We were to interact with our African counterparts in magical exchanges.

Standing for the first time on African soil, I remembered Countee Cullen's poem, "What Is Africa to Me?"—and suddenly, I knew! As I wandered down to the sea, I received answers from the waves and rocks in "Whispers from the Continent." It was *heavy!*

The cavernous halls of Dakar's Musée Dynamique, major site of the conference, were filled with imposing masks, sculptures, ceremonial objects, and powerful, colorful patterns in fabrics and tapestries. Giants, like Leopold Senghor, spoke of "Negritude." What did it mean? (A recognition of spirituality and uniqueness and pride in being *black*.) We talked of animism, the presence of spirit

Malkia Roberts, 1994. Photo courtesy of Edward Shaw.

in all things. The talking drums underscored it; the graceful women in their colorful geles and bubas let me know that my painting palette would be stronger, more vital, more brilliant and exciting from that time forward. (This trip was the progenitor to similar trips made by other African American artists for Festac in 1977, the National Conference of Artists in 1984, and others.)

Out of these experiences came visual testimony to the reclamation of legacy and heritage, which denied previous negative stereotypes of mass media and brought a dignity and spiritual vibrancy to the dimensions of the African experience. Scores of African American artists have since traveled to Africa to see, to study, to create, to become living links with the cultural legacy still intact in Africa.

I, too, made four more trips to Africa. Friends kidded me about my "pilgrimages," but I wouldn't exchange these experiences—my study at the University of Ghana in Legon, the Kumasi Institute of Technology; yet another exploration to Nigeria, where the sculptor Lamidi Fakeye proved to be an invaluable guide to the riches of Yoruba sculpture, the brilliant colors, swirling forms, and textural riches of the young contemporary Nigerian artists working at Oshogbo.

Other trips took me to East Africa—to Tanzania, Kenya, and, yes, Uganda! Thence to Ethiopia and Egypt (naturally spanning a few years!) The major impact was to be in my own painting—from traditional Western realism to simplified—extended, exaggerted forms—blazes of color with gestural forms—great excitement to explore!

There have been so many fellow artists on this journey, each working to the beat of his own drummer. Space can permit only a small sampling. Let's start with Renee Stout, whose magical works still resonate in the MAA and invoke the sacred and the secular. Ed Sorrells-Adewale's piece, "Short Story Concerning Regeneration," likewise evokes in its sense of "accumulation" a relation to Congo Power Figures and underscores a feeling of mystery and spirituality.

But if one were to begin to explore the work of pioneers in African American art (with African influence), one could not begin without the great muralists, Aaron Douglas, Hale Woodruff, and certainly the glowing magical murals of John Biggers in Houston and Hampton.

Romare Bearden's later work in his photomontages magically intersected pieces of Benin and Ife masks with figures from the inner cities. *Prevalence of Ritual* is powerful.

Jacob Lawrence, though not primarily concerned with African themes, is unmistakably African American in his flat color simplifications and strong, moving patterns. For forty years Elizabeth Catlett, a strong poignant painter, sculptor, and lithographer, has been making searing social statements that speak of family. (A powerful relief of Catlett's may be seen on the facade of the Architecture and Engineering Building at Howard University in Washington, D.C.).

Ed Love, strong master sculptor, has monumental sculptures of steel that strongly recall powerful African deities. His recent work, *The Orkestra,* explores the Africa-Caribbean diaspora and the visual resonance of reggae music and the bright colors of that areas.

David Driskell, eminent art historian and painter, is a most articulate spokesman for African American art and its genesis in Africa. He authenticated his African ties during a year's visiting professorship at the University of Ife.

Winnie Owens Hart, ceramic artist, also spent a year as apprentice to the women potters in the Nigerian village of Ipetimodo. The imposing forms of her vessels and clay sculpture reflect this discipline.

Fabric artists, such as Faith Ringgold and Viola Burley Leake, recall in their works the patchwork traditions in Dahomey and make transfer of the quilting expressions in the intricate polyrhythmic spaces based on African designs.

These artists are only a "mini-sample" of African American expression in recent years— expressions of *authentic* connections of ethnic and cultural identity—visual testimony of the growing consciousness of a people no longer afraid to make expression of deeply felt connections with their past.

Major museums and galleries in this area, such as the Smithsonian's National Museum of American Art, Anacostia Museum, Howard University Gallery of Art, and the Evans/Tibbs Gallery afford the viewer opportunities to explore.

We are aware of the indigenous religious and spiritual component in much of African art on the continent. There has been, however, influence from the Christian legacy also. On this continent perhaps the most striking expression might well be *The Throne of the Third Heaven of the Nations Millennium General Assembly* by African American artist and visionary James Hampton. Hampton created this incredible piece over a number of years (1950-64) from discarded pieces of gold and silver aluminum foil, colored Kraft paper, and plastic sheets. This awesome labor of love may be seen on permanent view at the Smithsonian National Museum of American Art. See it, be awestruck, and draw your own conclusions as to its spirituality and African heritage.

One word of caution—beware of some of the commercial shops that spew out "multi-reproductions" of so-called black art. Recently some of these "mall shops" have been pushing pieces that unfortunately have a minimum "connection" to the authentic African experience. Value judgments are strongly personal, but the collector who would affirm connections of African symbolism and motifs should be sure that the work speaks in unmistakable language of both aesthetics and context.

* * *

Malkia Roberts cites the late 1960s, that explosive period of black consciousness and awakening, as the turning point for her art. During this and later decades African American artists, among others, engaged in a process of self-discovery and in doing so served notice that they would express themselves and no longer accept the marginal status imposed upon them by society. Attending the first World Festival of Negro Arts in Senegal, West Africa, in 1966 catalyzed Roberts's transformation. Indeed, she was "totally saturated with the uniqueness of black culture and the need for positive images to replace the negative stereotypes." Subsequently, her art became dedicated to "the cultural liberation of Black people and celebration of their unique experience."

While African and African American imagery is the bedrock of Roberts's work, she also has explored Native American culture and that of Japan, Australia, New Guinea, and the South Pacific as a means of connecting peoples of color to their shared similarities. Prior to these explorations her work reflected the traditional Western training she had received in the arts while studying in the United States and in Paris. To this extent Roberts felt that her work did not reflect who she was or the culture from which she had evolved. Nor was her work informed by the African or other Third World visual elements now primary to her concerns.

Roberts firmly believes that "black art must be decidedly functional and spiritual, speaking to, for and of the 'soul forces' which have survived within the world of Blackness. Imagery in traditional African art has always served functional, symbolic purposes, standing as a magnificently rich language to be readily read and understood. . . . Art permeates every facet of traditional African life, but strangely enough in none of these languages was there a word for 'art,' because the images and objects were not created for 'art' in the Western concept, but as vital parts of everyday communal life."

By 1969 the artist was producing such works as *Black Heritage* and *Black Madonna,* which mined her newly found consciousness. Her once straightforward realism was giving way to an expressionistic approach with a decidedly Afrocentric iconography. There is a certain magical and metaphysical element at play in these works. After all it is the cultural essence of spiritual and emotional experience that she is translating into her work—ancestors against a backdrop of ancient symbols read as obscure figures engaged in traditional tribal rituals. Roberts's brisk brush strokes dance across the canvas, folding the past into the present, the mythical into the modern, the tribal into the technological. Her richly colored palette sometimes includes other materials such as textiles, found objects, and mixed media. Whether she creates collages or works in oil, acrylic, or watercolor, the figure remains the primary form in her work, although cubist angles embedded in her colors both texturize and energize the figures' movement within the picture plane.

In the 1970s Roberts's art became much more abstract. Without compromising her use of color, her work came to solidly embrace an abstract expressionist sensibility. By incorporating the benefits of her extensive travels into such paintings as *Natural Woman* (1972), Roberts combined East Asian spatial elements with an expressive use of color and with African, Asian, and African American imagery. In such later work as *Gonna Spread These Wings and Fly* (1985) and *Africa Oye'* (1990) one can see the confidence of her mature brush stroke, one that is reminiscent of Hale Woodruff, with whom Roberts studied in the 1960s.

In addition to African, African American, Amerindian, and other sources informing her work Roberts says that it also "takes shape around the images, ideas and feelings that [she has] experienced as a black woman at this point in our history. [My art] is a response to events—places witnessed and felt—past and present; symbolic rites shaped by their own meaning. It is ceremony enacted again—because I *must,* out of my need to extend our boundaries—deepen our insight and recharge our energies."

After Roberts retired from Howard University as a professor of painting and design, she remained active as a painter. She has also continued to participate in docent programs at the Smithsonian Institution's National Museum of African Art and Hirshhorn Museum and Sculpture Garden and as a lecturer at the National Gallery of Art.

—Crystal Britton

ROBINSON, John H(arold) D(eVon)

American painter

Often mistakenly referred to as T.H.D. Robinson. **Born:** Jamestown, New York, 20 September 1895. **Education:** Jamestown Public Schools, New York; U.S. Army E & R School, Columbus, New Mexico, graduated 1920; Brooklyn Art School, New York, 1927; Arts Students League, New York, 1929-1935; New York University. **Military Service:** U.S. Army: Commissioned Second Lieutenant, Officers Reserve Corps, 1920-29. **Career:** Investigator, 1923-28; doorman, 1929; guard, United States Customs Service, 1930. **Died:** 8 June 1970.

Individual Exhibitions:

1929   135th Street Branch, New York Public Library

Selected Group Exhibitions:

1928   135th Street Branch, New York Public Library
1929   135th Street Branch, New York Public Library
1931   *Exhibition of the Work of Negro Artists,* The Art Center, New York
1933   Washington Square Outdoor Art Exhibit, New York
1934   Roerich Museum, New York
         Harmon Foundation, Washington, D.C. (traveling)
1935   *Annual Exhibition,* Society of Independent Artists, New York

Publications:

On ROBINSON: Book—*Negro Participation in the Texas Centennial Exposition* by Richard F. Howard, Christopher Publishing House, Boston, 1938.

*   *   *

Only a part-time painter after the 1940s, John H. D. Robinson was a noted exhibitor in New York's black and integrated art circles during the 1930s. His color and design sensibilities elicited comments from his audiences, who were stirred by the individual and refreshing character of his works.

A student of art from 1927, Robinson learned the fundamentals at New York institutions, first at the Brooklyn Art School and then at the venerable Art Students League. At the Art Students League, Robinson studied briefly with Boardman Robinson, a social realist painter, muralist, and political cartoonist, and it may be that his color sensibility was advanced under this prominent artist's tutelage. Thomas Hart Benton was another of Robinson's instructors, and his classmates included Joseph Delaney and Jackson Pollock. As Delaney related in interviews and memoirs before his death in 1991, Benton exposed his students to European Renaissance and nineteenth-century French art, offering the compositional and color strategies of those eras as paradigmatic guides. At the same time Benton encouraged students to discover their own modes and vehicles of expression.

For Robinson this meant figure painting, Benton's preferred genre, as well as still lifes. Although only a small portion of Robinson's work from the 1930s has been viewed since its execution, it can be gathered from exhibition catalogs listing his submissions that he was interested in the everyday elements of American life. Titles of early paintings included *Landscape with Red Truck, The Plowman, The Blacksmith's Shop,* and *Workday End.*

Portrait, a painting shown at the Harmon Foundation's all-Negro exhibition in 1931, is likely a self-portrait. The light-skinned male subject with parted wavy hair resembles a photograph of Robinson taken around this time. The figure, moreover, wears a short-sleeved jacket that is probably an artist's smock and is posed before a quadrilateral form that may be read as a blank canvas. Stark and simplified, the artist's studio is designed in clean and yet expressive lines. The wall and window visible in the picture's rear passage are modernist distortions of subtle curves. The human form of the artist is slightly exaggerated, with sharply sloping shoulders and a planar presentation. In *Portrait,* Robinson displayed the willingness to adopt modernist touches to a traditional genre.

Critics and peers noted the adventurism in Robinson's art. In a still life painting of the 1930s, a work whose title is not known, Robinson assembled a ceramic jug, a glass bottle, and an egg on a table, and before the objects he propped a mirror. The painting, which was exhibited at the Washington Square Outdoor Art Show in New York City in 1933, is a challenging compositional exercise in representing light, depth, and volume. Both viewers and critics were struck by the artist's technical skill, and they praised his paintings as "symbolic" and "slightly modernistic."

One of the few black American artists appointed to the federal government's Public Works of Art Project, Johnson completed four easel works during the nine-month project (1933-34). He later taught (1935-43) in the Federal Art Project of the Works Progress Administration. During this period Robinson continued to exhibit at the Roerich Museum (1934) and with the Society of Independent Artists (1935) and the Harmon Foundation-College Art Association joint venture (1934-35). He was an early member of the Harlem Artists Guild (1935-41), an activist group that lobbied for black inclusion in government arts projects.

Sometime during the 1940s, Robinson ceased his efforts in professional painting. He became a chiropractic doctor and worked for many years at a Long Island hospital. Nonetheless, he pursued creative expression for the rest of his life, and he was a familiar presence in classes at the Art Students League after his retirement in 1968.

—Jacqueline Francis

RYDER, Mahler (Bessinger)

American painter and sculptor

Born: Columbus, Ohio, 7 July 1937. **Education:** Columbus College of Art and Design, 1955-58; Ohio State University, Athens; Art Students League, New York; School of Visual Arts, New York. **Family:** One daughter. **Career:** Teacher/instructor, Army Special Services, Germany, 1960-63, New School for Social Research, 1969, Providence School Department, Providence, Rhode Island, 1971-72. Worked at Rhode Island School of Design, 1969-91. **Awards:** Ford Foundation grants, 1965-66; National Endowment for the Humanities grant, 1973. **Died:** 27 February 1992.

Individual Exhibitions:

1965	Satori Studio, New York
1973	Whitney Museum of American Art, New York
1987	Bannister Gallery, Rhode Island College, Providence

Selected Group Exhibitions:

1968	Minneapolis Institute of Art, Minnesota
1970	Museum of Fine Arts, Boston
1971	Whitney Museum of American Art, New York
1973	New York Cultural Center and Fairleigh Dickinson University
1976	Suzette Schochet Gallery, Newport, Rhode Island
1980	Museum of the National Center of Afro-American Artists, Boston
1990	Newport Art Museum, Newport, Rhode Island

Collections:

Columbus College of Art and Design, Columbus, Ohio; The Guibel, Kaiserlauten, Germany; Wisconsin State University, Superior.

*   *   *

The painter, sculptor, art educator, and musician Mahler Ryder defined himself as a humanist. His artistic vision was forged in the civil rights era. The experience of participating in a high school art exhibition hosted by a country club in Columbus, Ohio, where blacks could not become members convinced Ryder that art had the power to penetrate racial barriers he himself could not. As a cultural activist he struggled to open up exhibi-

tion opportunities for black artists, helped to establish the Studio Museum in Harlem, and implemented community-based art education projects. Ryder developed the concept for the American Jazz Hall of Fame and was instrumental in the restoration of Edward M. Bannister's grave.

Ryder's early works were figurative social protests rendered in narrative format. His subjects reflected his interest in sports, especially boxing, and in history, geography, and popular culture. During the 1970s Ryder fabricated sculpture from wood, metal, plastic, fiberglass, and found objects. Exposure to a plastic resin jeopardized his health, which forced him to abandon what had been his favorite medium. He also used collage as a vehicle for expanding his interest in social, political, cultural, and historical events. Ryder incorporated text from letters, notes, advertisements, almanacs, sales slips, and newspapers along with photographs and fragments of road maps as metaphors for recycling, collective memory, self-identity, and cultural heritage.

Throughout Ryder's career he worked in a series format. His best-known series were "The Great American Subway" (1969), in pen and ink; "The Bi-Centennial Series" (1976), collage; "Beaux Reves," collage; "The Garden Series" (1977), collage; "American Pugilist" (1984), collage; "The Women's Series" (1984); and several assemblages on jazz themes, including "Jazz Piano," "Homage to the Guitar," and "Jazz Composers" (1980-89).

By the 1980s Ryder's art had become less political and more abstract. It is no surprise that jazz was a major influence in his work, for both he and his father were jazz musicians. Ryder's association with Rahsaan Roland Kirk, Don Patterson, and Nancy Wilson solidified his belief that the abstract elements of painting and jazz were complementary. He was also inspired by the paintings of Stuart Davis and by Romare Bearden's collages centered on jazz rhythms. Bearden in particular helped Ryder to understand the relationship between music and color.

Interest in the language of jazz influenced the compositional structure of several series that Ryder created over a ten-year period. He constructed large mixed-media assemblages to which he attached found objects, including fragments of musical instruments, that disrupted, punctuated, intersected, and extended into space. The push-and-pull relationship of shape, texture, collaged materials, and color suggested the improvisational aspect of jazz. He was interested, however, not only in the representation of musical notes but also in the silent intervals between them. He used color to define space and the overlapping and interpenetration of color to suggest sound. His surface effects alternated between stippled hues, splatter motifs, blotches, and the blending of colors. This treatment of color, characteristic of Ryder's late style, suggests that he understood color relationships well.

Ryder's exploration of a visual language culminated in his mixed-media wall relief series "Jazz Composers," in which rendered his personal response to the styles of nine musical personalities. His visual interpretation captured the aesthetics of the jazz sound and the elements of abstract painting.

—Claude L. Elliott

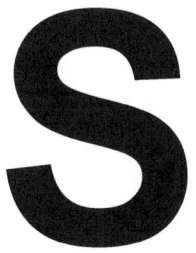

SAAR, Alison
American sculptor and printmaker

Born: Los Angeles, California, 1956. **Education:** Scripps College, Claremont, California, B.A. 1978; Otis Art Institute, Los Angeles, M.F.A. 1981. **Awards:** National Endowment for the Arts Fellowship, 1988; John Simon Guggenheim Memorial Foundation Fellowship, 1989. **Agent:** Jan Baum Gallery, 170 South La Brea Avenue, Los Angeles, California 90036, U.S.A.

Individual Exhibitions:

1982	Jan Baum Gallery, Los Angeles
1983	Peppers Gallery, Redlands University, California
	Jan Baum Gallery, Los Angeles
1984	Creative Time, New York
	Monique Knowlton Gallery, New York
1985	Artpart, Niagara Falls, New York
	Jan Baum Gallery, New York
	Roswell Museum of Art, New Mexico
1986	Monique Knowlton Gallery, New York
1987	Jan Baum Gallery, Los Angeles
	Zeus-Trabia Gallery, New York
1988	Thomas Barry Fine Art, Minneapolis, Minnesota
	The New Gallery, Calgary, British Columbia
	Jan Baum Gallery, Los Angeles
1990	Jan Baum Gallery, Los Angeles
1991	Jan Baum Gallery, Los Angeles
1992	Museum of Contemporary Art in Baltimore, Maryland
	Whitney Museum at Philip Morris, New York
	Neuberger Museum, Purchase, New York
	Bellvue Art Museum, Washington
	Cleveland Center for Contemporary Art, Ohio
1993	Virginia Museum of Fine Arts, Richmond
	High Museum, Atlanta, Georgia
	Hirshhorn Museum, Washington, D.C.
	Allbright College Center for the Arts, Reading, Pennsylvania
1994	Virginia Museum of Fine Arts, Richmond
1995	Newhouse Center for Contemporary Art, Staten Island, New York
	Phyllis Kind Gallery, New York
	Brooklyn Museum, New York
1997	Swarthmore College, Pennsylvania

Selected Group Exhibitions:

1988	Queens Museum, New York
1990	Wight Art Gallery, University of California, Los Angeles (traveling)
1991	Aldrich Museum, Ridgefield, Connecticut
	Maryland Institute of Art, Baltimore, Maryland
1992	University Art Gallery, San Diego State University
1993	Whitney Museum of American Art, New York
1994	Museum of Contemporary Art, Sydney, Australia
1996	New Museum of Contemporary Art, New York
	Bearing Witness: Contemporary Works by African American Women Artists, Spelman College Museum of Fine Art, Atlanta (traveling)
1997	Santa Monica Museum of Art, California

Collections:

Arkansas Art Center, Little Rock; Artworks, Los Angeles; Fine Arts Museum, Houston; Hirshhorn Museum and Sculpture Garden, Washington, D.C.; Kresge Art Museum, East Lansing, Michigan; Metropolitan Museum of Art, New York; Newark Art Museum, New Jersey; New Jersey State Museum, Trenton; Studio Museum of Harlem, New York; Trenton Museum, New Jersey.

Publications:

On SAAR: Articles—"Alison Saar at Jan Baum Gallery" by Peter Clothier, in *L.A. Weekly* (Los Angeles), 7(47), 18-24 October 1986; "Alison Saar" by Amy Gerstler, in *Artforum,* January 1989, p. 123; "Radical Differences in Two Black Artists" by Cathy Curtis, in *Los Angeles Times,* 29 June 1989; "The Bewitching Works of the Saars" by Kristine McKenna, in *Los Angeles Times,* 11 January 1990, pp. F1,9; "Heredity and Environments: The Artistic Visions of Betye and Alison Saar" by Ben Marks, in *Angeles,* January 1990; "On Compiling Relics: The Magic of Works by Alison and Betye Saar Transcends Postmodernism" by Betty A. Brown, in *Artweek,* 21(4), 1 January 1990, pp. 1, 20; "Artist's Alliance Dates Way Back" by Ginny Holbert, in *Chicago Sun Times,* 29 July 1990, p. 11; "Mother and Child Reunion" by Katherine Cook, in *Artweek,* 3 August 1991; "A Conversation with Betye and Alison Saar" by Mark Van Proyen, in *Artweek,* 15 August 1991; "Alison Saar: Refined Savagery" by Diane Weathers, in *Essence,* 24(5), September 1993; "Alison Saar: Fertile Ground and Crossroads," in *Virginia Museum of Fine Arts Bulletin,* 54(3), January-February 1994, p. 8; "Art with Conscience" by Vivien Raynor, in *New York Times,* 7 January 1996.

*   *   *

Alison Saar began having one-woman exhibitions in 1982, when she was just twenty-six years old, and since then they have been an almost yearly occurrence. Some years she has had as many as five one-woman exhibitions at a time. She is a very fine sculptor and also makes artists' books. In 1978 she received a dual degree in art history and studio art from Scripps College in Claremont, California. Among African American women artists, a degree in both these fields is rare.

Saar has been developing ideas around wooden sculptures in her more recent work. In 1991 she created *Terra Firma* (wood, tin, tar, and found objects, 24" x 72" x 22"). It is a life-size image of an African American male reclining on the earth, using his right hand to cradle his face and head. The body language is that of a drained and weary individual. Absent from the face are refined features and details. There is a kinship between the choice of materials and the political statement inherent in Saar's piece. *Terra Firma* was included in the controversial exhibition at the Whitney Museum of American Art in New York City in 1994, *Black Male: Representations of Masculinity in Contemporary American Art.* Curator Thelma Golden suggests that the figure "[w]hen viewed in the light of classical odalisques . . . seems languid and serene. When approached with the references of contemporary culture he seems desperate, despairing , and perhaps even dead." *Tree Souls* (1994) is another wooden piece, larger-than-life, which rests on tree roots. The 1993 piece *Clean House* has limbs growing from the body of a female form. Both *Clean House* and *Tree Souls* are covered with metals. *Tree Souls* is covered with small squares of copper, and *Clean House* is covered with tin and aluminum paint. The eyes are mirrors. It is obvious that underneath the metal is carved wood with a textured surface.

The artist has always acknowledged her interest in the Middle Passage and the impact of Africa in the diaspora. Thus it is to this culture we turn in order to apprehend the meaning of these two works. Saar is, perhaps, revealing the sanctity of nature and the creatures that dwell in and within natural objects. Additionally curator Charlotta Kotik suggests that in these works Saar may be referencing nineteenth-century African slaves, who escaped through swampy terrain and concealed themselves in the roots of large trees. Women slaves are especially interesting in this regard, since their plight is usually overlooked or marginalized.

As the progeny of celebrated artist Betye Saar, Alison and her two sisters observed up close the location of the black woman artist in the United States. Alison and her sister Lezley have worked from this site with confidence and success.

—Jontyle Theresa Robinson

SAAR, Betye
American assemblage artist

Born: Los Angeles, 30 July 1926 **Education:** University of California, Los Angeles, B.A. 1949; California State University, Long Beach; University of Southern California; California State University, Northridge. **Family:** Married Richard W. Saar in 1951 (divorced 1968), three daughters. **Awards:** National Endowment for the Arts Fellowships, 1974, 1984; J. Paul Getty Fund for the Visual Arts Fellowship, 1990; Twenty-Second Annual Artist Award, Studio Museum in Harlem, New York, 1990; Guggenheim Memorial Foundation grant, 1991; honorary doctorate degrees, Otis/Parson, Los Angeles, San Francisco Art Institute, Massachusetts College of Art, Boston, 1992; Distinguished Artist Award, Fresno Art Museum, California, 1993; honorary doctorate degree, California Institute of the Arts, 1995.

Individual Exhibitions:

1972	Multi-Cul, Los Angeles
1973	California State University, Los Angeles
1975	Whitney Museum of American Art, New York
1976	Monique Knowlton Gallery, New York
	Wadsworth Athenaeum, Hartford, Connecticut
1977	San Francisco Museum of Modern Art
	Baum-Silverman Gallery, Los Angeles
1979	University of California, San Diego
	Baum-Silverman Gallery, Los Angeles
1980	Studio Museum in Harlem, New York
1981	Monique Knowlton Gallery, New York
	Baum-Silverman Gallery, Los Angeles
1982	Quay Gallery, San Francisco
1983	Canberra School of Art, Australia
	Woman's Art Movement, Adelaide, Australia
1984	Georgia State University Art Gallery, Atlanta
	MOCA, Los Angeles
1987	List Visual Arts Center, Massachusetts Institute of Technology, Cambridge
	Pennsylvania Academy of the Fine Arts, Philadelphia
1988	House of Fortune, Manila, Philippines
	Taichung, Taiwan
1989	Artspace, Auckland, New Zealand
	Wellington City Art Gallery, New Zealand
1990	MOCA, Los Angeles
1991	Objects Gallery, Chicago
1992	University of Connecticut, Hartford
	HypoBank, New York
1993	Fresno Art Museum, California
1994	Santa Monica Museum of Art, California
1996	Desaisset Museum, Santa Clara, California
	Palmer Museum of Art, Penn State College, Pennsylvania

Selected Group Exhibitions:

1977	National Gallery, Smithsonian Institution, Washington, D.C.
1982	*Ritual and Myth,* Studio Museum in Harlem, New York
1987	Fresno Center and Museum, California
	Montclair Art Museum, New Jersey
1988	Shoshanna Wayne Gallery, Santa Monica, California
	The Poetic Object, San Antonio Museum of Art, Texas (traveling)
1990	Banff Centre for the Arts, Canada
1992	Municipal Art Gallery, Los Angeles
1993	Center for the Arts at Yerba Buena Gardens, San Francisco
1995	*Africus Johannesburg Biennale,* South Africa

Collections:

Boston Museum of Fine Art; High Museum, Atlanta, Georgia; Hirshhorn Museum and Sculpture Garden, Washington, D.C.; Kresge Art Museum, East Lansing, Michigan; Los Angeles County Museum of Art; Montclair Art Museum, New Jersey; New Jersey State Museum, Newark; Oakland Museum, California; Palmer Museum of Art, University Park, Pennsylvania; Pennsylvania Academy of Fine Arts, Philadelphia; Philadelphia

Museum of Art; San Francisco Museum of Modern Art; Santa Barbara Museum of Art, California; Seattle Arts Commission; Smith College Museum of Art, Northampton, Massachusetts; Smithsonian Museum of American Art, Washington, D.C.; State Museum of New Jersey, Trenton; Studio Museum in Harlem, New York; University Art Museum, Berkeley, California; University of Massachusetts, Amherst; Walker Art Center, Minneapolis, Minnesota.

Publications:

On SAAR: Books—*Art Talk: Conversations with Fifteen Women in Art* by Cindy Nemser, Icons Editions, 1975 (revised, 1995); *Lives and Work: Talks with Women Artists* by Lynn F. Miller and Sally S. Swenson, Scarecrow Press, Inc., 1991, pp. 177-84; *The Art of Betye Saar and John Otterbridge,* exhibition catalog, Brazil, United States Information Agency and Twenty-Second International Bienial of São Paulo, 1994; *Personal Icons and Crystallizing Forms: The Recent Work of Betye Saar,* exhibition catalog, Missouri, Exhibits USA and Lizzetts LeFalle Collins, 1995. **Videos**—"Spiritcatcher: The Art of Betye Saar" produced by Perry Miller Adato, in *The Originals: Women in Art Series,* New York, WNET, 1978; "Similar Differences: Betye and Alison Saar," *in Fellows of Contemporary Art,* California, Long Beach Museum of Art, 1990; "Betye and Alison Saar: Conjure Women of the Arts" produced by Linda Freeman, L & S Video, 1994.

*

Betye Saar comments:

(1995)There has been an apparent thread in my art that weaves from my early prints of the 1960s through later collages and assemblages and ties into the current installations. That thread is a curiosity about the mystical. *Personal Icons* is the result of a conscious investigation of this thread.

I am intrigued with combining the remnants of memories, fragments of relics, and ordinary objects with the components of technology. It's a way of delving into the past and reaching into the future simultaneously. The art itself becomes the bridge.

The recent works of 1993 to 1995 are examples of my increased interest in the painted surface, specifically the palette and forms of Tantric art. Also I began to integrate my experimental "altered" Polaroid photos into the assemblages. The resulting works become documentation of places, visual clues to feelings, memories, and dreams.

> Curiosity
> about the unknown
> has no boundaries.
> Symbols, images, place and cultures merge.
> Time slips away.
> The stars, the cards, the mystic vigil
> may hold the answers.
> By shifting the point of view
> an inner spirit is released.
> Free to create a personal icon.

*   *   *

Celebrated artist Betye Saar, born in 1926, has been creating art for several decades. She is perhaps best known for her assemblages, which she started creating when her three daughters were born. Two of her daughters, Alison and Lezley, are now accomplished artists. Saar and artists like Faith Ringgold, Elizabeth Catlett, Lois Jones, Jean Lacy, Valerie Maynard, and Emma Amos are indisputable role models for generations of younger black women artists. Saar, Catlett, Ringgold, and Jones have had control over their lives and careers and enjoyed financial success.

Saar's career has been marked by certain phases or themes. The assemblages and altars, however, have been present over several decades. During the 1960s and 1970s she responded to the turmoil and political activism of the civil rights movement with *The Liberation of Aunt Jemima* (1972, mixed media, 11 3/4" x 8" x 2 3/4"). Saar's work deals with issues such as gender, oppression, race, ethnicity, sexual orientation, slavery, ageism, and body politics. Saar's sensitivity regarding the woman of color and where she is located in terms of the masculinized, patriarchal civil rights movement and the marginalization and devaluation of black women since their arrival on American shores in 1619 is striking and incisive. The *Liberation of Aunt Jemima* is angry and confrontational. In the decades since, her subject matter and iconography have reflected a post-civil rights era; nevertheless, some of her statements about race and gender remain powerful and chilling.

Another work from the 1970s is *Spirit Catcher* (1976-77, 3'9" x 18 1/2" x 18"). Like *The Liberation of Aunt Jemima,* it is an assemblage. Saar created a series of spirit catchers. They have secret parts and are endowed with mystery and accumulative energy, i.e., the different parts utilized to create the assemblage have energy and power from their previous existence, and all these energies combine in their new existence. Saar rarely searches for anything specific to employ in her assemblages and altars, she goes by her intuition and waits for objects to beckon her. She acquires objects for her works at swap meets, antique shops, or junkyards.

Watching is a work dated 1995. It was created on a recycled furnace grate. It is a mixed-media collage of paper, fabric, and acrylic paint and measures 13 1/2" x 9 1/2". It is a self-portrait of the artist peering out from behind the recycled furnace grate, on which Jim Crow is resting and watching. It is a poignant comment on where, she has been, where she is, and where she is going. Born only one year into the second quarter of the twentieth century, Saar is the youngest member of the trio of first generation, financially successful black women artists. She has much to tell us through her art about the past and the new millennium.

—Jontyle Theresa Robinson

ST. BRICE, Robert

Haitian painter

Born: Petionville, Haiti, 1898. **Died:** August 1973.

Individual Exhibitions:

1960	New York City
	Musée d'Art Haitien du Collège St. Pierre, Port-au-Prince, Haiti
1968	Centre d'Art, Port-au-Prince, Haiti

Selected Group Exhibitions:

1969	Davenport Art Gallery, Davenport, Iowa
1974	Milwaukee Art Center, Wisconsin
	Davenport Art Gallery, Davenport, Iowa
1978	Smithsonian Institution Traveling Exhibition Service, Washington, D.C. (traveling)
	Brooklyn Museum, New York (traveling)
1983	Chicago Public Library Cultural Center
	Davenport Art Gallery, Davenport, Iowa
1985	Davenport Art Gallery, Davenport, Iowa
1989	Museum of Art, Fort Lauderdale, Florida
	Musée du Panthéon National, Port-au-Prince, Haiti

Collections:

Centre d'Art, Port-au-Prince, Haiti; Davenport Museum of Art, Iowa; Flagg Collection, Milwaukee, Wisconsin; Musée d'Art Haitien du Collège St. Pierre, Port-au-Prince, Haiti; Perry E.H. Smith Collection, New Orleans Museum of Art; Selden Rodman Collection of Popular Art, Ramapo College, Mahwah, New Jersey.

*　　*　　*

The Haitian artist Robert St. Brice was introduced to painting in 1948 by Alex John, an American abstract painter who rented a room in St. Brice's house in Bizoton. St. Brice was already forty-eight years old at the time, when his mentor provided him with painting materials and encouraged him to create works out of his own imagination. It is not known if John provided him with technical instruction, but it is certain that St. Brice's technique of impressionistic abstraction was derived from John's style of painting. John later introduced St. Brice to DeWitt Peters, whose Centre d'Art, founded in 1944, was an important locus for the development of an indigenous art style in Haiti during the second half of the twentieth century. In this new environment St. Brice developed a consistent style of painting, one whose imagery and themes were mainly derived from Haiti's voodoo religion and rituals. His most accomplished paintings represent the ambiguous ritual universe of voodoo in an equally ambiguous pictorial format.

St. Brice's first works were images drawn on paper and cardboard sheets using charcoal and graphite. His later pictures, done in oil paints, usually consisted of one or two main figures situated in an indeterminate space suffused with dabs of contrasting colors applied in an obvious pointillist manner. Eyes and other facial features of his figures are loosely indicated, and their faces are painted a characteristic dark shade. In addition to the indeterminate spaces in St. Brice's compositions, his figures, devoid of arms and legs and rendered in curvilinear, biomorphic shapes, seem to float like spirits or shrouds. The artist, however, grounded each image by providing his pictures with specific titles, thus drawing attention to the *loas* (deities of the voodoo pantheon) they represent and, within their liminal spaces, providing an explanation for the activities of these supernatural beings. He claimed that the images were revealed to him in dreams. St. Brice ascribed his use of dots and lack of distinction between foreground and background to the fluid state of the deities he painted. In voodoo rituals these deities are able to possess human subjects at will and are capable of assuming different shapes or forms.

In *Two Spirits* (1957?) St. Brice's images are better delineated, and the artist pays greater attention to details of dress and orna-

mentation. The two central figures enclose an amorphous form whose presence is indicated only by swift brush strokes that signify its facial features. The picture is painted in bright spots of yellow, red, and dark brown colors. Another work—*Voodoo* (1965)—painted in muted tones, is considered more characteristic of St. Brice's palette and represents the major technical shift of his late period. Apart from some earlier paintings such as *Flowers and Bird* (1949), however, St. Brice's themes and imagery remained consistent throughout his career.

St. Brice's art has received different critical reactions. Some critics deride the artist for his repetitive, amorphous images. Others see in his works the most expressive and spiritually evocative images to have come out of the Centre d'Art and the Haitian indigenist (naive or popular) movement. At his best St. Brice's works achieve evocative mystery and subtle beauty through his focus on voodoo spirit imagery and a minimalist aesthetics that eliminates physical attributes in a search of the psychological center of his precisely themed objects. While his works never achieved the fame or frenzy of pictorial compositions by Philomé Obin or Hector Hyppolite, two major figures of the Haitian indigenous art movement, St. Brice's pictures are unusual for their rejection of the conspicuous imagery and overdetermined themes that characterize much Haitian popular art.

—Sylvester Okwunodu Ogbechie

SAMBA, Chéri

Zairian painter

Work also appeared under the name Samba wa Mbimba Nzinga Nunimasi Ndombasi. **Born:** Kinto-Mvuila, Zaire, 30 December 1956. **Career:** Worked as an assistant to a local painter, Kinshasa, Zaire, 1972. Since 1977 freelance artist.

Individual Exhibitions:

1989	Galerie Jean-Marc Patras, Paris
1990	Annina Nosei Gallery, New York
	Galerie Jean-Marc Patras, Paris
1991	Provinciaal Museum voor Modern Kunst, Ostende, Belgium
	Chicago Museum of Modern Art
	Miro Foundation, Barcelona, Spain
	ICA, London
	Portikus, Frankfurt, Germany
1992	Kunsthalle, Basel, Switzerland
	Studio Rafaelli, Tranto, Italy
	Wadsworth Atheneum, Hartford, Connecticut
	Stadt Museum, Munich, Germany
1993	Galerie Apunto, Amsterdam
1994	Galerie des Extravagances, Montbéliard, Paris
1995	Arndt und Partner, Berlin

Selected Group Exhibitions:

1978	Académie des Beaux-Arts, CIAF, Kinshasa, Zaire
1982	Musée des Arts Décoratifs, Paris
1985	L'Art vivant d'Afrique Centrale, University Laval, Quebec
	History Department, University Laval, Quebec

1986   *Contemporary Zairian Painters,* Festival d'Avignon,
        France
1989   *Magicians of the Earth,* Centre Georges Pompidou-La-
        Villette, Paris
1991   Museum for Contemporary Art and Center for African
        Art, New York
        Atlantic Center of Modern Art, Las Palmas, Canary Islands
1992   Galerie Apunto, Amsterdam
1993   Trevi Flash Art Museum of Contemporary Art, Italy

Collections:

Institut des Musées Nationaux du Zaire.

Publications:

On SAMBA: Books— *Chéri Samba/Matrix 117,* exhibition catalog, Connecticut, Wadsworth Antheneum and Andrea Miller-Keller, 1992. **Articles—**"Chéri Samba," in *Kanal Magazine,* October 1989, p. 70; "Chéri Samba Images That Color the Whole Ethnic Question" by Jan Avgikos, in *Flash Art,* October 1990, p. 150; "Chéri Samba: Griot of Kinshasa and Paris" by Miriam Rosen, in *Art Forum,* March 1990, pp. 137-40; "Chéri Samba, Aninna Nosei Gallery," in *The New Yorker,* 7 May 1990, p. 52; "Painting in Zaire: From the Invention of the West to the Representation of Social Self" by Bogumil Jewsiewicki, in *Africa Explores: Twentieth Century African Art* edited by Susan Govel, New York, Center for African Art, 1991, pp. 130-51; "Chéri Samba" by Bernard Marcadé, in *Galeries,* 1991, pp. 84-87; "Chéri Samba and the Postcolonial Reinvention of Modernity" by Jean-Pierre Jaquemin, in *Callaloo,* 16, 1993, pp. 772-95.

                              *

Chéri Samba comments:

(1990)Impressions: through my travels I find that all countries share certain key characteristics. In the industrialized countries or in the third world, there is always poverty; many people cannot eat their fill.

We should be organizing "Restaurants du Coeur," those who have made it helping the ones who have not had any luck yet. The hungry of the Third World are at the gates of Europe, which are closed to them even if half-open to the East.

Even in the land of Uncle Sam, that world power that spends billions of dollars on arms, the wealth and greatness of Manhattan stands side by side with the poverty of Harlem. Man looks for his personal honor and profit and does not give a thought to his neighbor.

Could our planet not be a paradise for its inhabitants?

                    *   *   *

Chéri Samba is a self-taught artist from southern Zaire who dropped out of school to become an apprentice sign painter in the capital of Kinshasa. After opening his own sign shop complete with assistants, he began painting on canvas.

With his roots firmly entrenched in sign painting, Samba produces large, colorful works loaded with text that often reads like the latest Madison Avenue advertising. Yet there is something peculiar in his work that is shared by sign painters and artists in other West African countries and in Haiti in the Western Hemisphere. This might be thought to be a Francophone influence, but in fact it goes back to the Mexican muralists—David Alfaro Siqueiros, José

Clemente Orozco, and Diego Rivera—and thus to social realism, both American and German, and to the French *Figuration Libre* movement of the early 1980s.

Flat, hard, figural painting has always been a development of the harsh reality of oppression, persecution, and injustice. This can be seen, for instance, in Édouard Manet's *The Execution of the Emperor Maximilian of Mexico* (1867) or in Eugène Delacroix's *Liberty on the Barricades,* which gave a strong visual account of the storming of the Bastille. The creation of such paintings was born of necessity. They serve history by giving a graphic depiction of an important event in the story of humanity, lest people forget. For without the pictorial people can leave history's ugliness to a never-never land where "it could have happened . . . but." Thus, before the invention of the camera painting had a practical purpose and presented a much stronger point of view. Since the camera painting has come to be allowed to present the painter's interpretation but not to provide firsthand documentation of the event.

Compare, for instance, the atrocities of the slave trade in the 1600s with those of the Holocaust in the 1940s. If the barbarity of the slave trade had been captured on videotape (as was the beating of Rodney King) rather than in fictional reinterpretation, the civil rights movement might have taken place much earlier. An integral component of the civil rights movement was the fact that when Eugene "Bull" Connor turned fire hoses on African Americans in the South people had vicious cruelty brought into their living rooms via technology. Had that technology not existed, this text would, more than likely, not exist.

For Samba's Africa technology still has a long way to go, and although his artwork may seem dull in the modernist sense, it is thoroughly of the moment. In his paintings big, bright, bold color provides the background for the depiction of everyday people caught up in tragedy. They combine humor with pathos. The paintings are morality tales played out on canvas and concerned with sex and sexuality, AIDS, colonialism, and poverty. In the 1989 painting *Le Sida* (*AIDS*), for instance, three topless women, two holding phalliclike capsules and one holding a globe, all covered with condoms, raise the objects to the sky as if in praise. The figures are erotically charged, as if they came from *Playboy* cartoons, although the subject is deadly serious. In text at the bottom of the painting Samba says, "AIDS IS STILL INCURABLE BUT PREVENTABLE." While he is occupied with the situation in his native country, he also drops wry commentary on France in a painting like *Paris est propre* (1989), in which three African street cleaners sweep dog excrement from the streets, with the Eiffel Tower glowing in the center.

Samba's somewhat retro style makes his paintings seem like large comic books chronicling the new Africa, free of colonialism but not of oppression. In their contemporaneity, however, they are necessary reminders of the power of paint and of Shakespearean comic relief in the face of tragedy.

                                        —M. Franklin Sirmans

SAUNDERS, Raymond
American painter and mixed-media artist

Born: 28 October 1934, Pittsburgh. **Education:** Carnegie Institute of Technology, 1959-60, B.F.A. 1960; California College of Arts and Crafts, 1960-61, M.F.A. 1961. **Awards:** Cresson European Traveling Scholarship, 1956; Eakins Prize, 1956; Thoron Oil Paint-

Raymond Saunders. Photo courtesy of Nancy Moran.

ing First Prize, 1956; First Prize in oil painting, Pennsylvania Academy of Fine Arts, 1957; Third Prize, *Pittsburgh Playhouse Gallery Invitational,* 1959; Schwabcher Frey Award, San Francisco Museum of Modern Art, 1961; Ford Foundation Purchase Award, 1964; Prix de Rome Prize, 1964-66; Lee Cultural Center Award, Philadelphia, 1968; Atwater Kent Award, 1970; Society of Four Arts Award, Palm Beach, Florida, 1972; KQED Art Award, San Francisco, 1975; Granger Memorial Award, Pennsylvania Academy of Fine Arts, Philadelphia, 1975; Guggenheim Fellowship, 1976; National Endowment for the Arts Award, 1977, 1984; Visual Arts Award, South Eastern Center for Contemporary art, 1989. **Agent:** Stephen Wirtz Gallery, Bankers Investment Building, 49 Geary Street, San Francisco, California 94108, U.S.A.

Individual Exhibitions:

1980   Triton Museum of Art, Santa Clara, California
        Stephen Wirtz Gallery, San Francisco
        Baum/Silverman Gallery, Los Angeles

1981	Hunter College, New York
	Traver/Sutton Gallery, Seattle
	Hunsaker-Schlesinger Gallery, Los Angeles
	Portland Museum Art School, Wentz Art Gallery, Portland, Oregon
	Seattle Art Museum
	Artmobile, Metropolitan Dade County, Miami
1982	Marion Porter Senson Art Gallery, University of California, Santa Cruz
	Dixie Park Library, Allapattah Library, Coral Gables Library, Florida (traveling)
	Miami-Dade Community College, North Campus, Miami
	Stephen Wirtz Gallery, San Francisco
	Arizona State University, Tempe
1983	Stephen Wirtz Gallery, San Francisco
	University of Texas, San Antonio
1984	Barnsdall Park, Los Angeles Municipal Art Gallery
1985	Boise Gallery of Art, Idaho
	Thomas Babeor Gallery, La Jolla, California
	Hunsaker/Schlesinger Gallery, Los Angeles
	Angles Gallery, Santa Monica, California
	Hunsaker/Schlesinger Gallery, Los Angeles
	Stephen Wirtz Gallery, San Francisco
1986	University Gallery of Fine Arts, Ohio State University, Columbus
	Terry Dintenfass, Inc., New York
	Pritchard Art Gallery, University of Idaho, Moscow
	Miami-Dade Public Library System
	Hearst Art Gallery, Saint Mary's College, Moraga, California
1987	Hunsaker/Schlesinger Gallery, Santa Monica, California
	Bank of America, San Francisco
	Addison Gallery of American Art, Phillips Academy, Andover, Massachusetts
	Cava Gallery, Philadelphia
	Stephen Wirtz Gallery, San Francisco
1988	Greenville County Museum, South Carolina
	Carlton College, Northfield, Minnesota
	Miami-Dade Public Library System, Florida
1989	Addison Gallery of American Art, Phillips Academy, Andover, Massachusetts
	San Marco, Dominican College, San Rafael, California
	Stephen Wirtz Gallery, San Francisco
1990	Pennsylvania Academy of the Fine Arts, Philadelphia
	Santa Monica College Art Gallery, California
	Galerie Resche, Paris
	Stephen Wirtz Gallery, San Francisco

Selected Group Exhibitions:

1983	Cleveland Museum of Art, Ohio
	38th Corcoran Biennial Exhibition of American Painting, Corcoran Gallery of Art, Washington, D.C.
1985	American Academy and Institute of Arts and Letters, New York
1986	David and Alfred Smart Gallery, University of Chicago
1987	Arkansas Arts Center, Little Rock
1989	Albright-Knox Art Gallery, Buffalo, New York
1990	Studio Museum in Harlem, New York
1994	Terry Dintenfass, Inc., New York

1995	Metropolitan Museum of Art, New York
1996	Contemporary Arts Center, Cincinnati

Collections:

Achenbach Foundation, Palace of the Legion of Honor, San Francisco; Addison Gallery of American Art, Andover, Massachusetts; Allentown Art Museum, Pennsylvania; Arizona State University, Tempe; California College of Arts and Crafts, Oakland; California State College, San Bernardino; Carnegie Institute, Pittsburgh, Pennsylvania; Crocker Art Museum, Sacramento, California; Dartmouth College, Hanover, New Hampshire; Elvehjem Art Center, University of Wisconsin, Madison; Fisk University, Nashville; Howard University, Washington, D.C.; Hunter College, New York; Long Beach Museum, California; M.H. deYoung Memorial Museum, San Francisco; Metropolitan Museum of Art, New York; Miami Dade Junior College, Florida; Mount Holyoke College, South Hadley, Massachusetts; Museum of Contemporary Art, Los Angeles; Museum of Modern Art, New York; National Institute of Arts and Letters, New York; Oakland Museum, California; Pennsylvania Academy of Fine Arts, Philadelphia; St. Louis Museum of Fine Arts, Missouri; San Francisco Museum of Modern Art; Seattle Art Museum; Sheldon Memorial Art Gallery, University of Nebraska, Lincoln; University Art Museum, Berkeley, California; University of Utah Art Museum, Salt Lake City; Walker Art Center, Minneapolis, Minnesota; Whitney Museum of American Art, New York.

Publications:

On SAUNDERS: Articles—"Blackboard Memories" by Mollie Malone, in *Artweek,* 17, 8 February 1986, p. 3; review (Terry Dintenfass, New York) by Robert G. Edelman, in *Art in America,* 75, February 1987, p. 146; "Improvisation in the Realm of Memory" by Jamie Brunson, in *Artweek,* 20, 27 May 1989, p. 1; review (Galerie Resche, Paris) by Miriam Rosen, in *Artforum,* 29, November 1990, pp. 178-79; review (Stephen Wirtz Gallery, San Francisco) by Rene Duer, in *Artweek,* 22, 6 June 1991, p. 11; review (Stephen Wirtz Gallery, New York) by Kenneth Baker, in *Art News,* 92, May 1993, pp. 146-47; "Raymond Saunders—Malcolm X: Talking Pictures at Stephen Wirtz Gallery" by Terri Cohn, in *Artweek,* 25, 20 October 1994, p. 17 (illustrated); "Raymond Saunders: Improvising with High and Low" by Gay Morris, in *Art in America,* 83, February 1995, pp. 89; "Raymond Saunders" by David Carrier, in *Artforum,* 35, October 1996, p. 122 (illustrated).

*   *   *

Since the 1960s Raymond Saunders has been at the forefront of the mainstream art world. While his work has a spiritual association with abstract expressionism and pop art, his complex imagery is largely autobiographical and frequently political, and it proclaims his racial heritage.

The academic background that shaped the development of Saunders's career included periods of study in his hometown of Pittsburgh and in Philadelphia, as well as in Oakland, California, where he now teaches. His early works were personal adaptations of the pop art culture of the 1960s. His paintings displayed bold colors, broad brush strokes, and stenciled and drawn letters, and the cartoon character Mickey Mouse frequently appeared. During that period Saunders also began depicting ragged crosses in his

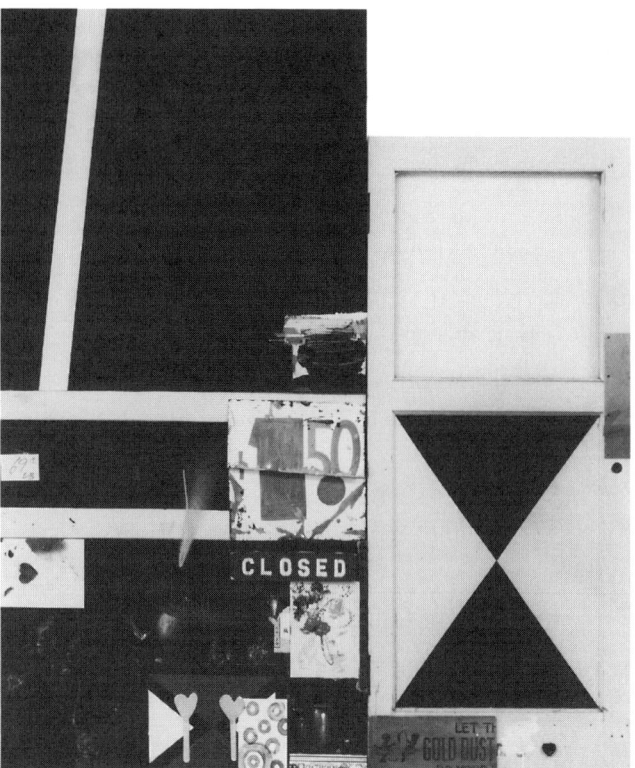

Raymond Saunders: *Things Were Never $1.50,* 1995. Photo courtesy of Ben Blackwell.

paintings, which he has described as "my still-life and still my life." Painted images of sidewalk hopscotch patterns appeared early on. He has stated that this persistent motif is inspired by his association with children in the art classes he sometimes teaches in an Oakland school.

Saunders's recent works include his large "Black Paintings," executed on wooden panels and doors. He applies bright colors, delicate contour drawings, graffiti, scribbled words, and various found objects against solid black wooden backgrounds. The resulting works are not actually paintings but rather mixed-media assemblages representing a rich historical, visual tapestry of the artist's philosophy and day-to-day experiences.

As is the case with many African American artists of his generation, Saunders is an avid jazz fan. He frequently incorporates the names of his favorite musicians into his assemblages, and his artworks reflect the same improvisational qualities. This improvisational character of jazz is probably the impetus for his two most famous trademarks, the constant reworking of pieces and the reincarnation, or re-creation, of others. Saunders seldom considers a work of art completed, and he is known to enter galleries and museums after his works have been installed to make changes or add what he considers finishing touches. He is also known for re-creating his works, sometimes more than once. Earlier paintings or assemblages are redesigned, repainted, and renamed. They use titles, however, that evoke memories of the earlier works, as in *I Don't Go to Church Anymore,* from the earlier *I Used to Draw in Church,* and *Once Dr. Jesus,* from *Dr. Jesus.*

Saunders travels constantly and maintains studios in Oakland as well as in Venice and Paris. He has visited Italy, France, Africa, and China and has made numerous trips to Mexico. He has often visited

Harlem. Saunders's travels figure prominently in his works, and during his journeys he considers himself a "streetwalker" who collects cast-off odds and ends, most of which eventually appear in his assemblages. He was especially inspired by his visit to China, and during the past several years Chinese calligraphy, signage, fortune cookie papers, symbols, and even titles, such as *Imperial Palace, Beijing,* have appeared in his works.

Drawing and color are two important elements of Saunders's paintings, drawings, collages, and assemblages. He carefully employs sensitive contour drawings, which are usually simply executed, in his works, and his figures sometimes appear to be inspired by children's drawings. He uses conté crayon and even blackboard chalk against dark backgrounds. His colors are bright and reflect the Kool-Aid palette—strawberry pinks, lime greens, and lemon yellows—of the 1960s Africobra group of Chicago. Saunders's colors may be thickly or thinly applied, static or reflecting a drip technique, but they always play against the black backgrounds and sharp white contrasts in a kaleidoscopic symphony.

Saunders grew up and has always lived in an urban environment, which has affected the symbols that appear most frequently in his art. He incorporates tin cans, discarded gum wrappers, parking signs, soft drink bottles, paint brushes, cut and torn paper, strips of wood, ticket stubs, and other urban detritus into his works. Other symbols include calla lilies, playing cards, fruit, and heart-shaped forms.

Saunders has the ability to combine and juxtapose figures with abstraction, vibrant colors with solid blacks and whites, painted surfaces with three-dimensional ones, and sensitive contour drawings with scrawled graffiti. His imagery reflects his African American heritage, love of jazz, and world travel, and it comments on the state of affairs in the United States and elsewhere This ensures Saunders an indelible niche in the history of modern art.

—Regenia Perry

SAVAGE, Augusta (Christine)
American sculptor

Born: Augusta Christine Fells, Green Cove Springs, Florida, 29 February 1892. **Education:** Tallahassee State Normal School (now Florida A & M), 1915; Cooper Union, New York, 1921; Académie de la Grande Chaumiere, Paris, c.1929. **Family:** Married 1) John T. Moore in 1907 (died), one daughter; 2) James Savage (divorced 1920s); 3) Robert Lincoln Poston c.1923 (died 1924). **Career:** Founded Savage Studio of Arts and Crafts, New York, 1932; assistant supervisor, Works Progress Administration Federal Art Project, beginning 1936. Commissioned portrait artist. Elected member, National Association of Women Painters and Sculptors, 1934. **Awards:** Scholarship, Italian-American Society, c.1923; travel grant, Rosenwald Foundation, 1929; grant, Carnegie Foundation, c.1930; commission award, World's Fair Corporation, New York. **Died:** 26 March 1962.

Individual Exhibitions:

Argent Gallery, New York (1932); Art Anderson Gallery, New York (1932); Grande Chaumiere, Paris (c.1929); Grand Palais, Salon Printemps, Paris; Harmon Foundation, New York; 135th Street Branch, New York Public Library; Société des Aristes Français Beaux Arts, Paris.

Collection:

Schomburg Center, New York.

Publications:

On SAVAGE: Book—*Augusta Savage and the Art Schools of Harlem,* exhibition catalog, New York, Schomburg Center for Research in Black Culture, 1988. **Articles**—"Harlem Goes in for Art" by Sophia Steinbach, in *Opportunity,* 14, April 1936, p. 114; "Art Comes to People of Harlem" by James H. Baker, in *Crisis,* 46, March 1939, pp. 78-80; article, in *Chicago Herald-American,* 9 May 1940; "The Art Notebook," in *Chicago Bee,* 10 May 1940; "Art and Artists" by Ernest Heitkamp, in *Chicago Herald-American,* 12 May 1940; "Augusta Savage—An Appraisal" by Elton C. Fax, in *American Society of African Culture Newsletter,* Schomburg Center Clipping file, n.d.; *Five Black Masters of American Art* by Romare Bearden and Harry Henderson, 1972, pp. 76-98; "Augusta Savage," in *A History of African-American Artists, from 1792 to the Present* by Romare Bearden and Harry Henderson, Pantheon Books, New York, 1993, pp. 168-80.

*   *   *

Augusta Savage was a sculptor of remarkable tenacity, will, and determination, in spite of issues of race, class, and gender in an era that did not encourage or recognize women who chose to work in a genre believed to be the domain of white males. She was also an ardent political activist and arts educator. Savage is responsible for contributing to the legacy of early modernist imagery as it reflected the quest for identity, beauty, and racial self-determination during the period commonly known as the Harlem Renaissance or the New Negro Movement of the 1920s.

Savage's artistic career was most active from the early 1920s until the 1940s. Between 1940 and 1951 her activity as a sculptor began to wane due to an absence of commissions, diminishing patrons, fewer opportunities to exhibit her work, and the onset of age, economic urgencies, and illness. Her first critical successes in the 1920s were portrait busts that concentrated on studies of racial identity and character in prominent individuals in the African American community of Harlem. Later she would receive critical recognition for portrayals of subjects who reflected the heroic stature, personality, and integrity of the common man. The dignity with which she imbued her subjects combined with a faithfulness to personality types and expressive characterizations became a hallmark of Savage's work, as she continued to study African American physiognomy, movement, and form. Her figurative portrayals were noted for the humanity of her subjects as well as for the dexterity of her skills in bronze, clay, and plaster. In 1939 her monumental achievement was a commission to produce *The Harp* for the New York World's Fair, which was inspired by James Weldon and Rosamond Johnson's song "Lift Every Voice and Sing." At the close of the World's Fair, no funds from patrons were raised and the sixteen-foot sculpture was destroyed. Savage's professional career as a sculptor then began to decline. Works after 1940 tended to be commissioned portrait busts.

Augusta Savage: *Gamin,* **1930. Photo by Manu Sassoonian; courtesy of the Schomburg Center for Research in Black Culture.**

Savage is also known for the art schools and organizations she founded in the 1930s in Harlem.

Among these were the Savage Studio of Arts and Crafts; the Vanguard, a salon of politically active Harlem intellectuals cofounded with Aaron Douglas and other artists; and the Harlem Artists Guild. She also served as director of the Harlem Community Art Center and as supervisor on the Works Progress Administration (W.P.A.). Her classes were open to anyone interested in learning about or experiencing art.

Young artists flocked to her studio workshops to study, and she is responsible for influencing the artistic careers of Norman Lewis, Marvin and Morgan Smith, William Artis, Ernest Crichlow, and Gwendolyn Knight. Savage's studio became a center of creative activity and intellectual exchange with the constant presence of W.E.B. DuBois, James Weldon Johnson, Claude McKay, Romare Bearden, Buford and Joseph Delaney, and Selma Burke. Jacob Lawrence credits Savage with signing him on to the W.P.A. and providing the opportunity for him to become an artist.

Savage was a passionate believer that art belonged to the community and fought to defend the rights and representation of the African American artist in the larger arena of American art. Her relentless intent to bring these issues to the forefront of the political and cultural arena did not win her the affections or support of patrons who were often put off by her aggressive and outspoken positions. Often Savage herself dismissed the importance of her own work and artistic contributions in deference to issues she believed to be critical to the survival and recognition of the African American artist. Savage was a true Renaissance woman.

—Leslie King-Hammond

SCOTT, Elizabeth (Talford)

American quiltmaker

Born: Chester, South Carolina, 2 August 1916. **Career:** Quilting instructor and demonstrator, AFRAM Festival, Baltimore, Maryland, 1977, Johns Hopkins Free School, Baltimore, Maryland, 1977, Smithsonian Institution, Washington, D.C., 1977, Cloister's Children's Museum, Baltimore, Maryland, 1977-78, Baltimore City Fair, Maryland, 1978, African American History Conference, Baltimore, Maryland, 1978, First African-American Crafts Conference and Jubilee, Memphis, Tennessee, NAACP Black Arts Festival, Maryland, 1979, Museum of African Art, Washington, D.C., 1979, University of Maryland, 1981. Artist-in-residence, Baltimore Bureau of Recreation, 1980-85, Maryland State Arts Council, 1980-85.

Selected Exhibitions:

1982   Studio Museum in Harlem, New York
1984   Pratt Manhattan Center Gallery, New York
1985   Maryland Art Place, Baltimore, Maryland
1989   *Stitching Memories: African American Story Quilts,* Cheekwood Museum, Nashville
        Family Traditions: Recent Works by Elizabeth T. and Joyce J. Scott, Pennsylvania Academy of the Fine Arts
1990   Baltimore Museum of Art, Maryland
        Steinbaum Krauss Gallery, New York

*   *   *

Through the wisdom of her experience Elizabeth Talford Scott has become the guardian of a heritage thought to be forgotten and lost. She articulates a history that speaks to the lineage of African American people in the New World through the use of material culture. When she began as a quilt maker, it was to provide functional objects to keep people warm, but through her imaginative artistry she has unwittingly connected the reality of the African American past and present. Scott has made a vital addition to the visual language black people use to contribute to the culture and character of the United States. She is the mother of the mixed-media performance and visual artist Joyce Jane Scott. They share a large studio and living complex in Baltimore, Maryland.

Growing up in Chester, South Carolina, the sixth of fourteen children, Scott helped sharecrop the land with her family. Her grandparents had been slaves. The tradition of quilting was then an integral and vital part of rural black American experience, and her father as well as her mother quilted. At the age of nine she began her first quilt. In her adult life she quilted only intermittently, never realizing the aesthetic importance of her efforts. In the early 1970s, however, she began to quilt more seriously. Her imagery not only recalled the continuity of African pieced, striped textiles but also

involved visual innovations in its displays of bright colors and complex patterns and in the incorporation of animals, insects, flowers, stars, and "monsters" to embellish the surfaces.

Life has held a series of ironic twists of fate for Scott, who had no formal intent or personal aspiration to become an artist of distinction in American society. Yet, despite the issues of class, race, and gender, she began to emerge in the 1970s as an artist of unique vision and exceptional artistry and creativity, as a person who captured the spirit, energy, realities, fears, hopes, and dreams of the African American characters in the narratives portrayed in her elaborately fabricated assemblages.

In 1981, nearly ten years after she had resumed making quilts in earnest, Carl Schottler observed in the *Baltimore Sun* that Scott was "a preserver of cultural history. She presents a cultural heritage spanning centuries through fabric, thread, and needles, creating a landscape of memories." Through her textile creations Scott has begun a long, complex process of redefining the traditional functions of the genre of fiber art.

In the early 1980s and the 1990s Scott's visibility began to increase dramatically, and she was recognized by numerous major museums. At the same time her work began to change in scale and content. Recurring problems with her eyes inspired new designs and visual interpretations in her works. Smaller works like lap quilts, pillows, or wall hangings, as opposed to larger bed-sized quilts, sometime became easier to execute. The materials used to embellish the surfaces increasingly began to include buttons, bells, beads, lace, tied and knotted fibers, metals, coins, mirrors, rocks, and small pebbles. The use of these materials recalls the Nkisi traditions of the Kongo that have survived in the United States.

Scott provides history with the critical challenge of addressing aesthetic continuances through traditions practiced over generations within the lineage of the extended family. Documentation of African American families with continuous histories of active involvement in the plastic arts has rarely been made. Whereas the creative energies of Scott and her family have become known, others have yet to be discovered. She represents a critical link to cultural and aesthetic sensibilities that exemplify the essence of African American artistic traditions in the New World.

Scott's education was limited because of the necessity for her to work at sharecropping. She has always been troubled by this so-called lack of education and has used quilts as her vehicle for communication. She informs, elevates, and gives new meaning to the heritage of African American culture through preservation, memory, storytelling, and the innovative use of common material artifacts routinely used in American culture but distinctly articulated in the artistry of her mediated compositions.

—Leslie King-Hammond

SCOTT, John T.

American sculptor, painter, and printmaker

Born: New Orleans, 30 June 1940. **Education:** Xavier University of Louisiana, B.A. 1962; Michigan State University, M.F.A. 1965. **Career:** Since 1965 professor of fine arts, Xavier University of Louisiana. Art department chairman, Xavier University of Louisiana, 1974-80. Visiting artist/lecturer, Southern Methodist University, Dallas, 1975, University of Maine at Orono, Michigan, 1978,

Benjamin Mays Academy, Indiana, 1984, Florida A & M University, Tallahassee, Florida, 1985; Albany State College, Georgia, 1985; Brandywine Workshop, 1988, Washington Project for the Arts, Washington, D.C., 1988; Monoprint Workshop, Michigan State University, East Lansing, 1990, Brandywine Print Workshop, Philadelphia, 1992; University of Southern Illinois, Evensville, 1996.

Awards: Fellowship in sculpture, Michigan State University, 1964; Phi Kappa Phi National Scholastic Honorary Fraternity, Michigan State University, East Lansing, 1965; Second Annual Mayor's Arts Award, New Orleans, 1980; Hand Hollow Fellowship, 1983; Strengthening the Humanities Fellowship, United Negro College Fund, 1983; Distinguish Scholar Award, United Negro College Fund, 1986; honorary Ph.D., Madonna College, Livonia, Michigan, 1987; Role Model Award, Youth Leadership Council, 1988; award for excellence in teaching, presented by President George Bush, 1992; genius award, John D. and Catherine T. MacArthur Foundation, 1992; Certificate of Merit, City of New Orleans, 1995; certificate, Special Congressional Recognition for Service to the Community, 1995; Governor's Arts Award, State of Louisiana, 1995; Outstanding Art Contributor Award, National Conference of Artists, 1995; Delta Region Preservation Commission for Distinguished Service, 1995; Monumental Discoveries Award, East Lansing, Michigan; arts award, New Orleans Chapter of the Links, Links, Inc., 1995; Lifetime Achievement in the Arts Award, Arts Council of Louisiana, 1995; Doctor of Humanities, honorary degree, Michigan State University, Lansing, 1995; Artie Award, Delta Sigma Theata Sorority, Inc., 1996; Delgado Society Award, New Orleans Museum of Art, 1996. **Agent:** Galerie Simonne Stern, 518 Julia Street, New Orleans, Louisiana 70130, U.S.A.

John T. Scott. Photo courtesy of Frank Methe.

Individual Exhibitions:

1967	Xavier University, New Orleans
1968	Florida A & M University, Tallahassee, Florida
1971	Laemmle Fine Arts Theatres, Santa Monica, California
	Experience Gallery, Brooklyn, New York
1972	Studio 8, New Orleans
1976	Sol Del Rio Gallery, San Antonio, Texas
1983	Rivet Gallery, Metairie, Louisiana
1984	Harris/Brown Gallery, Boston (traveling)
1986	Harris/Brown Gallery, Boston
1988	Kipp Gallery, University of Pennsylvania, Indiana
	Masur Museum, Monroe, Louisiana
	Galerie Simonne Stern, New Orleans
1989	Nexus Gallery, Atlanta, Georgia
1990	Stoner Museum, Shreveport, Louisiana
1992	Southern University of Louisiana, Baton Rouge
	Galerie Simonne Stern, New Orleans
1993	Galerie Simonne Stern, New Orleans
1994	McIntosh Gallery, Atlanta, Georgia
	National Museum of American Art, Washington, D.C.
	Southeastern University, Hammond, Louisiana
1995	Galerie Simonne Stern, New Orleans

Selected Group Exhibitions:

1987	Boston Museum of Fine Arts
	City Gallery of Contemporary Art, Raleigh, North Carolina
	Liz Harris Gallery, Boston

1989	New Visions Gallery, Ithaca, New York
1991	*John Scott, Josef Staub, Glenn Watson,* Vistor Fischer Galleries, San Francisco
1992	George N'Namdi Gallery, Birmingham, Mississippi
1993	*John Scott and Richard Johnson,* Alexandria Museum of Art, Louisiana
1995	Studio Museum in Harlem, New York
	Twentieth Century American Sculpture from the Permanent Collections of Southern Museums, White House, Washington, D.C.
1997	Smithsonian Institution (traveling)

Collections:

Arts Council of New Orleans; Dallas Museum of Art; Fisk University, Tennessee; Florida A & M University; Kresge Art Museum, Michigan State University, East Lansing; Loyola University of the South, Louisiana; National Museum of American Art, Smithsonian Institution, Washington, D.C.; New Orleans Museum of Art; One Canal Place, New Orleans; Prairieview A & M University, Texas; Tulane University Law School, New Orleans; University of New Orleans.

Publications:

By SCOTT: Articles—"Remembering a Friend," in *Arts Quarterly,* 11(1), New Orleans Museum of Art, February/March 1989. "Quality: Who Defines It and How," in *Connections Quarterly,* 8(5), June 1989.

John T. Scott: *Ocean Song,* **1989. Photo courtesy of Galerie Simonne Stern.**

On SCOTT: Articles—"An Artist and His Cause" by Larry Bartlett, in *Dixie Roto Magazine,* 7 June 1970; "Portfolio of Drawings by John Scott" by Jo G. and Clifton Webb, in *New Orleans Review,* 4(1), 1974; "John Scott's Quest for Unity" by Roger Green, in *Times Picayune,* 1978; "John Scott in Duncan Plaza and Art in New Orleans" by Alan Huard, in *Xavier Gold,* Spring 1981; "John T. Scott and the Black Aesthetics" by Evonne Edwards-Tucker, in *International Review of African American Art,* 6(2), 1985; "Life, Work and Thoughts of an Artist/Teacher" by Iris Kelso, in *Xavier Gold,* May 1986.

*   *   *

John T. Scott's abstract sculptures of painted steel and aluminum use tension—formal, technical, and conceptual—as the structuring principle behind works that, while derived from the uniqueness of the artist's New Orleans-based African American cultural experience, convey universal resonance through the suggestion of ritual. During the early years of his career in the 1960s and 1970s, Scott worked in cast bronze and prints to create figurative pieces that reflected the political and social concerns of the black arts movement. In 1983, however, two events precipitated a shift of direction in the artist's work. The events formed the aesthetic and methodological underpinnings for Scott's subsequent production.

During 1983 Scott's research as the chief designer for the African American pavilion for the 1984 Louisiana World Exposition led him to an African myth that described hunters turning over and restringing the bow used to kill an animal, an act that transformed the weapon into a musical instrument. The hunter then played a lyrical memorial to the spirit of the animal he had killed. The *diddlie* bow, as the instrument was called, was formed by the tension of the wire strung between two points. It spoke to Scott formally as a visual tool and culturally as a reclamation of African history that also suggested the ongoing significance of music in the African American experience, especially in New Orleans. Also in that year, at the invitation of the kinetic sculptor George Rickey, Scott spent six weeks working at the Hand Hollow Foundation in East Chatham, New York. Scott had a long-standing interest, one that Rickey encouraged, in moving sculpture, and he used the time at Hand Hollow to begin developing what he calls a "kinetic vocabulary."

Akhanaten's Rowboat (1983) is a transitional work that exhibits Scott's developing visual language. The wood and brass sculpture is held in balance by the tension in the wire and wood elements. The artist suggests the upturned *diddlie* bow with the contour of the ship's bottom. He represents the historical reality of the middle passage even as he strips the form of the slave ship to its most essential linear elements. The conceptual tension between the historical past and the present is invoked and transformed by the implied lyrical and visual honor made to the spirits of the dead. The act of remembering becomes a transformative event, one that connects the slave traders and the enslaved in a common history.

The artist's later works demonstrate the continued development of the visual language begun in *Akhanaten's Rowboat.* In 1995 Scott produced a series of works on "the way that language treats women," collectively called "Urban Ibeji," a reference to the cult of twins found in Yoruba culture. The *ibeji,* or twins, are believed to bring luck to the house in which they are born. In Yoruba society a mother of twins prepares special foods for the children in order to placate their unpredictable spirits. If one of the twins dies, the mother often has a statue commissioned to commemorate the child, carrying it with her and providing ritual feedings. Like *Akhanaten's Rowboat* the "Urban Ibeji" series is derived from a ritual practice in African culture.

Scott also uses the concept of twinning to highlight the dual identities of whores and virgins inflicted on women by language. In the series the conceptual and formal tensions beginning to be explored in the early 1980s have been complicated to the point that Scott is probing multiple themes even as he returns to figural representation. In *Confined Two-Step* (1995), for example, Scott represents two figures dancing in a house. The three-dimensional polychromed aluminum deceives the eye in the shifting tension between two and three dimensions. The reference to a two-step and Scott's interest in representing the spirit and expressive qualities of jazz through the visual arts exploit the tensions between the visual and the musical. The figures contained within the house spill out of the boundaries of the structure; the interior and exterior are juxtaposed and related concepts. Women's containment and restraint are called into question by the dynamism of figures and the broken boundaries of the confining home structure. If such containment is acknowledged and represented in a modified ritual context, the troubled spirits of the restrained figures and their models in the physical world can begin to be soothed.

—Nicole Gilpin

SCOTT, Joyce (Jane)
American sculptor and performance artist

Born: Baltimore, Maryland, 15 November 1948. **Education:** Maryland Institute, College of Art, Baltimore, B.F.A. 1970; Instituto Allende, San Miguel Allende, Guanajuato, Mexico, M.F.A. in crafts 1971; Haystack Mountain School of Crafts, Deer Isle, Maine, 1976. **Awards:** National Endowment for the Arts Fellowship, 1980; Maryland State Arts Council Fellowship, 1981 and 1987; Mid-Atlantic Arts Consortium Award, 1990; National Printing Fellowship, 1992; Art Matters Award, 1994; Mid-Atlantic Arts Foundation Award, 1994; Pace Roberts Fellowship, 1994.

Individual Exhibitions:

1981	Washington Project for the Arts, Washington, D.C.
1985	Cultural Center, Chicago Public Library
1988	Textile Center for the Arts, Chicago
	Walker Point Center for the Arts, Milwaukee

1990	Washington County Museum of the Fine Arts, Hagerstown, Maryland
	Susan Cummins Gallery, Mill Valley, California
	University of Oklahoma, Tulsa
1991	Mobilia, Cambridge, Massachusetts
	Corcoran Gallery of Art, Washington, D.C.
1992	Brooklyn College Art Gallery, New York (traveling)
	Esther Saks Fine Art, Limited, Chicago
	Frostburg Art Gallery, Frostburg State University, Maryland
	Wellington B. Gray Gallery, Jenkins Fine Arts Center, Greenville, North Carolina
	Helen Drutt Gallery, Philadelphia
1993	City Gallery of Contemporary Art, Raleigh, North Carolina
	Shippenburg Gallery, Pennsylvania
1994	Esther Sake Fine Art, Limited, Chicago
	Susan Cummins Gallery, Mill Valley, California
	Sybaris Gallery, Royal Oak, Michigan
	Okun Gallery, Santa Fe
	Laumeier Sculpture Park, St. Louis
1995	Susan Cummins Gallery, Mill Valley, California
	Joanne Rapp Gallery, Scottsdale, Arizona

Selected Group Exhibitions:

1989	Arkansas Arts Center, Little Rock
	American Crafts Museum, New York (traveling)
1990	New Orleans Contemporary Arts
1991	Spoleto Festival U.S.A., Charleston, South Carolina
1992	Bellevue Art Museum, Washington
	Craft Alliance and Washington University Gallery of Art, St. Louis, Missouri
1993	Taft Museum, Cincinnati, Ohio
	Hokkaido Museum of Modern Art, Sapporo, Japan
1994	Cleveland Center for Contemporary Art, Ohio
1995	Bronx Museum of the Arts, New York

Selected Performances:

1988	*Women of Substance,* Edinburgh Festival, Scotland
1989	*Generic Interference/Genetic Engineering,* University of Maryland, Catonsville
1990	*Honey Chil'Milk,* Maryland Art Place, Baltimore
1993	*Generic Interference/Genetic Engineering,* Diverse Works, Houston
1994	*The Body Politic: Creative Time,* Cooper Union, New York

Collections:

Baltimore Museum of Art; Detroit Institute of Arts; Kruithuis Museum, Hertogenbosch, Netherlands; Mint Museum, Winston-Salem, North Carolina; Pennsylvania Convention Center Authority, Philadelphia; Philbrook Museum of Art, Tulsa, Oklahoma; Spirit Square Center for the Arts, Charlotte, North Carolina.

Publications:

By SCOTT: Articles—"Carrying On," in *Spirit, Space and Survival: African American Women in (White) Academe* edited by Joy

James and Ruth Farmer, New York and London, Routledge, 1993; "The Fleck," in *New Breezes of 1994: An Anthology of African American Literary Voices* edited by Alma Robertson, Baltimore, New Breezes, Inc., 1994.

On SCOTT: Books—*Joyce Scott: I-con-nobody/i-con-o-graphy,* exhibition catalog by Terrie Sultan, Washington, D.C., Corcoran Gallery of Art, 1991; *Crossing Over/Changing Places,* exhibition catalog by Jane M. Farmer, Washington, D.C., United States Information Agency, 1992. **Articles**—"Portfolio," in *American Craft,* 47, December/January 1988, pp. 56-57; review (Textile Arts Center, Chicago) by Diane Douglas, in *New Art Examiner,* 15, Summer 1988, pp. 42-43; "Joyce Scott: Beaded Jewelry and Small Sculpture" by Roberta Floden, in *Metalsmith,* 10, Summer 1990, p. 45; "Joyce Scott, I-con no body/I-con-o-graphy" by Barbara Hamaker, in *Ornament,* 15, Winter 1991, p. 33; "Joyce Scott: Migrant Worker for the Arts" by Karen Searle, in *Ornament,* 15, Summer 1992, pp. 46-51 (illustrated). **Video**—*The Legacy of Elizabeth and Joyce Scott* directed by Rebecca Crumlish, Osiris Productions, Washington, D.C., 1990.

*   *   *

In the family of Joyce J. Scott, there are renowned artists and artisans. Her mother, Elizabeth Scott, is a quilt maker; her maternal grandfather was a blacksmith, who made Afro-Carolinian sweetgrass baskets; and her paternal grandfather carved and decorated canoes. Both grandmothers were quilt makers. In the multifaceted art of Joyce J. Scott, these creative traditions have merged and been transformed. Scott is a multitalented artist, who makes room-size installations, dazzling jewelry, spectacular quilts, unique sculpture, and beaded work. She is a performance artist, known for such presentations as *The Body Politic, Genetic Interference/Genetic Engineering, Honey Chil' Milk, Women of Substance,* and *Bite and Smile.* Along with Kay Lawal in 1982, she cofounded *Thunder Thigh Revue,* a multimedia performance piece that interrogates the location of the full-bodied, ample black woman and the pain and passion she feels in being an outsider or the "other" in this society. Her innumerable lecture presentations, the workshops she has conducted, and her many residencies as an artist have been very impressive. She has a national and international reputation.

Born in Baltimore, Maryland, on 15 November 1948, Scott probably received her first art training from grandmothers, grandfathers, and her mother. Later she attended the Maryland Institute's College of Art and received her B.F.A. in 1970. She received her M.F.A. in crafts from the Instituto Allende in San Miguel Allende, Guanajuato, Mexico, in 1971. She conducted further study at the Haystack Mountain School of Crafts in Deer Isle, Maine, in 1976.

As a result of her extensive travel and study in international institutions, her art has a very cosmopolitan quality as observed in the 1995 installation *Images Concealed* at the Walter/McBean Gallery at the San Francisco Art Institute. Made of aluminum foil, beads, glass rice, coal, wire, monofilament, and thread, the installation measures 18' 6" x 54' 6" x 40'. Her knowledge of African, Mexican, Caribbean, Native American, and African American traditions is revealed in this powerful, overwhelming tour de force.

Scott can also create seemingly delicate pieces of glass beadwork, which she designs so that they cannot be seen from a distance.

Nevertheless, these apparently precious pieces are deceptive and chilling. They actually carry the same powerful, awesome quality as her magnificent room-size installations. Some of her smallest and most delicate pieces have a paradoxical quality in that they are at once violent and passionate, dealing with hard-hitting, problematic issues such as race, gender, religion, ethnicity, sexual orientation, the physical body, the erotic, racism, and sexism.

Jar Woman #4 (1995 beadwork, mixed media) is an amalgam of Scott's ancestry, heritage, training, and travels. Loaded down with amulets and relics, Scott's work is at once elegant and macabre, winsome and frightening. In her own inimitable way, she draws you close to *Jar Woman #4* and compels you to look at this exquisitely detailed, disarmingly beautiful image.

Scott also creates images in blown glass. Although it is not a medium that African American women often utilize, Scott enjoys the medium because it is translucent and because it pushes her to the limits of her technical skill and knowledge. *P-Melon #1* (1995) is a recent glass work.

—Jontyle Theresa Robinson

SCOTT, William Edouard
American painter, illustrator, and muralist

Born: Indianapolis, Indiana, 11 March 1884. **Education:** Art Institute of Chicago, 1904-09; Julian Academy, Paris; Colarossi Academy, Paris. **Career:** Studied under Henry O. Tanner in Paris. **Awards:** First prize, Indiana State Fair, 1914; Harmon Gold Medal, Harmon Foundation, 1927; Rosenwald Foundation Fellowship, 1931; Jesse Binga Prize, 1931; Municipal Art League traveling scholarship; Frederick Manus Brand Prize, Art Institute of Chicago (twice). Legion of Honor, Government of Haiti. **Died:** 1964.

Exhibitions:

American Negro Exposition, Chicago (1940); Art Institute of Chicago (1932); Autumn Salon, Paris; Harmon Foundation (1928, 1933); Harmon College Traveling Art Exhibit (1934-35); Howard University, Washington, D.C. (1945); Johannesburg, South Africa; Los Angeles Museum; New Jersey State Museum, Trenton (1935); Port-au-Prince, Haiti (solo, 1931); James A. Porter Gallery (1970); Royal Academy, London (1912); Salon de Beaux Arts Toquet; Salon la Tourquet; San Diego Museum; Smithsonian Institution, Washington, D.C.; South Side Community Art Center, Chicago (1941); Texas Centennial (1936).

Collections:

135th Street YMCA, New York; Anthony Hotel, Ft. Wayne, Indiana; Bethesda Baptist Church, Chicago; Betsy Ross Junior High School, Chicago; Binga State Bank, Chicago; City Hospital, Indianapolis, Indiana; Court House, Ft. Wayne, Indiana; Court House, Lafayette, Indiana; Davis Square, Chicago; First Presbyterian Church, Chicago; Government of Argentina; Herron Art Institute, Indianapolis, Indiana; Illinois State House; John Shoop School, Chicago; lobby, *Chicago Defender*; Metropolitan Community Center, Chicago; Municipal Tuberculosis Sanitarium, Chicago; National

Archives, Washington, D.C.; Paris Salon; Pilgrim Baptist Church, Chicago (murals); Port-au-Prince, Haiti; Royal Academy, London; Schomburg Center, New York; schools in Institute, West Virginia, and Charlestown, West Virginia (murals); South Park M.E. Church, Chicago; Stanford Fieldhouse, Chicago; Truly Park, Chicago; YMCA Indianapolis, Indiana.

Publications:

On SCOTT: Articles—"Art," in *Crisis,* 1, February 1911, p. 10; "Music and Art," in *Crisis,* 5, February 1913, pp. 169-70; "William Edouard Scott" by Francis C. Holbrook, in *Southern Workman,* February 1924, pp. 72-75.

*　　*　　*

When William Edouard Scott graduated from the Art Institute of Chicago in 1909, he received an award to study in France. Notwithstanding the skills he acquired in French art schools from 1910 to 1913, it was the impressionistic style of his mentor, Henry O. Tanner, that became apparent in his work during this period. Scott gained recognition for a 1912 painting, *La Pauvre Voisine,* which was accepted by the Salon in Paris. Acceptance at this major exhibition was important, for Scott was only the second black to be so recognized, his teacher Tanner having been the first. This particular work by Scott was well reviewed in French newspapers and was purchased by the government of Argentina for six hundred francs.

Scott, who had been born in Indianapolis, Indiana, held an exhibition at the studio of his high school art teacher, Otto Stark, in November 1912. A painting from the exhibition was purchased by a group of Indianapolis blacks, who donated the work, *Rainy Night, Etaples,* to the Herron Art Institute. The painting, done in the style of impressionism, was the first piece of work by a black to become part of the institute's collection. Scott's success continued in Europe when, in 1913, a painting entitled *La Misere* was awarded the Tanqueray Prize of 125 francs. The Salon at Paris-Plage also included paintings by Tanner, the first time two African American artists had appeared in a major European exhibition.

In 1915 Scott spent several months in Tuskegee, Alabama, studying and documenting the everyday activities of blacks in the South. His hope was to effect a change of attitude within the American artistic community, which continued to portray blacks in stereotyped images.

While at the Art Institute of Chicago, Scott developed a reputation as a muralist who understood the intricacies of painting large, complex panoramic scenes. He used a classic triangular composition for one of his first murals, *Commerce,* done at Lane Technical High School in Chicago in 1909. In 1915 he was the only black selected from among outstanding Indiana artists to paint a number of murals at the Indianapolis City Hospital. The majority of his murals there were religious in subject matter. In 1927 Scott was awarded a special medal by the Harmon Foundation for his mural paintings.

In preparation for the *American Negroes Exposition: Celebrating 75 Years of Negro Achievement,* which opened in Chicago on July 4, 1940, and closed on September 7, Scott painted sixteen hours a day for three months to create twenty-four murals. Reflecting the shift in art during the Great Depression to social realism, he told stories of black achievement in the murals. He was one of seven artists selected in a 1943 national competition to produce murals

William Edouard Scott: *Blind Sister Mary.* Photo by Manu Sassoonian; courtesy of the Schomburg Center for Research in Black Culture.

for the Recorder of Deeds Building in Washington D.C. The seven murals done there depicted the positive contributions blacks had made to the United States, with the title of Scott's mural being *Frederick Douglass Appealing to President Lincoln and His Cabinet to Enlist Negro Soldiers in the Civil War.*

In 1931 Scott took advantage of a Julius Rosenwald fellowship to document everyday life in Haiti. Departing from the cool palette of impressionistic blues to use warm yellows, reds, and browns, Scott produced more than 140 works of art in less than a year, the majority having as their subject the working people of Haiti. He also taught classes to young Haitian artists, encouraging them to use indigenous subject matter and styles rather than imitating French academic painting. Scott thus influenced the perspective of many artists there, and the Haitian government bestowed upon him membership in the Order of Merit for his contributions.

Despite having both legs amputated in the mid-1950s because of diabetes, Scott continued to teach and paint until his death in the 1960s. He had no job outside art and taught only occasionally, existing on commissions and the sales of his works, an achievement that was unusual for a black during the period from 1910 to 1960. What was important for Scott was to be assured that his own people had a voice and an audience, which he helped create.

—William E. Taylor

SEARLES, Charles

American sculptor and painter

Born: Philadelphia, 11 July 1937. **Education:** Pennsylvania Academy of Fine Arts, 1968-72, B.A. 1972; University of Pennsylvania, 1973. **Family:** Married 1) Mary McDaniels in 1957 (divorced 1972), two daughters and one son; 2) Kathleen Spicer in 1986. **Career:** Instructor, Ile-Ife Cultural Center, Philadelphia, 1970-73, Philadelphia Museum of Art, 1971-73, Bloomfield College, New Jersey, 1992, University of the Arts, Philadelphia, 1973-94. Since 1995, instructor, Pratt Institute, New York. Traveled in Nigeria, 1972, 1977, Haiti, 1974, Ghana, Morocco, 1972. Member of Recherché (African American artist group in Philadelphia). **Awards:** Cresson Memorial Traveling Scholarship, Pennsylvania Academy of Fine Arts, 1971; Ware Memorial Traveling Scholarship, Pennsylvania Academy of Fine Arts, 1972; certificate of recognition, Lagos, Nigeria, 1977; National Endowment for the Arts Fellowship, 1979; Creative Artists Project Service (CAPS, New York), 1981. **Agent:** June Kelly Gallery, 591 Broadway, New York, New York 10012, U.S.A.; Sande Webster Gallery, Philadelphia, Pennsylvania, U.S.A. **Address:** 640 Broadway #3W, New York, New York 10012, U.S.A.

Individual Exhibitions:

1973	Philadelphia Museum of Art
1974	Howard University, Washington, D.C.
1984	Sande Webster Gallery, Philadelphia
	Sande Webster Gallery, Philadelphia
1978	Newman Gallery, Philadelphia
1981	Landmark Gallery, New York
1982	Pennsylvania Academy of Fine Arts, Philadelphia
1983	Sande Webster Gallery, Philadelphia
1986	Sande Webster Gallery, Philadelphia
1988	Sande Webster Gallery, Philadelphia
1989	Montclair Art Museum, Montclair, New Jersey
1992	June Kelly Gallery, New York
	Sande Webster Gallery, Philadelphia
1993	Malcolm Brown Gallery, Shaker Heights, Ohio
1994	Sande Webster Gallery, Philadelphia

Selected Group Exhibitions:

1981	Arnot Art Museum, Elmira, New York
1986	Charlottesborg Museum, Denmark
1988	Sande Webster Gallery, Philadelphia

Charles Searles, 1990.

1990   Sande Webster Gallery, Philadelphia
        High Museum of Art, Atlanta, Georgia
1991   Richmond Museum of Fine Art, Virginia
        Art Alliance, Philadelphia
1992   Sande Webster Gallery, Philadelphia
        Ellipse Arts Center, Arlington, Virginia
1993   Berneice Steinbaum Gallery, New York
        Drawing Center, New York
1994   State Museum of Pennsylvania, Harrisburg
1995   Museum of American Art, Washington, D.C.

Collections:

Alvin Ailey American Dance Company, New York; Dallas Museum of Art; Federal Railroad Administration; Howard University, Washington, D.C.; Montclair Art Museum, New Jersey; Museum of the National Center of Afro-American Artists, Boston; National Museum of American Art, Washington, D.C.; New York State Office Building; Philadelphia Museum of Art.

*   *   *

Charles Searles began as a painter. In 1978, however, after moving to New York City, he came to devote his energies completely to sculpture, although he paints the surfaces of his forms in bright colors and exciting patterns. Perhaps the combination of color and constructed forms is natural for Searles, for his father remodeled homes and his mother was very conscious of color in her approach to decoration and the home. Searles remembers always making things, even as a child, and he carved masklike forms before becoming a painter. It took a while, however, before his sculptural tendencies became the dominant force in his art.

Searles remembers his earliest artistic inspiration and influence to have been African sculpture, and his first paintings were inspired by the works of Jacob Lawrence. In Philadelphia during the 1960s Searles worked at the Ile-Ife Cultural Center, and came to know James Phillips, Barkley Hendricks, Ed Sorrells, and other Philadelphia artists. From 1969 to 1975 his house became a meeting place for a number of black artists traveling or returning to Philadelphia, including Phillips, Adger Cowans, Frank Smith, Alfred Smith, James Dupree, and Nelson Stevens.

Searles studied at the Pennsylvania Academy of the Fine Arts, and while there, he won a fellowship that he used in 1972 to visit Ghana, Nigeria, and Morocco. From this trip came the inspiration, subjects, and colors found in many of his paintings of the period, including *Filas for Sale* (1972) and the series "Dancers" (1975). These works combined Searles's interest in color, pattern, mask forms, and dance movement. In the late 1960s he had lost a daughter, and his grief and pain led to introspection and a commitment to reach for positive directions in his work. Abandoning the political subjects and the civil rights frame of earlier work, he looked to Africa for positive ideas and connections, which became one of the motivations for his trip there. Five years later Searles participated in Festac in Nigeria, another major event affecting him and his work.

African experiences and ideas influenced Searles's work and awakened certain sensibilities within him, but once the process was complete, he no longer looked to Africa for subjects and ideas. The colors, patterns, and sensibilities of his work express his place in the world as a person of African descent, but he gives his creative impulse free reign so that the cultural resonances that occur do so because of his being rather than through conscious effort. He also

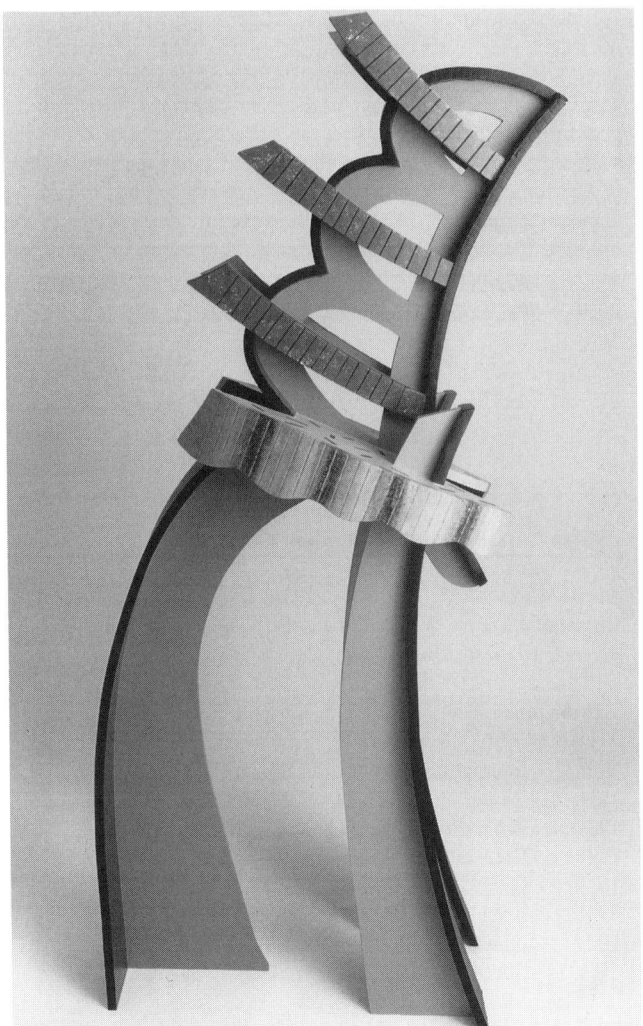

Charles Searles: *Strutting, 1996.*

feels free to draw ideas and inspiration from non-Western cultures around the world.

From the beginning Searles's sculptural forms and spaces have been extracted from his paintings. The imagery in the paintings, however, has been abstracted into curvilinear elements with rhythmic relationships and syncopated patterns. Some works, like *Strutting* (1996), seem to approximate the movements and gestures of dance, and others, such as *Caribbean Sun* (1996) and *Forest Dance* (1994), appear to intersect fragments of tropical landscapes and flowing movement. Everywhere in his work—whether it is freestanding, intersects with the floor and wall, or is mounted on the wall—there are rhythmic elements that give a musical pulse.

Searles has played percussion instruments for many years, and he says that his work often concerns itself with rhythm, the swing and sway of things, and is sometimes organized to reflect a four-beat or triple phrase. He listens to music throughout the process of creating art, and when a work is completed, he plays the drums in front of it in its honor. He listens to world music, including that of the Pygmies of Central Africa and that of East Africa, Morocco, Cuba, and Brazil. The patterns, colors, and forms found in Searles's sculpture appear to bring together both common and unique characteristics from world music.

Searles's sculptures begin in sketchbooks, and with their many open areas they retain calligraphic linear qualities when completed. They are cut out with a jigsaw and then worked and constructed before being painted. When he completes them, Searles applies a coat of polyurethane to protect the surface. Several of his earlier sculptures use birdlike forms with a sense of wings and flight (*Flight of My Fathers,* 1980) or have biomorphic suggestions of animals (*Fantasy Animal,* 1978). Always, however, there are rhythms, colors, and patterns. Always there is the suggestion of dance and spatial freedom, and often there are surprising forms and a playful, positive character to the work.

—Michael D. Harris

SEBREE, Charles

American painter and illustrator

Born: Madisonville, Kentucky, 1914. **Education:** Art Institute of Chicago. **Career:** Worked in easel division, Illinois Federal Art Project, 1936-38. **Died:** 27 September 1985.

Exhibitions:

1935	International Watercolor Society
1936	Katherine Kuh Gallery, Chicago
1937	Federal Art Project Gallery, Chicago
1938	Breckenridge Gallery
1939	Grace Horne Gallery, Boston
1940	*American Negro Exposition,* Chicago
1941	Howard University, Washington, D.C.
	South Side Community Art Center, Chicago
	McMillen Galleries, New York
1943	Institute of Modern Art, Boston
1945	South Side Community Art Center, Chicago
1949	Roko Gallery, New York
1967	City College of New York
1970	James A. Porter Gallery

Collections:

Atlanta University-Countee Cullen Collection; McBride Collection, Chicago; National Archives, Washington, D.C.; Renaissance Society Collection; Schomburg Center, New York; Thornton Wilder Collection; University of Chicago.

Publications:

By SEBREE: Book—*Mrs. Patterson* (or *Dry August* , play, opened New York 1954).

On SEBREE: Book—*Exhibition of Book Illustrations by Jacob Lawrence, Charles Sebree, Vernon Winslow,* exhibition catalog, Chicago, South Side Community Art Center, 1941.

*   *   *

Though formally trained as an artist, Charles Sebree lists his uncle, John Robinson, as one of his early artistic influences. Robinson drew cartoons and stick figures in his spare time, and Sebree characterizes this activity as the inspiration for his interest in art. Once Sebree's family moved to Chicago, he had a much broader range of exposure to art but much of the cartoonlike qualities of "doodling" remained in his work.

Sebree studied at the Art Institute of Chicago and at the Chicago School of Design. (Formerly the German Bauhaus School of Applied Arts, the Chicago School of Design was disbanded, renamed, and relocated to Chicago by Laslo Moholy-Nagy in 1937.) The primary Bauhaus influences in Sebree's work are those of the expressionists. Influences from The Blue Rider (Der Blaue Reiter) group, which incorporated abstract or naive painting techniques penetrated with intense color, can be seen in paintings such as *Village* and *Man in the Temple.* Influences from The Bridge (Die Bruke) group, which used a more representational yet still distorted style, often modeled after African sculptural forms, can be seen in paintings such as Sebree's *Blue Jacket.*

Charles Sebree has also been influenced by his many personal associations with artists from other mediums, particularly theater and literature. Among his many friends were such luminaries as Countee Cullen, Owen Dodson, Katherine Dunham, Langston Hughes, Eartha Kitt, and May Miller Sullivan. He has provided book and cover illustrations for his literary friends and has designed costumes and sets for the productions of his performance friends.

It is seemingly his aptitude as a cross-cultural/cross-medium artist that makes his paintings optimistic and immediately striking. "I'm still trying to probe into the mysteries of Byzantine and African art," he has said, "I think I've caught something in these works." His paintings are not solutions to mysteries, of course, but mysteries in their own right, intriguing compositions to be explored and appreciated by the next generation of artists and art lovers. His paintings are something like a wish for the future.

—Terry Bain

SEKOTO, Gerard

South African painter

Born: Botshabelo, Middelburg, Transvaal, 12 September 1913. **Education:** Botshabelo Training Institute, 1928-29; Diocesan Training College, Pietersburg, South Africa, 1930; Anglican Teachers' Training College, Pietersburg, 1933; Académie de la Grande Chaumiere, Paris, 1948. **Career:** Teacher, Khaiso Secondary School, near Pietersburg, South Africa, 1934-38. Freelance painter, Sophiatown, South Africa, District Six Cape Town, South Africa, and Eastwood in Pretoria, South Africa, 1939-45, Paris, 1945-49. Lived in Senegal, 1967-68. **Awards:** Prize (bible and five shillings) for school badge design, Botshabelo Training College, 1928; Second Prize, May Esther Bedord Competition, 1937; Poster Selection Award for Exhibition of South African Paintings, Drawings and Sculpture, Tate Gallery, London, 1948; Poster Selection Award for Second Congress of Negro Writers and Artists, Rome, 1958; Exhibition of African Art Prize, Nemours, France; diplome officiel, *XIX Prix International de Peinture de Deauville,* 1968.

Exhibitions:

1939	Gainsborough Gallery, Johannesburg, South Africa

Selborne Hall, Johannesburg, South Africa

Pretoria, South Africa (solo)

1940   Selborne Hall, South Africa Academy, Johannesburg, South Africa

1941   Duncan Hall, South Africa Academy, Johannesburg, South Africa

1945   Cape Town, South Africa

1948   Tate Gallery, London (traveling through 1949)

1949   Galerie Else-Clausen, Paris (solo)

1966   Salon d'Automne, Paris

1973   Galerie du Marais, Paris

1975   Atlantic Gallery, Burg Street, Cape Town, South Africa

1978   *Galerie Art Premier,* Paris France

1980   Maison de L'Afrique, Paris

1988   Cassirer Fine Arts, Johannesburg, South Africa

Collections:

South Africa National Gallery; National Art Gallery, South Africa; UNISA; University of Wits Galleries.

*   *   *

The Bantu artist Gerard Sekoto was trained at the Anglican Teachers' Training College in the Pietersburg area of South Africa, where he came into contact with art and chose to pursue art classes. He received encouragement from the Reverend Roger Castle, "Brother Roger," of Saint Peter's School in Rosettenville in Johannesburg. Brother Roger conducted art classes for Bantu students in his own room and is acknowledged to be the first to offer such instruction in the Johannesburg area at a time when art was not viewed as a suitable profession for the Bantu. Sekoto's work gained the attention of those conscious of art, making him the first Bantu to receive notice for developing skills in a European painting tradition. His paintings were viewed as colorful yet primitive, and he was seen as a self-taught artist.

Artists initially paint what they know, what is closest to them. Artists like Sekoto were denied access to other worlds and situations, and so they built up a reservoir of themes that they painted time and again. *Fruit-seller* (c.1939) suggests Sekoto's preference for the common scenes of everyday life in his township. His genre scenes of the township portrayed a peaceful village, not the harsh realities of life under apartheid. The poignant emotion he expressed for his people caught the eye of the powerful, and after one-man exhibitions in Pretoria and Johannesburg a patron arranged for him to travel to Paris in 1947 for study.

Although many expatriates then in Paris suffered from too little money, inadequate accommodations, and poor health, one thing they shared was a freedom to be artists and to explore European as well as other traditions. Like African American artists such as Albert Alexander Smith, who had been in Paris earlier, Sekoto joined the cabaret scene, playing the piano and guitar at nightclubs to supplement his income. He also frequented the bohemian area in Montparnasse. He became friends with a community of expatriates who enjoyed meeting in cafés and bars to discuss art. One friend and colleague was the African American abstract painter Herbert Gentry, who had come to Paris in 1946 and by 1949 was teaching at the Académie de la Chaumiere.

Sekoto continued to paint recollections of his home in South Africa and scenes of his adopted environment, exhibiting his works in both European and American cities. He had earlier been praised in his native South Africa for his "fearless [use of] color . . . unconventional viewpoint . . . and awkward handling of familiar forms that were refreshingly original and honest." One South African critic, however, now writing almost with a sense of betrayal, stated that "he was led to modify his individual style by adopting a number of conventions fashionable in Parisian painting but possibly less valid to his emotional needs. Aesthetically, he became a 'displaced' person, teetering between two disparate cultures." This view of Sekoto's work and art processes suggest that he would not have been allowed to grow as an artist in South Africa, that expectations for his development would have always been in the narrow frame of a self-taught township artist.

In France, however, Sekoto saw things differently, and his experiences and friendships with an international group of artists that included Europeans, African Americans, and South Americans changed his outlook on life and informed the themes and processes of his paintings. That he teetered between two cultures is questionable. Such a judgment was not made of Pablo Picasso or of other artists who chose the excitement of Paris and its freedoms instead of oppressive governments at home. Sekoto surely realized this and freely chose to remain in Paris.

—Lizzetta LeFalle-Collins

SHIBRAIN, Ahmad Mohammed

Sudanese painter

Born: Barbar, Sudan, 1931. **Education:** College of Fine and Applied Art, Khartoum, 1955; Central School of Art and Design, London 1957-60. **Career:** Lecturer, Department of Graphic Arts and Design, College of Fine and Applied Art, Khartoum, Sudan, 1956-70; chair, Department of Graphic Arts and Design, College of Fine and Applied Art, Khartoum, Sudan, 1970-75; dean, College of Fine and Applied Art, Khartoum, Sudan, 1975-80; director, National Council of Arts and Letters, 1983-90; deputy director, Minister of Culture and Information, 1990-91. Designer, Sudanese banknotes, stamps, murals and woven rugs.

*   *   *

Ahmad Mohammed Shibrain is a leading figure in modern Sudanese art who has turned extensively to Arabic calligraphy as the basis for his expression. Like other pioneering artists who formed what came to be known as the Khartoum school, Shibrain visualizes letterforms as living elements, and he has been attracted by the elegant shapes of the forms and their intricate weaving in space.

Arabic calligraphy has been used symbolically within the Khartoum School to emphasize the Arabic-Islamic aspects of Sudanese culture. This can be traced to the early days of the movement as a tradition pioneered by Osman Wagialla. Shibrain has taken the use of Arabic calligraphy a step further, however, with his extensive explorations of its aesthetic potential. His adventurous spirit has led to the evolution of a unique style.

Ahmad Mohammed Shibrain: *Untitled calligraphic formation,* 1986.

Shibrain graduated from the College of Fine and Applied Arts in Khartoum in 1955 and went on to study at the Central School of Art and Design in London between 1957 and 1960. Upon his return to the Sudan in 1960, Shibrain assumed several influential positions, including lecturer and chair of the department of graphic arts and design in the College of Fine and Applied Arts until 1975 and a dean in the same college from 1975 until his retirement in 1980. Throughout this long period of involvement in teaching in the Sudan, Shibrain came in contact with a whole generation of younger Sudanese artists who were influenced by his style.

Shibrain uses the potential of Arabic calligraphy within an Africanized Sudanese framework, and as he has often said about his work, it is a mixture of images, African-Arabic and Islamic. He uses other elements along with Arabic calligraphy as part of the overall design. In several of his paintings, for example, he includes traditional Islamic decorative motifs such as the rosette and crescent and floral-like arabesques. In his work Arabic letters gain their fully plastic aesthetic value. Individual characters are barely decipherable, and letters are shortened or elongated, compressed or expanded, to become part of a larger abstract composition. Shibrain's innovative use of calligraphy can be seen in *Calligraphic Abstraction,* a pen-and-ink work in which Arabic-like characters are arranged in a Kufic style on a plain background.

Although Shibrain's favorite technique is pen and ink, he has also experimented with oil painting, wood, and other media. He stresses a symbolic use of the colors seen in the Sudanese landscape. For him blue and bluish green are colors of the Blue Nile, and red and yellow or brown are those of the earth and of traditional Sudanese architecture.

Shibrain is also a designer and an interior decorator who has enjoyed commercial success and who has had several commissions for public works, including projects at the Jiddah airport in Saudi Arabia and at international hotels and company offices in the Sudan. His public commissions include calligraphic designs as their basic elements and are executed in low relief in wood with paints, mixed-media murals, and woven rugs. He has also designed several Sudanese banknotes and stamps.

In addition, Shibrain is a writer and a journalist who has made regular contributions to journals, magazines, and newspapers. Several of his essays are valued for their theoretical contributions to the dialogue on Sudanese art and culture. He has participated in a number of one-man exhibitions and in more than a dozen group exhibitions in the Sudan and other countries, including Egypt, Nigeria, the United States, Britain, and Germany. His works are included in several private and public collections in the Sudan and elsewhere.

—Salah Hassan

SIHLALI, Durant

South African painter and sculptor

Born: Germiston, 1935. **Education:** Art Centre, Moroka, 1953-53; Polly Street Art Centre, 1953-58; studied with Sdoya and Goldblatt, 1955-58; Villason Art School, Nice, France, 1986. **Career:** Muralist for businesses and private individuals, c.1950-60; jewelry designer, 1956-70; teacher, FUBA Art Center, Johannesburg, 1978-83. Beginning 1983 head of fine arts, FUBA. Participant, Thupelo workshops. **Awards:** First Prize, School Art Competition, Queenstown, South Africa, 1947; First Prize in painting, Mariannhill Institute, 1978; Second Prize in sculpture, *UZ African Arts Festival,* 1982; First Prize in graphics, *UZ African Arts Festival,* 1983; French Government Scholarship, 1986.

Individual Exhibitions:

1966	Lidchi Art Gallery, Johannesburg
1967	Adler Fielding Galleries, Johannesburg
1969	Gallery Michelangelo, Johannesburg
1974	Triad Gallery, Johannesburg
1975	Elizabeth Art Gallery, Johannesburg
1976	Elizabeth Art Gallery, Johannesburg
1977	Pieter Wenning Gallery, Johannesburg
1978	Everard Read Gallery, Johannesburg
1987	FUBA Art Center, Johannesburg

Selected Group Exhibitions:

1972	Gallery 101
1974	National Arts Society, Johannesburg
1979	Gallery 21, Nuremberg, West Germany
	Renaissance II, SAAA, Johannesburg
1982	National Museum and Art Gallery, Gaborone, Botswana
1983	Milner Park, Johannesburg
1985	FUBA Art Center, Johannesburg
1986	Gallery 21

Collections:

AFRICANA; AMCOL, Witbank; FUBA Art Center, Johannesburg; Kagiso Hospital, Krugersdorp; National Museum and Art Gallery, Gaborone, Botswana.

*　　*　　*

The South African painter Durant Sihlali began his formal training in art in 1950 at the Chiawelo Art Center in Moroka and later studied at the Polly Street Art Center. During this time he was also painting murals in businesses and private homes. By 1965 he had begun designing jewelry and selling it to shops in South Africa and abroad to support himself, but in 1970 he began a full-time career as a painter. Most of his paintings are in watercolor or ink wash and reflect his training at the Polly Street Art Center. His work has been done in what is known as "township style," in which black South African artists specialize in recording specific sites in the townships in which they paint.

The Polly Street Art Center used European and American techniques in art education, following the model that had been successful in other African and Caribbean nations. This was the type of training that had particular success in the development of Haitian naive painting, for example. Among other things the students were taught still life techniques using the traditional European media, including charcoal, graphite, watercolor, and oil paint. The intent of the workshops was to develop a marketable form of art in which the artists could establish professional careers. The content of the compositions and their marketability to white patrons were, therefore, of great concern. Nonetheless, the director of the Polly Street Art Center, Cecil Skotnes, discouraged students from pursuing Eurocentric themes. In his attempt to refrain from altering the aesthetic sensibilities the students brought to the center, Skotnes encouraged them to paint the environments of their own townships and the everyday lives of their people.

Sihlali's work stands out because, unlike many other township painters, he did not copy from existing paintings or photographs. He is known to visit places so that he can paint on-site. In addition to painting township scenes, he also has painted vignettes showing interior views of households, as in *Round 7 Payneville* (n.d.). These works give a sense not only of the hardships of life but also of its simple pleasures. In doing so, he has hoped to capture a changing South Africa as it has moved closer to a new order and to greater freedom for its black and colored populations.

In 1978 Sihlali began teaching at the newly founded FUBA Art Center in Johannesburg. This was one of the community-based art centers in South Africa that were established in the 1970s and 1980s to offer alternative educational programs, as well as a place for people to voice their resistance to apartheid and to vent other concerns. In 1983 Sihlali was appointed as the head of the fine arts section at FUBA, but he continued to pursue his own training in visual arts through workshops in South Africa and abroad. In 1995 he was one of the South African artists featured in the first Johannesburg International Biennale.

—Lizzetta LeFalle-Collins

SILLS, Thomas Albert
American painter

Born: Castalia, North Carolina, 20 August 1914. **Family:** Married Jeanne Reynal. **Career:** Laborer. **Award:** William and Norma Copley Foundation Award, 1957. **Address:** 240 West Eleventh Street, New York, New York 10014, U.S.A.

Selected Exhibitions:

1955	Betty Parsons Gallery, New York (solo)
	Stable Gallery, New York
1956	New School for Social Research
	Camino Gallery, New York
1957	Betty Parsons Gallery, New York (solo)
1959	Betty Parsons Gallery, New York (solo)
	Whitney Museum, New York
1961	Betty Parsons Gallery, New York (solo)
1962	Paul Kantor Gallery, Los Angeles
1964	Bodley Gallery, New York
	Fairleigh-Dickinson University
1967	Bodley Gallery, New York
	Creighton University, Omaha, Nebraska
1968	Wilson College Chambersberg, Pennsylvania
	Minneapolis Institute of Art
1969	Brooklyn College, New York
	Museum of Modern Art, New York
	Philadelphia Civic Center Museum
	Mount Holyoke College, South Hadley, Massachusetts
	Bodley Gallery, New York
	Ruder and Finn Fine Arts, New York
1970	Boston Museum of Fine Arts
1972	Bodley Gallery, New York

Collections:

Bodley Gallery, New York; Finch College Museum, New York; Fisk University, Nashville; Fordham University, New York; Hofstra University, New York; Krannert Art Museum, University of Illinois; Los Angeles County Museum; Museum of Modern Art, New York; Norfolk Museum of Arts and Sciences, Virginia; Phoenix Art Museum, Arizona; Rockefeller University, New York Rose Museum, Brandeis University, Waltham, Massachusetts; San Francisco Museum; Sheldon Memorial Gallery, Lincoln, Nebraska; Syracuse University Museum, New York; Whitney Museum of American Art, New York; Williams College Museum, Williamstown, Massachusetts.

Publications:

On SILLS: Articles—"Reviews and Previews—Thomas Sills" by Gerrit Henry, in *Art News,* 69, March 1970; "Now I'm Boss" by Jay Jacobs, in *Art Gallery,* April 1970; "The Rupture" by Frank Bowling, in *Arts,* Summer 1970; "Exhibition at the Betty Parsons Gallery," in *Pictures on Exhibit,* 30 (5); "The Flowering of Thomas Sills" by Lawrence Campbell, in *Art News,* March 1972.

*　　*　　*

From about 1952 to 1971 the painter Thomas Sills, who had no formal education, maintained an active career showing his abstract works in major New York City galleries and in national exhibitions. He developed a style of painting that reflected the abstract expressionist movement of the mid-1940s and the 1950s. His gestural style was developed from a series of brushless techniques arrived at through experimentation with various materials.

Sills did not begin painting until relatively late in life, when he was in his midthirties, after he had married Jeanne Reynal, a wealthy collector and artist who worked in mosaics. Very little is known about Sills's early experience. It can be supposed, however, that his contact with the art in Reynal's collection—which included paintings by Arshile Gorky, Jackson Pollock, Matta Magritte, Barnett Newman, Elaine de Kooning, Willem de Kooning, Ad Reinhardt, Yves Tanquy, and Mark Rothko and sculpture by David Hare, Alberto Giacometti, and Isamu Noguchi—had a significant impact on Sills's aesthetic. He not only had the benefit of living with the works of these artists, who were critical to the evolution of abstract expressionism, but he also had direct contact with Gorky, Pollock, Newman, and Willem de Kooning, who greatly encouraged his efforts in painting.

The earliest works Sills created were in magnesite, a cement substance used by Reynal in her mosaics. He later worked in oils to create imagery that played against the grain of wood panels or that flowed in flat asymmetrical forms of color when applied to the surface of canvas with rags. Sills's aesthetic was grounded in his passion for color and its relationship to form. He developed a highly sophisticated sense of artistry that was often incorrectly labeled as "folk" abstraction. His persistent evasiveness to comment on his work was revealed in a 1972 interview in *ArtNews:* "I paint something, but I don't know what I'm painting. What comes out, comes out."

Sills's career otherwise remains an enigma. Given his resistance to discuss his work, one can only say that he remains a part of the abstract expressionist movement and most probably the only African American to have any direct contact or relationship with those artists who represented the prominent aesthetic voice of the era.

—Leslie King-Hammond

SIMMONS, Gary
American sculptor

Born: New York, 14 April 1964. **Education:** School of Visual Arts, New York, B.F.A. 1988; California Institute of the Arts, Valencia, California, M.F.A. 1990. **Awards:** National Endowment for the Arts grant, 1990; Penny McCall Foundation grant, 1991. **Agent:** Metro Pictures, 150 Greene Street, New York, New York 10012, U.S.A.

Individual Exhibitions:

1989   Roy Boyd Gallery, Santa Monica, California
1990   White Columns, New York
1991   Roy Boyd Gallery, Santa Monica, California
        Simon Watson Gallery, New York
1992   Roy Boyd Gallery, Santa Monica, California
        Jason Rubell Gallery, Miami

The Garden of Hate: Gary Simmons, Whitney Museum
        at Philip Morris, New York
1993   Galerie Philippa Rizzo, Paris
        Metro Pictures, New York
1994   *Urban Paradise: Gardens in the City,* Paine Webber Art
        Gallery, New York
        Residence Secondaire, Paris
        Hirshhorn Museum and Sculpture Garden, Washington,
        D.C.
1995   Metro Pictures, New York

Selected Group Exhibitions:

1990   Kryoier/Landau Contemporary Art, Santa Monica, California
        New Museum of Contemporary Art at Marine Midland
        Bank, New York
        Espace de Dieu, Paris
        Simon Watson Gallery, New York
1991   *Interrogating Identity: The Question of Black Art,* Grey
        Art Gallery, New York (traveling)
        Meyers/Bloom Gallery, Santa Monica, California
1992   Tory Shafrazi Gallery, New York
1994   Randolph Street Gallery, Chicago
        Whitney Museum of American Art, New York
1995   Fabric Workshop/Museum, Philadelphia

Collections:

Hirshhorn Museum and Sculpture Garden, Washington, D.C.; Portland Art Museum, Oregon; Whitney Museum of American Art, New York.

Publications:

On SIMMONS: Book—*Dissent, Difference, and the Body Politic,* exhibition catalog, Oregon, Portland Art Museum, 1993. **Articles**—"Gary Simmons" by Michael Anderson, in *Art Issues,* March/April, 1990, p. 23; "Gary Simmons" by Colin Gardner, in *Artforum,* March 1990; "Articulating Subjectivity" by Doug Ischer, in *Artweek,* 18 January 1990; "Interrogating Identity" by Roberta Smith, in *New York Times,* 17 March 1991; "The Subversive Stitch" by Roberta Smith, in *New York Times,* 12 July 1991; "Interrogating Identity" by Lois Nesbitt, in *Artforum,* Summer 1991; "Gary Simmons" by Yazmin Ramirez, in *Art in America,* December 1992, p. 116; "Gary Simmons" by Gene Ray, in *Flash Art,* January/February 1993, p. 94; "Art with an Attitude" by A. Wallach, in *New York Newsday,* 5 March 1993, pp. 52-53; "A Showcase for Political Correctness" by Deborah Solomon, in *Wall Street Journal,* March 1993, p. A7; "Gary Simmons, Metro Pictures" by Holland Cotter, in *New York Times,* 8 October 1993, p. C30; "Gary Simmons at Metro Pictures" by Jen Avgikos, in *Artforum,* 32(5), January 1994 (illustrated); "Black Like Whom?" by Peter Plagens and Ellis Cose, in *Newsweek,* 14 November 1994, pp. 64-67; "Arrested Childhood" by Bonnie Clearwater, in *Art Press,* December 1994, pp. 33-40; "Learning from Black Male" by Linda Nochlin, in *Art in America,* March 1995, pp. 86-91; "Gary Simmons: Erazures" by George Howell, in *Art Papers,* March/April 1995, pp. 39-40.

*   *   *

Gary Simmons's early works include autobiographical data and delve into racism and the affirmation of identity. Nonetheless, he clings to concepts of postconceptualism and has a many-sided aesthetic. He shifts from imagery alluding to black popular culture and racial subjects to landscapes and aerodynamically executed drawings of stars. He conveys his subject matter overtly and covertly with many formalist and innovative techniques.

Simmons does not want to be considered a black artist but rather an artist who draws on multiple sources for his work. Nonetheless, his entrance into the mainstream art scene was the result of work heavily laden with autobiographical references to race and identity. He has also functioned as a recorder of popular culture and as an informant of the realities of being black. His installations of advertising logos, sports paraphernalia, and aspects of hip-hop culture allude to his identification with the complexities of existence in the urban United States.

For example, Simmons's boxing ring work, presented in the Whitney Museum of American Art's *Black Male* show in 1993, holds a multiplicity of meanings depending on the viewer. The installation was constructed with diagrams of dance steps etched in black on the floor. According to one critic Simmons had rendered vestiges of personal memory, and the dance floor painting was a "method of conveying previous movements of meaning in our hypercommodified culture." It may be, however, that Simmons was broaching paradoxes of existence as a black male by using popular forms as symbols of that struggle. The writer Ishmael Reed has said that the careers of black boxers are analogous to the careers of black males: "Every day is like being in the gym, sparring with impersonal opponents as one faces the rudeness and hostility that a Black male must confront in the United States, where he is the object of fear and fascination." Simmons may have been embracing Reed's radical view, or he may merely have been referring to the dominance blacks have achieved in the areas of sports and entertainment. On the other hand, he may have intended all of these references to converge to summarize both the travails and the triumphs experienced by blacks over the generations.

Simmons's classroom installations have autobiographical roots. A work in a 1991 exhibition in Santa Monica, California, originally planned as a static environment mocking schoolroom education, became an active and highly charged installation. A cockatoo, which was supposed to perch on a podium in a classroom complete with chalkboard and clock, never sat still. It squawked incessantly, flew around the gallery, and left its droppings everywhere. The autobiographical element in the work, however, was ironic. Simmons's father had relocated the family from New York City in order to provide his offspring with a better education. For Simmons, however, the new school was less than idyllic, for he was acutely aware of being different and he found it difficult to conform to the stifling restrictions of suburbia. It was clear that his comfort zone existed within the context of a culturally rich, albeit tumultuous, urban environment. His representation of the classroom was thus inextricably linked both to American pedagogy and to the sting of prejudice he himself felt. The classroom is a microcosm of social values.

The "Erasure Drawing" series, prompted by Simmons's interest in the education of children, is based on his study of cartoons. Early on in his study Simmons realized that his analysis of the images and characters in cartoons was starkly different from that of whites. He has created a body of work derived from stereotypical depictions of blacks as jiving crows with pop-eyed, big-lipped facial expressions. His drawings with white and colored chalk are executed di-

rectly on the wall. Although he has eliminated the chalkboard, he approximates its surface through the application of slate paint. Through the process of erasing he represents the fragmentation in the construction of histories in which information is deleted. Here Simmons obscures political overtones yet gives testimony to the racial stereotyping that permeates all levels of American popular entertainment.

Influenced by the mark-making systems of Cy Tombly and the conceptualists, especially Joseph Beuys, Simmons has built his own visual vocabulary. It resembles notes or the rough draft of a script yet to be finished, however.

—A. M. Weaver

SIMMS, Carroll (Harris)
American sculptor, painter, jewelry designer, and ceramist

Born: Bald Knob, Arkansas, 29 April 1924. **Education:** Hampton Institute, Hampton, Virginia, 1944-45; University of Toledo, Ohio, 1946-47; Toledo Museum Art School, 1945-48; Cranbrook Academy of Art, Bloomfield Hills, Michigan, 1948-50, B.F.A. 1950; Wayne State University, Detroit, 1949-50; Slade Art School, University College, London, 1954-56; Royal College of Art, London, 1955; British Museum, London, 1955-56; Central School of Arts and Crafts, London, 1955-56; Morris Singer Bronze Art Foundry, London, 1955-56; Cranbrook Academy of Art, Bloomfield Hills, 1959-60, M.F.A. 1960; Swedish Institute, Stockholm, 1964; private study with Jeremy Leach, London, 1964; Michigan Institute of African Studies, University of Ibadan, Nigeria, University of Ife, Ile-Ife, 1968-69; Ife Museum, Ile-Ife, Nigeria, Bennin Museum, Bennin, Nigeria, Museum of Antiquities, Lagos, 1968-69. **Career:** Professor of art, Texas Southern University, 1950-87. Member, Slade Society, University College, London; associate life member, Michigan Institute of African Studies, University of Ibadan, Nigeria. **Awards:** First award, Toledo Museum of Fine Arts, 1949-50; purchase award, Cranbrook Museum of Art, 1953; Fullbright Fellowship, 1954-56; Swedish Institute Stockholm Survey of Contemporary Ceramic Pottery scholarship, 1964; Certificate of Recognition for Exemplary Representing of African American Artistic and Cultural Expression, Second World Black and African Festival of Arts, 1977; Carroll Simms Day proclaimed in Houston, 22 September 1977; Griot Award, Southern Conference on Afro-American Studies, 1984. **Address:** 3861 Blodgett Street, Houston, Texas 77004-6501.

Selected Exhibitions:

1951	Toledo Museum of Fine Arts, Ohio (solo)
1979	Huntsville Museum of Art, Alabama
1980	Texas Southern University, Houston
1981	National Conference of Artists, Dallas City Hall
1982	California Museum of Afro-American History and Culture, Los Angeles
1983	Houston Public Library
1984	Harambee Arts and Cultural Heritage Festival, Tallahassee, Florida
	Art Institute of Houston Gallery

Carroll Harris Simms: *A Tradition of Music.* **Photo courtesy of Earlie Hudnall.**

Collections:

California Afro-American Museum, Los Angeles; Texas Southern University, Houston.

Publications:

By SIMMS: Books—*Ancestral Origin of Classical Yoruba Pottery,* Houston, Texas Southern University, 1973; *Black Art in Houston* by John Biggers and Caroll Simms with John Edward Weems, Texas A & M University Press, 1978.

On SIMMS: Articles—"Public Program is Local Benchmark for Sculptor Simms," in *Houston Post,* 18 February 1979, p. 12AA; "Carroll Simms' Work Reflects in Art What He's Seen, Where He's Been" by Bill Minutaglio, in *Houston Chronicle,* 12 February 1982, Section 5, p. 5.

*

Caroll Simms comments:

During the late thirties, while looking at pictures in a magazine in Arkansas, my home, I first became acquainted with the sculpture of Jacques Lipchitz and Jacob Epestein. Later due to the patronage of Mrs. Jane Blaffer Owen, of Houston, Texas, I first met Mr. Lipchitz in his studio at Hastings on the Hudson and next at his studio on East Hampton, Long Island. Having received a Fulbright Scholarship (1954-56) to study sculpture at the Slade in London, I first met Mr. Epestein in his studio at the Royal College of Art and later at the Morris Singer Bronze Foundry, where I was apprenticed to learn techniques of bronze casting where his sculpture was cast. It was there that almost on a daily basis (1955-56) I was privileged to experience the wisdom of his thoughts about his sculpture, relative to the struggle and humanities of everyday life. As a freshman at Hampton Institute, Virginia, (1944-45) my painting teacher, Dr. Viktor Lowenfeld (as did the two before him) gave image to the expression "your concept of art—to have value—must reveal how you react to the struggle and problems of everyday life." Their thoughts and teachings having intrinsic value far beyond the view of my first teachers. And as the result, throughout the years till now, I acknowledge the classical tradition of the Negro spiritual, the church, gospel music, dance, poetry, jazz, and the blues, symbolically existing as vessels and proverbs, which are artistically, genetically, imbedded with the wisdom and knowledge of the black experience, all of which directs my struggle to create concepts of painting and sculpture (as well as pottery and jewelry smithing), which I trust shall make a worthy contribution to the presence, permanence, and continuity of black African American history and culture.

*   *   *

Carroll H. Simms synthesized the spirituality of poor black people in the rural South with that of the peoples of western Africa in very modern and unusual sculpture. Focused on teaching most of his life, with African folklore as a subject for sculpture, Simms simply tuned out publicity and gallery shows. Although he created a striking eight-foot crucifix for an external wall of Saint Oswald's Church in Coventry, England, and designed a garden of sacred Yoruba pottery in Nigeria, most of his work is public sculpture in Houston, Texas, particularly on the campus of Texas Southern University. Private collectors hold some of his smaller works.

Born in Bald Knob, Arkansas, on 29 April 1924, Simms has a genuine feeling for the beliefs expressed in African art. His ability to absorb feelings began in childhood, when he watched his grandmother "piece" together a quilt. His first ideas about design arose in this context. Later a scholarship brought him to Hampton Institute, where Victor Lowenfeld, head of the art department, stressed self-identification in art. This contributed to Simms's confidence and has continued throughout his career. At Hampton, Simms also met John Biggers, an enthusiastic follower of Lowenfeld's approach. Later Biggers, Simms, and Joseph Mack created the art department at Texas Southern University, which has supplied most African American art teachers for Texas schools.

A scholarship at Cranbrook Academy of Art near Detroit introduced Simms to modern art movements in sculpture. His studies also included jewelry making. In 1948 and 1949 he won first prize for sculpture at the Toledo Museum exhibitions. At Cranbrook he met and talked with nationally known visiting artists and writers, among them Alexander Archipenko, Yasua Kuniypshi, and writer John Steinbeck. These talks helped him shed his southern-bred timidity and realize his individuality.

Abroad on a Fullbright Scholarship in 1955-56, Simms studied sculpture at the Slade School in London with Sir Henry Coldstream. This led to a casting apprenticeship with Sir Jacob Epstein, one of the great figures in twentieth-century sculpture. Epstein was delighted when Simms called peanuts "goobers." Simms's massive *Prophet and Son,*

Carroll Harris Simms: *The Sow Hog Has Looked at the Moon,* 1967. Photo courtesy of Lloyd Koenig Studios, Houston, Texas.

carved in walnut, reflects Epstein's influence. Later Simms spent six weeks with Jacques Lipchitz, another major sculptor of the twentieth century, at his Hastings, New York, studio..

In the British Museum, Simms's fascinated study of Ashanti gold weights attracted William Fagg, a leading authority on African art. Fagg began a series of conversations with Simms on the religious and social beliefs and attitudes expressed in African art. These talks had a profound impact on Simms, who then spent two years in Nigeria (1968-69) studying these relationships, absorbing the meaning of fetishes and shrines in fields and the characters that enliven African folk tales. This became a central influence on Simms's work as a teacher, sculptor, and jewelry maker.

Simms always considered pottery the aesthetic equal of sculpture. In Nigeria he was delighted to find that various jars and large vessels were considered "sacred objects." The leading Nigerian museum official, Dr. A.A. Akinanwa, instructed him to refer to both pottery and sculpture as either "sacred objects" or "antiquities." Simms designed a garden for such objects.

Simms's work is unique and unmatched in its relationship to African folklore. His largest work, *The African Queen,* twelve feet tall and seventeen feet long, is a reclining female figure in a reflecting pool. Her outstretched arms become her breasts. One hand holds aloft a star, while her face symbolizes the moon. Her lower torso is symbolically a spider. She rests on the form of an alligator, and the entire figure sits on a beetle. Simms says the figure is based on an African folk tale, in which crocodiles formed a bridge that allowed peaceful villagers to escape invading warriors. Simms retired from teaching at Texas Southern University in 1987. While many African American artists have used African designs in their work, Simms appears to be the only one who has made extensive use of the characters in African folklore in his sculpture. Even his jewelry is alive with spiders, crocodiles, and beetles.

—Harry Henderson

SIMON, Jewel Woodward

American painter, sculptor, and printmaker

Born: Houston, Texas, 28 July 1911. **Education:** Atlanta University, Georgia, A.B. (summa cum laude) 1931; private study with B.L. Hellman, 1934, Hale Woodruff, 1946, Alice Dunbar, 1947;

Commercial Art, graduate certificate, 1962; Atlanta College of Art, Georgia, B.F.A. 1967; Tamarind Institute, 1981. **Family:** Married Edward Lloyd Simon in 1939 (died 1984), one son and one daughter. **Career:** Math department head, Jack Yates High School, 1931-39. **Awards:** Second Prize in sculpture, Atlanta University, Georgia, 1949; Bronze Woman of the Year in Fine Arts Award, 1950; Second Prize in watercolor, Atlanta University, 1953; Second Prize in sculpture, Atlanta University, 1955; First Prize in watercolor, Atlanta University, 1957, 1962, 1968; NCA Award, Mental Health Association, 1958; First Prize in sculpture, Atlanta University, 1964; Alumni Award, Atlanta University, Georgia, 1966; John Hope Prize, 1966; Arts Service Award, Phoenix Arts and Theater Company, Arizona, 1978; Golden Dove Heritage Award, Kappa Omega Chapter, AKA Sorority, 1979; Bronze Jubilee Award, 1981; Golden Girl Award, Alpha Kappa Alpha Founders Day Celebration, 1991.

Individual Exhibitions:

1968	Atlanta Jewish Community Center, Georgia
1971	Atlanta Jewish Community Center, Georgia
1973	Clark College, Atlanta, Georgia
1974	Carver Museum, Tuskegee, Alabama
1979	Huntsville Museum of Art, Alabama
	International Society of Artists, New York
	Chicago Museum of Science and Industry
	Ariel Gallery, Soho, New York

Selected Group Exhibitions:

1943	Atlanta University, Georgia (through 1973)
1953	Tuskegee Arts Festival, Alabama
1957	Houston Fine Arts Museum, Texas
1960	Invitational, Howard University, Washington, D.C.
1964	High Museum, Atlanta, Georgia
1966	University of California, Los Angeles
	Oakland Museum, California
1970	Stillman College, Tuscaloosa, Alabama
1971	Carnegie Institute
1972	Georgia Institute of Technology, Atlanta

Collections:

Atlanta University, Georgia; Carnegie Institute; Chicago University; Clark College, Atlanta, Georgia; National Archives Slide

Collection; University of Maryland; University of South Alabama.

*   *   *

Jewel Simon draws on her love of nature and strong spirituality to create art she likes to refer to as "enduring, quiet comments on the social scene." Classic still lifes and natural landscapes were a major part of her early work. As she has grown as an artist, so has her approach to her work. Over the years Simon—a painter, sculptor, and printmaker—has become known for her mastery in depicting the world and its inhabitants in simple, naturalistic terms with true grace.

Simon's *The Early Birds,* painted in 1969, is a perfect example of her simple yet beautiful style. The work celebrates family and natural beauty as one. The classic scene of a family enjoying a picnic lunch on a warm spring day is framed by interlocking trees to provide a snapshot of the joys and simplicity of family life. In *The Eternal Hills,* Simon explores another theme—eternal life. As in most of her work, nature takes center stage, but the artist's use of atmospheric embellishment in the painting separates it from her classical approach to landscape. *The Eternal Hills* reflects the mystical through her depiction of a mist that hangs above the mountains, suggesting a heavenly, ethereal image and peacefulness.

Simon, however, strays from her classic theme in her 1969 *Apparition,* which uses almost dreamlike figures that recognize and celebrate the beauty and sensuality of women. The reds and oranges in the painting come together in a burst of vibrant dancing flames. She also employs an abstract expressionist approach in the painting by simply hinting at the facial characteristics of her subject.

Simon and her work often reflect an ever present and understated beauty and forceful strength. Her sculpture *Tusi Princess* illustrates this theme. The viewer is drawn to the elegant bust of the beautiful black woman by her piercing eyes, expertly crafted by Simon. The sculpture appears to convey a message of hope and pride.

Simon is the embodiment of the strength she conveys through her art. In 1967 she became the first black to graduate from the Atlanta (Georgia) College of Art. She also studied under the noted artists Alice Dunbar and Hale Woodruff at Spelman College. She has been exhibiting her work nationally and internationally since 1934, and her art is held in some of the most distinguished collections in the world.

—Coria Holland

SIMPSON, Lorna

American photographer

Born: Brooklyn, New York, 1960. **Education:** School of Visual Arts, New York, B.F.A. 1982; University of California, San Diego, M.F.A. 1985. **Awards:** Arts Management Fellowship, National Endowment for the Arts, 1985; Workspace Grant, Jamaica Arts Center, 1987; Louis Comfort Tiffany Award, Louis Comfort Tiffany Foundation, 1990. **Agent:** Sean Kelly, 43 Mercer Street, New York, New York 10013, U.S.A.

Individual Exhibitions:

1985	Alternative Gallery, 5th Street Market, San Diego
1986	Just Above Midtown, New York
1988	Jamaica Arts Center, Queens, New York
	Mercer Union, Toronto
1989	Wadsworth Atheneum, Hartford, Connecticut
1990	Denver Art Museum
	Portland Art Museum, Portland, Oregon
	Museum of Modern Art, New York
	University Art Museum, California State University, Long Beach
1991	Josh Baer Gallery, New York
	Center for Exploratory and Perceptual Art, Buffalo, New York
1993	John Berggruen Gallery, San Francisco
	Shoshana Wayne Gallery, Santa Monica, California
	Josh Baer Gallery, New York
	Contemporary Arts Museum, Houston
1994	Whitney Museum of American Art at Phillip Morris, New York
	Fabric Workshop, Philadelphia
	Rhona Hoffman Gallery, Chicago
1995	Sean Kelly Gallery, New York
	Albrecht Kemper Museum of Art, St. Joseph, Missouri
	Cohen/Berkowitz Gallery, Kansas City, Missouri

Selected Group Exhibitions:

1987	New Museum of Contemporary Art, New York
1988	Museum of Fine Arts, Boston (traveling)
1989	Whitney Museum of American Art, New York
1990	Milwaukee Art Museum (traveling)
1991	Contemporary Art Museum, Houston
1992	Rhona Hoffman Gallery, Chicago
1993	Bonner Kunstverein, Bonn, Germany
1994	Walker Art Center, Minneapolis, Minnesota
1995	Whitney Museum of American Art, New York
1996	Museum of Modern Art, New York

Collections:

Baltimore Museum of Art, Maryland; Brooklyn Museum of Art, New York; Corcoran Gallery of Art, Washington, D.C.; Denver Art Museum; Department of Cultural Affairs, Chicago; Milwaukee Art Museum, Wisconsin; Museum of Contemporary Art, Chicago; Museum of Contemporary Art, San Diego, California; Museum of Modern Art, New York; High Museum of Art, Atlanta; Israel Museum, Jerusalem; University of New Mexico, Albuquerque; Wadsworth Atheneum, Hartford, Connecticut; Walker Art Center, Minneapolis, Minnesota; Whitney Museum of American Art, New York.

Publications:

On SIMPSON: Book—*Lorna Simpson: Untitled 54* by Deborah Willis, San Francisco, Friends of Photography, 1992. **Articles**—"Lorna Simpson" by Haun Saussy, in *Arts,* December, p. 84; "Emerging in the 90's: Lorna Simpson Conceptual Artist" by Kelly Jones, in *Emerge,* 2(3), January 1991, p.40; "Lorna Simpson" by Terry Myers, in *Lapiz,* 72, November 1991; "Interview with Lorna

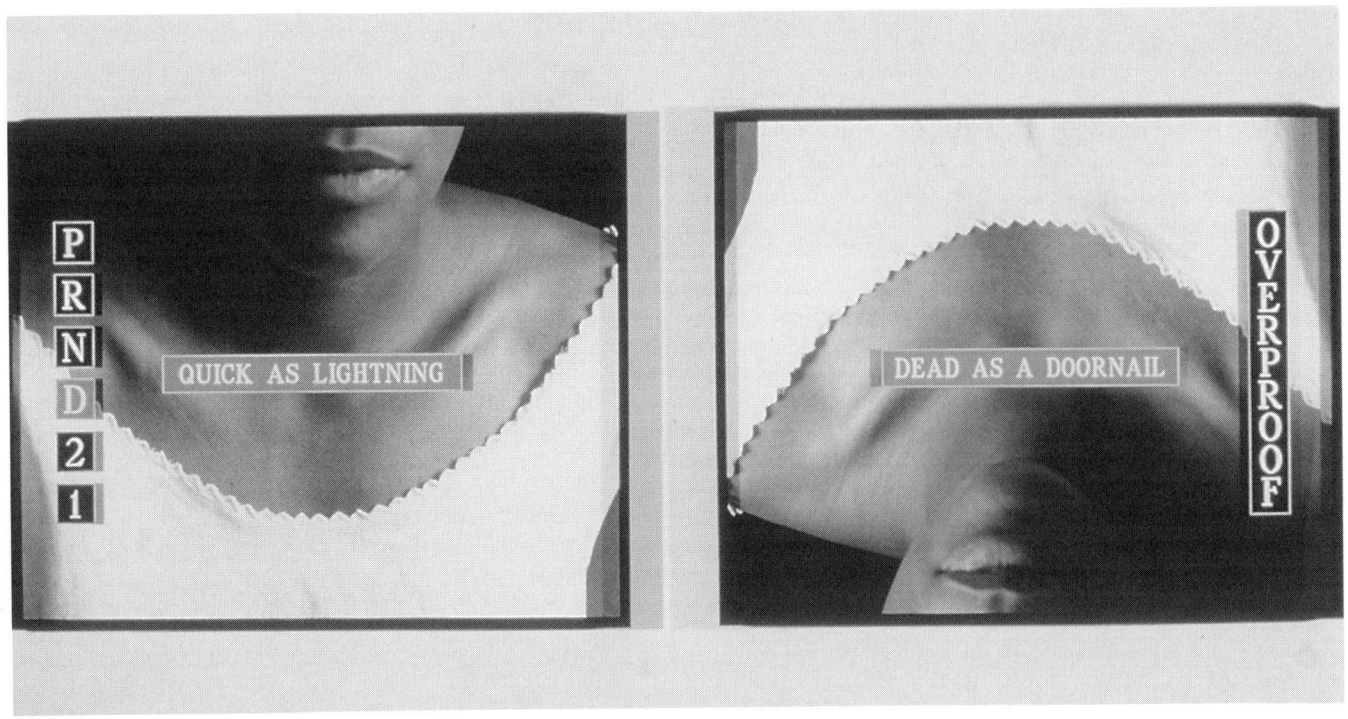

Lorna Simpson: untitled, 1989. Photo courtesy of Sean Kelly, New York.

Simpson" by Regina Joseph, in *Balcon* (Madrid), (5/6), 1991; "Lorna Simpson: Stop and Think," in *MS.*, May/June 1991, pp. 48-53; "Lorna Simpson" by Gretchen Faust, in *Arts,* September 1991, p.80; "Lorna Simpson" by Eugenie Bruno, in *Shift* (7), 1991, pp. 36-39; "Lorna Simpson" by Jan Avgikos, in *Artforum,* October 1992, p. 104; "Lorna Simpson" by Alice R. Gray, in *ARTnews,* October 1992, pp. 124, 126; "Lorna Simpson: Words and Images" by Dolores, S. Slowinski, in *Michigan Photography Journal*, 5, 1992, pp. 18-19; "Olympia's Maid: Reclaiming Black Female Subjectivity" by Lorraine O'Grady, in *Afterimage,* Summer 1992, pp. 14-15, 23; "Lorna Simpson" by Kim Levin, in *Village Voice,* 5 October 1993, p. 75; "Lorna Simpson: Waterbearer" by bell hooks, in *Artforum,* September 1993, pp. 136-37; "Lorna Simpson, Standing in Water" by Holland Cotter, in *New York Times,* 18 March 1994; "Premature Emancipation: African American Artists and Time Magazine" by Bill Gaskins, in *New Art Examiner,* February 1995, p. 14-18.

* * *

Lorna Simpson, born in 1960, is thirty-seven years of age. In this brief number of years, relatively speaking, she has achieved a great deal. In 1990, when she was thirty years of age, she was the first African American woman artist to represent the United States at the prestigious Venice Biennial, and in that very same year she had a one-woman exhibition in the Projects Room of the Museum of Modern Art in New York City. Noted for her powerful and provocative installations, Simpson has focused much of her recent work on black women and how they are treated within a masculinized tradition in the construction of knowledge, which is characterized by a number of assumptions. Simpson acknowledges in her art the invisibility, devaluation, and marginalization of black women. But she does not just stop there, she confronts gender-defining institutions; the tradition of male prerogative; and the male hegemonic worldview that presumes its own view of the universe constitutes reality.

Born in Brooklyn, New York, she received a B.F.A. from the School of Visual Arts, New York, in 1982 and her M.F.A. from the University of California, San Diego, in 1985. She is well known for installations that combine photographs and small blocks of text. Such an installation is *Wigs*. Created in 1994 this installation is made up of twenty-one image panels and seventeen text panels. Text and image panels are printed on felt using the waterless lithography process. Overall the installation measures a whopping six feet by thirteen feet. *Wigs* is a critical probe into issues such as oppression, class, sexual orientation, and physical or handicapping conditions. The brief statements that accompany the images are complicated and cerebral. One needs wisdom, patience, intellect, and wit to decode Simpson, but once that is accomplished (though I believe the multiple layers of dialogue are not easy to fathom), her work is sheer joy.

Another work from the 1990s is *9 Props*. In this work the photographer pays homage to James VanDerZee, a Harlem photographer active from the 1920s through the 1980s. Other important works include *Waterbearer* (1986 silver print, 40 ½" x 70"), which is the subject of a lengthy essay by bell hooks in her book *Art on My Mind: Visual Politics;* her work also adorns the cover of *Afrekete,* an anthology of black lesbian fiction, essays, and poetry. The 1985 work *Gestures/Reenactments* was included in the 1994 exhibition *Black Male: Representations of Masculinity in Contemporary American Art* at the Whitney Museum of American Art, which was curated by Thelma Golden. Ms. Simpson provides a vision of black male masculinity from a black female perspective in this work, which is a whopping 76" x 252" overall and contains six gelatin silver prints and seven text panels. Using a Polaroid camera Simpson created *Self-Possession* in 1992. Iconography here includes images of a woman's torso dressed in black, with hands covered in red gloves on either side of her stomach, on which are found the words "9/10ths of The Law." Simpson has also pushed the edge of her medium by doing collaborative work with others. *Places with a Past,* an evocation of the slave trade in South Carolina, combines audiotapes, relics, and photographs. Simpson joined forces with actress Alva Rogers to create this tour de force.

—Jontyle Theresa Robinson

SIMPSON, Merton (Daniel)

American painter

Born: Charleston, South Carolina, 20 September 1928. **Education:** New York University; Cooper Union Art School; University of Charleston, South Carolina. **Military Service:** United States Air Force, 1951-54: artist. **Family:** Married Beatrice Houston, two sons. **Career:** President and owner, Merton D. Simpson Gallery, Inc. **Awards:** Award, Tenth Annual Exhibition of Negro Artists, Atlanta University, Georgia, 1951; Young American Painters Award, 1954; American Negro Art Prize, 1960; Contemporary Artists of South Carolina Award, 1970; Afro-American Artist Award, 1973. **Address:** Merton Simpson Gallery, Primitive and Modern Arts, 1063 Madison Avenue, New York, New York 10028, U.S.A.

Individual Exhibitions:

1960	Krasner Gallery, New York
1978	Edward Merrin Gallery, New York
1982	Langston Society, New York
1983	Charleston County Library, South Carolina
	Allan Stone Gallery, New York
1984	William Halsey Gallery, Charleston, South Carolina
1990	Twining Gallery, New York
1992	Noir d'Ivoire Gallery, Paris
1993	Tambaran Gallery, New York

Selected Group Exhibitions:

1952	Metropolitan Museum of Art, New York
1954	Guggenheim Museum, New York
1956	Museum of Art, University of Michigan, Ann Arbor
1979	Huntsville Museum, Alabama
1984	Simmons Center for the Arts, Charleston, South Carolina
	Bucknell University, Lewisburg, Pennsylvania
1986	Bucknell University, Lewisburg, Pennsylvania

Collections:

Atlanta University, Georgia; Detroit Institute of Arts; Fisk University, Nashville; Gibbes Art Gallery, South Carolina; Howard University, Washington, D.C.; Rogers Engraving Company, New York; James J. Sweeney Collection; Scott Field Museum, Chicago; South Carolina Arts Commission; St. Lawrence University, Canton, New York; University of Michigan, Ann Arbor.

Publications:

On SIMPSON: Articles—"New Yorkers Win Honors at Atlanta Show," in *Art Digest,* 25, 15 April 1951, p. 13; "Merton Simpson, Artist" by A.C. Hollingsworth, in *Black Art,* 3(2), 1979.

*   *   *

Merton Simpson has had two careers in the arts. He is an accomplished painter and a successful gallery owner. He began as a painter, and he continues to be a productive artist. He has built up a considerable following and a name for himself in the mode of lyrical abstract expressionism, and he has exhibited widely.

Born in South Carolina, Simpson later moved to New York City, where he made his career. He studied at New York University and at Cooper Union. He became a member of the Spiral Group and thus was one of the politically active artists who were concerned with their relationship to the struggle for civil rights. He worked closely with Romare Bearden and Hale Woodruff.

Among the early works for which Simpson is known is the "Confrontation" series. In the series his expressionist style became a backdrop for the passion and anger seen in two opposing faces, presumably those of a black and a white person. The two faces appear throughout the series.

In 1995 a major retrospective of Simpson's work was mounted in South Carolina. The exhibition, titled *Merton Simpson: The Journey of an Artist,* started in Charleston, and parts of it subsequently traveled to Columbia and to Clemson. The lengthy and comprehensive essay written by Angela Mack for the exhibition catalog recalls major events in Simpson's life and the stages of his artistic development. Although it was not the first time Simpson had received acclaim in his native state, the exhibition was, nevertheless, a personal triumph of tremendous proportions.

Simpson has spoken in detail of the early importance of William Halsey as a mentor and source of inspiration and acknowledges that his going to New York to study was important in his maturation as an artist. But he also has spoken about the importance to him of a seemingly minor job he held in a frame shop owned by Herbert Benevy on East Fifty-Second Street. The job brought him into contact with many leading members of the New York School of painters who came to national prominence during the 1950s. Many of them, including Willem de Kooning, Robert Motherwell, and Jackson Pollock, went to the shop to have their works framed.

Simpson's second career in the arts has also been significant, and he is well known as a dealer in modern and African art. As such, he has built up a successful gallery on Madison Avenue, at the heart of the mainstream art world in New York. Even today, however, he is one of only two African Americans who own galleries in Manhattan. He maintains that the gallery came about purely by chance as a way to cope with a personal problem and that his true purpose has always been to work as an artist.

As an art dealer Simpson is known for connoisseurship based on his refined taste and good eye. At the first National Black Fine Art Show, held in New York from 31 January to 2 February 1997, one of the works he handled as a dealer was a painting by Henry O. Tanner.

—Thomas M. Shaw

SIMPSON, William H.
American painter

Born: Buffalo, New York, c.1818. **Education:** Studied under Matthew Wilson. **Career:** Portrait painter, Boston, 1854-72. **Died:** 1872.

Exhibitions:

1942   Downtown Gallery, New York
1945   Howard University, Washington, D.C.
1967   Howard University, Washington, D.C.

Collection:

Howard University, Washington, D.C.

*   *   *

William H. Simpson is known for his work as a portraitist. Although he produced several portraits in his career, only two paintings are known to exist today. The ardent and devoted writing of author William Wells Brown, a contemporary of Simpson, has provided what little the public knows about Simpson's works of art and his life. Simpson's interest in art began early in life. It is documented that, as a schoolboy, he often got in trouble for drawing instead of doing his schoolwork. As an adult, Simpson apprenticed with the artist Matthew Wilson. Simpson was listed in the Boston directories as an independent artist, and he attracted many patrons from the northern United States and from Canada. According to Brown, Simpson was known for painting whole families or groups of people, placing his subjects in natural poses, as if they were having a conversation.

The two paintings of Simpson's that still exist are portraits of Jermain Loguen and his wife, Caroline Loguen. Although these paintings have faded, it is obvious that the colors were once very rich. A comparison with a photograph of Loguen reveals that Simpson was highly skilled at capturing the expression and attitude of his subject. Jermain Wesley Loguen was a fugitive slave, a prominent leader in the Underground Railroad, a bishop of the African Methodist Episcopal church, and involved in antislavery groups. It is interesting to note that most early African American artists were obliged to produce art confined to the Eurocentric aesthetic, and while Simpson may have conformed stylistically, he chose to paint some of the early African American leaders, such as Loguen and John Hilton.

—Christine Miner Minderovic

SLIGH, Clarissa (T.)
American photographer and mixed-media artist

Born: Washington, D.C., 30 August 1939. **Education:** Hampton Institute, Virginia, B.S. 1961; Howard University, Washington, D.C., B.F.A. 1972; Skowhegan School of Art, Maine, 1972; University of Pennsylvania, M.B.A. 1973; International Center for Photography, New York, 1979-80. **Career:** Computer programmer and financial analyst, Wall Street, New York. Instructor, City College of New York, 1986-87, Lower Eastside Printshop, New York, 1988-90. Visiting artist, Minnesota College of Art and Design, Minneapolis, 1988-89, Carleton College, Northfield, Minnesota, 1992. **Awards:** National Endowment for the Arts Fellowship, 1988; New York State Council on the Arts Award, 1990; Artist en France Award, Greater New York Links, French Government, 1992; President's Award, National Women's Caucus for Art, 1994; Jerome Foundation grant, Women Artists of Color Leadership Workshops, 1994. **Address:** 465 West Broadway, New York, New York 10012, U.S.A.

Individual Exhibitions:

1987   C.E.P.A., Satellite Space, Buffalo, New York
1990   Meridian Gallery, San Francisco
1992   Boliou Art Gallery, Carleton College, Northfield, Minnesota
        YMI Cultural Center, Asheville
        Center for Photography, Woodstock, New York
        Art in General, New York
        Walker Art Center, Minneapolis (traveling)
1993   Afro-American Historical and Cultural Museum, Philadelphia
        Whitney Museum of American Art, New York
1994   Deluce Gallery, Northwest Missouri State, Maryville
        Toronto Photographers Workshop
        Atlanta College of Art, Georgia
        Houston Center for Photography (traveling)
        San Francisco State University
        Forum for Contemporary Arts, Saint Louis, Missouri
        National African American Museum Project, Smithsonian Institution, Washington, D.C.
1995   Atlanta College of Art, Georgia

Selected Group Exhibitions:

1982   Parsons School of Design Gallery, New York
1984   P.S. 1 Gallery, Long Island City, New York
1985   *Artists as Filmmakers Series,* A.I.R. Gallery, New York
1986   Moonmade Space, New York
1986   Photo Center Gallery, New York University
        Life Stories, Minneapolis College of Art and Design, Minnesota
1987   Hera Gallery, Wakenfield, Rhode Island
        herstory, Castillo Gallery, New York
        With Her Body in Mind, Hera Gallery, Wakefield, Rhode Island

Collections:

Museum of Modern Art, New York; National Museum of Women in the Arts, Washington, D.C.; Schomburg Center, New York.

Publications:

By SLIGH: Article—"On Being an American Black Student," in *Heresies,* 7(1), 1990, pp. 29-33 (illustrated).

On SLIGH: Articles—"Black and White Photography" by David Trent, in *Afterimage,* 13(10), 16 May 1986; "Not a Pretty Picture: Can Violent Art Heal?" by Arlene Raven, in *Village Voice,* 17 June 1986; "Reinscribing the Self" by Laura U. Marks, in *Afterimage,* 17, December 1989, pp. 6-9; review (Meridian Gallery, San Francisco), in *Artweek,* 21, 1 November 1990, p. 17 (illustrated); "Clarissa Sligh (Photographer's Work)" by Deborah Willis-Thomas, in *Aperture,* 138, Winter 1995, pp. 4-11 (illustrated); "Reading Deeper: The Legacy of Dick and Jane in the work of Clarissa Sligh" by Carla Williams, in *Image* (Rochester, New York), 38, Fall/Winter 1995, pp. 2-15.

*   *   *

Throughout her career Clarissa Sligh's work has challenged conventional divisions between the personal and the political and has reckoned with the gaps between cultural myth and lived experience. Combining family photographs with handwritten autobiographical text, Sligh displays a remarkable penchant for storytelling while delving into some of the darker secrets of family and cultural life. Her work explores the ways in which sexism and racial oppression reveal themselves through personal and familial narratives and also explores the potential for these narratives to unearth and even heal the psychic wounds inflicted by oppression.

A photographer and mixed-media artist, Sligh is best known for her artist's books and her works on paper that use nonsilver photographic processes, as, for example, Van Dyke Brown printing. In the book *Reading Dick and Jane with Me* (1989) she creates a disturbing and moving juxtaposition between the traditional portrayal of Euramerican childhood and her own childhood growing up poor in the South. Photographs of herself and other black children contrast with line drawings of Dick and Jane and refer to the suppression of uniqueness in the face of a two-dimensional ideal. On some pages she recontextualizes appropriated phrases such as "we go up," repeating them obsessively to evoke meanings hidden behind the original context of the words. Relying on a recognizable and accessible format, Sligh thus provides an entrance into difficult subject matter such as social iniquity, incest, and the pain of childbirth.

Some of Sligh's more powerful and ambiguous pieces, such as *Slept with Brother* (1984) and *Waiting for Daddy* (1987), communicate an underlying sadness that is palpable but unnamable. They speak to that existential state of childhood in which one cannot identify clearly the source of sorrow or even of joy. In *Slept with Brother* two photographic figures—a young girl and boy—are placed in the foreground of a sketch of a bedroom interior. A text overlay tells a story not provided by the photographic information ("she slept with her brother . . . whenever he took a piss in his dreams, she woke up soaking wet"). The story is both a detail in memory and a telling observation about relationships. *Waiting for Daddy* takes the form of a frontal snapshot of the artist's family in a collage of a story about a visit to her grandmother's. Although the story is a happy one, the somber bearing of the little girl, the way the image divides the text, and the longing implied by the title suggest a deeper subtext—speculation about which relies solely upon the viewer's imagination.

The style of Sligh's work is unique in several ways—her use of handwritten text and he scrapbook look that comes from her collages of words, snapshots, and sketches. It also stands out from the more polished and commercial look of other celebrated postmodern feminist artists such as Barbara Kruger and Lorna Simpson. Sligh's style represents not the naïveté, lack of skill, and obsessive vision used to characterize (often falsely) so-called outsider art, but rather it insists on the value of memory and experience as legitimate sources and on personal mark making as a meaningful aesthetic practice.

Sligh's work, however, is distinctly postmodern in its use of text as a way of undermining the authority of the singular photograph. It acknowledges the constructed nature of identity through the very self-consciousness of its own layered construction. Sligh presents identity as a contested territory whose boundaries resist clear definition, as in the pieces *Who We Was* (1984) and *Who She Was* (1987). The texts for these works are "We didn't know who we was, but we knew we wasn't who you all said we was" and "She didn't know who she was, but she knew she wasn't who you all said she was." By using both the singular and plural pronouns, Sligh acknowledges the complexity of both individual and collective identity—with regards to race, gender, and otherwise.

—Audrey Mandelbaum

SMITH, Albert Alexander

American graphic artist and painter

Born: New York, 17 September 1896. **Education:** Ethical Culture Art School, New York; National Academy of Design. **Career:** Worked as jazz musician, Paris. **Awards:** Ethical Culture Art School Scholarship, 1911; Tanner Gold Medal, 1916; Suydam Medal 1917, 1919; Chaloner Prize, 1919; Bronze Medal, Harmon Foundation, 1929; National Academy of Design Award; Wolfe Scholarship, Ethical Culture Art School; three honorable mentions for draftsmanship, National Academy of Design; Amy E. Springarn Prize. **Died:** Paris, 1940.

Selected Exhibitions:

1921	135th Street Branch, New York Public Library (solo)
1922	Tanner Art League
1927	Art Institute of Chicago
1928	Ethical Culture Art School
	Harmon Foundation
1929	Smithsonian Institution, Washington, D.C.
1932	Veterans Exhibit, Paris
	Boston Museum of Fine Arts
1933	Harmon Foundation
1935	Harmon Foundation
1938	Paris
1939	*Contemporary Negro Art,* Baltimore Museum of Art
1940	American Negro Exposition
1935	New Jersey State Museum, Trenton
1935	Harmon College Art Traveling Exhibit
	Harmon Traveling Exhibition
1936	Texas Centennial
1945	South Side Community Art Center, Chicago

Collections:

Harmon Foundation; Schomburg Center, New York.

Albert Alexander Smith: *Portrait of Arthur Schomburg,* **1928. Photo by Frank White; courtesy of the Schomburg Center for Research in Black Culture.**

Albert Alexander Smith: *The Laugh,* **1928. Photo courtesy of the Schomburg Center for Research in Black Culture.**

Publications:

On SMITH: Article—"Our Young Artists" by Cleveland G. Allen, in *Opportunity,* 1, June 1923, pp. 24-25; "Music and Art," in *Crisis,* 35, May 1928, p. 163; "Albert Alexander Smith" by Jean McGleughlin, in *Opportunity,* 18, July 1940, p. 209.

*   *   *

Albert Alexander Smith was best known as a graphic artist. His portraits of famous blacks were sensitive as well as beautiful. His illustrations often appeared in *Opportunity* and in *Crisis,* one of the earliest, *The Fall of the Castle* (1917), in 1920, when he was still a student. His early prints were in an illustrative style and centered on injustices to blacks in the United States. *The Reason* and *They Have Ears But They Hear Not* were published in *Crisis* in February

and November 1920, respectively. Whether in the image of a Southern Negro fleeing to the North, the image of a black man hanging in the background, or the image of a chained black on trial in a Southern court with the jurors, the judge, and the law itself wearing earphones so that they cannot hear his plea, Smith clearly focused on injustice.

There is, however, a body of work by Smith that is quite curious. He did a number of etchings that focus on African Americans frolicking as they have a good time. In *Plantation Melodies,* for example, which was accepted for the 1920 spring exhibition of the National Academy of Design in New York City and reproduced in *Crisis* in the same year, the facial expressions and gestures border on buffoonery. The gyrations and uncontrollable laughter of the participants recall the many late nineteenth-century portrayals of African Americans as carefree, fun-loving minstrels who avoided work and were always ready for a good time. Smith continued to create such works throughout the 1930s, including the painting *Dancing Time* (1932) and the etching *Darktown Strutters* (1939), both exhibited in museums. In a review of the Harmon Foundation's exhibition of 1930 a critic for the *New York Herald-Tribune* wrote of Smith's *Friends* (c.1929), an oil painting on canvas, that his "group portrait that includes two rural Negro men, a bright-eyed pickaninny holding a bunch of daisies, and a litter of puppies, is a vivid scene that would touch the heart of any Southerner."

How Smith came to create such works calls for explanation. He was born and raised in New York and entered the National Academy of Design in 1915, where he won many student prizes. After serving in the army in 1918-19, he returned to the academy, where he was influenced by the teachers William Auerbach-Levy and Joseph Pennell. Smith then worked as a chauffeur and radio musician and in recording studios. Before traveling to Europe in about 1922, he was awarded a gold medal for his etchings at the Tanner Art League exhibition in Washington, D.C. In Paris he first worked as a cabaret entertainer, a profession that was readily open to people of color who needed to supplement their income while practicing their art. In 1929 he won a Harmon Foundation bronze medal for his paintings and prints, and in 1938 he exhibited three paintings at the Salon of American professionals in Paris and was reviewed in *La Revue Moderne.* According to the review, "His mountain countrysides, the scenes where he evokes Spain . . . his pictures consecrated to the nobility of the work of the peasant and the laborer, his familiar scenes of everyday life, his landscapes of all countries, are all marked by the individuality of his character, an exactness of light and color, and an originality, finally, which denotes an artistic temperament of great power."

One critic has suggested that, although Smith was a musician and a cabaret entertainer, little of that life can be seen in his work. A closer analysis, however, reveals that his scenes of African Americans not specifically created for *Crisis* often were portrayals of blacks as musicians or entertainers. Further, he was clearly aware of the minstrel tradition, as is evident in the titles of genre paintings such as *Plantation Melodies, Dancing Time,* and *Darktown Strutters.* In these works on blacks as entertainers, Smith seems to have accepted the stereotypes that had long been acceptable and popular, and he produced works reminiscent of the nineteenth-century images that had been created by white artists.

Smith's technical skill and, perhaps even more so, the subject matter of many of his etchings and paintings may account for their acceptance into exhibitions at important institutions. These included the Museum of Fine Arts in Boston in 1932 (sponsored by the New England Society of Contemporary Art) and the Baltimore

(Maryland) Museum of Art's 1939 exhibition of Negro art (in conjunction with the Harmon Foundation).

—Lizzetta LeFalle-Collins

SMITH, Al(fred J. Jr.)

American painter, sculptor, and muralist

Born: Montclair, New Jersey, 9 July 1948. **Education:** Boston University, M.F.A., B.F.A. **Career:** Since 1972 professor, Howard University, Washington, D.C. **Awards:** National Endowment for the Arts craftsman grant, 1975; Faculty Research grant, Howard University, Washington, D.C., 1980-81; National Endowment for the Arts building arts grant, 1980. **Address:** 3407 Welthem Street, Suitland, Maryland 20746, U.S.A.

Individual Exhibitions:

1975   Howard University, Washington, D.C.
1976   *Chant for the Sun,* Florida A & M University, Tallahassee

1976   National Center of Afro-American Artists, Boston
        Studio Museum in Harlem, New York
1981   Miya Gallery, Washington, D.C.
        Nyangoma's Gallery, Washington, D.C.
1987   Norfolk State University, Virginia
1988   Bedford Stuyvesant Restoration Corporation, Brooklyn, New York
1989   Franz Bader Gallery, Washington, D.C.
1990   Wendell Street Gallery, Cambridge, Massachusetts
1991   Franz Bader Gallery, Washington, D.C.
1993   Susquehanna Art Museum, Harrisburg, Pennsylvania
1994   Franz Bader Gallery, Washington, D.C.
1995   Ramapo College Art Gallery, New Jersey
        American Association for the Advancement of Science, Washington, D.C.

Selected Group Exhibitions:

1972   Studio Museum in Harlem, New York
1975   Boston Museum of Fine Arts
1979   Preibe Gallery of Art, University of Wisconsin, Oshkosh

Al Smith: sculpture. Photo courtesy of Ronald Beverly.

Al Smith: *Oshun & Shango.*

African American Historical and Cultural Museum, Philadelphia
1986   Torpedo Factory Art Center, Alexandria, Virginia
Maryland Institute College of Art, Baltimore, Maryland
Nassau County Museum of Fine Arts, Roslyn Harbor, New York
1989   Hood College, Frederick, Maryland
1990   *Art Against Aids,* Kornblatt Gallery, Washington, D.C.
1992   Ellipse Arts Center, Arlington, Virginia

Collections:

D.C. Commission of the Arts, Washington, D.C.; Florida A & M University Gallery, Tallahasse; Howard University Gallery, Washington, D.C.; Museum of the National Center of Afro-American Artists, Boston; North Carolina A & T Gallery, Greensboro; Studio Museum in Harlem, New York.

Selected Murals:

Boston University; Harvard University, Cambridge, Massachusetts; Northeastern University, Boston; Saint Paul's A.M.E. Church, Cambridge, Massacheusetts.

Publications:

On SMITH: Book— *Black Artists of the New Generation* by Elton Fax, New York, Dodd Mead and Company, 1977. **Articles**—re-

view by Florece Rubenfeld, in *Museum and Arts,* February 1989; review by Dianne Hendy, in *B.E.* (Black Elegance), 1991.

*   *   *

Al Smith is an artist with great talent and relentless creativity. Throughout his career he has been willing to experiment and make radical shifts in his approach. Although he is primarily a painter, Smith also has created carved musical instruments, and in recent years he has developed works that straddle the line between painting and sculpture.

Smith's father and grandfather were noted sign painters in New Jersey, and as a youth Smith watched his father work. This may have instilled in him the love of calligraphy that became so important in his paintings in the 1980s and 1990s. After college Smith attended graduate school in Boston. While trying to learn to play the saxophone, he saw a demonstration by the renowned Nigerian carver Lamidi Fakeye. The rhythmic, musical quality in Fakeye's carvings convinced Smith that he could find music in art. After receiving his master's degree, he moved to Washington, D.C., to teach at Howard University, where he has remained.

Smith's earliest paintings of note were from a series linking Africans and African Americans by showing each group in its own setting but emphasizing their similarities. He used colorful, patterned settings and clothing and often placed the figures in communal and performance arrangements. An African king, for example, might be accompanied by musicians and dancers, and an African American musical group in African garb be playing African instruments and accompanied by dancers. His visits to West Africa in 1973 and 1975 convinced Smith that African art thrived in communal settings, whether in carving workshops, public celebrations and masquerades, or performances involving calls and responses with the audience. These visits also made him more sensitive to pattern and its potential for suggesting music.

Smith's African visits also convinced him that he was an African American, not an African, and he did a series of paintings exploring an African American cultural phenomenon—the barbershop. These paintings were not as symbolic or as patterned as his earlier work.

Smith did several carvings in the early 1970s and spent time studying at Fakeye's workshop in Ibadan during his African travels. By the end of the decade he had begun to carve a series of innovative musical instruments, one a slit drum five feet tall with a stylized human head at the apex and several others using strings.

In the 1980s Smith began to study tai chi and turned to nonrepresentational forms in his paintings. Using gridlike structures, he experimented with rhythm and began to incorporate calligraphic elements that approximated gestures he had learned in tai chi. Toward the middle of the decade Smith again turned to painting figures, but they became more photorealistic than in his earlier stylized works. In the later works Smith attempted to explore polyrhythmic patterns in an urban setting. For example, he played the rhythm found in the windows of a high-rise building off the vertical patterns of objects like lampposts and newspaper boxes. Smith's exploration of rhythm became so consuming that by the end of the 1980s he had taken up drumming. He came to believe that music and rhythm had metaphysical potentials, ideas that became elements in his art.

Smith soon abandoned the figure again for more direct explorations of pattern, rhythm, and gesture in a series of more three-dimensional works. Some involved turning calligraphic forms into mobiles, as if musical gestures had been frozen in space. He painted each form with color and patterns so that the linear forms played off one another as polyrhythms. He also began to develop works with a flat base of woven strips that were painted various colors, with calligraphic marks atop the strips used to create contrast and tension. These works suggested the structure of music and the gestures of playing, with harmonics suggested through color relationships. In the case of *Bembé Clavé* the instruments themselves were implied.

Smith's most recent series of paintings explores the calligraphic forms similar to those he created as mobiles and wall sculptures, but the three-dimensional qualities are created visually on canvas through the use of color and through complex illusions of transparency where the linear forms overlap. These gestural forms emerge from solid dark ground, and while they seem at first to be less complex than earlier works, they actually may be more complex.

Throughout his career Smith has experimented and made jumps in the imagery and forms of his work, but gradually these seemingly disparate explorations have merged. He has multiple talents and an insatiable curiosity.

—Michael D. Harris

SMITH, Alvin
American painter, illustrator, and mixed-media artist

Born: Gary, Indiana, 27 November 1933. **Education:** University of Iowa, B.A.; University of Illinois; Kansas City Art Institute; New York University; Columbia University Teachers College, New York. **Career:** Art teacher, New York City public schools. Lecturer in art education, Queens College, Flushing, New York. **Awards:** Painting Award, *Chicago Tribune,* 1954; Dow Award, 1967. Purchase prizes: Dayton Art Institute, Ohio, 1961-66, Atlanta University, 1962-67 (four awards), The Living Arts Center, 1969, Columbia University, New York, 1969, Mount Holyoke College, 1969. Newbery Medal (for illustrations in the book *Shadow of a Bull*), 1965.

Selected Exhibitions:

1961	Toledo Museum, Ohio
	Dayton Art Institute and Museum, Ohio
1962	Toledo Museum, Ohio
	Dayton Art Institute and Museum, Ohio
	Contemporary Arts Gallery, New York
1963	New York University
1964	Dublin Gallery, Knoxville, Tennessee
	Purdue University, Lafayette, Indiana
	Ruth Sherman Gallery, New York
1965	National Academy Galleries, New York
1968	American Academy of Arts and Letters, New York
	Queens College Art Education Faculty Show, Flushing, New York
1969	Brooklyn College, New York
	Community Gallery, Brooklyn Museum, New York
	Mount Holyoke College, Massachusetts (solo)
	Living Arts Center, Dayton, Ohio
1970	Community Gallery, Brooklyn Museum, New York
	Gallery Museum, Saratoga, New York
1971	Musée Rath, Geneva, Switzerland

Collections:

Atlanta University, Georgia; Dayton Museum, Ohio; Mount Holyoke College, Massachusetts; Public Library, Gary, Indiana; Tougaloo College, Mississippi; University of Minnesota.

Publications:

On SMITH: Articles—"A Triumph Rather than a Threat," in *New York Times,* 27 April 1969; *Art International Magazine,* October 1969; *Art Gallery,* April 1970; "Not Judicious," in *The New York Times,* 19 April 1970; *Art in America,* September/October 1970; "Alvin Smith: Artist-Scholar Par Excellence" by Henri Ghent, in *Crisis,* 82, June/July 1975, pp. 211-13.

* * *

Alvin Smith's paintings are characterized by his use of pure color, smooth texture, and attention to the edges rather than the center of the canvases. The emotional quality of his paintings is produced by the clarity of his pigment and his unusual and evocative color pairings, as in *White on White* (1975) and *Beige and Terra Cotta* (1975). He also varies the emotional effect of his works by the way in which he finishes them—pulling the pigment to one or more edges of the canvas in smooth or ragged thin coats.

Over the course of his career Smith has largely eluded categories. He was less didactic than his contemporaries who began their careers in the black arts movement of the late 1960s and the early 1970s. He has made the following comment, in relation to his "Amherst" series, about his reliance on color and pure painting: "The leading edges of this series of paintings strive to replicate a variety of growth patterns one so readily associates with evolution in nature. I pursue this course, as opposed to a direction that gives considerable importance to the invention of so-called emblematic and symbolic forms because I find the latter no longer challenging." Lacking obvious symbolism, Smith's paintings are still vehicles for introspection and wonderment.

In the early 1970s Smith was among a group of African Americans artists to capture the attention of mainstream New York museums and galleries. Even though he was a young black artist, his concerns consisted of explorations of space, color, and nature rather than racism and other forms of oppression. He was less interested in manufacturing new cultural icons than in using his paintings and sculptures to ponder beauty and human emotion. It was for this reason that Smith was selected, along with seven others, to take part in the exhibition *Eight Afro-American Artists.* The exhibition also included works by Romare Bearden, Robert Thompson, Senga Nengudi (Sue Irons), Marvin Harden, Frederick John Eversley, Wilbur Haynie, and Ruth Tunstall. It was curated by Henri Ghent, then the director of the Brooklyn Museum's Community Gallery, and was assembled for the Rath Museum in Geneva, Switzerland. *Eight Afro-American Artists* was the first exhibition of contemporary black artists to be assembled for viewing in a European museum.

In a 1971 issue of *Art International,* Ghent commented on his reasons for curating African American art, and his remarks provide an apt description of Smith's paintings and sculptures: "To copy for so-called contemporary African sculpture to gain a sense of form, or to repeat the mass produced 'dashiki' designs, only negated the existence of authentic art that is to be found. By doing so, black artists not only deny themselves the experience of being truly confronted by inspired great art, they also rob themselves of a knowledge of their real negritude, which they constantly profess to be seeking. Instead the Afro-American artist should call upon the best aspects of his African heritage, together with a temperament that has emerged out of his experience of forced acculturation in America."

Smith teaches art in the public schools in New York City, and he is also a prolific illustrator of children's books. His illustrations for *Shadow of a Bull* won the book the Newbery medal for 1965.

—Deirdre Cross

SMITH, Frank

American printmaker, painter, and mixed-media artist

Born: Chicago, 15 June 1939. **Education:** University of Illinois, B.F.A. 1958; Howard University, Washington, D.C., M.F.A. 1972. **Career:** Art instructor, Illinois Board of Education, Chicago, 1959-67; instructor, art and science PS85 (special education for socially maladjusted male students, grades 7-12), City of New York Board of Education, 1967-70. Since 1970 associate professor of fine arts/ lecturer, Howard University, Washington, D.C. Consultant, Waterbury, Connecticut, Board of Education, 1973, D.C. Commission on the Arts and Humanities, Washington, D.C., 1978-84; prepared guidelines for *Artists in the Schools* program, Board of Education, Washington, D.C., 1970-74, *Art in Public Places*, Washington, D.C., 1985. **Awards:** FESTAC Award, Nigeria, 1977; Service to the Arts Award, City of Washington, D.C., 1981; DAAD German Academic Exchange Fellowship, 1981, 1983, 1988 and 1990; DCCAH Fellow, 1985 and 1987; United States Department of State Art in Embassies Award, 1989; D.C. Commission on the Arts and Humanities Award, 1988; Maryland State Council on the Arts Award, 1992; Brandywine Fellow, 1987 and 1994. **Address:** Howard University, Washington, D.C. 20059, U.S.A.

Selected Exhibitions:

1986	High Museum, Atlanta, Georgia
	California Museum of Afro-American Culture, Los Angeles
	Museum of Fine Arts, St. Petersburg, Florida
1987	Addis Ababa, Ethiopia
	Cigna Museum, Philadelphia
	Print Club, Philadelphia
1988	National Museum of Fine Arts, Kinshasha, Zaire
	Montgomery College, Rockville, Maryland
1989	Touchstone Gallery, Washington, D.C.
	California Museum of African American Art, Los Angeles
1990	Duke University, Durham, North Carolina
	Bronx Museum, New York
	African American Museum of Fine Arts, San Diego
1991	Museum of Science and Industry, Chicago
	Touchstone Gallery, Washington, D.C.
1992	Howard University, Washington, D.C.
	Maryland Institute, Baltimore, Maryland
1994	Parish Gallery, Washington, D.C.
	Black Art Group International, Chicago
1995	Emerson Gallery, McLean, Virginia
	Japan Information and Cultural Center, Washington, D.C.
	Saint Mary's College, Maryland

*   *   *

Frank Smith is the son, brother, and nephew of musicians. His brother Warren is a jazz percussionist who has been a part of Max Roach's all-percussion ensemble M'Boom. Smith himself plays the piano, but his dislike of playing in front of an audience kept him from going further with his musical talent.

For as long as he can remember, Smith has played music and made art. He has said that music was the way his family handled life. When he was young, the family stayed up to hear his father, who also played reed instruments, sing on the radio. His mother played the harp and piano. The siblings of both parents played musical instruments. Besides, Smith was born and raised in Chicago, a city that teemed with jazz and blues clubs, artists, and galleries. When he was older, Smith became enamored with the work and ideas of Wassily Kandinsky, who associated art and music, an association that has informed Smith's visual expression for most of his adult life.

Smith recalls spending nearly every weekend when he was young visiting the Art Institute of Chicago to look at paintings. There he saw Pablo Picasso's *Old Guitarist* and Georges Seurat's *Sunday Afternoon on the Island of La Grande Jatte*. He came to enjoy the works of the impressionists and of Toulouse-Lautrec, the latter especially because they gave visual importance to nightlife. He also liked Vincent van Gogh and others who developed textured surfaces. While he was an undergraduate at the University of Illinois, where Al Loving was a classmate, Smith came to admire the work of Hans Hofmann, who taught there at the time.

In 1967 Smith moved to New York City, and in 1970 he met the members of Africobra during their exhibition at the Studio Museum in Harlem. He already knew Jeff Donaldson, Napoleon Jones-Henderson, and Murray DePillars from Chicago. Soon afterward, Smith moved to Washington, D.C., where Donaldson had become chairman of the art department at Howard University, and, after completing his M.F.A. degree at Howard, he joined the faculty there, where he has remained since.

Since the 1960s Smith's work has shown a concern for abstraction, expression, and surface texture. In the mid- to late 1970s he worked with patterns and tried to make the object indistinguishable from the ground by giving each equal importance and color intensity and by gradually breaking down spaces. His practice of working patterns against one another and his penchant for working with several paintings at the same time soon led him to lay one atop another. He found that he liked the way the patterns played off one another, which led him to attach two works together by sewing them. During this process he discovered ways to use the sewing machine to draw, and he eventually incorporated fabric and leather into his work. The abstraction and syncopated patterns, along with the color relationships in these works, can be interpreted musically in ways similar to Kandinsky's efforts.

During the 1980s Smith began to create patterns and images on ceramic tiles for large public works, his first major work in this form being a mural for the Washington Convention Center in 1984. He also began to explore ways to lift his works from the wall by creating pieces to be suspended in space and with imagery on both sides. Surface texture have remained of interest to Smith, and he has experimented with a variety of media and techniques, including printmaking, painting, and the use of fabric, mixed media, and ceramic tile. The nature of his work, however, has maintained continuities across media.

Smith is a member of Africobra, and his work vibrates with the color, pulse, and rhythm of black music, but he does not feel a need to create "black" work. He believes that his work reflects his life experiences and the person he is, and because he has lived life as a black man in the United States, that perspective is present by default.

Having grown up in an environment in which everyone in his family was an artist, Smith never contemplated anything else. Smith defines himself by art, music, and teaching. He says that this always has been the case, and he intends it always to be so.

—Michael D. Harris

SMITH, Vincent (Dacosta)

American painter and printmaker

Born: New York, 12 December 1929. **Education:** Arts Students League, New York; Brooklyn Museum Art School, 1954-56; Skowhegan School of Painting, 1953-56, M.E. 1956; Empire State College; State University of New York, Saratoga, 1980. **Military Service:** United States Army, 1948-49: private. **Family:** Married Cynthia Linton in 1972. **Career:** Instructor, Whitney Museum Art Resources Center, 1967; artist-in-residence, Smithsonian Conference Center, 1967, Cite des Arts International, Paris, 1978. Participant, Second World Black African Festival of Arts and Culture, Lagos, Nigeria, 1977. **Awards:** Skowhegan School of Painting and Sculpture Scholarship, 1955, Brooklyn Museum Art School; John Hay Whitney Foundation Fellowship, 1959-60; National Institute of Arts and Letters grant, 1968; Childe Hassam Purchase Prize, American Academy of Arts and Letters, 1973, 1974; Thomas B. Clark Prize, National Academy of Design, 1974; commissioned (for four murals), New York City Board of Education, 1975. **Address:** G.W. Einstein Company, 591 Broadway, New York, New York 10012, U.S.A.

Individual Exhibitions:

1955	Brooklyn Museum Art School Gallery, New York
1956	Macon Street Library, Brooklyn, New York
1967	Larcada Gallery, New York
1968	Larcada Gallery, New York
1969	Studio Museum in Harlem, New York
1970	Fisk University, Nashville
1971	New Muse Community Museum, New York
1972	Whitney Museum Art Resources Center, New York
1973	Larcada Gallery, New York
	Allegheny College, Pennsylvania

Vincent Smith. Photo courtesy of G.R. N'Namdi Gallery.

	Emory University, Atlanta, Georgia
	John Jay College, New York
	Kibo Art Gallery, Kilimanjara, Tanzania
	Chemchemi Creative Arts Center, Arusha, Tanzania
	Paa Ya Paa Gallery, Nairobi, Kenya (traveling)
1974	Studio Museum in Harlem, New York
	The Reading Public Museum, Pennsylvania
	Portland Museum of Art, Portland, Maine
1975	Larcada Gallery, New York
	North Carolina A & T State University, Greensboro, North Carolina
	Burke Art Center, Carnegie Institute, Pittsburgh, Pennsylvania
1976	Whitney Museum Art Resources Center, New York
	Livingston College, Salisbury, North Carolina
1977	Erie Art Center, Pennsylvania
	Gallery 7, Detroit
	"African Series II," Larcada Gallery, New York
1978	Franklin and Marshall College, Lancaster, Pennsylvania
1979	Cooper Square Gallery, New York
1981	New York Community Folk Art Gallery, Syracuse, New York
	Storefront Museum/Paul Robeson Theatre, Jamaica
1982	"Journey to the Source," Spectrum IV Gallery, New Rochelle, New York
1983	Capital East Graphics, Washington, D.C.
	Center for Art and Culture of Bedford Stuyvesant, Brooklyn, New York
	Capital East Graphics, Washington, D.C.

Vincent Smith: *Wailing for the Funk Dealers (Fly Me to the Moon),* **1983. Photo courtesy of G.R. N'Namdi Gallery.**

1984	"Dry Bones," Randall Gallery, New York
1988	Art Galleries of Ramapo College, Mahwah, New Jersey
	Spiral Gallery, Brooklyn, New York
	Hamilton Hill Art Center, Schenectady, New York
1989	Schenectady Museum, New York
	Mid Hudson Arts and Science Center, Poughkeepsie, New York
1990	G.W. Einstein Company, Inc., New York
	Picker Art Gallery, Colgate University, Hamilton, New York
	Anderson Gallery, Virginia Commonwealth University, Richmond
	Hammonds House Galleries and Resource Center of African American Art, Atlanta, Georgia
	Davidson Art Center, Middletown, Connecticut
	NCCU Art Museum, Durham, North Carolina
	Milwaukee Art Museum, Wisconsin
	Louis Abrons Arts Center, New York
	G.W. Einstein Company, New York
1991	G.R. N'Namdi Gallery, Birmingham, Michigan
1993	Fire House Gallery, Nassau Community College
1994	Robeson Gallery, Rutgers University, New Jersey
	G.W. Einstein Company, Inc., New York
	G.R. N'Namdi Gallery, Birmingham, Michigan

Collections:

Ackland Art Museum, Chapel Hill, North Carolina; Art Institute of Chicago, Illinois; Baltimore Museum of Art, Maryland; Bayly Art Museum, Charlottesville, Virginia; Boston Museum of Art, New York; Brooklyn Museum, New York; Chemchimmi Creative Arts Center, Arusha, Tanzania; Columbus Gallery of Fine Art, Ohio; Detroit Institute of Arts; Dorsey Gallery, Brooklyn, New York; Kibo Art Gallery, Kilimanjaro, Kenya; Library of Congress, Washington, D.C.; Museum of Fine Arts, Boston; Museum of Modern Art, New York; National Museum of Afro-American Artists, Boston; National Museum of American Art, Washington, D.C.; New Muse Community Museum, Brooklyn, New York; Newark Museum, New Jersey; Paa Ya Paa Gallery, Nairobi, Kenya; Snite Museum of Art, Notre Dame, Indiana; Southeast Arkansas Arts and Science Center, Pine Bluff, Arkansas; Studio Museum in Harlem, New York; Yale University Art Gallery, New Haven, Connecticut.

Publications:

On SMITH: Books—*The Lower East Side, Literary and Arts Movement of the 1960's,* edited by Norman Morgan, New York, African American Review, 1993; *Lenten Meditations,* New York, Trinity Church, 1989 (illustrated); *In This Particular Gumbo . . . Jazz in Art and Literature,* Smithsonian Institution, Washington, D.C., 1994. **Videos**—*Artist in the Studio,* New York, Studio Museum in Harlem, 1974; *Acstract Expressionism, The Missing Link* by Beryl Wright, New York, Jamaica Art Center, May 16, 1988. **Films**—*Works on Paper,* eight-minute color film on the opening of exhibition, Jamaica, New York, Storefront Museum/Paul Robeson Theatre, 1981; *CBS Artists Panel Discussion: Bearden and His Contemporaries, Black Artists in Harlem and the World,* New York, Studio Museum in Harlem, May 17, 1991. **Audiocassette**—*Afro-American Art in the Twentieth Century* by Hamilton Bryan, New York, Bronx Museum of Art, 1980.

*   *   *

Vincent Smith, best known as a painter of geometric and symbolic paintings that show an affinity with African art, has also channeled his energy into drawing and printmaking. Exhibitions like *Riding on a Blue Note: Monoprints and Works on Paper, on Jazz Themes* represent his presentational and objective style and a return to his roots. Created from 1983 to 1991, the pieces in the exhibition bring him back to his initial development as a painter while maintaining the high standards he has always set for himself.

Smith has worked with the subject of jazz since the 1950s, when he was hanging out in New York City with top performers. As with many other black visual artists who came of age in the postwar period—Romare Bearden, Robert Thompson, and Jacob Lawrence are examples—the music of jazz has always been an important part of Smith's life, regardless of its influence on his artistic output. Throughout the 1950s he was a permanent fixture on the New York avant-garde scene and in the cultivation of the black arts movement that came to fruition in the latter part of 1960.

During this time Smith met Lester Young, Charlie Parker, Thelonious Monk, Art Blakey, and Max Roach, as well as the painters Edward Clark, Arthur Monroe, and Norman Lewis.

The scene downtown, which was filled with the activities of the Beat generation, was developing in a way similar to the Harlem of the 1920s. In addition to the musicians who received recognition at the time, black poets such as LeRoi Jones (Amiri Baraka), Don L. Lee (Haki Madhubuti), Mari Evans, and Bob Kaufman were coming into their own. The downtown bars were frequented by these literary artists, whom Smith befriended. Of the painting entitled *Hoo Doo Hollerin BeBop Ghosts: For Larry Neal* (1987), Smith recalls: "We were a strange group because people didn't know what to make of us. They were used to black musicians and performers, but the visual arts were sacred territory. . . . We used to have marathon sessions rapping about art, politics, literature, religion, aesthetics and women."

Against the dominant abstract expressionist style Smith incorporated his New York experiences into his representational paintings. Jazz in his paintings is an "incredible synthesis of inherent interests and formal training," biographer Sharon Patton has said. The image of jazz musicians is common throughout the paintings, but most important is the representation of movement, with the instruments being the tools of this movement. In *Scrapple from the Apple* (1989), for example, the horns bend and curve across the paper as they provide composition to the work.

Fused into some of the images of smoke-filled nightclubs are women, who are portrayed as seductive, beautiful, and sophisticated. In *Dancing in the Dark* (1989) woman is seen as sheer beauty, as the desired, with the circular repetitions of the women's faces, breasts, and buttocks evoking similarities with Henri Matisse's *The Blue Nude* of 1907. The black woman is also seen as refined elegance, as represented by great blues and jazz singers like Ma Rainey, Bessie Smith, and Billie Holiday in *I Gotta Right to Sing the Blues* (1989) and *Dr. Feelgood* (1987).

The one-time-only application of paint on a Plexiglas plate to create a monoprint is comparable to the improvisations that are essential to jazz. Each brush stroke is representative of the improvisatory method. The bright colors and masklike faces that appear in Smith's work also testify to the influence of the German expressionists—for example, Emil Nolde and Otto Dix—coupled with the effect of art in the African diaspora, which Smith has always been interested in.

—M. Franklin Sirmans

SMITH, William E.
American printmaker

Born: Chattanooga, Tennessee, 22 August 1913. **Education:** John Huntington Poly Art Institute, 1932-40; Cleveland School of Art, Ohio, 1939-41. **Family:** Married Frances Mae Palmore in 1951. **Career:** Member and president, Arts West Association; art coordinator, Authors Study Group, 1964-67. **Awards:** Certificate of Merit, Cleveland Museum of Art, Ohio; first prize, Val-Verde Art and Hobby Show, California.

Individual Exhibitions:

Benedict Art Gallery, Chicago; Florenz Gallery, Los Angeles; Lyman Brothers Gallery, Indianapolis; YMCA, Los Angeles.

Selected Group Exhibitions:

1935	*Cleveland May Show,* Ohio (through 1939)
	Cleveland Museum of Art (through 1941)
1938	Connecticut Academy of Fine Arts
1939	Dayton Art Institute, Ohio
1940	*American Negro Exposition,* Chicago
1942	Association of American Artists Galleries
	Atlanta University, Georgia
1943	Library of Congress, Washington, D.C.
1966	National Academy of Design
1968	Oakland Museum, California
1969	Atlanta University, Georgia

Collections:

Cleveland Museum of Art, Ohio; Golden State Insurance Company, Los Angeles; Howard University, Washington, D.C.; Library of Congress, Washington, D.C.; Oakland Museum, California.

Publications:

On SMITH: Articles—*Bulletin of the Cleveland Museum of Art,* 25, May 1938, pp. 81, 93, 96; *Art Digest,* 16, 15 January 1941, p. 19; *Magazine of Art,* 34, August 1941, p. 19; *Chicago Schools Journal,* 30, January/February 1949, p. 140; "Negro Artists Gain Recognition after Long Battle" by James Porter, in *Pittsburgh Courier,* 29 July 1950; *Charlotte Observer,* 16 August 1968, p. C-10; *Black Art: An International Quarterly,* 1, Winter 1976, p. 12.

*   *   *

William E. Smith has worked exclusively as a printmaker for several decades. He was part of the well-known Karamu House in Cleveland, Ohio, which was started in 1915 for the cultural education of African Americans. Its purpose was to encourage African American artists to communicate their unique experiences through their art and to direct the talent of African Americans into mainstream America. Among Smith's artistic peers during the time he was involved with Karamu House were Hughie Lee-Smith and Charles Sallee. Smith became a prominent artist while at Karamu House, and early in his career his work was sought by collectors and praised by critics. Smith's work was widely exhibited and attracted the attention of African American leaders such as Alain Locke and James Porter.

Smith's style is unmistakable, and many of his linocuts are well known. The subjects in his prints appear as if only one direct light source were illuminating them, so there are large areas of white and black, but detail is not lost. His prints are very dramatic. Smith's images impart a feeling of sadness and of being downtrodden. *Sulking Boy* (1938) depicts a half-clothed young man sitting on a stool, peering out of a window. The viewer realizes the boy is sad but also notices a sense of contemplation. This linoleum was boldly cut, with very few fine lines cut in. The detail in the print is found in the overall gesture and facial expression of the subject. Smith uses a similar technique in *Native Son* (1938) and *Bill Johnson as Emperor Jones. Native Son* depicts a forlorn young man with patched clothing who is half leaning against a wall. Again the linoleum was cut with bold lines, but the young man's expression imparts a deep, sad softness. More stark yet more soulful is *Bill Johnson as Emperor Jones,* a profile of a man.

Not all of Smith's images portray depressed people. *Pay Day* (1941) is a frontal view of a happy and proud-looking man who, judging from the title, has just gotten paid. The image has high contrast, and the viewer's eye is drawn to the lightest and darkest areas. The most noticeable areas are the man's forehead, nose, cheeks, teeth, and chin. The way in which the linoleum was cut for this image makes the man's face appear to be glistening. Two arced lines above the head suggest a hat. The neck area is extremely dark and his shirt color is bold white. The overall effect makes his face stand out even more.

Smith is a master of gesture and line. His ability to represent the richness of complex and powerful human emotions by using the fewest lines possible seems to match his suggestiveness in acquainting the viewer with poignant life situations.

—Christine Miner Minderovic

SNOWDEN, Gilda

American painter and mixed-media artist

Born: Detroit, Michigan, 29 July 1954. **Education:** Wayne State University, Detroit, B.F.A. 1977, M.A. 1978, M.F.A. 1979. **Career:** Since 1981 associate professor of fine art, Center for Creative Studies College of Art and Design, Detroit; gallery director, Detroit Repertory Theatre Lobby Gallery. Grant panelist, Michigan Council for the Arts and Cultural Affairs, 1994. Artist representative, *Biennial National Black Arts Festival,* 1994. Member, Forum for Contemporary Art. **Awards:** Graduate professional scholarship, Wayne State University, Detroit, 1977-79; Michigan Council for the Arts Individual Artists grants in painting, 1982, 1985, 1990; Michigan Council for the Arts Individual Artists grants in sculpture, 1988, 1995; Tannahill Faculty grant, Center for Creative Studies, 1990; Arts Midwest National Endowment for the Arts Regional Fellowship, 1990.

Individual Exhibitions:

1981	Willis Gallery, Detroit
1982	Detroit Artists Market
1984	Detroit Council for the Arts
1985	55 Peterboro Gallery, Detroit
1987	Paint Creek Center for the Arts, Rochester, Michigan
1988	Broadway Gallery, Detroit
1995	*Out of Sight, Out of Mind,* Center for Creative Studies, Detroit

Selected Group Exhibitions:

1982	J. L. Hudson Gallery, Detroit
	Park West Gallery, Southfield, Michigan
1984	Artcite Gallery, Windsor, Canada
1989	Pontiac Art Center, Michigan
	Meadowbrook Art Gallery, Oakland University, Rochester, Michigan
1990	Artemisia Gallery, Chicago
	Signature Images, Detroit Institute of Arts
	Art in General, New York
1991	Detroit Institute of Arts
1996	*A Detroit Tradition: Collecting African American Art,* Community Arts Gallery, Wayne State University

Collection:

Detroit Institute of Arts.

Publications:

On SNOWDEN: Book—*The Art of Black American Women: Works of Twenty-Four Artists of the Twentieth Century* by Robert Henkes, MacFarland Press, 1993. **Articles**—"Creative Artist/Instructor Seeking to Encourage Others" by Jocelyn Brown, in *Michigan Chronicle,* 12 September 1982; "Artist Calling" by John Sinclair, in *The Metro Times,* 18 January 1984; "One Person Show at 55 Peterboro Gallery" by Helen Shannon, in *Detroit Focus Quarterly,* December 1985; "Interview: Gilda Snowden" by Mark Puls, in *The South End,* 5 and 12 October 1985; "Gilda Snowden/Chris Whittey at the Michigan Gallery" by Joy Hakanson Colby, in *Detroit News,* 11 November 1985; "Her Challenges in Art Has Layers of Secrets" by Betsey Hansel, in *Detroit Free Press,* 4 December 1986; "Working: She Stretches the Boundaries of Her Art" by Jim Gustafson, in *The Detroit News,* 15 March 1987; "Gilda Snowden Gives Tornadoes a Good Image" by Joy Hakanson Colby, in *The Detroit News,* 7 September 1988; Review (Broadway Gallery, Detroit) by Sandra Yolles, in *Art News,* 87, December 1988, p. 169; "Art by Committee: Local Artists Draw Battle Lines over DIA's Michigan Program" by Joy Hakanson Colby, in *The Detroit News,* 23 April 1989; "A Rumbling Inside" by Michelle Biggs, in *City Arts Quarterly,* Fall 1989; "Ugly Reality Takes Walk in Shoe Sculpture" by Betty DeRamus, in *The Detroit News,* 6 March 1990; "Catalyst: Gilda Snowden" by Dawn Jones, in *Art Midwest Monthly Magazine,* October 1990; "Hot Dates: Luchs and Snowden Exhibition" by Neil Olivierra, in *The Metro Times,* October 1990; "Gilda Snowden" by Thomas Wojtas, in *Art Papers,* 20, March/April 1996, pp. 46-47.

*   *   *

A painter and self-described abstractionist (though probably more adequately classified as an abstract expressionist), Gilda Snowden blurs or distorts objects in her works, sometimes enough so that objects are unrecognizable except by the work's title or by a repetition of images from piece to piece. A recurring subject for her is the storm or tornado, represented by dynamic swirls and vigorous strokes of color and shade. Her tornadoes are transformed by abstraction from the objects of violence in the real world to the perfections of pastel and paint in the work; captured, they are no longer a danger but live in a world of their own—to be observed as aesthetic objects entirely separate from actual tornadoes.

Though not precisely "pictures" of anything recognizable in the world, Snowden's works may nonetheless be viewed as snapshots. If these snapshots, created largely in pastel or oil, can be said to depict anything, it would be Snowden's feelings about the outside world at a given time and in a given place. It is her intent to create something imaginary from within herself by abstracting and combining that which is concrete outside herself; in turn she tries to create something visionary from sensory impression, intuition, and emotion.

Storms seem to have special importance to the artist and have even become an integral part of her self-portraiture. In *Self in Storm* (1991), a silhouetted figure (head and shoulders, hair wildly twisted in the wind) is anchored in the center of a multidirectional maelstrom. The figure is seemingly strong enough not to be injured—or even tossed about—but is no doubt influenced by the storm, especially given its importance throughout Snowden's work. The storm may indeed be inseparable from the figure in the drawing, reflecting, it seems, the artist's goal of exploring and illustrating her feelings about her own environment.

—Terry Bain

SNOWDEN, Sylvia (Frances)
American painter and printmaker

Born: Raleigh, North Carolina, 21 April 1946. **Education:** Howard University, Washington, D.C., B.A.; Le Grande Chaumier, Paris, France, certificate; Skowhegan School of Painting and Sculpture, Maine, certificate; Howard University, Washington, D.C., M.F.A. Studied with Leonard Bocour, John Button, Robert Cronbach, Willard Cummings, David Driskell, Zubel Kachadoorian, Alex Katz, James Kearns, Lois Jones Pierre-Noel, James A. Porter, Ben Shahn, and James A. Wells. **Family:** Married John Butler in 1970 (divorced 1987), one daughter and one son. **Career:** Instructor/lecturer in painting, design, and art history at various universities (including Cornell University, Ithaca, New York, and Howard University, Washington, D.C.), 1965-92; director, Washington Women's Arts Center, 1983; administrator, JTPA Contracts, ARTs D.C., Washington, D.C., 1984-88. Artist-in-residence, University of Sidney, Australia, 1975, California Institute of the Arts, Valencia, 1989; visiting artist, University of Colorado at Boulder, 1990, Cornell University, Ithaca, New York, 1991-92, Brandywine Workshop, Philadelphia, 1994, Howard University, Washington, D.C., 1995, Corcoran Gallery, Washington, D.C., 1995. Traveled in England, France, Germany, and Holland, 1989. **Awards:** Lois M. Jones Award for Recognition, Fondo del Sol Gallery; individual grant, District of Columbia Commission on the Arts and Humanities, Washington, D.C.; Lois Jones Pierre-Noel Award for Water Color; scholarship, Skowhegan School of Painting and Sculpture; first place award for oil painting, Skowhegan School; first place award for painting, Association for Black Arts/East. **Address:** 465 M Street, N.W., Washington, D.C. 20001, U.S.A.

Individual Exhibitions:

1965	Delaware State College, Dover
1970	Johns Hopkins University, Baltimore, Maryland
1979	Zenith Gallery, Washington, D.C.
1985	James Hurd Gallery, Washington, D.C.
1987	Brody's Gallery, Washington, D.C.
1992	National Museum of Women in the Arts, Washington, D.C.
1993	*Burns Series,* Zenith Gallery, Washington, D.C.
1995	*Portraits of Frances,* Addison/Ripley Gallery, Washington, D.C.

Sylvia Snowden: *"G"* (painting of artist's father, Dr. George W. Snowden).

Sylvia Snowden: *Jessie* (painting of artist's mother, Jessie B. Snowden).

Selected Group Exhibitions:

1979   *Emerging Artists,* Washington Projects for the Arts, D.C.
1983   *Afro- and Latin American Women,* Georgetown University, Washington, D.C.
1986   *Myth and Ritual,* Touchstone Gallery, Washington, D.C.
1987   *Afro-American Art, Now,* George Washington University, Washington, D.C.
1989   *Introspective: Contemporary Art by American Brazilian Artists of African Descent,* California Afro-American Museum, Los Angeles
1990   *Art and Conscience,* Dadian Gallery, American University, Washington, D.C.
1994   *Off the Mall,* Corcoran Gallery of Art, Hemicycle Gallery, Washington, D.C.
1995   Howard University Gallery of Art/Fondo del Sol Art Center, Washington, D.C.
        African-American Women: Prints, Brandywine Workshop, Washington, D.C.
        1995 Contemporary Print Fair, Baltimore Museum of Art, Maryland

Publications:

On SNOWDEN: Books—*Sylvia Snowden: A Black American Female Painter,* Sydney, Australia, University of Sydney Press, n.d. **Articles**—"Galleries: High Voltage Intensity in Paintings from

the Inner City" by Benjamin Forgey, in *Washington Star* (D.C.), 4 May 1979; "Curtain Call" by Charles Farrow, in *Washington Afro-American* (D.C.), 3 March 1979; "Sylvia Snowden" by J.W. Mahoney, in *New Art Examiner*, December 1985; "The Experience Exhibited" by Elizabeth Lazarus, in *Washington Post* (D.C.), August 1986; "Separate But More Than Equal" by Alice Thorson, in *Washington Times* (D.C.), 29 January 1987; "Sylvia Snowden: Engaging Expressionism" by Alice Thorson, in *New Art Examiner*, 16(2), October 1988; "Optical Illusions: Images of Miscegenation in Nineteenth and Twentieth Century Art" by Judith Wilson, in *American Art* (Oxford), S(3), Summer 1991; "Painter Sylvia Snowden's Visceral Expressionism" by Mary McCoy, in *Washington Post* (D.C.), 26 December 1992.

* * *

Sylvia Snowden belongs to the expressionist lineage of twentieth-century painters, a multinational group that includes Oskar Kokoschka, Chaim Soutine, Beauford Delaney, and Willem de Kooning, each trying the very limits of representation in order to express essences. Like them, Snowden has developed a distinctive style that dissects and distorts the figure and in the process lays bare human emotions.

An artist trained in American and French institutions, Snowden made her debut as a printmaker in a 1957 exhibition. Since the 1970s, however, she has applied her energies to painting the nude. Many of her subjects are female—*M Street: Connie* (1978), *Mamie*

Harrington (1985), and *Michelle Haberon* (1985) are among the titles of her works—and they are active, loose-limbed forms in leaning, squatting, and bending poses set against monochromatic backgrounds. What so effectively communicates the force of her subjects is the artist's physical handling of the paint medium. She customarily uses acrylic pigment as plaster, building densely impastoed surfaces on canvas, hardboard, and paper supports. Her technique challenges the two-dimensionality of conventional painting, presenting works that are textured and plastic. Furthermore, her drawing of the body seems to mock standardized means of illusory representation. Breasts are plotted at different latitudes, feet turn inward toward the knees, and fingers bend at unnatural right angles. Rather than foreshorten the appendages of figures to make them seem more real, she extends their lengths. Arms and legs undulate and gesticulate wildly like cooked spaghetti strands, enlivening the overall imagery.

Snowden also makes aggressive decisions with regard to her palette so that the colors seem to advance beyond the picture plane and enter the viewing space. She uses bright reds and blues liberally to describe broad areas of the figures, but she judiciously mixes secondary colors and tones into the Technicolor emulsion. As a result both the external and internal body appear exposed and accessible to the audience. If flesh, blood, skin, bone, and muscle could be seen simultaneously when the human form is examined, this is how the heterogeneous mass would appear. Yet Snowden's work is more like landscape and cartography than anatomical drawing or figure painting. She regards the body as a varied terrain, with parts that are drifting islands, vast oceans, peninsulas, and mountain ranges.

Critics have discussed Snowden's art in terms of portraiture and, because they suspect the figures to be versions of her creative personality, self-portraiture. Nonetheless, she has described her works in terms of experience and documentaries, for they are named for people she has met on M Street in Washington, D.C., a urban stretch of poverty and deprivation. However grotesque, the figures spew forth palpable energy, signifying strength in lives that lie hidden from circumscribed views.

—Jacqueline Francis

SOARES, Genilson (da Silva)

Brazilian painter and sculptor

Born: Joao Pessoa, Brazil, 1940. **Education:** Modern Art Society, Recife. **Career:** Advertising and graphic arts, Brazil. **Awards:** Research prize, *Fifth Contemporary Art Exhibition,* Contemporary Art Museum, São Paulo, Brazil, 1971; Acquisition Prize, *Eighth Contemporary Art Salon,* Campinas, São Paulo, Brazil, 1972; prize, *XII Bienal Internacional de São Paulo,* Brazil, 1973; prize, *XIV Bienal Internacional de São Paulo,* Brazil, 1977; Elebra Informatica Prize, *Overview of Contemporary Brazilian Art,* Modern Art Museum, São Paulo, 1985.

Individual Exhibitions:

1972   No Sobrado Gallery, São Paulo
1979   Espaço Max Pochon, São Paulo
1980   Pinacoteca do Estado, São Paulo
1981   *Projects for the Morning,* Espaço NO, Porto Alegre, Brazil
1982   Deco Gallery, São Paulo, Brazil
1985   *Passage through the Solstice,* Modern Art Museum, São Paulo, Brazil
1987   Paulo Figueiredo Gallery, São Paulo
1989   Paço das Artes, São Paulo
1990   Ribeirao Preto, São Paulo

Selected Group Exhibitions:

1972   Contemporary Art Museum, Campinas, São Paulo
1973   *XII Bienal Internacional de São Paulo*
1975   Estudio Actual, Caracas, Venezuela
         Fluxus Gallery, Selb, Germany
1976   Modern Art Museum, Rio de Janeiro
1977   *Editions and Communications in Latin America,* Le Havre, France
         XIV Bienal Internacional de São Paulo
1979   Cranbrook Academy of Art, Bloomfield Hills, Michigan
1989   California Afro-American Museum, Los Angeles
         Bronx Museum of Art, New York
1993   Brazilian Art Museum, São Paulo
1994   A Culture Confluence, Frankfurt, Germany
1995   Centro de Cultura de Belo Horizonte, Bahia

*   *   *

Genilson Soares is a small, quiet man, soft-spoken, gentle, and reserved. He is also intensely serious about his work and the thought that gives it shape. His colors and visual playfulness are equally gentle. They do not strike aggressively but rather are meant to dawn on people gradually as they contemplate them. The colors very much express the artist's personality.

Genilson Soares. Photo courtesy of Camila Pedral.

Genilson Soares: *Between Us* (installation view). Photo courtesy of the Sao Paulo State Museum.

Soares grew up in northeastern Brazil and studied art in Recife, where he was first influenced by the social realism of the Mexican muralists. Later, after he had moved to São Paulo, he decided that his art should be separate from politics since "art cannot change the world . . . only perceptions."

Although he was brought up in a strictly Roman Catholic household, Soares dislikes institutionalized religion. He was taught that Afro-Brazilian faiths such as Candomblé "were not religions," and he was made to fear them. As a result he explored Zen Buddhism and Jungian theory. He has found that people around the world can relate to his work, and "so there must be universals."

The stress on universals is reflected in Soares's works that play with the perception and experience of space. He forces the viewer to see things in new ways by altering the interactions of three-dimensional (real) and two-dimensional (illusory) space. He designs installations and environmental works that include his "corrective perspectives—a kind of joke with the space," involving plays on positive and negative volumes, inside and outside spaces, straight walls that appear to bend, and wall outlets (one real, one painted).

Despite the illusion of purely visual plays with perception and a lack of content, Soares's works contain other things as well. Fragments of childhood memories sometimes appear, as in his series of wall pieces based on the Brazilian pastime of kite flying. And despite the denial of social or political commentary in his work, he created *River without End* (1987) to protest the construction of a nuclear power plant that would have destroyed a virgin forest.

Soares's installation entitled *Fragile Equilibrium* combines many of his interests in space and perception. The work is simple, direct, and clear, and his colors muted, soft, and subtle—like his visual illusions and his personality. Two pieces—a bisected sphere on a copper bar and a nonparallelogram of painted wood, copper, and plastic—exemplify his corrective perspective, his play with real

and imagined space. Two other pieces—a tall square column with a serpentine line running through it and a circle of velvet cloth, a square sheet of glass, and oval stones—suggest movement, the passage of time, and, most importantly, a "fragile equilibrium." Soares explains, "My work searches for the equilibrium, the fragile equilibrium that lives in the world. It is a way to see movement abstractly, the primitive movement in atoms, the basic movement of life."

Soares's works challenge us to see anew and to question our notions of reality. His words reveal his spirituality and his efforts to assert the unlimited potential of humans with free minds: "My life is my work. It has changed much since my childhood in Recife. I am older now. . . . I am like dust in the universe . . . like a spider in the forest who is small but continues to do his work, to weave his web. I fight to do my work in Brazil even though conditions make it very hard. I use my work to make people think differently about space . . . a space that appears very restricted . . . a wall becomes glass—so that people can look *beyond* it."

—Henry John Drewal

SOW, Amadou

Senegalese painter, sculptor, and graphic artist

Born: Mamadou Sow, Saint Louis, Sénégal, 17 November 1951. **Education:** École des Beaux Arts, Dakar Sénégal, 1979-73; École des Beaux Arts, Vienna, 1979. **Family:** Married Veronika Sow in 1982, one daughter and one son. **Awards:** Vienna Academy of Arts Award, 1975, 1995. **Address:** 1030 Vienna, Blattgasse, 3/3/18, Austria.

Individual Exhibitions:

1981   Art Contemporain Gallery, Dakar, Senegal
1982   Afro-Artist Institute, Vienna, Austria
1983   Studio Moliere, Vienna, Austria
1988   Gallery Espace, Dakar, Senegal
1992   Gallery 39, Dakar, Senegal
1993   Gallery 8F, Dakar, Senegal
1994   Gallery 8F, Dakar, Senegal
1995   Gallery Kajaroma, Abidjan, Senegal
1996   Gallery Lesard, Dakar, Senegal

Selected Group Exhibitions:

1974   Grand Palais, Paris
        Academy of Arts, Vienna
1975   House of Culture, Stockholm, Sweden
        Palazzo Braschi, Rome
        Palais des Affaires, Florence
1976   Bonn Center, Bonn, Germany
1979   Palacio des Bellas Artes, Mexico
1980   Corcoran Gallery, Washington, D.C.
1992   International Biennale, Dakar, Senegal
1996   International Beinnale, Dakar, Senegal

Publications:

On Sow: Books—*Portrait of the Artist,* exhibition catalog, Vienna Austria, Academy of Arts, 1974; *Amadou Sow,* exhibition catalog, by Monica Liedl, Vienna, 1996. **Articles**—"Un sculpteur remarquable" by Jean F. Briere, in *West African,* 1974; "Art a Dakar" by Francine Normese, in *Elle,* Paris, 1996.

*

Amadou Sow comments:

I was very lucky to grow up on the island of Gorée, a place whose atmosphere made me look closely at the world around me, which seems essential for encountering art. I was part of the earth, the sand, and the stones of my world, materials which were my first means of expressing myself through art. Already at an early age I decided to become an artist. My academic studies in painting, sculpture, and graphics were then important for my further development, and materials such as stone, wood, glass, cloth, paper, aluminum, or clay were to become an interesting challenge. Earth and sand, however, have remained my favorite materials.

While working I do not think about what I am doing, but I am guided by my soul and my ancestors.

*   *   *

In 1996 the painter Amadou Sow provided the official emblem for the Dakar Art Biennial. The choice of his work to represent contemporary Senegalese art reflects his importance within and dedication to the art history of his country and his concern with defining a place for the work of African artists in the international arena. His design, broadly in the shape of a draped canvas in bright reds and greens, emerged from a series of works with acrylic on Plexiglas. The series, which Sow has exhibited in Europe as well as Senegal, shows connections with a traditional painting practice in Senegal and the Maghreb that is widely known as *sous verre,* or

glass painting. The technique, which arose originally to tell Koranic stories banned from print by French colonial authorities, has become an important popular art form. Sow's works are more transparent than the earlier forms, which are typically opaque. Moreover, he does not paint his compositions in reverse on the back of the glass, as is the tradition. In Sow's compositions the light filters through, providing illumination from behind and giving greater emphasis to the details of the designs. His use of single colors in bright hues recalls the glass-painting technique, however, and his deliberate reference to these earlier forms is indicative of his interest in traditional artistry.

Like many other painters of his generation just beginning art school in the years after Senegalese independence in 1960, Sow trained at the École des Beaux Arts in Dakar. His early training and the professional and personal contacts he made in this milieu are keys to understanding his aesthetic choices and his place within the larger history of the Senegalese arts scene. In the 1970s Sow came under the patronage and influence of the French mathematician, amateur painter, and art teacher Pierre Lods. Because of the interest he had shown in the artistic traditions of the continent while teaching in the French Congo, Lods had been recruited to teach in Dakar by president Léopold Senghor. Like Papa Ibra Tall, Lods believed in the philosophy of Negritude, the importance of traditional motifs and working methods, and the innate creativity of his African students. He held a private atelier in which Sow, Mohammadou M'Baye, and Kré M'Baye were his most favored and successful students.

The early works of Sow show a preoccupation with stereotyped, schematic images of African sculpted figures and spirit

Amadou Sow, 1974.

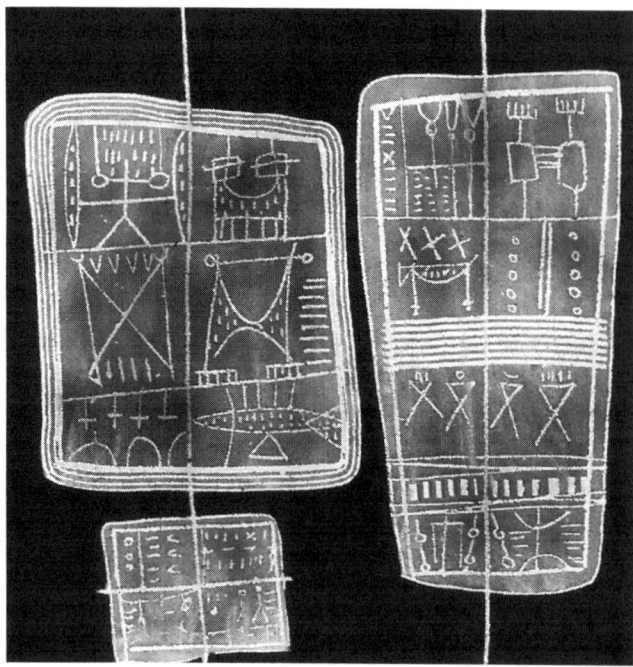

Amadou Sow: untitled, 1995.

forms. His *Power* (1974) and *Femme et l'oiseau* (1973) are typical of his artistic output during the period. Both compositions make full use of the picture space, filling it with interlocking flat forms executed in strong, often earthy tones. While his mentor did not teach directly, preferring to let the artists create in isolation, Lods did provide paints and advice. Sow has insisted that Lods's methods of instruction were characterized by *dire rien* (saying nothing). Some critics have suggested, however, that Sow's work illustrates a Senegalese school of Lodsian followers similar to that formed in Poto-Poto in the French Congo.

Like many of his contemporaries, during the 1970s Sow contributed several designs to the Manufacture Sénégalaise des Arts Décoratifs (Tapestry Center) and showed his works in large government-funded traveling exhibitions. With his permanent relocation to Vienna in the 1980s, Sow has been able to distance himself from his early roots in the Negritude school and begin to experiment in other media and artistic practices. He has described his artistic life in Vienna as a double-edged sword, however. Although he has access to a greater market, he also must confront the exotic preconceptions of his European patrons, who look for an essential Africanness in his works. Sow forms part of a large and growing diaspora of Africans working in both Africa and Europe and changing the conceptions of contemporary African artistry.

—Elizabeth Harney

STATOM, Therman
American sculptor

Born: 1953. **Education:** Pilchuck Glass School, Stanwood, Washington, 1972; Rhode Island School of Design, Providence, Rhode Island, B.F.A. 1974; Pratt Institute of Art and Design, Brooklyn,

New York, M.F.A. 1980. **Career:** Instructor, University of Rhode Island, Kingston, 1976, Pratt Fine Arts Center, Seattle, 1980-81, Colorado Mountain College, 1983, University of California, Los Angeles, 1983-85, Pilchuck Glass School, Stanwood, Washington, 1984-86, Pitzer College, Claremont, California, 1985. **Awards:** Ford Foundation Award, 1977; Pratt Institute Fellowship, Brooklyn, New York, 1978; National Fellowship Fund Award, 1978; National Endowment for the Arts fellowships, 1980, 1982, 1988; Brody Arts Foundation Fellowship, 1985. **Address:** 2349-D South Santa Fe Avenue, Los Angeles, California 90058, U.S.A.

Individual Exhibitions:

1977	Anne Hathaway Gallery, Washington, D.C.
1978	Pratt Institute of Art and Design, Brooklyn, New York
1981	Rubin/Mardin Gallery, Seattle
1984	Los Angeles Contemporary Exhibitions
1985	Kohler Art Center, Sheyboygan, Wisconsin
1987	Bluxome Gallery, San Francisco
	Habatat Gallery, Boca Raton, Florida
1988	Pittsburgh Center for the Arts, Pennsylvania
	Clare Scremini Gallery, Paris
	Habatat Gallery, Boca Raton, Florida
	Marilyn Butler Gallery, Scottsdale, Arizona
1989	Habatat Gallery, Boca Raton, Florida

Selected Group Exhibitions:

1981	Rubin/Mardin Gallery, Seattle
1983	Montclair Art Museum, New York
	Meyer Breier Weiss Gallery, San Francisco
1984	Jan Baum Gallery, Los Angeles
1985	Traver/Sutton Gallery, Seattle
1986	Los Angeles County Museum of Art
	Oakland Museum, California
1988	Denver Art Museum, Colorado
1989	Traver Gallery, Seattle
	Nielson Gallery, Malmo, Sweden

Collections:

City of Seattle; Detroit Institute of Arts; High Museum of Art, Atlanta, Georgia; Los Angeles County Museum of Art; Oakland Museum, California.

*   *   *

Therman Statom challenges the medium of glass by conceptualizing its architectonic uses and melding them into structures that weave angular sheets with blown curvilinear, organic shapes to create calligraphic gestural forms. A graduate of New York's Pratt Institute in 1978, he also studied glassblowing and taught at the Pilchuck Glass School in Washington State in the 1980s.

Statom thrives on the contrasts created by using different glassmaking techniques in one composition, and because of his atypical use of glass, he has been described as possessing an anticraft aesthetic. His glassworks often seem painted as he creates fluid blown shapes alongside angular manufactured ones. In the 1980s he created a series of small glass houses that he painted and then marked with expressionistic strokes of pastel crayons and decorated with broken shards of beautifully colored irregular glass shapes, reminding the viewer that "he who lives in glass houses shouldn't throw stones." This type of humorous lyricism is often present in Statom's work. In addition, he likes to include the element of play. In an untitled work of around 1993, solitaire is being played on the surface of a game table. The faces of the cards have expressionistic markings that hold hidden messages the viewer must unravel, thereby making the spectator a participant in Statom's playful antics.

Statom has also created walk-in rooms that enclose collections of glass forms such as vases, jars, beads, and ladders, all fashioned by the artist. These pieces, for example, the ladders, can and have stood by themselves as works of art, but when they are housed in glass, they work as precious jewel-like forms for closer examination and appreciation by the viewer. The work *Map Room* (1994) recalls Statom's interest in borders that have been imposed for political motives. He seeks to reveal the cultural significance of artificial demarcations, which can be devastating. In *Map Room* he sealed four land maps and two astronomical maps in glass boxes. Blue green water floats in an adjacent box, evoking the mythologies and legends of buccaneers' maps and island treasures. Statom invokes a sense of discovery by frosting the glass panels so that the viewer must read the images through a screen. Exploration of secretive spaces parallels his investigation of mythologies and the world of metaphysics, in which his own evolving mythology holds a reverence for light and water. Statom also has used painted panels to create works that range from realistic landscapes to a collection of painted or cast glass shapes adhering to a surface, as in *China Queen* (1992) and *La Melon* (1993).

Statom created three fanciful chandeliers for the renovated Los Angeles Public Library. The chandeliers are a collection of colored glass jars, vases, ladders, and figures that appear to be suspended by an invisible energy. The objects were created by carving out Styrofoam molds and pouring liquid glass into them. The glass forms were then refined and polished. Each is eighteen feet in diameter and weighs 1,750 pounds. The three chandeliers can be viewed from ground level or as one ascends from lower floors to upper ones, echoing the three historic chandeliers that are suspended at the opposite end of the main lobby hallway. The older chandeliers are decorated with stars and moons to reflect the theme of the solar system. Building on this theme, Statom chose to focus on three main subjects—man-made endeavors, natural phenomenon, and spiritual ideas—saying that he wants them to serve as the heart of the overall visual, architectural, practical, and spiritual purpose of the building. Each chandelier represents one of the three worlds. The chandeliers are decorated with glass motifs of hearts, eyeglasses, angels, a self-portrait of Statom, a turtle, and other symbols.

Statom has pushed and expanded the expectations for glass in shape as well as scale. Respectful of its fragility but not bound by it, he has developed a process that exhibits the physical strengths of glass and that belie our preconceived notions of the possibilities of this industrial medium.

—Lizzetta LeFalle-Collins

STETH, Raymond
American printmaker and graphic artist

Born: Norfolk, Virginia, 1917. **Education:** Pennsylvania Museum School of Industrial Art (now the University of the Arts), 1941-43;

Barnes Foundation, Philadelphia, 1942-44. **Family:** Two sons. **Career:** Sign painter, Philadelphia; member, vaudeville theater company, Philadelphia; artist, Graphic Arts Division, Works Progress Administration, Philadelphia, 1938. Cofounder and director, Philographic School of Art, 1948-53; instructor, Pennsylvania Museum School of Industrial Art, 1949-51. Artist-in-residence, Pennsylvania Academy of the Fine Arts, Philadelphia. Guest curator, Philadelphia Print Club, 1942-43. Worked with Dox Thrash, the inventor of the Corborundum print process, and helped develop its potential. **Died:** Philadelphia, 6 February 1997.

Selected Exhibitions:

1940   Library of Congress, Washington, D.C.
1941   South Side Community Art Center, Chicago
1943   Fort Huachuca, Arizona

Collections:

Corcoran Gallery of Art, Washington, D.C.; Library of Congress, Washington, D.C.; Metropolitan Museum of Art, New York; Philadelphia Museum of Art.

Publications:

On STETH: Book—*Alone in a Crowd: Prints of the 1930s-40s by African-American Artists from the Collection of Reba and Dave Williams,* New York, 1993, pp. 4ff. **Articles**—"Chicago's New Southside Art Center," in *American Magazine of Art,* August 1941; "Negro in Art," in *Art News,* 19 December 1941, p. 24; "Papers of Raymond Steth" by Marina Pacini, in *Archives of American Art Journal,* 29(3)(4), 1989, p. 73; "Raymond Steth" by Rolando Corpus, in *Philadelphia Museum of Art Bulletin,* 90, Winter 1995, pp. 14-15 (illustrated).

*   *   *

Raymond Steth was a member of the Philadelphia graphics division, a community center that was designated for fine prints during the Works Progress Administration (WPA) in the early 1940s. He was in the company of Dox Thrash (the originator of Carborundum print), Claude Clark, and Samuel Brown. Even though Steth did some Carborundum prints, his focus was on lithography, and he produced some great prints. In her essay in the *Alone in a Crowd* catalog, Leslie King-Hammond described Steth as a master of content and commentary, a natural storyteller in the tradition of the African griot. What makes his prints unique is his ability to compose and tell a complete story of his people on the very small space of a lithograph plate.

His ability to produce and create prints that look monumental is also notable. The prints entitled *Beacons of Defense* (c.1944) and *Evolution of Swing* (c.1943) look massive. The draftsmanship, the scale, and the value of the prints are testimonies to Steth's technological skill. The multiple images in the *Beacons of Defense* prints convey the energy of integrated American war workers that resulted when President Roosevelt, under threat of protest march in Washington, ordered desegregation of the defense industries. These prints have enabled us to look at the role that African Americans played in the military not only at the war fronts but also in the military industries.

In *The Evolution of Swing,* Steth traced the history of music, beginning in an African village. The print shows drums, singing slaves, and dancers "swinging" to a jazz band. One can see the music beamed through the towers around the world. As Leslie King-Hammond has pointed out, "Steth celebrates the development of swing as a part of African American history; in the same spirit, African American printmakers glorified their heroes and heroines."

Steth also shows the importance of religion among African Americans. In his *Heaven on a Mule* (1944), the artist says, "The people are so devout that religion is first and foremost in their lives. They did everything they could according to the Bible. The families are so religious that when they were ready to go to heaven they were wearing wings. The women bowed their heads because they could not see the face of the lord, while the man was so fervent that he thought he saw an angel." Religion was the source of energy for the slaves and their families. After slavery it remained the great force that educates and unites African Americans.

Steth's *Boys* (1942) in the collection of Morgan State University depicts the activities of young boys in the neighborhood—basketball, fist fights, cart wheels, and other mischievous activities.

Raymond Steth was a devoted printmaker who also helped to develop the Philadelphia Philographic School of Art, an independent printmaking/graphics workshop where he taught classes, and the printmaking department for Morgan State College in Baltimore (now Morgan State University). Steth made his mark among the printmakers of the world in every aspect of the medium.

—Gabriel Tenabe

STEVENS, Nelson (L.)

American painter

Born: Brooklyn, New York, 26 April 1938. **Education:** Ohio University, B.F.A. 1962; Kent State University, Ohio, M.F.A. 1969. **Career:** Instructor, Cleveland Public Schools, 1962-66, Cleveland Museum of Art, 1966-68; assistant professor of art, Northern Illinois University, DeKalb, 1969-72. Beginning 1972 associate professor of art, University of Massachusetts, Amherst. Publisher, Spirit Wood Productions. Album illustrator, *The Cry of My People,* Archie Shepp album, ABC Dunhill, 1972, *There is a Trumpet in My Soul,* Archie Shepp album, Arista, 1975. **Address:** 81 Florida Street, Springfield, Massachusetts 01109, U.S.A.

Selected Exhibitions:

1970	National Center of Afro-American Artists, Boston
	Studio Museum in Harlem, New York
	Howard University, Washington, D.C.
1972	Karamu House, Cleveland, Ohio (solo)
	Studio Museum in Harlem, New York
	National Center of Afro-American Artists, Boston
	Howard University, Washington, D.C.
	Kent State University, Ohio
	Neighborhood Art Center, Akron, Ohio
1977	Afri-Cobra, Philadelphia
	FESTAC 77, Lagos, Nigeria
	Janet Carter Gallery, New York

Collections:

Fisk University, Nashville; Karamu House, Cleveland, Ohio; Kent State University, Ohio; Northern Illinois University, De Kalb.

Publications:

On STEVENS: Articles—"Where Down Home Meets Back Home" by Jean B. Grillo, in *Boston After Dark,* September 1970; "Performing Arts for the People" by Robin C. Smith, in *Black Art Quarterly,* Winter 1978, pp. 17-27.

*　　*　　*

Nelson Stevens, a native of Brooklyn, New York, has become a recognized and respected African American artist. He was one of the first members of Africobra in Chicago in the early 1970s, and his colorful, complicated figures have become recognizable as signature works.

After running track at Ohio University, Stevens taught in the Cleveland public schools and at the Cleveland Museum of Art before going to graduate school at Kent State University. While in Cleveland, Stevens regularly went to the Jazz Temple, where he heard, among others, John Coltrane. Throughout his career as an artist, his form and subject matter have reflected his interest and understanding of jazz, and he has forged a close relationship with Max Roach and come to know Archie Shepp, both of whom have been his colleagues at the University of Massachusetts in Amherst. He has done album covers for both musicians, and musicians regularly are the subject of his paintings and drawings. In many ways Stevens's complex imagery is a syncretism of music (sound), kinetic performance, and visual expression. Although actually static, his images seem to vibrate with sound in ways not unlike Coltrane's work filled auditory space with energy.

Nelson Stevens.

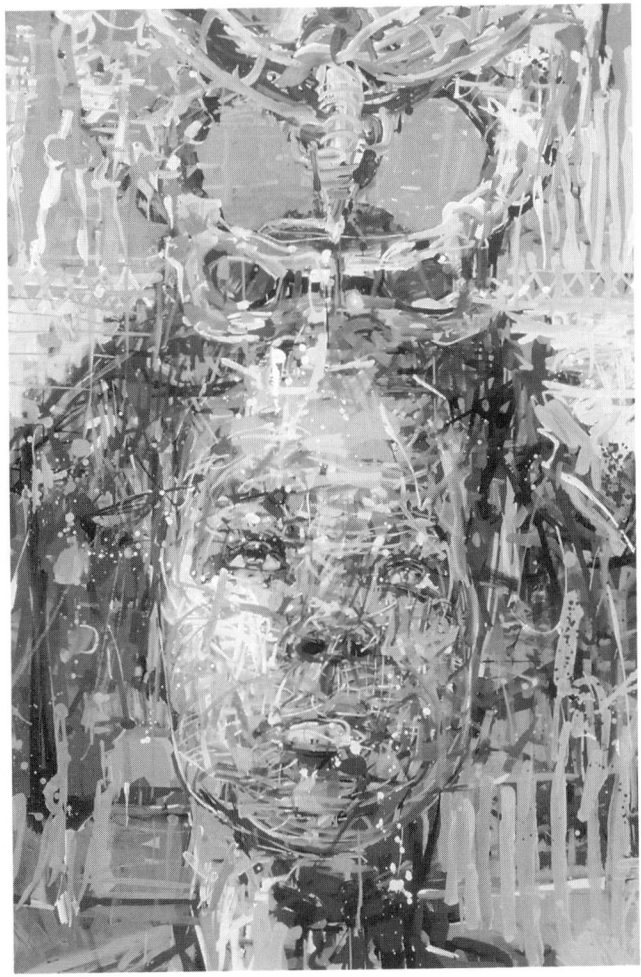

Nelson Stevens: *Bonnie* ("Hoo Doo Bone" series). **Photo courtesy of Robert Arruda.**

As a member of Africobra, Stevens participated in the creation of an aesthetic approach that included Kool-Aid colors, positive imagery, African aesthetics, and the objective of making artworks accessible and acceptable to the black community. The heroic, monumentalized heads for which Stevens became known early on evolved into more complex groupings of figures and into studies of women, particularly the long-running "Hoodoo Bone" series that involved the female pelvic bone in a composition with a nude figure. He also has created images of notable blacks like Bob Marley, Stevie Wonder, Malcolm X, and Angela Davis. His early heads were often situated slightly above the viewer, a perspective that emphasized their heroic status. One of his more notable works from 1970, *Sister Spirit*, was filled with the face and large Afro of fellow artist Valerie Maynard.

For many years Stevens produced *Drum* magazine at the University of Massachusetts, a publication devoted to black culture, and more recently he originated the *Art in the Service of the Lord* calendar, which uses Christian art done by black artists from a black perspective. He included work by such artists as James Phillips, Jon Lockard, Pheoris West, and Paul Goodnight in this endeavor. The project is consistent with the political consciousness that motivated his Africobra paintings and with his understanding of publishing and the impact of the popular media learned from working with *Drum*. Throughout his career Stevens also has developed note

cards, posters, reproductions, and prints from his works, thereby making his images available to the public.

Stevens also has produced numerous murals, continuing the philosophy behind the 1967 *Wall of Respect* in Chicago of making art the property and inspiration of the black community. One of his most important murals was the 1980 *Ascensions,* produced at Tuskeegee University for the hundredth anniversary of the institution and linking the history and notable people of the school—Booker T. Washington, George Washington Carver, Chappie James, and the Flying Tigers air squadron that trained there during World War II—with other people from black history, including Ida B. Wells, Malcolm X, Marcus Garvey, Martin Luther King, Jr., and Mary McLeod Bethune.

Like that of Romare Bearden or Jacob Lawrence, Stevens's work remains recognizable because of his unique use of complex color lines and pieces to create solid-looking forms that are actually not solid at all. In this way his work implies the underlying subatomic reality of matter, which is composed primarily of space and energy. Like Lawrence, Stevens has improvised and evolved a particular approach to the figure and the image during his long career.

—Michael D. Harris

STOUT, Renee
American sculptor and assemblage artist

Born: Junction City, Kansas, 1958. **Education:** Carnegie-Mellon University, Pittsburgh, Pennsylvania, B.F.A. 1980. **Awards:** Afro-American Master Artists in Residency Program, Northeastern University, Boston, 1984-85.

Individual Exhibitions:

1987	Chapel Gallery, Mount Vernon College, Washington, D.C.
1991	B.R. Kornblatt Gallery, Washington, D.C.

Selected Group Exhibitions:

1982	Pennsylvania State University, State College, University Park
1984	Pennsylvania State University, State College, University Park
1985	Fitchburg State College, Fitchburg, Massachusetts
	Massachusetts College of Art, Boston
	Museum of Science and Industry, Chicago
1986	California State University, California
	Sixth Annual Atlanta Life Insurance Company Juried Art Exhibition, Atlanta
1987	Bloomers Gallery, Pittsburgh
	Carlow College, Pittsburgh
1988	Marie Martin Gallery, Washington, D.C.
1989	Dallas Museum of Art

Collections:

Allegheny Community College, Pittsburgh, Pennsylvania; Columbia Hospital, Pittsburgh, Pennsylvania; Coraopolis Health Center, Pittsburgh, Pennsylvania; Dallas Museum of Art.

Publications:

On STOUT: Book—*Dear Robert, I'll See You in the Crossroads: A Project by Renée Stout* by Marla Berns, Santa Barbara, University Art Museum, 1995. **Article**—"Resonance, Transformation, and Rhyme: The Art of Renée Stout" in *Astonishment and Power* by Michael D. Harris, Washington, D.C., Smithsonian Institution, 1993, pp. 105-59.

*   *   *

Renee Stout recalls that, while growing up in Pittsburgh, she was exceedingly interested in art and nature. She began drawing during her childhood and enrolled in art classes at the Carnegie Museum. While studying there, she saw two objects that exerted a profound and lasting influence upon her development as an artist—a *minkisi* (Kongo power or fetish figure) and a group of shrunken heads from South America. Trained as a photo-realist painter, Stout graduated from Carnegie-Mellon University in 1984, and her early works were still life compositions and figural cityscapes in the spirit of Edward Hopper. A year after graduating Stout became an artist in residence in Boston, and in 1985 she moved to Washington, D.C.

Shortly after Stout settled in Washington, her style changed dramatically. She abandoned two-dimensional Hopper-like paintings and began creating small boxes and fetish forms to reflect her African American heritage. She was particularly influenced by Kongo *minkisi* and still makes regular pilgrimages to the Carnegie Museum to view the example that intrigued her during her youth. Stout has created a series of fetish figures, and *Fetish #2,* a life-size version molded from her own body, was the work that first gained her national attention.

Stout is a deeply spiritual person, and much of her work examines her African and African American heritages, Caribbean religions, and her own individuality. Many of Stout's works are autobiographical and are created as part of a healing process. Family members figure prominently. She has been influenced by the works of one of her uncles who was an artist, her grandmother's death, a now-resolved conflict with her only sister, and both fulfilled and unfulfilled love relationships. Stout keeps a diary, and she has developed a cryptic script that appears in some of her works. She says that the symbols have no meaning and are an unconscious, automatic type of writing.

Another key aspect of Stout's work is the fictional narratives she writes to accompany her works. The narratives are written after the works are created, with the characters based on real-life people. Her first fictional characters were a Colonel Frank and his girlfriend Dorothy, to whom she dedicated a series of works completed in 1989. Colonel Frank is a roaming cultural anthropologist, and his girlfriend is a seamstress. Madam Ching, a later figure in Stout's narratives, is a combination fortune-teller, root doctor, and psychic inspired by an eccentric lady who lived in Stout's neighborhood in Pittsburgh.

Music is also important in Stout's works, and she recalls that her grandfather was a local blues musician who frequently hosted music parties and socials at his home for mixed black and white audiences. One of Stout's series, which includes a narrative, is dedicated to the Mississippi bluesman Robert Johnson, whose early death ended his brilliant career. In the exhibition catalog, entitled *Dear Robert, I'll See You at the Crossroads* (1995), Stout composed a letter to Johnson in which she shares her frustrations concerning an unfulfilled love affair and her yearnings for a particular sweetheart.

The suite of works in the series attempts to re-create the life of Johnson through a guitar, juke joint, dress suit, and provocative man trap. Stout is also interested in the Haitian pantheon of gods, and she has created individual works and a series that symbolize each of the seven gods, with her favorites appearing to be Elegba and Erzulie.

Stout has discovered a spiritual and cultural link to New Orleans, and she travels there regularly. She is interested in voodoo, which is still practiced in New Orleans, and she is a devotee of Marie Leveau, the mid-nineteenth-century African American voodoo queen. Found objects from New Orleans appear in some of Stout's works.

Although Stout's reputation rests primarily upon her provocative mixed-media works, she is also an extremely talented draftsman and realistic painter in a trompe l'oeil style. In addition, she has produced a suite of prints based on some of her three-dimensional works and paintings. Several years ago Stout moved to a studio in downtown Washington, which allows her a firsthand glimpse of the violence and activities of the drug culture. As a result, her work has assumed a more rugged character, and she has returned to painting in combination with the use of found objects.

In 1993 Stout became the first African American to have a one-person exhibition at the Smithsonian Institution's National Museum of African Art as part of *Astonishment and Power.* Her exhibition was titled *The Eyes of Understanding: Kongo Minkisi and The Art of Renee Stout.* She is an artist whose works reflect her African American heritage in a deeply personal way.

—Regenia Perry

STREAT, Thelma Johnson
American painter

Born: Yakima, Washington, 1912. **Education:** Art Museum School, Portland, Oregon, 1934-35; University of Oregon, 1933-36. **Died:** 1959.

Selected Exhibitions:

1940	*American Negro Exposition,* Chicago
1941	M.H. de Young Memorial Museum, San Francisco
1942	Raymond and Raymond Galleries, New York
	San Francisco Museum of Art
1943	American Contemporary Gallery
	Little Gallery, Beverly Hills, California
1945	South Side Community Art Center, Chicago
1971	Newark Museum, New Jersey

Collections:

Museum of Modern Art, New York.

On STREAT: Articles—"At 17 Her Painting Won Prize," in *Silhouette Magazine,* 1939; "Painter's Death of a Black Sailor Attracts Attention," in *Black Dispatch,* December 1943.

*   *   *

Born in Yakima, Washington, of African American and Cherokee parentage, the painter and designer Thelma Johnson Streat sought to elevate the power of otherness in her work. She was fascinated with non-European forms and explored the visual traditions of Northwest Indian, Pacific, and African cultures. Like an ethnologist, she familiarized herself with the visual designs of these cultures, but she also studied their music and dance and incorporated such traditions into her artwork and performances.

Most of Streat's works are small paintings on paper or board. *The Holy One* (1939) and *Robot* (1942), which was an illustration for a children's book, both suggest self-contained ritualized figures. The facial features and extremities in both are minimalized, as they are in the traditional art forms of Native American, Oceanic, and African cultures. The use of heavy outlines recalls the work of Sargent Claude Johnson, who worked in San Francisco during Streat's time there. Like Johnson, Streat was employed as an artist by the Works Progress Administration, and she debuted her choreography at the San Francisco Museum of Art in 1946.

An early proponent of multiculturalism through her fascination with the music and dance of the indigenous peoples of the Pacific Rim countries, Streat traveled with her husband to Hawaii, Mexico, and Canada to study dances and to promote the creative expressions of the inhabitants. Thus, although her paintings are composed of abstract designs, the images, especially the animal forms, are interpretations of the art of indigenous peoples. Her *Rabbit Man* (1941), for example, is a painted multitiered mask on paper. A stylized rabbit head is decorated with geometric patterns and has slits for eyes, reminiscent of the designs of the Coast Salish Indians of British Columbia. Atop the rabbit head is a smaller spherical head of a man, also with geometric patterns but with glaring eyes. This two-part mask, one part human and the other animal, is characteristic of Coast Salish practices.

Streat claimed her heritage in Africa and the Americas and among Africans and Native American peoples. Like other African Americans, she capitalized on the interest of her mainly white patrons in the indigenous arts, which hold both mystery and terror for them. She accepted her role as a mediator who can interpret in her own words the insider's knowledge of the so-called primitive. Hence, as the other she was associated in an exotic way with masks and other forms of indigenous artistic expressions. Streat's embrace of abstraction and minimalized forms stemmed from her direct knowledge of such objects, as well as from her investigations into cubism and other modern art forms. Her attraction to cubist shapes was actually the realization that she could go to the source of the form and deconstruct it for herself, as she did with dances. Her interpretation of indigenous forms was, therefore, a personal quest to broaden her cultural knowledge and to claim her cultural roots within a modernist context that, although it also embraced the forms, trivialized the context in which they were originally created.

—Lizzetta LeFalle-Collins

STROUD, Richard

American painter

Born: Clifton Forge, Virginia, 22 January 1933. **Education:** School of the Boston Museum of Fine Arts, B.F.A.; Cummington School of the Arts, Massachusetts; New School of Social Research, New York; Brook-

lyn Museum of Fine Arts, New York; National Academy of Design, New York. **Family:** Married Martha Labell in 1976, one son, two daughters. **Career:** Formerly teacher, DeCordova Museum of Art, Lincoln, Massachusetts, The School We Have, Concord, Massachusetts; associate professor, University of Massachusetts, Boston; professor, Massachusetts College of Art, Boston, Boston Museum School of Fine Arts, Boston. Presently instructor in drawing, Massachusetts Institute of Technology, Cambridge, Massachusetts; teacher of drawing, painting, and scupture, Charles River School Dover, Massachusetts; teacher of aikido, Cambridge School of Weston, Massachusetts. Served as counselor, Metropolitan State Hospital, Waltham, Massachusetts; project director, Prison Art Project, Walpole State Prison, Massachusetts; visiting artist, Massachusetts College of Art, Boston. **Awards:** Traveling Scholarship, Boston Museum School of Fine Arts; Boston Museum School of Fine Arts First Prize in painting, second year, fourth year; Boston Museum School of Fine Arts, Second Prize in painting, third year; National Academy of Design First Prize in painting; American Friends Society Prize, National Academy of Design. **Address:** 46 Waltham Street, Boston, Massachusetts 02118, U.S.A.

Selected Exhibitions:

Armenian Museum, Waltham, Massachusetts; Art Resources, Cambridge, Massachusetts; Harcus Krakow Gallery, Boston; Massachusetts Institute of Technology, Cambridge; Museum of Fine Arts, Boston; Museum of the National Center of Afro-American Artists, Boston; Naga Gallery, Boston; Rose Art Gallery, Brandeis Univer-

Richard Stroud, 1978.

Richard Stroud: *Homage to Goua.*

sity, Waltham, Massachusetts; Sonnabend Collection, Boston; Weeden Gallery, Boston.

*   *   *

Richard Stroud received both undergraduate and graduate degrees at the School of the Museum of Fine Arts in Boston. He also studied at the Cummington (Massachusetts) School of the Arts, New School for Social Research, School of the Brooklyn Museum of Fine Arts, and National Academy of Design. In addition to his extensive training in the fine arts, Stroud also holds a third-degree black belt in aikido, the Japanese martial art.

Stroud is an artist of great interest who has distinguished himself as both a draftsman and a painter. His drawings, frequently executed in charcoal and colored pastels, are disciplined and spare and tend toward classicism in their feeling. They suggest a distillation, precise but lyrically expressive, like the work of a seasoned poet. The most striking of his drawings are large-scale works that, by combining the use of charcoal with casein, sometimes bridge the boundary between drawing and painting. Stroud's paintings are sometimes executed in oil or enamel but more frequently done in casein. They generally feature large singular forms floating on a light plane, with a light ground occasionally articulated by overmarkings or drawings. The surface is matte and sometimes suggests reworked passages.

The titles of Stroud's works are generally self-evident, as in *Two Figures* or *Cityscape.* Often, however, he challenges the viewer's wit by including images that seem to require explanation, such as the sunglasses that adorn the face of a black bear in one of his paintings. These touches clearly bring another dimension to Stroud's work, requiring that the viewer not only appreciate its aesthetic resolutions but also ponder its meaning.

Stroud has taught at the Massachusetts Institute of Technology, Massachusetts College of Art, University of Massachusetts at Boston, School of the Museum of Fine Arts in Boston, and School of the DeCordova Museum in Lincoln, Massachusetts. He has also been an artist in residence for the city of Cambridge, an art instructor in programs at Walpole State Prison, and a counselor for the Metropolitan State Hospital in Waltham, all in Massachusetts.

—Edmund Barry Gaither

STULL, Robert (J.)
American sculptor and ceramist

Born: Springfield, Ohio, 4 November 1935. **Education:** Ohio State University, Columbus, B.S. 1962, M.A. 1963; New York University, Japanese Language School, 1964-65; Fulbright Resident Scholar in Ceramics, Japan, 1965-67. **Military:** United States Air Force: sergeant. **Career:** Manager, Greenwich House Pottery, New York, 1963-65, 1967-68. Associate professor in ceramics, University of Michigan, 1968-72; professor in ceramics and visual communications, Ohio State University, beginning 1972; chairman, art department, Ohio State University, 1975-79; associate dean, Ohio State University, 1979-86. Since 1974 founder and general partner, JDS Associates, Columbus, Ohio. Lecturer, Kyoto City College of Fine Arts, Japan, 1966-67. Cofounder, Gallery 7, Detroit; director and founder, Gallery 7, Columbus, Ohio. Boardmember, National Conference of Artists, 1976; chairman of the board, National Conference of Artists, 1978. **Awards:** Fulbright Fellowship, 1965, 1967; Outstanding Achievement Award, African Studies Center, University of Michigan, 1975; Elizabeth Catlett Moro Award, National Conference of Artists, 1978; Virginia Kiah Award, National Conference of Artists, 1978. **Address:** 2287 Brookwood Road, Columbus, Ohio 43209, U.S.A.

*   *   *

Robert Stull studied at Ohio State University, where he earned both undergraduate and graduate degrees. He subsequently studied at the Japanese Language School at New York University and at the Kyoto City College of Fine Arts in Japan, where he was a Fulbright research scholar in ceramics. After teaching at the University of Michigan, Stull joined the faculty of Ohio State as a professor of art and black studies, and he eventually rose to become dean of the College of Art. In 1980-81 he also served as interim director of the university's art gallery. In many cases his ceramic works, like his paintings and drawings, drew on themes associated with black culture and nationalism.

Stull was a person with wide-ranging interests. He enjoyed science, architecture, history, and the visual arts. His scientific knowledge was especially useful, for it allowed him to create his own glazes for his large-scale and often daring ceramic works. A careful and disciplined artist, he produced an expansive body of clay works that included teapots, cups and settings, bowls, and jars. They ranged from dramatic Japanese-inspired containers such as *Kyoto* (forty-eight inches) in black glaze to African-inspired megajars such as *Queen Mother* (twenty-nine inches). In the latter work Stull used brilliant warm colors and an inverted pear shape to suggest aspects of an African royal woman. *Nommo,* named for the ancestral figures of the Dogon of Mali, was one of a number of ceramic sculptures created by Stull. Several of his early sculptures took the form of wall-mounted platters, with wire or other materials added. Building on his interest in three-dimensional structures, Stull used tubular, arching pipes rendered in bright colors for the design of an elegant swing for an Atlanta playground.

Stull's paintings were generally done on a large scale and frequently were works on shaped canvas based on fully resolved drawings. Using colored inks and the tools of an architectural draftsman, he composed his drawings and precise diagrams with circular, triangular, and other geometric forms. He later re-created the drawings as paintings, folding the canvas edges over the shaped frames as if to emphasize their structural integrity. Lending still greater emphasis to this architectonic approach was his use of broad areas of flat color between sharply defined borders. These works, as is evident in titles such as *Malcolm Is, Bakota,* and *Shango Rising,* were inspired by Stull's deep interest in his African heritage as well as the forces affecting his African American experience.

As an artist Stull mastered both the science and esthetics of ceramics to create a body of extraordinarily beautiful objects characterized by a fertile imagination and exquisite artistry. His drawings and paintings, like his ceramic works, were carefully constructed and expertly rendered, capturing a rich awareness of the shaped-canvas movement counterbalanced by a deeply felt commitment to art that was expressive of his experiences as a black man.

—Edmund Barry Gaither

SULLIVAN TWOTREES, Kaylynn
American performance artist

Work also appeared under the name Kaylynn Sullivan. **Born:** Des Moines, Iowa, 1945. **Education:** Rambert School of Ballet, London; Sorbonne, Paris; University, Des Moines, Iowa. **Career:** Administrator and dramaturge, International Ballet Caravan, London, 1971-73; dancer and administrator/teacher, United States and Europe, 1973-76; founder/president of management, booking, and production company for performing artists, including Meredith Monk, Martha Graham Dance Company, KLS Management, New York, 1976-80; production director, Meredith Monk's *Vessel,* Schaubühne, Berlin, 1980; project director, *Afro-American Pop Culture,* Just above Midtown, New York, 1981-82. **Awards:** Committee for the Visual Arts Award, 1981; Beard's Fund Award, Goethe House, New York, 1982; New York State Council on the Arts grant, 1984; Frank Furnace Fund grant for performance arts, Jerome Foundation, 1986; Lila Wallace-Readers Digest International Artist Fellowship, 1993.

Selected Performances:

1974	*Split Ends,* City Literary Institute, London
1976	*Bubble Gears,* De Moines Art Center, Iowa
	Simpson College, Osceola, Iowa
1980	*Victims,* Perry Street Apartment, New York
1981	Just above Midtown, New York
	Marina Dinkler Galerie, Berlin
1982	Fashion Moda, Bronx, New York
	Lower Manhattan Cultural Council, Battery Park, New York
	Beauty, ABC No Rio, New York
1983	*The Square Rap,* City Gallery, Department of Cultural Affairs, New York
	Civic Plots—'if the shoe fits . . .', Art on the Beach, Creative Time, New York
	Feet, feet, get me out of here, Sarah Lawrence College, Bronxville, New York
	Tillar Latino Americano, New York
1984	New Museum of Contemporary Art, New York
	P.S. 122, New York
	Fandango, Nuvo Recluse, New York
	Nighttrippers, New York City Public Baths, Fairview Baptist Church, Harlem, New York, Oscar Hammerstein Opera House, New York

1985   *even in my house,* Central Hall Gallery, New York
        Shortcut to Paradise, Just above Midtown, New York
        Me without J.P., Exit Art Gallery, New York
        women without air conditioning/man with a fever, Queens
            Museum, New York
1986   *Fandango,* Just above Midtown, New York
        . . . and he had 6 sisters, Just above Midtown, New York
        Love and Free Will, Contemporary Art Center, New Or-
            leans

Selected Group Exhibitions:

1983   Sculpture Center, New York
        City Gallery, New York
1984   galerie de resistance, New York
        New Museum of Contemporary Art, New York
1985   *Honey, I'm Home!* Midtown Art Center, Houston, Texas
1986   The Clocktower, New York
        Contemporary Art Center, New Orleans

Publications:

On SULLIVAN TWOTREES: Articles—"Bits" by Robert Massa,
in *Village Voice,* 29 September 1981; "See No Evil" by John Howell,
in *Soho Weekly News,* 29 September 1981; "On the Beach" by Kay
Larson, in *New York Magazine,* 5 September 1983; "Engaging Experiments Transform a Sandy Site" by Grace Glueck, in *New York
Times,* 31 July 1983; "Pencilvania or Bussed" by Sally Banes, in
Village Voice, 29 January 1985.

*   *   *

Kaylynn Sullivan Twotrees is part of a growing cadre of African
American women who are well known for performance art. Lowery
Stokes Sims (in her essay "Aspects of Performance by Black American Women Artists" in *Feminist Art Criticism: An Anthology*) suggests
two reasons for the lure of African American women to performance
art: first, the fact that African American art is overwhelmingly male and
might not be able to accommodate an expressive form dominated by
women; and second, "The act of performing also plays provocatively
into certain stereotypes about women, black women in particular."
Ms. Sullivan Twotrees was trained in dance and theater. Her performance repertory recognizes and reveals her desire to extend the limits
of performance. According to Stokes Sims, Twotrees has incorporated
"olfactory impressions and nonnarrative sound."

Consistently providing her audiences with cutting-edge presentations throughout the 1980s and 1990s, Sullivan Twotrees has
dealt with issues that are temporally and artistically provocative.
A chronology of these presentations is instructive: 1980 *Victims;*
1981 *Open Clothes;* 1982 *Beauty;* 1983-1984 *Civic Plots—if the
shoe fits; Night Trippers* (3 parts); *women with air conditioning;*
1983 *Diminished Capacity;* 1986 *Fandango; . . . and he had six
sisters; Half-Way to Jesus; Love and Free Will;* 1993 *Maka Wicasa-
Earth People.*

In her entry in *Gumbo Ya Ya: Anthology of Contemporary African American Women,* Sullivan Twotrees eschews the designations
"feminist" and "black" as uncomfortable for her. She resists these
terms as defining who she is and what she does. Instead she addresses healing as the term that "gives me my place, whether it
takes the form of teaching, laying on of hands, or performing."
Perhaps closer scrutiny is necessary in understanding why her
work is so significant to these audiences. In her book *Fugitive
Information: Essays from A Feminist Hothead,* author Kay Leigh
Hagan explains that feminism is "a simple matter of human rights—
that women are entitled to equal pay, equal opportunity, equal
protection under the law, control over our bodies, and safety from
male violence." Such themes emanate from the work of Sullivan
Twotrees. It is no wonder that individuals of certain ethnicities and
persuasions align themselves with Sullivan Twotrees's work because she presents, so forcefully, her dissatisfaction with oppression, subordination, and domination.

In *Victims,* the personal and familial is political. Wearing apparel
is the focus of *Open Clothes* and *Beauty.* Sullivan Twotrees brilliantly tackles a monied-economy run amuck in *Civic-Plots—if the
shoe fits.* Time and place are the themes in the tripartite *Night
Trippers.* Lack of harmonious and clear communication is explored
in *women with air conditioning* and *Fandango.* Junk food and murder have congruent applications in *Diminished Capacity.* The piece
. . . and he had three sisters examines nonconformity. Women's co-
option with their own oppression and destruction is treated in
Love and Free Will. Half-Way to Jesus and *Maka Wikasa—Earth
People* explore nature, the physical, and the metaphysical.

Often assuming the persona of Ms. Carol Fugate in her performance pieces, Sullivan Twotrees is an exceptional artist of wide-
ranging talent who has a large following. The breadth of her performances is mesmerizing, and the politically charged, woman-centered themes attract vast and diverse audiences.

—Jontyle Theresa Robinson

T

TALL, Papa Ibra
Senegalese painter and fiber artist

Name also spelled Papa Ibra Taal. **Born:** Tivaouane, Senegal, 1935. **Education:** École spéciale d'acrchitecture, Paris, 1959. **Career:** Founded Section de recherches en arts plastiques nègres at the École des Beaux Arts, Dakar, 1960. Director, Manufacture sénégalese des arts décoratifs, Thiès.

Individual Exhibitions:

1956	Grenoble, France
1960	Maison des Arts de Dakar, Dakar
1965	Moscow, Leningrad, and Yerevan
1967	Senegal Pavillion, Expo 1967, Montreal
1977	Best of Africa Gallery, Toronto
1991	Galerie Nationale, Dakar

Selected Group Exhibitions:

1964	Centre des Études Afro-Orientales, San Salvador, Brazil
1965	*8th Biennale of São Paulo,* São Paolo, Brazil
1966	*Premier Festival Mondial des Arts Nègres,* Dakar
1968	*Cultural Program of the Olympic Games,* Mexico City
1969	*Premier Festival Panafricain,* Algiers
	Biennale de Paris
1987	Galerie Nationale, Dakar

*   *   *

Papa Ibra Tall. Photo courtesy of Harold Armstrong.

Papa Ibra Tall: *Rêve de Grandeur.*

Papa Ibra Tall is often referred to as the doyen of the Senegalese arts scene. Although best known for his large-scale tapestries and richly colored oil paintings, Tall began his artistic career in the 1950s as a student of architecture in Paris. Evidence of his early training as a draftsman resonates throughout his oeuvre, in which an attention to detail, a delicacy of line, and an innovative use of space are apparent. Both at home and abroad, Tall is regarded as a crucial figure in the development of a postindependence visual aesthetic in Senegal that focused on pan-African themes.

Tall's interest in pan-Africanism stemmed from a deep involvement in and commitment to the philosophy of Negritude. Tall spent his time in Paris not only studying to be technically proficient in oil painting, architectural design, ceramic work, graphic arts, and tapestry making but also, in his own words, as "an errand boy for the big thinkers of the Negritude movement." He returned to Senegal to teach art at the request of the first president, the poet and Negritude theorist Léopold Sédar Senghor. It was through the development of a curriculum for the École des Beaux Arts and the Manufacture Sénégalaise des Arts Décoratifs (Tapestry Center) that Tall began to fine-tune his own unique style and vision of the African heritage. In his teachings Tall propagated certain ideas about the nature of Africanness and the importance of preserving and contributing to a shared cultural and racial heritage. This agenda found its visual translation in typical objects of Africa, such as masks, carved combs, statues, and drums, and in an overall patterning effect in rich colors, reminiscent of textile designs.

In 1964 Tall and his workshop began to design painted models of narrative stories to be transferred into large-scale woolen tapes-tries. Tall found the medium of tapestry useful in bringing art to the masses. Most of the narratives focused on local and pan-African sources. Ironically, most of his works and those of his center became the property of foreign states or government dignitaries. After 1966, when Tall became involved in the Africobra movement, he extended his themes to include images of figures of the diaspora and of other artistic forms, such as jazz. While the stories and motifs of these tapestries emphasized an African viewpoint, the technology and materials used were imported from France and Belgium. In this way Tall's teachings and creations exemplified the wishes of Senghor, his cultural mentor, who insisted that the artistic output of modern Africa should combine the traditions of Africa with the latest technology available internationally.

The designs of Tall's tapestries and of those attributed to his followers are characterized by large tracts of bright colors and stylized figures. Works such as *Judu bu rafet* (1978) illustrate the mastery Tall developed in the medium. The consistency of the design of the tapestries was the result, in part, of the constraints of the weaving technology, which would not allow for the subtleties possible in other media. Thus, some of Tall's unique graphic design talents were lost when his painted and drawn forms were transferred to tapestry.

Despite the high profile of his tapestries, many of which welcomed visitors to the first World Festival of Negro Arts in 1996, Tall has also continued to indulge his passion for meticulous detail and the powerful line in drawings such as *Projection Spatialle* (1976) and *Zimbanzania* (c.1970s). In the latter Tall alluded to the troubles in Anzania (South Africa) and Zimbabwe through interwoven forms that resemble both landscape and human beings, thus underscoring the people's intimate relationship to the land. As they swirl around the composition to embrace the figures within it, the lines of Tall's work resemble the threads of a textile

In his oil paintings Tall seems to have found a way in which to combine his penchant for design, liberal use of pictorial space, and love of bright colors. In works like *La Lutteur* (c.1970s) the movements of the subject, a wrestler, are illustrated through a complex play of interconnecting arcs of color and black outlines of form.

Tall has not exhibited recently, and the Negritude aesthetic he so eloquently advocated has fallen out of fashion. Nonetheless, his work and commitment to defining and celebrating African creativity has left a legacy that both Senegalese and black artists worldwide must contend with.

—Elizabeth Harney

TANKSLEY, Ann Graves
American painter and printmaker

Born: Pittsburgh, Pennsylvania, 1934. **Education:** Carnegie Institute of Technology, Pittsburgh, B.F.A. 1956; Art Students' League, New York; Parsons School of Design; Bob Blackburn's Printmaking Workshop. **Family:** Married, two daughters. **Career:** Adjunct art instructor, Suffolk County Community College, 1973-75. **Awards:** Harlem Cultural Council grant, 1981. **Address:** 18 Carlton Road, Great Neck, New York, 11021, U.S.A.

Individual Exhibitions:

AC-BAW Center for the Arts, Mount Vernon, New York; Acts of Art Gallery, Mount Vernon, New York; Barnes-Little Gallery, Washington, D.C.; Black History Museum, Hempstead, New York (1972); California College of Arts and Crafts, Oakland; Campbell Gallery, Sewickley, Pennsylvania; Carnegie Institute, Pittsburgh, Pennsylvania; Dorsey Gallery, Brooklyn, New York (1986); Langston Hughes Library, Queens, New York; Jamaica Art Center, New York (1987); Isobel Neal Gallery, Chicago (1990); Savacou Galleries, New York; Spectrum IV Gallery, New Rochelle, New York; Spiral Gallery, Brooklyn, New York (1988).

Selected Group Exhibitions:

American Women in Art, Nairobi, Kenya; Bratten Gallery, New York; Brooke Alexander, New York; Christie's New York; Hudson River Museum, Yonkers, New York; Indianapolis Museum of Art; Isobel Neal Gallery, Chicago; Kenkeleba House, New York; Mount Holyoke College, South Hadley, Massachusetts; Purdue University, Lafayette, Indiana; Salmagundi Club, New York; Samuels's Gallery, Oakland, California; Union Theological Seminary, New York; University of Maryland, College Park, Maryland.

Publications:

On TANKSLEY: Books—*Ann Tanksley,* exhibition catalog, Mount Vernon, New York, AC-BAW Center, 1991; *Tanksley Art Exhibit*

Pictures the World of the Black Woman, exhibition catalog, Mount Vernon, New York, Acts of Art Gallery, 1991; *Ann Tanksley,* exhibition catalog, New York, Kenkeleba House, 1991. **Articles**—"Artist Comes Home," in *Pittsburgh NB News,* 28 January 1987; "Standing Out: Artist Puts Pointed Ideas in Soft Hues" by Jean Bryant, in *The Pittsburgh Press,* 10 February 1987; "Ann Tanksley at the AC-BAW Center" by Raymond Steiner, in *Art Times,* March 1991.

*   *   *

Ann Tanksley paints ordinary events in an extraordinary manner. The people in her paintings are doing such things as building canals, dancing, walking home, recovering from an illness, or dressing a chicken, but the perspectives and proportions of their bodies and faces and their surroundings do not appear as might be expected. Dark outlines surround relatively flat portrayals of three-dimensional objects, and the two-dimensional world makes the paintings seem extremely direct. Tanksley sets the painting—foreground, subject, and background—close to the viewer, almost as if the entire painting were caught somewhere in the foreground, near the point at which the viewer is looking at it. Her methods are reminiscent of the unsophisticated or child artist, the elegant simplicity of which has an immediate impact on the viewer.

The focus of attention—where the eye is supposed to land or move to—is usually easy to recognize. Tanksley's paintings are often simple enough that the focus is simply the figures represented, as in the painting *Black Dancers* (1985). Five dancers appear, hands raised and linked in a circle, a hill and sky directly behind them, with little evidence of perspective. Dancers meant to be close to the viewer overlap the dancers meant to be farther away, and those that appear behind are also slightly higher in the painting. The eye naturally travels around the circle of dancers, as if joining the dance, and it is the scene's simplicity that enhances the illusion of focus and motion.

Tanksley's style is easy to recognize from painting to painting. Even within a single painting, subjects may appear in regular patterns or pairs, rarely veering outside the canvas or without echo—similar clothing, body shape, or expression—in another part of the painting. In *Pickin Chickens* (1986), for example, the three subjects are similar, but their varying levels of interest in the activity seem to represent different levels of world-weariness. The central figure is busily picking chicken feathers. The figure on the right holds the chicken by the neck and rests her head on her other fist, gazing outside the canvas as if not interested in the task. The third, to the left, has set the chicken aside and also gazes away, and her body language clearly shows an even greater disdain for the task. Entire lives dare to be guessed at from such direct and emphatic gestures, which is precisely what Tanksley seems to be trying to get the viewer to do. She draws people in as if the worlds in her paintings are far more engaging than their own.

—Terry Bain

TANNER, Henry Ossawa
American painter

Born: Pittsburgh, Pennsylvania, 21 June 1859. **Education:** Pennsylvania Academy of Fine Arts under Thomas Eakins, 1880. **Fam-**

ily: Married Jessie Macauley Olssen in 1899, one son. **Career:** Owned photography studio, Atlanta, Georgia, 1888; professor, Clark College, c.1888-89. Traveled to Egypt, Morocco, and Algeria. Member, American Art Club, Paris, 1891, American Art Association, Paris, 1897, Paris Society of American Painters, 1909, Societé Internationale Peinture et Sculpture, Paris, National Academy of Design, New York; president, Societé Artistique de Picardie. **Awards:** Third Class Medal, Salon des Artistes Francais, 1897; Second Medal, Universal Exposition, Paris, 1900; Second Medal, Pan-American Exposition, Buffalo, New York, 1901; Second Medal, Salon des Artistes Francais, Paris, 1908; Bronze Medal, National Arts Club, 1927. Chevalier of the French Legion of Honor, Government of France, 1923. Knight, French Legion of Honor. **Died:** 25 May 1937.

Selected Exhibitions:

1894	Salon des Artistes Francais, Paris (and annually through 1924)
1900	12th Annual Exhibition of Philadelphia Art Club
1904	Exhibition of Society of American Artists
1914	Anglo-American Art Exhibition, London
1921	New York Public Library
	Vose Galleries, Boston
1927	National Arts Club Galleries, New York
1933	Century of Progress, Chicago
1945	Philadelphia Art Alliance
1966	University of California at Los Angeles Art Galleries
1969	Frederick Douglass Institute and National Collection of Fine Arts, Washington, D.C. (traveling retrospective)
1991	Philadelphia Museum of Art (traveling retrospective)

Collections:

American National Red Cross, Washington, D.C.; Atlanta University, Georgia; Carnegie Institute, Pittsburgh, Pennsylvania; Chicago Art Institute; Des Moines Art Gallery, Iowa; Fisk University, Nashville; Frederick Douglass Institute, Washington, D.C.; French Government; Grand Central Art Galleries, New York; Hampton Institute, Hampton, Virginia; High Museum of Art, Atlanta, Georgia; Houston Museum of Fine Arts; Howard University, Washington, D.C.; Hyde Collection, Glens Falls, New York; Isaac Delgado Museum of Art, New Orleans; Los Angeles Art Gallery; Los Angeles County Museum of Art; Louvre, Paris; Metropolitan Museum of Art, New York; Milwaukee Art Center, Wisconsin; Pennsylvania Academy of Fine Arts; Philadelphia Museum of Art, Fairmont Park; Schomburg Center for Research in Black Culture, New York Public Library; Spelman College, Atlanta, Georgia; Wilstach Collection.

Publications:

On TANNER: Books—*Henry Ossawa Tanner: American Artist* by Marcia M. Mathews, University of Chicago, 1969; *The Art of Henry O. Tanner, 1859-1937,* exhibition catalog, Washington, D.C., Frederick Douglass Institute and Smithsonian Institution, 1970; *Six Black Masters of American Art* by Romare Bearden and Harry Henderson, New York, Doubleday and Company, 1972; *The Art of Henry Ossawa Tanner,* Hyde Collection, 1972; *Henry Ossawa Tan-*

ner, Philadelphia Museum of Art, 1991; *Henry Ossawa Tanner* by Dewey F. Mosby, New York, Rizzoli International and Philadelphia Museum of Art, 1991; *Across Continents and Cultures—The Art and Life of Henry Ossawa Tanner* by Dewey F. Mosby, University of Washington Press and Nelson-Atkins Museum of Art, 1995. **Articles**—"Henry O. Tanner, Painter" by Helen Cole, in *Brush and Pencil,* June 1900, pp. 97-107; "Henry O. Tanner" by W.S. Scarborough, in *Southern Workman,* December 1902; "Henry O. Tanner, Exile for Art's Sake" by W.R. Lester, in *Alexandra's,* 15 December 1908, p. 69; "An Afro-American Painter Who has Become Famous in Paris," *Current Literature,* October 1908, p. 405; "Henry O. Tanner's Biblical Pictures," in *Fine Arts Journal,* March 1911, pp. 163-66; "Notes: Henry O. Tanner," in *Chicago Art Institute of Art Bulletin,* July 1911, p. 11; "An American Painter of the Resurrection" by William E. Barton, in *Advance,* 20 March 1913, p. 2011; "A Poet Painter of Palestine" by C.T. MacChesney, in *International Studio,* July 1913; "Henry Ossawa Tanner" by Jessie Fauset, in *Crisis,* April 1923, pp. 255-58; "Henry Ossawa Tanner" (interview) by Jessie Fauset, in *Crisis,* 27, April 1924, pp. 255-58; "Henry Tanner 77 Dies in Paris, Was American Negro Painter," in *New York Herald Tribune,* 25 May 1937; "Henry O. Tanner" by James A. Porter, in *Negro Caravan* (New York), Dryden, 1942; "Work of Henry Ossawa Tanner," in *Carnegie,* November 1945, p. 157; "Henry Ossawa Tanner, American Artist," *South Atlantic Quarterly,* Autumn 1966, pp. 1-10; "The Art of Henry O. Tanner," *Ebony,* October 1969; "The Art of Henry O. Tanner" (Washington, D.C.), Smithsonian Institution, 1969; "My Meeting with Henry O. Tanner" by Hale Woodruff, in *Crisis,* 77, January 1970, pp. 6-12; "Henry Ossawa Tanner," in *African-American Artists* by Romare Bearden and Harry Henderson, New York, Pantheon Books, 1993, pp. 78-110.

*   *   *

Henry Ossawa Tanner is best remembered for his poignant genre paintings of African Americans during the last decade of the nineteenth century. Well-known works include *Old Couple Looking at Lincoln* (c.1892-93), with the couple gazing humbly and admiringly at a portrait of Abraham Lincoln; *The Grateful Poor* (1896), with a father and son at a modest table engaged in prayer; and the famous *Banjo Lesson,* in which an aged black man teaches a young barefoot boy how to play the banjo. All were painted as the new century approached, at a time when African Americans were engaged in an effort to redefine themselves.

In his genre paintings Tanner attempted to redefine and recontextualize the former slave, whose economic condition had not dramatically improved since emancipation. In their poverty his subjects show a dignity that was not often afforded them in nineteenth-century art or even in later twentieth-century paintings. Tanner studied with Thomas Eakins, one of the few nineteenth-century white American artists who sensitively humanized his portrayals of blacks and did not exaggerate or treat their physiognomy as laughable. Tanner respected Eakins for placing black people in the realm of humanity, and when Eakins suggested that Tanner go to the South to paint his people, he complied.

Tanner came from a prominent middle-class Pittsburgh family that moved to Philadelphia when he was a child. He was an early example of the new Negro in the late nineteenth century, one who had access to education and who promoted cultivated tastes and proper deportment. His upbringing in the church and the teachings

Henry Ossawa Tanner: *Still Life with Fruit,* c. 1910. Photo by Manu Sassoonian; courtesy of the Schomburg Center for Research in Black Culture.

of his father, a bishop in the African Methodist Episcopal Church, also affected his work, tearing him between pursuing a career in art and a life in the ministry. He tried, therefore, to make his artwork relevant to his Christian beliefs, which included helping those who were less fortunate than he was. *The Banjo Lesson* is a prime example of this. Tanner began with an image of black males—demeaned, romanticized, and made laughable—that was common in the fine and popular arts in the nineteenth century. Many portrayals of black males also suggested that music was an innate gift that should be pursued in place of reading. Tanner subverted this characterization, casting his black man in the role of educator. Perhaps the older man may not have known how to read or write, but he knew how to play the banjo, something of value and a gift that he passed on to the young lad.

Leaving the United States in 1891 to study in France, Tanner shunned European and early American modernism. American modernists found the art of the academies, for example, the Pennsylvania Academy of the Fine Arts, where Tanner had trained, to be old-fashioned. Tanner, however, was more interested in

exploring his Christian beliefs in his art, and by the mid-1890s he was concentrating almost exclusively on religious subjects. His academic painting style is evident in works like *Three Marys* and *Daniel in the Lion's Den,* which employed the same sense of yellow blue light he had used in *The Banjo Lesson*. Tanner then traveled to North Africa, which placed him closer to the world of the Holy Land. The sunlight there bathed him in a type of white light that was not available in Paris, and the people—their garments and way of life—recalled characters from Bible stories. In the paintings he did in North Africa, Tanner personalized his compositions further. He moved from the academic style he had learned under Eakins to a style that not only reflected his Christian beliefs but also substituted mysteriously vague shapes for what had formerly been defined figures, causing the works to transcend the text of the Bible and become mystical. Tanner continued to develop this personal sense of mysticism throughout the remainder of his career.

—Lizzetta LeFalle-Collins

TERCILIANO, JR.
Brazilian painter

Born: Terciliano Domingos, Salvador, Brazil, 1939. **Address:** Av. Pinto de Aguiar, 5, Patamares-Salvador, Brazil.

*   *   *

The spiritual aura of Candomblé has spiraled outward to touch many Afro-Brazilian artists. Such is the case with Terciliano, Jr. And like the gods who have many qualities and personalities, artists work in different ways at different times.

Terciliano asserts his Afro-Brazilian heritage in large paintings devoted to the ritual arts of Candomblé. His abstractions are related to the ineffable qualities of the gods and their spiritual essence, or *ase*. As he explains, "I try to do work that is truly representative of Black people, not caricatures of Black culture." But a certain pragmatism emerges when he says that he wants to "situate [his work] in a wider space, in a subtle and lyric way."

Terciliano grew up in a large and poor family. Over the years he took many jobs in order to survive—blacksmith's apprentice, fabric salesman, receptionist, soap opera actor, and poet—before deciding to live by his art. His devout family has always been deeply involved in the Angolan Candomblé called Bate-Folha, which has been a source of spiritual as well as artistic inspiration. Terciliano states, "As an artist, I see African religion in a different way from my family, not without the same respect, but also as a cultural source from where I can find elements for research and expression. . . . It is a strong form of resistance that survived slavery, racism and still today struggles to maintain its identity."

Terciliano's art has gone through major stylistic changes over the years. His early work centered on genre scenes of Bahia—street and market scenes and the dress, movement, and color of Salvador. His figures were often simplifications of their sources, soft and loose, like quick glimpses of the life around him. All were sensitively rendered, especially a tender portrait of his mother.

In the late 1980s Terciliano became bolder, transforming his partial figures into strongly colored solid ones, moving toward abstraction and overall pattern, and working on a large scale. There were reasons for his increasing abstraction. For one, he explains that he was exploring new ways to express the realities of Candomblé, "to situate it in a wider space, in a subtle and lyric way, blending my art and life experience." Too, he was dealing with intangible ideas of the sacred—life force and *ase,* gods and goddesses, and religious rites and offerings.

Rituals—persons, actions, and objects—fill Terciliano's works. A large, shallow wooden bowl, known as a *gamela,* is an important and recurring motif. The bowl has many uses in Brazilian life, but in the context of Candomblé it is primarily a receptacle for offerings made to the gods. Just as worshipers express their love, respect, and devotion by contributing to the god's power, the deity in turn assures their well-being. In one painting the fluid bodies of devotees bent to the will of the gods during ceremonial occasions fill the canvas to give a sense of movement and energy. In such works on Candomblé, Terciliano celebrates his family, his ancestors, and the generations of Afro-Brazilians who have kept the gods of Africa alive and well in the hearts and minds of Brazilians today.

—Henry John Drewal

THOMAS, Alma (W.)
American painter

Born: Columbus, Georgia, 22 September 1891. **Education:** Howard University, Washington, D.C., B.S. 1924; Columbia University, New York, M.A. 1934; American University, Washington, D.C., 1950-60; Tyler School of Fine Arts, Temple University, Tour of the Art of Western Europe; Miner Teachers Normal School, Washington, D.C. **Career:** Teacher, Shaw Junior High School, 1924-60. Vice President, Barnett-Aden Gallery, Washington, D.C. Organized the School Arts League Project. **Awards:** 1st prize, watercolor, Community Art Show; 3rd prize (purchase award), Howard University, Washington, D.C. **Died:** 1978.

Selected Exhibitions:

American University, Washington, D.C. (two-woman); Anacostia Neighborhood Museum-Smithsonian Institution, Washington, D.C.; Franz Bader Art Gallery, Washington, D.C. (solo); Baltimore Museum, Maryland; Boston Museum of Fine Arts (1970); Carnegie Institute; Corcoran Gallery of Art, Washington, D.C. (1972); Howard University, Washington, D.C. (1966, retrospective); Jackson State College, Mississippi; La Jolla Museum of Art, California (1970); National Collection of Fine Arts, Smithsonian Institution, Washington, D.C.; Nordness Galleries, New York; James A. Porter Gallery, New York; Society of Washington Artists, D.C.; State Armory, Wilmington, Delaware (1971); United Negro College Exhibition, D.C. Art Association; Wesleyan University Center for the Arts; Whitney Museum of American Art, New York (1972).

Collections:

Corcoran Gallery, Washington, D.C.; Franz Bader Gallery, Washington, D.C.; Howard University, Washington, D.C.; La Jolla Museum, California; Metropolitan Museum, New York; National Museum of American Art, Smithsonian Institution, Washington, D.C.; Whitney Museum, New York.

Publications:

On THOMAS: Books—*Alma W. Thomas: Recent Paintings,* exhibition catalog, Nashville, Tennessee, Carl Van Vechten Gallery of Fine Arts, Fisk University, and David Driskell, 1971; *Alma Thomas Paintings* by Joshua C. Taylor, Martha Jackson West Gallery, New York, 1973; *Alma W. Thomas: Recent Painting, 1975-76,* exhibition catalog, New York, Marsha Jackson West Gallery and Robert Doty, 1976; *A Life in Art: Alma Thomas, 1981-1978* by Merry A. Foresta, Smithsonian Institution, Washington, D.C., 1981. **Articles**—"Approaches to Inhumanity" (interview) by H.E. Mahal, in *Art Gallery 13,* April 1970; "Alma Thomas" by Warren Marr, in *Crisis,* 77, May 1970, pp. 189-93; "Alma W. Thomas," in *A History of African-American Artists, from 1792 to the Present* by Romare Bearden and Harry Henderson, Pantheon Books, New York, 1993, pp. 447-53.

*   *   *

Alma Thomas's vibrant abstract canvases, filled with color and light, reflect the engagement of a vital personality with the world of art, nature, and ideas throughout a long and varied life. In 1972 Thomas became the first black woman to be given a solo exhibition at the Whitney Museum of American Art in New York City. In 1924 she became the first graduate of Howard University's newly formed art department. But it is the unbridled energy with which she embarked on a full-time career as a painter at the age of sixty-nine that stands alongside her paintings as perhaps her most remarkable achievement.

Thomas was born in 1891 in Columbus, Georgia, to a well-established, progressive middle-class family. When she was in her midteens, the family moved to Washington, D.C., and settled in the house on Fifteenth Street, NW, that the artist was to inhabit for most of the rest of her life. Raised to be a proper young lady, Thomas nonetheless possessed a fiercely independent, unconventional spirit, as Adolphus Ealey has said, "a personality forever torn between a passion for freedom of self-expression and a reluctance to betray the values handed down to her by an older generation of black pioneers into the mainstream of American life."

Following her graduation from Howard, where she studied under James Herring, Thomas began teaching at a junior high school. Despite thirty-six years of full-time teaching, Thomas managed to earn a master's degree in art education from Columbia University, to produce costumes, stage sets, and marionette plays, and to lecture on art history. Seeking to expand her already broad outlook and to improve her technique, Thomas enrolled in painting classes at American University when she was in her fifties. Her paintings from this period, although traditional in subject matter, show Thomas to have had the ability to adopt modernist styles, a particular adeptness at handling color, and a growing tendency toward abstraction. By the early 1960s Thomas was exploring the emotional and psychological effects of color in an abstract expressionist idiom and absorbing influences from Washington color school artists such as Gene Davis, Kenneth Noland, and Morris Louis.

After retiring from teaching in 1960, Thomas began to paint with increasing confidence and seriousness. During this period she began to experiment with watercolor. The luminosity, freshness, and spontaneity of the medium suited Thomas's temperament and gave momentum to her growing affinity for bright, pure color. She began to suspend translucent cascades of loose brush strokes against the rough white ground of the paper, varying the positions and patterns of the strokes in the twenty or more studies she often made for a single canvas. These small studies took as their subject distillations of closely observed natural phenomena—blossoming trees, flower beds, sunrises, the shimmering patterns of leaves in the wind.

Thomas's mature style coalesced in the series "Earth Paintings," which she first exhibited in the late 1960s. In an acrylic work on canvas, *Evening Glow* (1972), sheer luminous swatches of orange red, yellow, and white appear to hover over an opaque blue field, making a patterned interplay of light and dark. Thomas actually painted the blue over the warm colors in short, irregular vertical strokes, the small interstices revealing the glowing hues or bare white of the canvas beneath. Along the left side of the canvas Thomas applied red over the blue again, creating a denser surface and a corresponding shift in weight and space.

The radiant series "Space Paintings," which was inspired by the Apollo 11 voyage of 1969, displayed more saturated colors, often in hotter color keys. The paintings alluded to solar phenomena, the great forces of energy that govern space, and man's own orbiting of Earth and Moon. In her later works the artist played freely with the structure of her patterns. In *Grassy Melodic Chant* (1976), for

example, the rhythms of the densely packed floating wedges of green imply a swelling that would seem to expand beyond the edges of the picture plane.

Despite their highly formal structures Thomas's canvases retain a strong sense of the handmade. They are at once forceful, direct, and highly nuanced. They depart entirely from natural forms, yet they convey a palpable sense of the transient effects of light and color on the visible world, acutely observed and deeply felt. They suggest the revelation of the transcendent moment and testify to the persistent, joyous vision of an artist determined to paint despite the limitations of age and time.

—Dorothy Valakos

THOMAS, Matthew
American painter and installation artist

Work also appeared under the name Matthew Manjusri Thomas. **Born:** Matthew Willis Thomas, San Antonio, Texas, 1943. **Education:** San Fernando Valley College, Van Nuys, California, 1961-63; Honolulu Academy of the Arts, Honolulu, 1963-64; Chouinard School of Fine Arts, Los Angeles, 1965-67. **Family:** Married in 1974 (divorced in 1984), one son and one daughter; married in 1991. **Career:** Art instructor, California State University, Los Angeles, 1985-87, Armory Center for the Arts, Pasadena, California, 1993-95, Otis College of Art, Los Angeles, 1990-94. Art instructor, Junior Arts Center, Los Angeles since 1979, Los Angeles County Museum of Art since 1989. Artist-in-residence, University of California at Los Angeles Extension, since 1990, Crossroads Outreach, Santa Monica, California, since 1995. **Awards:** California Arts Council grants, 1983-87; Helen Lundeberg-Lorser Feitelson Art Fund Fellowship, 1989. **Agent:** Eric Atken, Proud Heritage Fine

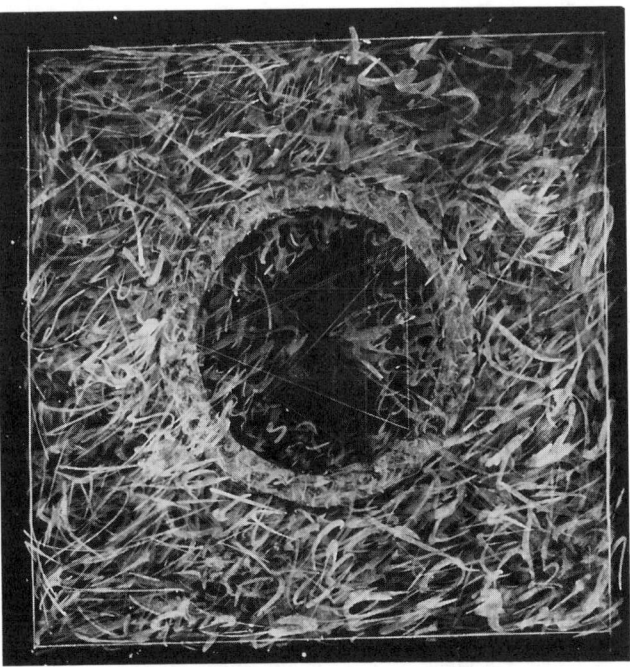

Matthew Thomas: *Elemental of Fire.*

Arts, 648 West Stonehurst Drive, Alta Dena, California 91001, U.S.A. **Address:** 1704 South Pacific Avenue, #17, San Pedro, California 90731, U.S.A.

Individual Exhibitions:

1989	Victor Fischer Galleries, San Francisco
1990	Simmonson Gallery, Los Angeles
1991	Ruth Bachofner Gallery, Santa Monica, California
1993	Watts Towers Art Center, Los Angeles
	Ruth Bachofner Gallery, Santa Monica, California
1994	Watts Towers Art Center, Los Angeles
1995	Gallery Eden, Rowland Heights, California
1996	Ruth Bachofner Gallery, Santa Monica, California
	University of California Polytechnic, Fullerton

Selected Group Exhibitions:

1994	Gate Gallery, Angels Gate Cultural Center, San Pedro, California
	Gallery Eden, Rowland Heights, California
1995	University of Judaism, Los Angeles
	Sabina Lee Gallery, Los Angeles
	Black Gallery, Los Angeles
	Luckman Fine Arts Gallery, Los Angeles
1996	Watts Towers Art Center, Los Angeles
Art Center, Williamson Gallery, Pasadena, California
	Armory Center for the Arts, Pasadena, California

Collections:

Arco, Los Angeles; Grunewald Center for Graphic Arts, University of California, Los Angeles; Kumbo Museum of Art, Korea; National Museum of Contemporary Arts, Seoul, Korea; Taiwan Museum of Art, Republic of China; University of Los Angeles.

*   *   *

Matthew Thomas received his art training in California and Hawaii, but the inspiration for much of his work comes from an inner spirituality that has its roots in Eastern religious practices. As a practitioner of Buddhism, he incorporates vestiges of the religion's iconography in his paintings, which are often done with a combination of sand and dry pigment. He has said that he strives for a oneness with "God, the Great Spirit," but he also strives for a oneness between heaven and earth, the natural and the man-made, and humility and arrogance. Standing in front of the bold concentrations of complementary colors in his paintings, the viewer is almost absorbed by their power.

Thomas's search for God has taken him to various Eastern religions and to Islam. In paintings from the early to the mid-1980s Thomas concentrated on the beauty and fluidity of Arabic calligraphy. Enlarging and abstracting from the characters of the Arabic alphabet, he created large calligraphic paintings that he then embellished with iridescent highlights, making them work as exquisite woven cloths. From these ornate surfaces Thomas turned to working with natural fibers, stones, and other earth materials to create paintings and sculptural installations. He became more interested in a muted finish than in the glistening surfaces of earlier years. The mixed-media triptych painting *Pathways* (1986) illustrates his con-

Matthew Thomas: *Symbol of Earth Soul,* 1988.

centration on matte but with bright colors. The work also illustrates his concept of the crossroads, using rust-colored pigment surfaces in which lines of string take alternate paths to form cross shapes in the lower portions of two of the canvases. Small bundles of twigs or a rock wrapped in twine dangle from the centers of the crosses, suggesting that the direction one follows in life must be a personal decision.

Since the early 1990s Thomas has been influenced by the sand paintings of Tibetan monks. The imagery of the Tibetan Wheel of Life, which is one of Buddhism's best-known iconographies, demonstrates basic doctrines regarding liberation from suffering and ignorance. Thomas uses aspects of Buddhist cosmology in his paintings and follows the monks' art processes and approach to the concept of spirituality. For the monks color is pure and unmixed. Intricate geometric designs are formed by patiently releasing sand through small tubelike applicators to make linear designs in large site-specific floor paintings. Upon their completion the paintings are ritually dedicated and the sand gathered and returned to the earth or sea. The idea of a return to the earth is also a primary concern for Thomas and is conceptually achieved in works such as *Drawing a Point* (1994).

Thomas employs colored pigment to create shapes on the floor like those of the Tibetan sand painters, but the shapes in his sand paintings seem closer to the sculpted pictographs that have mysteriously appeared in farm fields in Europe and the United States. These mysterious shapes suggest the presence of a cosmic visitor traversing the Earth's immediate space. Like these shapes Thomas's paintings should be viewed from above if one is to receive the full impact of their design.

Along with Thomas's paintings, swaths of colored cloth and metal strips punctuated with symbolic shapes are elements in his installations. Small objects are thoughtfully placed on adjoining walls as if offering vessels to an unknown deity. As in his other works, one feels a spiritual presence in his installations that is deeply rooted in Thomas's art and life.

—Lizzetta LeFalle-Collins

THOMPSON, Mildred

American sculptor, painter, and printmaker

Born: Jacksonville, Florida, 1936. **Education:** Howard University, Washington, D.C., B.A. 1957; Brooklyn Museum School, New York, 1958; Hamburg Hochschule fur Bildende Kunst, 1959-61. **Career:** Assistant professor, Agnes Scott College, Decatur, Georgia. Artist-in-residence, Spelman College, Atlanta, Georgia, Morehouse College, Atlanta, Georgia, Tampa Bay Arts Center, Florida, 1974-77, and Howard University, Washington, D.C., 1977-78. Art and set director of numerous films, including *The Life of Paula Modersohn-Becker.* Resided in West Germany, 1964-74, and in France, 1979-85. **Awards:** National Endowment for the Arts grant, 1974; Florida State grant for *Arts Expansion,* 1974; Tampa Arts Council grant for *Arts Expansion*, 1974.

Selected Exhibitions:

1961   Howard University, Washington, D.C.
1970   Howard University, Washington, D.C.
1977   Howard University, Washington, D.C.

Collections:

Brooklyn Museum, New York; Duerner Hoesch Museum, West Germany; Museum of Modern Art, New York; National Collection of Fine Arts, Washington, D.C.; University of Lagos, Nigeria.

Publications:

On THOMPSON: Articles—"Mildred Thompson, Sculptor," in *Black Art Quarterly,* 1, Spring 1977, pp. 20-31; "Mildred Thompson" by Sidney Perkowitz, in *Art Papers,* 20, September/October 1996, p. 49 (illustrated).

*   *   *

In her mind and in her art Mildred Thompson does not separate black American experience from American experience. In fact, the artist, who has lived the life of an expatriate, no longer even thinks of herself as an American. Throughout the years she has spent in the United States, Europe, and Africa studying and rediscovering herself, her art has moved from the figurative to the abstract, steadfastly exploring themes of love, sexuality, spirituality, physics, and, most recently, music.

In the 1950s Thompson studied at Howard University, where she was deeply influenced by James Porter and where she made her commitment to art. Porter gave her confidence and encouraged her

to find a voice of her own. "I owe all of what I am to James Porter and his influence," she has said. "He carried me." More than twenty years later, after having spent ten years teaching art in Germany and three years teaching in Tampa, Florida, she returned to Howard for a year.

It was on Porter's recommendation that Thompson left the United States for Germany at a time when black artists were placing themselves at the service of the black arts movement—an exercise that ran the risk of implying that art was trivial unless it was politically motivated. What might have started as an exercise only in self-development, however, ultimately gave her work universal appeal. Her series of etchings "Psychological Studies" (1970s), based on her reading of Carl Jung, shows people with many faces and people in conflict. In the series she defines and reveals, and she discovers and expresses truths that reach beyond temporal values.

Like many other black artists working in expressive social realism in the 1960s and 1970s, Thompson adopted the figure for a brief period as a mainstay of her work. Her early etchings are reminiscent of Henri Matisse, with a strong figurative quality. In the early 1970s she moved away from the figurative mode, and her etchings, paintings, and sculpture then developed an abstract quality.

An oil painting that predates the transition, *Coney Island* (1958), demonstrates Thompson's uncanny ability to capture urban scenes. Brash brush strokes, an intricate play of light and dark, and overlapping geometric shapes lend a busy, even chaotic feel appropriate to the subject. It has been said that her feel for the United States created developments in art that were new, interesting, and American.

Thompson's "Open Window" silk screen series (1974-75) is a colorful study of light that she produced in Tampa. While it explores a widespread fancy—peeping through open windows—it makes use of a truly American technique in doing so. Thompson's later series "Music of the Spheres" is an innovative exploration of music prompted by her belief that as she grows older she grows less visual and more auditory. The series delves into Pythagorean theories of octaves and the movement of planets away from the Sun and their relationships to sound.

Thompson's paintings, which are just as powerful as her drawings and sculptures, have received the most attention from the art world. Nonetheless, in all of her work she makes penetrating statements about people and the worlds around them that ring so true that she must be regarded as an artist of considerable significance.

—Joanne Harris

THOMPSON, Robert (Bob)

American painter and sculptor

Born: Louisville, Kentucky, 26 June 1937. **Education:** Boston University, 1955; University of Louisville, Kentucky, 1956-58. **Family:** Married Carol Penda in 1960. **Awards:** Allan R. Hite Arts Scholarship, University of Louisville, c.1957; Walter Gutman Foundation grant, 1961; John Hay Whitney Fellowship, 1962. **Died:** 30 May 1966.

Individual Exhibitions:

1958   Arts in Louisville, Louisville, Kentucky
1960   Delancey Street Museum, New York

1961	Superior Street Gallery, Chicago
1963	El Cosario Gallery, Ibiza, Spain
	Martha Jackson Gallery, New York
	Drawing Shop, New York
1965	Donald Morris Gallery, Detroit
	Richard Gray Gallery, Chicago
	East End Gallery, Provincetown, Massachusetts
1968	Martha Jackson Gallery, New York (retrospective)
1969	New School Art Center, New York (retrospective)
1971	JB Speed Museum, Louisville, Kentucky
1974	University of Massachusetts at Amherst
1975	National Collection of Fine Arts, Smithsonian Institution (retrospective)
1978	Studio Museum in Harlem, New York
1983	Wanderwoude-Tananbaum Gallery, New York
1986	Wadsworth Atheneum, Hartford, Connecticut
1987	Jamaica Arts Center, Jamaica, New York

Selected Group Exhibitions:

1960	Zabriskie Gallery, New York
1969	Brooklyn College, New York
1971	Musée Rath, Geneva, Switzerland
1984	Center Gallery, Bucknell University, Lewisburg, Pennsylvania (traveling)
1988	Newport Harbor Art Museum (traveling)
1989	Washington Project for the Arts, Washington, D.C. (traveling)
1990	California Afro-American Museum, Los Angeles (traveling)
1992	National Museum of American Art, Smithsonian Institution, Washington, D.C. (traveling)
1994	San Antonio Museum, Texas (traveling)

Collections:

Guggenheim Museum, New York; Hirshhorn Museum and Sculpture Garden, Washington, D.C.; Metropolitan Museum of Art, Washington, D.C.; Museum of Modern Art, New York; National Museum of American Art, Washington, D.C.; Wadsworth Atheneum, Hartford, Connecticut.

Publications:

On THOMPSON: Books—*Bob Thompson,* exhibition catalog, by Paul Mossanyi, New York, New School Art Center, 1969; *Bob Thompson,* exhibition catalog, by Nelson Stevens, et al., Amherst, Massachusetts, University of Massachusetts, 1974; *The World of Bob Thompson,* exhibition catalog, by Gylbert Coker, New York, Studio Museum in Harlem, 1978; *Bob Thompson,* exhibition catalog, by Judith Wilson, et al., Jamaica, New York, Jamaica Arts Center, 1987; *Novae: William H. Johnson and Bob Thompson,* exhibition catalog, Los Angeles, California Afro-American Museum Foundation, 1990. **Articles**—"For Thompson, a Triumph Too Late" by Peter Schjeldahl, in *New York Times,* 23 February 1969; "Myths and Memories: Bob Thompson," in *Art in America* (New York), 71, May 1983, "Bob Thompson's Beauty and the Beast," in *Artist and Influence* (New York), 6, 1988, both by Judith Wilson.

*   *   *

Taking his cues from the signposts of art history canons, Robert Thompson made figuralism exciting just as abstract expressionism was becoming the institutional style of painting in the 1960s. His innovation was to re-vision mythic and religious themes in a contemporary language—hot, wild, and un-self-consciously naive looking. Once he arrived at his flat, rhythmic style in 1960, he painted obsessively. Within six years he had done nearly a thousand drawings and paintings, many of which have been exhibited posthumously.

Thompson's interest in the paintings of the old masters dated to his student days at the University of Louisville in Kentucky, where he made copies from reproductions. In a thesis on Piero della Francesca, Thompson analyzed the chromacentric strategy of the Italian Renaissance, admiringly noting the use of unifying color and adapting it to his own work. He also was influenced by the San Francisco figurative painters Elmer Bishoff and Richard Diebenkorn and by the German expressionist tradition, handed down from his émigré teachers at the University of Louisville.

Drama further defined his canvases. His sense for performance was fueled by a passion for bebop and by the happening, the interactive improvisational art form that burgeoned in the New York and Provincetown, Massachusetts, circles he traveled in from 1958. A participant in a happening organized by Red Grooms in 1960, he translated the spontaneous energy of the event into his paintings.

Moving to New York City in 1959, Thompson haunted area collections, including that of the Barnes Foundation near Philadelphia to see the art of Paul Gauguin, Paul Cézanne, and Henri Matisse. The centrality of the human figure in their works convinced Thompson that it was the only form that mattered. He began to travel to Europe in the early 1960s, and the representational art he saw in French, Italian, and Spanish museums shored up his commitment to the figure.

While Thompson's conceptions often began with paradigmatic works, his approach of reducing detail and paring down the compositional elements to bare essences made his paintings vastly different from the ones that inspired them. He consistently compressed the internal picture space and positioned the broadly painted, colorful elements in close proximity to one another. Objects and lines democratically share the same flat space, and even his large paintings evoke the eloquence of stained glass art.

Thompson's desire to energize his compositions through distortion and simplification extended to his treatment of figures. Although some wear the capes and hoods of ancient costumes, the figures are often naked and boldly colored. In *Descent from the Cross* (1963) the nude forms of Jesus, the Virgin Mary, and Mary Magdalene are portrayed in red, light blue, and yellow.

Biblical allegories inspired *Nativity* (1963-64) and *Angel* (1964), while ancient myth and history were the bases for *Perseus and Andromeda* (1964), *Satyr and Maiden* (1965), and *Blue Daphne* (1966). In his version of these stories Thompson communicated the tense psychology of relationships between the sexes. Female and male figures pair up in bare landscapes, some sylvan, pastoral, and idyllic, and yet their stances are often confrontational, if not aggressive. Watched by supporting actors—imps and instigators that could be stand-ins for the artist himself—the male and female characters enact repressed human emotions and inexpressible fantasies and fears.

Many of Thompson's paintings lend themselves to such readings, which are encouraged by the facts of his biography: a black artist, born in the segregated South, who left the region for the

North and entered bohemian and predominantly white art circles. His success in this environment and gusto for living failed to mitigate his obsessions with the memories of his father's death, however, and with his own fatalism. Hard living precipitated the early end of a brilliant career when, following a series of illnesses, he died in Rome in 1966. His admired body of work survives.

—Jacqueline Francis

THRASH, Dox
American printmaker and painter

Born: Griffin, Georgia, 22 March 1892. **Education:** Studied art through correspondence school until 1909; School of the Art Institute of Chicago, 1914-17; Graphic Sketch Club, Philadelphia, 1918-23. **Military Service:** American Expeditionary Force, 1917-18. **Career:** Printmaker, Pennsylvania Federal Arts Project, 1934-1942. Coinventor of carborundum print process. Worked as a railroad porter, elevator operator, house painter, steward, dancer, and advertising designer. **Awards:** Graphic Sketch Club Exhibition honorable mention, Philadelphia, 1933. **Died:** 1965.

Individual Exhibitions:

1942   Philadelphia Museum of Art, 1942
        Howard University Gallery of Art, Washington, D.C.
1944   Philadelphia Art Alliance

Group Exhibitions:

1939   Baltimore Museum of Art, Maryland
1940   New York World's Fair
        American Negro Exhibition, Chicago
        Tanner Art Gallery, Chicago
1941   South Side Community Art Center, Chicago
1942   Atlanta University, Georgia
1946   Pyramid Club, Philadelphia
1948   Smithsonian Institution, Washington, D.C.
1970   James A. Porter Gallery
1971   Newark Museum, New Jersey

Collections:

History Society of Pennsylvania, Philadelphia; Library of Congress, Washington, D.C.; National Archives, Washington, D.C.; Philadelphia Museum of Art; Philadelphia Public Library; Smithsonian Institution, Washington, D.C.

Publications:

By THRASH: Article: "History of My Life" edited by Ruth Fine Lehrer, in *Philadelphia, Three Centuries of American Art,* Philadelphia, 1976.

On THRASH: Books—*Black Printmaker and the W.P.A.,* exhibition catalog, New York, Lehman College Art Gallery, 1989; *Alone in a Crowd: Prints of the 1930s and 1940s by African American*

Artists from the Collection of Rebe and Dave Williams, exhibition catalog, by Rebe and Dave Williams, New York, 1994. **Articles**—"Originator Describes New Copper Etching Process at Howard University," in *Evening Star* (Washington, D.C.), 31 January 1942; "Carborundum Tint, a New Printmakers Process" by Richard Hood, in *Magazine of Art,* November 1938, p. 643; "Bridging Identies: Dox Thrash as African American and Artist" by David R. Brigham, Washington, D.C., Smithsonian Studies in American Art, 1990.

*   *   *

Dox Thrash, printmaker and painter, is chiefly remembered for his invention (along with Michael Gallagher and Hubert Mesibov) of the carborundum print, while he worked for the Philadelphia graphics division of the Works Progress Administration's Federal Arts Project between 1934 and 1942. Thrash resurfaced lithographic stones with carborundum, a coarse, granular industrial product made of carbon and silicon crystals, to produce images with soft, expressive hues and great tonal variation. His carbographs, or Opheliagraphs (named after his mother), depict a wide range of subject matter, including urban and rural landscapes, industrial laborers, portraits, Philadelphia street and slum life, and other genre scenes.

Thrash first studied art in 1900 through correspondence courses in rural Georgia. He left the South in 1909 for Illinois, where he took part-time art classes at the School of the Art Institute of Chicago and received private tutoring from William Scott. After Thrash was wounded in action while serving with the American Expeditionary Force in France (1917-18), his disability pension allowed him to resume courses at the Art Institute until 1923. He then lived an itinerant life in Boston, Connecticut, and New York, "hobo-ing . . . and painting people of America, especially the 'Negro,'" according to his autobiography. Settling in Philadelphia, Thrash studied privately with Earl Hortor of the Graphic Sketch Club and painted signs for a living in the early 1930s.

Among Thrash's earliest known work is a series of African American portraits and ideal heads, posed in full-front, three-quarters, and profile views and executed in carborundum print, etching, aquatint, lithography, watercolor, ink wash, pastel, charcoal, and graphite. Most have a moody, introspective quality, such as *Abraham* (n.d.), *My Neighbor* (1937), and *Marylou* (c.1940), all carborundum prints that depict sculptural black faces emerging from shadows and staring into the distance. Despite their titles, the artist conceived of them less as individual portraits and more as types, given their masklike qualities and subtle range of tonal variation. Other works, such as the etching *Silas* (before 1943) and the graphite drawing *Man with Harmonica* (n.d.) demonstrate Thrash's skill in employing broad, gestural lines in carefully modeled facial structures.

Occasionally Thrash employed a deeper message in his portraits, as in at least four works that suggest a connection between reading and success. (With his fourth-grade education, the artist's own literacy was limited.) In the carbograph *Life* (c.1940), a pigtailed girl quietly scans a magazine, while in the etching *Morning Paper* (before 1943), a bespectacled, middle-aged man in suit, hat, and bow tie peruses a newspaper. Here Thrash followed such artists as Cassatt, Homer, Chase, Eakins, and Bellows in the American artistic tradition of representing people reading.

Complex darks illuminated by translucent lights are evident in Thrash's carbographic rural landscapes, such as *Georgia Cotton Crop* (c.1938), *Cabin Days* and *Deserted Cabin* (both c. 1939), and

Boats at Night (1940). In the manner of the regionalists, such as Thomas Hart Benton, these refer to the artist's birthplace and the lives of black sharecroppers. In *Georgia Cotton Crop,* a family of six pause forlornly in front of a shadowed, ramshackle shotgun house among scattered piles of picked cotton under darkening skies. Thrash also depicted the horrors of racial persecution in the South, as in *Untitled* (c.1938-40), in which huddled survivors mourn a lynching victim carried by two men.

Similar smoky atmospheres dominate Thrash's urban landscapes, as in the lithograph *Freight Yard* (n.d.), where two nameless, faceless workers stand near a train pulling out of the yard in the shadow of Philadelphia's city hall and skyscrapers. In contrast, an anonymous jackhammer laborer, given monumental scale and seen from below in the carbograph *Defense Worker* (before 1943), shows Thrash's adaptation of a theme treated by social realists, that of the heroic proletarian.

Among those influenced by Thrash's printmaking techniques and subject matter were his colleagues Claude Clark, Raymond Steth, and Samuel Brown, as well as Charles White, Elizabeth Catlett, and Robert Blackburn.

—Theresa Leininger-Miller

TOLLIVER, Mose

American painter

Work also appeared under the name Mose T. **Born:** Pike Road, Alabama, 4 July 1915. **Family:** Married Willie Mae in 1941 (died 1992), 12 children. **Career:** Mover, McClendon Furniture, 1930-65; self-employed gardener, 1930-65. **Agent:** Anton Haardt, Anton Haardt Gallery, 2714 Coliseum Street, New Orleans, Louisiana 70130, U.S.A.

Individual Exhibitions:

1981   Philadelphia College of Art
        Montgomery Museum of Fine Art, Alabama
1993   Museum of American Folk Art, New York

Selected Group Exhibitions:

1982   Corcoran Gallery of Fine Art, Washington, D.C.
1992   Anton Haardt Gallery, Montgomery, Alabama
1994   New Orleans Museum of Fine Art

Mose Tolliver: *Kinto Bird,* **c.1978. Photo courtesy of Anton Haardt.**

Collections:

African American Museum, Dallas; Montgomery Museum of Fine Art, Alabama; Museum of American Folk Art, New York; National Museum of American Art, Washington, D.C.; Philadelphia College of Art; New Orleans Museum of Fine Art.

Publication:

On TOLLIVER: Article—"Mose Tolliver" by Anton Haardt, in *Raw Visions* (London), 1995.

*

Mose Tolliver comments:

I just want to paint my pictures!

I learned to paint by myself when I was recovering from an accident at work. The owner of the store took me to an art exhibit and asked me if I ever tried to paint a picture. And I said I would try.

I use pure house paint.

* * *

Mose Tolliver is the classic example of a folk artist whose career began following his retirement, which resulted from a work-related accident. During the 1960s, while employed in the shipping department of a furniture company, a heavy load of marble fell from a forklift and crushed both of his feet. He was unable to walk without crutches and forced to retire. In the early 1970s an amateur painter took Tolliver to a painting exhibition and encouraged him to study art. Tolliver decided to teach himself and began painting around 1973.

Masonite and plywood panels are used almost exclusively for Tolliver's paintings, but he has also painted on bottles, gourds, birdhouses, furniture, mirrors, clocks, and a variety of other objects. Because he usually paints while seated on the side of his bed with the panel supported on his thighs, the scale of Tolliver's paintings is limited. The surfaces must be small enough to fit comfortably on his lap. He has, however, completed some large-scale pieces, including the exterior of a small cargo van.

Ordinary house paint is the medium for Tolliver's paintings. He attempted to surround his earlier paintings with rudimentary wooden strip frames, but he currently frames each painting with a border painted in a contrasting color. Metal rings from beverage containers serve as hanging devices.

The majority of Tolliver's paintings are compositionally very simple. They include self-portraits, birds, dogs, camels, sharks, moose, turtles, flowers, fruit, cutaway buses and cars, imaginary creatures, and standing males and females. Some of his most popular paintings depict erotic females with their legs encircling their heads to reveal their genitalia and females with spread legs resting on phallic forms. Although Tolliver teasingly insists that these forms are scooters, bicycles, or exercise machines, the sexual connotations are evident. All of Tolliver's human subjects are dominated by enormous heads resting on bodies, with small eyes placed near the heart-shaped voids created by the outline of the foreheads and vertical noses.

Tolliver's choices to employ cast-off pieces of wood and paneling, paint his frames directly on the panels where they form a part of the design, and use beverage containers for hangers are all folk art

Mose Tolliver: *George Washington,* 1992. Photo courtesy of Anton Haardt.

improvisations created for reasons of economy. Another aspect of Tolliver's style is his finesse in incorporating a knot or flaw in a piece of wood into the total design rather than discarding the material. Wooden panels that are splintered during the sawing process are cleverly accented with paint by Tolliver to produce interesting color and textual highlights.

Perhaps the most powerful aspect of Tolliver's paintings is his extraordinary, successful use of color. Although he paints exclusively with inexpensive house paint, his flat tones are never garish or discordant. He mixes his paint to achieve an incredible range of values and seldom uses more than three colors in the same painting. His color combinations are unusually sophisticated for a folk artist and include turquoise with light and medium gray, aqua with orange and brown, mauve with lavender and gray, aqua with mauve and gray, and rose with blue and gray.

A prolific painter, Tolliver often completes ten paintings a day. He paints when the "spirit moves him" and some days does not paint at all. The fact that he is dyslexic accounts for his distinctive signature with a reverse *S*. This signature also serves to complement the naivete of his style.

Tolliver is currently at the height of his career and is producing paintings that are simpler in composition than many of his earlier works. Some of his self-portraits form what is probably the most unusual category of his work. They are also the most dramatically abstract of his heads, with almost terrifying faces viewed in illogical perspective, eyes placed vertically, and teeth bared in large open mouths. The spirit of these horrific representations is totally different from the lyricism of his gentle turtles, spotted birds, and buses with wobbly wheels and the erotic overtones of his ladies on scooters. In 1981 at the Montgomery Museum of Art, Tolliver was one of the first African American folk artists of his generation to hold a one-man exhibition at a major museum. His works have since been widely exhibited and collected in the United States and abroad.

—Regenia A. Perry

TRAYLOR, Bill

American painter

Born: William Traylor, George Traylor plantation, Benton, Alabama, 1854. **Career:** Slave and farm hand, George Traylor plantation, Benton, Alabama. **Died:** 1947.

Individual Exhibitions:

1940	New South Art Center, Montgomery, Alabama
1941	Fieldston School, New York
1979	R.H. Oosterom Gallery, New York
1982	Vanderwoude Tananbaum Gallery, New York
	Hammer and Hammer Gallery, Chicago
	Montgomery Museum of Fine Arts, Alabama
	Arkansas Art Center, Little Rock (traveling)
	Karen Lennox Gallery, Chicago
1983	Mississippi Museum of Art, Jackson
	Gasperi Gallery, New Orleans
	Hill Gallery, Birmingham, Michigan
1984	Acme Art Gallery, San Francisco
1985	Luise Ross Gallery, New York
1986	Hirschl and Adler Modern, New York
1988	Randolf Gallery, Chicago Library Cultural Center (traveling)
	Luise Ross Gallery, New York
1989	Hirschl and Adler Modern, New York

Selected Group Exhibitions:

1979	R.H. Oosterom Gallery, New York
1982	Southern Arts Federation, Atlanta, Georgia
	City College of New York
	Corcoran Gallery of Art, Washington, D.C. (traveling)
	Fleisher Gallery, Philadelphia
1983	High Museum of Art, Atlanta, Georgia
	University of Illinois, Chicago
	Hammer and Hammer Gallery, Chicago
1984	University of New Orleans
	Fleisher Gallery, Philadelphia
1987	Luise Ross Gallery, New York
1989	Rooseum, Malmo, Sweden

Collections:

Abby Aldrich Rockefeller Folk Art Center, Williamsburg, Virginia; Arkansas Arts Center, Little Rock; Evans-Tibbs Collection, Washington, D.C.; High Museum of Art Atlanta, Georgia; Menil Collection, Houston; Montgomery Museum of Fine Arts, Alabama; Museum of American Folk Art, New York; National Museum of American Art, Smithsonian Institution, Washington, D.C.; New Jersey State Museum, Trenton; Newark Museum, Newark, New Jersey; Schomburg Center, New York.

Publications:

On TRAYLOR: Book—*Bill Traylor: His Art, His Life* by Frank Maresca and Roger Ricco, New York, Knopf, 1991. **Articles**— "Art—not—art" by Joann Burstein Hays, in *Artweek,* 5 January 1985, p. 6; "History and Bill Traylor" by Dan Cameron, in *Arts Magazine,* October 85, pp. 45-57; "Bill Traylor's Triumph (How the Beautiful and Raucous Drawings of a Former Alabam Slave Came to Be Known to the World)" by Charles Shannon, in *Art and Antiques,* February 1988, pp. 60-65+; "Bill Traylor's Descendants Located," in *Folk Art,* Winter 1992-93, pp. 29-30; "On Traylor's Trail" by Judd Tully, in *Art and Antiques,* April 1993, p. 15; "Traylor Lawsuit Settled," in *Art in America,* November 1993, p. 152; "Forum: Untitled (Man in Blue Shirt) by Bill Traylor" by Joseph Jacobs, in *Drawing,* March/April 1995, pp. 130-31.

*   *   *

When Bill Traylor was born a slave on a plantation near Montgomery, Alabama, the Emancipation Proclamation was almost a decade away. Following his emancipation, Traylor remained on his master's plantation and worked as a farmhand until he was eighty-four years old, widowed, and most of his children had left the area. He then moved to Montgomery and worked briefly in a shoe factory prior to assuming a hobo-like existence. He had no fixed address, slept in the storage room of a funeral parlor, and spent his days seated on the sidewalks of downtown Montgomery.

Around 1939, when he was eighty-five years old, Traylor's artistic impulses erupted suddenly and unexpectedly. Perhaps the most remarkable aspect of Traylor's art is that his style apparently emerged fully developed, and the quality of his enormous output is remarkably even. Employing only a pencil and straight edge, Traylor often began his compositions by drawing a simple geometric form on any material at hand—paper, cardboard scraps, and shirt cardboard from laundries. These simple geometric shapes were filled with color and became the vortex for the creation of human and animal figures. Animals figure prominently among Traylor's designs and include large, red-tongued dogs, spotted cats, green goats, yellow birds, purple rabbits, and opossums. Scenes depicting dancers, merry drinkers, men driving mules, men leading dogs, and women milking cows may also be seen among Traylor's hundreds of drawings. These were the experiences of Traylor's childhood and adult life.

Traylor's works may be best described as colored drawings since line is their most important element. His compositions are of two types: those with single animal or human figures and those with pictorial compositions populated with animals and humans engaging in vigorous and often humorous anecdotal activities.

Although Traylor exhibited his drawings frequently by suspending them with string on a fence behind his "studio" on the sidewalk, his sales were few during his lifetime. He was extremely prolific and drew constantly, almost excessively, as if he were attempting to compensate for the late beginning of his career as an artist.

Traylor's artistic activities in Montgomery were interrupted during World War II. He moved to the North in 1942 and during the following four years lived with relatives in Detroit and Washington, D.C. No drawings from that period are known. In 1946 Traylor returned to Montgomery, minus a leg that had been amputated due to a gangrene infection, and quickly resumed drawing, as well as his hobo lifestyle. A short time later he became ill and lived in a nursing home until his death. The majority of Traylor's known drawings were produced in Montgomery between 1939 and 1942.

The birds, animals, reptiles, and people in the drawings of Bill Traylor are among the most delightful in the area of American folk art, and by the 1990s their prices had skyrocketed. Whimsical and light-hearted, the simple yet spirited creatures that people Traylor's drawings appear light-years removed from the serious iconography of the spirit world of West African art.

Traylor's attitude, as revealed through his drawings, was that of a total optimist who delighted greatly in the simple pleasures of life. Employing pencils, charcoal, wax crayons, and poster paints, Traylor created a world of delightful imagery that stylistically shares a great deal in common with prehistoric cave paintings and the sensitive artifacts of Paul Klee. The works of Bill Traylor, however, are far removed from prehistoric man's need to depict hunting and animal scenes on the walls of caves and from the famous paintings of a sophisticated artist such as Paul Klee. Traylor's drawings were intensely personal, sometimes imaginative, and profoundly inspired by the experiences of his long life.

—Regenia A. Perry

TUCKER, Curtis (Dee)

American ceramist

Born: Austin, Texas, 26 September 1939. **Education:** California Western University, 1957-58; University of Zaragoza, Spain, 1962-63; Otis Art Institute, 1966-68. **Family:** Married Yvonne Edwards Tucker in 1967, three children. **Career:** Instructor, Miami-Dade Community College, 1968-69; director, ceramic workshops, Florida A and M University, 1973-75; instructor, Haystack Mountain School of Crafts, Deer Isle, Maine, 1974; art director, Raquette Lake, New York, 1985. Member, Southern Arts Federation. **Awards:** Merit Award, Metropolitan Art Museum, Florida Craftsmen, Miami, 1969; Best in Show, Lowe Art Museum, Black Artists of Florida, Coral Gables, 1970; Best Use of Clay Award, Hollywood Museum of Art, Southeast Florida Craftsmen, Hollywood, Florida, 1972; Best in Show, Tallahassee Society of Arts and Crafts, 1979; first place award, KUUMBA Statewide Exhibition, Daytona, Florida, 1981; Best in Show, Harambee Festival, Tallahassee, Florida, 1984; Purchase Award, Tallahassee City Hall, Florida, 1985; second place, Seventh Annual Atlanta Life Insurance Company, Atlanta, Georgia, 1987; Purchase Award, Mammoth Life and Accident Insurance Company, J.B. Speed Museum, Louisville, Kentucky, 1988; second place, WFSU, Collector's Board, Tallahassee, Florida, 1989; Purchase Award, Syracuse University Afro-American Ceramics Collection, 1989; Merit Award, Florida State University Center for Professional Development, Tallahassee, 1990; Merit Award, Arts Festival of Atlanta, Georgia, 1990; Best in Show, Art in the Park, Memphis, Tennessee, 1990; Purchase Award, Panoply of the Arts, Huntsville, Alabama, 1991; Award of Distinction, Deland Outdoor Art Festival, Florida, 1991; Award of Merit, Waterside Art and Blues Festival, Louisville, Kentucky, 1991; Best in Show, Starke Festival of the Arts, Florida, 1991; first place, Fine Crafts, Hall of Fame ArtFest, Canton, Ohio, 1991. **Died:** 16 July 1992.

Selected Exhibitions:

1968   Contemporary Gallery of Fine Arts, Dallas
1972   *Curtis and Yvonne Tucker,* Micanopy Gallery of Fine Arts, Florida
         AFRO-RAKU: Ceramics by Yvonne and Curtis Tucker, North Florida Junior College, Madison

1974   *Yvonne and Curtis Tucker,* Foster Tanner Fine Art Gallery, Florida A and M University, Tallahassee
1979   North Florida Junior College, Madison
         Brooks Memorial Art Museum, Memphis, Tennessee
1980   Gulf Coast Community College, Panama City, Florida
         Craftsman's Gallery, Scarsdale, New York
         Tennessee State University, Nashville
         Curtis and Yvonne Tucker: Ceramics, Evans-Tibbs Gallery, Washington, D.C.
         Florida A and M University, Tallahassee
1982   California Museum of Afro-American History and Culture, Los Angeles
         Museum of the National Center of Afro-American Artists, Boston
1987   Community Folk Art Gallery, Syracuse, New York
1988   J.B. Speed Museum, Louisville, Kentucky
1989   School #33 Art Gallery, Baltimore, Maryland
         Gallery Antigua, Miami
1991   Florida State University, Tallahassee

Collections:

Albany State University, Georgia; Evans-Tibbs Collection, Washington, D.C.; Fisk University, Nashville; Lincoln Theater, Columbus, Ohio; Syracuse University Afro-American Ceramics Collection, New York; Tennessee State University, Nashville.

Publications:

By TUCKER: Articles—"Black Art Theatre," in *Afro Arts,* 1970; in *African, Indian and Oriental Influences in the Aesthetics of Two Contemporary Craftspeople: First National African-American Crafts Conference: Selected Writings,* Shelby State Community College, 1980; "John T. Scott and the Black Aesthetic," in *International Review of African American Art,* 6(2), 1985.

On TUCKER: Book—*Double Visions: Yvonne and Curtis Tucker,* exhibition catalog, Tallahassee, Florida, LeMoyne Art Foundation, 1995. **Articles**—"Afro-Raku: The Ceramics of Yvonne and Curtis Tucker" by Ellen A. Ashdown, in *Black Art: An International Quarterly,* 3(4), New York, 1979, pp. 36-44; "The Ceramics of Yvonne and Curtis Tucker" by Ellen A. Ashdown, in *Art/Craft* (formerly *Art Voices),* 1(2), 1980, pp. 22-23.

*

Curtis Tucker comments:

I am deeply spiritual in my approach in my art, although not a church-goer. I am inspired by thoughts of the power but invisibility of the spirit. As we can feel the soul of the invisible wind as it shapes the air and moves the trees, I also throw a pot from the inside because then the outside takes care of itself. The inside is the spirit of the vessel, the intangible part. The surface of my works mirrors the range of my experiences and captures symbolically the key impressions in my life and/or collective experiences in our culture—aspects that we can all sense or recognize. For example, a lidded jar titled *The Feather is Still Strong* refers to the symbolism of the feather in African, Egyptian, and Native American culture and refers to the unbroken line of strength in these cultures in spite of the terrifying pressure to break in their spirit.

When a wise man was asked about life, he said, "Go down to the potter and he can tell you about life." You understand what he meant when you work with clay because when you work intimately with clay, you can understand life.

*   *   *

Curtis Tucker grew up in Lubbock, Texas, and spent summers on his grandfather's farm in Mexia, Texas. These summers at the farm had a great impact on his personality and gave him an independent spirit and love of the land recognizable by all who knew him. Tucker grew greens and beans and other foods on small plots while living in northern Florida, where he and his wife, Yvonne, moved in 1973 after spending five years in Miami. The fact that he became, along with Yvonne, one of the most significant African American ceramics artists is entirely consistent with this background and his love and respect for the earth.

Tucker moved to southern California at sixteen and from there visited Tijuana and Ensinada, Mexico, where he was influenced by Latin culture. Tucker had always been interested in music and developed a salsa band at his high school in San Diego. Never comfortable in the academic world, he dropped out of college and joined the air force, which led to a duty tour in Spain for several years. There he learned to paint with the help of Jose Val Verde, a bullfighter and painter he met in Zaragosa. It also is significant that he had a love of chemistry in school. After the air force tour, Tucker met Yvonne in Los Angeles, while she was doing graduate study at the Otis Art Institute and, through her, became interested in ceramics.

Curtis Tucker's ceramics most often took the form of pots thrown on a wheel and tended to be characterized by swelling oval forms and geometric designs or stylized characters. Over the years, he experimented with firing and glazing techniques, and his painting experience affected the imagery and colors used on his pots. His early work involved high-temperature stoneware glazes and was influenced by Chinese Sung dynasty pottery. He was also affected by the Japanese concept of *shibui*—simplicity of form, glaze, and weight for an inner radiance, quietness, and purity. He was influenced by the southwestern Pueblo pottery of Maria and Julien Martinez and the spiritual shine of African sculpture, and he was affected stylistically by the West Coast revolution in pottery (looking at clay as art rather than craft) through the work of Peter Volkous and the raku work of Paul Soldner. A demonstration by Michael Cardew and African ceramist Ladi Kwali also had an impact on Tucker and led to explorations with African techniques and new ideas in his work.

In 1975 the Tuckers were without their kiln for a while because it needed repairs, and they turned to raku techniques they had learned from Soldner in California. Tucker built a simple raku kiln from an oil drum and lined it with Fiberfrax, a refractory material developed in the space program at NASA. The mastering of raku techniques led to a new visual style and allowed the Tuckers to develop the rich black surfaces that are so notable in their work. During a teaching experience at the Haystack Mountain School in Maine one summer, Tucker worked with Nigerian potter Abbas Ahuwan, and together they developed a new technique called "Afro-raku" that combined African techniques with innovative cooling and reduction processes to yield new surface qualities.

Many of Tucker's works had narrative or symbolic images drawn from his African and Native American heritage, his social consciousness, his musical background and interests, or his sensitivity to black cultural experiences and practices. Tucker developed his own unique style, using joken temoku glazes, Afro-raku pots with crackled glazes, or slips and burnished surfaces. He was also part of a communal style that developed from a long history of artistic collaborations with his wife, Yvonne. Her work was more sculptural than his, more vertical, and her imagery was more figurative, but their collaborations led to a style different from either of their individual styles. Often they worked on each other's objects, and their collaborative pots were often thrown by Curtis with Yvonne's drawings and sculptural additions.

Curtis Tucker was a vibrant, extroverted person who told stories in the Texas tall-tale tradition, loved to cook, and saw spiritual aspects in his artistic expression. His work combined the influences of Zen, African ideas and techniques, West Coast innovation, and his own creativity to develop something completely new in African American art. Clay gave him a great sense of the earth, and it seems to be almost a metaphor for the rich personality and creative spirit of this very earthy man.

—Michael D. Harris

TUCKER, Yvonne Edwards
American ceramist

Born: Chicago, Illinois, 1941. **Education:** School of the Art Institute of Chicago, 1962; University of Illinois, Urbana, B.F.A. 1962; University of California, Los Angeles, 1962-64; California State College, Los Angeles, 1964-65; Otis Art Institute (now Otis/Parson's School of Design), Los Angeles, B.F.A. 1968; Otis Art Institute (now Otis/Parson's School of Design), Los Angeles, M.F.A. 1968; University of Miami, 1971-72; Florida State University, 1979-80. **Family:** Married Curtis D. Tucker in 1967, three children. **Career:** Assistant professor, Miami-Dade Community College, South Campus, 1968-73. Since 1973 associate professor, Florida A and M University, Tallahassee. Visiting artist, Tallahassee Arts Council and Leon County Board of Education, 1979-77, First National African-American Crafts Conference, Memphis, Tennessee, 1979, Tennessee State University, Nashville, 1980, Albany State College, 1983 and 1979, University of Mississippi, Oxford, 1986, Gulf Coast Community College, Panama City, Florida, 1989, North Florida Community College, Madison, 1981-90, New Orleans Jazz and Heritage Festival, 1987-90. Panelist/lecturer, Florida A and M University, Tallahassee, 1981, 1984, 1985, Indian River Community College, Florida, 1989, Florida State University, Tallahassee, 1988-90. Cofounder, Harambee Council of Tallahassee. Administrator and project director of folk and fine arts festivals annually from 1980-90. **Awards:** Educators to Africa Travel Award, African American Institute and Howard University, Washington, D.C., 1975; National Endowment for the Humanities fellowships, 1978, 1981-82. **Address:** 3007 Kevin Street, Tallahassee, Florida 32301, U.S.A.

Selected Exhibitions:

1968   Contemporary Gallery of Fine Arts, Dallas
1972   *Curtis and Yvonne Tucker,* Micanopy Gallery of Fine Arts, Florida

AFRO-RAKU: Ceramics by Yvonne and Curtis Tucker,
North Florida Junior College, Madison

1974   *Yvonne and Curtis Tucker,* Foster Tanner Fine Art Gallery, Florida A and M University, Tallahassee
1975   Morgan State College, Baltimore, Maryland
1978   *Transitions: Works of Yvonne Tucker,* Alabama State University, Montgomery
1979   North Florida Junior College, Madison
        Brooks Memorial Art Institute, Memphis, Tennessee
1980   Gulf Coast Community College, Panama City, Florida
        Tennessee State University, Nashville
        Curtis and Yvonne Tucker: Ceramics, Evans-Tibbs Gallery, Washington, D.C.
1981   Malcolm Brown Gallery, Shaker Heights, Ohio
1987   *Rhythm of Women: Kabuya Bowens and Yvonne Tucker,* Gallery Antigua, Miami
        Community Folk Art Gallery, Syracuse, New York
        Florida A and M University, Tallahassee
1988   J.B. Speed Museum, Louisville, Kentucky
1989   Contemporary Art Center, Kansas City, Missouri
        School #33 Art Gallery, Baltimore, Maryland
        Gallery Antigua, Miami
1991   Florida State University, Tallahassee

Collections:

Alabama State University, Montgomery; Albany State College, New York; Caleb Center, City of Miami; Evans-Tibbs Collection, Washington, D.C.; Fisk University, Nashville; Florida A & M University Black Archives, Tallahassee; Miami-Dade Community College; North Florida Community College, Madison Otis Art Institute of Parson's School of Design, Los Angeles; Syracuse University Afro-American Ceramics Collection, New York; Tennessee State University, Nashville; University of Illinois, Champaign-Urbana.

Publications:

By TUCKER: Articles—"African, Indian and Oriental Influences in the Aesthetics of Two Contemporary African-American Craftspeople," in *First National African-American Crafts Conference: Select Writings* edited by David Driskell, Memphis, Shelby State Community College, 1980, pp. 56-63; "The Afro-Raku Ceramics of Yvonne and Curtis Tucker," in *National Council on Education for the Ceramic Arts,* 10, 1989-90, pp. 51-54.

On TUCKER: Book—*Double Visions: Yvonne and Curtis Tucker,* exhibition catalog, Tallahassee, Florida, LeMoyne Art Foundation, 1995. **Articles**—"Afro-Raku: The Ceramics of Yvonne and Curtis Tucker" by Ellen A. Ashdown, in *Black Art: An International Quarterly,* 3(4), New York, 1979, pp. 36-44; "The Ceramics of Yvonne and Curtis Tucker" by Ellen A. Ashdown, in *Art/Craft* (formerly *Art Voices),* 1(2), 1980, pp. 22-23.

*

Yvonne Tucker comments:

As blues and jazz musicians reveal depths of the human spirit through syncopated rhythms, harmonics, and improvisation, I am also challenged to touch others through the language and warmth of hand-formed clay. When throwing or hand building, I often hold my breath while centering myself in the moment in order to dance in partnership with my silent teacher, clay. It is then that I often feel my hands and mind becoming a conduit for greater forces from the inner realm of the spirit.

It is through process and philosophy that my work is connected in spirit to traditions stemming out of Africa and Native America, as well as Japan. As in traditional West African sculpture, my vessels' aim is to function symbolically as receptacles for the spirits of ancestors and griots of American culture. As such, they go beyond decoration to function as "power objects," becoming silent metaphors for deep memories and feelings. As in Japanese and Korean Zen-inspired raku, my work can become a focal point for personal contemplation, for "being and becoming" in a point in time.

*   *   *

Yvonne Tucker grew up in Chicago and originally thought of herself as a painter. Her mother had, for a while, gone to the same school in Texas as the father of her husband and art partner, Curtis Tucker. Yvonne went to graduate school in Los Angeles at the Otis Art Institute in the mid-1960s, where she studied drawing with Charles White and ceramics with Helen Watson. Peter Volkous, who was the focal point of the new movement in ceramics that emphasized clay as art, had been at Otis for a while, and his influence was felt, too. While in Los Angeles, Tucker talked with and was inspired by African American artists, such as Herman "Kofi" Bailey, just back from Ghana, Samella Lewis, Noah Purifoy, John Outterbridge, and others.

Curtis and Yvonne were married in 1967 and collaborated as artists for the rest of his life. Both Tuckers came from storytelling traditions, but Yvonne, because of her strong background in painting and drawing, developed a style that involved inscribing images, often figurative, on her ceramic works. She was more interested in the natural surfaces and colors of the clay than in glazes, though she enjoyed temoku and celadon glazes. Her work tended to have a vertical thrust, sculptural treatments, lidded vessels, and figurative imagery. Her works were often smaller than some of her husband's because she could manage only about twenty pounds of clay, while Curtis could work with up to fifty pounds. He did help her develop larger works by working the clay for her. She also preferred hand-built sculptural forms to the functional, wheel-thrown forms preferred by Curtis. She has been fascinated with lidded vessels since the early years, and they have evolved into "Spirit Vessels" with both thrown and hand-built elements.

Tucker's early work involved stoneware and earthenware traditions using lusters and overglazes, West Coast ceramics, and Japanese or Chinese influences. A demonstration she attended by Michael Cardew and African potter Ladi Kwali inspired a change of focus and the inclusion of African techniques and elements in her work. Also, travel to Ghana, Togo, and Dahomey affected Tucker, and she came to enjoy the unglazed, burnished surfaces and textures of West African and Congolese pottery. Eventually she began to study correlations between Zen and West African spirituality and saw her work as having spiritual, as well as social, political, and artistic implications.

Yvonne was recruited to teach in Miami at Miami-Dade Community College in 1968 after graduation from Otis Art Institute. The Tuckers then moved to Tallahassee in 1973, where she joined the faculty of Florida A & M University. In 1975 the Tuckers lost the services of their stoneware gas kiln, so they turned to raku firing techniques they had learned in Los Angeles from Paul Soldner. The spontaneity of raku was appealing as were the new surface qualities it produced in their work. Eventually techniques were developed involving bisque-firing works in an electric kiln and then raku firing in a makeshift gas kiln. The works were glazed as greenware after burnishing, and then she performed freehand drawings on them prior to firing.

As she and Curtis were developing new techniques, Yvonne continued exploring philosophical and aesthetic issues. Her exploration of the parallels between Zen thinking and African spiritual ideas led to an understanding of art functioning on multiple levels. She recently has developed a series of lidded vessels addressing notions about African American women, and in the late 1980s she did a series with elaborate sculptural lids including *Spirit Vessel: Bird of Ganier Coming Home*, and *Spirit Vessel: For Kofi Bailey, Who Knew to Know the History*. She has acknowledged African deities like Oshun in her work and exalted heroic African American women like Zora Neale Hurston and Sojourner Truth.

As her own style evolved, so did the style she shared with Curtis. Usually their collaborative works involved pots thrown by him with her drawings or sculptural additions. Sometimes Curtis would create spirit vessels and she would coil or throw large rounded pots, so there was a borrowing in their competitive collaborations, each partner pushing and lifting the other to new heights of creative expression. Yet Yvonne retained her own sensibilities and maintained her own aesthetic explorations in a complimentary relationship.

The clay work of Yvonne Tucker is unique and recognizable in the history of African American expression, but her explorations with Japanese, Chinese, Native American, American, and African ceramic traditions and techniques has made her work international in scope. Her foundations in black Chicago, her location in the midst of the black West Coast art community, and her constant commitment to the black community have given her art the heart and soul of African America, a center which rearticulates the global influences in her native tongue.

—Michael D. Harris

TWIGGS, Leo (Franklin)

American painter

Born: St. Stephen, South Carolina, 13 February, 1934. **Education:** Claflin College, Orangeburg, South Carolina, 1952-56, B.A. (suma cum laude) 1956; Art Institute of Chicago, 1960; New York University, 1962-64, M.A. 1964; University of Georgia, Athens, 1967-70, Ed.D in art education and art criticism 1970. **Military Service:** Signal Corp, 1956-58: Sp4c. **Family:** Married Rosa Johnson in 1961, three sons. **Career:** High school art instructor, Sumpter School District, Orangeburg, South Carolina, 1964-71; instructor/professor/chair, art department, South Carolina State University, Orangeburg, 1964-80. Since 1980 executive director, I.P. Stanback Museum, and chair, art department, South Carolina State University, Orangeburg. **Awards:** Elizabeth O'Neal Verner Award (governor's trophy), State of South Carolina, 1980; National Art Education Southeastern Region Award, 1981. **Agent:** Hampton III, Ltd., 10 Gallery Centre, Taylors, South Carolina 29678, U.S.A. **Address:** 420 Woodlawn Drive, Orangeburg, South Carolina 29115, U.S.A.

Leo Twiggs: *Extended Family Portrait*, 1985.

Individual Exhibitions:

1972	Ashville Museum, North Carolina
1977	Towson Art Gallery, Baltimore, Maryland
1978	Schenectady Museum, Schenectady, New York
	Studio Museum in Harlem, New York
1980	Louisiana Technical University Gallery, Ruston
1983	University of South Alabama, Mobile
1984	Delta Fine Arts Center, Winston-Salem, North Carolina
1990	Greenville Museum, Greenville, South Carolina
1993	Hampton III Gallery, Taylors, South Carolina
1996	African American Gallery, Charleston, South Carolina

Selected Group Exhibitions:

1971	New Jersey State Museum
1972	Carnegie Technical Institute, Pittsburgh, Pennsylvania
1973	High Museum, Atlanta, Georgia
1978	Cornell University, Ithaca, New York
1984	Nexus Gallery, Atlanta, Georgia
	Palazzo Venezia, Rome
1986	United States State Department (traveling through 1990)
1990	South Carolina State Museum, Columbia
1992	Columbia Museum of Art, Columbia, South Carolina
1994	National Afro-American Art Center and Museum, Wilberforce, Ohio

Collections:

American Crafts Council, New York; Atlanta University, Georgia; City of Atlanta, Georgia; Columbia Museum of Art, Columbia, South Carolina; Cornel University, Ithaca, New York; Gibbes Museum, Charleston, South Carolina; Greenville Museum of Art, Greenville, South Carolina; South Carolina State University, Orangeburg; Winston-Salem State University, Winston-Salem, North Carolina.

Publications:

By TWIGGS: Articles—"The Black Artist as Teacher and Pan Africanist," in *Negro Educational Review,* 1972; "The Museum and the Black Community," in *Museum News,* American Museum Association, 1972; "Painting with Dyes, Some Experiments in Batik," in *Design,* Spring 1972, pp. 24-25; "Reflections of a Southern Heritage, Twentieth Century Artists of the Southeast," in exhibition catalog (Charleston), Gibbes Art Museum, 36(2), 1979, p.12; "Black Journey," in *History News* (Charleston, South Carolina), Association for American Life and History, February 1981; "On Art and Testing in a Period of Educational Reform," in *Design for Arts in Education,* 88(1), 1986, pp. 51-54; "The Arts Are Basic," in *Artifacts,* South Carolina Arts Commission, III, November, December, January 1989, p.5; "Teaching Art to Disadvantaged Black Students: Strategies for a Learning Style," in *Art, Culture and Ethnicity* edited by Bernard Young (Reston, Virginia), National Art Education Association, 1990, pp. 1-15; "The McDonald Collection Heirlooms of a People," in *Collections* (Columbia, South Carolina), Columbia Museum of Art, 1992; "Adapting African American Culture into the School Curriculum: Developing the Real McCoy," in *Perspectives,* South Carolina Art Association, Spring 1993.

On TWIGGS: Book—*Leo F. Twiggs: Down Home Landscapes,* New York, Studio Museum in Harlem, 1978. **Articles**—"Signature in Wax: Batik Artist Leo Twiggs" by Harriet Green, in *Columbia Museum* (Columbia, South Carolina), 4, 1986; "Leo Twiggs: Artist as Teacher" by Charles Twady, in *State Newspaper* (Columbia, South Carolina), 1987; "South Carolina's Hidden Treasure," in *Ebony,* September 1988.

*   *   *

Leo Twiggs's successful employment of batik as a communicative medium rather than as a decorative craft device characterizes the unique quality of his work. Expressive manipulation of this ancient, wax dye-resist technique, which dates to Egyptian cultural antiquity, to investigate issues of history and heritage creates extraordinary, irony-filled implications in his oeuvre that stem from the medium per se, in combination with his often Afro-centrist subject matter.

Formal affinities with his mentor-teachers, Hale Woodruff and Arthur Rose, are sometimes evident in Twiggs's images by virtue of his progressively exotic, tertiary palette, innovative use of color and form, and precarious balancing of abstract and figurative elements. Despite the consistently representational content of Twiggs's images (for his are always paintings of *something*), compositional arrangement, spontaneity, and control—not figuration—are the principal aesthetic issues that he emphasizes. Thus, the figures who populate his canvases are more significant as elements of composition and abstract embodiments of social concepts than as representational renderings of particular personalities.

Motifs of youth and age, looming and powerful mother icons, and images of mystical old men and of regional culture are presented as a means of telegraphing ideas of universal significance. They are devices Twiggs uses with authority and ingenuity to create formal and aesthetic contributions unlike those of any other American painter. While his subject matter is often centered in an African American subcultural context and may incorporate principally African American imagery, the essential themes of life, decay, death, and renewal and the interweaving of literary and intellectual concepts in what often appear at first as deceptively simplistic visual images constitute his forte.

In paintings from his "Commemorations" series of the 1970s, Twiggs's images of the naval battle jack of the Confederacy raise many questions pertaining to the heritage of Americans of African descent and their position in the culture of the South, specifically, and in America as a whole. The inherently faded, aged, folded, and crinkled quality of the medium of batik elicits a series of conceptual associations regarding perception of this particular commemorative device. These associations with the Confederate flag include its symbolism, antiquity, and continued iconographic and ideological importance in the South for its allusions to racial injustice, obtuse social values, and the intricately paradoxical relationships that have evolved from the Southern American experience and its institutions, specifically the institutionalized trading in human beings—slavery. Thus, Twiggs's batik paintings in the "Commemorations" series, by using a traditional African craft form in an expressive context, examine both the losses of the Southerner of European heritage as well as the cultural losses of the African American. This examination of loss is accomplished in part through the medium, but also through the choice of subject matter. The survival of this African craft form is a metaphor for the survival of the African American and the subcultural traditions retained from an African past, subsumed (sometimes almost invisibly) under the larger American cultural conglomerate.

Another of Twiggs's series that pertains to the African American experience, the "We Have Known Rivers" group of paintings, is concerned with the foundations of civilization, cultural dispersal, and not only the African diaspora but also the fragmentation and dissemination of any culture relying on the cyclical nature of our common human experiences. The series also pays homage to the African American literary and intellectual tradition, specifically the work of poet Langston Hughes, celebrating a people and a heritage that encompasses all peoples and traditions in the power of its continuity and survival under adverse circumstances. Rivers, as cradles of civilization, are used as a metaphor for the continued flow, transition, and movement of human existence.

The "Hugo Series," centered on a regional natural disaster, Hurricane Hugo, examines the frailty of human existence before the power of nature and expands the cyclical concepts that underlie much of Twiggs's imagery.

A new direction in Twiggs's works of the 1990s is his use of the painted assemblage. The work *Blues for B.B.*, for example, combines contextually similar but culturally disparate forms of the sacrificial reliquary, a form used in traditional Christian (particularly Roman Catholic) iconography, which is equally popular in many traditional African tribal cultures.

Twiggs's exceptional batik paintings incorporate a sociopolitical statement on the tenacious survival of a particular ethnic group

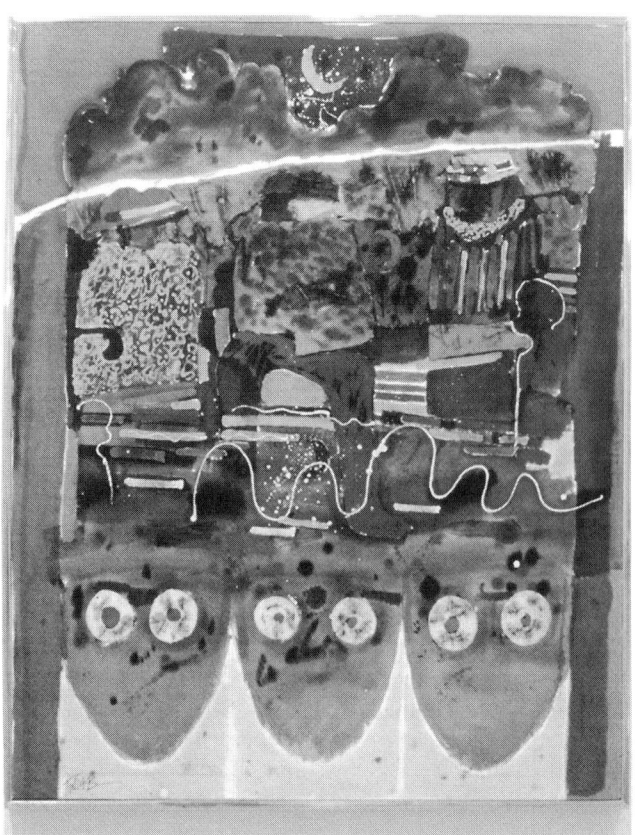

Leo Twiggs: *We Have Known Rivers: Trio of the Gods*, 1992.

(African Americans) as a metaphor for the endurance of humanity. His works demonstrate exceptional compositional subtlety, sophistication, and visual richness, while incorporating his regional experiences and cultural heritage as universal metaphors of the human condition.

—Frank Martin

(Prince) TWINS SEVEN-SEVEN

Nigerian painter and sculptor

Also known as the Amuludun of Ilobu. Work has appeared under the name Olaniyi-Oyewale Osuntoki. **Born:** Taiwo Olaniyi-Oyewale Aitoyeje; Toyeje Oyakale Osuntoki, Ibadan, Nigeria, 3 May 1944. **Family:** Married, children. **Career:** Teacher, Institute of Contemporary Art, London, and Italian Cultural Institute, Lagos, Nigeria. Teacher, Merced College, California, 1972; lecturer, Haystack Mountain Crafts School, Deer Isle, Maine, 1974; artist-in-residence, National Black Theatre, New York. Operates Art Man's Gallery, Oshogbo, Nigeria. Well-known musician and performer, producing several albums. Member Osun State Chamber of Commerce. **Awards:** Institute of Corporate Art Award, 1967; Merced City College Award, 1972; Key to the City of Philadelphia, Key to the City of Los Angeles, both 1975; International Recognition Citation, Mayor of Philadelphia, 1992; Merit Award, University of Nsukka, 1994; African Youth Congress Award, 1995; Heritage '95 Award, LAUTECH, 1995; musical award, University of Ife. **Agent:** Dr. Harriet Schiffer, 1657 The Fairway, Jenkintown, Pennsylvania 19046, U.S.A. **Address:** Keke Elemuy Cultural Centre, P.O. Box 68, Osogbo, Osun State, Nigeria.

Individual Exhibitions:

1967 Institute of Contemporary Art, Dover Street, London
Institute of African Studies, University of Sussex
1970 Commonwealth Institute, London
Camdem Arts Centre, London
Studio Museum in Harlem, New York
Third Anniversary Celebration of Mbari Mbayo, Oshogbo, Nigeria
Goethe Institute, Lagos
USIS, Ibadan, Nigeria
1971 Virginia Union University, Richmond
Goethe Institute, Lagos
Merton D. Simpson Gallery, New York
1973 Elma Lewis School of Fine Arts, Boston
Colorado State University, Fort Collins
Goethe Institute, Lagos
1974 National Museum, Lagos
Goethe Institute, Lagos
1975 Goethe Institute, Lagos
1977 Goethe Institute, Lagos
1990 Italian Cultural Institute, Lagos
1992 Ludwig Forum, AACHEN
1993 Jantzen Gallery Eshweiller, Germany (retrospective)
1994 Heildberg, Germany
Iserlon Catholic Academy, Germany (retrospective)
Airport Hotel, Hamburg, Germany (retrospective)

Selected Group Exhibitions:

1972 *New African Art in Czechoslovakia,* Naprstek Museum
1972 *Africa Creates '72,* Union Carbibe Gallery, New York (traveling)
1973 Egg and Eye Gallery, Los Angeles
1974 Museum of African Art, Washington, D.C.
Los Banos Community College, California
1976 Carnegie Institute of Arts, Pittsburgh, Pennsylvania
1977 Howard University, Washington, D.C.
1985 Commonwealth Institute Art Gallery, London, and Edinburgh, Scotland
1990 San Jose State University Gallery, San Jose, California
1991 Moderno Institue de Art, Las Palmas, Spain

Collections:

African Art Now, Mordernano, Institute of Art, Las Palmas, Spain; Contemporary Art Museum, Houston; Elf Oil, Lagos, Nigeria and Paris; Hampton University Museum, Hampton, Virginia; Iwalewa-Haus, Bayreuth, Germany; Mbari Art, Washington, D.C.; Musée de l'Homme, Paris; Museum für Volkerkunde, Frankfurt, Germany; Museum of Man, Ottawa; Museum of Modern Art, New York; National Museum of Africa Art, Washington, D.C.; Studio Museum in Harlem, New York; Tropical Museum, Amsterdam; University of Southern California, African Art Center, Los Angeles; Volkerkunde Museum, Rotterdam, Netherlands.

Publications:

On TWINS SEVEN-SEVEN: Book—*The Paintings of Twins Seven-Seven*, exhibition catalog, Ibadan, Nigeria [USIS Auditorium exhibit], 1970. **Articles**—"Seven Seven" by Ulli Beier, in *Black Orpheus* (Ibadan), 22, August 1967, pp. 45-48; "Twins Seven-Seven" by A.C. Mundy-Castle and Vicky Mundy-Castle, in *African Arts* (Los Angeles), 6(1), Autumn 1972, pp. 8-13; "Two African Artists; Amir I. M Nour and Twins Seven-Seven" by Irwin Hersey, in *African Arts* (Los Angeles), 10(1), October 1976, p. 82; "Nike Twins Seven-Seven: Nigerian Batik Artist" by Betty Laduke, in *Sage* (Atlanta, Georgia), 4(1), Spring 1987, pp. 61-64; "Chief Twins Seven-Seven Art" by Ulli Beieer, in *Culturen* (Amsterdam), 1, 1987, pp. 12-18 (illustrated; color); "Twins' Art and Dance" by Tam Fiofori, in *West Africa* (London), 3689, 25 April 1988, p. 738 (illustrated); "Chief Councillor Twins Seven-Seven, A Seamless Yoruba Personality" by Ulli Beier, in *Three Yoruba Artists: Twins Seven-Seven, Ademola Onibonokuta, Muraina Oyelami*, Bayreuth, Germany, Bayreuth University (Bayreuth African Studies Series, 12), 1988, pp. 5-40.

*   *   *

Taiwo Bamidele Huseini Olaniyi Oyewale, or simply Twins Seven-Seven, is a painter from the Oshogbo school, whose multifarious names, careers (i.e., dancer, painter, musician, and politician), and lives are as numerous as the possible interpretations for his fantastically detailed drawings, paintings, etchings, and multimedia works. He draws subject matter from Yoruba religion and mythology, everyday life, and literature. Regardless of the subject, Twins always populates his Boschian worlds with mutant gods, goddesses, spirits, and mortals that often emerge from his dreams. These works are as surreal as the unique circumstances surrounding Twins' birth: he is the only survivor of seven sets of twins born to his mother. The Yoruba regard twins as supernatural beings, who at one time rarely survived birth. It is believed that Twins was born seven times to the same mother, and finally, after the seventh birth, decided to stay.

His very individualized style developed out of the experimental Oshogbo workshops, which were started in the early 1960s by Ulli and Georgina Beier, Suzanne Wenger, and Dennis Williams. They encouraged artists and ordinary people to create from their imagination and not be confined by technical directives. Consequently, technical instructions were minimal. The artists or would-be artists were at liberty to paint from their personal visions. At the time many academically trained Nigerian artists and critics voiced skepticism about an approach they saw as condescending and artistically infantalizing. Although their methods differed, artists from both the Oshogbo school and the academic world encouraged students to reconnect with and celebrate traditional culture, artifacts, and values that had been discarded during British rule. Charged with a freedom to express himself and examine his cultural heritage, Twins made visible in two dimensions the masks and the super-real

dealings of the *orisha,* or Yoruba divinity, and legends from folklore.

Before the 1964 Oshogbo workshop, Twins had never drawn or painted. He had studied music prior to leaving school. Twins' earliest artworks were detailed pen and ink drawings on paper. *Devils Dog*, from 1964, is one of his first drawings and typifies this early stage. At first glance the six figures depicted seem to float in space, but a closer look reveals that they each stand firmly in separate realms, something like simultaneous realities. What connects them is the patterned background of thin lines tracing their forms. The largest of these is a multipod, part-amoeba, part-mammal dog that advances into its space from the upper left corner of the drawing. On it live smaller, seemingly magnified microorganisms and abstract shapes. Below it to the left is a similar yet smaller creature with two horns atop his head. There is a spaciousness in this work that disappears in the densely packed later works on wooden panels.

About ninety percent of Twins' work has to do with Yoruba religion and the *orisha. Esu-Odara's Giant Domestic Animals Shade on the Wood* from 1967, *308 Pictures from the Grad Plan of Creation,* and *Devil's Dog* are examples of works with direct references to the *orisha.* Esu is a Yoruba *orisha,* and when he is depicted with a knife or feather projecting from his head, signifying that a display of power has begun, he is called Esu-Odara (Wonder-Worker). *Devil's Dog* is also a representation of Esu, often referred to by Christians as the devil. Twins has given Esu an extra head projection and called him by his Christian name. The large multipod, part-amoeba, part-mammal dog described earlier is one of the offerings used to appease Esu.

Twins' visual imagery feeds on the same elements of plurality and simultaneity of the beings as do the stories and characters created by Nigerian writer, Amos Tutuola. Tutuola's text *My Life in the Bush of Ghosts,* given to Twins by Ulli Beier, inspired the titles and some of the subjects for many of Twins' early works. In 1965 he painted an oil on board, entitled *Amos Tutuola's Head in a Pitcher on Top of a Coconut Tree,* in which he pays homage to the writer. Although his themes and signature, large amorphous figures with claw-like hands and feet have remained consistent throughout his production, Twins' later paintings grew in size and started to incorporate cast-off objects. In these works disembodied eyes, forests of ghosts, and plants fill every inch of the space. Where there was once white space in *Devil's Dog,* there are now repetitions colored in mazelike and mosaic patterns.

Twins' 1984 etching, *God's Sketchbook,* calls to mind a taxonomist's data book of creatures categorized by species. In this etching Twins has catalogued the various species that inhabit his works. Perhaps like the great Yoruba divinity Orisa-nla, who was sent by Olodumare (God) to give form and life to human beings on earth, Twins has been sent to give form to new worlds of beings, and *God's Sketchbook* represents the blueprint that he was given to follow.

—Regina L. Woods

UDECHUKWU, Obiora
Nigerian graphic artist, illustrator, and painter

Born: Onitsha, Anambra State, Nigeria, 4 June 1946. **Education:** Central Art School, Onitsha, Nigeria; Ahmadu Bello University, 1965-66; University of Nigeria, B.A. 1972, M.A. 1977; protegé of Uche Okeke. **Family:** Married Ada Udechukwu. **Career:** Teacher, Onitsha, Nigeria, 1965; assistant commercial artist, Ministry of Agriculture, Enugu, Nigeria, 1965; graphic designer, Ministry of Information, Aba, Umuahia, 1968-69; assistant art organizer, Biafran Cultural Workshops, Alaenyi-Ogwa, 1969-70; traveled in Belgium, Denmark, England, France, Germany, and Norway, 1972. Art editor, Onitsha and Enugu, 1972-73; arts and production editor, *Okike,* Nsukka, Nigeria, 1976-82; art editor, *Nsukkascope: A Journal of Opinion,* Nsukka, Nigeria, 1977. Since 1977 lecturer/senior lecturer, University of Nigeria, Nsukka. Artist-in-residence, Iwalewa-Haus, Bayreuth, Germany, 1985. Member, African Literature Association, AKA Circle of Exhibiting Artists, Arts Council of the African Studies Association, Association of Nigerian Authors, Society of Nigerian Artists. **Awards:** Shell d'Arcy Cup, painting, Eastern Nigeria Festival of Arts, 1965; Department of Fine and Applied Arts Fasuyi prize, painting, University of Nigeria, Nsukka. **Address:** Department of Fine and Applied Arts, University of Nigeria, Nsukka, Enugu State, Nigeria.

Individual Exhibitions:

1975	*Obiora Udechukwu: Genesis of His Art,* Onitsha, Nigeria
	British Council, Enugu, Nigeria
1976	Gong Gallery, Lagos
1977	Gong Gallery, Lagos
1980	Goethe Institute, Lagos
1981	*No Water,* Nsukka, Enugu, and Lagos, Nigeria
1982	Iwalewa-Haus, Bayreuth, Germany
1984	National Theatre, Lagos
1985	Italian Cultural Institute, Lagos
	Bhownagree Gallery, Commonwealth Institute, London
1988	P.G. Gallery, National Gallery of Zimbabwe, Harare
1989	Italian Cultural Institute, Lagos
	University of Erlangen, Nürnberg, Germany
	Eric Clark Library, Dennis Memorial Grammar School, Onitsha, Nigeria
1990	Altstadt Galerie, Bamburg, Germany
	Mbari Art, Washington, D.C.

Selected Group Exhibitions:

1988	Ana Gallery, University of Nigeria, Nsukka
	Italian Cultural Institute, Lagos
	Hotel Presidential, Enugu, Nigeria
1989	Iwalewa-Haus, Bayreuth, Germany (traveling)
	Centro Wifredo Lam, Havana
	Bonn, Bocholt, and Mönchengladbach, Germany
1990	Continuing Education Centre, University of Nigeria, Nsukka
	Hotel Presidential, Enugu, Nigeria
	National Museum, Lagos
	National Theatre, Lagos

Collections:

Asele Institute, Nimo, Nigeria; Bradford City Museum and Galleries, Bradford, England; Centre for Culture Studies, University of Lagos; Enugu State Council for Arts and Culture, Enugu, Nigeria; Federal Ministry of Information, Cultural Division, Lagos; Goethe Institute, Lagos; Iwalewa-Haus, Bayreuth, Germany; Museum für Volkerkunde, Frankfurt, Germany; National Council for Arts and Culture, Lagos; National Gallery of Modern Art, Lagos; State House, Lagos.

Publications:

By UDECHUKWU: Book—*What the Madman Said: Poem by Obiora Udechukwu,* Bayreuth, Germany, Boomerang Press-Norbert Aas, 1985 (illustrated). **Articles**—"Functionality, Symbolism and Decoration: Some Aspects of Traditional Igbo Art," in *Conch* (New York), 3(2), September 1971, pp. 89-96 (illustrated; bibliography); "Observations on Art Criticism in Nigeria," in *Nigeria* (Lagos), 126-27, 1978, pp. 35-43; "Obiora Udechukwu: Towards Essence and Clarity," in *Nigeria* (Lagos), 132-33, 1980, pp. 43-46 (illustrated); "Line, Space, Simplicity and Spontaneity: Aspects of Igbo and Chinese Drawing and Painting," in *Ugo* (Enugu, Nigeria), 1(4), July-December 1981 (illustrated; bibliography; notes).

On UDECHUKWU: Books—*Obiora Udechukwu: Genesis of His Art, Drawings, Paintings, and Prints: 1960-1970,* exhibition catalog, Nsukka, Nigeria, Obiora Udechukwu and Dennis Memorial Grammar School, Onitsha, 1975 (illustrated); *Rhythms of Hunger: An Exhibition of Recent Work by Obiora Udechukwu,* London, Bhownagree Gallery, Commonwealth institute, 1985 (illustrated). **Articles**—"An Interview with Obiora Udechukwu" by Ulli Beier, in *Okike* (Nsukka, Nigeria), 20, December 1981, pp. 53-68 (illustrated); "Interview," in *Guardian* (Lagos), 20 July 1983, p. 11; "International Acclaim for Nigerian Artist," in *Africa Now* (London), 14, June 1982, pp. 80-81; "Woman as Metaphor in Obiora Udechukwu's Art" by Olu Oguibe, in *Kurio Africana: Journal of Art and Criticism* (Ile-Ife, Nigeria), 1(2), 1989, pp. 42-51 (bibliography).

*   *   *

Since the 1950s many of the modern artists associated with the University of Nigeria at Nsukka have looked to traditional art for inspiration. It is thus that Nsukka Uli art has become one of the established movements in Nigeria. The pioneers of the movement were C. Uche Okeke, Chuka Amaefuna, and Chike Aniakor. Obiora Udechukwu, one of the leading contemporary Nigerian artists, is the foremost of the second generation of the Nsukka Uli school.

Udechukwu is a painter whose secondary media are printmaking and poetry. Like other Africans who believe that a true artist always expresses himself in whatever medium is available, Udechukwu also practices playwriting, singing, and dance. His art has gained broad acceptance because of its political and social significance. He also has been energetic and selfless in promoting the works of other artists.

Udechukwu began his formal art training at Bello University, but because of the Biafran civil war he transferred to the University of Nigeria. Upon his graduation he joined the staff of the Nsukka campus, where he has continued to teach painting.

Traditional Uli body painting and mural paintings by Igbo women have been the most noticeable influences on Udechukwu's work, but he has transformed them into his personal language. Copying is not the basis of his work. His art is a poetic lament about the human psyche and the collective failure of leadership in Nigeria. He exemplifies the artist at the vanguard of society, someone who uses art to motivate people for social change.

In the early 1970s Udechukwu began experimenting with the traditional Uli art of Igbo women, and this influence remained dominant in his work until the late 1980s. Like traditional Uli art, which is essentially a female tradition, his is a minimal art. It is similar to poetry in which economy of language and spontaneity of execution are paramount. He relies on lyrical forms and economy of means to state his social and political messages, thus imitating the traditional role of Igbo satirical songs.

From 1973 to 1977 Udechukwu's adaptation of Uli to his line drawings was calligraphic. From the late 1970s through the mid-1980s, he used motifs and large circular shapes, and the descriptive treatment of linear forms became important in his work. Between 1981 and 1985 he produced a number of drawings in ink wash and prints. Udechukwu's studies of Nsibidi symbols, Chinese art, and works of Sudanese artists, especially Ibrahim El Salahi, have also enhanced the pictographic character of his work.

To Udechukwu watercolor or drawing on paper is a thinking process. He often starts with a blank sheet, one spontaneous form leading to another until the end is resolved. The result is usually a panoramic reference to various aspects of the subject matter. His forms may be elongated, stretched to magnify the force of their communication.

Udechukwu's association with the Enugu Mbari Artists and Writers' Club was crucial to the character of his 1967-69 haunting images of Nigeria's Biafran tragedy. *Refugee Family, Silent Faces at Crossroad,* and *Lament of the Unsilenced* are instances of works that indicate his transition from naturalism to distorted representations of social reality. Works such as *Homage to Christopher Ohigbo* (1975), *No Water* (1981), *Onye Ndidi* (1985), and *Rhythm of Hunger* (1985) denote the humanistic range of his art.

Since the late 1980s there has been a resurgence of interest by Udechukwu in easel painting in oil, acrylic, and gouache. The linear emphasis has begun to dissipate, and form and color seem more important than subject matter. His colors are vibrant and massive, giving an impression of collage. *Spirit in Accent, What the Weaver Wove,* and *In the Beginning* illustrate this change in emphasis.

In 1993 a retrospective exhibition of Udechukwu's drawings, paintings, and prints was held at the Italian Cultural Institute in Lagos. The exhibition spanned three decades and included works the artist had produced during his secondary school years. The exhibition revealed his remarkable skill in painting and drawing.

—Barthosa Nkurumeh

VALENTIM, Rubem

Brazilian painter

Born: Salvador, Brazil, 1922. **Education:** Self-taught painter. **Career:** Assistant professor, Instituto Central de Artes, University of Brazil. Participant, New Movement of Art, Bahia. **Awards:** Travel Award, Salao Nacional de Arte Moderna, Rio de Janeiro, 1961; Purchase Prize, *Tenth Biennial of São Paulo,* 1969. **Died:** 1991.

Selected Exhibitions:

1949	*Salao Baino de Belas Artes,* Salvador
1950	Institute of History and Geography, Bahia
1955	*Salao Baino de Belas Artes,* Salvador
	Bienal de São Paulo
1956	*Salao Nacional de Arte Moderna,* Rio de Janeiro
1958	*Salao Nacional de Arte Moderna,* Rio de Janeiro
1959	*Bienal de São Paulo*
	Salao Nacional de Arte Moderna, Rio de Janeiro
1960	*Salao Nacional de Arte Moderna,* Rio de Janeiro
1961	*Bienal de São Paulo*
	Salao Nacional de Arte Moderna, Rio de Janeiro
1963	*Bienal de São Paulo*
1967	*Bienal de São Paulo*
1969	*Bienal de São Paulo*

*   *   *

The art of Rubem Valentim is precise, meticulous, strong, and straightforward. He worked with geometry, and his paintings, reliefs, and three-dimensional sculptures are filled with endless recombinations of geometric, hard-edged shapes—triangles, spheres, arcs, stars, parallelograms, arrows. Most are strictly symmetrical, supremely balanced arrangements. The shapes are rendered with extreme care, giving the sense of having been mathematically, scientifically created. His colors reinforce this impression. They are bold and flat and are essentially primary and secondary hues juxtaposed with their complements to produce dramatic optical effects—again the science of seeing at work.

Yet, despite the impression of coldly objective forms presented solely for their optical effects, works by Valentim express spiritual matters. As he explained, "Today physics approaches both religion and aesthetics. . . . I am creating a new metaphysics." He achieved a true synthesis of the physical and the spiritual, for all of his seemingly meaningless forms are in fact signs and symbols of spiritual forces at the heart of Candomblé, the Afro-Brazilian religion that was a part of his childhood in Bahia, a region he described as being "very strong in mysticism, religiosity."

Even Valentim's working process was a synthesis of science and spirit. He began every day by making a series of small studies or models in a systematic and disciplined way. He described these as both "laboratory experiments" and "devotions"—daily efforts to evoke and invoke spiritual forces that inhabit his thoughts, his world, and his work.

When one becomes aware of this metaphysical synthesis in Valentim's work, it takes on many unexpected aspects. Forms become meaningful. The persistence of threes, for example, is not simply a matter of composition, for three is also a sacred number that invokes spiritual forces. A blood red color and hard-edged forms in some of his works signal the ax of Shango, the Yoruba god of thunder. Such boldness strikes the viewer like a flash of lightning.

Other geometric motifs and colors reveal additional African spiritual presences. Works bathed in whiteness signal the calming presence of Oxala, lord of creation. Multitiered shafts evoke Oxala's staff of authority, the *opasoro*. Oxala is an appropriate subject, for he is the divine artist who shapes all existence. Strong, stable forms and a cool color visibly and symbolically capture the essence of Oxala.

While deeply rooted in African sacred signs and cosmological concepts, elements of Valentim's compositions visualize cosmic shapes and forces that come from other, universalizing intentions. He explained that he wanted to "popularize," that is, reach beyond specific symbolic, meaningful systems to "signs" that are "pure" forms expressing "feelings and rhythms" universally. His work is often described as being full of Jungian archetypes, things stored in the human subconscious. Thus, Valentim was an artist who combined many seemingly contradictory attributes to create powerful images: science, religion, and aesthetics to create a new metaphysics; a semiotic system based on language to create a visual vocabulary; and signs and symbols rooted in Africa and his early life as a Brazilian of color to create a universal imagery that can touch people everywhere.

—Henry John Drewal

VAN DER ZEE, James (Augustus Joseph)
American photographer and painter

Born: Lenox, Massachusetts, 29 June 1886. **Education:** Lenox Public Schools, Massachusetts; self-taught in photography. **Family:** Married 1) Kate Brown in 1960 (divorced 1914), two daughters (both deceased); 2) Gaynella Greenlee in 1920 (died 1970); 3) Donna Mussenden in 1978. **Career:** Busboy, waiter, elevator man, New York, 1906-07; dining-room waiter, Hotel Chamberlain, Old Point Comfort, Virginia, 1907-09; waiter and musician, Fletcher Henderson Band and John Wanamaker Orchestra, New York, 1909-15; darkroom assistant and photographer, Gertz's Department Store, Newark, New Jersey, 1915-16; owner, Guarantee Photos, and GGG Photo Studio, New York, 1916-68. **Awards:** American Society of Magazine Photographers Award, 1969; Metropolitan Museum of Art Life Fellowship, New York, 1970; Pierre Toussaint Award, 1978; President's Living Legacy Award, Washington, D.C., 1978; honorary doctorate, Howard University, Washington, D.C., 1983; James Van Der Zee Institute established by Reginald McGhee and

Charles Innis, now under care of Metropolitan Museum of Art, New York, 1969. **Agent:** Howard Greenberg Gallery, 120 Wooster Street, New York, New York 10012, U.S.A. **Estate Address:** James Van Der Zee Institute, 103 East 125th Street, New York, New York 10035, U.S.A. **Died:** 1983.

Individual Exhibitions:

1970　Lenox Library, Massachusetts
1971　Studio Museum in Harlem, New York
1974　Lunn Gallery/Graphics International, Washington, D.C.
1979　*The Legacy of James Van Der Zee: A Portrait of Black Americans,* Alternative Center for International Arts, New York
　　　Delaware Art Museum, Wilmington
1983　Camera Club of New York
　　　Idaho State University, Pocatello
1987　Deborah Sharp Gallery, New York
1994　*Retrospective,* National Portrait Gallery, Washington, D.C.
　　　Howard Greenberg Gallery, New York

Selected Group Exhibitions:

1969　*Harlem on My Mind: Cultural Capital of Black America 1900-1968,* Metropolitan Museum of Art, New York
1978　Lunn Gallery, Washington, D.C.
1979　San Francisco Museum of Modern Art
　　　Fleeting Gestures: Dance Photographs, International Center of Photography, New York (traveling)
1982　Rheinisches Landesmuseum, Bonn
1985　San Francisco Museum of Modern Art
1987　Studio Museum in Harlem, New York (traveling)

Collections:

Baltimore Museum of Art, Maryland; Center for Creative Photography, University of Arizona, Tucson; Cleveland Museum of Art; Library of Congress, Washington, D.C.; Metropolitan Museum of Art, New York; Minneapolis Institute of Arts; Museum of Fine Arts, Houston; University of California, Los Angeles; University of Michigan, Ann Arbor; University of Nebraska, Lincoln.

Publications:

By VAN DER ZEE: Books—*The World of James Van Der Zee: A Visual Record of Black Americans,* New York, 1969; *James Van Der Zee* edited by Liliane De Cock and Reginald McGhee, New York, 1973; *James Van Der Zee: Eighteen Photographs,* portfolio, Washington, D.C. and New York, 1974; *The Harlem Book of the Dead,* with Owen Dodson and Camille Billops, Dobbs Ferry, New York, 1978.

On VAN DER ZEE: Books—*Harlem on My Mind: Cultural Capital of Black America, 1900-1968,* exhibition catalog, New York, Allon Schoener, 1969; *The Legacy of James Van Der Zee: A Portrait of Black Americans,* exhibition catalog, New York, Gino Rodriguez and Robert W. Brown, 1977; *Van Der Zee: Photographer, 1886-1983* by Deborah Willis-Braithwaite, New York and

London, 1994. **Articles**—"Harlem's 'Picture-Taking Man'" by Val Wilmer, in *The Observer Magazine* (London), 21 September 1980; "James Van Der Zee Dies: Photographer of Harlem," in *New York Times,* 16 May 1983; "James Van Der Zee, 1886-1983," in *Afterimage* (Rochester, New York), June 1983; "Obituary," in *Art in America,* 72, August 1984, p. 47; review (Deborah Sharpe Gallery, New York) by Klaus Ottmann, in *Flash Art* (International Edition), 136, October 1987, pp. 107-08; "Trail Blazers in Harlem" by Mark Van Proyen, in *Artweek,* 19, 6 February 1988, p. 1; "Black Photography in America" by Alain Dister, in *Cimaise,* 35, November/December 1988, pp. 85-120 (illustrated); "James Van Der Zee's Harlem Book of the Dead: A Study in Cultural Relationships" by Diana Emery Hulick, in *History of Photography,* 17, Autumn 1993, pp. 277-83 (illustrated); "Black and White (Walker Evans and James Van Der Zee)" by Charles Hagen, in *Art and Antiques,* 17, Summer 1994, pp. 68-75 (illustrated); review (Howard Greenberg Gallery, New York) by Laurel Berger, in *Art News,* 93, September 1994, p. 172.

*   *   *

The photographic career of James Van Der Zee spanned three cities, two World Wars, and the Great Depression of the 1930s. Recognized as the dean of African American photographers, he spent more than seventy years in the Harlem section of Manhattan in New York City, which remains America's most distinctive African American community.

Van Der Zee's earliest formal body of photographs were taken between 1907 and 1910 in Phoebus, Virginia, and in his hometown of Lenox, Massachusetts, prior to establishing his studio in New York City. Van Der Zee's Virginia photographs include lucid portraits of teachers, pupils, and classroom scenes at the Whittier Preparatory School of Hampton Institute and views of everyday life in Phoebus. The photographs from the Tidewater region of Virginia reveal Van Der Zee's keen eye for composition, a great sensitivity to texture and light, and an affinity for genre subjects. The Lenox photographs of the same period comprise the second group of Van Der Zee's early works. To this category belong the intimate glimpses of Van Der Zee's friends and relatives and the splendid outdoor portraits of himself, his wife, their toddler daughter, and friends. The Lenox landscapes posed challenging problems for Van Der Zee in the treatment of figures in outdoor light that he solved successfully long before the advent of the light meter. In contrast to the crisp handling of light and darks in the Virginia photographs, Van Der Zee employed light more softly in the Lenox landscapes. It gently caresses and defines form and literally sparkles among the myriad leaves and blossoms of the picturesque Lenox woodlands.

The most prolific period in Van Der Zee's career was in Harlem between 1920 and 1945, when he photographed the majority of African American celebrities who lived in or traveled to New York. Joining the famous among his customers were hundreds of people from less celebrated walks of life. Van Der Zee photographed almost every aspect of life in Harlem and also served as the official photographer for Marcus Garvey and the United Negro Improvement Association. The majority of Van Der Zee's portraits are of women and children, his favorite subjects, and he was probably the earliest African American to treat the female nude as an artistic subject in 1923.

Multiple-image photographs provide an intriguing aspect of Van Der Zee's work. They were achieved by sandwiching two negatives together or by the multiple exposure of a single native. Although the earliest examples of these techniques appeared in American photography during the 1940s, Van Der Zee was unaware of such experiments by others.

"James Van Der Zee-Artist and Photographer" was the title Van Der Zee used for advertising, and it was evident that he considered himself an artist first. He composed his photographs as carefully as a painter and arranged his sitters in a variety of poses that captured something of their personalities. He employed light to its maximum advantage, and he was a master printer with a fine sense of detail and texture. Many of his vintage prints still retain a remarkable degree of clarity.

Van Der Zee's extensive use of retouching and additional embellishments using a wide variety of props and dramatic lighting distinguish his photographs from those of his contemporaries. Among the numerous props employed by Van Der Zee were two dogs—a cardboard cocker spaniel and a ceramic bull dog—that appear so frequently they may be regarded as trademarks, almost as commonplace as Van Der Zee's signature.

Essentially self-taught, Van Der Zee began his career in the early 1900s, when American photography was still in an early stage of technical development. During that time the photographer's basic equipment consisted of heavy glass plates, flash powder, and glass caps. Van Der Zee used Eastman, Stanley, and hammer dry plates with a speed of around 40 compared to the 200 to 400-plus speeds of contemporary photographic equipment.

By the early 1950s the advent of inexpensive Kodak and Polaroid cameras diminished Van Der Zee's clientele greatly. During the next fifteen years, he primarily shot photographs for taxi licenses and passports and recopied old photographs through mail order commissions. Van Der Zee lived in relative obscurity until 1969, when he provided the largest number of photographs for the "Harlem on My Mind" exhibition at the Metropolitan Museum of Art, and the Van Der Zee Institute was formed to house his archives and provide a library and research center for African American photographers.

Van Der Zee resumed photographing in 1980 after an eleven-year hiatus. His return to photography during the last three years of his life afforded a number of people the distinction of reliving the spirit of the Harlem Renaissance of the 1920s. The settings in the late portraits recall Van Der Zee's classic photographs of the 1920s and 1930s, since he used the painted backdrops, furniture, and props that he had used originally. Shot with Van Der Zee's favorite 8 x 10 format camera and developed in sepia or black and white, most of the late photographs bear a remarkable similarity in spirit and quality to his finest earlier works.

A Renaissance man in the truest sense of the term, Van Der Zee was an accomplished painter, pianist, violinist, poet, and master photographer. He was the last surviving giant of the Harlem Renaissance and provided the most comprehensive view of African American life in Harlem during the first fifty years of the twentieth century.

—Regenia A. Perry

W-Y

WADDY, Ruth (G.)
American printmaker

Born: Lincoln, Nebraska, 1909. **Education:** Famous Artists Home Study Course, 1962; Los Angeles City College; Otis Art Institute, Los Angeles; University of Minnesota. **Career:** Worked in defense plant, Los Angeles; ran small business; worked for U.S. Postal Service. Founder, Art West Associated North. First president, Art West Associated, 1962. **Awards:** National Association of College Women Award, Los Angeles, 1963; Certificate of Merit, National Conference of Artists 1968; Ruth Waddy Testimonial Award, Los Angeles, 1972. Honorary degree: Parsons School of Design, New School for Social Research, in fine arts, 1988.

Selected Exhibitions:

1963	Art West Associated Black History Month Exhibitions, Los Angeles (annually through 1969)
1964	Jimmy Crawford's Frame Shop, Los Angeles
1965	Safety Savings and Loan Association, Los Angeles
	International Buchkunst-Aussellung, Leipzig
	Los Felis Jewish Community Center, Los Angeles
1966	University of California, Los Angeles
	Friendship House in Moscow (traveling)
1968	Jewish Women's Council House
1969	Independence Square, Los Angeles (solo)
1972	Rainbow Sign Gallery, Berkeley
	Oakland Art Museum, California
	Black Artists of Southern California, Compton College
1979	Museum of African American Art, Los Angeles
1982	National Urban League Conference
	William Grant Still Community Art Center, Los Angeles
1985	University of California, Los Angeles
1987	*Impressions/Expressions,* Smithsonian Institution, Washington, D.C. (traveling)

Collections:

Brand Library, Glendale, California; Howard University, Washington, D.C.; Metropolitan Museum, New York; Oakland Museum, California.

Publications:

By WADDY: Book—*Black Artists on Art,* coedited with Samella Lewis, Contemporary Crafts Publishers, 1969.

On WADDY: Article—*Los Angeles Times,* 9 July 1966.

*　　*　　*

For Ruth G. Waddy art is a spiritual and socially conscious activity "for the benefit, growth and improvement of the human animal." This personal philosophy is consistent with Waddy's artistic output of strong, vibrant, bold works that express cultural pride and convey beauty, distinction, and power. Waddy consciously chose printmaking as her medium because prints are affordable, can be made widely available, and demand precision and patience to achieve the desired image.

Waddy's early retirement from the post office allowed her to pursue a life-long love affair with art. As a young girl she lived near and often visited the Minneapolis Art Museum. It was not until she had married, raised children, and moved to Los Angeles that her interest in art manifested itself through an attempt to mount an exhibition of black artists in celebration of the 100-year anniversary of the Emancipation Proclamation in 1963. Waddy was fifty-three years old, when this attempt to have a juried exhibition of African American artists in Los Angeles propelled her into the art world. She has continued to promote African American artists by organizing exhibitions, writing essays, editing books, and preserving the artists and their work for future generations.

After completing a home study course in art and taking classes at Los Angeles City College and Otis Art Institute, Waddy began painting and drawing. It was while working on a printmaking exhibition of contemporary African American printmakers in 1965 that Waddy became a printmaker. After talking to the artists and studying with them during collaboration on the exhibition, she found her medium of choice to be printmaking, linocut to be specific.

Waddy's work is deeply informed by the 1960s, the decade from which she emerged as an artist. Her work is Afro-centric, as demonstrated in her 1969 linocut *The Exhorters.* This print depicts a group of African Americans, some in traditional African garb, actively listening to a modern-day griot. *Untitled* is an abstract linocut with a large design in the center of the paper, reminiscent of the Akwaba doll (West African symbol of fertility) and bathed in rich earth tones with strong bold lines, both curving and linear, suggesting an interesting landscape. This seminal work boldly displays Waddy's skill as a printmaker, her keen sense of design, her reverence for African culture, and her vision as an artist. *Untitled* looks fresh and contemporary, as if it could have been made today.

Waddy says in the catalog *New Perspectives in Black Art from the Oakland Museum Art Division Kaiser Center Gallery,* published in 1968: "The role of the artist has many aspects. He portrays society, bounded as it is by its economic and social development. He prophesies. He comforts with his quiet scenes. The Black Artist also portrays humans subjected to a humanistic environment of false and unnatural values. The intention in my work is message more often than not. I hope that I make an emotional impact first, then upon continued looking the viewer becomes aware of color, line and shape." Waddy's work does produce a powerful emotional impact. Her print *Matter of Opinion* jolts the viewer with its bright orange background and draws the viewer closer to inspect the "bamboo poles and logs," where *X* marks the spot.

An arts activist and mentor, in addition to being a printmaker, Waddy has been informed and inspired by the spirit of activism and social consciousness that permeated the 1960s. Her art and heart speak boldly and loudly, as she proclaims in her work the beauty, dignity, and struggle of her beloved African American community.

—Delores Jackson Radney

WANGBOJE, S(olomon) Irein

Nigerian printmaker and graphic artist

Born: Avbiosi, Uleha, Edo State, 16 August 1930. **Education:** Nigerian College of Arts, Science and Technology, Zaria, Nigeria, diploma in graphic and commercial design 1959; Cranbrook Academy of Art, Bloomfield Hills, Michigan, M.F.A. in advanced design 1963; New York University, Ed.D. in art education 1968. **Career:** Publications artist/graphic arts officer, Federal Ministry of Information, 1959-64; design and art supervisor, Nigerian Broadcasting Corporation TV, 1964-65; senior lecturer, Ahmadu Bellow University, Zaria, Nigeria, 1971-73; professor/head of Department of Fine Arts, Ahmadu Bello University, Zaria, Nigeria, 1973-78; dean, Faculty of Arts and Social Sciences, University of Benin, Benin City, 1982-86. Since 1983 deputy vice-chancellor, University of Benin, Benin City, Nigeria. Lecturer, Yaba Technical Institute, Lagos, 1963-65; research fellow, University of Ife, Ile-Ife, Nigeria, 1968-71; founder/director, Ori-Olokun Cultural Centre's Arts Workshop, University of Ife, Ile-Ife, Nigeria, 1969-71; visiting professor, School of Art and Design, University of Illinois, Urbana-Champaign, 1987. Illustrated *A Crocodile has me by the leg* (1967) and *Animals mourn for da leopard and other West African stories* (1970). Member, Zaria Art Society, International Society for Education Through Art. Founding member, Society of Nigerian Artists. **Awards:** Fellow, Asele Institute, 1985; Ziegfield International Award in Art Education, 1988. **Address:** Creative Arts Centre, 9 Utomwen Owoseni Street, New Benin, Benin City, Edo State, Nigeria.

Individual Exhibitions:

1963	Grinnell Galleries, Detroit
	Exhibition Centre, Marina, Lagos
1971	USIS, Lagos
1979	Goethe Institute, Lagos

Selected Group Exhibitions:

1977	National Theatre Lagos
1978	*Exhibition of Nigerian Traditional and Contemporary Art,* Lagos
	National Theatre, Lagos
	Goethe Institute, Lagos (traveling in Germany, through 1979)
1980	National Theatre, Lagos
	Exhibition of Nigerian Contemporary Art, Dakar, Senegal
1984	National Center of Afro-American Artists, Boston
1985	National Theatre, Lagos
1989	National Theatre, Lagos
1990	National Gallery of Crafts and Design, Lagos

Collections:

Hampton University Museum, Hampton, Virginia; Mbari Art, Washington, D.C.; National Council for Arts and Culture, Lagos; National Gallery of Modern Art, Lagos; National Museum of African Art, Washington, D.C.

Publications:

By WANGBOJE: Articles—"Functional Arts in the Traditional Past," in *Nigeria* (Lagos), 119, March 1976, pp. 34-49; "Western Impact on Nigerian Arts," in *Nigeria* (Lagos), FESTAC '77 edition, 122/123, 1977, pp. 111-12 (visual supplement, 113-24; illustrated); "Cultural Identity and Realisation through the Arts: Problems, Possibilities and Projections," in *Journal of Art and Design Education* (United Kingdom), 5(1,2), 1986, pp. 23-31 (illustrated); "Art Education and the National Policy on Education," in *Creative Dialogue: SNA at 25,* Lagos, Society of Nigerian Artists, 1990, pp. 7-10.

On WANGBOJE: Articles—"Solomon Wangboje: Art Forges a Link of Pride with the Past" by Yahne Sangare, in *Topic* (Washington, D.C.), 36, 1968, pp. 11-12 (illustrated); "Art Personality: Irein Wangboje" interview by Toyin Akinosho, in *Daily Times* (Lagos), 14 April 1990, 21 April 1990, p. 12.

*   *   *

Solomon Irein Wangboje is a printmaker, art educator, and administrator. He was one of the key individuals who helped change the direction of art education in Nigeria. His commitment to art education through the years has hampered his work as an artist, and he has not been prolific.

Until the turn of the century art was not part of the Nigerian school curriculum. The objective of art at this period was to achieve a mimetic representation of subject matter, for in the view of the colonialists no African could appreciate or create art in a naturalistic style.

The formation of the Zaria Art Society in the late 1950s was in response to the colonial art curriculum. The contention of the society was that art should evolve from the artist and that art education should include the learner's knowledge of self, not an imposed alien culture. This led to a formulation of numerous cultural approaches to art, and new forms, media, and techniques were introduced that have continued to influence the national art of Nigeria.

Wangboje was one of the ten members of the Zaria Art Society. He views art and education as inseparable parts of African life. The art educator, he believes, has a social role. His duty is not only to stimulate creativity but also to inculcate the cultural pride that is essential to the development of a nation.

Like some of his Zaria colleagues, Wangboje has helped establish art centers, and he has held numerous administrative posts, ranging from art department head to university assistant vice-chancellor. He is the administrator of the Creative Arts Center at the University of Benin. He ran a similar institution, the Ori Olokun Cultural Center, from 1969 to 1971. Ori Olokun was essentially an informal arts workshop aiming at the stimulation of personal artistic growth, with demonstrations of techniques as the instructional method.

Wangboje and Bruce Onobrakpeya are the most eminent of the pioneering printmakers in modern Nigerian art. Wangboje is a versatile artist, having started as a sculptor. Exploration with color led him to painting, printmaking, and textile design. His use of tones of blue, deep green, brown, and yellow ocher lends resilience to his work. His semiabstract compositions are derived from everyday activities in Nigerian society, which may include a camel caravan, milk seller, laborer, or music maker or even masks. The life of northern Nigeria is dominant in his prints, with embellishments adapted from the geometric Islamic art of the Hausa people.

—Barthosa Nkurumeh

WARBURG, Eugène

American sculptor

Name sometimes spelled incorrectly as Warbourg. **Born:** New Orleans, c.1825-26. **Education:** Studied with Philippe Garbeille, French sculptor, New Orleans, c.1841-49, Paris, c.1852-53. **Family:** Married Louise Ernestine, c.1853-57. **Career:** Co-owned studio in New Orleans and worked as an independent sculptor. **Died:** 12 January 1859.

Individual Exhibitions:

1850   Hall's Gilding Establishment, New Orleans

Selected Group Exhibitions:

1855   Beaux Arts Universal Exposition, Paris
1967   *Ten Afro-American Artists of the Nineteenth Century,*
            Howard University, Washington, D.C.

Collections:

Virginia Historical Society, Richmond.

Publications:

On WARBURG: Books—*Ten Afro-American Artists of the Nineteenth Century,* exhibition catalog, Washington, D.C., Howard University and James A. Porter, 1967. **Articles—**"The Warburg Brothers: New Orleans Sculptors" by Patricia Brady, in *Historic New Orleans Collection,* 1989; "The Cities of the Dead: Free Men of Color as Tomb Builders in 19th Century New Orleans" by Patricia Brady, in *Cross, Crazier, and Crucible,* Lafayette, Center for Louisiana Studies, 1993; "Eugene Warburg and Pierre Soule" by Patricia Brady, in *Quarterly,* (New Orleans), Summer 1994.

*   *   *

A critical appraisal of the sculpture of Eugène Warburg must be based almost entirely on one surviving major work—a portrait bust of U.S. Minister to France John Young Mason, executed in 1855. Sculpted of fine white marble, the Virginia diplomat is depicted in the classical Roman style esteemed by nineteenth-century political leaders. His shoulders and chest are bare, unsullied by any sign of contemporary life, and his eyes gaze sightlessly forward. The bust, however, is an extremely persuasive individual likeness, as Warburg successfully interpreted the sitter's personality in stone. The large balding head with midlength fluffy hair, the brows knitted over a large nose, the firm full lips over a decided cleft chin, the double chin and general fleshiness of a successful middle-aged man—all contribute to a convincing portrait, reflecting the strong will and determination of the sitter. Mason himself considered it an excellent likeness; after allowing the piece to be displayed at the Universal Exposition, he carried it home, where it now resides in the Virginia Historical Society.

Most of the remainder of Warburg's work is known only at second hand. His *Ganymede,* executed in New Orleans in 1850, was highly praised by the local press for its beautiful design and creditable execution. Its whereabouts are unknown, as are those of the bas-reliefs of Uncle Tom's Cabin said to have been carved in England for the duchess of Sutherland in 1856 and the fine funerary sculpture and tombs, allegorical pieces, and busts which he is said to have created in New Orleans prior to 1852. There are tombs and wall vaults signed "Warburg" in the Saint Louis cemeteries, but they are relatively modest. The attribution is shaky, as they could have been carved by Warburg's brother or nephew, also marble cutters.

That his sculpture and marble cutting were well regarded in New Orleans is clear. In 1851 during the extensive rebuilding of the Saint Louis Cathedral, the churchwardens invited the young Warburg to submit a bid and plans for the central aisle of the nave. His simple design—black-and-white marble squares in a checkerboard pattern—was apparently accepted and installed within the next year. Well-cut and fitted, Warburg's marble central aisle is still in use in the cathedral nearly 150 years later.

The artist died young, already a master of his craft. The discovery of another of his technically proficient, finely imagined sculptures would be an important addition to the history of black art in the United States.

—Patricia Brady

WARD, Barbara

American sculptor, fiber artist, and mixed-media artist

Born: Boston, 24 March 1940. **Education:** Billie Pope School of Dance/Percussion and Theatre Arts, Boston, 1960-68, certificate of completion (dance choreographer/percussionist), 1968. **Family:** Lives with William Howard Armstrong. **Career:** Billie Pope School of Dance and Theatre Arts, Boston, instructor, 1968-71, costume designer, 1971-75; freelance doll maker, 1975-78. Since 1984 artist/educator, Piano Factory, Boston. Artist-in-residence, AAMARP, Northeastern University, Boston, 1978-84. **Awards:** Design 25 Merit Award, Calendar of Children's Art, Boston, 1980; community artist recognition, Federal Women's Program, National Park Service, Boston, 1986; Massachusetts Council on the Arts and Humanities Award, 1988, 1989; Geron Excellence Award, 1990; Museum of African American History Award, 1992. **Address:** Piano Craft Guild, 791 Tremont Street, Studio E515, Boston, Massachusetts 02118, U.S.A.

Barbara Ward. Photo courtesy of Paul Foley.

Individual Exhibitions:

1978	Craftery Gallery, Hartford, Connecticut
1979	*Dolls and Soft Sculpture,* Barnard College Gallery, New York
1980	Brown University, Churchill Providence, Rhode Island
	Sarah Doyle Gallery, Providence, Rhode Island
1982	*Fabric Art,* Trustman Gallery, Simmons College, Boston
1983	Boston Children's Museum
	New Race, Phoenix Cultural Arts Gallery, Atlanta, Georgia

Selected Group Exhibitions:

1982	Weidner Library, Harvard University, Cambridge, Massachusetts
1985	Sherman Gallery, Boston University
1986	Fashion Moda Gallery, New York
1987	Boston Museum of Fine Arts
1990	Bunker Hill Community College, Charlestown, Massachusetts
1988	California Afro-American Museum, Los Angeles
	Museum of the National Center of Afro-American Artists, Boston
1996	Pine Manor College, Chestnut Hill, Massachusetts

Collections:

Boston Children's Museum; Boston YWCA Gallery; Harriet Tubman Gallery, United South End Settlements, Boston; Museum of Afro-American History, Boston Museum of the National Center of Afro-American Artists, Boston.

Publications:

On WARD: Articles—"Woman of Power: Art as Activism" by Char McKee, in *Woman of Power, Inc.* (Massachusetts), 1987; "Fiberarts" by Kate Mathews, in *Nine Press* (Asheville, North Carolina), 1987; "Drum" by Martha Grier-Deen, in *New Africa House* (Massachusetts), 1987; "Be Black Elegance" by Sharyn J. Skeeter, in *Starlog Telecommunications, Inc.* (New York), 1990.

*

Barbara Ward comments:

I consider my art to be the "fabric scraps of my life," a medium through which I tell my stories. I began making cloth-stuffed dolls as a child, and as doll groupings they became my make-believe family and friends. I am currently focusing on the creation of life-size multicultural soft sculpture and cloth West African ceremonial masks known as "Okakagbe."

My background in African and Balinese dance and theater has played a major influence on the rhythm and visuals of my art. My intuition towards the fabric and ornaments that celebrate my art is also connected to my Native American heritage. Most importantly I thank my grandmothers who gave me my first hands-on cloth experiences and who never criticized my individuality as an eccentric child.

This artistic journey has kept me healthily grounded—intellectually, emotionally, and spiritually. It has made me realize the importance of giving back to our communities. Nana taught me to strive to be a conscience of my time, to be a mentor, to remember my ancestors. My inspiration comes from living, it comes from you. My drive is to visually integrate social awareness with artistic integrity and to reveal a spiritual philosophy through emotions and intellects. My soft sculpture is a visual determinant for history, reflective of circumstances, and it is the tool I use to aid in the survival and visual remembrance of Third World people. It is a medium through which all people can share personal experiences and differences for mutual growth. Barbara Ward's soft sculpture and masks celebrate their African heritage and at the same time question the masks behind which we all hide.

*   *   *

Barbara Ward's early career as a principal dancer in a modern dance company is reflected in the strong command of gesture and pose she incorporates in her life-size soft sculpture figures. Evocative of human figures, these works draw upon puppet making and masking traditions—Eastern, Western, and African—in their stylized, articulated silhouettes and dramatically configured features and facial planes. Ward is a persistent observer of both the myriad facial masks we present to the world each day and the body language which she has found speaks across boundaries of race and culture in ways that can advance or restrain honest communication.

Along with dance, Ward worked in costume design for many years. Her command of the skills of cutting and tailoring different

Barbara Ward: *New Race,* **1986-87. Photo courtesy of Rogier Gregoire.**

fabrics lends a particular subtlety of technique to the intricate construction of her figures. She understands human anatomy and the ways in which the drape and form of fabric are affected by underlying physical structures. As a result her work displays the highly sophisticated uses of distortion, scale, proportion, and angle of vision required for work in less malleable sculptural media. In particular, her command of anatomy heightens the effects she is able to produce in the construction of masks.

In much of Ward's work, fabric in vivid, glowing color, used to both aesthetic and symbolic ends, is layered upon dark or muted body forms. Highly saturated pinks, oranges, purples, and aquas deliberately echoing African, Caribbean, South American, and other folk art palettes and patterns vibrate against deep brown, gray, and matte black bodies. A constant play of textures is established in each sculpture through the use of a variety of textiles, such as braided wool, taffeta, moiré fabrics, *kente* cloth, and leather. Layers of appliquéed fabric along with beads, raffia, and metallic strips add to the complex designs.

The figures in her "New Race" series, I and II, from the 1980s incorporate all of these elements, suggesting both the rich spectrum of African American skin colors and an extension of that variety into the realm of imaginative characterization with the construction of, for instance, the turquoise-colored *Diva* with her cloud of curly purple hair, evidence of Ward's tongue-in-cheek humor and her occasional visual puns. In other works, such as her female figure commissioned for exhibition in the sanctuary of the historic African Meeting House in Boston, Ward incorporates authentic period garments and accessories into her work, eloquently evoking the physical presence of men and women whose names are lost to history.

In the 1990s Barbara Ward began an extended exploration of the technical and aesthetic connections between her work and the West African art of *Okakagbe,* a form of appliqué mask design. During a period as artist in residence at the Massachusetts Institute of Technology in 1996, Ward worked with students in creating their own versions of these deeply personal representations of one's inner essence and identity. Used as ceremonial proclamations of the wearer's role in the community and, after death, as memorial images, these masks always incorporate selected personal belongings into their construction.

Faith Ringgold, the pioneer African American maker of soft sculptural figures, and later Marie Calloway-Johnson have both emphasized the political and sociological dimensions of this idiom, depicting heroic figures and representing scenes from black life and history. Ward, who has taken a less narrative direction, considers her work a means of recording creative, historical, and spiritual aspects of the struggles and survival of Third World peoples.

—Marilyn Richardson

WARD-BROWN, Denise

American sculptor

Born: Denise Delia Ward, Philadelphia, 25 May 1953. **Education:** Tyler School of Art, Temple University, Philadelphia, 1971-75, B.F.A. 1975; Howard University, Washington, D.C., 1981-84, M.F.A., 1984. **Career:** Instructor, Prince George's Community

College, Largo, Maryland, 1988-91, Howard Community College, Columbia, Maryland, 1990-91. Since 1991, associate professor, Washington University School of Art, St. Louis, Missouri. Served residencies at Ragdale, Lake Forrest, Illinois, 1994, University of Colorado, Boulder, 1995. Jury panelist, Arts In Transit, Saint Louis, Missouri, 1993-96, United States General Services Administration, Saint Louis, Missouri, 1995, Regional Arts Commission, Saint Louis, Missouri, 1995. **Awards:** Penland School of Crafts study grant, North Carolina, 1973; Haystack Mountain School of Crafts study grant, 1973-74; Ford Foundation study grant (Howard University), 1982-83; Graphic Development grant, Washington, D.C., Commission on the Arts and Humanities, 1984-85; Washington, D.C., Commission on the Arts and Humanities Artist-In-Education grant, 1985; Fifth Annual Mayor's Outstanding Emerging Artist Award, Washington, D.C., 1986; Commission on the Arts and Humanities Individual Artist grant, Washington, D.C., 1989 and 1991; Regional Artists' Projects grant, 1994; National Association of Women Business Owners Salute, St. Louis, Missouri, 1995; Bunting Institute of Radcliffe College Fellowship, Cambridge, Massachusetts, 1995. **Agent:** Madeline Rabb, 161 East Chicago Avenue, #34A, Chicago, Illinois 60611, U.S.A. **Address:** 3927 Juanita Street, St. Louis, Missouri 63116-3911, U.S.A. **Online Address:** ddwardbr@art.wustl.edu.

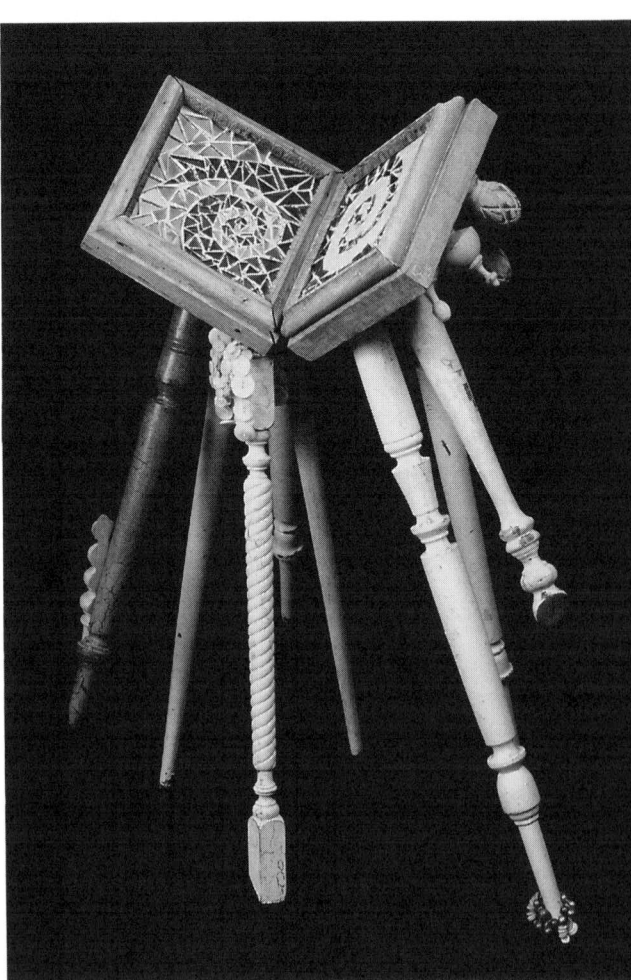

Denise Ward-Brown: *Sing Praises,* **1992. Photo courtesy of Re⊠ Elf.**

Individual Exhibitions:

1984   Washington Project for the Arts, Washington, D.C.
1986   Bethune Museum and Archives, Washington, D.C.
        Smithsonian Museum Mall, Washington, D.C.
        Sojourner, New York City College
        Washington Project for the Arts, Bozeman, Montana
1989   "O" Street Gallery, Washington, D.C.
        Montgomery College, Tacoma Park, Maryland
        Jones, Troyer, Fitzpatrick Gallery, Washington, D.C.
1991   University of Maryland, Eastern Shore, Princess Anne,
            Maryland
1993   *Holding East and East,* Pierce-Arrow Gallery, Saint Louis,
            Missouri
1995   Saint Louis Art Museum, Missouri

Selected Group Exhibitions:

1986   *Myth and Ritual,* Touchstone Gallery, Washington, D.C.
1987   Corcoran Museum of Art, Washington, D.C.
1988   Strathmore Arts Center, Rockville, Maryland
1989   Northern Virginia Community College, Arlington, Virginia
1990   *Other Rooms,* The Kunstrum, Washington, D.C.
1992   Art Saint Louis, Saint Louis, Missouri
1993   Lindenwood College, Missouri
        Murray State University, Eagle Gallery, Murray, Ken-
            tucky
1994   University of Wisconsin, Eau Clair
1996   Saint Louis Design Center, Missouri

Collections:

Ariel Management Corporation, Chicago; Artary Corporation, Bethesda, Maryland; Mayor's Office, Washington, D.C.

Publications:

On WARD-BROWN: Book—*Myth and Ritual,* exhibition catalog, Washington, D.C., Touchstone Gallery, 1986. **Articles**—"Isolation/Saturation: Washington, D.C./Montana Artists Exchange," in WPA newsletter, I(1) (Washington, D.C.), 1987; "Denise Ward-Brown" by Curtia James, in *New Art Examiner* (Washington, D.C.), 1 December 1989; "Art Collector for Hire" by Tracey Clark, in *American Visions* (Washington, D.C.), 1 April 1993; "A World of Black Sculptors" by Mary McCoy, in *Washington Post* (Washington, D.C.), 16 February 1994; "Art Review" by Debra Kiley Parr, in *Saint Louis Post Dispatch* (Missouri), 25 May 1995; "Six Artists in Search of a Curator" by Robert Duffy, in *St. Louis Post Dispatch* (Missouri), 20 October 1996. **Videos**—*City of Sculpture* by Race Young, Saint Louis, Missouri, 1993; *Spectrum* (interview) by Robin Royce, KETC, Channel 9, 1994.

*

Denise Ward-Brown comments:

I layer fragments of architectural objects to create my sculptures. Over the past sixteen years, I have developed a visual language based on the concept that architecture is a language of spatial symbolism signifying a culture's sense of place in the universe.

A dominant visual element in my artwork is pattern, which I define to include three-dimensional, structural form as well as sur-

face treatment. I have a passion for pattern based on my investigation of pattern as a cultural and expressive vehicle. I feel the predominant aesthetic element throughout the African diaspora is the use of invigorated, polyrhythmic patterns. It's found in the syncopated rhythms of jazz and the "call and response" of gospel music; the patterns of speech in patois and rap; and the body movements of Katherine Dunham, carnival, and the martial art form, caporeia; the exuberant compositions of Romare Bearden and William H. Johnson; and the quilts, carvings, and paintings of folk artists.

The intention of my sculpture is to celebrate the aesthetics of the African diaspora. I am searching to create art not as "art for art's sake" but as "art for life's sake."

*   *   *

Denise Ward-Brown is a sculptor who symbolically relays the mysteries and secrets within the African American culture that build connections with an African past. Immersed in abstraction, she attributes the sense of spirituality that exudes from her work and the accumulative process in her use and construction of materials to an African heritage. For Ward-Brown, African art is a principal wellspring of source material; her research into its cosmological roots is an ongoing endeavor.

Ward-Brown's sculpture and installations do not reflect a direct appropriation of indigenous African forms. She uses abstraction as a vehicle to construct personal mythologies to which she gives poetic articulation. Giving life to readymades is another component of her aesthetic. She collects and scavenges materials, such as doors, bottles, window frames, furniture, and fragments of old buildings, which she carefully transforms into structures that merely allude to her underlying theme or idea. Ward-Brown's passion for found objects pertains to her perception of them as the embodiment of secrets. Objects with a past possess heightened forms of energy embedded within. Ward-Brown intends for her readymades to be viewed symbolically and as objects recalling their obsolete functions. A kitchen table was once the focal point for family gatherings, and windows, which now exist in the context of an installation, served as vehicles to illuminate a home. Multiple manifestations of sign and symbol are inherent in Ward-Brown's use of the found object.

Her mature works stand, austere and stoic, as singular objects or in clusters of asymmetrical formations. They exist simultaneously on two diametrically opposed levels—formal and intimate. One is aware first of the sheer impact of the presence of the objects; upon closer scrutiny surfaces rich in texture and detail are revealed.

Ward-Brown embraces the sensibilities of asymmetry and accumulation. The presence of accumulation as exemplified in votive N'Knisi objects from the Congo inform her aesthetic. She understands the reference to imbuing an object with power through accumulation and embraces its underlying relationship to varied levels of knowing. According to Ward-Brown, asymmetry is the method through which she invokes rhythm. Her fragmented, asymmetrical constructions render in physical terms the concept of syncopation.

Her attitude toward process and her aesthetic inclinations directly correlate with modes of creation prevalent during the black art movement of the 1960s. Within this movement there was a conscious effort to dissect aspects of African American life and culture derived from African origins, ascribing to them particular qualities that comprise a rich aesthetic hierarchy. Although Ward-Brown's resulting aesthetic is not Afro-centric on the surface, she

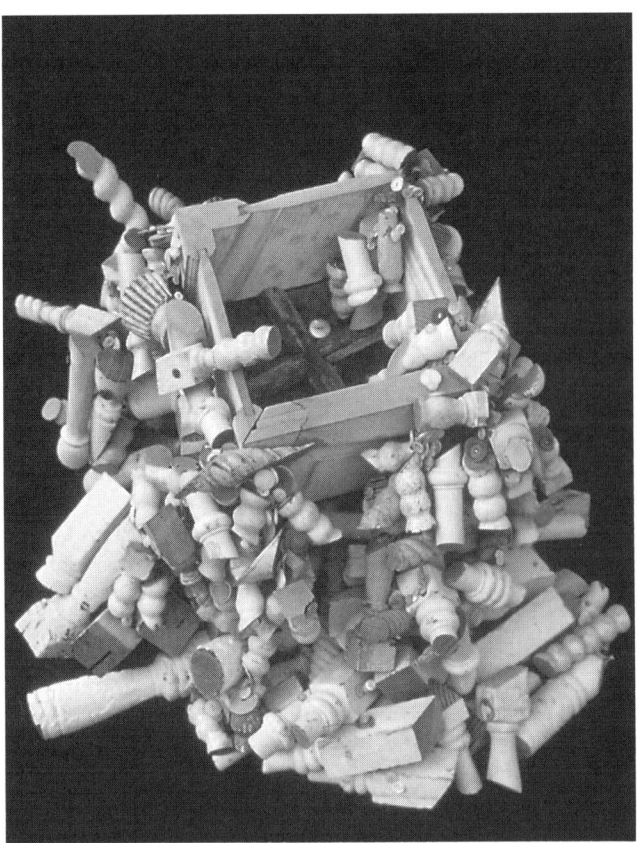

Denise Ward-Brown: *Blue Road Evolving,* **1994. Photo courtesy of Adelia Parker Castro.**

symbolically invokes her quest for a heightened cultural awareness and sense of identity. Robert Douglas asserts that the indigenous African cultural trait in the visual arts, dance, and music is the ability to entertain a series of dominant elements simultaneously. Ward-Brown, deeply grounded in this modality, achieves a multivalent presence in her sculpture through her use of texture, asymmetry, and symbolism.

—A.M. Weaver

WARING, Laura Wheeler

American painter and illustrator

Born: Hartford, Connecticut, 27 May 1887. **Education:** Boston Institute of Normal Methods, 1912; Pennsylvania Academy of Fine Arts, Philadelphia, 1907-10; Harvard summer school, Cambridge, Massachusetts, 1918; Columbia summer school, New York, 1920; L'Academie de la Grande Chaumiere, Paris, 1924-25. **Career:** Art instructor, 1906-25, director, 1925-48, art department, Cheyney State Teachers College, Cheyney, Pennsylvania. **Awards:** Harmon Gold Medal, Annual Harmon Foundation Salon, 1927. **Died:** 3 February 1948.

Individual Exhibitions:

1928   Miner Normal School, Washington, D.C.
1949   Howard University, Washington, D.C.

Selected Group Exhibitions:

1929   Galerie du Luxembourg, Paris
1940   Howard University, Washington, D.C.
1944   National Portrait Gallery, Smithsonian Institution, Washington, D.C. (Harmon Foundation traveling exhibit through 1954)
1945   Brooklyn Museum, New York
1967   New York Public Library
1973   Murphy Fine Arts Center, Morgan State College, Baltimore, Maryland
1982   Center for Visual Arts Gallery, Illinois State University, Normal
1989   Newark Museum, New Jersey
1994   National Museum of American Artists

Collections:

Barnett-Aden Collection, Museum of African-American Art, Tampa, Florida; Cheyney State University, Cheyney, Pennsylvania; Evans-Tibbs Gallery, Washington, D.C.; Howard University, Washington, D.C.; Laura Wheeler Waring Junior High School, Philadelphia; National Portrait Gallery, Smithsonian Institution, Washington, D.C.

*   *   *

The art of Laura Wheeler Waring was irrevocably molded by her middle class, socially conscious family. Rev. Robert F. Wheeler, her father, was a graduate of Howard University Theological Seminary and served various churches, including Talcott Street Congregational Church in Hartford, Connecticut. Her mother, Mary Christiana Freeman Wheeler—an amateur artist and teacher in the Brooklyn public schools (which she sought to desegregate)—was the daughter of Rev. Amos Noe Freeman, a teacher, minister, and conductor in the Underground Railroad.

Waring began painting water colors in her early teens. With the support of her family, she developed into a skillful artist, winning several awards during high school. In 1906 she became a teacher at Cheyney State Teachers College in Pennsylvania, where she would remain, eventually as director of the art department, until 1945.

Waring's mainstay during the 1920s was illustrations for *The Brownies Book* and for the cover of *The Crisis.* She also worked for Harcourt, Brace and Howe, Inc., illustrating numerous children's books, including *Boy and the Bayonet* and *The Dog and the Clever Rabbit.*

Although Waring's portraits are typically described as realistic, her art also shows impressionistic, traditional, and academic influences. For example, *Jacob's Ladder* (c.1940), part of a series interpreting Negro spirituals, was painted in a Japanese perspective reminiscent of Degas. *Harriet* and *Portrait of a Painter* (both painted in 1922) are Whistlerian with soft pastel tones and chromatically modulated color.

Beginning in 1924 Waring studied a year and a half in Paris at L'Academie de la Grande Chaumiere, where she abandoned her Whistlerian imitation and began to use a more vivid approach to light, color, and atmosphere, producing a powerful melding of styles, as in her *Houses at Semur, France* (1925).

In Paris Waring was under the tutelage of Boutel de Monvel, Robert Henri, and Delacluse. Reflecting their influence (and in the manner of Manet and Henri), she began to use swift strokes and a loaded brush to accentuate transient light upon faces. She captured the color contrasts of both the composed and natural worlds with spontaneous vigor, enlivening her subjects.

It was during her studies in Paris that Waring began to gain fame among an emerging group of noteworthy African American artists. Henry Ossawa Tanner introduced her to such artists as Palmer Hayden, Malvin Gray Johnson, Nancy Elizabeth Prophet, Augusta Savage, and Hale Woodruff. She was also introduced to the writers Countee Cullen, Eric Walrond, Langston Hughes, and Jessie Fauset and such singers and performers as Lillian Evanti, Roland Hayes, and Paul Robeson.

In 1927 Waring won the Harmon gold medal prize for the portrait *Anne Washington Derry,* which illustrates a mastery of finely adjusted tones and articulated planes (in contrast to the unrestrained brush work and characterization in much of her previous work). Also reflective of her discerning eye is the portrait *Mother and Daughter* (c.1929) in which she transcribed with fidelity the contrast in complexions of the former, a mulatto, and the latter, a quadroon.

Among Waring's most famous works are her portraits of the prominent African Americans Harry T. Burleigh, Jessie Redmon Fauset, George Edmund Hayes, James Weldon Johnson, W.E.B. Du Bois, and Marian Anderson. All were eventually placed in the permanent collection of the National Portrait Gallery at the Smithsonian Institution. Originally part of the 1944 Harmon Foundation Traveling Exhibit, they were designed to combat the stereotypical portrayals of blacks commonly found in museums throughout the United States. The thirty-two-city Harmon exhibit continued until 1954, the year when the U.S. Supreme Court, in the case *Brown vs. the Board of Education,* declared illegal the maintenance of segregated public schools.

—Madeline Wheeler Murphy

WARMACK, Gregory

American sculptor, mixed-media artist, and jewelry designer

Also known as Mr. Imagination. **Born:** Chicago, 1948. **Career:** Visiting artist, DuSable Museum of Afro-American Art, Chicago, Expressway's Children's Museum, Chicago, 1986, Boston College of Art, 1987, Illinois State Museum, Lockport, 1988, University of Chicago, 1989, Dallas Museum of Art, 1990, Field Museum, Chicago, 1991, Sibell-Wolle Fine Arts, University of Colorado, 1992, TASA Conference, University of Texas at Tyler, 1995, Museum of International Folk Art, Sante Fe, New Mexico, 1996. Artist-in-residence, Wabash College, Crawfordsville, Indiana, 1994. **Award:** Children's Defense Fund Award, 1995. **Agent:** Carl Hammer Gallery, 200 West Superior Street, Chicago, Illinois 60610, U.S.A.

Individual Exhibitions:

1983	Carl Hammer Gallery, Chicago
1986	Carl Hammer Gallery, Chicago
1990	Art Talk at Cairo, Chicago
1991	*The Eye Stands for Mr. Imagination: A Retrospective Show,* University of Illinois, Chicago
1992	Sibell-Wolle Galleries, University of Colorado, Boulder Illinois State Museum, Springfield

1993	*The Eye Stands for Mr. Imagination,* Carl Hammer Gallery, Chicago
1995	Wustum Museum, Racine, Wisconsin University of Montana, Missoula
1996	Carl Hammer Gallery, Chicago Modern Primitive Gallery, Atlanta, Georgia

Group Exhibitions:

1985	Janet Fleischer Gallery, Philadelphia
1986	Carl Hammer Gallery, Chicago
1987	Mia Gallery, Seattle
1988	Massachusetts College of Art, Boston
1989	Dallas Museum of Art (traveling)
1990	High Museum of Art, Atlanta, Georgia
1991	Columbia College, Chicago
1994	William Benton Museum of Art, University of Connecticut, Storrs
1995	Society for Contemporary Craft, Pittsburgh, Pennsylvania
1996	Bend Regional Museum of Art, South Bend, Indiana (traveling)

Gregory Warmack (Mr. Imagination), 1991. Photo by Ron Gordon; courtesy of Carl Hammer Gallery.

Gregory Warmack: Untitled Construction, 1996. Photo courtesy of Carl Hammer Gallery.

Publications:

On WARMACK: Articles—"Stone Carvings by Mr. Imagination Embody the Black Folk-Art Tradition," in the *Chicago Sun-Times,* 22 May 1983; "He Has a Dream: Mr. Imagination Takes First Steps Toward Fame," in *Uptown News,* 6 November 1984; "Mr. Imagination to Share His Secrets: Folk Artist/Sandstone Sculptor an Expert in Visual Story-Telling," in *The Houston Post,* 29 September 1991; "The Magic of Mr. Imagination," in *Springfield Magazine,* February 1992; "Discards Pop Up in Artwork," in *Southtown Economist,* 11 June 1992; "Portraiture with Inventive Twists," in *Boston Globe,* 16 July 1992; "Making a Statement with Castoff Objects," in *The Providence Journal-Bulletin,* 18, 4 March 1994; "Treasure from Trash: Self-Taught Artists Recycle Their Way through an Exhibition," in *Chicago Tribune,* 17 April 1994, p. 12; "Partnership Promotes Exhibition and Beautification," in *Spotlight Chicago,* 10 May 1994, p. 12; "Imagination Gives Junk Artistic Life," in *Journal North* (Albuquerque, New Mexico), 15 May 1996; "Mr. Imagination Pounds Away on North Side" by Dave Horkstra, in *Chicago Sun-Times,* 14 July 1996.

*   *   *

Known to his friends, neighbors, and fans as "Mr. Imagination," Gregory Warmack is as much a personality as an artist. During his childhood he searched alleys in his South Side Chicago neighborhood looking for used furniture and other discarded objects. He had a talent then, as he does now, for converting cast-off objects into art. In 1980 Warmack saw a truck dump a load of sandstone foundry molds on a lot near his former home in Chicago. He picked up several pieces, took them home, and rubbed them together to extract powder that he hoped to use on the roof of a miniature house that he was constructing.

Warmack decided to carve his name in the soft stone using a found nail, and his career as a sandstone carver was born. After carving his own name, he began to carve other large-scale names that resembled large nameplates in relief, using a four-inch long nail and a keyhole saw blade. Many of Warmack's early nameplates were presented as gifts to celebrities and well-known local personalities in Chicago. His subjects progressed from nameplates to figures, heads, Moses and the Ten Commandments, portraits of African kings, Egyptian queens, self-portraits, grimacing gargoyles with bared teeth and horns protruding from the foreheads, and Old Testament prophets. Other subjects included monolithic eyes (his trademark), hands, and fragments of human and animal feet that bear a remarkable resemblance to terra cotta sculptures from the ancient kingdoms of Nok and Ife in Nigeria, West Africa. Since Warmack is not familiar with West African art history, the similarities are more spiritual than stylistic.

Egyptian royalty is a subject that fascinates Warmack greatly because of the Egyptians' belief in reincarnation. He envisions his own personal history as a succession of reincarnations, and he has commemorated them in a series of self-portraits that sometimes evoke his past lives. In 1978 Warmack was critically injured by an armed robber and was not expected to recover from his gunshot wounds. Following his remarkable recuperation, his belief in reincarnation intensified.

The second stage in Warmack's artistic career was the creation of his paintbrush figures. Instead of discarding a group of old worn paintbrushes, he converted them into human figures. Utilizing the bristles for hair, and modeling facial features in plaster on the metal band between the bristles and the handles, the paintbrush handles became the bodies for his limbless creatures. Each paintbrush figure has a unique personality, and they were made to be viewed singly, in pairs, or in groups. From the small paintbrush figures, Warmack progressed to creating larger figures of the same type using worn broom heads. Found objects and costume jewelry were frequently used to embellish these figures.

The third and current stage of Warmack's career involves beverage bottle caps, which he uses to cover, embellish, and construct two- and three-dimensional works. Employing an abundance of beer bottle caps provided by numerous bars in his current neighborhood, Warmack created a trademark ensemble for himself by covering a denim jacket, hat, and ornate staff with bottle caps. In addition, he created two large bottle cap-covered thrones, on which he sits while receiving the numerous visitors who flock to his studio.

Warmack's bottle cap objects have been the most celebrated among his works of art, and he has used bottle caps to cover, embellish, or accent figures of humans, animals, fish, birds, costume jewelry brooches, large totems, picture frames, and even the pedestal stand holding the guest book that visitors to his studio are urged to sign. His largest commissions, from a beverage company and a distillery company, have been in the form of gigantic bottles covered with bottle caps.

The recent closing of a bowling alley in Chicago resulted in Warmack's receiving dozens of bowling pins that he quickly transformed into bowling pin figures—singles, couples, and groups—all of whom are decorated with bottle cap accents.

Above all, Gregory Warmack is a fervent publicist, and his public relations activities are an important part of his persona. From the beginning of his career, when he carved his name and the date of his birth repeatedly in his sandstone creations, to the numerous public appearances, lectures, and school workshops in which he participates, Mr. Imagination calls attention to himself again and again. This persistent self-advertisement, the two national commissions that he has received, and the constant workshops, lectures, and demonstrations that he presents result in his being the most visible self-taught artist of his generation.

—Regenia Perry

WATSON, Barrington
Jamaican painter

Born: Lucea, Jamaica, 9 January 1931. **Education:** Kingston College, Jamaica; London School of Printing and Graphic Art, London; Royal College of Art, London; Rijiks Academie, Amsterdam, Holland; Academie de la Grande Chaumiere, Paris; Academia de Belle Arti, Rome; Academia de Las Bellas Artes, Madrid. **Career:** Instructor, London School of Printing and Graphic Art, 1959-60, Maidstone College of Art, Kent, England, 1961, University of the West Indies, Kingston, Jamaica; director of studies, Jamaica School of Art, Kingston, 1962-66; visiting professor of art, Spelman College, Atlanta, Georgia, 1972-73; instructor, Harvard University, Boston, 1974, Paine College, Augusta, Georgia, 1976. Artist-in-residence, Spelman College, Atlanta, Georgia, 1971-72. Founder, Young Commonwealth Artists' Association, London, 1958, Contemporary Jamaican Artists Association, Kingston, 1964, Gallery

Barrington, Kingston, Jamaica, 1974, Contemporary Art Center, Kingston, Jamaica, 1985, Jamaica Art Foundation, Kingston, 1987, Orange Park Trust, Yallahs, Saint Thomas, Jamaica, 1991. **Awards:** British Council Scholarship, 1957; Jamaican Government Scholarship, 1958-59; German Government Scholarship, 1960; Dutch Government Scholarship, 1960; Jamaican Government Travel Scholarship, 1961; Special Award, Spanish Biennial, First Barcelona International Exhibition, 1967; Fulbright Professorship, 1971; Gold Medal, Jamaica Festival, 1974; Centenary Medal, Institute of Jamaica, Kingston, 1980; Prime Minister's Award for Excellence, 1984; Commander of the Order of Distinction, 1984. **Address:** 1 Liguanea Avenue, Kingston 6, Jamaica.

Individual Exhibitions:

1959	West Indian Student Center, London
1960	Royal College of Art, London
	West Indian Student Center, London
1961	West Indian High Commission, London
	Kingston and Saint Andrew Parish Library, Kingston, Jamaica
1964	The Gallery, Contemporary Jamaican Artists Association, Kingston
1965	The Gallery, Contemporary Jamaican Artists Association, Kingston
	Institute of Art, Panama City, Panama
1966	The Gallery, Contemporary Jamaican Artists Association, Kingston
1968	Greer Gallery, New York
	City Hall, Toronto, Canada
	Jamaican Embassy, Washington, D.C.
1970	The Gallery, Contemporary Jamaican Artists Association, Kingston
	Spelman College, Atlanta, Georgia
1971	Embassy of Trinidad and Tobago, Rio de Janeiro, Brazil
1972	Atlanta University Center College, Georgia
	Talladega College, Alabama, Georgia
	Spelman College, Atlanta, Georgia
	Olympia Hotel, Kingston, Jamaica
	Courtleigh Manor Hotel, Kingston, Jamaica
1974	Olympia International Art Center, Kingston, Jamaica
1975	Gallery Barrington, Kingston, Jamaica
1976	Gallery Barrington, Kingston, Jamaica
1979	Georgian House Gallery, Montego Bay, Jamaica
	Rizzoli's Gallery, Omni International, Atlanta, Georgia
	Astoria Gallery, Ottostrasse, Munich, Germany
1980	Gallery Barrington, Kingston, Jamaica
	Richmond Hill Inn, Montego Bay, Jamaica
	Giammaica Gallery, Venice, California
	Jamaican High Commission, London
1981	Gallery Barrington, Kingston, Jamaica
	Richmond Hill Inn, Montego Bay, Jamaica
1982	Richmond Hill Inn, Montego Bay, Jamaica
1983	Gallery Barrington, Kingston, Jamaica
	Richmond Hill Inn, Montego Bay, Jamaica
1984	Richmond Hill Inn, Montego Bay, Jamaica
1985	Richmond Hill Inn, Montego Bay, Jamaica
1986	Contemporary Art Center, Kingston, Jamaica
1987	Richmond Hill Inn, Montego Bay, Jamaica
1988	Contemporary Art Center, Kingston, Jamaica
1990	Contemporary Art Center, Kingston, Jamaica
1991	Contemporary Art Center, Kingston, Jamaica
1992	Contemporary Art Center, Kingston, Jamaica
1993	Contemporary Art Center, Kingston, Jamaica

Selected Group Exhibitions:

1958	Commonwealth Institute, London
1960	Royal Academy, London
1963	Jamaican Pavillion, Chicago
	Tea Center, London
1969	O'Keefe Center, Toronto, Canada
	Thirty Years of Jamaican Art, Spelman College, Atlanta, Georgia
1974	Museum of the National Centre of Afro-American Artists, Boston
1981	*Annual National Exhibition,* National Gallery of Jamaica, Kingston
1986	Museum of Modern Art, Rijka, Yugoslavia
1992	National Gallery of Jamaica, Kingston

Collections:

Gallery Barrington, Kingston, Jamaica; Institute of Art, Panama City, Panama; Institute of Jamaica, Kingston; Lyndon B. Johnson Memorial Library, Austin, Texas; Museum of African Art, Washington, D.C.; National Gallery of Canada, Ottawa; National Gallery of Jamaica, Kingston; Olympia Collection, Kingston, Jamaica; Richmond Hill Inn, Montego Bay, Jamaica; Spelman College, Atlanta, Georgia; University of Alberta, Edmonton, Canada; University of the West Indies, Mona Campus, Kingston; Whitney Collection, New York.

Publication:

On WATSON: Book—*Barrington,* exhibition catalog, Kingston, Jamaica, Gallery Barrington, 1993.

*   *   *

There is something oddly heroic about Barrington Watson's commitment to the painting of Jamaica and its people. He paints for posterity. In the vein of French salon painters, such as Eugène Delacroix or Alexandre Cabanel, he documents the culture's history, myths, and fantasies. Although he might balk at being described as a painter steeped in the European academic tradition, he has no qualms about being described as a figurative painter. He is steadfast in his efforts to paint figuratively and to accurately depict what he calls the Caribbean's temperate influences—its light, color, tropical feel, and the vagaries of Caribbean flesh tones. Of course, he relishes working with oils, since no other medium could so obviously suggest his respect for tradition. In a similarly traditional manner, each major work is supported by a series of preliminary charcoal drawings and watercolors, demonstrating his deft draftsmanship and his commitment to a historically validated process of painting.

Of all these concerns, the pursuit of Caribbean light has been his most compelling challenge. In recognition that the quality of light in the Caribbean cannot be conveyed in the manner of the Dutch masters, since his return from his studies in Europe in the 1960s, he has explored the peculiar quality of Caribbean light using numerous hybrid techniques combined with a sensitivity to be expected from a "son of the soil." His handling of pigment is deft and light. He builds his surfaces by gently applying color in swaths that allow a shimmering build-up of tonalities. Sometimes his application is so sheer that the white of the canvas surface reinforces the notion of inner light. Sometimes his techniques are more deliberate and controlled, as he creates devices to focus on the subject of a painting.

Women, whether staunchly matriarchal or seductively pubescent, are often the subject of his work. His penchant for merely draping their bodies in sheer garments demonstrates his accomplishment in rendering the female form while at the same time charging it with erotic overtones. In this sense his female paintings can be likened to those of the nineteenth-century impressionist Auguste Renoir—worldly, robust, and engaging.

Yet to view Watson's work purely within a European art historical tradition would be to recount only a portion of his concerns. His work represents a fusion of cultural interests, both European and Caribbean. Viewed from a Caribbean perspective, his need to visualize images of cultural and historical significance in his work might parallel the storytelling and oral traditions of the West African griot, whose narratives are so crucial to continuity within black culture.

Watson's commitment to social concerns was evidenced as early as the 1960s, when as a young man returning from Europe, he placed himself at the center of an artistic movement that promoted art as a vehicle for social change. Unlike his colleagues in the Contemporary Artists Association, Eugene Hyde and Karl Parboosingh, Watson remained wholly committed to representational painting, never abandoning figuration for modernist abstraction, which was at the time alien to the Jamaican man in the street. His popularity garnered further patronage from corporate companies and banks establishing art collections during the 1970s and 1980s.

Today Watson is the only surviving member of that 1960s triumvirate and operates the Contemporary Art Centre, which he established in the early 1980s. Considered a master of the Caribbean genre scene, he is increasingly able to imbue his paintings with significance and to execute the grand historical themes to which he has always aspired. He is creating a visual repository for future generations.

—Petrine Archer-Straw

WATSON, Osmond

Jamaican painter and sculptor

Born: Kingston, Jamaica, 13 June 1934. **Education:** Junior Centre Art Class, Institute of Jamaica, Kingston, 1947-52; Jamaica School of Art and Crafts, Kingston, 1952-58; St. Martin's School of Art, London, 1962-65. **Family:** Married Daphne Small in 1956, one daughter. **Career:** Art teacher, Munro College, St. Elizabeth, 1966-68, Ardenne High School, Kingston, Jamaica, 1968, Jamaica School of Art, Kingston, 1968-69, 1972-74, 1975, Morant Bay High School, St. Thomas, 1968-70, Sts. Peter and Paul High School, Kingston, Jamaica, 1970-72, Clarendon College, Clarendon, 1974, Womer's Boys School, Kingston, Jamaica, 1976. **Awards:** First prize, National Painting Exhibition, Institute of Jamaica, 1957; Bronze Medal, National Festival Exhibition, 1968; First Prize, National Painting Exhibition, Institute of Jamaica, 1969; Gold Medal, National Festi-

val Exhibition, 1971; First Prize (shared), National Painting Exhibition, Institute of Jamaica, 1972; Silver Musgrave Medal, Institute of Jamaica, 1972; Centenary Medal, Institute of Jamaica, 1980; Order of Distinction, National Honour of Jamaica, 1986; Gold Musgrave Medal, Institute of Jamaica, 1992. **Agent:** Mrs. Diane Fredricks, Hi-Qo Galleries, No. 1 St. Lucia Avenue, Kingston 5, Jamaica, West Indies. **Address:** P.O. Box 27, Lawrence Tavern Post Office, St. Andrew, Jamaica, West Indies.

Individual Exhibitions:

1959	Hills Gallery, Kingston, Jamaica
1960	Hills Gallery, Kingston, Jamaica
1961	Hills Gallery, Kingston, Jamaica
1966	Hills Gallery, Kingston, Jamaica
1972	Institute of Jamaica Art Gallery, Kingston, Jamaica
1981	Mutual Life Gallery, Kingston, Jamaica

Selected Group Exhibitions:

1970	Museum of Modern Art, Rijeka, Yugosalvia Medellin, Columbia
1971	Commonwealth Institute, London
1975	Casa de las America, Cuba Commonwealth Institute, London
1979	Bronx Museum of Arts, New York
1983	National Gallery of Jamaica, Kingston (traveling through 1985)
1986	*4th Wifredo Lam Bienale,* Havana, Cuba
1993	International Trade Centre, Curacoa, Netherlands
1995	Center for the Fine Arts, Miami, Florida

Collections:

Case de las America, Havana; Eagle Commercial Bank, New Kingston, Jamaica; Frame Centre Gallery, Kingston, Jamaica; Hi-Qo Gallery, Spanish Court, Kingston, Jamaica; Kingston Paris Church, Jamaica; National Gallery of Jamaica, Kingston; Olympia Art Centre, Mona, Kingston, Jamaica; St. Judes Church, Stony Hill.

Publications:

On WATSON: Articles—"Osmond Watson Talks to Alex Gradussov" by Alex Graddussov, in *Jamaica Journal* (Kingston), Institute of Jamaica, 3(3), September 1969; "The Works of Watson and Gonzales" by Basil McFarlane, in *Sunday Gleaner* (Kingston), *Daily Gleaner,* 13 November 1977; "Osmond Watson (A Profile)" by Deryck Roberts, in *Sunday Gleaner* (Kingston), *Daily Gleaner,* 7 June 1981; "Osmond Watson's Masquerades" by Gloria Escoffery, in *Jamaica Journal* (Kingston), Institute of Jamaica, 16(1), February 1983; "Jamaica Journey: Mystery of Slavery, African Religion, and Redemption" by Tekla Meket, in *Sunday Gleaner* (Kingston), *Daily Gleaner,* 28 February 1993.

*   *   *

From an early age Osmond Watson demonstrated a precocious talent for drawing. Between the ages of fourteen and eighteen, he attended the art classes of the Junior Centre of the Institute of

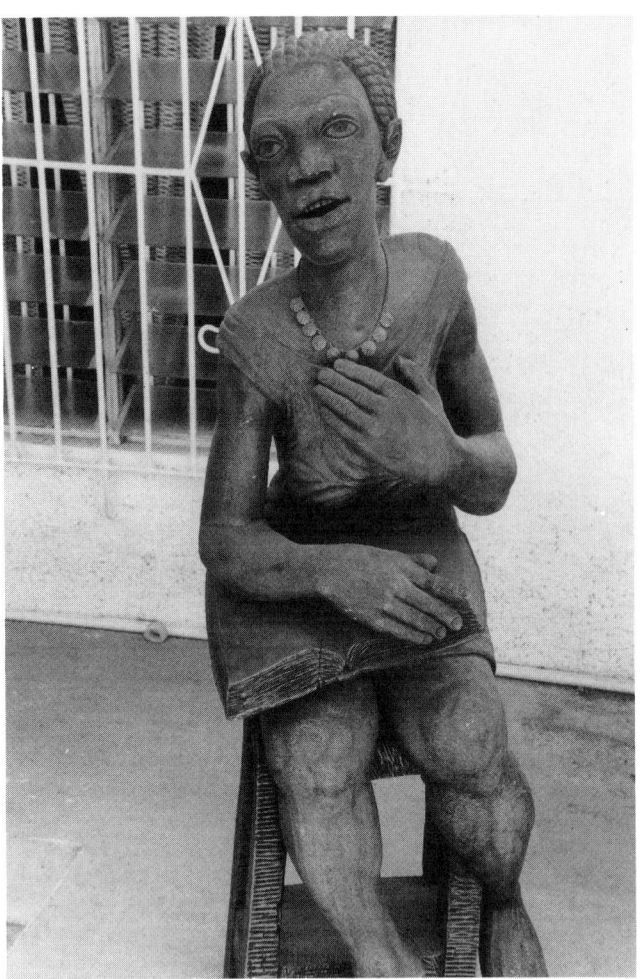

Osmond Watson: *Hope, 1973.*

Jamaica, and at eighteen he entered the Jamaica School of Art and Crafts. On graduation in 1958 he began exhibiting his work with some success. His early works—although in the naturalist tradition of Jamaican artists of an earlier generation such as Albert Huie, David Pottinger, and Ralph Campbell (with whom he served an apprenticeship)—revealed an artist of uncommon boldness. To further his studies, he traveled to London in 1962 and enrolled at Saint Martin's School of Art.

London was a liberating experience. Even more than classes at Saint Martin's, it was visits to the British Museum and exposure to its great collection of African art that stimulated Watson. An immediate outcome of his exposure to African sculpture was that he began to explore wood carving as a medium for his creativity. It is clear that he was also drawn to the cubism of Pablo Picasso, probably because of cubism's own dependence on African art. The stylistic benefits are obvious, and a cubistlike structuring form and simultaneity are evident in many phases of Watson's subsequent work. But more than this, it was a new awareness of self and of self as a black man, a black man with a history and a glorious artistic heritage, that began to inform his work.

On his return to Jamaica in 1965, Watson resumed exhibiting. He quickly rose to prominence, largely through his gaining a string of medals for both painting and sculpture in the All Island and National Festival exhibitions. His prize for sculpture in the 1969 exhi-

bition at the National Festival was the first gold medal ever awarded in that competition.

Watson's return home was also marked by a more conscious involvement with the ideas of Rastafarianism and the philosophy of Marcus Garvey. Religion, especially as expressed in the Jamaican Afro-Christian cults of Pocomania and Revivalism, also gained in importance. Some of Watson's key works from this period—such as the carvings *Hallelujah* (1969), done as a hymn of praise after his wife's recovery from a serious illness, and *Revival Kingdom* (1969), which represents the Revival shepherd Kapo surrounded by a host of followers in the spirit—show this influence. These two carvings, considered by many to be his finest, are both bas-reliefs, with the figural elements massed within a hierarchical composition in a manner that recalls certain African, especially Yoruba, traditions.

In the late 1960s Watson began what was to become an extended series, continuing well into the late 1970s, based on the traditional Jonkonnu, a Jamaican Christmas masquerade. A neocubist technique informs most of these works, but there is a pronounced emphasis on movement and on the symbolic masks. Actual small objects, such as mirrors and coins, are occasionally introduced, and the paintings are highly finished with enamel-like surfaces. The painting of self-portraits also became increasingly significant, even obsessive. In many of these Watson is seen in Rastafarian guise, as a revolutionary (as in the 1974 *Freedom Fighter*), or as a black Christ. In one of his best-known paintings, *Peace and Love* (1969), Watson depicts himself as a blessing Christ wearing Rastafarian locks. In an allusion to the crown of thorns, the painted frame is encircled by protruding nails.

In the 1970s and 1980s Watson began delving into Jamaica's precolonial past and did a series of paintings that celebrate the existence of the Jamaican Taino, the aboriginal Jamaicans who had been exterminated by the Spaniards. These are his most abstract paintings, and they use an imagined language of abstract signs and symbols to portray the felt spiritual vibrations of a vanished people. Perhaps the best known of these "Arawak" paintings is the enigmatic *Secret of the Arawaks* (1977).

The recipient of many awards, including the prestigious Gold Musgrave medal, Watson lives and works near Kingston. Although he now exhibits only rarely, he has been an important inspirational source for a generation of younger Jamaican and Caribbean painters.

—David Boxer

WEEMS, Carrie Mae
American photographer

Born: Portland, Oregon, 1953. **Education:** California Institute of the Arts, Valencia, B.A. 1981; University of California, San Diego, M.F.A. 1984; University of California, Berkeley, M.A. 1987. **Career:** Teaching assistant, University of California, San Diego, 1983-84; teacher, San Diego City College, California, 1984; teaching assistant, University of California, Berkeley, 1987; assistant professor, Hampshire College, Amherst, Massachusetts, 1987-91; assistant professor, California College of Arts and Crafts, Oakland, 1991. Artist-in-residence, Visual Studies Workshop, Rochester, New York, 1986, Light Work, Syracuse, New York, 1988, Art Institute of Chicago, 1990, Rhode Island School of Design, 1990; visiting professor, Hunter College, New York, 1988-89. **Awards:** Los Angeles Women's Building Poster Award, 1981; University of California Fellowship, 1981-85; University of California Chancellor's grant, 1982; California Arts Council grant, 1983; Massachusetts Artists Fellowship (finalist), 1988, 1989; Louis Comfort Tiffany Award, 1992; Photographer of the Year Award, Friends of Photography, Ansel Adams Center, San Francisco, 1994; National Endowment for the Arts Visual Arts grant, 1994-95. **Agent:** P.P.O.W., 532 Broadway, New York, New York 10012, U.S.A.

Individual Exhibitions:

1984	*Family Pictures and Stories,* Multi-Cultural Gallery, San Diego
1987	Hampshire College Art Gallery, Amherst, Massachusetts
1989	Rhode Island School of Design, Providence
1990	CEPA Gallery, Buffalo, New York
	P.P.O.W., New York
1991	Institute of Contemporary Art, Boston
	Trustman Gallery, Simmons College, Boston
	And 22 Million Very Tired and Very Angry People, New Museum of Contemporary Art, New York
	Matrix Gallery, Wadsworth Athenaeum, Hartford, Connecticut
	Family Pictures and Stories, Albright College, Reading, Pennsylvania
	University of Southern California, Irvine
	Art Complex Museum, Duxbury, Massachusetts
1992	Greenville County Museum of Art, South Carolina
	Walter/McBean Gallery, San Francisco Art Institute
	Cleveland Center for Contemporary Art, Ohio
	Sea Islands, P.P.O.W., New York
1993	Linda Cathcart Gallery, Santa Monica, California
	Rhona Hoffman Gallery, Chicago
	New Langton Arts, San Francisco
	The Fabric Workshop, Philadelphia, Pennsylvania
	National Museum of Women in the Arts (traveling)
1994	Hood Museum of Art, Dartmouth College, Hannover, New Hampshire
	Dakar Biennial, Senegal
	Sarah Moody Gallery of Art, University of Alabama, Tuscaloosa (traveling)
1995	J. Paul Getty Museum of Art, Malibu, California
	Museum of Modern Art, New York

Selected Group Exhibitions:

1980	Brockman Gallery, Los Angeles
1986	*Social Concerns,* Maryland Institute of Art, Baltimore, Maryland
1988	Houston Center for Photography,
1990	CEPA Gallery, Buffalo, New York
	New Museum of Contemporary Art, New York
1991	Whitney Museum of American Art, New York
1992	*Vote,* Terry Dintenfass Gallery, New York
	Mis/Taken Identities, University Art Museum, University of California, Santa Barbara (traveling through 1994)
1993	Weatherspoon Art Gallery, University of North Carolina, Greensboro (traveling)
1994	Museum of Modern Art, New York

Publications:

On WEEMS: Books—*And 22 Million Very Tired and Very Angry People,* exhibition catalog, New York, New Museum of Contemporary Art and Laura Trippi, 1991; *Family Pictures and Stories: A Photographic Installation,* exhibition catalog, Pennsylvania, Freedman Gallery, 1991; *In These Islands: South Carolina, Georgia,* exhibition catalog, University of Alabama and Houston Baker, 1995. **Articles**—"Carrie Mae Weems: The Right Questions" by Marguerite van Cook, in *Village Beat,* December 1990, p. 12; "Carrie Mae Weems/Matrix 115, Wadsworth Athenaeum," in *Journal of the Print World,* Spring 1991, p. 49; "Carrie Mae Weems" by Lois Tarlow, in *Art New England,* August/September, pp. 10-12; "Down-Home Look Belies Power of Carrie Mae Weems' Works" by Cathy Curtis, in *Los Angeles Times,* 21 October 1991; "The Isms Brothers, Carrie Mae Weems at SFAI" by Jeff Kelley, in *Artweek,* 23(15), May 1992, p. 4; "Lessons in the Stories: The Engaging Voice of Carrie Mae Weems" by Jo Ann Lewis, in *The Washington Post,* 7 January 1993, p. C2; "Weems's World" by Rudy Rich, in *Mirabella,* February 1993, p. 109; "Review" by Debra Bricker Balken, in *Art in America,* April 1993, pp. 129-30; "Carrie Mae Weems: Indictments of Racism in Black and White" by David Hamilton, in *Art and Antiques,* September 1993.

*   *   *

In Carrie Mae Weems's photographs, history and solutions meld into herstory. Weems's herstory always confronts the past with solutions for the future. Thus she does more than simply record or document. She is able to distinguish, analyze, differentiate, appraise, calculate, criticize, question, relate, examine, and solve history's conundrums. Weems's photographs document the past and offer a plan for the future. Sometimes Weems will use one photograph, often more than one photograph, to recall how black people have been represented in photographic history. In the herstory that Weems weaves, she makes those who would malign accountable for the misery they spread. Nothing is sacred with Weems; she interrogates everything. For those who are unclear about any message in Weems's herstory, she often superimposes text over the image. This has the effect of a "double whammy." Often Weems's succinct text provides recognizable entry into her chilling and biting reportage.

Born in 1953, Weems received her M.A. in folklore from the University of California, Berkeley. She earned her M.F.A. in photography from the University of California, San Diego. With these two degrees, natural mother wit, profound eyes that see more than most, and an uncanny sense for unmasking myths and outright "lies," she has had a very successful career. Her work is in the most prestigious collections worldwide. Two examples of her most recent work include *Mirror, Mirror* (silver print 20" x 16") from her "Ain't Jokin'" series and *Field Yard House Kitchen* from the installation *From Here I Saw What Happened and I Cried* (1996, monochromatic color photographs with sand-blasted glass, each 26 3/4" x 22 1/4"). The irrepressible Weems serves up questions about standards of beauty and the black woman in *Mirror, Mirror,* which created a stir of controversy when it first appeared. While polemical the photograph is also didactic and confrontational. A black woman is staring into a mirror, and Weems's text reads

LOOKING INTO THE MIRROR, THE
BLACK WOMAN ASKED, "MIRROR, MIRROR ON

THE WALL,
WHO'S THE FAIREST OF THEM
ALL?" THE MIRROR SAYS, "SNOW
WHITE YOU BLACK BITCH, AND
DON'T YOU FORGET IT!!!"

Field Yard House Kitchen is similar to *Mirror, Mirror.* Weems is interrogating the same issues of place and standards in history. Because of the size, multiplicity (this installation has more than twenty-five images), color, and arrangement of the photographs, Weems weaves herstory in a magical and magnificent manner. She recalls the tragic past of black people at the hands of avaricious folk. But in *her* telling of the *story,* she clarifies what will occur next. With Weems as the soothsayer viewing the history and placing it before a knowing and willing audience, the occurrence of such evil doings will be prevented. While looking at Weems's photographs one can always see her reflection.

—Jontyle Theresa Robinson

WELLMAN, Joyce

American painter and printmaker

Born: New York, 1950. **Education:** City College of New York, B.S. 1972; University of Massachusetts, Boston, M.A. 1977. **Career:** Education specialist, Wider Opportunities for Women in Washington, D.C.

Selected Individual Exhibitions:

First American Bank; Gallery 900; Howard University Gallery of Art; University of the District of Columbia.

Publications:

On WELLMAN: Articles—"A Washington Celebration: Let the Art Be First" by Karen Ritter, in *Women Artists News,* 11, June 1986, p. 16 (illustrated); review (Howard University Gallery of Art, Washington, D.C.) by Curtia James, in *New Art Examiner,* 19, June/Summer 1992, pp. 41-42.

*   *   *

Throughout her career Joyce Wellman has journeyed back and forth from the concrete to the cryptic. Much of her work until 1985 was in graphic printmaking, and an extreme example of her illustrative—though still organic and fantastic—work is her 1979 print *Creation,* which combines images of the Adam, Eve, and Serpent story with "becoming" tales from the Akan people of Ghana. In her 1984 work *Pathway Dancers,* Wellman employed stark black-and-white linocuts to illustrate the passage of life of an anthropomorphic, female form. The four stages of life found in the piece are those of a little girl, an adolescent girl, a young adult, and a sensuous, enlightened adult woman.

Later, especially when Wellman started painting again in 1985, she seemed to explore the surface of the work more intuitively during the process of creation, in the process discovering the path to more exotic, abstract, other-worldly compositions. Paintings such as *Undersea Life,* which depicts a gestural, theoretical ocean-space, contain such seemingly out-of-place objects as messages ("S.O.S." appears here and in other Wellman paintings), accent marks, and disassociated body parts.

Joyce Wellman's paintings seem to divulge the course taken to create them. "My work involves the use of imagery that reveals itself through an unconscious process of placing color, form, cryptic signs and marks onto the surface of my paintings," she says. "The real challenge begins as I push and pull these abstractions in order to create visual sensations that evoke from the viewer an emotional response." The process of pushing and pulling, as well as the process of the work revealing itself to the viewer and evoking an emotional response, is much like a journey, which is a recurring theme for Wellman. Whether it be the journey from infancy to adulthood or the journey from the act of painting to the emotional reaction in the viewer, it is the traveling that is represented in her work—the act of making the excursion. The destination might be important but perhaps only in the context of the pilgrimage, in which "getting there" is but a fragment of the whole.

—Terry Bain

WELLS, James Lesesne

American printmaker and painter

Born: Atlanta, Georgia, 1902. **Education:** Lincoln University; National Academy of Design; Florida Industrial and Collegiate Institute, c.1914; Columbia University's Teachers College, 1924-29, B.S. 1929. **Career:** Professor, Howard University, Washington, D.C., 1929-68. Director, Harlem Art Workshop and Studio, New York, 1933. Worked briefly in Paris. **Awards:** Florida Normal and Industrial Institute Scholarship, Jacksonville, 1914; Florida State Fair Drawing Prize, 1915; Harmon Gold Medal, 1931; George Haynes Prize, 1935; honorable mention, Sixth Annual Area Exhibit, Corcoran Gallery; Second Prize, Federations of Churches Exhibit; George F. Muth Prize, Washington Watercolor Club; First Prize in graphic arts, Washington Area Religious Art Exhibition; honorable mention, Society of American Artists. **Died:** 20 January 1993.

Individual Exhibitions:

1932	Delphic Studios
	Barnet Aden Gallery
	Brooklyn Museum, New York
1987	Washington Project for the Arts and Studio Museum in Harlem, New York (retrospective through 1988)

Selected Group Exhibitions:

1921	New York Public Library
1930	Montclair Y.W.C.A.
1931	Harmon Foundation
1932	Brooklyn Museum, New York
1933	Art Center, New York
	Harmon Foundation
1935	Studio House, Washington, D.C.
	State Museum, Trenton, Ohio

James L. Wells: *Provincetown Street.* Photo by Frank White; courtesy of the Schomburg Center for Research in Black Culture.

1936   Texas Centennial
1937   Howard University, Washington, D.C.
1940   Negro Exposition, Chicago
1943   Smith College, Northampton, Massachusetts
        Institute of Modern Art, Boston
1968   Sheraton Hotel, Philadelphia
1970   James A. Porter Gallery
1971   State Armory, Wilmington, Delaware
        Smith-Mason Gallery

Collections:

Fisk University, Nashville; Hampton Institute, Virginia; National Archives; Phillips Memorial Gallery, Washington, D.C.; Smithsonian Institution; Spelman College, Atlanta, Georgia; University of Kansas; Valentine Museum, Richmond, Virginia.

Publications:

On WELLS: Books—*Paintings and Prints by James L. Wells,* exhibition catalog, Washington, D.C., Howard University, 1965; *Paintings and Prints by James L. Wells, Series #2,* Atlanta, Georgia, Spelman College, 1966; *Alone in a Crowd,* exhibition catalog, New York, from the collection of Reba and Dave Williams and the Metropolitan Museum of Art; *James Lesesne Wells: Sixty Years in Art* by Richard Powell and Jock Reynolds, Washington Project for the Arts, 1986. **Articles**—"Harmon Foundation Exhibit," in *Art Digest,* 15 February 1931, p. 7; *Art Digest,* 1 March 1933; "Harlem Library Shows Negro Art," in *Art News,* 20 May 1933, p. 14; "Black Artist" by Virginia Kiah, in *Savannah Magazine,* April 1972, p. 16; review (Washington Project for the Arts) by Daniel Barbiero, in *New Art Examiner,* 14, May 1987, p. 54; review (Hammonds House, Atlanta) by Curtia James, in *Art in America,* 78, December 1990, pp. 176-77.

*   *   *

James Wells was an accomplished painter early in his career. He won major prizes such as the Harmon Gold Medal in 1931 for *The Flight into Egypt* and in the same year sold his *Journey to Egypt* to Duncan Phillips, the founder of the first gallery in America devoted to modern art. Despite this early success, he made the conscious decision to dedicate the rest of his artistic life to the medium of printmaking. Wells, commenting on his life's work, said, "I was one of the country's early printmakers, not black printmakers necessarily."

Several critics and artist colleagues have indicated his mastery of the various types of techniques and media within printmaking. Jacob Kainen, a well-known painter and former curator of the Smithsonian Graphic Arts Division, said "Certainly his late color linoleum prints are among the more memorable ones made recently in this country." Color linoleum became his special forte. Wells was an innovative pioneer in the use of color in printmaking. Romare Bearden concluded that "His expressionistic use of brilliant color has increased the impact of his woodcuts and lithographs." This use of color is beautifully shown in *The Flight into Egypt*, a print in which the mother and child ride on a yellow donkey led by Joseph through a very simple landscape background of blue and green.

German expressionism and African art are the two major influences on the body of prints that Wells created. He was exposed to German expressionism by his professors at Teachers College, Columbia University, who introduced him to the woodcuts and lithographs by Albrecht Durer. The German expressionists believed that the print medium was a great but neglected classic art form. Wells particularly liked the lithographs by Otto Muller, who used African motifs. Wells's study of German expressionism made him aware of its impact on cubism, which was profoundly impacted by African art in general and African sculpture in particular. In fact Wells was one of the African American printmakers to use African art concepts to help simplify the design of his prints. This African influence is exemplified by the woodcut *The Primitive Boy*.

African art was an enduring influence on Wells's printmaking. While a student at Columbia, he visited an exhibition of African sculpture at the Brooklyn Museum of Art and was so enthralled that he returned to the exhibition many times. This initiated his life-long love affair with African art.

Wells was also deeply influenced by the writings of Alain Locke, especially his classic volume, *The New Negro*. Locke argued that African American artists needed to turn to African art and cultural traditions for content and sources of creative inspiration. Wells later joined Locke on the faculty of Howard University. They collaborated on many projects until Locke's death. Wells's decision to focus primarily on printmaking was in part due to Locke's opinions and support.

After his retirement from the department of arts at Howard University, Wells received an invitation to visit West Africa, where his son Jim was a photographer on contract with Time-Life. Wells was so impressed with West Africa that he extended his trip for three months. He commented that "I have never been so impressed with my environment as I was in Africa . . . . I stood in awe of Dakar's marketplace, teeming with colors and activity." This trip to West Africa gave Wells a new burst of creative energy that was stimulated by the brilliance of color and by African imagery. *Bus Stop, Ghana* and *Young Heardsmen with Flowers* are products of this experience. This was the other bookend, matching his repeated visits to the Brooklyn Museum of Art in 1923.

James Lesesne Wells died on 20 January 1993. His colleague at Howard, James A. Porter, wrote in 1943 that the "dean of Negro printmakers is James L. Wells." How prophetic was his assertion. His name has appeared on every list of notable black artists of the twentieth century, and he has taught many other outstanding printmakers, including Lila Oliver Asher, Elizabeth Catlett, David C. Driskell, Eugene Frederick, Lloyd McNeil, Stephen Pogue, Richard Powell, and Lou Stovall. The fact that those artists have achieved such great heights is not in small part due to the fact that they stood on the shoulders of a giant. That giant was James Lesesne Wells.

—Robert Steele

WEST, Pheoris

American painter

Born: Albany, New York, 17 August 1950. **Education:** Brockport, State University, Brockport, New York, 1968-70; Pennsylvania Academy of Fine Arts, Philadelphia, 1970-74, professional certificate; Yale University, New Haven, Connecticut, 1974-76, M.F.A. **Family:** Married 1) Louise Calio in 1972 (divorced 1976); 2) Michele Hoff in 1979, three sons (triplets) and one daughter. **Career:** Since 1976 professor of art, Ohio State University, Columbus. Art director, Inner City Enrichment Program, Philadelphia, 1974; artist-in-residence, Hillhouse High School, New Haven, Connecticut, 1975-76. **Awards:** Popular Prize, Philadelphia Museum of Art, 1971; James A. Porter Grand Award, National Exhibition of Black Artists, 1971; First Prize in oil painting, Chautauqua Art Festival, 1971; Alexander Prize, Pennsylvania Academy of Fine Arts, 1973; William E. Cresson Memorial Traveling Scholarship, Pennsylvania Academy of Fine Arts, 1973; Henry Scheidt Traveling Fellowship, Pennsylvania Academy of Fine Arts, 1974; teaching fellowship, Yale University, 1974; Connecticut Commission for the Arts grant, 1976; Ohio Arts Council mini-grant, 1978; Ohio Arts Council Fellowship, 1988. **Address:** 756 Seymour Avenue, Columbus, Ohio 43205, U.S.A. **On-line Address:** west.1@osu.edu.

Individual Exhibitions:

1974	Glassboro State College, New Jersey
	Studio Museum in Harlem, New York
1976	Peg Alston Arts, New York
1977	Uniworld Group, New York
1978	Ohio University, Athens
	American International College, Springfield, Massachusetts
1979	Museum of African and African-American Art and Antiquities, Buffalo, New York
	Ohio State University, Marion
1980	Ohio State University, Newark
1983	Central State University, Wilberforce, Ohio
1987	Peg Alston Arts, New York
1988	Garret Gallery, Fairfield County Public Library, Lancaster, Ohio
	Benjamin-Marcus Gallery, Columbus, Ohio
1989	Bricker Hall, Ohio State University, Columbus
	Morris Brown College of Atlanta, Georgia
	Peg Alston Arts, New York
1990	Columbus Cultural Arts Center, Ohio
	Worthington Arts Council, Worthington Community Center, Ohio
1992	Paul Robeson Center, Central State University, Wilberforce, Ohio
1994	Purdue University Galleries, West Lafayette, Indiana
	Peabody's Art Factory, Columbus, Ohio
1996	Middle Tennessee State, Murfeesboro, Tennessee

Selected Group Exhibitions:

1976	Balch Institute, Philadelphia
1980	Galerie Mitakal, Abidgan, Ivory Coast
	National Center of Afro-American Art, Boston

Pheoris West: *The Garden,* **1992. Photo courtesy of Michele Hoff West.**

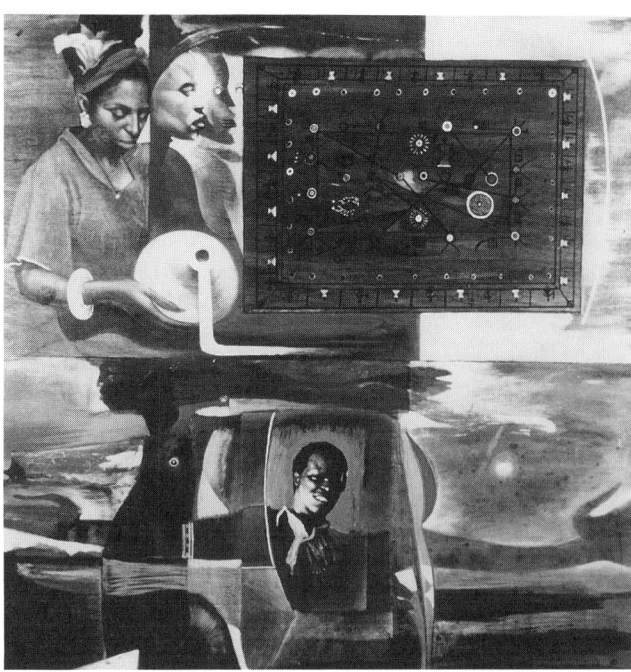

Pheoris West: *Libation,* 1994. Photo courtesy of Michele Hoff West.

1987	*Art of Black America,* Osaka, Japan
1988	Salvador da Bahia, Brazil
1989	Museo Civico d'Artes Contempraneo, Palermo, Italy
1992	Philadelphia Art Museum
	APEX Museum, Atlanta, Georgia
	Oslo, Norway (traveling)
1993	National Civil Rights Museum, Memphis, Tennessee

Collections:

APEX Museum, Atlanta, Georgia; Black Enterprises, New York; Central State University, Wilberforce, Ohio; Charles Drew Health Center, Dayton, Ohio; Frank Hale Black Cultural Center, Ohio State University, Columbus; Howard University, Washington, D.C.; Lower Washington Heights Health Center, New York; Morris Brown College, Atlanta, Georgia; Mount Vernon AME Church, Columbus, Ohio; Museum for the National Center for Afro-American Art, Boston; North Carolina Central University, Durham; Studio Museum of Harlem, New York.

Publication:

On WEST: Video—*More Than Color,* Athens, Ohio, Ohio University Telecommunications Center, 1992.

*

Pheoris West comments:

In my artwork I'm always striving for an ideal image, one that is based on balance and harmony. The choice for representing the human form is deliberate and extremely important. I celebrate humanity as godly images, the embodiment of the four essential elements of earth, air, fire, and water. The formats that I choose for representing my compositions (the square and the rectangle) are just as essential. Activities in my paintings generally are based on horizontal and vertical axes; the axis lines further emphasize my concerns for balance. My prime motivation for making art is considerably selfish (because it is a pleasurable experience). I also see art as the "great communicator." Therefore I use the medium as a conveyor of ideas. Each color, method of mark making, spatial concern, and developed form (or character) uses physical means for communication of a message. Activities within the paintings are not only symbolic but functional as part of our visual language. The paintings, then, are not simply to be read but also to be felt.

*   *   *

Pheoris West cites the major influences on his early development as the works of Romare Bearden and Henry O'Tanner and the 1970s African American arts collective Africobra. Immersion in the vibrant black art scene in Philadelphia during the late 1970s also had a significant impact. At the age of twenty-two, West endeavored to construct a visual language that embodied the concept of blackness. His paintings of contemporary genre scenes were ennobled renditions of the common and hip folk. Their regal bearing and defiant poses, stances, and gestures harbored the energy and poise contained within a vibrant urban culture. During this period West relied heavily upon representationalism; however, he managed to infuse abstract sensibilities through the employment of overlapping forms and translucent layering of paint. His intent was to create a deluge of imagery celebrating the presence of African Americans. Captured in these early works were not only a dignity of spirit but also an expressed sensitivity to the disclosure of the varying dynamics and factions within the black community.

Since 1975 West has traveled extensively throughout Europe and West Africa. His experiences have heavily influenced the direction of his work. Form and process in creation of the art object were major concerns. The opportunity to analyze Rembrandt's and Vermeer's various compositional strata in the construct of painting and the technique of chiaroscuro had a tremendous effect on West's stylistic development. Also, the work of Ingre and his relationship to classicism further expanded West's investigation of form in painting. The works of these artists reinforced his directives in the use of paint and laid the foundation for the formal qualities retained in his mature work.

His research of works from African cultures extended beyond surface admiration of artifacts. His pursuit of an in-depth understanding of cultural factors and their role in the creation of art resulted in the formal study of traditional religions of various African cultures and their retention in the African diaspora. West proclaims that living in Ghana for an extended period of time literally altered his perception of the world.

West continued to pursue his research, tracing the historical connections between the legacy of Western art traditions and their Egyptian origins. His study of Egyptian art and philosophy began an odyssey that culminated in the exploration of West African pantheons. He began to create works that embodied signs and symbols representative of aspects of indigenous African belief systems, which are involved in the codification and revelation of knowledge and worldviews.

Multiple layers of paint and translucent modeling of muted tones with an overall brilliant color scheme became West's trademark as a painter. Realistically rendered figures surface through multivalent fields of marks. There, figures materialize as floating forms, wafting in and out of focus, or serve as stoic and powerful focal points. In

West's work there is constant interaction between abstract and realistic modes. His marks, whether visible brush strokes or linear delineations of specific forms, are infused with a vital life force. Varied painting techniques, metaphysical compositions, and marks signifying charts and divination symbols are essential elements within the precepts of his unique visual language system; a conglomerate of data converges to formulate a harmonious whole.

Tracing his life path, West's works range from the documentation of the inner sanctums of urbanity to the sacred. His current work is a vehicle for the expression of spiritual growth, giving insight into the essence of that process of discovery. Painting for West is not a means to an end but an excursion into the region between human existence and the realm of the ephemeral.

—A.M. Weaver

WESTBROOK, Rene

American painter, mixed-media artist, and photographer

Born: New York. **Education:** Massachusetts College of Art, Boston, B.F.A. 1980.

Selected Exhibitions:

Boston Center for the Arts; Derrick Joshua Beard Fine Arts, West Hollywood, California (1992, solo); Harvard University Science Center, Cambridge, Massachusetts; Jamaica Arts Center, New York (1988); Longwood Gallery, Boston; Museum of the National Center of Afro-American Artists, Boston; Nile Gallery, Boston; Office of the Mayor, Washington, D.C.; Harriet Tubman Gallery, Boston; University of Connecticut, Storrs.

Collections:

Museum of the National Center of Afro-American Artists, Boston; Paige Academy, Boston; Harvard University, Cambridge, Massachusetts.

*

Rene Westbrook comments:

My specific approach to art is one that explores and develops a means by which several methods of self-expression are used to convey ideas. To this end I have spent many years working in a number of mediums and now wish to combine them into unified visual statements. Painting, photography, writing, and video have

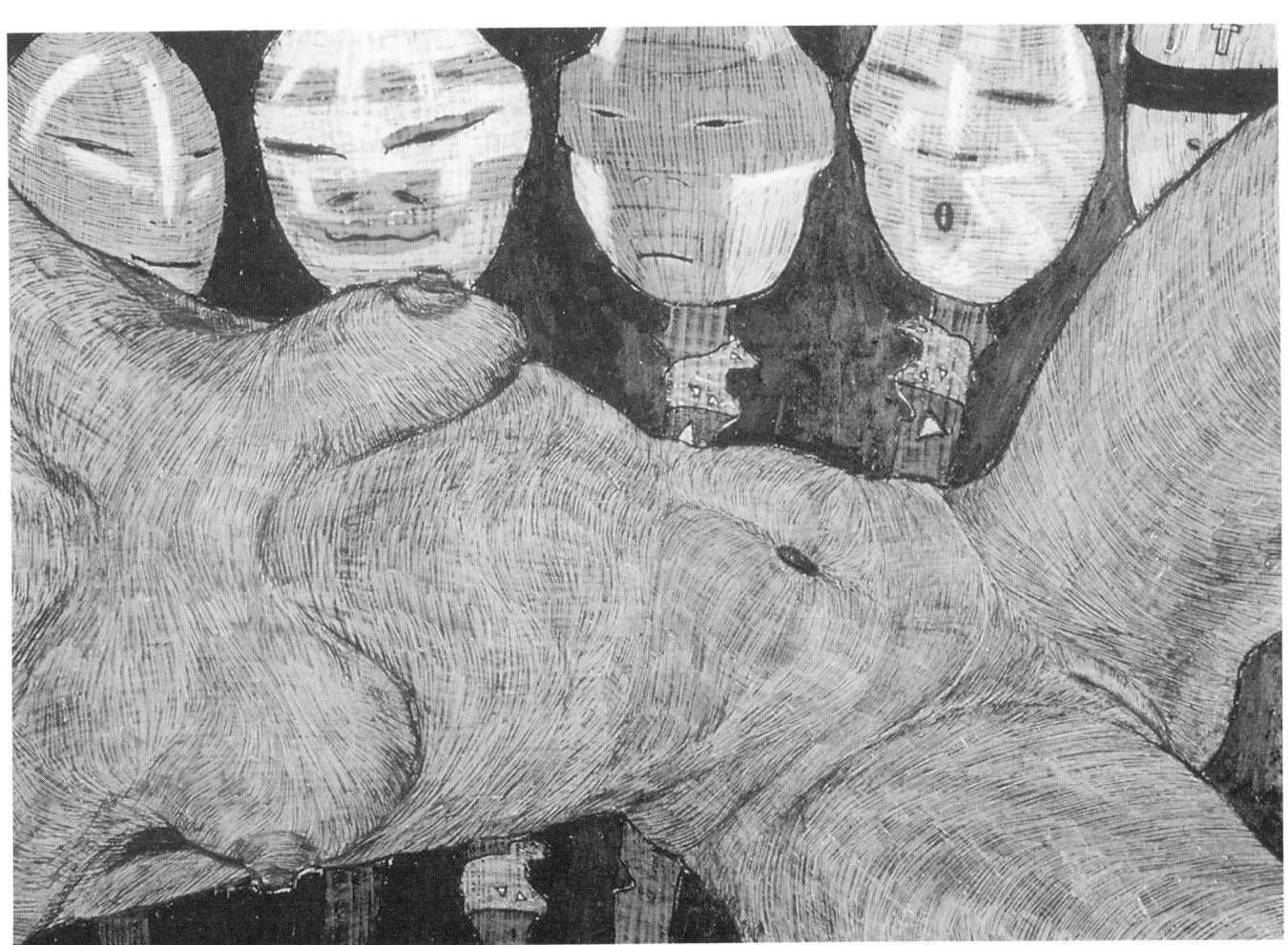

Rene Westbrook: *The Speculators,* 1985. Photo courtesy of Hakim Raquib.

Rene Westbrook: *The Veil,* 1985. Photo courtesy of Hakim Raquib.

become the spectrum from which to blend and combine difficult concepts into artistic presentations.

I love the narrative process, whether it be explored in visual terms or in text. My expressed aim during the next two years in graduate school will be to develop an already well-defined interests into a strong working knowledge of multimedia presentations that deliver powerful imagery balanced with the language of form and content.

The themes of my artwork during the past five years have dealt with social issues. I fully expect to continue this difficult yet rewarding commentary on culture and society. I do not, however, define my work as espousing any one racial or cultural dimension. My goal is to develop presentations that include a variety of imagery skillfully rendered.

Finally, I wish to teach. My experience to date on the college level as one visiting teacher and judge during review boards has been a good one. Feedback from and evaluations of my work have revealed that I am a challenging learner-teacher for my students. My unconventional style and approach to art/life makes me a useful candidate to bridge the burdensome exercise of imparting perspective and technique to both young and older art students today. I believe I will be able to aid students to conceptually confront the possibilities of their innate talents with skillful technique which can then be explored as self-expression.

*   *   *

Born in New York to parents of Caribbean background, Rene Westbrook studied at the Massachusetts College of Art. She has a probing intellectual personality, and she has applied her creative energies in several directions. While working as a researcher at Harvard University, she developed several concepts and scripts for area television stations. She also distinguished herself as a creative and technical writer and as an actor and dramatic reader. Never content with her achievements, she moved to California and then the Pacific Northwest, where she has continued to explore various creative areas.

As an artist Westbrook has had an abiding interest in textured surfaces and in experimentation. In the early 1980s these interest were expressed though a preference for crayon paintings, in which she employed rich blues and magentas to create vibrant figurative compositions that seemed almost fabriclike on their surfaces. Later, using techniques such as scraping over thickly applied crayon markings, Westbrook produced works that achieved astonishing figurative references. During this period she favored a heavily painted, almost monochromatic surface that suggested a primordial organic wall. These more brooding paintings are very different in spirit, often combining various materials in a manner reminiscent of the cleverness and sharp wit of the assemblage and constructivist movements. Her works have often explored gender themes.

Westbrook has also experimented with photography. Using large-format Polaroid cameras, she has produced a series of remarkable and unique color prints using masks and featuring herself as well as other people. These prints testify to her inventive imagination and her comfort with new technologies and approaches.

—Edmund Barry Gaither

WHITE, Charles (Wilbert)

American painter, muralist, printmaker, and draftsman

Born: Chicago, 2 April 1918. **Education:** Art Institute of Chicago, 1937; Art Students League, New York; Taller de Grafica, Mexico. **Family:** Married 1) Elizabeth Catlett (divorced); 2) Frances White, one son, one daughter. **Career:** Teacher, South Side Community Art Center, Chicago, 1939-40; artist-in-residence, Howard University, Washington, D.C., 1945; teacher, Otis Art Institute, Los Angeles, until 1979. Member, executive board, Black Academy of Arts and Letters, Otis Art Association, National Conference of Artists, Pasadena Society of Artists, National Academy of Design, board of directors, National Center of Afro-American Artists. **Awards:** Art Institute of Chicago Scholarship, 1937; National Scholastic Award, 1937; Julius Rosenwald Foundation Fellowship, 1941-43; Edward B. Alfred Award, 1946; Purchase awards, Atlanta University, 1946, 1951, 1959, 1961; National Institute of Arts and Letters grant, 1952; Atlanta University Award, 1953; John Hay Whitney Fellowship, 1955; Gold Medal, International Show, Germany, 1960, 1965; Purchase Award, Howard University, 1961; Childe Hassam Award, American Academy of Art, 1965; City Council Award, 1968; Adolph and Clara Obrig Prize, 1971 and 1975; Isaac N. Maynard Prize, 1972. Honorary doctorate: Columbia University, 1969. **Online Address:** http://www.artnoir.com. **Died:** 3 October 1979.

Exhibitions:

1938	Paragon Studios, Cincinnati
1939	Howard University, Washington, D.C.
1940	Tanner Art Galleries, Chicago
1941	ACA Gallery, New York
	South Side Community Art Center, Chicago
1943	Institute of Modern Art, Boston
1944	University of Chicago
1949	Roko Gallery, New York
1966	First World Festival of Negro Arts, Dakar, Senegal
1967	Palace of Culture, Warsaw
	Howard University, Washington, D.C.
	Morgan State College, Baltimore, Maryland
1968	Fisk University, Nashville
	University of Dayton, Ohio
	Wright State University, Dayton, Ohio

	Otis Art Institute, Los Angeles
	Kunstnernus Hus, Oslo
	Pushkin Museum, Moscow
	Heritage Gallery, Los Angeles
	Whitney Museum of American Art
	Florida A and M University, Tallahassee
1969	Boston Museum of Fine Arts
	New School of New York
1970	La Jolla Museum of Art, California
	Spelman College, Atlanta, Georgia
1971	Los Angeles County Museum of Art
	Heritage Gallery, Los Angeles
	Whitney Museum of American Art

Collections:

Atlanta University, Georgia; Barnett Aden Gallery, Washington, D.C.; Deutsche Academie der Kunste, Berlin; Dresden Museum of Art; George Cleveland Branch, Chicago Public Library; Howard University, Washington, D.C.; Library of Congress, Washington, D.C.; Los Angeles State University; Metropolitan Museum of Art, New York; Oakland Museum, California; Syracuse University, New York.

Publications:

By WHITE: Book—*Images of Dignity: The Drawings of Charles White,* Ward Ritchie Press, Los Angeles, 1967.

On WHITE: Books—*Portfolio of Six Drawings—The Art of Charles White,* New York, New Century, 1953; *Portfolio 10/Charles White,* Los Angeles, Pro-Artis, 1961; *Three Graphic Artists: Charles White, David Hammons, Timothy Washington* by Joseph E. Young, Los Angeles County Museum, 1971; *Images of Dignity: A Retrospective of the Works of Charles White,* exhibition catalog, New York, Studio Museum in Harlem, 1982. **Articles**—"The Remarkable Draughtsmanship of Charles White" by Janice Lovoos, in *American Artist,* 26, June/July/August 1962, pp. 96-102; "Charles White, Artist" by Hoyt W. Fuller, in *Black World,* 12, July 1963, pp. 40-45; "Images of Dignity: The Drawings of Charles White," in *Black World,* 16, June 1967, pp. 40-48; Charles White: Portrayer of Black Dignity" by Louie Robinson, in *Ebony,* July 1967; "Charles White, Painter of Black Dignity" by Evelyn Wolfe, in *Urban West,* 3, December 1969, pp. 21-23; "Charles White/A Retrospective" by Bert Hammond, in *Black Art Quarterly,* 2, Fall 1977, pp. 18-21; "Charles White in Person" (interview) by Sharon G. Fitzgerald, in *Freedomways,* September 1977, p. 116; "Jubilee for Charlie," in *Ebony,* 35, February 1980, pp. 68-70; "A Charles White Bibliography" by Ernest Kaiser, in *Freedomways,* 20, March 1980, pp. 206-27; "Charles White: Art and Soul," in *Freedomways,* 1980, pp. 133-227; "Charles White," in *A History of African-American Artists, From 1792 to the Present* by Romare Bearden and Harry Henderson, New York, Pantheon Books, 1993, pp. 405-17.

*   *   *

Charles White was foremost a great draftsman and painter of history. He first became known through his volumetric renderings of African American historical figures, who became the main characters of his murals and prints in the 1940s. There were few paintings to historicize the deeds of African Americans on easels or

Charles White: *Head of a Young Girl,* 1960. Photo by Manu Sassoonian; courtesy of the Schomburg Center for Research in Black Culture.

walls before White embarked on mural painting. He had been encouraged by other social realist mural painters, such as Clay Sporin and Robert Millman, themselves influenced by the Mexican muralists, who began painting murals in North America in the 1920s. For them and White, the Mexican muralists presented a valid form of "history painting" that many painters, including African American painters, subsequently emulated. In mural paintings, the narrative form required in history paintings could be realized. In an interview in 1940 with Willard Motley, Charles White stated: "I do know that I want to paint murals of Negro history. That subject has been sadly neglected." He continued, "I am interested in the social, even the propaganda angle in painting."

White's idea of figuration was for it to communicate in a direct way rather than in an abstract way. After his tenure in Mexico, he returned to the United States and printed works at the Workshop for Graphic Art in New York in 1946 and in 1949. Contributing works for these two mass-produced portfolios was in line with his philosophy that art should be accessible to a broad classless society and that it was one of the necessities of life.

White continued to document aspects of African American life through his figurative work. After relocating to southern California due to failing health, he concentrated on drawings and prints. He was unable to continue with mural painting, but the large charcoal and ink wash drawings of solitary figures on paper could have very well stepped out of one of his murals. The themes of the drawings are struggle, courage, and triumph over adversity—the core themes present in his murals. While most figures suggest a marginal exist-

ence, they also suggest hope for the future. White found his medium in charcoal and ink wash. His strong figurative studies show a boldness of design and contemplation. They stand in silence with questioning stares as in *J'Accuse.* Their rounded and volumetric arms reach out into the air as if supported by some unknown force and are often contrasted with a light diaphanous cloth that has the feathery lightness of the wings of a dragonfly. White's earlier figures from the murals and prints of the 1940s protested with stridently animated movements; in the later works, however, their protest is a silent dignity, suggesting that no matter what has been done to them, no matter what hardships they may face, their inner spirit could not be crushed. In these large black-and-white drawings, White has adopted the position that less is more, that he no longer needs a cast of figures to make a statement of position or protest in his work. His work has grown so that the image is more than a representation of an epic hero; now he finds heroism in the common person. His history paintings have given way to psychological vignettes that tell their stories without all of the action of the murals but nonetheless encompass all of the pain and suffering of a people in a single earthbound form or poignant stare.

—Lizzetta LeFalle-Collins

WHITTEN, Jack

American painter

Born: Bessemer, Alabama, 5 December 1939. **Education:** Tuskeegee Institute, Alabama, 1957-59; Southern University, Baton Rouge, Louisiana, 1959-60, Cooper Union for the Advancement of Science and Art, New York, 1960-64. **Career:** Adjunct lecturer, Queens College, New York, 1968-69, Manhattan Community College, New York, 1970-75, Fordham University at Lincoln Center, New York, 1978-83. Since 1971 adjunct professor, Cooper Union for the Advancement of Science and Art, New York. Since 1979, adjunct professor School of Visual Arts, New York. Visiting instructor, Pratt Institute, Brooklyn, New York, 1979-80; visiting artist, Brooklyn College, New York, 1991-92; visiting professor, Hunter College, New York, 1992-93. **Awards:** John Hay Whitney Opportunity Fellowship, 1964; National Endowment for the Arts Fellowship, 1973; Xerox Corporation grant, 1974; New York State Council on the Arts CAPS grant, 1975; Guggenheim Fellowship, 1976; Sambuca Romana Contemporary Art Fellowship, 1984. **Address:** 36 Lispenard Street, New York, New York 10013, U.S.A.

Individual Exhibitions:

1969	Alan Stone Gallery, New York
	Art Gallery, State University of New Art at Stoney Brook, New York (traveling)
1970	Alan Stone Gallery, New York
	American Federation of Arts, New York (traveling)
1971	Museum of Modern Art, New York
1972	Whitney Museum of American Art, New York
	Aldrich Museum of Contemporary Art, Ridgefield, Connecticut (traveling)
	Vassar College Art Gallery, Poughkeepsie, New York
1973	Poindexter Gallery, New York

1974   Pratt Institute Gallery, Brooklyn, New York
       Aldrich Museum of Contemporary Art, Ridgefield, Connecticut
       Soho Center for Visual Arts, New York
       Whitney Museum of American Art, New York
1975   Fine Arts Gallery, New York State University College, Brockport
       Bedford-Stuyvesant Restoration Corporation, Brooklyn, New York
1977   Aldrich Museum of Contemporary Art, Ridgefield, Connecticut
       Metropolitan Museum of Art, New York
       Montclair State College, New Jersey
1978   Robert Miller Gallery, New York
1983   Studio Museum in Harlem, New York
1984   Onyx Art Gallery, New York
1989   G.R. N'Namdi Gallery, Detroit
1990   Cure Gallery, Los Angeles
1992   Horodner Romley Gallery, New York

Selected Group Exhibitions:

1973   Poindexter Gallery, New York
1974   Soho Center for Visual Arts, New York
1977   Metropolitan Museum of Art, New York
1988   Eric Siegeltuch Gallery, New York
1989   California Afro-American Museum, Los Angeles
1990   Museum of Modern Art, New York
1991   Kenkeleba Gallery, New York
       New York Academy of Art, New York
       Brooklyn College Art Gallery, New York
1992   Horodner Romley Gallery, New York

Collections:

Larry Aldrich Museum, Ridgefield, Connecticut; Metropolitan Museum of Art, New York; Museum of Modern Art, New York; Newark Museum, New Jersey; Palm Springs Museum, California; Studio Museum in Harlem, New York; Virginia Commonwealth Museum, Richmond; Wadsworth Atheneum, Hartford, Connecticut.

Publications:

On WHITTEN: Books—*Recent Works by Manuel Hughes, William T. Williams and Jack Whitten* by Robert H. Browning, New York, Alternative Center for International Arts, 1979; *Jack Whitten: New Works,* exhibition catalog, New York, Onyx Art Gallery and David Driskell, 1984; *Jack Whitten: Ten Years 1970-1980,* exhibition catalog, New York, Studio Museum in Harlem and Henry Geldzahler, 1984; *Jack Whitten: Spirit and Matter,* exhibition catalog, New Jersey, The Newark Museum and Beryl Wright, 1990. **Articles**—"Reviews and Previews: Jack Whitten, Exhibition at Stone Gallery" by Natalie Edgar, in *Art News,* February 1965, p. 20; "In the Galleries: Jack Whitten" by Miriam Brumer, in *Arts,* March 1969, p. 64; "Review and Previews: Jack Whitten, Exhibition at Stone Gallery" by Harris Rosenstein, in *News,* April 1970, p. 76; "In the Galleries: Whitten at Allan Stone" by Susan Ryan, in *Arts,* April 1970, p. 66; "It's Not Enough to Say 'Black Is Beautiful'" by F. Bowling, in *Art News,* April 1971, pp. 53-55, 84-85;

"Jack Whitten at the Whitney" by Peter Schjeldahl, in *Art in America,* November 1974, p. 120; "Jack Whitten: Ten Years 1970-1980" by Morgan Lewis, *At Cooper Union,* Winter 1984, pp. 21-22; "Opposing Forces in Jack Whitten's Art" by Will Grant, in *Artspeak,* October 1984; "Tyrone Mitchell/Jack Whitten" by Terry Myers, in *Arts Magazine,* March 1991, p. 84.

*   *   *

In his lengthy career on the New York scene, Jack Whitten has sought and discovered new ways to organize the picture space and to work paint. The result of ceaseless experiment and intellectual curiosity, his canvases are veritable "energy fields" that glow with internal light.

Whitten arrived in New York in 1960 and joined an avant-garde culture that was reckoning with the legacy of abstract expressionism. That group's gestural painting became his adopted mode, and their interest in uncovering one's relationship to the collective unconscious deeply affected Whitten's thinking. Personal identity and experience are themes in his art, and they are translated in his expression regarding the universal and global. *Look Mom, Look, See the Funny People,* a mid-1960s painting, drew its symbolic title from a caption written above a sea of bestial forms. His commentary reflected growing antagonisms in the United States and his dismay extended to the violent conflicts and polarized attitudes that have roiled many societies.

A 1965 series of black-and-white paintings solidified Whitten's commitment to process art. Never exhibited, these canvases were made by screening paint through diaphanous fibers and discovering abstract and yet suggestive imagery once the excess paint had been removed. After the private experiment he continued to manipulate his medium, combing pools of acrylic with Afro-picks, brooms, saw blades, and homemade rakes. Using these tools, which he called his "developers," he alternately spread paint into thin bands of

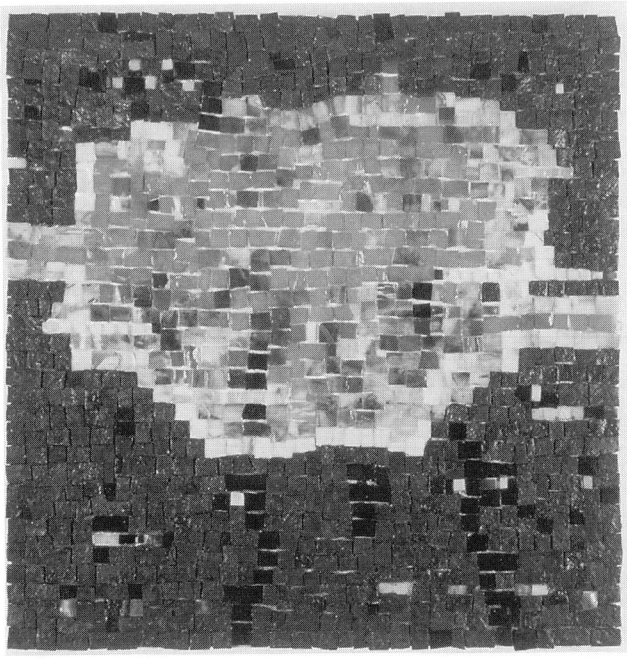

Jack Whitten: *Little Red,* **1993. Photo courtesy of G.R. N'Namdi Gallery.**

color and made incisions in thick buildups of it. The former paintings, among them *Golden Spaces* (1971), evoke the abstract expressionist work of Mark Rothko, while the latter impastoed types generally relate to late modernist preoccupations with surface as a site of optical illusion and plastic presence. Whitten confronted this paradox of space, convinced that it was the key to understanding deep mysteries of time and place. The "Annunciation" series, begun in the late 1970s, *Norman Lewis Triptych* (1983), and *Charkra* (1986) verify his engagement with spiritual and canonical art.

Dissatisfied with the immediacy of fast-drying acrylic, Whitten briefly turned to oils in the 1980s. *Dead Reckoning* (1980) combines a minimalist diagram with the painterly gesture, and this rare oil work helped the artist paint more deliberately and reassert his analytic and conceptual approach. Yet after a 1980 studio fire, acrylic again became his preferred medium. Since then he has poured acrylic into molds, cut it into tiles, and made both mosaiclike paintings and mixed-media collages on canvas. Examples of this unique practice—*28 Black Holes* and the "Amazing Popcorn" series, both made in 1994—incorporate ordinary elements of coffee, tinfoil, and hair. The additions enrich pictorial texture, space, volume, and chromatic character. With a sense of wonderment wedded to his artistry and impeccable craftsmanship, Whitten has found that the very process of art making girds his thinking about the nature of beauty, existence, and knowledge.

—Jacqueline Francis

WILLIAMS, Aubrey

Guyanese painter

Born: Georgetown, Guyana, 1926. **Education:** Studied with Burrowes, a Guyanese painter; studied and traveled extensively in Europe, 1952-54, Saint Martin's College, London, 1952-53. **Career:** Lived for two years with the Warrau, an Amerindian tribe in the Northwest jungle of Guyana while an agronomist for the Guyana Civil Service. Member, Caribbean Artists Movement, 1966. Participated in the Working People's Art Group. **Awards:** Commonwealth Prize for Painting, London, 1964; Golden Arrow of Achievement Award, Guyana, 1970; Real Aula Mallorquesa seu Esquela Miramar, 1979; Cross of Merit of Saint Anthony of the Desert, 1980; Cacique Crown of Honour, Guyana, 1981. **Died:** 1990.

Individual Exhibitions:

1954	Archer Gallery, London
1958	New Vision Center, London
	Ferens Art Gallery, London
	Blanden Art Gallery, England
	Peterborough Museum, England
	Cavendish Gallery, Dublin
	Redcliffe Gallery, England
	Galerie Collette Allendy, Paris
	Portal Gallery, London
1959	Contemporary Art Society, London
1960	A.I.A. Art Gallery, London
	Towner Art Gallery, England
1961	Caravan Gallery, New York
	The Walcheturm, Zurich
1962	Irish Living Art, Dublin
1963	Grabowski Gallery, London
1964	Pater Gallery, Milan, Italy
	Commonwealth Institute, London
1967	Richmond Hill Gallery, London
	Oxford University, England
1968	House of Commons, London
1969	Royal Albert Memorial Museum, Exeter, England
1970	John Peartree Gallery, Kingston, Jamaica
1971	Camden Arts Center, London
1972	Nicholas Treadwell Gallery, London
	Carifesta, Festival of the Creative Arts, Guyana
1974	Olympia International Arts Center, Jamaica
1976	Contemporary Arts Center, Jamaica
1977	Festival of the Arts, Lagos, Nigeria
1981	Commonwealth Institute, London
1984	Royal Festival Hall, London
	October Gallery, London
1985	Goldsmith College, London
	Commonwealth Institute, London
1986	Contemporary Arts Center, Jamaica
1987	October Gallery, London
1989	De Graaf Fine Art, Chicago
	October Gallery, London
1994	Sotheran's Antiquarian Books, London
1995	October Gallery, London

Selected Group Exhibitions:

1960	Museum of Modern Art, San Francisco
1968	Dutch Informal Group, Holland
	Hessenhuis, Antwerp, Belgium
	De Warande, Ghent, Belgium
	Gallery Orex, The Hague, Holland
	Leyden University, Holland
	Gallery Glassin, Kassel, Germany
1970	Contemporary African Painting, Nigeria
1973	XI São Paulo Biennale, Brazil
1989	Hayward Gallery, London

Collections:

Arts Council of Great Britain; Castellani House, Guyana; Elliot College, Kent University; Exeter Museum; National Gallery of Jamaica, Kingston; Guyana House of Assembly; Guyana Museum, Colgrain House; Olympia Art Center, Jamaica; Marlborough House, London; Royal Albert Memorial Museum, Exeter; Rutherford College, Kent University; Saint Catherine's College, Oxford; Sussex University; Tate Gallery, London; University of Warwick; University of the West Indies, Jamaica; University of York; Van Mildert College, Durham University; York Art Museum.

Publications:

On WILLIAMS: Book—*Guyana Dreaming* edited by Anne Walmsley, Dungaroo Press, 1990. **Film**—*The Mark of the Hand*, Arts Council of Great Britain, 1986.

*   *   *

The first thing to strike someone looking for the first time at the work of Aubrey Williams is the explosive vibrancy of color that oozes from his canvases like eruptions of viscous volcanic lava; the second is an overpowering sense of movement and energy, as fire, burning structures, dismembered bones, and pre-Columbian artifacts dance across his paintings. But the soothing warmth of his works is ephemeral. What appears on the surface to be warm, sensuous, and exciting is overshadowed by a darker, more sinister suggestion of violence and destruction. Williams referred to this duality as "tragic excitement." His memories of his Guyanese homeland ravaged by a brutal history were intertwined with a nostalgic reverence for the land of his birth. His vision was, he felt, a South American syndrome. "I'm talking about the thing that I have in my work—the fire in the belly; this anxiety. It's a South American thing. I feel it. . . . It's the smell of old blood. It's the smell of a loss, and a replacement of less than what was destroyed. It's a quality coming out of forced change, a displacement of identity."

If one looks at the work of certain other South American artists, the same violent shape is shared by the Mexican Rufino Tamayo, the Chilean Roberto Matta, and the Cuban Wifredo Lam, all of whose work Williams was exposed to in London during the 1950s and 1960s. Williams' work likewise captures the spirit of the vast South American landscape, delving into the pre-Columbian world of the civilizations of South America—the Mayas, Aztecs, and Incas, and the Guyanese indigenous peoples—the Warrau, Carib, and Arawak Amerindians. But his use of the pre-Columbian goes further than just reviving the myths of forgotten cultures. His vision is an apocalyptic one. In his series "The Olmec-Maya and Now" (1985), he uses the Mayan civilization as an analogy for the destruction of the modern world zooming towards ecological disaster. The ancient books of the Maya warned of impending catastrophe, but these warnings were ignored, and the once populous cities completely vanished within thirty to fifty years. Williams believed he was caught in a modern world impregnated with greed, materialism, and lack of respect for the environment, and he was trying to tell us to look back to history and to learn from our mistakes.

Looking back to these folk traditions and recapturing their beliefs and rituals was not an easy task. Many had not been recorded but instead were gathered from a series of oral traditions. These long-buried memories became distorted over time and merged together; they became, Williams believed, naturally "abstract." It is not surprising, then, that Williams, studying art in London during the mid-1950s, gravitated towards the American abstract expressionist school. "Pollock was our god! All those artists—Kline, Newman, Rothko, de Kooning! They were all great," said Williams, who shared a similar philosophy with many of the artists from that movement. He was an "outsider" in the United Kingdom like many of the abstract expressionists who arrived in the United States in the 1930s, and in his search for a new authentic identity, he retreated from reality through abstraction.

This mythical search for roots was shared in the 1950s and 1960s by some of his British contemporaries, such as Alan Davie, Peter Lanyon, and Roger Hilton, who adopted the language of abstract expressionism as a means to exploring their themes subjectively. But Williams, along with many Afro-Asian artists in Britain, has not had the same international acclaim enjoyed by his white counterparts. Williams' work was revered when he first joined the British art scene. He has been awarded honors and prizes, has hosted nearly fifty one-man shows, and has contributed to nearly as many group shows throughout Europe, America, Africa, and Japan. Yet he has never been truly recognized as part of the mainstream "British" art movement. Until recently there were no representatives of "ethnic" art in Tate Gallery, and if we look at books or accounts of postwar art in Britain, there is scant reference to artists whose origins are outside the United Kingdom. The Tate has now purchased two Williams paintings to hang alongside the works of other British artists of the twentieth century, and a major retrospective of his "Cosmos" series was shown to great acclaim at the October Gallery in 1995. Aubrey Williams has now found himself a place within the boundaries of a British cultural heritage.

—Stephanie Harvie

WILLIAMS, Frank (J.)
American painter and printmaker

Born: Chicago, Illinois, 17 February 1959. **Education:** South Side Community Art Center, Chicago, 1975-78; Saint Edward's University, Austin, Texas, 1978-80; University of Oklahoma, Norman, 1980-84, B.F.A. (painting and drawing) 1984, B.F.A. (printmaking and design) 1984; University of California, Los Angeles, 1985-88, M.F.A. 1988; Skowhegan School of Painting and Sculpture, Maine, 1989. **Family:** Married Rebecca Williams, 1991. **Career:** Laboratory assistant, 1986-88, and teaching assistant, 1986-89, University of California, Los Angeles. Instructor, Santa Monica College, California, 1990-91; teacher, Salesian High School, Los Angeles, 1992-94; chairperson, art department, Salesian High School, Los

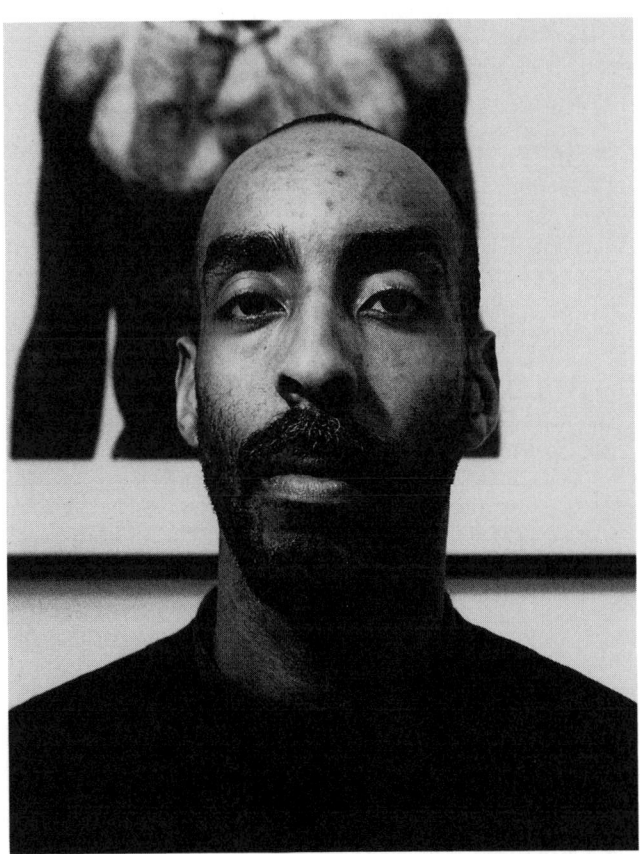

Frank Williams, 1997. Photo courtesy of Rebecca Williams.

Angeles; instructor, California Afro-American Museum, Los Angeles, 1995. Lecturer, Santa Monica College, California, 1989, Los Angeles County Museum of Art, 1990, California Afro-American Museum, Los Angeles, 1995, Crenshaw Christian Center, Los Angeles, 1996. Curator, designer, and preparator for numerous California museums, 1989-95. Museum assistant, Museum of Art, Norman, Oklahoma, 1983-84. **Awards:** Clyde Clark Scholarship, University of Oklahoma, Norman, 1982; Roxie Scott Scholarship, University of Oklahoma, Norman, 1983; Ben Y. Barnett Trust Scholarship, University of Oklahoma, Norman, 1982; Purchase Award, Museum of Art, Norman, Oklahoma, 1983, 1984; Graduate Opportunity Fellowship, Los Angeles, 1985; Art Department Scholarship, Hortense Fisbaugh Memorial Scholarship, and Sydney A. Temple Scholarship, University of California, Los Angeles, all 1988; Skowegan School of Art Fellowship, New York, 1989. **Address:** 1709 Monte Vista Street, Pasadena, California 91106, U.S.A.

Individual Exhibitions:

1989	Santa Monica College Art Gallery, California
1995	California Afro-American Museum, Los Angeles

Selected Group Exhibitions:

1978	South Side Community Art Center, Chicago
1981	Museum of Art, Norman, Oklahoma
1983	Light Well Gallery, University of Oklahoma, Norman
1988	Frank Wight Art Gallery, Los Angeles
1990	Pauline Hirsch Gallery, Los Angeles
	California Afro-American Museum, Los Angeles
1992	Biola University Art Gallery, La Mirada, California
	Alitash Kebede Fine Art, Los Angeles
1994	Korean Cultural Center, Los Angeles
1996	Pasadena Art Space, California

Collections:

Broadway Federal Savings and Loan, Los Angeles; Museum of Art, Norman, Oklahoma; Southern California Gas Company, Los Angeles.

Publications:

On WILLIAMS: Book—*New Expression,* exhibition catalog, California Afro-American Museum and Lizzetta Collins-Lefalle, October 1990, pp. 49-52 (illustrated); *Three Worlds One Art,* exhibition catalog, Biola University Art Gallery and Duncan Simcoe, August 1991 (illustration). **Articles**—"Creative Lives" by Jane Ellison, in *Pasadena Magazine,* Spring 1996, pp. 1, 2, 12, 13; "Enlarging the Cultural Vocabulary" by Susan Geer, in *Los Angeles Times,* September 10, 1990; "Galleries" by Lynell George, in *LA Style,* September, 1990, p. 52 (illustration).

*

Frank Williams comments:

I work in a narrative style of painting and drawing, creating pictures of urban and rural life. I like to paint portraits, landscapes, and things that surround me. I also try to capture a quiet emotion in my art through intense realization of the essence of the scene. My work reflects my experiences on both a conscious and a spiritual level.

Frank Williams: *Meditate, Day and Night,* 1996.

I carefully select fragments from both my past and present experiences. Each situation or character portrayed reveals a human emotion caught in transition. They are "frozen moments" that seem timeless. I try to convey a universal feeling from within me that raises the consciousness of others.

I work in a variety of styles, from silhouette paintings to abstraction. I sometimes combine these styles to help convey an idea. In each painting and drawing, I am searching for a specific emotional response through the interplay of light and shadow.

Light empowers my work. It creates the magic. The interplay of light and mysterious shadows tends to abstract things. Color on the other hand vibrates, making things more descriptive. The light that illuminates the objects in an environment creates a rhythm of pattern and a texture of color. Light comes from various directions and adds intensity, excitement, and drama. In my work light becomes the principal actor, modeling forms, creating a quality of movement, and conveying the mystery and excitement of both the urban and rural environments.

My use of color is essentially symbolic. The highlights of dark and light color in my paintings intensify the emotional impact of my images and heighten the psychological drama. Color expresses a state of mind. It embraces form for its associative value rather than as a direct reference.

I have been influenced by such great historical masters as Rembrandt, Inness, Van Gogh, and Henry O. Tanner. I have also relied on more modern references like Edward Hopper, Charles White, and Jacob Lawrence. These artists have affected my work through good draftsmanship, a sense of space, and their use of color and application of paint. However, what I like most about their work is its spiritual quality. Their art is for the people, it is about the people, and it communicates to the people. As other artists in other times who look back in order to go forward, I also choose to take this path.

*   *   *

Frank Williams's art is more narrative than conceptual. An artist who is capable of using a myriad of artistic styles, Williams often combines various styles in one work, and his drawings and paintings present an intriguing fusion of his academic study of design, graphics, and printmaking and of his broad exploration of both historical and modern masters. Williams's use of light and color remind the viewer of Vermeer, Rembrandt, and Van Gogh, but his subject matter and composition are contemporary. Essentially his works are a culmination of his academic, intellectual, and spiritual experiences.

Williams's decisions about style, medium and its particular application, color, subjects, and light are always deliberately made in order to tell a particular story in a particular way. He uses color, light, and objects as symbols to convey a specific meaning or emotional state. In order to express the paradoxical relationship between nature and civilization, Williams often portrays more than one plane of existence within his canvas. In his pastel drawing *Environment* (1987), Williams depicts what appears to be, at first glance, a nighttime landscape. On closer examination one notices that the drawing appears to be viewed through an opening. There is a brick wall in the background, and there are two doorways in the wall. Beyond the wall are triangular structures—perhaps rooftops. Toward the top of the picture is a diagonal line emerging from the trees, and while the continuation of the line goes off the picture plane, one assumes that the line originated on the other side of the wall and is connected to what could be a light pole located in the foreground. The foliage in the drawing has the depth of carved objects, with deep curving crevices. The use and application of the pastels impart a rich, velvety, and sensual otherworldly quality. The colors are intense—too intense for a nighttime setting.

In *City Life* (1988) Williams juxtaposes the organic with the inorganic, graphic design with figurative and landscape, and light with dark. The left portion of the painting is angular. The viewer peers through a brick wall, and the eyes rest upon a man dressed in sneakers, blue jeans, a blue jacket, and a blue knit cap. Does his choice of clothing reflect the desire to blend in? Light shines down on the figure, illuminating the right side of his face. Is the figure emerging or receding? Behind the figure is a window comprised of several panes. The right side of the painting is curvilinear. Behind several red concentric rings (a target?) is a source of light and what appears to be foliage. The graphic structures in the foreground are bold red, while the organic structures are recessed and enveloped in darkness, their colors subdued.

Rhythm (1988) is a triptych. The center panel is a grouping of tree trunks. The outer panels are figurative—one animate, one inanimate. The left panel is an African mask, while the right is a nude female in fetal position. Both outer panels are edged with hieroglyphic symbols, with the ankh (the ancient Egyptian symbol for life) at the top.

Works of art are a means of communication, and Williams strives to use his creations to describe the spiritual connections and parallels between nature and the urban setting or between the organic and the inorganic. His paintings, whether a landscape, an urban setting, or a figurative, provoke a strong emotional reaction from his viewers.

—Christine Miner Minderovic

WILLIAMS, Michael Kelly
American sculptor and printmaker

Born: American Hospital, Neuilly-Sur-Seine, France, 8 March 1950. **Education:** Michigan State University, East Lansing, 1969-71; Wayne State University, Detroit, 1971-72; University of Michigan, Ann Arbor, 1973-75, B.F.A. in printmaking (cum laude), 1975; University of Chicago, Illinois, 1977-78 (Near Eastern languages and civilizations); Robert Blackburn's Printmaking Workshop, New York, 1979-83; Krishna Reddy's Color Print Atelier, New York University, New York, 1980; Skowhegan School of Painting and Sculpture, Maine, 1988; Brooklyn College, University of New York, 1993-96, M.F.A. in sculpture, 1996. **Career:** Art teacher, Metro Arts Complex, Detroit, 1972, Children's Art Carnival, New York, 1979-84, Printmaking Workshop, New York, 1979-94, Studio in a School Association, New York, 1995-96; art instructor, Pittsburgh Public Schools, 1978-79, Cooper Union for the Advancement of Science and Art, New York, 1996; shop monitor, printer, foreman, and assistant to the director, Printmaking Workshop, New York, 1979-83. Visiting artist, Berkshire School of Contemporary Art, North Adams, Massachusetts, 1991. **Awards:** Grant and residency, Wayne State University and Etruscan Foundation, Santa Lucia di Rosia, Sienna, Italy, 1972; Asilah fellowship and residency, Morocco, 1983; grant, Jerome Foundation, 1984; residency, New York State Council on the Arts, 1984; Print Club Selection award, 1987; residency, Studio Museum in Harlem, 1986; Purchase Award, Ann and Donald W. McPhail Philadelphia Museum, 1987; Skowhegan Fellowship, Skowegan School of Painting and Sculpture, 1988; Artist Equity grant (for attending Fifth International Biennial, Cairo, Egypt), 1994. **Address:** 409 Edgecombe Avenue, Apartment 3i, New York, New York 10032, U.S.A.

Individual Exhibitions:

1978	Paul Robeson Gallery, Detroit
1985	Bronx Museum Satellite Gallery, New York
	Front Room Gallery, Detroit
1986	John Jay College, New York
	Arts Extended Gallery, Detroit
	DeLawrence Maine Gallery, Detroit
1987	Cinque Gallery, New York
1988	June Kelly Gallery, New York
1991	Scarab Club, Detroit
	June Kelly Gallery, New York
1992	Art Extended Gallery, Detroit
1994	Jamaica Art Center, New York

Selected Group Exhibitions:

1991	*Walter O. Evans Collection,* Beach Institute, Savannah, Georgia

1992   *Recent Acquisitions,* Detroit Institute of Arts
        Poetic Utility, Jamaica Art Center, New York
1993   *Public Art in the Bronx,* Lehman Art Gallery, Bronx, New
            York
        Family Ties, Krasdale Foods Gallery, Bronx, New York
        Crossroads, Kingsborough Community College, New
            York
1995   *Art en Route,* Paine Webber Art Gallery, New York
1996   *Group Exhibition,* Eight Floor Gallery, New York
        Form with an Attitude, One Night Stand Gallery, New
            York
        450 Broadway Gallery, New York
1994   *Twenty-Five Years of African-American Art,* Studio Mu-
            seum in Harlem, New York (traveling)

Collections:

Detroit Institute of Arts; Library of Congress, Washington, D.C.;
Museum of Contemporary Art, Asilah, Morocco; Philadelphia
Museum of Art; Studio Museum in Harlem, New York.

Publications:

On WILLIAMS: Articles—"Juss Jazz: Correlations of Painting
and Afro-American Classical Music" by Frieda Jones, in *Guardian*
(New York), 7 December 1983; "From the Studio: Artist-in-Resi-
dence, 1986-1987" by Grace Stanislaus, in 1986-87 catalog, Studio
Museum in Harlem (New York); "Michael Kelly Williams Has a
Gift" by Soho Eye, in *Art World* , 21 December 1988; "Art of the
African World" by Samella Lewis, in *The Black Collegian,* Novem-
ber/December 1990; "Art: African-American" by Samella Lewis, in
Handicraft Studios catalogue (Los Angeles), 1990; "Daughter of
the Dust" by Valerie Boyd, in *American Visions,* February 1991;
"Forms with an Attitude" by Raul Zamudio, in 450 Broadway
Gallery catalogue, 1996.

*   *   *

Black America's pervasive attitudes find expression in Michael
Kelly Williams's abstractions—his meditative responses to the
vibrancy of black urban culture, with an emphasis on music.
Since the 1960s, when he began creating prints and sculptures,
he has defined blackness by forging connections between strong
black images and historical legacies. His monoprints, murals,
and sculptures are collages, combining improvisation, innovation, and traditional African art and folk art forms. His technique of using abstraction simplifies forms, reducing their detail
to overlapping shapes and figures that carry joyful messages of
love, hope, and reverence for our past. His sculptures are imbued with the multiple identities of the found and recycled materials that compose them. Williams's father, who ran a community-based art school in Detroit, greatly inspired his career not
only by encouraging him to be an artist but also by exposing him
to a creative environment. For example, the walls of his father's
studio were a collage, reminiscent of old houses in the South,
where magazines and newsprint served as wallpaper.

Williams graduated in 1975 with a bachelor of fine arts degree in
printmaking and went on to study and teach at Robert Blackburn's
Printmaking Workshop in New York City, the oldest nonprofit
lithography workshop in the United States. Blackburn became
Williams's master teacher and mentor. In the 1970s, Williams found

himself caught up in the surge of interest in folk art. During that
same period, he rejected the revolutionary stance of the black nationalist movement, which identified abstract art as purely a white
form of art. He has worked in a lyrical abstract style ever since.
Williams spent two decades focusing his attention on monoprints,
working by hand, and freely using stencils and color viscosity to
imbue his creations with an element of unpredictability. He has
always found it important to seek out and work with the experts. In
1984 he worked with master printmaker Krishna Reddy, who had
developed with Stanley Hayter the viscosity technique used by
Williams in his monoprints. For Williams, 1984 was a landmark
year. His love of collage, his interest in surface printing, and his
work with Reddy propelled his art to another level. *Around Bout
Midnight* (monoprint, 1984) explores the relationship between man
and music. It has a singing energy suggestive of jazz.

Williams recently returned to sculpture, making it the focus of
his 1996 master of fine arts degree. In his sculptures he has taken
traditional folk art into a modern context, in the process collapsing
perceived differences between "high" art and "low" art in single
works. His favored materials are wood, clay, metal, plastic, and
rubber, each one significant for its previous use. At the top of
Amulet of Light (metal and plastic, 1996), cable wires are woven and
wrapped in a fashion characteristic of basket weaving or quiltmaking.
The metallic elements, charged with power, signify currents of
energy. The plastic elements—including telephone parts, segments
of water hose, and bottle caps—stand for communication. Energy,
currents, communication; these modern-day fascinations have become a way of life. Despite its twentieth-century message, the
overall effect of *Amulet*—a colorful sculpture of varied textures—
recalls traditional Yoruba beadwork of the nineteenth century. Williams feels a familiarity with black culture and uses it boldly in his
prints and sculptures to establish his artistic and cultural fluency.
Through his trans-Atlantic continuum of material culture, we feel
it, too.

—Joanne Harris

WILLIAMS, Pat Ward

American photographer

Born: Philadelphia, 19 March 1948. **Education:** Cheyney State
University, Pennsylvania, B.A. in psychology 1982; Moore College of Art, Philadelphia, B.F.A. 1982; Maryland Institute College
of Art, Baltimore, Maryland, M.F.A. 1987. **Career:** Teacher, Baltimore School for the Arts, Maryland, 1984-87; instructor, Notre
Dame College of Maryland, Baltimore, beginning 1987. Presently
associate professor of art, University of California, Irvine. Artist-
in-residence, Snow Hill Middle School, Maryland, Easton High
School, Maryland, Lake Clifton High School, Baltimore, 1987. Official photographer, North Avenue Centennial Project, 1989. Initiated the photography program, Baltimore School for the Arts.
Awards: Ford Foundation grant, 1985, 1987; Best News Photographer Award, National Newspaper Publishing Association, 1985,
1986; City Arts Individual Artist's grant, Mayor's Advisory Committee for Arts and Culture, Baltimore, Maryland; National Endowment for the Arts Fellowship, 1988; Fulbright Fellowship to
South Africa, 1996-97. **Address:** Downey Museum of Art, 10419
Rives Avenue, Downey, California 90241, U.S.A.

Selected Exhibitions:

Antioch University, Philadelphia; Artquest (1988); Bechtler Gallery, Charlotte, North Carolina; Cameraworks, San Francisco; Forum Gallery, Saint Louis, Missouri; Fox Gallery, Maryland Institute College of Art, Baltimore (1985); Getehouse Gallery, Washington, D.C. (solo, 1987) Hunter College, New York; INTAR Gallery, New York (1986, 1988); Maryland Art Place, Baltimore (1987); Montpelier Cultural Arts Center, Laurel, Maryland (traveling, 1986); Moore College of Art, Philadelphia; Painted Bride Arts Center, Philadelphia; PPOW Gallery, New York; Santa Monica Museum of Art, California (1992-92); *Seventh Annual National Art Exhibit,* Atlanta, Georgia (1986); Smith College, Northhampton, Massachusetts; J.B. Speed Museum, Louisville, Kentucky (1987); Temple University, Philadelphia.

Publications:

On WILLIAMS: Articles—Review (Gormley Gallery, College of Notre Dame of Maryland, Baltimore) by Carol Wood, in *New Art Examiner,* 16, September 1988, p. 51; "An Interview with Pat Ward Williams" by Moira Roth and Portia Cobb, in *Afterimage,* 16, January 1989, pp. 5-7 (illustrated); review (INTAR Gallery, New York) by Eleanor Heatney, in *New Art Examiner,* 16, February 1989, p. 54; "Sigalert: A Project for Artforum," in *Artforum,* 30, October 1991, p. 100 (illustrated); "Pursuit of Power" by Lane Barden, in *Artweek,* 3 September 1992 (illustrated); "Social Sights" by Celeste Connor, in *Artweek,* 25, 5 May 1994, pp. 27-28 (illustrated); "Some Thoughts on African American Representations of Masculinity: A Conversation with Pat Ward Williams, Photographer" (interview) by M. A. Greenstein, in *Artweek,* 26, July 1995, pp. 21-22 (illustrated).

* * *

Twentieth-century African America art is memorable for its powerful social and historical commentary. Such luminaries as Aaron Douglas, Hale Woodruff, Charles White, Elizabeth Catlett, Jacob Lawrence, and many others have used their talents to chronicle the lives and struggles of their people in the face of racist violence and oppression. The civil rights explosions of the 1960s encouraged a younger generation of black artists to intensify this commitment to political art. Adrian Piper, Dana Chandler, Faith Ringgold, David Hammons, Murray DePillars, Joe Overstreet, and several more have added impressively to the burgeoning history of American socially conscious art.

A key contemporary figure in this tradition, Pat Ward Williams is a photoconstructionist, whose dramatic works have blazed new formal and thematic artistic paths. Known especially for her personal responses to the history of her people, she focuses on past events to offer perceptive commentary about African American history, family, and personal life. Above all, her art communicates a vision of the human consequences of American racism and sexism.

Her family promoted a sense of black pride, which has infused her mature artwork. In 1974 she learned photography at the Haystack Mountain School of Crafts in Maine, where she also met and worked with black artists who encouraged her artistic pursuits. Continuing her formal studies at Philadelphia's Moore College of Art, she resolved to augment the African American photographic tradition. Influenced especially by the work of Roy DeCarava, she

has sympathetically documented the lives of her fellow African Americans.

Her 1981 trip to Nigeria magnified her social and historical perspective. Throughout the 1980s she refined her techniques, moving from the single-shot photograph to multiple images combined with textual and sculptural elements. She also discovered the work of Mexican muralist Diego Rivera and was influenced by his fusion of art and politics. Williams saw how she too could use art in the broader struggles against injustice.

Completing her M.F.A. at the Maryland Institute College of Art, she began to integrate photographic images into a larger installation format. Her works reflect her personal experiences as a black woman in an often hostile environment. Her objective is to encourage viewer confrontation with the issues she raises in her artworks.

One of Williams' major themes is the power of memory. Various installations incorporate family snapshots, providing a memorial to the artist's family history, especially to the women whose dignity and strength have been instrumental to black survival in America. Her installations join the personal and political, providing a robust enthusiastic portrayal that counters the widespread media accounts about the disintegration and depravity of the black family.

Pat Ward Williams also draws heavily on African American history to offer even more direct visual political commentary. Her signature artwork, a three-dimensional, freestanding installation entitled *32 hours in a Box . . . Still Counting,* showcases the story of Henry Brown, who in 1856 had himself nailed in a box and shipped from Richmond, Virginia, to Philadelphia. This homage to a famous abolitionist whose dramatic escape from slavery has become legendary enables Williams to personalize larger historical and political issues in her art.

The artist's other major installations in the 1980s and 1990s focus on such themes as lynching and public indifference, police brutality against African Americans, and the questionable exercises of American political and military power throughout the world. These works successfully impel audiences into an active engagement with the art, a deliberate negation of the passivity that often characterizes conventional museum and gallery visits. In the process Williams has emerged as a major postmodern artist, combining new techniques and audience strategies with the long historical tradition of social commentary in African American art.

Williams' Fulbright Award in 1996-97 to spend the year in South Africa enabled her to extend her artistic vision to the past and present struggles in that land. Her documentation of black South African family life complements her earlier visual efforts on similar themes in her own country. Like her distinguished predecessors and contemporaries, she encourages viewers to understand the intensely human dynamics of political struggle, therefore fulfilling the central premise of political art throughout history.

—Paul Von Blum

WILLIAMS, William T(homas)
American painter and printmaker

Born: Cross Creek, North Carolina, 17 July 1942. **Education:** City University of New York/New York City Community College, A.A.S. 1962; Pratt Institute, B.F.A. 1966; Skowhegan School of Painting and Sculpture, 1965; Yale University, M.F.A. 1968. **Fam-**

ily: Married Patricia A. DeWeese, two children. **Career:** Professor/instructor of art, Pratt Institute, 1970, School of Visual Arts, 1970. Since 1971 professor of art, City University of New York, Brooklyn College. **Awards:** National Endowment for the Arts grants, 1965, 1970; faculty research awards, City University of New York, 1973, 1984, 1987; Guggenheim Memorial Foundation Fellowship, 1987. **Address:** City University of New York, Brooklyn College, Brooklyn, New York 11210, U.S.A.

Selected Exhibitions:

1969	Aldrich Museum, Ridgefield, Connecticut
	American Embassy, Moscow
	Museum of Modern Art, New York
	State University at Stonybrook
	Studio Museum in Harlem, New York
	Whitney Museum of American Art, New York
1971	DeMenil Foundation, Houston
	Kolner Konstmarkt, Cologne, Germany
	Reese Palley, New York (solo)
	Rice University, Houston
	Whitney Museum of American Art, New York
1970	Foundation Maeght, St. Paul, France
1972	Indianapolis Museum of Art
	Museum of Modern Art, New York
	Utah Museum of Fine Arts, Salt Lake City
	Whitney Museum of American Art, New York

Collections:

Fisk University, Nashville; Museum of Modern Art, New York; Rice University, Houston; State of New York, Albany Mall; University of Maine; Whitney Museum, New York.

Publications:

On WILLIAMS: Book—*Fourteen Paintings,* exhibition catalog, Montclair [New Jersey] Art Museum, 1991. **Articles**—"Discussion on Black Art-II" by Frank Bowling, in *Arts Magazine,* May 1969; "Problems of Criticism" by Frank Bowling, in *Arts Magazine,* 46(7); "To Black Artists" by Walter Jones, in *Arts Magazine,* April 1970; "652 Broadway" by David Shapiro, in *Art News,* 70, April 1979, pp. 52, 85-86.

*   *   *

From the outset of his successful career, William T. Williams has worked in abstract modes. While he has kept his imagery nonobjective, his paintings, constructions, and prints both communicate the emotional affect of color and reference his meditative states of mind.

His earliest influences arose from the modernist canon: Russian constructivism and suprematism, and the Dutch de Stijl, all early twentieth-century movements concerned with the essential and spiritual qualities of basic forms. He also absorbed Bauhaus theories of ideal composition and design at Yale University, where Josef Albers was a formidable presence. In the late 1960s Williams's acrylic paintings were hard-edge style abstractions, in which flat surfaces were activated by clashing colors and dynamic geometries, such as the diamond and the diagonal. The broadly painted patterns of his canvases provoked critics to compare him to Frank Stella and

William T. Williams: *T.A.,* 1974. Photo by Manu Sassoonian; courtesy of the Schomburg Center for Research in Black Culture.

Al Held, prominent painters of the post-abstract expressionist era, who insisted that art's power was strictly formal and internal rather than referential. Yet for Williams abstraction was a revolutionary manner, inherently capable of reflecting society and its transformations.

Some of Williams's early paintings, though nonrepresentational, did not erase his engagement with the external world. The large pendant pair of 1969, *Elbert Jackson, L.A.M.F., Part II* and *Sophie Jackson, L.A.M.F.,* is named for Williams's relations, whose characters are invoked via chromatic intensity and tensions of intersecting shapes and lines. He also worked in mixed media, integrating his paintings with the stuff of everyday life. This fact situates him in the Western art historical lineage of collagists that includes Henri Matisse and Pablo Picasso and in the popular tradition of interior decoration schemes. *George Washington Carver Crossing the Du Pont River, May 17, 1954* (1970) is a stark construction of two components: one a vee-shaped steel trough, the other a wood board covered with a patterned piece of linoleum. On top of the latter platform stands a simple scaffold from which a bare lightbulb hangs. Devoid of conventional portraiture, the piece summons the inventive capabilities of the scientist Carver, and its spare imagery of the historical plays against the conceptual language of contemporary art.

In the early 1970s Williams increasingly sought to add more personal touches to his work. He abandoned the machine look, so critical to the movements of the previous decade, in favor of the painterly mark and craft signature. The palette of his art changed from high-key colors as he investigated tonal relationships, first in black, white, and gray, then in metallic and iridescent hues. This revision is manifest in the "Equinox" series (c.1973-75). Since then his stated ambition has been to produce art that would appeal to audiences across cultural, national, and racial boundaries. The prints of the "Ellington" series (1976-82), which are graphically translated sketches, illustrate his process of precisely recreating the mental image on paper and canvas. The drawings lay bare his investigation of common symbols and signs, and as a result Williams has emerged as a poised expressionist.

The unified pictorial surfaces of his early career have given way to heterogeneous and textured ones. His inspiration comes in part from African textiles, which he began to study in the late 1960s and observed closely during a visit to Nigeria in 1977. These densely worked canvases were achieved through a layering technique. By adding wet pigment into wet pigment, Williams discovered rich and elemental colors, which he separated into discrete panels and accentuated with rhythmic strokes of the brush and palette knife. No less insistent than his early work, these rugged landscapes are finely attuned to the dramatic energy of the organic world.

—Jacqueline Francis

WILLIAMSON, Philemona

American painter

Born: New York, 1951. **Education:** Bennington College, Vermont, B.A. 1973; New York University, New York, M.F.A. 1979. **Career:** Teacher, Harlem School of the Arts, New York, 1978-83, Metropolitan Museum of Art, New York, 1983, Arts Connection, 1986-89; adjunct faculty, Rhode Island School of Design, 1989-90, Bard College, Annandale-on-Hudson, New York, 1991, Milton Avery Graduate School of the Arts, 1991, Cooper Union, New York, 1991-92, Parsons School of Design, 1991-92. Supervisor of student teachers, School of Visual Art, 1988-89. Since 1989, advisory board member, Getty Center for Education in the Arts. Visiting artist, Norfolk State University, Virginia, 1982, Centre D'Art, Port-Au-Prince, Haiti, 1987, University of North Carolina, Chapel Hill, 1992, Parsons School of Design, 1994; artist-in-residence, Very Special Arts, 1987-88. Served as panelist, National Endowment for the Arts, 1990, Flushing Council on Culture and Arts, New York, 1990, New York State Council on the Arts/Visual Arts, 1994-96. Served as juror, Pennsylvania Council on the Arts, 1992. **Awards:** National Endowment for the Arts Fellowship, 1987-88; Artist Space exhibition grant, 1988; Pollock-Krasner Foundation grant, 1989-90; New York Foundation for the Arts Fellowship, 1991; Arts in Transit Poster commission, Union Square Station, New York, 1992; Ludwig Vogelstein grant, New York, 1993-94. **Address:** c/o June Kelly Gallery, 591 Broadway, New York, New York 10012, U.S.A.

Individual Exhibitions:

1988   Queens Museum of Art, New York
1989   Wenger Gallery, Los Angeles

1990   Southampton College Gallery, New York
        June Kelly Gallery, New York
1991   African American Museum, Hempstead, New York
1992   Powers Art Gallery, East Stroudsburg University, Pennsylvania
        New Paintings, June Kelly Gallery, New York
1993   Pennsylvania State University, University Park
        Inaugural Exhibition, Flushing Council on Culture and Arts, New York
1994   Hypo-Bank, New York
1995   June Kelly Gallery, New York

Selected Group Exhibitions:

1986   Nohra Haime Gallery, New York
1988   *Artist in the Marketplace,* Bronx Museum of the Arts, New York
        Bernice Steinbaum Gallery, New York
1991   Pepsico Gallery, Purchase, New York
        Mint Museum of Art, Charlotte, North Carolina
1992   Fine Arts Gallery, University of Wisconsin, Milwaukee
1993   *Child's Play,* Art in General, New York
1994   *IV Internacional de Pintura,* Cuenca, Ecuador (traveling)
1996   Kingborough Community College Art Gallery, Brooklyn, New York
        Bearing Witness: Contemporary Works by African American Women Artists, Spelman College Museum of Fine Art, Atlanta (traveling)

Collections:

Mint Museum of Art, Charlotte, North Carolina; Reader's Digest, Pleasantville, New York.

Publications:

On WILLIAMSON: Articles—"Whimsical Art of Philemona Williamson" by Marlena Donohue, in *Christian Science Monitor,* 81(224), October 16, 1989; "Philemona Williamson: Through the Looking Glass," in *The International Review of African American Art,* 9(2), October 1990; "Review/Art: Philemona Williamson" by Michael Brenson, in *The New York Times,* 2 November, 1990; "Review/Art: Philemona Williamson" by Peggy Cyphers, in *Arts Magazine,* January 1991; "Philemona Williamson at June Kelly" by Carl Little, in *Art in America,* March 1991; "Philemona Williamson, June Kelly Gallery" by Adam McGovern, in *Cover Magazine,* February 1991; "Philemona Williamson: Painting at the Juncture of Past and Future" by Helen Shannon, in *American Visions,* April/May 1993; "Paintings by Philemona Williamson," in *The Gettysburg Review,* Spring 1994.

*   *   *

Traditionally children and adolescents are portrayed sentimentally in art, with an emphasis on their physical beauty and innocence. Philemona Williamson casts aside such a honeyed approach to portray children in a way that evokes memories of the explorations and discoveries of childhood in activities such as crawling under a table. While unsentimental, her paintings are not without sentiment. Through memory, with all its real and fantasied events, Williamson has opened a new pathway for the provocative portrayal of the experiences of growing up. Her paintings tell stories but do not illustrate them. They provoke questions, not answers. They have already won her a place of distinction among contemporary artists.

Growing up as an artist when abstract expressionism was dominant in the United States and when hard-edge, pop art, color-field, and a handful of other movements stuttered into existence, Williamson went her own way. One of her most difficult decisions was whether figures would be part of her paintings. After some seesawing deliberations, she decided that figures were part of her life and had to be in the paintings. As an African American, she also had to decide what bearing race might play in her work. Because she grew up in an unusual multiracial household, her paintings often have a multiracial character.

What Williamson captures is the innocence and enthusiasm of children, their freedom from stereotypes, and their encounters with evil, combined with the wisdom of adulthood. Her paintings often confront the viewer with a puzzle or mystery. Something is going on in each painting. The question is *what,* and the answer is *there is no one answer.*

The children in her paintings appear in an undefinable, dreamlike world. They may soar through the air a la Chagall or crawl among unusual objects spilled helter-skelter. Their poses are unusual, not due to distortion by the artist's brush but due to their difficult anatomical poses. These poses add to the provocative and individual character of the work. There is no mistaking a Philemona Williamson painting. She has established a strong identity that defies categorization.

Williamson's own childhood is the source of her work, although her paintings are not autobiographical. Instead, her memories are the springboard for the issues, conflicts, and anxieties of children and adolescents. She grew up in the New York home of a wealthy Greek family. Though her parents worked as domestics in the home, they were not treated as subservient. Nor was Philemona. The family had two daughters who were her playmates, and Williamson remembers with great clarity their playing together and their discoveries and fears. She was considered by everyone in the family to be the brightest. Sometimes she used the servants' entrance, sometimes the front door. It made no difference. Her father drove her to school in the family limousine.

Only when she reached junior high school did she become acutely aware of social and racial restrictions—and how greatly her family situation differed from that of other African Americans. She also had to deal with the fact that her father had begun a scary ten-year bout with cancer. These experiences tended to separate and individualize Philemona Williamson and account for her strong presence.

Contact with two capable professional women artists, Joan Thorne and May Stevens, in junior high school helped her decide to become an artist. She liked their attitude toward themselves and their feeling of caring about what they were doing, plus the fact that they accepted her and her ideas. Although years of training followed at the New York High School of Music and Art, Bennington College, and New York University's M.F.A. program, they were merely a means of helping Williamson express what she remembered and valued and how these memories and values had been tempered by her life as an adult and mother.

In *Single Foot Pirouette* (1944) an outgrown toy horse is in the foreground. One child soars upward, abandoning a childhood garment, while the other, also abandoning a garment, apprehensively and awkwardly balances on one foot. Does the awkward balancing

of one child while the other flies through the air represent the state of race relations in America for adolescents? What do you think?

Many of Williamson's paintings imaginatively reflect our interracial shuffling. Not all focus on childhood. One concerns the desperate seagoing risks of Haitian "boat people." Having lived briefly in Haiti, she knew the terrible problems Haitians sought to escape, problems that drove them into the open sea in flimsy boats—only to be turned back by the U. S. government. Another painting, burning with red, deals with the anxieties created in children by the televised Gulf War. Could it happen here, to us?

—Harry Henderson

WILSON, Ed(ward N., Jr.)
American sculptor

Born: Baltimore, Maryland, 28 March 1925. **Education:** University of Iowa, Iowa City, 1946-51, B.A., M.A.; University of North Carolina, 1961. **Military Service:** United States Air Force, 1943-46: private first class. **Family:** Divorced; two children. **Career:** Chairman and vice-chairman, Department of Art, North Carolina College (now North Carolina Central University), Durham, 1953-64, State University of New York at Binghamton, 1968-72, 1974-77, 1982-85. Artist-in-residence, Yaddo, 1966, Western Michigan University, 1969. Traveled in Italy, 1975-76. **Awards:** Carnegie

Ed Wilson: *Medgar Wiley Evers, 1925-1963* (work in progress), 1990.

Foundation grant, 1952-53; Maryland Artists Annual Prize for Portraiture, Baltimore Museum of Art, 1956; research grants, North Carolina College, 1956, 1957, 1958, 1960, 1961, 1962; State University of New York Fellowship, 1966, 1968. **Died:** 26 November 1996.

Individual Exhibitions:

1966   State University of New York at Binghamton
1970   Harlem School of the Arts, New York

Selected Group Exhibitions:

1951   University of Iowa, Iowa City
1959   Chapel Hill Art Gallery, North Carolina
1961   Howard University, Washington, D.C.
1966   University of California at Davis
1969   Rhode Island School of Design, Providence
        San Francisco Museum of Art
1970   New Jersey State Museum, Trenton
1979   Huntsville, Museum of Art, Alabama
1982   Studio faculty exhibitions, State University of New York,
        Binghamton (through 1991)
1986   Kenkeleba Gallery, New York

Collections:

Howard University, Washington, D.C.; San Francisco Museum of Modern Art; State University of New York.

Publication:

By WILSON: Article—"CAA and Negro Colleges," in *Art Journal,* XXVIII(2), Winter 1969, p. 228.

*

Ed N. Wilson comments:

I am an older African American sculptor (seventy-one), and I harbor a resentment of my having been "assigned" an invisible existence by the majority segment of this republic for the majority of my life.

My sense of aesthetics has been formed mainly by jazz and black literature, both disciplines having been shaped by the black experience as it has responded to oppression, racism, invisibility, and all those ingenious nuances of intellectual, physical, psychological, social, political, and economic violence made so continuous and certain by the majority of the republic.

My strength to make sculpture for forty-five years (to date) without a developed existence of a body of critical literature on the black visual artist (until very recently) comes from the spiritual re-energizing that is derived mainly from other black artists' work (African and American), black literature, black history, black poetry, and dance. There is a profound sense of humanism contained in these works that provides, for me, an identity, a spiritual focus, sustenance, and will to productively counter the otherwise dehumanizing impact of the republic at large.

Fortunately social invisibility (and all that that means) does not cripple the mind, the spirit, and expression of one who rejects the

majority's concepts of omnipotent intolerance and social acceptance and, in so doing, becomes the one who visualizes and brings alive the silent memory of all those African and African Americans gone.

*   *   *

Ed Wilson's philosophy of humanism has shaped his art, the role of which is to make people aware of their spiritual and perceptive natures. He was raised in a totally segregated environment in Baltimore, Maryland, and his early experiences were affected by a repressive system that methodically worked to subvert the creative potential of African Americans and to limit their humanity. The years between 1949 and 1960 were particularly trying because he experienced a "psychic split," a condition of rebelliousness that drove him into direct confrontation with the racist structures of power. Wilson credits the influence of Ralph Ellison's and James Baldwin's writings with giving him a strong and balanced sense of direction. Political activism helped, too. Working with the Congress of Racial Equality (CORE) provided a constructive avenue for initiating social change in the South. From 1958 to 1964 Wilson actively participated in the civil rights protests in the Durham-Chapel Hill area of North Carolina.

In 1964 Wilson moved to Binghamton, New York, to head the art and art history department at the State University of New York. While there he executed a number of major sculpture commissions for public spaces. These include the *J.S. Bassett Memorial Bust* (1965, bronze) for Duke University; the granite and bronze sculpture in *JFK Memorial and Park* (1969) for the city of Binghamton; *Second Genesis* (1969-71, aluminum) for Lake Clifton School, Baltimore; *Falling Man* (1973, bronze) for Binghamton University; and the bronze bas-relief composition of *Jazz Musicians* (1982-84) for the city of Baltimore. From 1974 on, Wilson executed commissioned bronze portraits of influential African Americans, namely Ralph Ellison (1974-75), Whitney Young, Jr. (1983-84, 1989), and Medgar Evers (1989-90).

Wilson's artistic sensibility tends toward abstraction. He prefers to interpret human issues through his own experiences in a nonliteral, nondocumentary mode as does jazz music. The *Board of Directors* (1969) is one such work that reflects this creative ideal. Wilson created the *Board of Directors* in a style closely reminiscent of the sculptural forms of *Falling Man*. The work is a highly polished bronze sculpture mounted on a highly polished reflective chrome base. Begun in 1968 after the death of Martin Luther King, Jr., the idea for the sculpture emerged from a study of the political, social, cultural, and economic relationship of Harlem to the rest of New York City, especially areas such as Greenwich Village and Manhattan. Two perplexing questions dominated Wilson's thoughts while he lived in Harlem to observe the effects of King's assassination. What is the central mechanism by which a sharply divided city of "haves and have-nots" is created? And how could an important segment of New Yorkers take vicarious pride in showing off Harlem to their out-of-town friends as the best slum in the world?

Wilson's answer to the questions was the *Board of Directors*. The work is a satirical statement on any organized group of people, such as city councils, legislative bodies, corporate bodies, or museum boards, that makes repressive decisions that significantly impact the quality of other people's lives. Taking a swipe at both the pomposity of such boards and the crassness of their decisions, Wilson created ten amorphous bronze figures huddled around a table in conspiratorial discussion. The figures are stripped of all

Ed Wilson: *Up from Slavery,* 1995-96.

particularizing human characteristics and of their human essences as well. The chrome-plated box to which the figures are attached and the chrome-plated base to which the box is attached reveals the shallowness of the board by exposing all aspects of the figures in its reflections. Specially selected by the 1993-94 United States Academic Decathlon (a national competition program for high school students) in its sparse art and artist review category that includes artists like Michelangelo and Pablo Picasso, the *Board of Directors* captures the complex, nuanced way Wilson presents his humanistic goals.

The *Seven Seals of Silence* (1969) are seven highly textured bronze plaques that are part of the memorial sculpture to John F. Kennedy. They are located at a triangular traffic island at J.F.K. Memorial Park in Binghamton. Commissioned by the city of Binghamton in 1966 and completed in 1969, the granite monument is ten feet high. It is basically a *trylon,* with three partial cubes projecting from each side. The seven bas-relief bronze seals are embedded in the vertical surfaces of seven cubes, with a quote and biographical data on Kennedy on the remaining two cube surfaces. The walks and seating in the memorial park were specially designed by Wilson to give the viewer a constantly changing elevation as he or she moves about the island and looks at the sculpture.

Middle Passage at New Boys High in Brooklyn is another of Wilson's significant works. Completed in 1977, two years after its commencement, *Middle Passage* is a bronze and concrete assemblage of three concave-shaped columns that measure ten by eight feet each. The spaces between the columns create narrow passageways through which students walk daily. The width of the passageways precisely parallels the narrow space between the deck floors, where captives were contained in the Atlantic crossing of slave ships. Bronze bas-reliefs, embedded at eye level in the concave columns, depict the horrors of the ships in which the ancestors of some students were brought across the Atlantic. The sculpture also resonates at the physical level, creating an atmosphere of containment and compression in a claustrophobic hollow. Wilson's objective here is to jog people's memories: "Young African Americans and a lot of other older people have no sense of the experience of slavery [and of the crossing]. I wish to be their memory. I want to preserve the memory of all that inhumanity related to Africans and also African Americans."

—Nkiru Nzegwu

WILSON, Ellis

American painter

Born: Mayfield, Kentucky, 30 April 1899. **Education:** Art Institute of Chicago; Kentucky State College, Frankfurt. **Career:** Cafeteria worker, YMCA, Chicago, c.1925; assistant, interior decorator, c.1925; messenger, sporting goods store, Wall Street brokerage house, New York, c.1928-33; artist, Works Progress Administration, c.1933; worker, aircraft engine factory, New York, c.1940. **Awards:** George E. Hoe Prize; Charles S. Peterson Prize (for African poster); Guggenheim Memorial Foundation Fellowship, 1944; award, Terry Art Institute National Competition, c.1953. **Died:** 1 January 1977.

Exhibitions:

African Art Center, New York; Albany Museum, New York; American Negro Exposition, Chicago (1940); Atlanta University, Georgia; Barnet-Aden Gallery, Washington, D.C. (1949); City College of New York (1967); Contemporary Arts Gallery, New York (1948, 1951); Detroit Museum; Dillard University, New Orleans; Fisk University, Nashville (retrospective, 1971); G Place Gallery, Washington, D.C.; Graves County Library, Mayfield, Kentucky (1949); Harmon Foundation; Howard University, Washington, D.C.; McMillen Galleries, New York (1941); 135th Street Branch, New York Public Library; James A. Porter Gallery (1970); Roko Gallery, New York (1949); Augusta Savage Studios (1939); Washington Square Exhibit (1939).

Collections:

Aaron Douglas Collection, Amistad Research Center, Tulane University, New Orleans; Clark-Atlanta University; Georgia; Howard University Gallery of Art, Washington, D.C.; National Museum of American Art.

Publications:

On **WILSON: Book**—*Paintings by Ellis Wilson, Ceramics and Sculpture by William E. Artis,* exhibition catalog, Nashville, Carl

Van Vechten Gallery of Fine Arts and David C. Driskell, 1971. **Articles**—"Mayfield Sees Its Artist's Work" by Harry Bolser, in *Louisville Courier-Journal*, 30 April 1947; *Art News*, 50, April 1951, p. 48; "Ellis Wilson," in *A History of African-American Artists, from 1792 to the Present* by Romare Bearden and Harry Henderson, Pantheon Books, New York, 1993, pp. 337-44.

*   *   *

Ellis Wilson, who was from a small town in Kentucky, went to Chicago as a young man after World War I. There he met the illustrator and artist Charles Dawson, as well as other African American artists. He studied commercial art at the Art Institute of Chicago and became aware of the work of artists like Jacob Lawrence, Aaron Douglas, and Horace Pippin, all of whom were to have profound influences upon his work.

Wilson painted in two styles, both reflecting his interest in the silhouette. His more familiar style, as in *Field Workers*, stemmed from his attraction to the way Lawrence and Douglas silhouetted their black forms, reducing them to basic angular shapes. After studying El Greco at the Art Institute, it was in New York City that Wilson gained an understanding of the elongation techniques that Douglas employed in his compositions. Studying Douglas helped Wilson develop an elongation of form that he then applied to his work. This helped release him from the academic techniques of the academy and set him on the road to developing his own style. The second major stylistic influence derived from Pippin, in whom Wilson found an appreciation for the basic day-to-day activities of black people.

Wilson sought to paint images of blacks in the South. With a Guggenheim fellowship he was able to return to his hometown in Kentucky to paint familiar scenes in which he had an emotional investment. He also traveled to Charleston, South Carolina, to paint black people in the markets there, for, with their straight, upright bodies and carrying bundles on their heads, they seemed to Wilson to be closer to Africans. He also was attracted to their poise and dignity.

The paintings that best embodied Wilson's silhouette style of representation and African forms were those he painted in Haiti. He first traveled there in 1950 with the Haitian artist and cabinetmaker Milo Pierre Antoine. Wilson said that he found the Haitian people "good-looking, very black, with small features and bones." These physical traits would characterize his figurative style for the rest of his career. *Haitian Funeral Procession* (1950s) is a composition composed of two horizontal bands of mourners as they proceed to the grave site. A zigzag tension is created by the processional, the group in the foreground moving toward the right while the group in the background proceeds to the left of the composition, suggesting a long line of mourners winding up a hilly path. This same horizontal movement through pictorial space is evident in *To Market* (c.1954), in which all of the people wear light-colored clothing that makes a striking contrast against their black skin. Their legs and bare feet create a sense of angular shuffling along a dusty path. The work *Lobster and Man* (1950s) is an example of Wilson's humor. A large figure of a kneeling man confronts a lobster of almost equal size. They spar in the sand, and as the man attempts to capture the lobster, it fights back.

Although Wilson lived most of his adult life in New York, his early paintings were centered on life in the South, especially portrayals of people who he felt were closely related to their African heritage. He later traveled to Charleston and then to Haiti to come closer to his African heritage and to arrive at an Africanness in his work.

—Lizzetta LeFalle-Collins

WILSON, Fred
American sculptor and installation artist

Born: Bronx, New York, 1954. **Education:** State University of New York, Purchase, B.F.A. 1976. **Career:** Served on the board of directors, Artists Space, 1988-92, National Association of Artist Organizations, 1988-92. Since 1994 boardmember, Artists/Homeless Collaborative. Since 1995 boardmember, Sculpture Center, New York. Since 1995 member of the board of governors, Skowhegan School of Painting and Sculpture. Panelist, Visual Arts Program, National Endowment for the Arts, 1989-91, InterArts Program, National Endowment for the Arts, 1989-91. **Awards:** New York Foundation for the Arts fellowships, 1987, 1991; New York State Council on the Arts Award, 1990; National Endowment for the Arts Award, 1990; commission, Percent for Art Program, Department of Cultural Affairs, 1991; commission, Riverside South Public Art, New York, 1992; National Endowment for the Arts Fellowship, 1994; Artist and the Community Award, Winston-Salem Foundation, Rockefeller Foundation and North Carolina Arts Council, 1995; New Jersey Transit and New Jersey Council on the Arts Award, 1995. **Agent:** Metro Pictures, 150 Greene Street, New York, New York 10012, U.S.A.

Individual Exhibitions:

1988	Public Art Fund, New York
1990	*The Other Museum,* White Columns, New York
1991	Metro Pictures, New York
	Washington Project for the Arts, Washington, D.C.
	Gracie Mansion Gallery, New York
1992	Biennial, Cairo, Egypt
	Metro Pictures, New York
	Contemporary and Maryland Historical Society, Baltimore
1993	Seattle Art Museum
	Indianapolis Museum of Art
	Beaver College Art Gallery, Glenside, Pennsylvania
	Capp Street Project, San Francisco
1994	Museum of Contemporary Art, Chicago
	"Insight: In Site: In Sight: Incite—Memory," Artist and the Community: Fred Wilson, Southeastern Center for Contemporary Art, Winston-Salem, North Carolina
1995	Metro Pictures, New York
1996	Beaver College Art Gallery, Glenside, Pennsylvania
	Rice University Art Gallery, Houston

Selected Group Exhibitions:

1981	A.I.R. Gallery, New York
1985	Kenkeleba Gallery, New York
1987	55 Mercer Gallery, New York
1990	Clocktower Gallery, New York

1993   Whitney Museum of American Art, New York
        Museum of Modern Art, New York
        Studio Museum in Harlem, New York
1996   The Drawing Center, New York
        Institute of Contemporary Art, Boston
        Museum of Art, Fort Lauderdale, Florida

Collections:

Baltimore Museum of Art, Maryland; Denver Art Museum; Kresge Art Museum, Michigan State University; New School for Social Research, New York; Seattle Art Museum.

Publications:

On WILSON: Articles— "Fred Wilson: White Columns" by Lois E. Nesbitt, in *Artforum*, October 1990, p. 172; "Fred Wilson: Metro Pictures" by Michael Kimmelman, in *New York Times*, 22 March 1991, p. C19; "Fred Wilson at Gracie Mansion and Metro Pictures" by Debra Bricker Balken, in *Art in America*, July 1991, pp. 113-14; "The Ghosts in the Museum: Artist Fred Wilson Mines History" by Als Hilton, in *The Village Voice*, 22 September 1992, p. 41; "Fred Wilson - Maryland Historical Society" by Sarah Tanguy, in *Sculpture*, September/October 1992; "Canon Fodder: Fred Wilson at the Seattle Art Museum" by Ron Carlowen, in *Artweek*, 8 April 1993; "Artist Finds IMA's Soul" by Nan Hoffman, in *Indianapolis News*, 21 January 1993, p. F15; "Mining Exhibit Shatters Records, Opens Eyes at Historical Society" by John Dodsey, in *Baltimore Sun*, 1993, p. 1D; "Fred Wilson: Mixed Metaphors at S.A.M." by Robert Mittenthal, in *Reflex*, January/February 1993, pp. 14-15; "Fred Wilson First in MCA's Op-Ed Series," in *Flash Art International*, 27(177), Summer 1994; "Interviews with Sherrie Levine, Louise Lawler, and Fred Wilson" in *October*, 70, pp. 109-12; "Making up Museums: Revisionism and Fred Wilson" by Reesa Greenberg, in *Parachute*, 76, October/November/December 1994; "Artist and the Community: Fred Wilson" by Linda Johnson Dougherty, in *Art Papers* (Georgia), 19(1), January/February 1995, p. 36; "Remembering Old Salem" (interview) by Curtia James, in *Art Papers* (Georgia), July/August 1995, pp. 28-31; "Interview: Race Matters" by Howard Halle, in *Time Out New York*, 6 December 1995, p. 85; "Fred Wilson: Mining the Memory" by Tony Whitfield, in *Sphere*, Spring 1996, pp. 17-18; "Fred Wilson" by T. J. Demos, in *New Art Examiner*, March 1996, pp. 42-43.

*   *   *

Fred Wilson's entrée into the New York art scene began when the conceptualist movement was in full swing. His aesthetic sensibilities and sociopolitical agenda, however, extend beyond the parameters of mere process. It is evident that Wilson is as much concerned with product, content, and audience as with instruments of intellectual systems. For him what is important is the ability to create paradigms in which the meaning is the message.

Wilson's early experiments involved site-specific outdoor installations. His "Platform" series consisted of horizontal structures bearing portraits of luminaries such as Pope John Paul II, Paul Gauguin, and John James Audobon. Through representational and symbolic modes, Wilson exposed vital political and sociological agendas evident in the lives and philosophies of his subjects. The pivotal work *No Noa Noa, Portrait of a History of Tahiti* (1987) was designed to evoke the travesties of imperialism, the dissolution of indigenous cultures, and the Western tendency to exoticize such people. Intent on creating works outside European-based ideologies, in the "Platform" series Wilson began to introduce cross-cultural references.

Wilson's horizontal constructions, intended to be viewed from above to symbolize a reverence for the earth, were inspired in part by the Native American practice of creating monumental mounds of earth as sacred spaces. One major influence was the Serpent Mound in Adams County, Ohio. By superimposing paintings on his platforms, Wilson also referred to the ancient earth drawings of great expanse from the Peruvian Nazca desert. Accompanying the portraits were objects related to the lives and concerns of the subjects. Contemplation of these works fostered speculation on issues beyond the historical and required delving into controversial sociopolitical areas.

Wilson's altar works were transitional, marking a turning point in his development. His sculptural portrait of Gauguin, for example, transcended a preoccupation with the portrayal of the individual and moved into broader investigations of cultural histories, ethics, and race. The type of employment Wilson pursued to maintain himself as a young artist—as a museum guard, curator, and arts educator—merged with his interest in history, philosophy, sociology, and anthropology to lead to work with museum collections. His life experiences and interests eventually led him to present art objects in a fashion opposed to Western traditions.

The opportunity to curate the exhibition *Rooms with a View: The Struggle between Culture, Content and the Context of Art* served as a stimulus for the formulation of these new directions in Wilson's work. His approach was to create separate spaces, with each room parodying a particular era of design practice. The artists remained nameless in the museum-style installation, the salon room was structured to connote status and wealth, and the contemporary space conveyed a modernist aesthetic. The exhibition marked a break with the construction of the individual object. From this point on he became more interested in history and began to carve a niche for himself as a promoter of museology from a multicultural perspective.

Regarding museums as imperialistic relics, Wilson reconstructs and recontextualizes their aesthetic and political agendas. His modus operandi is to present views that extend beyond Eurocentric paradigms. He is distrustful of the museum's basis, which is heavily laden with imperialistic overtones indicating how historical artifacts and art objects are to be characterized. Wilson uses the museum environment to expose the deletion of information in the construction of false historical narratives. He challenges the way in which museums misrepresent indigenous art forms from the Americas and elsewhere and misconstrue the context of contemporary art. He redefines the role of the artist by appropriating, reusing, and combining things that already exist, creating for the viewer an enriched field of interpretation and meaning.

In 1993 Wilson was invited by the Contemporary Museum to work with any museum in Baltimore having a permanent collection. He chose the Maryland Historical Society, based on the fact that it lacked presentations reflecting the contributions of blacks and Native Americans and thus misrepresented history. In his tour de force exhibition *Mining the Museum*, Wilson reconfigured major installations to reexamine Maryland's history. He rummaged through archives, excavating artifacts never displayed and discovering holdings unknown to the museum staff. He integrated displays of Early American and European artifacts with museum items identified with African Americans of the same period. Iron slave shackles were mounted along with embossed silver containers, giving voice to those traditionally excluded from the museum's displays. Objects from Liberia in the museum's holdings were also installed. It was not commonly known that the Maryland Historical Society had been affiliated with the Colonization Society, a national organization responsible for the establishment of a colony in Liberia for the return of freed slaves. Thus, Wilson reconstructed a history previously hidden or allowed to remain dormant.

The presence of the Native American was also addressed in *Mining the Museum,* as were the relationships of African Americans to white inhabitants. These dynamics were explored and examined through a multiplicity of devices—juxtaposing images, objects, and sound with text, labels, and signage—that challenged museum-style classifications. Wilson restored obscure identities and the historical presence of groups once portrayed in the shadow. *Mining the Museum* not only fulfilled the mission of the Contemporary Museum but also openly confronted issues of race.

Art that challenges mainstream values is still an arena of debate. Even within the current body of museum-based works by artists who resist the standardized canon of museology, however, few attempt to wage battle with institutionalized racism.

—A. M. Weaver

WILSON, John
American sculptor, painter, and printmaker

Born: Boston, 14 April 1922. **Education:** School of the Museum of Fine Arts, 1939-45, diploma (with highest honors); Tufts University, Medford, Massachusetts, 1947, B.S. in education; Fernand Leger's School, Paris, 1949; Institute Politecnico, Mexico City, Esmeralda School of Art, Mexico City, 1952; Escuela de las Artes del Libro, Mexico City, 1952-55. **Career:** Since 1965 professor of art, Boston University. Instructor/teacher, Boris Mirski School of Modern Art, Boston, 1945-47, School of the Museum of Fine Arts, Boston, 1950, Pratt Institute Evening School New York, 1958, New York City Board of Education, 1959-64. **Awards:** Popular Prize, Annual Pepsi-Cola Exhibit, 1945; James William Paige Fellowship (for study in Europe), School of the Museum of Fine Arts, Boston, 1946; John Hay Whitney Fellowship (for study in Mexico), 1950-51; International Institute of Educational Exchange Student Fellowship (for study in Mexico); best lithograph, Silvermine Guild, 1956; Purchase Prize, Hunterdon Art Center Annual Exhibit, 1958; Merit Citation, Society of Illustrators, 1964; Best Cover Design, International Federation of Periodicals Press, Paris, 1964; Massachusetts Arts and Humanities Foundation Fellowship, 1976; Purchase Award, American Academy and Institute of Arts and Letters,

John Wilson, 1983.

1979; winner, Dr. Martin Luther King, Jr. Monument Competition, Buffalo Arts Commission, 1982; winner, Roxbury Community College monument competition, 1985; winner, Dr. Martin Luther King, Jr. memorial statue competition, U.S. Capitol, Washington, D.C., 1985; Artists Foundation Fellowship, 1986; American Academy and Institute of Arts and Letters Purchase Prize, 1995. **Address:** 44 Harris Street, Brookline, Massachusetts 02146, U.S.A.

Individual Exhibitions:

1967	Joseph Gropper Gallery, Cambridge, Massachusetts
1970	School of the Museum of Fine Arts, Boston
1971	American International College, Springfield, Massachusetts
1983	Art Space, New York (retrospective)
1987	Museum of the National Center of Afro-American Artists, Boston
1990	Tufts University, Medford, Massachusetts

Selected Group Exhibitions:

1992	Newark Museum, Newark, New Jersey
	Boston Public Library
1993	Fuller Museum of Art, Brockton, Massachusetts
	Institute of Contemporary Art, Boston
1994	Boston Museum of Fine Arts
1995	Amherst College, Massachusetts
	University of Vermont, Burlington
	American Academy of Art and Letters, New York
	Mead Art Museum, Amherst College, Massachusetts

Collections:

Atlanta University; Bezalel Museum, Jerusalem; Boston Public Library; Boston University; Brooklyn Museum, New York; Carnegei Institute, Pittsburgh, Pennsylvania; City of Boston; City of Buffalo, New York; Department of Fine Arts, French government; Fitchburg Art Museum, Massachusetts; Florence Heller School of Social Work, Brandeis University, Waltham, Massachusetts; Gibbes Museum of Art, Charleston, South Carolina; Howard University, Washington, D.C.; Morgan State University, Baltimore, Maryland; Mugar Library Collections, Boston University; Museum of fine Arts, Boston; Museum of Modern Art, New York; Museum of the National Center of Afro-American Artists, Boston; Rose Art Museum, Brandeis University, Waltham, Massachusetts; Smith College Museum of Art, Northampton, Massachusetts; Tufts University, Medford, Massachusetts; University of Vermont, Burlington, Vermont.

Publications:

On WILSON: Articles—"Reality is Not a Fad" by Alicia Faxon, in *Boston Sunday Globe,* 5 September 1971; "John Wilson, A Painter Turned Sculptor" by Lori Calabro, in *Bostonia Magazine* (Boston), 59(4), July/August 1985; "John Wilson," in *Art, New England,* February 1988; "Interview with Sculptor John Wilson," in *Reunion,* 3(2), December 1994, both by Edward Strickland; "Dialogue; John Wilson/Joseph Norman" by Sandy Coleman, in *Boston Globe,* 16 July 1995.

*   *   *

During the mid-1940s John Wilson began to discover works by African American artists and was further stimulated by Alain Locke's treaties on art. These two things encouraged him to visually document the consequences of oppression and to offer a means to resisting it or exposing the vile social conditions that caused it. After reading Richard Wright's *Uncle Tom's Children,* he was ready to produce pieces that would have an impact on a social and economic revolution led by black Americans.

Looking for a tangible visual form, Wilson considered mural painting. While at the Boston Museum School he applied for a fellowship to travel to Mexico to study with muralists, but at the time the fellowships were approved only for Paris. He had not yet "discovered" the work of other African American artists but thought the Mexicans were doing in Mexico what he wanted to do in the United States. He revered Jose Clemente Orozco's work and philosophy and read everything that he could about him. He was impressed by the theatricality and starkness in Orozco's paintings and murals and was "inspired by his sense of profound compassion for the oppressed Indians and peasants of Mexico. Orozco's work seemed less driven by a didactic political ideology than the work of David Alfaro Siqueiros and Diego Rivera." Wilson was not to go to Mexico yet. First he landed in Paris, where he studied painting with Ferdinand Leger.

Back in the United States in 1950, he applied for and received a Whitney fellowship to study in Mexico, where he remained until 1956, supplementing his income as a graphic artist. In Mexico he studied fresco painting and responded again to the conditions of poverty and despair. In the 1940s he created a series of ink and wash drawings on the themes of lynching and oppression. The "Incident" series (1946) chronicled the reality of a black man being captured and lynched by a mob of white men. Wilson says that his black-and-white and ink drawings and prints were done in a period when he was very angry with the unequal treatment of blacks in the United States. *Deliver Us From Evil* (1943), a study for a mural, attempted to bring some understanding to what life was like for black people in America. *The Trial* (1952), which was done in Mexico, attacked the notion of white supremacy, a philosophy that he says attempts to dehumanize all black people and uses the technique of lynching to destroy black men in particular. The falseness of racism to disguise one's humanism, Wilson says, is exhibited in this composition because both judge and jury wear white masks.

Wilson has subsequently created sculptural pieces that do not possess the hard-edge realism of his early works. These later works are more rounded in their quiet lyricism and represent a sense of hope rather than despair. In the 1930s and 1940s he was driven by a personal sense of living in a society that dehumanized him, when racism was blatantly clear and the only references to black people were negative stereotypical images in movies and other popular arts. These images were at odds with life in his black community.

Wilson is also attracted to the timeless, deeply human qualities of Asian and Egyptian art, specifically Buddhist figures that suggest for him a kind of universal consciousness. He says that African sculpture, like Asian sculpture, possesses a colorful and intense energy that is summed up in a simple head or figure. These figures contain a complex kind of truth. For example, Wilson says that "Baule masks and figures hold a deep black density, a built in vitality, a life force that imbues the statue with power, like a bomb which is a simple shape, but has explosive power." Power comes from an intangible inner force and seems to emanate from the statues. His earlier drawings such as *Angry Man* had this density, but

John Wilson: *Eternal Presence*, 1987.

later the two-dimensional works weren't enough for him, and he began to explore three-dimensional pieces. *Eternal Presence or Monumental Head* (1987), a seven-foot head of a black person that can be interpreted as male or female, was cast in bronze and placed at the Elma Lewis Center for the Arts in Boston. Wilson chose bronze because he wanted the head to last "forever." Another work, *Father and Child* (1990), also seven feet high, shows a seated man and child reading a book and is installed at Roxbury Community College. This piece was inspired by a print that Wilson completed in the 1960s entitled *Father and Child Reading*. Wilson conceives many of his sculptures from his prints, continuing his signature of dark, dense shapes.

—Lizzetta LeFalle-Collins

WINSLOW, Vernon

American painter and illustrator

Born: Dayton, Ohio, 1911. **Career:** Director of the art department, Dillard University, New Orleans. **Awards:** Second Purchase Award, Atlanta University, Georgia, 1944. **Died.**

Selected Exhibitions:

1941	South Side Community Art Center, Chicago
1942	Atlanta University, Georgia
1943	Fort Huachuca, Arizona
	Atlanta University, Georgia
1944	Atlanta University, Georgia
1945	Albany Institute of History and Art, New York

Collection:

Atlanta University.

Publications:

By WINSLOW: Articles—"Making the Negroes' Art Practicable," in *Opportunity,* 18, September 1940, pp. 262-63, 277-78; "Negro Art and the Depression," in *Opportunity,* 19, February 1941, pp. 40-42, 62-63; "The Negro Artist and Modern Art," in *The Negro in Music and Art* edited by Lindsay Patterson, Publishers Company, New York, 1969.

On WINSLOW: Book—*Exhibition of Book Illustrations by Jacob Lawrence, Charles Sebree, Vernon Winslow,* Chicago, 1941. **Article**—"Fort Huachuca, Arizona Art Show," in *Art Digest,* 1 August 1943.

*   *   *

Vernon Winslow is possibly better known for his philosophical contributions than for his art. In his writings he addressed the plight of the African American artist during the Great Depression and promoted the essential interdependence of arts and industry. As an educator he emphasized the commercial arts as a means of building and supporting autonomy in the African American com-

munity. Much of Winslow's writing reflects ideas similar to those of other leading African American thinkers of the early twentieth century.

In 1938, while a faculty member at Tennessee State College, he was commissioned to illustrate a primer for African American schoolchildren living in the rural South. In the illustrations he used light as a pictorial element to fuse two or more areas or objects. In the watercolor *The Mailman,* for example, Winslow used every area in the picture plane to refer to some aspect of a country setting. In the central, middle ground is a vehicle and driver passing mail to a young boy standing beside two mail boxes along the edge of the road. The illustrations demonstrate his technical proficiency as a painter and his mastery of color and design. Affirming his abilities as an artist is the fact that he received a purchase award in one of the annual Atlanta University exhibitions curated by Hale Woodruff during the mid-1940s.

While living in Chicago, Winslow served as an arts instructor in the federal government's Works Progress Administration program. In 1943 his designs were accepted by the Harmony Musical Instrument Company of Chicago, an affiliate of Sears, Roebuck and Company, to adorn the faces of ukuleles for distribution among U.S. servicemen. These successes and other ventures demonstrated his interest in and dedication to the importance of commercial crafts.

Winslow referred to weaving, pottery, carving, and leather work and metalwork as rural crafts. In larger urban communities he emphasized the interface of arts and industry through vocational trades such as printing, show-card writing, typesetting, wood turning, and photography. He supported Alain Locke's position that handicrafts are an essential basis for starting the artistic education of individuals within communities. Winslow also believed that artistic development usually begins with and runs parallel to economic development, and he saw a connection between general poverty within the African American community and the lack of sufficient vocational training.

During his tenure as an art instructor at Dillard University, Winslow encouraged his students to learn to use a variety of media. He was proficient in printmaking, sculpture, and painting and placed great emphasis upon color technology. As a teacher and chairman at Dillard, he was well acquainted with many artists of the Harlem Renaissance, including Richmond Barthé, and often invited them to the university as visiting artists.

During Winslow's career of twenty-two years he established himself as a leading figure in promoting commercial art as a means of building African American economic independence. The visual and written legacy left by Winslow is a record of his sensitivity to African American life in the rural South.

—Regina Holden Jennings

WOODARD, Beulah (Ecton)

American sculptor and painter

Born: Near Frankfort, Ohio, 11 November 1895. **Education:** Los Angeles Art School; Otis Art Institute; University of Southern California, Los Angeles. **Family:** Married Brady E. Woodard. **Awards:** First Prize for sculpture, *Third All-City Art Festival,* Los Angeles, 1953. **Died:** 13 July 1955.

Individual Exhibitions:

1935   Los Angeles County Museum (solo)
        Office of *California News,* Los Angeles
1965   Municipal Museum, Munich, Germany

Publication:

On WOODARD: Article—"Art Should Inspire Us Says Woman Artist of Los Angeles," in *California News,* 22 February 1935.

*   *   *

Beulah Woodard sought realism in her sculptures and concentrated mainly on busts, which recall the work of August Savage and Richmond Barthé. Her bronze *Bad Boy* (1936) is markedly similar to Savage's *Gamin* (c.1930), yet the poignancy achieved by Savage escaped Woodard's almost comic characterization. Her works have a static solidity about them, never achieving the kinetic energy or drama that characterizes Barthé's engaging, elegantly sculpted figures with elongated limbs and rotating hips, such as *Blackberry Woman* (1932) and *Wetta* (c.1934). Like Barthé, however, she was interested in visually referencing an African heritage for African Americans.

She promoted a consciousness of an African heritage with *Fulah Kunda* (African Man) (c.1935) and *African Woman* (c.1935) and followed stereotypical characterizations of African Americans with *Maudelle* (c.1936) and *Bad Boy.* One of her most important achievements was a group of nineteen African masks, which possessed great detail and were based on studious research. These sculptures were a direct result of her interest in ethnology. She once declared that "In the so-called 'primitive' African there is much of which Negroes today should be proud. I am recording types as rapidly as I can. They are at once interesting, picturesque, dramatic and colorful."

Woodard was after a definitive racial identity in her work. Her purpose was to instill pride in being black for those black people who were to view it and to promote the race to nonblacks. Realism, therefore, was a main element in her work. With ethnological zeal she attempted to be true to what she believed were phenotypical characteristics of black people. Like other artists, Woodard also did studies of masks; however, her approach to mask making was scholarly. She studied ancient and modern methods of mask making, as well as African tribes and customs. Memorizing photographs of Africans from books, she sculpted lifelike masks with varied headdresses and realistic details. She was concerned that her masks be used as a teaching tool that stressed the people of Africa rather than a faraway continent. She exhibited them in American museums and schools so that students could gain a more intimate knowledge of the people of this continent.

Her approach to sculpture was direct, foregoing preliminary models or drawings. Recognizability of the form seemed to be her driving force. There were no experiments with abstraction, nor did truth to materials and their inherent properties affect her quest for reality. She was more educator than artist in her constant attempts to make black people aware and proud of their African heritage.

Her first public exhibition was in an office window in 1935. This was followed by exhibitions in libraries and, finally, a solo exhibition at the Los Angeles County Museum in the fall of the same year. She was the first African American artist to be invited to exhibit at the museum. The exhibition was covered in all the metropolitan newspapers, where Woodard was lauded for the "exact anthropological detail of her primitive African masks."

Woodard's focus was on educating through her art, which became self-limiting and prevented her from creative explorations of materials and expanding her themes. Because of her early death, we cannot say if she, like others who became mature artists, might have delimited herself and explored more abstract forms.

—Lizzetta LeFalle-Collins

WOODRUFF, Hale (Aspacio)
American painter, printmaker, and muralist

Born: Cairo, Illinois, 26 August 1900. **Education:** John Herron Art Institute, Indianapolis, Indiana, c.1918; Fogg Art Museum, Cambridge, Massachusetts; Academie Scandinavia, Paris; Academie Moderne, Paris. Studied with Henry Ossawa Tanner in Paris. Worked on frescoes with Diego Rivera in Mexico, 1936. **Family:** Married Theresa A. Barker, one son. **Career:** Professor, Atlanta University, 1931-45; art instructor, New York University, 1947-68; professor emeritus, New York University, 1968-70. Initiated annual art shows for Black artists, Atlanta University, Georgia, 1941. Traveled in Europe, Africa, and Mexico. **Awards:** Second and third awards, Diamond Jubilee Exposition, Chicago; first prize, High Museum, Atlanta, Georgia; Bronze Medal, Harmon Foundation, 1926; Rosenwald Fellowship, 1943-45; Purchase Prize, Atlanta University, 1951; Great Teacher Award, New York University, 1966. Honorary doctorate: Morgan State College, Baltimore, 1968. **Died:** September 1980.

Individual Exhibitions:

Eastern Michigan State Teachers College, Ypsilanti; Hampton Institute, Virginia; International Print Society, New York; Kansas City Art Institute; Bertha Schaefer Gallery, New York; State Museum of North Carolina, Raleigh; Studio Museum in Harlem, New York (1976); Tuskegee Institute, Alabama; University of Michigan, Ann Arbor; University of North Carolina, Chapel Hill; University of North Carolina, Greensboro; University of Southern Illinois, Carbondale.

Selected Group Exhibitions:

1958   Bertha Schaefer Gallery, New York
1967   City College of New York
        Howard University, Washington, D.C.
        Museum of Fine Arts, Boston
        San Diego Art Museum
        Los Angeles County Museum of Art
        New York University
1971   Newark Museum, Newark, New Jersey
1976   Los Angeles County Museum of Art (traveling)
1985   Bellevue Art Museum and the Art Museum Association
        of America (traveling)

Collections:

Newark Museum, Newark, New Jersey; IBM Corporation, New York; Atlanta University, Georgia; Howard University, Washing-

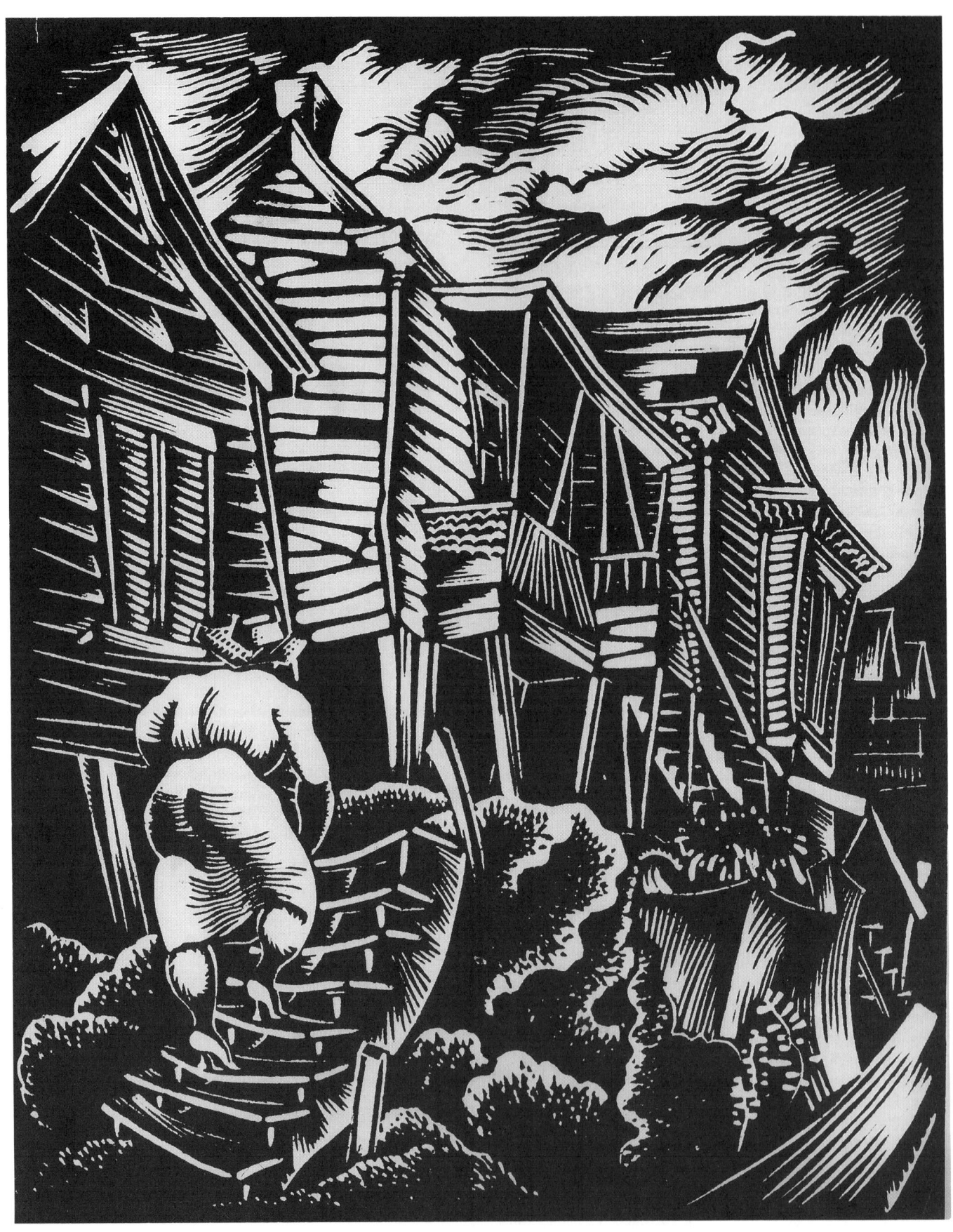

Hale Woodruff: *Returning Home.* **Photo by Manu Sassoonian; courtesy of the Schomburg Center for Research in Black Culture.**

ton, D.C.; Spelman College, Atlanta, Georgia; New York University; Lincoln University, Lincoln University, Pennsylvania; Harmon Foundation, Talladega College, Alabama; Texas Southern University, Houston; Johnson Publishing, Chicago.

Publications:

By WOODRUFF: Article—"My Meeting with Henry O. Tanner," in *Crisis,* 77, January 1970, pp. 6-12.

On WOODRUFF: Articles—"Frontpiece," in *Opportunity,* 8, February 1930, p. 38; "Survey of the Month—Art," in *Opportunity,* 9, October 1931, p. 320; "Hale Woodruff" by Alain Locke, in *American Magazine of Art,* January 1934; "Hale Woodruff" by Ralph McGill, in *Atlanta Constitution* (Georgia), December 1935; "Hale Woodruff" by Ralph M. Pearson, in *Forum Magazine,* June 1940; "American Negro Review in New York Show," in *Art Digest,* 15 December 1941; "Negro Art Scores without Double Standards" by Ben Wolf, in *Art Digest,* 1 February 1945; "Six Paintings of City Life," in *Arts Quarterly,* December 1939, pp. 13-19; "Why Spiral" by Jeanne Siegel, in *Art News,* 65, September 1966, p. 48; "Five Black Artists" by Charles Giuliano, in *Boston After Dark,* 4 March 1970; "Hale A. Woodruff," in *A History of African American Artists, from 1792 to the Present* by Romare Bearden and Harry Henderson, Pantheon Books, New York, 1993, pp. 200-215; "Reexamining Hale Woodruff's Talladega College and Atlanta University Murals" by M. Akua McDaniel, in *International Review of African American Art,* 12(4), 1995, pp. 4-17.

*   *   *

During most of his adult life Hale Woodruff wore two hats. He was a successful artist whose body of work spanned more than fifty years, and he was a teacher whose methods and manner became an exemplar for art departments at black colleges and universities throughout the South. The dual roles Woodruff played during his lifetime had an impact on his productivity as an artist. He lamented the fact that he seldom had time to paint, yet after he retired from New York University, he continued to teach part-time. Teaching was evidently a source of satisfaction in his life.

While Woodruff struggled to reconcile the artist-teacher combination, over the years he remained an artist committed to a never ending search for an aesthetic framework, synthesized from both African and African American elements, that black artists could pursue. He often spoke of Pablo Picasso's *Guernica* (1937), how it expressed the horrors of war while being connected to the Spanish heritage established by Francisco de Goya and how Picasso had transcended the local to make something universal. As he sought converts among his students, Woodruff told this story frequently and with a kind of missionary zeal.

A book on African sculpture that Woodruff received as a gift when he was quite young stimulated his interest in the subject. His study of how the African artist orchestrated formal elements to produce majestic sculptures had a pervasive influence on his work. Perhaps it was in African sculpture that he saw the factors he could use to begin to define the framework that was so much a part of his creative passion. Even in the early landscapes of the 1930s and 1940s, his brush strokes imitated the marks of a chisel, as if he were sculpting the forms out of a thick board. The pronounced brush strokes add both solidity and energy to these works.

Hale Woodruff: *Encounter II.* Photo by Dawoud Bey; courtesy of the Schomburg Center for Research in Black Culture.

Woodruff's apprenticeship with the Mexican muralist Diego Rivera seems to have helped him synthesize many of the disparate elements suggested in his earlier works. The series of "Amistad Mutiny" murals, completed at Talladega College in 1939, showed that Woodruff could do thorough research and use it to tell a powerful story. But it was in the Atlanta University murals of 1950 that Woodruff was most successful in synthesizing African sculptural elements. His brush strokes are magnified, reminiscent of earlier sculptural treatments in his work, and the images move freely among various shapes. Although most forms are recognizable, there is a pervasive sense of the abstract. The works are not windows the viewer looks through; rather, their energy dances on the surface or shimmers back and forth in a shallow depth. Edges protrude and recede to create a pulsating rhythm that seems to echo the murals of Aaron Douglas at Fisk University, yet Woodruff's works build upon them.

In the body of abstract work that Woodruff did when he went to New York University in the late 1940s he continued his African connections. His "Celestial Gates" series drew from Dogon relief sculpture and Ashanti gold weights, but he reduced the images to strange primordial-like symbols. For Woodruff the images seemed to suggest passageways to a higher existence.

Woodruff's artistic journey reflected his passion for doing the necessary research, for experimentation, and for maintaining the quality of the art form. As a teacher Woodruff understood that his students needed to study the local sources that nurtured the black experience. But as an artist he recognized that his role, and the role of those he taught, was to sort out these experiences and to create from them artworks that possessed the transcendental quality to make them universal. In this sense Woodruff, perhaps unknowingly, reconciled his role as both artist and teacher. This is the legacy that lives on in all those he taught.

—Leo Twiggs

WOODSON, Shirley

American painter

Work also appeared under the names Shirley Reid and Shirley Woodson Reid. **Born:** Pulaski, Tennessee, 3 March 1936. **Education:** Wayne State University, Detroit, Michigan, 1955-58, B.F.A. 1958; School of Art Institute of Chicago, 1960; Wayne State University, Detroit, 1960-64, M.A. 1965. **Family:** Married Edsel Reid in 1967, two sons. **Career:** Art educator, Detroit Public Schools, Michigan, 1958-65; art instructor, Highland Park Community College, 1966-78; art educator, Highland Park Schools, Michigan, 1978-92; visiting professor, Eastern Michigan University, Ypsilanti, 1988-89. Since 1992 supervisor, art education, Detroit Public Schools. Since 1995 adjunct professor, Wayne State University, Detroit. **Awards:** MacDowell Colony Fellowship, 1966; Artistic Excellence Award, National Conference of Artists, 1977; Outstanding Contribution to Visual Arts Award, Michigan Women's Foundation, 1988; Arts Achievement Award, Wayne State University, Detroit, 1995; Creative Artist Award grants, Michigan Council of Arts, 1984 and 1987; artists grant, Detroit Council for Arts, 1987. **Agents:** Barbara Wallace, 544 West Queen Lane, Philadelphia, Pennsylvania 19144, U.S.A.; Sherry Washington, 1274 Library, Detroit, Michigan 48226, U.S.A.; Darice Wright, 230 West Superior, Chicago, Illinois 60612, U.S.A.. **Address:** 5656 Oakman Boulevard, Detroit, Michigan 48204, U.S.A.

Individual Exhibitions:

1988	Impressions Five Museum, Lansing, Michigan
1989	Flint Gallery, University of Michigan, Flint
1992	Jacobson's Home Store, Dearborn, Michigan
	Sherry Washington Gallery, Detroit
	CAAS Gallery, University of Michigan, Ann Arbor
1995	Wayne State University, Detroit
	Thoughts, Dreams, Visions, Satori Fine Art, Chicago
	Detroit Artists Market
1996	*Recent Paintings,* Parish Gallery, Washington, D.C.
	Sherry Washington Gallery, Detroit

Selected Group Exhibitions:

1968	*Childe Hassam Foundation Purchase Exhibition,* Academy of Arts and Letters, New York
1977	National Museum, Lagos Nigeria
1981	*Forever Free: Art by African American Women 1862-1980,* Illinois State University, Normal
1987	Detroit Institute of Arts
1990	Art in General, New York
1991	Beach Institute/King Tisdell Museum, Savannah, Georgia
1993	*I Remember . . . Thirty Years After the March on Washington: Images of The Civil Rights Movement, 1963-1993,* Corcoran Gallery of Art, Washington, D.C.

1994	National Arts Club, New York
	National Conference of Artists Gallery, Detroit
	Firehouse Art Center, Philadelphia

Collections:

Museum of African American History, Detroit; Museum of National Center of Afro-American Art, Boston; Studio Museum in Harlem, New York; Wayne State University, Detroit; White House, Washington, D.C.; Your Heritage House Museum, Detroit.

Publications:

By WOODSON: Articles—"History of Black Art in Michigan," in *City Magazine,* March 1987; "Middle Passage: Matrix and Memory, The Art of Richard Hunt," in *Walter O'Evans Collection of African American Art* (Georgia), King Tisdell Cottage Museum, 1991.

On WOODSON: Books—*New Initiatives: Five Michigan Artists,* exhibition catalog, Michigan Council For the Arts, 1989; *Coast to Coast: Women of Color,* exhibition catalog, Virginia, Flossie Martin Gallery, 1990. *The Art of Black American Women: Works of Twenty-Four Artists of the Twentieth Century* by Robert Henkes, McFarland and Company, North Carolina, 1993. **Articles**—"Black Artists—Interview Shirley Woodson/Alvin Loving" by Ruth Rattner, in *Detroit Tribune,* April 1968; "Art: Woodson—Randall" by Joy Hankanson, in *Detroit News,* April 1969; "Painter and Poet Team for Gallery Exhibit" by Joy Hankanson, in *Michigan Chronicle,* April 1969; "Analysis/New Works By Shirley Woodson" by Charles Finger, in *Automobile Club of Michigan* magazine, October 1982; "Profile of an Artist" by Lula Charleston, in *City Magazine* (Michigan), November 1986; "Portfolio: Shirley Woodson" by Anthony Murphy, in *American Visions Magazine,* August/September 1992; "Open Letters and Other Collages by Shirley Woodson" by Bamidele Demerson, in *National Conference of Artists, Michigan Chapter* (Michigan), 24 February 1992; "Self-Contained Works Become Bios in Boxes" by Catherine Fox, in *Atlanta Journal,* 29 July 1994; "Work Depicts African American Family" by Marsha Miro, in *The Detroit Free Press,* 12 February 1995, p. 4G; "Filament, Wanting, Memory: Woodson's World of Kinship" by Bamidele Demerson, in *Detroit Artists Market Journal of Exhibitions,* 8(1), September 1995; "Artist Uses Bright Colors, Faceless Figures as Hallmark" by Rhonda Bater-Rudd, in *The Detroit News,* 3 April 1996.

*

Shirley Woodson comments:

My current paintings explore iconography arrived at over the last fifteen years. In these works figurative elements have moved from scenic member to central theme. These paintings underscore my desire to have color approximate sound. Music is an essential participant in my palette and directs the interplay of images and color. The figurative environment of landscape, seascape, and interior are composed to intensify the relationship between the work and the viewer. My icons have evolved as water, wave, cloud, mountain, tree, pyramid, star, horse, flower, hand, fish, shield, boat, farmhouse, family, mirror and faceless bather. These images are developed in my paintings, drawings, collages, graphics, boxworks and fabric designs.

*   *   *

A hidden intellectualism marks the work of the abstract expressionist artist Shirley Woodson, whose narrative paintings, drawings, collages, and assemblages are at once fresh, complex, and energetic. Since the 1950s, when she began her career, her work has moved from the figurative to the abstract and then back to elements of realism. Combining figurative painting with abstractionism has allowed her to incorporate African history, spiritual journeys across time and distance, and varied artistic techniques into her work.

More critical to Woodson's recent development, however, was a trip home to Pulaski, Tennessee, in 1991, to the farmhouse her family still occupies. Adept at looking over her shoulder and carrying the viewer with her into her people's history, Woodson has begun casting her view over her own past. The series "Ancestors Known" is a direct response to the Tennessee trip. It consists of boxes covered with images from old family photos and carrying inside them relics significant to her ancestry. The boxes, or box works as the artist calls them, are a format that helps her deal honestly with her past.

Exuberant colors, decisive brush strokes, energetic movement, human figures, and sheer joy continue to characterize Woodson's work, but the stories she has begun telling are more intimate—possibly even more engaging—because of their personal force. The painting *Portrait with Red Cloud* (1992), for example, is a penetrating but affectionate glimpse of a young woman deep in thought. The viewer does not know what is on the woman's mind, but the erratic scribbles surrounding her head, the white chalk on her face and upper lip, and the blues and greens converge to create an introspective, perhaps even tense, moment. The bursts of color define shapes that seem at war with one another, but they also define a structure, reflecting a controlled improvisation Woodson nurtured in the 1980s, that is fundamental to the energy—sometimes anxious, sometimes excited, sometimes quiet—she projects.

Woodson used the 1980s to blend the influences in her past: her travels throughout Europe, her studies of Africa through research and collecting art and artifacts from the continent, her 1960s exploration of music through portraits of singers and musicians, and her 1970s experimentation with color contrasts and emphasis on shadows and reflection. What she achieved during the 1980s has elicited comparisons to Paul Gauguin's Tahiti paintings for their striking colors, graceful movement, and mysterious figures that blend harmoniously into the backgrounds.

The painting *Within* (1982) is an image of a threesome barely discernible from their abstract background. It represents Woodson's 1980s experimentation in oil and acrylic, an improvisational technique allowing her to change her mind while putting preconceived ideas on canvas. The more the viewer looks at her paintings, the more her sense of resonance and magnetism defies description.

Woodson conceived *Flight into Egypt II* (1982) during the same period as *Within,* and it became a precursor to her ambitious series "Shield of the Nile" (1984-89), which has been labeled a pilgrimage of renewal, or Woodson's journey home. Here the Nile River stands for purity and revitalization. Woodson's fascination with water stems from its necessity as a basic element of life and from the challenge of capturing its refractive qualities. Other symbols present in the "Nile" series are the camel (perseverance), the serpent (wisdom), the fish (prosperity), and the bird (freedom).

Woodson has always worked in series, which for her are ongoing. (*Flight into Egypt III* was created as recently as 1995.) "Once they're in, they're in," she says. The "Shield of the Nile" series has begun to turn into the "Niagara" series, however, a response to Woodson's 1995 family reunion at Niagara Falls, and her most recent series of

Shirley Woodson: *Red Pool, Blue Waves,* **1992. Photo courtesy of Bill Sanders.**

collages, "The Woven Landscapes," is an abstract exploration of the fabric of life.

Woodson has steadily honed her craftsmanship, enabling her to create panoramic views of cultural heritage that explode with feeling so strong that they thunder into thoughtful silence. Her paintings are her prose, her collages are her poetry, her drawings are her dialogue, and her box works are her essays.

—Joanne Harris

YARDE, Richard

American painter

Born: Massachusetts, 29 October 1939. **Education:** Boston University, Massachusetts, 1958-62, B.F.A. 1962; Boston University, Massachusetts, 1962-64, M.F.A. 1964. **Family:** Married Susan Donovan in 1967, two sons. **Career:** Assistant professor, Boston University, Massachusetts, 1965-71; associate professor, Wellesley College, Massachusetts, 1971-76; professor, University of Massachusetts, Boston, 1981-90. Since 1990 professor, University of Massachusetts, Amherst. Visiting artist, Amherst College, Massachusetts, 1976-77, Massachusetts College of Art, Boston, 1977-79, Mount Holyoke College, South Hadley, Massachusetts, 1980-81. **Awards:** National Endowment for the Arts grant, 1976; Childe Hassam Purchase prizes, American Academy of Arts and Letters, New York, 1977, 1982; Henry W. Ranger Fund Purchase Prize, National Academy of Design, New York, 1979; Adolph and Clara

Richard Yarde, 1992. Photo courtesy of Stephen Long.

Obrig Prize, National Academy of Design, New York, 1983; Massachusetts Artist Fellowship, Boston, 1985; William P. and Gertrude Schweitzer Prize, National Academy of Design, New York, 1987; Certificate of Merit, National Academy of Design, New York, 1995; Academy Award in Art, American Academy of Arts and Letters, New York, 1995. **Agent:** June Kelly, June Kelly Gallery, 591 Broadway, Third Floor, New York, New York 10012, U.S.A.

Individual Exhibitions:

1970	Carl Siembab Gallery, Boston
1972	Thayer Academy, Braintree, Massachusetts
1974	The Gallery, Boston
1975	Wellesley College Museum, Wellesley, Massachusetts
1976	Studio Museum in Harlem, New York
	Museum of the National Center for Afro-American Artists, Boston
1977	University of Connecticut, Storrs
1978	Smith College Museum of Art, Northampton, Massachusetts
1979	Williams College Museum of Art, Northampton, Massachusetts
	Harcus-Krakow Gallery, Boston
	Meredith Long Gallery, Houston
1982	Studio Museum in Harlem, New York
	Savoy: An Installation by Richard Yarde, Mount Holyoke College Art Museum, South Hadley, Massachusetts (traveling)

1983	Exeter Academy, Exeter, New Hampshire
1985	Philadelphia Art Alliance
	Wendell Street Gallery, Cambridge, Massachusetts
1986	Utah Museum of Fine Arts, Salt Lake City
	Galerie Tension, Paris
1987	Springfield Museum of Fine Arts, Massachusetts
	CRT'S Craftery Gallery, Hartford, Connecticut
1990	Zone Art Center, Springfield, Massachusetts
	Museum of the National Center of Afro-American Artists, Boston
1993	*Recent Watercolors,* June Kelly Gallery, New York
1996	Massachusetts College of Art, Boston

Selected Group Exhibitions:

1970	Museum of Fine Arts, Boston
1976	*American 1976,* Department of the Interior, Washington, D.C. (traveling)
1988	Morris Brown Gallery, Atlanta, Georgia
1990	Boston Center for the Arts
	Newport Art Museum, Rhode Island
1993	Bomani Gallery, San Francisco
1995	*Twenty-Five Years of African-American Art,* Studio Museum in Harlem, New York (traveling)
	Boston University Art Gallery
	National Academy of Design, New York
1996	Canal Gallery, Holyoke, Massachusetts

Collections:

Allen Memorial Art Museum, Oberlin College, Oberlin, Ohio; Butler Institute of American Art, Youngstown, Ohio; Fisk University, Nashville; Johnson Museum of Art, Cornell University, Ithaca, New York; Herter Gallery, University of Massachusetts, Amherst; Mount Holyoke College Art Museum, South Hadley, Massachusetts; Metropolitan Museum of Art, New York; Museum of Art, Rhode Island School of Design, Providence; Museum of Fine Arts, Boston; Museum of Fine Arts, Houston; Museum of Fine Arts, Springfield, Massachusetts; National Academy of Design, New York; Newark Museum of Art, New Jersey; Rose Art Museum, Brandeis University, Waltham, Massachusetts; Smith College Museum of Art, Northampton, Massachusetts; Smithsonian Institution, Washington, D.C.; Studio Museum in Harlem, New York; Utah Museum of Fine Arts, Salt Lake City; Wellesley College Museum, Wellesley, Massachusetts.

Publications:

On YARDE: Articles—"Richard Yarde, Painter" (interview) by Lois Tarlow, in *Art New England,* October, 1980; "Wreaths" by Marilyn J.S. Goodman, in *Worcester Magazine*, March, 1981; "Richard Yarde" by Robin Karson, in *Art New England,* May, 1982; "Richard Yarde: Recent Watercolors" by Lynette Benton, in *Art New England*, July-August, 1985; "Boston Curator Defends Black Artist's Exhibition" by Allan R. Gold, in *The New York Times,* January 26, 1988.

*

Richard Yarde comments:
My first influence was my older brother Edgar, who taught me to draw from comics. My godfather, Amos Gibson, was also an inspi-

ration. He operated a portrait photography studio in Boston's South End. I loved to watch him hand tint black-and-white photographs. I would try to imitate him by adding watercolor to newspaper photographs that interested me. My mother, Enid, supported me in my art by bringing home art materials, even though she had her heart set on my becoming a minister. When I was nine I took Saturday morning classes in watercolor and sculpture at the Museum of Fine Arts in Boston. There I was drawn to William Blake's watercolors. They reminded me of the comic books I loved. The ritual and religion of Blake's work really stuck with me. Gaugin is the painter who made me realize I could be an artist. In his painting *Where Do We Come From? What Are We? Where Are We Going?* I saw people of color as the subject of painting. It wasn't, however, until I got to Boston University and studied with Conger Metcalf and Walter Murch that my resolve to become an artist became fixed. Both men were great teachers who had a tremendous influence on me.

There was a rigorous commitment to Western European Art. Cezanne and Matisse most impressed me. When I graduated I set out to study on my own: African, Oriental, and Indian Art. At the time, I was rejecting the Western Art tradition partly because of my rage at racial oppression, which I associated with Western European culture, and partly from a hunger for a wider vocabulary as a visual artist. At present my influences come largely from outside formal art. I am exploring imagery from old game boards, medical charts, X rays, Braille, etc.

Like many African Americans, I have had high blood pressure for most of my adult life. Complications of treatment led to kidney failure. My work has become one of the sources of my continual recovery and healing. Through my illness, I have become interested in the ideas of transformation: positive and negative.

As the son of immigrant parents, I have had lifelong pressure on me to be strong, to achieve, and be a role model. My illness forced me to confront another aspect of my humanity: My need and dependence on other people and on my spiritual resources. The early work is all about African American pride, heroism, and the struggle to be creative. Now I am dealing with the contradictions: the fragility. In this society there are tremendous contradictions in the roles required of African-American males that contribute to the pressure we live under. They can be deadly. These contradictions are in the very fiber of my work.

First and foremost, just to work is an assertion against tremendous odds and is a healing in itself. I am fortunate to have state-of-the-art medical care. I feel I have put my intellect, heart, and soul all into my work. I am asserting that I am nothing but a man on the same journey as any other human being. When all is said and done, I see the most important thing I have to offer is my art, which is an act of mediation between myself and the awesome mystery of creation.

*   *   *

One of the greatest American watercolorists of the twentieth century, Richard Yarde is, according to some critics, as much a master of the watercolor medium as the nineteenth-century artist Winslow Homer. Yarde is a powerful and original painter whose thirty-year career has been concerned with an exploration of identity around themes of African American cultural history and personal mythology. A native of Boston, he is best known in the New England area, where he has had great influence as both a practicing artist and professor of art.

Yarde's works are rich in social insight, historical awareness, and imagination. The focal point of Yarde's compositions—gestures of men and women, architectural details, domestic interiors such as parlor rooms and barber shops, and neighborhood streets—is organized into narrative composites that reflect the warmth and charm

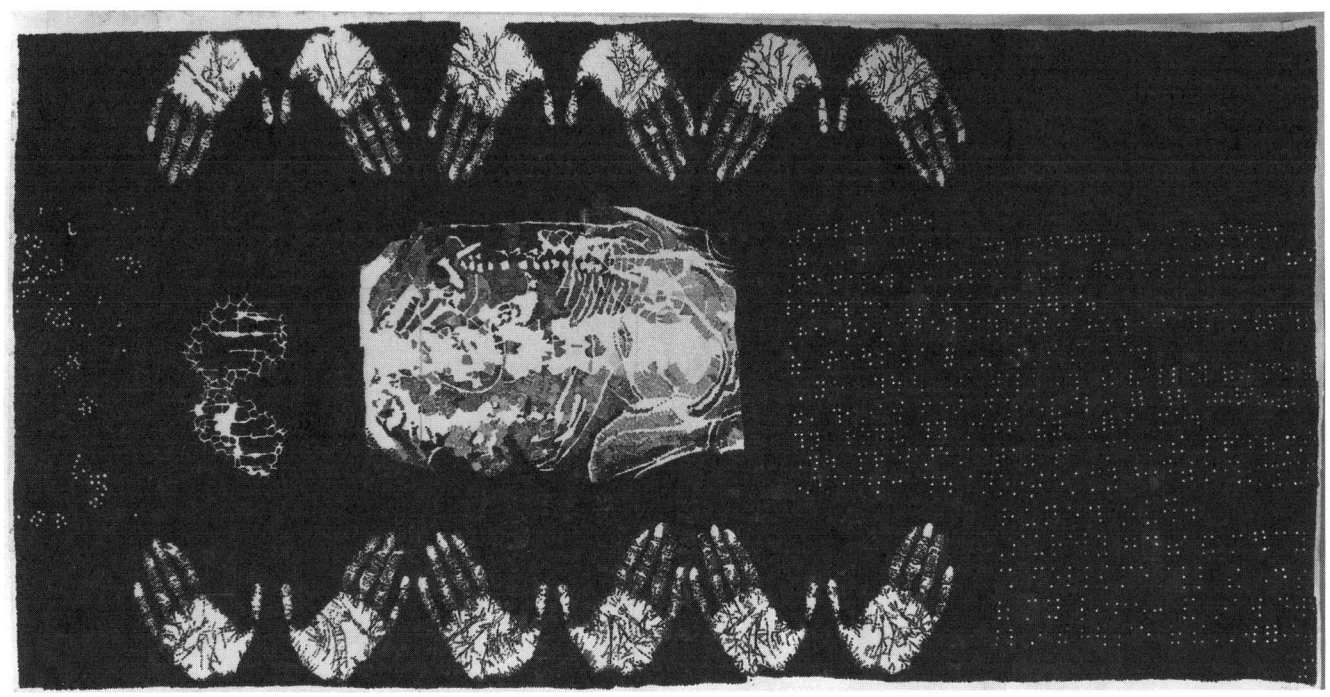

Richard Yarde: *Mojo Hand,* **1996. Photo courtesy of Clive Russ.**

of family members and aspects of his community during his youth in the 1940s and 1950s. His paintings are characteristically built up with loosely painted irregular shaped squares of monochrome color on large sheets of white paper; typically he works with a large-scale format. Sometimes he even collages additional paper to achieve spatial shifts and to intensify the action.

Yarde's artistic vocabulary evolved from abstractions to architectural settings to people and personalities to three-dimensional installations of cultural landmarks and to universally symbolic imagery based on intensely personal issues. The figure was added in the 1970s and is distinguished in particular by two early bodies of work—"The Apartment" series, which most often refers to family history, and a series of memorial portraits of heroic figures (the messianic Marcus Garvey, the evangelical Sweet Daddy Grace, heavyweight champion Jack Johnson, and Paul Robeson as Emperor Jones). His exploration of cultural history and his foray into physical space was launched with the monumental installation *Savoy* (1982), a three-dimensional re-creation of the legendary Savoy Ballroom. In 1991 his art turned more toward self-definition (a shift due to a nearly fatal illness), though his work continues to be consistent in the theme of exploration.

—Deirdre Bibby

A SELECTED BIBLIOGRAPHY
ON BLACK ARTISTS

COMPILED BY BETTY KAPLAN GUBERT

GENERAL REFERENCE

Albany Institute of History and Art. *The Negro Artist Comes of Age: A National Survey of Contemporary American Artists.* Albany, New York: Albany Institute of History and Art, 1945, unpaged.

Brown, Evelyn S. *Africa's Contemporary Art and Artists: A Review of Creative Activities in Painting, Sculpture, Ceramics, and Crafts of More than 300 Artists Working in the Modern Industrialized Society of Some of the Countries of Sub-Saharan Africa.* New York: Harmon Foundation, 1966, 136 p.

Cederholm, Theresa Dickason. *Afro-American Artists: A Bio-Bibliographic Directory.* Boston: Boston Public Library, 1973, 348 p.

Contemporary African-Caribbean, Asian and African Art in Britain: Individual Artists: A Bibliography of Material Held in the Library, Chelsea College of Art & Design (The London Institute). London: The Library, 1991, 81 leaves.

Davis, Lenwood G. *Black Artists in the United States: An Annotated Bibliography of Books, Articles, and Dissertations on Black Artists, 1779-1979.* Westport, Connecticut: Greenwood Publishing Group, 1980, 138 p.

Gumbo Ya Ya: Anthology of Contemporary African-American Women Artists. New York: Midmarch Arts Press, 1995, 368 p.

Henkes, Robert. *The Art of Black American Women: Works of Twenty-Four Artists of the Twentieth Century.* Jefferson, North Carolina: McFarland & Co., 1993, 274 p.

Holmes, Oakley N., Jr. *The Complete Annotated Resource Guide to Black American Art: Books, Doctoral Dissertations, Exhibition Catalogs, Periodicals, Films, Slides, Large Prints, Speakers, Filmstrips, Videotapes, Black Museums, Art Galleries, and Much More.* Spring Valley, New York: Black Artists in America, 1978, 275 p.

Igoe, Lynn Moody. *250 Years of Afro-American Art: An Annotated Bibliography.* New York: R.R. Bowker Company, 1981, 1,266 p.

Keen, Melanie. *Recordings: A Select Bibliography of Contemporary African, Afro-Caribbean and Asian British Art.* London: Institute of International Visual Arts and Chelsea College of Art & Design, 1996, 133 p.

Kelly, Bernice M. *Nigerian Artists: A Who's Who and Bibliography.* London: Hans Zell, for the Smithsonian Institution, National Museum of African Art, 1993, 600 p.

Miller, Judith Von D. *Art in East Africa: A Guide to Contemporary Art.* London: Frederick Muller Ltd., 1975, 125 p.

St. Louis Public Library. *An Index to Black American Artists.* St. Louis, Missouri, 1972, 50 p.

AFRICAN

Adepegbe, Cornelius O. *Nigerian Art: Its Traditions and Modern Tendencies.* Ibadan: Jodad, 1995, 168 p.

Africa Now: Jean Pigozzi Collection. Groningen, Netherlands: Groninger Museum, 1991, 224 p.

Beier, Ulli. *Contemporary Art in Africa.* New York: Praeger, 1968, 173 p.

Contemporary African Artists: Changing Tradition. New York: Studio Museum in Harlem, 1990, 148 p.

Fosu, Kojo. *20th Century Art of Africa.* Zaria, Nigeria: Gaskiya Corporation, 1986, 230 p.

Fusion: West African Artists at the Venice Biennale. New York: Museum for African Art, 1993, 96 p.

Home and the World: Architectural Sculpture by Two Contemporary African Artists: Abroudramane and Bodys Isek Kingelez. New York: Museum for African Art, 1993, 91 p.

Kennedy, Jean. *New Currents, Ancient Rivers: Contemporary African Artists in a Generation of Change.* Washington, D.C.: Smithsonian Institution Press, 1992, 204 p.

La Duke, Betty. *Africa through the Eyes of Women Artists.* Trenton, New Jersey: Africa World Press, 1991, 148 p.

Levinson, Orde. *The African Dream, Visions of Love and Sorrow: The Art of John Muafangejo.* New York: Thames and Hudson, 1992, 120 p.

Mount, Marshall Ward. *African Art: The Years since 1920.* Bloomington: Indiana University Press, 1973, 236 p. Reprinted in 1989 by Da Capo Press, New York.

Seven Stories about Modern Art in Africa. Paris: Flammarion, 1995, 319 p.

Vogel, Susan. *Africa Explores: 20th Century African Art.* New York: Center for African Art, 1991, 295 p.

Wahlman, Maude. *Contemporary African Arts.* Chicago: Field Museum of Natural History, 1974, 124 p.

AFRICAN AMERICAN

19 Sixties: A Cultural Awakening Re-evaluated, 1965-1975. Los Angeles: California Afro-American Museum Foundation, 1989, 63 p.

Adele, Lynne. *Black History Black Vision: The Visionary Image in Texas.* Austin: University of Texas Press, 1989, 94 p.

African American Works on Paper from the Cochran Collection. Atlanta, Georgia: Double Density, n.d., 69 p.

Afro-American Artists: New York and Boston. Boston: Museum of the National Center of Afro-American Artists and Museum of Fine Arts, 1970, unpaged.

Afro-American Artists: North Carolina USA. Raleigh, North Carolina: North Carolina Museum of Art, 1980, 93 p.

Alone in a Crowd: Prints of the 1930s-40s by African-American Artists, from the Collection of Reba and Dave Williams. N.p.: Washburn Press, [1993], 58 p.

Another Face of the Diamond: Pathways through the Black Atlantic South. New York: INTAR Latin American Gallery, 1988, 68 p.

The Arts of Black Folk. New York: Schomburg Center for Research in Black Culture, New York Public Library, 1988, 96 p.

Atkinson, J. Edward. *Black Dimensions in Contemporary Art.* New York: New American Library, 1971, 126 p.

Baking in the Sun: Visionary Images from the South. Lafayette: University of Southwestern Louisiana, 1987, 146 p.

Barnett-Aden Collection. Washington, D.C.: Smithsonian Institution Press, for the Anacostia Neighborhood Museum, 1974, 190 p.

Bearden, Romare and Harry Henderson. *A History of African-American Artists, from 1792 to the Present.* New York: Pantheon Books, 1993, 542 p.

―――. *Six Black Masters of American Art.* New York: Zenith Books, 1972, 119 p. (Joshua Johnston, Robert S. Duncanson, Henry Ossawa Tanner, Augusta Savage, Jacob Lawrence, Horace Pippin.)

Bearden, Romare and Carl Holty. *The Painter's Mind: A Study of the Relations of Structure and Space in Painting.* New York: Crown Publishers, 1969, 224 p. Reprinted by Garland Publishing, 1981.

Biggers, John Thomas. *Black Art in Houston: The Texas Southern*

University Experience Presenting the Art of Biggers and [Carroll] *Simms and Their Students.* College Station: Texas A&M University Press, 1978, 106 p.

Black Art, Ancestral Legacy: The African Impulse in African-American Art. New York: Abrams and Dallas Museum of Art, 1989, 305 p.

Bomani, Asake and Belvie Rooks. *Paris Connections: African American Artists in Paris.* San Francisco: Q.E.D. Press, 1992, 95 p.

Chase, Judith Wragg. *Afro-American Art & Craft.* New York: Van Nostrand Reinhold, 1971, 142 p.

Davis, Donald Fred. *Contributions of 4 Blacks to Art Education in the South 1920-1970.* Ph.D. dissertation: Arizona State University, 1983, 221 p. (Aaron Douglas, Hale Woodruff, James Porter, John Biggers.)

Deacon, Deborah A. "The Art & Artifacts Collection of the Schomburg Center for Research in Black Culture," in *Bulletin of Research in the Humanities,* New York Public Library, Summer 1981, pp. 145-261.

DePillars, Murry Norman. *African-American Artists and Art Students: A Morphological Study in the Urban Black Aesthetic.* Ph.D. dissertation: Pennsylvania State University, 1976, 245 p.

Doty, Robert M. *Contemporary Black Artists in America.* New York: Whitney Museum of American Art, 1971, 64 p.

Dover, Cedric. *American Negro Art.* Greenwich, Connecticut: New York Graphic Society, 1960, 186 p.

Driskell, David C. *African American Visual Aesthetics: A Postmodernist View.* Washington, D.C.: Smithsonian Institution, 1995, 140 p.

———. *Amistad II: Afro-American Art.* Nashville, Tennessee: Fisk University, 1975, 92 p.

———. *Contemporary Visual Expressions: The Art of Sam Gilliam, Martha Jackson-Jarvis, Keith Morrison, William T. Williams.* Washington, D.C.: Smithsonian Institution Press, 1987, 79 p.

———. *Hidden Heritage: Afro-American Art, 1800-1950.* San Francisco, California: Art Museum Association of America, 1985, 104 p.

———. *Two Centuries of Black American Art.* New York: Alfred A. Knopf with the Los Angeles County Museum of Art, 1976, 221 p.

East/West: Contemporary American Art. Los Angeles: California Afro-American Museum, 1985, 56 p.

The Evolution of Afro-American Artists 1800-1950. New York: City College with the Harlem Cultural Council and New York Urban League, 1967, 70 p.

Explorations in the City of Light: African-American Artists in Paris, 1945-1965. New York: Studio Museum in Harlem, 1996, 100 p.

Fax, Elton C. *Black Artists of the New Generation.* New York: Dodd, Mead, 1977, 370 p.

———. *Seventeen Black Artists.* New York: Dodd, Mead, 1971, 306 p.

Ferris, William. *Afro-American Folk Art and Craft.* Boston: G.K. Hall & Co., 1983, 436 p.

Fine, Elsa. *The Afro-American Artist: A Search for Identity.* New York: Holt, Rinehart and Winston, 1973, 310 p.

Fonvielle-Bontemps, Jacqueline. *Art Departments in Selected Predominately Black Institutions of Higher Education in the United States.* Ed.D. dissertation: Illinois State University, 1976, 104 p.

Forever Free: Art by African-American Women 1862-1980. Alexandria, Virginia: Stephenson Incorporated, 1980, 214 p.

Freeman, Roland L. *A Communion of the Spirits: African-American Quilters, Preservers, and their Stories.* Nashville, Tennessee: Rutledge Hill Press, 1996, 396 p.

Fry, Gladys-Marie. *Stitched from the Soul: Slave Quilts from the Ante-Bellum South.* New York: Dutton Studio Books with the Museum of American Folk Art, 1990, 101 p.

Gaither, Edmund Barry. *Massachusetts Masters: Afro-American Artists.* Boston: Museum of Fine Arts with the Museum of the National Center of Afro-American Artists, 1988, 50 p.

Golden, Thelma. *Black Male: Representations of Masculinity in Contemporay American Art.* New York: Abrams and the Whitney Museum of American Art, 1994, 223 p.

Goode-Bryant, Linda. *Contextures.* New York: Just above Midtown, 1978, 103 p.

Greene, Jr. Carroll. *American Visions, Afro-American Art, 1986.* Washington, D.C.: Visions Foundation, 1987, 57 p.

Hall, Robert L. *Gathered Visions: Selected Works by African-American Women Artists.* Washington, D.C.: Smithsonian Institution Press for the Anacostia Museum, 1992, 54 p.

Harlem Renaissance: Art of Black America. New York: Abrams with the Studio Museum in Harlem, 1987, 200 p.

The Harmon and Harriet Kelley Collection of African American Art. Texas: San Antonio Museum of Art, 1994, 68 p.

Hartigan, Lynda Roscoe. *Sharing Traditions: Five Black Artists in 19th Century America.* Washington, D.C.: Smithsonian Institution Press, 1985, 120 p. (Joshua Johnson, Robert Scott Duncanson, Edward Mitchell Bannister, Edmonia Lewis, Henry Ossawa Tanner.)

Herbert F. Johnson Museum of Art. *Directions in Afro-American Art.* Ithaca, New York: Cornell University, 1974, 81 p.

Kraskin, Sandra. *Wrestling with History: A Celebration of African American Self-Taught Artists from the Collection of Ronald and June Shelp.* New York: Baruch College, City University of New York, 1996, 72 p.

Leon, Eli. *Who'd a Thought it: Improvisations in African-American Quiltmaking.* San Francisco: San Francisco Craft and Art Museum, 1987, 87 p.

Lewis, Samella. *Art: African American.* Los Angeles, California: Hancraft Studios, 1990, second edition, 298 p.

———. *Black Artists on Art.* Los Angeles: Contemporary Crafts Publishers, 1969, 2 volumes.

Livingston, Jane and John Beardsley. *Black Folk Art in America: 1930-1980.* Jackson: University Press of Mississippi, 1982, 186 p.

Locke, Alain. *Negro Art Past and Present.* Washington, D.C.: Associates in Negro Folk Education, 1936, 122 p.

———. *The Negro in Art.* Washington, D.C.: Associates in Negro Folk Education, 1940, 224 p.

Logan, Oscar Levon. *Concepts and Values Affecting the Transmission of a Black Visual Aesthetic: Study of Art Instructors in Historically Black Colleges and Universities.* Ph.D. dissertation: University of Wisconsin/Madison, 1982, 158 p.

McElroy, Guy C. *Facing History: The Black Image in American Art 1710-1940.* San Francisco: Bedford Arts with the Corcoran Gallery of Art, 1990, 140 p.

Morrison, Keith. *Art in Washington and Its Afro-American Presence 1940-70.* Washington, D.C.: Washington Project for the Arts, 1985, 109 p.

New Black Artists. New York: Harlem Cultural Council, 1969, 54 p.

Next Generation: Southern Black Aesthetic. Winston-Salem, North Carolina: Southeastern Center for Contemporary Art, 1990, 163 p.

Perry, Regenia A. *Free within Ourselves: African-American Artists in the Collection of the National Museum of American Art.* Washington, D. C.: Smithsonian Institution with Pomegranate

Artbooks, 1992, 205 p.

———. *What it Is: Black American Folk Art from the Collection of Regenia Perry*. Richmond: Virginia Commonwealth University, 1982, 72 p.

Porter, James A. *Modern Negro Art*. New York: Dryden Press, 1943, 272 p. Reprinted by Howard University Press, 1992.

Powell, Richard J. *Black Art and Culture in the 20th Century*. New York/London: Thames and Hudson, 1997, 256 p.

Ransaw, Lee Andrew. *Black Mural Art and Its Representation of the Black Community* [Chicago]. Ed.D. dissertation: Illinois State University, 1973, 117 p.

Reynolds, Gary A. and Beryl J. Wright. *Against the Odds: African-American Artists and the Harmon Foundation*. Newark, New Jersey: Newark Museum, 1989, 298 p.

Robinson, Jontyle Theresa. *Bearing Witness: Contemporary Works by African-American Women Artists*. New York: Rizzoli International Publications and Spelman College, 1996, 176 p.

The Search for Freedom: African American Abstract Painting 1945-1975. New York: Kenkeleba Gallery, 1991, 139 p.

Shaw, Luke Alfred. *Rating of Black Artists' Works and the Degree of Their Inclusion in Selected University Courses*. Ed.D. dissertation: Illinois State University, 1978, 124 p.

Since the Harlem Renaissance: 50 Years of Afro-American Art. Lewisburg, Pennsylvania: The Gallery, 1985, 124 p.

Smith, Alvin. *A Selective, Illustrated Survey of Fine Art by African Americans: 1945-1973*. Ed. D. dissertation: Columbia University, New York, 1973, 319 p.

The Studio Museum in Harlem: 25 Years of African-American Art. New York: Studio Museum in Harlem, 1994, 56 p.

Taylor, William E. *A Shared Heritage: Art by Four African Americans*. Indianapolis: Indiana University Press with the Indianapolis Museum of Art, 1996, 196 p. (William E. Scott, John W. Hardrick, Hale Woodruff, William Majors.)

Teilhet, Jean. *Dimensions of Black*. La Jolla, California: La Jolla Museum of Art, 1970, 154 p.

Tradition and Conflict: Images of a Turbulent Decade 1963-1973. New York: Studio Museum in Harlem, 1985, 100 p.

Uncommon Beauty in Common Objects: The Legacy of African American Craft Art. Wilberforce, Ohio: National Afro-American Museum and Cultural Center, 1993, 112 p.

Vlach, John Michael. *The Afro-American Tradition in Decorative Arts*. Cleveland: Cleveland Museum of Art, 1978, 175 p.

Walter O. Evans Collection of African American Art. Savannah, Georgia: Beach Institute, King-Tisdale Museum, 1991, 93 p.

Weld, Alison. *Dream Singers, Story Tellers: An African American Presence*. [Japan: Yoshida Kinbundo], 1992, 238 p.

Welsh-Asante, Kariamu. *The African Aesthetic: Keeper of the Traditions*. Westport, Connecticut: Greenwood Publishing Group, 1993, 263 p.

Williams, Hobie L. *The Impact of Atlanta Exhibition of Black Artists (1942-1969) on Black and Non-Black People*. Ed.D. dissertation: University of Pittsburgh, 1973, 135 p.

Willis, John Ralph. *Fragments of American Life: An Exhibition of Paintings*. Princeton, New Jersey: The Art Museum, 1976, 75 p.

Yet Still We Rise: African-American Art in Cleveland, 1920-1970. Cleveland, Ohio: Cleveland Artists Foundation, 1996, 93 p.

CARIBBEAN

Apraxine, Pierre. *Haitian Painting: The Naive Tradition*. New York: American Federation of Artists, 1973, 64 p.

Archer-Straw, Petrine. *Jamaican Art: An Overview with a Focus on Fifty Artists*. Kingston, Jamaica: Kingston Publishers, Ltd., 1990, 167 p.

Bomani, Asake and Belvie Rooks. *Paris Connections: African and Caribbean Artists in Paris*. San Francisco: Q.E.D. Press, 1992, 56 p.

Carib Art: Contemporary Art of the Caribbean. [Curacao]: Unesco, [1993], 374 p.

Caribbean Visions: Contemporary Painting and Sculpture. Alexandria, Virginia: Art Services International, 1995, 228 p.

Christensen, Eleanor Ingalls. *The Art of Haiti*. South Brunswick: A.S. Barnes, 1975, 76 p.

Davenport Museum of Art. *Tracing the Spirit: Ethnographic Essays on Haitian Art*. Seattle: University of Washington Press, 1995, 112 p.

Drot, Jean-Marie. *An Encounter between Two Worlds as Seen by Haitian Artists*. Paris: Afrique en Creation Foundation, 1994, 195 p.

Forty Years, the Edna Manley School for the Visual Arts and the National Gallery of Jamaica. Kingston, Jamaica: The Gallery, 1990, 2 vols.

Girouard, Tina. *Sequin Artists of Haiti*. New Orleans: Contemporary Arts Center, 1994, 114 p.

Haiti, Three Visions: Etienne Chavannes, Edger Jean-Baptiste, Ernst Prophete. Mahwah, New Jersey: Ramapo College of New Jersey, South Gallery, 1994, 93 p.

The Intuitive Eye: National Gallery of Jamaica, August 20th - October 5th, 1979. Kingston, Jamaica: The Gallery, 1979, 48 p.

Milwaukee Art Center. *Haiti, the Naive Tradition: The Flagg Tanning Corporation Collection*. Milwaukee, Wisconsin, 1974, 120 p.

New World Imagery: Contemporary Jamaican Art: David Boxer, Margaret Chen, Albert Chong, Albert Daley, Ras Dizzy, Milton George, Anna Henriques, Omari Ra. Manchester: Cornerhouse Publications, 1995, 72 p.

Pataki, Eva. *Haitian Painting: Art and Kitsch*. Jamaica Estates, New York: E. Pataki, 1986, 161 p.

Rodman, Selden. *Artists in Tune with Their World: Masters of Popular Art in the Americas*. New York: Simon & Schuster, 1982, 222 p.

———. *The Miracle of Haitian Art*. New York: Doubleday, 1974, 95 p.

———. *Renaissance in Haiti*. New York: Pellegrini & Cudahy, 1948, 134 p.

———. *Where Art Is Joy: Haitian Art, The First Forty Years*. New York: Ruggles de Latour, 1988, 236 p.

Stebich, Ute. *Haitian Art*. New York: Abrams, 1978, 176 p.

———. *A Haitian Celebration: Art and Culture*. Milwaukee, Wisconsin: Milwaukee Art Museum, 1992, 176 p.

Walmsley, Anne. *The Caribbean Artists Movement 1966-1972: A Literary and Cultural History*. London: New Beacon Books, 1992, 256 p.

NATIONALITY INDEX

American

Terry Adkins
Tina Allen
Charles Alston
Amalia Amaki
Emma Amos
Benny Andrews
William Ellisworth Artis
Ellsworth Ausby
Herman "Kofi" Bailey
Malcolm Bailey
James Ball
Ellen Banks
Henry Bannarn
Edward Bannister
Ernie Barnes
Richmond Barthé
Jean-Michel Basquiat
Gloretta Baynes
Romare Bearden
Phoebe Beasley
Gwendolyn Bennett
John Biggers
Camille Billops
Willie Birch
Robert Blackburn
Betty Blayton-Taylor
Leslie Bolling
Shirley Bolton
David Bustill Bowser
William Ernest Braxton
Grafton Tyler Brown
Samuel Joseph Brown, Jr.
Vivian Browne
Beverly Buchanan
Selma Burke
Calvin Burnett
Millie Burns
Margaret Burroughs
David Butler
Carole Byard
Elmer Simms Campbell
Arthur Carraway
Carol Ann Carter
Nanette Carter
Yvonne Pickering Carter
George Washington Carver
Yvonne Parks Catchings
Elizabeth Catlett
Dana Chandler
Barbara Chase-Riboud
Claude Clark
Ed Clark
Irene Clark
Robert Colescott
Houston Conwill
Eldzier Cortor
Ernest Crichlow
Allan Rohan Crite
Emilio Cruz
Bing Davis

Alonzo Davis
Charles Dawson
Roy DeCarava
Avel DeKnight
Beauford Delaney
Joseph Delaney
Nadine DeLawrence
James Denmark
Murry DePillars
Milton Derr
Thorton Dial
Jeff Donaldson
Aaron Douglas
Robert M. Douglass, Jr.
John Dowell
David Driskell
Robert S. Duncanson
William Edmondson
Melvin Edwards
Minnie Evans
Frederick Eversley
Malaika Favorite
Thomas Fleet, slave of
Sherman Fleming
Frederick Flemister
L'Merchie Frazier
Allan Freelon
Robert Freeman
Roland Freeman
Meta Vaux Warrick Fuller
Reginald Gammon
Herbert Gentry
Sam Gilliam
Paul T. Goodnight
Russell Gordon
Rex Gorleigh
Gladys Barker Grauer
Renée Green
Jefferson Eugene Grigsby, Jr.
David Hammons
James Hampton
Marvin Harden
Inge Hardison
John Wesley Hardrick
Edwin Harleston
William A. Harper
Michael D. Harris
Bessie Harvey
Maren Hassinger
Cynthia Hawkins
Palmer Hayden
Vertis Hayes
Benjamin Hazard
Barkley Hendricks
Janet Oliva Henry
Leon Hicks
Freida High
Adrienne Hoard
Alvin Hollingsworth
Charnelle D. Holloway
Varnette Honeywood

Earl J. Hooks
Humbert Howard
Mildred Howard
Julien Hudson
Manuel Hughes
Margo Humphrey
Richard Hunt
Clementine Hunter
Martha Jackson-Jarvis
Harlan Jackson
May Howard Jackson
Oliver L. Jackson
Suzanne Jackson
Wadsworth A. Jarrell
Wilmer Jennings
Malvin Gray Johnson
Marie E. Johnson
Sargent Claude Johnson
Stephanie A. Johnson
William H. Johnson
Joshua Johnston
Napoleon Jones-Henderson
Barbara Jones-Hogu
Ben Jones
Loïs Mailou Jones
Paul Keene
Gwen Knight
Laura Jean Lacy
Doyle Lane
Jacob Lawrence
Hughie Lee-Smith
James Lewis
Joseph Lewis
(Mary) Edmonia Lewis
Norman Lewis
Samella Lewis
Glenn Ligon
Arturo Lindsay
Thomas Lloyd
Jon Lockard
Juan Logan
Ed Love
Al Loving
Kerry James Marshall
Richard Mayhew
Valerie Maynard
Yvonne Cole Meo
Tom Miller
Lev Mills
Priscilla Mills
Evangeline Montgomery
Scipio Moorhead
Clarence Morgan
Norma Morgan
Archibald Motely
Teixeira Nash
Nefertiti
Senga Nengudi
Joseph Norman
Ademola Olugebefola
Mary Lovelace O'Neal

Hayward Oubre
John Outterbridge
Joe Overstreet
William Pajaud
Gordon Parks
Marion Perkins
James Phillips
Delilah Pierce
Elijah Pierce
Anderson J. Pigatt
Howardena Pindell
Adrian Piper
Rose Piper
Horace Pippin
Michael B. Platt
Stephanie Pogue
Prentice Herman Polk
Charles Ethan Porter
James Porter
Georgette Powell
Harriet Powers
Debra Priestly
Nelson Primus
Nancy Elizabeth Prophet
Noah Purifoy
Martin Puryear
Rachelle Puryear
Helen Ramsaran
Patricia Ravarra
Patrick Henry Reason
Robert Reid
John Rhoden
Gary Rickson
John Riddle
Faith Ringgold
Haywood Rivers
Malkia Roberts
John H. D. Robinson
Mahler Ryder
Alison Saar
Betye Saar
Raymond Saunders
Augusta Savage
Elizabeth Scott
John T. Scott
Joyce Scott
William Edouard Scott
Charles Searles
Charles Sebree
Thomas Albert Sills
Gary Simmons
Carroll Simms
Jewel Woodward Simon
Lorna Simpson
Merton Simpson
William H. Simpson
Clarissa Sligh
Albert Alexander Smith
Al(fred) Smith
Alvin Smith
Frank Smith

Vincent Smith
William E. Smith
Gilda Snowden
Sylvia Snowden
Therman Statom
Raymond Steth
Nelson Stevens
Renee Stout
Thelma Johnson Streat
Richard Stroud
Robert Stull
Kaylynn Sullivan Twotrees
Ann Graves Tanksley
Henry Ossawa Tanner
Alma Thomas
Matthew Thomas
Mildred Thompson
Robert Thompson
Dox Thrash
Mose Tolliver
Bill Traylor
Curtis Tucker
Yvonne Edwards Tucker
Leo Twiggs
James Van Der Zee
Ruth Waddy
Eugène Warburg
Barbara Ward
Denise Ward-Brown
Laura Wheeler Waring
Gregory Warmack
Carrie Mae Weems
Joyce Wellman
James Lesesne Wells
Pheoris West
Rene Westbrook
Charles White
Jack Whitten
Frank Williams
Michael Kelly Williams
Pat Ward Williams
William T. Williams
Philemona Williamson
Ed Wilson
Ellis Wilson
Fred Wilson
John Wilson
Vernon Winslow
Beulah Woodard
Hale Woodruff
Shirley Woodson
Richard Yarde

Bahamian
Amos Ferguson

Barbadian
Karl Broodhagen

Brazilian
Aleijadinho
Emanoel Araújo

Octávio Araújo
Antônio Bandeira
José Barbosa
Raimundo da Costa e Silva
Manuel da Cunha
Mestre Didi
Leandro Joaquim
Maria Magliani
Abdias do Nascimento
Genilson Soares
Terciliano, Jr.
Rubem Valentim

British
Sonia Boyce
Eddie Chambers
Keith Piper

Canadian
Artis Lane

Cuban
Pastor Argudin y Pedroso
Tomás Esson
Wifredo Lam
Manuel Mendive
Teodoro Ramos-Blanco

Dominican
Tam Joseph

Ethiopian
Skunder Boghossian

French
Jules Lion

Ghanaian
El Anatsui
Ablade Glover
Vincent Kofi

Guyanese
Frank Bowling
Philip Moore
Aubrey Williams

Haitian
Rigaud Benoit
Wilson Bigaud
Edgar Brierre
Murat Brierre
Édouard Duval-Carrié
Hector Hyppolite
Serge Jolimeau
Georges Liautaud
Philomé Obin
Robert St. Brice

Ivory Coaster
Christian Lattier
Ouattara

Jamaican
Carl Abrahams
David Boxer
Everald Brown
Albert V. Chong
John Dunkley
Milton George
Christopher Gonzalez
Kapo
Kofi Kayiga
Edna Manley
Ronald Moody
Keith Morrison
Petrona Morrison
Omari Ra
Barrington Watson
Osmond Watson

Kenyan
Gregory Maloba

Mozambican
Valente Malangatana Ngwenya

Nigerian
Tayo Adenaike
Jimoh Buraimoh
Sokari Douglas Camp
Felix Eboigbe
Uzo Egonu
Erhabor Ogieva Emokpae
Ben Enwonwu
Lamidi Fakeye
Agboola Folarin
Ovia Idah
Akinola Lasekan
C. Uche Okeke
Asiru Olatunde
Aina Onabolu
Bruce Onobrakpeya
Twins Seven-Seven

Obiora Udechukwu
S. Irein Wangboje

Puerto Rican
Henry DeLeon

Senegalese
Souleymane Keita
Iba N'Diaye
Amadou Sow
Papa Ibra Tall

South African
Mhlaba Zwelidumile Mgxaji Feni
Gerard Sekoto
Durant Sihlali

Spanish
Rashid Diab

Sudanese
Rashid Diab
Ibrahim El Salahi
Mohammad Omer Khalil
Khalid Kodi
Amir Nour
Ahmad Mohammed Shibrain

Tanzanian
Lubaina Himid

Trinidadian
LeRoy Clark
Geoffrey Holder

Zairian
Bodys Isek Kingelez
Moke
Chéri Samba

Zimbabwean
Thomas Mukarobgwa

MEDIUM INDEX

Assemblage
David Boxer
Yvonne Pickering Carter
Barkley Hendricks
Janet Oliva Henry
Lev Mills
Petrona Morrison
Noah Purifoy
Betye Saar
Renee Stout

Ceramics
William Ellisworth Artis
Bing Davis
El Anatsui
Earl J. Hooks
Martha Jackson-Jarvis
Sargent Claude Johnson
Souleymane Keita
Doyle Lane
Carroll Simms
Robert Stull
Curtis Tucker
Yvonne Edwards Tucker

Collage
Phoebe Beasley
James Denmark

Drafting
Marvin Harden
Patrick Henry Reason

Drawing
Benny Andrews
Octávio Araújo
Malcolm Bailey
Gloretta Baynes
John Biggers
Karl Broodhagen
Beverly Buchanan
Calvin Burnett
Robert Colescott
Thorton Dial
Tomás Esson
Malaika Favorite
Mhlaba Zwelidumile Mgxaji Feni
Russell Gordon
Marvin Harden
Geoffrey Holder
Earl J. Hooks
Oliver L. Jackson
Suzanne Jackson
Paul Keene
Norman Lewis
Glenn Ligon
Juan Logan
Ed Love
Maria Magliani
Edna Manley
Joseph Norman

Michael B. Platt
Al Smith
Vincent Smith
Papa Ibra Tall
Matthew Thomas
Bill Traylor
Osmond Watson
Pheoris West
Charles White
Jack Whitten
Frank Williams
John Wilson

Engraving
Patrick Henry Reason

Filmmaking
Camille Billops
Henry DeLeon

Graphic
Tayo Adenaike
Vivian Browne
Jimoh Buraimoh
Uzo Egonu
Erhabor Ogieva Emokpae
Agboola Folarin
Herbert Gentry
Benjamin Hazard
William H. Johnson
Tam Joseph
Khalid Kodi
Bruce Onobrakpeya
Stephanie Pogue
Albert Alexander Smith
Amadou Sow
Raymond Steth
Obiora Udechukwu
S. Irein Wangboje

Illustration
William Ellisworth Artis
Gloretta Baynes
Gwendolyn Bennett
Shirley Bolton
Elmer Simms Campbell
Ernest Crichlow
Allan Rohan Crite
Charles Dawson
Murry DePillars
Aaron Douglas
Uzo Egonu
Loïs Mailou Jones
Khalid Kodi
Akinola Lasekan
Jon Lockard
C. Uche Okeke
Adrian Piper
William Edouard Scott
Charles Sebree
Alvin Smith

Henry Ossawa Tanner
Obiora Udechukwu
Laura Wheeler Waring
Vernon Winslow

Installation
David Boxer
Sokari Douglas Camp
Carol Ann Carter
Albert V. Chong
Houston Conwill
Nadine DeLawrence
Renée Green
Mildred Howard
Margo Humphrey
Marie E. Johnson
Khalid Kodi
Glenn Ligon
Arturo Lindsay
Juan Logan
Ed Love
Senga Nengudi
John Outterbridge
Patricia Ravarra
Matthew Thomas

Jewelry
L'Merchie Frazier
Charnelle D. Holloway
Evangeline Montgomery
Carroll Simms
Gregory Warmack

Mixed Media
Amalia Amaki
Gloretta Baynes
Romare Bearden
Betty Blayton-Taylor
Sonia Boyce
Beverly Buchanan
Carol Ann Carter
Nanette Carter
Eddie Chambers
Bing Davis
El Anatsui
Michael D. Harris
Mildred Howard
Suzanne Jackson
Stephanie A. Johnson
Ben Jones
Laura Jean Lacy
Evangeline Montgomery
Raymond Saunders
Clarissa Sligh
Alvin Smith
Frank Smith
Gilda Snowden
Barbara Ward
Gregory Warmack
Rene Westbrook

Mosaics
Jimoh Buraimoh

Murals
Charles Alston
Pastor Argudin y Pedroso
Dana Chandler
Aaron Douglas
Erhabor Ogieva Emokpae
Agboola Folarin
Edwin Harleston
Vertis Hayes
Christian Lattier
Norman Lewis
Jon Lockard
James Phillips
Gary Rickson
William Edouard Scott
Al Smith
Charles White
Hale Woodruff

Painting
Carl Abrahams
Tayo Adenaike
Tina Allen
Charles Alston
Emma Amos
Benny Andrews
Octávio Araújo
Pastor Argudin y Pedroso
Ellsworth Ausby
Herman "Kofi" Bailey
Malcolm Bailey
Antônio Bandeira
Ellen Banks
Henry Bannarn
Edward Bannister
José Barbosa
Ernie Barnes
Richmond Barthé
Jean-Michel Basquiat
Romare Bearden
Phoebe Beasley
Gwendolyn Bennett
Rigaud Benoit
Wilson Bigaud
John Biggers
Willie Birch
Betty Blayton-Taylor
Skunder Boghossian
Shirley Bolton
Frank Bowling
David Bustill Bowser
David Boxer
William Ernest Braxton
Edgar Brierre
Karl Broodhagen
Everald Brown
Grafton Tyler Brown
Samuel Joseph Brown, Jr.

Vivian Browne
Beverly Buchanan
Jimoh Buraimoh
Calvin Burnett
Margaret Burroughs
David Butler
Carole Byard
Arthur Carraway
Carol Ann Carter
Nanette Carter
Yvonne Pickering Carter
George Washington Carver
Yvonne Parks Catchings
Elizabeth Catlett
Dana Chandler
Claude Clark
Ed Clark
Irene Clark
LeRoy Clark
Robert Colescott
Houston Conwill
Eldzier Cortor
Raimundo da Costa e Silva
Ernest Crichlow
Allan Rohan Crite
Emilio Cruz
Manuel da Cunha
Bing Davis
Alonzo Davis
Charles Dawson
Avel DeKnight
Beauford Delaney
Joseph Delaney
Nadine DeLawrence
James Denmark
Murry DePillars
Milton Derr
Rashid Diab
Thorton Dial
Jeff Donaldson
Aaron Douglas
Robert M. Douglass, Jr.
David Driskell
Robert S. Duncanson
John Dunkley
Édouard Duval-Carrié
Uzo Egonu
Ibrahim El Salahi
Erhabor Ogieva Emokpae
Ben Enwonwu
Tomás Esson
Minnie Evans
Malaika Favorite
Amos Ferguson
Sherman Fleming
Frederick Flemister
Agboola Folarin
Allan Freelon
Robert Freeman
Reginald Gammon
Herbert Gentry

Milton George
Sam Gilliam
Ablade Glover
Christopher Gonzalez
Paul T. Goodnight
Russell Gordon
Rex Gorleigh
Gladys Barker Grauer
Jefferson Eugene Grigsby, Jr.
David Hammons
Marvin Harden
John Wesley Hardrick
Edwin Harleston
William A. Harper
Michael D. Harris
Cynthia Hawkins
Palmer Hayden
Vertis Hayes
Benjamin Hazard
Barkley Hendricks
Janet Oliva Henry
Freida High
Lubaina Himid
Adrienne Hoard
Geoffrey Holder
Alvin Hollingsworth
Varnette Honeywood
Humbert Howard
Julien Hudson
Manuel Hughes
Richard Hunt
Clementine Hunter
Hector Hyppolite
Harlan Jackson
Oliver L. Jackson
Suzanne Jackson
Wadsworth A. Jarrell
Wilmer Jennings
Leandro Joaquim
Malvin Gray Johnson
Marie E. Johnson
William H. Johnson
Joshua Johnston
Ben Jones
Loïs Mailou Jones
Barbara Jones-Hogu
Tam Joseph
Kapo
Kofi Kayiga
Paul Keene
Souleymane Keita
Mohammad Omer Khalil
Gwen Knight
Khalid Kodi
Laura Jean Lacy
Wifredo Lam
Artis Lane
Akinola Lasekan
Jacob Lawrence
Hughie Lee-Smith
James Lewis

Joseph Lewis
Norman Lewis
Samella Lewis
Glenn Ligon
Arturo Lindsay
Jules Lion
Jon Lockard
Juan Logan
Al Loving
Maria Magliani
Edna Manley
Kerry James Marshall
Richard Mayhew
Manuel Mendive
Yvonne Cole Meo
Tom Miller
Priscilla Mills
Moke
Ronald Moody
Philip Moore
Scipio Moorhead
Clarence Morgan
Norma Morgan
Keith Morrison
Archibald Motely
Thomas Mukarobgwa
Abdias do Nascimento
Teixeira Nash
Iba N'Diaye
Valente Malangatana Ngwenya
Joseph Norman
Philomé Obin
C. Uche Okeke
Ademola Olugebefola
Omari Ra
Aina Onabolu
Mary Lovelace O'Neal
Bruce Onobrakpeya
Ouattara
Hayward Oubre
John Outterbridge
Joe Overstreet
William Pajaud
James Phillips
Delilah Pierce
Elijah Pierce
Howardena Pindell
Rose Piper
Horace Pippin
Michael B. Platt
Charles Ethan Porter
James Porter
Georgette Powell
Debra Priestly
Nelson Primus
Patrick Henry Reason
Robert Reid
Gary Rickson
John Riddle
Faith Ringgold
Haywood Rivers

Malkia Roberts
John H. D. Robinson
Mahler Ryder
Robert St. Brice
Chéri Samba
Raymond Saunders
John T. Scott
William Edouard Scott
Charles Searles
Charles Sebree
Gerard Sekoto
Ahmad Mohammed Shibrain
Durant Sihlali
Thomas Albert Sills
Carroll Simms
Jewel Woodward Simon
Merton Simpson
William H. Simpson
Albert Alexander Smith
Al(fred) Smith
Alvin Smith
Frank Smith
Vincent Smith
Gilda Snowden
Sylvia Snowden
Genilson Soares
Amadou Sow
Nelson Stevens
Thelma Johnson Streat
Richard Stroud
Papa Ibra Tall
Ann Graves Tanksley
Henry Ossawa Tanner
Terciliano, Jr.
Alma Thomas
Matthew Thomas
Mildred Thompson
Robert Thompson
Dox Thrash
Mose Tolliver
Bill Traylor
Leo Twiggs
Twins Seven-Seven
Obiora Udechukwu
Rubem Valentim
Laura Wheeler Waring
Barrington Watson
Osmond Watson
Joyce Wellman
James Lesesne Wells
Pheoris West
Rene Westbrook
Charles White
Jack Whitten
Aubrey Williams
Frank Williams
William T. Williams
Philemona Williamson
Ellis Wilson
John Wilson
Vernon Winslow

Beulah Woodard
Hale Woodruff
Shirley Woodson
Richard Yarde

Performance
Terry Adkins
Yvonne Pickering Carter
Houston Conwill
Emilio Cruz
Sherman Fleming
L'Merchie Frazier
Maren Hassinger
Geoffrey Holder
Arturo Lindsay
Senga Nengudi
Adrian Piper
Faith Ringgold
Joyce Scott
Kaylynn Sullivan Twotrees

Photography
James Ball
Beverly Buchanan
Millie Burns
Albert V. Chong
Bing Davis
Roy DeCarava
Roland Freeman
Inge Hardison
Barkley Hendricks
Adrienne Hoard
Earl J. Hooks
Jules Lion
Evangeline Montgomery
Teixeira Nash
Gordon Parks
Prentice Herman Polk
Lorna Simpson
Clarissa Sligh
Henry Ossawa Tanner
James Van Der Zee
Carrie Mae Weems
Rene Westbrook
Pat Ward Williams

Printmaking
Charles Alston
Emma Amos
Octávio Araújo
Herman "Kofi" Bailey
John Biggers
Robert Blackburn
Grafton Tyler Brown
Samuel Joseph Brown, Jr.
Calvin Burnett
Millie Burns
Yvonne Pickering Carter
Eldzier Cortor
Allan Rohan Crite
Murry DePillars

Rashid Diab
Jeff Donaldson
John Dowell
David Driskell
Uzo Egonu
Malaika Favorite
Thomas Fleet, slave of
Allan Freelon
Reginald Gammon
Russell Gordon
Rex Gorleigh
Jefferson Eugene Grigsby, Jr.
David Hammons
Michael D. Harris
Maren Hassinger
Leon Hicks
Margo Humphrey
Richard Hunt
Oliver L. Jackson
Wilmer Jennings
Sargent Claude Johnson
Napoleon Jones-Henderson
Barbara Jones-Hogu
Souleymane Keita
Mohammad Omer Khalil
Gwen Knight
Artis Lane
Norman Lewis
Glenn Ligon
Jules Lion
Juan Logan
Edna Manley
Yvonne Cole Meo
Lev Mills
Evangeline Montgomery
Norma Morgan
Keith Morrison
Nefertiti
Joseph Norman
Ademola Olugebefola
Mary Lovelace O'Neal
Bruce Onobrakpeya
Michael B. Platt
Stephanie Pogue
Rachelle Puryear
Helen Ramsaran
Patrick Henry Reason
Faith Ringgold
Alison Saar
John T. Scott
Jewel Woodward Simon
Frank Smith
Vincent Smith
William E. Smith
Sylvia Snowden
Raymond Steth
Ann Graves Tanksley
Mildred Thompson
Dox Thrash
Ruth Waddy
S. Irein Wangboje

Joyce Wellman
James Lesesne Wells
Charles White
Frank Williams
Michael Kelly Williams
William T. Williams
Fred Wilson
John Wilson
Hale Woodruff

Quiltmaking
Napoleon Jones-Henderson
Harriet Powers
Faith Ringgold
Elizabeth Scott

Sculpture
Terry Adkins
Aleijadinho
Tina Allen
Charles Alston
Emanoel Araújo
William Ellisworth Artis
Henry Bannarn
Richmond Barthé
John Biggers
Camille Billops
Willie Birch
Leslie Bolling
Edgar Brierre
Murat Brierre
Karl Broodhagen
Everald Brown
Samuel Joseph Brown, Jr.
Beverly Buchanan
Selma Burke
David Butler
Carole Byard
Sokari Douglas Camp
Elizabeth Catlett
Barbara Chase-Riboud
Albert V. Chong
Houston Conwill
Charles Dawson
Nadine DeLawrence
Henry DeLeon
Thorton Dial
Mestre Didi
David Driskell
John Dunkley
Felix Eboigbe
William Edmondson
Melvin Edwards
El Anatsui
Erhabor Ogieva Emokpae
Ben Enwonwu
Tomás Esson
Frederick Eversley
Lamidi Fakeye
Agboola Folarin
Meta Vaux Warrick Fuller

Christopher Gonzalez
James Hampton
Inge Hardison
Bessie Harvey
Maren Hassinger
Vertis Hayes
Benjamin Hazard
Charnelle D. Holloway
Earl J. Hooks
Margo Humphrey
Richard Hunt
Ovia Idah
May Howard Jackson
Suzanne Jackson
Martha Jackson-Jarvis
Sargent Claude Johnson
Serge Jolimeau
Ben Jones
Barbara Jones-Hogu
Tam Joseph
Kapo
Bodys Isek Kingelez
Vincent Kofi
Laura Jean Lacy
Artis Lane
Christian Lattier
James Lewis
Joseph Lewis
(Mary) Edmonia Lewis
Georges Liautaud
Arturo Lindsay
Thomas Lloyd
Juan Logan
Ed Love
Gregory Maloba
Edna Manley
Valerie Maynard
Tom Miller
Evangeline Montgomery
Ronald Moody
Philip Moore
Petrona Morrison
Thomas Mukarobgwa
Senga Nengudi
Amir Nour
C. Uche Okeke
Asiru Olatunde
Bruce Onobrakpeya
Hayward Oubre
John Outterbridge
Marion Perkins
Elijah Pierce
Anderson J. Pigatt
Keith Piper
Nancy Elizabeth Prophet
Martin Puryear
Teodoro Ramos-Blanco
Helen Ramsaran
Patricia Ravarra
John Rhoden
John Riddle

Faith Ringgold
Mahler Ryder
Alison Saar
Augusta Savage
John T. Scott
Joyce Scott
Charles Searles
Durant Sihlali
Gary Simmons
Carroll Simms
Jewel Woodward Simon
Al(fred) Smith
Genilson Soares
Amadou Sow
Therman Statom
Renee Stout
Robert Stull
Mildred Thompson
Robert Thompson
Twins Seven-Seven
Rubem Valentim
Eugène Warburg
Barbara Ward

Denise Ward-Brown
Gregory Warmack
Osmond Watson
Michael Kelly Williams
Ed Wilson
Fred Wilson
John Wilson
Beulah Woodard

Textiles
Gloretta Baynes
L'Merchie Frazier
Ablade Glover
Michael D. Harris
Napoleon Jones-Henderson
Teixeira Nash
Papa Ibra Tall
Barbara Ward

Woodcarving
José Barbosa
James Denmark

INDEX TO ILLUSTRATIONS

The following index lists the titles of works illustrated in the text, followed by the name of the artist in whose entry the illustration can be found. Artist portraits are not indexed here, nor are untitled works that appear in the text.

NOTES ON
ADVISERS and CONTRIBUTORS _____

ARCHER-STRAW, Petrine. Lecturer, Courtauld Institute, University of London. Coauthor, *Jamaican Art: An Overview with a Focus on Fifty Artists,* Kingston: Kingston Publishers, 1990. **Essays:** Eddie Chambers; Christopher Gonzalez; Barrington Watson.

BAIN, Terry. Freelance writer. Author of articles and short stories in many publications, including *Prize Stories 1994: The O'Henry Awards.* **Essays:** Ellen Banks; Phoebe Beasley; Millie Burns; Yvonne Pickering Carter; Yvonne Parks Catchings; Nadine DeLawrence; Agboola Folarin; Gladys Barker Grauer; Maren Hassinger; Cynthia Hawkins; Janet Oliva Henry; Ovia Idah; Gregory Maloba; Yvonne Cole Meo; Thomas Mukarobgwa; C. Uche Okeke; Bruce Onobrakpeya; Marion Perkins; Patricia Ravarra; Charles Sebree; Gilda Snowden; Ann Graves Tanksley; Joyce Wellman.

BARKER, Dedria A. Humphries. Editor, *Take Care Magazine,* East Lansing, Michigan. **Essays:** Marie E. Johnson; Barbara Jones-Hogu.

BIBBY, Deirdre. Executive director, Amistad Foundation, and curator of African American art, Wadsworth Atheneum, Hartford, Connecticut. Coeditor of *The Arts of Black Folk,* Schomburg Center for Research in Black Culture, 1991. **Essays:** Ademola Olugebefola; Richard Yarde.

BOXER, David. Chief curator and director emeritus, National Gallery of Jamaica, Kingston, Jamaica. See his own entry. **Essays:** Carl Abrahams; John Dunkley; Milton George; Kapo; Edna Manley; Omari Ra; Osmond Watson.

BRADY, Patricia. Director of publications, Historic New Orleans Collection, New Orleans, Louisiana. Author of numerous books and articles, including *Encyclopaedia of New Orleans Artists, 1718-1918* and "The Cities of the Dead: Free Men of Color as Tomb Builders in Nineteenth-Century New Orleans," in *Cross, Crozier, & Crucible: A Volume Celebrating the Bicentennial of a Catholic Diocese in Louisiana (1793-1993).* **Essays:** Julien Hudson; Jules Lion; Eugène Warburg.

BRITTON, Crystal. Freelance writer. Author of *Art, African American, the Long Struggle,* Smickmark Press, 1996, as well as essays on African American artists. **Essays:** Allan Freelon; Suzanne Jackson; Arturo Lindsay; Gary Rickson; Malkia Roberts.

CHAMBERS, Eddie. Curator-in-residence, University of Sussex. See his own entry. **Essays:** Frank Bowling; Lubaina Himid; Tam Joseph.

CROSS, Deirdre. Program coordinator, Center for African American History and Culture, Smithsonian Institution, Washington, D.C. **Essays:** Benjamin Hazard; Anderson J. Pigatt; Alvin Smith.

CUMMINS, Alissandra. Director, Barbados Museum & Historical Society, St. Michael, Barbados; founding president, Museums Association of the Caribbean; vice president, Commonwealth Association of Museums; and vice chairman, Advisory Committee, International Council of Museums. Author of *Art in Barbados and the Lesser Antilles in 1492-1992: A New Look at the Caribbean,* Courbevoie, France: L'Espace Carpeaux, 1991, and "European Views of Aboriginal People" in *The Indigenous People of the Caribbean,* University Press of Florida, 1996. **Essay:** Karl Broodhagen.

CURNEN, Monique G. Programming coordinator, Arts Festival of Atlanta, Atlanta, Georgia. Contributor to *Santería Aesthetics in Contemporary Latin American Art,* Washington, D.C.: Smithsonian Institution Press, 1996. **Essays:** LeRoy Clark; Robert Freeman; Souleymane Keita.

DARISH, Patricia J. Assistant professor of art history and African and African American studies, University of Kansas, Lawrence. Author of essays in *Cloth and Human Experience,* Smithsonian Institution Press, 1989, *The Scramble for Art in Central Africa,* Cambridge University Press, 1997, and other publications. **Essays:** Bodys Isek Kingelez; Moke.

DODSON, Howard. Director, Schomburg Center for Research in Black Culture, New York Public Library. **Essay:** Preface.

DREWAL, Henry John. Evjue-Bascom Professor of Art History, University of Wisconsin, Madison. Author of numerous books and articles, including *Introspectives: Contemporary Art by Americans and Brazilians of African Descent* (with David Driskell), Los Angeles: The California Afro-American Museum, 1989, and *Yoruba Art: Nine Centuries of African Art and Thought* (with John Pemberton III and Rowland Abiodun), New York: Alfred Knopf and The Center for African Art, 1991. **Essays:** Octávio Araújo; Emanoel Araújo; Jimoh Buraimoh; Mestre Didi; Maria Magliani; Genilson Soares; Terciliano, Jr.; Rubem Valentim.

DRISKELL, David. Professor of art, University of Maryland, College Park. See his own entry.

DURHAM, Carolyn Richardson. Associate professor of Spanish and Latin American studies, Texas Christian University, Fort Worth, Texas. Author of *Finally...Us: Contemporary Black Brazilian Women Writers* (with Miriam Alves), Colorado Springs: Three Continents Press, 1995, and articles in numerous magazines, including *Letras peninsulares, Journal of Interdisciplinary Literary Studies, Callaloo, Hispania,* and *Afro-Hispanic Review.* **Essays:** Aleijadinho; Antônio Bandeira; José Barbosa; Raimundo da Costa e Silva; Manuel da Cunha; Leandro Joaquim; Abdias do Nascimento.

ELLIOTT, Claude Ledell. Consultant, Modern Prints and Drawings, National Gallery of Art, Washington, D.C. **Essays:** Henry Bannarn; Wilmer Jennings; Mahler Ryder.

FITZPATRICK, Laurie. Senior arts editor, *Art & Understanding* magazine. **Essays:** Jean-Michel Basquiat; Bessie Harvey; (Mary) Edmonia Lewis; Al Loving; Scipio Moorhead; Faith Ringgold.

FRANCIS, Jacqueline. Member, Department of Art History, Emory University. Contributing writer, *The American Collection: Selected Works from the Norton Museum of Art Collection,* West Palm Beach, Florida: The Museum, 1995, and author of essays in *Callaloo* and other publications. **Essays:** Charles Alston; Malcolm Bailey; Frederick Flemister; William A. Harper; Vertis Hayes; Norman Lewis; Richard Mayhew; Joe Overstreet; Georgette Powell; Nelson Primus; Haywood Bill Rivers; John H. D. Robinson; Sylvia Snowden; Robert Thompson; Jack Whitten; William T. Williams.

GAITHER, Edmund Barry. Director, Museum of the National Center of Afro-American Artists, Boston, Massachusetts, and special consultant/adjunct curator, Museum of Fine Arts, Boston.

Author of *Massachusetts Masters: Afro-American Artists,* Boston: Museum of Fine Arts with the Museum of the National Center of Afro-American Artists, 1988, as well as articles in many publications, including *Museums and Communities, Views, Encyclopedia of the City of New York, Journal of Museum Education, American Visions, Convergences: 8 Photographers,* and *Black Art: Ancestral Legacy,* Dallas Museum of Art, Dallas, Texas. **Essays:** Gloretta Baynes; L'Merchie Frazier; Paul T. Goodnight; Napoleon Jones-Henderson; Nefertiti; Joseph Norman; Richard Stroud; Robert Stull; Rene Westbrook.

GILPIN, Nicole. Member, Department of the History of Art, University of Michigan. **Essay:** John T. Scott.

GUBERT, Betty Kaplan. Art editor, *Multicultural Review,* and formerly head of reference, Schomburg Center for Research in Black Culture, New York Public Library. Author of *Early Black Bibliographies, 1863-1918,* New York: Garland, 1982, *Nine Decades of Scholarship: A Bibliography of the Writings of the Staff of the Schomburg Center, 1893-1983,* New York: New York Public Library, 1986, *Invisible Wings: An Annotated Bibliography on Blacks in Aviation, 1916-1993,* Westport, Connecticut: Greenwood, 1994, and articles in *African Arts, Notable Black American Women, Encyclopedia of African-American Culture and History,* and other publications. **Essays:** Amos Ferguson; Barkley Hendricks; Rose Piper; John Rhoden; bibliography.

HANKS, Eric. Owner and director, M. Hanks Gallery, Santa Monica, California. **Essays:** Tina Allen; Emilio Cruz; Artis Lane.

HARNEY, Elizabeth. Fellow, Art and Liberal Studies, New York University. Author of articles in *Oxford Art Journal, African Arts, Eastern Art Report,* and various catalogs. **Essays:** Amadou Sow; Papa Ibra Tall.

HARRIS, Joanne. Executive editor, American Visions Society, Washington, D.C. **Essays:** Thorton Dial; Teixeira Nash; Mildred Thompson; Michael Kelly Williams; Shirley Woodson.

HARRIS, Michael D. Assistant professor of art history, University of North Carolina, Chapel Hill. See his own entry. **Essays:** Sokari Douglas Camp; Wadsworth A. Jarrell; Jon Lockard; Lev Mills; Charles Searles; Al Smith; Frank Smith; Nelson Stevens; Yvonne Edwards Tucker; Curtis Tucker.

HARVIE, Stephanie. Researcher, British Broadcasting Corporation, London. Author of articles on art, including an essay on Aubrey Williams in *Cosmos Series.* **Essay:** Aubrey Williams.

HASSAN, Salah. Assistant professor of African and African American art history, Cornell University, Ithaca, New York. Author of *Art and Islamic Literacy among the Hausa of Northern Nigeria,* Mellen Press, 1992, and coauthor, *Seven Stories about Modern Art in Africa,* Flammarion, 1995. Editor, *NKA: Journal of Contemporary African Art,* consulting editor, *African Arts,* and member, editorial board, *Atlantica.* **Essays:** Skunder Boghossian; Rashid Diab; Jeff Donaldson; Meta Vaux Warrick Fuller; Khalid Kodi; Amir Nour; Ahmad Mohammed Shibrain.

HENDERSON, Harry. Contributor to many magazines, including *Harpers, Redbook,* and *Reader's Digest.* Author of *War in Our*

Time (with Sam Shaw and H.C. Morris), 1942, *Your Inner Child of the Past* (with Hugh Missildine), 1963, *Six Black Masters of American Art* (with Romare Bearden), 1972, and *A History of African-American Artists from 1792 to the Present* (also with Romare Bearden), New York: Pantheon Books, 1993. **Essays:** Carole Byard; Robert Reid; Carroll Simms; Philemona Williamson.

HICKS, Kyra E. Freelance writer and nationally exhibited quilter. **Essay:** Sonia Boyce.

HIGH, Freida. Professor of Afro-American studies, University of Wisconsin, Madison. See her own entry. **Essays:** Ibrahim El Salahi; Erhabor Ogieva Emokpae; Vincent Kofi; Iba N'Diaye; Valente Malangatana Ngwenya.

HOLLAND, Coria A. Media relations specialist, Northeastern University, and freelance writer. Author of articles in the *Bay State Banner, The Worcester Telegram and Gazette, The Beverly Times,* and *The Springfield Union-News.* **Essays:** Dana Chandler; Allan Rohan Crite; Henry DeLeon; Malaika Favorite; Kofi Kayiga; Jewel Woodward Simon.

HOLUBIZKY, Ihor. Senior curator, Art Gallery of Hamilton, Hamilton, Ontario. Author of articles in *Next, Canadian Art, Etc.,* and other publications. **Essay:** James Hampton.

JENNINGS, Regina Holden. Curator, The Mattye Reed African Heritage Center, Greensboro, North Carolina, and formerly assistant to the director, Hampton University Museum, Hampton, Virginia. Contributor to *Homecoming.* **Essays:** Tayo Adenaike; Selma Burke; Robert S. Duncanson; Russell Gordon; Gwen Knight; James Phillips; Helen Ramsaran; Vernon Winslow.

KING-HAMMOND, Leslie. Dean of graduate studies, Maryland Institute, College of Art, Baltimore, Maryland, and president, College Art Association. Author of numerous essays in books and catalogs, including *Celebrations: Myth and Ritual in African American Art,* 1982, *The Intuitive Eye,* 1985, *Art as a Verb,* 1988, *Black Printmakers and the WPA,* 1989, *Masters, Mentors, and Makers,* 1992, *Gumbo Ya Ya: An Anthology of African American Women Artists,* 1995, and *Three Generations of African American Women Artists: A Study in Paradox,* 1996. **Essays:** David Driskell; Harlan Jackson; Juan Logan; Tom Miller; Augusta Savage; Elizabeth Scott; Thomas Albert Sills.

KIRSCHKE, Amy. Senior lecturer in African American and African art, Vanderbilt University, Nashville, Tennessee. Author of *Aaron Douglas: Art, Race, and the Harlem Renaissance,* Jackson: University Press of Mississippi, 1995, as well as articles in several magazines, including the *International Review of African American Art.* **Essays:** Elmer Simms Campbell; Aaron Douglas.

KULTERMANN, Udo. Ruth and Norman Moore Professor of Architecture, Washington University, St. Louis, Missouri. Author of many books, including *New Architecture in Africa,* 1963, *History of Art History,* 1966, 1981, *The New Sculpture,* 1969, 1977, *The New Painting,* 1969, 1977, and *Contemporary Architecture in Eastern Europe,* 1985. **Essay:** Robert Colescott.

LAWAL, Babatunde. Professor of art history, Virginia Commonwealth University, Richmond, Virginia. Author of *The Gèlèdé Spec-*

tacle: Art, Gender, and Social Harmony in an African Culture, University of Washington Press, 1996, as well as articles in the *British Journal of Aesthetics, Studio International, Journal of African History, Africa, Journal of the International African Institute, Current Anthropology,* and other publications. **Essays:** Murry DePillars; Asiru Olatunde.

LeFALLE-COLLINS, Lizzetta. Member, department of art history, University of California, Los Angeles; fellow, Center for Black Studies, University of California, Santa Barbara, and independent curator. Author of articles in catalogs and journals, including the *International Review of African American Art, Visions Art Quarterly, Art Week, American Visions,* and the *Michigan Quarterly Review.* **Essays:** Herman "Kofi" Bailey; Grafton Tyler Brown; Arthur Carraway; George Washington Carver; Albert V. Chong; Claude Clark; Alonzo Davis; Charles Dawson; Roy DeCarava; Édouard Duval-Carrié; Herbert Gentry; Michael D. Harris; Humbert Howard; Mildred Howard; Oliver L. Jackson; Malvin Gray Johnson; Sargent Claude Johnson; William H. Johnson; Wifredo Lam; Doyle Lane; Joseph Lewis; Ed Love; Keith Morrison; John Outterbridge; Mary Lovelace O'Neal; Stephanie Pogue; Charles Ethan Porter; Noah Purifoy; John Riddle; Gerard Sekoto; Durant Sihlali; Albert Alexander Smith; Therman Statom; Thelma Johnson Streat; Henry Ossawa Tanner; Matthew Thomas; Charles White; Ellis Wilson; John Wilson; Beulah Woodard.

LEININGER-MILLER, Theresa. Assistant professor of art history, University of Cincinnati, Cincinnati, Ohio. Author of articles in *Notable Black American Women, Gumbo Ya Ya: Anthology of Contemporary African-American Women Artists, Encyclopedia of African American Culture and History,* and other publications. **Essays:** Pastor Argudin y Pedroso; William Ellisworth Artis; James Ball; Gwendolyn Bennett; David Bustill Bowser; Nancy Elizabeth Prophet; Patrick Henry Reason; Dox Thrash.

LEWIS, Samella. Professor emerita of art history, Scripps College, Claremont, California. See her own entry.

LINDO, Nashormeh N. R. Lecturer in African American history, art, and photography. Author of articles in *The African Presence in the Americas: 1492-1992, Coast to Coast: A National Women of Color Artists Book Project, The Encyclopedia of African-American History and Culture,* and other publications. **Essays:** William Ernest Braxton; Samuel Joseph Brown, Jr.; Mohammad Omer Khalil; Norma Morgan.

LONG, Richard A. Atticus Haygood Professor of Interdisciplinary Studies, Emory University, Atlanta, Georgia, and member, advisory board, *International Review of African American Art.* Author of *African Americans: A Portrait* and *The Black Tradition in American Dance.*

LONG, Worth W. Freelance writer. **Essays:** Roland Freeman; Prentice Herman Polk.

MANDELBAUM, Audrey. Freelance writer. Contributor to *New Art Examiner.* **Essay:** Clarissa Sligh.

MARTIN, Frank. Curator of exhibitions and collections, I.P. Stanback Museum & Planetarium, South Carolina State University, Orangeburg, South Carolina. Author of articles in various publications, including *American Visions* and *American Artist Magazine,* as well as in the catalogs *Conflict and Transcendence: African-American Art in South Carolina, 1790 to the Present,* Columbia Museum of Art, 1992, and *Moments from the Past: An Exhibition in Celebration of the Penn Center of the Sea Islands,* I.P. Stanback Museum, 1993. **Essays:** Avel DeKnight; Teodoro Ramos-Blanco; Leo Twiggs.

MINDEROVIC, Christine Miner. Freelance writer. Contributor to *Contemporary Artists* and other publications. **Essays:** Camille Billops; Vivian Browne; Calvin Burnett; Irene Clark; James Denmark; Robert M. Douglass, Jr.; Frederick Eversley; Thomas Fleet, slave of; Marvin Harden; Palmer Hayden; Leon Hicks; Clementine Hunter; Loïs Mailou Jones; Archibald Motely; Delilah Pierce; William H. Simpson; William E. Smith; Frank Williams.

MURPHY, Madeline W. Freelance writer. Author of *Madeline Murphy Speaks,* C.H. Fairfax, 1989; a forthcoming book on Laura Wheeler Waring; and numerous articles in newspapers, including the *Baltimore Times.* **Essay:** Laura Wheeler Waring.

NKURUMEH, Barthosa. Assistant professor of art, Cheyney University, Cheyney, Pennsylvania. His drawings and poems have appeared in *Okike, Nsukka Journal of Humanities, Anthill Annual,* and *West Africa.* **Essays:** Ellsworth Ausby; Uzo Egonu; Ablade Glover; Obiora Udechukwu; S. Irein Wangboje.

NZEGWU, Nkiru. Associate professor of art history, Binghamton University, Binghamton, New York. Contributor to the *International Review of African American Art, Matriart: A Canadian Feminist Art Journal, NKA: Journal of Contemporary African Art, American Anthropologist,* and many other publications. **Essays:** El Anatsui; Ben Enwonwu; Akinola Lasekan; Evangeline Montgomery; Aina Onabolu; Ed Wilson.

OGBECHIE, Sylvester Okwunodu. Fellow, Smithsonian Institution. Author of articles in various publications and catalogs, including *Ben Enwonwu Retrospective,* Lagos, Ben Enwonwu Retrospective Exhibition Organizing Committee, 1991, and *Tribute: Emeka Ezera Memorial Exhibition,* Lagos, United States Information Agency, 1991. **Essays:** Wilson Bigaud; Adrienne Hoard; Christian Lattier; Manuel Mendive; Robert St. Brice.

PERRY, Regenia A. Professor emerita of African and African American art, Virginia Commonwealth University, Richmond, Virginia. Author of *James Van Der Zee,* New York, Morgan and Morgan, 1973, *Free within Ourselves,* Washington, D.C., Smithsonian Institution, 1992, and *Harriet Power's Bible Quilts,* New York, Rizzoli International, 1994. **Essays:** Edward Bannister; Leslie Bolling; David Butler; Houston Conwill; William Edmondson; Minnie Evans; David Hammons; Jacob Lawrence; Elijah Pierce; Harriet Powers; Raymond Saunders; Renee Stout; Mose Tolliver; Bill Traylor; James Van Der Zee; Gregory Warmack.

PIERCE, Aaronetta Hamilton. President and owner, Premier Artworks, Inc., San Antonio, Texas. Author of articles in *American Way* magazine and other publications. **Essay:** Joseph Delaney.

POUPEYE, Veerle. Lecturer in the history of art, Edna Manley College, Kingston, Jamaica. Author of books, magazine articles, and catalog essays on Jamaican and Caribbean art. **Essays:** David Boxer; Everald Brown; Tomás Esson; Ronald Moody; Philip Moore; Petrona Morrison.

POWELL, Richard J. Chairman and associate professor, Department of Art and Art History, Duke University, Durham, North Carolina. Author of *James Lesesne Wells: Sixty Years in Art,* Washington, D.C.: Washington Project for the Arts, 1986, *From the Potomac to the Anacostia: Art and Ideology in the Washington Area,* Washington, D.C.: Washington Project for the Arts, 1989, *The Blues Aesthetic: Black Culture and Modernism,* Washington, D.C.: Washington Project for the Arts, 1989, *Homecoming: The Art and Life of William H. Johnson,* New York: Rizzoli International, 1991, *Jacob Lawrence,* New York: Rizzoli International, 1992, *Black Art and Culture in the Twentieth Century,* London: Thames and Hudson, 1997, and numerous essays in journals and catalogs.

RADNEY, Delores Jackson. Director, Center for African American Culture, Memorial Art Gallery of the University of Rochester, Rochester, New York. **Essay:** Ruth Waddy.

RICHARDSON, Marilyn. Independent curator. Author of *Black Women and Religion,* G.K. Hall, 1980, *Maria Stewart, America's First Black Woman Political Writer,* Indiana University Press, 1987, and articles in the *International Review of African American Art, Encyclopedia of African American Culture and History,* and *Oxford Companion of African American Literature.* **Essay:** Barbara Ward.

ROBERTS, Brady M. Curator of collections and exhibitions, Davenport Museum of Art, Davenport, Iowa. Author of numerous publications, including "The Spiritual Art of Haiti" in *Tracing the Spirit: Ethnographic Essays on Haitian Art,* Seattle: Davenport Museum of Art in association with the University of Washington Press, 1995. **Essays:** Rigaud Benoit; Murat Brierre; Hector Hyppolite; Serge Jolimeau; Philomé Obin.

ROBINSON, Jontyle Theresa. Associate professor of art history, Spelman College, Atlanta, Georgia. Author of *The Art of Archibald J. Motley, Jr.,* Chicago, Chicago Historical Society, 1991, *Bearing Witness: Contemporary Works by African American Women Artists,* Atlanta: Spelman College and Rizzoli International, 1996, and numerous articles in catalogs and other publications, including the *Christian Science Monitor, The Black Collegian* magazine, and the *Encyclopedia of African American Culture and History.* **Essays:** Amalia Amaki; Emma Amos; Shirley Bolton; Beverly Buchanan; Nanette Carter; Elizabeth Catlett; Barbara Chase-Riboud; Freida High; Charnelle D. Holloway; Varnette Honeywood; Stephanie A. Johnson; Laura Jean Lacy; Priscilla Mills; Debra Priestly; Rachelle Puryear; Alison Saar; Betye Saar; Joyce Scott; Lorna Simpson; Kaylynn Sullivan Twotrees; Carrie Mae Weems.

SHANNON, Helen M. Independent scholar and formerly fellow, National Museum of African Art, Smithsonian Institution. Author of essays in *African Masterworks in the Detroit Institute of Arts, Masterpieces of African Art from Private Collections,* and the *Encyclopedia of African American Culture and History.* **Essay:** May Howard Jackson.

SHAW, Thomas M. Associate professor and coordinator of art history, Kean College of New Jersey, Union, New Jersey. Author of *Bayard Rustin as Art Collector: A Study of Sections of African, Asian and European Art in the Collection of a Prominent African American* (exhibition catalog), Kean College of New Jersey, 1989, *The Fulani Matrix of Beauty and Art in the Djolof Region of Senegal,* Lewiston, New York: Edwin Mellen Press, 1994, *What Manner of Men?* Lanham, Maryland: University Press of America, 1997, and articles on African and African American art. **Essays:** Richmond Barthé; Robert Blackburn; Edgar Brierre; Melvin Edwards; Mhlaba Zwelidumile Mgxaji Feni; Rex Gorleigh; Inge Hardison; Ben Jones; Georges Liautaud; Gordon Parks; Merton Simpson.

SHULTZ, Neale Anda. Freelance writer. **Essay:** Geoffrey Holder.

SIRMANS, M. Franklin. Author of articles and reviews in many publications, including *Publishers Weekly, Oneworld Magazine, Quarterly Black Review of Books, ARTnews,* and *American Visions.* **Essays:** Terry Adkins; Eldzier Cortor; Renée Green; Ouattara; Keith Piper; Chéri Samba; Vincent Smith.

STEELE, Robert E. Associate dean, College of Behavioral & Social Sciences, University of Maryland, College Park, and founding president, National Black Arts Festival, Collector's Guild. Contributor to numerous periodicals, including the *Journal of Black Psychology, Contemporary Psychology,* and the *American Journal of Community Psychology.* **Essays:** Margo Humphrey; James Lesesne Wells.

STINSON, Sonya. Freelance writer and editor. Formerly editor of the *Black Collegian* magazine. **Essays:** Carol Ann Carter; Milton Derr.

STONE, Louise D. Freelance writer and formerly feature writer and critic for the *Washington Post, Washington Afro-American,* and *Chicago Daily Defender.* Editor of *Pennsylvania's Black History,* Portfolio Associates, 1975. **Essays:** John Dowell; Richard Hunt; Hughie Lee-Smith; Hayward Oubre.

TAYLOR, William E. Lecturer in African American visual art history, University of Indiana, Bloomington, and Indiana University-Purdue University at Indianapolis. Author of articles in the *International Review of African American Art, Art Documentation, Encyclopedia of Indianapolis,* and other publications. **Essays:** John Wesley Hardrick; William Edouard Scott.

TENABE, Gabriel. Director, Office of Museums (James E. Lewis Museum of Art and Lillie Carroll Jackson Museum), Morgan State University, Baltimore, Maryland. Founder, Association of Professional Artists of Nigeria, and cofounder, Association of African Artists in North America. **Essays:** Benny Andrews; Margaret Burroughs; Ed Clark; Ernest Crichlow; Bing Davis; Beauford Delaney; Alvin Hollingsworth; Paul Keene; James Lewis; James Porter; Raymond Steth.

TOWNES, Glenn. Associate editor and writer, the *PitchWeekly Newspaper,* Kansas City, Missouri. Author of articles in *Essence, Kansas City Star, Miami Herald, YSB* magazine, and many other publications. **Essays:** Betty Blayton-Taylor; Reginald Gammon; Earl J. Hooks.

TWIGGS, Leo. Executive director, I.P. Stanback Museum & Planetarium, South Carolina State University, Orangeburg, South Carolina, and chair of art department, South Carolina State University. See his own entry. **Essays:** Edwin Harleston; Hale Woodruff.

VALAKOS, Dorothy. Associate educator, Baltimore Museum of Art, Maryland. **Essays:** Romare Bearden; Sam Gilliam; Joshua Johnston; Horace Pippin; Martin Puryear; Alma Thomas.

VON BLUM, Paul. Lecturer, Center for African American Studies, University of California, Los Angeles. Author of *The Art of Social Conscience,* 1976, *The Critical Vision: A History of Social and Political Art in the U.S.,* 1982, *Stillborn Education,* 1986, and *Other Visions, Other Voices,* 1995, as well as contributor to various journals on art, culture, and politics, including *American Visions, Z,* and *The Dictionary of Art.* **Essays.** Ernie Barnes; Jefferson Eugene Grigsby, Jr.; William Pajaud; Pat Ward Williams.

WALKER, Roslyn Adele. Director, National Museum of African Art, Smithsonian Institution, Washington, D.C. Author of articles, reviews, and chapters in various publications, including *African Textiles and Decorative Arts, Humanities through the Black Experience, African Women/African Art, African Arts, The Yoruba Artist: New Theoretical Perspectives on African Arts,* and *Africa: Art of a Continent.* **Essays:** Felix Eboigbe; Howardena Pindell.

WEAVER, A.M. Director of visual and media arts, Painted Bride Art Center, Philadelphia, Pennsylvania. **Essays:** Willie Birch; Sherman Fleming; Manuel Hughes; Martha Jackson-Jarvis; Glenn Ligon; Kerry James Marshall; Valerie Maynard; Clarence Morgan; Senga Nengudi; Adrian Piper; Michael B. Platt; Gary Simmons; Denise Ward-Brown; Pheoris West; Fred Wilson.

WOODS, Regina L. Freelance writer and curator. Contributor to *African Arts, Flash Art,* and *Guggenheim Magazine.* **Essays:** Twins Seven-Seven; Lamidi Fakeye; Thomas Lloyd.

ZEIDLER, Jeanne. Director, University Museum, Hampton University, Hampton, Virginia. **Essays:** John Biggers; Samella Lewis.